ALSO BY IRVING KOLODIN

The Guide to Long Playing Records: Orchestral Music
The Musical Life
The Story of the Metropolitan Opera: 1883–1950

These are Borzoi Books
published in New York by Alfred A. Knopf

THE
Metropolitan Opera
1883–1966

THE

Metropolitan Opera

1883–1966

A CANDID HISTORY

BY

Irving Kolodin

Library of Congress Catalog Card Number: 66-19384

THIS IS A BORZOI BOOK
PUBLISHED BY ALFRED A. KNOPF, INC.

The first edition of this book was titled *The Metropolitan Opera, 1883–1935,* published by Oxford University Press, Inc., in 1936; the second was *The Metropolitan Opera, 1883–1939,* published by Oxford University Press, Inc., in 1940; the third was *The Story of the Metropolitan Opera, 1883–1950,* published by Alfred A. Knopf, Inc., in 1953. The present, fourth edition has been revised, expanded, reset, and printed from new plates, November 1966.

TO

IRMA

MY WIFE

PREFATORY NOTE

WHATEVER THE FATE of the physical frame that has now inevitably come to be known as the Old Met, its aura and its lore are apt to endure as long as opera is performed. Like any arena that has seen the birth and also the death of many notable careers, it came to possess a personality and a character that will outlive all but the most illustrious of those humans who came and went upon its boards. It was not for want of effort that the works born within its walls have yielded less that is durable than those who performed in them. The observation of W. J. Henderson in his much-valued foreword to the first version of this survey[1] —"Historically the most important new production in the long list was that of Puccini's *Girl of the Golden West*"—remains as true today as when it was written, though thirty years have passed.

The amalgam of performers, what they performed, and those for whom they performed it supply the substance of such a history as this. However much we might have preferred the order of importance to be other than it was, it is with what it was rather than what it might have been that this volume is concerned. Now and then the thin line separating what was from what might have been invites the kind of editorial heat that is generated more in sorrow than in anger. But by and large one may paraphrase a familiar maxim of government to say that a public gets the kind of opera enterprise it deserves. If this is a hint to those who will assist in making a home of the new house in Lincoln Center, it is accompanied by an abundance of evidence.

With the Gala Farewell of April 16, 1966, in which the Metropolitan Opera Company lowered the curtain on a span of activity extending over eighty-three years, there ended a term of occupancy hardly imagined by those who called the building into being. It was, perhaps, providential that of all the innumerable incidents recorded within it one of the most dreaded never came to pass—the loss of a patron's life as a result of the peculiarities of its construction, deterioration of staircases and hand railings during the years, the lack of the margin for safety deemed essential today. Oddly, the possibility of such a happening arose only days before the closing, when a youthful onlooker at one of the final student matinées

[1] *The Metropolitan Opera, 1883–1935* (Oxford University Press, 1936).

stumbled and pitched over a railing. Fortunately he fell only to the tier of boxes below, escaping with bruises rather than broken bones or worse.

With this last retrospective view I ever expect to write of the subject should go an inclusive expression of thanks to those who have contributed to it. However, any such expression would be inadequate to take in the innumerable persons, dead as well as living, who contributed an insight, shaped an impression, or corrected a misimpression. I can, however, direct an expression of gratitude to those readers whose acceptance of the previous volumes has made this final one possible. It would not, in any case, have been what it is without the continuing devoted interest of Herbert Weinstock, whose understanding of the subject fulfilled—again— an author's ideal of what an editor should be. Gerald Fitzgerald has rendered inestimable assistance in collating, checking, and correcting myriad statements of fact.

IRVING KOLODIN

July 1, 1966

CONTENTS

ILLUSTRATIONS

b) Jussi Bjoerling as Manrico in *Il Trovatore*
   (LOUIS MÉLANÇON)

c) Titta Ruffo as Rigoletto
   (CULVER SERVICE)

d) Leonard Warren as Rigoletto

e) Lawrence Tibbett as Simon Boccanegra

f) Carlo Bergonzi as Riccardo in *Un Ballo in maschera*
   (ANDREA PAGLIARANI)

g) Giulietta Simionato as Azucena and Franco Corelli as Manrico
   in *Il Trovatore*
   (ERIO PICCAGLIANI)

XVIII. *Tosca* and *Madama Butterfly*
   a) Maria Jeritza as Floria Tosca
      (MARIE TSCHIEDEL, VIENNA)

   b) Geraldine Farrar as Floria Tosca
      (CULVER SERVICE)

   c) Enrico Caruso as Cavaradossi
      (BROWN BROTHERS)

   d) Antonio Scotti as Scarpia

   e) Geraldine Farrar as Cio-Cio-San
      (THE METROPOLITAN OPERA GUILD)

   f) Licia Albanese as Cio-Cio-San

   g) Maria Callas as Floria Tosca and Tito Gobbi as Scarpia
      (METROPOLITAN OPERA PRESS DEPARTMENT)

XIX. *Faust*
   a) Nellie Melba as Marguerite

   b) Geraldine Farrar as Marguerite
      (CULVER SERVICE)

   c) Édouard de Reszke as Méphistophélès

   d) Pol Plançon as Méphistophélès
      (METROPOLITAN OPERA GUILD)

   e) Nicolai Ghiaurov as Méphistophélès
      (METROPOLITAN OPERA PRESS DEPARTMENT)

   f) Gabriella Tucci as Marguerite and Nicolai Gedda as Faust
      (LOUIS MÉLANÇON)

XX. *Carmen*
   a) Emma Calvé as Carmen
      (THE METROPOLITAN OPERA GUILD)

   b) Maria Gay as Carmen
      (THE METROPOLITAN OPERA GUILD)

XXIV. *Boris Godunov*
    a) Feodor Chaliapin as Boris Godunov
       (THE METROPOLITAN OPERA GUILD)
    b) Ezio Pinza as Boris Godunov
    c) Alexander Kipnis as Boris Godunov
    d) Kerstin Thorborg as Marina
       (ALFREDO VALENTE)

XXV. *American and English Opera*
    a) Lucrezia Bori as Mary, Edward Johnson as Peter Ibbetson, in *Peter Ibbetson*
       (CARLO EDWARDS)
    b) Act II scene from *Peter Grimes,* with Polyna Stoska
    c) Eleanor Steber as Vanessa and Rosalind Elias as Erika, with Regina Resnik as the Baroness
       (LOUIS MÉLANÇON)

XXVI. *Sopranos*
    a) Marcella Sembrich
    b) Luisa Tetrazzini
    c) Claudia Muzio (as Norma in *Norma*)
    d) Rose Ponselle (as Santuzza in *Cavalleria rusticana*)
       (CULVER SERVICE)
    e) Amelita Galli-Curci (as Violetta in *La Traviata*)
    f) Geraldine Farrar with Mary Garden, right, who wears costume for film of *Thaïs* she was then making at the Goldwyn studios in Hollywood
       (CULVER SERVICE)

XXVII. *Sopranos and Contraltos*
    a) Emma Eames
       (BROWN BROTHERS)
    b) Louise Homer (as Orfeo in *Orfeo ed Euridice*)
       (BROWN BROTHERS)
    c) Gladys Swarthout (as Stephano in *Roméo et Juliette*)
       (THE METROPOLITAN OPERA GUILD)
    d) Marion Talley (as Philine in *Mignon*)
       (THE METROPOLITAN OPERA GUILD)
    e) Ernestine Schumann-Heink as guest at a "Surprise Party" of 1932, with Michael Bohnen
       (CARLO EDWARDS)

XXVIII. The Metropolitan from First to Last
    a) Guests at party honoring Antonio Scotti in 1933 include Marcella Sembrich, who sang on the second night of the

Elisabeth Schumann as Marzelline, Carl Braun as Rocco, Albert Reiss as Jaquino
(CULVER SERVICE)

b) Final scene from *L'Amore dei tre re* (1917–18 season), with Pasquale Amato as Manfredo, Claudia Muzio as Fiora, José Mardones as Archibaldo
(CULVER SERVICE)

XXXVII. Productions—III

a) Act III scene from *Il Barbiere di Siviglia* (1940–41 season), with Irra Petina as Berta, Josephine Tuminia as Rosina, Ezio Pinza as Don Basilio, Salvatore Baccaloni as Doctor Bartolo, John Charles Thomas as Figaro, Bruno Landi as Almaviva

b) Opening scene from *Le Nozze di Figaro* (1948–9 season), with Alessio de Paolis as Basilio, Jarmila Novotna as Cherubino, John Brownlee as the Count, Bidú Sayão as Susanna
(LOUIS MÉLANÇON)

XXXVIII. Productions—IV

a) Joan Sutherland as Amina and Nicolai Gedda as Elvino in *La Sonnambula*
(LOUIS MÉLANÇON)

b) Maria Callas in *Lucia di Lammermoor,* with Nicola Moscona as Raimondo, Paul Franke as Arturo, and Thelma Votipka as Alisa (background)
(LOUIS MÉLANÇON)

XXXIX. Productions—V

a) Otto Wiener as Hans Sachs and Karl Doench as Beckmesser in Act II of *Die Meistersinger.* At left, Sándor Kónya as Walther and Ingrid Bjoner as Eva
(LOUIS MÉLANÇON)

b) Risë Stevens (Carmen) and Richard Tucker (Don José) in Act I of *Carmen*
(GJON MILI)

XL. Productions—VI

a) Entrance of Butterfly in Act I of *Madama Butterfly,* with Antonietta Stella as Cio-Cio-San, Eugenio Fernandi as Pinkerton, and Mario Zanasi as Sharpless
(LOUIS MÉLANÇON)

b) Birgit Nilsson as Turandot (Act II). In the background, Alessio de Paolis as the Emperor
(LOUIS MÉLANÇON)

I

Patrons and Purposes

OPERA WAS GIVEN continuously at the Metropolitan Opera House, 1423 Broadway, New York City, for nearly eighty-three years—from its first season of 1883. During that time no work by a native American —indeed, no work created on the North American continent—had any lasting success in its repertory. In this as well as in other ways, the Metropolitan took on a coloration peculiarly American.

As opposed to those countries (recently including England) where opera is given largely in the vernacular, opera at the Metropolitan was given largely in the language of its original text. As opposed to those countries (now, also, including England) where opera is state or municipally supported, opera at the Metropolitan struggled along with only marginal assistance from governmental groups. Mostly this assistance took the form of tax relief. Though the budget of the city of New York is larger than that of many European countries, it gave not one penny of aid to this world-celebrated institution.

The international tinge of the Metropolitan and its lack of subsidy thus denominate it "American," though it gave opera for seven seasons in German only, reached its greatest glory under the direction of two Italians, and has most recently been directed by a Canadian and an English subject of Austrian birth. One American, Herbert Witherspoon, interrupted this sequence; but he died before his work was fairly begun.

The first Metropolitan was oddly American, too, in outliving the circumstances that brought it into being—indeed, the whole mental atmosphere that determined its location, size, and structure. Like the national Capitol in Washington (once a central point of a concentrated federation), it became a relic of another day's thinking, no longer suitable for the purpose it served, and vastly more costly to maintain for that reason. It had eaten up its original cost many times over in deficits that persisted for lack of plan or direction in meeting the changes, social and economic, of more than eighty years.

Few of us today could imagine a society in which a mere whim could determine the existence of such a structure as the Metropolitan. Lilli Lehmann has recorded the circumstances in her memoirs, *My Path through Life* (New York: G. P. Putnam's Sons; 1914): "As, on a particular evening, one of the millionairesses did not receive the box in which she intended to shine because another woman had anticipated her, the husband of the former took prompt action and caused the Metropolitan Opera House to rise."

The box denied was, of course, in the Academy of Music, on Fourteenth Street, the fashionable home of opera in New York from 1849. The person denied was a Vanderbilt, most probably Mrs. William H. Her husband had but recently inherited a fortune from the family founder, Commodore Vanderbilt. Virtually all the boxes in the Academy were held by older elements of New York society, sufficiently venerable to be known as the Knickerbocker gentry. Their money dated from the Revolution; those whose money dated only from the War between the States were considered tainted, no matter how much of it they had.

William H. Vanderbilt came into most of the family fortune (ninety-four million dollars) when his father died in 1877. The heir lived only until 1885, by which time he had doubled the stake entrusted to him. In a time of such untaxed accumulation of wealth, the hundreds of thousands of dollars required to create the most lavish theater were barely consequential.

Vanderbilt could doubtless have done it by himself and held the theater as a physical chattel, as his heirs did as a social chattel through the long life of his daughter-in-law, Grace Orme Wilson Vanderbilt (at her death in 1953, she was the last recognized *grande dame* of New York society). But he was willing enough to share the burden with other eager millionaires excluded from the Academy of Music's box-list.

The critical period may be dated from April 4, 1880, when it was noted in *The New York Times* that George H. Warren, a lawyer and broker affiliated with Vanderbilt, had conferred with a group of Academy stockholders: August H. Belmont and Messrs. Lorillard, Van Hoffman, and Dinsmore. All the Academy people could offer was a plan to add twenty-six boxes to the existing thirty. Obviously the old box-holders would remain the inner brotherhood. The offer was rejected.

Within the week (on April 7) Warren announced to the press that $800,000 had been subscribed to create a new opera house. He identified the leading participants in the plan as: "The two Roosevelts, Iselins,

Goelets, the Astors, the three Vanderbilts, the Morgans, myself, and others." Had the building been erected on the first site chosen, the first Metropolitan for all of its years would have stood on Vanderbilt Avenue, adjacent to Grand Central Terminal (between Forty-third and Forty-fourth Streets); but the deeds to some plots forbade erection of a theater where the Biltmore Hotel now stands.

In mid-March 1881 the original site on Broadway between Thirty-ninth and Fortieth Streets was secured at an investment of $600,000. At the same time the capitalization was increased to $1,050,000. The rumor that this was a Vanderbilt project was dealt with in *The New York Times* of March 9, 1881: "Of the 10,500 shares, W. H. owns 300, W. K. 300, and Cornelius 150." This gave the one faction five boxes, however, not to mention those possessed by in-laws and business dependents. A more realistic view is offered on page 56.

Delays in taking possession of the site and ousting stubborn leaseholders made completion of the project by the target date of October 1882 impossible. Even after construction had begun, with a foundation costing $125,000, increased costs of building materials caused gossip that the whole venture would be abandoned, or an apartment building substituted. At a meeting called to decide the issue in 1882, only fifty-one of the seventy stockholders appeared. Thirty-seven (a narrow majority of the whole) voted to go ahead on a capitalization now of $1,700,000. The final expenditure was $1,732,478.71.

Perhaps because of the added expenditure, it was decided to fill in the corners of the structure (originally indented for a modest kind of eye-appeal) with rent-yielding apartments. As it was not unknown for a single ball, wedding-reception, or other social function of the day to cost the host $200,000, the factor of cost alone could not have been considered crucial in this decision. Rather, it was that same concept of "good business" which impelled the elder Vanderbilt to haggle over the charge for a load of manure when he was a traction tycoon, and a struggling truck-farmer (his son William H.) was the customer.

There are those who would cite the old Met's exterior as no uglier, really, than that of the Bayreuth Festspielhaus. Aesthetically the margin between them is narrow. But if severity is a characteristic of Wagner's exterior design, utility is a criterion of its interior planning. No such balance can be found in the American structure of 1883. At that, its instigators cannot be held wholly blamable. They can hardly have imagined that it would survive into an era of telephone, wireless, television, and jet planes. That it would survive such then still unbuilt marvels as the New Theater—thirty years younger—the Hippodrome, the Ritz Hotel (a construction of 1914), and even the Center Theater (built in 1931) would have been regarded as palpable nonsense.

Whatever the majority sentiment, at least one member of the board of directors had a grasp of the business realities inherent in operating an opera house. Following one meeting to increase capitalization, James A. Roosevelt (fourth cousin of Franklin Delano) told a *Times* reporter on March 14, 1882: "We never expected that it would pay. No opera house in the world has ever paid as an investment, and none ever will."

If payment was lacking, other compensations were not. The house was first used on May 24, 1883, when the stockholders met to apportion the boxes. In a gambling spirit, location went by chance. From one hat, young Miss Warren drew a name; from another, Miss Townsend drew a number. As there were three less stockholders than the seventy boxes in the two tiers, Nos. 9, 24, and 35 remained unassigned. At the same meeting, an assessment of $5,000 was placed on each stockholder to underwrite completion of the business properties. And, to relieve the "pressure" on the dauntless millionaires, the Bowery Savings Bank granted a mortgage of $600,000.

2

Having gone so far as to provide New York with its most magnificent gaslit structure, the innovators intended to go no farther. Operation of the theater was obviously the province of a professional who would entertain the public as Colonel Mapleson entertained it at the Academy of Music, and possibly make a profit as well. At that, the proposition was an inviting one, for the stockholders posted a guarantee of $60,000, against possible losses in a season of sixty-one performances. "All" the operator had to do was dress the stage and engage an orchestra, stars, and supers.

The contract was finally awarded to Henry E. Abbey, well known as a theatrical entrepreneur and manager of concert artists. His adviser on operatic matters was Maurice Grau, well versed in producing operettas and musical comedies. What Grau learned was of considerable value when he came into prominence a decade later; but it was an expensive education for Abbey. Henry H. Krehbiel (in *Chapters of Opera*) quotes an Abbey associate (Schoeffel) as saying that the loss of the single season was $600,000. Doubtless this included the seventy-four road performances.

In any case, the expense of outfitting nearly a score of operas would have placed a staggering burden on any single season's income. As well as paying Christine Nilsson and Italo Campanini one thousand dollars a performance, Abbey's lavish hand provided a wardrobe in which "every costume, every shoe and stocking was provided . . . by Worth of Paris."

The witness to this extravagance was Lilli Lehmann, who came to New York two seasons later. Such matters could not fail to impress the unpretentious Lilli, whose frugality, when a reigning prima donna, extended to riding the horse car to and from the theater rather than engaging a hack.

The directors met the obligation of their guarantee to Abbey, and also granted him the use of the theater for a benefit. This remarkable show (see page 85) added $16,000 to his personal fortune, but solvency was far away. He offered to run the theater for a second season without compensation of any kind if the stockholders would absorb his losses of the first, but the offer was laughed aside.

Had Ernest Gye, impresario of Covent Garden, London, not been married to the soprano Emma Albani, the history of the next decade could have been quite different. Gye had been in the running for the lease before Abbey was selected, and negotiations were resumed with him on the assumption that he might still be interested. His wife, he replied, would have to be considered in any plans he might take, which brought an end to the conversations. The stockholders were loyal to Nilsson, and no company then could comfortably accommodate more than one prima donna.

In the end the stockholders had neither Nilsson nor Gye. Faced with the penalty of keeping the theater dark (and meeting tax charges anyway) while the Academy of Music crowd enjoyed a triumph, they accepted from Leopold Damrosch an offer that transformed the Metropolitan, for a period of seven years, into a German opera house. A moving spirit in the musical life of New York since his arrival from Germany ten years before, Damrosch proposed his own services as conductor and director for a season's salary of $10,000. The orchestra would be his own Symphony Society; choristers from the Oratorio Society (which he also conducted) could be utilized; and he would recruit his principals from central Europe, thus avoiding the expensive stars of the Italian and French theaters. An appeal to the quarter-million persons of German extraction in New York would be made by attention to the long-neglected Wagner repertory.

Damrosch was authorized to proceed in early August. Despite the handicap of this late date, his knowledge of the situation on both sides of the Atlantic supported his program. He gathered a company able to perform (in German) *Rigoletto, Tell,* and *La Juive,* as well as the promised Wagner (see page 87). At a four-dollar top (Abbey had asked seven), the public response was keen. By January 1885, business was running so far ahead of the previous year that Damrosch was encouraged to plan a second season. His salary was reduced to $8,000, but he would share in the profits.

Damrosch did not live to see his scheme prosper, however. The overwhelming work load of opera performances, plus his concert routine, made him an easy victim to pneumonia, and he died on February 15, 1885. The fight for the open post was both ugly and unpleasant, with a prominent member of the company, Anton Schott, making noisy claim to recognition. He later claimed credit for directing attention to Anton Seidl, who was engaged as music director to succeed Damrosch; he did not otherwise add luster to the meager record of tenors for sagacity.

As executive, the stockholders appointed Edmond C. Stanton, already serving as secretary to the board of directors. Young Walter Damrosch was sent abroad to negotiate with Seidl, and to give glamour to the roster by adding Max Alvary, Emil Fischer, and Lilli Lehmann to the company.

The reduction in loss from $40,000 in the first Damrosch year to $25,000 in the first year under Seidl was gratifying. The ecstatic approval of the largely German-dominated press was welcome. When Mapleson gave up the fight at the Academy of Music in 1886, the Metropolitan stockholders could relax in contentment. Even his aspersions against the "new yellow brewery on Broadway" could be shrugged aside; likewise his historic farewell: "I cannot fight Wall Street." Seidl was given a three-year contract, and the Germanization of the theater proceeded.

As too frequently in the pattern of Metropolitan operation, expedience and convenience took precedence over any other considerations of how a representative opera house should be conducted. If Abbey was willing to risk his fortune, Italian opera sufficed. If Damrosch and Seidl could save money by giving German opera, German opera sufficed. Many of the difficulties that beset the Metropolitan in those early years were inherent in the ill-assorted coterie that had produced the money in the first place. They accepted a yearly assessment as part of the expense of social position, but with more than a few mental reservations about other responsibilities.

So it was German opera for the next little while. When the time came for another decision in the spring of 1889, the advance sale for the next season stood at $80,000. This impressive figure could not be denied, and a vote to continue opera in German was upheld, 43 to 3. As may be noted, twenty-five stockholders did not even bother to vote.

So long as there was no alternative to German opera at minimum losses, impatience, indeed boredom, with its "heavy" intellectual pressures, were endured. When the novelty of the Wagner repertory wore off, and damaging experiments with such minor composers as Nessler, Brüll, Smareglia, even the Duke of Saxe-Coburg, aroused objection in the press, a change became inevitable. The box-holders were all for getting out of the responsibility of opera-producing as soon as possible.

The alternative that presented itself could have been much worse. Abbey had recovered from his first season's losses and was again making money with such singers as Patti, Albani, Nordica, and Del Puente. Grau, now in his early forties, did most of the planning and direction of the company. When the company presented a season of old favorites in the Metropolitan in the spring of 1890, the tunes and their singers cast their usual spell. When the existing commitments to the German group were fulfilled, the lease was given to Abbey and Grau, to begin with the fall of 1891.

This decision was by no means unanimous, nor was it welcomed by that part of the press which represented the interests of the German-descended public. Without opera in German, they reasoned, there would be no German opera, a matter of distress to those wedded to contemporary ideas of Italian opera being "old-fashioned," and Wagner representing "the music of the future." In addition, many of the box-holders who had joined up in the first flush of social enthusiasm for the new meeting-place were finding the continuing responsibilities irksome.

As sometimes happens (if the participants are fortunate enough), a cumbersome situation was resolved by *force majeure*. For the Metropolitan stockholders it was the fire of August 27, 1892, which consumed, along with wood and walls, the softer elements of the membership. Only those who cared enough about opera not to count its cost or those who had so much money that the cost did not matter took up the burden of refinancing and reconstruction. Most of the stockholders of the newly formed Metropolitan Opera and Real Estate Company were in the second category, and they soon evolved a formula whereby important money losses were held to a minimum for three decades.

Through the terms of the lease with each producing group (until the sale of the property in 1940), the stockholders waived a rental charge, taking instead the use of the boxes for all subscription performances. Thus the opera-producing faction had no fixed rental to meet. On the other hand, those who occupied the most desirable seats in the theater—the only ones to which special prestige was attached—were relieved of any obligation or responsibility for the quality of work done. The contradiction inherent in this division of function complicated much of the succeeding history of opera at the Metropolitan.

3

When the scheme was first devised, however, and as long as the national economy remained substantially that of the 1890's, it was well suited to the problem of the Metropolitan. Boxes-for-rent was a kind of subsidy—in the American tradition of tenant-farming, for example—in which, relieved of one item of overhead, the operating company could devote itself wholly to keeping the expense of opera *below* the income. Automatically a profit would follow.

Not for fifteen years did the idea emerge that opera of the Metropolitan's pretensions should *not* return a profit, that there was always a phase of opera to be improved if money was available to be spent on it. Grau's company prospered in spite of primitive staging, often execrable orchestral playing, and a uniform emphasis on star singers and stars alone. When he died and the control of the theater passed to a group headed by Heinrich Conried, the shortcomings of his predecessor were recognized and acted upon in a fashion—but always with the profit motive in mind.

The transition from Grau (recognized as an entrepreneur and pretending to be nothing else) to the producing company headed by Conried (a theatrical manager with pretensions to intellectual leadership) introduced a new factor into the affairs of the Metropolitan. Grau's own capital had been augmented by investments, for profits, of persons in the theatrical world. Conried's backers were men of means with some social standing, if several rungs below those of the box-holders. To assure the box-holders against a fiasco on the Abbey order, Conried was required to post a guarantee of $150,000. Among the patrons of his Irving Place Theater (see page 160) was Henry Morgenthau, Sr., who related the circumstances in his reminiscences, *All in a Lifetime* (New York: Doubleday, Page & Company; 1922).

Morgenthau scanned Conried's projected list of backers (Thalman, Guggenheim, Guggenheimer, and Ickelheimer) and scoffed at it as "a winelist." He proposed the addition of such men as James Hazen Hyde, vice-president of the Equitable Life Insurance Company, Eliot Gregory, Henry Rogers Winthrop, George J. Gould, and J. Henry Smith. To give further solidity to the membership, several of the box-holder group who were not averse to making a profit on the productions at the Metropolitan if it could be arranged—Alfred G. Vanderbilt, H. P. Whitney, and Robert Goelet (an Astor kinsman)—"gambled" ten thousand dollars apiece. By the narrow margin of one vote—seven to six—the Conried Metropolitan Opera Company was awarded the lease in 1902. Had the deciding vote been cast differently, the Metropolitan might have remained under a single leadership from 1903 until 1951. One director alone prevented the lease from going to a company headed by Walter Damrosch, a man of forty then, who became one of music's hardiest patriarchs, living until January 1951.

The group that backed Conried for profit in 1903 was the genesis of the board of directors that, sixty years later, had the task of keeping the Metropolitan open and operating. When Conried was bought out in 1908, his erstwhile associates established the principle that profits would no longer be expected from the operation of the Metropolitan. A principal propagandist for this view was Otto H. Kahn, who had been nominated by Jacob H. Schiff (his business partner) to take the place on the Conried board originally set aside for him. (Schiff pleaded lack of time.)

Thus the Metropolitan Opera Company, which came into being in 1908, not only engaged Giulio Gatti-Casazza, who remained general manager until 1935; it also comprised the individuals who either themselves or through successors engaged Edward Johnson in 1935, conducted the campaign for the funds to buy the building in 1940, and eventually engaged Rudolf Bing in 1949. The long-term trend, then, was to take ownership out of the hands of the group that had built the opera house as a place for social display and transfer it to a group interested primarily in the production of opera. The way had many tortuous turnings, and the path was anything but direct, but if there is a single line of evolution in the running of the theater, that is it.

A rather fascinating instance of time and circumstances accomplishing what man's wit could not achieve may be found in the unquestionable status of the Metropolitan today as the single major opera-producing entity in the country. It was the hope and desire of Kahn and his associates that this end could be accomplished through their financial resources in 1910, 1911, or 1912. It was first necessary to eliminate the local competition of Oscar Hammerstein at the Manhattan Opera House, at a cost of $1,200,-000. Next his artists would be formed into a Philadelphia-Chicago Opera Company, with members of the Metropolitan board of directors sitting in on the planning for those cities. Next, Boston would be serviced from the main office in New York. After that, presumably, other places would be added to the chain, as business opportunities took shape.

Chicago, however, rebelled against the intrusion of New York millionaires, and Philadelphia soon proved itself unable to support more than an occasional visit. When these facts became evident, Kahn and Company made an amicable arrangement for an occasional exchange of artists with Chicago and, for a while, welcomed the Western singers and repertory on visits to the Metropolitan. This arrangement did not endure for long, and for half a dozen years beginning in 1917 the Chicagoans' visits made embarrassing competition—both financial and artistic—for the Metropolitan. With the entry of Samuel Insull into the affairs of the Chicago company, the New York visits ended. The two companies made a quiet arrangement not to compete in the European market for the same artists.

The scope of these plans is indicative of the new spirit that had come into

the Metropolitan along with Conried, and it took firmer hold of its management as his time ran out. It is hard to imagine that Grau had other than
a businessman's pride in giving opera that made money. When Conried's
replacement by Giulio Gatti-Casazza was announced on February 12,
1908, the management's evaluation of its artistic pretensions could be read
clearly: "To the high standards they [the directors of the Metropolitan
Opera and Real Estate Company] have set is due the credit for having
made the Metropolitan Opera House what it now is universally conceded
to be—the 'Blue Ribbon' of the operatic world."

The intermingling of the two groups had now become almost complete.
Of Conried's original backers there remained Goelet, Gould, Gregory,
Hyde, Kahn, Mackay, Whitney, and Winthrop. Alfred Vanderbilt had been
succeeded by his brother W. K. From the ownership company had been
added W. Bayard Cutting and Hamilton McK. Twombly. Closely linked to
the box-holder faction, though not actually part of it, were several other
new members: Edmund L. Baylies, Rawlins L. Cottenet, Frank G. Griswold and T. De Witt Cuyler.

Thus by 1908 one phase of the Metropolitan's historic cycle was completed. After twenty-five years of operation it had been determined that
opera should not make money, that it had a place of artistic responsibility
to fulfill in the community (if not in the country), and that it should be
operated by salaried professionals with only an objective interest in the
box-office takings. To provide New York with a broad program of opera
in all its forms, the New Theater had been created on Central Park West
where *opéra-comique* and other works too intimate for the vaster auditorium could be performed. Unfortunately, this desirable separation of
activity did not survive a trial period during which Hammerstein was still
active and the potential audience divided among three theaters. Thereafter
it was decreed that the acoustics of the New Theater were unsuitable for
"serious" music, even in its lighter manner of *opéra-comique*.

4

With the elimination of Hammerstein, the abandonment of the New
Theater, and the concentration of Kahn's complete interest in opera on the
Metropolitan, Gatti—for a time with Arturo Toscanini as his artistic collaborator—entered upon a period of financial and musical well-being which
has had no parallel in opera production elsewhere. In place of the fifty- or
sixty-thousand-dollar advance sale of the German opera period, the three
or four times that amount of the Grau seasons, or even the half-million-
dollar pre-season income of Conried, the subscription sale mounted steadily

toward the million-dollar mark, eventually to reach it and continue well beyond.

The proud program that had been installed on Gatti's arrival was altered more than a little, however. The double orchestra engaged to carry the work load of performances at two New York theaters or in New York and Baltimore or Philadelphia simultaneously was abandoned; the separate German and Italian choruses were merged into one. Although profits from the operation were no longer distributed as dividends to the stockholders, Gatti was not discouraged from budgeting his seasons in such a way as to make profits possible. Indeed, though the books show that income exceeded expenses in 1910–11 by $34,915 and in 1911–12 by $52,075, a rise in prices from $5 to $6 for orchestra seats was instituted for the 1912–13 season. For this season the credit balance reached the imposing sum of $133,858.

These profits totaled well over $200,000, but it was not until the spring of 1914—following a season that left the company with a $66,609 balance —that the public had some intimation of these "favorable" developments. As he left for Europe on April 30, Gatti acknowledged: "Contrary to custom, the Metropolitan actually showed a financial profit during the season just completed." Impresarios, even as politicians, can be loose with the truth and still be considered to be serving "higher" purposes.

For if it was commonly known that a profit existed, would it not follow that the artists would discover that they had, all along, been underpaid? When Gatti was released from cares of this sort, he could state in his book (*Memories of the Opera,* page 304) the case the record supports: not until 1930, in the first year of the depression, did the twenty-year run of opera without a deficit under his direction come to an end.

To be sure, the promise made to him on arrival: "In two or three years, a new Metropolitan Opera House will be built, answering all needs" (*Memories of the Opera*) was not kept. As long as he remained in the theater, Gatti could congratulate himself that he had at least insisted on the construction of a roof-stage for rehearsals (at the Seventh Avenue and Fortieth Street corner of the building) at a cost of $25,000. Otherwise, as in Johnson's time (and still in Bing's), a daytime visitor to the theater could hear the sounds of music being rehearsed in such unlikely places as the smoking-room on the grand-tier floor and the ladies' parlor.

All this argues a certain adaptability on Gatti's part, a careful sensing of where money should be spent to advantage, a willingness to compromise where it might not show too much. The twin pillars of the structure he had created were Caruso and Toscanini. It was his good fortune that Caruso was satisfied with a top fee of $2,500 a performance from 1914 on. No pittance, to be sure, but substantially less than a man of his popularity might have demanded. This not only assured Gatti of a satisfied star, but put him in an advantageous bargaining position with lesser artists. Toscanini's nature was otherwise. Neither adaptable nor inclined to compromise where artistic standards were at issue, he could not bear with restrictions on the free exercise of his talent when the money was available to assure that freedom.

Already Toscanini had served the first contract of three years, with an extension through the season of 1914. When the break came, it was explained that only the outbreak of war prevented his reappearance. But rumors of his displeasure had been frequent, as had flat statements, from year to year, that each would be his last. Of the multiple factors that influenced his decision—some private, some artistic—the unquestionably overriding one was contributed by Kahn and his associates. Given the conditions that prevailed upon his arrival and for several years thereafter, it is altogether possible that his high standards would have continued to dominate the theater for ten, twenty, even thirty years *longer* than they did. Riverdale, on the fringe of Manhattan, would have been as convenient to the Metropolitan as it later was to Studio 8H in Radio City and to Carnegie Hall.

In common with most conscientious conductors, Toscanini had a violent dislike for the repertory system of opera-giving, in which the effects of rehearsal are dissipated by changes in personnel. When policy dictates such changes, there is rarely time—even if there is money—for fresh rehearsal of such works in midseason. A study of the casts of the revivals and novelties Toscanini conducted between 1908 and 1914 yields clear proof of his preference.

Unlike most other conductors, even the most conscientious, Toscanini made his dislike operative not by fretting or "making do," but merely by giving up the thing he disliked. Having failed in his efforts to make Gatti withdraw with him—arguing that a joint action would assure them all they asked—he departed alone, and saw little of his old friend for seventeen years thereafter. Gatti's creed, often quoted, was Verdi's dictum: "The theater was not built to be empty." Toscanini's *idée fixe,* if never articulated in words, was that, empty or full, the theater, like the concert hall, is the place for maximum effort or nothing. The points of view were not reconciled until the emotional occasion of 1932, when Toscanini conducted the Ninth Symphony of Beethoven in Carnegie Hall as a benefit for unemployed musicians, and the two men embraced in a banishment of old disagreements.

Having measured the situation and the men involved, Toscanini was immune to pleas for reconsideration. In *The New York Times* of June 21, 1931 Olin Downes wrote: "Very suddenly, however, the end came and Toscanini was on the wharf. The Metropolitan, as one member of the organization [Kahn] put it, awakening too late to the true situation, followed him there and threw its purse and its pride out of the window. Toscanini was definitely finished, and the wealth of the Indies would not have returned him to the fold."

A fuller statement of the same petition comes from another source. As reproduced by Krehbiel, a cable to Toscanini after his return to Italy read:

Am happy to hear that you are considering Gatti-Casazza's proposition which has my fullest approval not only because it is meant as a public expression of our admiration and gratitude for what the Metropolitan owes to your unique genius, but also because it will give still greater scope and effect and force to your great personality in shaping the artistic development of the Metropolitan. I voice the sentiments of the Board and New York public and myself in expressing sincerest hopes that we may continue to enjoy the inspiration of your splendid art. You may rest assured that anything in my power to make your work here sympathetic and satisfactory to you will be cheerfully done. Kindest regards.

OTTO H. KAHN

The "proposition," it is commonly believed, was accession to all his demands, plus title of Artistic Director. There is no evidence that Toscanini ever replied to the cable.

5

Toscanini's turn to the left at this crossroad was no more drastic than Gatti's to the right, toward financial stability and artistic conservatism. The revision of business methods begun by Gatti was continued with the engagement of Edward Ziegler, formerly of the *Herald* musical staff, as "administrative secretary." The job attracted to it whatever functions in the opera house Ziegler gradually deemed himself qualified to oversee, from negotiating contracts and supervising rehearsal costs to inventing means of supplementing the Metropolitan's income beyond box-office receipts.

Ziegler more than earned his own salary at once by selling the Metropolitan's endorsement of a piano for $15,000. Since phonograph records first had begun to be made in Grau-Conried days, the Metropolitan had derived an income from those made by its members. In 1916 this amounted to $23,000, and it remained close to that level until 1925, when it soared to $50,663. No longer, however, was this wholly from records. Radio had now become a factor in the entertainment world, and the use of Metropolitan stars drove the entry in this column to $98,000 in 1927. The same column was utilized for the income from broadcasts when it began ($173,000) in 1931.

A further source of revenue was the levy on artists' earnings in concert appearances. The custom was of long standing, derived from the period when Grau or Conried actually booked a tour for a Nordica or Caruso. It ended in the early 1930's, when a central plank in the platform on which the American Guild of Musical Artists (AGMA) was founded was elimination of this impost. In the bookkeeping scheme, the income from the sale to a sponsor of rights to the Metropolitan Auditions of the Air eventually took its place.

These points are introduced, not as digressions, but to stress two facts: labor costs were still so low that capacity business or close to it, plus the shrewd utilization of Metropolitan prestige, made for a healthy financial picture. Qualified management, such as Gatti provided, left virtually no financial burden for the stockholders either of the producing company or of the ownership group.

Nevertheless, it was considered sound policy for the management to proclaim the staggering problem of opera-giving at every opportunity, with the implication that only such selfless assistance as was rendered by Kahn and his associates made possible the maintenance of the Metropolitan title to the blue ribbon of the operatic world. A clear statement of this sort was made in 1926, when one of the periodic renewals of Gatti-Casazza's contract prompted an editorial in the *Herald Tribune* (doubtless written by its then music critic, Lawrence Gilman) proposing that it be extended for life. The editorial also suggested that if the current impression of financial well-being was accurate, certain artistic deficiencies could be remedied.

Ziegler's reply stated that the difference between income and expense "shows, and always has shown since Mr. Gatti-Casazza assumed control, a very considerable deficit, the precise amount of the deficit for last season being $226,991. It is only through skillful utilization of sources of revenue other than those which the opera-going public supplies that this deficit has been diminished or covered, or at times somewhat more than covered."

One of the times was the year of the "deficit" quoted, in which, actually, there was a book profit on the year's operation of $35,277. As Gatti's statement elsewhere confirms, the other times were every year from 1910 to 1930.

As well as taking credit for what they did not do to support the opera, the "patrons" were not averse to taking credit for not supporting other ventures in which they were interested. When the Diaghilev Ballet Russe toured the country in 1916, the "educational service" of presenting the great works of the Russian repertory was nationally attributed to Kahn and his associates. The cash loss of $300,000, however, was charged against the books of the opera company. I know: I have seen them. Thus the lights and shadows in the picture of patrons and purposes.

6

With Toscanini gone and the war over, production of opera on an assembly-line system reached its greatest efficiency during the twenties. Though the death of Caruso (1921) and the retirement of Farrar (1922) deprived Gatti of two infinitely serviceable performers, Gigli and Jeritza —also Chaliapin and Galli-Curci—were of sufficient stature to make his program work. Earnings during the 1920's may be tabulated as follows:

1921	$ 48,201
1922	49,141
1923	66,872
1924	53,809
1925	35,277
1926	142,041
1927	144,378

With so steady a rise of income over expenditures, Kahn could well afford a courteous but firm no-thank-you to an offer of aid in 1924 from the then new Juilliard Foundation. In the rising market the Metropolitan kept pace, with longer seasons at higher prices. The twenty-four-week subscription season became an established custom in 1926, and, with all technical problems mastered, Gatti could schedule eight operas in six working days (plus a Sunday-night concert) while manipulating a repertory of forty-eight works. "Coolidge prosperity" being the order of the day, an $8.25 top for Metropolitan seats was the order of the night. It even rose to $8.50 in 1929.

All these trends were centralized in one major manifestation: Kahn's most serious attempt to make a "new" Metropolitan a reality. With the income of his producing group at an all-time high (over $3,000,000 from 1926 to 1929), and the public more evidently interested than ever, Kahn undertook to carry out his promise, first made in 1908 and periodically repeated.

A catalogue of the reasons why the old house was ill suited to its purpose may be found elsewhere (Part II). Press, public, and artists were in agreement from the first *Faust* of 1883 that it was misshapen and badly designed. It served only one function perfectly: display of those who occupied the boxes for which it was built. The decline of the opera as a social function and the equalization of interest among performers, *mise en scène,* and orchestra emphasized anew the failings of the structure. As theaters came and went on adjacent Broadway, air-conditioning became a commonplace and movie audiences reveled in luxuries denied lovers of Verdi, Wagner, or Strauss, the static situation of the Metropolitan marked its lack of modern stage and lighting resources as a community disgrace.

While boom-time economy prevailed, the penalties were vitally but exclusively artistic. Lurking in the background were days to come when labor would demand higher rates to offset the effects of mechanization. It was the dreary fate of the Metropolitan not to profit from mechanization, but still have to pay the vastly increased rates imposed by intractable unions. Lacking space for storage of scenery, it had to meet charges for off-premises warehousing, plus staggering costs for trucking, as these elements, too, followed a national pattern of reward to unskilled labor. Between the Scylla and Charybdis of taking in and taking out, hundreds of thousands of hard-earned dollars were churned into the dirt and grime of the "strait of Messina" where this endless process went on, day and night.

Had Kahn's lead been followed, at least this aspect of the Metropolitan's plight would have been eliminated for generations to come. He first set forth the proposition that a new house was a "necessity" in 1924, affirming this position in a pamphlet distributed to subscribers at the season's end. Two major problems had to be resolved before serious thoughts of removal could be entertained: agreement on a site for the new building and adoption of a *modus operandi* for liquidating the existing holdings and directing to new construction the funds thus realized. Delicate problems of timing were involved to prevent a lag between the date of leaving the old theater and that of entering the new.

The behind-scenes activity was noted in the press of November 1925. An offer of seven million dollars had been made for the old site, but the Opera and Real Estate Company was holding out for ten. The new theater, it was rumored, might be on Seventy-second Street, facing Central Park (both Fifth Avenue and Central Park West were mentioned), or on Fifty-seventh Street between Eighth and Ninth Avenues. The usual denials (December) were followed by the usual confirmation (January) that Kahn had assembled the required space in the Fifty-seventh Street area and that the Metropolitan Life Insurance Company had underwritten a loan of $1,900,000 for the purchase.

Rather than welcoming the news, one powerful faction in the ownership company remained aloof, not to say hostile. It was a faction sufficiently powerful to make its will the will of the majority and to authorize a statement that for snobbishness and stubborn defense of entrenched authority can serve as a model in bad manners:

If the music lovers of New York want a new opera house they are entitled to have one and the trustees of the present property will certainly not oppose any obstacle or competition to such a project. They are not, however, of the opinion that the present house is antiquated or that its site is undesirable. It is producing opera more superbly than anywhere else in the world. The acoustic properties of its auditorium are unsurpassed. . . .

No doubt several of its characteristics could be improved and its superiority to other similar institutions still further enhanced. If it is desirable that the building should be replaced by one larger and more scientifically equipped, I presume the company of which Mr. Kahn is the chairman will undertake the project.

Fulton Cutting,
Chairman of the Board of Directors
Metropolitan Opera and Real Estate Company

The plain implication was that Kahn as a dilettante in the production of opera could be tolerated; Kahn as the leader in a social hegira would not be (see page 21). No doubt Kahn, with his long indoctrination in the politics of the institution, had expected such a rebuff. At any rate, he went ahead with plans to interest younger members of the box-holding faction. The substance of his plan, when fully revealed, was epoch-making for the Metropolitan. Owned boxes would be abolished. Instead, the single tier to be included in the new house would be leased to a list of eligibles totaling one hundred and fifty, the list to be composed by consultation between the Cutting and Kahn groups.

By January 1926 Kahn could claim a substantial group of recruits to his general proposal. Vincent Astor, Edward S. Harkness, Robert L. Gerry, E. Roland Harriman, and Frederic Potts Moore were added to the board of the producing company. All but Moore were box-holders or related to box-holders. The hopeful attitude was that the house could be completed by January 1928.

Nothing consequential occurred for more than a year. The development, when it came, was important enough to justify the time of negotiation involved. In February 1927 Kahn stated that the board of directors of the Opera and Real Estate Company had accepted the substance of his plan. The details, however, diverged greatly from his in one crucial respect: the box-holders would still form an ownership group. They would have undisputed sway on Monday nights and either Thursday evenings or Saturday afternoons. For other performances the boxes would be available on rental to a group approved by a "box committee."

This scheme would be financed through liquidation of the original property, with each of thirty-five shareholders reinvesting $145,000. (This was substantially below the price at which boxes were selling in the 1920's. See Part II.) The total thus available for construction would be $4,640,000. Other than settling the all-important question of boxes, the statement proposed a theater seating nearly five thousand, with an abundant number of cheaper seats that would all command a good view of the stage—a detail, it was acknowledged, in which "the present auditorium is sadly deficient."

To assure protection of their interests, the box-holders nominated as architect Benjamin Wister Morris, whose works include the Morgan Memorial in Hartford and the annex to the J. Pierpont Morgan Library on Madison Avenue in New York. He would look out for the Morgan interests. Joseph Urban, who designed more than forty Metropolitan productions between 1917 and 1933, was appointed "assistant architect." (His enduring monument is the handsome Ziegfeld Theater on Sixth Avenue.) Good will reached its high point in April 1927, when it was announced that a majority of the Metropolitan stockholders had agreed to turn in their stock and permit the Opera House Committee to proceed.

The liaison, grudgingly accepted, barely survived the summer. By an odd irony, Deems Taylor—who had been handsomely favored by the Metropolitan in the production of two of his operas—was the *deus ex machina*. On a casual visit to Urban's studio, he discovered the architect deep at work on his version of a desirable theater, and asked leave to make his own sketch for reproduction in *Musical America,* of which he was then editor. Its appearance, in the issue of October 8, 1927, though carefully described as in no sense "official," brought an immediate reaction from the Real Estate group. The Morris idea, it was said, was much more severe than the cathedral-like interior projected by Urban. Morris himself promoted further confusion with the words: "There are no plans yet for the new opera house. The site has not yet been selected, and until it is there can be no plans."

Although this plainly contradicted all that Kahn had said, he could do no more than keep his pride in check and work for the object he cherished. When the Opera and Real Estate Company announced on October 1 that J. P. Morgan, Fulton Cutting, Cornelius N. Bliss, Jr., Robert S. Brewster, and De Lancey Kountze had been nominated to find a "suitable" site, Kahn said merely: "Mr. Urban's plans have not received the approval of, and their publication has not been authorized by, either Mr. Morris or the two organizations concerned." He offered no comment on the attitude that Fifty-seventh Street was undesirable because of the near-by elevated railway, which was then scheduled for removal and has long since vanished.

Between October and January the committee was said to be interested in locations at Fifty-ninth Street and Central Park South, 110th Street facing the Park (and presumably backing on Harlem), the old New Theater site on Central Park West, and half a dozen other locations, all purely conversational. In January, Kahn offered to hold his own site available for another month or two, but digressed into a little "background" that just about scuttled the sinking ship. He said that the Fifty-seventh Street site, the plan for the distribution of the boxes, and the scheme for financing had all "been approved last February by the unanimous vote of the boards." The common belief now is that a concerted effort to overthrow that vote, unanimous though it was, was successfully led by Mrs. Cornelius Vanderbilt III through her nephew Robert Goelet (see page 257). At the end of January 1928 Kahn announced that his brokers had put the property on the market.

As a commentary on the question whether a site had been agreed upon or not, one may cite an entry in the Metropolitan's ledger for 1927: "Architect's fees for 57th Street site—$40,000." Eventually the plot was utilized for an apartment development called the Parc Vendome. Kahn's second mortgage of $1,600,000 was a complete loss in a reorganization of the 1930's, and represents his heaviest contribution to opera in New York.

Finally, though the action of the Metropolitan Opera and Real Estate Company had deprived the public of its long-cherished hope, there was no indication that it owed anyone anything, even an explanation. It was left to the salaried secretary Frank Dodd to tell the press in an off-hand way that his employers "objected to the commercial features of Mr. Kahn's scheme." Presumably the reference was to a skyscraper tower that would provide rent-bearing space to lessen the financial burden on the theater's operation. Their own ancestors were hardly so fastidious in 1883 when the corners of the long-standing building were filled in for exactly the same reasons.

7

Conversationally if not concretely the stockholders found the subject of a "new" Metropolitan hard to drop. A focus for the conversation was provided by John D. Rockefeller, Jr. Although not specifically interested in opera, he was sufficiently imbued with community spirit to interest himself in the whole problem. In August 1928 he announced that his brokers had assembled a considerable plot of land between Fifth and

Sixth Avenues, bounded by Forty-ninth and Fiftieth Streets—the earliest form of what became known as Rockefeller Center, or Radio City.

In the *Herald Tribune,* Rockefeller's motivation was explained thus: "The deal was consummated primarily to provide a new location for a new Metropolitan Opera House." Kahn professed to know nothing about the plans. Cutting, however, did. "Everything looks very promising," he said.

How far the realities of the situation had been canvassed one cannot say at this time; but it appears doubtful that they had been very thoroughly explored. For one thing, the Opera and Real Estate Company was looking for a purchaser who would pay $13,000,000 for the Broadway property, whereas current opinion then was that $8,000,000 would be high. Moreover, the Rockefeller plan would have required the box-holders to build a theater and then pay him ground rent—there was no provision for the builders to have their boxes rent free.

Time raced ahead as the opera people looked for a purchaser to pay top dollar for their land, and Rockefeller resorted to legal action to clear out the speakeasies that crowded the area. Eventually October 29, 1929, arrived, the bottom dropped out of the real-estate market, and the value of the Broadway property declined sharply. Not even the addition to the board of directors of Ivy Lee (public-relations counselor for the Rockefellers) could reverse the general trend.

Thus passed the moment of opportunity, which had struck not once, but twice. Not until another three decades had produced a renewed cycle of buying and building did the Metropolitan's property regain the value it possessed in 1929. And even then it was only the initiative of another Rockefeller (John D. III) which made the dream a reality (see page 261).

In the elaboration of the Radio City scheme, a place remained earmarked for an opera house, and plans to that end were actually filed on April 8, 1932. It was explained, however, that this was a mere incident in the routine of filling out the original project and signified nothing. A building of fifteen stories was projected, containing an opera house that would seat 4,042 and cost approximately $4,500,000. When the land was eventually utilized, it bore a parking garage—which, at least, probably has no deficit.

When the final words on the Radio City prospects were spoken, they came not from Otto H. Kahn, but from Paul D. Cravath, his lawyer and associate in many cultural ventures, who had succeeded him as chairman of the opera-producing board in October 1931. "I should not feel very disappointed," he said, "if we had to stay on in the old house. It has associations and traditions which attach audiences to it." Not only the man but the ideas had changed: for a prospect of comfort was substituted a continuation of the miserable sight-lines and the side-saddle, neck-craning posture that were the real tradition of the old Metropolitan for those who could not afford expensive seats or were not fortunate enough to secure the small proportion of desirable ones at cheaper rates.

Whatever Cravath's suitability to act as spokesman for the Metropolitan at any time, it was an unquestionable hardship for him to act as its spokesman in a period as difficult and in some ways discreditable as any in its long history. The small loss for the year 1929–30—subscriptions, of course, had been paid for prior to the crash—was but a straw in the wind: $14,743. This left virtually no mark on Gatti's celebrated surplus of $1,000,000, much of it rolled up in the 1920's when the promise of a new theater resulted in cutbacks of normal spending on scenic replacements—with results that were still being felt twenty years later.

The deadly parallel of slipping income and rising losses grew alarming in 1930 and 1931:

	Income	Losses
1930	$2,667,062	$322,231
1931	2,175,911	497,213
1932	1,165,996	339,901

(The 1932 season had been shortened to sixteen weeks, the top ticket price reduced to $7).

By contrast with losses in the era after World War II, when labor costs and non-musical expenses hungrily swallowed the maximum income from capacity business, these losses were caused in large part by severe decline in attendance, coupled with expenditures based on the expectations of boom years. The first steps toward retrenchment were taken early in the 1931–2 season, when Gatti proposed a "voluntary" cut of ten per cent—in the fashion of the time—for all salaried employees. The intent was to save $200,000. None demurred save Beniamino Gigli, the company's leading tenor and heaviest earner at the time. The unionized employees were saved from making a decision by their superiors, who denied the request. For the musicians, the secretary of Local 802, Edward Canavan, declared that a lower wage than the existing minimum of $128 a week would impair the ability of employed musicians to aid unemployed ones.

Although Cravath denied rumors that the company might suspend— "no one could explain how the company could avoid the obligations of its contracts and subscriptions without going into bankruptcy"—the position of Gigli (who had total earnings of $275,000 coming to him over a four-year period) and the unions prompted drastic action. The Metropolitan Opera Company ceased to exist, and the Metropolitan Opera Association took its place.

The magnitude of the calamity that had come upon the institution was not yet realized by directors, artists, or union functionaries. Not a change, but an upheaval impended. It took half a dozen years, at least, for all the factors at work to assert themselves and for the situation to be re-created with some promise of stability. In the meantime it was inevitable that all concerned would seek to preserve some shred of vested interest and act in a way that history might judge, objectively, as rather bad.

In midwinter Gatti informed his company that he had offered to serve without salary if necessary, and added: "In such a critical and decisive moment, it would be petty . . . to raise questions of *contracts and rights*" (italics mine). A generous offer, so it seemed, but hardly in the light of facts now known: that his original salary of $25,000 a year had been raised to $30,000 in 1915, after Toscanini's departure, and remained at that level until 1928, when it was doubled to $60,000, and moved up to $67,057 for the season of 1930–1, in which the company lost $322,231. It remained at $59,169 for 1931 and $57,736 for 1932, but after this "offer" he still drew $43,108 for 1933! Nor was this all the Metropolitan paid to Gatti or his dependents. His second wife, ballerina Rosina Galli, received $224,000 for her services during the period 1921–30.

How much of this was known to Gigli and his lawyer, the late Fiorello H. La Guardia, it is hard to say; more than a little, if opera secrets were then what they are now. In any event, acrimony was intensified when at the season's end Gigli returned his contract, which still had three years to run, and informed the press that his "sincere efforts [to work out a solution] had been met with conditions and impositions which would have diminished my dignity as a man and an artist."

In reply, Gatti exposed a letter dated April 12, signed by all the re-engaged personnel, in which Gigli's conduct was described as "inexcusable" and he was accused of "lack of co-operation and *esprit de corps*." The general belief is that the re-engaged artists were offered a new contract with one hand, the petition with the other, with the understanding that they were to sign both. As Gigli phrased it, the signatures were "not written spontaneously." On a later occasion (Rome, January 1934) he was quoted as saying: "I would have been one of the first to accept a cut of even 30% had I not been told point-blank that . . . the contract, Gatti-Casazza informed me, was 'not worth the paper it was written on.'"

Hard times require hard measures. But they do not require the hard measures to be applauded for their wisdom ($43,000 remains a large sum for an opera manager who had volunteered to serve for nothing) or that those who endorse them be admired as art patrons and social leaders. All the forces of respectability were marshaled behind Gatti in a letter of thanks from the board on May 18:

I wish to express to you my satisfaction as chairman of the board and that of the board of directors of the Metropolitan Opera Association, with the masterly manner in which you have performed this task. . . .

Sincerely yours,

PAUL D. CRAVATH

Chairman

That the structure Gatti and Kahn had so cunningly contrived over a twenty-five-year period was to be cast into the discard by three seasons' adversity was doubtless a tragedy to both of them. Gatti has written that it had been an unpleasant experience for him to learn, in 1908, that "his predecessor had left a deficit." Doubtless it would have been the deepest kind of satisfaction for him to leave the Metropolitan one million dollars richer than when he arrived. That much would have been tangible, whatever the carping of the critics; but it was not to be.

8

In the blessed wisdom of hindsight, it would clearly have been better for the newly formed Metropolitan Opera Association to start afresh with a new general manager as well as a new corporate structure. In electing Franklin D. Roosevelt President in 1932, the people of the United States had not merely "turned the rascals out," as they proverbially do in so-called "bad times." They had given assent to a program of social-economic change which vastly enhanced the bargaining power of labor, in the arts as well as in the factory. In a national picture so small an item as an opera budget is hardly consequential; but if it is the only full-scaled opera we have, it mounts in importance. An opera budget geared to the "free market" days of the 1920's would not bear the strain of newly powerful labor pressure. Something would have to give, and eventually it did in 1935, when $1,000 a performance became the top fee for Metropolitan personnel, and the number of artists in that bracket was sharply limited until the return of "normal" conditions.

Gatti's contract, however, had three seasons to run still, on its latest renewal (presumably it could have been abrogated as were all others, but he was in a position to protect his own interest), and his long career argued for the opportunity to steer the ship to safe waters. Had not he proved his sagacity with profit-making opera? What man could do better?

No one could see that the situation had altered radically, and that it would never again be as it had been.

As Cravath had said on the previous December 15, "bankruptcy . . . was quite out of the question." But the convenient substitute of the time —reorganization—was not. In place of the old Metropolitan Opera Company, with stockholders and, now, empty coffers, the Metropolitan Opera Association was created. It acquired the scenery, costumes, and other effects of the predecessor group for the traditional dollar, while waiving all the Company's obligations, as to Gigli. More important still, as an "educational institution," it was granted exemption from federal amusement taxes. Thus it could make its ticket prices more attractive to a depression-wise public without reducing its own share of the income.

The singers accepted new contracts, well aware they had no alternative. The public accepted the new company placidly, if it was at all aware that a change had occurred. (Actually, public and press continued to refer to the Metropolitan Opera "Company" long after it had ceased to exist.) One who did not accept the change without speaking his mind was Artur Bodanzky. On his arrival from Europe, the press informed him that opera enterprises in Philadelphia and Chicago had closed down for lack of financial backing. "That is not like your real Americans," said Bodanzky, "but it is decidedly like those who use opera for their own social ends. Gentlemen, upon my word, I had no intention of discussing the finances of the Metropolitan. But you have brought it up, so perhaps it is just as well. I say it was the artists who saved this distinctly great American institution from going to the wall. The bankers and the backers —why, they quit!"

Bodanzky intimated that there was a "plan afoot" to take the Metropolitan out of the hands of the "wealthy few" and put it in the hands of the "appreciative public." He suggested that the reporters take it up with Ziegler and Gatti. Nothing further was available from those sources. Possibly Bodanzky visualized some such development as occurred in 1940, when the box-holders relinquished their holdings for a price. If so, he did not live to see its realization.

Despite the lowered prices and the shortened season, the stretches of empty seats at almost every performance argued dire things when the returns for the year would come in. There were rumors that the company would give up the old, uneconomic house and move to the Center Theater (the "small" house in the Rockefeller development, replaced by offices in 1954–5). The rumors implied that backers not welcomed in the old home would pay the bills in the new one. Nothing ever came of these suppositions, for perhaps the simplest of reasons. The Center Theater had a handsome auditorium and fine lighting facilities, but it was even less suitable, backstage, for a repertory opera company, with its need for scenic elbow-room, than the old Metropolitan. Finally, it backed directly on Forty-eighth Street, and enlargement of its facilities was impossible. In 1950 it found a destiny, temporarily, as a home for elaborate TV productions, before being replaced.

The decision finally taken by the Metropolitan Opera Association was historic, for it charted the course regularly taken thereafter when costs exceeded income—that is to say, almost annually for the next twenty years. In substance, it followed the format of the Cutting letter to Kahn (if a new opera house is desirable, presumably you will build it), with the difference that it now read: if continued production of opera is desirable, presumably the public will pay for it.

There can be no objection to this as a principle. There can be objection to it, as there was, when the boxes still remained the property of a privileged few, and the conduct of the institution remained in the hands of those who did little to deserve their positions of prominence. The first situation was amended in 1940, but it is not too harsh to say that the second still persists.

Cravath's communication to Cutting (February 10, 1933) dripped with self-justifications that there is no present need to repeat. In a typical pattern of evasion, it mentioned the $1,000,000 surplus amassed by Gatti and confounded reason by proclaiming this was done "without profit to the stockholders, who never received a dollar in dividends." (The Company was organized on that basis!) To meet the losses of the 1932–3 season—$150,000—a "guaranty fund of $150,000 was subscribed by various directors of your company and ours and by other patrons of opera." To judge from the inclusive description, the per capita contribution could not have been very large. It stands as the only spontaneous contribution by the so-called "backers" in a quarter of a century.

Cravath might have mentioned, but did not, the example of Chicago, where Harold F. McCormick underwrote the single season of 1921–2, directed by Mary Garden, at a cost of $1,100,000. Or the Chicago deficit of $450,000 met by a group of underwriters in 1928, *before* the depression. Or the construction, during this same decade, of the modern theater on Wacker Drive. All of this did not result, at once, in the establishment of opera on a durable basis in Chicago, but it left memories of results in quality rarely matched at the Metropolitan.

An unfortunate consequence of the propaganda thus spread was the public impression that the operations of the Metropolitan should, somehow, be profit-making—unlike those of any other first-class opera in the world. If the directors did not siphon dividends from it in good days, that was proof of their greatheartedness. If the management piled up a surplus, that was proof of its success. The fact, of course, is that both premises were false.

What is "good opera"? It is not a static quality, like a peck of potatoes or a loaf of bread. It is always and ever susceptible to improvement, and that improvement—in our unionized, mercantile civilization—can be accomplished only by spending money: money for rehearsals, money for scenery, money for better artists. Yes, and money for decent, workable, livable surroundings. The widely acclaimed foresight by which Gatti accumulated his $1,000,000 did enable opera to go along two years longer in losing years; but it also left an inheritance of shabby scenery and outmoded facilities which remained a staggering handicap for many times two years.

Cutting's answer to the Cravath letter was to propose a committee of box-holders—Bliss, Brewster, Myron C. Taylor, and himself—to meet with a group of Association board members and three senior artists: Lucrezia Bori, Edward Johnson, and Lawrence Tibbett. Together the groups comprised a "Committee for Saving Metropolitan Opera."

With Edward Johnson as the first speaker, and a pledge to "reduce expenditures to the lowest possible point consistent with the high artistic standards which have always prevailed at the Metropolitan," the campaign began with a radio broadcast on February 25, 1933. Present and past members of the company (including the long-retired Geraldine Farrar) spoke at some intermission of every performance for the remainder of the season.

One consequence of rather far-reaching importance which resulted from this campaign was the reminder that A. D. Juilliard, wealthy textile manufacturer and a box-holder for many years, had left a sizable fortune in 1919 to be used for musical philanthropy. A first proviso of his will was: "To aid by gift or part of such income at such times and to such extent and in such amounts as the trustees of such foundations may in their discretion deem proper, the Metropolitan Opera Company . . . providing that suitable arrangements can be made with such company so that such gifts shall in no way inure to its monetary profit."

As previously noted (page 17), the trustees had fulfilled Juilliard's desires by making an offer of aid in 1924, which Kahn refused. Thereafter they devoted virtually all of the $13,000,000 realized from the liquidation of Juilliard's assets to the creation of the Juilliard School of Music, with its manifold investments in property, buildings, teaching facilities, and so on.

The "reminder" was set forth in a letter to *The New York Times* on March 1 by William Mattheus Sullivan, a lawyer acquainted with Juilliard and his interest in opera. Almost immediately John Erskine, then president of the Foundation, affirmed the intention of himself and his associates to "see the Metropolitan through," though he denied that the Sullivan letter had any part in this decision. Eventually it developed that the gift was only $50,000, that the public campaign must continue on its hortatory way. With the aid of benefit performances, a ball in a Second Empire setting, and a gift of $25,000 from the Carnegie Corporation, the sum was raised by mid-April.

Some recommendations accompanied the Juilliard donation—more American singers were to be engaged; a supplementary season of *opéra-comique* was proposed; Juilliard students were to be admitted to rehearsals —but these could scarcely become operative while the old hands guided the theater in the old way. For example, it did not become known until several years later (*The New York Times,* June 16, 1935) that the Company's leading conductor of the Italian repertory, Tullio Serafin, received $58,000 in salary during the first of Gatti's losing years. After successive reductions, mutually agreed upon, he received $34,000 for the season of 1933–4. In both instances—though Serafin did not bother to mention this—he was paid at a rate of $2,425 a week: for by 1933–4 the work period had shrunk to fourteen weeks.

Whether a disproportionate payment to a single artist of $34,000—one tenth of the sum required to finance an entire season—was consistent with a pledge to "reduce expenditures to the lowest possible point" may be doubted. But it indicates the kind of earnings that had burgeoned at the Metropolitan during the 1920's, and the magnitude of the task that confronted Herbert Witherspoon and then Edward Johnson, when Gatti retired.

One more campaign for funds was necessary before Gatti's contract expired, for the 1933–4 season used up $317,582 of the Company's resources. It was not conducted on a scale similar to that of the first, for the Philharmonic-Symphony Society was engaged in a campaign for a million-dollar subsidy, and the New York public—on which both institutions depended primarily—could scarcely support two such competing ventures. The campaign was conducted largely in the opera house and by private solicitation among members of the boards and their friends. An all-star vaudeville show—called a "Surprise Party"—helped, and there was another ball, this time in a Louis XIV setting. The Juilliard Foundation again contributed, this time $40,000. Presumably about $250,000 was raised, though no figure was published: the last Gatti season lost

$230,538, in any case. This brought the cost of opera over income to $1,705,465 during the final five years of his direction.

While these losses, caused in some degree at least by the antiquated working conditions of the theater, were being made good by the public, another sizable sum was poured into the bottomless pit at Thirty-ninth Street and Broadway to perpetuate its costly existence. A routine investigation of the building in the spring of 1934 drew an adverse report on the electrical wiring of the stage area. It was as it had been since 1903, but the recent transfer of supervisory functions from the Fire Department to the Superintendent of Buildings had invoked the judgment of electrical engineers. Their standards were different from those of the Fire Department members.

At an expense of $1,500,000, in those prewar days, the Opera and Real Estate Company could have underwritten a thoroughgoing modernization of stage and auditorium, thus making amends for the neglect of thirty years. But a compromise was decreed. The all-important air-conditioning system, which would have made the theater usable twelve months in the year, was deemed too expensive. (The construction of the theater has to be considered in this connection: its walls actually bore a heavy part of the support of the superstructure, and thus were massively thick. Burrowing through them to install the ducts for a conditioning system would, in fact, have been uncommonly expensive.)

For the summer of 1934 attention was concentrated on the urgently needed electrical work, including a new switchboard. A new curtain was installed, and the front, only, of the building sandblasted. The Seventh Avenue façade remained, to the end, as dirty as it had been for fifty years. In the summer of 1935 an air-*circulating* system—which merely substituted street air of nature's own temperature for the murk of the auditorium— was installed. These half measures were accomplished at no cost to the box-holders. It was no problem to raise $600,000 by a mortgage on the building, which had been unencumbered for sixteen years. Surprisingly, it had never occurred to anyone to do this rather than appeal to the public for money when opera-giving was in jeopardy.

9

The imminent departure of Gatti as his last season began in 1934, and the probability that a successor could be induced to take a more flexible part in amending the long-standing patterns of operation, led at this time to new activity aimed at finding a long-range solution to the problems that had cost the Metropolitan over one million dollars in losses during the years from 1930 to 1935. To be sure, national recovery was prerequisite to the success of any plan, but the business brains involved with the arts had begun to doubt that the lush days of the 1920's would return. Steady tax rises were already making clear the decline of private philanthropies on the large scale of old, and labor had not yet begun to play the cards in its hands.

Mention has been made of the financial problems that faced the New York Philharmonic-Symphony Orchestra in this period. Beyond the deficits incurred in its normal plan of operation, there was the harrowing threat, periodically renewed, that Carnegie Hall—of which it was the steadiest user of space—might be sold for more profitable construction on its site or converted into a film theater. It was a mere matter of time before a scheme emerged to consolidate New York's two principal music-making activities under a single roof, with financial savings to both.

Bruno Walter, arriving in the fall of 1934 to begin a series of guest engagements, bravely declared that the largest city in the world could and should support the two institutions independently. But enough sentiment for the merger existed for an emissary to be sent abroad to sound out Arturo Toscanini, who held a power of decision as the Philharmonic's musical director since his return to New York in 1925. When Bruno Zirato, assistant manager of the orchestra, had laid the plan before the Maestro and reported back to New York on December 12, 1934, this road of escape was closed. Toscanini cited, first, the unfavorable acoustics of the Metropolitan for symphony concerts; second, his belief that the smaller repertory necessary under the changed system would not satisfy the New York public; third, his fear that Philharmonic standards would suffer.

The first of these was a physical fact hard to disregard; the second a mere opinion (later proved wrong, first by Johnson, more radically by Bing); the third only a speculation. Thus the one fixed question was: under which roof could the plan be carried out? Because the Metropolitan's was the only one available, it could not be carried out. Speaking for his father, Walter Toscanini told the *Times:* "My father does not think the merger will work because the Metropolitan is too old a theater. They should have a new Metropolitan. Father advised this some time ago." Those who later taxed Johnson for not inducing Toscanini to conduct some gala or other at the Metropolitan must have forgotten the succeeding words: "It is absolutely to be excluded that my father would ever resume direction in the Metropolitan."

Nothing further was done. That only an undesirable setting was available remained a liability of the desirable features of the plan. Sober thought must be, however, that a modern Music Center to house both activities would be the ideal solution for the problems of each. Thus the eventual creation of Lincoln Center was inherent in the problem.

Along a line of commercial reasoning, the firm known as Trade Ways, Inc., was retained to survey the Metropolitan's books and determine which operas were most popular and what length of season was most advantageous. That both might be gravely influenced by who sang what or in what style the operas were conducted was apparently not considered material.

In the end it was the Juilliard Foundation that took a responsible view of the situation, this time providing more than token aid. The negotiations resulted not only in the appointment of Herbert Witherspoon, a recent member of the Juilliard faculty, as Gatti's successor, but also in the establishment of some philosophic principles that strongly influenced the Metropolitan for years to come. The conditions under which the aid was forthcoming are worth examining in some detail.

After restating at length the circumstances that had brought the members of the Metropolitan board to solicit assistance, and the prior commitments that made such assistance difficult to provide, the lengthy statement of March 7, 1935 set forth the preconditions on which aid would be provided:

A budget that would have "every promise of operating without a deficit."
A substantial increase in subscription sales.
Increased opportunity for young American talents, particularly through the device of a supplementary season at modest prices ($3 was suggested as the price for the most expensive seats).

The financial aid provided by the Juilliard Foundation was $150,000, toward a total fund of $250,000. Its aid would be contingent on an increase of at least ten per cent in the subscription sale for the 1935–6 season. Costs of both the regular and the supplemental season would be prorated against the separate contributions.

As further protection for its interests, the Juilliard Foundation requested the addition to the Metropolitan's board of directors of John Erskine, president of the Juilliard School, Ernest Hutcheson, its dean, and two of its trustees: John M. Perry and Felix Warburg. As Witherspoon's associates in conducting the Metropolitan, the two groups agreed that Edward Ziegler should continue his long-standing functions, and that Edward Johnson should organize and direct the supplemental season.

Little time remained for Witherspoon to work out details of his first season, and he devoted himself to it tirelessly. On the eve of leaving for

Europe, he collapsed in the manager's office of a heart attack on May 10 and died almost immediately. In this wise Edward Johnson was elevated to the position he held for the next fifteen years.

Among the devices called into being to carry out the Juilliard stipulations was an Opera Management Committee, with John Erskine as chairman and Lucrezia Bori, Cornelius Bliss, and Allen Wardwell (lawyer for the Foundation) as co-members with Johnson. Its functions were absorbed by the Metropolitan's board of directors within a few seasons, but another group organized at the time still endures and steadily grows more influential.

This was The Metropolitan Opera Guild, organized in August to stimulate subscription sales and attendance generally. Mrs. August Belmont was its chairman, a post she held till 1942. Her fellow officers were Mrs. Myron C. Taylor, Mrs. Herbert Witherspoon, and Harvey D. Gibson. The two thousand members of its first year have increased thirty fold, with all the states of the Union now represented. Along with promoting interest in the Metropolitan among the younger element of New York's population, the Guild has done much useful work in raising funds during several campaigns, underwriting the restaging of the *Ring* cycle in 1947 and of many other new productions thereafter.

As a mental review of the Johnson seasons will suggest, much of the thinking represented in the Juilliard stipulations became firm Metropolitan practice. Outstanding, perhaps, if not spelled out, was the revision of fees paid to principal artists, with a top of $1,000 a performance. World conditions permitted the retention of this ceiling until nearly the mid-fifties, when the broadening of European activities after the war and the creation of a higher American financial standard in Chicago compelled an increase in kind (see page 621 note). For the while, however, it made one aspect of the problem manageable.

On the other hand, the supplemental season idea did not work out at all. Artistically (see page 396), the management could find too few "young" singers who could sing acceptably in the big house, whose requirements are as formidable in May as in January. Moreover, the capricious spring climate of New York—it may often be as sultry as November or as chilly as June—was a sorry liability. The air-circulating system made little difference, though a pipe line to the air-conditioned lobby of the Roxy Theater would have. After two seasons' trial the efforts were abandoned. Opera at the City Center was eventually evolved on a sounder foundation (European and American artists plus air-conditioning in a more compact auditorium) to fill the need clearly visualized in the Juilliard proposals.

10

The downward trend of receipts, which had reached its lowest point in modern history in 1933, made its first significant upward turn in 1935–6. Incomes for the two final Gatti seasons were virtually equal—$1,085,036 in 1933–4 and $1,090,970 in 1934—but a trend for the better emerged in 1935, when the income was $1,231,333. This increase of about $140,000 comfortably surpassed the condition of the Juilliard contribution, both in subscription sales and in single tickets.

Thereafter the gain was steady for five years:

> 1936—$1,437,385
> 1937—$1,645,329
> 1938—$1,780,704
> 1939—$1,780,861
> 1940—$1,860,511

The impact of the war, blackouts, curtailed rail service, and rationing of gasoline had inevitable effects in 1941 and 1942, with a decline to $1,645,784 in 1941 and a further slip to $1,502,708 in 1942. By then the general acceptance of altered habits of travel and the so-called "war prosperity" gave new stimulation to Metropolitan attendance. The new trend was as follows:

> 1943—$1,805,530
> 1944—$1,911,655
> 1945—$2,251,069

There can be little doubt that the five-year period 1935–40 was a crucial one in Metropolitan affairs. Without the upward trend of income, indicating a slow revival of more general interest in the company, it is possible that the *Operndämmerung* would have finally come. There was a question in 1892 whether a home for opera on the Metropolitan scale could be maintained after the fire. The question of 1940 was whether a home for opera could be maintained at all. Having showed that it did not propose to let opera die, the long-suffering public was given another chance to help it meet a crisis.

Succinctly, the Metropolitan Opera and Real Estate Company succumbed to the inevitable cycle of death and taxes. It had endured beyond the lives of its founders and the interest of their descendants. By 1939 half of the boxes were held by the estates of original investors, who could be neither shamed nor coerced into meeting the obligations that went with the privileges. On July 19 it became the unhappy responsibility of Robert Brewster, president of the box-holding group—as the minds of most persons were absorbed with the Sudetenland and when Hitler would march into Danzig—to inform the Opera Association: "Certain stockholders have refused to pay the assessment levied on their shares, and in spite of repeated requests have persisted in this refusal." What this meant, merely, was that the company lacked funds to pay its taxes, though it represented the wealthiest—or at least the most exclusive—segment of New York society.

Brewster acknowledged that the income from the annual assessment ($4,500 per box) and that from the rent-bearing properties in the building were together sufficient for taxes, interest on the mortgage, and other costs of maintenance. There was no outwardly induced crisis. The crisis was internal and could have been resolved by the simple device of reorganization. The possibility that the remiss minority might be succeeded by other persons was covered by Brewster with the single statement: "The only recourse of the company is the sale of such shares, for which at present there appears to be no market." The immemorial clannishness of the box-holders (see page 68) leaves little doubt that possible purchasers were limited to those who had already withdrawn their trade.

No doubt all the arrangements proposed by Bliss in his public reply had already been rehearsed *in camera:* the opera-producing company would take an option for purchase of the building with a deposit of $100. It would agree to provide by the following May 31 (1940) a total of $1,970,000 (the old, magic figure of original construction), $500,000 to be paid in cash, the mortgage of $470,000 outstanding from the renovations of 1934-5 to be assumed by the Association, and bonds to the amount of $1,000,000 to be issued for the rest of the sum.

Beyond the $100 deposit, Bliss surmised that the funds "in a substantial amount" would "probably involve a public appeal." Although the advantage to the public of retaining in existence a house long deemed uneconomic was dubious, the initiative for a clean break was lacking. "Fix it up, wear it out, make it do," was a war slogan that might have originated at the Metropolitan.

The graceful and public-spirited thing, of course, would have been for the box-holders—very few of whom had personally invested in the stock held in their names by inheritance—to have counterproposed liquidation at a far more nominal amount, to earn some measure of gratitude from the public that had paid the upkeep of their social setting for so long. The reverse, rather, happened, with one group of "patrons" banded into a dissident faction that disapproved this settlement and demanded a more favorable one.

This became public knowledge in January 1940, when the Bliss proposal was accepted by 68½ per cent of voting shares, a bare few points more than required for such a decision. The decision had been delayed, according to the *Herald Tribune* of December 10, 1939, because the minority had threatened court action to make "the value of the property" the condition of sale, and the majority had hoped to persuade them otherwise. The dissenters were identified as Robert Goelet, Frazier Jelke, Mary W. Harriman, and Forsyth Wickes, and representatives for the estates of James B. and Henry Clews (co-owners of No. 12), Georgine Iselin, Elbridge T. Gerry, and Mrs. Arthur Little. As may be noted elsewhere, Miss Iselin frequently made a profit by subletting her box in good years (page 66), and Goelet had been an active opponent of the Kahn plan for a new house. Jelke had some justice on his side, for he had paid $200,000 for the Harold Vanderbilt box in 1926, and thus had enjoyed relatively short return on his investment.

The position of the dissenters was that the assessed valuation of building and land was $5,000,000, that a sale on the open market would yield a much larger return than the less than $2,000,000 proposed by the Association. Plainly they had no interest in the continuance of opera in New York. They were interested only in a liquidation at the highest possible price, whether the money was provided by the public or by a real-estate speculator. Their suit was eventually carried to the Appellate Division (May 1942), where the appraisers appointed by the Supreme Court presented a majority opinion that $75 a share—*less* than the amount provided in the sale contract—was a fair valuation. Jelke's attorney, Harold B. O'Neill, contended that the minority report of the third appraiser ($202.61 a share) should be granted, because the assenting stockholders had received $144 a share for their stock—$47 in cash, the rest in four per cent bonds. The court was not impressed.

Although the purchase itself required only $500,000 in cash, it was decided to make a campaign for twice that amount. It was patiently explained by George A. Sloan, who conducted the campaign, that the future of the enterprise had to be assured when title was taken to the building. In addition to this requirement for operating capital, plans called for replacement of the no longer salable grand-tier boxes with several hundred individual seats, installation of more comfortable chairs in the balcony, some badly needed building repairs, and improvement of the backstage sanitary facilities, which for fifty years had been the despair of stars and supers.

A vast force of public opinion was harnessed to raise the necessary amount. It was not promised that another appeal for funds would never be necessary, but it was implied that purchase of the house would put the Association on "a sound financial basis." (Black figures finally appeared in the books in 1944, but the accountants have bought considerably more red ink than black since then.) With the Guild and AGMA co-operating, ten governors serving on a committee of 175 civic and educational leaders, of which Fiorello H. La Guardia was chairman, and fifteen foundations making contributions, it was nevertheless the radio audience that provided the largest sum from a single source when the results of the campaign were tabulated in May: $327,000. Something less than the equivalent of four box-holders returned the sale price of their holdings to the Association, in a contribution of $144,400. Other important categories were identified as follows:

Fifteen foundations	$149,482	(Juilliard, $70,000
		Carnegie, $50,000)
Business and financial concerns	$143,517	
Opera subscribers	$ 86,000	
Directors of the Association	$ 70,621	
Out-of-town opera groups	$ 61,186	
Artists, management, and employees . . .	$ 36,496	
Metropolitan Opera Club members	$ 20,429	
Labor and theatrical groups	$ 6,745	
Grand total	$1,042,000	

When the title of the area designated on the real-estate map of New York City as Block 815 passed to the Metropolitan Opera Association on June 28, 1940, a full cycle had been completed. The property had been bought and the building erected by a group that desired to provide a home for opera, but had no interest in the production of it. Fifty-seven years later, after a slow but perceptible progression, it passed to the control of a group interested in the production of opera, but not particularly interested in owning the home for it—save as ownership became a necessary protection of its primary interests.

It was the completion of an evolutionary process that the house should be owned by those who operate it, for there was no longer any valid social cachet attached to the audience side of the theater. Those "who own it" were, in fact, the people of the state of New York. The theater, under its charter, could not be sold save to provide for the continuance of operation elsewhere, and any funds realized from a liquidation and not needed for payment of outstanding debts would revert to the Secretary of the State of New York. In such circumstances, those who make its command decisions and hire the employees to carry them out are in no sense patrons of the arts: it is the public that must be pleased, the unions that must be reckoned with. Even the press must be heeded. For the present Association to utter such stiff-necked statements as a Cutting could issue with impunity or a Cravath without it would make it not merely offensive but ridiculous as well. Thus the "cancellation" of 1961, when rescinded under pressure from Washington, marked the final frustration of such pretensions.

II

The circumstances that decreed that the Opera Association should own its own home have also encumbered it with certain notable disadvantages. For the inconvenience of being a tenant it had substituted the inconvenience of being a landlord. There were problems to be solved, changes to be made before the latent gains became actualities; then new problems to be solved when the financial easement gained by temporary measures was subject to new pressures.

The hope, for example, that the change in status of the ownership would result in immediate relief from real-estate taxes was ill-founded. When such a bill was passed by the New York State Legislature in 1941, it was vetoed by Governor Herbert Lehman at the behest of Mayor Fiorello La Guardia, who had his philosophical reasons for deciding that it would establish "a vicious precedent." The bill was eventually signed into law by Governor Thomas Dewey in April 1943. He asserted that "a matter so vital to the culture of this state, the nation and the world, transcends home rule"—the principle that La Guardia had invoked.

Before the relief became operative, the Metropolitan was forced to meet several years' tax bills, cutting heavily into the money earmarked for operating capital after the sale. Also the decline of attendance in the first years of American participation in the war upset calculations. Hence another public appeal was decreed in 1943–4, from which $316,793 was collected.

The resumption of touring at the war's end and the exemption from real-estate taxes, together with a high level of attendance, enabled the Metropolitan to conduct its affairs without loss through the season of 1946–7—but without new productions to replace those which had been through the mill of twenty and thirty years' use. Affairs took an ugly turn again in 1947–8, with a net deficit of $233,357 despite an increase of $195,000 in income over the previous season's.

The significant fact was that the Metropolitan had in this year achieved a $3,000,000 income for the first time in twenty years. In 1928 an income of $3,111,805 during a season of twenty-four weeks (plus a brief tour) permitted a credit balance of $90,937, as well as the mounting of four works never given at the Metropolitan before, and a new *Manon* (not replaced until 1963). In 1947–8 an income slightly larger (produced in part by a lengthy tour) resulted in a loss of $233,357—a spread of $320,000. The clear inference was that restoring the income to what it was in the best of boom times would not offset the multitudinous ways in which the production of opera had become more expensive, even without the sums paid to such stars as Jeritza, Chaliapin, Gigli, and Serafin.

Some of this deficit—about $50,000—was attributed to miscalculation on the cost of Lee Simonson's *Ring* productions. The Guild had raised $149,245 for the purpose, but the cost was closer to $200,000. A heavy rehearsal schedule for the Wagner works and Benjamin Britten's *Peter Grimes* also was costly. And the unions, which had settled for periodic small increases during the war years, were clamoring for certain guarantees they had waived during a period of great labor progress in other fields: social-security protection and state unemployment insurance as specifics, with a pension system as a desirable, if more remote, possibility.

As late as August 24, 1948, there was no agreement on a contract to cover the 1948–9 season; it had, in fact, been written off by the Association's board of directors. Eventually pressure of public and press compelled a compromise, by which the Association promised to provide the desired benefits as soon as possible and the unions agreed to hold wages at the high level of 1946. It became Rudolf Bing's problem to settle in the spring of 1950, at an immediate cost of $60,000, and an annual addition to the budget of close to $100,000. In return for adjustment in the size of the chorus and concessions on some desired replacements, a wage increase was granted to this group at about the same time.

In the closing year of Edward Johnson's direction, a semi-public appeal was conducted by the Opera Guild to raise $250,000 for several new productions to embellish his last weeks. Most of the amount was consumed in the production of Mussorgsky's *Khovanshchina* and Puccini's *Manon Lescaut,* plus the touching up of several works taken from the warehouse. Meanwhile agitation had been instituted for a bill to relieve the Metropolitan of the amusement tax levied in wartime and still in force as of 1950. With its performances in New York and on the road yielding over $3,000,000, relief of the ten per cent tax would enable the company to retain over $300,000 paid annually in federal taxes. Just as passage of the bill seemed assured in June 1950, the outbreak of the Korean War changed the whole national taxation problem, and Metropolitan relief was forgotten. Not until the fall of 1951 was the subject given sympathetic consideration. In the meantime pressing budgetary problems and the prospect of future ones made another appeal for funds mandatory in the spring of 1951, this time for $750,000.

Among the gratifying signs of public accountability the Association has given in recent years are its annual financial statements. Instituted in 1944, they have provided the interested portion of the public with a clarifying insight into the operations, the problems, and the peculiar difficulties that confront the Metropolitan. Embellished though they are with such self-flattering phrases as "one of the great opera houses of the world," "a bulwark of culture in an uncertain world," "opera of Metropolitan quality"—as though that quality had any consistency from day to day—they talk, at least, of opera and nothing else. In January 1949 Chairman Sloan made history by telling a radio audience—while asking for money for the latest "crisis": "A new opera house with modern technical and storage facilities and a larger seating capacity would undoubtedly contribute to an easier financial picture. Extensive alterations of our present house, both backstage and in the auditorium, plus the installation of air conditioning offer another possibility." Thus the antiquity of the structure was finally given its proper place in the mottled picture.

The flame of hope that a "new" Metropolitan might indeed come into being in the 'fifties flickered fitfully and disappeared like all the others not long afterwards. At the prompting of Robert Moses, Chairman of the Triborough Bridge and Tunnel Authority, the Metropolitan's board was encouraged to believe that a large site at Columbus Circle—running west between Fifth-ninth and Sixtieth streets—could be made available to the Metropolitan as part of condemnation proceedings for a housing project. Word of this was first heard in 1951. The Metropolitan would be required to raise $1,200,000 to pay for the site before the price of construction could be considered. With forty per cent of the amount guaranteed by one anonymous donor (who may well have been Eleanor Belmont), the required amount was nearly assured when word came from Washington in March 1952 that the arrangement did not conform to the law governing housing projects.

However, the area to which Moses had directed attention eventually provided the locale of the Promised Land toward which the Metropolitan's well-wishers had long aspired. Somewhat north and west of Columbus Circle, it took in a many-acred expanse of crumbling brownstones and other antiquated dwellings serving many more than their contemplated quota of residents. The southern boundary was Sixty-first Street, the northern perimeter Sixty-fifth Street, between Amsterdam Avenue on the west and Columbus Avenue on the east. This time, it may be assumed, the requirements of the legislation providing for municipal, state, and federal assistance (under the Urban Renewal program) were studied in advance and the participating elements selected accordingly. To provide the necessary educational adjunct, Fordham University was invited to establish a downtown annex at the south end of the property; eventually, a new Juilliard School was provided at the north end, with the area for reconstruction extended accordingly (to Sixty-sixth Street). The new "Musical Arts Center" (as it was then known) would serve the needs of both the Metropolitan Opera and the New York Philharmonic Orchestra.

However, before this Ancient Mariner of opera houses could conclude its weary life-in-death course across troubled financial waters to the safe harbor of Port Rockefeller, one final link to the past remained to be severed. For a decade and a half after 1423 Broadway and the building upon it had become the property of the Metropolitan Opera Association in 1940 (see page 37), interest continued to be paid on outstanding bonds representing shares acquired from box-holders in the Metropolitan Opera and Real Estate Company. During the 1944 appeal for funds, Sloan stated that such paper to the amount of $755,100 was still outstanding: $400,800 of it held by estates, $354,300 by living individuals. To the question: "Would the gift of these bonds to the Metropolitan Opera Association be welcomed?" Sloan replied: "As welcome as flowers in May."

Initially only four box-holders were public spirited enough to waive both cash and bonds: a few returned the cash and kept the bonds or kept the cash and returned the bonds. As of 1950, the list of those contributing all or part of their bonds included the estate of E. H. Harriman, Myron C. Taylor, Cornelius N. Bliss, Mrs. John T. Pratt, Mrs. Francis P. Garvan, Mrs. Margaret Haggin, Lady V. Gabriel, the heirs of Otto H. Kahn and Arthur Curtiss James, R. V. N. Gambrill, H. E. Manville, Olivia M. Cutting, R. Thornton Wilson, G. Beekman Hoppin, Mrs. H. Havan Wickes, Mrs. Cornelius Vanderbilt, and the Mary Owen Borden Memorial Foundation (the last representing Harriman interests). The phrase "all or in part" was, obviously, as broad as it was vague— Mrs. Vanderbilt for example remitted only $5,000.

When the Bing administration and its new complement of financial officers began to study their financial prospects, the total of bonds outstanding had been reduced to $604,000. Of the quantity held by the Association ($394,000), $130,500 had been acquired in the settlement of the suit by the dissident elements, $264,000 in gifts from the persons listed above. At the customary interest rate of four per cent, this levied on the institution an annual carrying charge of $25,000, which, in the prevailing economy, might very well have been used, year by year, for a modest new production of a one-act opera (*Gianni Schicchi,* say, or one of the "twins"), for sandblasting the Seventh Avenue end of the building, or for underwriting some urgently needed repair.

After five more years, the outstanding amount was reduced to $525,000, but there was little prospect that it would ever go below $400,800 (the amount held by estates, whose trustees were powerless to dispose of "assets," however hypothetical). It was then (1955) determined that in the best interests of the institution, a bank loan secured by the Association's credit should be taken out and the bonds retired.

It could have been coincidence, but probably was not, that this action occurred in the year when discussions looking to the development of a "Musical Arts Center" (see page 41) became public, meaning that they had been private for some time previously. The possibility—which *this time* could be construed as the probability—that a new Metropolitan would finally come into existence naturally gave rise to thoughts of what might be done with the old one. Whatever the direction of these thoughts, it could be taken more readily if all the symbols of ownership—theoretical as well as factual—were concentrated in the hands of those responsible for converting thoughts into decisions. Thus it was desirable to eliminate forever the financial links to the past, even if only by the transfer of interest payments from individuals to a bank. With a first mortgage of $470,000 remaining from the alterations of 1934 (see page 30), this brought the total indebtedness of the Metropolitan to $995,000 as the end of 1955 brought good prospects for an end also to the old cycle of expensive discomfort.

What should happen following the fall of the final curtain on the performance of opera at the Metropolitan and once the building reverted to its status as Block 815 on the Real Estate map of Manhattan Island was productive of far from unanimous opinion. Those who were attached to the old building by ties of sentiment stretching back through decades and generations felt as keenly about an overt act of destruction as they might have felt toward an elderly, ailing relative. But when the question of alternatives was raised, the choices narrowed alarmingly.

To preserve it as a going theater, on behalf of such visiting attractions as ballet, or as the scene for ceremonial celebrations of some suitable state occasions would be to deny every reality of its misbegotten theatrical past.

To maintain it as a museum to past glory after everything related to that glory had been transferred to the scene of present and future history would be a contradiction in terms.

To make a match of utility and sentiment by preserving the *interior* under provisions of the Landmark Commission's function would have been a welcome solution to the double dilemma created by sentiment and reality. A resolution in favor of putting it in the Landmark category was narrowly defeated in November 1965, and the suggestion that a commercial structure be created *around* the old auditorium posed problems of a foundation (the property is surrounded on four sides by traffic-laden streets and two subways pass under it) for which there was no known solution.

Finally, to propose that the city equal its value to the owners as it had in the instance of Carnegie Hall several years before, thus making it a community heritage, overlooked two factors: Carnegie Hall, beautifully designed for its primary purpose, was as qualified to serve that purpose in 1961, when city action saved it from demolition, as it had been at any time in its seventy-year history; the antiquated Metropolitan, with its grave liabilities of construction and even graver liabilities of maintenance, would have required more than three times the outlay for Carnegie Hall.

In the formula finally devised, which provided for lease rather than sale, the opera-going public of New York could take comfort from as close an approach as humanly possible to the time-honored equivalent of the impossible: to eat one's cake and have it too. It would be able to have its new opera house and derive continuing benefit from its investment in the old. Unlike prior schemes for a new Metropolitan, which had required the new construction to be financed from the *sale* of the old, the plan for the "Musical Arts Center" (the name soon became Lincoln Center for the Performing Arts) proposed that construction costs as well as cost of the ground would be provided for in the Metropolitan's participation as a constituent member of the Center.

The important reality of this was that income from the old property could be applied to the creation of an Endowment Fund, an asset that the Metropolitan had never been able to amass in any meaningful size. The income—unlike the sums provided by the Opera Guild, the National Council, the "Voluntary" contributions programs, Corporate Sponsors, etc.— could thus be applied not to meet deficits arising from ordinary operations, but to underwrite activities which *would not have been possible otherwise:* expansion of the repertory, revivals of works with marginal box office potential, productions of contemporary works, etc.

Even this sound program of self-help was not without the share of hazard and threat of pre-emption which seems to hang over any endeavor to increase the means to support opera on the Metropolitan scale. When the formula for the use of the old site was disclosed in March 1961, it provided for a ground lease (ninety-nine years' duration) to Jack D. Weiler, Robert H. Arnow, and Irwin S. Chanin (of New York) and Benjamin Swig (of San Francisco). It was then assumed that the property would be vacated in late 1964 or early 1965, with a yearly fee of $200,000, payable on delivery, to commence at that time). Thereafter, payments would be on a rising scale, as the commercial building to be constructed on the site was completed and rented. The top amount of $600,000 per year would be reached in the fifth decade. It was then made known to the Metropolitan's board of directors that Lincoln Center would "welcome" a substantial contribution from this amount (above and beyond the sums that had been subscribed to its building fund by Metropolitan patrons, including board members, as individuals). How this was made known, how often, and with what degrees of urgency may be left for others to spell out.

Whatever the deprivation caused by the Metropolitan's stolid resistance, Lincoln Center was able to announce in early 1966 that its enterprise had resulted in the raising, in barely more than a decade, of the unprecedented sum of $160,000,000 plus an overage of $4,500,000 (the first estimates of cost had been $75,000,000). Thus, the Metropolitan's nest still contained its jealously guarded golden egg, as yet unhatched, but with every prospect that it would remain intact—at least until birth.

Just what form it would take remained uncertain, however. Stokowski's plea to "save this beautiful house" at the final performance of April 16, 1966 (see page 745), found a responsive echo in the voices of many others, some of whom (such as the two senators from New York and assorted other politicians) were merely rendering lip service, and others of whom (such as choreographer Agnes de Mille) spoke out of conviction and from the heart. Eventually the point of pressure became the State Legislature in Albany, where legislation was introduced to empower the Buildings Commissioner of New York to delay the issuance of a demolition permit for 180 days in order to allow the Old Met Corporation added time in which to raise the $8,000,000 it considered a fair price for the property. It was passed in mid-May by the Senate with hardly a dissenting vote (62 to 2) and by the Assembly on May 16, by the much narrower margin of 89 to 42. The bill stipulated that the Old Met Corporation would have to post $200,000 as security to gain the extension of time. Originally it had agreed to raise $100,000 for this purpose, but when the Metropolitan Opera Association, through Charles M. Spofford, chairman of its executive committee, protested that this was insufficient to indemnify the Association against loss, should the fundraising be unsuccessful, the amount was doubled. It came out, thus, to an amount equal to the first year's rental payment under the agreement with the lessees (see page 44). The legislation became law when Governor Nelson D. Rockefeller signed the bill on June 24.

Just what the law provided, beyond the delay of 180 days, also remained uncertain. Most in dispute was the amount proposed by the Old Met Corporation (which had sprung up barely weeks before the end of the 1965–66 season). It was the Corporation's contention that this amount, advantageously invested, would eventually produce a larger income than was stipulated in the rental arrangement. But it did not stress, as it should have, that the rental arrangement provided for the Opera Association to *retain ownership* of a valuable parcel of land which constituted the closest thing to a tangible asset that it possessed. Under the Old Met Corporation proceedings, title would pass to the non-profit corporation acting under that name. For its part, the Opera Association protested that $8,000,000 was far too little (it would, indeed, have returned the value of the property to the level of 1928—see page 22— when the dollar had considerably greater purchasing power), and argued for at least $12,000,000. Wherever the judgment should finally fall, the Old Met Corporation would have to provide many more millions for renovation of the auditorium, restoration of the rentable portions of the building, and installation of safety precautions long unprovided for. This presumed that a sum of at least $15,000,000 could be raised by public subscription, a formidable program regardless of how many times the 180-day period might be extended.

The first meeting of the board of trustees appointed by Mayor John V. Lindsay to oversee the activities of the Old Met Corporation was called for July 15, 1966.

II

House and Home

THE CIRCUMSTANCES that decreed the creation of the old house have
been amply described (page 3); but their effect on the structure, if
almost to be termed indescribable, cannot be lightly disregarded. As certainly as the pews of a church are ranged in lines ordained by the purpose
of the structure, so the Metropolitan was built around the tiers of boxes
which were its original sin. All attempts to reconcile the structure to changing times were balked by the idea and its execution.

In what seemed to them wisdom, the founding fathers were not to be
convicted of such a parsimony in boxes as caused them to leave the Academy of Music. More than eighty years of use so affected the arrangement of
space in the unchanging interior that many persons did not realize that
there were two full tiers of boxes as late as 1940. Many fewer are aware
that the auditorium was built with a third tier of boxes (soon converted
into the final dress circle). In addition, the area given over to the orchestra
circle and the standing space behind it provided another type of box in the
original design. They were called *baignoires* (from their resemblance to
bathtubs). Some cherished them for the curtains and hangings that
almost hid the occupants from view, but their utility was hardly as
great as their novelty. When the house was rebuilt after the fire of 1892,
they were replaced with seats. In the renovations of 1953, these seats
were replaced by extending the rows of orchestra chairs toward both
walls.

The emphasis on these original details is no mere matter of whimsy.
They were a deeply significant part of the whole space distribution. Because
the balcony and family circle were occupied by persons of inferior status,
those who paid the way for opera could ignore their complaints of poor
visibility. The poor visibility endured, however, long years after any one
group or social caste accepted the responsibility. If the sponsors were aware

at all of the shocking inadequacy of the structure, it was most likely under the circumstances described by Robert Goelet in his memoirs, *The Old Order Changeth,* privately published in 1940: "From the uppermost rows, known as the 'peanut gallery' in common jargon, only about one quarter of the seats had a view of the stage. The writer can vouch for this fact, having had to sit in them on various occasions when he served on committees to see if the situation could not be ameliorated."

It will hardly surprise those acquainted with matters Metropolitan that the plans were originally drawn for another site than the one finally utilized (see page 4). Four firms of architects had been invited to submit plans, and the accepted one of Josiah Cleaveland Cady shows little reworking from the design for the Vanderbilt Avenue site—a square block—for the Broadway site, which was decidedly rectangular (205 feet on Broadway, 197 feet on Seventh Avenue, 284 feet on Thirty-ninth Street, and 229 feet on Fortieth Street).

	Vanderbilt Avenue	*Broadway*
Boxes	674	732
Parquet	800	600
Balcony	580	735
Gallery	1,100	978
Total	3,154	3,045
Stage	70 ft. deep	86 ft. deep
	120 ft. wide	101 ft. wide

In its final season, 1965–6, the totals were:

Boxes		280
Orchestra		1185
Grand Tier		288
Dress Circle		519
Balcony		647
Family Circle		706
	Total	3,625*
Standing Room	(Orchestra)	164
Standing Room	(Family Circle)	60
	Total	224
	Grand Total	3,849

* The total number of seats available for sale was restricted to 3,613 because of the subtraction of eight seats in the General Manager's box and of four orchestra seats reserved for staff use.

Cady's position among New York architects was an illustrious one, and some monuments to his memory remain—the American Museum of Natural History, St. Andrew's Church, the Hudson Street Hospital. But the only one that has the slightest relation to a theater was the Metropolitan; hardly the appropriate qualification for designing the largest venture of the kind undertaken in America to that time.

When the finished structure met with some dissatisfaction, Cady responded rather plaintively in the New York *Tribune* of November 12, 1883: "Probably no other building in the country has received so much care and thought." Hundreds of drawings were made before the final sight-lines were decided upon, though the final result certainly underlined the incompatibility of design and site. Among European theaters studied was Covent Garden; indeed, its plans were made available to Cady by Ernest Gye, its lessor, who had hopes of securing the same rights in New York. Those who have seen the London theater know its similarity to the old Metropolitan.

To invoke such non-American influence was, of course, absurd: the nineteenth-century European houses were built to suit the hierarchy that supported them. Imperial boxes, and others arranged at reasonable distances from the throne, were appropriate enough in theaters that endured through the bounty of one class. It could be contended that the Vanderbilts and Morgans regarded themselves in somewhat the same light; but it is apparent that only the display appealed to them, not the attendant responsibilities.

The insufficiencies of the auditorium were at least the outgrowth of a specific plan, however maladroit; the crippling inadequacy of the backstage area could only be charged to ignorance of theatrical requirements. Most hampering, and ever more costly, was the lack of space to store scenery. Cady imagined that an area below the stage could serve this purpose. This was not only inadequate, but a hazard that had contributed so much to the fire of 1892 that its use thereafter was forbidden.

Because the building stood as an island in a sea of traffic, alterations could be effected in only one direction—up. Periodically, as plans for a new house waxed and waned, there was a revival of sentiment for renovation rather than relocation. This called for demolition of the area from the proscenium to the back wall, and the erection of twin towers—five or six floors each—on either side of the stage. (Construction laws in New York forbade building over a stage.) The lower area on either side would serve as scene docks, with adequate dressing-rooms, rehearsal space, offices, and so forth on the upper floors. In the end, of course, relocation prevailed.

The shortcomings of the Metropolitan for theatrical purposes were not merely a consequence of its age and the vast improvements in designing since its construction. In the first review of a Metropolitan performance ever written by Henry T. Finck, the long-time critic of the New York *Evening Post* said on October 23, 1883: "From an artistic and musical point of view, the large number of boxes . . . is a decided mistake." When the first season ended, Italo Campanini (the company's leading Italian tenor) told a *Times* reporter: "The reason why the performances failed largely of their proper effect is that the house is unfit for music. . . . When Mr. Fabbri [a banker related by marriage to the Vanderbilt family] first spoke to me about plans for the new opera house I suggested that he should examine the new Costanzi Theater at Rome. It cost about $600,000 to build but it is incomparably finer . . . than your Metropolitan. I should advise the directors of the Metropolitan to tear out the inside . . . and re-build. . . . No half measures . . . will do any good." Half measures, how-ever, were the only ones that were ever applied to the problem.

2

The considerations that were to influence eight decades of Metropolitan opera hardly concerned the audience that gathered for the opening *Faust* on October 22, 1883. The choice of opera was doubtless a compliment to the company's prima donna, Christine Nilsson (she had been the first Marguerite at the Paris Opéra); it also suited the occasion, though some critics deemed it "old-fashioned." During the long intermissions of a per-formance that began, a half hour late, at 7:15 and lasted until 12:45, the audience had ample opportunity to marvel at the magnificent gas chan-delier, to admire the murals of Francis Lathrop and Francis Maynard, to study the interior decorations of E. P. Tredwill. Many in the theater brought along the day's papers, in which diagrams were published docu-menting the two tiers of stockholders' boxes. The custom of publishing such pertinent data in the house program was not begun until 1886.

Much was made of the simultaneous opening of the Academy of Music season with Etelka Gerster in *La Sonnambula*. In place of the "monop-olists" (as the New York *Dramatic Mirror* described the Metropolitan box-holders), the Academy audience included Astors, Belmonts, Cuttings, Bayards, Beekmans, and Schuylers, the proudest of Knickerbocker aristoc-racy. Dr. Leopold Damrosch and Theodore Thomas, New York's most prominent resident musicians, were faithful to the established order. Maple-son invoked a Parisian analogy to compliment his patrons as "the Faubourg St. Germain of the town," sniffing at the Metropolitan crowd as "a number of rich persons who want some new way of spending money."

Mapleson might have justly called them very rich persons, for along with the Vanderbilts and others already identified with the project (see page 4), the box-owners included Ogden Goelet, Adrian Iselin, Elbridge

T. Gerry, George F. Baker, William C. Whitney, Cyrus Field, G. G. Haven, J. W. Drexel, William Rhinelander, and Luther Kountze. Still others, regarded as "new" millionaires, were Jay Gould, C. P. Huntington, James Gordon Bennett, D. Ogden Mills, James Harriman, and William Rockefeller.

How much interest most of these had in opera will be indicated in the pages to come; certainly they had substantially less interest when it became exclusively German opera. They endured it because it was economical, because the public responded in sizable numbers, and because the enthusiastic reception of the press for the unfamiliar masterpieces of Wagner gave them a flattering status as art patrons. This was somewhat clouded by charges of immorality when the relationship of Siegmund and Sieglinde was a new discovery. Elizabeth Drexel Lehr has written (*King Lehr and the Gilded Age*): "I remember my uncle, Anthony Drexel, once holding forth on the subject at a dinner party. . . . 'There's going to be a concert next week and I want no child of mine to go to it. Some fool whose name is Dam . . . Dam . . . some kind of bug or other . . . Roach, that's what it is . . . Walter Damrosch, and he's going to play the music of that miserable Wagner! None of you go to it, you understand.' "

As the novelty of these works wore off, and the prospect of sitting through still another *Tristan* or *Tannhäuser* was endured with diminishing grace, some of the box-holders were moved to outspoken rebellion. They were particularly outspoken during the performances themselves, with the result that the following notice was posted in the boxes on January 15, 1891:

Many complaints having been made to the directors of the Opera House of the annoyance produced by the talking in the boxes during the performance, the Board requests that it be discontinued.

By order of the
BOARD OF DIRECTORS.

This crisis was resolved by the return to solvency of Henry Abbey and the transfer to him of the lease for the purpose of resuming Italian opera (see page 103). With him came Maurice Grau, with his flair for building casts about such artists as the De Reszkes, Lassalle, Nordica, and Eames. He provided the box-holders with something of the brilliance and charm they expected in an opera house. He was a man to be encouraged.

This happy transition had hardly been effected when the stockholders were presented with the ugliest news in the ten-year history of the theater. Most of them learned at second hand, and at a considerable distance from the Metropolitan, that a fire had broken out on the morning of August 27, 1892. It was extinguished by noon, but not before it had spread from the stage to the auditorium, leaving little more than the basic structure. One by one the elaborate precautions provided to prevent such a catastrophe had been abandoned—a tank of water to feed a primitive sprinkler system had been emptied because it froze in winter; a fireproof curtain to prevent a fire on stage from spreading to the auditorium had been hoisted out of use—and the appalling fact emerged that only $60,000 in insurance could be collected against a damage of at least $250,000.

In Bar Harbor and Newport the stockholders were incredulous. Was not their building fireproof? They were not aware—as few laymen are, even today—that, in risk circles, a "fireproof" building is merely one of which something—walls and roof—will be left when a fire occurs. In the end, two things determined the future: stubborn pride and a considerable appreciation in the value of the land since the building had been constructed.

The first factor was inherent in the reaction of Luther Kountze, Henry Marquand, Calvin S. Brice, and Robert Goelet, the second in the statement of broker Henry C. Clews: "The opera property is a good investment. The original cost, building and all, was about $2,000,000. Now the ground alone is worth that much."

In less than a month the solution was worked out. Most of the "new" millionaires had been, in literal fact, burned by the social fire and were willing to leave opera to others. The property would be put up for sale, to be bid on by those whose plans for the future were already formulated. At a cost of $1,425,000—well under Clews's estimate of the land value alone —the newly formed Metropolitan Opera and Real Estate Company acquired the assets of the Metropolitan Opera Company Ltd. When this was distributed among the 70 stockholders, each received $20,000, or not greatly less than the original investment.

Membership in the Opera and Real Estate Company was restricted to thirty-five—the number of the boxes in the single tier they planned to occupy as owners and social aristocracy. Each member subscribed to 300 shares of stock at a par value of $100 per share ($30,000). Each subscribed an additional $30,000 for purposes of reconstruction. All participated in the distribution of money from the sale, of course; so the requirement from each, in fresh capital, was $40,000. When the property was liquidated in 1940, each of those whose families retained the original 300 shares received $43,200 in cash and bonds.

This was not at all an unreasonable recovery on an investment that permitted them to write into the by-laws of the company: "No transfer of shares shall be made except to a person or persons previously approved by the Board of Directors. . . ." Nor was this approval lightly granted or imposed by weight of numbers by an influential majority on a recalcitrant minority. Indeed, the requirement for approval was all but unanimous agreement. Under Article VII, from which the foregoing was extracted, the conditions under which alterations in the inner circle of boxholders could be effected were spelled out as follows: "On all resolutions, regarding the names proposed for the transfer or leasing of boxes, the vote shall be by ballot: and two negative ballots shall prevent the approval of any such transfer or lease." For nearly half a century not merely the ownership company as a whole but any two members of it remained a self-appointed, self-perpetuating judge and jury of what persons were socially acceptable in a city of mounting millions.

3

Millions of persons lived and died happily in New York after 1892 with no more than minor awareness of such an institution as the Metropolitan. Some hundreds of thousands of others were its patrons at one time or another and decided it would be a much better place in which to see and hear opera were there no boxes at all. A few thousand others doubtless yearned to be box-owners for all the privileges that status conferred; fewer than twenty aspirants realized this ambition in nearly fifty years. It was this power to scrutinize and reject, to include or exclude, that made opera-patrons of non-music lovers. Whether it was worth $4,500 a year in assessment may be judged from the facts that follow.

Of course, one could have "a box at the opera" without being a stockholder—by payment of the charge of the moment. For this purpose, the new owners set aside the second floor grand-tier boxes for whoever chose to lay out the necessary thousands of dollars. But the distinction was clear in the minds of those who made it, if not always realized by the general public. Herbert Satterlee, a Morgan son-in-law, put it clearly in his worshipful biography of that *magnifico:* "They were all getting rich. Gates was speculating in Wall Street. Judge Moore began to buy fine horses. . . . Converse, Reid and the others invested in large country estates and big houses which were in sharp contrast to the old-fashioned Cragston [the 'modest' ancestral aerie of the Morgans at Highland Falls, New York]. Some of these 'steel magnates' indulged in rented boxes in the Metropolitan Opera House, and their wives and family figured largely in the society columns of the newspapers."

If you "owned," you were "in"; if you merely "rented," you were more than out—you were socially nonexistent. Needless to say, those who "rented" swallowed their unhappiness with this caste system, but extended it a bit farther by looking down on those who neither owned nor rented, but merely bought tickets. Some place in the house there was a dividing line between those who looked down on each other and those who looked at the stage, but I have not, in thirty years of research, been able to determine just where it began.

Because those who took this seriously at all took it very seriously indeed, it might be well to appraise the elements which, surviving the fire, brought themselves into a much tighter alignment than had previously prevailed. Nineteen of the original group persisted. Among those who took their $20,000 each and retired were Cyrus Field, Collis P. Huntington, James Harriman, Jay Gould, and William Rockefeller. Those who remained can be grouped into three categories: Vanderbilt and Morgan, as two major factions, and as a minor but powerful source of prestige the leading elements of the old Academy of Music "Knickerbocker" society: Astor, Belmont, Cutting, and so on.

As shown in the table on pages 59-62, nineteen original stockholders retained their boxes. Of the sixteen new stockholders, more than half had a decided Morgan or Vanderbilt orientation. There were, to begin with, two boxes in the name of Cornelius Vanderbilt, and W. K. held another. Related by marriage were R. T. Wilson, one of whose daughters married a Vanderbilt (Cornelius III) and another Ogden Goelet. W. D. Sloane and H. McKown Twombly, the wives of both of whom were Vanderbilts, shared box 17. Another Vanderbilt was married to W. Seward Webb, who owned box 22.

The Morgan line was of another sort. The progeny were fewer, especially in women to be absorbed by other names. But there were numerous Morgan partners, chosen—as both Satterlee and another biographer, John K. Winkler, attest—as much for social acceptability as for business acumen. A sign of favor for a good-looking product of the right school and family would be the gift of a collie from Junius Pierpont's private kennel. In turn would come an invitation to join the firm and, eventually, the opportunity to buy a box.

God's will was working well at the second drawing for boxes: first choice went to Morgan and he chose number 35 at the direct center of the Horseshoe. Seventeen Vanderbilts at one side or seventeen Astors to the other might have to turn their heads to observe his arrival, but from his point of eminence he could survey all without effort. In social circles it ranked as the most desirable box, though it was at the greatest distance from the stage.

To balance the family of Vanderbilts, Morgan's friends and business associates included Levi P. Morton (an old friend, a one-time partner, and a Vice President of the United States) in box 16; J. Hood Wright, a

Morgan partner, in 21, which was bought and sold only within the firm; G. S. Bowdoin, a Morgan partner, in 27; and Cornelius Bliss, a former partner, in 8. From the general financial world closely tied to Morgan were George P. Wetmore, banker, Governor of Rhode Island, and eventually a Senator, in 5; George F. Baker in 10; and C. T. Barney, president of the Knickerbocker Trust, in 9. S. O. Babcock, one of Morgan's earliest friends in New York, held 26.

In the new alignment one may note several names identified with the Academy rather than the Metropolitan on the simultaneous opening night of 1883—J. J. Astor, Perry Belmont, W. Bayard Cutting, A. T. Van Nest. Although they were greatly outnumbered by the other factions, they did include the unquestionable *doyenne* of New York Society, Mrs. Caroline Astor. The interest that attaches to the Vanderbilt-Morgan-Astor domination is twofold: first as a permanent restraint against social interlopers; second as a governing force in the affairs of the Metropolitan.

In the first instance, the influence is more amusing than censurable. Those who approached the fort could only invoke the tool that had built it—money in the largest possible quantity, plus a mingling of blood lines that created prestige. Aside from Otto Kahn, who finally acquired box 14 in the 1920's—after two decades of work on behalf of the institution—there is no indication that any Jew was welcome. By then, in any case, Kahn was a worshipper at St. Thomas's Episcopal Church.

Morgan's standard of acceptability was defined by Satterlee thus: "The people in his social world were of his own kind, and the bankers and business men with whom he came into contact had, for the most part, the same standards of ethics and point of view that he himself had." Another phrasing of the same thesis is quoted by Winkler, with Maxine Elliott the speaker: "Why, you men in Wall Street are like a lot of cannibals. You devour anything that comes along—if it is edible!"

While still a student at Göttingen, Morgan had clearly formulated his notion of a woman's place in a man's life. Writing to a friend at Harvard, who had confided his love for a girl with thoughts of a career as a singer, the nineteen-year-old Morgan counseled: "Our courses . . . will both be in the mercantile sphere and from this cause it becomes our duty to select for our wives those who, when we go home from our occupations, will ever be ready to make us happy and contented with our homes." The Lillian Russells and Maxine Elliotts had their place, but neither in the home nor in the Diamond Horseshoe.

As an influence on the artistic course of the Metropolitan the Morgan tie was somewhat more absurd. Although his interest, according to Satterlee, was limited to the "old, familiar, romantic tuneful operas," he was invariably consulted in policy decisions from 1892 until his death in 1913. "His special favorite," continues Satterlee, "was 'Il Trovatore,' He always went when it was given and was very discriminating as to how the different numbers were sung. . . . In later years he generally would not go to the opera except on the opening night or for some gala performance. When he had to go, he often took naps in the back of the box."

It was Morgan's influence, nevertheless, that caused the ban on *Salome* (in 1907), perhaps in accord with Satterlee's observation. "He had no use at all for the pictures of impressionists, for 'modern' music, or for the writers who dealt with morbid themes or social problems." It is plain how little such a canon could include *Salome*. Nevertheless, it was to the Morgan library that the directors were summoned for many important decisions, as were his actual employees when matters of gravity in the financial world merited his personal attention.

Not only did Morgan bestride the world of finance with its ramifications in politics, the social scene with its influence on the everyday happiness of thousands more than the "400," and the little world of the Metropolitan Opera. He saw fit, in 1873, to join William E. Dodge and a group of others in organizing the New York Society for the Prevention of Vice, which sought to tell New Yorkers during the next fifty years what they should see, read, and hear.

4

As well as fitting a mental concept of "kind," it was a physical necessity for the main social currents of the box-holders to flow in the same direction. Taken as a group, the box-holders were people with like interests, who went "on" to the same parties or balls, and had friends—not to mention relations—in common. Each hostess knew whom she would see at the opera of a given evening, reserving for the intermission or dull stretches the necessary social planning, small talk, and confidences.

For the generation that lived between 1893 and 1913, the winter's social life revolved about the Opera as never before or since. From the opening of the Opera or the Horse Show—they exchanged priority from year to year—dated the social round of parties and balls which had for its serious purpose the pattern of coming-out, engagement, and wedding. For those with a proprietary interest in the house, it served as the interim point of almost every evening's activity. Dinner over, there was little other diversion to occupy the time before appearance at a ten-o'clock ball. As Henry James noted in *The American Scene* (1907): "There was nothing, as in London or Paris, to go 'on' to; to 'going on' is, for the New York aspiration, always the stumbling block. . . . Its presence is felt unmistakably, for instance, in

THE DIAMOND HORSESHOE IN 1892

BOX OWNER	VANDERBILT	MORGAN	ACADEMY
1* Ogden Goelet (landowner)	cousin by marriage (Wilson)		
2 A. D. Juilliard (textiles)			
3* R. T. Wilson (cotton broker)	daughter Grace married Cornelius III		
4* Cornelius Vanderbilt III			
5* George P. Wetmore		business associate	
6* W. K. Vanderbilt			
7* J. J. Astor			Academy box-holder
8 Cornelius Bliss		former partner	

* Retained investment from 1883.

THE DIAMOND HORSESHOE IN 1892 [continued]

BOX OWNER	VANDERBILT	MORGAN	ACADEMY
9 C. T. Barney (banker)		business associate	
10* George F. Baker (financier)		business associate	
11 Perry Belmont			Academy box-holder
12* Henry Clews (financier)		business associate	
13 Edward Cooper H. T. Sloane	marriage		
14* Mrs. George H. Warren			
15* Adrian Iselin			
16* Levi P. Morton		former partner	
17 W. D. Sloane H. McK. Twombly	married Emily T. Vanderbilt married Florence A. Vanderbilt		
18 Calvin S. Brice (financier)		Nickel Plate R.R.	

* Retained investment from 1883.

		Academy box-holder
19	Mrs. H. I. Barbey	
20*	D. Ogden Mills	
21*	J. Hood Wright	partner
22	W. Seward Webb	married Elizabeth O. Vanderbilt
23	E. T. Gerry	(mother a Goelet)
24*	Robert Goelet	(see box 1)
25*	G. G. Haven	partner of Babcock (see 26)
26	S. O. Babcock	longtime friend
27	G. S. Bowdoin	partner
	Charles Lanier	banker

* Retained investment from 1883.

THE DIAMOND HORSESHOE IN 1892 [continued]

BOX OWNER	VANDERBILT	MORGAN	ACADEMY
28 W. Bayard Cutting			Academy box-holder
29 A. T. Van Nest			Academy box-holder
30* W. C. Whitney	marriage (his son Harry Payne Whitney married daughter of No. 31)		
31* Cornelius Vanderbilt			
32* Luther Kountze			
33 Thomas Hitchcock		Friend	
34 Heber R. Bishop			
35* J. P. Morgan			

* Retained investment from 1883.

the general extravagant insistence on the Opera, which plays its part as the great vessel of social salvation, the comprehensive substitute for all other conceivable vessels."

Even those who were not box-owners participated, vicariously if need be, in the ceremonial procedures. As Mrs. Lehr has written: "My mother . . . regarded the Opera purely as a social function and never failed to occupy her box [rented] on Monday evenings, like everyone else with any claim to being fashionable. On those nights the house would be crowded, every box in the 'Diamond Horseshoe' would present the spectacle of two women superbly gowned and bejewelled sitting in the front row, while four men grouped themselves behind." She does not forget to tell us, too, that Lily Hamersley (later the Duchess of Marlborough) had the walls of the anteroom to the box "concealed by festoons of orchids."

According to accepted custom, the social leader—in this period Mrs. Astor—would appear at the opera promptly at nine, regardless of what was being given or when it started. During a convenient intermission she would "receive," in order of eminence, her own set, perhaps accompanied by out-of-town or European guests. Rarely, if ever, did she leave her box to visit any other.

Not all the visitors, of course, came from other boxes. There were some "accepted" people who chose to be only subscribers, and there was a whole category of young people who did not necessarily have access to a box. Indeed, with the proper costume—tails, white tie, white gloves—and a dollar for standing-room admission, a well-connected young man could easily find himself a haven in exchange for conversational service during the intermission.

Often enough Mrs. Astor would have departed by the next intermission. When her place was vacant, others would begin to drift away. Leaving before her was scarcely thinkable, not merely as a violation of protocol, but even more because some bit of byplay might occur which would be the next day's justification for having spent the previous evening at the opera.

The personal aspect of social leadership was reflected in Harvey O'Connor's comment in *The Astors* (New York: Alfred A. Knopf; 1941): "Unfeeling people said Mrs. Astor was intent only on a vulgar display of wealth as she sat, bejewelled, in the Diamond Horseshoe. They forgot she was a mother, that she had four daughters and a son, plain of face and mind, who must be married off into the rank suitable to their exalted station in the American aristocracy." This had been accomplished, and to her satisfaction, when she died, on October 30, 1908, at the age of seventy-seven.

The power aspect of social leadership and the contest for recognition as Mrs. Astor's successor have been touched upon by Mrs. Lehr in her reminiscences. Even in her later years Mrs. Astor commanded the prestige to decide whether a friend's daughter could marry the man of her choice without jeopardizing social standing. There was no conceivable objection to the man—James Speyer—save the fact that he was a Jew, and none such had ever been invited to an Astor party.

Considering the question in all its gravity, and studying the anxious face of the girl (Ellin Dyneley Prince), Mrs. Astor pronounced her verdict: "We are all so fond of you. Marry him dear, if you want to. I for one will invite you to my parties, and I think everyone else will do the same." For Mrs. Astor to "think" a thing was for others to accept it: the shattering precedent was established.

The possible candidates for succession were five: the daughter-in-law of the deceased (Mrs. John Jacob Astor) had heritage, but "no talent for social leadership" (the opinion is Mrs. Lehr's). For Mrs. Mills, having too many friends was a liability; for Mrs. Oliver H. P. Belmont (a Vanderbilt by a former marriage, and the mother of Consuelo Vanderbilt), having too many enemies was the same. Mrs. Stuyvesant Fish had supporters, but even they gave up the cause after the famous "monkey dinner." In collusion with Harry "King" Lehr, society's most celebrated practical joker, she tendered a formal dinner for an unknown "Prince del Drago." When the "Prince" turned out to be a monkey in evening dress who was seated at Mrs. Fish's right for the evening, the guests were hugely entertained. Not so, however, the press, which chided her circle to remember that "New York society represents America in the eyes of the foreign world, and we should behave with a becoming sense of dignity."

Not only by elimination but also by attraction the honor went to Mrs. Cornelius Vanderbilt, III, born Grace Wilson, who had a "flair for social intrigue," says Mrs. Lehr, and "all the qualities that make a ruler." Nearly forty years later her arrival at a Metropolitan opening still carried awe for those who were more impressed by the performance in the boxes than that on the stage. The picture of her arrival at the 1949 opening, shaking a cane at a photographer who "took her" (literally) unaware, is its own commentary on the health of the tradition she represented. Likewise, her opposition to the Kahn-led plans for a new theater (page 21) throws vivid light on the power she could marshal to continue a social tradition, even when it conflicted violently with every sensible consideration of art and economics.

5

In this conflict lies the only compulsion to dwell, now, on the glitter and display that have long since vanished together with those whose pretensions they conveyed. What was necessary to preserve the auditorium as the home for a social circle was invariably done; what was necessary to adapt it to house an artistic endeavor adequately was never done.

The reconstruction after the fire provided a scheme in which the walls were cream-colored. Although this proved to be disadvantageous for the favorable display of gowns and jewelry, it was suffered until 1903, when Heinrich Conried's plan to present *Parsifal* made some primitive stage machinery mandatory. At a cost of $150,000, the overhauling of the stage (counterweights to fly scenery were introduced, and a new stage floor with traps for the disappearance of Klingsor's castle was provided) was extended to include redecoration of the auditorium in the gold and deep maroon (the Vanderbilt house color) which has now become traditional. Also, for the first time, a foyer was created on the grand-tier floor for the convenience of those who did not hold boxes. Previously they had had no gathering-place during the intermissions except the drafty lobbies.

At the same time the familiar proscenium arch, with the front of the stage cut back on a line with it, was constructed, with panels bearing the names of Mozart, Verdi, Wagner, Beethoven, Gluck, and Gounod. Formerly the base of the pillars at either side had contained doors from which the performers could emerge for bows. These were closed up, and ornamental bases—for the pillars created in their places. Another change of administration, in 1908, brought some further minor changes in the theater —particularly the removal of a block of seats at either side of the orchestra pit, which was thus widened to its final dimensions. Then, at last, the elevators woefully needed to carry patrons to the lofty balcony and family circle were installed.

There were no further alterations in the physical plant of the Metropolitan until the legally decreed improvements of 1934. Such a necessary piece of equipment as a cyclorama (a canvas hanging on which light can be thrown to suggest sky or distance) was lacking until the Opera Guild raised the money to buy it in 1936. Most of the later worthwhile improvements were underwritten by public contributions (see page 37).

Despite this evidence of limited concern about the Metropolitan as an opera house, there was never any hesitation on the part of the boxholders to put forth the kind of self-justification dearly beloved by the rich when their motives are questioned. As we have seen, they divorced themselves as quickly as possible from the problem of presenting opera in New York. It is equally evident that they did not strain their resources to make the Metropolitan a theater the city could be proud of. Nevertheless, in 1929, when some talk of sale and removal brought up a problem of new capital for rebuilding, a representative of the Opera and Real Estate Company told a reporter for the *Herald Tribune:* "The directors of the Metropolitan Opera and Real Estate Company have contributed more than $5,000,000 in thirty-five years to keep the opera going. Opera is not a paying business. It is a donation to the public. Every year an assessment has to be made to continue to give opera in New York. The directors are reluctant to take a step which would increase this assessment."

It is an elementary principle of society that membership in any club carries with it an assessment for maintenance. For the box-owners, the Metropolitan was essentially a club, if perhaps one that had outlived its time of utility. The amount of $5,000,000, when properly apportioned, shows a total assessment in the period mentioned of $142,847 per box. For this the box-holder received the use of six seats for *every performance* of opera given.

Taking the very moderate average of 78 performances a season (in some there were as many as 176), the cost per box per performance was $52.32. Each of the six seats thus cost the box-holders $8.72, or very little more than the going price of those on the orchestra floor.

There is ample evidence, however, that, rather than being out of pocket by payment of the assessment—assuming that neither the prestige of patronage nor the enjoyment of music was adequate compensation—some box-holders made a financial profit on their holdings, especially in the prosperous days of the 1920's. During a tax investigation by the government of Miss Georgine Iselin's affairs in 1926, the *Times* reported the following facts:

In the season of 1920–21, Miss Iselin sub-leased her box for 47 performances, for a total return of $9,525. Her assessment was the usual $4,500. She thus made a profit of $5,025, and had the use of the box *free* for the other 80-odd performances. The prices she charged were broken down as follows:

Opening night	$550
11 Mondays	$275 each ($3,025)
11 other Mondays	$200 each ($2,200)
23 Fridays	$150 each ($3,450)
Prince of Wales gala	$300

Considering both the high and the low quotations, Miss Iselin received the average sum of $33.77 per seat for what cost her $8.72. As the practice of subleasing was by this time quite general, it is possible that others made deals to their advantage, even if one doubts that they were quite as venal as Miss Iselin. If proper accounting were made to the government, only the lessor and the lessee needed to know of the money that changed hands.

Another aspect of the assessment as a "contribution" may be derived from a consideration of prevailing practice when boxes were sold, as they were on some twenty occasions between 1892 and the liquidation of 1940. Whether people are rich because they are financially minded or financially minded because they are rich is a riddle to which one who is neither cannot provide the answer. But the theory involved in such sales may be deduced from the comment accompanying the first discussion I can trace. (The books of the Opera and Real Estate Company were never open to the public: after the sale, they became the property of the Metropolitan Opera Association, in whose custody they now repose.) This was in 1903, and a price of $100,000 was mentioned. Although this would seem a reasonable return for an investment of $60,000 ten years before, the owner was asking $120,000. Apparently $120,000 was a commonly held figure, for the sub-leasing rate at this time was $6,000 per half season—or interest at five per cent on the $120,000 supposedly tied up in a box. When the first recorded transaction occurred in 1913, the price, for publication, was $120,000.

The properties that changed hands were box 26, purchased by William Ross Proctor from the S. O. Babcock estate, and box 33, purchased by Henry E. Hoyt from the estate of Thomas Hitchcock. In 1921, in an affidavit filed in connection with the appraisal of the Henry Clews estate, Frank Dodd, acting for the Opera and Real Estate Company, specified the value of the 10,500 shares in the company to be $3,977,000, or $378.76 each. Presumably this reflected the increased value of the site. Thus a box representing 300 shares of stock would have been worth $113,628. That amounts as high as $200,000 were reported to have been paid during the 1920's indicates the premium that the sellers were able to place on their property.

Between 1913 and 1924 there were five further sales. Box 34 passed from Heber R. Bishop to James B. Haggin; box 11, originally owned by Perry Belmont, was purchased by Archer M. Huntington and Arthur Curtiss James jointly; box 19 was sold by the estate of Henry I. Barbey to Henry C. Frick, whose estate sold it to Judge Elbert H. Gary in 1924 at a quoted price of $200,000. In the same period Otto Kahn finally became a box-holder by acquiring number 14, originally owned by Mrs. George Henry Warren.

During the boom period of 1924–7 there were transactions almost yearly. In 1925 Johnson L. Redmond (who had recently married the niece of G. G. Haven, a box-holder for many years) purchased a one-fourth in-terest in box 29. In the same year box number 11, held by the estate of August Belmont (it was originally the property of Perry Belmont), was purchased by Paul H. Helm, president of the General Baking Company.

Apparently he was not happy with it, for he sold it the following year to Robert S. Brewster.

Two Vanderbilts chose an advantageous moment to sell. Harold Vanderbilt's number 6 went to Frazier Jelke in 1926, and the jointly held number 7 (Mrs. H. McKown Twombly and Mrs. Henry White were the owners) was acquired by H. E. Manville in 1927. Both transactions had their interest, for Jelke paid $200,000, and fought vigorously to recover an appreciable amount of it when the liquidation occurred in 1940 (see page 37). The documentation of the Manville purchase included the fact that J. Pierpont Morgan had recently arranged the investment of $7,000,-000 in the Johns-Manville corporation.

This sign of Morgan "influence" was underscored when the estate of H. P. Davison, a past Morgan partner, disposed of a half interest in box 21 to Charles R. Steele, a current partner. In commenting, casually, on the transfer of ownership from one member of the firm to another, Secretary Dodd of the Opera and Real Estate Company cast a beam of light on the thinking that governed the choice of "eligibles." "It is more difficult," he said, "to find a purchaser acceptable to the Board . . . for boxes in the central portion of the sides of the opera house than for those near the stage or in the rear."

The unconscious humor of this is both overpowering and saddening. Not only, then, did a chasm separate owners from renters and lessees, but even greater chasms within the ownership separated the hardy elite from the naked aspiring. Hidden in their boxes "near the stage or in the rear," the ones who had been granted mere squatters' rights found themselves forced to accept an inferior status. That they were labeled so, publicly, shows how secure the core of the inner circle felt itself.

At the same time it underscores fully the fact that lack of purchasers was not the whole, or the real, reason why almost half the boxes were held by estates when the collapse came. As the older investors died, the boxes on the market multiplied not alone in number, but also in desirability. If a Morgan partner rejected, as neighbor, an interloper from Milwaukee, the estate holding the "desirable" box continued to hold it, while resisting payment of the annual assessment. In the end it was the dead hand of the dead past that stifled the corporate life and transferred the burden to the public. At that, the by-laws had to be amended to make sure that none of the "dissident stockholders" (pages 35–6) could seek to assert rights they no longer possessed. The final addition to the by-laws, adopted May 8, 1940, reads:

"Each holder or holders of three hundred shares of stock shall have a license to use a designated box upon the parterre tier of the opera house so long as

the Company shall be the owner of the opera house.* . . . *No stockholder who is indebted to the Company shall be allowed to use his box until such indebtedness is fully paid."*

In other words, all rights were canceled by the sale, and those who were delinquent (estates included) had no rights prior to the sale unless back assessments were paid up.

6

The panorama of social change which accompanied the lives and deaths of the Metropolitan's founders can be observed acutely in the successive openings, from 1892 on. At first every night was fashionable, and society went to the opera regularly when it was "in season." Soon enough, however, the season grew so long, the schedule so onerous, that, by common agreement one evening a week was set aside as "fashionable."

To judge from the *Tribune* of December 8, 1894, it was not immediately Monday: "It seems to be the policy of the Metropolitan management to reserve the old-fashioned Italian repertory for the most fashionable night of the week, that is, Friday." The trend to Monday, if gradual, was also logical. It invariably served to open the season, and thus was a ritual of high degree; and conflicting social obligations of an evening-long character were more likely to occur in the middle or latter part of the week.

By the time Conried became director in 1903, the Monday custom was firm. A stipulation of his lease was that the number of Wagner operas presented on Monday should not exceed four. Some might consider this expressive of a continuing prejudice against the "immorality" of Wagner's works or their musical weight. But there was just as strong or stronger objection to the number of dimly lit scenes they contained, which were prejudicial to display or scrutiny of a fashionable wardrobe and its gems.

As the concentration on Monday determined one pattern of Metropolitan activity, so it had a considerable influence on another—the custom of subleasing. If "everybody" went on Monday, there was little reason to be there when "nobody" went. Hence a greatly widened circle of persons had the use of the boxes on the less fashionable nights, for a price. In the twenty or so years prior to World War I, it was often confined to a family circle, or to accommodate a friend whose business took him to Europe for the winter. Thereafter, as the instance of Miss Islein shows (page 66), it could be pursued as a profitable avocation, at whatever rates the market would bear.

By the 1920's the society pattern had so expanded that its journalistic historians referred not to the traditional *grandes dames,* but to the "Thurs-

* Emphasis in the original.

day night" hostess in this box or the "Friday night" hostess in another. Typical reportage (*Town Topics,* December 3, 1923) was: "Mrs. William A. M. Burden was the hostess in the White-Twombly box, and she did not escape the scrutiny of the opera glass battalion, for she wore the longest and most magnificent chain of diamonds seen in the parterre for several years." One would have to be well versed in genealogy to know that Messrs. Burden, White, and Twombly were all married to members of the Vanderbilt family.

Each opening, however, as the symbol of a new beginning, an augury of things to come, has its enduring interest. The second gala *Faust,* on November 27, 1893, may be accepted as the first, historically, of the modern era. In view of the smaller number of owned boxes, there was an understandable emphasis on who occupied them. It is not improbable that the jewels thus displayed cost more than the financing of the reconstruction.

The social life of New York as reflected at the Metropolitan marked an occasion of occasions on February 25, 1902, when Prince Henry of Prussia, brother of the Kaiser, was entertained. The tide of American money engulfing foreign titles was running high, with Consuelo Vanderbilt's marriage to the ninth Duke of Marlborough a recent memory, and such other unions as a Whitney with the Baron Queensborough, a Gould with Count Boni di Castellane, and a Morton (daughter of Levi P.) with the Duc de Valençay et de Sagan ushering in "the century of the common man."

Elaborate decorations inside and outside were matched by a spectacular program, for an admission charge of thirty dollars a seat. The lower floors were well filled, but both the balcony and the family circle were nearly one-third empty. Most members of the fashionable audience timed their arrival to coincide with that of the royal party, at nine o'clock. Thus there were less than one thousand people in the theater when a series of acts from various operas began at eight. Actually, the royal party did not arrive until 9:40 and departed well before the program was completed. When many in the theater did likewise, Marcella Sembrich decided that her dignity had been affronted and refused to appear in the first act of *La Traviata.* Among the dignitaries who came and went to strains of Wagner and Verdi were Admiral von Tirpitz (some of those present had reason to remember him bitterly a decade later), Mayor Seth Low, Chauncey Depew, and Rear-Admiral Robley Evans (a hero of the recently concluded Spanish-American War).

A custom of long duration was introduced on November 23, 1903, when Enrico Caruso made his debut in *Rigoletto.* It was also the occasion for the first viewing of the newly decorated auditorium. Caruso was accepted with applause, but Carrere and Hastings, who had supervised the redecoration.

received a letter of commendation from the board of directors of the Real Estate and Opera Company.

Caruso openings were invariable thereafter, save for November 26, 1906, when Geraldine Farrar made her debut in *Roméo*. From 1908, when *Aida* on November 16 also brought Emmy Destinn, they were Caruso-Toscanini openings, except in the 1912–13 season, when other affairs kept the conductor abroad until midseason. Society considered the 1908 historic for the absence from the Diamond Horseshoe for the first time of any member of the Astor family. (They were mourning the late Caroline, who had died shortly before.) The music-minded did not consider the *Aida* for this reason dull.

La Gioconda was the choice for 1909, *Armide* for 1910, *Aida* again for 1911. With Toscanini absent, the 1912 audience had to content itself with *Manon Lescaut* sung by Caruso, Scotti, and a new soprano, Lucrezia Bori. For the Maestro's next opening—*La Gioconda* again—1913 provided "the largest audience ever in the house" on a first night and a parterre "ablaze with jewels."

The last Toscanini opening was on November 16, 1914, when he conducted a performance of *Un Ballo in maschera* with Caruso, Destinn, Hempel, Matzenauer, and Amato. Thenceforward, till his death, Caruso carried the burden himself. For the 1915 opening (*Samson et Dalila*) the audience began to gather at three in the afternoon, and standing room went in twenty minutes. While seeking new words to describe the splendor of the audience, the *Times* observed: "Paquin, Worth and Poiret were in their glory." *Les Pêcheurs de perles* was elected for November 13, 1916, then the third Caruso *Aida* on November 12, 1917, and *Samson et Dalila* once more on November 11, 1918. The associations of the last date made for jubilation on the stage as well as in the house. At the end of the first act the curtain was raised amid cheers for the sight of Allied banners in the hands of the principals, while all the choristers fluttered small American flags.

The absence of Wagner during the war years blemished no opening, for his works were not considered suitable by Gatti. In any case, the *Tosca* that opened the 1919 season found society merely rehearsing for the Prince of Wales gala the following evening, November 18. The Prince, or Edward VIII, or the Duke of Windsor, as one prefers, was met by Otto Kahn and Clarence Mackay, who escorted him to the Morgan box. Viscount Grey, Assistant Secretary of War William Philips, and Admiral Halsey (a predecessor of the later famous "Bull") were also in the box. During the intermission Edward encountered General John J. Pershing in the corridor and invited him to spend the remainder of the evening as his guest. Mrs. Grover Whalen and Mrs. Rodman Wanamaker were similarly honored.

The advent of the 1920's brought a new factor in the musical world to rub some of the social luster from the Metropolitan. In four weeks of this winter there were as many orchestral concerts as there had been in three months a decade before. Such personalities as Mengelberg and Stokowski, Koussevitzky and Toscanini brought into being a "Philharmonic crowd," a "Philadelphia crowd" (the Boston audience could under no circumstances be called a "crowd"), which competed, at least, with the prestige of the opera's box-holders. Otto Kahn once told a colleague of mine that the fault for this was with the press, for making heroes of the "prima donna" conductors. Even the press could not persuade a prominent orchestra, resident or visiting, to venture a Monday-night series.

For his last opening, on November 15, 1920, Caruso in *La Juive* was not in his best voice (see page 290), but only the hypercritical complained. Barely a month later (December 24), he sang on this stage for the last time.

With his unquestionably premier singer and most valuable asset gone, Gatti had a new and perplexing problem to resolve. No longer was there the automatic opening choice for the indisputable lion; all the beasts of the musical jungle now clamored for recognition. Usually it went, by courtesy, to a female of the species, to Galli-Curci on November 14, 1921 (*La Traviata*), Jeritza in *Tosca* in 1922, Jeritza in *Thaïs* in 1923. Whether Rethberg or Martinelli dominated the *Aida* that opened the 1924 season is questionable, though Tullio Serafin, who made his debut that night, would doubtless contend that he did. A new pattern was established with his arrival, for he conducted every opening thereafter until 1934, when he was no longer with the company. Ponselle and *La Gioconda* served in 1925, Ponselle and *La Vestale* in 1926.

The glittering performance of *Turandot* on October 31, 1927, might have marked the end of an era, had the movement to Fifty-seventh Street proceeded by Kahn's timetable. As it did not, the opening, with Jeritza and Lauri-Volpi, may be considered historic only because smoke from the flash-powder used to photograph arriving celebrities drifted into the theater, and a fire alarm was turned in. Some regretted that the engines, on arrival, were not needed.

Gatti's most daring choice of an opening was doubtless *L'Amore dei tre re* with Ponselle, Martinelli, Pinza, and Danise on October 29, 1928. Fortunately the date of the next opening was October 28, 1929, rather than the 29th of the famous stockmarket crash. (The house was dark on that Tuesday). On the previous evening, Lucrezia Bori had the place of honor in *Manon Lescaut,* thus repeating the circumstance of her debut in 1912. *Aida* was again chosen for 1930 (Maria Müller and Martinelli), with an audience that showed little influence of the deepening depression.

In the years that followed, the inevitably "brilliant" opening night did not guarantee a successful season. Those who came when the photographers were present found reason to be elsewhere in the weeks to come. Gradually, the *haut monde* had been outnumbered by the smart set, the bon ton, or whatever prevailed in a given decade. When it became "café society," its luster was more artificial than real.

Gatti's losing year of 1931–2 opened on November 2 with a Ponselle, De Luca, Lauri-Volpi *Traviata.* It was the last season for six years to open at the accustomed early date, for two months had been eliminated from the schedule for 1932, which began on November 21 with Tibbett in *Simon Boccanegra.* To honor the beginning of Gatti's twenty-fifth year, Arturo Toscanini was his guest.

By 1933, when the season began on December 26, it was clear that the old society function of the opening had vanished. Whatever the merits of the performance of *Peter Ibbetson,* with Bori, Tibbett, and Johnson, it was clear that no "season" (other than opera) could wait so long to begin. Staunch to the end, Gatti began his last season, on December 22, 1934, as he had his first, with *Aida.* Rethberg, Martinelli, and Tibbett were as close as he could provide to the Destinn, Caruso, and Scotti of old.

It was a major task in readjustment to reverse the trend of late openings and short seasons. How Edward Johnson approached the problem is discussed elsewhere (see page 405). In the present context it is sufficient to say that two more December openings—in 1935 on the 16th it was *La Traviata* with Bori, Crooks, and Tibbett; in 1936 on the 21st it was *Die Walküre* with Flagstad, Melchior, Schorr, and Rethberg—were to pass before November became feasible again. In 1937 it was more a technicality than an accomplished fact, the season opening on November 29 with Flagstad, Melchior, and Thorborg in *Tristan.* It moved back to the 21st in 1938, and it was middle-late November through the Johnson years save for 1940, when *Un Ballo in maschera* opened on December 2.

In the light of after events, the opening of the 1939 season was heavy with symbolism. Formal agreement on the mechanism of liquidation was yet to be reached, but it was accepted as fact that November 27, 1939, would be the last time the Horseshoe would have the homogeneous character of old. Whatever interest there was in this fact or in the performance of *Simon Boccanegra* was dimmed by the antics of an over-extroverted Texan named Richard A. Knight, who decided to liven the scene by cartwheeling through the bar, tails flying.

When the eager photographers followed him to the street, he obliged with a handstand (top-hatted) in front of a Metropolitan signboard. Thus was ushered in an era of rowdy, noisy, pushing, impolite, publicity-seeking exhibitionists, of whom the hundred or two worst made their seasonal appearance at the Metropolitan on this one occasion alone.

On this November 29, 1939, the boxes showed the following terminal occupants. Asterisks indicate those finally held in whole or part by estates.

1893–4	1939–40
1. Ogden Goelet	1. Robert Goelet Duke of Roxburghe
2. A. D. Juilliard	2. F. A. Juilliard* E. Pennington Pearson (*Fridays*)
3. R. T. Wilson	3. Mrs. Cornelius Vanderbilt III Mrs. Orme Wilson
4. Cornelius Vanderbilt	4. Robert S. Brewster Mrs. O. G. Jennings (*even Mondays, odd Fridays*)
5. George P. Wetmore	5. George P. Wetmore* Mrs. Harold Brown
6. W. K. Vanderbilt	6. Frazier Jelke
7. J. J. Astor	7. Vincent Astor
8. Cornelius Bliss McC. D. Borden	8. C. N. Bliss Bertram H. Borden Gen. Howard S. Borden Cornelius W. Dresselhuys (*Mondays, opening night*)
9. C. T. Barney	9. E. H. Harriman*
10. George F. Baker H. C. Fahnestock	10. George F. Baker* Mrs. John Hubbard
11. Perry Belmont	11. Archer M. Huntington Arthur Curtiss James
12. Henry Clews	12. James B. Clews* Henry Clews*
13. Edward Cooper H. T. Sloane	13. Myron Taylor George Henry Warren
14. Mrs. George H. Warren	14. Otto H. Kahn* Mrs. Christian R. Holmes (*Mondays, opening night*)

1893–4 (Cont.)	1939–40 (Cont.)
15. Adrian Iselin	15. Miss Iselin Mrs. Watts Sherman
16. Levi P. Morton George Bliss	16. William Willis Reese Mrs. Walter P. Bliss Joseph E. Davies (*opening night*)
17. W. D. Sloane H. McK. Twombly	17. H. Edward Manville
18. Calvin S. Brice	18. Miss Helen O. Brice Winthrop W. Aldrich Sheldon Whitehouse Arnold Whitridge Mrs. Marius de Brabant (*odd Mondays, opening night*)
19. Mrs. H. I. Barbey	19. Elbert H. Gary*
20. D. O. Mills	20. Elisabeth Mills Reid* Ogden L. Mills*
21. J. Hood Wright	21. Charles Steele* Mrs. Herbert Satterlee Mrs. Morgan Hamilton
22. W. Seward Webb	22. Mrs. W. Seward Webb* Mrs. J. Watson Webb (*Mondays, matinees, opening night*) Mrs. David S. Gamble
23. E. T. Gerry	23. Robert L. Gerry Peter G. Gerry Miss Angelica L. Gerry Mabel Drury* Miss Juliana Cutting (*matinees*) Miss Cottone (*matinees*)
24. Robert Goelet	24. Robert Walton Goelet Mrs. Henry Morgan Tilford (*Mondays, opening night*)
25. G. G. Haven	25. G. G. Haven* Forsyth Wickes John Parsons* Mrs. James Lees Laidlaw

1893–4 (Cont.)	1939–40 (Cont.)
	Mrs. John C. Hughes
	Mrs. T. J. Mumford
26. S. O. Babcock	26. Mrs. Vernon H. Brown
	William Ross Proctor
	J. Allen Townsend
27. G. S. Bowdoin	27. Mrs. John T. Pratt
Charles Lanier	R. Fulton Cutting*
28. W. Bayard Cutting	28. Mrs. W. Bayard Cutting
29. A. T. Van Nest	29. R. V. N. Gambrill
	Mrs. Johnson L. Redmond
	Mrs. Arthur Little
30. W. C. Whitney	30. H. P. Whitney*
	Mrs. Francis P. Garvan
31. Cornelius Vanderbilt	31. Alice G. Vanderbilt*
32. Luther Kountze	32. Henry Walters*
	de Lancey Kountze
	Grafton Minot
	Mrs. Beverly Bogart
	(*opening night, odd Mondays, matinees*)
	G. Lauder Greenway
	(*odd Wednesdays*)
	Hoyt A. Moore
	(*part Fridays*)
33. Thomas Hitchcock	33. G. Beekman Hoppin
	E. Farrar Bateson
34. Heber R. Bishop	34. James B. Haggin*
35. J. P. Morgan	35. J. P. Morgan

It is of this group that Robert Goelet in his memoirs, *The Old Order Changeth* (1940), wrote: "'The old order changeth, yielding place to new.' But for those who follow, lest they forget, let it be recorded that each individual family which took part in the construction of the original opera house and retained its box ever since . . . has contributed to the date of this writing upwards of $312,000 to the support of opera in New York in return for the privilege of occupying a box."

These figures extend those previously cited by Dodd (page 66) from the thirty-five-year history of the Metropolitan Opera and Real Estate Company (in 1927) to the whole fifty-eight-year history of the house itself (1940). Subtracting the sum of $43,200 accepted as settlement in the liquidation, the net amount is $268,000, or $4,633 per year.

In recalling her Newport days, Elizabeth Drexel Lehr wrote: "The line of sumptuous villas—the 'cottages' as they were ironically called by their inhabitants—which stretched the length of Bellevue Avenue along the cliffs and over Ochre Point, was Newport's glory. . . . One splendid villa after another, each owned by men whose names made history in the world of finance, who thought nothing of spending ten million dollars for a house in which they lived for six weeks in a year. . . . Among them was 'Ochre Court' where Mrs. Ogden Goelet, who was an enormously rich widow, had more suitors than she could count, lived in an atmosphere of luxury and magnificence. . . . I remember Mrs. Pembroke Jones telling me that she always set aside $300,000 at the beginning of every Newport season for entertainment."

For another view of the same circle, let us consult Dixon Wecter's *The Saga of American Society* (New York: Charles Scribner's Sons; 1937): "Of even greater social luster are the Goelets, whose name is pronounced with no Gallic frills. They derive from Peter Goelet, ironmonger during and after the Revolution, who also had the good judgment to buy several acres on what were then the northern fringes of the young city. . . . These Goelets became a byword for parsimony, and transmitted their habits to the third generation—even though from 1850 to 1870 with the great migration uptown, their tract of land reaching from the present Union Square to 47th Street and Fifth Avenue advanced their fortune to well over a hundred million. . . . They at last welcomed the social tradition, ordered steam yachts, sent their sons to Harvard, and began to entertain at Newport."

What was that sum again, Mrs. Lehr? Three hundred thousand dollars in one year for upkeep of opera? Three hundred twelve thousand dollars in fifty-eight years for summer entertainment? Or was it the other way round? Who kept up with what Joneses? Was the hundred million exhausted by the steam yachts or by the $4,633 per year for a box assessment?

Think of what these people might have done had they really *cared* about opera.

7

In the decade after the sale, there was an attempt, though a gradually declining one, to keep the material inheritance of the Metropolitan alive by allusion to the cherished names that had meant so much in the past. In the immediate aftermath of the sale, the opening of the 1940 season with *Un Ballo in maschera,* there was a strong showing of Vanderbilt, Astor, Bliss, Goelet, Whitney, and Cutting names among subscribers for boxes. Single series were the rule, Monday the preference. Mrs. Vanderbilt was unique in retaining her box for all performances in this year and for several thereafter. Absent from any participation were J. P. Morgan, H. Edward Manville, Frazier Jelke, and such former Metropolitan names as Clews, Harriman, and Baker. The Morgan box, for Mondays, passed to Thomas J. Watson.

Among those who moved in to fill the vacuum that the nature of press photographers abhorred was Mrs. George Washington Kavanaugh, encrusted with jewels. It was this woman who insisted on a full display of her valuables at the first opening after Pearl Harbor, in the fall of 1942. Most of those at the performance of *La Fille du régiment* with Lily Pons on November 23 accepted a blackout on such ostentation. But in characteristic fashion Mrs. Kavanaugh stifled criticism by saying: "I'm not unfeeling, but what shall we do with these things if we don't wear them?" The surety company could have told her, especially when she chose to appear for the 1946 opening in all her mineral glory and managed to lose one of her numerous diamond bracelets (it was found and returned to her).

In the next year she permitted a photographer to snap her counting her bracelets as she entered the theater, perhaps inspiring a rival to outdo him by persuading the aged Mrs. Betty Henderson to be pictured with her leg resting on a table.

As a result of the more blatant views of society at play, George A. Sloan, chairman of the Metropolitan's board of directors, issued a statement declaring his concern about "certain news photographs." He deplored that they had been reproduced "in some cities abroad, including Moscow." This nervous shudder did not affront the photographers, long used to being insulted after the fact. It would have been far more effective to confine the photographers to the outside lobby—the custom prior to 1944—rather than to permit them the freedom of the bar, whose name, Sherry's, had nothing to do with that mild beverage.

In part, the concentration of attention elsewhere than on the stage at these openings was a consequence of the limited interest of the musical fare provided for them. In 1941, on November 24, it was Mozart's *Nozze di Figaro,* the first time a score by this composer had served for ceremonial purposes at the Metropolitan. The wartime openings of 1942, 1943, and 1944 were much more subdued—save for Mrs. Kavanaugh— than the counterparts of 1917–18. New York was considered a vulnerable area, with blacked-out electric signs and blue-lit theater marquees as the dulled evidence of a world at war. Following *La Fille du régiment* in 1942, *Boris Godunov* was chosen in 1943 to observe the Diamond Jubilee of the building. There was little that was jubilant in the performance of November 22, however. As a tribute to what the *Times* called "the gallantry and heroism of the Soviet Union's fighting forces and people," it earned a transoceanic greeting from Dmitri Shostakovich, whose fervor was not echoed when he visited the United States a few years later.

Faust was chosen for the opening on November 27, 1944, and *Lohengrin* for November 26, 1945, when Miss Margaret Truman attracted some attention, and Mrs. Vanderbilt's reappearance was noted approvingly. For the first time the opening was broadcast. With Mrs. Kavanaugh on November 11, 1946, when she appeared for *Lakmé* were two bodyguards. The drab *Ballo in maschera* of the 1947 opening had the front-page consequences noted previously (see above), a forewarning of what was to happen on November 29, 1948, when the opening *Otello* was televised for the first time. This provided a new field of exhibitionism for those who craved the notoriety of being looked at by people they would never look at in turn. The cameras were also present when the last Johnson season opened on November 21, 1949, with *Der Rosenkavalier*. The viewers were told what dressmakers were responsible for the more showy creations; those in the theater could only guess.

Those who found the disorder and display of these openings a plague on both house and home found a reminder of their origin in the news stories detailing the death of the hand-standing Knight on January 10, 1949. Reciting the glories of a career that had included disbarment from the law and kidnapping his own child from his wife to compel her to stop a divorce suit against him, some accounts related the reactions of the Metropolitan's press representative, Frank A. Wenker, when his original drunken display was pictured in 1939. "Well," said Wenker, "he walked away with the show, didn't he? That's good enough for us." Director Johnson, he added, "laughed until his sides hurt."

In a commentary on the 1949 opening, I proposed (the New York *Sun,* November 22, 1949) setting aside the first performance of the season as a benefit for the institution, at raised prices,[1] letting those who insist on making a spectacle of themselves pay the piper as well. It had ceased to be a part of anything—social life or artistic record. The artistic work of the season could begin the next night, as the artistic portion of this record now begins.

[1] Such a policy was instituted by Rudolf Bing for the beginning of his first season as director on November 6, 1950. He made the professional's improvement on the amateur's suggestion by combining the opening with two other galas in a package of "three firsts" at a total of $60 per orchestra seat.

III

Operas and Artists

1

THE METROPOLITAN OPERA
AND REAL ESTATE COMPANY

THE HENRY ABBEY OPERA COMPANY, 1883–1884

THE COMPANY THAT Henry Abbey brought together to open the first season of the Metropolitan's long history had more to do with the past of opera in New York that with its future. According to custom, it gave all its performances—whether the work was *Faust, Lohengrin,* or *Carmen*—in Italian. The nominal prima donna was Christine Nilsson, who sang Margherita*[1] in the opening *Faust* on October 22, 1883. In the cast with her were Italo Campanini as Faust,* Franco Novara as Mephistopheles,* Giuseppe del Puente as Valentino,* and Sofia Scalchi as Siebel.* Augusto Vianesi, a maestro as well known in London as in Italy, conducted.

Of rather more enduring consequence was the debut on the second night, October 24, of Marcella Sembrich as Lucia,* with Campanini as Edgardo,* in Donizetti's *Lucia di Lammermoor.* Only twenty-five years old, and with her debut in London but a few years behind her, Sembrich was characterized by H. E. Krehbiel in the *Tribune* as: "A lovely singer [with] nearly all the graces of beautiful singing in the old Italian sense." Circumstances prevented her from reappearing in New York until 1898, but she was, for the whole of the decade thereafter, one of the great favorites of the Metropolitan public.

Among other roles sung by Sembrich in her first season were Elvira* in *I Puritani* on October 29, Violetta* in *La Traviata* on November 5, Amina* in *La Sonnambula* on the 14th, Gilda* in *Rigoletto* on the 17th, Rosina* in *Il Barbiere* on the 23rd, and Zerlina* in *Don Giovanni* on the 28th. The last of these marked the first performance of a Mozart score in the Metropolitan. For the time the cast was outstanding: Nilsson

[1] The symbol * indicates that the role so marked was sung by the artist named for the first time at the Metropolitan on this date.

(Elvira*), Emma Fursch-Madi (Donna Anna*), Guiseppe Kaschmann (Don Giovanni*), Giovanni Mirabella (Leporello*), and Roberto Stagno (Ottavio*), with Vianesi conducting.

Whatever the quality of the singing, the standard of conducting and orchestral playing may be judged from the comment by Krehbiel that "the instrumentalists made a sad mess of the orchestral score." On an occasion when Sembrich sang *"Gli angui d'inferno"* (from *Il Flauto magico*) during the lesson scene of *Il Barbiere,* the report read: "Mme Sembrich [ended] a dazzling feat of vocalization to the discordant scrapings of a half dozen fiddlers."

Perhaps Abbey was getting no more from his orchestra than he paid for. Vianesi recruited the players in Italy, Leipzig, and London, sixty-five of the eighty-odd from Venice and Naples. The pay scale ranged from one hundred to one hundred and fifty dollars a *month,* much less than their equivalents of today receive per *week.* On the other hand, such stars as Nilsson received one thousand dollars a night, vastly more, by comparative standards—even if the figure is smaller—than the Nilssons and Sutherlands of the mid-twentieth century.

Another young musician who, like Sembrich, was to leave a mark on later New York music-making was Cleofonte Campanini, younger brother of the tenor star Italo. At twenty-three he was but a once-a-week substitute for Vianesi. His steady progress through touring companies dominated by his famous brother led him eventually to musical direction of the Hammerstein company and then to the rank of impresario in Chicago. During the Hammerstein period (1906–10) he won the kind of commendation usually associated in Italian opera with Arturo Toscanini—who was engaged, within a year or so, to give the Metropolitan what was so greatly admired at Hammerstein's Manhattan Opera House.

The single unfamiliar work of the first Metropolitan season was the perpetually revived, but rarely vivified *La Gioconda* of Ponchielli, on December 20. The work was prepared in nine days, and provided a scenic spectacle regarded by the contemporary press as "without precedent" on the American stage. Nilsson was the first Gioconda,* with Fursch-Madi as Laura Adorno,* Scalchi as La Cieca,* Stagno as Grimaldo,* Del Puente as Barnaba,* and Novara as Alvise Badoero.* Malvina Cavalazzi had the honor of leading the first Metropolitan "Dance of the Hours." The work was given three times later, then not again until 1904.

Otherwise, the repertory was largely that of the Academy of Music, if more spaciously mounted on the expanse of the Metropolitan stage. *Don Giovanni* and *Lohengrin* (with Nilsson and Campanini) were the most ambitious operas musically. *Robert le Diable* of Meyerbeer and *I Puritani* of Bellini exploited the vocal virtuosity in the small company—twenty men and twelve women—which called for the kind of versatility shown by Zelia Trebelli's range from Carmen to Nancy in *Martha* or Martha and Pantalis in *Mefistofele*.

Mapleson's serious effort to keep his Academy of Music patrons adequately entertained was expressed by a company boasting not only Etelka Gerster, who appeared in the opening *La Sonnambula,* which shared the night of October 22 with the Metropolitan's *Faust,* but also Adelina Patti. This illustrious soprano returned to New York in Rossini's *La Gazza ladra* on November 10, singing thereafter in two extreme varieties of Verdi—*La Traviata* and *Aida.* The Ricci brothers' *Crispino e la comare* occupied her on several occasions, with an invariable afterpiece—a performance of Arditi's *Il Bacio,* with the composer conducting. She was also heard in Rossini's *Semiramide,* Meyerbeer's *Les Huguenots,* and Gounod's *Roméo* (all in Italian).

One of the notable American singers of this generation began her operatic career in New York on November 26 at the Academy when Lillian Norton Gower was heard as Margherita in *Faust.* She was regarded as the best of Mapleson's artists next to Patti and Gerster, hardly surprising in view of her later celebrity as Lillian Nordica.

Abbey's commitments to his artists spun his costly season through a Boston holiday recess from the Metropolitan, a return to New York in mid-January, and a long tour, followed by a spring season beginning on March 10. All of this ran his losses to over half a million dollars (see page 6). As a sympathetic gesture, the stockholders of the Metropolitan granted him the use of the theater for a benefit on April 21, 1884, at which the following program was performed:

PART I

I. *Guglielmo Tell* Overture ROSSINI

II. Selection from the second act of *Lucrezia Borgia* DONIZETTI
Lucrezia Fursch-Madi
Duca Alfonso Novara

III. Selection from the third act of *Il Trovatore* VERDI
Leonora Goldini
Ruiz Grazzi
Manrico Stagno

IV. Second act of *Il Barbiere*   ROSSINI
    Including the Lesson Scene in which
    Mme Sembrich *will sing*
    (A) PROCH's "Air and Variations"
    (B) Solovej (ROSSIGNOL) Russian National Air

Almaviva	Capoul
Figaro	Del Puente
Don Basilio	Mirabella
Dr. Bartolo	Corsina
Rosina	Sembrich

    (*To conclude with the Quintet*)

V. Selection from *Aida*   VERDI

Aida	Fursch-Madi
Amneris	Trebelli
Amonasro	Kaschmann
Radames	Campanini

VI. Concerto for violin No. 7 (Adagio and Rondo-finale)   DE BERIOT
    (with orchestral accompaniment)
    Mme Sembrich, who, out of personal compliment
    to Mr. Abbey and on this occasion only, has consented
    to play

PART II

VII. Overture and Chorus from *Dinorah*   MEYERBEER

VIII. *Ave Maria* (on Bach's "Prelude")   GOUNOD

Voice	Mme Nilsson
Violin obbligato	Mme Sembrich
Pianoforte	Sig. Vianesi
Harmonium	Sig. Azzoni

IX. Fourth act of *Les Huguenots*   MEYERBEER

Raoul	Campanini
St. Bris	Kaschmann
de Nevers	Del Puente
Valentine	Nilsson

X. Fourth act (trial scene) from Shakespeare's comedy *The Merchant
    of Venice*

Shylock	Henry Irving
Duke of Venice	Howe

Antonio	T. Wenman
Bassanio	W. Terriss
Salanio	Lyndall
Salarino	Harburg
Gratiano	F. Tyers
Clerk of Court	Louther
Nerissa	Miss Payne

and

Portia	Miss Ellen Terry

XI. Grand Ballet Divertissement   MASCHERONI
    ("Farewell")
    (Arranged especially for this performance by Cav. Vianesi)
    Mme Cavalazzi and corps de ballet

As may be noted, Abbey called upon such stars of his theatrical ventures as Ellen Terry and Sir Henry Irving to make the evening more
attractive, and the profits to him were $16,000. Musically, the evening
remains historical for the versatility displayed by Sembrich, who had
been trained as a violinist and pianist before settling on a career as a
singer (it was Liszt who decided that, of her three talents, singing was the
exceptional one). Her playing of the De Beriot concerto being warmly
applauded, Sembrich went to the piano and played a Chopin mazurka.
Then, to the delight of her audience, she sang *"Ah, non giunge"* from
Sonnambula. Such a qualified eyewitness as W. J. Henderson told
me that her artistry was hardly less as an instrumentalist than as a vocalist.

OPERA IN GERMAN, 1884-1891

The economic and temporal factors that determined the next direction of
Metropolitan history were clearly in the pattern of its major design—
expedience. Abbey's refusal to continue without restitution of his first
season's losses left the stockholders with several alternatives (see page 6)
none of which materialized. At the latest possible moment—August—
they accepted the proposal of Leopold Damrosch to give a season of
German opera, stressing the little-known works of Wagner. With a knowledge of the New York public gained by direction of the New York
Symphony Orchestra, Damrosch was convinced that the losses would
be modest, especially as the services of the singers he engaged did not
come high. These would necessarily be Germans, for it was as yet unknown
for French or Italian artists to sing Wagner except in their own tongue.
If French or Italian works were included in the repertory, they would
be sung in German.

The seven seasons that succeeded planted some strong ideas about opera in the minds of those who lived through them and passed their thinking on to others. The conviction that Wagner should be sung only in German was perhaps to be expected; less expectable but no less a conviction was the agreed fact that Italian works should be sung in Italian, French works in French. Such conviction then flourished only in Anglo-Saxon countries, which, lacking an operatic literature of their own, can be objective about the best way of presenting the literature of others. After some vacillation, it has again become the "policy of the house" at Covent Garden. The trend at La Scala is also in that direction. For the most part, the Metropolitan stands on the same ground, though with more exceptions than one would like.

1884–1885

The Metropolitan's first season of opera in German was an experiment not only in type, but in detail. What made its success possible was two basic factors: a large German-speaking population in New York (a quarter of a million, according to contemporary estimates) and a Wagner literature that it was eager to hear. Such singers as Amalia Materna and Marianne Brandt (both had sung Kundry in Bayreuth performances of *Parsifal*), Adolf Robinson (a baritone who made a later mark as teacher of Leo Slezak), and Anton Schott were well equipped to serve as liaison. One suspects that the results would have been approximately the same even with lesser singers.

In the circumstances, one might have expected the Academy to burst into renewed vigor with the Italian and French works and singers excluded from the Metropolitan. Mapleson's beginning on November 10 with Patti in *Il Barbiere* was promising, but he had few male singers of quality to support Patti, Emma Nevada, Scalchi, and Fursch-Madi. Moreover, the owners of the property had made little effort to keep the house in proper repair, with the result, according to Krehbiel, that more than one dramatic climax was ruined "by the collapse of a stall." By Christmas time the Academy season was over.

In such circumstances the new Metropolitan was obviously a pleasanter place in which to spend the evening, almost in spite of what might be happening on the stage. For that matter, there was the excitement of novelty in the playing of the New York Symphony Orchestra under Leopold Damrosch for the performance of *Tannhäuser* with which the season opened on November 17. Auguste Kraus (known also as Seidl-Kraus after she married conductor Anton Seidl) was a capable Elisabeth (d),[1]* Anna Slach a suitable Venus (d).* As Wolfram (d),* Robinson was better than either woman. Schott's shouting as Tannhäuser (d)* was disturbing to an audience that thought Campanini's Lohengrin the right sound for Wagner. Krehbiel vouches that an audience of five thousand attended this opening, though we wonder where it was put.

The second-night *Fidelio* was a notable success for Brandt, whose Leonore (d) was greatly admired. The only portion of the house not filled, according to the *Tribune,* was the stockholders' boxes. A week later Weber appeared in the Metropolitan repertory for the first time, when *Der Freischütz* was given with Kraus as Ännchen,* Marie Schröder-Hanfstängl as Agathe,* Kögel as Caspar,* Robinson as Ottokar,* and Anton Udvardy as Max.* The spoken dialogue fared poorly in the large house. Despite one revival in 1909 and another in the 1920's, *Der Freischütz* has barely had more hearings in all the Metropolitan history than, say, *Peter Ibbetson.*

Along with a typical repertory of *Les Huguenots, Guillaume Tell* (in which Brandt surprised the public by accepting the minor role of Tell's wife), *Lohengrin* (in which the same Brandt left a high mark for other Ortruds* to challenge), and even *Rigoletto* (Schröder-Hanfstängl was Gilda,* Robinson the Rigoletto*), the company ventured *Don Giovanni* on December 10. In this the remarkable Brandt turned up as Donna Elvira,* with Schröder-Hanfstängi as Donna Anna* and Hermine Bely as Zerlina (d). Robinson sang the Don,* with Udvardy as Don Ottavio.* A rather more musicianly affair than the one of the year before, it was still given a black mark for the use of a German text.

Materna made her debut on January 5 as Elisabeth* in *Tannhäuser,* spending most of the remainder of the month in preparation for the first performance of *Die Walküre* on January 30. Several appearances as Valentine* in *Les Huguenots* and Rachel* in *La Juive* were scattered along the way, but none made so deep an impression as her "impetuous, exultant Brünnhilde"* (Krehbiel), with its "deep feeling, majestic appearance" (Henderson, the *Times,* January 31). Schott was the Siegmund,* Kraus the Sieglinde,* Kögel the Hunding,* and Staudigl the Wotan.* Such quality was not unexpected of Materna, for she had come to New York several years before to sing in concert performances of Wagner directed by Theodore Thomas. No one, however, expected Brandt to turn from the prominent role of Fricka to the minor one of a Valkyrie (Gerhilde*) in Act III. If these singers had pride, it was not for what they did, but for how they did it.

[1] The symbol (d) indicates the Metropolitan debut of the performer so designated.

Bayreuth procedure was claimed as the model for Stage Director Wilhelm Hock's action, though we may note one deviation that remained a perverse Metropolitan "tradition" for decades to come: in place of the "great door" that springs open midway in Act I, a curtain fell to the floor. Withal, *Die Walküre* was a huge success, with six more performances in this season.

Damrosch's formula was endorsed as sound in mid-January, when he was re-engaged for another year. At a ticket scale barely half of Abbey's, twice as much money had come to the box office as in the first two months of the previous season. Damrosch agreed to go on for a fee of $8,000 (his first contract, for managing and conducting, had been $10,000) plus a share of the profits. But there was no second season for Leopold Damrosch, for he died of pneumonia on February 15, after a brief illness. The intellectual community of New York paid honor to the fifty-three-year-old native of Breslau in impressive ceremonies at the opera house on February 18. In addition to music, there were verbal tributes by Henry Ward Beecher and Felix Adler.

During his father's illness Walter Damrosch made his debut as conductor on February 11, when *Tannhäuser* was given. He also directed *Die Walküre* the next day. During the period of family mourning, John Lund, the company's chorus master, took over in the pit, and he shared the post-season tour with the younger Damrosch.

Despite the noisy contention of Anton Schott that he was the man to succeed Damrosch as managing director, the stockholders eventually selected their executive secretary, Edmund C. Stanton. He was obviously chosen to supervise business details, with the musical supervision entrusted to others. Walter Damrosch, at twenty-three, was not ready for such responsibility, but there was a logical candidate who was—Anton Seidl. Schott had put his name into a letter arguing his own cause, and thereafter claimed credit for Seidl's engagement. It may be assumed that Seidl, as Wagner's trusted disciple and the husband of a member of the Damrosch company, was known favorably to others than Schott.

The season's breakdown showed that Damrosch had kept his production costs to an average of $3,400 a performance (in 1965 they averaged nearly nine times as much). The loss for the year was about $40,000, hardly imposing when spread among seventy stockholders.

1885–1886

Largely speaking, the six seasons of opera which followed the death of the senior Damrosch adhered to the scheme he had conceived. Wagner *premières*, plus the introduction of other works successfully presented in

Berlin and Vienna, were the basis of the repertory. The singers were of much the same type as those in the first German season, save that New York had the good fortune to hear Lilli Lehmann, the greatest of her generation, from the beginning of her period of greatest glory through the peak years of her career.

If her work left one standard of comparison by which future sopranos were judged, Anton Seidl's conducting marked the beginning of a tradition in another category of effort. From the opening performance of *Lohengrin* on November 23, 1885, which was remarkable if only for the number of errors (180 or more) in the printed score which he corrected during rehearsals, Seidl won an enduring esteem not only for scholarship, but also for temperament. He was one of the younger disciples of Wagner —he was only thirty-five when he came to America—and his sudden death in 1898 left a void that was not filled until Gustav Mahler arrived in 1908. Such generally respected men as Felix Mottl, Franz Schalk, and Alfred Hertz did not, in the intervening decade, give discriminating New Yorkers what they had learned to expect from Seidl.

How his *Lohengrin* differed from those to which New Yorkers were accustomed may be illustrated by Seidl's comment a few years later when a group of musicians were exchanging opinions on various approaches to Wagner. "In the property room of the Metropolitan Opera House," he said, "is a helmet . . . very much like other helmets save for the *Schwanen-ritter* emblem which it bears. It was made for *Lohengrin,* and my dear friend Campanini wore it in a truly magnificent performance . . . if you were to find that helmet today, you would discover that in addition to the prescribed dimensions and insignia, Campanini had put on it a blue plume, probably three feet in length. That, my dear gentlemen, is Italian opera [*see* illustration]."

Seidl's second opera, on November 25, was *Carmen.* Lilli Lehmann made her debut in the title role, in German, of course, and with the spoken dialogue. At thirty-five she was just beginning to make the transition from a lyric singer of high distinction to a dramatic one of even greater stature. The later Bayreuth favorite, Max Alvary sang José (d), with Robinson as Escamillo* and Seidl-Kraus as Micaëla.* *Carmen* was repeated on the Saturday afternoon of this week, with the same cast, following which Lehmann returned to the theater in the evening for a full rehearsal of *Die Walküre.* This unusual procedure was necessary because the orchestra was paid a higher rate for a Sunday rehearsal. The conductor for *Die Walküre* in this season was Walter Damrosch, Seidl being engaged first with the preparation of Goldmark's *Die Königin von Saba* and then with *Die Meistersinger.*

Lehmann had the leading role of Sulamith* when *Die Königin von Saba* was given for the first time on December 2. Krehbiel found the score "highly spiced" (the *Tribune,* December 3), but admired Goldmark's handling of the text and the lavishness of the production. It was said that the work cost $75,000 to produce, a sum for which considerable scenery and costumes could be purchased in those days. Apparently it was the spectacle that justified a total of fifteen performances in this single season (a house record until the oft-repeated *Die Fledermaus* of the first Bing season). Four performances satisfied public curiosity in 1886, and it was revived with negligible results in 1889 and 1905. Lehmann appeared in most of the performances in the first season, one, on December 4, being followed by a Brünnhilde in *Die Walküre* the next afternoon. In a period of ten days she made six appearances in three operas, taking part also in numerous rehearsals.

During the Christmas interval the company played a two-week engagement in Philadelphia and continued its arduous rehearsing of *Die Meistersinger.* The dominant impression of the first performance on January 4 was the picturesquely burgherish Hans Sachs* of Emil Fischer, a Dresden favorite who became much beloved in New York. For a later Sachs to be praised in terms of Fischer—as Friedrich Schorr eventually was—was to receive the highest praise a critic could find. Seidl-Kraus was well received as Eva* and Brandt as Magdalene,* but it was the conducting of Seidl that carried the others. The score was known to the concert-going public from performances by Theodore Thomas and Leopold Damrosch, but even the best-disposed members of the press thought a knowledge of German life and customs essential to enjoyment of the work on the stage. *Town Topics,* the organ of the society element, complained that "taking numbers . . . are unfortunately not very abundant." Apprehensions to the contrary, *Die Meistersinger* was given eight times this season, with cuts that reduced the playing time to four and one-quarter hours.

The repertory was limited to nine operas this season, each preceded by a dress rehearsal. Lehmann sang in all but two or three, appearing as Bertha* in *Le Prophète* on December 9, as Marguerite* in a five-act version of *Faust*[1] on January 20 (with Fischer as Méphistophélès* and Brandt as Siébel*), and as Irene* when *Rienzi* had its first American performance on February 5. Lest the later portion of the season seem a mere breathing-spell for Lehmann, it may be mentioned that the last *Tannhäuser* on March 3 found her cast as Venus.* The records for the year also show a concert performance of *Parsifal* directed by Walter

[1] Generally considered the longest performance of opera given in New York till that time; later exceeded only by *Parsifal.*

Damrosch on March 4, with the untiring Brandt as Kundry, Fischer as Gurnemanz, and Krämer as Parsifal. The assisting Oratorio Society Chorus performed in English.

Although society's pleasure with the new trend of things was not profound (see page 8), the year's loss was only $25,000—much of it incurred during the Philadelphia visit—with paid attendance averaging 2,666 at *Die Königin von Saba*, 2,500 at *Die Meistersinger*. To guarantee such musicians as Seidl, Lehmann, Fischer, and Alvary reasonable tenure in New York—most of them had given up pension rights and other court-theater prerogatives to come to the Metropolitan—an extension of three years was voted to German opera early in March. It might almost be said that along with building a theater in Bayreuth, Richard Wagner had created the means to keep one open in New York and close another.

For while Seidl was promoting the Germanic revival at the Metropolitan, Mapleson came to the end of his string at the Academy of Music. He could offer his customers neither Patti nor Gerster, and even the vivacious Minnie Hauk as Carmen disappointed his opening audience on November 2, 1885. Twenty years of singing had elapsed since she was first heard in New York, and her voice was badly worn. The notable event of a season limited to three weeks occurred after a short tour, when Mapleson selected Massenet's *Manon* for a manager's benefit on December 23. For its first North American performance Hauk sang Manon, with Del Puente as Lescaut, Ferruccio Giannini as Des Grieux, and a Signor Cherubini as his father. Mathilde Bauermeister, the incomparable *seconda* of the later Grau company, was Poussette; the language was Italian.

With his once flourishing enterprise bereft of support, Mapleson announced his withdrawal from opera in New York with the historic words: "I cannot fight Wall Street."

1886–1887

Wall Street and Wagner were, indeed, a formidable if fortuitous combination. *Tristan und Isolde* was the missionary work of this season, and Seidl attacked it with all the zeal of a prophet. His introductory performance on December 1 was rated by Krehbiel as "finer than those of Bayreuth" in a review that ran serially in the *Tribune* on December 2, 3, and 5. Lehmann's Isolde* was "beyond praise," Brandt as Brangäne gave "real pleasure," and Fischer was an admired Marke.* More magnetic than any of his younger colleagues, if well worn in voice, was the fifty-seven-year-old Tristan,* Albert Niemann.

A central figure in Wagnerian lore—he was the Tannhäuser of the famous Parisian incident of 1861 and the first Bayreuth Siegmund in

1876—Niemann came to New York at a time when stage presence and a superb sense of declamation were his last dependable resources. All contemporaries are agreed that he was an artist of profound impulse, whether as Siegmund* in *Die Walküre* (in which he made his debut on November 10), Tannhäuser* on the 26th, or Florestan* in *Fidelio* on January 14. In fact, when he sang his final Tristan on February 7, the *Evening Post* compared the response to "the triumphs of Patti and Lind," and seats with a face value of four dollars were sold by speculators for fifteen. All this was accomplished despite a voice dry and unresonant, which might, as it did in his first Tannhäuser, break in mid-phrase.

As Chaliapin attracted an audience for *Boris* which had no special sympathy for Russian opera, so Niemann's powerful personality did its work on behalf of Wagner. Eight performances of *Tristan* in this season were more than it had in any following one at the Metropolitan until the late 1930's, when Flagstad and Melchior were another generation's counterparts of Lehmann and Niemann.

Lehmann and Niemann, however, could not sing every night, and the bright success of *Tristan* could not obscure the dim side of the season's schedule, which this year included fourteen works. As a successor to the previous year's successful *Die Königin von Saba* (it had its sixteenth performance on the opening night, November 8, 1886), *Merlin*, also by Goldmark, appeared on January 3. Although Lehmann sang Viviane,* with Alvary as Merlin,* it had the unhappy distinction of being the first of many one-season "novelties" at the Metropolitan. On the other hand, the most popular of all operas in the Metropolitan's history was poorly served by the German performers when *Aida* had its first performance in the theatre on November 12. W. J. Henderson, ordinarily an outspoken admirer of Seidl, found his direction responsible for "unconscionable dragging of the tempi" (the *Times*, November 13), and took issue with the "excessive emphasis" of such singers as Theresa Herbert-Förster (wife of Victor Herbert) as Aida,* Brandt as Amneris,* Robinson as Amonasro,* and Fischer as Ramfis.* Radames* was sung by Carl Zobel.

There was, of course, no sensible reason why New Yorkers should listen to *Aida* in German or why they should be invited to so Germanic a "light evening" as the double bill of *Vienna Waltzes* (a ballet to music arranged by Josef Bayer) and Ignaz Brüll's *Das goldene Kreuz*, given first on November 19. This was obviously as much operatic imbalance as the Italian *Carmen* or *Lohengrin* of the first season, and doomed to fall in the same category of limited interest. Seidl could scarcely be blamed for an unidiomatic *Aida*, for this was not his idiom. One should not be too surprised to discover that he brought to it something of the "freshness" that Walter Damrosch brought to a *Trovatore* he conducted in this period. Asked by Henderson: "For goodness' sake, Walter, where did you get those tempi?" he replied: "I don't know. I never conducted it before."

A reminder of another kind of operatic art came at the end of the German season when a touring company starring Patti played a short season at the Metropolitan in April and May. She was now working for the undiscourageable Abbey, with a typical stock company of the time— Scalchi, Del Puente, Galassi, and so on. With a repertory of *La Traviata, Carmen, Semiramide, Faust, Lucia,* and *Marta,* Abbey did a spectacular business at seven dollars for his best seats. Henderson might scoff: "Everyone knew that Carmen was a cat, but Patti made her a kitten," but Abbey had a better phrase with which to fight back. This, the public was told, was Patti's farewell in opera. One can imagine the mournful state of mind with which Krehbiel wrote, in his Chapters of Opera (1908): "I have just been reading the same legend again in the London newspapers —twenty-one years after it served Mr. Abbey a turn." Voice and legend were good enough to attract $70,000 for six operas, and a repetition of *Lucia* on May 6. This was *addio,* but not *senza encore.*

1887–1888

In the circumstances thus far detailed, the time might have seemed ripe for a revision of the thinking that had resulted in three years of German opera. Why, one might have said, with an Abbey company available could there not be a collaborative effort, in which Seidl would go on with his production of German opera and the public be served otherwise by Italian performances of Italian works?

Aside from such a matter as the extension of lease voted to Seidl and his German artists the year before, there was a more practical factor to consider. By restricting the company in size and encouraging the kind of ensemble which flourished in the court theaters from which the singers came, ticket prices could be kept to a top of four dollars. Nothing of the sort would be possible with a company built around stars. And, remembering their last experience with such a company, in 1883, the stockholders felt no disposition to risk heavy losses.

Hence Seidl proceeded with *Siegfried* and *Götterdämmerung* as the new Wagner ventures of this season, balanced by *Euryanthe,* Spontini's *Fernand Cortez,* and Nessler's *Trompeter von Säkkingen.* In *Siegfried* on November 9, Alvary showed his attractively youthful Siegfried,* with Lehmann as Brünnhilde.* In a *Times* review (the column was headed "Amusements," with the subheading "Another Wagner Opera") Henderson said: "There is no doubt that the brilliant array of society people . . .

were extremely bored." Others in the audience were "unquestionably pleased" by Lehmann's "magnificent singing" and Fischer's "noble" Wotan.* Alvary was "surprisingly good," but Ferenczy was "execrable" as Mime.*

In the two months that elapsed before *Götterdämmerung* (the program called it *"Die" Götterdämmerung*) was given on January 25, the Metropolitan Siegfried* had aged more than the Wagnerian one. In Bayreuth, Niemann had been forbidden to appear as Siegfried, for Wagner considered it undesirable (for illusion) for the same performer to play both Siegmund and his son. His death scene, however (as in *Tristan*) sent "magnetic shocks" (the *Tribune,* January 26, 1888) through the audience and Lehmann was "a benediction to the memory." Henderson endorsed Seidl's omission of the Norn and Waltraute scenes as "judicious pruning," of which one consequence was that Brandt had nothing to sing but a Rhinemaiden (Wellgunde*). Not until Franz Schalk came in 1898 was *Götterdämmerung* given entire.

With the trilogy at last in the repertory (*Das Rheingold,* it will be remembered, is officially a "prelude"), Seidl offered his public a pseudo-Bayreuth ceremonial beginning on January 30, continuing on February 1 and 3. Lehmann sang the three Brünnhildes in five days, and Niemann pleased himself, if not the memory of Wagner, by playing Siegmund and the elder Siegfried. The sequence was repeated the following week, and there were three later hearings of *Götterdämmerung* before the season ended on February 18.

With all this indication of public favor, the kind and character of the performance should not be overvalued. In a summing up at the season's end Henderson commented (the *Times*) that *Götterdämmerung* is full of opportunities for scenic effects, "none of which have been advantagageously used." In part "the lack of mechanism and properly arranged space" of the stage was blamed for this, but it was also felt that too much money had been spent on *Fernand Cortez.* Niemann sang Cortez* when it was first given, on January 6, with a largely male cast (Meisslinger as Amazily* was the single exception), with results that Krehbiel described as very much like "trying to resuscitate a mummy." Henderson admired the "vigor and sweep" of the writing, but did not find its effect "deep or lasting." Aside from the "glittering production," the project offered little, and it disappeared after three repetitions.

In the press of more important affairs, Nessler's *Trompeter* was given in a way Henderson termed "slovenly," for all its "tuneful" qualities. Louise Meisslinger was heard as the ex-Countess of Wildenstein* in the first performance on November 23, showing a voice the same critic termed "clear and fresh, if rather acid." The work was repeated six times in this season.

Along with her week of three Brünnhildes, Lehmann found time to sing several Isoldes (the first, on November 2, being the opening performance of the season, in the presence of the Secretary of the Navy and a delegation from the Chinese Embassy), several performances of Leonore in *Fidelio*, and Euryanthe* on December 23. Despite the splendid work of Brandt as Eglantine,* Alvary as Adolar,* and Fischer as Lysiart,* the Seidl production (with the tableau during the overture) fared much the same as Toscanini's of 1914–15—four performances in the earlier season, five in the later.

Near the end of the season Brandt let it be known that she would not return, though her services were highly valued. Her choice of *Fidelio* for a farewell on March 17 recalled an incident of the previous year, when her performance of the dungeon scene had been interrupted by raucous laughter from a box, and Seidl had to begin *"O namenlose Freude"* a second time. The blame was attached to Lilli Lehmann, something of a Leonore herself, and the relations of the two thereafter were very cool. Unfortunately, for all her greatness as an artist, Lehmann did not get along well with some female colleagues. In the 1890's, Nordica—by then an artist of distinction—approached Lehmann deferentially in a foyer at Bayreuth and asked when she might call to pay her respects. In a voice that could be heard for yards, Lehmann replied: "I am not taking pupils this season."

The itinerant companies that used the Academy of Music at this time left little of note save for the United States *première* of Verdi's *Otello* on April 16, with Cleofonte Campanini conducting for a company headed by his brother, and Eva Tetrazzini (sister of the still-to-be-heard-from Luisa) as Desdemona. Italo Campanini did not take the title role, however, until April 20, Francesco Marconi preceding him. Henderson and Krehbiel were at variance in their reports of this affair, the former describing "tumults of applause," repetitions of the *"Credo"* (sung by Galassi) and the *"Ave Maria,"* and a final opinion that it was "a great work and one that ought to live long." Krehbiel thought the public attitude "apathetic," declared that the tenor, Marconi, did not "please," and called the music "not of the kind expected from Verdi." Inasmuch as Henderson went back for the Campanini performance to marvel at his acting ("rarely seen on a lyric stage in this country"), one may assume that his attitude was more receptive than that of the strongly pro-Wagner Krehbiel.

1888–1889

Among the ironies with which the history of the Metropolitan is sprinkled, few are more diverting than the quirk by which the works of Wagner written for his "modern" stage at Bayreuth were made to serve as saviors of a theater barren of such resources. The complaints aroused by the manner in which *Götterdämmerung* had been given in the previous season were much surpassed when the turn of *Das Rheingold* came on January 4, 1889. As excuse for presenting the work with a quarter-hour intermission between the second and the third scenes, the "practise of the Imperial Opera House in Vienna" was cited. How this made it better, the explanation did not explain.

No precedent could be cited, however, for lowering the curtain after the Nibelheim scene. Krehbiel politely attributed this to the "structural peculiarities" of the stage (*Tribune,* January 5). Henderson, more forthright, said: "The house has a badly constructed stage," ill-adapted to anything requiring "heavy mechanical operations." Despite a Loge* by Alvary which was "sadly lacking in subtlety," Henderson had hearty admiration for Seidl's treatment of the score, the Wotan* of Fischer, and the Alberich* of Joseph Beck, a Bayreuth stalwart. None of the women was outstanding. To take advantage of the interest aroused by the scenic illusions, the other repertory was suspended for a while, with repetitions of *Rheingold* on January 5 and 7.

There were, in all, nine performances of *Das Rheingold* in this season, including two as part of complete cycles, the first beginning March 4, the second March 15. Lehmann sang the Brünnhildes in most of these, plus extra performances of *Götterdämmerung* on March 16 and 22. In fact, between March 16 and 22 Lehmann sang a major role every day except the 17th and 19th.

She did not arrive this season until January, but she repeated a greatly admired role in a new setting on January 30, singing Venus when the Paris version of *Tannhäuser* was introduced. Niemann's American career having ended and Alvary being ill, Tannhäuser (d) was sung by Lehmann's husband, Paul Kalisch. He was favorably known as a concert singer in New York, but had not previously ventured into opera. Not gifted with a notable voice, he was nevertheless an artist of quality, and a singer of "fine taste" (Krehbiel). Opinions varied on the comparative merits of the Paris *Tannhäuser* and the Dresden one, then better known in New York. Some missed the "noble climax" of the overture as it passed directly into the Venusberg scene; others thought that the second scene had lost some of its simplicity. Eventually the Paris version became standard at the Metropolitan, even to the season when Fritz Busch of Dresden was its conductor. (It reappeared briefly in 1953–4 with Szell and again in 1965–6).

With most of the major Wagner repertory explored, Stanton had a thought of giving *Parsifal* in this season, despite the well-known objections of the Wagner family. More influential, perhaps, were the objections of his principal singers, most of them Bayreuth-oriented, with a keen idea of what would happen to their future relations with Cosima should they take part in a *sub rosa Parsifal.* Lehmann has recorded (*My Path through Life,* page 380) her strong advice to Stanton to "leave it to Bayreuth."

With the tenure of German opera up for renewal, it is perhaps easy to understand the trend in repertory toward a German *Trovatore* (as well as *Aida*), a new mounting of *L'Africaine,* and more attention to *Les Huguenots* and *Le Prophète* than in the previous season. On one occasion when *La Juive* was given, the ballet in Act III tripped lightly to the *"Pizzicato"* from Delibes's *Sylvia.*

The season began with *Les Huguenots* on November 28, with Fanny Moran-Olden a new Valentine (d), Felicie Kaschowska a new Urban (d), and a vigorous tenor, Julius Perotti, making his debut as Raoul.* Considering the German influence of the day, it is hardly surprising that the *Times* identified Fischer, the Marcel, as "Maxel." *Guillaume Tell* was revived on on December 3 to show off Perotti's high C sharp in the role of Arnold.* When the trio with Robinson and Fischer was heartily applauded, Perotti walked to the footlights for a bow while his German-trained colleagues held their poses.

Perotti also had a triumphant time with the top notes of Vasco da Gama* when *L'Africaine* was presented on December 7. Henderson spoke well of the scenery, especially the "ship scene . . . a fine specimen of marine architecture." Robinson (Nelusko*) and Fischer (Don Pedro*) did their work well, but the ladies (Moran-Olden as Selika* and Sophie Traubman as Inez*) were wanting. Seidl was the conductor. Perotti made a contribution of sorts to history by singing both Faust* (December 26) and Siegmund* in *Die Walküre* (February 15), a pair of tenor roles not attempted even by Jean de Reszke. Perotti was also involved, as Manrico,* in a *Trovatore* of February 6 in which Henderson accused Damrosch of taking the "Anvil Chorus" at a "break-neck tempo."

The patience of the box-holders with opera in German was fraying badly—some unusually loud conversation during a flute solo in the opening *Huguenots* was "hissed down," said the *Times*—but it had not quite reached the breaking-point. Midway in the season a statement of plans for the next year was circulated, offering a choice of continuing German opera at an assessment of $3,200 a box or keeping the theater dark at an assessment of $1,000 a box. Italian opera was ruled out because "it would entail a much larger assessment upon the stockholders than to give German opera." On March 17 the stockholders voted to continue German opera, forty-three in favor, three opposed.

The only performance of Italian opera in Italian at the Metropolitan in this season came late in April, when Italo Campanini arranged a benefit performance of *Lucia* with Clementine de Vere, a later Metropolitan favorite, as Lucia, and Del Puente as Enrico. The worthy object of the benefit was Campanini himself.

Not to be scorned in any chronicle of musical events at the Metropolitan was a concert on March 27, in which Hans von Bülow, currently favoring New York with a "cyclus" of Beethoven piano sonatas, conducted a program of Berlioz's *Benvenuto Cellini* Overture, the Fourth Symphony of Brahms, the Eighth of Beethoven, and the *Tannhäuser* Overture. Along the way Fursch-Madi sang arias from *Hérodiade* and *Samson et Dalila*. A rather breathless account in the *Times* concluded: "Dr. von Bülow displayed his remarkable musical memory by conducting the four orchestral numbers without score."

1889–1890

The two final years in which opera was given exclusively in German at the Metropolitan show a pair of trends, sharply opposed, but equally intense: a growing resistance on the part of the stockholders to more and more Wagner, an increasingly desperate effort on the part of Stanton and his associates to vary the fare while preserving the basic cuisine. When the two attitudes reached a climax of tension, the decision was made, on January 14, 1891, to turn the house over to Abbey and Grau for a fresh start on opera in the old manner.

How little some of the stockholders had come to care for their responsibilities as "art patrons" was shown midway in this season by an article in the *Times* of February 2, 1890. Titled "Opera House Rights," it began: "The annual dispute as to the rights of man to talk in an opera house has broken out with its customary severity. Persons who have come to New York to see the sights . . . are surprised when they hear a sudden outburst of sibilant sounds not down in the score. These are the admonitory hisses of the three-dollar men and women who sit in the orchestra stalls and grow weary under the constant down-dropping upon their heads of diamonds of speech from the thirty-two-hundred-dollar ladies and gentlemen in the boxes."

The provocation for these comments was the open statement of Henry Clews and Elbridge T. Gerry that the stockholders were tired of being rebuked by the ticket-buyers and would conduct themselves as they pleased.

"Mr. Gerry agrees with Mr. Clews," the *Times* continued, "that all persons who hiss the licensed conversationalists should be put out." It offered the suggestion that a simple solution would be for the house to be closed to such interlopers. "It will cost them only $7,000 each to run the opera" and "enjoy their conversations without the interruption of hissing." The notion of such an investment doubtless appealed to them as little as the ironic tone of the writer, W. J. Henderson.

What was being talked through, moreover, was on frequent occasions some of the most amazingly versatile singing that the Metropolitan had heard or would hear. With no remaining Wagner roles to explore, Lilli Lehmann assumed a repertory staggering in both breadth and inclusiveness —not only the three Brünnhildes, Isolde, Venus, and the Queen* in *Die Königin von Saba,* but also Donna Anna* in *Don Giovanni* on December 4, Amelia* in *Ein Maskenball* (*Un Ballo* in German) on December 11, Rachel in *La Juive* on December 20, Aida* on January 15, and climactically, Norma* on February 27.

The last of these was chosen by Lehmann for a performance arranged for her own benefit, rousing infinite admiration in some quarters, a little resistance in others. The Wagnerians, led by Krehbiel, hailed it as proof beyond dispute that constant singing of Wagner did not, as some contended, permanently impair the voice: "It . . . served to disprove in part the assertion . . . that devotion to the lyric drama in its latest and most significant phase does not necessarily preclude excellence in the old domain of beautiful singing." Henderson thought that *Norma,* hastily got up for a benefit, was a rather egotistical gesture by Lehmann, but concurred in the judgment of the art displayed. "Her voice possesses far more flexibility . . . and a greater command of the pure ornamentation of singing than anyone suspected." Some of the earlier singers of the Italian stage performed with more assurance, Henderson suggested, "but so long is it since this public has heard so excellent an exhibition of this sort that the audience was fairly carried away" (the *Times,* February 28). It was a long time between Normas for the Metropolitan, for the next was Rosa Ponselle, thirty-eight years later. Kalisch was the Pollione* in his wife's benefit, with Damrosch conducting.

Earlier, Henderson had judged Lehmann's Amelia, in December, as "equal to anything that could have been done by a great Italian singer . . . her acting far beyond that which the Italian stage had been in the habit of associating with Verdi's earlier works." Her Aida was also of exceptional quality, closer to the ideal established by Clara Louise Kellogg in 1874 than anything heard in the interim. Her Donna Anna, in a poorish cast

(Reichmann was the Don,* with Kalisch as Ottavio,* and Sonntag-Uhl as Elvira [d]), was admirable, though not the forceful performance of a few years later. Seidl's conducting, it was said, gave a new insight into "the composer's instrumental design." This year's *Tristan** to the Lehmann Isolde on January 22 was Heinrich Vogl, a Viennese. The judgment was short but comprehensive: "an earnest man, but he cannot sing."

Aside from the work of Lehmann, the season was notable only for the introduction of the zestful *Barbier von Bagdad,* by Peter Cornelius, a Wagner disciple. It was well received at its *première* on January 3, 1890, though Seidl had become ill after directing all the reheasals and Damrosch took his place. The *Times* spoke well of its "wonderfully faithful" musical characterization, and Krehbiel thought that the judgment of New York might reverse the work's previous failure in Europe. Fischer was the Barber,* with Kalisch as Nureddin* and Traubman as Margiana.* The disruption of the German repertory in the next season delayed further attention to Cornelius for a while—until 1925, in fact.

In a pre-season prospectus there had been talk of *La Gioconda* and Lalo's *Roi d'Ys* to vary the repertory further, but neither was given. The *Ring* returned, distinguished largely by Lehmann's Brünnhildes, for Vogl was a further step down from Niemann and Alvary. The additional Wagner included *Der fliegende Holländer* (with which the season began on November 27) and *Rienzi.*

Abbey's tourists returned to the Metropolitan for a month of Italian opera in better form than ever to challenge the good judgment that insisted on German opera for New York. Francesco Tamagno in *Otello,* with Albani as Desdemona and Del Puente as Iago, was a rousing start on March 24, with Patti in *Semiramide* on March 25, Nordica, Tamagno, and Del Puente in *Il Trovatore* two days later, and Patti in *La Sonnambula* on the day following.

Between the clarion voice of Tamagno and the agile one of Patti, the critics held to a course that included, in either instance, superlatives. "One of the most manlike men ever to stride the stage," said the *Times,* ". . . his 'Sangue Sangue!' was given *parlando* with a fierce shout . . . his B and C are immensely powerful." Of Patti: "This was vocal art that would draw in 'The Bohemian Girl.'" Apparently Abbey was not altogether certain that it would continue to draw in *Lakmé, Lucia, Roméo et Juliette,* for by April 26 it was advertised that this was, again, Patti's farewell. The categorical statement was: "It is certain that this public will never again hear her in the roles with which her name and fame are identified." Never again, actually, until the spring of 1892.

1890–1891

Whatever the abuses the hosts of the Metropolitan visited upon their paying guests, one could scarcely condemn them for calling "Enough!" when the season Stanton had contrived for his seventh was halfway along. There was no Lehmann, no Materna, no Brandt; no Niemann, Alvary, or even Vogl. Aside from Andreas Dippel, who was to find his way to an executive's chair before his Metropolitan career ended, the enduring Emil Fischer, and a thin-voiced Minnie Hauk, the names on the season roster are of the sort known only to specialists in bygone opera lore.

Even more offensive, if possible, was the repertory, which blossomed with such "novelties" as Baron Alberto Franchetti's *Asrael,* which had its *première* on the opening night, November 26, with Dippel as Asrael (d); Smareglia's *Der Vasall von Szigeth,* and *Diana von Solange* by Ernest II, Duke of Saxe-Coburg. "Bewildering" was the term of the *Times* (November 27) for the libretto of Ferdinand Fontana on which the German-influenced Franchetti based his score, a "sup of horrors" the description of Krehbiel for *Der Vasall von Szigeth,* during which "volleys of talk and laughter" (the *Times*) echoed from the boxes.

These, at least, were professional works of competent writers, however imitative or banal. Neither novel nor professional was *Diana von Solange,* which was thirty years old in 1891 when Stanton elected to put it on for reasons related to the well-known "lavishness of the Duke . . . in the distribution of orders, especially among musicians." The diligent Dippel sang Armand* in a score described by Henderson as "simply rubbish." The critic's prophecy that *Diana* would not see a third performance was borne out when a petition protesting a repetition on January 17 was delivered to the management with three hundred signatures. As a species of tit for tat, its replacement was fairly remarkable: *Fidelio.*

It was during this series of days that the management came to the conclusion that opera in German, however cheap, was no replacement for desirable opera, however costly. On January 14 it was decided to give Abbey another chance with a full season's presentations. On the next day the famous card (page 53) commanding silence was posted in the boxes. Presumably the rebuke could be issued when the issue was decided. And with the issue decided, the management could even be magnanimous and let the German public have its fill of Wagner for the remainder of the season.

Only *Lohengrin,* the *Holländer,* and *Tannhäuser* had been heard during the weeks of the controversy. On this same January 14 the opera was *Die Meistersinger,* with Heinrich Gudehus as Walther,* Reichmann as Sachs, and Marie Jahn as Eva.* *Siegfried* came along on January 28 (with Antonia Mielke as Brünnhilde*), *Walküre* on February 6, *Götterdämmerung* on the 13th, and *Tristan* on the 25th. From March 7 to the closing date of March 21 nothing but Wagner was given. Every performance had its vociferous demonstration for Wagner and Seidl, and at the closing *Die Meistersinger* (with Dippel as Walther) Fischer's Sachs was cheered until he spoke a few words in English. Seidl and Stanton shared the post-curtain calls, which continued for half an hour.

To judge from the Krehbiel documentation, this demonstration was a measured objection by the whole operatic, non-stockholder public; but access to the Henderson files has cast another light on the emerging picture. Reviewing the opinions expressed by "our esteemed contemporaries," he said in the *Times* (January 26, 1891) that they were "based on an assumption that the Directors of the Opera House are flying in the face of public demand. This seems a little severe. . . . The Germans, who comprise three-fourths of the present patronage of the Metropolitan, will seldom darken its doors next season. Whether or not there is a public to take their places is the problem."

The answer seemed clear to Henderson, even if no known company was capable of providing it. "The modern French school, which has endeavored to make a fusion of the styles of Wagner and Gluck . . . has been shut out of the Metropolitan, probably on account of the expense. . . . The Italian and German novelties have not found favor with the public with the exception of Cornelius's charming 'Barber of Bagdad,' and the patrons of the house have refused to attend performances of the threadbare Meyerbeer operas. . . . The result is that the public has literally limited the paying repertoire . . . to the Wagner list and 'Fidelio.' Now it is quite as impossible to run an Opera House on such a list as this as it is on a list composed of 'Lucia,' 'Il Trovatore,' 'La Sonnambula,' 'Rigoletto,' *et id omne genus*. The safest way out of the difficulty was to produce some of the French operas often promised but never forthcoming."

Plainly what Henderson had in mind was a fusion of the operatic elements at large in the world, each of valid interest when provided in reasonable proportion. How this could be achieved within the framework of a resident repertory company was a question that took nearly all of a decade to answer.

Characteristic of the epoch was the Metropolitan "career" of Minnie Hauk, who appeared as a member of the company for the first time on February 20. This favorite of New York, where she was born, was thinner of voice than in her Academy days, but the opera, almost automatically, was *Carmen*. With Damrosch conducting, and Dippel singing "the weakest

José I have ever encountered" (Henderson), Hauk sang this and two other performances of Carmen,* for her own countrymen, in her native city, in German.

EPILOGUE

In purely musical terms no period in the history of the Metropolitan saw so much accomplishment as the seasons given over to the production of opera in German. The first performances of the *Ring, Tristan,* and *Die Meistersinger* were inevitable happenings in America, as they had recently been in London; but it was much to America's gain that they were produced with Niemann, Brandt, Materna, Lehmann, and Fischer, under so capable a conductor as Anton Seidl. The period was inordinately prolonged after the work foreordained for it was completed; but that was not to be charged against the artists who made it memorable.

As witness to collateral conditions in the other great English-speaking city in which opera flourished, one may invoke the observations of Bernard Shaw. Writing of *Die Meistersinger* in July 1889, he notes: "How Johannistag sounds as 'solenne di' and Wahn! Wahn! as 'Si, Si' may be imagined." From Bayreuth a little later he wrote: "After the scratch representations we are accustomed to in London, at which half the attention of the singers is given to the prompter, half to the conductor, and the rest to the character impersonated, the Bayreuth plays seem miracles of perfect preparedness" (*London Music in 1888-89*).

For that matter, Shaw wrote that the Covent Garden underwriters of the "season" were hardly less rude than their American counterparts: "They delay the rise of the curtain until half-past eight and then come late. . . . They waste invaluable space with their comfortless dens of boxes. The percentage of inconsiderate persons among them is so high that there are always at least three parties disturbing the audience by talking and laughing at full pitch during the performance."

The beginning made in New York was reflected in tours organized by Walter Damrosch and others. The German artists brought to the Metropolitan were heard and admired in other centers, and their standards became ours. When there was a reversion to earlier practices, enough experience had been amassed to prove that the "music of the future" was, in truth, the music of the present.

To be sure there was a veneration of the ponderous to the neglect of the merely pleasurable. The later Verdi languished, Mozart was barely noticed, Gluck and Handel were ignored. But a definite responsibility to the public was discharged, if involuntarily; the cornerstone laid, if the building was never really completed.

THE DE RESZKES AND THE "GOLDEN AGE OF SONG,"
1891–1903

Among those with a reasonably wide view of the operatic world of the 1890's, the reaction to the new policy of the Metropolitan was not all lamentation and despair. Abbey's company was to be, in the first place, not merely Italian but Franco-Italian. In the second place, it promised, among its principal artists, Édouard and Jean de Reszke, of whom Henderson said (in the *Times* article quoted previously, page 102): "So far as the De Reszke brothers are concerned, the public may rest satisfied. . . . These gentlemen are real artists and while they sing like angels, they do not forget to act like men."

It was inevitable that personalities of this magnitude should come to America; in fact, they had all but committed themselves to Mapleson for a tour in 1888 (Clara Leiser: *Jean de Reszke and the Great Days of Opera.* New York: Minton Balch & Company; 1934, p. 64). That impresario's determination not to "fight Wall Street" put an end to his American activities, which was just as well for the De Reszkes. When they came, it was not in a touring company of dubious artistic possibilities, but as generative forces in a new operatic development.

The pattern did not emerge at once, but the elements that entered into it may be indicated here. Two factors had to be reconciled. One, a question of musical style, involved the capacity of singers trained in the "old" school of Gounod and early Verdi to adapt themselves to the "new" requirements of Wagner. The second, a matter of language, posed the necessity for the best singers of the day to be equally adept in Italian, French, *and* German if the whole repertory were to profit from their talents.

It was the signal contribution of the De Reszke brothers, in the fullness of time, to lead the way in that historic evolution. And historic it was, not only for the time in which they lived and functioned, but also as a model on which the seriously ambitious singers of the future might form their own careers. The contribution would have been a notable one had they been lesser men; that they were, as well, the idols of London, New York, and Paris gave them leadership in what was the first truly international period of operatic performance.

Something might be said about the odd fact that this new concept of versatility was led by two Poles—the De Reszkes—seconded by such Americans as Eames, Nordica, and Bispham. But what could be more natural? Neither Polish nor English being an "operatic language," it was a matter of little moment whether such nationals learned Italian and French or Italian, French, and German. When the period had passed, and its lessons could be evaluated, the conclusion was that the key language and training was French; that facility in French and the training of the Opéra vastly enhanced the work these people did in Italian and German. In years to come, many important singers of German background learned to perform in French and Italian; fewer of the standard Italian artists were so diligent. Doubtless temperament and training were important in this; but it is also a fact that Italian opera-singers could find a lifetime's employment in their own theaters without learning even one additional language.

The Abbey–Schoeffel–Grau Opera Company, 1891–1897

1891–1892

The break with the period of German opera was accompanied by several other musical happenings that put what followed in a much more contemporary frame of reference. October 1, 1891 was marked by a competition in New York *premières* of *Cavalleria rusticana.* The victory went to Rudolph Aronson, who put his version on the stage of the Casino Theater in the afternoon. In the evening Oscar Hammerstein, then associated with the Harlem Opera House on 125th Street, produced *Cavalleria* in the Lenox Lyceum. The competition seemed futile in any case, for the American *première* had occurred on September 10 in Philadelphia, and none of the performances did justice to the score. The only name worth noting other than Hammerstein's was that of Heinrich Conried, who was stage manager for Aronson.

During the next few weeks the record of musical performance in New York gained such familiar names as Olive Fremstadt (the *t* came off later), who made her debut in a concert directed by Seidl in the Lenox Lyceum on November 8; and Ignace Paderewski, who made three appearances with orchestra and gave three recitals between November 17 and December 2. Thus the musical public was alert for fresh experiences when the Abbey company came to the Metropolitan on December 14, after five weeks in Chicago.

Vianesi, who had conducted most of the performances of the 1883–4 season, was in charge of the opening *Roméo et Juliette,* and the orchestra greeted him with a fanfare when he took the podium. For the first time French was heard in the Metropolitan, and the choral prologue to the opera was included. The youthful Emma Eames (only twenty-six, but with Parisian success to her credit) made her debut as Juliette,* as did Jean de Reszke as Roméo,* Édouard as Frère Laurent,* Mathilde Bauermeister as the Nurse,* and Jean Martapoura as Mercutio.* The *Tribune* described Eames as a "strikingly beautiful Juliette" and Jean de Reszke's artistic instincts as "most admirable," though "his voice is not sensuously beautiful." Henderson, in the *Times,* echoed the compliments for Eames (her waltz was "one of the . . . most finished bits of coloratura singing lately heard"), termed De Reszke's voice an "agreeable though not a surprising organ," and concurred in recognizing his "genuine artistic feeling." The highest praise went to Édouard de Reszke, who demonstrated "in a single scene" (Act II) that he was a "really great artist."

In an honest effort to combine the best of the old with the new, Abbey engaged Lilli Lehmann for this season, and had serious intentions of presenting her in a German *Walküre* with Seidl conducting and Fischer (Wotan) *als Gast,* during February. She found herself out of voice as the time approached, however, and the project was dropped. She began her work for the season on the second night (December 16), as Leonora* in an Italian *Trovatore,* with Kalisch as Manrico,* and a current London favorite, Giulia Ravogli, as Azucena (d). Lehmann's dramatic power "interested her listeners more than any . . . Leonora in many years" (the *Times*), but Ravogli lacked the low tones New York liked in the role.

Lillian Nordica's Metropolitan debut came on December 18, when she replaced the ailing Albani as Valentine* in *Les Huguenots,* with Jane de Vigne as Urbain.* With Jean de Reszke as Raoul* and Édouard as Marcel,* the night was alive with fine singing, though not enough to make Henderson indifferent to a performance of the viola obbligato to Raoul's first air, which was "one of the most discomforting performances ever heard in the Opera." (The Symphony Society had left the house with the end of German opera.)

One of the favorite experiences of this era was introduced on Christmas Day when Jean de Reszke was heard for the first of many times as Faust,* with Eames as Marguerite,* Scalchi as Siébel, and Bauermeister as Marthe.* Enrico Serbolini was a stand-in for the indisposed brother De Reszke as Méphistophélès.* When Édouard appeared in the part for the first time on February 1 it was Henderson's opinion that *"Veau d'or"* had "never been sung on the Metropolitan stage as he sang it." For reasons of convenience, apparently, this opera continued to be given in Italian, as was *Carmen.*

The full impact of the company Abbey had engaged was not evident until mid-January, when the great baritone Jean Lassalle made his debut as Nelusko* in *L'Africaine,* with Nordica (Selika*), Jean de Reszke (Vasco da Gama*) and Édouard (Don Pedro*). Even the reluctant Krehbiel rejoiced: "To see three such splendid representations of physical and artistic manhood . . . on the stage was in itself a unique sensation." Lassalle's second role, on January 18, was a Don Giovanni* "in strict accordance with the traditions of the Paris Grand Opera" (the *Times*), with Édouard de Reszke a "wholly delightful" Leporello,* and Lehmann's Donna Anna now of "gigantic stature." None of the other performers matched such standards, nor was Vianesi a Seidl.

Along with Roméo, Faust, and Vasco da Gama as noted, Jean de Reszke's range in this season encompassed John of Leyden* in *Le Prophète* on January 1, 1892 (with Lehmann as Bertha, Édouard de Reszke as Zacharias*), Radames* in *Aida* on December 28 (with Lehmann, and with Serbolini replacing Édouard as the High Priest*), Lohengrin* on January 4 (Eames as Elsa* and Édouard as the King*), Otello* with Albani on the 11th, and Walther* in an Italian *Meistersinger* on March 3. He was admired for most of these, though his Otello, by the standard of Tamagno, was deemed "small" in voice, if well acted. Unfortunately, he did not sing the part in later years.

In the Wagner roles Jean had varying success. Although Lohengrin is recalled as one of his greatest, the *Times* thought his first attempt "sentimental," if "remarkably handsome," his grail knight no more than a "charming gentleman." His "sincere, fervent and thoughtful" performance as Walther in *I Maestri Cantori* was admired, as was the Sachs of Lassalle, but even with Seidl on hand to conduct, the *Times* found the "frequent inappropriateness" of the whole enterprise too much to condone.

Although Lehmann could not manage Brünnhilde in this season, she could sing Philine* in *Mignon* in Italian on February 6—probably the first time in operatic history the two roles have been associated with the same artist. "Stalwart both physically and vocally," was Henderson's phrase for the great lady, who spent her time otherwise in this season in such roles as Norma on December 19 and Leonore in *Fidelio* on January 13 (with Édouard de Reszke as Rocco* and Kalisch as Florestan*). In Italian, and with Louis Victor Saar as conductor, *Fidelio* did not tempt many of those who had given it avid attention in the German period.

The pattern of versatility demonstrated by the De Reszkes and Lehmann was a spur to such younger singers as Eames, who was Santuzza* when *Cavalleria rusticana* was first given in the Metropolitan (December 30), with Giulia Ravogli as Lola;* Elsa and Marguerite, as mentioned, and Micaëla* on March 4. The Mascagni score made less than the expected impression on the public, though Eames was admired for a "forcible and well-considered" impersonation. Most of the comment was expended on the "curtain raiser": a performance of Gluck's *Orfeo,* with Giulia Ravogli condemned for the "vices" of her vocal style in the title role and her sister

Sofia hardly better liked in her debut as Eurydice.* Odds and ends from *Merlin* and *Asrael* were utilized to dress the stage for *Orfeo.*

Two further French operas were introduced in this season: *Hamlet* on February 10, with Lassalle as Hamlet,* Édouard de Reszke as Claudius,* and an American soprano, Margaret Reid, as Ophelia (d); and *Lakmé* on February 22, in which the composer's own choice for the title role, Marie van Zandt, sang with "excellent command of staccato," and Édouard de Reszke as Nilakantha* won a repetition for his second-act solo. The "Bell Song" was also repeated.

Apparently Abbey was satisfied with the response to his company, for he brought it back for an extra two weeks beginning on March 28. Farewell or no, Patti was able to sing in *La Traviata, Martha, Lucia,* and *Il Barbiere,* the last on April 9 including probably the longest "lesson scene" on record: the "Swiss Echo Song," "Home, Sweet Home," and "The Last Rose of Summer." Still the applause went on, and she responded with "Comin' through the Rye."

The effort to satisfy the Wagner public, if not the requirements of the language, went forward in this supplementary season with an Italian version of *Der fliegende Holländer* on March 31. Seidl was the conductor, Édouard de Reszke sang Daland,* Lassalle was the Dutchman,* and Albani was Senta.* It was not repeated, which was no tragedy for a generation that could choose, on April 6, between a matinee *Faust* with Eames and the De Reszkes and an evening *Lucia* with Patti. So sated was the press with vocal miracles that no account of these performances appeared in the *Times.* "Music" for April 7, 1892 was the report of a piano recital by Franz Rummel in the concert hall of Madison Square Garden.

1893–1894

The effects, on the corporate structure of the Metropolitan, of the fire that consumed the interior on August 27, 1892 have been described elsewhere (page 9). The lapse of one year in the presentation of opera had a like effect, if hardly of so long a duration, on the artistic well-being of the enterprise. The principal outcome of the first Abbey-Grau season and the breathing-spell that followed was to tie opera at the Metropolitan much closer than it had been before to Covent Garden. Eventually, indeed, Maurice Grau became director of both theaters (1897).

As of the mid-nineties there was a problem common to London and New York: how to admit the immense push of the Wagnerian literature to the common repertory without making it, as it had been in New York during the 1880's, an exclusively *German* enterprise, or as it had been in London—and still was—an exclusively non-German enterprise.

The influential press of both places thus acted, atypically, in concert, if not exactly in harmony.

As early as 1891 Shaw was abusing Jean de Reszke for his "petulant laziness" (the *World*, July 22, 1891), resulting in the repetition of worn-out operas when "we might have been listening to *Siegfried* and *Otello*." The comment accompanied Jean's singing of Otello for the first time, a creation Shaw found worthy, if not a complete success. Prophetically he added: "When the rivalry of younger men and the decay of his old superficial charm . . . force him to make the most of all his powers, he may yet gain more as an actor than he will lose as a singer." Krehbiel and Henderson both joined the chorus with increasing vigor as the brothers became more closely identified with the local scene, more inclined to consider its problems their problems.

For the moment, the De Reszkes continued to be, primarily, glamorous figures in the era now fondly remembered as the "golden age," though for the older music-lovers of the 1890's, the true golden age was the vanished era of Mario and Rubini, Lind and Faure. Few today, however, would dispute the attractions of the *Faust* that opened the newly decorated, freshly hung theater on November 27, 1893. Under the terms of his new agreement with the management, Abbey was required to include two from a stipulated group of six performers in each presentation. The box-holders need not have worried. *Faust* with the two De Reszkes, Lassalle (Valentin), Eames, and Olympia Guercia (Siébel, [d]) was typical of the occasions to come when Grau cast six stars for almost every performance.

With Luigi Mancinelli conducting, the phrase that had begun to creep into reports in the spring of 1892 was now heard on all sides: the era of the "ideal cast" had arrived. Without endorsing arson as an artistic principle, the *Times* guardedly remarked: "Fire is sometimes a blessing in disguise. Last night we had not only a new Opera House, but new scenery and costumes." It was probable, though not explicitly stated, that this *Faust,* finally, was in French. With such singers as Pol Plançon and Emma Calvé added to the company, its resources of French singers moved ever higher, as did the cost of engaging them.

They made their debuts on the second night of the season, November 29, with Plançon's "sonorous bass . . . suave and finished style" (Krehbiel) booming through the role of Jupiter* in Gounod's *Philémon et Baucis*. Sigrid Arnoldson was Baucis (d). Even Plançon's notable art, however, had to defer to the commotion created by Calvé as Santuzza.* For the first time the full force of Mascagni's desperate heroine was liberated by "a dramatic soprano of the first rank" (the *Times*). Krehbiel marveled at this "woman with hot blood in her veins, whose voice takes color from the situation and occasionally sets one's finger-tips to tingling." Even a commonplace group of associates and routine conducting by Enrico Bevignani could not dim Calvé's luster.

There were no such complaints on December 20 when Calvé sang her Carmen* in the first performance of the work in French to be heard at the Metropolitan. With her were Jean de Reszke (José*), Lassalle (Escamillo*), and Eames (Micaëla), with Mancinelli conducting. Appropriate, then, Henderson's comment: "If any cast offered this season has justified the epithet of 'ideal,' it was this one." Calvé's Carmen he measured as a "creature of unbridled passion, with a sensuous, suggestive grace . . . careless of all consequences." Krehbiel, in the *Tribune,* was magnetized by the frankness of her playing, which would satisfy "the most ardent lover of realism." He did not discourage attendance with the remark: "It has but one prototype . . . and of that impersonation . . . the Prefect of Police took cognizance in Paris." Presumably he referred to Marie-Célestine-Laurence Galli-Marié, the creator of the role.

The De Reszke José was admirably contrasted with the Calvé Carmen, "full of eloquence and grace," said Henderson, "one of the very best . . . ever seen on the American stage." Neither Lassalle's "picturesque" toreador nor the charming Micaëla of Eames left much to be desired. In this year of multiple *Carmen* performances, Arnoldson sometimes replaced Eames, with Fernando de Lucia and Mario Ancona as alternates for De Reszke and Lassalle.

Grau had engaged Calvé at a relatively small fee, and the numerous *Cavallerias* and *Carmens* were warmly profitable to him. Not so, however, Mascagni's delightful *L'Amico Fritz,* which had its Metropolitan introduction on January 10, with De Lucia (Fritz*), Calvé (Suzel*), and Ancona (Rabbi*). Of the rather slim attendance, the *Times* remarked: "It requires a powerful cast in a strong opera to attract the public." The cast barely qualified; the work did not. After one repetition it was not heard again until 1923.

One more typical artist of the time came to contribute her share to the "strong cast" requirement when Nellie Melba sang Lucia* in her debut on December 4. Krehbiel honored the memory of Sembrich by describing Melba as the "finest exponent of vocalization" heard since 1883, while Henderson hedged but slightly in saying: "If she is not the foremost coloratura soprano . . . she is certainly in the very first rank." (He cited her vocal lineage approvingly by mentioning that Melba, like Eames and Calvé, had profited from the guidance of Mathilde Marchesi.) Vignas (Edgardo*), Bauermeister (Alisia), and Carbone (Raimondo*) were lost in a footnote, but Mancinelli's conducting drew the comment: "the orchestral part was never better played here."

Despite the critical enthusiasm, Melba was slow to become a favorite with the New York public. Her next appearance, in Thomas's *Hamlet* (with Lassalle as Hamlet, Plançon as Claudius*) on December 6, gave the *Times* "great delight," and she was well liked as the first Metropolitan Nedda* when *Pagliacci* was introduced on December 11 (De Lucia was Canio [d]; Ancona was Tonio [d]), in *Rigoletto* on December 29, and in Rossini's *Semiramide* on January 12. (Several postponements preceded the last of these.) But it was her first Juliette* to Jean de Reszke's Roméo which gave her general success with the public. The *Times* reported nothing notable in her dramatic conception of the role, but had outspoken praise for "the exquisite smoothness" of her singing and a delivery of the waltz that "fairly delighted her hearers." After great applause, she repeated the aria. Few companies could post a notice of substitution for Édouard de Reszke without a good deal of audience discontent. This one managed well enough by offering Plançon as Frère Laurent.

Though the roles enumerated may suggest that Melba was far from the Wagnerian trend of the time, she sang both Elisabeth* in *Tannhäuser* on January 29 (the Paris version in Italian) and Elsa* in *Lohengrin* on February 6. Neither satisfied Metropolitan standards for Wagner, though Melba surpassed expectations in both parts, and Plançon was an "entirely satisfactory" Landgraf Hermann* in *Tannhäuser*. Ancona as Telramund* and Édouard de Reszke as King Henry were worthy enough, but the casts were otherwise spotty, the choral work was poor, the staging inept. Olga Pevny, who was called upon to replace the scheduled Venus in *Tannhäuser*, sang in German. The only other Wagner of this season was an Italian *Meistersinger* first given on January 8, with Jean de Reszke and Lassalle as before, plus Eames as a "charming" Eva.* Mancinelli's conducting proved him a "broad-minded" artist, but Plançon was a "stilted" Pogner." Bauermeister as Magdalena and Maugiere as David* fell short of Wagner's requirements. "Timid" was the *Times'* word for the staging.

Lovers of Meyerbeer had a series of *Les Huguenots* performances to delight them this season, with such notable singers as Nordica, the De Reszkes, Lassalle, Arnoldson (Marguerite*), and Scalchi on December 18. Lovers of an operatic bargain noted December 22 as historic, for it offered the first pairing in Metropolitan history of *Cavalleria* and *Pagliacci*, with Calvé in the first, Melba in the second. (This time, *Pagliacci* came first.)

Also historic was the appearance of two works by Mozart in the same season. *Don Giovanni* on December 27, with Mancinelli conduct-

ing, was marked, said Henderson, by De Lucia's "miserable" Ottavio*
and Kate Bolla's "mediocre" Elvira. Fursch-Madi (Donna Anna),
Arnoldson (Zerlina), Lassalle (Don), and Edouard de Reszke (Leporello)
were in various respects better, but the chorus had small idea of what
it was supposed to do, the stage band in the ballroom scene was rarely
together with the pit players. *Le Nozze di Figaro* went much better
in its first Metropolitan performance on January 31, possibly, as Henderson noted, because "its traditions are familiar to the Italian stage." Eames
gave high promise of things to come with her Countess,* Nordica was an
"intelligent" Susanna,* Arnoldson a "most dainty" Cherubino.* The men
were Édouard de Reszke, a splendid Almaviva,* and Ancona, a Figaro*
"deficient in grace and lightness." Enrico Bevignani, who enraged Shaw
on more than a few occasions, conducted.

A post-season fortnight that began on April 16 after an interval
of touring, recapitulated the favorite operas and casts, and added *Werther*
to the Metropolitan repertory on April 19. Jean de Reszke as Werther*
was considered the "star of the piece," with Eames an "excellent"
Charlotte,* and Arnoldson a capable Sophie.* In a final one-night recapitulation of the year's impressions, Abbey and Grau instituted the
custom of season-ending "galas" on April 27, with favorite acts from
Roméo (Eames and both De Reszkes), *Carmen, Aida,* and *Werther.*
Melba concluded with the "Mad Scene" from *Hamlet.* "Society was out in
full force," reported the *Times* "and the boxes gleamed with satin . . .
and jewels. Of course, Lassalle had to sing the Toreador song twice."
All the stars spoke, in English or French, and Melba finally "quieted the
turmoil" by singing "Home, Sweet Home."

Although it was contended, through the German period, that "Italian"
opera could not be given for less than a seven-dollar top, the price scale
in this year ranged from one dollar to five. Many economies were
practiced, of course, in staging. The choral singing and orchestral playing
were often inept, but the complaints were not severe enough to persuade
Abbey and Grau to adopt other methods.

A loud echo of the German period was provided on March 28 when
Walter Damrosch engaged the theater for a performance of *Götterdämmerung* with Materna, Schott, and Fischer. Although it was the first
time he had conducted the work, the *Times* declared that he "acquitted
himself with great credit."

1894–1895

The interest aroused by that echo was soon enough to have its influence on
the Metropolitan as Damrosch, without operatic employment in New

York, proceeded with plans for a company that would carry the gospel of Wagner to America. In the meantime, Abbey and Grau did quite enough for the music-loving operagoer in this season by offering Victor Maurel in the North American *première* of *Falstaff,* reviving *Otello* with Tamagno, and adding many more to the long list of "ideal" casts.

As tends to happen in the routine of repertory opera, first things do not always come first. *Falstaff* had to be rehearsed before it could be given, with the result that Maurel made his debut, on December 3, as Iago (d) to Tamagno's Otello,* rather than in his most celebrated role. He was by no means unknown to New York, for as a young man he had been the Amonasro of the first American *Aida* twenty years before. But his Metropolitan debut as a mature artist earned him credit in the *Times* as "a truly great singing actor." His voice was deemed not more than "good," but it was "backed by a very fine art and an uncommon dramatic instinct." Eugenia Mantelli as Emilia* and Eames as Desdemona* were both better than previous performers of these roles, and Tamagno made his usual deep impression as Otello. Mancinelli's conducting and the staging were relatively inferior.

Not being what the Italian operagoer expected at a time when few others went to Italian opera, *Otello* and its splendid cast had but three further performances this season. Commenting on the spare attendance at one of these, the *Times* said: "With all its pretensions this is not really a profoundly musical city . . . 'Otello' is not a work for the fashionable masses; it is too sombre, too tragic, too utterly in earnest." By contrast then, the gaiety and sparkle of *Falstaff* should have won a warm response on February 4, when (two years after Buenos Aires) New Yorkers had an opportunity to hear the last of Verdi's scores—and the surprising fact seems to be that it did.

To be sure, the cast was close to perfection, with Maurel in the part he had created at La Scala, Giuseppe Campanari a fine Ford,* Eames a notable Mistress Ford,* and Scalchi as good a Dame Quickly* as could be imagined. The press did its share with reviews that recalled the impact of *Tristan*—Henderson, in the *Times,* packed two and three-quarters agate columns with such expressions as "Happy are we to sing the praises of this inspired old man, who carols in second childhood with all the freshness of his first youth and is worthy to be acclaimed, like Mozart, a 'glorious boy.' " Krehbiel likened the score to a "perfect sea of melodic champagne" and spoke of the "throb of delight" that surged through the theater as one situation succeeded another.

At the season's final matinee on February 16, the theater was "packed to suffocation" (the *Tribune*), and cheers for Maurel at the final curtain brought him out, eventually, in a dressing-gown, minus paunch. He spoke a sentence of thanks in French and then withdrew. Despite this evidence of overwhelming response (repeated in the supplementary weeks), the work was given but four times in the next season, and not again until 1908 and 1909. The next revivals were more than a dozen years apart. As the most recent effort, begun in 1963–4, attested, it was not the fault of the public that *Falstaff* was long in coming to the esteem of *Figaro* and *Don Giovanni*. It was, rather, the lack of proper production values and the failure of management, which privately asserted its admiration for a masterwork, to offer (at the cost of a few empty seats) a reasonable opportunity for the public to become acquainted with it.

Of the other "novelties," one was not an opera in one sense, and the other was not an opera in any sense. The lack of dramatic action which has penalized most efforts to make Saint-Saëns's *Samson et Dalila* palatable on the stage was quite evident on February 8 when the oratorio had the services of Tamagno as Samson,* Mantelli as Dalila,* Plançon as both Abimelech* and the Old Hebrew,* and Campanari as the High Priest.* The great tenor's trumpet tones were deemed "cold" for this music (the *Times*), and Mantelli did not come up to previous singers heard in the concert-hall performances. Caruso and Matzenauer had more success in 1915.

Hermann Bemberg's *Elaine* was rather gently treated at its *première* on December 17, for it was known to be a gesture of the De Reszkes toward a favorite friend. As in the London *première* on July 5, 1892, Melba sang Elaine, Plançon was Astolat,* with Jean de Reszke as Lancelot* and Édouard de Reszke as L'Ermite.* "Grace" and "gentle charm" were granted to the score (the *Times*); its lack of "passion or power" was mildly deplored. It came and went with a single repetition.

Worthier, though not so prominent, was the first French *Manon* at the Metropolitan on January 16. Puccini's rival work being as yet unknown, it was described, using more of the full title of the Abbé Prévost's *nouvelle,* as *Manon Lescaut*. A principal provocation was the appearance as Manon (d) of Sibyl Sanderson, a thirtyish native of Sacramento, California, who had won a Parisian success with her remarkable range (to G above C), for which Massenet wrote *Esclarmonde*. She was too slight in sound, however, for the Metropolitan, and the performance was memorable for Jean de Reszke's Chevalier des Grieux,* one of his most admired impersonations. Presumably he had never sung it elsewhere, a claim Henderson regarded with skepticism: "If it was, indeed, his first performance . . . it was remarkable for its freedom and certainty . . . it reached a height of passion which called forth . . . an irresistible demand for a repetition of the principal air." Plançon as Comte des Grieux* and Ancona as Lescaut* were satisfactory enough, but objection was entered to Bevignani's "cast-iron" conducting and Miss Sanderson's determination to wear her jewels en route to the convent in Act I.

With Calvé absent in this season—the small financial return that accompanied her sensational success doubtless determined her to stay away until her worth was better appreciated—emphasis was more than ever on the men in the company. If "matinee idol" was a term still for the future, "mash note" was not. The De Reszkes (and Lassalle, when he shared quarters with them at the bygone Gilsey House) received them in every mail. In such roles as Arnold (d)* in *Guillaume Tell* on November 21, Radames* on November 23, Manrico* on November 30, and Da Gama* on February 13, Tamagno added to the furore, while Maurel invaded some of the older hearts with his artful Rigoletto* (Shaw thought it the dramatic equal of Edwin Booth's Triboulet) on December 7 and his incomparable Don Giovanni* on December 31.

Tamagno's Guillaume Tell almost did not happen, for Lucille Hill was unable to sing Mathilde,* and the only alternate, Libia Drog, had never performed it in public. At the evening's end there was doubt that she had performed it this time, for she came to a dead stop in *"Sombre forêt"* and walked off the stage. Tamagno led her back for the succeeding duet, and again she walked off. Meanwhile the audience applauded. In Italy, the *Times* commented, "they would have torn up the seats and thrown them on the stage." Thankfully, there were Édouard de Reszke (Fürst*) and Ancona (Tell*) to help out, and when the tenor "proceeded to electrify the house with [his] magnificent declamation on a high note . . . Mme. Drog was thenceforward a nonentity." She had the fortitude to come back two nights later to sing Aida* with "fire" and a "powerful voice . . . of excellent quality," but the cheers went to Tamagno. "The manner in which he enunciated several syllables, as in 'Io rest' a te,' on one high B flat was simply astonishing," Henderson reported. On the other hand, he had no compunction about "hanging over the footlights and hurling his voice into the audience with the metallic penetrativeness of an eight inch shell" (same source). The evening marked the debut of Eugenia Mantelli as Amneris (d),* the beginning of a career founded on "a substantial contralto voice of fine quality."

Maurel's forte, of course, was subtlety, as in the Don Giovanni* of December 31. The *Times* described his work "in passages calling for delicacy and finesse" as "the perfection of dramatic art," and deemed the Don and Leporello (Édouard de Reszke) "a pair never surpassed on the local stage." Russitano was a barely respectable Ottavio,* and though the women were Nordica (Donna Anna*), Eames (Elvira*), and De Lussan (Zerlina*), none satisfied, for one reason or another.

The era of ideal casts was running toward all-star casts on such occasions as December 26, when *Les Huguenots* reunited not only the De Reszkes, Plançon, Nordica, and Scalchi as before, but also added Melba (Marguerite*), and Maurel (De Nevers*). Melba was considered "the best Marguerite ever heard on the Metropolitan stage," Maurel, if vocally limited, a fine figure of dramatic credibility. Grau asked, and got, seven dollars for orchestra seats—on a theory, perhaps, of one dollar per star. When a repetition was announced for January 3, the *Times* noted: "It is not often that any opera house offers such an array of celebrities . . . the lion's share of the credit for the . . . remarkable company . . . is due to Mr. Maurice Grau."

At ordinary prices, Grau combated the apathy of theatergoers toward Christmas Eve performances with an *Aida* in which Nordica, Tamagno, Plançon, and Mantelli were "bolstered" by Maurel's first Amonasro* in several years. The voice was light; the "fire and energy" of the performance (the *Times*) were compelling. Or, lacking Calvé for *Carmen* on November 26, he atoned with Édouard de Reszke as Escamillo* and Melba as Micaëla* in an "ordinary" cast, with Jean de Reszke and Zélie de Lussan (Carmen [d]).

It is hardly surprising that in this era of "the best ever," Mathilde Bauermeister should rank as the "best ever" among secondary singers. In an article of 1891 in the *World,* Shaw named her as "probably the most indispensable member" of the Covent Garden company, and she showed why at the Metropolitan on February 13, 1895, when the ill-fated Lucille Hill fainted during the second act of *L'Africaine.* Bauermeister— "she knows all the other roles as a matter of course," calmly reported the *Times*—switched from Anna to Inez, and the performance proceeded.

The Wagner of this season was sparse indeed—*Lohengrin,* on December 5, with Nordica offering the Elsa she had sung the previous summer at Bayreuth, but still in Italian—Jean de Reszke, Plançon, Mantelli as Ortrud,* and Ancona as Telramund; and *Die Meistersinger* in a supplementary season on April 22, with Édouard de Reszke as Sachs,* Eames, Jean de Reszke, and Plançon. It was the lull before the storm, for as early as December 23 the *Times* printed a rumor that plans were in the making for a German *Tristan* with Nordica and Jean de Reszke, adding: "de Reszke has set his heart on appearing here in this music drama."

His serious intentions came out into the open when the Grau company went touring as February ended, and the Damrosch German Opera

Company moved in for twenty-one performances. De Reszke asked Krehbiel and Henderson to keep him posted on the public response to the venture, saying to the latter: "I go to Boston to sing Faust, but I will cry."

The Damrosch company was more than respectable, with such former favorites as Emil Fischer and Max Alvary, and such favorites-to-be as the young Johanna Gadski and Marie Brema. After the opening *Tristan* on February 25, Henderson wrote to De Reszke: "The sooner you and Édouard sing in German, the better it will be for you, for Wagner, and for the public." Without publishing any of this at the time, he stated in a *Times* article of March 3, 1895 the philosophical framework of the impending decision: "The great names of the Wagnerian genesis are already falling into the historical past . . . Winkelmann, Scaria, Niemann, Vogl, Materna, Sucher, Brandt. . . . In all human probability the time is now too close to us when the later dramas of Wagner will become a part of the repertory of the advanced dramatic singers of the French and German stages." Urging the case of Wagner in German, sung by the international artists of the day, he concluded: "The performance of the Wagnerian music drama *and* the French and Italian opera will be improved. The former will benefit by the delivery of its perfectly singable music—once foolishly called unsingable music—with the most beautiful vocal art. The latter will gain, from the importation into its performance of German traditions . . . the dramatic illusion which is now too frequently absent. Thus a transfusion of blood in both directions will develop the general vitality of art."

Under the spur of such writing and the warm response to the Damrosch repertory (the *Ring* minus *Das Rheingold, Tristan, Die Meistersinger, Lohengrin,* and *Tannhäuser*), a petition was delivered to Abbey and Grau requesting one evening a week of German opera in the next season. While they pondered the future, the company returned for a supplementary fortnight, beginning with a *Falstaff* on April 15. It went "splendidly," according to the *Times,* which called it a "great opera" that "should live as long as *Le Nozze di Figaro*." Maurel was called upon to sing *"Quand' ero paggio"* three times. *Figaro* itself was heard in this post-season on April 2, with Maurel as Figaro,* Eames as the Countess, Nordica as Susanna, and Édouard de Reszke as Almaviva. Maurel's Figaro was artistically done, but he was not really suited to the part, lacking lightness.

In return for the gifts of song the company had given New Yorkers in this winter, admirers lavished it with tokens of esteem at a monster gala on April 30. Jean de Reszke received a silver candelabrum, his brother a fish fork (with a Mephisto handle), Melba a gold wreath mounted on velvet, and Tamagno a gold medallion. Bauermeister was remembered by the gentlemen of the Opera Club with a gold watch, and, accepting it in the midst of an applauding stage of "mastersingers"— Melba, the De Reszkes, Eames, Maurel, Tamagno—the peerless *seconda* hugged her prize and burst into grateful tears.

1895–1896

Grau's approach to the problem of opera in German was much the same, in the case of *Tristan und Isolde,* as his approach to *Les Huguenots:* get the strongest possible cast and let them sing. At the urging of some of his journalistic advisers, and with the tangible proof of interest by some two thousand petitioners that opera in German be made a Thursday-night feature (the subscription series did not include either Tuesday or Thursday), he engaged Anton Seidl[1] to conduct.

Thus, for the next few years, the Metropolitan had a reprise of the excitement that had attended the introduction of the Wagner works a decade before. Now, however, the revelation came not from the work itself (*Tristan* in this season, *Siegfried, Götterdämmerung,* and *Die Meister-singer* in the several seasons soon to come) but from the curve of line, the accent of phrase that could be imparted to the "unsingable" music by artists who knew how.

As Lehmann still preferred Germany to America, the first Isolde* of the new order, on November 27, 1895, was Lillian Nordica, with Jean de Reszke as Tristan*. Her performance, said the *Times,* "simply amazed those who thought they had measured the full limit of her powers." The credit to both principal artists embraced clarity of word as well as purity of tone. "Never before," wrote Krehbiel in the *Tribune,* "have we had a Tristan able to sing the declamatory music . . . with correct intonation, to say nothing of the duet of the second act. . . . Together they gave the text with a distinctness . . . they enabled those familiar with the German tongue to follow the play." For Henderson, Édouard de Reszke's Marke* was "vocally stupendous," and Seidl conducted "gloriously." Brema and Kaschmann completed the cast.

Something of the De Reszkes' approach to the task they had assumed should be known, if only to explain the time lag until the urging of their well-intentioned critics took effect. Paderewski, as we have seen (page 107) came to America for the first time in 1891. As of that time, the De Reszkes did not speak German, for when the pianist returned

[1] Seidl had a hand in another event of consequence this year, when he directed the first American performance of Humperdinck's *Hänsel und Gretel* at Daly's Theater on October 8. The cast was poorish, however (only Jacques Bars as Peter was of sizable repute) and an English text was used. The score was much admired.

shortly after this *Tristan* and heard a mutual friend express admiration for the fluency of Jean's German, he exclaimed: "But that is not so. Jean does not speak German." A few moments later De Reszke joined the group, was greeted by Paderewski in German, and conversed fluently with him.

In other words, they were not content merely to learn the words of the part, but felt obligated to know and speak the tongue—which, it was later disclosed, they had done in private for *two years* before this *Tristan*. Seidl's contribution to the musical success of the undertaking could hardly be overvalued. He worked tirelessly with them in rehearsals. An eyewitness (Henderson) painted a word-picture of such an occasion when, he related: "Jean, in morning coat and bowler hat was declaiming a passage and Seidl stopped for a correction. De Reszke walked to the footlights, removed the hat and said 'Yes, Herr Direktor?' Then he went back and did it the way Seidl suggested."

Shortly after the performance (November 30), the *Times* printed a lengthy analysis by Henderson of the way in which Jean de Reszke's Tristan differed from his predecessors'. "Not even Niemann showed a truer conception of the part . . . he never approached the Polish singer in the tenderness, the melting fervency of his love-song. . . . The splendid dignity and mournful power of . . . de Reszke's . . . 'War Morold dir so werth' . . . has never been surpassed." Act II was made for the great Faust and Roméo. In Act III, he continued: "This final scene of Tristan has been presented . . . as a series of painful shouts and ejaculations . . . de Reszke's incomparable skill in the management of the vocal organs overcame all . . . difficulties. . . . It is enough. M. de Reszke has demonstrated that Wagner can be sung."

This overshadowing event was repeated five times with, if anything, increasing effect. The first of the ten Thursday performances occurred on December 5, in the presence of a largely German-speaking audience, which, according to the *Times,* "passed expert opinion on the performance" and did not find it lacking. The successive performances in German, however, were sadly inferior. Adolf Wallnöfer was an indifferent Siegmund* for *Die Walküre* on January 9, and Kaschmann a poorish Wotan.* Rosa Olitzka (Fricka*) and Marie Brema (Brünnhilde*) sustained a reasonable standard, but the comparison with the *Tristan* was painful. An audience that came to a special performance on December 19 and found notice that Jean de Reszke, Nordica, and Brema were ill might well have felt cheated. Georgine von Januschowsky sang a passable Isolde* and Olitzka's Brangäne* was even praised. But to say Wallnöfer was no De Reszke would be distortion; he was also no Tristan.* *Tann-*

häuser, Fidelio, and *Lohengrin* also turned up in the Thursday sequence, mostly ill sung.

As a new variant, *Lohengrin* was given in both Italian and German this season. Nordica and the two De Reszkes sang in an Italian performance on November 22 (Seidl conducting), in a German one on January 2. The choice of language seemed to turn on the singers of Ortrud and Telramund; they were Mantelli and Ancona in the first, Brema and Kaschmann in the second. *Die Meistersinger* remained steadfastly in Italian in its only performance on February 10. Lola Beeth sang Eva* in a cast otherwise similar to that of the previous season. "When," plaintively inquired the *Times,* "are we going to have Melba as Eva?" The unrequested Brünnhilde in *Siegfried* came before it—and no other Wagner after it.

Calvé's return as a recognized star provided not only a full quota of splendid Carmens and Santuzzas, but also the investigation of such additional specialities as Anita* in *La Navarraise* (Massenet had written it for her) on December 11, Leila* in *Les Pêcheurs de perles* on January 11 (the first two acts only, *La Navarraise* following), and the two roles of Margherita* and Helen of Troy* in Boito's *Mefistofele* on January 15. Mantelli sang Martha* and Pantalis,* and Édouard de Reszke was as remarkable an Italian Mefistofele* as a French Méphistophélès. In all of these, Calvé's ability to color her voice, especially her use of the "*voix blanche,*" was deeply impressive, her gamut as an actress widely admired. She succeeded, even, in giving interest to Thomas's *Hamlet* with her acting virtuosity as Ophelia* on December 4, showing a conception quite different from the merely spectacular vocalization of Melba or Van Zandt. When a chorus girl picked up the bouquets tossed to Calvé as she lay unconscious and buried her amid a shower of flowers, the critics thought the action suspiciously "unpremeditated," but the public became greatly attached to her version of the part.

In place of "ideal casts" (oddly, no one thought of referring to *Tristan* thus), Grau contrived a new spurt to business at "Patti prices," as they were called. Foreshadowed by the seven-dollar top for the *Huguenots* of the previous season, they were billed as "Nights of the Seven Stars," and included the same list of singers in the same work on January 8: Nordica, Melba, Scalchi, the De Reszkes, Plançon, and Maurel. Maurel's season was scarcely a triumph, for his vocal shortcomings left him "merely a name" as Escamillo in *Carmen* on November 23, and his Valentin in *Faust* on December 21 did not match expectations. "His days of *bel canto,*" observed the *Times,* "are over."

On the other hand, he was still the master fat knight when *Falstaff* came back on January 22. Frances Saville, who had made charming use of a light voice at the opening of *Roméo* on November 18, was an attractive Mistress Ford,* with Scalchi and Campanari as before. This perperformance fared well, but a repetition on February 8 unfortunately followed a star-studded *Les Huguenots* in the afternoon. Commenting on the crowded auditorium for Meyerbeer, the *Times* noted: "Several people were carried out in a fainting condition." In the evening "one of the most artistic . . . works of recent years was given to an audience which occupied less than one-half the auditorium."

Manon* was added to the Melba repertory on January 27, when the combination of her ease and De Reszke's striking Des Grieux "made the public cup of happiness run over," according to the *Times*. All was not so pleasant to the reviewer. "Mme. Melba," he wrote "has the voice of a lark, and—so far as her singing is evidence—the soul of one also." For Mantelli, Grau arranged the first Metropolitan performance of *La Favorita* on November 29. Her Leonora* struck fire with a powerful performance of *"O mio Fernando"* despite "a great tremolo" (the *Times*). Plançon was Baldassare;* Giuseppe Cremonini showed a pale voice of light caliber in his debut as Fernando;* and the durable Bevignani conducted.

A temporal tempest raged in the press of this winter because of Grau's refusal to lease the Metropolitan to Damrosch for another season, mostly of Wagner, while the resident company toured. Not to be daunted, Damrosch took his company into the absurdly inadequate Academy of Music on March 2 for several weeks. Two new singers of great qualities came to the attention of New Yorkers during this series. Katharina Klafsky made her debut as Leonore (d) in *Fidelio* on the opening night, and Milka Ternina sang in *Lohengrin* on March 4 in a way to make the *Times* say that "the only Elsa to compare with her was Christine Nilsson." Oddly, these two luminaries were destined to shine but a short while: Klafsky died suddenly the following September in Germany at the age of forty-one, and Ternina, who had a brilliant career at the Metropolitan for several seasons, had to retire because of ill health while still a young woman. As well as the customary *Ring* dramas, *Tannhäuser,* and *Die Meistersinger,* Damrosch's season included his own *Scarlet Letter* on March 6, with Gadski as Hester Prynne. It was Henderson's view that "criticism . . . ought to be friendly and encouraging," and the matter may be left at that.

Such a list of artists as Abbey and Grau offered the New York public this season (with the famous *Tristan*) might seem a reasonable answer to a critic's dream. Henderson, however, had his own complaint to register in a *Times* article of February 22. The season was devoid of novelties, save the unimportant *La Navarraise,* leaving the critics "with nothing to criticize except singing. . . . If the managers of the opera, instead of offering great star casts alternating with 'off nights,' were to engage a company of less celebrated, but competent artists, and make the production of operas the central feature of their system, the course of the critics would certainly change. . . . But, as Messrs. Abbey and Grau say . . . they are not 'in the operatic business for their health.' They frankly say they cannot afford to comply with the demands of the critics, when the paying public is making a wholly different demand."

Gatti, perhaps, had the answer—on a much later occasion—when an assistant informed him of adverse reviews of a performance to which his company had given much effort. "The critics—pah!" he said. "They have to criticize."

1896–1897

In the season of his first appearance as Tristan, Jean de Reszke had also sung Lohengrin (German and Italian), Roméo, Faust, Radames, the Chevalier des Grieux, Don José, and Raoul in the language of the composer, also Walther von Stolzing in Italian. Singular though this repertory was, and remains, it was but the beginning of the task he had set for himself: to interpret all the great Wagnerian roles before he retired.

The objective for this season was *Siegfried,* with Jean in the title role and Édouard de Reszke as the Wanderer.* For them, December 30 marked a triumph; for Melba, who sang her first and only Brünnhilde,* it was a disaster. For Grau, it was but one among many blows that made this season his most difficult.

He was in a desperate way for a dramatic soprano even before the season began, for Nordica declined a contract when she discovered that Melba insisted on exclusive rights to Brünnhilde. Lehmann, though available for America again, was committed to Damrosch, and Klafsky, who might have solved the problem, was dead of an operation for a head injury suffered from a fall during the previous season. On October 17, 1896, Grau's partner, Henry Abbey, died.

As if all these problems were not enough, Melba's preparation for Brünnhilde limited her availability in the early weeks of the season, and the strain she suffered (plus an attack of influenza) permitted but a single appearance thereafter. When she felt unable to sing for the *seventh* time on January 18, she asked to be released from her contract. Only then could Grau utilize Eames, for example, as Juliette; for that, too, was reserved for Melba.

Much as has been written about the Melba Brünnhilde, her reasons for undertaking a role so foreign to her equipment and experience are still obscure. The contention of Jean de Reszke's biographer, Clara Leiser, that he meant her to sing the Forest Bird, and that she misunderstood, has an element of plausibility. Those who were nearer the scene, however, thought otherwise. Even *before* the event, the *Times* took note of Nordica's appearance in concert to say: "Whether M. Jean de Reszke advised that Mme. Melba should sing Brünnhilde or not, it is wrong that anything should come between the public and Mme. Nordica."

The mystery extends, actually, to the kind of performance Melba gave. *Siegfried* Brünnhildes traditionally receive short shrift in the daily press because they appear so late and are on stage for a relatively short time. Henderson, in the *Times,* referred to the singer's "nervousness," then said: "The quality of her voice and her style of singing are not suited to a complete embodiment of Brünnhilde . . . her ambition . . . was more potent than wise." Krehbiel took another tack: "Mme. Melba's share in the performance cannot be discussed even in general terms." Writing in *Chapters of Operas* years later (1908), he speaks of the "difference in power and expressiveness between the higher and lower registers" of her voice as "pitifully obvious."

In an unsigned review in the *Evening Post* the picture was much brighter. There is no reason to doubt that the writer was Henry T. Finck, who said (after twelve hundred words devoted to the De Reszkes): "Mme. Melba made such a wide departure from her specialty that it would have been a marvel had she risen fully to the occasion. . . . The difficult awakening scene was somewhat constrained but in the love scene she caught the inspiration from the tenor's radiant countenance and youthful ardor. . . . Her voice, too, while as yet hardly strong enough for the climax . . . had an unusual touch of fervor and a beauty all its own. Her success with the public was undoubted."

If the success was "undoubted," it was nevertheless unrepeated. My contribution to the clouded picture is a quotation from her biography, Percy Colson's *Melba, an Unconventional Biography* (London: Grayson & Grayson; 1932). Exhausted and tearful, Melba asked for Grau after the curtain fell and implored him: "Tell the critics I am never going to do that again. It is beyond me. I have been a fool." If these words were repeated, it would explain why kindness prevailed in the published accounts.

In any case, there was the welcome alternative of extolling the new triumphs of the De Reszkes. For the *Times,* Jean's young Siegfried* was "one of the greatest successes of his career." The *Post* (Finck) noted: "Jean de Reszke loves his Siegfried as one loves a bride. For that character he sacrificed what neither Lohengrin nor Tristan made him give up—his moustache." On a later occasion (see page 143) De Reszke was not so meticulous.

By contrast with the *Siegfrieds* of the previous decade, this splendid production was notable for its lack of native German singers. Only Adolph von Hübbenet (Mime [d]) was German-born. Of the others, both David Bispham (Alberich*) and Sophie Traubman (Forest Bird) were American, Castelmary (Fafner*) was French, and Seidl, who conducted, Hungarian.

That this season of *Siegfried* should also be the year in which Henderson invented his famous description of the Metropolitan as *das Faustspielhaus* may seem more than ordinarily incongruous. However, Melba's control of certain other roles and a sequence of happenings that drove the repertory in odd directions were all involved in inordinate repetitions of Gounod's masterwork. It opened the season on November 16, with Melba, the usual number of De Reszkes, and Lassalle as Valentin; Eames had her turn on December 23, and Calvé was Marguerite* on January 4. This being the night of Mrs. Astor's annual ball, the audience was more than usually bejeweled. Perhaps by contrast, Calvé's singing of the "Jewel Song" seemed, to the *Times,* "positively bad." There was the making, however, of an unusual characterization in her transformation from "girlish innocence" to a "pathetic figure of a remorseful woman," and it grew to be one of her most admired roles.

Even when the De Reszkes were inactive on January 29, Grau found it profitable to give *Faust* with Calvé, Thomas Salignac (Faust*) and Plançon. "The audience heard the *Veau d'Or* twice," commented the *Times,* "so why should one find fault?" When *Faust* was given for the tenth time on February 17, with Calvé once more, Henderson was ready. The heading was innocent enough: "Faust the last time. Heard by an audience which jammed the Opera House." Then without further warning:

> *"Far hence in the future when a guide of cosmopolitan misinformation is escorting Macaulay's New Zealander through the excavations on Manhattan Island, they will pause at the ruins of a vast auditorium on upper Broadway, and the New Zealander will say: 'I suppose this was the arena.' The guide will reply: 'No, it was the sacred Faustspielhaus.' Macaulay's New Zealander, knowing German, will say: 'You mean Festspielhaus, don't you?' And the guide will answer: 'No, honored Sir, the Festspielhaus was in Germany, where they played dramas by one Vogner. Here, they played "Faust," and it is, therefore, the Faustspielhaus.' And the New Zealander will marvel greatly."*

Perhaps it was sheer desperation that impelled the same writer, in the *Times* of February 24, to suggest a project for Grau's next season: a revival of *H.M.S. Pinafore,* with Melba (Josephine), Eames (Hebe), Calvé

(Little Buttercup), Jean de Reszke (Ralph Rackstraw), Lassalle (Captain Corcoran), Bispham (Sir Joseph Porter), Édouard de Reszke (Dick Dead-eye), and Ancona (Boatswain's Mate), with Seidl conducting. "There is available," he appended, "a translation in German."

This season was well remembered because of Melba's failure in *Siegfried*, but it might have been recalled for a triumph in *La Traviata* had she been content to leave well enough alone with her Violetta* on December 21. "She sang superbly," reported the *Times,* "at times gloriously, and with an utter freedom of style." Her acting was not remarkable, but "as good as it was unexpected . . . it can be said that the new Violetta is quite competent to fill the place of the one [Patti] who has passed her prime." Cremonini (Alfredo) and Ancona (Germont) were no more than routine.

With neither Nordica nor a reasonable replacement at hand, the Wagner repertory labored from the very start. The logic of having Mancinelli conduct *Meistersinger,* even in Italian, when Seidl was available, did not appeal to the press, nor did Plançon's Pogner on November 18. The fine artist David Bispham was hailed in his debut as Beckmesser (d), a part in which he was to be admired many times in the future. *Tannhäuser,* two nights later, was given in a mixture not only improbable, but unfathomable: basically, it was French (Eames as Elisabeth, Plançon as the Landgraf, Lassalle as Wolfram*), but Engle sang Venus* in Italian, and Jules Gogny, the Tannhäuser (d) varied from one to the other. The first appearance of Eames as a singer of German occurred in a *Lohengrin* on November 27, her singing of Elsa's music in the balcony scene being described as "flawless musical perfection" (the *Times*). Her enunciation of the text was rather less expert. Here, too, may be noted the beginning of the great admiration for Jean de Reszke's Lohengrin. Reconsidered "in the light of his Tristan," the *Times* said, "it is no longer a sentimental chevalier but a devoted hero." The chorus, singing in Italian, was both pathetic and apathetic.

With or without Melba, *Siegfried* had to be given to justify the time and money spent on its preparation. On January 2, Félia Litvinne (the sister of Édouard de Reszke's wife) went on, also singing Isolde* on January 15. An earnest artist, she nevertheless performed "with all the faults which we used to bear so patiently in those German days following the departure of Lilli Lehmann," the *Times* complained. Matters were even worse, however, on February 6, with Litvinne ill, and a sold-out theater for the matinee. Georgine von Januschowsky (see page 121) was alerted to take her place, but it was hardly Wagner of the kind the audience expected. On the same evening Eames sang a German Elsa in

Lohengrin, the rest of the cast singing Italian. Louis Victor Saar conducted.

The notion that the Metropolitan public would support a midweek matinee was investigated by Grau with a series of performances on Wednesdays, beginning with Melba and the De Reszkes in *Faust* on November 21. Even at reduced prices, the attendance was limited. The sequence ended with *Don Giovanni* on December 16, which at least had the effect of testing Bauermeister's resourcefulness once again. With Engle ill, she went on as Zerlina.*

To appease the critical appetite for "novelties," Grau offered Massenet's *Le Cid* on February 12. It also exhibited the De Reszkes in two roles they had created in Paris ten years before (Jean as Rodrigue,* Édouard as Don Diègue*) and the original Comte de Gormas,* Plançon. This, the *Times* made clear, was not the kind of novelty wanted, terming the score "a deadly piece of weariness," redeemed only by the singing and an attractive ballet.

For a season that began in dissension and proceeded with disaster, only the worst could suffice; and it occurred during a performance of *Marta* on February 10. For the first time in a history of countless stage deaths at the Metropolitan, a performer expired in public view, and so ironically pertinent was his collapse that Armand Castlemary was loudly applauded as he gasped his last. The action at the end of Act II calls for Tristano to run about the stage and stumble. The exertion was too much for the sixty-three-year-old singer, and he died in the arms of Jean de Reszke, who had been watching the performance from the wings.

What with the death of his partner, the collapse of Melba and the general feeling that reorganization of the company was called for, Grau decided to suspend activities at the Metropolitan for one year. A brief post-season series concluded on April 20 with a benefit for Miss Kitty K. Abbey, daughter of the late co-manager, and the news that Grau's lease had been renewed for a three-year period.

It was perhaps with a view to having a tenant for part of the next season that Grau opened the house to the Damrosch company on March 8 for a spell of opera in German. Lehmann, "grown to the proportions of Materna," the *Times* had to recognize, sang Brünnhilde in the opening *Walküre,* with Gadski, Fischer, and a reputable artist of the day, Ernst Kraus as Siegmund (d). Other persons and events that foreshadowed later happenings were Gadski as Elisabeth in *Tannhäuser* on March 12, a *Lohengrin* on March 15 in which Lehmann sang Ortrud to Nordica's Elsa, and a *Siegfried* on March 24 in which Nordica showed what she might have done as Brünnhilde. The casts were otherwise of erratic quality, with a persistent indisposition of Kraus causing Kalisch to appear in roles (Sieg-mund particularly) which he would have preferred not to sing. One of the attractions of the season was meant to be Xaver Scharwenka's *Mataswintha,* with Kraus as King Witichs. It was finally given with Gerhard Stehmann, a baritone, in the role, and the composer—unfortunate man!—conducting "with authority." The date was April 1.

The Maurice Grau Opera Company, 1897–1903

1897–1898

The year's interval in the work of the resident company allowed for many things, not the least of them innumerable articles in the press analyzing the state of Metropolitan opera and, for the most part, finding it not good. To the last, it was imagined that Grau would give a season after all; when he did not, there were rumors that he was influenced by the unavailability of Melba or Jean de Reszke or both.

This merely confirmed the onlookers in their opinion that the present star-system was even worse than the preceding one, when the public would go to hear Patti or Albani regardless of the work in which they appeared. "That was bad," contended the *Times,* "but it was practical." In the program evolved by Abbey and Grau, the previous mediocrity of staging, orchestral playing, and ballet was not measurably improved; now the public would respond only to four, five or six stars. Others, no matter how able, would not be accepted in a "Melba part" or a "Calvé part."

Perhaps the commentators were too close to the whole epoch to value its virtues as well as to evaluate its shortcomings. At our distance, the high points may stand out with greater clarity. But it is quite clear that the modern concept of a repertory theater had not emerged. *Rigoletto, Lucia,* and *Il Trovatore* were damned as "old" works whose day had gone, rather than valued as vital expressions that would be welcome in just proportion to other kinds of writing. Wagner was not a unique master, but an "advanced" writer in whose image future opera would have to be created. "Italian" singers would not learn new roles; "German" singers would. Lurking in the wings were the forces of a new era—Puccini, Strauss, Debussy; but to the musical thinkers of New York in the nineties Puccini was an imitation Mascagni, Strauss a composer of ridiculously over-orchestrated tone poems, Debussy barely a name.

Walter Damrosch had his most extensive opportunity up to this time to show his hand as an opera impresario when the Damrosch-Ellis Grand Opera Company undertook a five-week series beginning on January 17, 1898. The hyphenation respected the presence in the company of Melba, whose services in the United States were controlled by the Boston manager Charles A. Ellis. She was, indeed, the Violetta of the opening *Traviata,* with Salignac and Campanari, Bimboni conducting. Although the *Times* acknowledged that "no such voice has been heard since Patti was in her prime," there was complaint about the "rough edges" of her legato. The old esteem for Marcella Sembrich, and the veneration to come, had lately been stimulated by her reappearance in concert (October 26) after thirteen years' absence. In that light, Melba's lapses were "the more notable just now because a perfect legato has recently been heard."

Mme Melba was both the pleasure and the pain of the non-German repertory of this company. Marguerite in *Faust* and Rosina in *Il Barbiere* were pleasures on the order of her Violetta, but there was no precedent for her Aida on January 24 save her Brünnhilde in *Siegfried.* It was alien to her "voice, her style, and her temperament," wrote Henderson in the *Times.* He thought the clue to the unfathomable mystery of Melba's abuse of "one of the most precious gifts that Heaven ever put in a human throat" was a desperate quest for new roles. "The public," he was convinced, "can no longer be beguiled to go . . . to old-fashioned Italian opera." That the savior for Melba would be such "new-fashioned" opera as Puccini's *La Bohème* could not yet have occurred to anyone.

For his part of the season, Damrosch conducted a *Tannhäuser* on the second night, January 19, in which Kraus, again in good voice, was a welcome associate for Gadski, Bispham, and Fischer; and Damrosch proceeded with most of the *Ring, Die Meistersinger, Der fliegende Holländer,* and so on. Nordica sang the *Walküre* and *Götterdämmerung* Brünnhildes for the first time this season. Both were warmly admired as instances of excellent singing, but the temperament of the young goddess was not hers. In *Götterdämmerung,* attention was directed to her "splendid vigor" in the opening duet and to her fine intelligence in the spear scene. Nothing needed to be said of her "Immolation Scene," as she had sung it often and well in concert. There was some disposition to tax the absent Grau company with the "German spirit" of the Damrosch-Ellis group, but it could not go too far. On the occasion of this *Götterdämmerung,* for example, the *Times* noted that the "orchestra played most of the music in a rather slovenly way." It was hardly surprising, for in its series of New York Symphony concerts the same orchestra had played that afternoon Beethoven's *"Eroica"* Symphony, the Serenade for Wind Instruments by Richard Strauss, and sundry other things.

Moreover, the *Times* found the "glorification" of individual singers "mere silliness." They were "almost as famous as prize fighters." Even Jean de Reszke was held in too high esteem, with such talk as opera "depending on

M. de Reszke. . . . Someday he will retire. . . . Shall there be no more cakes and ale? Nonsense! There will still be men to sing Faust and there will be people who never heard Jean de Reszke and who will think these men great."

The year of opera was at an end, but not the events of influence on opera. After but the briefest illness, Seidl died of food-poisoning on March 28, 1898. There had been no place for him at the Metropolitan during the Damrosch season, but he had been prominent as conductor of the Philharmonic. He introduced Dvořák's "New World" Symphony to New York, of course, and was admired for his conducting of Tchaikovsky, Brahms, and other "contemporaries." Summing up the influence on musical taste in New York of a man not yet fifty, the *Times* said: "His death could never have been timely. It could not have been more untimely than it was. . . . The work must go on, though the worker is silent. . . . Those of us who remain must try to do what we can to make the future bloom with fruit from the labors of Anton Seidl." Virtually every prominent musician in New York took part in the funeral services at the opera house on March 31.

The contention that Italian singers would not learn new roles was rather shaken in the later weeks of this music season when *La Bohème* was given for the first time in New York in Wallack's Theater on Herald Square. The grandly titled Royal Italian Grand Opera Company that gave New Yorkers their first experience with the much-beloved music on May 16 was wholly Italian, with Giuseppe Agostini as Rodolfo, Linda Montanari as Mimi, and Cleopatra Vincini as Musetta. Some obvious parallels between *La Traviata* and *La Bohème* were drawn in the *Times,* which described the music as "of the new Italian school. It is like that of Mascagni and Leoncavallo. Yet one can fancy he sees Verdi smiling through his beard. . . . He knows that when these things are dead and buried beyond all redemption, foolish people will go to hear his 'Traviata' and wise ones will shout bravo at his wonderful 'Falstaff.' " Yet the *Times* noted "an abundance of melody in this 'Boheme.' There is grace, there is force, there is even passion at times. But there is not much soul to it after all." The performance, loud and crude, made an effect; a "refined" performance, it was surmised, would make a much better one.

It was nearly three years before Melba discovered that she could do with Mimi what she could not do with Brünnhilde and Aida. Then, in fact, a new influence came to bear on the Metropolitan, where it not only abided but also flourished.

1898–1899

The creation of the Maurice Grau Opera Company to replace the dissolved firm of Abbey, Schoeffel, and Grau wrought changes more profound than those concerned only with business and finance. The direction of Covent Garden (at the suggestion of Jean de Reszke) had come under Grau's control in 1897, and the actual if informal connection of opera in New York and London became factual and formal. Thus he was better able to command the best singers of the world than any individual before or since.

Of the day's major celebrities, only Calvé was not on this season's roster. But Melba and Sembrich were, also Lehmann and Nordica, Marie Brema and a new contralto, Ernestine Schumann-Heink; not only the De Reszkes and Maurel and Plançon, but also Anton Van Rooy, one of the greatest of Wagnerian baritones, and Ernst Van Dyck, the Dutch tenor to whom Shaw had referred (see page 111) in 1891 as one of the "younger men" who might spur Jean from his "lethargy."

This powerful personnel made some mourn more than ever the passing of Seidl; but Grau went to extremes to provide a suitable replacement for him in Franz Schalk. At thirty-five, Schalk was just the age at which his predecessor had come to New York, and he would rise to eminence as director of the Vienna State Opera. Schalk's way of conducting Wagner was not always what the critics deemed appropriate, but he was an important factor in some long-cherished experiences.

Among these was the first complete *Ring* cycle in Metropolitan history. It was Seidl's conviction that uncut performances were appropriate only at Bayreuth, Munich or another festival. Henderson stated his view on January 22, 1899: "I am first, last, and all the time in favor of the customary cuts." He also complained, however, when the Norn scene was omitted from a noncyclical performance of *Götterdämmerung* on February 3, posing the perennial problem not only of whether to cut, but also of what. No ready formula exists for pleasing everyone.

One of the revelations of the *Rheingold* that began the sequence on January 12 was the Loge* of Van Dyck, quite the best ever heard till that time from "an actor of rare and brilliant skills" (the *Times*). Van Rooy's Wotan* left "nothing to be desired," likewise Schumann-Heink's Erda.* Eames gave a fresh impulse to her career with an unexpectedly emotional Sieglinde in the *Walküre* of January 17, with Brema as Brünnhilde, and Lampriere Pringle (Hunding) joining Van Dyck and Van Rooy (Wotan). Lehmann was the *Siegfried* Brünnhilde on January 19, with Dippel (Siegfried) and Van Rooy (the Wanderer); Nordica took the part in the *Götterdämmerung* of January 24, in which the De Reszkes (Jean as Siegfried,* Édouard as Hagen*) appeared for the first time. Despite this awaited happening, Schumann-Heink's Waltraute* compelled the *Times* to declare: "No greater piece of declamation has ever been heard on the stage here."

Praise of Édouard's Hagen was equally lavish, but the first appraisals of Jean's elder Siegfried were much more guarded. The music of the first act lay low for him (though he was originally a baritone, he chose not to sing Siegmund for the same reason), but he improved in the second act. The death scene, wonderfully characterized, had the memory of Niemann's to contend with. Schalk's conducting was better liked than in previous *Ring* dramas. He was uniformly respected for knowledge and precision, but found wanting in temperament—by the Seidl standard.

That lack could not have been a grievous one, for he was the conductor of one performance, at least, remembered through the lifetime of some who were present. That was a *Tristan* on January 7, with De Reszke and Lehmann, Brema as Brangäne, and Van Rooy as Kurvenal.* Years later, in Berlin, Henderson asked the aging Lehmann if she remembered an afternoon *Tristan* when (as quoted by Leiser) "everything was perfection, when the audience seemed breathless. . . .' 'I remember it well,' said the great Isolde. 'It was the ideal *Tristan* performance of my life.' " She and de Reszke sang together in no other season in New York, and in no other matinee *Tristan*.

In his account the next day Henderson wrote: "Not a sound could be heard in the auditorium save the music. . . . After such a performance, criticism is weak for want of superlatives. [Lehmann's] voice was simply marvelous in its beauty of tone, its radiant color, its breadth, its tenderness. . . . In the duet she and M. de Reszke gave such an exhibition of masterly singing as has never been excelled." Only one other audience, on February 1, shared the experience. Lehmann was thereafter busy with other things, and Nordica sang Isolde.

Between the two Isoldes, Lehmann took up a singular kind of challenge and met it with her unfailing distinction. Brema found herself in dubious voice for Fricka in *Das Rheingold* on January 27, and decided at three in the afternoon that she could not perform. The only possible alternates were Rhinemaidens, who could not be spared. Lehmann, who had studied the part but never sung it, agreed to try. She was, according to the *Times,* "eminently satisfactory." So far as I know, this was the beginning and end of Lehmann's history as Fricka* in *Das Rheingold*.[1]

It is easy to comprehend, in the impact of such events, why Krehbiel should have written, after a *Lohengrin* on January 9: "Fortunate public, destined to be the envy of future generations!" Nordica and the De Reszkes

---

[1] Actually, Lehmann took on the task rather than let her sister Marie, who was spending the winter in New York, jeopardize her pension rights in Vienna by singing an unauthorized performance for Grau. "Riezl" was a thoroughly experienced Fricka, and helped Lilli get the part in hand.

were the keystones of the cast, as on numerous occasions before; but Schumann-Heink made her debut as Ortrud* in a manner to merit comparison with Brandt, Fursch-Madi, and Lilli Lehmann. The Wagnerian emphasis was present from the opening with *Tannhäuser* on November 29, with Van Dyck (Tannhäuser [d]), Nordica (Venus), Eames, Plançon (now a German Landgraf), and Albers (a rather poor Wolfram). Mancinelli's conducting was of a familiar, not very stimulating sort. Matters improved when Schalk made his debut in *Die Walküre* on December 14.

The advent of Sembrich gave Grau no less than six able-to-brilliant Juliettes to join such men as the De Reszkes and Saléza; and the Gounod score took up the box-office slack left by the absence of Calvé and *Carmen*. Sembrich was the soprano on December 26 when Jean de Reszke was welcomed, after an absence of a year and a half, with "a loud and prolonged burst of applause . . . seldom . . . heard in any theater in New York." After the balcony scene the new Juliette* and the old Roméo were called out eight times. Melba (no longer dictating casts to Grau) sang it on December 2, Suzanne Adams followed on January 4, and Eames on January 14. Adams was greeted by Krehbiel as "one of the latest illustrations of America's capacity for producing lovely voices," but Henderson termed her "generally immature." In after years the latter critic cited her on several occasions as the kind of singer who would have been a star in the 1920's, but was just a satellite in this particular constellation.

Sembrich's first season as a mature artist was a series of musical and dramatic triumphs which clearly explains why she became such a favorite with the public and the press. Her Rosina on November 30 gave her rank as a charming comedienne, and as Violetta on December 5 she was likened to "Adelina Patti . . . in her palmy days" (the *Times*). "*Sempre libera*," ending with "clear, mellow E flat in alt," had to be repeated. Her art added to the attractions of *Le Nozze di Figaro* and *Don Giovanni*, both given with remarkable casts. In the former, on December 17, her Susanna* matched Eames's Countess superbly, and Sembrich even made sense of an "inescapable" repetition of the letter duet by showing the audience that a blot of ink on the page made it necessary to rewrite the letter. Bevignani waved a rather limp stick at such other singers as Édouard de Reszke (Almaviva), Campanari (Figaro*), and De Lussan (Cherubino). Save for relying on the same undistinguished conductor, Grau spared no cost to make his *Don Giovanni* distinguished on January 2, 1899. Lehmann's Donna Anna no longer had the ease of old, but "the nobility of her style remains," said the *Times*. Nordica's Elvira was not at her best in the arias, for she was vocally out of form, but the ensembles went splendidly. Zerlina was a role that Sembrich had sung fifteen years before, but not nearly so well. The men were Salignac (a "tolerable" Ottavio), Maurel, and Édouard de Reszke (Leporello).

How did these performances compare with those of the fine court theaters of the day: Dresden, Vienna, Munich, Berlin? In the view of one with the necessary knowledge (Henderson), Grau "solved the problem in a very satisfactory manner by omitting those factors usually found in the subsidized opera houses—namely fine chorus, orchestra, ballet, and *mise en scène*—and providing what the kindly aid of Government never secures—namely, the services of the world's greatest singers." This was spoken of a *Don Giovanni* on January 21, in which Sembrich was replaced by the relatively little-remembered Frances Saville as Zerlina.

Sembrich was also included in the season's extra-price attraction, a version of *Les Huguenots* in which she sang Marguerite on February 20, with Nordica,[1] Mantelli (Urbain), the De Reszkes, Plançon, and Maurel. On January 18 the cast included Lehmann as Valentine and Adams as Marguerite,* and on February 7, when Jean de Reszke was not available, Saléza was a more than able replacement. Lucia, Harriet in *Martha,* and Gilda were other roles sung by Sembrich during these weeks.

A kind word might be entered here for Albert Saléza, a tenor whose career was spent first in the shadow of De Reszke, then in that of Caruso. "He has a pure, mellow tenor voice of admirable quality," wrote Henderson of his debut as Roméo on December 2, and there was praise also for his "elegant diction," the "finish of the Gallic school" in his phrasing. His Don José* on December 21 was rated "very fine" by the same writer. A rather short man, with a plain face, Saléza came to high esteem among devotees of fine singing, if not with the general public.

Twenty-seven works were given in the seventeen-week period, with fewer of the "off nights" previously scorned. *Manon* gave much pleasure when it was sung on January 14 with Saville (Manon*), Van Dyck (Des Grieux*), Albers (Lescaut*), and Plançon, and if the De Reszkes plus Nordica and Plançon were not enough reason for going to *L'Africaine* on February 27, Grau provided a fillip by offering Maurel as Nelusko.* "He is thoroughly acquainted with the traditions of 'L'Africaine,'" said the *Times,* "being something of a tradition himself."

Along with a heavy burden of conducting, Luigi Mancinelli prepared his own *Ero e Leandro* for a *première* on March 10, thus becoming the first composer to direct his own opera in a Metropolitan season. Much attention

[1] In the week thus begun, Nordica sang the same role the next night in Philadelphia, an emergency Donna Anna in place of Lehmann on Wednesday, and her scheduled Isolde on Saturday afternoon. The *Times* observed that the exertion left no effect on her tones, though it "apparently cost a little more effort than usual to produce some of them."

was directed to Arrigo Boito's libretto, generally judged the worthiest part of the venture. Krehbiel found the score "eclectic," with moments of "passionate intensity." Even with Mantelli singing the prologue when Schumann-Heink was indisposed, the cast was hardly improvable— Eames (Ero*), Saléza (Leandro*), and Plançon (Ario-farne*). The public was not impressed, but Grau tried two further performances in 1902.

The passage of eighteen months or more since Nordica and Eames had been heard in a full season's repertory (the first, of course, had been part of the Damrosch-Ellis company) had added stature to both. Constant references in the press reflected the increasing freedom and ease of Nordica in her greatest roles—the Brünnhildes, Isolde, even Donna Anna—and the confidence that she would fill the place of the departing Lehmann. Nevertheless, when Bauermeister fell ill on March 4 (a new twist to an old story), Nordica did not hesitate to add the music of the off-stage Priestess to her on-stage chore of Aida. Nobody ever heard *that* music better sung.

As for Eames—once described by Shaw as "intelligent, ladylike and somewhat cold"—her Sieglinde* on December 14 was valued by the *Times* as "womanly and tender," acted with "unexpected wealth of beautiful detail." When she sang "With verdure clad" (from Haydn's *Creation*) at a Sunday-night concert, the mating of voice and material seemed impossible of improvement. Her coming of age, artistically, was given official status by the presentation of *Faust* with Eames and the De Reszkes on March 13—ten years, exactly, since her Paris Opéra debut with the same stalwart support.

For Lehmann there was a round of farewells as the season ended and her decision to forego opera in America became general knowledge. She was lustily applauded and presented with a diamond pendant at a song recital in Carnegie Hall on April 10, and sang her last at the Metropolitan in a post-season gala on April 21, choosing the last half of the first act of *Die Walküre* with Dippel. On the following afternoon she honored a protégé of the late Seidl, Franz Kaltenborn, by singing *"Abscheulicher"* from *Fidelio* and the *"Liebestod"* in a concert he conducted in Carnegie Hall. Lehmann came to America for a concert tour the next winter, and then decided that eighteen crossings of the Atlantic had sufficed. When she was prominently mentioned in the press again, it was as the moving spirit in the organization of the Salzburg Festival, and then as mentor for Geraldine Farrar.

1899–1900

Taking all things together, the season of 1898–99 probably marked the high point in Grau's career as an impresario. For one thing, it had been two years in the making, and virtually every contingency was anticipated to make the chosen repertory work. For the season that followed it, two mighty personalities had to be replaced: Lehmann, whose absence had been anticipated, and Jean de Reszke, whose return had been expected despite some hints that he, too, was looking forward to retirement. In the end he decided that Paris and London were closer to his country home in Poland than New York was, and Grau had to manage as best he could for this winter without him.

One consequence was a project to outdo anything Grau had previously undertaken in all-star casts. This was a production of *Die Zauberflöte*— not previously heard in the theater—of which the *Times* anticipated no great public interest in the music, but thought "large audiences can be attracted by putting as many of the principal members of the company as possible into the cast." As a production, too, it promised more than Grau's average, for the designs of a greatly successful revival in Munich the summer before were utilized.

When it finally came to the stage on March 30, it did not immediately compete with Munich, for at least the reason of text—the Metropolitan knew it first as *Il Flauto magico*. If it did not have quite the ten stars of both sexes rumored to be in store, there were more than enough for all ordinary purposes. Sembrich (Queen of the Night*), Eames (Pamina*), Plançon (Sarastro*), De Lussan (Papagena*), Campanari (Papageno*), and Dippel (Tamino*) were a fair enough start. To them were added Milka Ternina, Mantelli, and Carrie Bridewell (Three Ladies*), and Suzanne Adams, Eleanore Broadfoot (later know as Eleanora de Cisneros), and Rosa Olitzka as the Three Boys. Mancinelli conducted.

Whatever the reason, the audience went "well-nigh wild" (the *Times*) when the principals lined up for a call after the first act, and there was commendation for the production, of which "the lions alone were worth the price of admission." The vocalization of Eames and her lovely appearance were the artistic summits of this occasion, for Sembrich was not in her best vocal condition. Plançon, however, was an impressive Sarastro, and Mancinelli's conducting satisfied. The house was full for the repetition on April 4, and there were three more performances in the closing days of the season. The casts remained largely the same, but Clementine de Vere replaced Eames on April 7, and Édouard de Reszke was Sarastro* on April 9.

The criticism applied to the look of Grau's stage resulted in a new production of *Roméo* when the Gounod score opened the season on December 18. Albert Alvarez, from Paris, made his debut as Roméo (d), and was greeted as a man of "splendid presence, an actor of unsurpassed grace . . .

[with] a very fine voice." Eames, Plançon and Édouard de Reszke were in this cast. Alvarez sustained a high standard as José* in *Carmen* on December 20, in which Calvé returned in splendid style, with Plançon a much admired Escamillo;* as Faust* on December 23; and as Radames* on January 3, when Eames added one of her best-remembered roles to a lengthening list.

The celebrated photograph of Eames's Aida* (see pictures) had its verbal parallel in the description of the *Times:* "an enchantment to the eye . . . a ravishingly beautiful spectacle." Costumes designed by her painter husband, Julian Story, were no small part of the total effect. Moreover, she sang the music "fluently and with an opulent loveliness of tone" (the *Times*). The picturesque Amonasro* was Antonio Scotti, whose thirty-three-year career began on December 27 in *Don Giovanni*. The *Tribune* found him "an artist in the highest sense of the word"; the *Times* pronounced him "immediately successful." Antonio Pini-Corsi, a well-liked buffo, was Masetto (d), with Nordica, Sembrich (Zerlina), and Adams on one side of the drama, Édouard de Reszke (Leporello) on the other. It was noted that real musicians took part in the ballroom scene on stage, not the usual supers.

Scotti, among a series of roles which included Valentin* in *Faust* on December 29 (Calvé a much more expert Marguerite than before), Malatesta* in *Don Pasquale* on January 18, and Alfio* in *Cavalleria* on March 21, won the greatest admiration for his Tonio* in *Pagliacci* on January 20. The *Times* described it as "one of the most admirable impersonations ever seen on the Metropolitan stage." By March 23, when he sang Escamillo,* Scotti was "the popular baritone." The curtain was dropped midway in the third act of this performance when Calvé fainted during the scuffle of José and Escamillo. She was revived, and continued.

Milka Ternina and Johanna Gadski began their Metropolitan careers this season with successful debuts, the first as Elisabeth (d) in *Tannhäuser* on January 27, the second as Senta (d) in *Der fliegende Holländer* on January 6. Both were known from their appearances with the Damrosch touring troupe, and Ternina, in particular, was found "full of intelligence" (the *Times*), with a voice "round, sweet and sympathetic." Gadski's Senta was praised for sincerity and sound style, thought she did not always sing on pitch. Her Eva* in *Die Meistersinger* on February 2 suffered by comparison with her alternates of this season, Eames and Sembrich. The latter sang this, the only Wagnerian part of her Metropolitan career, on March 19, with customary finesse; she knew Elsa, but did not sing it in New York. Theodore Bertram, a new baritone this season, was the able Sachs,* as Van Rooy had been before.

Ternina grew steadily in esteem from a rather small-scaled Isolde* (with Van Dyck, Van Rooy, Schumann-Heink, and Édouard de Reszke) on March 2, to a series of Brünnhildes—March 20, March 22, and March 27—of which the climaxing *Götterdämmerung* earned the epithet "glorious" from the *Times,* with additional commendation for "an overwhelming plenitude of warm, mellow tone."

This year's Wagner was directed by Emil Paur, who, in the manner of Seidl, was also conductor of the Philharmonic Society. He appealed to current taste more than Schalk had, winning praise at his debut on December 23 for a performance of *Lohengrin* "intelligent, sympathetic and enthusiastic," and for orchestral playing "vigorous, flexible and at times brilliant" (the *Times*). He led an uncut *Ring* cycle that began on February 21 with a *Rheingold* in which Van Dyck's Loge was valued by the *Times* as "a finer creation than Edwin Booth's Iago." Brema's Fricka was admired, but the deficiencies of the staging were deplored. Schumann-Heink sang both Erda and a Rhinemaiden. The later works presented Nordica unvaryingly as the Brünnhilde, with a surprising success for Ternina as Sieglinde* in *Die Walküre* on February 22. This was, in the view of the *Times,* no more nor less than "the most complete and convincing interpretation of the Volsung's bride" New York had experienced. In the *Götterdämmerung* of March 1, Schumann-Heink exceeded all records for busy service by singing not only the First Norn and Waltraute, but a Rhinemaiden as well.

Paur was also offered an opportunity to show his hand in another kind of German repertory when Nicolai's *Die lustigen Weiber von Windsor* was heard on March 9. Fritz Friedrichs was an undelightful Falstaff,* while Bertram (Fluth*), Pringle (Reich*) and Dippel (Fenton*) were not of the usual Grau standard. Only Sembrich (Frau Fluth*) and Schumann-Heink (Frau Reich, or Mistress Page*) were. There was no repetition—the size of the house, the spoken dialogue in German, and the unbalanced cast were all liabilities.

The favor to German was accidental, the available singers being mostly of that background. In giving *Die Zauberflöte* in Italian, convenience still prevailed, as it did in the instance of a German *Fidelio* on March 16, with the chorus singing in Italian, or a *Carmen* on February 14 with Olitzka using Italian because Calvé and De Lussan were ailing. Ternina's Leonore* was far from Lehmann's (last heard in 1892) in dramatic stature, but she sang "with no little beauty of tone" and a "complete understanding of [the role's] significance" (the *Times*). The cast did not measure up to previous standards, and Paur's rough handling of the score called for remonstrations. He prefaced the opera with the *Fidelio* Overture, playing the "Leonore" No. 3 before Act II.

This was the first season to offer three works of Mozart, *Don Giovanni* and *Le Nozze di Figaro* continuing in the repertory now graced by *Il Flauto magico*. Scotti's Don added considerably to the force of the first (page 138), but the *Figaro* cast was not always what it had been. Eames, Campanari (Figaro), and Édouard de Reszke (Almaviva) continued to be excellent, but when Sembrich could not sing on December 22, Clementine de Vere was a Susanna* "unusually deficient in sonority," the *Times* reported. On occasions when Mancinelli conducted, there was more Mozart in the air than Bevignani provided. There was least of it on March 24, when Édouard de Reszke could not appear as Almaviva, and Dufriche, the Antonio, took his place. Whether he actually sang both parts is questionable, thought the *Times* reported: "M. Dufriche was permitted to exhibit his famous feat of singing two roles at once." It is a certainty that Eames became hoarse during the evening and *"Dove sono"* was omitted.

So far as versatility is an index to the ability of a singer, Sembrich and Nordica found common ground in Violetta, which the great Isolde and Brünnhilde sang on February 17, when her colleague was indisposed. Nordica, who had sung the *Walküre* Brünnhilde a few days before in Philadelphia, gave her listeners what the *Times* described as "a genuine treat. . . . It is because she began her career in the school which teaches the treatment of such parts that she is now able to sing the music of Wagner so notably. . . . She never sang 'Ah fors e lui' with such breadth . . . the facile ornamentation of her 'Sempre libera' had gained in subtle significance." Sembrich made her contribution to good will among *prime donne* by singing an excellent Marguerite* on April 2 in place of Calvé.

Despite the favor Sembrich enjoyed with the press and some elements of the public, she did not provide the kind of "star" quality that some box-holders thought desirable. Thus, the comment in Henderson's column of the *Times* on April 25: "It is not generally known but it is a fact that Mr. Grau is at the beck and call of the Amusement Committee of the stockholders, and the most active member of this committee is, to put it as courteously as possible, not a judicious guide.[1] Certain changes which are to be made in next season's company are the result of this influence. Mme. Melba, for example, is to come back and Mme. Sembrich is not." After noting that the ticket demand, in a season without Melba and De Reszke was not what it had been, there came the invariable question of novelties: "Mr. Grau cannot compel his singers to study new roles and with the multitudinous activities of a season divided between New York and Phila-

[1] Inferentially, the reference is to the then president of the Opera and Real Estate Company, G. G. Haven.

delphia, he cannot find time for the rehearsal of new works." Dates change, but not the immemorial problems and promises of managers!

1900–1901

Just as Philadelphia and the rehearsal problem were immutable factors of Metropolitan Opera, so is the "controversial" issue of opera in English. Would it interest a larger public—though its well-meaning advocates ignore the fact that the "popularity" of opera is no part of its recent problems— and thus help to make ends meet? What has apparently been forgotten is that it was actually put to the test, at the Metropolitan itself, prior to the regular season of 1900.

Henry Savage was the impresario. He was allowed to call his company the Metropolitan English Grand Opera Company, and the productions came out of Grau's warehouse. Of the singers, only Clarence Whitehill (a splendid Sachs, Wotan, and Amfortas-to-be) obtained later celebrity, and only Zélie de Lussan was a current "name." Emphasis was on repertory— a characteristic sequence of *Roméo, Tannhäuser, Il Trovatore, Lohengrin, Carmen,* and *Mignon,* with *The Bohemian Girl* and *The Mikado* to flavor the mixture—and a top price of one dollar and a half.

The press was indulgent, but the severest critic of all—the auditorium— remained inflexible. The small voices and the limited experience of most of the singers proved no bargain, at whatever price. What could not be heard could not be enjoyed, whether in English or any other tongue. The lack of public response was interpreted to mean that operagoers preferred to save their money for one performance by the established favorites rather than attend two performances by others. The season struggled on to the end, when most of the performers returned to the Castle Square Opera Company, which toured during the winter and played in New York during the off season in such a theater as the Casino or the Broadway.

In the framework of the time, the day that saw the actual turn of the century—December 31, 1900—had an almost unbearable importance. For months rumors had been circulated that Jean de Reszke would never sing again, or if he did, would sing with little of the quality of old. He had, in fact, sung little during the whole of 1900; but he assured Henderson in a private communication that this was merely to conserve his strength against another New York winter, and he would show in good time just how well he would sing.

Grau's selection of the date was not without interest, for it had been set aside, many months before, for a Sembrich recital in Carnegie Hall, which would begin an extended tour for this artist. (She was not a member of the company this season.) Fearful that a lesser attraction might not draw,

Grau put the issue beyond doubt by announcing it as the occasion for Jean de Reszke's reappearance. In a *Times* report the Sembrich audience was described as "large and happy." In another column of the same paper Henderson stated that De Reszke was greeted "by an immense audience . . . with every manifestation of . . . interest in his vocal welfare." The performance was interrupted by cheers when De Reszke appeared in the Swan Boat, and when it was stilled, Henderson continued: "Though the famous singer was palpably suffering . . . from nervousness, he sang the farewell with delicious beauty of tone and that consummate mastery of phrasing and declamation which make his every vocal utterance a delight."

The reception during Act I has long ranked as one of the most prolonged in Metropolitan history—half an hour, by some estimates. After Act II, Nordica (singing Elsa) slipped from sight to permit De Reszke to face "cheers and bravos" from his admirers. He ended the evening with the same kind of performance with which he began—but no longer nervous. Actually the contemporary reports suggest that Édouard, singing King Henry, and Nordica were more overwrought than the tenor. The postmortems declared that Jean realized that there would be an outburst when he appeared, and if he allowed it to distract him from the trying task of singing *"Nun sei bedankt, mein lieber Schwan,"* the evening might be a fiasco. When he had sung it successfully and walked to salute the King, he found himself facing a monarch—his brother, after all—with tears in his eyes. As the act continued, Nordica—once more his friend after the Melba-Brünnhilde misunderstanding—encouraged him with whispers of "Bravo, Jean!" For the first time in a De Reszke performance at the Metropolitan the conductor was Walter Damrosch.

For this last season in America, De Reszke received $2,500 for each of the thirty performances, and responded with a review of virtually every major role in his repertory, plus Walther von Stolzing in German. In sequence came Faust on January 4 (with Melba, Édouard as Méphistophélès, and Scotti as Valentin); Radames in *Aida* on January 7; a revival of *Le Cid* on January 16, in which Lucienne Bréval made an equivocal impression in her debut as Chimène, and Melba was the Infanta; with Da Gama, Tristan, Siegfried, and Walther later on.

The *Aida* was notable not only for De Reszke's inclusion of *"Celeste Aida"* (which he preferred to omit because he found it trying to sing so early in the performance), but also for a strong Aida* by Gadski, Louise Homer's Amneris, and an Amonasro by Scotti which was judged "the finest . . . since Pantaleoni." Phillippe Flon got more out of the orchestra than had been customary with his predecessors, and the future of *Aida* began to look brighter.

Roméo, on January 30 (with Melba, Plançon, and brother Édouard) was, as a matter of course, a "unique interpretation" (the *Times*) for Jean, as was his Raoul in *Les Huguenots* on March 11. Some concern was expressed when Jean contracted *"la grippe"* following a draughty exposure during the third act of *Tristan* on February 11 (the superstitious remembered that a similar happening had cost the life of Schnorr von Carolsfeld, the first Tristan), but he recovered after a three-week interruption of work.

The staggering season continued for Jean de Reszke with the young Siegfried on March 19. He had not sung the role since April 14, 1897, and the weight he had put on in five years was not easily disguised. But the singing art was in splendid order (he had bothered to go to a Philadelphia performance with Dippel as Siegfried a few weeks earlier to refresh his ear for the score), and the *Times* marveled at his "freedom of movement, grace and youthfulness of bearing." This time, however, the young Siegfried had a mustache. Walther von Stolzing, in German, was finally accomplished on March 25, with Gadski, Schumann-Heink, Édouard as Sachs, and Bispham. Two performances of *Götterdämmerung* (one with Nordica, one with Ternina) were followed on March 29 by a return to *Lohengrin.* Only his friends knew that he did not intend to sing another season in America, but the public could not have been more demonstrative at a formal farewell. He made his final appearance on the Metropolitan stage in a postseason gala on April 29, singing the second act of *Tristan* with Nordica, Schumann-Heink, and Édouard as King Marke.

Thus the De Reszke era, as it applied to the brothers at the Metropolitan. Édouard returned for two more seasons, but Jean sang sparingly thereafter, not, as some intimated, because of trouble with his vocal organs, but simply because he found it increasingly difficult to control his weight and resultant shortness of breath. He gave up all public performances in 1903, and made his home in Nice, where he taught as much as suited his fancy and received old friends from all over the world till his death in 1925. He had but one unfulfilled ambition: to sing Parsifal. He might have gone to Bayreuth to do so, but one of his dearest friends was the Princess of Wales, who could not imagine why he should give pleasure to the Kaiser, whom she described as a "horrible old man." Rather than do so, De Reszke did not sing Parsifal. That, I suppose is the meaning of being an artist and a gentleman.

There is a legend—spread only after both men were dead—that De Reszke heard Caruso at Covent Garden in 1902 and said: "That is the boy who will take my place," but it can be scarcely believed that he thought the Italian, no matter how great a vocalist, the type to shoulder his encompassing repertory. As De Reszke was departing the scene in Wagner, however, the Metropolitan was welcoming the works of Puccini, in which

Caruso was to have some of his most splendid successes. Mimi entered with Melba on December 26, 1900, in a performance of *La Bohème* that tempted Krehbiel to describe it as "foul in subject . . . futile in its music." Henderson judged the work as "episodic," while admiring the "fine duet" of Act III. He could not see "permanent success for an opera constructed as this one is." Melba lacked acting skill as Mimi, but he thought that her "cold, silvery voice suited the music perfectly." Saléza, as Rodolfo* "frequently evoked something like a frenzy of enthusiasm" (Krehbiel). Charles Gilibert (Schaunard*), Campanari (Marcello*), and Marcel Journet (Colline*) were others in the cast, but Fritzi Scheff was unable to appear as Musetta, causing Grau to engage a Signora Occhiolini from a touring Italian company. She sang in a thin, tremulous voice, much inferior to the "pert and vivacious" Scheff admired by the *Times* as Musetta* on January 11. Henderson began to hear more in the score with its repetitions, remarking the "beauties of the orchestration" and finding even the xylophone used "with ingenuity and appropriateness." *Bohème* was not given in 1901–2, but it returned in 1903 and did not miss a season during the next fifty.

Perhaps this increasing familiarity with Puccini's methods favored the greater respect with which *Tosca*[1] was received at its introduction on February 4. "Repulsive" was the *Times'* word for the subject, "hideous" the *Tribune's*. Henderson, however, found *"Recondita armonia"* a "really seductive piece of cantilena," the orchestration throughout "solid, picturesque, ingenious." Ternina as Tosca* was "almost great" as an actress, "highly expressive" as a vocalist. For the moment nothing could be said of Scotti's Scarpia save that it was admirable, but in a week-end article Henderson called it a "brilliantly vigorous and aggressive impersonation . . . with a full appreciation of the brutality of the character." Nothing then being known as *"Vissi d'arte,"* the writer directed attention to "the one cantabile of the second act," in which Ternina "makes a fascinating point." It would have been repeated for the "unreasonable Italian contingent" had Ternina not been "a true artist."[2] Cremonini was but fair as Cavaradossi. Scotti sang *every* performance of Scarpia in *Tosca* until 1909, when Amato had a chance, and most of those till his retirement in 1932.

The season's other novelty was Reyer's *Salammbô* on March 20, not denied by Grau to be the most expensive production he ever offered, as

[1] The incorrect billing *La Tosca* is still too often repeated. It is correct for Sardou's play, but the librettists deleted *"La"* from the opera, which is inscribed simply *Tosca*.
[2] This same column of February 10, 1901, contains the first mention I have found in the *Times* of the name Toscanini. Just so, neither Arturo nor Signor. It relates Siegfried Wagner's pleasure with a production of *Tristan* at La Scala, especially with the details of lighting supervised by Toscanini.

copied by Homer Emens from the Parisian original. The stimulus for it was the promotion of Lucienne Bréval (born Berthe Schilling, of Swiss parents, in Berlin), who had not won much favor in *Le Cid* (see page 142), *Les Huguenots,* or *L'Africaine* despite an appearance "ideal" for Selika* (Henderson). As Salammbô,* a role she created in Paris, Bréval "wore gorgeous gowns and ran the gamut of her semaphoric poses," but her singing "was again not a source of pleasure" (the *Times*). Saléza made something of the "crepitant" music with his Mathos,* and Scotti (Hamilcar*) and Journet (Narr-Havas*) performed in customary fashion. Two repetitions ended the career of a production "seldom equaled" in an American theater (Henderson). Bréval had a long career to come in Paris, but it was the judgment of the *Times* that she sang "rudely and without finish."

Boito's *Mefistofele* had a brief return in this season on behalf of Marguerite MacIntyre, an English favorite who made her debut as Margherita (d) on January 14, with Cremonini (Faust) and Plançon as Mefistofele,* one of his great parts. MacIntyre, however, had only a worn voice to withstand comparison with Calvé's, and little of the latter's dramatic art.

Among the artists, besides Scotti, launched on long careers during this transitional season were Louise Homer, Marcel Journet, Fritzi Scheff, and Charles Gilibert. Homer was the least skilled of them when she was first heard as Amneris (d) in *Aida* on December 22, being described as having "a rather hard voice of plentiful volume," but not "gifted with much temperament" (the *Times*). She made a place for herself, however, as one of the better American artists of this era. Journet, the Ramfis* of this same *Aida,* was heartily endorsed for his "smooth, sonorous, extensive, and well-placed" voice. It endured long enough for him to sing Méphistophélès in the first complete recording of *Faust* thirty years later. This year he went on to the big bass roles in *Roméo, Il Trovatore, Les Huguenots* (Marcel) and even *Das Rheingold* (Fafner), always with creditable artistry.

Scheff's debut should have been as Musetta (see page 144), but she was vocally unfit, and appeared first, instead, as Marcelline (d) in *Fidelio* on December 28. She brought a "whiff of the Viennese style" to the evening, according to the *Times,* and also pleased as Zerlina* in *Don Giovanni* (the only Mozart of the year, on January 23, with Nordica, Gadski, Scotti, Salignac, and Édouard de Reszke), the Forest Bird* in *Siegfried,* Nedda* in *Pagliacci,* and a *Walküre*—Helmwige—in the gala on April 29. Gilibert, best remembered for his Father in *Louise* with the Hammerstein company, made his debut as the Duke of Verona (d) in the *Roméo* that opened the season on December 18. This was an uncommonly splendid first night, and the description of Mme. Bauermeister carrying off the bouquets tossed to Melba after her waltz usurped the space that might have been given to the new baritone. He wore well, however, until his sudden death in 1910.

Verdi's death, on January 27, 1901, was mourned in a full two columns of obituary in the *Times,* and the same evening's concert at the opera paid him tribute. How much it might have pleased him is questionable, for Walter Damrosch honored his memory with the Funeral March from *Götterdämmerung.* Something more appropriate was organized for February 17, when Mancinelli conducted the first performance in the Metropolitan of the "Manzoni" Requiem, with Nordica, Schumann-Heink, Salignac, and Plançon.

The custom of an uncut *Ring* cycle was abandoned this season, not to return until Bodanzky undertook the task in 1929–30. The four works were given in sequence, however, beginning on February 25, with casts much the same as the year before. Without Eames, Calvé, Sembrich, or Lehmann, among recent favorites, Grau had problems in organizing all-star casts of former quality. Instead, he tempted the cautious opera-lover with couplings of Melba in *Bohème* followed by Melba in the "mad scene" from *Lucia* on March 18, and still did not fill the house. (The *Times* reported that the cast supporting Melba was not composed of singers "who excite public curiosity." They were Cremonini, Scheff, Campanari, and Journet.) He did better on March 22, when he coupled Melba in *Rigoletto,* with Gadski, Scotti, and Dippel in *Cavalleria.*

Grau's company toiled extensively for him this season, beginning on November 9 in Los Angeles, with six Western cities visited before the New York opening in December, and four Eastern ones in the spring. Philadelphia saw the group twenty times this winter. The final impression was that after meeting expenses for the new productions of *Salammbô, Tosca,* and *Bohème* he had come out about even.

1901–1902

As was inevitable with a singer of Jean de Reszke's celebrity, rumors were frequent during the next half-dozen years that he had changed his mind about retirement and would sing again in New York. He was considered a possibility as general director when Grau had to retire because of ill health in 1902–03; and the shrewd Oscar Hammerstein did not omit his name from the list of artists with whom he was "negotiating" when the opening of the Manhattan Opera House approached.

Had Grau held on until 1903, when his contract with Caruso became operative, he might well have entered another era of all-star casts. But the distinction between "all-star" and "ideal casts" is at once apparent. Lacking a tenor of Jean de Reszke's special distinction—which is to say lacking Jean de Reszke—the "ideal" cast became a figure of speech, implying a wish rather than a prospect, a memory rather than a promise.

In the pattern of the previous season, this one opened late—indeed, as late as December 23. Sixty-nine performances were compressed into a ten-week playing schedule, which meant, with Tuesdays and Thursdays not in the subscription cycle, that two performances on some days were more frequent than usual. Grau's choice of *Tristan und Isolde* for the first night might look at this distance to have some æsthetic significance, but the reasons were wholly practical. Van Dyck was now the first tenor, and the honor of opening the season might enhance his prestige. By saving *Roméo,* with Eames as Juliette, for the second playing night—Christmas —Grau would, in effect, have two *premières.*

All this careful planning misfired badly when the W. K. Vanderbilts decided to spend the holiday week-end in the country, and the people subordinate to him, according to the *Times,* "decided it would never do for them to be seen at the opera on either the opening night or Christmas evening." Those of the society stratum who did come to *Tristan*—with Ternina, Édouard de Reszke, and Schumann-Heink—arrived late, and left after Act II. So dark an opera for so bright an occasion was generally deplored, though a fresh setting for Act I was approved. On Christmas evening half a dozen boxes were not used at all, and others were filled by what was described as the "below stairs" aristocracy. Attendance elsewhere in the house was below par, a condition attributed by the *Times* to the "enormous extravagance which marks the holiday season . . . these days [and] leaves people with little money to spend on . . . musical performances."

Evaluation of the works in which Jean de Reszke had usually appeared vacillated between two tendencies: to accept without comparison what was offered in the general spirit that opera did not end with De Reszke; to mourn, after all, that things were not what they had been. *Roméo,* with Alvarez on December 25, and *Faust,* with Dippel on December 28 (Eames was the soprano on each occasion) were in the former category; *Les Huguenots* on January 29 definitely in the latter. Journet's fine Méphistoph-élès ("Sonorous voice and excellent style"), Scotti's Valentin—even minus what was still called *"Dio possente"*—helped Gounod; but of *Les Huguenots* the *Times* commented: "Of the celebrated cast of which Jean de Reszke was a member, only Édouard de Reszke remains . . . [his] was really the most enjoyable performance of the entire cast." Those encompassed in secondary status were Gadski (Valentine*), Emilio de Marchi (Raoul*), Suzanne Adams (Marguerite*), Scotti (De Nevers), and Journet (Saint-Bris), with Flon conducting.

The division of Jean de Reszke's duties among Dippel, Alvarez, Van Dyck, and De Marchi left varying complaints against all. The last named was of interest because he had been the first Cavaradossi* in Rome two years before. His Metropolitan debut (he had sung briefly at the Academy of Music half a dozen years before) in a *Tosca* of January 3, 1902, with Ternina and Scotti, earned praise for the size and freshness of his voice and his manly bearing. Likewise praised was his Radames* on January 17, in which attention was directed to his *"Celeste Aida,"* for he sang it in the original key. He appeared in Grau's last company, but did not return after Caruso's debut.

Sembrich was in this season, and Melba out, with several influences on the repertory, especially the presentation of *Le Nozze di Figaro* and *Il Flauto magico* and the first hearing of Donizetti's *La Fille du régiment*. Sembrich reappeared in *Don Pasquale* on December 27 (*Il Barbiere* had been scheduled, but Campanari was out of voice and "the company does not contain another Figaro," the *Times* reported), with Scotti as Malatesta and Salignac as Ernesto. Sembrich was still mourning the death of her young son, but she gave great pleasure with her singing. She also sang in *Nozze di Figaro* on January 1, with Eames a "picture of inspiring beauty" and Scheff a good-looking Cherubino* of "reedy tones," and in *The Magic Flute* on January 27. She was warmly applauded for her *"Gli angui d'inferno,"* and repeated it. Although Ternina was a much more prominent artist than in 1900, she again sang the First Lady, with Homer and Bridewell as the other Ladies. Scheff was a lively Papagena,* Eames a charming Pamina. Dippel as Tamino and Édouard de Reszke as Sarastro were not so well suited to their roles. Mancinelli being busy this year composing another opera (*Francesca da Rimini*), Armando Seppilli conducted the *Figaro,* Damrosch the *Flute,* neither with distinction.

Sembrich had "one of the prettiest triumphs of her American career" (Krehbiel) on January 6 when *La Fille du régiment* had its first French performance in the memory of those who had not been alive when a troupe from New Orleans gave it in 1843. All later Maries known to New York had sung in Italian. Henderson declared: "Only those who saw Patti at her best ever enjoyed such an exhibition of buoyant, bubbling comedy, such a display of gorgeous singing." Save for Salignac ("a ligneous and untuneful Tony," said the *Times*), the cast of Gilbert (Sulpice*), Van Cauteren (the Marquise*), and Dufriche (Hortensius*) was fair enough. Flon's conducting was deemed "not capable" by the *Times.* To "fill out the evening," Grau offered *Cavalleria* with Calvé.

As well as providing Sembrich with a beloved role, this *Fille du régiment* stimulated a critical sentiment that led to the eventual construction of the New Theater. In the *Tribune* of January 6, Krehbiel declared: "The city needs an Opera Comique as a companion to its grand opera," an opinion endorsed by Henderson a week later. It came within a decade—not at all a bad time lag for acceptance of a critical suggestion—but at the worst possible juncture, when the public was being tempted by both the Metropolitan and the Manhattan opera companies, and rarely found its way to Columbus Circle in satisfying numbers.

Also part of a continuing pattern was the reaction to Isidore de Lara's *Messaline,* when Calvé appeared on January 22 for the first time in a work that had considerable success abroad. Previous complaints against "foul Mimi" and "repulsive" Scarpia became more strident as Henderson denounced this new "brazen display of impure passion," and Krehbiel sought for words to convey his displeasure with this "new low in harlotry." It was not long before *Salome* and *Elektra, Sapho,* even *Der Rosenkavalier,* were to run a gauntlet of critical objection based on morality. One may judge from the survival of the Puccini and Strauss works whether the unconventional stories utterly damned the operas deemed musically weak as well.

For the press, De Lara's music lacked pith, pungency, or picturesqueness, but Calvé's Messaline* wrung praise from the most reluctant. She "acted and sang the role with consummate dramatic art," wrote Henderson. "The more's the pity." Her use of vocal coloration he compared to Bernhardt's, but the total effect was "deplorable." Alvarez was praised, or condemned, for a Helion* full of "unbridled passion"; Scotti and Gilibert were deemed good in what was asked of them. Flon conducted. *Messaline* had two repetitions this season, and has had no revival since.

Liabilities of another sort made the other novelty of this season, Paderewski's *Manru,* equally short-lived. The general esteem in which the pianist-composer was held as man and artist made the task of the reviewers an uncomfortable one after the *première* of February 14, and Henderson began the letting-down process by describing Alfred Nossig's libretto as "unskillful in construction and unpoetic in diction." Thereafter came the unpleasant truth that the vocal utterance was "not direct," that leitmotivs were used, but "not with real mastery," and that heavy orchestral scoring in the Wagner manner obscured the voices. Paderewski was cordially urged to learn from these miscalculations and proceed with operatic writing, but he never attempted another stage work. As Ulana,* Sembrich had an uncommon success in a dramatic role, and Alexander van Bandrowski, a tenor engaged for this task, made a "pleasing impression" as Manru (d). Damrosch conducted. There were fifteen curtain calls for the composer after Act II, but there were no repetitions after the two of this season.

Some talk appeared in the press of a Verdi cycle to honor the memory of the recently deceased master, but the only addition to the usual *Traviata, Aida,* and so on was a revival of *Otello* on January 31, with Alvarez, Eames, and Scotti. Our perceptions are blurred, but those nearer the events could see in *this* score the genesis of what is called the *verismo* school of *Cavalleria, Pagliacci,* and *Tosca.* Eames's Desdemona showed again the "perfect suitability" of her voice to the music; Alvarez survived comparison with Tamagno to be termed a "splendid, virile figure, passionate and affecting"; and Scotti's Iago,* if a little unsubtle, was "crafty, malignant, intense." (All the comments are from the *Times.*) In this work, Seppilli's conducting was apropos. For a novelty, there were no standees in the theater; a new fire regulation prohibited their presence. Because the opera could no more thrive without them than without the on-stage chorus, prudence soon gave way to necessity.

The gala for Prince Henry of Prussia as a social event has been described elsewhere (page 170); in its musical dimensions, it was remarked particularly for the inconveniences it visited on the previous day's performances of *Das Rheingold* and *Les Huguenots* (February 24). The Wagner score had been insufficiently—if at all—rehearsed, and the Meyerbeer became a problem when Suzanne Adams reported ill. Sembrich knew her role (Marguerite), but begged off to save herself for the gala. Estelle Liebling (d) (identified as "the daughter of the accompanist Max Liebling") was called upon, and obliged—in German. As is well known, the royal party came late and left early, with the result that Sembrich decided not to sing after all.

Of *Das Rheingold,* the *Times* reported that "the orchestra wabbled through the score in uncertain fashion," with Damrosch conducting. This being a year without Nordica, Ternina sang Sieglinde in *Die Walküre,* and Bréval—given a second chance—Brünnhilde.* Good appearance and excellent German enunciation were her salient qualities. Ternina sang the later Brünnhildes in splendid style, but the performances were disrupted by a stubborn ailment that prevented Bispham from appearing as Alberich in either. As a result, Alberich's scene was omitted from *Götterdämmerung.* Moreover, Scheff was ill when time came for the Voice of the Forest Bird in *Siegfried,* and Grau called in Sophie Traubman, of German days, to help out. Dippel was a poor young Siegfried, Van Bandrowski scarcely better as the elder Siegfried. Amidst all this, Albert Reiss, who had made his debut as the Shepherd (d) in the opening-night *Tristan,* sang "the best Mime we have yet had" (the *Times*). He remained a very able impersonator of such parts for two decades.

Grau's company continued to make money for him, but its members did not, other than as individuals, make friends for their artistry. The *Flute* production, for all its notable names, would have been improved had not some of the "names" refused to attend rehearsals. The orchestra (now often prefaced by the word "overworked") sometimes had to meet a schedule such as that of two January days that called for a *Manru* rehearsal at 11 a.m., a *Tannhäuser* rehearsal at 2 p.m., departure for a Philadelphia performance at 4, return to New York at 4 a.m., and a *Messaline* rehearsal at 11. Apparently the efforts Grau had made to revise his productions in the two or three previous seasons had slackened. The description, in the *Times* of December 21, has a familiar ring (see page 124): "bad scenery in most of the operas, a poor chorus, a wretched ballet, a mediocre orchestra, and general laxity and carelessness in all departments." Nor did "a list of prominent singers such as can be found in no other opera house in the world save Covent Garden" seem as much compensation as theretofore.

1902–1903

The preceding comment points the way in which, without leaving his desk, Grau might have considerably bettered the kind of opera he was giving; but he had his own view of what the public cherished, and he acted accordingly. Indeed, by remaining at his desk and improving the general quality of opera rather than scouring the theaters of Europe for new talent to bolster the specific, Grau might have spared his health and averted the collapse that cost him control of the Metropolitan before this season was over.

Henderson painted his searches vividly in the *Sun* [1] of February 1, 1903, when the choice of a successor to Grau still hung in the balance: "Where are the new singers to be found? What is the almost insoluble problem which will confront any new impresario. . . . It is the problem which has given Mr. Grau many a sleepless night and made his summer 'vacations' into hideous nightmare. . . . Into a train and ride four or five hours to hear a tenor in Gath. No good! Into another train at midnight and ride all night to hear another tenor at Gilead! No good! First express out for Tyre to hear a dramatic soprano. . . . And so forward through the weary days and restless nights."

[1] The critic changed his affiliation from the *Times* on September 21, 1902.

Yet it was not a prospect wholly adverse. Grau could look forward to Caruso, who had made a great success at the season in Covent Garden the preceding summer, for 1903; Olive Fremstadt would soon be ready for America; and the Berlin successes of Geraldine Farrar must have made him smile, for she was in some respects a Grau protégée and could have been singing at the Metropolitan already had her advisors not decided that a period of European experience would be to her advantage.

For this season Grau finally organized the Verdi tribute talked about the preceding season, but not accomplished. *Otello* was retained, and actually opened the season on November 24, with Eames, Scotti, and Alvarez, Mancinelli conducting. To the usual fare of *Aida, Trovatore, Traviata,* and *Rigoletto,* he added *Ernani* and *Un Ballo in maschera.* The opening night turnout was a very large one, and Henderson noted as its components: "High-bred women . . . men who are called 'robber barons' by those who hate them and 'railroad magnates' by those who merely envy them: young bucks . . . half weaned boys . . . swell gamblers and other 'sporty men' . . . half-crazed women reporters, terrified lest a Vander-bilt or Astor escape their count . . . all in that motley mob which consti-tutes the American equivalent of *tout Paris.*"

When *Ernani* was given its first Metropolitan hearing on January 28 (it had been dormant since an Academy season of 1882), Sembrich sang her first Elvira* anywhere, with delightful style; De Marchi was an earnest Ernani,* Scotti an explosive Don Carlos.* The undercurrent of dissatis-faction with the work of Édouard de Reszke during his last Metropolitan season drew the comment from Henderson that his " 'Infelice' was extremely infelicitous." On the whole, the work seemed static, with the few airs, such as *"Ernani involami,"* insufficient to carry the evening. Richard Aldrich, new critic of the *Times,* doubted whether it was "all worth while."

Un Ballo was a somewhat fresher memory when it came along on February 23 (the German season of 1889–90 had included it), but Grau's production provided novelty in the restoration of an Italian locale for the action (Naples) and, of course, the original language. The names in the cast—Gadski as Amelia,* Homer as Ulrica,* De Marchi, Campa-nari (Renato*), Édouard de Reszke (Sam*), and Journet (Tom*)—were moderately promising, but few of them had sung the parts elsewhere, and the total was not impressive. By this time Grau had given over direction of the company to his associate, Frederick Latham,who did not challenge the good-natured contempt of the press with a repetition.

Falstaff had been planned for the Verdi sequence, but a misguided attempt by Eames to sing Tosca* in December left her with a strained voice and deprived *Falstaff* of a necessary performer. The other Verdi performances were not of notable quality, though luster was added to Scotti's repute with a fine Germont* in *Traviata* on November 29, and a spirited Rigoletto* on December 5. Three names were associated with Amneris in the *Aida* of November 27: Homer, who was announced, but did not sing; Bridewell, who was appointed to replace her, but could not, breaking down midway in Act II: and Eugenia Mantelli, singing this season in vaudeville, who was finally brought on to finish the tomb scene. The single performance of *Il Trovatore* on March 11, with Nordica, Homer, De Marchi, Campanari, and Journet did not receive much critical attention, for it shared the evening with Ethel Smyth's *Der Wald,* Grau's last novelty.

Due attention was directed to the fact that no opera by a woman had previously been given at the Metropolitan, and the record remained unchanged after sixty-five years. Dame Ethel's one-acter had an interesting intellectual structure, following the form of a French *ouverture,* with a slow section at the beginning and end, a fast one between. The "solemn dryness" of the writing, however, inclined the *Sun* to describe *Der Wald* as "an academic grove." Questions were raised why the new work was not either Charpentier's *Louise* or Puccini's *Manon Lescaut,* with rather pointed implications that friends in high places had influenced the choice of this composer's work rather than another's. It was given once again, with Gadski, Bispham, and Georg Anthes, this time on a bill with *La Fille du régiment.*

Perhaps the most notable thing about *Der Wald* was the conductor, Alfred Hertz. After experiments with Schalk, Paur, and Damrosch, Grau finally found, in Hertz, a musician who satisfied the situation for a decade, until he left, with regrets, when the San Francisco Symphony beckoned in 1915. *Parsifal, Salome,* and *Der Rosenkavalier* were among the works New Yorkers heard first under the direction of Hertz. He made his debut with *Lohengrin* on November 28, "ridding the performance of much of its perfunctoriness," said the *Sun.* Georg Anthes [1] made his debut as Lohengrin (d), singing well enough, but without the distinction to please a public still mindful of Jean de Reszke.

Perfunctory Hertz never was, but there were often complaints that he loved Wagner's sonorities too keenly for the best interests of the singers. The objections were heard after both *Siegfried* and *Götterdämmerung* of a *Ring* cycle that began on January 14. Nevertheless, the ebb and flow of

---

[1] For Anthes this single season in New York was memorable, if not pleasurable. He tipped over the Swan Boat in a *Lohengrin* of January 10, and in *Siegfried* on January 19 the anvil fell apart while his sword was still poised in the air.

the music were more strongly present than for some time. Anthes made something of a record by singing the leading tenor part throughout the *Ring*—Loge, Siegmund, and the two Siegfrieds. He was, needless to say, not equally suited to all, his young Siegfried in particular being deficient. Nordica sang the Brünnhildes in casts that deviated little from those of the several preceding seasons. Although *Das Rheingold* is hardly long enough to require cuts, Hertz risked critical displeasure by eliminating Alberich's renunciation of love before the rape of the gold. Omitting the Norns in *Götterdämmerung* was not disapproved.

A new line of critical thinking about Wagner was disclosed this season when Alois Burgstaller, with a Bayreuth background, came to sing Siegmund* in *Die Walküre* on February 12. His background was not a virtue, for the local attitude was that the real Wagner tradition had been brought to New York by Seidl, that what was practiced at Bayreuth had been corrupted by the "Meister's" wife, Cosima, and his son, Siegfried. Burgstaller was admired for a fresh young voice and a good lithe figure, but, said the *Sun,* "he was as innocent of the art of tone production as a child." He sang the two Siegfrieds* on February 14 and 28, eventually winning more favor than either Anthes or Emil Gerhäuser, who was actively disliked at his debut as Tannhäuser (d) on December 1 and soon vanished. Burgstaller sang the first Parsifal at the Metropolitan a year later, and flourished for several seasons thereafter.

With neither Ternina nor Melba in the company, the public demand for Puccini resulted in the Tosca by Eames, and Sembrich's first Mimi. Neither came close to replacing the absent divas, though for quite different reasons. When Eames appeared in the new role on December 12, Henderson granted that it was better than anticipated, but added: "There is no blood in her performance. It was impeccable in design, icy in execution . . . lyric sweetness . . . perfect poise . . . the lovely but immobile face . . . were elements in a portrait of surpassing beauty but not of tortured womanhood." She managed three further performances, but missed several other assignments between. Finally suffering from what one paper termed "Toscalitis," she gave up singing for the season, and save for the post-season gala was absent from the Metropolitan until 1904.

Sembrich managed the music of Mimi* handily enough, but the judgment, on December 15, was that it was no role for her. Her conception, said the *Sun,* was "based on the assumption that the girl was modest, retiring and naturally refined" (a long step from "foul Mimi"). Archness or coquetry were not in her Mimi, nor the qualities that made Henderson term Scheff a Musetta "chic to her finger tips."

Grau's gradual separation from active participation in the company, and the new duties assumed by Eames and Sembrich, left the company in short supply of what had formerly been its principal asset: brilliant singers of Marguerite and Juliette. Suzanne Adams, Camille Seygard, even Fritzi Scheff had the chance to distinguish themselves as singers of Gounod, but did not. Adams was still a woman with an "exquisitely beautiful voice" (the *Sun*), but little gift for dramatic action. Finally, acting manager Latham called on Nordica to sing Marguerite on February 18, which she did with a dazzling display of "demivoice and a cold tone" (in the first scene), "chest tones and a warm color" (in the love duet), then the "full power of her voice" (in the church scene). The witnessing words are Henderson's. The week before she had sung Isolde and the *Walküre* and *Siegfried* Brünnhildes.

A pseudo-stellar *Le Prophète* on December 10, with Alvarez, Journet, and Édouard de Reszke, left the memory of little that was notable save Schumann-Heink's Fidès. Her singing of *"Ah! mon fils"* was ranked among the broadest, most noble feats of vocalization heard in the best of Metropolitan days. Also long remembered as a Metropolitan criterion was Scotti's Almaviva,* when *Figaro* was first given on December 17. With Eames, Sembrich, and Scheff as good as ever or better, Campanari a fine Figaro, and Gilibert (Bartolo*) and Reiss (Basilio) superior to the customary singers of those parts, the performance was endorsed as close to the best *Figaro* heard in the house. It was not given even once again, however, for Eames became involved with *Tosca* and the company had no other qualified Countess.

The other Mozart of this season was not outstanding, though both *Il Flauto magico* and *Don Giovanni* were performed. Gadski sang Pamina "unsteadily" in the former on February 25, and Donna Elvira without "the velvety smoothness necessary for . . . Mozart's music" on March 8, said the *Sun*. Critical compassion was exercised because Gadski had helped to take up the Eames slack by singing, in this season, Aida, Pamina, Elvira, Röschen in *Der Wald,* Eva in *Die Meistersinger,* Elsa, Elisabeth, Valentine in *Les Huguenots,* Sieglinde, Amelia in *Un Ballo,* Ero in a brief restoration of Mancinelli's *Ero e Leandro,* and even Santuzza.

As a gesture to the departing Grau, Gadski sang a thirteenth role in a gala for him on April 27, appearing as Senta in the second act of *Der fliegende Holländer.* Sembrich sang the first act of *Traviata,* Eames came back for the last act of *Faust* with Alvarez and Édouard de Reszke—his farewell to the Metropolitan—and there were other excerpts from *La Fille du régiment, Les Huguenots,* and *Lohengrin.* Mrs. Grau accepted the tribute on behalf of her husband, who was inconspicuous if present (the reports do not agree).

The decision to accept the group headed by Heinrich Conried as the new lessors of the theater was made on February 14 (see page 10). A strong faction for Walter Damrosch had powerful support in the press, which contrasted his musical capabilities with the lack of any in Conried, and warned: "Whether Mr. Conried is acquainted with these matters remains to be seen. One thing may be prophesied with perfect assurance: if he is not, he is going to get a whole lot of experience and some one is going to pay a whole lot of money for it" (editorial in the *Sun* of February 15). As an influence in the decision that favored Conried by seven votes to six, one may cite a remark by G. G. Haven, president of the Opera and Real Estate Company, which appeared in an announcement of Conried's victory: "The men who are back of him are men who it is very advantageous for us to interest in the enterprise."

The principal assurance offered by Conried to his landlords was that he "believed more in ensemble than in stars." To assist his aim of improving the staging of Metropolitan opera, the ownership company proposed to rebuild the stage "to bring it up to the standards of the best Continental houses." In the end, the emphasis of Conried was placed on new mechanical devices and old singers. Both Jean and Édouard de Reszke would sing again, also Eames, Sembrich, Schumann-Heink, Scotti, and Journet. The productions would be handsomely staged, well lit, and, above all, rehearsed. In a comment not without interest some sixty years later, the *Sun* remarked on March 22, 1903: "Mr. Conried has not explained yet how he is going to compel Mme. Sembrich and M. de Reszke to go to rehearsals nor how he is going to make them obey his stage manager if they do go. Under the star system which he intends to retain, no one has any authority over the principals: they do as they please. . . . This state of affairs is an utter absurdity, of course; but there it is."

So far as the De Reszkes were concerned, the solution was a relatively simple one: they did not come either to rehearsals or to New York. An irony of all the brave talk about abolishing the star system is its timing. It was scarcely six months later when the most illustrious star of the whole long Metropolitan history (as a public favorite and a drawing power) came to New York.

EPILOGUE

The quality of opera presented at the Metropolitan during the period when Maurice Grau was in command (1891–1903) is self-evident from the list of names which decorated the roster from the opening *Roméo* to the closing *Meistersinger*. In no other period have so many of the greatest singers of the day been systematically presented to the New York public.

The sole exception of consequence was Mattia Battistini, whose aversion to ocean travel, after one trip to South America in young manhood, is well known.

Nordica, Eames, Sembrich, the De Reszkes, Lassalle, Scotti—these are indeed the symbols of fine singing for any age. Yet in that listing we have not mentioned Calvé, Melba, or Ternina; Salignac, Saléza, or Alvarez; Plançon, Journet, or Tamagno. And there are as many more unnamed as named: Gadski, Brema, Schumann-Heink, Lilli Lehmann, Scalchi, Mantelli, and Arnoldson among the women; Campanari, De Marchi, Maurel, Bispham, Van Rooy, Van Dyck, and Reiss among the men.

The distinction of the era was thus not merely the quality of the singers, but the profusion of them. There have been, in every period of the Metropolitan, artists of fine voices, presence, and superior intelligence. At no other time were they so abundant or the sources of supply so productive of replacements in any given category. They were, essentially and predominantly, *opera*-singers, who worked hard at their trade and knew it well. Twenty or thirty appearances were by no means unusual for a Melba or a Plançon; there were later years when Lily Pons made two, Jussi Bjoerling four. In conformity with their standard, such secondary singers as Suzanne Adams, Camille Seygard, Fritzi Scheff, Zélie de Lussan, and Mathilde Bauermeister were equally superior to their present-day counterparts.

Given this historical group of singers, Grau nevertheless followed the unvarying course of every director with a public to please: expediency. Novelties appeared as they suited the convenience of his stars, and were as quickly abandoned when the public failed to respond. Traditional methods prevailed without scrutiny or change. Vocal excellence there was, and it was worth paying to hear. As for conductors, it was Grau's convinced opinion that "No one ever paid a nickel to see a man's back."

About the only manifestation to indicate that there was an æsthetic somehow, somewhere latent in opera was the urge, expressed through the De Reszkes, to sing the Wagner literature in German. With it came a preference for French works in French, largely because the salable exponents of the roles—Eames, Calvé, Melba, Nordica, Sembrich—had such background to call upon. Deviations from both patterns were by no means unusual, but they at least established the basic habits of thought from which emerged the Metropolitan's signal distinction for half a century— the presentation of its major repertory in the language set by the composer. The *Ring* was given uncut for a while. *La Bohème* and *Tosca* were successfully launched. *Otello* and *Falstaff* were introduced, but the continuous effort for both was slight.

To a second-hand opinion of what was well done in this period and why, what was shabby and how, the words of one who lived through it are much more pertinent. Writing in the *Times* of December 22, 1901, as the Grau impulse was running downhill, W. J. Henderson said:

> *"When an opera is performed in which there is no chorus and no ballet, in which the scenic attire is not vital to the general effect, in which stage management is powerless to work destructive evil, and in which the devotion and personal ambition of several great artists work together for good, we sometimes get admirable results, as we have in . . . 'Tristan and Isolde.' Probably nowhere in the world have more impressive performances been given than those in which Mmes. Lehmann, Ternina, Nordica, Brema and Schumann-Heink were united with the Reszke brothers and Mr. Bispham or Mr. Van Rooy.*
>
> *"Similar results have been obtained in 'Die Walküre' and 'Siegfried,' though in the former they were always attained in spite of stupid and even ridiculous stage effects. But . . . 'Romeo et Juliette,' for instance, is never adequately done at the Metropolitan, and as for 'Les Huguenots' what is there in our performances but the imposing line-up of celebrities before the curtain at the end of the garden scene?"*

If Grau read these words, as he doubtless did, he would probably have repeated that he was "not in business for his health"—which became bad while business remained good—and pointed to the record of receipts as indicative of what the public wanted. Reserved, even-tempered, capable on many occasions of what would seem an extravagance today (such as offering Eames, at $800 a performance, as Micaëla, when a much cheaper singer would have sufficed), Grau nevertheless had an unfailing instinct about where a line should be drawn. He paid Jean de Reszke $2,500 a performance in his final season because the box office would justify the extravagance, but he would not spend an extra dollar for a first-rate conductor.

When he made a mistake, he took the blame squarely, as on the occasion when a disastrous tour westward ended with the company rolling homeward through the picturesque hills of New York State. "Look well, my children," he said. "You will not see this view again at my expense." When he died in Paris in 1907, still short of sixty, Nordica grievingly said: "He was so good and kind. I sang with him for years and we never had a written contract." In a summation of his curious blend of generosity and prudence, Jean de Reszke said: "He will give you a cigar, but he won't give you a match."

In a time when choristers worked for fifteen dollars a week and orchestral players for less than fifty, when four conductors drew a total sum of $20,000 for a season's work, and a whole ballet half as much, the kind of relations Grau enjoyed with his stars was a key to successful operations.

According to one partner, Henry B. Dazian of the costuming firm, Grau left over $600,000, virtually all of it acquired—after earlier bankruptcy—from his last years at the Metropolitan. Some of it came from well-advised investments, but most of it from the following earnings:

Year	Earnings	
1898–9	$137,766	(The average cost of raising the curtain was then $5,984. In the 1940's it stood at $13,000, and by 1960 was nearly $30,000.)
1899–1900	111,834	
1900–1	15,290	The year of Jean de Reszke's return, the expensive *Salammbô* production, and an unprofitable tour.
1901–2	185,022	
1902–3	142,948	
	$592,860	

Besides drawing a large share of these profits plus earnings from galas, Grau received an annual salary that went from $10,000 in 1898 and $12,000 in 1899 to $20,000 for his last seasons. The company also profited from the concert tours it booked for its prominent personnel.

THE CONRIED METROPOLITAN OPERA COMPANY
1903–1908

The narrow margin by which Heinrich Conried and his associates became the successors of Maurice Grau in the production of opera at the Metropolitan foreshadowed the rather troubled time they had in the next five years. Much of the press felt that the choice was ill considered, and the relations between the director and his critics were more subjective than they should have been (see page 164).

A few words about Conried himself might help to clarify certain subsequent happenings. His productions of *Parsifal, Die Fledermaus,* and *Salome*—defensible as they might have been as theatrical ventures—were all shadowed by some lapse of judgment which afflicted the worthwhile end with the curse of questionable means. Not the least of these was the clause in his contract by which the artists signed contracts with him, not with the company, and were thus obligated for an annual "manager's benefit." His abuse of this prerogative was one of his signal affronts to the position such an institution as the Metropolitan should occupy in public affairs.

An actor by trade, Conried was Silesian-born, Viennese-trained. In his twenties he turned to stage management and supervisory work in general, coming to America at twenty-three to help run one of several German-language theaters then flourishing in New York. Within a few years he had secured backing from some of its patrons to open a competitive theater. He exercised a considerable business acumen to secure American rights for various popular works of Johann Strauss and Millöcker, which he produced with success and leased, on royalty, to others. He also earned a comfortable side-income by providing the Hamburg-American line with steamer chairs, which were rented to its passengers.

Conried was best known in the 1890's for his direction of the Irving Place Theater, where works of Sudermann, Fulda, and Hauptmann were given years before Broadway knew them. He built an imposing patronage from the German-speaking public, conceived a plan of subscription sales much like that which the Theater Guild utilized later, and founded an able, well-disciplined stock company. From time to time prominent personalities of the German stage would be brought to star in a special production. Out of this background grew the movement for a national theater which produced the New Theater on Central Park West as a home for spoken drama and the *opéra-comique* repertory not suitable to the Metropolitan. An eminently self-made man, Conried was remembered by an associate of his younger days as "lacking in those small courtesies which people like " (Montrose J. Moses, *Life of Heinrich Conried,* page 37).

As an opera impresario, Conried was as ill equipped as he was well equipped to run a theater. He had scant technical knowledge of voices, little grasp of the problems of operating an international repertory, rather limited acquaintance with music itself. To be sure, he saw clearly the theatrical shortcomings of Grau's productions and could well see how they could be improved—by overhauling the chorus and orchestra, providing more rehearsal time, and, as the immemorial saying goes, abolishing the star system. How well he succeeded, the detailed record will reveal. Certainly his business sense did not fail him: he received a yearly salary of $20,000, and the income from his benefit almost doubled that sum. Nearly half the profits of $300,000 earned by the company in its first three years went to Conried. When he retired, his investment of $75,000 was bought out by W. K. Vanderbilt for $90,000. His total income for running the Metropolitan between 1903 and 1908 was close to $400,000.

While talking about abolishing the star system, Conried accepted the stockholders' decree that two from a list of six specified singers should appear in every performance, also agreeing that the number of performances of Wagner operas on Monday nights should be severely restricted.

Moreover, he pledged that the total of Wagnerian performances should be no more than forty per cent of the season's total.

1903–1904

Whether for reasons of business or art, Conried's decision to produce *Parsifal* had far-reaching consequences. To flout Bayreuth was by no means a new idea (see page 99), but those who had considered it previously, in New York or London, had come, finally, to the conclusion that Wagner had willed some sort of proprietary right to his family in restricting the work to Bayreuth. More than this was not granted: as Bernard Shaw had written as long before as March 25, 1891 (the *World*), when a Londoner thought *Parsifal* should be restricted to the "religious atmosphere" of Bayreuth: "In front of the Bayreuth Theatre, then, on the right, is a restaurant. On the left there is a still larger restaurant. . . . The little promenade in front . . . is crowded with globe trotters . . . quite able to hold their own in point of vulgarity, frivolity, idle curiosity and other perfectly harmless characteristics, with the crowd in the foyer of Covent Garden or the Paris Opéra."

For its part, the Wagner family made, without success, every possible effort to prohibit the planned performance. When an informal appeal to the Kaiser yielded nothing worth while, a civil suit was instituted in the New York courts. No copyright agreements were in effect between Germany and the United States; hence none was being violated. Thus an appeal for an injunction could not be acted upon favorably. For that matter, Conried offered to pay a performance fee, which was curtly rejected by the Wagner heirs.

In non-musical circles the desirability of *Parsifal* was hotly argued, with most heat by those most ignorant of its content. One Protestant worthy stated his objection, in the *Sun* of November 15, to a work in which "not only is Christ's person represented, but the blood." The music critic (Henderson) demonstrated clearly that no such action takes place in *Parsifal,* whereupon the attack veered to the whole idea of "profanation" of a sacred subject. The Catholic Church, much more reserved, though also misidentifying *Parsifal* with a "personation of Christ," stated through a spokesman, Father Hughes: "We will not take our ideas of what is sacred and what is not from these Protestant clergymen" (the *Sun,* as above).

Meanwhile, plans went forward for a December *première,* with intensifying objections from the clergy and even a petition to Mayor Seth Low that he suspend the Metropolitan's license. Some part of the objection was incurred by Conried because he had scheduled his first performance for Christmas Eve. He had, doubtless, no intention of further offending those who thought of Christmas as a religious ceremonial as well as a season of good cheer; he was merely looking for an attraction for the worst theatrical night of the season. In terms of what would now be called "public relations," it was an inspired piece of bad judgment.

For those who had paid up to ten dollars apiece for tickets, the problems were of another order. What was the appropriate dress for a performance beginning at five in the afternoon? It was finally determined that evening dress had been elected in London the previous summer by King Edward and Queen Alexandra for an afternoon-evening *Ring* cycle at Covent Garden. The precedent sufficed for New York.

In the aftermath of the great event the New York press was concerned primarily with the production. The score had been heard in concert performances periodically since it was new, and excerpts were occasional occurrences on symphony-orchestra programs. As a spectacle *Parsifal* was acclaimed an overwhelming success. The new stage devices (mostly traps) installed under the supervision of Carl Lautenschläger of Munich were admired, as was the stage direction of his Bavarian associate, Anton Fuchs.

Henderson thought the Metropolitan's *Parsifal* "better than any production ever given in Bayreuth," the scenery "beautiful, imposing, and illusive." Even the moving "panorama" (the unrolling back-piece rarely used these days to suggest change of location as Gurnemanz leads Parsifal to the Halls of the Knights in Act I) was handsomely painted and "moved properly." In the opinion of Aldrich (the *Times*), it was "the most perfect production ever made on the American stage." Krehbiel was especially impressed with the treatment of the Flower Maidens.

Among the cast, Ternina was outstanding as Kundry,* even if her voice showed the beginnings of the unhappy condition that would shortly cause her retirement. Burgstaller, as Parsifal,* outdid any previous accomplishment, and Otto Goritz (Klingsor, [d]) began a career terminated only by the curtailment of the German repertory when America entered World War I. Robert Blass, of American birth, was a poorish Gurnemanz,* meaning that the garrulous tended toward the tiresome. Van Rooy did nobly as the afflicted Amfortas.*

Whatever the fine points of the performance—the conducting of Hertz did not please all tastes, some of his tempos, for an oddity, being considered overfast—the interest of thousands had been stimulated. Ten repetitions were completely sold out, for total receipts of $183,608. Allowing for production costs and the expenses of the cast, it was guessed that close to $100,000 could be reckoned as profit. Conried pocketed the takings from a full house on April 23 when he specified a performance of *Parsifal* as his "manager's benefit."

There were few cast changes in the numerous *Parsifals,* the important ones being restricted to the appearance of Marion Weed as Kundry* on January 7 and 21 and February 4, and Dippel as Parsifal* on February 16. The stimulation of interest encouraged Henry Savage to announce that he would send a touring company of *Parsifal* (in English) across the country in the fall, and Walter Damrosch presented a series of excerpts, with Nordica as soloist, on March 12. David Mannes was also violin soloist in a transcription of the Good Friday Music which the *Sun* properly rejected as "cheap claptrap."

Parsifal was the musical event of this season with the largest share of pre-performance interest, but the debut of Enrico Caruso on November 23 set in motion a chain of events still misinterpreted, embellished, and romanticized many years after his death. Rather than being "discovered" by Conried from a phonograph record, Caruso was committed as long as two years before to appearing in New York during the winter of 1903. Henry Dazian, of the Grau company's board of directors, heard the tenor at Monte Carlo in 1901 and advised Grau to engage him at once. Although he was not available at all in 1902, Caruso was engaged to come in 1903 for forty performances at 5,000 francs each—$960 as the franc then was quoted. When Grau retired, the contract lapsed. It was Conried's dilemma to make a choice between Caruso and the rising Alessandro Bonci. Fortunately for the Metropolitan, Conried made the commercially sound decision, for if Caruso rather than Bonci had been left for Oscar Hammerstein, the Manhattan Opera might have had a longer and more irritating history than it had. Conried did, finally, hear a record of Caruso's voice, but it was after a contract for twenty-five performances had been signed. He was impressed enough to cable Caruso, in Buenos Aires on May 12, 1903, asking for restoration of the original forty performances of the Grau contract, but the tenor's time was already committed.

Caruso's debut in *Rigoletto* with Sembrich and Scotti found the attention of the audience divided among the freshly decorated theater (see page 7), the new maestro from La Scala—Arturo Vigna—in the pit, and the happenings on the stage. It was possibly the least effective of Caruso's six hundred seven appearances in the theater. *"La donna è mobile,"* was redemanded only once, "not . . . more times," as Aldrich noted in the *Times* "than is usual from tenors of much smaller repute." In a bold venture of opinion, he thought Caruso's singing and acting "gave reason to believe in his value as an acquisition to the company." The *Tribune* objected to his "tiresome Italian mannerisms," but commended him as "a manly singer, with a voice of fine quality." For Henderson (the *Sun*), the voice was "pure . . . of fine quality." His "clear and pealing high tones set the bravos wild with delight, but connoisseurs . . . saw more promise of his *mezza voce* and his manliness."

Richard Genée Conried, son of Heinrich, told me that Caruso felt that he had not done himself justice at his debut, and was let down at the evening's end. To show his confidence in the tenor's future, Heinrich Conried offered to sign a five-year contract controlling his services, world-wide, on a rising scale that would reach $2,000 a performance in the fifth year. Caruso, apparently, was not depressed enough to accept.

The succeeding series of Caruso appearances were steadily more secure and relaxed: as Radames for the first of sixty-four times in Aida on November 30, with Gadski, Scotti, Plançon, and Edyth Walker (Amneris [d],); as Cavaradossi* in *Tosca* on December 2; as Rodolfo* three days later, and as Canio* in *Pagliacci* on December 9. The startling freshness of his voice made him the best Cavaradossi yet heard in New York, even if his acting was "bourgeois" (the *Times*). Some of the press remembered this occasion for non-musical reasons. They were at work on reviews of the evening's performance during the latter phases of the second act when Conried appeared in the press room (a space on the grand-tier floor finally occupied by the Guild Room) and threatened them with banishment from the house if they did not listen to Caruso sing *"E lucevan le stelle."* The incident was unreported in the next day's reviews, but in a week-end article Henderson commented (the *Sun*): "Heinrich Conried has added to his other numerous duties that of supervisor of the press of New York. He walked into the press room . . . the other night and practically issued an order to the experienced critics of the morning newspapers as to how they should listen to the performance." This incident underlines the special situation that prevailed between director and press. Damrosch, as director, would probably not have been so bold—or so tactless.

Caruso continued to thrive, in any case, with a Canio (see above) that was "very beautifully sung" (the *Sun*), though he went through the act-ending agony of *"Ridi, Pagliacci,"* a second time when the audience demanded a repetition. Sembrich was the sweet-voiced Nedda.* At a repetition of *Tosca* on December 11 Caruso took rank as "the best Italian tenor we have had here in years" (Henderson), and his Edgardo* in *Lucia* on January 8 (with Sembrich) left a comparison with Campanini the only measurement for a performance that had "manliness, vigor, passion, and withal a beauty of tone and vocal style that left nothing to be desired." Caruso showed one of his most prized, if then unsuspected, talents when he clowned through the part of Nemorino* in *L'Elisir d'amore* on January 23 with rich comic effect, and sang *"Una furtiva lagrima"* so beautifully it had to be repeated. In this first hearing at the Metropolitan of Donizetti's delightful score Sembrich was a charming Adina,* Scotti a handsome Belcore,* and Rossi an amusing Dulcamara,* but the evening was Caruso's. His farewell for the season, in *Lucia* on February 10, attracted the largest audience of the year, except for *Parsifal*.

Among the contracts acquired by Conried from Grau was one that named Felix Mottl, of Karlsruhe, the first *Generalmusikdirektor* in Metropolitan history when he made his debut as conductor of *Die Walküre* on November 25. How descriptive this title was of Mottl's function is difficult to say, for he did not return for a second season. He had, certainly, a considerable supervisory hand in the preparation of *Parsifal* (it was his score, with interpolations of Wagner's own comments, that Hertz used), and some attempt was made to give the Sunday-night concerts, with Mottl conducting, the stature of concerts of the Symphony Society or the Philharmonic, but this effort was soon abandoned.

His most notable production was the first performance of *Die Zauberflöte* in German which the Metropolitan had known, on January 11; when it became *Il Flauto magico* again on January 20, Mottl's displeasure was not concealed. The change became necessary when Goritz, who sang Papageno* in the German version with Sembrich, Gadski, Dippel, and Kloepfer, was replaced by Campanari. Ternina sang the First Lady rather poorly in the German version, and Seygard replaced her in the Italian. Critical praise was lavish for the lightness and spirit of Mottl's direction, but the old level of splendid voices throughout the cast was considerably depressed. One performance of *Le Nozze di Figaro on* March 4, with Gadski, Sembrich, Seygard, Scotti, and Campanari, was all the other Mozart that Mottl conducted at the Metropolitan.

As a Wagner conductor, Mottl was admired as the best since Seidl, with whom he had served his apprenticeship under Wagner and Richter. New settings for *Die Walküre on* November 25 also introduced a new Sieglinde (d), Olive Fremstad, whose "warm mezzo voice" was a little taxed by the top of the role, but whose performance was "thoroughly artistic" (the *Sun*). Ernst Kraus returned a better tenor than ever, and Gadski sang her first Brünnhilde* with poise and sufficient vocal resource. For a change, Grane was visible and Fricka* (Homer) was towed from the stage in a chariot preceded by a pair of stuffed rams. This kind of literal faithfulness to Wagner's stage directions was regarded as more a distraction than an illusion.

Fremstad sang a splendid Venus* in *Tannhäuser* on December 4 (with Kraus* and Ternina), but the steady succession of *Parsifals* and Ternina's uncertain vocal condition made the season's other Wagner performances rather hit-or-miss. A *Tristan* of January 9 found Ternina unable to appear, Marion Weed's a small-scaled voice for Isolde,* and Walker a variable Brangäne* to go with Kraus. Ternina recovered to sing Isolde on January 22, with Homer winning new respect as Brangäne, and Mottl, finally given a cast he could depend upon, stirring a steady surge of drama in the first act and winning approval for the exceptional mood he created in the second act. The *Ring* cycle was given during the last week of the season, without distinction. Hertz conducted the first and last works, Mottl the intermediate two. After a post-season tour, a final *Götterdämmerung* on April 25 provided an opportunity for the public to show its feeling for Ternina, whose health made her return doubtful. She did not sing at the Metropolitan again, but her later career as a teacher in Zagreb had unforeseen consequences when she singled out a young girl named Zinka Kunc in 1921 and urged her on to an operatic career: it was the first step toward fame of Zinka Milanov.

For an oddity of the Mottl career, it was he who was in charge of *Carmen* when Calvé returned to the company on February 1. Dippel as José took a good bit of roughing from Calvé, in a performance that found her in a chair-throwing mood. The naturalistic creation of old was now self-conscious exhibitionism and not as well sung as before. On February 17, when Gustav Hinrichs was the conductor for *Cavalleria,* Calvé stamped her foot impatiently when he would not take her tempo. For a final demonstration of "star" temperament in this non-star ensemble, Calvé chose the Sunday-evening concert of April 24, when Mottl agreed to accompany her at the piano in a group of Provençal songs. As they were about to begin, she turned and asked him to transpose the music a tone lower. When he refused, she walked off the stage and out of the Metropolitan's history. When she reappeared in New York, it was with Hammerstein (1907).

To the presence of Mottl may be traced the only occurrence in Metropolitan history of the name of Boieldieu among its composers: his *La Dame blanche* was given in German on February 13 as *Die weisse Dame.* Its pretty tunes were neatly suited to the light voice of Fran Navál, who made his debut as Georges Brown (d), but the general opinion was that such people as Gadski, Homer, and Reiss were wasted in so tenuous a work. It was not repeated.

The direction the repertory was to take under the influence of Caruso was already beginning to attract attention. Ten operas were given in Italian, only three in French, with Aïno Ackté, whom the *Sun* described as "intolerable," singing the Juliette of *Roméo et Juliette.* The strictures against

Exterior from southeast (1940)

Exterior from southeast (1966)

Interior (about 1933), showing Grand Tier Boxes and Orchestra
Circle Seats prior to re-arrangement

Panorama of audience before Gala Farewell, Leopold Stokowski at the conductor's desk (April 16, 1966)

View of the stage at student performance of *La Fanciulla del West* in the Lincoln Center Metropolitan Opera House (April 11, 1966)

Lilli Lehmann as Brünnhilde

Lillian Nordica as Brünnhilde

Margarete Matzenauer as Brünnhilde

Ernestine Schumann-Heink as Waltraute

Der Ring des Nibelungen—I

Max Alvary as Siegfried

Set Svanholm as Siegfried

Friedrich Schorr as Wotan

Ernst Van Dyck as Siegmund

Anton Van Rooy as Wotan

Der Ring des Nibelungen—II

Lillian Nordica as Isolde

Olive Fremstad as Isolde

Helen Traubel as Isolde

Albert Niemann as Tristan

Jean de Reszke as Tristan

Kirsten Flagstad and Lauritz
Melchior as Isolde and Tristan

Birgit Nilsson as Isolde

Tristan und Isolde

Italo Campanini
as Lohengrin

Johanna Gadski as
Elisabeth in *Tannhäuser*

Elisabeth Rethberg as
Elisabeth in *Tannhäuser*

Karin Branzell as Brangäne
in *Tristan und Isolde*

Clarence Whitehill as
Amfortas in *Parsifal*

Margarete Matzenauer
as Kundry in *Parsifal*

George London as
the Flying Dutchman

Leonie Rysanek as Senta
in *Der fliegende Holländer*

Wagner

Frieda Hempel
as the Marschallin

Florence Easton
as the Marschallin

Emmanuel List
as Baron Ochs

Der Rosenkavalier
and *Arabella*

Maria Olszewska as Octavian

ë Stevens as Octavian, Lotte
hmann as the Marschallin,
ing a curtain call

Elisabeth Schwarzkopf
as the Marschallin

Lisa della Casa as
Arabella and Anneliese
Rothenberger as Zdenka

Olive Fremstad as Salome

Ljuba Welitch as Salome

René Maison as Herod

Salome and *Elektra*

Rose Pauly as Elektra

Astrid Varnay as Elektra

Inge Borkh as Salome

Birgit Nilsson as Salome

Victor Maurel
as Don Giovanni

Maurice Renaud
as Don Giovanni

Antonio Scotti
as Don Giovanni

Ezio Pinza as Don Giovanni

Don Giovanni—I

Tito Schipa as Ottavio

Editha Fleischer as Zerlina

Elisabeth Schwarzkopf as Donna Elvira, Rosalind Elias
as Zerlina, and Cesare Siepi as Don Giovanni

Don Giovanni—II

Grau's ballet resulted in a new prominence for this ensemble, with an abbreviated *Coppélia* given four times as part of a double bill. On the first occasion (February 12), it followed a *Cavalleria* delayed twenty-five minutes till Calvé decided that a sufficient number of boxes was occupied for her to sing. Enrichetta Varasi (Swanilda), Tekla Braun (Frantz), and Augusto Francioli (Coppelius) were the principal dancers.

In a seasonal retrospect on April 24, Henderson rated the coming of Fremstad as the third most important happening of the season (*Parsifal* and Caruso naturally took precedence). Aside from a Santuzza* of January 15, which was beyond her vocal range, there was nothing but good to be said of her: "She has great magnetism, a rich and temperamental voice, a warm and eloquent face . . . a finely wrought dramatic style of singing and high intelligence."

With an income of $1,107,068, the season showed a profit of $60,000. It would have been larger had it not been Conried's policy to charge off productions to the budget of the year in which they were introduced rather than amortizing them over a period of years.

1904–1905

The power latent in *Parsifal* and the power active in Caruso provided the twin impulses for Conried's second season. The slight decline in public interest was reflected in the total of eight performances of the Wagner work in this season, rather than the dozen of the year before; but eight is a considerable number of *Parsifal* performances for any fifteen-week season. [1] Caruso's contract now stood at thirty performances, meaning that about half the total of operas given in this season were either *Parsifal* or with Caruso. No doubt Conried was the first to deplore that they could not be combined.

Parsifal was freshened by the first Kundry* of Lillian Nordica when it was given on the evening of Thanksgiving Day (November 24) in the presence of Prince Friedrich Karl and Prince Johann von Hohenlohe-Öhringen. As between the two American exponents of the part (Fremstad had her first chance on December 1), there was strong division of sentiment in the press, though it was universally agreed that both were excellent. Krehbiel preferred the seductive youthfulness of Fremstad despite a little strain on her top tones in the garden scene; Henderson inclined toward the subtler intellectual concept of Nordica, who also sang the music

[1] Beginning on October 30, the English production sponsored by Henry Savage played eight performances in New York before going on tour. Walter Rothwell conducted, and the cast included Francis Maclennan (he later married Florence Easton), Putnam Griswold, of later Metropolitan fame, as Gurnemanz, and Louise Kirkby-Lunn (of the silent second K) as Kundry.

with greater breadth and power. Neither had the lyric line of Ternina, but a long dissertation by Henderson in the *Sun* of January 8, 1905 makes the basic point that New Yorkers would hear a splendid Kundry on any occasion *Parsifal* was given. In this season it was five of Nordica, three of Fremstad.

As a reaction to the extravagances that had come into Calvé's Carmen in recent years, the first performance by Fremstad on November 25 earned rapturous approval from all sections of the press. Aldrich in the *Times* commended its "bewitching grace," Henderson (in the *Sun*) termed it the "Carmen of Bizet and Mérimée, not the traditional Carmen of the Metropolitan." Saléza, in splendid voice after an absence of three seasons, sang a fine José, with Journet as Escamillo and Ackté as Micaëla.* Fremstad was also scheduled for the *Carmen* of January 7, but she was out of voice and Anna Arnaud, an instructress in the newly established Opera School, took her place. She received virtually no credit for her soundly routined performance, for this was the evening when the stage bridge collapsed during Act I. Fifteen members of the chorus fell eight feet to the stage, amid confusion and screams. Fortunately, the injuries were confined to cuts, bruises, and a few broken limbs.

The advent of Caruso and the strong restraints placed on Conried's choice of operas for the Monday-night series gave it even brighter luster as the accepted night for socializing and display. Its official status was discussed by Henderson in the *Sun* of March 5: "The smart set, which is a very stupid set indeed . . . dislikes anything so serious as the great tragedies of Wagner. . . . So Mr. Conried was informed . . . that he would not be permitted to give Wagner on Monday night, the fashionable night of the week." The exceptions, which are *not* among the "great tragedies," were *Die Meistersinger* and *Lohengrin*.

Of the other thirteen Mondays, Caruso was heard on nine, in a review of all the roles he sang in this season save Edgardo in *Lucia*. For the opening on November 21, it was Radames in Aida,[1] with Eames, Walker, and Scotti, followed by such previous roles as Alfredo, Cavaradossi, Canio, and Rodolfo. When Caruso was absent, Saléza was present, in *Carmen, Faust,* and *Roméo.*

The Monday-night audience also saw the first performance of Donizetti's *Lucrezia Borgia* on December 5, with Caruso as Gennaro,* Scotti as Alfonso,* and Walker as Maffio Orsini.* Maria de Macchi was engaged, at Caruso's suggestion, to sing Borgia.* All of Caruso's art could not make the work interesting, though Walker sang the famous *Brindisi*

---

[1] For the first time the ballet in the temple scene was included.

extremely well. The handsome stage production attracted favorable attention, but the work was not repeated, nor has it been since.

More durable was a revival of *La Gioconda,* for which Grau had commissioned the production, in his last season, for Ternina. Neither was present when it reached the stage on November 24, 1904, with much the best cast Ponchielli's music had ever enjoyed in New York. Caruso as Enzo Grimaldo* sang *"Cielo e mar"* with "gorgeous tone and fine sentiment" (the *Sun*), and Nordica (Gioconda*), Walker (particularly admired as La Cieca*), Homer (Laura*), and Plançon (Alvise*) made a generally strong showing. Also good was the ballet. Eugenio Giraldoni, however, in his debut as Barnaba (d) belied the repute he had won as the first Scarpia in *Tosca* by singing in a disappointingly crude manner. As may happen with *Gioconda* revivals, this one ran its course after a total of eight performances in two seasons. Nordica's remark, late in her career, may have its pertinence: after studying the role and singing it dozens of times, she still could not relate the story.

Caruso's singing was also a "continuous joy" (Henderson) when *Un Ballo in maschera* was given on February 6, with Eames a splendid Amelia,* Scotti an excellent Renato,* and Homer, Journet, and Plançon completing a strong cast. This effort had twice the success of Grau's revival in 1902—that is, it was given twice rather than once. Again, for reasons having to do largely with the complexity of the libretto, the able voices had no further chance to sing the inviting music until 1913.

The special qualities that marked Caruso's unique place not only in the esteem but also in the affection of his public may be seen gradually emerging in this season. His voice and personality restored the importance of Edgardo in *Lucia* to its rightful place so that, in Henderson's words, " 'Lucia, ending with the mad scene,' is no longer seen on the theater bills." Thanks to his superb singing of the tomb scene, Edgardo was now a character with an end as well as a beginning. "He is the owner of a glorious voice," ran the comment in the same paper on another occasion, "and he is today at the height of his popularity. He deserves all his honors and wears them with charming modesty."

That modesty and the general artistic stature of Conried's principals made it seem even more an indignity that they should be required to participate in a glorified vaudeville show for the manager's benefit when *Die Fledermaus* was given for the first time on February 16. As the merely excellent cast of Sembrich (Rosalinda*), Dippel (Gabriel*), Walker (Orlofsky*), Bella Alten (Adele*), Reiss (Alfred*), and Goritz (Warden*) would hardly justify the raised prices charged the previous year for *Parsifal,* Conried required all other star members of the company to participate in a concert during the ball scene. Scotti sang *"Quand 'ero paggio"* from *Falstaff,* Fremstad offered Delibes's *"Les Filles de Cadix,"* Eames joined Plançon and Francisco Nubio in the trio from *Faust,* and Nordica was required to pretend she was Gilda in the *Rigoletto* quartet with Caruso, Homer, and Giraldoni. There have been later occasions when self-respecting artists did incongruous things on the stage of the Metropolitan, but not for the profit of one individual.

The general tone of the press was of more than casual regret that the manager had chosen this device for his benefit purposes, and it spilled over into a reaction against *Fledermaus* itself. Sembrich's lively Rosalinda and Dippel's capable Eisenstein were approved, but not the conducting of Nahan Franko or the suitability of the theater for a work with spoken dialogue. In the aftermath of the reviews, Conried attended a public dinner at which he said the critics took themselves too seriously. When his off-the-record remarks were published, he declared that, in the phrase of the day, he had been "misreported." Misreported or misquoted, he did not serve the theater's interest best by his action in giving *Die Fledermaus* as he did, or by his reaction to the reaction of the press.

Also retrogressive, in the view of the press, was the production of Meyerbeer's *Huguenots* with an all-star ensemble, though Caruso did not know the role of Raoul* and would consent to study it only in Italian. Thus it was *Gli Ugonotti* when it was heard on February 3, with such old favorites as Nordica (Valentine), Sembrich (Marguerite), Scotti (De Nevers), and Plançon (Saint-Bris) in familiar places. Caruso's performance was tonally superb, and Sembrich, though not in best voice, sang her florid air so well that her colleagues on stage joined in the applause. That intangible called "style," however, was in short supply, and Conried ventured no more Meyerbeer after three repetitions of this revival.

With Mottl gone and no replacement for him yet engaged, virtually all the Wagner in this season was conducted by Hertz. Most of the personnel he had to work with was the same as in the several previous seasons, but one newcomer of quality was Heinrich Knote, from Munich. His debut as Walther* in *Die Meistersinger* on December 3 won him the praise of Henderson as "the best lyric tenor we have yet received from Germany." "Temperament . . . elegance . . . warmth" were among the attributes that made him welcome. More admired even than the generally able vocal work of Ackté (Eva*), Van Rooy (Sachs), Goritz (Beckmesser*), and Reiss (David) was the staging by Fuchs. It bettered not only the inept procedures of Grau days, but also the previously admired productions of the German seasons in detail, plausibility, and harmonious adjustment to the music.

Knote was consistently admirable in his other roles, which included

Tannhäuser* on December 7, Lohengrin* on December 10, and a Tristan* on January 11 with Nordica, Walker, and Van Rooy. Rarely had the tenor's music of the first act of *Siegfried* sounded as well as it did when Knote appeared on January 19, with Van Rooy, Reiss, and Goritz. The Brünnhilde* of Senger-Bettaque (she had sung lighter roles in 1888–9 as Katti Bettaque) was well below the acceptable. Knote was welcome in the next several years whenever he could secure leave from Munich, and was still admired for musicianship when he came back, a much older man, with a traveling troupe in the twenties (see page 314). Some remembered him fondly for reasons other than his qualities as a performer. On arrival in New York he told an interviewer that his stay would be memorable whether the public liked him or not, because he had the chance, at last, to hear Caruso.

To satisfy public demand as well as private necessity, Conried offered two *Ring* cycles this year outside the subscription series, on Thursday evenings beginning with January 5. Hertz was the conductor throughout. When the scheduled singers were in voice, the quality of production was about as it had been. When they were not, as in the *Götterdämmerung* of January 26, when Burgstaller was ill and replaced by Dippel, and Nordica had to sing though she would have preferred not to, the thinness of the company was evident.

Dippel's reputation as a replacement *par excellence* was often tested, in these circumstances, and rarely found wanting. He had occasion to sing *sixteen* different roles in three languages this year, in a variety of musical styles ranging from *Traviata* to *Tristan*. The appalling sequence is worth repetition: in order of occurrence the cast of characters in Dippel's personal drama included Alfredo, Ernesto (*Don Pasquale*), Almaviva (*Il Barbiere*), Parsifal, Florestan (*Fidelio*), Froh (*Rheingold*), Don José, Turiddu, Edgardo, Cavaradossi, Rodolfo, Siegfried (*Götterdämmerung*), Walther, Tristan, Eisenstein (*Fledermaus*), and Tannhäuser. On one occasion (February 18) he was asked to sing Tannhäuser in place of Burgstaller, but begged off, pleading indisposition himself. Burgstaller began, but broke down during Act I, and Dippel was brought to the theater—having downed a hearty meal—as one indisposed tenor replacing another. After this, his fame as a "one-man opera company" was secure.

Somewhat like the season of Melba's Brünnhilde and the onstage death of Armando Castelmary, this one of the collapsed bridge in *Carmen* struggled through various untoward incidents. Melba herself came back for a *Bohème* on December 16, pleading bronchitis and singing *sotto voce* through most of the performance with Caruso, Journet, Scotti, and Alten (Musetta*). She failed to appear for a scheduled Gilda on December 31

(Alma Webster-Powell took her place not very successfully, while Caruso sought to compensate the audience for its disappointment by singing a high D flat at the end of the second-act duet), and was never again a regular singer at the Metropolitan. There was no fatality, but Saléza narrowly escaped a serious accident in *Roméo* on February 4 as he was disappearing off-stage after the garden scene. A sharp twang attracted his attention roof-ward, and he was barely able to scurry aside before a 600-pound counter-weight plunged past him, through the stage floor, and into the cellar.

Beethoven and Mozart were reduced to a total of three performances this season: a poor *Fidelio* on December 24 (Senger-Bettaque was the Leonore*) and an erratic *Nozze di Figaro* on November 30 and December 31. Sembrich (Susanna) and Eames (Countess) were excellent as ever, and Bella Alten, making her debut as Cherubino (d) had to repeat *"Voi che sapete."* Blass was a thick-voiced Figaro,* Scotti the flexible Almaviva. The most that could be said for Nahan Franko's conducting was that he was the first native-born American to lead an opera in the Metropolitan.

Whatever the patchy picture this season presents in retrospect, it made considerable money ($125,326) for Conried and his associates. The following summary of expenditure, as against a typical Grau year, was published a year later when intimations in the press that he was cutting corners to amass profits angered Conried. It was his contention, supported by the figures, that he was spending on the average ten thousand dollars *more* a week than Grau had spent. Whatever their contemporary significance, the figures on the following page have pertinence today, in any discussion of operatic costs.

1905–1906

The principle that no beginning at the Metropolitan is official unless it has to do with *Faust* was proved on January 3, 1906 to apply even to labor relations. According to Conried's planning, this date was set aside for the first appearance of Caruso in a French opera and the presence of Eames as Marguerite, one of her favorite roles. It remains memorable today as the first[1] in the long line of union negotiations that rewrote the kind of budget quoted (on the following page) and transformed the whole problem of giving opera at the Metropolitan.

For their evening's work in this *Faust,* Eames would receive $1,500, Caruso $1,344, Scotti $600, and Plançon $500, a total of more than $3,900 for the four principals. For their evening's work, the choristers would receive whatever part of fifteen dollars would be *prorated* from a

---

[1] A brief walkout of the German chorus in 1884 failed for lack of organization.

week's work of seven performances. It would not, in any case, be more than $2.14 per night.

According to custom, the members of the chorus had been engaged individually by Conried before the season started. It was not until it was under way that the union was formed and the demands presented. An increase of wages to twenty-five dollars per week was sought, also an end of the practice of transporting choristers on overnight trips in day coaches.

	Grau	*Conried*
PRODUCTION	*1902–3*	*1904–5*
Artists and staff	$522,315.13	$544,153.11
Chorus, ballet, and supers	41,386.13	66,212.13
Orchestra and stage band	85,569.29	95,083.40
Steamship transportation	16,799.29	20,656.07
Railroad transportation, etc.	36,209.52	72,687.30*
Costumes, wardrobe, wigs	18,110.59	15,953.33
Music and royalties	3,517.16	3,499.67
Commissions and sundries	2,356.62	4,371.54
Advertising	16,566.91	25,167.42
Totals	$742,830.64	$847,783.97

* Includes the post-season tour to the Pacific coast.

MAINTENANCE		
Rent, taxes, and insurance	$ 57,078.85	$ 60,300.23
Box office, ushers, doormen	5,844.50	5,723.65
Cleaners, porters, etc.	7,422.86	10,275.95
Engineer's depar't	9,934.79	9,763.43
Electrician's depar't	8,255.55	10,758.66
Scene painters	13,894.56	7,173.15
Carpenters and stagehands	22,723.38	45,894.59
Property depar't	9,487.19	16,365.95
Gas and electricity	8,626.34	14,372.84
Storehouse expenses	1,551.29	3,040.00
Tickets and sundries	2,559.61	4,140.46
Opera School	....	5,712.04
Director's and office salaries, general and European expense accounts, etc.	41,779.12	43,497.58
Repairs, stage reconstruction, costumes from Europe	2,228.54	98,257.66
Grand totals	$934,217.22	$1,183,060.15

Conried countered with an acknowledgment that the wages were too low, and that he would consider an increase on an individual basis. He refused, however, to deal with the union, contending that it had not existed when the choristers agreed, freely, to the contracts then offered.

In the belief that they had the support of the Musical Mutual Protective Union (orchestra players) and the Theatrical Protective Union (stagehands), the chorus people informed Conried at six in the afternoon that they would not perform that night.

When the curtain went up, however, the orchestra and stagehands were in place, as were six choristers who decided to honor the contracts they had signed. Although the night was stormy, the theater was crowded, especially the standing space. Caruso as Faust,* even in French, was something his countrymen could not resist. Conductor Franko had spent the day editing the passages in which the chorus appeared and, when they could not be cut, assigning its music to woodwinds and brass. During the first interval, Conried read a statement setting forth his resistance to the union demands as "a matter of principle, of respect for art and respect for this art-loving public." The references to "art" drew howls of derision from the standees.

For Caruso the evening was undoubtedly trying, not alone for the omissions and distractions in the score—no Soldiers' Chorus, of course, and only an organ in the church scene—but he used his voice considerately, with splendid sound on *"Je t'aime"* and the climax of *"Salut demeure."* "His Parisian accent," commented the *Sun,* "was imported from a quarter where perfection does not prevail." A Buster Brown wig and white gloves tended to accentuate the unintentionally comic.

For the first *Tristan,* on January 5, Conried recruited a sailors' chorus from German singers not on duty, including Knote, Muhlmann, and Goritz. Caruso offered to help from off stage, but it was decided his German was not good enough. Burgstaller's Tristan* went very well, and with Nordica in fine form, the evening was a success. With Édouard de Reszke gone, King Marke had reverted to his traditional status of a bore, as sung by Robert Blass.

Denied recognition by Samuel Gompers (president of the American Federation of Labor) because of the contract situation, the choristers decided to accept Conried's compromise offer and go back to work the next day. Salaries were raised to twenty dollars per week and better transportation facilities were guaranteed. In addition, the choristers were paid for the whole week of the strike. Not much progress toward strong organization was made until 1920, when the management agreed to hire choristers only from the Grand Opera Choral Alliance. It was not until the formation of the American Guild of Musical Artists, in 1933 that the chorus had real bargaining power at the Metropolitan.

In his second Faust, on January 6, Caruso wore a more becoming wig, and he took off his white gloves before breaking into the jail to rescue

Marguerite (Eames). With all his fine sound, the press did not endorse these changes as the final touches to qualify him as Jean de Reszke's successor. Altogether, Caruso's conscientious effort to make himself useful in the French repertory had more success in Don José* on March 5. His version of the *"Air de fleur"* was marked by "unexpected delicacy and finish," said the *Sun,* with a "warmth of passion" not surpassed by any previous José. The storm of applause it aroused tested Caruso's restraint severely and, rather than repeat the air, he finally rose, bowed, and slumped back to his knees beside the plainly nettled Fremstad. Her alluring, dramatically cogent performance pleased all save those convinced that without chair-throwing and disheveled hair, Carmen was not Carmen. Bessie Abott sang a rather timid Micaëla,* Journet a vocally gruff Escamillo that was attributed to a bad cold. Vigna conducted.

Caruso's performances climbed to forty in New York this winter, causing Henderson to write on March 18: "The public has gone to the opera in the season just ended almost solely for the purpose of hearing Enrico Caruso. . . . The invariable request . . . at the box office has been 'Can you let me have seats for Caruso's next performance?' "

To accommodate those who preferred the tenor in a varied repertory, Donizetti's *La Favorita* was revived on November 29; likewise *La Sonnambula* on December 15 and *Marta* on February 9. All had the central focus of celebrated tenor airs, of course, and Caruso's dazzling ease in *"Spirto gentil,"* his artless fooling as Elvino, and his impassioned *"M'appari"* as Lionel kept the audiences content. None of these was sung with the kind of lightness the discriminating critics thought desirable, but the vocal flow could hardly be resisted. Edyth Walker's fine singing of *"O mio Fernando"* added to the pleasures of *Favorita,* as did Sembrich's Amina and Lady Harriet in the other works. In *Marta,* the soprano's interpolated "Last Rose" was charmingly sung, and there were kind words also for Walker's Nancy,* if not for the excessively debonair Plunkett* of Plançon.

The coming of *Hänsel und Gretel* on November 25, with Humperdinck in the audience, was marked by some learned analysis that must have made the composer wonder whether he had, in fact, "meant all that." Henderson saw the *Hexenritt* as a take-off on the "Ride of the Valkyries," the laughter of the children a reminiscence of the Rhinemaidens. Nevertheless, he found it "masterly," "charming," and "delightful" as sung by Bella Alten (Gretel*), Goritz (Peter*), and Marion Weed (Gertrude*). Lina Abarbanell, then a soubrette of the Irving Place Theater, later well-known for collaborating in the production of musical plays on Broadway, acted Hänsel* appealingly, though her voice was small for the big auditorium. Hertz made the most of his able cast, which included Homer as the Witch.*

Much comment was aroused by Conried's decision to present, as Sulamith (d) in a revival of *Die Königin von Saba* on November 22 the youthful Brooklyn-born soprano Marie Rappold. Not only did she have no European training; she had not sung on any stage prior to her Metropolitan debut. Seven years of study with Oscar Saenger had given her a firm vocal foundation, and Conried's personal coaching in dramatic action prepared her for a performance of quite acceptable quality. The judgment was that European training was not indispensable for success on the operatic stage, but the legion of novices who have followed Rappold rarely came with so much deliberate preparation. A variable cast, including Walker, Knote, Van Rooy, and Alten, could not revive the previous interest in Goldmark's score. It has not been produced since.

Rappold lacked the repertory to appear frequently in her first season, singing (according to the *Sun*) a "singularly sweet and fresh" Elsa* in *Lohengrin* on December 30, and also taking part in *Der Zigeunerbaron* when Conried added it to the Metropolitan repertory on February 15. For the customary purposes, the action was suspended in Act III and most of the company's stars were led in, as captives of Baron Barinkay, to sing for their freedom—and Conried's benefit. Nordica was announced, but pleaded illness (induced perhaps by the memory of the previous year's *Rigoletto* quartet), but there was easily ten dollars' value in the sequence of solos by Journet, Sembrich, Fremstad, Eames, Plançon, Caruso, and Scotti, the last two singing their famous version of the duet from *La Forza del destino*. At the end, four eminent Wagnerians—Burgstaller, Knote, Van Rooy, and Blass—presented themselves in costume as a Bavarian quartet.

The critical abuse this year was taken in silence by Conried, who could endure complaints in the warmth of his twenty-thousand-dollar profit. In *Der Zigeunerbaron*, Rappold (Arsena*) headed a cast that included Homer (Czipra*), Dippel (Barinkay*), Alten (Saffi*), and Goritz (Zsupan*), with Bauermeister singing her last new part (Mirabella*) in her last Metropolitan season. There was no repetition, and only one offering of *Die Fledermaus*, on Thanksgiving night, November 30. Both Strauss works were conducted by Nahan Franko.

The well-regarded Knote came early and stayed late, beginning with *Tannhäuser* on November 25, with Jeanne Jomelli a new and small-voiced Elisabeth (d). Caruso would not sing Manrico at this period of his career (he contended that it was "all shouting"), and Knote obliged with his first Italian role anywhere on January 19, enjoying a considerable success. The *Sun* commended his "pleasing lyric quality" in *"Ah, si ben mio"* and noted

that *"Di quella pira"* (lowered in pitch) was "boldly given." The management was saved from the most dismal of all operatic happenings, a change
of bill,[1] by using a Helene Noldi as Leonora in place of the ailing Nordica.
Although identified as "lately prima donna of the Italian Opera in Mexico
City," Noldi did not match the Metropolitan standard, and was not heard
again.

Knote was the *Götterdämmerung* Siegfried* on December 22, which the
Sun—now rather persistently harassing Conried—termed a "dress rehearsal" for the full cycle to be given the following week. The Norns and
Alberich were omitted, but Knote's "thoroughly dignified . . . musical"
singing and the commanding Brünnhilde of Nordica atoned for much that
was lax in the stage direction and rough in Hertz's conducting. As a new
departure, the season's first cycle was given during five days, beginning on
the afternoon of Christmas and ending on December 29. Consequently, the
Brünnhildes were all different (Walker, Weed, and Nordica), the tenor
roles sung by Dippel (Siegmund), Knote (young Siegfried) and Burgstaller
(Loge and the elder Siegfried). Fremstad sang the *Siegfried* Brünnhilde*
on December 13 with the usual lack of critical review. When it was repeated on March 8, it was described by the *Sun* as an "improvement over
her former very questionable performance."

The two-season run of *Parsifal* at extra prices was now over: it was given
on January 11 at the usual five-dollar top before an audience of modest
size and conventional attire. Fremstad's Kundry, in the words of Henderson, rose in the second act "to a level of thrilling power . . . seldom reached
at the Metropolitan," and Burgstaller's Parsifal showed the refinements
that may come with repetition. Of the season's four performances, the most
attention was directed to one on Washington's Birthday. Many persons
from out of town were present, applause was discouraged, and the whole
performance had the ceremonial air now associated with Good Friday.
The other Wagner casts of this season were familiar and of routine quality.
At a Sunday-night concert on February 25 Hertz included the rarely heard
original version of the prelude to Act III of *Tannhäuser,* known as "Tannhäuser's Pilgrimage."

This was the year in which the one hundred and fiftieth anniversary of
Mozart's birth was widely celebrated in European theaters, but the Metropolitan offered only *Don Giovanni,* twice. The first performance, on January 27, brought testimonials to "the vitality of Mozart's genius" (the
Sun), but only Scotti as the Don and Sembrich as Zerlina matched the

---

[1] Nonsubscribers may ask for a refund in such circumstances. Subscribers have no
privilege in any circumstances.

occasion. Nordica was less good as Donna Anna than she had been as Elvira, and Jomelli as Elvira* was not so good as Eames would have been. The latter, however, had sung Aida the day before and was not available. For a change, the staging was approved, save for the ever-perplexing ball. Musicians played on stage, as the score directed, but the three styles of dancing required by the action were sadly muddled. *Le Nozze di Figaro* was announced for March 12, but canceled when Eames begged off. The only possible alternative was Fremstad, who knew the part only in German. This being a "Sembrich night," the audience was asked to feast instead on Acts II and III of *Don Pasquale* (Sembrich, Scotti, and Dippel), with Caruso, Campanari, and Alten following in *Pagliacci*. This was not the most remarkable of the season's double bills, however. On January 31 Alten sang Gretel and Nedda in the same evening, and on March 17 Act II and the lesson scene of *Il Barbiere* were preceded by two acts of *Tosca*. The excuse for the Rossini-Puccini combination was the seasonal farewells of Eames and Sembrich. For Dippel, it was just an evening's hard work—he sang both Cavaradossi and Almaviva-Lindoro.

The profit figures quoted previously for the Conried seasons were swelled by earnings of $111,018 in this one. The bright picture thus presented was considerably dimmed in mid-April when the company had the misfortune to be playing in San Francisco and lost its entire stock of scenery, costumes, and properties in the earthquake and fire. Considerable loss was incurred when the remainder of the long tour had to be canceled and the company transported back to New York. Among the worst afflicted were the orchestral players, whose instruments were damaged beyond salvage. Sembrich deepened the special niche she held in the affections of her public by announcing, on her return to New York, that she would give a benefit concert to help the musicians replace their instruments. Carnegie Hall was crowded for the program on May 6, for which she and her pianist, Isidore Luckstone, contributed their services. The proceeds to the musicians were nearly $9,000.

Among those who watched the money-making activities of Conried at the Metropolitan with a thoughtful eye was Oscar Hammerstein. He had sold his old Manhattan Opera House at Thirty-fourth Street and Broadway (the Macy corner) for commercial construction and taken over a site farther west on Thirty-fourth Street. On February 13, 1906 he informed the press that the new theater would bear the same name, that he would begin operatic production in the fall, and the artists with whom he was "negotiating" included the De Reszkes. The musical sophisticates treated this with the skepticism it merited, knowing that even a fee of $3,500 a performance—as Hammerstein airily offered—could not lure Jean de Reszke[1] from Nice. As the summer progressed and Hammerstein let it be known that Bonci and Melba, Renaud, and Clotilde Bressler-Gianoli, and Cleofonte Campanini as musical director, were committed to him, skepticism gave way to anticipation.

In Conried's private book for the season 1905–6 there are these notations:

Artists	Number of performances or length of season	Fee per performance
Alten, Bella	60 performances	$100
Eames, Emma	9, plus 10 on tour	$1,500
Fremstad, Olive	6 months' season, 10 performances per month	3,333.33 marks per month
Homer, Louise	5 months' season, 10 per month	$1,500 per month, plus $1,000 at season's end
Nordica, Lillian	20 performances	$1,250
Sembrich, Marcella	45 performances	$1,000

(The artist also to have "two orchestra seats for each performance in which she sings")

Walker, Edyth	40 performances	$500
Blass, Robert	60 performances	$150
Burgstaller, Alois	20 performances	$500
Caruso, Enrico	40 performances	7,000 francs
Goritz, Otto	7 months' season, 70 performances in New York and elsewhere	40,000 marks for entire season
Journet, Marcel	63 performances	$10,000 for season ($158 a performance)
Knote, Heinrich	40 performances	$1,000 per performance
Plançon, Pol	15 weeks, 10 performances per month	2,500 francs per performance
Scotti, Antonio	40 performances	$600 per performance
Van Rooy, Anton	40 performances	$500 per performance

It was further stipulated that Van Rooy was not to sing these parts in succession: the Dutchman, Der Wanderer, Hans Sachs, and Telramund.

The name of Luisa Tetrazzini (written "Louisa") also occurs in the book; Conried had acquired an option on her services, but neglected to exercise it before she made other plans (see page 193).

[1] The first of innumerable "De Reszke pupils" to reach New York was Bessie Abott (see page 175), who was admired for a voice of "lovely timbre" and "impeccable purity" of execution (Krehbiel) as Mimi on January 20.

1906–1907

In a backward look at the success of Oscar Hammerstein's Manhattan venture in its second season, Krehbiel (*Chapters of Opera,* page 364) recalls his easy discouragement on an earlier occasion (1893) and adds: "It was not strange that many observers refused to believe that he was of the stuff out of which opera managers are made. He did not seem illogical enough." A dozen additional years in the theater had taught Hammerstein tenacity at least. He hung on just a little longer than the Metropolitan dared gamble he would. In consequence he came out of the four-year venture not only with a glorious reputation for musical innovation, but also with cash in hand, all his debts discharged—and still owner of the Manhattan Opera House.

A formidable bill of particulars against Conried has accumulated from various sources, tending to show that had he done this or that, Hammerstein's competition would have been materially weakened if not wholly prevented. His oversight in the matter of Tetrazzini has been mentioned, and so great a singer as Maurice Renaud, according to the words of Conried's own biographer, Montrose Moses (page 217), could have been secured for the Metropolitan "if he [Conried] had been a judge of singers." In his *Memories of the Opera* (New York: Charles Scribner's Sons; 1941), Giulio Gatti-Casazza recorded his belief that Conried had been remiss in not reserving all the French works later produced by Hammerstein. They had been offered by the Parisian agent Gabriel Astruc (ibid., page 168) and rejected by Conried with "a contemptuous wave of his hand." As for Hammerstein, Conried would not even discuss him with Astruc.

Nevertheless, it is not easy to grant that even the most astute manager could have signed up every desirable artist of the day or secured the rights to every producible opera just (as Gatti suggested) "to keep them in the desk drawer." Doubtless Hammerstein would have had less immediate success had the Metropolitan been less vulnerable; but his flair, his gambling instinct, and his uninhibited showmanship would have created a problem for the Metropolitan at almost any period of its history. Nor was Hammerstein's bias toward a French repertory wholly the result of Conried's oversight. As we have seen, weakness in this category was an inherent shortcoming of the Metropolitan repertory in its early years. The forces Hammerstein set in motion made Gatti more receptive to it for a while, but French opera has gradually dwindled to the virtual vanishing-point again.

Even in the best of circumstances it is unlikely that Conried's command of the Metropolitan would have lasted longer than it did, but it is somewhat ironic that ill health and the Hammerstein menace began to creep up on him as he began to get a firmer grasp of how a first-rank theater should be conducted. In this season, for example, he added two durable works to the repertory—*Madama Butterfly*[1] and *Salome*—experimented with two others of quality—Puccini's *Manon Lescaut* and Giordano's *Fedora*—and gave the only hearings in Metropolitan history to Berlioz's *La Damnation de Faust*.

Conried's ailment (sciatic neuritis, affecting his legs) was common knowledge even before the season began. Caruso's greatly important part in the Metropolitan scheme of operation was threatened by his arrest and temporary jailing, and this brought Conried to the brink of a breakdown. The opening night was little more than a week off when Caruso was arrested in the monkey house of the Central Park Zoo on November 16, charged with annoying a passer-by, Mrs. Hannah Stanhope. The charges were not spelled out, but the implication was that the tenor had made "improper advances," even unto pinching. The tenor protested that his ignorance of English had been imposed upon and he had been victimized. The complainant did not appear in court, but the evidence of the arresting officer was credited, and Caruso was convicted and fined. Worry about the public reaction and alarm over the possible consequences to the box office aggravated Conried's ailment, and he went to the opera house infrequently in the early weeks of the season.

The public regard for Caruso was affirmed at the earliest opportunity, when he sang Rodolfo in *Bohème* on November 28. The standees and gallery patrons applauded the sight of him when the curtain rose, but he was a very nervous singer until he launched into the *"Racconto."* It was superbly delivered, and the theater rang with applause. Thereafter the evening and Caruso's part of the season proceeded without incident.

Geraldine Farrar's illustrious career at the Metropolitan had been initiated two days before, as Juliette (d) in the season-opening performance of *Roméo* on November 26. With her was Charles Rousselière as Roméo (d) and a new conductor from France, Samuel Bovy. The twenty-four-year-old Farrar's successes in Berlin, both musical and romantic, had been well publicized, and critical resistance to her was more than moderate. The *Tribune* described her as a "beautiful vision," with "a voice of exquisite quality in the middle register." The *Sun* report concurred in valuing the voice as "a full bodied lyric soprano, with tendencies toward the dramatic," but declared "Miss Farrar has yet thrown but a pebble into the vast sea of

[1] The first American performance, in an English-language version, was given in Washington, D.C., early in November by the Henry Savage company. The same company presented *Butterfly* at the Garden Theater, New York, on November 12, with Elza Szamosy in the title role, Joseph Sheehan as Pinkerton, and Winifred Goff as Sharpless. Walter Rothwell conducted.

vocal art." M. Simard (not identified by a first name) made his debut as Mercutio (d), and the Nurse was Von Januschowsky of earlier seasons, now known as Georgine Neuendorff. Both Rousselière and Bovy were commended for their work.

Other singers introduced in this first week were Katherina Fleischer-Edel as Elisabeth (d) and Carl Burrian as Tannhäuser (d) on November 30, and Riccardo Stracciari as Germont (d) on December 1, with Sembrich and Caruso. Fleischer-Edel's career was brief, but Burrian endured till the outbreak of the First World War, after the 1913–1914 season. Although Stracciari became a well-esteemed baritone of the Italian school, his debut was inauspicious—"throaty, tremulous . . . pallid" were Henderson's first words for him, replaced later by more favoring ones.

Hammerstein intended to open his new theater in direct competition with the Metropolitan opening, but its interior still lacked some finishing touches when the audience assembled for *I Puritani* on December 3. Official "society" paid little attention to the upstart venture, but the social set was sufficiently represented by H. H. Flagler, Rawlings Cottenet, Miss May Callender, E. Berry Wall, James de Wolf Cutting, and Mrs. Charles Childs to give West Thirty-fourth Street an uncommon clog of "wagonettes and automobiles." More than 3,100 crowded in to see the house and hear *I Puritani,* and there were great cries of *"Viva Bonci!"* when Mario Ancona, a New York favorite of ten years before, made his entry as Riccardo. The more knowing shushed them to silence, saving their greeting for a roaring welcome to the tenor when he did appear. Light as his voice was, he used it "like a great artist," said the *Sun,* adding encomiums for his "delicacy, refinement, grace, and elegance." Cleofonte Campanini conducted ably a cast that included Regina Pinkert (Elvira), but it was clear that orchestra and principals were still feeling their way. In characteristic humor, Hammerstein made a speech declaring his sole responsibility for what was done. It had been his desire to establish "opera for the masses," but New York standards were too high for that to be done at low prices. Hence he was concentrating on "the best and greatest." The Metropolitan was crowded on the same night for a performance of *Marta* in which Sembrich sang "The Last Rose of Summer" twice. Caruso did not repeat *"M'appari."*

Maurice Renaud made his debut at the Manhattan on December 5 in a *Rigoletto* that marked him as "a big man physically who has a voice of great power" (the *Sun*). Bonci was a splendid Duke, Pinkert a satisfactory Gilda. The Metropolitan offering was Giordano's *Fedora* for the first time in America with the beautiful Lina Cavalieri as Fedora (d) winning acclaim for a "very pretty" voice, an "exquisite figure," a face that was "a delight to see" (all the praise is Henderson's). There was too little for Caruso to do as Loris Ipanow,* however, or for Scotti as De Siriex.* The opera was given six times more in Conried's last two seasons, but not again until 1923, with Maria Jeritza.

Farrar was heard both as the Berlioz Marguerite* when *La Damnation de Faust* was introduced on December 7 and in a new production of the conventional Gounod *Faust* on December 31. Rousselière and Plançon were philosopher and devil in both. The stage arrangement devised for Berlioz's "dramatic legend" by Raoul Gunsbourg of Monte Carlo in 1894 was used, with enough applause for the ballet of the sylphs to be repeated. The general judgment, however, was expressed by Henderson, who said "the work is deficient in action and its pictures have no valid connection." Of the two Marguerites, Farrar was happier in the music of Gounod. Her performance was characterized in the *Sun* as "Dramatically, one of the finest . . . seen on the Metropolitan stage" and "exquisitely sung" in the garden scene. Hammerstein introduced his own *Faust* (Gounod's) as a counterattraction to the Berlioz, with Charles Dalmorès a sweet-voiced Faust and Pauline Donalda a convincing Marguerite.

In the unfolding panorama of Hammerstein's activity, not the least pleasure was provided by the always vital and sometimes fervent conducting of Campanini. Neither *Don Giovanni* nor *Carmen* nor *Aida* had recently been done at the Metropolitan with the verve Campanini imparted to them in a single week beginning on December 12. Bonci's Ottavio added to the "real joy" the *Sun* found in the playing of *Don Giovanni*, though the cast was otherwise indifferent. December 15 was the occasion of Renaud's first Don, and "a handsomer, more dashing and captivating conqueror has not been seen in this part," wrote Henderson.

Campanini conducted *Carmen* with Calvé, and the Bizet score was given nineteen times at the Manhattan this season, but the credit was not wholly hers. Much interest was aroused by the "elemental, frank, physical Carmen" of Clotilde Bressler-Gianoli, the orchestral playing, and well-drilled ensemble that "rose to notable heights." With so fine a French tenor as Dalmorès to sing José, and Donalda as Micaëla, the major pattern of Hammerstein activity began to be evident. A demonstration in which Campanini and Hammerstein were both called out for bows followed *Aida* on December 19 (with Eleanora de Cisneros, Amadeo Bassi, and Ancona). When Vigna sought to arouse the same effect in a Metropolitan performance on December 21, with Caruso, Stracciari (Amonasro*), and Celestina Boninsegna a lovely-sounding Aida,* the results were judged to be merely boisterous.

If there was no place for Melba at the Metropolitan, there was a great audience to hear her sing Violetta at the Manhattan on January 2, with

Bassi and Renaud, though Eames, Caruso, and Scotti managed to fill the Metropolitan for *Tosca* the same night. Two nights later Bonci was singing to even more people in *L'Elisir d'amore* than were attracted to a repetition of *Lakmé* which Conried was offering in a poorish revival with Sembrich. Rousselière was an explosive Gerald, Journet a ponderous Nilakantha, and Bovy failed to animate a performance that moved "like a river of oil" (the *Sun*). When Renaud returned to France, Hammerstein had, in Mario Sammarco, another baritone New York was glad to hear. He commanded attention in *Pagliacci* (Tonio) for "a fine, fresh, vigorous . . . voice of most excellent quality." He was also commended for his Marcello in *Bohème* on March 1, with Bonci, Melba, Gilibert, and Emma Trentini (Musetta). This was one performance Campanini did not conduct. Conried claimed exclusive rights to the Puccini scores, and this one was given with orchestral parts "remembered" by an unidentified scholar. To avoid reprisals against him in Italy by Ricordi, Campanini sat in a box while Tanara conducted.

Having proved without question his ability to give first-class opera, Hammerstein ended his season with boasts of subscription for his second season already totaling $200,000. Half of this was from the public, half from ticket-brokers, who in those days invested heavily in opera seats for resale to regular customers (see pages 241–2). It was Hammerstein's contention that his first season had brought $750,000 to the box office, a figure decried by Krehbiel, in his *Chapters of Opera* (published in 1908), with these words: "If all that Mr. Hammerstein himself said could have been accepted . . . the lesson of the season would have been that the people who live in New York and come to New York in the winter season were willing to spend . . . one and three quarter million dollars . . . for this one form of entertainment."

Exaggeration or not, a like figure was quoted to me thirty years later by his son Arthur Hammerstein, who also set the profit of that first season at $100,000. What Krehbiel could not have known as the events were happening was the extraordinary growth of New York's population during the first years of the century. The march of figures[1] shows

1890	2,507,414
1900	3,437,202
1910	4,766,883

The growth was especially pertinent to opera. Between 1900 and 1910 the foreign-born elements of that population increased by 700,000. Specifically, the Italian-born in New York increased from 145,000 in 1900 to 340,765 in 1910. Adding first-generation children of Italian-born parents,

[1] 13th Census, Report by States, Volume III, page 216.

the total rose to 523,310 people with the strongest kind of orientation to the subject of this volume.

If all this appears to be a digression, it is by no means so. The figures suggest not only the general reasons why New York could provide support for two opera enterprises, but also the specific reasons why the less pretentious but by no means unworthy Manhattan Opera House developed a public largely its own, as the City Center did several decades later. It also indicates one arm of the pincers that was closing about Conried in a nagging competition. The other arm was made up of some untoward events in his own theater, including the "affair *Salome.*"

The record shows that Conried had reason to suppose that he would have difficulties with *Salome,* for he used as a pretext to persuade Strauss to reduce his royalty fee the possibilities of objections to its subject. Fortunately, Farrar had rejected Conried's preposterous suggestion that she should sing Salome (Moses: *Life of Heinrich Conried,* page 219), but the manager determined to profit fully from any performance that might be given by electing the first public showing on January 22 as his annual benefit.

This materialistic attitude toward so important an event as the first performance of a Strauss opera in America might have passed unnoticed had not Conried selected the preceding Sunday, January 20, for the dress rehearsal. Moreover, he threw the theater open to more than one thousand persons, many of them just come from church. The spectacle of Fremstad as Salome* fondling the severed head of John the Baptist naturally offended more in these circumstances than it would have otherwise. Actually it is hard to determine, from the published reports, whether the objections of Mrs. Herbert Satterlee (J. P. Morgan's daughter) were to the first performance or to the dress rehearsal. In his résumé on January 22, Henderson wrote in the *Sun:* "Miss Fremstad . . . coddled the severed head a good deal more [in the rehearsal] than she did on Tuesday. . . . On Tuesday she moderated her transports so that even little girls . . were not shocked. As for the society women, they viewed the spectacle with perfect calmness." He commended the "perfect adaptation of the musical expression to the scene," declared that Fremstad's performance put her "in the front rank of great dramatic singers," and ranked Burrian's Herod* with Van Dyck's Loge as a character study. Finally, he felt, if "this sort of degeneracy is to become popular," it should depend "entirely on the theater goer."

The picture presented by Walter Prichard Eaton (then a twenty-five-year-old reporter) for the *Tribune*'s readers was quite different: "Many voices were hushed as the crowd passed out into the night, many faces were white . . . many women were silent and men spoke as if a bad dream were upon them." Krehbiel thought the reviewer should be "an embodied conscience stung into righteous fury by the moral stench with which *Salome* fills the nostrils of mankind." Nevertheless, he directed attention to three "supremely beautiful musical moments" in *Salome:* the brooding at the cistern, the Dance of the Seven Veils, and the finale. Aldrich, in the *Times,* labeled the subject abhorrent, but gave lavish praise to the production and the conducting of Hertz. As is well known, the dance was performed, not by Fremstad, but by the company's ballerina, Bianca Froelich. According to Henderson, "She spared the audience nothing in . . . active and suggestive detail."

In other reports, the early departure of some of the public was interpreted as a gesture of antagonism. The opera, however, in Conried's beneficent manner, had been preceded by a long, miscellaneous concert. Thus *Salome* did not begin until nearly ten, and the homeward trend did not begin any earlier than it does for some members of the audience at any performance in the theater. As Edward Ziegler, then writing for the *Theater Magazine,* remarked: "The silly concert and the long intermission had wearied most of the listeners."

Whatever the combined public reaction, the influential private opinion decreed that *Salome* was "objectionable, and detrimental to the best interests of the Metropolitan Opera House." This was the phraseology of a resolution by the board of directors of the Metropolitan Opera and Real Estate Company addressed to Conried on January 27. According to the press, "the objections started in the family of one of the most influential and powerful of the box-holders." This was the *Tribune's* way of characterizing the Morgan position at the Metropolitan.

Conried petitioned first to have the work restricted to non-subscription performances, and was denied this salvation. Then, he threatened to present it in another theater, a course his own directors deemed unwise. Finally, after a meeting with a representative group from the Opera and Real Estate Company, *Salome* was dropped from the repertory. Much of the talk in the press recounted the expense incurred in producing *Salome,* the commitments to the composer for several years' performing rights. Morgan personally offered to reimburse Conried and his group, but they declined with thanks. They preferred the record to read that the forbidden *Salome* had been at their expense.

One critical vacillation in the valuation of *Salome* may be mentioned as indicative of the influence that the heat of the moment may exert on a usually unbending mind. Henderson's original reaction has been indicated on page 185. On February 2 he described *Salome* as "operatic offal" and declared the prohibition of it had "removed a stench from the nostrils. Mr.

Strauss," he continued, "stands convicted . . . of having found his inspiration in a low subject." In a later review of the season *Salome* had sunk to the level of "a deadly bore."

The vexing problem of morality was not present when Puccini's *Manon Lescaut* had its first Metropolitan hearing on January 18, but it was latent in *Madama Butterfly,* introduced on February 11. Both were given in the presence of Puccini, and he was warmly applauded whenever he showed himself. With Caruso in *Lescaut* were Cavalieri (Manon*), Scotti (Lescaut*), and Rossi (Geronte*), a cast that reads better than it sounded, for Cavalieri was not suited to Manon, and Rossi was weak. *Butterfly,* with Farrar (Butterfly*), Caruso (Pinkerton*), Scotti (Sharpless*), and Homer Suzuki*), was decidedly better, though Krehbiel's objection to the "carnality" of the story was not wholly offset by "Love conjugal and love maternal" (the *Tribune*). At its previous showing in the Garden Theater, Aldrich had thought the appearance of Kate Pinkerton in the last act would be "atrocious taste" in reality. Musically, the virus of Puccini was working its wiles. Henderson referred approvingly to the "exquisite instrumentation" of the score and the "ravishing" beauty of the climax to Act II, and Krehbiel concurred with references to "haunting tenderness and poetic loveliness" in the score.

The upward surge of Puccini in the Metropolitan repertory was reflected in a total of twenty-one performances of his works this season, second only to Wagner with twenty-four. Few of the latter were worthy of more than passing notice, for the effort expended on *Salome* had virtually frozen the services of several important principals. Fremstad, for example, was due to sing her first Isolde in this season, but bypassed it in favor of Salome. Consequently, Gadski was the Isolde* on February 15, with hardly the command of the part which was later to be hers. In addition, Hertz was in a mood to drive the orchestra with untoward consequences for the vocalists (Burrian as Tristan,* Homer, Van Rooy, and Blass). Gadski's first act was admired, her second less so. When she sang again on March 6, Schumann-Heink was the Brangäne (a role she had not sung in some time). In addition to appearances in the *Ring,* she performed the Witch* in *Hänsel und Gretel* on March 22.

The last of these shared an evening with *Pagliacci,* in which Farrar sang Nedda* delightfully, and Caruso made his experiment with public perceptions by singing the off-stage serenade of Beppe in Act II. The famed tenor being invisible, there was no more applause than if it had been sung by Reiss, whose name was on the program for the part. There was in fact, no applause at all. A final credit for Farrar in her first season was an Elisabeth* in *Tannhäuser* on February 6, in which the *Sun* commended the "breadth and certainty" of her performance and paid tribute to the "benefit of Lilli Lehmann's coaching."

For a while, Caruso interrupted his pursuit of French style (he did not sing either Faust or José this season), but he added to Des Grieux (*Manon Lescaut*), Pinkerton, Loris in *Fedora*—and Beppe—the role of Da Gama* when *L'Africaine* was given on January 11. Journet (Grand Inquisitor*) and Plançon (Don Pedro*) reversed the roles they had sung in the last prior revival with results that were well matched by the superior vocalizing of Caruso. Fremstad, however, was uncomfortable in the music of Selika*; Stracciari as Nelusko* and Rappold as Inez* were below the approved standard. Most at fault was the ill-balanced ensemble, crudely conducted by Vigna.

This conductor's qualities had sufficed in his first seasons, when he seemed an improvement over his immediate predecessors. The problems of such "new" scores as *Tosca* and *Butterfly,* however, and the advent of Campanini at the Manhattan had showed his limitations. That much can be reconstructed from the Gatti memoirs, which relate an offer from Conried to Toscanini late in 1906. On March 17, 1907 a rumor of this offer was discussed in the *Sun,* with the comment: "His conducting of *Tristan und Isolde* is said to be a dream. . . . He is almost equally great in *Die Meistersinger.* Unless he is to conduct such works he will not come."

For this year no further progress was made—publicly. But a good deal was going on out of view. Conried was advised by the directors of the Opera and Real Estate Company that "under no circumstances would the theater again be conducted as it had been last winter when for days at a time Mr. Conried was too sick to transact any business" (the *Sun,* August 1, 1907). In July, Conried had met Gustav Mahler in Berlin and concluded negotiations begun some time before for him to come to New York. But even then Conried's tenure was drawing to an end. In the same month Gatti-Casazza met Otto Kahn in Paris—after preliminary soundings had been carried on through intermediaries—and accepted, in principle, Conried's position, should Conried be forced to retire by illness. He also made it clear that Toscanini would come with him "willingly" (as Gatti-Casazza relates it in *Memories of the Opera*). As he would not come *without* Gatti, the relation of one to the other is clear.

Upon Kahn's return to America, he was queried by the press about the progress of the rumored changes, but would not discuss them. The *Sun* then printed the status of Conried's position (see page 180), adding its catalogue of possible successors: Jean de Reszke (not desirable because he might fill the house with his pupils), André Messager (late head of Covent Garden, and probably too French), Anton Fuchs (the admired

producer of *Die Meistersinger* for Conried, and probably too German),
Tito Ricordi (with his bagful of Puccini scores), and Andreas Dippel.
In an editorial of the next day, the same paper—doubtless acting on
information that Dippel was well favored by an ownership faction—
urged his case, declaring he was the one man who could "protect the
cosmopolitanism that Maurice Grau had given to the Metropolitan." His
experience in opera on both sides of the Atlantic was praised, as was
his standing as "a man of widest artistic sympathies as well as a keen
business man."

Little as the *Sun* knew of Gatti, so little did Gatti know of Dippel. They
met in not the best of circumstances. By then another new element in the
situation was Gustav Mahler. His contract extended beyond Conried's
final year, and Kahn considered it appropriate to protect Mahler's standing as an artist before a crisis should arise. Hence, when he made a formal
offer to Gatti and Toscanini in January 1908, he asked assurance, by
cable, that the latter would not find this situation difficult. Gatti quotes
(*Memories of the Opera,* page 148) Toscanini as answering: "But of
course I will have no difficulty at all. There is room at the Metropolitan
for several conductors and I am very happy to find myself with an artist
of Mahler's worth. I hold Mahler in great esteem and would infinitely
prefer such a colleague to any mediocrity."

Mahler found himself not so "happy"—and eventually out of the
Metropolitan. It was an instance of an irresistible force meeting a not
quite immovable object. Dippel came, saw, and did not conquer.

1907-1908

The most active season of operatic production New York had yet known
began on November 4, 1907 and continued for six months. It opened
at the Manhattan Opera House with *La Gioconda* and finished 237 performances later with *Götterdämmerung* at the Metropolitan. Activity was
virtually equal in the two places, the Metropolitan offering seven more
performances than Hammerstein's total of 115.

It was the year for New Yorkers to become acquainted with Feodor
Chaliapin, Mary Garden, Jean Périer, and Gustav Mahler, but it began
with the reappearance of an old favorite, Lillian Nordica, in the Manhattan *Gioconda*. This was Hammerstein's first reply to the lavish expenditure by which Conried hoped to attract his rival's principal singers to the
Metropolitan. He had succeeded with Bonci, morally if not legally committed to Hammerstein. Rather than waste time on legalities, Hammerstein simply produced new and better singers than Conried seemed to
know existed. For this first *Gioconda,* for example, Hammerstein imported

the brilliant young tenor Giovanni Zenatello to sing Enzo, found Adamo Didur for Alvise, borrowed Jeanne Gerville-Réache from Paris to be La Cieca, and combined them with Nordica, Ancona, and De Cisneros to provide Campanini with what the *Sun* temperately described as "on the whole, a competent cast." The same report declared: "Mr. Hammerstein is still engaged in his cheerful pastime of showing that . . . persons who say there are no more good singers in Europe are evasive, Machiavellian and empiric."

Mindful of his previous season's success with *Carmen,* especially with the pleasure provided by the excellent ensemble, Hammerstein inclined ever more strongly to the French works and singers with which his name is durably linked. *Carmen* on the second night brought Armand Crabbé as Escamillo with Bressler-Gianoli and Dalmorès, followed by deliberate comparison with the Metropolitan's *La Damnation de Faust* on November 6. The sophisticated ear rejoiced in the apt direction of "the continuous conductor," as Henderson termed Campanini, and the striking Méphistophélès of Renaud—a "brooding, world weary devil who goes about his business with all the infinite pathos of despairing satiety." Dalmorès and Jomelli were also excellent, but a prime attraction for the public was the elaborate "aerial ballet." It was larger in numbers and less clothed than Conried's, thus proving conclusively Hammerstein's superior understanding of Berlioz.

Unlikely as it seems for a work twenty-six years old, Offenbach's *Les Contes d'Hoffmann* was virtually unknown in New York when it was given at the Manhattan on November 15.[1] It was thus a new, delightful experience, especially as sung by a cast rarely surpassed since, with Dalmorès (Hoffmann), Renaud a perfect embodiment of the three spirits of evil (Dr. Coppelius, Dappertutto, and Miracle), Zepilli (Olympia), Jomelli (Giulietta), and a Mme Francisca (Antonia). De Cisneros, as tends to be the case with altos, was rather stalwart for Nicklausse. The *Sun* described the score as "extremely good in its kind and its kind is one that most people are wise enough to enjoy." Prophecy of success was supported by ten repetitions this season and a warm welcome whenever it has been produced since.

The Metropolitan had double competition when its turn came to open on November 18. For a novelty, the season began with a novelty, Cilèa's *Adriana Lecouvreur,* in which Caruso sang Maurizio* as he had at the Milan *première* in 1902. Hammerstein countered with *Hoffmann,* and the Horse Show was inconsiderate enough to open the same evening. Society

---

[1] An *opéra-bouffe* company operated by the young Maurice Grau had given it, briefly, during 1881.

took some of *Adriana* and then proceeded to the Madison Square Garden for the equestrian display, a decision not difficult in the face of what Henderson termed a "commonplace, trite, and wearisome" score. Caruso had his usual success with *"L'anima ho stanca,"* and Scotti was a first-class Michonnet.* Cavalieri, "good to see, bad to hear," in the judgment of the *Sun,* left more than a little wanting in her performance, and the conducting of Rudolph Ferrari was not much above the level of Vigna, who had succumbed to the Campanini competition.

Caruso also lent his art to the cause of Mascagni's *Iris* when it was given in the Metropolitan on December 6, with Ferrari conducting. This was not the first hearing of the score in the house, for Mascagni himself had conducted it as a private venture on October 16, 1902, prior to Grau's last season. It was then rated by Henderson as "a real opera" with "spectacular effects" and orchestrated with "wondrous tonal tints." On second hearing it still commanded the same writer's respect for its "riotous energy," though he found it short of the "directness and compressed interpretative power" of *Cavalleria*. Eames as Iris,* Scotti as Kyoto,* and Journet as the Father* gave performances of quality. A between-lines reading suggests that Puccini and *Butterfly* had absorbed as much interest as New Yorkers could muster for an opera with a Japanese locale.

Conried's most aggressive tactic to combat Hammerstein was the presentation of Caruso fifty-one times and Bonci twenty-five times. As they shared only two roles (Rodolfo and Alfredo), it was one tenor or the other in virtually all the non-Wagnerian repertory—76 performances out of 122. When they were inactive, it was likely to be an occasion when Feodor Chaliapin left little room on the stage for competitive personalities in any case. His debut, in *Mefistofele* on November 20, roused admiration in the *Sun* for "sustained power, consistency and coherence" in his acting and for an "exceptional" vocal technique. By contrast with Renaud's devil, however, Chaliapin's descended to actions Krehbiel called "disgusting frankness" and Henderson rated as "cheap claptrap." On Aldrich of the *Times* Chaliapin made "a deep impression . . . if not always a wholly agreeable one." Farrar sang Margherita* with charm, and Rappold (Helen*) and Jacoby (Pantalis*) divided the parts previously sung by one soprano. A new tenor of quality was the Kentucky-born Riccardo Martin (d), singing Faust* with "a true tenor of pretty quality" (Henderson) and evident lack of background.

Although Chaliapin left America with bitter complaints of a press cabal and a determination never to return (it was a dozen years before he relented), it is more likely that the unified reaction was merely against his naturalistic acting, a rude shock to a generation reared on the refinement of the De Reszkes, Plançon, the elegant Maurel, and Scotti. When he sang Basilio* in *Il Barbiere* on December 12, his "mugging" (the *Sun*'s word) did not please, nor did his nose-blowing through the fingers. "Acceptable" was all that could be said of his singing. As the Gounod Méphistophélès* in *Faust* on January 6, the *Sun* found him "hoarse . . . raucous in tone . . . rude . . . boisterous . . . without respect for the manner of the composer." Of his post-debut roles, Leporello in *Don Giovanni* roused not acclaim, but perhaps the least objection (see page 195).

Some apprehension attended Bonci's debut as the Duke* in *Rigoletto* on November 22, for it was assumed he would be hard to hear in a theater as large as the Metropolitan. Henderson's comment on this point is instructive: "The art of the singer who knows how to focus his voice and how to sustain it with a steady column of air made every note float through all the spaces of the house." Exquisite diction and the perfect use of vowels and consonants in an unbroken legato made his second-act duet with Sembrich "one of the most perfectly balanced pieces of singing" in Metropolitan history. Ferrari, it was noted, was happier in this old-fashioned music than in the "newer" Cilèa and Boito scores. Rodolfo, Lionello in *Marta,* Almaviva in *Il Barbiere,* and Ottavio in *Don Giovanni* were other roles sung with distinction by Bonci in this season.

An era of operatic experience in America may be dated from November 25 when, after several postponements, Mary Garden made her debut at the Manhattan in *Thaïs.* For the New York press to acknowledge that so famous a performer was "in almost every way worthy of her reputation," as the *Sun* did, is a measurement of accomplishment rarely equaled. "Captivating" in appearance rather than merely beautiful, "alive with magnetic temperament," Garden failed in only a single respect. "Whatever Miss Garden might have been in the sweet summertime long ago," wrote Henderson, "she cannot now be called a singer. . . . There may have been a voice once, but it and that method could not long dwell together." Renaud's masterly Athanaël, Dalmorès's picturesque Nicias, and Campanini's conducting made the most of what the *Sun* called "a good market place opera."

Within a few weeks Garden had given New Yorkers a concept of what was meant by the new term "singing actress," with her Louise on January 3 and her Mélisande on February 20. Campanini, as musical director, had imported virtually complete casts of key performers for *Louise* and *Pelléas,* with the result that a theatrical integration hardly known to New York opera in the past was achieved after relatively short rehearsal periods. Garden's touchingly acted Louise was but one element in a beautifully balanced cast that included Dalmorès (Julien), Bressler-Gianoli (the Mother), and, above all, Charles Gilibert as the Father— "a compendium of blighted love, blasted hope, human agony," wrote Henderson. By now Puccini had become a paragon, and Charpentier's melodic flow was compared, disadvantageously (by the same writer), with the Italian's. But there was keen appreciation of the "excellent tone painting" in the score and warm endorsement for the "masterly . . . convincing" last scene. Apparently Krehbiel's cries of "immorality," "vulgarity," "licentiousness," aroused less—or more—attention in opera-going quarters than he imagined. *Louise* was given ten times in all, with few empty seats.

The advent of *Pelléas et Mélisande* stimulated Aldrich, in the *Times,* to a critical evaluation that recalls the columns claimed by *Tristan* and *Falstaff* when they were new, but his older colleagues Henderson and Krehbiel were measurably less sympathetic. It was well known that Campanini had let the cast teach him the score rather than vice versa, but it was Aldrich's judgment that "only a musician of the highest powers" could have contributed as much as Campanini did to the success of the work. With Garden, who rose "to a height of tragic power" (Aldrich), were Périer (Pelléas), Gerville-Réache (Geneviève), and Dufranne (Golaud), all participants in the world *première* of 1902. The last of these, in Henderson's estimation, was "one of the greatest artists who ever came here from France," but he found the first two acts of the score "deadly dull, monotonous, wearisome." Krehbiel's objection was directed to "combinations of tones that sting and blister and . . . outrage the ear." In non-journalistic circles, in the monthly reviews and periodicals, *Pelléas* easily ranked as the most consequential of Hammerstein's innovations. He was easily forgiven the limited interest of Giordano's *Siberia,* which came and went with little attention after its first showing on February 5, with Zenatello (Vassili) and Sammarco (Gleby).

The shrewdness that had carried Hammerstein from small theatrical ventures to somewhat larger ones and finally to singlehanded competition with the richest enterprise in the United States had a typical illustration in the introduction of Luisa Tetrazzini. Although Conried protested that she was bound, in some way, to him, by the negotiations previously mentioned (see page 179), Hammerstein proceeded with plans to present her in the fall of 1908. Convinced by reports of her London success in November 1907 that she was ready for New York—and acting, no doubt, under the urging of Campanini, who was married to her sister, Eva—

Hammerstein decided to exercise his option at once, and announced her New York debut for January 15, 1908,[1] in *La Traviata*.

As the history of opera proves, from Lind to Pons, and from Patti to Galli-Curci and Sutherland, there is an aural appetite that only the highest notes and the swiftest scales satisfy. In Tetrazzini, the New York public had its first fresh serving of the sort since Melba was new, and the response dazed even the well-versed press. "It is useless to discuss the phenomenon," wrote Krehbiel. "The whims of the populace are as unquestioning . . . as the fury of the elements." Henderson began with some disparagement of the audience reaction, but soon surrendered to the appeal of "a clear fresh voice of pure soprano quality," in "perfectly unworn condition," with a "splendid richness in the upper range." The "lower medium," he continued, was marred by a pallid color and a tremolo so pronounced that it sounded like "the wailing of a cross infant," but she took rank as a "remarkable technician," if not quite capable of "supreme vocal art." Bassi (Alfredo) and Ancona (Germont) were also present.

In all, Tetrazzini appeared twenty-two times this season, frequently in *Lucia* with Zenatello and Sammarco, in *Rigoletto* with Bassi and Renaud, occasionally in *Crispino e la Comare,* once in *Dinorah.* Henderson's blow-by-blow account of a cadenza following *"Spargi d'amaro"* in *Lucia* is typical of the kind of thing her listeners doted on: "There were leaps, runs, staccati, double swells from piano to forte, twice repeated, and a finish on the high E flat." All this led to loud cries for the repetitions usually denied by Campanini, though the same critic found it wanting in "abandon, daring, dash." When Campanini relented to allow a second hearing of *"Caro nome"* on January 29, the public felt well treated indeed by Hammerstein. Considering the variety and excellence of the diversion Hammerstein offered his public, it is not unbelievable that he actually made the quarter of a million dollars quoted to me by Arthur Hammerstein as the season's profit. Nor is it hard to understand why Conried sought out a vocal phenomenon named Ellen Beach Yaw to give his public a Tetrazzini-like show in *Lucia* on March 21. Yaw was a concert artist who drew audiences to hear her sing C above "high" C, but she went no higher than G (in alt) during *"Quando rapito,"* and was not asked back.

The march of events at the Manhattan, reflected in attainments both artistic and commercial, clearly left the directors of the Conried Metropolitan Opera Company in an uncomfortable position. With the director a sick man and the end of his five-year contract almost at hand, the simplest solution was to separate "Conried" from "Metropolitan Opera

[1] Her American debut occurred in San Francisco two years before, when a company with which she was appearing in Mexico City ventured north for a short tour.

Company" and start afresh under new auspices. Negotiations to this end were under way even before Tetrazzini's debut on January 15.

The last of Conried's endeavors to make his company worthy of its surroundings was one that earned him enduring credit when Gustav Mahler conducted for the first time on January 1, 1908. Convinced that opportunities for the kind of work he wanted to do no longer existed in Vienna, this troubled yet potent spirit came to New York with anticipation if not with eagerness, and, for a while at least, found conditions much to his liking. For his introductory *Tristan* he had ample rehearsal time, a fresh-voiced Isolde,* and one eager to follow his guidance, in Fremstad, who had not sung the part previously. With Knote an excellent Tristan, Mahler achieved a performance "filled with vitality and voicing a conception of high beauty" (the *Sun*). In the line of what was written about her when her conception was fully matured, Fremstad's Isolde was already "a deeply studied and poetically conceived characterization . . . beautiful in its tenderness and melting passion . . . not a raging Isolde but a woman smothering a yearning love" (Henderson). As might have been expected from her mezzo beginnings, a few top tones were a little inhibited, but on the whole the music was gloriously sung.

Along with other superior performances of Wagner, Mahler found time to acquaint New York with the revaluations of *Don Giovanni* and *Fidelio* for which his years in Vienna will be ever remembered. On January 23, *Don Giovanni* became what it had almost never been at the Metropolitan: a completely integrated unit, in which all concerned, as Henderson observed, contributed to making the score move "swiftly, steadily, even relentlessly toward its great climax." Mahler's superbly flexible hand on the orchestra molded it into a rich fabric with the voices of Bonci (Ottavio*), Scotti (Don Giovanni), Chaliapin (Leporello*), Eames (Donna Anna*), Gadski (Elvira), and Sembrich (Zerlina). On a later occasion Farrar sang Zerlina* with "personal charm and piquancy," and Chaliapin's broad playing was held within tolerable bounds. According to Henderson, "he sang '*Madamina*,' at any rate, with humor." It was twenty years before the Metropolitan gave *Don Giovanni* again.

Fidelio came on March 20, not only with Mahler's preference for the "Leonore" Overture No. 3 after the dungeon scene, but also with a replica of the massive Roller sets that Mahler had commissioned for his Vienna revival of 1904. Although New Yorkers had more than a fair familiarity with *Fidelio* as a result of the German seasons, success, for the first time, was measured by more than how well a soprano sang Leonore. Berta Morena certainly was inferior to Lehmann and Materna, but with staunch performers such as Burrian, Goritz (Pizarro*), and Van Rooy (Minister of

Justice*), the action blended smoothly from one scene to another, and the "breathless intensity" of Mahler's conducting made for an experience the *Sun* termed "altogether absorbing."

Mahler also had a share in the season's *Ring* cycle, producing on February 7 a *Walküre* that was notable especially for the "torrent of glorious, vivifying tone" the orchestra produced in Act II, and on February 19 a *Siegfried* that impressed the same commentator (Henderson) as "more scholarly than passionate." Fremstad was the Brünnhilde in the latter, Gadski in the former. The cast adhered to arrangements familiar during the recent Conried seasons—Burgstaller, Van Rooy, Blass, etc. (with Kirkby-Lunn as Fricka*). Hertz had charge of *Rheingold* and *Götterdämmerung* in a post-season cycle beginning on April 13, and also conducted *Lohengrin, Die Meistersinger,* and a rather poor revival of *Der fliegende Holländer*. Conried's staging of the last named was praised more than the singing of Gadski, Knote, Van Rooy, and Dippel (the Steersman).

Among matters of more import, Farrar won praise for her Violetta* in *La Traviata* on February 28, 1908, an occasion she recalled in conversation nearly forty years later. Speaking of Conried, she said: "He could be so distant and yet so kind. I remember when he said to me: 'I have a present for your birthday. How would you like to sing Violetta?' " February 28 did, in fact, mark the popular soprano's twenty-sixth birthday. She won praise not only for her "willowy physique," but also for the "communicative warmth" of her singing (the *Sun*). This production, in modern dress, also presented Stracciari and Caruso. The latter, incidentally, overcame his objections to Manrico* in this season, singing in a *Trovatore* of February 26 with Eames (Leonora*), Homer, and Stracciari. He gave particular attention to the lyric music of the role, and did not disdain transposition down in *"Di quella pira,"* whose top tone was B.

Alma Mahler's reminiscence of her husband's career, *Gustav Mahler, Memories and Letters* (New York: Viking Press; 1946), shows rather clearly that as late as the end of December 1907 Conried fully expected to continue as Metropolitan director. She described their visit to the impresario at his home shortly after arrival in America, where he received them "on a divan in the middle of the room with a baldachino and convoluted pillars." His assurance that he was going to "make" Mahler rather amused both visitors.

Rawlins Cottenet, of Conried's board of directors, however, was en route to negotiate a contract with Gatti and Toscanini in January 1908. Alma Mahler states: "It is fair to say that Mahler was offered the post but declined it," though contemporary accounts indicate, if anything, a possible joint arrangement with Dippel as administrator and Mahler as musical director. This was unacceptable because both were considered Teutonic in background. Dippel's status was revealed in the press of February 15. He was described as "administrative manager," with Gatti-Casazza as "general manager." Rightful objections to the "ambiguity" of these terms was entered, the whole arrangement suggesting that Dippel was imposed upon Kahn and his associates by a faction that thought Conried should be allowed to name his successor. Gatti did not become acquainted with either his associate or the fact that he had an associate until his arrival in New York in May to examine at first hand the problems with which he was confronted.

While the affairs of the Conried Metropolitan Opera Company were being worked out, one privilege remained for Conried. That was the annual manager's benefit, which occurred this year on March 24. The repertory lacking an expensive novelty for which satisfying rates could be charged, he ordered, instead, a gala concert, in which Mahler conducted the "Leonore" Overture No. 3 and virtually the whole company appeared in excerpts from *La Bohème, Butterfly, Il Trovatore, Faust,* and *Die Meistersinger.* Van Rooy, Reiss, Goritz, and Blass, who took part in an abbreviated version of Act III of the Wagner work, may be said to have put themselves out considerably for Conried. They went to Philadelphia on a 9.25 train that morning, sang a performance of *Siegfried* with Fremstad beginning shortly before noon, and caught a five-o'clock train back to New York for the benefit. The receipts amounted to $19,119; there were tiers of flowers for the retiring director; and the affectionate directors of the Conried Metropolitan Opera Company presented him with a silver cup eighteen inches high.

EPILOGUE

A cold impartial judgment would inevitably come to the conclusion that there should never have been a man named Heinrich Conried in the Metropolitan's succession of policy-makers and influence-shapers. Too little qualified with special skills, too greatly disqualified by special inabilities, he stands forth between the self-justifying Maurice Grau and the obviously professional Giulio Gatti-Casazza as an intermediate experiment, a man who was not quite either.

The essential error of judgment was not his, of course, but that of lessors and lessees who, between them, shared the opinion that money could be made from opera less exclusively vocal than Grau's. It is not only conceivable but demonstrable, in certain years of the Gatti direction, that opera could be given without loss; but not in a framework of profit-sharing, dividends on stock, managerial benefits, and the like. Profit, in short, could be the result when the economic setting was favorable; but it could not be the motive.

To Conried's credit is the initiation of the systematic broadening of the repertory which produced the widely varied season to come. *Parsifal, Salome, Madama Butterfly, Hänsel und Gretel, La Damnation de Faust* may seem all too obvious additions to the repertory. But if Conried is to be scorned for ignoring *Louise, Thaïs, Pelléas, Les Contes d'Hoffmann,* and *Elektra,* he should be commended for the risks he ventured. *Die Fledermaus* and *Der Zigeunerbaron* would have been remembered more happily in other circumstances than the ones that governed their production.

One sound way in which Conried affected the continuing history of the Metropolitan was in the replenishment of the basic company by such notable additions as Farrar, Fremstad, Mahler, Bonci, and Burrian. Caruso, Sembrich, Eames, Journet and Scotti he owed to Grau, but several of them served Gatti well. Had either New York or Chaliapin been more flexible, Chaliapin's career might have been longer associated with Conried. It was to Conried's credit, certainly, that he sponsored the engagement, even if the wedding was short-lived.

Even to those unborn at the time, there is something unsavory and ill-judged about the double-price *Parsifal* benefit, the exploited (for profit) *Salome,* the benefit-concert *Fledermaus.* It reveals a perilously materialistic evaluation of opportunity for a man who was receiving a salary of $20,000 when such a wage was formidable.

As a practical theater man, Conried instituted some procedures both desirable and long delayed, and the general tone of comment honors this influence. They were not sufficiently accompanied by musical awareness to yield the benefits they might have brought. The directors knew better what they wanted when they chose his successor.

INCOME, PROFIT, AND LOSS
OF CONRIED METROPOLITAN OPERA COMPANY

Year	Income	Profit	Loss
1903	$1,107,000	$ 60,000	
1904	$1,285,000	$126,326	
1905	$1,209,000	$111,018	
1906	$1,312,000		$84,039 [1]
1907	$1,340,173		$95,806

[1] The decline in income for 1905 was owing in part to the abbreviated tour as a result of the San Francisco earthquake. The next year's loss is in part attributable to the cost of replacing nineteen productions destroyed in the earthquake, and in part to the *Salome* investment.

2

THE METROPOLITAN
OPERA COMPANY

THE YEARS OF TOSCANINI, 1908–1915

THE VERY REAL apprehensions with which some supporters of Metropolitan opera viewed the arrival of Gatti-Casazza and Toscanini must
seem absurd today. But there were at least two factors to create uneasi-
ness. One was the outspoken antagonism to Wagner of a substantial element
in the ownership group. The other was the national background of the
two men, and the affinity of Gatti with the house of Ricordi. I would not
say that Gatti abused his position in producing a list of hopeless works
by Zandonai, Laparra, Catalani, Riccitelli, Leoni, and others, but it could
be said that he had monumental patience with failure after failure while
Mozart languished and Beethoven was forgotten.

Toscanini, of course, needed no more than an orchestra, a cast, and
an opera to establish his place as a factor in Metropolitan history. It was
by no means a unanimous accolade he won in the works of all schools,
but his aims were so consistently high that differences of opinion could
only be with details. Gatti, who was accepted rather more grudgingly,
eventually rose to a position of pre-eminence among Metropolitan directors.

The confusion and cross-purposes that confronted Gatti with a hitherto
unknown "collaborator" upon his arrival in New York in May 1908
had more than administrative ramifications. References to the terms on
which "Toscanini would come" (see page 188) were supported by his
expectations when he did come. In correspondence with Mahler before
the season of 1908 began, Dippel spoke of Toscanini's desire to do *Tristan*
with a new production from Milan. Mahler reacted to this with the
utmost vigor: it was "inconceivable" to him that a new *Tristan* should
be planned without his knowledge, and he refused his consent (*Gustav
Mahler, Memories and Letters,* page 255). For this year Mahler prevailed;

but when *Tristan* was first given in the 1909 season, Toscanini conducted. I have been informed that Toscanini denounced Alma Mahler Werfel's recollection of events of this period as false and malicious, but the evidence is quite clear that conflicting promises were made in the name of the divided authority.

Furthermore, the circumstances of the transition made for difficulties. Many of the stars were retained on contracts negotiated with Conried in which promises of preferential possession of certain roles were implied if not stated. It is not improbable that the singers looked to Dippel to protect their interests, and when his tenure was threatened, they became alarmed (see page 202). Both Eames and Sembrich retired from the Metropolitan after Gatti's first season, though neither was even approaching retirement from singing.

On the other hand, the reorganization of the company to carry out the Gatti-Dippel plans—and, if possible, put Hammerstein's competition completely to shame—was far more ambitious than anything previously contemplated. Separate choruses, of one hundred voices each, were organized for the Italian-French and the German repertory. Giulio Setti, from La Scala, was engaged to direct the first, Hans Steiner of Munich was brought over to train the second. A pool of one hundred and thirty-five orchestra musicians was maintained, not only to relieve the "overworked" personnel of the Metropolitan itself, but to accommodate an expanded activity in the new Brooklyn Academy of Music and in Philadelphia.

The paper planning also extended to revision of operations in the Metropolitan, with eight of the twenty Saturday nights set aside for "revivals of classical works by such composers as Mozart, Beethoven and Wagner." The previously unused Tuesday was also to be incorporated into this scheme. Although Conried had restaged nineteen productions after the San Francisco earthquake, a completely new scenic program was launched, to be executed in Italy. To facilitate rehearsals, Gatti recommended the construction of a roof stage.

All this was to be done with no thought of profit-sharing by the salaried employees or the directors of the Metropolitan Opera Company. It was to be done, moreover, with no change in the price scale of five dollars for orchestra seats established by Grau and perpetuated by Conried (save for well-remembered deviations). In descending order, dress-circle seats were three dollars, balcony seats two dollars and a half and two dollars, family-circle seats one dollar and a half and one dollar. Grand-tier boxes were rented for all the performances of the season for six thousand dollars, for one performance a week for twelve hundred dollars, or sold for a single performance for sixty dollars. These prices remained without change through the 1911–12 season.

1908–1909

1907 was a panic year and 1908 a period of "hard times," but the evidence is hard to trace in the operatic activity offered to New Yorkers and supported by them. Hammerstein had no contractual or administrative problems to deal with in his venture. Indeed, the change at the Metropolitan had been to his advantage, for Conried's retirement freed the Puccini works that he had reserved under a personal contract, and the "West Side house" (as it was often described) could offer its customers a *Tosca* conducted by Campanini for its opening on November 9. Zenatello (Cavaradossi) and Renaud (Scarpia) were both performers of tested worth who gave their new roles fresh color and accent, and if Maria Labia was not the best Tosca New York had heard, she was a vigorous actress. Special attention was directed to the audience, by far the most representative Hammerstein had attracted. Winthrop Ames, Bourke Cochran, and Miss Beatrice Mills came with the Clarence Mackays, and the society reporters noted Justice and Mrs. James W. Gerard, George F. Baker, Jr., Lady Northcliffe, Mrs. Cadwalader Jones, and August Belmont in the audience.

Within the week Hammerstein offered Garden in *Thaïs,* Gerville-Réache in a more imaginative staging of *Samson et Dalila* than the Metropolitan had yet known (with Dalmorès and Dufranne, on November 11), and Tetrazzini's first Rosina in *Il Barbiere,* with Sammarco, Gilibert (Bartolo), and Andrés de Segurola as Basilio. (Segurola's brief appearance with the Grau company in the last days of the 1901–2 season had apparently been forgotten, for he was treated as a new, welcome artist.) Tetrazzini did not decorate the airs as lavishly as Patti, but she earned a right to the coveted comparison, especially in her light playing of the comedy episodes with Gilibert.

Gatti's first venture was the traditional *Faust,* not in the home house, but in the Brooklyn Academy of Music, on Saturday evening, November 14. By the measurement of the Metropolitan, this new theater was "intimate," the pleasure in the singing of Caruso and Farrar enhanced. A Hammerstein discovery, Adamo Didur was now under Metropolitan contract and admired as Méphistophélès. The conductor was Francesco Spetrino. Despite the suggestions of his name, he came from Vienna, with Mahler's endorsement.

Minus an Astor for the first time in history (see page 71), the Metropolitan opening on November 16 made the happiest kind of musical news —for Toscanini's conducting of *Aida,* of a scope not known to New York before, for Emmy Destinn's "great power, body and vibrant quality" (the *Times*) as Aida,* and for the prodigal fervor of Caruso's Radames. Aldrich thought the Egyptology of the production from Milan more splendid than consistent with "accepted ideas" of that landscape, and Henderson preferred his Radames unbearded, but there was wholesome accord on one point: Toscanini. Aldrich termed him "a strenuous force, a dominating power, a man of potent authority"; Krehbiel proclaimed him "in the best sense, an artist, an interpreter, a recreator"; and Henderson added to an optimistic forecast of a few days before ("his advent . . . ought to mark the beginning of an era in the history of Italian opera") the encouraging confirmation that "Even the principals who have sung the same roles here before showed . . . that they had subjected themselves to a general plan." Scotti (Amonasro) and Homer (Amneris) marked, with Caruso, the smooth merger of the old order with the new (Destinn, Didur as Ramfis,* Giulio Rossi as the King [d], and Leonora Sparkes as the Priestess [d]).

A performance of *Butterfly* (described by the *Sun* as "masterful") on November 19 was followed on November 25 by more Toscanini-led Puccini, when Spetrino suffered an accident prior to *Tosca* and his colleague replaced him. For the first time Toscanini's habit of conducting without score was noted. In Henderson's view, it was evident that "the conductor knew the score thoroughly and rejoiced in emancipation from the printed page." The rising graph of esteem for Toscanini took a downward turn on December 3 when his treatment of *Carmen* was described (the *Sun*) as "a misdirected attempt to refine things by eliminating most of the life from Bizet's piquant rhythms." Maria Gay made her debut as a "no more than tolerable" Carmen (d), and Farrar's Micaëla* found her in a mood of uncommon reserve.

The latter's state of mind may have well been affected by an episode of which the public had only limited knowledge at the time. In the first excitement attending the success of Gatti as producer and Toscanini as conductor, rumors spread that their one-year contracts had been superseded by exercise of options covering two further years. The implication was that Dippel would soon be dismissed. On November 25 a letter was delivered to the board of directors of the Opera Company over the signatures of Caruso, Eames, Farrar, Sembrich, and Scotti. It specified the rumors mentioned above, and expressed the "desire" of the signers "in the protection of our artistic interests and the welfare of the Metropolitan Opera House" that Dippel's contract be extended likewise. The reply of

December 6 was full of conciliatory phrases, but it confirmed Gatti as "supreme executive head" and stated Dippel's functions to be "subordinate to those of the general manager." The final effect was to leave Farrar in the bad graces of the management, for Sembrich and Eames soon left the company and Caruso and Scotti made peace with their countrymen, protesting that they had only signed out of regard for the others. Farrar has written in her autobiography, *Such Sweet Compulsion* (New York: Greystone Press; 1939) that Gatti was "quite consistently courteous," but "never could quite forget this first sign of rebellion." Her own leave-taking, years later, was not without a suggestion of such unforgetfulness.

The foreknowledge, in informed quarters, of Toscanini's rank as a conductor of Wagner was tested in *Götterdämmerung* on December 10. Some who came as skeptics remained to cheer a reading of breadth and imagination, in which Fremstad moved to command of a new Brünnhilde* with customary intelligence. Erik Schmedes, from Vienna, was rather lacking in voice for Siegfried,* and there were objections to the omission of the Waltraute episode and the restoration of the Norns. Henderson judged Toscanini prone to "dwell unduly on the phrase, to exaggerate the rhetorical pause, to smooth out all the rugged edges of the declamation"; but he found cause for greater enthusiasm in a repetition of February 24, in which a different Siegfried and Brünnhilde (Burrian and Gadski) gave "inspiriting vigor" to the duet. He commended the orchestral playing as "worthy of a Bayreuth festival."

What is now known as the typical energy of Toscanani, but was then a day-to-day phenomenon, found him mingling, with the repertory just mentioned, the productions of two works new to the Metropolitan— Puccini's *Le Villi* on December 17 and Catalani's *La Wally* on January 6—a revival of *Falstaff* on March 20, and a Good Friday performance of Verdi's "Manzoni" Requiem on April 9. Both new works were in the nature of sentimental gestures, for the Puccini one-acter was hardly more than a student work, which even a cast of Bonci (Roberto*), Pasquale Amato (Wolf*), and Frances Alda (Anna*) could not make convincing. Some opinion held that the following *Cavalleria,* magnificently conducted by Toscanini and sung with unprecedented power by Caruso (Turiddu*), Destinn (Santuzza*), with Amato (Alfio*) merited the seven-dollar top price more than the Puccini *première.* Toscanini's devotion to Catalani, one of the formative influences of his career, is well known (he labored mightily to make *La Wally* a Metropolitan success and he named one of his daughters Wally). With Destinn (Wally*), Amato (Gellner*), and Riccardo Martin (Hagenbach*) as performers of quality, Henderson thought the work might win a "tolerable measure of popular success," but it was no more durable than the early Puccini score. Neither was heard in a second season.

The old critical affection for *Falstaff* and its puzzling evanescence in the repertory were freshly revealed when "Toscanini . . . breathed into the entire representation the life of Verdi's conception" (the *Sun*) on March 20. Scotti had an "artistic triumph" as Falstaff*; Campanari was once again a spirited Ford; and such new personalities as Destinn (Alice*), Maria Gay (her Dame Quickly* was admired for "humor and brisk glee-fulness"), and Alda (Nanetta*) made for a production "in every way an honor to the house." Rinaldo Grassi was, as many Fentons* are, "pale." The venture seemingly survived what the *Sun* termed its "severest test" when a repetition on March 29, with a "most thoroughly 'smart' Monday night audience" in attendance, echoed the applause of the previous occasion. A third performance, on April 2, encouraged a hope that this time the verdict would be different, that Toscanini might make the differ-ence. There were two performances in the next season and none again until 1924.

The old clamor for "novelties" was abundantly satisfied at the Metro-politan in this season, with Hertz and Mahler supplementing the efforts of Toscanini. The first was charged with the responsibility for Eugen d'Albert's *Tiefland* when it was given on November 23, to a mixed critical reaction. Henderson deemed it a "strong and vital music drama," though doubting its future "in this Caruso-ridden town." Krehbiel deplored its "Vienna commonplaces" and the lack of authentic folk music for the Spanish subject. There was little but praise for the cast of Destinn (Marta*), Schmedes (Pedro*), and Fritz Feinhals (Sebastiano*).

Those who were fighting the Dippel-Gatti battle as well as the Metro-politan-Hammerstein competition rejoiced in the overwhelming success of Smetana's *Verkaufte Braut* on February 19, with Mahler conducting and Dippel associated in the production. The overture was a concert-hall favorite and so honored as a classic that it was played before Act II to avoid interruption by late-comers. With Mahler's Bohemian blood as one affinity and Destinn's (Marie*) as another, the words of praise ranged from Henderson's esteem for a "specimen of genuinely artistic comic opera" to Krehbiel's acclaim for a "masterpiece" given with "vivacity and lustiness." Carl Jörn was a splendid Hans,* Didur an amusing Kezal,* and Reiss an excellent Wenzel.* Ottokar Bartik directed the ballet, made up of dancers imported from Prague blended with others from New York's Bohemian-descended population.

Dippel was likewise honored for his part in a staging of *Le Nozze di*

Figaro which Mahler conducted on January 13, especially for the innovation of an interior stage that gave the illusion of bringing the action closer to the audience. Twenty rehearsals were not quite as many as Mahler was accustomed to in Vienna, but many more than New York was accustomed to in its Mozart; the "fine unity of style" he achieved was admired, as were the "clean, accurate, elastic and transparent" playing of the orchestra and the "happy issue" of the whole (the *Sun*). The cast was quite the best for a Mozart work at the Metropolitan up to this time, with Eames, Sembrich, and Farrar (Cherubino*) all in form, and Didur (Figaro*) to join Scotti (Almaviva) in the principal male roles. Didur's selection accorded with the German preference for a basso rather than a baritone in this part, and it worked out, the *Sun* observed, "better than his method would have led [one] . . . to expect." For all its luster, this *Figaro* was something of a sunset glow to a whole era of Mozart, for Sembrich and Eames sang no more after this season, and it was not until 1916–17 that the work was ventured again.

With the works freshly prepared by Toscanini and Mahler added to those carried over from the latter's first season, the day-by-day level of conducting and orchestra performance was higher than it had been at the Metropolitan for years, perhaps ever. An exceptional concurrence of critical and professional opinion can be noted in the aftermath of a *Tristan* directed by Mahler on March 12. Beginning with a headline calling it a "great performance," the *Sun* account continued: "Some years ago there was a wonderful . . . *Tristan und Isolde* at the Metropolitan. Lilli Lehmann was the Isolde. One beautiful summer day in Berlin, looking back over her past, she said 'That was the memorable Tristan performance of my life' [see page 133]. There was an Isolde [Fremstad] last night who may sometime remember with a great glow of joy her performance of March 12, 1909. A superb, a queenly, a heroically tragic Isolde this, but she was not alone in her glory. . . . Mr. Mahler hurled all petty restraints to the four winds . . . and turned loose such a torrent of vital sound as he had never before let us hear. . . . The advent of Tristan became genuinely heroic: the crash of the death motive when Isolde raised the cup to her lips was cataclysmic."

In her *Gustav Mahler, Memories and Letters* (page 119), Alma Mahler provides the echo to this in 1945: "Mahler said after a performance of *Tristan* with Fremstad and Burrian: 'The stars were kind. I have never known a performance of *Tristan* to equal this.' " "A" performance should read "the" performance, for the singers did not appear in another *Tristan* this season with Mahler. In fact, he did not conduct the work again in New York. A further interest of this performance was the advertisement of it as "complete," which no previous Metropolitan *Tristan* had been. It began at 5:30, and an intermission from 6:55 to 8:45 followed Act I. When the curtain fell on Act III, however, the press decided that cuts had been made in the last act nevertheless. A similar profession about *Die Meistersinger* on March 23 was not critically contradicted. Hertz conducted and Jörn was a well-liked Walther, with Gadski, and Walter Soomer (Sachs). The opinion was that presenting *Die Meistersinger* complete was of special benefit to the Beckmesser, on this occasion Goritz.

The other Wagner of this season was not notably different from what it had been, possibly because the orgy of scenic replenishment did not go quite so far as promised. *Die Walküre* was much as before when it was given on November 18, though Fritz Feinhals, of Munich, brought a "glorious voice" (the *Sun*) to his debut as Wotan (d). Of other interest was the debut, as Pogner in the final scene of *Die Meistersinger* at a Sunday-night concert on November 22, of Herbert Witherspoon, a basso who was destined to be the successor (briefly) of the man who engaged him. He had another opportunity to display his sonorous voice as Titurel* when *Parsifal* was presented on November 26 after a season's absence. Fremstad's Kundry was as magnificent as ever, but Erik Schmedes was an indifferent Parsifal.* Any temptation to use Mahler as conductor of *Parsifal* was forestalled by a provision of his contract, and Hertz continued as the only interpreter of this music the Metropolitan had known. The German list was rounded out by a single *Fidelio* on February 20, with Morena no more appealing than the year before.

The effort of Kahn and his associates to restore the center of operatic attention to the Metropolitan was valiant and well planned, but Hammerstein had much to offer by pursuing a program suggestive of Voltaire's: "Let us cultivate our garden." Hammerstein's Garden was cultivated first in *Thaïs* on November 11, and was still bearing fruit when *Salome* was given for the tenth time on March 26. Her first new role in this season was the modified role of Jean in Massenet's *Le Jongleur de Notre Dame* on November 27, judged by Henderson to convey "a feminine archness" more sophisticated than the "boyish innocence" of the character merited. Nevertheless, it was a remarkable piece of stagecraft, complemented by Renaud's artful Boniface and Dufranne's Friar.

Hammerstein's French production of *Salome* on January 28, with a predominantly French cast and Campanini conducting, set up inevitable comparisons with the German version of the Metropolitan. Fremstad was remembered by the *Sun* as "strange, inexplicable, complex, psychic." Garden, by contrast, was "volatile, sinuous of mind and body, quivering with emotions that lie upon the pearly surface of her flesh." Nevertheless, it added up to a "dance with commentary, for . . . Miss Garden cannot sing a phrase of Strauss's music." Save for the three musical climaxes previously admired, Henderson thought the music "a prodigious bore," and all the efforts of "Mrs. Glynn, Eugene Walters and others to persuade the community to forget childish ideas of morals" did not sway his belief that Strauss had "perpetrated an indecency." Mixing disdain with suspicious relish, Krehbiel commented: "In the climax of the dance the utmost limit of disrobing ever reached by an . . . actress . . . within a long memory was attained." By general agreement, Dalmorès was less effective as Herod than Burrian had been, Doria a fair Herodias. Dufranne sustained his usual level as Jochanaan. Campanini gave a suaver, less strenuous accent to the music than Hertz. In all, Garden and *Salome* attracted ten large audiences in this season, and Philadelphia also saw it despite clerical objections. Boston would not have it.

In addition to Garden (who sang thirty-three times, including, on March 6, an afternoon *Louise* and an evening *Jongleur*) and Tetrazzini, Hammerstein persuaded Melba to return for another season. After an exquisite Mimi in *La Bohème* on December 14 (in the able company of Zenatello, Sammarco, Gilibert, and De Segurola), Melba appeared for the first time as Desdemona in *Otello* on December 25. Campanini's flair for the score was even more pronounced than it had been twenty years before; Zenatello produced "precisely the right kind of voice for this role, a hard, brilliant, pealing tenor, with far reaching high notes," to Henderson's ear; and Sammarco gave fine vigor if not much subtlety to his Iago. After their second-act duet "the audience burst into such a storm of applause as is rarely known in an American opera house." Melba's contribution was delightful vocalization throughout, but little characterization; but her tones were so fresh and appealing that little more was looked for by the audience. On the same evening Sembrich and Bonci shared the applause of a Metropolitan audience for *L'Elisir d'amore,* followed by a Toscanini-directed *Cavalleria,* with Destinn, Gay, Martin (Turiddu*), and Amato.

The advent today of such a baritone as Pasquale Amato would be cause for cheers, and there were some when he made his debut as Germont* in *La Traviata* on November 20 with Sembrich and Caruso. His "fresh sonorous style" (the *Sun*) and his "taste in style" were approved, but a strange suspicion attached to him. He had sung some Wagner roles in Italy, and there were forebodings that he might be the first in a series of principals designed to turn back the clock to Wagner in Italian. Amato sang Amfortas* in *Parsifal* on February 22 and remained a member of the company, with occasional intervals, until 1933: but the dread thing never happened. As Marcello* on November 21, Rigoletto* on November 28, Alfio* in *Cavalleria* on December 17, through a succession of leading baritone roles (Di Luna in *Trovatore,* Tonio, Sharpless, Amonasro, Valentin, and Enrico Ashton in *Lucia*) Amato's art was staunch, his voice appealing.

Destinn's success was assured from her debut in the opening *Aida.* The greatest interest, in a series of well-liked impersonations, attached to her Butterfly, a Covent Garden sensation five years before. How might it compare with the favorite New York one of Farrar? The background of rivalry between them, from Berlin, further fed such anticipations. They were answered on February 6 as follows (the *Sun*): "Destinn does not look the childish *Cio-Cio-San* [but] the artistic glory of her impersonation is found in . . . wonderfully eloquent singing of the music, to which her dramatic voice is perfectly suited."

For Frances Alda the way was a good deal more difficult. She did not match "the standard of the house" in Henderson's opinion of her debut as Gilda (d) in *Rigoletto* on December 7, though her voice had "a pretty enough natural quality." Her Marguerite* in *Faust* on January 1 was similarly discouraging, but the critic thought it "useless" to waste words on her performance as she was going to sing for three years "no matter what is said."[1] As an alternate for Farrar when *Manon* was given on February 26, she did not quite qualify. Her best success in this season was as Nanetta in *Falstaff* (see page 204).

An artist of quality who did not have quite the American career he merited was Florencio Constantino, a Spanish tenor discovered by Hammerstein for the Bonci roles. His debut on December 6 at the Manhattan Opera House with Tetrazzini in *Rigoletto* earned him honors for "a voice of lovely quality" used "with many charming morendo effects and other ornaments of the lyric art," said Henderson. As Alfredo, Edgardo in *Lucia,* Don José, Rodolfo, even Lord Arthur in *I Puritani* (with Tetrazzini), he was consistently admired for a "voice of the most engaging quality." He made trouble for himself, however, with a notoriously difficult personality, and fared better in South America than in New York or Boston.

Sembrich and Eames both came to the end of their Metropolitan careers this season, but the manner in which they departed could hardly have been more contrasted. Each of Sembrich's final appearances in a favored role was reverently tucked away in verbal moth balls, leading to a formal farewell of February 6 in which she sang favorite portions of *Don Pasquale,*

[1] The attachment to Gatti that resulted in their marriage in the next year was well known.

Il Barbiere, and *La Traviata,* the Strauss *"Voci di primavera"* (dedicated to her), and, of course, *"Ah! non giunge"* from *La Sonnambula.* There were gifts in profusion, and Eames, Gay, and Destinn paid her the compliment of posing as guests in the first act of *La Traviata,* in which Farrar sang the small part of Flora, with Scotti, Didur, and Amato, as, respectively, Barone Douphol, Dottore Grenvil, and Marchese d'Obigny. On the following evening Sembrich was honored at a dinner at the Hotel Astor, the guest list extending from Mr. and Mrs. Richard Aldrich to Dr. Ludwig Wüllner.

For Eames there was no ceremonial and no dinner. Of her parting *Tosca* on February 15, the *Sun* said: "The career of a prima donna has not been one of unqualified pleasure to Mme. Eames. . . . She has also suffered from great nervousness and has been overanxious about her voice. . . . It would be natural for her now to seek . . . recreation." Many flowers and a wreath from Gatti were lavished on her, and after the second act she was repeatedly recalled, finally telling her audience: "This is good-bye. . . . You have been very kind, but you have been very exacting. You have called for the best I commanded, and whatever is good in me you have brought out. Therefore I owe much to you. My love I leave with you and I go."

Gatti offered his public thirty-one works this season, Hammerstein twenty-five. Several promised novelties—Converse's *Pipe of Desire,* Goldmark's *Cricket on the Hearth,* Laparra's *Habanera,* and Tchaikovsky's *Pique-Dame*—were laid over for another year. The Metropolitan lost $205,201, or more than in any year since its very first; Hammerstein made, according to his son Arthur, $229,000. A final incident of the long season came on April 27, when Heinrich Conried's death was reported from Meran, Austria. Having kept in force an insurance policy on his life, Kahn and his associates collected $150,000. When $58,000 had been disbursed to Conried's widow for settlement of various claims, the Metropolitan Opera Company still had a sizable sum to apply to the losses of 1906–7 and 1907–8.

1909–1910

The last season for years in which New York was to be flattered by two resident companies in simultaneous operation provided it, paradoxically, with opera in three places. The New Theater, under construction since 1907, was now completed; the geographical spread of operatic action extended from Thirty-fourth Street and Eighth Avenue to Sixty-first Street and Central Park West. "New" as it was, the uptown theater had a grave liability from the start, being "on the wrong side of town," socially speaking. In time this objection might have been overcome, but the multiple activity elsewhere and some fundamental objections to the acoustic properties of the auditorium closed its history, for serious music-making, almost before it had begun.

The famous restlessness of Hammerstein asserted itself in a variety of ways, beginning with a season of "educational opera" in the Manhattan late in August,[1] and extending to an operatic venture in Philadelphia that brought him close to bankruptcy. He was an influential factor in establishing a Chicago Opera also, for when news came to Otto Kahn, in Paris, during October, that Hammerstein was about to make a deal with local underwriters for an opera company, he proposed a counter-deal that resulted in a season beginning in the Auditorium Theater on November 3, 1910 (see *How Grand Opera Came to Chicago,* by C. J. Bulliet). How two erstwhile competitors in New York—Andreas Dippel and Cleofonte Campanini—became collaborators in Chicago was but an incident of this unprecedented winter.

Actually, Campanini succumbed to the Toscanini competition, as Vigna had succumbed to the Campanini competition. There was no decline in esteem for the popular Cleofonte, but he demanded additional rehearsal time to meet the improved Metropolitan standard, and Hammerstein rejected the request. Thus the final Manhattan season began on November 8 without Campanini for the first time, if with still another novelty, Massenet's *Hérodiade.* According to the *Sun,* the "production bedazzled the eye and beguiled the ear," thanks in part to the return of Lina Cavalieri, whose art showed "very considerable" improvement, as Salome. Henrique de la Fuente was the new conductor who led skillfully a cast that included Renaud as Hérod and Dalmorès as John the Baptist (reversing the tenor-baritone arrangement of the roles in Strauss), with Gerville-Réache as Hérodias. Further comparisons between Strauss's hard-bitten Salome and the "affectionate sentimentalist" drawn by Massenet left only such words as "pleasant" and "ingenious" for the latter.

In the framework of the time this was just one more performance of an opera, but it had a significance not appreciated until much later. As well as being an appreciably talented opera singer, Cavalieri was a woman who not only fascinated men, but married them as well. One of her numerous conquests was Robert Winthrop Chanler, of the Astor kin,

---

[1] He declared it a success, in his usual way, by saying it "lost only $50,000 instead of the $150,000" he expected. The repertory included such characteristic works as *Louise, Les Contes d'Hoffmann, Le Prophète,* and *Carmen,* and introduced a number of artists of quality, among them Marguerite d'Alvarez, Marguerite Sylva (who sang both Nedda and Santuzza in a double bill on September 17), Alice Baron, and Alice Gentle. Giuseppe Sturani was the usual conductor.

born in 1872, who succumbed to Cavalieri in Paris after her early Metropolitan appearances (1907-8). As Harvey O'Connor puts it in *The Astors:* "For 'one week of joy and terror' he lived with Lina, who demanded he sign over his entire fortune to her. . . . A friend lent him fare to escape to America, where to his relief he found that his trustees —his older brothers—refused to recognize his deed of gift to Lina. She was forced to be satisfied with only a part of Bob's million and a divorce." She was hardly welcome at the Metropolitan after that, and when Hammerstein persisted in presenting her in New York, the threatened "reprisals" culminated in the plan to buy him out.

On this November 8, the Metropolitan began its Brooklyn season with Farrar and Jörn in *Manon,* and the new Boston Opera House opened with *La Gioconda.* Constantino had been hired away from Hammerstein to perform for Henry Russell, the Boston impresario. Russell then enjoyed an amiable relation with the Metropolitan which allowed him to present Nordica, Homer, and Anna Meitschik (one of Gatti's new singers, as La Cieca). A Baltimore season using Metropolitan talent was also ventured. Before it was over, opera had radiated from New York as far south as Atlanta and overseas to Paris (see page 221). It was an epoch of empire-building, and if in railroads, why not in opera? All one could lose was a fortune—and some did.

That, however, was hardly a deterrent to the men "of high social position and almost fathomless financial means" observed by the *Sun* at the Metropolitan opening of November 15. This *Gioconda,* a more splendid one than Boston's, was imported from Milan and dubbed "remarkable." Under Toscanini's urgent baton the orchestra was found "to be worthy of a great lyric theater." Caruso sang *"Cielo e mar"* with "beautiful cantilena," and Destinn, Amato, Meitschik, and De Segurola collaborated in a "vital interpretation . . . rare at all times and in all places."

Here, certainly, was a crossroad. As the critical ear harked back to other Giocondas, Enzos, Barnabas, to Nilsson, Fursch-Madi and Del Puente, the eye and the mind had to agree that something closer to the whole of Ponchielli's invention was being experienced. A page had been turned, and on it was inscribed a new set of standards by which the presentation of opera was to be measured. As big and bold as John Hancock's, the signature thereto was plainly Arturo Toscanini's.

The Manhattan Opera offering of this November 15 was *Lucia* with Luisa Tetrazzini, and a tenor of "very pretty quality," John McCormack, as Edgardo. He had made his debut on November 10, in a *Traviata* with Tetrazzini, and won encouragement from the *Sun* for "a lyric tenor voice of much natural beauty," and from the *Tribune* for its quality of "rare sweetness." His acting was almost as naïve as Caruso's had been in his early years, but he sang many a fine operatic performance before deciding that concert-singing was his true métier.

On Tuesday night, November 16, the third ring of New York's operatic circus swung into activity with Massenet's *Werther,* the first opera to be given in the New Theater. Farrar sang Charlotte* and the young Alma Gluck had an amazing success as Sophie,* in a surpassingly fine cast with Edmond Clément (Werther*) and Dinh Gilly (Albert*). Lest he be thought remiss, Hammerstein initiated an *opéra-comique* season of his own on the same night, with *La Fille de Mme Angot.* The cast lacked notable names, but there were many who preferred Lecocq to Massenet.

Guarded opinions about the qualities of the New Theater became more outspoken after a Hertz-directed *Verkaufte Braut* on the following afternoon provided a more dependable measurement of its properties. In some spots the voices predominated; in others, the orchestra. Most seriously, the hoped-for intimacy had not been achieved, largely because of that endemic New York ailment, too many boxes. "What a pity," commented the *Sun* of November 20, "that the wealthy men who so generously contributed the money for the erection of the house were not a little less liberal in their ideas. If they had been less concerned about providing an auditorium large enough to furnish themselves and society with a certain element of exclusiveness while at the same time offering abundant accommodations for 'the people,' we should have had a smaller theater and perhaps conditions more favorable to both drama and opera bouffe." (The boxes were at the rear of the orchestra, but no small liability to its design nevertheless.) The ensuing contrast with the Munich Residenz Theater and its "revolving stage" (in 1909) is more than I can bear to reproduce.

Lamentations were short-lived, however, in a week that brought Leo Slezak's debut as an Otello* of "prodigious physical height and lofty artistic stature" (the *Sun*) on November 17, in a performance under Toscanini that "gave the significance of this noble score to a degree perhaps never surpassed here." Scotti was Scotti as Iago, but Alda was not Melba as Desdemona.* The harried journalists spent as much of the evening as they could allot at the Manhattan, where Massenet's *Sapho* was having its American *première* with Garden. Her Fanny Le Grand was a "tone poem of costuming," in Henderson's view, and brilliantly acted, the score without a page that would withstand "searching examination." Krehbiel, however, found much of it "admirable and ingratiating." Dalmorès (Jean), D'Alvarez (Divonne), and Dufranne (Caoudal) were all dependable.

The withdrawal of Sembrich and Eames left several of their favorite roles open for qualified replacements, but the coloratura parts fared more poorly than the dramatic. Lydia Lipkowska was offered as Violetta* in *La Traviata* on November 18, but her light voice and pretty appearance did not satisfy yearnings for Sembrich. On the other hand, *Tosca* with Farrar on November 22 and Fremstad on December 11 offered something of interest with each new impersonation. Farrar, a "beauteous vision in vermilion and grey," left for the future a full realization of "The Appeal to the Virgin" (still not called *"Vissi d'arte"*), but the reasons for Scarpia's (Scotti's) interest were quite evident. Fremstad's Tosca* was "interesting, because she is too intelligent to do anything badly" (Henderson), and artistically composed, if not successfully costumed. Amato was the new Scarpia,* and a promising one. Fremstad had a greater success in a part long associated with Eames when she sang Elsa* in *Lohengrin* on December 18 with "a skill that commanded not only admiration but even astonishment." Recalling her beginnings as a mezzo, the *Sun* described her management of the high tones "as clever in the extreme."

While Tetrazzini was drawing applause for Marie in *La Fille du régiment* (with McCormack, Gilibert, and Duchène), for Gilda in *Rigoletto* (with McCormack and Renaud), and in *Lakmé* (with McCormack and Huberdeau), the Metropolitan had no more than Lipkowskas under other names. One was Bernice de Pasquali, who had sung briefly in the previous season, and returned, without critical urging, in *L'Elisir d'amore* and *Don Pasquale;* another was Elvira de Hidalgo, who made her debut as Rosina (d) on March 7. The *Sun* recognized that she was "young and inexperienced," and was "expected to show promise, which she did," but doubted that "old frequenters of the Metropolitan . . . [considered] the institution as a nursery for little girls." On January 14, Jane Noria "assisted in lowering the standard of the prima donna to a point never known" in Metropolitan history with her Marguerite* in *Faust*. The *Sun*'s sweeping judgment was not without a background: Mme Noria, who had sung as Jane Ludwig with various small opera companies, was now the wife of Gatti's secretary, Centanini. Her right to sing was thus suspect.

The low estate of the high voice was an undoubted matter of concern, but there was a rising line of esteem to meet and surpass this falling one. Gluck's *Orfeo* had been given at the Metropolitan in 1891, and 1893, and 1895 without setting any standards save for ineptitude. Its presentation on December 23 with Toscanini conducting invoked some dusty comparisons with a concert version by Theodore Thomas in 1896, but even this could not match the "taste, enthusiasm, and musicianship" that governed the present production, its possession of both "repose . . . and the tragic note." Henderson further described Homer's Orfeo* as the "most satisfactory vocal art she has exhibited at any time," and Aldrich in the *Times* found

Gadski's Eurydice* "admirable in style." Alten was Amor.* An enchanting bit of song was provided by Alma Gluck as the Happy Shade.* Toscanini amended the Gevaert version by inserting *"Divinités du Styx"* from *Alceste* as a climax to Act I, adding a trio from *Paride ed Elena* after *"Che farò,"* and substituting a chorus from *Echo et Narcisse* for Gluck's finale. On January 20 a well-regarded French contralto, Marie Delna, sang Orfeo (d), with results that prompted Henderson to say: "Her respect for rhythm was slight . . . which must have taxed Mr. Toscanini's skill to keep the accompaniment in union with her." The general regard for her beautiful voice did not alter Delna's feeling that she had been ill-used, and she left the company, complainingly, after four further appearances. The incident, however, was not quite closed (see page 221). As for *Orfeo,* it remained a Metropolitan honor almost as long as Toscanini did.

The inexorable fulfillment of the predestined conditions on which Toscanini "would come" to the Metropolitan occurred in this season when he conducted a new production of *Tristan* on November 27 and his first *Meistersinger* on March 26. Mario Fortuny, described as "a one time friend of Wagner," was the designer of the former, which was given with Gadski, Burrian, Homer, Blass, and Amato (Kurvenal*). Of this generally familiar cast, none had previously sung with so much "finish of phrase, tone and nuance" said the *Sun.* The orchestral direction, "unexpectedly subdued" in Act I, "surged in inspiring grandeur" in Act II, and the climax of Act III was brought out "with superb power." On December 8 Nordica reappeared to sing her last Metropolitan Isolde,[1] to Krehbiel's ear "very near to what it was a decade ago in beauty of tone . . . and dramatic intensity." On December 27 Fremstad's Isolde was commended by Henderson as "one of the loveliest portraits in the Metropolitan's Wagnerian gallery."

There were no major disagreements about Toscanini's *Tristan,* but his *Meistersinger,* with Gadski, Slezak (Walther*), Soomer (Sachs), Goritz, and Reiss, was more controversial. For Aldrich, in the *Times,* it was his Metropolitan masterwork, a "profoundly beautiful and poetical performance" that reached "a pitch of perfection . . . of instrumental color . . . unique of its kind." In Henderson's opinion, the very Italianness of the treatment was inimical to "German thought, custom and feeling." The lyric episodes were read with "insight and sympathy," but the lighter moods suffered from "the manifest inability of the conductor to saturate himself with the spirit of the scene . . . from his failure to follow every nuance of

---

[1] This ill-starred singer did not sing again in opera at the Metropolitan, and rarely in public after a nervous breakdown that kept her inactive until 1913. She was en route to Australia for a concert tour when she became ill and sought hospitalization in Java, where she died on May 10, 1914, at fifty-seven.

the dialogue." This included the Dance of the Apprentices—"heavy, tame and angular"—and the gathering of the guilds. The second act, Henderson agreed, was "musically wonderful." Few Walthers since De Reszke had approached Slezak for vocal power, pride of bearing, or rightness of action.

This remarkable tenor, of the towering figure, the sizable girth, the eloquent voice, and the effervescent spirit, came with little forewarning and dominated a series of roles both exacting and various. Otello, as mentioned (page 212), was the first, followed by Manrico* in *Il Trovatore* on December 1, Radames* in *Aida* on December 29, Tannhäuser* on January 17, and several novelties before the climactic Walther von Stolzing. The *Sun* (not Henderson, who was busy elsewhere on that night) termed him "the most impressive Radames in years," and Aldrich found some of his performances "superb." When he sang his Tannhäuser, after a series of Italian parts, Henderson resorted to terms rarely used since the German seasons to commend his "beautiful devotion to high dramatic ideals." His "splendor of voice, skill in tone production [and] clear enunciation" were worthy testimonials to his studies with Adolf Robinson and Jean de Reszke. In an article of January 23 the same writer likened him to the fabled Niemann, arguing that this "youthful giant" (Slezak was then thirty-seven) might rise to a like "commanding position."

Slezak's part in the novelties to which he was assigned was universally commended, their ephemeral place in the repertory being in no way his fault. Flotow's *Alessandro Stradella* was new to New York when given on February 4 at the Metropolitan, though it was destined for the repertory of the New Theater. The "shallow and facile melodies" (the *Sun*) lacked the appeal that made Flotow's *Marta* an occasional pleasure, all to the disadvantage of Slezak's handsome, well-sung Stradella,* the Leonore* of Gluck—sung with a "beauty of tone that is valuable beyond price," said Henderson—and the Malvolio* of Goritz. Max Bendix was the conductor.

Tchaikovsky's *Pique-Dame* might have lasted longer in the repertory had it not been an enthusiasm of Mahler which did not survive his abbreviated association with the Metropolitan. When it was first given on March 5, Henderson admired its "singularly insinuating musical power," while confessing doubt that its elements of the supernatural would interest an American audience. Krehbiel was also sensitive to the Russian's "genius for dramatic expression," and praised the "splendidly sung and beautifully staged production," which duplicated the Viennese revival of 1902 pioneered by Mahler, with Slezak. The "remarkable finish, delicacy and finesse" of the orchestral playing were especially appealing to Aldrich. For the cast of Slezak, an imposing Hermann,* Destinn, a powerful Lisa,* Meitschik (Countess*), Didur (Tomsky*), and Gluck (Chloe*), only praise was written. Russian being no more a Metropolitan language then than now, *Pique-Dame* was sung in German.

The Toscanini novelty of this season was Franchetti's *Germania,* which left more perplexity than pleasure when it was heard on January 22. Why such high-powered talent as Amato (Worms*), Caruso (Federico Loewe*) and Destinn (Ricke*) should be combined with Toscanini's was not demonstrated by a work Henderson described as "utterly Italian, bewilderingly historical and weightily realistic." Krehbiel granted it the polite praise of the damning "effective," but it was soon abandoned. As well as the two Wagner works and the Gluck, Ponchielli, Verdi, and Franchetti operas already mentioned, Toscanini also directed *Aida, Butterfly,* and *Falstaff* this season. The last was heard twice, on February 16 and 21. By Henderson's word, "the performance as a whole lacked the musical incisiveness" of the year before. Scotti and Destinn remained of the previous cast, and Jeanne Maubourg was admired as Meg.* Homer (Dame Quickly*), Clément (Fenton*), and Pini-Corsi (Ford*) were not. *"Vecchio John"* was silent thereafter until 1924.

As early as the first week of January, indications were clear that time was running out for Hammerstein. Business was good, but Hammerstein continued to make curtain speeches threatening a program of vaudeville if it did not improve. In other public statements he complained that operasingers were so much in demand that managers had to come to them instead of vice versa. That, obviously was bad—for the managers. On January 10, he half-jokingly offered to give up his own venture and produce French opera for the Metropolitan. A few days later he denied rumors that he would soon give up opera in New York, on payment of one million dollars. The "rumor" was remarkably close to the truth.

In an editorial the *Sun* took account of these unfolding developments and declared "the chief obstacle in the way of making opera self-supporting" was that stars were "too highly paid." The Metropolitan's problem would "without doubt be greatly simplified" if Hammerstein were bought out, but the *Sun* hoped this would not happen. His competition, the editorial continued, "has built up a public interested in operas in addition to the interest in singers," with compulsive effect on the Metropolitan to raise its standards in "chorus, orchestra and *mise en scène.*" For the Metropolitan to expand into other markets would be a better solution than for it to purchase "a golden silence of the loquacious Mr. Hammerstein."

Whatever impended, Hammerstein went cheerfully ahead with his program, which included the introduction of Massenet's harmless *Grisélidis* on January 19, with Garden, Dalmorès (Alain), Huberdeau (Méphistophélès), and Dufranne (Saluzzo), and the long-awaited *Elektra* of Richard Strauss on February 1. It had been scheduled and postponed several times, as rehearsals revealed the need of prolonged preparation. When it occurred, the immediate reaction was an upsurge of esteem for Mariette Mazarin, whose previous appearances as Aida and Elisabeth (in a French *Tannhäuser*) had suggested nothing like the capacities to sing, as Henderson put it, "with astonishing accuracy an interminable series of notes" scarcely related to old concepts of harmonic sense. For Aldrich, no previous effort showed "the dramatic power, the intensity of conception . . . that shine in this achievement of hers."

The opera was another matter. Estimates of the text ranged from Henderson's denunciation of its "putrid morbidity" to Krehbiel's contention that it ventured "into the madhouse." The power of Strauss's score at its climaxes was acknowledged, along with early stretches Henderson found "deadly dull." To Aldrich, *Elektra* at its greatest "scarcely rises to the splendors that mark the great climaxes of *Salome*" (the so-recently-denounced *Salome*!), while Krehbiel compiled what seemed a scholarly allusion by calling *Elektra* "as unHellenic as Bernard Shaw's notion of Cleopatra is un-antique—or rather, let us say, was, for all of these artistic abortions fortunately pass away quickly." Gerville-Réache as Clytemnestra and Huberdeau as Orestes were both excellent, but it was imagined that the score might sound quite differently under a conductor less polite, gentle, and considerate than De la Fuente.

Not the least reported occurrence of the *première* was the collapse of Mazarin as she was taking her curtain calls with Hammerstein, Jacques Coini, the stage director, and De la Fuente. She was quickly revived, however, and continued her season's work with performances of Elektra on February 7 and 12. The latter performance, on a Saturday afternoon, found Hammerstein faced with an emergency, Cavalieri being unable to appear in the evening's *Hérodiade*. Mazarin volunteered to sing Massenet at night after Strauss in the daytime, and Hammerstein quickly had a gold watch inscribed for her to honor the double duty. On March 24, the Manhattan gave its last day of Hammerstein opera—Garden as Salome in the afternoon, Mazarin as Elektra at night. According to the *Sun,* "he issued Richard Strauss commutation tickets by the purchase of which the user could attend both performances for the price of one."

As if anticipating the events to come, Hammerstein left New Yorkers with the memory of a gigantic gala, which began at 8:20 with Cavalieri and Gentle in an episode from *Les Contes d'Hoffmann* and was in progress at 11:30 when Garden had finished an excerpt from *Roméo et Juliette,* with an hour's music still to come.[1] Hammerstein kept up his bold front, promised better things for "next year," and twitted the Metropolitan for losing more money than he had.

Despite the apprehensions expressed about the future of German opera, especially Wagner, under the Gatti-Toscanini influence, the Metropolitan gave all of that composer's works commonly included in the repertory (excepting only *Rienzi* and *Der fliegende Holländer*), including a restaged *Lohengrin* as well as the new *Tristan*. Hertz was the conductor on November 20 of a performance endorsed by the *Sun* for its stress on "interpretation of a music drama as a whole rather than on the vocal glories of the famous singers in the cast." The cast included Gadski, Jörn (Lohengrin*), John Forsell (Telramund [d]) and Homer (Ortrud). The first *Parsifal* on November 25 marked the debut of Clarence Whitehill as Amfortas (d), beginning a twenty-year career with notable promise. He sang a much-admired Wanderer* in *Siegfried* on December 16, and a Wotan* in *Die Walküre* on January 8 praised by Henderson for "beauty of tone, musical phrasing and nuancing . . . much nobility . . . and dignity of style." He also sang a fine Gunther* in a *Götterdämmerung* on February 1, which concluded a *Ring* cycle begun a week earlier. Hertz conducted the whole cycle this year, and also prepared a revival of *Der Freischütz,* first heard on March 11. Gadski's Agathe* was well liked; not so the Max* of Hermann Jadlowker or the stodgy Caspar* of Blass. Admiration for the "beautiful and expressive" set pieces was not great enough, in Henderson's opinion, to make a "contemporary audience" endure the spoken dialogue.

Quite conceivably *Der Freischütz* would have sounded much better in the New Theater, but it was not given there. In all, the hodgepodge of works, aspirations, and purposes revealed by its repertory (see page 220) makes a mockery of its pretensions. No work of Mozart was given there or at the Metropolitan itself this winter, though Gustav Mahler of the superb *Don Giovanni* and the matchless *Figaro* was in New York, and on call.

A review of the New Theater repertory shows, after the opening *Werther* (see page 212), a sequence of *Il Barbiere* on November 25 (Lipkowska, Campanari, and De Segurola), Lortzing's *Zar und Zimmermann* on November 30, with Goritz as Van Bett, sprinkling the German text with what the *Sun* called "gags" in "Metropolitan Opera House English," and Paër's *Il Maestro di Cappella* on December 9 as works properly associated with an "intimate" theater. The audience that admired Pini-Corsi's laughable Com-

---

[1] Garden sang at least one complete opera of Gounod—a composer not usually associated with her New York career—when she appeared as Marguerite in *Faust* on December 8, 1909. The best-known critics were busy with Nordica's final Isolde on the same night, but the *Sun* described it as "surprisingly effective," marked by "significant phrasing and nuance."

poser and Alma Gluck's piquant Gertrude in the Paër *bouffe* was not likely, however, to care much about *Cavalleria,* which followed with a Metropolitan "second cast"—Noria, Martin, Wickham, and Gilly.

The admired productions of this season also included *La Fille de Mme Angot* on December 14, with Jeanne Maubourg a tall, vivacious Mlle Lange, and Clément an excellent Ange Pitou. Despite the inferior De Pasquali as Norina, *Don Pasquale* on December 23 was a connoisseur's delight as sung by Bonci, Scotti, and Pini-Corsi. An uneven revival of *Fra Diavolo* on January 11, with Clément rather unsuited for Diavolo, but Maubourg an attractive Lady Pamela, preceded the production of Bruneau's *L'Attaque du moulin,* which was remembered by some as the most memorable experience of the New Theater season. Delna (Marcelline) and Clément (Domique) sang roles for which they were celebrated in Paris, with De Segurola and Gilly in the supporting cast.

The first in Gatti's long series of experiments with native opera came to the New Theater on March 31, when Frederick Converse's *The Pipe of Desire* shared a triple bill with two ballet *divertissements.* It had first been given downtown on March 18, with a critical reaction that foreshadowed a pattern of reaction to such works to come: the handicap of a "hopeless text"(in Henderson's estimation) expressed through a melodic invention sometimes pleasant, but more often "wanting in rhythmic contour." Martin (Iolan*), Homer (Noia*), Whitehill (the Old One*), and Witherspoon (First Gnome*) were as able a native cast as Gatti could provide, but the lack of intelligibility in the singing was held against the setting of the text, not the singers.

On eighteen occasions ballet was a part of a Metropolitan double bill this season, most satisfactorily when the principal dancers were Anna Pavlova and Mikhail Mordkin. They made their debut on February 28 after a performance of *Werther* that ran well past eleven o'clock, but those who remained for a one-act version of *Coppélia* saw the finest dancing yet offered in New York. Glazunov's *Hungary* was given four times by them in their series of Metropolitan and New Theater appearances.

The approaching solution of New York's unbalanced operatic equation was intimated by the resignation on April 1 of Andreas Dippel and his subtraction from the factors involved. He was to become head of the Chicago Grand Opera Company, it was stated, and rumors that he was leaving the Metropolitan because of the fiasco at the New Theater were declared false. Gatti's *Memories of the Opera* is categorical on this point: Dippel insisted on the New Theater program, and opera in Brooklyn and Philadelphia and Baltimore, as his area of operation. Gatti reluctantly agreed, on the condition that Dippel would withdraw if it failed. It failed, and Dippel withdrew. A covering statement from the Metropolitan Opera Company praised Dippel for his part in "bringing about a very considerable increase" in audience interest "in the Wagnerian performances" of the last two seasons, and pledged that Gatti's "eclectic taste" would support the "traditions of internationalism in art" for which the Metropolitan stood. One may wonder whether Dippel himself did not draft this salutation, which concluded with thanks to him from the group, via a comforting Germanicism, "in whose services you have been since twenty years."

The headline-writer who counted out the spaces and then wrote over a *Sun* story of April 28: "METROPOLITAN A MONOPOLY BY PAYING $2,000,-000" exaggerated nothing but the sum paid to Hammerstein in the long-expected, oft-denied plan of settlement. The cash that changed hands was $1,200,000, out of which Hammerstein paid his debts to E. T. Stotesbury of Philadelphia and surrendered to him ownership of the theater he had built at Poplar and Clarke streets. He also agreed not to engage in the production of opera in New York for a period of ten years, a restriction also binding on his son Arthur. The indomitable Oscar was in Europe when news of the hardly hoped-for settlement was cabled to him. He made plans almost immediately to use the money left from the payment of his debts to build a massive theater on the Kingsway in London—for opera. As Stoll's, it remained in use until the 1950's.

STAGE WORKS

GIVEN DURING THE 1909–1910 SEASON

[1] Metropolitan Opera House
[2] Manhattan Opera House
[3] New Theater

Aida [1, 2]	Elisir d'amore, L' [1, 3]
Alessandro Stradella [1, 3]	Falstaff [1]
Attaque du moulin, L' [3]	Faust [1, 2]
Barbiere di Siviglia, Il [1, 3]	Fille du Mme Angot, La [2, 3]
Bohème, La [1, 2, 3]	Fille du régiment, La [2]
Carmen [2]	Fra Diavolo [1, 3]
Cavalleria rusticana [1, 2, 3]	Freischütz, Der [1]
Cloches de Corneville, Les [2]	Germania [1]
Contes d'Hoffmann, Les [2]	Gioconda, La [1]
Don Pasquale [1, 3]	Götterdämmerung [1]
Dragons de Villars, Les [2]	Grisélidis [2]
Elektra [2]	Hänsel und Gretel [1]

Hérodiade [2]

Jongleur de Notre Dame, Le [2]

Lakmé [2]

Lohengrin [1]

Louise [2]

Lucia di Lammermoor [2]

Madama Butterfly [1, 3]

Maestro di cappella, Il [3]

Manon [1, 3]

Mascotte, La [2]

Meistersinger, Die [1]

Navarraise, La [2]

Orfeo ed Euridice [1]

Otello [1]

Pagliacci [1, 2, 3]

Parsifal [1]

Pelléas et Mélisande [2]

Pipe of Desire, The [1, 3]

Pique-Dame [1]

Rheingold, Das [1]

Rigoletto [1, 2]

Salome [2]

Samson et Dalila [2]

Sapho [2]

Siegfried [1]

Sonnambula, La [1, 3]

Tannhäuser [1, 2]

Thaïs [2]

Tosca [1, 2, 3]

Traviata, La [1, 2]

Tristan und Isolde [1]

Trovatore, Il [1, 2]

Verkaufte Braut, Die [1, 3]

Walküre, Die [1]

Werther [1, 3]

Zar und Zimmermann [3]

TOTALS

Number of works	60
Performances at the Metropolitan	138
Performances at the New Theater	40
Performances at the Manhattan	109
Total of performances	287

Aside from the $1,200,000 raised from various sources to buy off Hammerstein the opera competitor, Hammerstein the importer of Cavalieri, and Hammerstein the interloper in Philadelphia, the Metropolitan supporters had to reckon with a loss of $248,795 on the manifold activities of the year. These did not end until late in June, for Kahn and company decided that the Metropolitan was ready for display in Paris, opening a month-long season at the Châtelet on May 21. Of the opening *Aida,* with Destinn, Caruso, and Homer, the press had a mixed view. It considered the ballet and settings of the Paris Opéra superior to the visitor's, but complimented the leading singers. Toscanini was greeted with hisses before Act II, thought by some to be inspired by the grievances of Delna. During his engagement, Lucrezia Bori appeared in several performances of *Manon Lescaut,* but could not yet accept a New York engagement owing to commitments at La Scala. Pierre Lalo's rounded view of the Metropolitan as a "casino company"—meaning the sort that a summer visitor might see in

Biarritz, Deauville, or Vichy—was indignantly refuted by the American press when the slur reached New York.

The excitement and interest that Oscar Hammerstein contributed to opera in New York can be gauged not only from the operas and artists he introduced, but also from the powerful forces he set in motion. First in Philadelphia and Chicago, then with Chicago as base, they continued to fertilize the operatic soil in a way unmistakably his for a full twenty years.

1910–1911

Having vanquished, in a mere matter of twenty-four months, both the internal and the external opposition to their ideas—as represented by such formidable names as Mahler and Campanini, Hammerstein and Dippel— Gatti and Toscanini entered upon a period of financial well-being—and for a time artistic accomplishment—without parallel in opera. Public acceptance of the product they provided was manifest in steadily mounting pre-season subscriptions. From the fifty- or sixty-thousand-dollar advance sale of the German period, the three or four times that amount of the Grau seasons, or even the half-million reached by Conried, the subscription sale mounted steadily toward and past the million-dollar mark.

Free of Dippel's contrary ideas and the irritating competition of Hammerstein, Gatti was able to plan, on a clean slate, the first of his twenty-five years of unencumbered management. Performances in Brooklyn and Philadelphia were restricted to the unengaged Tuesdays; the double chorus and orchestra were reduced to less expensive numbers. To accommodate the tastes stimulated by Hammerstein, the new Philadelphia-Chicago Opera Company was welcomed on a series of Tuesday nights while it was based in Philadelphia. For the first time the Metropolitan season was extended to twenty weeks. Gatti's planning to make the Metropolitan a prime center of opera produced the first world _premières_ [1] in its history—Puccini's _La Fanciulla del West_ and Humperdinck's _Königskinder_. There was some talk, too, of _Così fan tutte,_ but the desired cast was not available.

How Toscanini thought a great opera house should function may be judged from his choice of Gluck's _Armide_ for the opening on November 14. A recent revival in Paris had stimulated interest in its possibilities for spectacle and ballet, fulfilled in a way to win the _Sun_'s praise as "worthy of a great art institution." Of particular quality were the designs of Puvis de Chavannes (he had done the previous year's _Orfeo_), for which Henderson had such words as "enchantingly unreal," "dark and forbidding," and "dazzling." Dominating the musical performance was the superb Armide*

---

[1] Converse's _Pipe of Desire_ had been given in Boston prior to its Metropolitan introduction.

of Fremstad, an accomplishment even more impressive than Homer's Orfeo. Krehbiel admired Caruso's adaptability in singing Renaud,* but to Henderson "he did not look happy" with the declamatory style or the recitatives. Dinh Gilly (Ubalde*) was well suited for the French manner, but Amato (Hidraot*) and Bada (Chevalier Danois*) decidedly were not. The basic fact deduced from every such sporadic attempt at restoration of a bygone style was plain in *Armide:* it is only the exceptional singer, a Fremstad or a Flagstad, who can slough off conventional mannerisms and strike a new, pure manner. No one, however, could decry what Henderson termed Toscanini's "affectionate sincerity and deep study," which gave profound pleasure to half a dozen more audiences in this and the next season.

Fremstad's versatility was warmly remarked when she turned from Gluck to Wagner to sing in the second night *Tannhäuser* on November 16. It provided "four towering artistic figures," said the *Sun:* Fremstad (Venus), Slezak (Tannhäuser), Soomer (Wolfram), and Morena (Elisabeth). After a year's absence Morena returned to sing "her music so beautifully that critical comment can only be a description of excellencies" (the *Sun*). Morena was also a fine Sieglinde in *Walküre* on November 18, but a new Hunding,* Basil Ruysdael,[1] performed his music in a "sepulchral, ejaculatory and tremulous" manner, and Lucy Weidt, from Vienna, did not overimpress in her debut as Brünnhilde (d). Hertz was sometimes guilty of his "old fashioned exuberance," but no one would call his conducting perfunctory.

This being a Puccini year, with the composer in New York from the season's start, Toscanini extended himself to show the best of which the theater was capable. When *Butterfly* was given on November 19, Henderson found Farrar "rich in captivating qualities," and the conductor's work full of "voluptuous coloring," though he also ventured the opinion (noting it as *lèse-majesté*) that the scale of orchestral sound was sometimes "not friendly to the voices." Presumably the composer approved a change of detail in the action before Butterfly's suicide. Farrar gave the child a doll and pushed it out in the garden before her hara-kiri. When Sharpless entered to find her dead, he had the child in his arms. As a compliment to Puccini, Toscanini conducted *Bohème* for the first time in New York on November 21. Jadlowker had a great success with Rodolfo,* and the "troublesome finale of the second act went wonderfully well and with great clearness" (the *Sun*).

Few things in Metropolitan history stimulated so much worldwide interest as the first showing of *La Fanciulla del West* on December 10. With the composer viewing the rehearsals, supervised by David Belasco, whose

[1] Radio provided this basso with a greater celebrity as an announcer, years later.

play was utilized, and Toscanini to conduct a cast including Caruso (Johnson*), Destinn (Minnie*), and Amato (Jack Rance*), every favorable factor was present. An enormous public response, even at doubled prices, created a stir that was reflected in the six-thousand-word review in the *Sun* and the scarcely shorter ones in the *Times* and *Tribune*.

When the embellishing phrases were reduced to essentials, several things emerged. Guelfo Civinini and Carlo Zangarini, the librettists, had taken Belasco's terse colloquial text and given it a coloration of Italian librettoese which warred with the familiar action. In the pattern of action, Puccini had not found opportunities to "permit his characters to sing out their thought in long phrases," according to Henderson. Aldrich, in the *Times,* agreed that "the new work shows considerably less fecundity of melodic inspirations . . . than Puccini's earlier one," but thought its lack of melodic flow a willful effort to put more of the drama into the orchestra. The collaborators—Belasco, Puccini, Gatti—were unanimous in praise of the performance, which Aldrich characterized as "one of Mr. Toscanini's masterpieces, so vitalized, so full of detail, so broad in its outlines." While he remained to keep these attributes fresh, *La Fanciulla* held its place in the repertory,[1] but it dropped away thereafter, and a revival of 1929 with Jeritza and Martinelli did not prosper. It had a surprising return to favor after the revival of 1961–2, possibly because the "West" no longer had realistic connotations and could be accepted in the same spirit of fantasy as any other operatic locale.

Farrar found one of her most characteristic parts, as the Goose-Girl,* when Humperdinck's *Königskinder* was presented on December 28, with the composer present and Hertz conducting. The original plan to present it the previous year at the New Theater had fallen through when the composer failed to meet the schedule, and the late delivery of the score prevented its presentation with an English text. Some opinion held that this was unfortunate, that a larger public would be reached in this kind of work with a vernacular text, but the "genuine sincerity" and "the imagination" that Henderson found in Farrar's performance worked its spell on many an audience till German works were banished during World War I. Krehbiel approved the "admirable characterization" in the score, if not all its "Wagnerisms." By general critical agreement, the first and third acts were quite fine, the second decidedly weak. Jadlowker (the King's Son*), Goritz (Spielmann*), and Homer (A Witch*) were outstanding in a generally good cast. Farrar's charm and enthusiasm won her lavish applause,

[1] Campanini conducted the Chicago *première* on December 27, 1910, in which the singers were Renaud (Rance), Carolina White (Minnie), Bressler-Gianoli (Wowkle), and Bassi (Johnson). The last-named was borrowed by the Metropolitan when Caruso became ill in March.

to which she responded, at the work's end, by appearing with a goose in her arms. For Humperdinck there was something more tangible: a silver wreath presented by Gatti.

The new estate of Farrar as a generative factor in Metropolitan productions may be seen in her participation on March 29 in the season's other substantial novelty, Paul Dukas's *Ariane et Barbe-bleue*. Among those who esteemed Debussy's *Pelléas,* it had something of the same *succès d'estime.* Henderson described it as "a good play and excellent opera," filled with "filamentous, funicular, festoons of music." For Krehbiel, the "excruciating dissonances" of *Pelléas* were again audible, and he did not approve the "Gardenish" impersonation of Farrar. By other count, she was a "gorgeous saffron clad figure" (Henderson), who read the text splendidly and sang the music with compelling effect. The skill and sympathy of Toscanini's conducting also fostered belief that Dukas's score would bear the test of repetition, but it was put aside after seven performances the next year. Maubourg (Sélysette*), Rothier (Bluebeard*), and Wickham (Nurse*) were others in the Farrar-dominated cast. Gatti's commendable policy of giving a second chance to works not commercially successful when first offered was sometimes rewarded by increased response, but it was not so with Franchetti's *Germania.* Two performances on February 1 and 6 closed its Metropolitan history.

For the most part Gatti's company this season was little different from what it had been. In more or less immediate prospect were two singers of the sort he needed: Lucrezia Bori and Frieda Hempel; but until they could be extricated from binding contracts, not much could be done. One recourse was to borrow Melba, Constantino, and Renaud for a *Rigoletto* on November 24, a cast that suggested, to the *Sun,* "an opening display of the goods acquired through the closing out" of the Manhattan. Melba's "silvery voice," in the same account, preserved "much of its early beauty." She appeared on November 29 in a *Traviata* that introduced John McCormack as Alfredo* and Carlo Galeffi as Germont.* A non-subscription affair, it left some empty seats, though what Melba did with *"Sempre libera,"* said Henderson, should have been "a dazzling revelation to many younger singers." Krehbiel was partial to McCormack's "delicate phrasing . . . the feeling and tenderness" of his art, but Henderson held him "a mild and inoffensive" Alfredo. Melba suffered one of her prolonged indispositions after this and did not sing again in the Metropolitan. In later seasons she appeared with the Chicago group at the Lexington Theater.

The decline in *bel canto* per se was marked in other directions. *Roméo et Juliette,* heard on January 13 in a new production for the first time since 1906–7, provided in Farrar a Juliette who sang "with many strange and warring qualities of tone," and in Dimitri Smirnoff a Roméo* "dead, flat, colorless" (Henderson's opinion). Dinh Gilly (Mercutio*) and Léon Rothier (Frère Laurent*) gave sound French schooling to what they did, but there were audible complaints that a return to the style of Eames and the De Reszkes was overdue. It seems rather more remote now.

Other glories there were, however. What the *Sun* called "the inspiration of the fervid and intelligent . . . Arturo Toscanini" illuminated his conducting of *Tristan* on four occasions, with Fremstad and Gadski as alternate Isoldes who excelled themselves from one performance to another. Destinn and Gadski were the alternating Evas in *Die Meistersinger,* and when the Walther was not Slezak, it was Jörn. Aside from a "methodical" treatment of the comedy, Henderson found Toscanini's *Meistersinger* full of "high and beautiful" qualities.

As long as Toscanini remained at the Metropolitan, he conducted no other works of Wagner—a neat fulfillment of the conditions stated as basic in his New York engagement. The public subsisted otherwise on a diet of Hertz, who presided when Slezak sang Lohengrin* [1] on December 9. "He was without question," said the *Sun,* "the largest swan knight ever seen in this town." He was also a singer of artistic dignity and fine expressiveness, who accorded admirably with Fremstad, Homer, and Goritz. The vexed matter of the Lohengrin-Telramund duel was at large again when Goritz fell to earth with no blow from Slezak's sword. According to the *Sun,* this reflected the influence of Bayreuth, where Cosima's "whims" rather than "the text of Wagner" were respected.

Doubtless to confute those who felt that Dippel's departure would adversely affect the quality of the German productions, Gatti and his staff produced a *Ring* cycle, beginning on February 2, which had something virtually unknown to this time at the Metropolitan—a smoothly functioning, convincingly pictorial production of *Rheingold.* "Lights shone in the proper places and with the proper degree of force," Henderson reported. ". . . Steam rose and ceased when it was right that it should do so, and it did not make too much noise." Not all the performers excelled previous standards, but the theatrical purpose was soundly achieved. On February 9, Fremstad sang Brünnhilde* in *Die Walküre,* with special success in the womanly attributes of the roles, though the high range of the *"Ho-jo-to-ho"* was uncomfortable for her. Morena and Gadski were the succeeding Brünnhildes, Burrian the Loge, Siegmund, and Siegfried. He also sang Parsifal on Thanksgiving Day, with Fremstad as Kundry and Amato as Amfortas.

---

[1] At the Metropolitan or elsewhere—legend is undependable on this point—Slezak as Lohengrin perpetrated one of his classic witticisms. Lingering over his farewell in Act III, Slezak turned to find that the swan had been towed off without him. Turning to a chorister he inquired: "When does the next swan leave?"

Amato added to a growing esteem with his singing of Iago—"bold, vigorous and inspiriting," said the *Sun*—on March 11 in one of five performances of *Otello* directed by Toscanini. Slezak was persistently convincing in what many considered to be his finest part, adding to clarion tone a heroic stature as Otello; but Rappold was a weak Desdemona. Scotti was the honored Iago at the first performance, on February 27.

The happy arrangement by which Campanini conducted the best of Hammerstein's repertory at the Metropolitan began on January 24 with *Thaïs*. Garden, Dalmorès, Renaud, and Bressler-Gianoli were received by an enormous audience, with Campanini singled out for special applause by some who remembered his youthful debut in the house twenty-seven years earlier. On January 31 *Louise* sounded in the Metropolitan for the first time, improved over its earlier hearings by the inclusion of the role of Le Noctambule, sung by Edmund Warnery. Garden and Dalmorès performed with familiar artistry, but the Father was sung by Dufranne. The cherished Gilibert had died suddenly in New York the previous October 11. *Pelléas* came on February 7, with *Les Contes d'Hoffmann* and *Carmen* thereafter.

For his final three operas Campanini chose works not previously heard in New York: Victor Herbert's *Natoma,* Wolf-Ferrari's *Il Segreto di Susanna,* and Jean Nouguès's *Quo Vadis?* Book trouble was a disturbing liability of *Natoma* when it was heard on February 28, though Henderson could not grant the admired operetta-composer[1] credit for more than "a sorry assault on this puerile nonsense." What stands out now, stood out then: the same critic found the Dagger Dance "really excellent." Garden made something thrilling of Natoma, for all its weak music, but McCormack's Lieutenant Paul Merrill was not merely as bad as the role: it was worse.

Wolf-Ferrari's *Secret of Suzanne* was quite another matter, once the critics had finished with the linguistic problem of a French play composed for a German translation (Max Kalbeck's) and sung in Italian. To Henderson it showed that "Italy still possesses a master capable of writing real opera buffa," and Krehbiel pronounced it "highly enjoyable," even "quite marvellous" in the way the composer turned "smoke into music or music into smoke." In the *première* on March 14, Sammarco was the Count, and Carolina White sang Suzanne. *Le Jongleur,* with Garden, Renaud, and Dufranne, followed. The Roman revels of *Quo Vadis?* as realized by Nouguès impressed Henderson, at its hearing on April 4, as lacking "all distinction of style or character," and Krehbiel gave it rank as second-rate Massenet, "inoffensive to good taste and judgment." Arimondi, a basso,

[1] Herbert's *Naughty Marietta* was concurrently making considerable money for Oscar Hammerstein in a production starring Emma Trentini.

was offered in the role of Nero, written for a tenor, and a full set of worthy names—Renaud (Petronius), Dufranne (Chilo), and Zepilli (Lygia)— could not redeem the workaday score.

Journalistic conjectures regarding the money-making results of the season were fended off by managerial contentions that the tour was "usually a financial failure," regardless of other factors. Kahn, embarking for Europe in April, said he would be content with "a modest loss." Actually the books showed a profit of $34,915. Stability was reflected in the announcement, as the year's activity was ending on April 15, that the next season's revivals and novelties would be chosen from a list of thirteen works, including *Così fan tutte* and Ravel's *L'Heure espagnole*. The Ballet Russe of Diaghilev was also promised. On May 18, 1911 the unhappy news reached New York that Gustav Mahler, whose ill-health had frequently interrupted his schedule of appearances with the New York Philharmonic Orchestra, had died in Vienna. His final Metropolitan appearance had been on March 21, 1910, when he conducted *Pique-Dame*.

1911–1912

Not all the promises indicated above were fulfilled by Gatti at once, or in the immediate future, but the world's operatic resources—of both operas and artists—were so plentiful that plans could be both altered and improved over a summer. If they had to be altered without being improved, facile explanations were always available from Gatti's new official intermediary, William J. Guard. The lank, bow-tied, bemustached flute-playing publicist and gentleman to the press had won friends as phrase-polisher for Hammerstein when that impresario's invention flagged—as it rarely did —but the more substantial area of operation now open to him did not find him wanting. When the press, lacking other operatic news, published a statement containing "the annual announcement of Farrar's rejection of Scotti's proposal of marriage," the fine Irish hand of Guard—a native of Limerick, no less—was unmistakably evident.

The ring of familiar names in greater profusion that tolled in the second decade of the century was mingled with another sound to become increasingly familiar. For the first time since 1891, prices were raised from five dollars to six for orchestra seats. As justification, the company's business controller, John Brown, pointed to greatly increased charges for services, if not for goods, since 1900: "Conductors' salaries have increased nearly 300 per cent," he said, "the orchestra one hundred per cent, the chorus and ballet from sixty to eighty per cent." With the additional revenue and the box office economies initiated by Earle E. Lewis (who stayed on for forty more seasons), Brown was confident that expenditures would not exceed income. Gatti's work justified that confidence, if not always the artistic values it implied.

The second of Toscanini's opening *Aida* performances, on November 13, could hardly exceed the effect of his first, three years before, his own standard now being thoroughly known. But it produced, in a cast with Caruso, Destinn, Amato, and Didur, an Amneris* of "imposing presence," with a "superb, rich and very flexible" mezzo used with "genuine vocal art" (Henderson). This was New York's introduction to Margarete Matzenauer, of whom nothing was known save that she came from Munich. When she had sung a dozen more leading roles in this season, her place in the Metropolitan hierarchy was very close to the top in her category.

Just what that category was, however, Matzenauer herself seemed not always quite sure. On November 17 she sang Brangäne* to Fremstad's Isolde in a performance marred by Burrian's hoarseness, but glorified by a new eloquence in Toscanini's conducting (Hermann Weil as Kurvenal and Lambert Murphy as the off-stage sailor made debuts of no special note). She sang a superb Waltraute* in *Götterdämmerung* on November 23, in a manner "intensely emotional, seldom overdone," said Henderson. In sequence came Ortrud* in *Lohengrin* on November 25, Hate* in *Armide* on December 16, and an unexcelled Orfeo* of "great repose and nobility" on Christmas Day. Her fine Erda* in *Siegfried* on December 30 lent character to a performance further embellished by a new setting for Act II (Hans Kautsky of Vienna was the designer). With Burrian, Reiss, Putnam Griswold (Wanderer*), and Gadski powerfully conducted by Hertz, contemporary judgment doubted that a better ensemble could be heard in Europe.

These were all accomplishments in an admirable but conventional pattern. Matzenauer moved beyond it in a rather majestic way on New Year's Day when Fremstad was indisposed for Kundry in *Parsifal*. Henderson's description conveys the character of Matzenauer's "substitution": she was a Kundry* "heroic in figure, moving with all the majesty of an ancient Oriental queen, large limbed, magnificent in frame and gesture, [who] nevertheless sounded the sweetest depths of sensuous tenderness." The magnitude of the accomplishment grows with the knowledge that it was Matzenauer's first Kundry anywhere. Aldrich observed that though "Matzenauer is so much a contralto, she has in her voice the higher notes to sing . . . Kundry . . . without obvious effort." Thus encouraged, Matzenauer ventured the Brünnhilde* in *Die Walküre* on February 26, without such friendly approbation. In all those sections relating to the "laughing Valkyrie," thought Henderson, "her singing was heavy, labored, and comparatively ineffective." Earlier she had sung the Frickas* of *Rheingold* and *Walküre* with great distinction. Her polished French style was valued as the Nurse* when *Ariane et Barbe-bleu* was given on January 31; and when it came to La Cieca* in *Gioconda* on February 16, the *Sun* found it "hardly necessary to add that this admired artist sang the music beautifully." In all, Matzenauer came to recognition as a paragon of the Schumann-Heink order, and more versatile.

The long-delayed debut of Tetrazzini as a member of the Metropolitan company finally occurred on December 27, when she and Constantino, of Hammerstein background, were blended with Amato and Witherspoon in a superior *Lucia*. Aldrich thought the voice had "gained in fullness and even in power," though what had been "a suspicion of tremolo" was now "confirmed." Henderson measured her as "a vocal virtuoso who has a small stock of extremely effective artifices," but the huge audience cherished what it heard, including the sextet twice. Her voice was finally blended with Caruso's on February 6 in a *Rigoletto* that, with Renaud and Rothier in the cast, gave the younger public a sample, at least, of the excitement that potent names created in Grau's day. None could remember, however, when a line of standees began to form at half past one in the afternoon (this was a Tuesday night, not included in the subscription series), and patience finally exceeded bounds when the doors were opened at seven o'clock. The line dissolved into a milling throng at the box office, the attending police wielded night sticks, and some standees were nursing bruised ribs as well as sore feet when the long day ended with what the *Sun* called "a good performance." It was estimated that two thousand more persons than the house could hold were turned away from this final appearance of Tetrazzini as a member of the Metropolitan company.

The systematic expansion of the repertory may be observed from the very first week of the season, which bracketed with the opening *Aida* and a well-sung *Tristan* such newer works as *La Fanciulla del West*, *Königskinder*, and the unknown *Lobetanz* of Ludwig Thuille, on November 18. This was apparently an enthusiasm of Hertz, for the score had not traveled widely since its *première* at Mannheim in 1898. Henderson granted the composer "facility in construction without large gifts of invention," while Krehbiel protested the "banal mood" that afflicted its tale of a sick princess and the wandering minstrel who revives her. Jadlowker (Lobetanz*) and Gadski (Princess*) were strong materials for Hertz to work with, and Lambert Murphy won special attention for "uncommonly pretty singing" in the brief part of a Youth.* The handsome production was seen no more after this season.

This year's foreign composer to attend a Metropolitan *première* in person was, in the aftermath of the previous year's successful introduction of *Il Segreto di Susanna,* almost inevitably Ermanno Wolf-Ferrari. Campanini's pioneering had earned him first call on the composer's latest work, *I Giojelli della Madonna,* and the Metropolitan had to content itself with *Le Donne curiose,* dating from 1903. Nevertheless it was a novelty of sorts, even to the composer, who said enthusiastically: "I have never realized what was in my opera until I heard it today for the first time in Italian." This seeming contradiction is easily explained: Wolf-Ferrari had been excluded from most Italian theaters because he did not care for the terms on which G. Ricordi offered to publish his works. He accepted, instead, the sponsorship of a Leipzig publisher (Rather), which was consistent with his own residence in Munich, where he had grown up musically. (His parentage was German on his mother's side, Italian on his father's.)

The composer's delight had been foreshadowed by the critical response to Toscanini's treatment of *Le Donne curiose* on January 3, which ranged from Krehbiel's endorsement of the whole project as possessing "great merit" to Henderson's enthusiastic response to "a treasury of brilliant delights, of musical inventions and fancies." The latter thought it should be "heard often, and the oftener it is heard the better it will be liked." Farrar was a delightful Rosaura,* working perfectly with a cast that included Jadlowker (Florindo*), Scotti (Lelio*), and Didur (Ottavio*). The full evening of lightness and bravura was rounded out by a showing of the Mordkin and Ekaterina Geltzer Imperial Russian Ballet (see page 234). Wolf-Ferrari had a warm reception when he arrived from Europe to attend the repetition on January 6, with ten curtain calls after each of the first two acts. Although he was already behind the schedule that called for him to assist in rehearsals for the Chicago *première* of *I Giojelli,* he lingered in New York for the excusable indulgence of hearing Toscanini conduct *Tristan* on January 8.

The accolade of a Chicago success was hanging over *The Jewels of the Madonna* when Campanini brought the work to the Metropolitan on March 5, but its qualities were too compelling for sectional frictions to assert themselves. "The opera has singular, sinister and striking power," wrote Henderson, "mingled with pure beauties of no uncommon order." Krehbiel's aesthetics judged that the composer had "followed the spirit of young Italy into the slums of Naples." He noted its "occasional beauty," but found much of it "quite as disreputable as part of that population." High praise was accorded Carolina White for her singing of the "appallingly exacting" (Henderson's phrase) music of Malielea, and the Hammerstein tradition of ensemble was honored by the work of Sammarco (Rafaele) and Bassi (Gennaro). Campanini's direction was brilliant, the response to the orchestral intermezzi prompting their repetition. For these "Jewels," James G. Huneker had the scathing word "Paste!" as the heading for his review in the *World,* but the public response was keen when the Chicago-Philadelphia company gave it again on March 19. On this occasion, Grenville Vernon, Krehbiel's associate on the *Tribune,* observed: "The final scene of the second act was made . . . much less offensive to the Roman Catholics in the audience by Miss Carolina White omitting to place the Virgin's crown on her head."

By this time the six new works promised in the schedules of the new companies had all been seen, and it was quite clear that Wolf-Ferrari's two works were the best of them. Leo Blech's one-act *Versiegelt* was noted with respect but no great affection when it was offered on January 20 with Gadski (Gertrud*) and Goritz (Lampe*), but the company's first full-length opera by an American, Horatio Parker's *Mona,* called for more extended consideration at its *première* on March 14. It was the product of a competition that enriched Professor Parker (he was head of the music department of Yale University) by ten thousand dollars and much printed tribute to his scholarship. For a change, the text by Brian Hooker was praised for literary qualities, though not as a model of dramatic craftsmanship. To Henderson, "Mr. Parker's musical design [was] fundamentally untheatrical," compromised by a "high minded but unrealistic avoidance" of usual theatrical devices. Krehbiel applauded the "fine capacities and high ideals" of both Hooker and Parker, deeming the work sound enough to profit from revisions. Homer's fine Mona* and the able Arth* of Witherspoon led a mostly American cast well conducted by Hertz, but all the first-night enthusiasm of friends and well-wishers could not provide *Mona* with momentum to carry it beyond a single season.

The apparently endless store of works by Massenet was drawn upon for still another unfamiliar to New York when Garden masqueraded as Prince Charming in *Cendrillon* on February 20. The contention of some German writers that Massenet was merely mimicking the Humperdinck of *Hänsel und Gretel* was reviewed by Henderson and rebuffed with the comment: "Humperdinck builded better than he knew; Massenet only as well." Krehbiel thought it "a pretty opera, but conventional," and "robbed of much of its musical and dramatic grace" by Garden's treatment of the male role. Maggie Teyte was praised by Henderson as "a sweet and simple" Cinderella; the supporting work of Dufranne (Pandolphe) and Louise Bérat (Stepmother) was also commended. Rosina Galli, whose future included rank as the second Mrs. Gatti-Casazza, was listed in the program as "Premiere Danseuse Etoile." A week before (February 13), *Carmen* brought a "seething mob," as the *Sun* termed it, to the Metropolitan for Garden's first New York Carmen. Henderson esteemed it "a serious and in some respects a successful attempt to sing the music," the dramatic conception showing more than "a trace of Catherine of Russia." "Harridan," "trollop," and "termagant" were also in his description. Dalmorès, Renaud, and Zepilli shared attention with Campanini's powerful conducting.

Massenet was flattered by an unprecedented care for the sum of his writing when Toscanini directed *Manon* for the first time on March 30, with Farrar, Caruso, Gilly, and Rothier (Comte des Grieux*). Fine singers of the individual roles had been frequent if not commonplace in Metropolitan history, but not such tight-knit weaving together of the many strands in the score. "It would be difficult to over-praise the beauty of the orchestral part," said the *Sun*. "It was full of spirit yet . . . charmingly treated in the details of nuance." It was to become even better as Toscanini impressed his conception on the performers, Farrar particularly. Another work commonly awarded casual treatment which was to be ennobled by this conductor's intensity and what the press now termed his "unflagging" energy was *Tosca*. On December 21 Destinn gave a new accent to Tosca,* making her "a woman of the people," in Henderson's phrase, "well-poised in her splendid independence." She was hardly endowed by nature to fill Sardou's image, but the "fine artistic intelligence" of her singing struck fire against Caruso's Mario and Amato's Scarpia. A distinction in Toscanini's direction was the clarification of the finale of Act I, which he made "go as he has not done before." He also persisted in his promotion of *Otello,* which had four performances this season, all with Alda (now known to some as the *padroncina*) as Desdemona. She had been absent for more than a year, and her reappearance on February 21 earned the *Sun*'s praise for "the simplicity and gentleness" of her characterization. It was beginning to be feared, however, that "Scotti's 'Iago' is not what it used to be vocally." Slezak was the usual, and able, Otello.

One of a steadily growing number of American singers who progressed from an apprenticeship abroad to a sound career at the Metropolitan was Putnam Griswold, who sang a notable Hagen (d) at his debut in *Götterdämmerung* on November 23. Another new singer of Wagner this season was Hermann Weil, a rather dry-voiced but well-schooled singer who was heard as Gunther* in the same *Götterdämmerung,* later singing such roles as Wotan, Wolfram, and Hans Sachs. He was Telramund in a *Lohengrin* on January 29 in which Destinn was Elsa.* Her treatment was more emotional than customary, but the *Sun* recorded that "the music lies well for her voice and its pure lyricism is well-suited to her style." Jadlowker and Homer were in this cast. In another *Lohengrin* on December 22, the tenor was Heinrich Hensel, liked both for his "naturally beautiful voice" and for the smart rap he delivered to Telramund's shield in the first-act duel. He was not ready, however, for such larger roles as Siegmund or the Siegfrieds, and did not return. Also members of the company but briefly were Theodora Orridge, an English contralto who sang La Cieca* with what Henderson termed a genuine "voce di teatro" in *La Gioconda* on November 29, and Mme Charles Cahier, who sang Azucena (d) in *Il Trovatore* on April 3 and Amneris in a post-season *Aida* on April 12. Well known on the concert stage under the name of Mrs. Morris Black, Mme Cahier was rated an intelligent singer, but not a compelling one theatrically. She became celebrated as a teacher and coach, her products of later Vienna years including Marian Anderson.

Though the promised Diaghilev Ballet was not produced, Mordkin was given prominence in a group called the Imperial Russian Ballet, this time with Ekaterina Geltzer as ballerina. In addition to *divertissements* or an abbreviated *Coppélia* after the shorter operas, it began a series of matinee performances on Tuesday, December 19, with Tchaikovsky's *Lac des cygnes.* By the *Sun* account, this was a novelty to New York, and the *Sun* warned that the popular Mordkin was "by no means the leading figure" of the four-act ballet. It added further: "If one goes to such an entertainment expecting to find himself in the presence of . . . high art he is going to be disappointed." Geltzer was reckoned a "charming dancer . . . well-equipped . . . in special 'steps.' "

The familiar pattern of the Sunday-night concerts—money-making combinations of operatic excerpts with a popular instrumentalist (De Pachmann, Zimbalist, or Spalding as guest artist)—was occasionally interrupted for more elevated music-making. On January 28 Wolf-Ferrari conducted his cantata *La Vita nuova,* and on April 14 Joseph Pasternack, an associate conductor of the opera company, directed a concert version of Monteverdi's *Orfeo.* This followed the precedent of one the year before in Rome (after a lapse of approximately three centuries since it was written), with Weil, a baritone, singing Orfeo, and Fornia, a soprano, Euridice. The musical edition of Giacomo Orefice and an English text were used.

The satisfaction of the management with Gatti and Toscanini was expressed in midseason by joint contracts for another three years. The off-the-record knowledge that the season was financially satisfactory prompted the *Sun* to say, editorially: "The disposition of a season of such magnitude without loss must be credited to great cleverness in the offering of the attractive features of the repertoire and company." There was, in fact, a profit of $52,075.

1912–1913

The gradual acceleration of the opera-producing mechanism that was to function with irresistible momentum for another dozen years was sharply stepped up in this one. A commitment of long standing kept Toscanini in South America till mid-December, but the able Giorgio Polacco was now at hand to replace him. Lucrezia Bori and Frieda Hempel were finally available for New York, and a cherished project of Gatti and Toscanini gave the Western Hemisphere acquaintance with a whole new school of opera when Mussorgsky's *Boris Godunov* was introduced.

The choice of Bori's debut for the opening-night performance of *Manon Lescaut* on November 11 was actually two stages removed from Gatti's intention. The honor was to have been the more celebrated Hempel's, in a new production of *Die Zauberflöte,* but it was decided that rehearsals for this could not be organized in the pre-season period. A change to *Les Huguenots* was decreed, but all thought of Hempel was banished when she became ill before sailing. Gatti's confidence in Bori was justified, however, by the reaction of press and public, if not uniformly at once, before many weeks passed. "Lucrezia Bori they call her," wrote Henderson in a pre-season comment, "but her real name is Lucrezia Borja." This was considered too sinister for stage use, and the familiar form substituted. On the evidence of her Manon* he deemed her "a light soprano of very moderate power," who was "not yet a consummate vocal artist," but sang "a phrase or two with perfect placing." Krehbiel's admiration was more pronounced: after a first act "pallid and infantile" in sound, she surprised "by exquisite diction, impeccable intonation and moving pathos." All were in agreement on her physical graces, complementary to a cast with Caruso as Des Grieux and Scotti as Lescaut.

Bori was heard "with pleasure, though perhaps not with rapture" (Henderson), as Nedda* to Caruso's Canio on November 20, with rising esteem as Mimi* on November 28 and Antonia* in *Les Contes d'Hoffmann* on January 11; but it was her Norina* in a Toscanini-directed revival of *Don Pasquale* late in the season (April 5) that changed reservations to raptures. Toscanini's feeling for the *opera buffa* style was quite without precedent, and he conveyed it masterfully to the cast of Scotti (Malatesta), Pini-Corsi (Don Pasquale), Umberto Macnez (Ernesto*), and Bori. Her Norina was acclaimed by Henderson for "brilliancy of style . . . understanding . . . and communicative temperament."

Despite Hempel's absence, Gatti proceeded with the newly prepared *Magic Flute* (the English name appeared on the program, though the German text was used), offering, as Queen of the Night,* Ethel Parks, whose debut the previous season had been prevented by what Henderson termed "a gift of the gods," and Krehbiel described as "the arrival of the stork." In either case, she provided a small voice distinguished only by brilliant staccati. Otherwise the event of November 23 was a revelation: Slezak's Tamino* showed Henderson "unsuspected mastery of elegant . . . musical style"; Destinn rose to "brilliant distinction" as Pamina*; and Edward Lankow, an unfortunately short-lived American, demonstrated the first "real basso profundo" the Metropolitan had heard in years in his debut as Sarastro (d). Goritz (Papageno) and Reiss (Monostatos) were veterans of the Conried-Mottl venture of 1904. Even without a Ternina for the First Lady (Vera Curtis was the present one), the Kautsky scenery and Hertz's painstaking direction produced, in Henderson's phrasing of the general view: "The only adequate presentation of this work that has ever been made in this city . . . without question the finest spectacle . . . the lyric drama has known" here. On December 29 Gadski was Pamina, and Jörn sang Tamino.* Hempel was finally heard as Queen of the Night* on January 10. This performance was quite creditable, but not an overwhelming success.

The facts in the Hempel case did not become clear until January 29, when she sang a Violetta whose first act was endorsed by Henderson for its "full bodied tone . . . immense buoyancy . . . and artistic attention to the meaning of the text." Previously she had sung Marguerite de Valois in *Les Huguenots* at her debut on December 27 with "thin and cold tone," and, to Krehbiel's ear, more "power and better quality" in the high range than the low; a Rosina* in *Il Barbiere* on January 1 complimented by Henderson as "very accurate" and with "facility in colorature" not surpassed "within the memory of the present generation"; and Olympia* in *Les Contes d'Hoffmann* on January 11.

If these words seem, on the whole, complimentary, it must be remembered that Hempel's advent had been awaited for nearly two years and that she came with a formidable reputation from Berlin. Her first Violetta and its repetition showed that the effects of her illness lingered long after her debut, and she had, for all the well-founded respect for her technical competence, not performed as she could and would. Her Gilda* on March 27 had "moments of grace" for Henderson, but even a new production of *Rigoletto* with Gilly (Rigoletto) and Macnez (the Duke*) could not stimulate much interest at this point of a crowded season.

The pleasures of Offenbach were admitted to the Metropolitan on almost regal scale when *Les Contes d'Hoffmann* took its place in the repertory on January 11. Fremstad sang a Giulietta* of ravishing physical beauty and suitable voice, Bori was credited with a "well-conceived" Antonia* sung in her "usual style," and Hempel performed with charm as Olympia.* No challenge was offered to Renaud's multiple mastery, for the roles he had performed were divided among Rothier (Dr. Miracle*), Gilly (Dappertutto*), and Didur (Coppelius*). Macnez was a weak Hoffmann,* and Maubourg no better than previous, unsatisfactory singers of Nicklausse.* But the serious attention to musical detail under Polacco, and the rich variety of characterizations provided by the leading ladies began a long history of Metropolitan success for *Hoffmann.*

The phrase might stand as well for *Boris,* when it was introduced on March 19, save that where *Hoffmann* merely titillated, *Boris* stimulated vastly. Despite the debatable emendations of Rimsky-Korsakov and the use of an Italian text, Toscanini's conducting and the "thoughtful, eloquent, well-studied" Boris* that Didur created gave a universal appreciation of Mussorgsky's genius hitherto unknown in America. In one way or another the critical view coincided with Aldrich's high valuation of "the novel and seizing imaginative quality of the music, often rude and unpolished . . . rising with relentless power to the tragic culmination." The production was the one executed by Golovine and Benois for Paris in 1908, bought abroad for use in New York. It remained in actual use until the late thirties, when a new painting was executed from the same designs. The well-chosen cast included Paul Althouse as the False Dimitri,* Homer (Marina*), Case (Theodore*), Segurola (Varlaam*), and Rothier (Pimenn*). One of Gatti's most laudable choices was to give the work without interruption for the next sixteen seasons, validating his statement when the work was new: "I consider *Boris* the most important performance artistically I have given at the Metropolitan."

Remarkable as it may seem, the production of *Boris* was but an incident —if a splendid one—of Toscanini's abbreviated season. He put a new price on company discipline, and made his artists pay it, if grudgingly, when he suffered a "sudden and violent" indisposition (in the *Sun*'s phrase) just before his season's first *Tristan* on December 20. *Götterdämmerung,* with Hertz conducting, was given instead. Actually, two members of the announced cast of Fremstad, Burrian, Matzenauer, Griswold, and Weil decided they would not attend a rehearsal, and Toscanini would not conduct without it. When *Tristan* was given on December 30, Gadski was Isolde and Homer sang Brangäne, and the reader is privileged to draw his own inference. On the other hand, when Jacques Urlus, of Holland, became voiceless after the first act of his debut as Tristan (d) on February 8—there being no Dippel or other convenient substitute—Toscanini shepherded him safely through the evening with no permanent effect on his vocal organs. Urlus made a welcome place for himself at the Metropolitan thereafter, as did Carl Braun (King Marke [d]).

With the new *Boris* and *Don Pasquale* productions barely launched in March and April, Toscanini took hold of another major task on April 13, a concert of symphonic music that included not only the Ninth of Beethoven but also Wagner's *Faust Ouvertüre* and Strauss's *Till Eulenspiegel*. "Too much is said about Mr. Toscanini's 'genius,'" wrote Henderson, "and not enough about his scholarship, his profound comprehension of orchestral tone values and skill in adjusting them." For Aldrich, "He revealed in the fullest measure the qualities of the great symphonic conductor," and prompted a phrase often paraphrased later: the performance was "devoted to the exposition of Beethoven and not of Mr. Toscanini." The splendid solo quartet (Hempel, Homer, Jörn, and Griswold) shared honors with the excellent choral singing. Years later, Henderson recalled as a new impact of Toscanini's treatment the sharply articulated attack on *"Freude!"* and the precision and marching force of the choral singing. The concert was repeated on April 18, with almost as large an audience as had been attracted by the first playing.

Under the stimulus of such events emerged what might be termed an era of good feeling with the press, strengthened by Gatti's clearly conscientious effort to find a stageworthy American opera. The venture of this year, on February 27, was an adaptation of *Cyrano de Bergerac,* for which W. J. Henderson was the librettist, Walter Damrosch the composer. Amato made a beautiful picture as the Gascon, Alda was an attractive Roxanne,* and Martin was a handsome Christian.* An intelligent condensation in which Cyrano died on the battlefield of Act IV (rather than at a later period in Act V of the original) was approved—the revelation of his secret came in a *Tristan*-like delirium—but Krehbiel found "Gallic esprit" missing in the English version, and the light touches of the original subdued by the Damrosch music. Moreover, Amato could not make his words intelligible, and the heavy orchestral writing was a further handicap. The unwieldy length [1] was somewhat reduced for a repetition on March 24, but Henderson (who had turned over scrutiny of his own work to William D. Chase at the *première*) thought the cut in Act III injurious to dramatic sense and that the act should be "partially rewritten." *Cyrano* had five performances this season, none thereafter.

Personal whim alone determined that this would be Leo Slezak's final

---

[1] When Damrosch told Henderson he had completed the setting, the librettist asked how long it would run. "Oh," said the composer, "four or four and a half hours." Aghast, the librettist exclaimed: "What!" "Well," said the composer, "take *Meistersinger*." "But, Walter," said Henderson, "you're not Richard Wagner."

season at the Metropolitan, for, at forty, he was in prime voice, qualified for roles as various as Tamino, Otello, or even Faust,* which he sang on December 7 in a manner described by Henderson as "sound in idea and honestly delivered," though not "great," perhaps not even "distinguished." He also sang Manrico, Walther, and Otello, taking part in the last performance ever given by Gatti of Verdi's great tragedy on January 31. "Slezak," the *Sun* observed, "was in his best voice and exerted himself to leave a fine memory. . . . He certainly succeeded."

Save for *Tristan*, all the Wagner works of this year were conducted by Hertz. The most impressive new singer for this repertory was Carl Braun, whose accomplishments included a Hagen* in *Götterdämmerung* on February 20 quite lavishly honored by Henderson as "the most commanding impersonation of the role ever disclosed to this public." Later (February 26) his Marcel* in *Les Huguenots*, in the same writer's opinion, was "one of the finest . . . the local stage has held." He was also admired as the King in *Lohengrin* and Wotan in *Die Walküre*. Willy Buers, a Leipzig artist, made his debut as Hans Sachs (d) in *Die Meistersinger* on February 13, singing tastefully and with an agreeable vocal quality. Urlus came along, after his unfortunate Tristan, singing both Siegfrieds in the *Ring* with, said Henderson, "rather more legato than Teutonic singers usually possess." One of the notable Wagner performances of this era occurred on December 16 when Slezak was Tannhäuser to Matzenauer's Venus,* with Destinn as Elisabeth. "Splendor of tone . . . imposing dignity of style" were found in Matzenauer's singing by Henderson, also "inspiring heights of expressiveness" in her scene with Slezak.

In a season that offered nine works of Wagner in thirty-five performances (the most, in both respects, for any composer and his works) there could scarcely be fears of "discrimination." *Parsifal* had settled to a pattern of holiday performances (Thanksgiving Day, New Year's, and Good Friday), at a level of execution uniformly high. If there was any complaint, it was that the centenary of Wagner's birth would fall in May 1913, when the theater would be closed.

The amiable relations by which activities in New York, Chicago, and Philadelphia were "co-ordinated" showed their first signs of approaching dissolution at this time. Dippel and Campanini had come to the end of their common road, and Campanini prevailed on his directors to pay a settlement of $25,000 to resolve their differences. It also assured the Chicago company further call on the services of Titta Ruffo, whom Dippel, in a practice of those days, had signed to a personal contract before selling him to the company of which he was an employee. (Garden and Dalmorès were likewise bound to Dippel at the time.)

The quality of Ruffo's personality and art was evident in the choice, for his Metropolitan debut on November 19, of Thomas's *Hamlet*, which had been in other days a means of displaying a Calvé. Henderson termed Ruffo's voice "hollow and cold" in its lower register, but "of magnificent power" in the middle and upper registers, with "enormous breath support" and "perfect" control. He had an ovation after the drinking song, which Campanini repeated. Aldrich described Ruffo in terms of "a voice of bronze," at its extreme power "a brazen clarion." The Italian esteem for Ruffo as an actor he thought inflated, terming his manner "tense and vivacious, restless and uneasy." The lightly regarded Ophelia was Zepilli, with Huberdeau (Claudius) and Cisneros (the Queen).

The success of Ruffo and the excited talk about him prompted Henderson to an article entitled "Get Rich Quick Singing" on December 3 which shows rather clearly what, in his opinion, had brought the golden age of the nineties to an end. The urge to make a big sound (Caruso was the model for the tenors, Ruffo for the baritones) had made for "hurried preparations for short careers." Nor did the house demand such power. "There was not a spot . . . where the moderato of Sembrich or the finest spun mezza voce of Bonci could not be heard." But that kind of mastery takes time, and singers are impatient. The outcome, in Henderson's view, was that "only a few singers are provided with a real vocal technic, and even some of these sacrifice their voices to . . . big tone. The others go to pieces anyhow in a few brief seasons . . . most become teachers of that which they never knew, namely, the art of bel canto."

The abbreviated season of Chicago-Philadelphia company visits resumed on February 4 with Mary Garden as Louise and ended on February 25 with Wilhelm Kienzl's *Le Ranz des vaches*. A gratefully written work for the cast of Helen Stanley (Blanchefleur), Huberdeau, Dalmorès, and Dufranne, it was rather light in texture, musically uneventful. A stronger reaction was earned by Riccardo Zandonai's *Conchita* on February 11, whose central figure, in Henderson's words, "enjoys life by tormenting the men who love her." Krehbiel thought the plot "all sordid and mean," but both critics admired the skill with which the score was wrought and Zandonai's real gift for orchestral writing. Tarquinia Tarquini, who was also the composer's wife, impersonated Conchita, with Dalmorès, Désiré Defrère (Tonio), and Stanley (Dolores) among the principals.

Hammerstein's hankering for the excitement and prominence of opera production came close to the point of creating a new competition for the Metropolitan in the fall of 1913, though all he proposed was "educational" opera in English. Some of the Metropolitan directors thought that this might be a good idea, but that they should be the ones to carry it out, in the Century Theater (a new name for the already old New Theater). When this became known, in March, Hammerstein announced that he would build another theater, on Lexington Avenue and Fifty-first Street, and resume opera on a grand scale in all necessary languages: he would no longer be "bulldozed," and anyway, all he had received for his Philadelphia house was $800,000,[1] nothing for "my scenery, my costumes, or my opera rights."

The Metropolitan's answer was to publish the pertinent clause of the agreement with Hammerstein which forbade him to produce for a ten-year period "in any language . . . any opera, operetta or comic opera that has ever been produced at the Metropolitan Opera House or the Manhattan Opera House." Hammerstein pursued various appeals to public sympathy for the conditions of duress that prevailed when he made the agreement; but the Metropolitan pursued the law instead, eventually winning an injunction and a ruling from the Appellate Division of the New York State Supreme Court that production of opera "was not trade or commerce" and thus not subject to penalties under the Sherman Anti-trust Act. Hammerstein persisted in building the Lexington Theater, which had some brief intervals of glory as a home for visiting opera. It then passed to the control of the Loew's movie chain, finally becoming the site for the Summit Hotel in 1959. Hammerstein, patiently awaiting the day when he could use it himself, died on August 1, 1919, a bare eight months before his commitment to the Metropolitan would have ended.

In the course of arguing its case against Hammerstein the Metropolitan's board issued a statement declaring: "Even with its enormous success of last year, the Metropolitan company made practically no profit; and better results are not expected for the current season." If $52,075—as the books show—was "practically no profit," what terms of belittlement could be applied to the black figure of $133,838 earned by the season under discussion? Probably a reprimand to Gatti.

1913–1914

Statistical proof that the Metropolitan was operating in this period with cash in hand and customers at the window can be read in the figures just cited. Although the figures were not known to the contemporary audience, the ticket-buying problem was, especially after it erupted into a scandal that brought the District Attorney to act before it was resolved.

At an earlier period of Metropolitan history (under Grau and Conried), the managers found the convenience of a large pre-season sale so welcome that ticket agencies were granted a fifteen per cent reduction on their

---

[1] He ignored the $400,000 paid to Stotesbury in settlement of debts.

purchases. When the general demand made such inducement no longer necessary, it was abolished, prior to the season of 1911. Nevertheless, the agencies continued to invest large sums of money in these pre-season "buys" for two reasons: many customers preferred to maintain charge accounts with the agencies from which they also purchased theater tickets; the agencies had access to superior locations,[1] for which they charged such "service" fees as they could command. It was not until 1919 that legal controls of any kind were imposed on the agencies, and not till years later that a uniform service charge was instituted.

The present dilemma involved a segment of the public which bought its season subscriptions through Tyson & Company, paying for them in advance in order to secure preferred locations. As the opening on November 17 approached and no tickets were remitted, complaints began to reach the Metropolitan management, which discovered that $220,000 worth of opera tickets had been pledged by Richard J. Hartman, director of Tyson & Company, as collateral with the Metropolitan Trust Company for loans to buy other theater tickets.

Although the opera company was not directly responsible to the Tyson customers, it had a share of the blame for endorsing the agency as a convenience (the opera's subscription department was not developed until several years later) and filing notices of price rises through the company's mailing lists. An indictment against Hartman was threatened, but the District Attorney permitted him time to raise the money to release the tickets, which he eventually did. Several years later Hartman was charged with misappropriation of a client's funds and received a jail sentence.

When the Tyson subscribers finally obtained their tickets for the opening-night performance a day or so in advance, they became part of a throng described by the *Tribune* as "the largest . . . ever in the house" on such an occasion. *Manon* had been scheduled, but was replaced by *La Gioconda* when Farrar came down with a cold that kept her inactive during most of December. Toscanini was the conductor, and the cast of Caruso, Destinn, Matzenauer, Amato, and Duchène responded brilliantly, though its most famous member's singing of *"Cielo e mar"* was not, to Henderson's ear, "even an echo of his delivery of the same number five or six years ago." The audience wanted it repeated, but Caruso did not.

The greatly strengthened repertory of the last few seasons was further enhanced in these weeks by the introduction of two of the most persistently repeated works created in the twentieth century: Strauss's *Der Rosenkavalier,* and Montemezzi's *L'Amore dei tre re.* Each gave the composer

---

[1] Fred Rullmann, who had been a Grau partner, operated one of these. His estate held the libretto concession for another fifty years (to 1963).

the satisfaction of knowing he had added durably to the world's (and the Metropolitan's) repertory before he died,[1] though valuations of both have fluctuated.

The European circumstances surrounding the works were as divergent as their receptions in New York. Strauss was a world-known master whose bizarre subjects and flamboyant personality often deflected calm evaluation of his creations. *Der Rosenkavalier* had been widely acclaimed when it was first heard in Germany and Austria in 1911. Montemezzi was virtually a new name (at thirty-eight), and the reception of *L'Amore* in Italy in 1913 had been equivocal.

At the Metropolitan the first Marschallin* in *Der Rosenkavalier,* on December 9, 1913, was Hempel, who had sung the role in the Berlin *première,* with Margarete Ober as Octavian. Anna Case was Sophie,* and Goritz sang Ochs.* Henderson wasted little time in terming it a "commonplace score," with some harsh words for the ending, which he thought "a piece of lamentable bungling. . . . After the story is complete they . . . maunder on for nearly ten more minutes and finish with a ridiculous piece of pantomime, evidently for the sake of doing something unexpected." To Aldrich, however, the trio was one of Strauss's "most successful passages," the pantomime at the end "a quaint touch." Both writers considered the Marschallin's monologues beautiful, though this did not dissuade Henderson from saying: "in the realm of poetic exaltation, Dr. Strauss is nothing better than a competent artisan."

Against Aldrich's confident assumption that "nobody will quarrel seriously" with the use of waltz rhythms unknown in Maria Theresa's time, was Krehbiel's complaint about this very "anachronism." He applauded Hertz for some cuts in the lengthy score, but added: "a greater debt of gratitude would be due (supposing the production . . . calls for gratitude) had he . . . [cut] 30 or more pages of the score."

The smooth performance was generally commended, Henderson noting Hempel's "style and diction" as "the best specimens of her art we have had."[2] Ober and Goritz also satisfied, but Case was in poorish voice, to which the same critic appended the note: "The part is written outrageously for the voice. To hear the little girlish *Sophia* screaming out her fluttering heart in high B's and even a C sharp is actually painful." A few days later he summed up: "The thing has no standing as a work of art. It is not even a good piece of workmanship."

The case of *L'Amore* was quite different. The critics attending the pre-

[1] Strauss in 1949, Montemezzi in 1952.

[2] The two great Marschallins of early Metropolitan history sang together at least once, when Lotte Lehmann, of later note, was the Sophie to Hempel's Marschallin, with Bohnen as Ochs and Beecham conducting, in London in 1914.

performance rehearsals were arrested, then absorbed, by the excitement created under Toscanini's direction. Querying a Ricordi representative during a lull, Henderson asked: "Why on earth wasn't this opera a success in Italy?" Nodding his head toward Toscanini, the man answered: "They never heard it in Italy."[1]

On turning to contemporary accounts, I find Henderson writing that "the opera had been a real success in Milan," though Aldrich termed it "quite unheralded by proclamations of European fame." On whichever side the error lay, it was unquestionably well received in New York on January 2, 1914. Krehbiel thought the score "would have delighted the soul of Verdi," and proclaimed the composer a "genius." Henderson observed that "Montemezzi writes . . . with dignity, with style, but . . . he makes some proclamations of riotous passion which sweep the hearer before them." Aldrich's view was crystallized in the statement that "the composer has attained his effects, even the most powerful, without finding it necessary to break with all . . . hitherto prized in music." Bori as Fiora* "astonished her most devoted admirers," said Henderson. Otherwise the greatest credit went to Edoardo Ferrari-Fontana (husband of Matzenauer), whose Avito,* sung with "a magnificent robust voice with pealing upper tones" (Henderson), suggested why he had been chosen to create the part in Milan. Amato as Manfredo* and Didur as Archibaldo* added measurably to the effect of Toscanini's mastery (Henderson noted that he had absorbed the score "in three weeks").

The question of "Monday-night approval" hitherto invoked (see page 204) was mentioned by Henderson on January 11 with the casual statement: "The work must stand or fall by the decree of the social leaders. If they do not like it the opera will be retired. This has always been the case with operas and always will be." He gave his own answer on January 13, with a heading that read, after mentioning the work and the cast: "APPROVAL SIGNIFICANT. Opera will Hold Place in Repertory of the House for a Long Time." If this was the yardstick by which other unfamiliar operas of the time were measured, it might be well for an enterprising manager to experiment with a few of them, now that we have escaped the mesh that Henderson conceived as having "always been."

Also worth considering, as a measurement of contemporary values, was a reply by Henderson to a correspondent who asked an opinion of

---

1 Alexander Smallens, widely versed opera conductor, was in Chicago when Montemezzi arrived some time after the success of *L'Amore* in New York. Learning that Smallens had heard the Toscanini version, with which the composer was unfamiliar, Montemezzi asked for a demonstration, and Smallens obliged on the piano with a likeness of Toscanini's vigorous treatment of the opening episode. "Stop!" cried Montemezzi. "Wrong! All wrong!" Much persuasion could barely convince Montemezzi that this was the way *L'Amore* had become a New York success.

the Metropolitan orchestra. Drawing on recent European experience, Henderson rated it—when thoroughly prepared by Toscanini—the equal of the best of the European ones, in Vienna and Dresden. Under Polacco or Hertz it was the equal of all but these two. To Vienna adhered one legendary, unfailing excellence: "The Vienna was better in strings."

L'Amore dei tre re and *Der Rosenkavalier* had almost identical histories during the twenty-two following seasons directed by Gatti: forty-two performances of Montemezzi in thirteen seasons, forty-six performances of Strauss in twelve seasons. The greater favor of recent years for Strauss does not have to do solely with merit. The singers suitable to his work and, perhaps even more, the conductors, have been more regularly available than those appropriate to Fiora, Avito, and the other Montemezzi characters.

After Gatti's considerable effort to secure the successor to Charpentier's *Louise*, it was exposed to scrutiny on February 27, when *Julien* had its American introduction. Here, however, was one case when a European verdict was neither reversed nor opposed. For all its mysticism, Henderson found the treatment "continually slow in movement, indefinite in rhythm, monotonous and heavy." Krehbiel did not review the first showing, but described it on a later occasion as "obscure in purpose, undramatic . . . inferior in melodic invention to its predecessor." Caruso's carefully detailed Julien* was honored as an effort in "one of the most difficult roles offered to a tenor at any period of opera" (Henderson), and Farrar as Louise* was "an artist to her finger tips." All the smaller roles were splendidly done and the production pleased, as did Polacco's conducting. No revival followed the five performances of this season.

The other additions to the repertory were similarly short-lived, though Wolf-Ferrari's *L'Amore medico,* at least, seems subject to reconsideration in view of Henderson's opinion that its two acts were "an opera bouffe of real beauty, of airy and playful humor, of ingenious workmanship." At its *première* on March 25, Bori as Lucinda* and Italo Cristalli as Clitandro* did humorous work under Toscanini's guidance. It was followed by Herbert's one-act *Madeleine,* first heard on January 24, and not even substantial enough to rate as *opéra comique.* The *Sun* called it an "operetta," in which Alda gave "genuine art" to the role of Madeleine.* Althouse sang Françoise* agreeably, also handling the English text ably. Polacco was the conductor.

Nothing more durable was provided in the last series of visits to the Metropolitan of the Philadelphia-Chicago Opera. New York made the acquaintance of the fine baritone Vanni Marcoux (a notable Boris and Scarpia), who was prominent in both of the new works—Massenet's

Don Quichotte on February 3 and Février's *Monna Vanna* on February 17. Of his Don Quichotte, Henderson wrote: "Vanni Marcoux proved
himself to be an artist worthy of respect. . . . He sang with so much
vocal resource, so much style . . . that he squeezed out of the role all
there was in it and put a little in that was not there before." Garden's
Dulcinea was admired, as was Dufranne's Sancho Panza. In *Monna Vanna,*
Lucien Muratore aroused admiration as Prinzivalle, the *Sun* describing
him as "a French tenor of the best type, artistic and fervent. He is an
excellent actor for a tenor." Garden's Monna Vanna was of her usual
excellence, though Henderson found little in the music to merit discussion.
"Who cannot," he asked, "mentally picture Miss Garden with one bare
shoulder, an occasional ankle, and a totally veiled voice?" Garden also
sang Louise in this series, on February 10, with Dalmorès and a usual
list of associates conducted by Campanini.

The contribution of Margarete Ober to the quality of performance heard
in *Der Rosenkavalier* was notable, but she was highly regarded also in
her other undertakings. As Ortrud* in *Lohengrin* on November 21,
with Fremstad, Urlus, Weil, and Carl Schlegel (the Herald [d]), she made
a debut that Krehbiel recognized as "the creation of a true tragic actress."
According to the Matzenauer pattern and in the mold Gatti sought to
impose on his new leading singers, she sang important parts in both
German and Italian, with Marina* in *Boris* and Erda* in *Siegfried*
preceding her Octavian* on December 9. Within a four-day period beginning on December 24, she sang Brangäne* in *Tristan,* Laura* in *La Gioconda,* and Amneris* in *Aida.* Her season of Wagner pursued the classic
plan of Erda* in *Rheingold,* Fricka* in *Die Walküre,* and Waltraute* in
Götterdämmerung, of which the last named on February 19 prompted
Henderson to term it "so beautiful in voice and so potent in poetic
utterance that she became . . . one of the grand figures of the drama."

Had the war not intervened, Ober might have remained a Metropolitan favorite as long, say, as Giovanni Martinelli, who made his debut as
Rodolfo* in *La Bohème* on November 20, with Bori and Scotti, the day
before Ober made hers in *Lohengrin.* Martinelli sang on and on, through
Caruso, Gigli, and Lauri-Volpi, when Ober and her wartime difficulties
(see page 270) were all but forgotten. Henderson described his voice,
at this debut, as "of unusually beautiful quality . . . in the high C of the
narrative—brilliant." As for Martinelli, Pinkerton* (with Farrar and
Scotti), Toscanini conducting, on November 27, and Cavaradossi* in
Tosca (with Fremstad and Scotti) on December 6, preceded his Radames*
in *Aida* on the 24th, of which the *Sun* said: "He lacks the . . . assurance
to make a commanding figure of Radames, but he sang . . . with a good

quality of tone." Krehbiel used such words as "splendid, clear, resonant" to describe his singing at this time, and Aldrich responded to his high range, used "naturally and easily."

Gatti added another artist of promise to his male roster in this season who could have had a long career save for unforeseen circumstances. This was Rudolf Berger, a tall, handsome Siegmund* in his debut in *Die Walküre* on February 5, whom Henderson endorsed as "manly, interesting and commendable." In physique if not in voice Berger had qualities, to quote Henderson, "such as the local stage has long lacked." He also sang Walther,* Tannhäuser,* Tristan,* and Lohengrin* in the ensuing weeks —with not too consistent vocal command, but in a developing pattern of artistry—as well as Parsifal.* Berger died suddenly, however, at the beginning of the next season. This was an ominous echo of the loss of Putnam Griswold, who died on February 25, 1914, after an operation for appendicitis.

Berger's Parsifal* on April 10[1] coincided with the final appearance of Olive Fremstad as Kundry. Her intention to leave the company at this season's end was no secret, and she had many curtain calls after Act II. As with Eames before her and Farrar to come, however, her farewell was something of an anticlimax. It was as Elsa—certainly not her best role— on April 23. The *Sun* hinted at "reasons" why this "distinguished soprano" is leaving, but did not go into details. The best explanation seems to be that Fremstad periodically threatened to leave when Gatti proposed a shorter season for her, and this time he took her literally. She cherished Isolde as her farewell to the Metropolitan; Gatti specified Elsa. Henderson's parting words paid tribute to her "splendid intelligence, genuine dramatic instincts, vivid and creative imagination." In a leave-taking speech Fremstad said she had lived "for but one purpose, to give you my best. . . . May we all meet in that far beyond where there is eternal peace and harmony. Good-by."[2]

A notable event in the Wagner repertory this year was the new *Ring* production by the Kautskys of Vienna, which remained in use almost *in toto* till the Simonson décor replaced it in 1948. (A new *Walküre* production by Jonel Jorgulesco was introduced in 1935–6.) The freshly dressed stage aroused general enthusiasm, though Krehbiel objected to a

[1] The Metropolitan was no longer alone in offering *Parsifal* outside Bayreuth. The copyright restriction, such as it was, expired at midnight on December 31, 1913, and performances were given that night or the day after in Berlin (Mörike conducting), Budapest (Fritz Reiner conducting), and Paris (Messager conducting). The London *première* occurred on February 2, Artur Bodanzky conducting.

[2] Fremstad was actually re-engaged for the 1917–18 season, but the war eliminated the repertory in which she would have been used.

curtain, rather than the specified door, as entrance to Hunding's tree-sheltered dwelling in *Die Walküre*. Jörn sang an excellent Loge* in *Das Rheingold* (better than any prior performer save Vogl and Van Dyck), and also did well as the young Siegfried.* At a noncyclical *Götterdämmerung* on March 13, Ruysdael sang Hagen,* "with great credit," said the *Sun*.

The new esteem for Hempel occasioned by her Marschallin in *Der Rosenkavalier* was heightened by her Eva* in *Die Meistersinger* on March 27, conducted by Toscanini, with Berger, Homer, and Weil. It was marked, said Henderson, by "freshness, fullness of tone, an ease of emission which went far toward giving the illusion of spontaneous utterance." A Lucia* on November 26 was admired for "grace" and "daintiness," but the comprehensive judgment was that Hempel was primarily a lyric artist whose skill in coloratura had been overstressed.

Nevertheless, Hempel as the Page* in *Un Ballo in maschera* was a decided treat when the early Verdi work was revived on November 22 as part of a tribute to the one-hundredth anniversary of the two giants born in 1813 (Wagner was honored with the restaged *Ring*). In the stern judgment of Henderson, Hempel performed with "spirit, personal charm, and certain musical excellence," though without rising above "the level of easy mediocrity" that had become standard in the last decade and a half. Caruso alone "stood forth as the artist commanding the respect of the connoisseur," for neither Destinn (Amelia*), nor Matzenauer (Ulrica*), nor Amato (Renato*) commanded the "schooling" for such music. Toscanini conducted, and "certainly did not miss any of Verdi's points." Illnesses prevented this fairly all-star cast from being seen again this season, Hempel and Matzenauer giving way to Alten and Duchène.

Two singers of later favor began their careers in small ways this season, when Sophie Braslau sang the off-stage Voice in *Parsifal* on November 24 and Theodore* in *Boris* on the next night; and Mabel Garrison was introduced at a Sunday-night concert on February 15. Of Miss Braslau the *Sun* said: "her charming voice made a pleasing impression." Of Miss Garrison the *Tribune* reported: "She possesses a light soprano voice of unusual purity and sweetness, a fluent and sure style."

The one-time perpetual *Faust* declined in this season to a single performance, on February 14, conducted by Richard Hageman as his debut. "Miss Farrar," the *Sun* observed, "now has a monopoly of the role of Marguerite, which she sings sometimes well, sometimes ill." With or without *Faust,* Metropolitan opera was so firmly entrenched that even a rumor that Toscanini might not sign another contract could be received by Henderson, "with equanimity." Hopes were expressed that he would change his mind, "for he is a very great conductor and his influence is invaluable in the opera house. But if he decides to leave us we shall do well to wait . . . till we see what Mr. Gatti-Casazza will do about it."

For his part, Gatti finally acknowledged that "contrary to custom, the Metropolitan actually showed a financial profit" when he left for Europe late in April. The tentative remark would hardly lead one to think it was as much as $66,609. It was consistent, however, with a system by which the manager kept two sets of books (according to Geraldine Farrar): one to show to a singer when a raise was requested, another to show the directors when credit figures were required.

1914–1915

The world that came to an end on July 28, 1914, when Austria declared war on Serbia, did not seem at all irretrievable when the Metropolitan began its season on November 16. America was very much that precious thing called a "neutral," and sentiment had by no means inclined heavily to the side of which we were later an ally. The problems of gathering singers[1] from the many European countries in which they customarily summered was reflected in Henderson's comment at the opening perform-ance of *Un Ballo in maschera:* "the culture, the refinement and the beauty of the town [were represented] as well as its wealth and prosperity. It was an audience well acquainted with opera music and opera singing . . . and its applause disclosed . . . a deeper and more serious satisfaction in the successful opening of a season which at one time seemed problematical." The performance earned warmer praise than the previous year's: "it is not likely anyone ever sang Riccardo better" than Caruso; Hempel was in nimble voice; Destinn and Matzenauer were stronger in their parts than before.

Toscanini's Verdi was a paragon, and this year his Bizet edged close to it when he presented a newly studied *Carmen* on November 19, with Farrar as Carmen,* Caruso (Don José), Amato (Escamillo*), and Alda (Micaëla*). Objections to Toscanini's tempos of 1908–9 were amended, as perhaps were the tempos also. Now Henderson found them "judicious," part of a conception that gave "great pleasure." For the first time a *Carmen* produced on the Metropolitan stage was wholly integrated from first to last, and it was properly appreciated. (The scenery was Kautsky-designed.) Farrar sang the music "better than any one since Emma Calvé," accord-ing to Henderson, and if the playing was slightly "artificial," she was never-theless a "vision of loveliness, never aristocratic, yet never vulgar, a

[1] Dinh Gilly, a French national interned in Austria, was, for the moment, the only important absentee.

seductive, languorous, passionate Carmen." Aldrich, however, missed what he described as "the smoldering Mediterranean fire" latent in *Carmen,* noted its lack of "rude elemental force." At that, it was "captivating" and "interesting." Caruso's stiffness in the dress uniform of Act I moderated thereafter, and his singing mellowed. Braslau added an effective Mercédès* to the ensemble, and Désiré Defrère[1] made his debut as Morales (d), as did Rosina Galli as *première ballerina.*

Although it was contrary to Toscanini's stated policies to rotate singers in the box-office-provoking manner impresarios love, this *Carmen* had an uncommon amount of it. On November 27 Bori was Micaëla,* Whitehill sang Escamillo* with style and dash, and Mabel Garrison made her stage debut as Frasquita (d). On March 18 and again on April 13, when Caruso's season was over, Martinelli sang Don José,* with Riccardo Tegani as Escamillo.* The *Sun* thought Martinelli "genuinely good" in some of his music, but Tegani was second-rate, with results noted on page 255.

The tempest of enthusiasm with which Toscanini attacked his work this season was uncommon even by his own standards—by any other's it was simply inhuman. *Il Trovatore* and *Iris* were revived besides *Carmen*; he gave the first performances anywhere of Giordano's *Madame Sans-Gêne,* restudied Euryanthe, and was deep in the final phases of *Prince Igor* when time ran out. After days at labor on these, he spent nights conducting *Boris, Aida, Butterfly, Tosca, Manon, L'Amore dei tre re, Un Ballo, Tristan,* and *Die Meistersinger.*

As preparation for the first *Euryanthe* on December 19, he directed *Tristan* on the 16th and *Tosca* on the 17th (all without score of course), with results Aldrich described in the Weber as: "tireless energy and burning enthusiasm." Henderson asserted that "nothing of the poetic beauty of the score escaped him." For all his mastery of "every nuance, every flash of orchestral color" (Krehbiel), Toscanini could not give Ober as Eglantine* the needed vocal virtuosity for Act II, though in the more straightforward singing she performed strongly. To Aldrich, Hempel was a "remarkably fine" Euryanthe,* and Henderson concurred with praise for both Hempel and Sembach (Adolar*). Krehbiel, as indicated, was most taken by the playing of "the marvellous orchestra," and indicated a dissatisfaction with the general repertory, even as conducted by Toscanini and Hertz, by saying that *Euryanthe* profited from "the kind of preparation of which all the German operas in the Metropolitan's list stand in great need." Toscanini omitted the tableau during the overture and bypassed the *Invitation to the Dance* (as ballet) in favor of a *pas de cinq* written)

---

[1] Defrère returned as stage manager in 1935, and acted in that capacity when *Carmen* was revived in 1952. He remained with the company until his death in 1964.

by Weber for Berlin. The overture came at the beginning. All five performances were given by the same cast, but the work was dropped when
Toscanini left.

The succeeding works restudied or newly produced by Toscanini came
at monthly intervals: *Madame Sans-Gêne* on January 25, *Il Trovatore*
on February 20, and *Iris* on April 1. Giordano's return to the milieu of
Andrea Chénier did not produce quite the virtue of that sometimes exciting score. Krehbiel thought it *opéra bouffe* rather below the Lecocq level,
and Henderson thought it would have to be carried by the performers
rather than vice versa, "in spite of the fact that Arturo Toscanini, the
foremost opera conductor of the world, has devoted . . . his unique
endowments and his inexhaustible energy" to it. Farrar's Caterina* was
described by the same critic as "too rude, too vulgar," and Amato's
Napoleon* as "a well composed character." Martinelli (Lefebvre*) and
Segurola (Fouché*) were singled out for praise in a generally good cast.
The work had a dozen repetitions in the next three years, but has had
none since 1918.

The notion of "restudying" *Il Trovatore* produced some welcome if
unexpected results, noted by Henderson as "style," in the melodic phraseology, "use of mezza voce effects too often neglected, and a generally
successful attempt to [give] . . . the numbers dramatic meaning." Toscanini's broadening of the waltz rhythms gave new surge to them, unfortunately not paralleled in the vocal resources of Martinelli, a Manrico* whose
"Ah, si ben mio" was outstanding, Destinn, Ober (Azucena*), and Amato
(Di Luna). Krehbiel stood outside the general critical area in regarding
Toscanini's treatment of the score as too symphonic.

The thirty-first of the operas conducted by Toscanini at the Metropolitan showed characteristic results when *Iris* was given on April 1. "Mr.
Toscanini literally transformed" the score, Henderson wrote (forgetful,
perhaps, that he had once called it "a real opera"). All his careful attention to detail did not make it a work "of the first importance," but it
came off as "rather impressive" nevertheless. Bori's Iris* was rated by the
same writer as "a creation of singular charm . . . and of delicate musical
beauty," with Luca Botta, a new tenor (Osaka*), and Scotti (Kyoto)
and Didur (Il Cieco*) filling out an excellent cast. On April 19, *Iris* had
its final performance of the season, without change of cast and without
need for critical coverage. The notice in the *Sun* read: "The final week
of the season began at the Metropolitan Opera House last night with
Mascagni's 'Iris.' The cast was the same as before, and Miss Bori[1]

---

[1] Bori underwent an operation for a nodule on the vocal chords during this summer and did not return to opera until January 28, 1921.

effected her last appearance. Mr. Toscanini being ill, the performance was conducted by Mr. Polacco." Thus passed Arturo Toscanini from the pit of the Metropolitan, where he appeared no more this season and did not conduct opera again.

The single non-Toscanini novelty this year was Franco Leoni's *L'Oracolo,* conducted by Polacco on February 4 with Scotti in his famous orange-rolling part of Chim-Fen,* in which he was seen some forty times before his retirement in 1933. Bori (Ah-Yoe*) and Botta (Win-San-Luy*) performed admirably in a work noted by Henderson to possess "fluidity without force," in Polacco's admired mustering of "lightness, transparency, and richness." As a variant from other one-acters, *L'Oracolo* was welcome as often as it permitted Scotti to show he was "among the foremost operatic actors of the time."

Gatti's far-ranging repertory included *Fidelio* under the direction of Hertz on January 30, with Matzenauer an unillusive Leonore,* but one who "conquered . . . by the beauty of her conception" and its emotional presentation. In the same Henderson review, highest praise went to Elisabeth Schumann, a lovely Marzelline.* For Aldrich, Matzenauer fared better than anticipated, giving in all "one of the most successful" performances of her New York career. Braun was an excellent Rocco,* Urlus a passable Florestan.* The Roller scenery was used again, as was the musical text as arranged by Mahler. Henderson and Aldrich were moved to write affectionately of the score, the latter declaring that its "poignant appeal to the heart" is unsurpassed in opera. The former summed up much of the greatness and the paradox in *Fidelio* by saying: "Of all the masters who ever wrote a music drama Beethoven was the least operatic and at the same time one of the most dramatic." When that distinction has been fully absorbed, *Fidelio* will have the place of esteem it deserves.

The waning of Meyerbeer's day was more than ever evident on December 30, when Gatti stocked *Les Huguenots* with the best names in his company—Destinn (Valentine), Hempel (Marguerite), Caruso (Raoul), Braun (Marcel), Scotti, and Rothier—and found them generally scorned by the older critics. Only Rothier as Saint-Bris offered a likeness of French style in this Italian presentation; Braun was "wholly German" in manner, the others in various degrees deficient, down to Garrison's Page* —"very well sung" for so young an artist, said Henderson, but "without the voice, the experience or the style demanded by the role." Polacco conducted commendably. Later, somewhat relenting, the same critic granted that Caruso sang "Raoul beautifully, but in the Italian style," Mme Destinn was "a good if not great Valentine, and Miss Hempel sings the music of the queen very well."

Where the vocal prowess of this generation abided may be read in the appearance of Melanie Kurt, of Berlin, who succeeded to the Fremstad roles in her debut on February 1 as Isolde.* Her training by both Lilli and Marie Lehmann was evident in Henderson's commendation of her voice, "fresh, unworn, youthful," and in a conception of Isolde that Krehbiel honored as "the work of a finished artist." She sang both the *Walküre* and *Götterdämmerung* Brünnhildes this season (the latter, said Aldrich, "had rarely been sung with a finer art"), Sieglinde, Elisabeth, Leonore in *Fidelio,* and Kundry. The last sustained the high level of Ternina, Fremstad, Nordica, and Matzenauer, and her Walküre's *"Ho-jo-to-ho"* on February 4 was singled out for praise by Henderson as being sung "precisely as it is written, without any of the familiar evasions." In this cast, Gadski was Sieglinde and Matzenauer Fricka, combining three better than average Brünnhildes on the same stage. The *Ring* cycle beginning on January 28 was full of excellent singing, with Sembach an admired Loge* in *Rheingold,* Braun a strong Wotan in the first two works, Whitehill a sonorous Wanderer in *Siegfried,* and Schumann providing an appealing voice for the Forest Bird. Berger's Siegfried in *Götterdämmerung* earned him honors for going on despite painful pleurisy, but it was a doubtful heroism. He died ten days later (February 28) of heart paralysis.

Johannes Sembach was liked for his introductory Parsifal on November 26 and for the agreeable lyric sound he produced as Walther von Stolzing* in *Die Meistersinger* on March 12 (Henderson still found Toscanini's conducting of this score "peculiarly inconsistent"), as Tamino in *Die Zauberflöte,* Siegmund in *Die Walküre,* and even Florestan in *Fidelio.* Elisabeth Schumann was less than thirty years old when she made her debut as Sophie* in *Der Rosenkavalier* on November 20, but what Henderson heard, as described in the *Sun,* was what her admirers heard through a career that ended with her death in 1952: "A light lyric soprano voice of beautiful natural quality . . . used . . . generally with fine technic. Her style had much taste and sentiment." Musetta, Papagena in *Die Zauberflöte,* and Gretel, during the next few weeks, passed without special notice, but her qualities as Marzelline in *Fidelio* have been noted (see page 252). She returned to Hamburg (where she had made her debut in 1910) after this season, and became more celebrated as a Vienna favorite in the twenties and as a recitalist.

A luxury not accessible to theaters of smaller repertory was the presentation, in this period, of both settings of *Manon.* Their coincidence in 1914-15 was heightened by the excellence of the specialists available for them—Farrar or Alda, Caruso, and Scotti in the Massenet when Toscanini conducted it, Bori, Caruso or Martinelli, and Amato (Lescaut*) in the Puccini *Manon Lescaut* when Polacco conducted it. The final judgment was that the Massenet version was the one preferred by the public, perhaps on sound musical grounds, or merely because it was the older work in the repertory, hence more familiar in a variety of impersonations.

Martinelli's Italian Des Grieux* on January 16 was an incident of a season's work that enhanced the good impression he had made the year before. Neither his Radames on November 21 nor his Pinkerton on November 30 drew more than pleasant phrases, but his Cavaradossi in a *Tosca* with Farrar and Scotti on December 4 prompted Henderson to say: "Mr. Martinelli has made decided progress since last season. . . . There was breadth and judgment in his phrasing, intelligent accent and color . . . general warmth in his style." Praising his industry in renewed studies since his debut, the account continued: "He has an uncommonly beautiful voice and he has ambition. His future looks bright." Luca Botta, a light-voiced tenor who lasted for three seasons, made his debut as Rodolfo* in *La Bohème* on November 21, and Riccardo Tegani was introduced as Schaunard (d) in the same performance.

As this season was approaching its end, the intention of Hertz to give up opera after thirteen Metropolitan seasons resulted in a ceremonial farewell for him at *Der Rosenkavalier* on April 24. Both management and artists honored him with gifts, and good wishes for his further career as conductor of the San Francisco Symphony. Simultaneously it was announced that Artur Bodanzky, a Mahler disciple active in Mannheim, would succeed him.

An atmosphere wholly unceremonial attended the departure of Toscanini. Rumors had come and gone that he would leave, the assumption being that a little extra urging would produce the desired results. One document bearing on that fallacy has been cited (see page 15); another that might have influenced it was the year's statement showing that profits had slumped from $66,609 in 1913–14 to $1,765 for the current year. This argued for retrenchment on rehearsals, to which Toscanini would not accede.

To give fine opera and make money was a double pride for Gatti; he thought, apparently, that the product could be cheapened a bit and still make money. Toscanini, it is reasonable to assume, thought it could be improved further, and had no interest at all in whether it made money.

Whatever the specific points of disagreement may have been, it is certain that the last performance of *Carmen* directed by Toscanini, on April 13, 1915, was the spark that ignited the explosion. According to the magazine *Musical America* (May 1, 1915), the performance was attended by Tullio Serafin of La Scala, Maria Gay, Giovanni Zenatello, and Titta Ruffo, en route to an engagement in Havana. Word of their presence was passed along, and Toscanini looked for the utmost in co-operation. However, Amato, who was ill, was replaced by Tegani (whose "doings, in these condition," reported the *Sun*, "shall be excused"); Farrar was in poor voice; and various things went wrong with the staging. Strained and put upon by personal difficulties, Toscanini conducted *Iris* the next night, and then no more. Although his absence was covered by mentions of "illness," he was seen in public places on nights when Polacco was conducting in his stead.

When the news finally came from Italy in September that he would not return, reactions were various. H. T. Parker, in the *Boston Transcript* (September 30) regretted, in an eloquent article, that neither Serafin nor Marinuzzi was listed to succeed him. A few days later Henderson in the *Sun* (October 10) calmly dismissed the whole matter thus:

"No reader of . . . THE SUN needs to be told that admiration for the masterly conducting of Mr. Toscanini was never wanting here. But there is no substantial reason for believing that the performances of the coming season will be lame and impotent because the maestro has become more interested in the singing of the bullet than in that of the prima donna.[1] The opera house has for several seasons possessed in Giorgio Polacco, a thoroughly competent conductor, who will now in all probability receive more of the general attention due to his merit. . . .

"To most observers the essentials of Toscanini's conducting were his blazing eyes, his spasmodically working features, his incessant singing, and his gesticulations. . . . Mr. Toscanini's conducting was appreciated by few. It was applauded by thousands who could not have given convincing reasons for their enthusiasm. If Mr. Polacco would wave his arms more vigorously, make more faces, and sing a bit, he would attract a wider measure of public attention."

This abdication of critical function can be merely exhibited, neither extenuated nor condoned. The only explanation is that Henderson resisted the emphasis on an individual in this case, as he did with both Jean de Reszke and Caruso, much as he admired them. But to substitute, for a conductor described in his own words as "the foremost in the world," one whom he rated no more than "thoroughly competent" is quite another matter. It shows a grievous unawareness of an axiom of opera production: while a bad conductor can do more to spoil a performance than a bad singer, a good conductor can do more to ennoble it than a good singer. And a great one can do more to set the tone of an opera house as high as it was at the Metropolitan in those several years than all the singers in the company combined. If New York's discriminating press did not more highly value what it had, it deserved no better than it eventually got.

[1] A reference to the management-disseminated excuse that Toscanini had stayed in Italy for wholly patriotic reasons.

Prior to his apparently unlamented departure, Toscanini performed the following works in the stated seasons:

1908–9: *Aida, Madama Butterfly, Tosca, Carmen, Götterdämmerung, Le Villi, La Wally, Cavalleria Rusticana, Falstaff,* Verdi's "Manzoni" Requiem, and the prologue to Boito's *Mefistofele.*

1909–10: *La Gioconda, Otello, Madama Butterfly, Tristan, Orfeo, Aida, Germania, Falstaff, Die Meistersinger.*

1910–11: *Armide, Aida, Madama Butterfly, La Bohème, La Gioconda, La Fanciulla del West, Orfeo, Tristan, Die Meistersinger, Germania, Tosca, Otello, Ariane et Barbe-bleue, Cavalleria and Pagliacci.*

1911–12: *Aida, La Fanciulla del West, Tristan, Madama Butterfly, La Gioconda, Tosca, Armide, Orfeo, Le Donne curiose, Ariane et Barbe-bleue, Otello, Die Meistersinger, Manon.*

1912–13: *Orfeo, Madama Butterfly, Tosca, Otello, Tristan, Manon, Le Donne curiose, Aida, Boris Godunov, Don Pasquale, La Fanciulla,* and the concert program of Wagner's *Faust Ouvertüre,* Strauss's *Till Eulenspiegel,* and Beethoven's Symphony No. 9.[1]

1913–14: *La Gioconda, Un Ballo in maschera, Madama Butterfly, Boris Godunov, Tosca, Aida, Tristan, Manon, L'Amore dei tre re, Die Meistersinger, Orfeo, L'Amore medico, Don Pasquale.*

1914–15: *Un Ballo in maschera, Carmen, Aida, Boris Godunov, Madama Butterfly, Tosca, Tristan, Euryanthe, Manon, Madame Sans-Gêne, L'Amore dei tre re, Il Trovatore, Die Meistersinger,* and *Iris.*

EPILOGUE

The remaking of the Metropolitan from the "star cast" house of Grau and Conried's *Hoftheater* to the smooth-running six-months-a-year, large repertory enterprise of Gatti had been virtually completed in the seven years of plenty with Toscanini. Much as Conried recognized the opportunity that the Metropolitan presented, he realized it only in part, and that part variably. Gatti's vastly superior technical knowledge, his acquaintance with the talent market, and his very strong sense of organization put the day-to-day functioning of the company on a historically high plane.

The ascent had not been without missteps. *Le Villi, La Wally, Germania, Stradella,* and *The Pipe of Desire* were dubious ventures no matter how regarded. *Die verkaufte Braut* was known to Conried and he thought about it, but its success was a credit to his successors. Certainly no earlier Metropolitan seasons had shown so balanced a repertory so well presented as those in which *Falstaff, Otello, Orfeo,* and *Der Freischütz* were revived,

---

[1] This was the year in which Toscanini did not report until mid-December. Hence the abbreviated list of operas he presented.

Armide was added to the repertory, and such unfamiliar works as *Boris, Der Rosenkavalier, L'Amore dei tre re* and *Ariane et Barbe-bleue* were explored for the first time. *La Fanciulla del West, Königskinder, Julien, Le Donne curiose, Il Segreto di Susanna, Madame Sans-Gêne,* and *L'Oracolo* were all valid experiments, however variable the results.

The total evidence is that, as samples of stagecraft, the standard repertory from *Aida* to *Zauberflöte* was abreast of the theatrical art of the period for the first time in Metropolitan history. It lacked the revolving stage that Munich knew in 1908—and did not acquire it in the nearly sixty seasons that followed—but scenery, costuming, and even lighting matched the best European models, being in most instances copies of them. When postwar thought brought a new impulse to European décor, the Metropolitan stood its ground—which soon receded underfoot.

The slow alteration, in type, of the available singers has been sufficiently documented not to require repetition. The addition in these years, however, of Bori, Hempel, Matzenauer, Slezak, Whitehill, Amato, Didur, Gluck, Kurt, Ober, Rothier, Martinelli, Witherspoon, Carl Braun, and Sembach sustained a fair standard at least in the German and Italian repertory. Marie Rappold never grew to the stature expected when she made her debut in Conried's time, and the younger Americans—Paul Althouse, Sophie Braslau, Mabel Garrison, and others—were still unproved.

In the aftermath of the Toscanini thunderbolt, the financial atmosphere may be described as "fair and cool." A fresh indication of the way the wind was blowing at that time may be found in the following observations. They were written to me in 1935 by Olin Downes, and can be given circulation at this time, now that virtually all the persons involved are dead.

"A few days after Otto Kahn's resignation as Chairman of the Board of Directors of the Metropolitan Opera Company,[1] *we had a talk in which he spoke with complete frankness of his relations to that institution. He said it was a good thing for him, and it was a good thing for the Metropolitan Opera Company that he had resigned his position with that organization. They were content to have him take much of the responsibility for the practical operations of the organization and to interest himself in the affairs of the company, as long as it gave them no trouble or additional burdens.*[2] *He said the primary cause, he believed, of their coolness to him was the fact he was a Jew, and that they were not wholly favorable to having a Jew as the chairman of their Board of Directors. As a result of this feeling, he continued, he had to work almost entirely alone, with very little cooperation from any but one or two of the members. If he had had cooperation and been given a greater amount of support than he*

[1] October 26, 1931.

[2] A checkpoint is provided in the *Sun* for January 3, 1915, in which Henderson wrote: "It is no secret that the present sound condition of the Metropolitan Opera House is due chiefly to his [Otto Kahn's] combination of artistic enthusiasms with business sagacity."

felt he would be likely to receive, he would have experimented more boldly than the Metropolitan had experimented, with repertory and in various aspects of stage presentation. Under the circumstances, he felt that the only advisable course to pursue would be one which guaranteed popular support of the Metropolitan performances and a balanced budget."

The observation of Blaise Pascal: "If the nose of Cleopatra had been shorter, the whole face of the earth would have been changed," is thus not without counterpart in the history of the Metropolitan.

THE FIRST WAR SEASONS, 1915–1921

1915–1916

If the turn of events that separated Toscanini and Hertz from the Metropolitan at the end of the same season severed a link with the distant past, the arrival of Artur Bodanzky forged one that endured till the recent present. His was, by far, the longest association with the old house of any conductor in its history, barely short of a quarter-century when he died on November 23, 1939.

His arrival, on October 8, 1915, found him speaking freely, even more than frankly, about the perplexed matter of cuts in Wagner. "One thing I firmly believe in," he said, "and that is in cuts. If the length of a Wagnerian music drama bores the public, it should be cut, and I intend to see that such cuts will be made in the works under my direction." It was the contention of the management, when objections were made to the Bodanzky cuts, that they were the same as those initiated by Seidl and perpetuated by Mahler, Hertz, and Toscanini. As has been demonstrated, however, their way of shortening such a work as *Götterdämmerung* was to delete the Norn scene or Waltraute's narrative, which, if offensive, at least left other sections of the score intact. Bodanzky's preference was to shrink the whole work, with results, the late Paul Bekker declared (*Musical America,* August 1935), such as "no German provincial stage of the second rank would offer."

The company line on Toscanini was enunciated by William J. Guard, on his return from Europe, with these words: "The Maestro is a burning bush of patriotism." It was echoed by Gatti a few weeks later: "No one regrets more than I do the failure of Mr. Toscanini to come to America. . . . Mr. Toscanini made his decision solely because of the war." To the growing rumors that German works might be discontinued, he replied: "Should we boycott the printers because Gutenberg, a German, invented printing?"

This was a problem for the future. A present one, whose importance was not yet evident, was the rise of films. Hollywood had not yet been heard of, but California had, and Gatti had to plan the weeks till mid-February without Farrar, who was busy with a celluloid version of *Carmen*. The long period without Bori had also begun.[1]

The impresario thus had special reason to be grateful for the health of Caruso, whose appearance as Samson* in the opening night *Samson et Dalila* on November 15 honored him as a strong man of more than one sort. With Matzenauer a warm-voiced Dalila,* able choral singing and orchestral playing well directed by Polacco, and a scenic production said to have cost $40,000, objections to lack of "French style" were overcome by a degree of theatrical power not previously generated on behalf of the work. Caruso's presence drew strongly on what Henderson called "the standing army of Italy," standees being much more numerous than for previous *Samsons*.

Had it not been for some spirited occasions late in his Metropolitan career, those who knew Bodanzky in the twenties as the strained conductor of the entire German repertory plus the Friends of Music series could hardly credit the enthusiasm that attended his debut on November 18. His cuts in *Götterdämmerung* (the Norns and Alberich were missing in this version) displeased the Wagnerians, especially Krehbiel, but Henderson thought the omissions "worth while" and the conductor himself a man of "temperament, taste, and fine judgment." A dynamic variety scorned by Hertz gave new profile to the score, and the excellent cast of Kurt, Matzenauer (Waltraute), Urlus, Weil (Gunther), and Braun had, in the words of Aldrich, "a chance to sing, not shout." Julia Heinrich made a quiet debut as Gutrune (d).

By contrast with the Hertz conception of *Der Rosenkavalier*, Bodanzky's moved with uncommon lightness in his second venture on November 20. The score had also been appreciably abbreviated, which may have contributed to Henderson's revised opinion that the delight "of the really fine pages of Strauss's score—and it contains some of his best" had never been more apparent. Edith Mason made her "very acceptable" (the *Sun*) debut as Sophie (d) in the otherwise integrated cast of Hempel, Ober, and Goritz. For this season Bodanzky prepared but a single novelty, and that was the innocuous setting by Hermann Goetz of *The Taming of the Shrew*,

[1] A fortnight of performances in the Manhattan Opera House by the Boston Opera Company began on October 23 with *La Muette de Portici*, in which Pavlova danced Renella, and Felice Lyne, Giovanni Zenatello, and Thomas Chalmers were the principal singers. Later events included *L'Amore dei tre re* with Luisa Villani, the original Fiora, Ferrari-Fontana, José Mardones, and Georges Baklanoff (Manfredo); a *Butterfly* with Tamaki Miura; *Tosca* with Fremstad, Zenatello, and Baklanoff; and *Otello* with the same men and Villani. Roberto Moranzoni was the principal conductor.

given on March 15 with the German text and title of *Der widerspenstigen Zähmung*. The pleasant qualities of the score (which had been heard with English text in New York in 1886), the spirit with which Whitehill (Petruchio*), Ober (Katherine*), and Rappold (Bianca*), entered into the lively Shakespearean action, and a production that gave full credibility to "the luxury of the life of the Florentine smart set" (Henderson) made it a welcome addition to what the same writer called "the regrettably impoverished" repertory of the Metropolitan.[1] Nevertheless, it was heard but once again in this season, not thereafter.

By default of Paris, where operatic activities were curtailed by war, the Metropolitan presentation of Enrique Granados's *Goyescas, o las Majas Enamoradas* on January 28 became its world *première*. This was a pleasure for New York, but a tragedy for the composer, who had made the long journey in understandable eagerness to see his work produced. With his wife he was homeward bound on the *Sussex* when it was torpedoed by the Germans in March, and neither survived. The reception of his work was respectful if not enthusiastic, partially a result of its patchwork construction. Much of the score had been put together from piano pieces, and the orchestration had been amended by unidentified hands when rehearsals showed it to be deficient. The since-familiar Intermezzo was singled out as the best music in the work, and there was high praise for the production by Rovescalli. Anna Fitziu made her debut as Rosario (d), with Martinelli (Fernando*), De Luca (Pacquiro*), and Flora Perini (Pepa*). The conductor was Gaetano Bavagnoli, who had come to share the Italian repertory with Polacco.

The latter gave much of his effort in this season to perfecting the preparation of *Prince Igor,* which had been brought to its final stages by Toscanini the previous spring. Gatti had intended to include the third act in his presentation on December 30, but its dullness discouraged this generosity, even as it had in Paris and in London. The eventual conclusion was that the camp scene, with its familiar dances and choruses (Kurt Schindler had introduced them to New York on March 3, 1911), was the strongest part of the score, but the other music did not measure up to that level. Amato was a dignified Igor,* Alda a likable Jaroslavna,* and Didur outstanding as Galitzky.* Henderson found Polacco's conducting "wanting in smoothness," Krehbiel thought the whole presentation an "event of unusual interest," but not likely to attract the public, and Aldrich missed, in the Italian text and settings, the "exotic note" that had resounded in *Boris.* Gatti persisted with it for two further seasons, but neither the splendid

[1] Thirty-four works were given in this twenty-week season.

choral singing nor the dancing of Galli and Bonfiglio could interest a sufficiently general audience to justify a place in the repertory.

The most durable new singer to join the company this season was Giuseppe de Luca, with a robust baritone voice in its prime and a dozen years of singing leading roles in Italy behind him. His first role[1] was Figaro* in *Il Barbiere di Siviglia* on November 25, with Hempel (Rosina), Giacomo Damacco (Almaviva [d]), and Pompilio Malatesta (Bartolo [d]), when he performed with a "voice of fine quality" and "abundant vivacity of action," by Henderson's standard. Also welcome was María Barrientos, a Spanish soprano who made her debut as Lucia (d) on January 31 with Martinelli and Amato. Melba-like evenness of registers was not hers, but the neatness and discipline of her singing, within a limited dynamic range, were approved.

Barrientos had a greater success with Rosina* when *Il Barbiere* was given on February 5 to celebrate the one-hundredth anniversary of its first performance. She rose to real esteem when *Rigoletto* was revived on February 11 with Caruso and De Luca (Rigoletto*). Her Gilda* had dramatic nuance as well as excellent vocal line, and De Luca was rated a "good" Rigoletto in a time when "good" meant more than "not bad." Neither Gatti nor Caruso thought the tenor should sing the Duke at this point of his career, but Kahn's persistence overcame their objections. As detailed in Gatti's *Memories of the Opera,* Caruso brought him the next day's notices as proof that they had both been wrong; but the concord was not all-embracing. Henderson emphasized that "questions of style might easily be raised, and they might be readily directed at Mr. Caruso, whose advances in the realm of robustness led him at times . . . close to the robustious." He further noted a decline in "the aërial quality of tone and elegant finish" of Caruso's early years, but he admired the "warmth" and "impassioned" conviction of his delivery. Polacco conducted, and the stage showed a new production by Vittorio Rota.

A final variation in Caruso's repertory brought a revival of *Marta* on December 11, for the first time since 1908. Hempel was a charming Lady Harriet,* and there was virtue in Ober's Nancy* and De Luca's Plunkett.* Bavagnoli provided what Henderson termed "a discreet accompaniment." *La Sonnambula* also returned after half a dozen years' absence, but Barrientos was no more than "tolerable" as Amina,* and Damacco a labored Elvino* in its first showing on March 3. Didur was admired for his Rodolfo. In a later performance *La Sonnambula* was followed by the Polovtsian Dances from *Prince Igor.*

The absence of both Farrar and Bori provided opportunities for several

---

[1] It was also his last, nearly twenty-five years later (see page 423).

singers who might not otherwise have reached Metropolitan eminence. One was Louise Edvina, borrowed from the Chicago Opera to sing Tosca (d) with Caruso and Scotti in her debut on November 27. No longer in the bloom of youth, she performed with skilled routine, but hardly with distinction in the company of the evening. She had few further opportunities, for Destinn was the Tosca on January 5, prompting Henderson to say: "No other Tosca since Mme. Ternina has sung the popular 'Vissi d'arte' as well," thus putting a stamp on both Destinn and the familiar terminology.[1] De Luca was an able Scarpia,* Martinelli an excellent Cavaradossi.

Others utilized in the Puccini repertory were Ida Cajatti, singing a "very unsteady . . . often white" Musetta (d) at her debut in *La Bohème* on November 19, and Luisa Villani, of Boston, borrowed to be a Butterfly* with Martinelli and Scotti on December 11. Farrar's reappearance on February 14 produced a "fairly dull" Tosca, by the *Sun*'s measurement, but her followers, stimulated perhaps by her new status as both a film star and the wife of Lou Tellegen, a handsome actor of the day, appeared in greater numbers than the theater could accommodate.

Whatever could be said of her Carmen on February 17, it could not be called "dull." Musically it conformed to convention, but she slapped Caruso smartly in the face during Act I, pushed one of the chorus girls roughly in Act II, and scuffled about in Act III with such vigor that she found herself in a position more singular than singable. At the end, Farrar let it be known that if Caruso didn't care for this "realism," the company could find another Carmen. "No," the tenor gallantly replied, "we can prevent a repetition of the scene by getting another José." Apparently conciliatory words had been spoken on both sides, for the waited repetition on February 25 went without incident. "She neither slapped Don José's face," reported the *Tribune,* "nor did she maul the unhappy chorus girl." The "disillusioning vulgarity" of the earlier occasion was not missed by the *Sun*. The only other roles sung by Farrar this season were Madame Sans-Gêne and Butterfly. The Giordano score was now a "respectable piece of mediocrity," in Henderson's opinion.

As an instrument of retrenchment, Bodanzky sufficed by being efficient, nonexigent, and virtually tireless. He moved steadily through a frightening assignment of scores that included not only *Lohengrin* (Erma Zarska of Prague made her debut as an unremarkable Elsa*) on November 26, *Parsifal, Tristan, Die Meistersinger,* and the *Ring,* but also *Der Rosenkavalier, Die Zauberflöte,* and the Goetz novelty (see page 260). In the Mozart score, Bodanzky's work, with a cast of Kurt (Pamina*), Hempel,

---

[1] The introduction of such designations seems wholly related to the increasing popularity of phonograph records, especially of operatic arias.

Mason (Papagena*), and Sembach on December 8, was admired principally for precision. A direct comparison with Toscanini was drawn by Henderson when Bodanzky directed *Die Meistersinger* on January 7. If Bodanzky lacked the "alternating sensuous languor and passionate poignancy" of Toscanini, he provided "a certain exuberance of feeling," and much more animation among the apprentices, whose "pranks seemed not to appeal to Mr. Toscanini's delicate sense of beauty." Hempel (Eva), Sembach (Walther), and Reiss (David) were all excellent; not so the "wooden and unsympathetic" Sachs of Weil.

The steady upward course of the *Ring* productions in recent years, especially of *Das Rheingold,* was reflected in its presentation for the first time in a quarter-century as a regular repertory work on February 18 and again on March 29. "Nothing else in the repertory," Henderson remarked, "has been quite so admirably done." Sembach as Loge, Matzenauer or Kurt as Fricka, Ober (Erda), Braun, and Reiss were elements of a smoothly functioning cast. In the *Ring* sequence, Gadski was the *Walküre* Brünnhilde, with Kurt singing the later ones. In *Siegfried* on February 17, Schumann-Heink returned after several years to sing Erda "as only she can," the *Sun* commented. With Germany's borders closed to normal traffic, few singers of that nation or its allies were in movement around the world. Aside from Zarska, the only new singer to sing major roles in the Wagner repertory this season was Maude Fay of San Francisco, who had been active in Munich for eleven seasons. She was praised for her intelligent work as Sieglinde (d) on February 28, and sang again in the following season. Most of her subsequent career was in Chicago.

In a summing up, Henderson found the season's "level of merit" by no means brilliant. "What has become," he inquired, "of 'The Secret of Suzanne.' 'Versiegelt,' 'L'Amore dei Tre Re,' 'Le Donne Curiose,' 'L'Amore Medico,' and 'Julien'? . . . The answer would probably be that they did not draw. But they drew as well as some of the works which are retained. . . . L'Amore . . . need not have been shelved because of Miss Bori's illness. Mme. Villani is in the country."

After repeated promises, the Diaghilev Ballet was brought to New York this winter, and the final four weeks of the opera subscription was filled by its repertory. Gatti thought this an unwise move, but apparently had no power to prevent it. When the ballet opened on April 3, much of the interest had been dissipated by an earlier season in the Century Theater during January,[1] and even the long-awaited arrival of Waslav Nijinsky did not stimulate attendance.

[1] The Catholic Theater Movement protested the "immoralities" of *L'Après-midi d'un faune* and *Schéhérazade* at this time, and the action was altered.

At the Metropolitan opening, the bill was *Les Sylphides, Petrouchka, Le Spectre de la rose* (with Lydia Lopokova and Alexandre Gavriloff), and the Polovtsian Dances. Nijinsky reached New York on April 5, after internment in Budapest, but spent a week arguing money with Diaghilev before making his debut in *Le Spectre* on April 12, with Lopokova. The program was not included in the subscription series, and the house showed more than a few empty seats. Dance criticism was then a matter more of description than of evaluation, and the *Sun* was content with a description of Nijinsky as "a stage artist of refinement, taste, direct method and conviction." He also danced Petrouchka on the same bill and appeared two evenings later in *Les Sylphides* and *Carnaval,* and on the 15th in *Schéhérazade* and the *pas de deux* from *Sleeping Beauty.* Repetitions of these roles sufficed for the two remaining weeks of Nijinsky's appearances, though *L'Après-midi* was anticipated. But Nijinsky insisted on Flora Revalles as the nymph, and Diaghilev would not allow Tchernicheva to be replaced. There was no *L'Après-midi* with Nijinsky at the Metropolitan. The inconspicuous but efficient conductor for the ballet was Ernest Ansermet.

A line of critical thought worth noting was offered in a ballet review by Aldrich in the *Times.* In his view, ballets danced to music written for the purpose were reasonable enough; but danced "interpretations" of music written for no such purpose were quite intolerable. The fusion of purpose now considered self-justifying was still unappreciated.

Although Gatti had signed a new contract the year before, extending his tenure till 1919, he was given further security until 1921 while this season was in progress. He also engaged Edward Ziegler as his assistant, beginning an association that identified Ziegler with the Metropolitan till his death in 1947 (see page 469). Coincidentally John Brown gave up his post as business controller and was succeeded by his assistant, Ernest Henkel.

With the full accounting for the Ballet Russe still to be rendered, the season showed a gratifying improvement over the previous year's meager profit of $1,765. The figure for 1915–16 was $81,719—a good solid sum, but not nearly so impressive as some to come.

A storied event that can hardly be omitted from any Metropolitan chronicle, though no opera was involved, was a benefit for the family of Granados on May 7 (see page 260). Kreisler, Casals, and Paderewski played the *"Geister"* Trio of Beethoven (opus 70, no. 1); Casals and Kreisler played solos, each acting as the other's accompanist; Kreisler played for McCormack, Coenraad van Bos for Julia Culp, Casals accompanied Barrientos, Paderewski played a group of solos, and Kreisler performed obbligatos to the singing of McCormack.

1916–1917

The growing probability that the United States would become a participant in the European war became a certainty before this operatic season ran its course. However distant the battle seemed from an audience that paid "fabulous prices" for tickets and expended "a small fortune on frocks" (the *Sun*) to attend the opening performance—*Les Pêcheurs de perles*—on November 13,[1] it was very much a reality to Gatti and his associates charged with planning. It was to become an even greater one before the year was over.

Previously conceived as an opera in which Leïla was the focal role (as it had been when last given, in 1896, with Calvé), *The Pearl-Fishers* is remembered now for its association, in this revival, with Caruso. The celebrated recording of *"Je crois entendre encore"* was, in the actuality, one of Caruso's most notable accomplishments, to judge from Henderson's opinion that he sang "with a lyric beauty recalling his earlier days." De Luca as Zurga,* was "a master . . . of delicate finish," and Hempel (Leïla*) delivered "ravishing" upper tones. Handsomely produced, and well conducted by Polacco, it was heard with pleasure two times again this season, and then joined *Armide, Ariane et Barbe-bleue,* and various other matters in puzzling silence.

Equally puzzling, even while audible, was *Iphigenia auf Tauris,* given on November 25 in a version by Artur Bodanzky based on the Richard Strauss edition of 1912. He utilized the three-act compression of Strauss, somewhat shortened in the earlier acts, but extended by two excerpts from *Orfeo* (the D-minor *lento* and a chaconne) for ballet purposes in Act III. Bodanzky's musical preparation was highly commended, but not the use of a German text and a cast largely of German background which had little contact with the style appropriate for a work first produced in Paris. Kurt was an impressive Iphigenia,* and Weil did some of his best work as Orestes.* Sembach (Pylades*), Braun (Thoas*), and Marie Sundelius (First Priestess [d]) were less suited to their assignment. Monroe J. Hewlett, one of the first American scenic designers to see his work on the Metropolitan stage, provided an excellent décor, but it did not survive for a second season.

A new work from the house of Ricordi bore the name of Tito Ricordi himself, as adapter of a D'Annunzio text, when Riccardo Zandonai's

[1] The Lexington Theater became a new site for operatic activity on November 6, when the Boston National Opera Company, again directed by Moranzoni, offered a short season of specialties including *Andrea Chénier* (Villani, Zenatello, Baklanoff, and Frances Peralta), *Iris* (with Tamaki Miura), and *L'Amore dei tre re* (Villani, Mardones, Baklanoff, and Riccardo Martin).

Francesca da Rimini was offered on December 22. Well orchestrated, as virtually every post-Wagner score has been, it "shot its bolt" in the first act, Henderson observed, with little in reserve for the third-act climax. Krehbiel likened it to *L'Amore,* but said that it lacked Montemezzi's individuality. He also thought Alda's Francesca* an "inadequate conception beyond her histrionic abilities." Musically the role was too heavy for her voice. Martinelli (Paolo*) and Amato (Giovanni*) performed ably. Queenie Smith, a later favorite of the musical-comedy stage, appeared as a Maid of Honor. Polacco conducted.

After a lapse of four seasons, Gatti offered another hearing to an American opera on March 8, when *The Canterbury Pilgrims* by Reginald de Koven and Percy Mackaye was given under Bodanzky's direction. Some opinion admired Mackaye's text and some found virtue in De Koven's music, but no one thought the latter's operetta mannerisms appropriate to the former's literary manner. Any temptation to charity was negated by the mangled delivery of the English text by Sembach (Chaucer*), Ober (Wife of Bath*), Mason (Prioress*), and Ruysdael (Miller*). Virtue did not always go by nationality, for Sembach's words came out more clearly than those sung by his American colleagues. James Fox, scenic artist for the company, shared credit for the production with Homer Emens. Richard Ordynski directed the stage action. At that, *The Canterbury Pilgrims* had six performances, one more than *Iphigenia auf Tauris.*

Mozart had greater honor in this season than in any earlier one directed by Gatti, with *Die Zauberflöte* retained in the repertory and *Le Nozze di Figaro* revived after eight years' silence. Garrison sang the Queen of the Night* fluently on November 20, when Hempel was ill, the other principals being the same as the previous year, including Urlus as a "depressing" Tamino (the *Sun*). From Mahler's notable *Figaro* cast there remained Farrar (Cherubino) and Didur, now singing Almaviva,* when the Mozartian masterpiece was revived on January 24. The new Figaro,* and a delightful one, was De Luca. His performance and the spirited Susanna* of Hempel alone gave real pleasure, for Matzenauer was a stolid Countess,* whose voice required transposition of some music, Farrar was no longer the picturesque Cherubino she had been, and she was now a less conscientious singer of Mozart's music. Neither work was pursued with much determination by Gatti, for *Figaro* had only five performances in this and the next season, while *Die Zauberflöte* lapsed at the end of the current one.

Fidelio, under Bodanzky, had three performances this season, in the version of Mahler and with largely the cast of Hertz: Kurt, Sembach, Goritz, and Braun (Rocco) were familiar figures in the performance of December 9. Mason sang Marzellina* well, and Kurt was a more convincing Leonore than previously, if no more successful with *"Abscheu-licher"* than the average soprano. When the curtain fell on the third performance, on January 19, it marked the last *Fidelio* New York was to hear for ten seasons.

In a year showing fewer new personalities than any, perhaps, in previous Metropolitan history, the introduction of Claudia Muzio on December 4 should have been more eventful than it was. Krehbiel thought her as fine a new singer as any the company had acquired since Bori; Aldrich added to his description of her as "young and beautiful" a characterization of her voice as "fresh and agreeable" and noted that she used it "artistically." Henderson heard "a good lyric soprano, full and vibrant in quality . . . but prone to become shrill when pinched." With her in *Tosca*[1] were Caruso (one of his infrequent Cavaradossis) and Scotti. Muzio was well received by an audience that included many professional musicians who remembered her father as a stage manager for Grau, Claudia as a child of eight lurking in the wings.

At twenty-two plus, Muzio was not yet the artist she later became, and a succession of roles which included Manon* in *Manon Lescaut* on December 9, Nedda* in *I Pagliacci* on December 15, Leonora* in *Il Trovatore* on December 18, and Aida* on January 27 was hardly to her advantage. Eventually Henderson spoke favorably of her "invaluable power to interest an audience" and her "fine and communicative enthusiasm," but the fact is plain that Muzio did not take the press by storm.

Thanks to the generosity of the Chicago company, which permitted the use of its scenery, *Thaïs* was added to the Metropolitan repertory on February 16. Farrar sang much of the music eloquently, if lacking the Garden forcefulness in action, but neither Amato (Athanaël*) nor Botta (Nicias*) gave to their roles what had been admired in Renaud and Dalmorès. A ballet omitted in the Manhattan presentation was included. The assumption that performers do not read what is written about them was proved untrue, at least in so far as Farrar's costuming was concerned. The reports of the first performance having suggested that Farrar was unduly conservative in dress, she appeared the next time in what the *Sun* described as "entirely . . . skirt. From the waist up it is exclusively Miss Farrar and two small groups of jewels . . . inconspicuous, but essentially located."

Another variation in customary repertory was provided by a revival of *L'Elisir d'amore* on December 30, with Caruso as Nemorino for the first time since 1905, Hempel (Adina*), and Scotti. The tenor's delivery of

---

[1] Aside from Cavalieri, who sang the role in an emergency, Muzio was the first Italian Tosca in the Metropolitan succession of Ternina, Eames, Farrar, Fremstad, Destinn, Edvina, and so on.

"Una furtiva lagrima" roused a storm of cries for an encore, but he out-lasted the applause, resuming with the interpolated words "To repeat is not allowable." Hempel sparkled as Adina, and Scotti was a delightful Belcore. Caruso and *L'Elisir* were Metropolitan favorites for the five years to come, to the day when the first symptoms of Caruso's fatal illness showed themselves in Brooklyn in *L'Elisir,* in 1920. Gennaro Papi, who had pre-viously been an assistant conductor, was in charge of the Donizetti score. Barrientos replaced Hempel as Adina* on February 15, acting with "gayety, ease and grace," said the *Sun,* and singing stylishly. She was also seen in a revival of *Lakmé,* with rather less satisfaction, on March 24. The Sembrich kind of ornamental singing was still remembered, to Barrientos's disadvantage, though she sang the first-act duet with Delaunois (Mallika*) very well. Martinelli (Gerald*), Rothier (Nilakantha*) and De Luca (Frederic*), were in the cast. The scenic production by James Fox and Polacco's conducting were both praised.

The year's performances of Wagner were even less eventful than those of the preceding season, when Bodanzky, at least, had given a fresh accent to the familiar casts. Of interest was the first appearance of the American mezzo Kathleen Howard as Magdalene* on January 17, a part she sang often in the future with musical effect and dramatic charm, and, on March 19, the long-awaited Hans Sachs* of Clarence Whitehill. The time he had spent in preparing the role was rewarded by Krehbiel's enthusiastic "Long may Clarence Whitehill sing . . . Hans Sachs . . . as he sang . . . last night." Henderson's admiration for "the deep undercurrent of poetic imagination" in the creation foreshadowed the day when it would be compared, without disadvantage, to the Metropolitan's Father Sachs of all, Emil Fischer. Urlus, Gadski, Mattfeld, and Reiss were in the cast of this *Meistersinger.*

Bodanzky conducted all the Wagner works as in the previous season, though he was spelled by Richard Hageman for some smaller chores, such as *Hänsel und Gretel* on Christmas Day. This departed from recent Metro-politan custom (dating from Humperdinck's visit in 1910) by which Albert Reiss, the tenor, sang the Witch, by offering Homer in the part. Raymonde Delaunois (Hänsel*) and Garrison (Gretel*) made a charming new brother and sister, and there were newcomers in the smaller roles. (The Sandman* was in Marie Tiffany* and the Dewman* was Odette Le Fonte-nay.) A customary *Ring* cycle began on February 1 with Gadski and Kurt as Brünnhildes. When *Siegfried* was repeated on March 29, the *Tribune* re-ported: "Mr. Bodanzky made several cuts in the interminable score which shortened the performance by almost half an hour." Needless to say, this was not written by Krehbiel, the pioneering Wagnerite, but by an assistant.

The rising pitch of international emotion was reflected at the Metropol-

itan during a performance of *Mme Sans-Gêne* on March 2. Amid cursory
attention to Farrar and Amato, the appearance on stage of the French flag
and the singing of *La Marseillaise* brought the audience to its feet. News
that war had been declared came on April 6, Good Friday, midway in a
performance of *Parsifal*. Earlier events of the week had prepared the
German members of the cast for the inevitable; the blow fell heavily none
the less. *Die Meistersinger* and *Tristan* were given as scheduled during
the remaining week of the season.

In the last of these, on April 13, the Metropolitan career of Johanna
Gadski came to a certain, if unofficial, end. She was allowed to announce
her "retirement," though the public was well aware of her marriage ties to
Captain Hans Tauscher, a reserve officer in the German army who represented the Krupp and other munitions firms in the United States. He was
accused of plotting to blow up the Welland Canal in 1916, but acquitted.
Gadski was also in disfavor because her home had been the scene of a
jubilant party after the sinking of the *Lusitania* (1915). Nevertheless, it
is hard to credit Henderson's view in the *Sun* that Gadski's engagement
was terminated because of "the deterioration of Mme. Gadski's voice and
art." His further allegation that she was merely "an honest, hard-working
. . . soprano," who has had "much admiration from easy going opera
patrons," did him no honor. Her farewell *Tristan* was marked by "a generous good-bye" and praise for the artistic Kurvenal* of Whitehill.

With the costly tour of the Diaghilev Ballet not yet counted against
Metropolitan earnings, Gatti's profit balance rose to new eminence this
year: $190,000. As noted elsewhere, amounts other than those received
at the box office were contributory to this (see page 5). They were more
than little bits, and all helped.

1917–1918

By common measurement, Gatti was pretty much the autocrat of Metropolitan affairs in this period, but there are several suggestions that he was
no more than a limited monarch, subject to suasion and suggestion of his
board—subject, in the final extremity, to direct order. Certainly he had
not wanted to present Caruso in *Rigoletto* (see page 261) or share his season with the Diaghilev Ballet Russe. These were relatively minor matters,
however, not worthy of being made issues. Such, however, was not the
abandonment of the German repertory in the first year of our participation
in World War I. Gatti's outspoken objection is clear from his *Memoirs,*
but he accepted the decision of the board when it was conveyed to him,
in the interest of keeping his job, if in no other.

Examination of the facts suggests that it was a decision hastily arrived at, and not wholly for the reasons given to the public. As late as September 15, the *Sun,* in an editorial, regarded the proposed action as "indeed a strange rumor." To discriminate against Bach, Beethoven, Wagner, and Brahms was pointless: "They belong to the world as do Shakespeare and Dante."

In the end the press condemned the timidity of the board and sympathized with Gatti, who had to find—at barely more than a week's notice— a way of replacing the normal forty to forty-five performances of works in German. No doubt he had made some tentative plans against an emergency, but hardly to substitute for one performance in every three.

The public was advised, a week before the opening on November 12, that the works were dropped "lest Germany should make capital of their continued appearance to convince the German people that this nation was not heart and soul in the war." In England, at closer quarters, where such propaganda might have counted for more, Beecham gave Mozart and Wagner (in English) in the midst of Zeppelin raids, and the French listened to Schubert while cursing the shells that dropped from the mouth of Big Bertha.

A secondary action, by which Kurt, Ober, Sembach, Braun, and Goritz were summarily dismissed from the company, suggests that backstage harmony was actually the issue at stake. Goritz, certainly, was outspoken in his Germanic fervor, and when Ober sued for $50,000 (she added to $24,000 due on her contract as much again for the expense and inconvenience of coming to this country), the Metropolitan's attorneys cited her "intense hatred" of the United States as a reason for breaking her contract. In any case, only Sembach was re-engaged after the war. A silent sufferer was Olive Fremstad, who was described in the *Sun* of November 10 as the "re-engaged Mme. Fremstad." She did not return during this season, or ever.

The heavy burden the season placed on Caruso and Farrar may be surmised from the number and scope of their appearances. The latter, at least, considered this a harmful expedient that might have been avoided, she recalled to me in conversation, had Gatti followed her suggestion that he assemble Garden, Muratore, Dalmorès, and several other "available"[1] artists to do *Louise, Le Jongleur, Monna Vanna, Pelléas, Werther,* and a few others half a dozen times each, thus filling the Wagner vacuum. Gatti's reply, as she remembers, was that it was too expensive and the board would not agree.

He did, however, undertake to repair some weaknesses in the French and

[1] By her recollection, though they seem to have been busy enough in Chicago (see page 281).

the Italian repertory performances by engaging Pierre Monteux to conduct the former, and Roberto Moranzoni for the latter (Polacco was gone, soon to reappear in Chicago). As with Italian conductors before and after, Moranzoni was introduced with *Aida* on November 12. The *Sun* took note of the simultaneous opening of the Horse Show, reporting "throngs of people distinguished in the ceremonial life of the city" in both places. Henderson also reported the customary enthusiasm for Caruso, though he "probably never sang 'Celeste Aida' so badly before." In the view of the same writer, Muzio was a "mediocre" Aida, but José Mardones made an impressive debut as the Priest (d), and Moranzoni conducted soundly. The curtain was raised after the triumphal scene, and the audience joined in the singing of the national anthem.

In place of the customary second-night Wagner, *Boris* was given on November 14, with Papi, a long downward step from Toscanini and Polacco, conducting. The *Sun* did not hear the "incisive accent" the music required. Papi was also the conductor of the next night's *Elisir d'amore* (Caruso and Hempel), prompting Henderson to describe him derisively as a conductor "who is held in high esteem in official circles" but in none other. Papi served the next night for Puccini, conducting a *Bohème* with McCormack as Rodolfo singing his first Metropolitan opera since *Natoma* in 1912. In the intervening years he had begun his long, successful career as a concert favorite, and the critical scrutiny was keener than it had been before. Aldrich doubted that McCormack was a Puccini tenor, but admired the finish of his singing, "of its kind unsurpassable." Henderson thought his style "excellently suited" to Rodolfo, and commended Alda for a "decided improvement" in her Mimi. The Musetta* was Ruth Miller, rather slender of voice.

"Well planned," "musicianly," and "finely wrought" were some of the terms applied by Henderson to the revival of *Faust* by which Pierre Monteux introduced himself on November 18. (How to give the measure of a conductor's contribution to an opera performance while not giving cause to deplore his departure was a delicate problem in critical adjustment.) Praise was high for Farrar's Marguerite, and the well-schooled Thomas Chalmers made his debut as Valentin (d) in a cast with Martinelli and Rothier. The settings, the first of many to be designed by Joseph Urban, were commended as "of great beauty, and of such design as to lend themselves to a complete shattering of the conventional stage business." Undoubtedly they looked better in 1917 than when *Faust* was being given in 1951 amid a dusty remnant of the same décor. For that matter, the new *Tosca* production by Mario Sala seen on November 19 served the house for more than forty years, freshened (if not improved) by repainting.

The muddled thinking that determined the inclusion or exclusion of works written between the Rhine and the Volga permitted Flotow's *Marta* on November 21 and Mozart's *Nozze di Figaro* on December 22, both sung in Italian, and Liszt's *St. Elizabeth* on January 3, in English, though all the composers, by nationality, were as much "enemies" as the interdicted Wagner. Whether as oratorio (its original form) or opera, Liszt's score was patently not dramatic; the English text by Constance Bache was a meager contribution to attentive listening. Florence Easton's singing of St. Elizabeth* gave her place "in the first rank of Metropolitan stars," said Aldrich, not alone for intelligent vocalization but also for her uniquely distinct English enunciation. Whitehill (Ludwig*), Matzenauer (Landgravine Sophie*), and Ruysdael (a Hungarian Magnate*) worked to little avail against a singularly unyielding score. The production was by Urban, and Bodanzky conducted.

On the whole, the absorbing innovations of this season were those directed by Monteux: Henri Rabaud's *Marouf* on December 19 and the endlessly delightful *Le Coq d'or* of Rimsky-Korsakov on March 6. Henderson found "an extraordinary amount of character, atmosphere and incidental significance" in Rabaud's score, and the qualified cast of De Luca (Marouf*), Alda (Princess*), Chalmers (Ali*), and Rothier (Sultan*) left few opportunities unexploited. Ernest Gros designed the scenery.

Measured words hardly sufficed for *Le Coq d'or,* one of the great productions of the whole Gatti period, with its imaginative décor by Willy Pogany, its marshaling of vocal and mime talent to fill the ingenious Fokine plan of double casting, and, of course, the insinuating leadership of Monteux. To be sure, *Coq d'or* did not fit into any convenient operatic category, which induced some critical hairsplitting, but the final judgment accorded with Henderson's conclusion: "Its influence on the listener is sure, while almost unnoticed." Barrientos sang the Queen's* music delightfully, and Galli performed the actions endearingly, with Didur a sonorous King* to hear, Adolf Bolm an amusing one to watch. Braslau sang Amelfa,* danced by Queenie Smith, and Ruysdael was the voice of the General,* acted by Bartik. An uncommonly apt performance of the Astrologer* by Rafael Diaz left a durable place in Metropolitan lore for this light tenor, who sang many other roles in a longish career (he made his debut as Nicias* in *Thaïs* on January 5), but none so creditably. Thirty-odd performances in the next half-dozen seasons gave public endorsement to *Le Coq d'or* as Gatti's happiest venture since *L'Amore* and *Der Rosenkavalier.*

L'Amore returned in gala style on March 14, with Muzio as Fiora* and Caruso as Avito,* neither matching the suitability of Bori and Ferrari-Fontana. The soprano persisted in the part, overcoming a physique not considered suitable for the childish heroine, but Caruso gave up after three further performances. Martinelli was his replacement on April 6, and sang it many times thereafter. Moranzoni's conducting was admirably energetic, and the cast had a sturdy Archibaldo* when Mardones appeared on March 22.

As a further departure from the days when "Italian singers would not learn new parts," Caruso added Flammen* in Mascagni's *Lodoletta* and Jean of Leyden* in *Le Prophète,* as well as Avito, to his repertory this season, while singing an almost endless succession of Nemorino, Radames, Samson, and so on. The Mascagni pastorale, at its hearing on January 12, was likened to his *L'Amico Fritz,* with Caruso superb in the melodic matter and Farrar (Lodoletta*), Amato (Gianotto*), and Didur (Antonio*) well liked. Easton had the title role on January 21. While speculating that "it ought to please," Henderson gave the full measure of its worth by saying: "There is not a wearisome moment in the vocal portions, nor is there a stirring one." In the same writer's opinion, Caruso's John of Leyden* was "one of his most artistic achievements" when the Meyerbeer score was given in Italian on February 7. Matzenauer was a noble Fidès* and Muzio a handsome Bertha,* but the presumptively all-star cast fell off badly from Didur (Oberthal*) and Mardones (Zacharias*) to Bloch, Schlegel, and D'Angelo.

Further explorations of the past included revivals of *I Puritani* for Barrientos on February 18 and *La Fille du régiment* for Hempel on December 17. The Spanish soprano's Elvira* was neatly sung, as was the Lord Arthur* of her countryman Hipólito Lázaro. De Luca's Sir Richard* and Mardones's Sir George* were on the order of acceptable, but the restless Gatti decided that the public had had enough of this after four performances. The martial suggestions of Donizetti were welcomed in wartime (as Johnson remembered twenty-five years later), and the able cast of Scotti (Sulpizio*), Carpi (Tonio*), and Mattfeld (Marchioness*) gave handsome support to the bright vocalization of Hempel. The language of this production was Italian, as was the conducting of Papi.

Though Gatti had good reason to be discouraged with the use made by American composers of the opportunities tendered to them, he continued his hospitality with the sponsorship of two short works. Certainly there was no bias to one school or another in the election of Charles Wakefield Cadman's *Shanewis* to be sung, and Henry F. Gilbert's *The Dance in Place Congo* to be mimed. At the first performance, on March 23, they were followed by *L'Oracolo,* thus offering a prismatic sequence of red man, black man, and yellow man. In none was beauty so much as skin-deep, though some considered Gilbert's score (a concert piece adapted by Bartik for ballet) more original than most previously heard in the Metropolitan. *Shanewis* (with Braslau as Shanewis* and Althouse as Lionel*) had the melodic charm of Cadman's "At Dawning" and "From the Land of the Sky-Blue Waters," but not much that was theatrically absorbing. Norman Bel Geddes designed the Cadman sets, Livingston Platt those for the ballet. Moranzoni conducted the opera, Monteux the ballet.

By measurement of years of service, Florence Easton was the important artist to begin a Metropolitan career this season, even though she had some years of drought to survive before the Wagnerian spring flowed again. As Santuzza (d) in *Cavalleria* on December 7, she was welcomed by Henderson as a singer with "a voice of beauty and no inconsiderable power," who gave "emotional value and theatrical picturesqueness" to the performance. As Ah-Yoe* in *L'Oracolo* on December 22, in *St. Elizabeth* and *Lodoletta*,[1] even as Nedda in the first act of *Pagliacci* at a benefit on March 21, Easton was complimented for assurance, musicianship, and intelligence. A singer subsequently prominent in the German repertory appeared for the first time in *Samson* on November 23, when Julia Claussen sang Dalila* to Caruso's Samson. Henderson's description of her as "entirely creditable and conventional" would be apt for anything she did. Monteux conducted with "verve and point," and the ever growing "dignity and virility" of Caruso's Samson were commended, as was Whitehill's High Priest.*

McCormack's ability as a singer of Mozart was not utilized at any time in his Metropolitan career, his appearances of this year being exclusively in Puccini—Rodolfo, Pinkerton, and Cavaradossi. Protestations that *Don Giovanni* had to be avoided for lack of a cast seem pointless when one imagines the results that could have been achieved by Scotti, De Luca (Leporello), McCormack, Easton (Donna Anna), Hempel (Elvira), and Farrar (Zerlina)—one of the best casts the Metropolitan never presented! Of other tenors, the roster showed two new ones: Morgan Kingston, who appeared first in *Il Trovatore* on December 1, and Hipólito Lázaro, who won some acclaim for daring a high D flat at the end of the second-act duet during his debut as the Duke (d) in *Rigoletto* on January 31. On February 8, as Cavaradossi,* Lázaro was judged by Henderson to have "one of the best tenor voices" heard in recent years. He later sang Turiddu in *Cavalleria* and Lord Arthur in *I Puritani* (see page 273).

The newly organized Chicago Opera Association (direction by Campa-

---

[1] This Monday-night subscription performance occurred on Tuesday, in compliance with an order by the Federal Fuel Administrator that theaters should be dark one night a week. Broadway agreed on Tuesday. By the next week it was agreed that the Metropolitan could save as much fuel on a dark Tuesday as on a dark Monday, and the opera resumed its traditional pattern.

nini, financing largely by the Harold McCormicks) challenged direct competition with the Metropolitan when it opened a lengthy season at the Lexington Theater on January 23 with Garden in *Monna Vanna* (Charlier conducting). Although Gatti was fond of contending that Europe was bare of singers he could use, Campanini introduced two whom the Metropolitan could have used at any time—Rosa Raïsa and Amelita Galli-Curci.

Of Raïsa's debut in *The Jewels of the Madonna* on January 24, Henderson said: "Her voice is full and rich and of large power . . . so genuinely beautiful that it cannot fail to give pleasure." The Raffaele was her husband, Giacomo Rimini, singing with "a light, dry voice." She also appeared as Santuzza on February 2, and they sang together in Mascagni's *Isabeau* on February 13, she in the title role, he as her father. Raïsa was sightly enough in this adaptation of the Lady Godiva legend, and sang superbly the indifferent music provided by Mascagni.

The measured praise that sufficed for Raïsa's excellence could hardly do for Galli-Curci's uniqueness. Not since Tetrazzini—the last time it had been "not since Melba"—had this special kind of audible phenomenon come to New York, and the response was in kind. Henderson did not temporize in describing her work as Dinorah on January 28: "She is an artist of brilliant abilities. Her voice is singularly smooth, deep colored and flexible. It is a pure flute voice . . . capable of much warm and tender expression." The "Shadow Song" provoked twenty-four recalls, and the curtain calls at the end ran close to sixty. Rimini, Huberdeau, and Octave Dua were in the cast, conducted by Campanini.

She was heard five times later, each performance drawing more patrons than the theater could hold. In addition to a second Dinorah, she sang Lucia on January 31, with Juan Nadal as Edgardo; Gilda in *Rigoletto* on February 9, with the same tenor and Stracciari, a far finer baritone than he had been a decade before; Rosina in *Il Barbiere* on the 13th; and Violetta, with Nadal and Stracciari, on the 15th. Her Gilda was a dramatic disappointment, but all the roles were beautifully vocalized, with an appropriate climax in a Violetta that Henderson described as "surpassingly beautiful . . . with rare beauty of tone and delicacy of feeling" and "deeper emotional power" than anticipated. To Aldrich, Galli-Curci represented "the moral value of art unspoiled," in the midst of a world at war. This being her farewell for the year, New Yorkers to the number of 10,000 (by police estimate) crowded the vicinity of a theater that held less than 3,000. A rainy night and snarled traffic found many who came in cars trudging through mud lest they miss *"Ah! fors è lui."* At the final curtain, the cheering audience would not leave until the soprano appeared close to midnight to sing "Home, Sweet Home."

Of necessity, the press queried Galli-Curci on approaches by the Metropolitan. She diplomatically contended that she had been sent directly to Campanini from Italy. Gatti's *Memories of the Opera* offers nothing relevant to the stories that he had heard her in 1916 and decided that she would not do. More recently I have heard that she did sing for him, but her inclination to sing flat was uncommonly evident in the audition.

The vast attention to Galli-Curci had its element of irony, for Melba returned to sing Marguerite on February 4 with Dalmorès and Baklanoff amid such press comments as Henderson's "the voice is no longer in its bloom . . . much of the famous soprano's singing could only cause regret." Garden had a relatively small part in this visit, following her *Monna Vanna* with *Thaïs, Pelléas* (with Alfred Maguenat), and *Carmen* (Muratore, Baklanoff, and Myrna Sharlow as Micaëla). Geneviève Vix was admired as Manon (d) in her debut on January 30, with special praise for Muratore's "impassioned, manly, graceful, and in the end, tragic" Des Grieux. Dufranne, Defrère, and Huberdeau completed the excellent cast.

The new works, beyond *Isabeau,* were of small merit. Henry Hadley directed his *Azora* on January 26, with Fitziu, Cyrena van Gordon, and Forrest Lamont; and Sylvio Lazzari conducted his *Le Sautériot* on February 11, with Germaine Manny, Dalmorès, and Dufranne. Neither was heard in New York again. Despite a loss (made good by Harold McCormick, who was responsible for any sums beyond the $100,000 subscribed by the guarantors), the company continued its New York visits for the next four years.

On the other hand, Gatti added $23,222 to his cash balance, though the company paid off in this and the next year the loss of $300,000 incurred by the Diaghilev Ballet. Publicly, Kahn and his associates accepted the honors tendered them as "guarantors" of the ballet tour; privately, they found it convenient to charge the cost against the account of the Metropolitan.

1918–1919

The end of the European war was still an uncertainty when Gatti arranged an opening-week schedule that elected Saint-Saëns and *Samson et Dalila* for the opening night. When the opening date of November 11, 1918 took a place in history of other sorts than musical, the *Sun* could well identify Gatti as "surely the son of a prophet" in arranging this glorification of the genius of France. Amid ceremonies and jubilation, the musical performance of Caruso, Homer, and Robert Couzinou (High Priest [d]) was on the dull side till Monteux and the ballet stirred cheers.

With or without hostilities, the demand for swift restoration of Wagner and other works with German texts was negligible. The sounds associated with the "arrogant" Hun and the "beast" who ravaged Belgium were scorned even in the concert hall, where lieder were welcome, if at all, only in English. In the curious circumstances that prevailed, *Oberon* was accepted on December 28 because it was written to an English text, though the composer's name was, after all, Carl Maria von Weber.

The splendid overture, such vocal high spots as *"Ozean, du Ungeheuer,"* and the airs of Huon gave to the evening a musical luster that Urban's artful designs complimented admirably. With Martinelli as Huon* and the newly acclaimed Rosa Ponselle as Rezia,* *Oberon* mustered a variety of attractions that kept it in the repertory for three seasons. To be sure, the young Ponselle was not the vocal trumpet needed to sound the full flourish of "Ocean, thou mighty monster," but her effort aroused Huneker's[1] "hearty admiration" and Henderson's "commiseration." Bodanzky introduced a new custom by providing recitatives made from Weberian motives, and by skillful reduction of the original twenty-one tableaux to seven earned Huneker's praise as "that rara avis, a musicianly conductor with temperament." Of the cast, Marie Sundelius earned special praise for exquisite singing of the Mermaid's song. Althouse was Oberon.*

Gatti's confidence in the young American soprano from vaudeville (the first program identified her as Poncelle) was manifest not only in his putting her forward on a stage with Caruso, De Luca, and Mardones on November 15, but also in his depending upon her for the exacting role of Leonora* in a revival of *La Forza del destino,* which had not been heard in New York since an Academy season of 1882. Recognition of the sumptuous voice was immediate. "It is vocal gold," wrote Huneker, "dark, rich, and ductile." Henderson regarded with some skepticism the statement that she had never sung in opera before; if so, he said "she must have been born with a ready made routine." In any case, she had "one of the most voluptuous dramatic soprano voices" ever heard, and, Henderson added, "doubtless some day Miss Ponselle will learn how to sing." Doubtless, too, her coming relieved Gatti of some liability for not presenting Raïsa or Galli-Curci. Further consideration of *Forza*—"welcome despite its curious shortcomings," said Henderson—or of the cast of Caruso (Alvaro*), De Luca (Don Carlos*), and Mardones (Abbott*) was understandably subordinate. Alice Gentle, as Preziosilla (d) made an inconspicuous debut.

Aside from Rezia in *Oberon,* Ponselle's only other role came in an American novelty. She sang Carmelita* when Joseph Breil's *The Legend*

[1] He served as critic of the *Times* during the war service of Aldrich.

was given on March 12. The composer's fame as writer of the incidental music for D. W. Griffith's *The Birth of a Nation* and *Intolerance* did not count for much in the opera house, though such a tune as his *The Perfect Song* (long associated with the Amos 'n' Andy radio program) would have helped. Also new on this bill was *The Temple Dancer,* by John Adams Hugo, with Easton (the Temple Dancer*) and Kingston (a Temple Guard*). The total, in Henderson's opinion, was "some sad moments" for advocates of opera in English. Norman Bel Geddes was the designer for *The Legend,* James Fox for *The Temple Dancer. Shanewis* followed, thus being the first American work to be heard in a second season.

The excitement that attended a Puccini *première* was hardly mitigated on December 14 by the division of the evening into a three-part triptych rather than a full-length work, for the public had the pleasure of hearing Easton, Muzio, and Farrar, plus numerous male singers, in new roles, and the press had three problems to consider rather than one. Least enthusiastic about the prospect was Gatti, who later wrote that he "never quite could understand" the juxtaposition of *Gianni Schicchi, Il Tabarro,* and *Suor Angelica,* and frankly deplored the need for putting three prima donnas to work on the same evening.

Ironically, the hardest to do won the most enthusiastic response and the most enduring popularity. Henderson's words for *Gianni Schicchi* were "uproarious farce," tinged with admiration for an orchestral style that suggested Puccini's study of the all-but-forgotten *Falstaff.* Krehbiel concurred that "uproariously funny" was the proper description, adding warm enthusiasm for Easton's Lauretta,* De Luca's Gianni Schicchi,* Giulio Crimi's Rinuccio,* and Didur's Simone.* Moranzoni had studied the work with Puccini during the summer and smoothed its ensemble problems with a knowing hand.

Toward the other pieces the critical attitude was no less uniform, but far less affirmative. *Il Tabarro* was skillful melodrama without sufficient power to be interesting, despite a strong cast of Muzio (Giorgetta*), Crimi (Luigi*), and Luigi Montesanto (Michele*). *Suor Angelica,* said Henderson, was "well composed . . . but without sustained utterance" for the voices of Farrar (Suor Angelica*), Perini (La Principessa*), and Sundelius (La Zelatrice*). Henderson nevertheless saw a binding theme in the three works (mad love, a retreat from the world, and a gibe at human greed), and thought it would be "false" for one to be separated from the others. That, however, is exactly how the one of superior merit has survived in most theaters.

The momentary trend to French works as novelties ventured nothing more controversial than Leroux's *La Reine Fiammette* (a Garden creation of 1903) on January 24 and the faded *Mireille* of Gounod on February 28. Thanks to what the *Sun* called "the blazing brush" of Boris Anisfeld, sixteenth-century Bologna was impressively invoked on Leroux's behalf, but the music Farrar had to sing as Orlanda* was, in Henderson's recollection of *Suor Angelica,* a "leap from the pan to the fire, and it is such a feeble fire." Lázaro (Danielo*) and Rothier (Cardinal*) did as well as circumstances allowed, and Mary Ellis, who had been barely noticed at her debut in *Suor Angelica,* won praise for the minor parts of Viola* and Angioletta.* The conductor was Monteux, who also directed *Mireille.* This had its share of designing interest also, for the sketches were made by the long-retired Victor Maurel, a product of its Provençal setting, who had been a student of painting before turning to the stage. Barrientos sang Mireille* agreeably, with Charles Hackett as Vincent.* It vanished after three repetitions.

Far more durable, and one of the ventures longest associated with Monteux, was the production of Stravinsky's *Petrouchka* on February 6. The ensemble could not compare with that of the Diaghilev company, but some preferred Galli's Ballerina* to Lopokova's, and Adolf Bolm's Petrouchka* ranked with the best. Bonfiglio was the Moor,* Bartik the Magician.* John Wenger's setting was apt, and Monteux's conducting of Stravinsky was praised for neither the first nor the last time.

A final novelty, for Hempel, was the Ricci brothers' *Crispino e la Comare,* not considered Metropolitan fare even in simpler days. Her singing of Annetta* was described as "fluent, luminous and elegant" by Henderson at its first performance on January 18. Scotti was Crispino,* with Braslau as La Comare.* For all the glitter of the interpolated *Carnival of Venice,* Hempel and the work were seen only twice again.

In its conventional aspects the season differed little from the wartime ones immediately preceding. Farrar and Caruso, Hempel and Muzio, Barrientos and Scotti were balance wheels of the mechanism. *Boris* was retained, but not *Prince Igor.* Other exceptions to the customary were *Marouf* and *Le Coq d'or, L'Amore* and the recently revived *Le Prophète.*

Among new singers of ephemeral careers were Mary Mellish, Xenia (d) in *Boris* on November 25 (with Papi a "notably uneven" conductor in the *Sun*'s judgment), and Margaret Romaine, who made a debut in *La Bohème* as Musetta (d) two evenings later, as did Luigi Montesanto (Marcello [d]). Much more consequential was the American tenor first called Carlo Hackett at his debut as Almaviva (d) in *Il Barbiere* on January 31. When Henderson heard him as Alfredo* in *La Traviata* on February 6, he commended his "mastery of mezza voce," and vowed that he sang "diminuendi with the skill of Bonci." When he sang the Duke* in *Rigoletto* on February 14, Hackett reverted to calling himself Charles, and so remained through an admirable career.

Also warmly approved in a brief venture into opera was the baritone Reinald Werrenrath, whose Silvio* in *Pagliacci* on February 19 was characterized by Henderson as "in respect of style, diction, phrasing and beauty of expression" the best he had ever heard. To be sure, voices such as Werrenrath's were rarely assigned to parts such as Silvio, but the credit stood. Werrenrath was also heard pleasurably as Valentin* in *Faust* on March 26. He devoted three years to a Metropolitan career, but operatic routine was never his forte so much as "Danny Deever," "Sylvia," and other morsels of the concert stage. Somewhat similar was McCormack, who reappeared as Pinkerton on December 26. "Inconceivable as a whale boat officer," said Henderson, "he sings the music surpassingly well."

Opportunity was available on several occasions to praise the steady development of Mabel Garrison, whose Lucia,* Queen in *Le Coq d'or,* and Gilda in *Rigoletto* all honored the "pluck and perseverance" the *Sun* valued in her equipment. At another extreme of honor was the tribute paid to Caruso on March 22 to commemorate the twenty-fifth anniversary of his operatic debut at the Teatro Bellini in Naples in 1894. He was both host and guest, entertaining a considerable audience (which paid a large sum into the Emergency Fund of the Metropolitan Opera Company) with excerpts from *L'Elisir d'amore, Pagliacci,* and *Le Prophète,* and receiving words of praise from Otto Kahn, as well as gifts from the management, his fellow artists, and the orchestra. He was also scheduled to receive the flag of the city of New York from His Honor Mayor John Hylan, but the Mayor's secretary, Grover Whalen, let it be known that the Mayor would not participate if James M. Beck, a political antagonist, took part in the ceremonies. Beck withdrew, with some sharp anti-Hylan words, and the presentation was made by Police Commissioner Enright.

Lacking *Parsifal,* Good Friday was observed in a manner both sacred and profane: Gounod's *Gallia* in the afternoon, directed by Setti, followed by Palestrina's *Missa Brevis* and Rossini's *Stabat Mater* (with Sundelius, Hackett, Matzenauer, and Mardones); *L'Amore dei tre re* was the evening attraction, with Easton, Martinelli, and Didur.

Whatever the financial outcome of the previous season, the underwriters of the Chicago Opera Association deemed a return visit to the Lexington Theater amusing if not profitable, and provocative of satisfying comparisons if nothing else. Although Raïsa was absent, Galli-Curci and Garden were not, and the list of roles with which the latter was identified added another when she appeared in the opening night *Gismonda,* on January 27. Another creation of Février, the composer of *Monna Vanna,* it had its interest while Garden was on stage, which was considerably but not quite enough. Charles Fontaine made his debut as Almerio, Alfred Maguenat was Zaccaria, and Marcel Journet in the role of the Bishop was welcomed as an old friend.

As an instance of the change that had come to New York's operatic life in a decade, the performance of Gounod's *Roméo et Juliette* on the following night was the first in nearly ten years. Yvonne Gall was a pleasingly Gallic Juliette, but John O'Sullivan sang a mediocre Roméo. Journet, as Frère Laurent, gave a lesson in style for those who cared.

No less than half a dozen operas not previously heard in New York were offered by the visitors, but their quality was scarcely exciting. Massenet took pre-eminence over Wagner and Verdi[1] as the most prolific opera-composer known to New York when *Cléopâtre,* on February 11, brought to twelve the number of his works produced there. As in several others, the justification was Garden, her Cléopâtre being seconded by Maguenat as Marc Antoine. Henderson described the dramatic writing as mostly "vapid arioso." What custom could not stale was dulled by the composer's lack of variety. Charlier was the conductor.

Giorgio Polacco, who had been superseded as "successor to Toscanini" by Moranzoni and Papi, recalled one of the Maestro's enthusiasms when he conducted Catalani's *Loreley* on February 13. The occasionally favored tenor air (*"Nel verde maggio"*) was well delivered by Alessandro Dolci, but Fitziu (Loreley), Florence Macbeth (Anna), Rimini (Hermann), and Virgilio Lazzari (Rodolfo) were indifferently suited to the music. On February 28 the one-act *Le vieil Aigle* by Raoul Gunsbourg, director of the Monte Carlo opera, shared an evening with *Cavalleria* and a ballet *divertissement.* This was the evening of the *Mireille* production at the Metropolitan, and Gunsbourg's creation passed without notice or repetition.

The attraction of Galli-Curci was almost as great as it had been the previous year, but the marriage of opinion among press and public was greatly strained. Her first opera was Donizetti's *Linda di Chamounix* on February 4, and though she sang its florid measures with ease and skill, critical ears found the voice dulled by overuse in a year of great activity, and the tendency to flat rather disconcerting. Stracciari (Antonio) and Lamont (Carlo) shared prominence in a work not heard for a twenty-nine-year period, Patti having been the earlier soprano. Following *Lucia* and *Il Barbiere,* Galli-Curci was heard in *Crispino e la Comare* on February 17. Direct comparisons with the Metropolitan production were not

---

[1] The advantage returned to Verdi during the next decade when *Don Carlos, Simon Boccanegra,* and *Luisa Miller* were revived.

drawn, but the evident undertone was that Galli-Curci was not so neat a singer as Hempel (in this part) or so clever a comedian. She also appeared in *Dinorah* and *La Traviata,* to profitable, but not overflow, attendance.

The season also promised several appearances by Melba, but she had a disagreement with the management, and Garden in *Pelléas* was substituted for her *Bohème* on February 27. The routine of the company also included *Isabeau,* with Fitziu, an inferior *Werther* (Irene Pavloska and O'Sullivan), *Fedora* (with Dorothy Jordan), *Butterfly* (with Tamaki Miura), *Manon* (with Gall) and *Le Jongleur* (with Garden). Because there was no amicable relation with the Metropolitan, the competition for customers produced a series of such occasions as Saturday, February 1, when the Metropolitan offered the Puccini triptych in the afternoon and *Le Coq d'or* and *L'Oracolo* in the evening, with *Thaïs* and *Les Contes d'Hoffmann* at the Lexington. Little wonder that Oscar Hammerstein looked ahead eagerly to the next February, when his agreement with the Metropolitan would expire. He died, however, on August 1, 1919, at the age of seventy-three.

When the final losses of the Diaghilev Ballet Russe were paid out of Metropolitan profits, the year showed a credit of only $3,701. It was the smallest since the bare $1,765 of 1914–15, but for quite different reasons.

1919–1920

The objections that would have to be satisfied before opera in German could be resumed at the Metropolitan were clearly revealed in another quarter before this season began. The former Metropolitan singers Goritz, Ober, and Braun were prominent in a plan to present a season of German opera in the Lexington Theater during October. Underwritten by persons who aspired, in the *Sun*'s words, to "restore German art to a position of prominence," the program was met with vigorous public protest. "The fact is," continued the same *Sun* article, "that people who have fought Germans do not at present like the sound of the German tongue." Possibly the reaction would have been different had the names and intentions not been so identifiable.

The opening concert program on October 19 was picketed by American Legion zealots and others more concerned with emotion than art. Inside, the choice of Hans Sachs's "Apostrophe to German Art" (sung by Hermann Weil) as the climax of the evening seemed notably provocative, and those who came with regard for art came away confused by emotion. An effort was made, after a few days, to continue the season in English, but the whole venture was soon abandoned.

Gatti's approach was to begin with what had been the most "controversial" of Wagner's works and was now the most sacrosanct. Contrary to some impressions, the production of *Parsifal* in English on February 19 was not conceived as a stop-gap, but as a serious attempt to persuade operagoers that a *good* translation would satisfy as much as the original. Krehbiel, a long-time advocate of opera in English, was commissioned to make the translation. To Henderson's ear, however, "it was easier to understand the text" when it was sung in German.

This was not necessarily an indictment of Krehbiel, for the longest role in the opera, Gurnemanz,* was sung by Rothier whose excellent French was long admired at the Metropolitan. Kundry was sung by Matzenauer, a Hungarian; Klingsor* by Didur, a Pole; and Titurel by Ananian, an Armenian. Of high credit were Orville Harrold (see page 286) as Parsifal* and Clarence Whitehill as Amfortas. Both American principals sang beautifully and in clear English, but the overwhelming lesson of an international opera house has been, and always will be, that strong casting will, almost inevitably, involve a principal[1] to whom English is as much a problem as Bengali would be.

On the whole, this *Parsifal* was an unhappy experience for most listeners. Urban's scenery, save for the massive interior for the Temple of the Grail, was not liked. Henderson thought the woodland lake of Act I "a cold and forbidding mountain sea," the Good Friday meadow lacking "mood." Also deplored was the elimination of the moving panorama, "one of Wagner's finest effects," said the same writer. Objection to the first scene was so general that it was repainted a few years later.

Aldrich found Bodanzky's conducting "masterly," but to Henderson much of it "moved heavily on leaden feet." Although liberally cut, the first act as led by Bodanzky took an hour and thirty-eight minutes against an hour and forty for Hertz, uncut. On Good Friday (April 2) Easton sang a splendid Kundry,* and Henderson referred to Bodanzky's conducting as "intellectual and scrupulously careful," adding that "it seldom attains heights of emotion."

For a generation born after 1932, one aspect of the season opening on November 17 must seem absurd indeed. It was the first in history in which, to quote Henderson, "immediate enjoyment" could not be guaranteed by consumption of "properly prepared grapes." In other words, the "choking blight of prohibition"[2] had settled on the land, and the opera bar was not excepted. *Tosca,* however, with Farrar, Caruso, and Scotti,

---

[1] As, thirty years later, Salvatore Baccaloni in *Gianni Schicchi,* Paul Schoeffler in *Alcestis,* Lorenzo Alvary in *Così,* or Leonie Rysanek in *Ariadne.*

[2] The Eighteenth Amendment was not national law until January 20, 1920, but local restrictions were already in force.

was more than moderately intoxicating, if but a dress rehearsal, in social terms, for the Prince of Wales's gala on the following evening (see page 71).

A further evidence of the times could be found in the rates for Metropolitan tickets in this first fully postwar season. The top price was advanced to seven dollars, and the bottom charge was raised, for the first time since Grau's day, to one dollar and a half.

By any standard, the artistic event of this year was Caruso's penetrating character study of Eléazar* in *La Juive* on November 22. By the measurement of Lehmann and Materna (for those who could recall their impressions of the '80's), Ponselle as Rachel* and Evelyn Scotney as the Princess (d) were, in Henderson's view, "but feeble representatives of the agonized women" of Scribe's play. By any measurement, Eléazar was one of Caruso's "highest flights," from the "exquisite" chanting in Act II to the inspired singing of *"Rachel! quand du Seigneur,"* which, said Henderson, "might have excited the envy of Nourrit[1] himself." Gatti gave Urban a free hand with the stage, and the production was rated splendid even by the expectations of the time. Bodanzky conducted, and the incidental attractions included a ballet led by Galli, the debut of Orville Harrold (Leopold [d]), Rothier as Cardinal Brogni,* and Chalmers as Ruggiero.*

Few singers of consequence were added to the roster, but one subtraction was generally deplored. In a pre-season commentary Henderson wrote in the *Sun* of September 27: "In looking over the list . . . this writer finds fulfillment of one prophecy made to him with no small vigor two years ago by a prominent member of the company that Mme. Hempel 'must go.' Well, she is gone and the art of singing is so much the poorer at the Metropolitan."

Of three Italian singers added to the company in a second-night *Aida* on November 19, none enjoyed lasting favor. Gabriella Besanzoni (Amneris*) is a name better known to history than Renato Zanelli (Amonasro*) or Giovanni Martino (Ramfis*), but for values others than those she displayed at the Metropolitan. Her voice had fine texture in the medium register, but no uncommon range. She had a prominent opportunity as Isabella* in a venture with Rossini's *Italiana in Algeri* on December 5, but her skill for florid music was limited, her comedy sense weak. This was a depressing influence on an otherwise excellent cast of Hackett (Lindoro*), Sundelius (Elvira*), De Luca (Taddeo*), and Didur (Mustafà*), lavishly surrounded by a brilliant Pogany décor. Besanzoni later sang Dalila* on December 10 with powerful voice but little seductive

---

[1] The original Eléazar, for whose text Halévy wrote the music of his most famous air.

suggestion, and Preziosilla* in *La Forza del destino* on January 26. She did not return.

When Albert Wolff made his debut with the traditional *Faust* on November 21, for the first time since Mahler and Mancinelli the Metropolitan had a conductor who was also a composer. He came to replace Monteux, who had moved to the Boston Symphony in succession to Henri Rabaud. He might have done well with *Boris* (better than Papi, certainly), but his talents were directed to a new production of *Manon*, a restudied *Carmen* (Farrar was prominent in both of these), and such repertory matters as *Samson* and *Marouf*, in addition to his own *L'Oiseau bleu*, as his setting of Maeterlinck's fantasy was known at its first performance on December 27.

First honors went to Boris Anisfeld's fanciful décor, for still another production more "opulent" than any the Metropolitan had previously offered. "Able and cohesive" expressed Krehbiel's opinion of the score, which, at its best, Henderson thought "good." The reservations were many, however, mostly concerned with stretches of text setting in which the score moved "slowly and placidly" (Henderson), with little melodic contour. Louise Bérat, a frequent visitor in the past with the Hammerstein company and its descendants, sang an excellent grandmother,* Delaunois was a charming Tyltyl,* Easton was a proper Mother Tyltyl,* with Rothier as Father Time.* The work had an even dozen performances this year and the next, but none thereafter, though Wolff remained as conductor for a third season.

The unpredictable fancy of operatic audiences gave Gatti an unexpected success for Farrar when *Zaza* was introduced on January 16, 1920, though it had no remarkable favor when Toscanini gave it first at La Scala in 1900, or in a Chicago revival of 1915. A large share of the credit may be ascribed to David Belasco, whose "master craftsmanship . . . moulded the Metropolitan production into a thing of vivid, scarlet, theatrical life," said Henderson, beyond the suggestions of Leoncavallo's score. *Zaza*, in Huneker's opinion in the *World*, was a "sensation." He scorned Leoncavallo's writing as "dry rot," but described Farrar as "a new 'Jerry' . . . who will enthrall the town for a long time to come." Whether by acting or by changing costumes in view of the audience, Farrar found in Zaza* a role perfectly suited, in the opinion of Aldrich, to her "gayety and recklessness." (Crimi as Dufresne* and Amato as Cascart* were also present, but hardly consequential.)

The role coincided with a new wave of popularity for Farrar, who sang it twenty times to few unsold seats during her three remaining seasons at the Metropolitan. The hysteria it provoked was provocative to Henderson, who wrote at the beginning of the second *Zaza* season, on November 20, 1920: "All the little gerryflappers were out last night striving to fill the Metropolitan . . . with their hysterical approval of everything done by the prima donna. . . . What is a gerryflapper? Simply a girl about the flapper age who has created in her own half baked mind a goddess which she names Geraldine Farrar." A new word had joined the language.

Mahler's sponsorship of Tchaikovsky's *Pique-Dame* was recalled in the choice of *Eugen Onegin* for production by his disciple Bodanzky on March 24. Huneker found the music "weak, pretty, inconsequential." Henderson was more taken by the scoring for orchestra, though admitting "the opera as a whole cannot send the listener away with a satisfied mind." In sum, the objection seemed to concern the theatrical values of the story, for which Muzio (Tatiana*), Martinelli (Lensky*), and De Luca (Onegin*) were conventional Italian opera figures, rather than characters at all Russian. In Henderson's opinion, De Luca's Onegin was a "contemptible prig," which may not be just what Pushkin intended. Urban designed the scenery, and the language was Italian.

For this year's American novelty, Gatti turned to Henry Hadley, one of the most prolific native writers of the day and one of the dullest. The libretto derived by Alice Leal Pollock from Gautier's *Une Nuit de Cléo-pâtre* was described by Henderson as "stilted and unnatural," but the action of *Cleopatra's Night* was contemporary in providing Alda (Cleopatra*) opportunity for those "unblushing candors of the body which are now practised on the stage." It was also Henderson's judgment, however, that Hadley had handled his situation as well as any other composer alive, save Puccini or Strauss. In the first performance, on January 31, Papi conducted, Harrold was Meiamoun,* Jeanne Gordon sang Mardion,* and Tiffany was Iras.* Norman Bel Geddes was the designer. On March 3 Hadley conducted his own work.

Gordon was one of several promising American singers to make debuts this season, being heard first as Azucena (d) in *Il Trovatore* on November 22, and later singing Fatima* in *Oberon,* Maddalena* in *Rigoletto,* and Preziosilla* in *Forza.* All these were creditably done. Rather older, but with limited experience in opera, was Orville Harrold, a Hammerstein discovery who had actually sung in his closing gala at the Manhattan Opera House ten years before. Aldrich thought his voice somewhat "light" for Léopold (d) in *La Juive* on November 22 (Harrold's debut), but the suggestion is that Harrold was still using cautiously a voice that had been rather hard-driven in the past and was still to regain its normal power. A Rodolfo* in *La Bohème* on December 29 convinced Henderson that the "big and powerful" tones of old were once more at his command.

Harrold was the False Dmitri* in a *Boris* of November 24 in which Krehbiel blamed Papi's conducting for "the accretion of perfunctoriness and carelessness [that] Signor Toscanini knew how to prevent . . . during his artistic administration." Win-San-Luy in *L'Oracolo,* Turiddu in *Cavalleria,* and Parsifal bear testimony to the valuable adaptability of Harrold.

The number and quality of American singers added to the roster in the several war seasons brought the first all-native casts for Italian and French works. In this period it was a rare phenomenon attesting to the abilities of the performers; more recently it has been a commonplace attesting to the limitations of the company. One of the earliest Puccini works to be sung with Americans in the leading roles was *Butterfly* on March 15, 1918, with Farrar, Althouse, and Chalmers. In this season Wolff had Farrar and Hackett for the leading roles of his *Manon* on March 6, and a full, qualified group of Americans on March 31 when Whitehill and Chalmers (Lescaut*) joined them to sing parts previously taken by Rothier and De Luca. (Wolff chose to omit the gambling scene and restore the *"Cours la reine"* episode.) On April 19 Whitehill was an "elegant and sardonic" (Henderson) Méphistophélès* in a cast with Farrar, Ellis, Harrold (Faust*), Chalmers (Valentin), and Howard (Marthe) which drew approving comment for its native excellence. In these later times an all-French cast would attract attention.

Emmy Destinn's return in *Aida* on December 8 was an occasion for warm praise of this able artist, who had been interned for three years in Austria. Her vocal state was good, and she was heard with pleasure several times as Santuzza. Considering her artistry, Destinn gave more and received less than any comparable performer of her time. Not for her was the honor of such revivals as that of *Il Barbiere* on November 27 for Mabel Garrison—it was only a few years since *Il Barbiere* had last been restaged, in 1916. Garrison's Rosina* was neat and well-disciplined but rather small in sound. In the cast were De Luca, Hackett (Almaviva), and Mardones (Basilio). The production was the one of Joseph Urban, which was not replaced until 1953–4.

As the increasingly frequent mention of his name suggests, Urban had won the durable esteem of Gatti, who continued to use his services till Urban's death in 1933. A versatile theater man, with special skill as an architect (the Ziegfeld Theater at Sixth Avenue and Fifty-fourth Street, New York, is his most durable monument), Urban often produced sketches more suggestive than the finished production—which did not seem to concern him unduly. He was able and easygoing, a combination of qualities which predestined him for the Metropolitan of the twenties.

For this year's visit by the Chicago Opera Association, Campanini had prepared by far the most ambitious repertory any visiting troupe ever undertook in New York—thirty-two operas in thirty-five days. His own part in the season that began in the Lexington Theater on January 26 was wholly spiritual, however, for he had died suddenly in Chicago of pneumonia on December 19. Herbert Johnson was his immediate successor, followed briefly by Gino Marinuzzi, and in the next year by Mary Garden.

In the opening *L'Amore dei tre re* on January 26, Garden sang Fiora for the first time in New York, and Edward Johnson made his debut as Avito. To Henderson, Garden's was a Gardenized Fiora, "sinuous, shifty of eye . . . tigerlike in stride," sung with a voice of many colors, but almost always off key. Johnson was commended as "a man of excellent figure, of virile and picturesque action, of moderately good voice." The *Tribune* thought him "altogether the artist that had been heralded." Baklanoff and Virgilio Lazzari were in the cast, well directed by the unfamiliar Gino Marinuzzi.

Johnson was later heard as Luigi in *Il Tabarro* and Rinuccio in *Gianni Schicchi* when the Puccini triptych was offered on February 11 with Raïsa in *Suor Angelica* and Carlo Galeffi singing Schicchi and Michele (in *Tabarro*). On February 27 Johnson sang Demetrios to Garden's Chrysis when Camille Erlanger's *Aphrodite* had its first New York showing. The prime interest concerned the promise that the operatic version surpassed in nudity the dramatic version that had recently scandalized New York at the Century Theater, and the house was sold out at ten dollars a seat. Henderson reported that "Garden displayed more of her person and about as much of her voice as in Thaïs," and Aldrich found much that was "not pleasant to the eye of decency, or to the ear, either." The season ended the next day without a repetition.

The other interests of the season were divided among new singers, such as Tito Schipa, in old parts, and old singers, such as Ruffo, in new ones. Henderson described the tenor, at his debut in *La Sonnambula* on February 5, as a singer whose voice possessed "power and resonance, a little reedy, but yet very pleasing in quality." Galli-Curci was in this cast, and not close to the vocalist she had been two years before. [1] Ruffo appeared with Schipa and Galli-Curci in a *Rigoletto* of February 20, described by Henderson as "without doubt the busiest Rigoletto the local stage has ever seen . . . and also the loudest." Galli-Curci had one of her fine nights as Gilda, and the crowded theater responded with

---

[1] On August 10, 1935, a goiter was removed from Galli-Curci's throat, which she said had been troubling her for fifteen years. It undoubtedly affected her singing, especially in pitch.

cheers. Ruffo had a great personal success in *Hamlet* on February 13, repeating the drinking song. For that matter, he began a performance of *Pagliacci* on January 28 by singing the prologue one and half times. The audience plainly enjoyed this more than the following *L'Heure espagnole* of Ravel, with Gall (Concepcion), Defrère (Torquemada), and Maguenat (Ramiro). Aldrich described Ravel's score as "finely wrought . . . subtle and suggestive," but Henderson did not consider it either "important or serious." Louis Hasselmans conducted.

Another new work of this visit, on January 28, was Messager's *Madame Chrysanthème* (based on a Pierre Loti story somewhat similar to that of *Madama Butterfly*). Tamaki Miura sang Chrysanthème, with Dufranne (Yves) and Warnery (Kangourou). Hasselmans conducted. On January 30 Alexander Smallens made his debut as conductor of Reginald de Koven's *Rip van Winkle,* with Baklanoff as Rip and Evelyn Herbert as Peterkin. There were also two ballets new to New York: Felix Borowski's *Boudour* on February 16 and John Alden Carpenter's *Birthday of the Infanta* on February 23. Carpenter's score and the dancing of Ruth Page (Infanta) and Bolm (Pedro) were all liked, but there was time for only a single repetition before the season ended.

Although the Metropolitan could not produce either *Norma* or *Falstaff* in this period, the Chicago company gave both with credit if not distinction on this visit. Almost thirty years had passed since Bellini's fine score had last been sung in New York (February 3, 1892), but Raïsa's "imposing and impressive" artistry measured fully up to older standards, Henderson describing her voice as "one of the most beautiful dramatic organs" New York had ever heard. Marinuzzi conducted well, but the associated singers (Sharlow as Adalgisa, Dolci as Pollione, Lazzari as Oroveso) were erratic. Raïsa did what she could to make *Falstaff* an occasion on February 6 by singing Alice, but Rimini lacked the comic touch for Falstaff. Defrère was an excellent Ford, Schipa a disappointing Fenton. Marinuzzi's conducting was praised by Henderson for "well considered tempi, a buoyant touch . . . and a general cohesion."

Beyond Johnson and Schipa, the company also offered Bonci in *Un Ballo in maschera,* in *La Bohème,* in *Lucia* with Galli-Curci, and in *L'Elisir d'amore.* Maeterlinck attended the performance of *Pelléas* on January 27, stating that he had never heard the work before. On leaving, he declared: "In spite of being tone-deaf, I passed a very pleasant evening."

Thousands of dollars were spent on the attractive fare offered by the Chicago company, but Gatti had profit figures to show again this year— $46,429. He would have been appalled at the idea that, less than a year in the future, he would be struggling through a season in which his most valuable property and greatest attraction would have but a nominal part. Miraculously, the profits continued even if Enrico Caruso could not.

1920–1921

In a winter of numerous happenings and diverse splendors in the Metropolitan Opera House, the most consequential event occurred on the stage of the Brooklyn Academy of Music on December 11, when Caruso broke down during a performance of *L'Elisir d'amore*. A few days before, on the 8th, he had wrenched a muscle in his side during a performance of *Pagliacci*. He had spent a week-end in bed to ease the pain. But even as he refused to consider himself a sick man after the *Pagliacci,* so he chose to laugh off the bloody warnings of the handkerchiefs that passed from hand to hand as he sought to finish *L'Elisir*. He sang three times again, against Gatti's protest, before he collapsed with a painful pleurisy on Christmas Day. He never sang again.

These are the familiar if sometimes distorted events in the foreground. Those in the background are no less absorbing. Consider, for example, the opening *La Juive* on November 15, which, for the sixteenth year in a possible seventeen,[1] presented the company's leading tenor in the leading role. Henderson noted "club land, automobiledom, and the mercantile realm" in the audience. For the first time a reference to "Park Avenue" indicated a new stratification in the social hierarchy. For the first time, too, it became the critic's duty to report that never before had Caruso "appeared at an opening performance in such a lamentable vocal state." Extensive pre-season touring had included one appearance in the Mount Royal Arena, Montreal, where amid sawdust and chill, Caruso had sung for eighty per cent of the $28,000 receipts.

Had Caruso been a lesser man, not so conscientious an artist mindful of Gatti's dependence upon him, he might have struggled a bit against his vocal miseries, given in to them, and after six months' rest, come back in prime health. But he insisted on proceeding with his normal sequence of Nemorino, Samson, and Alvaro in *Forza* before the painful *Pagliacci* and the disastrous *L'Elisir* in Brooklyn. "Happiness reigned supreme," noted Henderson[2] when Caruso braced himself for *La Forza del destino* on the 13th and sang through it successfully. He managed *Samson* without incident on the 16th, but missed *L'Elisir* on the 22nd, his complaint now being diagnosed as lumbago. Two days later Caruso

---

[1] The one interruption was in 1906, when Farrar made her debut in *Roméo et Juliette,* with Rousselière.

[2] In one of the mergers in the newspaper realm of the day, his writings now appeared in the *Herald*.

decided he was well enough to sing *La Juive,* with Easton, Harrold, and Rothier. It was his 607th Metropolitan performance, and his last.

In a summary on January 2, Henderson observed: "When Caruso supposedly wrenched his side in Pagliacci, he may have been suffering from the beginnings of the disturbance in his lungs. At any rate there is ground for at least a suspicion that he may not have been wholly well at any time the season opened. Such a theory would account for some very bad singing." The fears that were allayed, the hopes that were roused, in the next nine months had, so far as one can determine, very little relation to basic physical facts. Mere common sense would have restored his health in a reasonable time, just as one of the recent "wonder drugs" would probably have cured his ailment in a length of time then considered impossible. A life became a legend for want of elementary prudence.

Those who had made the vagaries of the vocal organs a lifetime concern were not put off by the stream of hopeful bulletins that dotted the season's course. Toward spring they were more optimistic than previously, causing Henderson to write on April 14: "Mr. Caruso (whom the gods protect) is recovering from a long and serious illness. He has been greatly missed." Observing, however, that such an illness would require a prolonged convalescence, that the Metropolitan might have to reckon without its special star for many more months, he posed the question: "What tenor has attracted the largest amount of public favor in the course of the season . . . ? We shall undoubtedly have to admit it was Mr. Gigli."

In normal circumstances, Caruso, then barely forty-eight, would have continued a favorite for a decade or more. Gigli, at thirty, would have served an apprenticeship in idolatry that would certainly have benefited his career. By a whim of fate, the younger man was elevated to a prominence for which he was not quite ready. The ultimate beneficiary was Martinelli, whose career continued to the splendid climax of a notable Eléazar in *La Juive* and a memorable Otello, though his natural endowment was—so far as such things can be measured in retrospect—probably inferior to Gigli's.

Beniamino Gigli's debut on November 26 was no more than an incident in a revival of Boito's *Mefistofele,* with Didur a more genteel archfiend than Chaliapin had been in 1907, Alda and Easton dividing the roles of Margherita* and Helen,* and Flora Perini as Pantalis.* Critical opinion was oddly divided, though not about the beauty of the newcomer's voice. The usually finicky Henderson deemed Gigli the possessor of a "fresh, well-delivered lyric tenor" who seemed "a servant of art and not a mere seeker after personal glory." But Aldrich was wary of his "persistent inclination to sing to the audience," his bent "to cultivate the high note." Krehbiel reacted strongly to what he called Gigli's "provincialism," and thought the bracing atmosphere of the Metropolitan might benefit him. It turned out to be, in the twenties, a hothouse for idiosyncrasies rather than a stern schooling in good musical manners. Moranzoni conducted this *Mefistofele* persuasively, and the splendid scenery of Boris Anisfeld was warmly admired.

As far as one can read in the press of the time, Gigli's first season was triumphant where mere vocalism was concerned, often a botch otherwise. On December 4 as Rodolfo* in *La Bohème* (Anna Roselle made her debut as Musetta [d]), he sang superbly but surprised some by advancing to the footlights midway in Act I to take his bows. Of his Cavaradossi* in *Tosca* on the 10th (with Destinn and Scotti), Henderson said: "His acting was merely a matter of form, and not very good form at that." His Avito* in *L'Amore* on January 1, however (Easton was the womanly Fiora), surprised for its "fine dramatic sincerity" (Henderson). He was also the first Metropolitan Chénier* when Giordano's opera was given on March 7, after weeks of waiting for Caruso to sing the part. Henderson endorsed him as "one of the best singers" recently heard in New York, who does "not belong to the inglorious company of shouters," thanks to his skill "in mezza voce." Muzio found special favor as Maddalena,* a role "thoroughly congenial" to her, and the new baritone Giuseppe Danise earned an uncommon accolade for his Gérard,* in which he "sang like an artist and acted like a man." Moranzoni conducted. Crimi was a substitute Chénier* on March 26 and April 20. In all performances Angelo Bada made a salient character of the small part of the Spy.*

The taunting shadow of Garden which hovered over Farrar each time she ventured a new French role (such as Thaïs) was again present when *Louise* came to the Metropolitan repertory on January 15. Farrar sang Louise* industriously, if with no overwhelming identity with the character. Henderson, for a detail, noted that "the good clothes, shoes and stockings" that Farrar wore did not convey the conviction of Garden's more authentically proletarian sewing-girl. Vocally, too, the performance was not so impressive as had been anticipated. Harrold was a prepossessing Julien,* but not a very dramatic one; Bérat as the Mother* and Whitehill as the Father* were both excellent. No fault could be found with the conducting of Wolff, but Aldrich detected "signs of age" in the score, judging *"Depuis le jour"*[1] as "only a picturesque episode added to

---

[1] His remark, in passing, that *"Depuis le jour"* was composed, as a piece by itself, before the opera, could explain much about *Louise*. A good starting-point, certainly; but not one from which Charpentier progressed very far.

the local color" rather than the "keynote of the whole" it had once seemed. As in the Chicago production of 1914, the Noctambulist (well sung by Diaz) was included (it had been omitted at the Manhattan Opera House).

The single wholly new opera of this season was, in fact, new only to the Metropolitan, for Karel Weis had written *Der polnische Jude* twenty years before it was heard in a translation by Spaeth and Cowdrey on March 9, 1921 as *The Polish Jew.* This treatment of the Erckmann-Chatrian story made famous by Sir Henry Irving as *The Bells* was pronounced by Henderson "without doubt the deadliest soporific ever administered to an operatic audience in this long-suffering town." Chief Caupolican, a vaudeville baritone engaged by Gatti because, it was said, no one else would learn the role, sang Mathis,* whose music was described by Henderson as "wretched." Mario Chamlee was Christian Brehm,* Gustafson had the title role, and Delaunois sang Annette.* Bodanzky conducted the *première* and one of two following performances, Paul Eisler the last, on March 25.

The Polish Jew was originally announced to follow a revival of *Il Segreto di Susanna* with Lucrezia Bori, but the order was inverted, for fear the theater would be half empty before the novelty was half over. Thus, said Henderson, "the audience had to swallow the bitter medicine in order to get the sweetmeat." As in all her appearances since Mimi on January 28, Bori sang more beautifully than ever, in a rare happy ending to an ominous series of events. Only rigid self-discipline in resisting the temptation to sing until medical science was sure her operation was climaxed by successful convalescence enabled Bori to resume her career. In fact, to Henderson's ear, the voice had lost its formerly "slightly acid quality," and was now "mellow, sonorous and smooth." Her "irresistibly charming" Mimi was matched by Gigli's Rodolfo, an "unqualified joy." Once launched, Bori sailed smoothly through such roles as Fiora in *L'Amore dei tre re,* Ah-Yoe in *L'Oracolo,* Nedda in *Pagliacci,* and a Micaëla "full of spirits and rich in charm" on March 11.

The first of several Verdi revivals in this decade was very much a qualified success when *Don Carlos* was heard on December 23, for the first time in New York since an Academy of Music season in 1877. Papi's version utilized matter from three editions authorized by the composer, with results that caused Henderson to complain of "altogether too much ponderous recitative." On the whole, he found the score "both tuneless and unvocal," "machine made from beginning to end," with a bare exception for "*O don fatale,*" which was "not a particularly fine air" in any case. Huneker thought it "worth seeing and hearing" as an illumination of Verdi's artistic evolution, but not otherwise. Papi's direction did not have desirable animation, and the description by Henderson of Ponselle's Elisabeth* as "neither queenly nor tear-compelling" is suggestive of the dramatic force provided by the cast of Martinelli (Don Carlos*), Matzenauer (Eboli*), De Luca (Posa*), and Didur (Philip II*). Urban's settings had their customary success. Chaliapin's fondness for the kingly role extended the interest in *Don Carlos* during the next two seasons, but it was nearly thirty years before the work was produced in a way to expose its particular beauties.

To provide the ballet with suitable occupation (Monteux's removal to Boston had, apparently, deprived the company of a conductor to deal with *Petrouchka*), Pick-Mangiagalli's *Il Carillon magico* was presented on December 2. As the characters suggest (Galli as Pierrot, Florence Rudolph as Columbine, and Giuseppe Bonfiglio as Harlequin), the work, set to over-pretty music, was derived from *commedia dell' arte*. Its first showing was part of a triple bill with *L'Oracolo* and *Cavalleria rusticana*. In the last of these Gigli was Turiddu,* singing, said the *Herald*, with "great vigor . . . real passion." *Il Carillon magico* served usefully to fill out double bills with *Pagliacci, Lucia,* even *L'Amore dei tre re* this season, but it disappeared without regret.

The cautious resumption of Wagner in English extended this year to *Tristan* on November 20 and *Lohengrin* on February 2, both in productions by Urban which remained in use for decades. Translations by H. and F. Corder, revised by Sigmund Spaeth and Cecil Cowdrey, were used. The Isolde* of Matzenauer posed a double problem, for in addition to struggling with an alien language, she sought, not too successfully, to adapt her heavy dark voice to the soprano requirements. Often, indeed, it was weightier than that of Gordon, the Brangäne.* Sembach, who had apparently kept clear of the Ober-Goritz group, sang a competent Tristan, and Robert Blass, of Conried days, returned as King Marke. The Kurvenal of Whitehill, it was agreed, was the most satisfactory character on the stage, and reasonably intelligible. Easton later sang Isolde,* to which Henderson's reaction was curiously similar to his words on Fremstad: it was "a lovely impersonation," neither "a termagant, nor a half civilized erotic, but a perfectly normal woman" carried away by emotion.

Both works were conducted by Bodanzky, whose *Lohengrin* was admired for its "wealth of detail," also—as a rarity—for the addition of a usually unheard ensemble in Act II rather than the subtraction of something usually heard. In the frame of an Urban production rated "the best the work has ever had here," Easton sang an Elsa* possessed of "supreme art and lovely tone," Whitehill was a Telramund* of "sinister power and vocal vigor," Matzenauer a fine Ortrud, as ever, and Sembach a plausible Lohengrin. Taken together, this was "one of the greatest achievements" of Gatti's direction. (All the opinions are Henderson's.) On March 3, Harrold sang Lohengrin to Julia Claussen's Ortrud.* The *Parsifal* performances were much as in the previous year, save that Blass, who had been the Metropolitan's first Gurnemanz seventeen years before, came back on December 10. A native American, if not a great singer, Blass was desirable while Wagner in English was inescapable.

Other than Gigli, the best new singer of this season was Giuseppe Danise, first heard as Amonasro (d) in *Aida* on November 17, and later admired for his part in *Andrea Chénier* (see page 292). In another *Aida* on December 25, Carolina Lazzari, of Chicago background, sang a very agreeable Amneris (d), but she did not return for another season. The American-born Mario Chamlee sang a Cavaradossi (d) in *Tosca* on November 22 which was commended by the *Herald* for the "fresh" sound of the voice and certain "lyric qualities of merit," but he was not of Martinelli-Gigli stature. With Caruso ailing and Gigli not yet accustomed to the New York winter, there were other opportunities for Chamlee as the Duke* in *Rigoletto* on November 27 (Nina Morgana made her debut as Gilda [d]), Pinkerton* in *Butterfly* on December 24, Edgardo* in *Lucia* on January 1, and Win-San-Luy* in *L'Oracolo* on January 10. A final new name was that of Cora Chase, a Boston soprano, who sang Gilda* on February 4 and a later Rosina of not more than mild interest. Easton's versatility endeared her to admirers of such a musical resource when she sang a "genuinely fine" Carmen* on December 9 in place of Farrar and two days later spelled Ponselle in *Oberon* by singing "Ocean, thou mighty monster," said Henderson, "with a firmer command of its style and its dramatic content" than any predecessor had provided.

The remarkable Mary Garden added a new distinction to her long list when she returned to the Manhattan Opera House in January as executive head of the Chicago Opera Company, thus making of *impresaria* a word both novel and exclusive. In personnel and repertory the company was much as it had been, though Garden's generosity in hiring singers—tenors especially—made for a payroll of amazing size (see page 306). Only two novelties were offered, neither of them consequential. On February 4 Gino Marinuzzi conducted his own *Jacquerie* (with Gall, Johnson, and Galeffi), which had, in Henderson's opinion, some "excellent pages" though the monotone of "misery, despair and rage" in the action became a little unbearable. Titta Ruffo's forceful personality made exciting the prospect of Leoncavallo's one-act *Edipo Re* (in which the baritone was on-stage for virtually all of its sixty minutes), but the "deadly" music undid him. The same star was a powerful voice for Iago's *"Credo"* when *Otello* was heard on February 1, but the whole of the impersonation lacked subtlety. Raïsa was a moderately satisfactory Desdemona, Charles Marshall a surprisingly strong Otello. The conductor was Pietro Cimini, for whose functioning Henderson found a new term—he conducted with "as much authority as the singers would allow."

A dozen years before, the debut of Rosina Storchio would have been a matter of moment, for she was the original Butterfly at La Scala in 1904. When New York heard her at the Manhattan on February 7, the voice was worn and tremulous, though Henderson noted that the "childish prattle" of Cio-Cio-San in Act I had never been done with quite so much artistry before. Joseph Hislop was Pinkerton, Baklanoff Sharpless. Galli-Curci (whose engagement for the following Metropolitan season was common knowledge) proved an uncommonly adept singer of Puccini on February 24, when her Mimi in *La Bohème* was commended by Henderson for its "command of fluent legato," the charm and grace of the acting. Bonci was the Rodolfo. She had a considerable success as Juliette on February 9 to Muratore's Roméo, but her Lakmé on February 15 was interesting only for the "Bell Song." Garden's parts were a review of such roles as Monna Vanna, Thaïs, Marguerite in *Faust,* Carmen, and Le Jongleur, but she astonished "her oldest admirers," in Henderson's phrase, when she sang Fiora in *L'Amore* on February 10 with "outbursts of vocal beauty." Johnson, Galeffi, and Lazzari contributed to a "decidedly interesting" performance under Marinuzzi.

The vagaries of criticism should surprise no one, but the capacity to learn from experience is well reflected in a Henderson comment after Toscanini's long-awaited return as conductor of the touring La Scala Orchestra on December 28. Having listened, with evident pleasure, to a program that included the A-minor Concerto of Vivaldi, the C-minor Symphony of Beethoven, Debussy's *Ibéria,* Respighi's *The Pines of Rome,* and two *Tristan* excerpts, Henderson concluded: "Mr. Toscanini ought to be caught and imprisoned, if he cannot be kept here any other way. He should never have been permitted to escape, even to serve his country. . . . There is always room in this country for such a consummate artist." Six years of lesser men at the Metropolitan had been eye-opening if not ear-filling.

Despite the long inactivity of Caruso and the intensified competition of symphony orchestras, the Metropolitan concluded its season with the usual credit balance. This time it was $39,782. Even more heartening was the decision of Caruso's doctors, in late May, that his condition was sufficiently improved for him to seek a warm climate for full recovery. It was Gatti's opinion, expressed as he was leaving for Europe, that "Enrico Caruso will without any doubt again take his glorious post at the Metropolitan." Somewhat against the wishes of his doctors, Caruso decided he could recuperate best in his native Naples. When another abscess developed in July, local medical opinion temporized until it was too late about the wisdom of an operation. He died on Tuesday, August 2, 1921.

Abbreviated though it was by his death at forty-eight, Caruso's was not only one of the longest careers in Metropolitan history, but also one of the most influential. When he arrived, the pre-season subscription was supported in large part by the ticket agencies. It is not unlikely that the difficulty of getting tickets for Caruso performances vastly stimulated the general habit of subscription. His effect on the repertory, in the establishment of the Puccini literature, in popularizing such works as *Pagliacci* and *Aida,* was equally basic. With all the temptation of easy success, the assurance of luxury by the repetition of a dozen popular roles, Caruso made himself a model among tenors by applying himself to such tasks as Renaud in *Armide,* Julien, Eléazar in *La Juive,* John of Leyden, and Samson. Such deeds are implicit in the evaluation of him published by Henderson on August 3, 1921: "In sincerity, in fervor, in devotion to his art, he was the peer of any opera singer in history. . . . He was an indifferent actor and a supreme singer when he came here. He finished his career a singer less flawless, but an operatic interpreter who commanded the respect and sympathy of the severest critics, even when they could not credit him with triumphant success."

During his New York career Caruso appeared in thirty-seven different roles, in as many operas. The works in which he appeared were: *Rigoletto, Aida, La Traviata, Il Trovatore, Un Ballo in maschera, Tosca, La Bohème, Manon Lescaut, Madama Butterfly, La Fanciulla del West, Lucrezia Borgia, La Gioconda, L'Amore dei tre re, L'Elisir d'amore, Lucia di Lammermoor, Pagliacci, Lodoletta, Cavalleria rusticana, La Sonnambula, La Favorita, Marta, Fedora, Le Prophète, Les Huguenots, Faust, Carmen, Germania, Armide, Adriana Lecouvreur, Manon, Julien, Samson et Dalila, Les Pêcheurs de perles, L'Africaine, Iris, La Forza del destino,* and *La Juive.*

The statistics of his eighteen seasons are appended. Caruso's earnings as a member of the Metropolitan Opera Company, both in opera and in concert, were:

Year	Fee	Appearances†		Total
1903–4	$ 960	29 in opera, plus	2	$　29,807.62
1904–5	1152	54 " " "	3	65,664
1905–6	1344	60 " " "	4	87,984
1906–7‡	1440	62 " " "	0	89,280
1907–8	2000	68 " " "	2	140,000
1908–9	2000	42 " " "	2	88,350
1908–9	2500	7 outside appearances		17,500
1909–10	2000	57 in opera, plus	1	116,350
1910–11	2000	28 " " "	2	61,000
1911–12	2000	50 " " "	0	100,000
1912–13	2000	50 " " "	1	103,000
1913–14	2000	50 " " "	0	100,000
1914–15	2500	28 " "		70,000
1915–16	2500	49 " "		118,000
1916–17	2500	49 " "		118,000
1917–18	2500	50 " "		125,000
1918–19	2500	49 " "		122,000
1919–20	2500	47 " "		117,000
1920	2500	10 " "		25,000

$1,693,935.62

† This table shows the number of opera performances sung by Caruso in New York and on tour, as well as the concerts given under contract with the Metropolitan. In later years his concerts were separately managed and are not included in this table. For several concerts Caruso received more than the fee for his opera performances, accounting for the discrepancies in the totals for 1903–4, and 1905–6.

‡ Previous to 1907–8, the figure expressed in dollars is the equivalent, at the prevailing exchange, of the francs stipulated in Caruso's contract. The number of these was: in 1903, 5,000; in 1904, 6,000; in 1905, 7,000; and in 1906, 7,500.

EPILOGUE

The ascending line of accomplishment which can be readily traced in the Metropolitan seasons from 1908 to 1914—in values other than merely vocal—is hardly perceptible in the six seasons that followed. At best, they comprise a plateau from which protrude a few peaks: *The Magic Flute* with Hempel, Caruso's *La Juive,* Monteux's *Petrouchka* and *Coq d'or,* perhaps Bodanzky's *Oberon.* On the whole, a methodical attention to detail exceeded a fanatical devotion to quality.

It would be absurd to undervalue the effect on the world talent market of a great war, hardly less in 1914 than in 1942. Unquestionably the constricted range of choice was a factor beyond reckoning. But it would be equally absurd to undervalue the effect of a factor within reckoning—the talent of Toscanini—in the altered tone and changed character of the institution.

If Krehbiel complained of the deficiencies of the Hertz-conducted Wagner, or later of the Papi-led Mussorgsky, it was a complaint against the memory of a readily accessible standard. The man named Toscanini was not indispensable; it was the standard for which the name and the man stood which was sorely missed when no other name with approximately equal authority took its place.

Some segments of the press still took the "enlightened" view of Grau that "Nobody ever paid a nickel to see a man's back." It was an attitude that carried over to the concert hall, where adulation for a Mengelberg or a Stokowski was met with the "sound" view that few people could recognize the difference between their Beethoven and Damrosch's, so why the fuss? But Seidl, in terms of results, was a *prima donna* conductor before the term was invented; Papi was honored with the title of Maestro, but did not honor it.

The ban on German works was of transitory effect in these seasons, long since absorbed in the long flow of works and years. Their slow return, however, cost the Metropolitan dearly in such singers as Maria Ivogün, Claire Dux, Lotte Lehmann, and Alexander Kipnis, who found a readier welcome in Chicago than existed for them at the Metropolitan. The waste of time and money on such matters as *The Polish Jew, St. Elisabeth, Lodoletta,* and *La Reine Fiammette* would be an embarrassment were not other more embarrassing matters in the offing.

For reasons not related to artistic merit such singers as Hempel, Barrientos, Ober, Kurt, and Schumann, and such conductors as Polacco, Monteux, Moranzoni, and—in a year or so—Wolff, came and went in this period. Muzio, Gigli, Easton, Hackett, De Luca, Ponselle, Garrison, and Gordon initiated important careers But who can recall the artistic measure of Edvina, Villani, Le Fontenay, Couzinou, Besanzoni, Montesanto, Martino, Zanelli, Cajatti, or Zarska—or recall the certainty which of these singers of leading roles was male, which female?

A tendency that became a trend was observable in the considerable number of American singers who were acceptable for leading or secondary parts but lacked the staying power to strive for durable careers. It is a long list, which grew longer with every decade. In this one it would include Mary Ellis, Mary Mellish, Cora Chase, Marie Sundelius, Reinald Werrenrath, Marie Tiffany, May Peterson, Cecil Arden, and Alice Gentle, who found other ways of earning a living more attractive. The one department of the Metropolitan to move steadily ahead in this period was the ballet.

Impelled first by the example of Mordkin and Pavlova, then by the visit of the Ballet Russe, it managed several creditable efforts of its own. But the fire subsided when the trade winds ceased to blow—hardly a healthy condition for an institution of the Metropolitan's pretensions.

Statistics may often be revealing when opinions are not. In Gatti's first season, 130 performances were given in 18 weeks. In his thirteenth, 167 were given in 23 weeks. The difference of 37 means that in 17 of the 23 weeks, an extra performance somehow had to be accommodated. Perhaps this was integral in a scheme of profit-making opera, or, at the least, a businesslike way of utilizing the eight "services" per week for which the orchestral players were paid, on union contract.

This reasoning was deficient in two ways at least: it deprived the company of a needed rehearsal period while lowering the general level with an increased work load. The institution not merely operated without loss, however, but—as extenuation of all shortcomings—continued to show a profit.

THE POST–CARUSO SEASONS, 1921–1932

1921–1922

Despite the positive public prophecy delivered by Gatti in the spring of 1921 (see page 297), there is every probability that he had profound private doubts about Caruso's possible reappearance. The suspended *L'Elisir d'amore* in Brooklyn, he relates in his *Memories of the Opera,* was the first such experience in his career; his premonition was that Caruso was "lost" to him. When pleurisy set in and operation followed operation, premonition gave way to harsh medical fact. His memoirs recount further that Dr. Antonio Stella informed him: "Mr. Gatti, Caruso will perhaps pull through, and he will keep his voice, for the voice has nothing to do with the pleurisy. But this man will never again have the necessary breath, with all these operations."

Confronted with this informed diagnosis, Gatti could only ponder the figures he knew so well. From 1911 to 1920, Caruso had averaged more than forty appearances per season in New York. In many of these he had been the dominant personality, the man around whom the performance was built. Prudence would have argued a turn in another direction; habit impelled Gatti to abide by the same formula, seeking new ingredients— if not Martinelli, Gigli; if neither, Lauri-Volpi, Fleta, Fullin, and so on, to make it work all over again. As he waited in vain for the new house he had been promised, staging methods and scenic design strode ahead elsewhere, leaving the Metropolitan not merely a static but a retrogressive institution. Habit settled into routine, routine soon enough into inertia.

The long-term problems were hardly visible in the success of the short-term solutions—the promotion of Gigli, the engagement of Galli-Curci, the sponsorship of Maria Jeritza, the integration into the company of Chaliapin and Ruffo when they became available. To the surprise of the best commercial thinkers, the public reaction to the uncertain condition of Caruso during the weeks when subscriptions were taken up was not to "wait and see." Instead of the expected slump, subscriptions actually rose as many who had held back previously decided this was the time to get the good seats they had been hoping for. Few of them got the good seats, but the subscription sale flourished remarkably.

The applause of the first-night audience on November 14 went to Galli-Curci in her debut as Violetta (d), to Gigli as Alfredo,* and to De Luca in a better than ordinary *Traviata*. But there were few without a thought, however fleeting, for the man whose part in the openings had become invariable, and many spent a moment before or after the acts in contemplation of Caruso's draped portrait on the grand-tier floor. A few weeks later the heroic bust that stood in the old house until the end was installed as a permanent reminder to operagoers and artists alike of one who was "the peer . . . of any . . . in history."

Galli-Curci's debut was a particular ordeal, and she began rather breathlessly. As the evening progressed, she had better control of what Henderson described as "one of the most beautiful voices this public has ever heard," and Gigli sang admirably while looking "a dignified family retainer." Stage and singers were dressed in new colors from the house of Urban. For all her prominence in the pre-season press, Galli-Curci appeared on relatively few occasions. Eleven performances were scattered in two sequences, with Lucia* on November 17 and Gilda* on November 26 sharing her early-season activity with Violetta, and with Rosina* in *Il Barbiere* as an additional role, on February 6 with Chamlee (Almaviva), De Luca, and Mardones (Basilio). She was especially liked in the last of these, Henderson describing it as "bewitchingly gowned," sung with "daintiness and charm." The *Rigoletto* and *Lucia* productions were newly imported from Italy.

Little was known of Maria Jeritza before November 19 save to diligent Continental travelers—and Gatti. She had first come to his attention in 1912, then aged twenty-five and a star of Reinhardt's *La Belle Hélène* in Munich. Her success in Vienna soon after led to plans for a New York engagement, but the war delayed it for almost eight years. The gradually growing tolerance for things German allowed her to be introduced in the twenty-two-year-old Erich W. Korngold's *Die tote Stadt,* and she did for it in New York what she had done for it in Vienna. By Henderson's valuation her Marietta (d) "smiled, danced and sang" its sinuous way into the affections of her listener, and her voice "flooded the auditorium with glittering tone." Aldrich was impressed by the "power-ful . . . youthful and sympathetic" quality of her tones, though he heard some "stridency" at the climaxes. Korngold's score was very well received, though the exceptional vocal demands it made—Harrold's energetic singing of Paul* is commonly held to have impaired his voice permanently —made it treacherous business for frequent repetition. Mario Laurenti had a notable success with Pierrot's song, and George Meader made an incon-spicuous debut as Victorin (d). Bodanzky was warmly praised for his conducting. The production was by Kautsky, of Vienna.

This was but a ripple, however, beside the splash Jeritza made with her Tosca* on December 1. Without calling attention to the prone posi-tion in which she sang *"Vissi d'arte"* Henderson saw a new life for the familiar work in her "enthralling vitality," the "luminous intelligence" that gave new meaning to hitherto choppy recitative. Deems Taylor, then critic of the *World,* noted that Jeritza "half fell, half slid" to the floor at the celebrated moment, to accomplish "a vocal feat as difficult as it was effective." By Gatti's recollection, the ovation that followed was the greatest he ever heard in a theater.

Some of the legalistic minds on the critical bench—such as Krehbiel—thought the device stagy, but the commentary must be that Jeritza had attempted a very difficult thing and done it well. Certainly many subse-quent Toscas must have been tempted to emulate her. That none has suggests, not restraint, but lack of ability. Scotti's "highly trained art" (Henderson) kept his Scarpia abreast of the drama in the new Tosca, but Aureliano Pertile, a tenor of considerable standing in Italy, was barely noticed as Cavaradossi (d). Moranzoni conducted.

A positive personality in *Die tote Stadt* or *Tosca,* or as Santuzza* when she was seen in *Cavalleria* on December 10, Jeritza made less impression as Sieglinde* when *Die Walküre* was resumed on December 16, or as Elsa* in *Lohengrin* on January 6 with German principals, but the chorus singing English. The long phrases of Sieglinde were embarrassing to her management of breath, and her Moravian dialect was oddly evident in the text. Others in the first postwar *Walküre* were Sembach, Gordon (Fricka*), and Matzenauer, with Whitehill a truly majestic Wotan. Aside from vocal limitations, Henderson thought Jeritza's Sieglinde worthy of "emphatic approval." *Tristan* was now given in German, with much the same cast as before, and Easton took the change of language in stride by singing Isolde, Elsa, and Sieglinde in German with authority and finesse. Julia Claussen, a routine mezzo, attempted Brünnhilde* in *Die Walküre* on April 19, but she was happier as Brangäne* in *Tristan* on the 21st.

All the old objections to bilingual opera and the unfortunate conse-quences of the star system might have been raised when Chaliapin sang Boris* on December 9, but the unspoken axiom was invoked that any liberty is tolerable if the justification is sufficient. Chaliapin singing Russian amidst others singing Italian, Chaliapin impressing everybody, including the supine Papi at the conductor's desk, was justified by what Henderson called a "powerful, symmetrical and convincing" characteri-zation, by what Aldrich deemed "a Russian Macbeth" enacted by a "great artist" who made a "profound impression." Aldrich found some of the "thrilling resonance" in the score unexpressed, nevertheless. Harrold, Gordon (Marina), Ananian (Varlaam), and Rothier (Pimenn) were in this cast. On December 14 Pertile (Dmitri*), Matzenauer (Marina), and Mardones (Pimenn) were heard. This was as much as Gatti had con-tracted for, but public interest was so great that three further perform-ances were added, on January 12, 21, and 26. By now it was apparent that Chaliapin had previously been in poor voice, and the new qualities in his art caused Henderson to describe him as "a singer of great skill, as well as an actor of the first order." Not since Niemann's death scene in *Götterdämmerung* had the writer seen anything "so thrilling in this line."

The introduction of Ruffo was planned for the role of Don Carlos* when *Ernani* was revived on December 8, but he was out of voice and was replaced by Danise. A splendid Italian scenic production, and a cast of Martinelli (Ernani*), Mardones (Don Ruy Gomez*), and Ponselle (Elvira) aroused the uncritical, but the soprano's "spasmodic" phrasing did not win Henderson's approval where such an air as *"Ernani involami"* was concerned. Papi conducted. Ruffo finally sang Don Carlos* impres-sively on January 28, after a debut as Figaro (d) in *Il Barbiere* on Janu-ary 19 which earned warm commendation for "great facility . . . elasticity . . . unction . . . color" (Henderson). Galli-Curci not being available, Cora Chase sang Rosina rather mildly. On a later occasion, Angeles Ottein, of Madrid, made her debut as Rosina (d). A fluent singer, she did not produce the kind of tone New York preferred, and soon departed.

The lustrous season that ushered in the twenties also brought the valida-tion of one of Gatti's long-standing promises: the first New York hearing of Mozart's *Così fan tutte,* promised since 1911, and finally performed on March 24, 1922, in a production by Urban utilizing an inner stage. In Henderson's judgment, it could be "placed beside the historic revelations which made the Metropolitan famous," and Aldrich pronounced the performance "thrice admirable" and Bodanzky's direction "finished, spirited, brilliant." Easton was a confident Fiordiligi,* Bori a charming Despina,* and Peralta a Dorabella* of unsuspected vocal resource. De Luca, in Henderson's view, met the requirements of Guglielmo* "triumphantly," Meader won esteem for his artful Ferrando,* and Didur was an amusing, if thick-sounding Alfonso.* The recitatives were much abbreviated, and Ferrando's two arias omitted. For all the long wait New Yorkers had endured for *Così,* and the evident response it aroused, Gatti did not burden his public inordinately with it. In this and the next three seasons it had eleven performances, and a final one in 1927–8.

The renewal of serious activity at the Metropolitan after a kind of wartime hibernation was manifest in the introduction of no less than four other works. Because the company was lacking just the voices desirable, *Le Coq d'or* had been put aside. Its place in the repertory was taken by Rimsky's *Snegurochka* on January 23, with Boris Anisfeld once more providing an admired décor. Henderson described the score as "fluent . . . but not impressive," full of "tender sentiment, burly travesty, merciless satire." Nevertheless, it lacked substance for an American audience, though Bori was a lovable Snegurochka,* Harrold excellent as the Tsar.* As always except for *Boris,* the Metropolitan's language for Russian works was French. Bodanzky was the conductor.

Among the works that came and went on almost an audition basis in these years (though fully costumed, rehearsed, and staged) were Catalani's *Loreley,* first seen on March 4, and Lalo's *Le Roi d'Ys* on January 5. Perhaps the choice of the first was impelled by a desire to show how much better it could be done by the Metropolitan than it had been done a few seasons before by the visiting Chicago company, but the demonstration did not convince the public. Muzio sang a fine Loreley,* and Gigli was a well-sounding Walter,* but the public did not respond. Moranzoni conducted. Albert Wolff gave admirable service to Lalo, but the innumerable minor distinctions of *Le Roi d'Ys*—economy, taste, skillfull orchestration—did not atone for its lack of major ones. Ponselle's treatment of Margared* was judged overstressed by Henderson, but the vocal virtue in her voice, in Gigli's as Mylio,* and in Alda's as Rozenn* was considerable. Wolff gave the familiar overture a place of honor before Act II. The opera was not heard in a second season.

On the eve of carrying out her intention to retire from the operatic stage, Farrar took a new role for the last time when she sang Anita* in Massenet's *La Navarraise* on November 30. It chanced that Emma Calvé was appearing in concert in New York during this winter, and Krehbiel, reminded of her tragic power in the part, noted Farrar's lack of it.

Henderson found the American's work "consistent, well-planned and theatrically effective." It was also well sung. Crimi was Araquil,* and Rothier the Garrido.* New production and all, it was dropped after three repetitions.

The coincidence of Farrar's withdrawal and Jeritza's arrival provoked some assertions that one happening was related to the other. If they were, it was merely Gatti's forehandedness in ringing in the new while the old still lingered on the scene, for Farrar had long planned to leave the opera stage at forty, and public life in every aspect at fifty. She adhered to both intentions. The public heard that this season would be her last at the Metropolitan just before a *Faust* on January 20, of which Henderson said "she never sang Marguerite more beautifully." Whitehill's Méphistophélès had reached a new point of eminence—ranked as the best since Plançon's—and Martinelli was a likable Faust. Louis Hasselmans, last noted with the Chicago company, made his debut as conductor.

A clamor for Farrar brought her forward at the end of the evening to inform some who alternately dabbed eyes and waved handkerchiefs: "Children, this is no occasion for a funeral." Her well-planned retreat found each favorite role buried in applause and flowers, such as had happened to no singer since Sembrich. After her Butterfly on January 23, she invited her listeners to nominate the role in which they would like to have her sing at a formal farewell, and the overwhelming sentiment was for Tosca (as rebuff to those who had swung to Jeritza as the company's reigning Tosca). Farrar reminded the audience, however, that it was, after all, Gatti's decision to make; and he tacitly reminded her of his long memory by deciding that her last appearance should be *Zaza,* on April 22. In the weeks between she was heard as Louise, Manon, Tosca, Marguerite, and Carmen, each occasion more hysterical than the last.

The singular fervor of the gerryflappers excelled all bounds when the last *Zaza* arrived, with banners hanging from boxes, balloons thrown in the air, even the presentation to the star, after Act II, of a crown, which she put on, and a scepter, which she carried off. A moment of real emotion was reached when the opera was over and Farrar finally spoke to the cheering audience. She reviewed her early career and recalled her prayers for a Metropolitan success. But, she said (indicating her mother and father in the front row), she had never dreamed it would "be like this." "Has George Cohan stopped crying?" she asked. "I don't want a tear in this house." She then stated, proudly: "I am leaving this institution because I want to go." Backstage she distributed her costumes and props to favored gerryflappers, to dispel any thought of a "comeback"; and donning a new outfit made for her by the loyal girls, she was escorted to a car and driven through cheering friends away from opera forever.

In addition to the *Faust* that introduced him, Hasselmans took over everything in the French repertory which Wolff chose not to conduct—*Le Roi d'Ys* on January 27, *Manon* on February 3, *Louise, Samson,* and so on. The epitome of a qualified *routinier,* Hasselmans vacillated between mediocrity and distinction for the next dozen years, rarely attaining either extreme. One more Musetta* joined a limitless supply of same when Yvonne d'Arle—a native American despite her name—made her debut in *La Bohème* on December 1. Viola Philo was the priestess in her debut in *Aida* on November 26, and Manuel Salazar, of the San Carlo company, was borrowed for several performances of Don Alvaro* in *Forza* (the first on December 31) when Martinelli was not up to singing it. His powerful high voice was heard intermittently in the next two seasons.

The oddly overlapping careers of Farrar and Garden (the latter's had begun a year later, in 1907) came to simultaneous ends, so far as New York was concerned, in the closing months of this season. Garden was in the second season of her brief career as directress of the Chicago Opera, well on the way to the million-dollar loss that brought about her (and the Harold McCormicks') retirement from posts of responsibility. In New York the company opened its Manhattan Opera House season on January 23 with D'Alvarez as Dalila and Muratore as Samson (especially admired for picturesque action), with Polacco conducting the Saint-Saëns score.

The last important novelty for which New Yorkers could thank Oscar Hammerstein, directly or indirectly, was Serge Prokofiev's *L'Amour des trois oranges,* conducted by the composer at its introduction on February 14. In the opinion of Aldrich, "There are a few, but only a very few, passages that bear recognizable kinship with what has hitherto been recognized as music." Henderson described the work as "an extravaganza," of which some elements were "riotous buffoonery," the music, on the whole, being "peculiar." Boris Anisfeld provided a "stunning" succession of designs, and the work was well sung by José Mojica (Prince), Nina Koshetz (Fata Morgana), Dufranne (Tchelio), and James Wolfe (Farfarello). Dua, as Truffaldino, won acclaim as a comedian. It was repeated once.

Those addicted to cynicism had occasion for laughter on February 4 when *Salome* was given as a benefit for a French charity headed by Anne Morgan, whose father's influence had been invoked to banish the work from the Metropolitan. It raised $22,000 for the charity, but no moral indignation. In Henderson's opinion, presentations on the spoken stage since 1910, when *Salome* had last been heard, made it nothing more or less than "utterly decorous." Polacco conducted a performance largely Garden, Riccardo Martin being notably weak as Herod.

Garden's final tour was Farrar-like for inclusiveness, Garden-like for exclusiveness—Mélisande, Louise, Thaïs, Le Jongleur, Monna Vanna, and a farewell Fiora in *L'Amore* on February 25, with Johnson, Baklanoff, and Lazzari. At the last of the last, Garden appeared in the somber shroud she wore as the dead Princess (it was her custom to be borne on-stage as the corpse, rather than passing the task over to a super) and told the audience: "We shall not come here again. We are going to take care of the Western territory, and it will be a hard thing to do." Garden reminded her friends of the easy journey to Chicago by Twentieth Century Limited, and assured them a courteous welcome on arrival.

Among a number of singers who made listening pleasant in Chicago during the remainder of this decade were Maria Ivogün, who won Henderson's approval for a voice of "beautiful quality and remarkable high range" when she made her debut as Rosina in *Il Barbiere* on January 28, and Claire Dux, the Nedda of *Pagliacci* on February 2. Ivogün was also honored for command of "every feat of the colorature soprano," and Dux was warmly praised. Joseph Schwarz sang an impressive Germont in *La Traviata* on January 24, with Schipa and Graziella Pareto, and Wolfram in *Tannhäuser* on February 8, with Raïsa (Elisabeth) and Richard Schubert (Tannhäuser). *Otello* had its last performance for more than a decade when it was given on February 22 with Raïsa, Marshall, and Rimini (Iago), Pietro Cimini conducting.

Commenting on the visiting activity versus the resident company at the Metropolitan, Henderson offered the view: "If we had two opera houses differing in character and styles as do the Grand Opera and the Opera Comique in Paris, perhaps there might be hope for both. . . . It might be possible to keep two opera houses going if one were the resort of society and the other a 'people's opera' exclusively. But then we should be confronted with that other difficulty, namely, that in this country the 'people' will not endure being set apart and soothed with something less than the very best. And without the boxes and high priced seats you cannot have the very best in opera."

For the directors of the Metropolitan, what Gatti provided was the "very best," as attested by extension of his services till May 1926. He reciprocated with a credit balance of $48,201. The seemingly innocent announcement, in midseason, that principals would be hired in the future on a half-season basis, in order to diversify casts and repertory as much as possible, had implications not realized at the time. From it emerged the vagrant comings and goings, the arbitrary impositions on management of times suitable to the stars, which later corrupted ensemble and weakened musical discipline.

1922–1923

The opening-night ceremony, which had been something of an artistic ritual in the Caruso period, passed, with his passing, into the category of a competition, a coveted reward for service rendered. The notion of *Armide* for an opening—as in 1910—was hardly less remote than the idea of *Armide* at all. In its place this time, on November 13, was *Tosca* with Jeritza, one of sixteen performances in the first two seasons of her arrival and Farrar's departure. Martinelli, Scotti, and Moranzoni did not fall below the level of "splendid vitality and pictorial beauty" recognized by Henderson in Jeritza's Tosca.

The integration of old and new so skillfully developed by Gatti in his dozen years of experience brought, within the first week, Edward Johnson's debut as Avito (d) in *L'Amore dei tre re* on November 16 to Bori's Fiora; a new production of *Der Rosenkavalier* with Paul Bender as Baron Ochs (d) on November 17, and Chaliapin in *Mefistofele* on November 18. Richard Mayr might have been preferable to Bender as Ochs, but this was otherwise close to the best the contemporary scene offered in all of these, with Bender rated a "vast improvement" over Goritz, Easton a compelling Marschallin,* and Jeritza a "fine upstanding" Octavian.* Gustav Schützendorf was an able Faninal* in his debut, Sundelius a passable Sophie,* and Harrold sang the Italian air in Act I. Henderson rated Bodanzky's treatment of the score productive of "changeful and even exciting delights," but the "crass and shameless realism" of the action still offended. The production, by Kautsky, endured as long as the theater itself, under a new covering of paint. The name of Wilhelm von Wymetal, as stage director, appeared for the first time.

The twenty-eight years of Edward Johnson's Metropolitan career (thirteen as performer, fifteen as director) began at a high point and rarely declined thereafter. As Avito,* Henderson thought, he "acted and sang with more finish and yet with more freedom" than before, and Aldrich complimented him as "a tenor who is something more than a voice." This was attested by his adaptability to a sequence of roles that included Dmitri in *Boris,* Des Grieux in Puccini's *Manon Lescaut,* Cavaradossi in *Tosca,* as well as José, Canio, Pinkerton, Roméo, and Faust within weeks.

Chaliapin's Boris, which had previously impelled Henderson to a comparison with Niemann's death of Siegfried, now prompted the same critic to say: "The operatic stage has furnished no such portrayal of the agonies of a soul since Tamagno's Otello." Matzenauer, Harrold and Mardones were somewhat overshadowed by this "huge operatic figure," and Papi conducted "with diligence but hardly with distinction." Chaliapin's Mefistofele, somewhat refined since 1907, was matched by Alda and Gigli in a performance described by Henderson as "the best the work has had in many years." Georges Clemenceau was noted in the very large audience.

Chaliapin's season also included two performances of *Don Carlos,* in which his enactment of King Philip II* on December 2 was more prominent than anything else in the moody score. His singing of *"Dormirò sol"* being heavily applauded, he inserted his own repetition, though the practice was now against the rules of the theater. In the words of Aldrich, "he finally came forward . . . told Mr. Papi where to begin again, and straightway repeated the last stanza . . . with what effect upon the dramatic illusion need not be described." If this was unexpected and uncontrollable this time, it need not have been on December 13, when the singer indulged the same self-esteem. In this version Act I was omitted, and the stirring scene between the King and the Inquisitor—which, apparently, had not always been given in prior performances at the Metropolitan—was restored. Rothier was the Inquisitor,* and Martinelli, Peralta (Elisabeth), and De Luca (Posa) filled out the cast, with Papi again the obliging *maestro.*

The leisurely return of the Wagner repertory to the Metropolitan extended this season to *Tannhäuser,* which provided (as did *Der Rosenkavalier)* a prominent role for Jeritza. Her Elisabeth* on February 1 did not make quite the impression on New York that it had made on Gatti when he saw it in Vienna in 1913, but it was one of her better Wagnerian roles, sightly and sometimes well sung. Save for Matzenauer as Venus, the cast was new, with Whitehill an excellent Wolfram,* Bender a qualified Landgrave,* and Curt Taucher a forceful Tannhäuser.* Bodanzky's conducting impressed some as long-winded. The then-admired Kautsky production remained in use until 1953–54.

The first new German tenor to reach this stage since 1914, Taucher was approved by the *Tribune* for a "dramatically and vocally thrilling" Siegmund in his debut in *Die Walküre* on November 23. Henderson's description of him as a "typical German tenor" is more in accord with personal recollection of his work a few years later. Bender was "a vocally sepulchral" Hunding* on this occasion, with Jeritza, Matzenauer, and Whitehill in familiar roles. Wymetal's direction was approved, save for allowing Siegmund and Sieglinde to "address their impassioned speeches to the subscribers" (Henderson).

Taucher's Tristan* on November 27 was moderately satisfactory for its "intelligent reading of the lines," but there was little beauty in the singing. Most of what there was of this was provided by Sigrid Onegin's Brangäne,* valued by Henderson as "beautiful to see, moving to hear." Matzenauer's Isolde was more strenuous than ever, Bender's Marke* ponderous. Taucher was Parsifal* in a German performance on December 8, Matzenauer and Whitehill resuming the original language without incident. Urban's repainting of his first scene was considered a thoughtful gesture (see page 283).

Onegin had been a New York success even before her Metropolitan debut as Amneris (d) on November 22, for she was sponsored by Stokowski at a Philadelphia Orchestra concert on October 23, singing "Andromache's Lament" from Bruch's *Achilles* and two Strauss songs in a way to remind Henderson of Marie Brema. "A truly noble voice . . . tragic intensity . . . large style" were among her attributes, rare then, even rarer now. With her as Aida (d) on November 22 was Elisabeth Rethberg, rather unsteady in her debut, but commended for a lovely voice and sound style nevertheless. Edmund Burke, the King (d), was also new. Onegin sang nothing else this season except Brangäne (see above) though she was in or near New York for many months.

The evident intention that Rethberg should be a favorite in the Italian as well as the German repertory gave her prominence as Nedda* in *Pagliacci* on December 2 before she sang Sieglinde* in *Die Walküre* on December 18. A little heavy for Leoncavallo, a little light for this Wagner, Rethberg had her warmest success this season as Sophie* in *Der Rosenkavalier* on December 23. Henderson noted that she sang her high-lying phrases in Act II with charm and ease, predicting, if she adhered to her schooling, "a position of considerable importance in her profession."

Two singers of solid German reputation made their debuts on March 1, 1923, when Michael Bohnen sang Francesco (d) and Barbara Kemp the Mona Lisa (d) in *Mona Lisa,* of which Kemp's husband, Max von Schillings, was the composer. Henderson admired the well-written book by Beatrice Dovsky, but thought the score the work of no more than "a mere musical mechanic." Neither role permitted an inclusive estimate of the vocal powers the performers possessed, but Kemp conveyed a remarkable likeness of Mona Lisa, and Bohnen was judged a singer of "much dramatic virility" by Krehbiel.[1]

The careers of Bohnen and Kemp followed closely parallel lines in this season, though with widely divergent results. They were Gurnemanz* and Kundry* in *Parsifal* on March 3, the King* and Elsa* in *Lohengrin* on March 8, and Marke* and Isolde* on April 4. Bohnen's Gurnemanz quickly established his exceptional feeling for this character and his high rank as a singing actor. Kemp's Kundry was interesting, but erratically sung. Her first Isolde, scheduled for March 14,[2] had to be postponed, and

---

[1] This was the last review written by Krehbiel in a career that began in Cincinnati in 1874, in New York in 1880. He died, in his seventieth year, on March 23, 1923.

[2] No alternate Isolde was available, and the bill was changed to *Butterfly*, to Gatti's great professional disgruntlement. No doubt this had a part in Kemp's troubles the following season.

when she did sing the part on April 4, the limitations of range and power in her voice were quite evident. Bohnen put his operatic aspiration in a clear light when he presented a ring to Chaliapin after the season's final *Boris,* and received a gold watch chain in return. The Chaliapin-like liberties that Bohnen permitted himself were singularly unsuited to such roles as Hagen, Wotan, or King Marke, and cost him the good will of many who held his talents in high esteem.

A final new singer in the German repertory this season was Delia Reinhardt, then the wife of Gustav Schützendorf. She sang an ingratiating Sieglinde* on January 27. She was scheduled for Butterfly on February 24, but illness intervened. Her other roles were Mimi* on January 31 and Elsa* in *Lohengrin* on April 20. They passed with little critical notice. Her replacement for *Butterfly* was Thalia Sabanieeva, described by Henderson as of "San Carlo" quality. (The reference was to the touring company in America, not the permanent one in Naples.) On another occasion, Butterfly was sung by Easton, when the latest, long-lived décor for this work by Urban was shown on November 24. Fifteen years before, Easton had been an affecting Cio-Cio-San; now she was a Kundry, a Marschallin, an Isolde. Something was missing and it was not only the gerryflappers. Easton was this season's Carmen on November 30, and when she was not available later in the year, Gatti offered Ina Bourskaya in her debut on March 2. This Russian alto had come to New York with a touring company, and gave intelligent service in smaller roles for numerous seasons; but she was rather dull of voice for leading roles.

The difficulties with *Butterfly* and *Carmen* give point to the opinion later expressed to me by Geraldine Farrar that her retirement and Caruso's death were happenings for which Gatti did not compensate in the boom years before the depression set in. (This was not prima-donna vainglory, but an objective evaluation.) In her opinion, artists of such background could "carry" performers of lesser experience and give the impresario a nucleus around which a performance could be built.

One, certainly, who filled that specification was Lucrezia Bori, who came to new prominence this season in three roles she had not previously attempted at the Metropolitan—Juliette* in *Roméo et Juliette* on November 25, Violetta* in *La Traviata* on November 30, and Manon according to Massenet on December 29. Memory is not belied by the record of her acceptance in these roles, for the fine Violetta and the touching Manon were immediately successful, less so the debatable Juliette. Henderson warned his readers not to expect anything of the Melba, Eames, or Sembrich variety from Bori's Juliette. Gigli as Roméo* lacked "poetic imagination . . . grace and aristocracy," and Didur was a Capulet* who "must have been at least 85 years old with a daughter of 15." The settings by

Urban remained in use through the forties. Queena Mario (born Helen Tillotson) was Juliette* on February 10. Hasselmans made what Henderson described as "a gallant and measurably successful effort" to weld an ensemble, but its high points were rather low.

Bori's Violetta,* however, was the occasion of a "brilliant success," said Henderson, blending "youth, beauty, vivacity, histrionic skill and a lovely voice." A familiar cadenza at the end of *"Sempre libera"* was omitted, but the offense was not considered serious. Gigli and Danise had the other principal roles, Moranzoni conducting. In her Manon, the same critic was impressed with the vocal "felicity of style" and "an indescribable charm" in her acting that made it an admired conception for a dozen years to come. Chamlee and Rothier were fellow performers.

Of other roles recently associated with Farrar, Thaïs* appeared in a new guise when Jeritza was heard on December 14, with an Urban production, possessing "all the sumptuousness" now common at the Metropolitan, seen for the first time. The soprano was a vision of beauty and sang with promising freedom, though she had learned the French text only a few months before. Harrold's Nicias* was acceptable, Whitehill's Athanaël distinguished. The afternoon of Christmas Day was one of seven occasions when *Thaïs* was given this season.

English was not heard at the Metropolitan this year, either in a translation or in an original score. A reasonable aversion for the kind of American work which had been available to date inclined Gatti to foreign novelties, *Mona Lisa* as representative of German craft, and Franco Vittadini's *Anima allegra* as a specimen of Italian writing. The *première* of the latter on February 14 inclined Henderson to describe the book as one that rose to "hitherto unsuspected heights of inanity" and the music as "one continuous flow of melodic treacle." Rovescalli's settings earned major praise; the cast of Bori (Consuelo*), Tokatyan (Lucio*), Lauri-Volpi (Pedro*), and Didur (Don Eligio*) general approval. Moranzoni conducted. Aldrich dissented from other opinion in finding the work "successfully gay." It had a two-season career, totaling nine performances.

Of the two new tenors, Giacomo Lauri-Volpi had made his debut as the Duke (d) in *Rigoletto* on January 26, singing with a voice of "excellent quality" by Henderson's standard, which stimulated "bright hopes" for his future. His health, however, was not of the best this season, and though he sang Rodolfo,* Alfredo,* Cavaradossi,* Almaviva,* Turiddu,* and Pinkerton,* no conclusive judgment emerged. Armando Tokatyan, of Armenian extraction, was a singer of less experience. He was introduced as Turiddu in a concert version of *Cavalleria* on Sunday, November 19 before taking the stage in the same work on February 3. He was later heard as Nicias* in *Thaïs* on February 28, being described as having a pleasant voice well used, but rather unformed art.

On behalf of Martinelli, who had rarely been favored with special honors, Rossini's *Guglielmo Tell* was brought out on January 5. In Henderson's judgment, the old-fashioned construction of the work and its lack of credible characters were debits that even Ponselle (Matilda*), Sundelius (Jemmy*), Martinelli (Arnold*), Danise (Tell*), and Mardones (Walter Furst*) could not redeem. Papi directed this better than most things, with a rousing performance of the overture before Act II. Rovescalli was the designer.

More welcome was Meyerbeer's *L'Africana,* whose last performances in 1907 were still closer to mind than those of *Tell* in 1895. The brilliance and effect of Meyerbeer's music were congenial to Gigli, who sang a fine Vasco da Gama* on March 21, and Ponselle's Selika* ranked high among her accomplishments. Danise (Nelusko*), Didur (Don Pedro*), and Rothier (Grand Inquisitor*) were all excellent; Mario was a successful Inez.* Urban was responsible for what Henderson described as "a splendid reincarnation," and Bodanzky's musical work was equally honored. With a series of performances in the next ten years, and three in 1933–34, *L'Africana* became the Meyerbeer work last applauded by a Metropolitan audience.

Both Galli-Curci and Ruffo were transient performers this season, the soprano singing Lucia, Rosina, and Mimi at scattered intervals, the baritone adding Amonasro* in *Aida* to his record on January 18. Gatti tended to use their services for so-called "benefits"—"so-called" because everybody was paid, with the seats sold at extra prices by any group that paid the company the fee for a full house—and thus they were rarely reviewed in the press.

The Wagnerian void left by the absence of the *Ring* and *Die Meistersinger* from the Metropolitan schedule was filled by a German company led by Leo Blech and Edouard Mörike of Berlin, which settled down at the Manhattan Opera House on February 12. The excellent conductors and some fine artists were impeded by makeshift scenery, an undependable orchestra, and primitive staging, but they left some durable impressions nevertheless.

Outstanding among them were those associated with Alexander Kipnis, the well-known but aging Friedrich Plaschke, and the younger, rising baritone Friedrich Schorr. Kipnis sang Pogner in the opening *Meistersinger,* with Plaschke (Sachs), Robert Hutt (Walther), and Meta Seinemeyer (Eva). Blech was the excellent conductor. Friedrich Schorr made his impressive debut[1] as Wolfram on February 13, and Elsa Alsen was a superior Venus. Seinemeyer was Elisabeth, Kipnis the Landgrave. Mörike conducted *Lohengrin* on the 15th, with Urlus, of the prewar Metropolitan company, as Lohengrin. Editha Fleischer, a charming singer for the Metropolitan for much of the following decade, sang Woglinde in a poor *Rheingold* on February 16, and Marcella Roeseler, who had a lesser Metropolitan career, was Rosalinde in a *Fledermaus* on the evening of the same day.

Some critical opinion thought the best work of this company to be its *Tristan,* directed by Mörike, with Eva van der Osten, Urlus, Kipnis as Marke, and Ottilie Metzger as Brangäne; others, such as Henderson, inclined to its *Walküre* conducted by Blech, whose "perfect tempos" had not been approached by Metropolitan conductors of Wagner within memory. Schorr was an "excellent" Wotan, Van der Osten a "splendid" Sieglinde, and Alsen an able Brünnhilde. Kipnis was honored after a *Götterdämmerung* on March 2 by a comparison with Édouard de Reszke, the nearest likeness, in Henderson's opinion, for his "subtle, sinister and commanding" performance. The high praise for Carl Braun had, apparently, been forgotten (see page 239).

The success of the Manhattan Opera House run encouraged an additional engagement at the Lexington Theater, during which Mörike conducted a poorish *Fidelio* on March 17 (Alsen, Schorr, Kipnis, and Fleischer were in the cast, but the performance had not been well prepared), and Heinrich Knote, of Conried days, gave surprising evidence of vocal preservation as Walther in *Die Meistersinger* and as Tristan. In the last of these, Alsen was Isolde, Schorr sang Kurvenal, and Kipnis Marke with Ernst Knoch conducting. Claire Dux and Maria Ivogün of the Chicago company also appeared as guests, the former singing Eva in *Die Meistersinger* and Lady Harriet in *Marta,* the latter performing Frau Fluth in *Die lustigen Weiber von Windsor.* Schorr's engagement at the Metropolitan was confirmed before the season ended, and Kipnis was engaged for Chicago, where he was a longtime favorite before coming to the Metropolitan years afterward (in 1940).

Despite a repertory that embraced forty productions, and the expense of four novelties and half a dozen standard works re-dressed (including *Tannhäuser, Der Rosenkavalier, Manon, Roméo,* and *Thaïs*), the Metropolitan profit for the year was $49,141. Including a week in Atlanta and the visits to Brooklyn and Philadelphia, the company gave 203 performances.

[1] He had actually sung briefly with the Chicago Opera in 1912, but he did not care to acknowledge this fact until his career was over.

1923-1924

The response to the seven-week season of German opera convinced the Metropolitan management that New York was ready for two things: more opera in general, and more German opera in particular. A week was added to the season, producing the twenty-four week pattern that remained without change till the decline of public support caused drastic abbreviation in 1932. The lengthened season had several unexpected consequences, however—of which the most important was an increase in the number of performances per week, with greater strain on all concerned, especially the orchestra.

An intimation of the sort was given on February 27, 1924, when Barbara Kemp asked to be released from her contract, pleading ill health. Gatti complied, with customary expressions of regret. A few days later her husband, Max von Schillings, decided that the press should know more about the affair, and charged that Gatti "had lost interest" in Kemp and was further dissatisfied because the singer had "not met all the conditions of her contract"[1] the previous season. Schillings added that when Kemp came to New York "she did not realize how heavy the work was or how short the time for rehearsal." He concluded that the differences were wholly "artistic," the plea of illness having been given out at Gatti's suggestion.

The director's reply was typically pointed. Kemp's trouble was, and he quoted her, "nervousness." He had kept her name on the roster only because of her "high reputation in Germany." Schillings, he concluded, had "lost a splendid chance to remain silent." Kemp, certainly, had not fulfilled the expectations of a leading soprano, but her charges of a "heavy" schedule and "short" time for rehearsal went unanswered, suggesting that the singers were well aware of the Metropolitan's shortcomings in these matters before they became generally evident a few seasons later.

Although time for another *Aida* opening had not quite arrived (*Thaïs*, with Jeritza, Tokatyan, and Whitehill had the honor on November 5), *Aida* made the first sensation of the new season when it was given on November 7 with a new Italian décor designed by Parravicini, executed by Rota and Rovescalli. "Such scenery cannot be described," said Henderson; "it must be seen." (It was seen for each of the next twenty-eight seasons, when it could not be described for other reasons.) Rethberg sang her Aida "extremely well," said the same writer, and the familiar Radames of Martinelli and the Amneris of Matzenauer were joined by James Wolfe,

---

[1] The canceled *Tristan* (see page 311) doubtless rankled.

formerly of the Chicago Company, as the King* and Phradie Wells as the off-stage Priestess (d). Moranzoni conducted.

The "Cherry Duet" and other melodic enticements of *L'Amico Fritz* were given a further chance for Metropolitan popularity on November 15 after a lapse since 1894. Henderson described it as "the incarnation of repose, one long sweet song of domestic affection," suggesting some lack of dramatic variety. For the performers there was nothing but praise. Bori, in a blond wig, was an affecting Suzel,* Miguel Fleta (who had made his debut as Cavaradossi [d] in *Tosca* on November 8) sang Fritz* well, and Danise was a picturesque Rabbi.* Merle Alcock performed creditably in the role of Beppe.* The new Urban production, warmly admired, was seen but twice more. Moranzoni's version of the score abbreviated it somewhat, and there was time for *L'Oracolo* to be included on the bill.

The total of works by Massenet seen in New York climbed steadily higher when *Le Roi de Lahore* (new in 1877) was introduced on February 29 amid an eye-filling décor by Boris Anisfeld. De Luca was an excellent Scindia,* Delia Reinhardt a tasteful Sita,* and Lauri-Volpi sang Alim* with fine vocal quality. Hasselmans conducted acceptably, and Galli led an elaborate ballet with traditional charm. The fault, and it was a fundamental one, was with Massenet's score, a weak suggestion of the man who was to write *Manon*. Four repetitions sufficed for *Le Roi de Lahore*.

Even less favored was a double bill of Raoul Laparra's *La Habanera* and Primo Riccitelli's *I Compagnacci*, first heard on January 2. Laparra's score had been on Gatti's agenda since 1908, and the first act earned Henderson's esteem for its "vivid and exciting dramatic action." It fell off badly as it progressed, however, with a third act, in the same opinion, "quite hopeless." Easton as Pilar,* Tokatyan as Pedro,* and Danise as Ramon* were worthy enough, as was the scenery of Rovescalli. But *La Habanera* was given only twice again. *I Compagnacci* had a pleasant tenor part well sung by Gigli (Baldo*), but the music did not escape the general mannerisms of post-Puccini writing. The scenery was the first to be credited to Joseph Novak, staff painter until 1950.

Relatively robust, by these standards, was the three-season run initiated by *Fedora* on December 8, with Jeritza the central figure, as Cavalieri had been in 1906, and with Scotti once more as De Siriex. The "radiant and ever vivacious Jeritza" (as Henderson dubbed her) did more for the opera than it did for her, and she was well partnered by Martinelli as Loris Ipanov.* The production was the work of Urban, as was a new *Carmen* on November 22, with Easton, Martinelli, Mardones, and Morgana (Micaëla) as principals under Hasselmans's direction. Bourskaya was a later Carmen; Fleta and Harrold appeared as Don José; and there was a

German Micaëla for a change, Delia Reinhardt appearing on occasions when Morgana, Mario, or Sundelius did not.

The total evidence is that in assembling his new company of German singers Gatti was making every effort to make them trilingual, capable of use also in the French and Italian works (as evident in the instances of Rethberg, Reinhardt, and Bohnen). This is eminently sound practice, but subject to the essential question: how successful? The use of Gustav Schützendorf as Mercutio in *Roméo et Juliette* on December 11 left a vast gap between his work and that of such earlier singers of the part as Albers or De Vries in a time when style was of the essence, and was commonly encountered.

Schützendorf, certainly, was more able to do himself justice as Beckmesser* when *Die Meistersinger* was restored on November 9 in a production by Kautsky which served long and well. Henderson thought Bodanzky had conducted no other work with "quite the insight" he showed in *Die Meistersinger,* for which Easton was an Eva* of "great charm and musical finish;" Meader an "unsurpassable" David;* Bender a heavy but able Pogner;* and Whitehill a Sachs well remembered and deeply loved. Rudolf Laubenthal made his debut as Walther (d), singing with the "good young fresh voice" admired on some subsequent occasions, and the "characteristically German style" that was not. Lawrence Gilman, who had succeeded Krehbiel as the *Tribune*'s music critic, hailed Schorr's Sachs* as a "truly great performance" when he sang the role for the first time on February 23, and Henderson spoke approvingly of its "fine manly quality." November 19 was the occasion for Rethberg's lovely Eva,* and Delia Reinhardt also sang it creditably on February 23. This singer's unfortunate Metropolitan career suffered one more black mark when she fainted after the quintet, but recovered to finish the performance.

Schorr's debut occurred on February 14 as Wolfram (d) in *Tannhäuser.* Henderson characterized him as "a *helden baryton*" who could also sing "lyrically." His steady sequence of well-sung parts included Telramund in *Lohengrin,* Kurvenal in *Tristan,* a Wotan* in *Die Walküre* on March 17, which Gilman termed "superbly sung," and Amfortas in Parsifal. Although Schorr's Wanderer was perhaps his best role when his voice was in its prime, the Metropolitan had no occasion to use him this season when *Siegfried* was brought back. Whitehill was the Wanderer on February 2, and Bohnen sang the part for the first time on February 28. Easton's womanly Brünnhilde* was warmly praised, and Meader's Mime* earned Henderson's accolade as "without question the best the Metropolitan has known." Taucher looked well but sounded badly as the young Siegfried,* and Matzenauer was, as ever, an impressive Erda. Kemp was announced for the *Siegfried* Brünnhilde of late February, but her sudden withdrawal from the company returned the part to Easton. Despite the expenditures for new scenery for *L'Amico Fritz, Fedora,* and other operas, the prewar *Ring* settings of Kautsky continued to be used.

As in the venture with *Oberon,* Bodanzky sought to overcome the long-standing objection to spoken dialogue at the Metropolitan by composing recitatives, save in the "Wolf's Glen scene," for *Der Freischütz* when it was revived on March 22. The value of this innovation was questionable, but not really questioned, for the focus of attention was Bohnen's magnificent Caspar,* "a magnetic force [whose] dramatic power vitalizes the whole performance," wrote Henderson. Rethberg's "lovely quality of voice which has given pleasure to so many audiences" was especially suited to Agathe,* and Mario sang Ännchen* creditably. Louise Hunter and Nanette Guilford were among the bridesmaids. The first had made her debut in a Sunday-night concert on November 11, the second as the Countess (d) in *Rigoletto* on November 10. In a *Freischütz* on April 10, Sabanieeva replaced Mario, and Meader sang a very intelligent, small-scaled Max.*

The other German works were briefly enhanced by Onegin, who sang a splendid Fricka* in *Die Walküre* on December 29 and again on January 25; and at greater length by Karin Branzell, beginning her first of twenty-two consecutive seasons on February 6, as Fricka (d) in *Die Walküre.* Henderson described her as "the fortunate possessor of a very beautiful mezzo soprano voice which has a vein of contralto in its timbre." "Poise" and "genuine grandeur of style" were also to her credit. Bohnen was the potent Wotan.* After Ortrud and Brangäne, Branzell attempted Brünnhilde* in *Die Walküre* on March 17, with more success than Matzenauer or Claussen, though the range was high for her. Her familiarity with the role was an asset at a Brooklyn Academy of Music performance of the work on January 27, 1925. Claussen lost her voice during Act II, and Branzell, who had finished her duties as Fricka, completed the evening as Brünnhilde.

Branzell was one of Gatti's discoveries of this period who could fill roles in the German, French, and Italian repertory with credit. Between April 7 and 19 she sang Amneris in *Aida,* Dalila in *Samson,* and Azucena in *Il Trovatore,* with musical sense if not the greatest abandon. In like manner, Rethberg was called upon for Butterfly (greatly admired for its vocal finesse) and Maddalena in *Andrea Chénier;* and Bohnen gave tigerish accent, if hardly the right vocal quality, to Amonasro on March 3. As for Easton, when not Brünnhilde or Kundry, she was Marguerite in *Faust,* or Fiordiligi in *Così,* the last mistress of so many styles the theater has known.

The brilliant career of Lawrence Tibbett began about as inconspicuously as possible on November 24, when he was noted as Lovitzky (d) in *Boris,* though not identified as a new singer. His first sizable role was Valentin* in *Faust* on November 30, when Chaliapin sang Méphistophélès for the first time since 1908, and chose to repeat part of *"Veau d'or."* The attention to a young baritone was thus minuscule, but Henderson observed his "light voice of agreeable quality" and thought he might "acquire at the Metropolitan" the stage experience he needed. The *Tribune*'s judgment was that Tibbett had made "a pleasant impression," with a "voice as light waisted as his physique." Both filled out in time. The stage experience was rigorously acquired in such parts as Marullo in *Rigoletto,* Fleville in *Andrea Chénier,* Silvio, and the Herald in *Lohengrin.*

The large repertory was further varied by the return of *Le Coq d'or* on January 21 with Galli-Curci singing the Queen* with excellent style and indifferent pitch, and Laura Robertson as the Voice of the Golden Cock.* Giuseppe Bamboschek conducted a cast otherwise very much as before, and the production was Pogany's. *Marta* had another round of performances beginning on December 14 with a new production by Urban. Alda, Gigli, De Luca, and Howard (Nancy*) were the principals.

As one was to notice with increasing frequency, the heavy schedule often resulted in cast changes that not merely deprived the audience of a favorite voice, but substituted one of notably inferior quality. Thus, Sabinieeva for Galli-Curci in *Le Coq d'or,* Marcella Roeseler for Rethberg as Elsa, Millo Picco for Danise as Rigoletto. In the week-end of January 4, 1924, Gatti gave a Friday-night *Tannhäuser; Bohème* and *Aida* on Saturday; two concerts on Sunday; *Thaïs* and *Marta* on Monday.

January 1, 1924, was a date set aside for a gala *Tosca* to honor Antonio Scotti's twenty-fifth consecutive season of Metropolitan appearances (he was Scarpia, with Jeritza and Fleta), but Otto Kahn made the date especially notable during a speech at a post-performance supper in the Biltmore Hotel. Reviewing Scotti's career, he added: "I hope that before very long all those concerned may agree upon the erection of an opera house which . . . shall be worthy of this great city . . . and . . . so arranged as to conform to the genuinely democratic sentiment which in many ways is and in all ways ought to be characteristic of America." This was one of the first public statements by Kahn on a subject on which he was something of an expert.

The German Opera Company, shorn of Schorr and Kipnis, began another engagement in the Manhattan Opera House on Christmas Day, but business was not what it had been the year before, and it suspended work on January 7. Events of some note were an opening *Meistersinger* with Editha Fleischer as Eva, and Hermann Weil (of the prewar Metropolitan company) as Sachs; a performance of *Rienzi* conducted by Mörike on December 26 with Knote as Rienzi; Fleischer as a charming Susanna in a German *Figaro* on December 27; and Wilhelm Kienzl's *Der Evangelimann* on January 1. Neither this last nor Eugène d'Albert's *Die toten Augen* on January 2 made much impression.

The vigorous expansion of the Chicago Opera Company gave rise to rumors that favored Metropolitan artists were being tempted westward, and finally to a statement from Gatti on February 20. He acknowledged conversations with Samuel Insull, but only confirmed that they had "talked seriously and frankly about various phases of the operatic situation, chiefly about the engagement of artists by both companies." Neither, he said, was negotiating for talent employed by the other. The evidence of the next few years is that a "gentlemen's agreement" prevailed, but it does not explain why such artists as Leider, Olszewska, Lotte Lehmann, and Kipnis were not engaged by the Metropolitan *before* they went to Chicago.

Two full years remained of Gatti's most recently renewed contract in March 1924, when he accepted a further extension of five years. Edward Ziegler's contract was likewise extended until 1929. After a season longer than any in history—November 5 to early May, including a tour to Atlanta, Cleveland, and Rochester—Gatti added $66,872 to the company's credit balance.

1924–1925

The comings and goings of conductors for the Italian repertory finally produced, on November 3, 1924, the man who had been publicly considered the most desirable replacement when Toscanini left in 1915. Tullio Serafin came not only as the unquestioned master of everything relating to the Italian repertory, but as something of a coequal with Bodanzky in the organization of the whole repertory. With Gigli and Bori, Rethberg, Ponselle, and Bohnen, Chaliapin and Galli-Curci as approximate likenesses of Caruso and Farrar, Destinn and Braun, one does not have to be clairvoyant to discern in Serafin further affirmation of Gatti's ambition to restore the high standards of the Toscanini era.

Praise for the scenic splendor of the Rovescalli-Rota *Aida* introduced the year before was lavished now on the musical production as well when Serafin made his debut conducting a cast that included Rethberg, Martinelli, Matzenauer, Danise, and Mardones. For Henderson, it was the most "vital performance" of *Aida* since Toscanini's last, and the credit was "chiefly due to Mr. Serafin." Principal attention was directed to his feeling for dynamics, in which the prevailing level was lower than customary. Thus at climaxes the singers did not have to shout to be heard. This virtue was still present when Serafin came to the City Center in 1952.

Some of the now forgotten forces that played upon the Metropolitan in the mid-twenties are recalled in a Henderson article of January 31, 1925. Predicting that his remarks would be contradicted, he said: "The theory of those engaged in the manufacture and production of operas in Italy is that it is the patriotic duty of Mr. Gatti-Casazza . . . to arrange the repertory in their favor." The subject of the moment was Boito's *Nerone*. According to Henderson, "immense pressure" had been put upon Gatti to produce it. However, the critic continued, it had been an "indisputable failure" in Milan under Toscanini, and it would be a waste of time to give it in New York. (By such reasoning, *L'Amore dei tre re* might never have been given in New York.)

Gatti resisted, permanently, the "pressures" connected with *Nerone,* and did not, in this season, show undue partiality for his "patriotic duty." In a schedule of ten novelties and revivals, the only one remotely related to contemporary operatic endeavor in Italy was Montemezzi's *Giovanni Gallurese*. This was undoubtedly owing to a bias of Serafin, who had conducted the *première* of the work (Montemezzi was a friend of his student days) in Turin in 1905. Regarding its Metropolitan *première* on February 19 as "a saddening revelation" of Montemezzi's musical past, Gilman could see little reason for a New York production. Henderson found admirable details in the score, but thought the style "unformed," lacking the individuality of *L'Amore*. Lauri-Volpi did not please as Giovanni,* and the German Maria Müller was an odd choice for Maria.* Montemezzi was present to be warmly applauded, but the venture disappeared after three repetitions. Giovanni Grandi of La Scala designed the settings.

Janáček's *Jenufa,* in which Jeritza sang the title role on December 6 as she had in Vienna in 1918, left a larger impression of quality than most of the novelties of this period. Henderson found much of the score interesting, though not easy to follow. However, he thought the book "dismal and repellent," the melodic line being corrupted by "shrieks and shouts." In the opinion of Ernest Newman, serving as guest critic of the *Evening Post,* Janáček was "only a cut above the amateur." Beyond Jeritza's striking Jenufa,* the best work was done by Matzenauer as the Sexton's Widow.* Carl Martin Oehmann made his debut to sing Laca Klemen (d), and the other tenor role of Stewa Buryja* was sung by Laubenthal. A German text was used, and the scenery was executed by Novak from designs by Hans Puehringer of Vienna.

Oehmann had a reputation for the lyric Wagner roles, but such abilities went without investigation save for a Sunday-night concert on December 28 in which he sang several *Meistersinger* excerpts. Gatti also used him as Samson on December 20. In later performances of *Jenufa* (there were only five in all), Meader was Laca Klemen,* and Branzell sang the Widow.*

Bodanzky's new formula for satisfying Wagnerites was exposed on January 31, when *Götterdämmerung* was restored after a lapse since 1917. All the scenes and characters of the drama were included, but bits were chopped here and there to allow the Norns, Waltraute, and Alberich to be seen and heard. Newman found the Norn Scene no more than a vocal accompaniment to a parade of late-comers, but reported that what followed was excellent. The scenery, though striking Newman as "old fashioned," was well lit. Nanny Larsen-Todsen made her debut as Brünnhilde (d), singing intelligently but with a hard voice that Henderson described as "affected through nearly its entire scale by a heavy tremolo." Newman thought Taucher a "bourgeois" Siegfried.* If such weakness in the leading roles could be overlooked, the cast could be rated highly, for Bohnen (Hagen*), Schorr (Gunther*), Branzell (Waltraute*), and Müller (Gutrune*) were all excellent. Laubenthal's Siegfried* on February 11 was his first on any stage, and hope was expressed that his good appearance might count for more with further opportunities to sing the music. The opportunities came, but not the hoped-for improvement.

The restoration of *Das Rheingold* on February 26 permitted the full *Ring* to be given for the first time in eight years, and Gatti embellished the occasion by instituting a new kind of Wagner cycle. In it the *Ring* was preceded by *Tannhäuser* on February 18 and followed by *Die Meistersinger* on March 26. This served the valuable purpose of gathering a homogeneous audience for these Wagner works and tended to set them aside from the season's routine, especially when (as after 1929) the *Ring* was given uncut. Lack of a first-rank dramatic soprano (Easton was unaccountably excluded from the cycle, though she sang such roles as Gioconda, Rachel in *La Juive,* Carmen, Isolde, Butterfly, and Fiordiligi in *Così* in the first half of the season) depressed the standard throughout, with Larsen-Todsen singing Fricka* in *Das Rheingold,* as well as the three Brünnhildes. Taucher was a poor Loge,* Laubenthal no delight as Siegmund.* The *Siegfried* performance of March 11 was one of famous consequence for Taucher. As he was making his way through the darkened stage to awaken Brünnhilde, he stepped into an open trap and fell twenty-five feet. Fortunately the trap was not fully depressed or he would have fallen another ten feet. He was helped back to the stage and continued the performance, but the shaking-up marred his work for the rest of the season.

Although Maria Müller was only twenty-seven when she made her debut in *Die Walküre* on January 21, her good looks and willowy figure made her Sieglinde,* in Henderson's opinion, "one of the most satisfying the Metropolitan has known." Possibly Müller's career might have gone more smoothly had she been permitted to specialize, but along with such roles as Elsa, Gutrune, Freia in *Das Rheingold,* and Eva in *Die Meistersinger,* she was called upon for Maria* in *Giovanni Gallurese* and even Mimi* in *La Bohème* (on March 30). She was not a Puccini singer by Metropolitan standards, but redeemed herself on April 11 by singing a charming Agathe* in *Der Freischütz.*

The range of operatic styles offered to New York this winter was remarkably wide, including Debussy's *Pelléas et Mélisande* for the first time by a Metropolitan company on March 21. (Previous performances in the theater had been by the Chicago-Philadelphia company.) Interior platforms compressed the area of stage action, and further illusion was provided by Urban's excellent décor. If the old charge was renewed that the Metropolitan was too big for such a work, it did not offset the superseding opinion that the work was worthy and should be heard, even at a disadvantage. In any case, the excellence of the cast headed by Bori and Johnson commanded respect for an artistic endeavor soundly accomplished. Henderson described Bori's Mélisande* as a "fitting companion" for her Fiora, and Gilman admired the "unity of plan and line" her performance conveyed. Comparisons with Garden are mutely conspicuous. Johnson had studied his Pelléas* with Périer, with results Henderson deemed "perfect in style and in delicate suggestion." With repetition it became the most memorable role of his New York career. Whitehill was an excellent Golaud,* and Rothier (Arkel*), Howard (Geneviève) and Hunter (Yniold*) blended into a consistent ensemble under the careful if hardly probing direction of Hasselmans. Having committed himself to *Pelléas,* Gatti made a serious effort to create a public for it by offering it at least twice in each of his remaining years.

For 1925, the whole repertory had a decently contemporary tinge, with *Petrouchka* restored under Serafin's direction on March 13 and Stravinsky present to be honored with applause and a wreath. A new décor by Serge Soudeikine replaced the previous, if hardly threadbare, one of John Wenger, and Galli, Bolm, Bartik, and Bonfiglio (the Moor) danced commendably. Also honored by Serafin's participation was a restoration of *Falstaff* on January 2, in which such older favorites as Scotti and Alda were joined by Bori ("an entrancing vision of beauty and grace," said Henderson) as Mrs. Ford,* Gigli an able Fenton,* Telva a capable if not dynamic Dame Quickly,* and the young Tibbett as Ford.*

Tibbett's "magnetic and authoritative" singing of "*É sogno*" was endorsed by others in different words than these of Gilman, but it was the pleasure of the audience to single him out for particular applause and to create the circumstances that made his name nationally known the next day. Scotti and Tibbett took the customary calls as the scene was being changed, but the audience only intensified its clamor with shouts of "Tibbett" until the young singer of Ford appeared alone. In all, this consumed fifteen minutes and many inches of front-page space in the next day's newspapers. The Metropolitan's board honored him with a letter of congratulations signed by Kahn, and his future was clearly brighter than it had been before.

At a subsequent *Falstaff* on January 17, Tibbett was allowed to take a solo bow after sharing one with Scotti, and the applause, though cordial, was far from boisterous. The attractive scenery by Urban was still in use when Tibbett became the next Metropolitan Falstaff in 1938, and when he was succeeded by Leonard Warren in 1944. Earlier, Tibbett had earned commendation for Schlemil* in a revival of *Les Contes d'Hoffmann* on November 13, Gilman describing it as "one of the best performances of the evening." This was not a singular feat, for aside from De Luca's skillful work as Coppelius,* Dappertutto,* and Dr. Miracle,* and Bori's Giuletta* and Antonia*, the cast of Morgana (Olympia*), Howard (Nicklausse*), and Fleta (Hoffmann*) was well below previous standards. In Henderson's view, the score was "tenuous" in the Metropolitan, and Hasselmans's conducting pointed the weak spots rather than the strong. Urban's later much-used settings were seen for the first time.

Ponchielli's *La Gioconda* entered on its longest period of Metropolitan favor when it was produced in a new scenic arrangement by Rovescalli and Rota on November 8. As with *Pelléas,* it remained current as long as Gatti did. Ponselle was a principal figure in Gatti's planning, but she was not available for the first performance, and was replaced by Easton, who sang Gioconda* rather uncertainly. Gigli's was a splendid voice for Enzo's *"Cielo e mar,"* Matzenauer a traditionally good Laura; Danise (Barnaba*) and Mardones (Alvise*) were both well qualified. Serafin's direction demonstrated him to be "an operatic conductor of fine skill" (Henderson). Ponselle's Gioconda* on December 19 was but one of many occasions when she sang this music beautifully. On January 9 Ruffo was a sinister Barnaba.* The work had more than fifty performances in the next eleven seasons.

In addition to the works he prepared afresh in this season, Serafin's authority and knowledge were beneficial to *Tosca, Andrea Chénier, Mefistofele, Madama Butterfly, La Traviata, Rigoletto,* and *L'Africana.* Among his numerous *Aidas* was a Christmas-evening one with Ponselle as Aida.* Her performance was notable for vocal strength, less for dramatic significance. She sang it only once more. On February 22 Serafin added his name to those of Mancinelli and Toscanini (also Giulio Setti) as conductors of Verdi's "Manzoni" Requiem in the Metropolitan. His feeling for the large line of the score was admired, as was his sense of nuance and dramatic contrast. Sundelius, Gordon, Gigli, and Mardones were the soloists, and in a repetition on April 6 Mardones was joined by Larsen-Todsen, Martinelli, and Alcock.

Much was expected from Toti dal Monte, an Italian soprano first heard in *Lucia* on December 5, and also as Gilda* in *Rigoletto* on February 23. Her facility was approved, but not her fondness for the white voice or her habit of pausing before attacking a difficult passage. A rehearing was offered to Elvira de Hidalgo as Rosina on November 27 and as Gilda* on March 6. The experience she had acquired since her appearances in 1910 was to her advantage, but she had lost much in vocal quality.

Galli-Curci remained the ranking, if not overactive, coloratura soprano of the company, with a revival of *Dinorah* in her honor on January 22. The Rovescalli production was more ambitious than anything usually offered for *Dinorah,* but the lack of brilliance in Galli-Curci's work ("fluently and agreeably" were Henderson's words for the way she sang) limited the opera to one repetition this year, and none thereafter. De Luca (Hoël*) and Tokatyan (Corentino*) were in the cast, conducted by Papi. A final addition to the repertory was *La Juive,* first seen on December 12. Martinelli offered an Eléazar* widely praised for its absorption of the Caruso model, as well as for his own expanding artistic capacity. Easton was not a proper voice for Rachel,* but Rothier sustained his responsibility as the Cardinal. Theater superstition, which had labeled Eléazar a fated role for its association with Caruso, was vindicated when Martinelli became ill of typhoid fever and did not sing again until March 5. He was in able voice, however, for Canio in *Pagliacci* (which, like *Cavalleria rusticana,* had new scenery by Joseph Novak this season). When he sang Eléazar again on March 25, the Rachel was Larsen-Todsen, described by Henderson as "entirely out of her element."

Those who heard Larsen-Todsen on one of the numerous occasions when she sang Isolde* in this period may be interested in Henderson's reaction to the first of them, on February 14. Out of his copious experience, he likened her to Katharina Klafsky of the nineties, a singer who "is likely to restore life to the long dead theory that operas can be given without good singing." Scope and vitality it had, also quavery, uncertain sound. With her were Taucher, Branzell, Schorr, and Bohnen, the last, as King Marke, indulging his fancy for walking off stage before the *Liebestod*. As Méphistophélès* in *Faust* on April 1, Bohnen affected a gray-tinged costume topped by a red plume. His Gurnemanz in *Parsifal* on April 10 was splendidly sung and admirably acted save for an inordinate amount of walking about in the Grail scene.

Newman's observation of the Metropolitan prompted some fresh views of its ways of doing things, including Gigli's ostentatious bids for applause "like a picturesque beggar appealing for alms." Guard, as the Metropolitan's publicist, sought to mollify the visitor with the claim that the management was making a "serious and honest endeavor" to provide the best that "physical conditions and available human elements" can furnish. Newman's lengthy answer centered on the premise that "with its human material and its financial resources, the Metropolitan could be very much better than it is." "Internal difficulties and troubles," he contended, were no more the concern of the operagoer than a shoemaker's sore hand would be for a customer who complained about a pair of bad shoes.

This exchange followed by hardly more than a week the confession by a leading American critic that there was no use, really, in criticizing the Metropolitan. Nothing would be done anyway. This remarkable statement came from Henderson in the *Sun* of November 28, in answer to a correspondent's accusation that he did not tell "the truth about the Metropolitan." Acknowledging the justice of the complaint, he said: "The experience of years has taught . . . that the Metropolitan is not deeply touched by newspaper criticism. The public which patronizes the institution regards its offerings as of supreme excellence. The commentator who decries any of them is likely to find he is as one decrying in the wilderness." Defending his own perceptions, he continued: "The writer is perfectly aware that . . . 'Carmen' on Wednesday was faulty from top to bottom . . . The Thanksgiving performance of 'Parsifal' was anaemic. . . . 'The Tales of Hoffmann' feebly done. . . . The opera is a place of resort for persons in search of relaxation. It is no place for antiquarians, historians, philosophers or psycho-analysis experts."

Little wonder, then, that when Newman was about to return to England, he mentioned as an outstanding lack in New York the absence of durable standards upheld by influential critics. Little wonder, that is, when one who knew, such as Henderson, did not think it worth while to say what he knew.

This was the year, it may be recalled, during which the Juilliard Foundation offered its aid, as stipulated in the Juilliard will, and was turned down because the Metropolitan's "normal program" might be impeded (see page 17). That "normal program" consisted in giving forty-four operas, plus *Petrouchka,* in a twenty-four-week season. In this time there were 205 performances (Philadelphia and Brooklyn included), or eight performances every week, nine every other week. The "normal program" also included a profit of $53,809.

1925–1926

The beginning of Gatti's final decade may serve as a point of vantage from which to observe the changes he had wrought in fifteen years of direction. The opening performance, on November 2, 1925, was convincing testimony to the stability the organization had attained. Late in the afternoon Jeanne Gordon reported her inability to appear as Laura in *La Gioconda.* Twenty years before this would have been a crisis of paralyzing proportions, resulting, perhaps, in a change of opera. Now there was a Matzenauer to call upon. Although she had not sung the role recently, she studied it as she dressed, and by curtain time was, in Henderson's opinion, "an impressive and colorful figure [who] sang with all her familiar opulence and richness of tone."

Among others "doing old things in the old way" were Ponselle and Gigli, with Serafin conducting. Opening night or not, "everything proceeded with the certainty and calm confidence of mid-season." To Gatti belonged the credit that the Metropolitan had become this kind of theater; to him, then, belonged the blame that too many of the forty-eight works in the repertory showed routine as well as certainty, complacence as well as confidence. The paradox of the period was that the works least done were likely to be the best done, for they had been freshly prepared. New settings for *Rigoletto* or *Carmen* did not guarantee better musical preparation than the old ones for *Tannhäuser* or *Die Walküre.*

Nevertheless, the market existed, and it was apparently insatiable. Another price rise (to $7.50 for orchestra seats and $4.95 for the dress circle, the cheapest prices remaining $1.65, as fixed in 1920) was absorbed without resistance, if with some complaint. A trend of a new sort was evident in the highly publicized debuts of Mary Lewis and Marion Talley. Doubtless the acclaim that had come recently to Lawrence Tibbett had a bearing on this. His publicity, however, had come after he sang, not before.

Mary Lewis, when she made her debut as Mimi (d) in *La Bohème* on January 28, was one of the first singers to come from the musical-comedy stage, though many—such as Fritzi Scheff, Emma Trentini, and

Mary Ellis—had followed the opposite course. Resisting both the theatrical crowd in the theater and Miss Lewis's background in the *Ziegfeld Follies,* Henderson rated her debut "creditable," but heard little to suggest "a distinguished operatic career." Johnson's Rodolfo made for a rather merciless contrast between raw talent and finished artistry. However, a new Musetta,* Elisabeth Kandt sang, said Henderson, "in such a way as to make Miss Lewis seem better than she was." Lewis later sang Nedda and Giulietta in *Les Contes d'Hoffmann* without important results. Her marriage to and divorce from Michael Bohnen were the most notable happenings of a five-year career at the Metropolitan.

A small delegation from Lewis's home in Hot Springs, Arkansas, was greatly outnumbered by the loyal Missourians who swarmed the Metropolitan for Marion Talley's debut as Gilda (d) in *Rigoletto* on February 1. The management disclaimed responsibility for this, but it did permit the Associated Press to install a telegraph wire backstage, on which Miss Talley's father, a telegrapher by trade, tapped out the story of his daughter's "triumph." This debut was presented differently in the news and the music columns. The critics refused to be overwhelmed by Talley's mere eighteen years. After all, Lind had come to public attention at that age, Lilli Lehmann at seventeen, Patti at sixteen. When the critics stated, as Henderson did, that her basically good material was marred by "radically incorrect placement," the reporters counted her recalls by a highly partisan audience, and the public was impressed. On February 22 a holiday matinee audience paid $14,000 to hear her sing Lucia* with Lauri-Volpi and De Luca, and her subsequent appearances were all well attended.

The pattern thus established became a continuing one during the twenties, whether the debutante was from Buffalo or Chattanooga, Minnesota or Massachusetts. When Dorothea Flexer made a relatively inconspicuous first appearance as the Old Mother (d) in *Andrea Chénier* on March 5, her personal claque from Allentown, Pennsylvania, was more modest in size, but not less partial in enthusiasm. Few returned for the occasions when Flexer merited their approval in larger measure.

Of the soundly musical ventures that Gatti sponsored this season, the most interest was aroused by Spontini's *La Vestale* on November 12. It illuminated two things: a school of classic opera-writing rarely heard at the Metropolitan, and the real range of Rosa Ponselle's gifts. Of her Vestale,* Henderson wrote: "She has ceased to content herself with splitting the ears . . . and gone in for real singing. . . . Hers is one of the most beautiful organs of tone that the Metropolitan has ever known."

He had praise, also, for the "broad, authoritative stride" of Serafin's conducting, the "superb spectacle" of Urban's scenery, the general good
work of Matzenauer (High Priestess*), Johnson (Licinio*), De Luca
(Cinna*), and Mardones (Pontifex Maximus*). Gilman also had admiration for the "splendor and massiveness" of Urban's production, but it
passed from view after eight performances during this and the next
season.

Interest in Giordano's setting of *La Cena delle beffe* was much of the
moment when it was given on January 2, for the Sem Benelli play was
a fresh memory as acted in English by John and Lionel Barrymore
(*The Jest*). Gilman found the musical treatment dull, but Henderson,
agreeing that "much of a critical nature might be said," termed the
score one that "acts and sings well." He also approved Ruffo's Neri* as
"brutal, savage . . . tortured," though others held it overdone and
crude. Gigli had a success as Giannetto,* Alda was an excellent Ginevra,*
and Serafin's conducting qualified for the flattering encomium "masterful."
The scenery was designed by Urban. On January 21, Tibbett sang Neri*
without the huge voice and tempestuous manner of Ruffo, but with
vigor and point that won praise for his developing art. Five repetitions
this season and two in the next were the history of *La Cena delle beffe* at
the Metropolitan.

A new kind of double bill was introduced on November 7 when Peter
Cornelius's *Der Barbier von Bagdad* was coupled with Ravel's *L'Heure
espagnole*. The artistic motivation for this may baffle, but it had practical
convenience when both were retired after five performances. In an odd
reconsideration of opinions previously registered on both works, Henderson found the Cornelius score a "hopeless bore," but pronounced Ravel's
"delightful." Bori, as Concepción,* was "beautiful, petulant, roguish,
seductive." Tibbett, as Ramiro,* "a very prince of operatic comedy."
Downes, in the *Times,* endorsed Ravel's work as a "truly Gallic effusion
. . . a masterpiece in little." Hasselmans, who had conducted the earlier
New York performances by the Chicago Opera Company, did his work
well. The scenery was by Joseph Novak. Some of the dissatisfaction
with the preceding *Barbier* doubtless derived from a ponderous playing
of the title role by Bender, but the style of writing retained little zest
for the audience in any case. Bodanzky directed, with Meader an outstanding Cadi,* and Rethberg as Margiana.* Urban was the designer.

A more suitable partnership was provided when Manuel de Falla's
music was heard in the Metropolitan for the first time on March 6,
pairing his *La Vida Breve* with Stravinsky's *Le Rossignol.* Henderson

ventured to predict that the attractive score, sung in Spanish to excellent effect by Bori (Salud*) and Tokatyan (Paco*) "may retain a place in the Metropolitan repertory for some time," but its disappearance after three repetitions can only be regarded as "some time!" Serafin conducted, and the usual Urban settings had the usual admiration. *Le Rossignol* persisted for a second season, not because of the fanciful music of Stravinsky (a truly charming score) or the delightful settings of Soudeikine, but because it employed Marion Talley as the Nightingale.* Serafin directed skillfully.

The richest musical revelation of this season was the gusty, brilliantly sung Kezal* of Bohnen when *Die verkaufte Braut* was revived on January 28. Henderson paid appropriate tribute to the "astonishing variety" of sounds, gestures, and grimaces that made Bohnen's creation a great piece of clowning as well as a superb vocal accomplishment. Laubenthal was an almost enjoyable Hans,* Müller a charming Marie,* Meader a delightful Wenzel*; and Schützendorf (Micha*), Telva (Kathinka*), and Hunter (Esmeralda*) gave full response to Bodanzky's zestful leadership. The ballet was well staged in the manner of the previous Mahler presentation (see page 204); the overture was played before Act II. Novak designed the suitable scenery. Despite the manifest virtue of the production and the brilliant comedy provided by Bohnen, the habit patterns of Metropolitan patrons left many paid-for but empty seats in the theater during this and the next two seasons when Gatti persevered with the work. It had a much warmer response a dozen years later in English.

Jeritza and Chaliapin were each favored by star parts in this season, a revival of *I Giojelli della Madonna* for the former coming on December 12, a production of Massenet's *Don Quichotte* on April 3 for the latter. The earlier respect for Wolf-Ferrari's score had dwindled after a dozen years, Henderson noting the second act as "quite dead." Jeritza's Maliella,* however, had "striking merit," Martinelli's Gennaro* was commended, and Danise sang well if appearing a "none too young" roué as Rafaele.* Rovescalli dressed the stage, and the costuming, to Henderson, "proclaimed the fact that the Metropolitan is an Italian opera house." Twenty recalls for Jeritza sent the work on a two-season span of favor. Chaliapin's enlivening art made Massenet's feeble score tolerable, permitting him to posture as, in Henderson's words, a Don Quichotte* striking for "burlesque hauteur . . . bland magnificence," amid Urban's effective stage settings. Easton made substantially less of Dulcinea* than Garden had, the second focus of attention being De Luca as Sancho Panza.* The latter also had a substantial success when *Gianni Schicchi* was restored on February 6, with Easton (Lauretta) and Lauri-Volpi (Rinuccio*). By general agreement this performance conducted by Papi (the scenery was by Novak) was the best Puccini's little comedy had yet had in its Metropolitan history.

The favorable press for John Alden Carpenter's *Birthday of the Infanta* (see page 289) doubtless was an influence in the choice, as a ballet for the Metropolitan, of the work introduced on February 19 as *Skyscrapers.* It was not written to be danced, but the choreographic plan of Robert Edmond Jones, who also designed the "modernistic" scenery, was well suited to the score and to the pride of Americans discovering that the big city, work and play, colored folk and spirituals were proof of exuberant vitality. Even measured by Gershwin's then new *Rhapsody in Blue,* Carpenter's jazz flavor was synthetic, but it pleased the Metropolitan palate. Sammy Lee designed the dance action, whose principal performers were Albert Troy (the Strutter*), Rita de Leporte (Herself*), and Roger Dodge (White Wings*). Hasselmans conducted. It had eleven performances in two seasons, or one less than *Così fan tutte* in five.

Although Lauritz Melchior's debut on the afternoon of February 17 was swallowed in the furore of Marion Talley's debut the same evening, he was unquestionably the most important artist introduced this season, or for several previous ones. He recalls two major occurrences of his debut: the hammering, backstage, to install a telegraph line (see page 328) as he performed, and the lack of rehearsal or even conversation with Bodanzky prior to his Tannhäuser.* Although some of the outbursts in Act I taxed his range, the beautiful head tone on *"Elisabeth"* was a sensation not provided by any of his contemporaries. Awkward and ungainly as he was and remained, Melchior possessed virtues as a singer which he steadily fostered. Downes noted that circumstances prevented his debut as Siegmund, and made no embracing comment; the *Sun* (not Henderson) ventured that he might be "a useful addition" to the company. Jeritza, Branzell, Schorr, and Bohnen were in the cast.

Siegmund* came along on February 20, but it was no notable success, Henderson describing Melchior's performance, with Larsen-Todsen, Easton, and Schorr, as belonging "to a day of small things, daily becoming smaller." His Siegfried* on March 10 (he had sung it only twice before) was better liked. His Parsifal* on April 2 was successful in the lyric passages, less so in the dramatic. Those who recall his fine recital in Aeolian Hall on March 30 need not be surprised that Henderson used the word "masterly" for some of Melchior's interpretations, though in praising his "taste, sensibility and feeling" the same reviewer declared "the song recital is Mr. Melchior's real field." He returned for limited service in 1926–7, but spent the following year abroad in study. [1] His real Metropolitan career thus dates from March 1929, when he was heard as Tristan for the first time, freed finally from the lingering influence of his early days as a baritone.

The *Ring* cycle that began on February 25 utilized a sharply restricted number of singers, with Larsen-Todsen again singing Fricka in *Das Rheingold* (Meader was an experiment as Loge,* and not very convincing) and the three Brünnhildes. Schumann-Heink was brought back to sing Erda with style but hollow sound (she had last appeared in opera in 1917), and Bohnen made his first venture as Hunding* on March 4 memorable by showing a half-bald skull of which the flesh did not match the color of his make-up. It was fully barbaric in action and sound, however. On the whole there was a stronger ensemble feeling in these performances than in the earlier ones of the twenties, but the orchestral playing was frequently coarse and inaccurate in exposed passages. Gilman, for example, wrote after *Siegfried* on March 12: "It is a pity that a conductor with so fine an ear, so true a musicianship [as Bodanzky's] should be hampered by so many inferior players." But the best players in the world (which the Metropolitan's were not) could not sustain quality in a winter's work that called for such exertions as *Tristan* at a Friday matinee, *L'Oracolo*, *Petrouchka*, and *Cavalleria rusticana* at night, *Madama Butterfly* and *Rigoletto* on Saturday, a concert Sunday night, and *Siegfried* on Monday evening (March 26–9).

Lawrence Tibbett made a rare venture into the German repertory when he sang the Herald in *Lohengrin* on November 30. Other unfamiliar impersonations included Rethberg's splendid Elisabeth* in *Tannhäuser* on January 7 and Laubenthal as Tristan* on January 16. The tenor's good looks and plausible demeanor were advantages not accompanied by adequate vocal technique, security of pitch, or sufficient range for the exactions of the music. Legends of the past or hope for the future seemed dim indeed when he was Tristan and Larsen-Todsen was Isolde. As for complaints of shabby scenery, they were silenced, as of January 1926, with Kahn's announcement that the "new" opera house was nearer than ever, as near, indeed, as West Fifty-seventh Street.

Several singers of indifferent character were heard this season, Mario Basiola singing Amonasro* in *Aida* on November 11, and Vittorio

---

[1] Melchior's carelessness in details of rhythm and accent was long the despair of conductors on three continents. In comparing him with an even more difficult tenor, however, one remarked: "Melchior anyway is dependable. He always makes the same mistakes."

Fullin venturing Radames* in the same work on November 19. Carmela Ponselle was Amneris* in still another *Aida* on December 5, but she made limited progress in an operatic career. Elisabeth Kandt made her debut as Annchen (d) in *Der Freischütz* on January 22, displaying what Henderson described as "an unsteady tone and a provincial style." The efforts to acclimate the German personnel to Italian roles continued with meager success in the instance of Müller as Aida* on February 12 or Schorr as Amonasro* on April 5. Larsen-Todsen attempted Gioconda* on April 17 (with Lauri-Volpi as Enzo*), netting little attention at this late point in the season. Scotti felt the wrath of his eleventh Metropolitan Tosca* on March 13, when Easton performed the murder with dignity but hardly the kind of sound the music needed.

Rumors that Gatti might not remain long enough to preside at a new theater led to a further renewal of his contract until May 1931. For the third year, Gatti would draw $60,000 in salary; for the fourth and fifth, $67,000 (needless to say, these figures were not published then, and not until now.) This long vista of Gatti-directed opera prompted the suggestion in the *Herald Tribune* that he be engaged for life (see page 16) and that various alterations be made in policy if the financial state of the institution was as good as it was rumored to be. As well as explaining how the Metropolitan managed to keep going, Edward Ziegler's reply rejected the contention of the editorial that its "critics" were its truest friends. Rather, he stated: "Between those 'friends' and the great opera-going public, the management . . . unhesitatingly chooses the latter and is proud of its unmistakable approval and steadily growing support."

For such a "normal" year as this, with a profit of $35,277, the reasoning was sound enough. When bad times came, it was much easier for the public to forgo inferior performances than to stay away from the kind of opera it had been offered a decade before. *Boris,* with Giuseppe Bamboschek conducting on April 10, may have been *Boris* to those interested only in Chaliapin. For those interested also in Mussorgsky, it was short measure.

1926-1927

The formula by which Gatti arrived at forty-eight productions as the ideal total for a twenty-four-week season has never been published, nor, indeed, do we know whether he did so regard it. But the mystic number persists during this period, suggesting that his thinking could have been that forty-eight works would accommodate, over a two-year period, the needs of two twenty-four-week subscription seasons *without* a repetition of any work. The reasoning is mine, but it has a spacious, Gatti-like sound to it.

Of the "48" in this season (well-tempered or otherwise), interest was plainly concentrated on Deems Taylor's *The King's Henchman*. For the first time in nearly ten years (since De Koven's *Canterbury Pilgrims* of 1917), Gatti risked the money and time to produce a full-length American opera, and the reception for it on February 17, 1927 made it seem almost worth while. Taylor was then not only the music critic of the *World,* but also a rising composer with creditable accomplishments for symphony orchestra, for choral groups, even in the legitimate theater, where his "A Kiss in Xanadu" had enhanced the appeal of the well-remembered *Beggar on Horseback.* His selection of Edna St. Vincent Millay as collaborator also encouraged hopes of a successful result.

What could be provided by planning and intelligent foresight made *The King's Henchman* in Henderson's opinion "the best American opera this public has heard." Resemblances in mood and plot to *Tristan* and *Pelléas* were too patent to dwell upon, but Miss Millay's libretto was, in the same opinion, "the best any American opera has had." If Henderson found no occasion to speak of "inspiration," he shared Downes's opinion that Taylor had succeeded in giving "his text musical form and organic musical rhythms." Sanborn, in the *Telegram,* bore heavily on the resemblances in the score to Puccini, Debussy, Massenet, and Mussorgsky before declaring: "For the most part *The King's Henchman* is based firmly on Wagner." Serafin's direction (he had studied the work from an Italian translation) was first class, and the cast was excellent: Tibbett (King Eadgar*), Johnson (Aethelwold*), and Easton (Aelfrida*). Urban's scenery was much admired.

Because the public response was encouraging and the attitude of the press (as Gatti termed it in his memoirs) "benevolent," Taylor was shortly commissioned by Kahn to proceed with a second work. "His genius alone," the generous expression ran, "can decide what the nature of his next opera shall be." Before the successor emerged as *Peter Ibbetson, The King's Henchman* had fourteen performances in a three-season run.

The season of Taylor's first Metropolitan opera was also the season of Puccini's last—an arrangement of emphasis that would be indefensible were *Turandot* not a flawed likeness of the composer's best abilities. Its production on November 16, 1926, followed as swiftly as possible its *première* at La Scala in April, and the cast of Jeritza, Lauri-Volpi (Unknown Prince*), and De Luca (Ping*) was pronounced superior to their Italian counterparts (Raïsa, Fleta, and Rimini). Serafin's conducting, a "gorgeous" production by Urban, and quantities of curtain calls provided an impetus for two hugely attended repetitions that prompted the *Sun,* on December 9, to describe *Turandot* in an editorial as "an almost sensational success."

This was not exactly the tone of the general critical response, which ranged from Gilman's description of the music as "bloated futility" to Downes's estimate of the whole as "a first night success and an ultimate failure." Henderson was impressed by the first scene, with its "promise of something new" in Puccini's treatment of the chorus, and the "magic spell of inspiration" he wove in the orchestra. Possibly the best summation is provided by Gatti in his memoirs. *Turandot,* he felt, suffered for lack of Puccini's self-critical review of the score after performance; his death robbed the work not only of a proper ending (Alfano's deferential sequences are certainly not that), but also of the changes the composer might have made on reconsideration of its shortcomings.

In addition to Jeritza's "amazing prodigality" of tone, Henderson endorsed George Cehanovsky, who sang the Mandarin* as "a barytone [with] an agreeable voice. . . . He will be heard from again." (He was, during every remaining season in the old house.) Pavel Ludikar made his debut as Timur (d), and Martha Attwood, similarly encumbered, had a hard time with the music of Liù (d). At a performance of December 6, conducted by Vincenzo Bellezza,[1] Henderson revised his earlier thinking to describe Jeritza as "a screaming scold," Lauri-Volpi as "her worthy companion," and De Luca as "utterly wasted" in his part. *Turandot* had twenty more performances in the four seasons it was given at the Metropolitan. Its revival at the City Center in 1950 preceded its triumphal return to the Metropolitan in 1960–1.

Gatti's long-standing contention that he would give Mozart operas when he could staff them properly was scarcely supported by this season's revival of *Die Zauberflöte** on November 6. Marion Talley sang the Queen of the Night's two airs, in Henderson's judgment, "mechanically and in an amateurish manner"; Laubenthal was a "ligneous" Tamino,* Schützendorf a "dry" Papageno,* and Bender a doleful Sarastro.* Quite the best Mozart style was heard in Rethberg's delightful Pamina,* and Whitehill was an imposing Sprecher,* but they had little assistance from the principals other than Meader as Monostatos.* Soudeikine's dazzling scenery, if not markedly Mozartian, was approved, as was Bodanzky's conducting. Editha Fleischer made her debut in commendable style as the First

---

[1] As accompanist for Caruso, Bellezza had directed two Sunday-night concerts in March 1918. He made his debut as a conductor of Metropolitan opera on November 4, 1926, directing *The Jewels of the Madonna.*

Lady (d), later singing Pamina* on December 18, when Meader was Tamino.* Gatti gave but five performances of *Die Zauberflöte*, however, and it was not heard again till the forties.

Other musical manna was provided on January 22, when *Fidelio* was heard (for the first time since 1917) in observance of the centenary of the composer's death. Urban's scenic production (in use till 1959–60) made its first appearance, as did Bodanzky's recitatives. To Henderson, his evocation of the noble spirit in the work amounted to "one of the most impressive" performances the work had had in New York. Of primary assistance was Laubenthal as Florestan,* whose singing in the dungeon scene was "the most successful" this veteran critic could recall. Larsen-Todsen was a grotesque figure as Leonore,* and a strident one in sound. Of stronger virtue were Bohnen's Rocco,* the excellent Marzelline* of Fleischer, Schorr's Pizarro,* and Meader's Jacquino.* A since-familiar name was invoked by Henderson on April 15, citing a letter from Richard Aldrich in Vienna describing Lotte Lehmann's Leonore there as "magnificent." Henderson continued, satirically: "Well, we need none of her magnificence here. The dollars can be drawn without it" (see page 339).

One of the notable careers of this era was initiated at the opening performance on November 1, when Ezio Pinza sang the Pontifex Maximus* in *La Vestale*. Henderson thought it probable he would be "useful," but Gilman described the new basso as a man of "imposing figure," who has an "excellent voice" used with "brains and discretion." His first season included Ramfis* in *Aida*,* Alvise in *Gioconda,* Sparafucile* in *Rigoletto,* the Abbot* in *La Forza del destino,* Basilio* in *Il Barbiere,* Pimenn* in *Boris*—in which he had a chance to study Chaliapin's conception as preparation for his own—and Raimondo* in *Lucia*. He was not singled out for special commendation in any of these, nor was there reason to suspect that he would be the singer to revitalize *Don Giovanni* and *Figaro* at the Metropolitan or, least of all, that he would become a reigning Broadway favorite twenty-five years later.

The shortish list of novelties (by recent standards) in this season's schedules very likely had to do with the expectations for a new theater. It was concluded by a revival of *Mignon* on March 10 (in French rather than the preceding Italian), with Talley as a Philine* "amateurish, very faulty in tone and technic" (Henderson), Bori an "entirely winning and lovely" Mignon,* if not one of much pathos, Gigli as Meister,* and Whitehill as Lothario.* Soudeikine designed the scenery, Ruth Page was the solo dancer, and Hasselmans conducted.

The excellent Page (who later established her own ballet company) was first seen on February 7 dancing the solos in the polka and furiante of *Die verkaufte Braut* with Bonfiglio. Although *Petrouchka* was absent, *Skyscrapers* was again performed, and Alfredo Casella's *La Giara* was introduced on March 19 in a staging by Rosina Galli, who appeared as Nela.* The bright, ingenious score was better liked than the choreography, which Henderson described as "conventional and depressingly dull." Serafin conducted, and the scenery was by Novak. *La Giara* was preceded by *Butterfly,* conducted with "much warmth, color, and discretion" by Bellezza, who also gave enlivening service to the other works he conducted, *La Bohème, Lucia,* and *Rigoletto* among them; but most of all to *Boris* on March 25, in which the choral work was stronger than it had been for some time.

Even more was expected of Serafin when on December 29 he undertook *L'Amore dei tre re* (of which he had been the original conductor in 1913 at Milan). Henderson thought it a "fine and inspiriting" reading, but Gilman found it wanting the force provided by either Toscanini or Moranzoni. Ponselle's Fiora* differed radically from the childlike creation of Bori, but the strength of her portrayal and the prismatic colors in her vocalization were warmly approved. Didur, a singer of vanishing voice, acted his Archibaldo well, with Gigli and Danise as the other kings. Another set of principals gave quite a different accent on January 29, when Bori and Johnson were joined by Tibbett as Manfredo* and Ludikar as Archibaldo,* both notably good.

The upward trend of Tibbett's career had a minor if conspicuous detour on November 3 when he sang Kothner* in *Die Meistersinger* in such a way as to prompt Gilman to write: "Mr. Tibbett's acting was amateurish, his singing the worst we have ever heard from him, and his makeup beyond belief." At that, Tibbett had a prominent if not worthy model in the matter of eccentricity in Michael Bohnen, whose so-called "archeological researches" this season produced the following guises for Hagen in *Götterdämmerung:* on January 14, a shaven skull from which protruded a single knot of hair; on January 26, a flaming red wig and beard; on March 18, something like the conventional black beard and wig. If the stage manager (the role of stage director virtually had lapsed at this time) had no firmer control of Bohnen, why should others be deterred?

The uncommon occurrence of an evening performance of *Das Rheingold* on January 28 was explained by the artistry and imagination of Walther Kirchhoff, who made his debut as Loge (d). Those who had not heard Vogl, Van Dyck, or Burrian were assured by one who had (Henderson) that Kirchhoff's Loge was quite in their class, "one of the finest" impersonations of the subtle and crafty schemer New York had seen. The applause for his narrative was, to Henderson, "unheard of." As in other recent *Ring* cycles, the one beginning on February 24 offered Larsen-Todsen in all the principal soprano parts. Kirchhoff's Siegmund* on March 4, like his later singing of the two Siegfrieds, Walther, and Tristan, was quite the artistic equal of his Loge, but their requirements of fresh and vital sound were not in the equipment of a tenor whose debut in Berlin had occurred in 1906. He was an impressive figure of a bearded Tristan* on April 4, with Easton, Branzell, and Whitehill, but a strained singer. On December 8 Easton sang the *Walküre* Brünnhilde,* with difficulty in the *"Ho-jo-to-ho,"* creditably thereafter, but not with distinction. This was something of an interim season for Melchior, who sang Siegmund on February 18 and nothing further till Parsifal on April 15. Description of the latter as "powerful, interesting and frequently poetic" (the *Sun*) was the most commendation Melchior had earned to this time.

As in the past, Bodanzky was the unvarying conductor for the Wagner works, also Mozart, Beethoven, and Smetana. On December 22, when he was ill, Bamboschek conducted *Lohengrin* in his place, without incident. Working the increasing number of new German singers into the repertory was something of a chore, especially as it was done almost wholly without rehearsal. Thus, in a *Rosenkavalier* of March 16, Bohnen was Ochs,* Müller sang Octavian,* and Fleischer was Sophie.* Both women were excellent, but the favorite Kezal and Caspar was a heavy, overstressed Ochs and a gruff-sounding one. Easton was the Marschallin.

The same German singers in the Italian repertory posed different kinds of problems. Müller, singing Butterfly* for the first time on any stage on February 16, was, to Henderson, "still in the chrysalis state." Rethberg as Mimi* on November 27 was a delightful vocal artist, a doubtful dramatic asset. On April 11, when Johnson sang Radames, Henderson noted a "delightful diversity of styles ranging from the elegance of Edward Johnson to the bumptiousness of the aggressive Mr. Bohnen" as Amonasro. Müller was the Aida; Claussen, Amneris; and Joseph McPherson the King.

McPherson, who had made his debut in the same role on December 30, was one of an increasing number of American singers with the minimum ability to qualify for the Metropolitan, but neither the perseverance nor the stamina to survive the trial by fire. Somewhat similar were Elda Vettori, who sang first as Santuzza* in *Cavalleria* on November 20, and Louise Lerch, who graduated from a Sunday-night concert on November 7 to the Countess* in *Rigoletto* on the 10th. Vettori later sang creditably as Gioconda, Lauretta in *Gianni Schicchi,* Aida, and Leonora in *La Forza.*

Relatively little excitement attended the return of Galli-Curci as Violetta on January 5, especially when the critics reported her vocal condition deteriorating. She sang, in Henderson's words, with "a small volume of tone and a dispiriting want of brilliance." Rosina, Gilda, and Lucia were other roles she sang during her month's engagement. Her fame still supported a strong demand for tickets, however, even if the quality of her performances did not justify it.

This year's tour extended not only to Atlanta and Cleveland, but also to Baltimore, Washington, and Rochester. On his return to New York on May 9, Gatti assured the press: "Never has the Metropolitan had its performances so largely attended. We have broken the record again." This was doubtless a source of comfort, if not the kind of season-ending review published by Henderson on April 15, 1926: "The venerable and shabby 'La Gioconda,' lamely done and inefficiently sung, had eight performances. 'Aida' had nine and the last of them was a truly sorrowful revelation. . . . The buffooneries of Mr. Bohnen are correct because they draw money. The colorless phantasms of Bruennhilde and Isolde which pipe their pallid woes into the awe-stricken auditorium are correct because they draw money. The dull and heavy footed interpretations of one work after another, with the great 'Meistersinger' hanging the most ponderous weight of all about the neck of the season, are correct because they draw money."

They all drew, indeed, to a profit close to the greatest in postwar Metropolitan opera—$142,041. When an interviewer for the *Herald Tribune* asked Gatti on April 11 when new settings for the *Ring* might be forthcoming, he replied with a reference to the possible new theater, but added: "Kautsky's [*Ring*] settings are almost new, owing to the marvellous quality of pre-war German materials. . . . The sets for *Meistersinger* and *Tristan,* made eight to ten years later, seem older than those for the *Ring.*" To be sure, the competition in unsightliness was close. But to describe as "almost new" the frayed *Walküre* and the dull *Götterdämmerung* of this period was virtually to say that the Wagner public would continue to patronize the Metropolitan because it had no alternative.

1927–1928

The season that marked a new high point of profit in postwar Metropolitan operations, and a more numerous repertory (forty-nine works) than any before or since, should be memorable for other reasons than statistical, but it is hard to find them. Two happenings provided promise, if not complete fulfillment: the long-waited appearance of Rosa Ponselle as Norma on November 16, and the debut of Grace Moore on February 7, 1928.

Because Moore was better known on Broadway than Mary Lewis had been, and was the favorite, particularly, of the Algonquin coterie, her debut as Mimi (d) in *La Bohème* was as near a family party as the Metropolitan had known. More than one hundred friends from Tennessee, Miss Moore's native state, were present, including its two United States Senators, Tyson and MacKellar. Of her performance Henderson wrote: "a pretty voice of lyric quality, the color tending toward mellowness . . . capable of more warmth than the singer knew how to evoke from it." Her acting inclined to simplicity: "Two or three rather constrained gestures . . . an alternation of facial expression from smile to no smile," were the limits of her dramatic powers. For Moore's Mimi, as for Lewis's, the Rodolfo was Johnson, with Bellezza conducting and Fleischer an excellent Musetta.* Kahn's comment that Moore's third act was the best he had ever heard may have had to do with qualities not apparent to everyone, but she survived the premature adulation to press ahead to a career still on its upward course when she was killed in a plane crash in 1946. In this first season her only other role was Lauretta in *Gianni Schicchi* on March 21.

A model to which Moore might have applied herself with profit was provided by Ponselle in her Norma.* Hers was vocal work, said Henderson, which matched the oft-flouted "tradition of the Metropolitan," and showed that "the ripening of her talent has been the result of a growing sincerity of purpose and earnest study." In his opinion, her *"Casta diva"* was a "genuinely beautiful piece of singing," though her mastery of recitative lagged behind her command of the melodic passages. The variable cast offered an excellent Oroveso* by Pinza, a capable Adalgisa* by Telva, and a questionable Pollione* by Lauri-Volpi. Serafin's ensemble, was greatly praised, especially the singing of the Setti-trained chorus, which, Henderson thought, "sang better than it had ever sung in an Italian opera." Urban was the designer. *Norma* was heard nineteen times during this and the next four seasons.

The illusion of *Turandot* as a popular if not a critical success was fostered by its choice for the opening on October 31. The profusion of money is attested by two occurrences of the time: a subscriber who found himself unable to attend the performance advertised his seventh-row tickets for sale at fifty dollars apiece (the District Attorney, Tuttle, could not take action because the season rate specified no price for the opening-night tickets); and an arrival of well-dressed patrons so heavy that smoke from the photographers' flash pans seeped into the Thirty-ninth Street corridor and a fire alarm was turned in.

Henderson now thought that the score "babbles but childishly of a grown up passion," that it was musically "all dressed up with no place to go." Liù* was better sung by Guilford than it had been by Attwood, the cast of Jeritza, Lauri-Volpi, and De Luca remaining as before. By contrast with the failure of *Turandot* to fulfill its large promise was the success of *La Rondine* in fulfilling its modest one when the Puccini comedy was given for the first time on March 10. In conformity with what Gatti declared to be Puccini's second thought after the Monte Carlo *première* in 1917, the role of Prunier,* written for a baritone, was sung by tenor Tokatyan, who made rich comedy of the posturing poet. Additional expert playing by Bori (Magda*), Fleischer (Lisette*), and Gigli (Ruggero*) made a light, charming experience of the entertaining score, effectively directed by Bellezza. Henderson warned his readers that *La Rondine* must be accepted "for what it is . . . a spruce and amusing afternoon off of a genius." Considering his further valuation of it as "a vivacious, high-class musical play" mingling farce and tender emotions in "delectable proportions," it is surprising that it has not been heard since Bori retired in 1935–6. Its sweeping staircase scene (Urban's) was frequently used to dress the Metropolitan stage on ceremonial occasions.

Something of quality was expected from *Madonna Imperia* (a treatment of Balzac's *La Belle Imperia*) when Franco Alfano's one-acter was heard on February 8. These were expectations based not on his completion of *Turandot,* but rather on his impressive *Risurrezione,* but they were ill founded in any case. Henderson described it as "a melancholy waste of drab dullness," and Gilman scorned Novak's scenery as resembling "a parlormaid's dream of the haunts of opulent debauchery." Müller was ill-cast as Donna Imperia,* the best singing being done by Frederick Jagel (new this season) as Filippo.* Pinza was the Chancellor,* and Serafin conducted. Pinza had one of the notable successes of his rising career as Dodon* in a revival of *Le Coq d'or* which completed the double bill, for Talley's voice (with which she had earned $350,000 in a two-year coast-to-coast barnstorming since her debut) was more pinched than ever, her singing of the "Hymn to the Sun" breaking precedent by drawing no applause at all. This was the last appearance of the work in its panto-mimed form (Galli, Bonfiglio, Bartik, Kosloff, and De Leporte were the principal dancers). At its reappearance in 1937 the conventional form was utilized.

The inordinate number of double bills favored by Gatti was further extended by a combination of Korngold's *Violanta* and Humperdinck's

Hänsel und Gretel, first given on November 5. A predecessor by four years of *Die tote Stadt,* the work of the seventeen-year-old Korngold had more of the manner of Strauss, less of the matter of Korngold, than was thought desirable. Jeritza repeated, with less effect, the Violanta* she had sung first in Vienna, and there were fine performances by Kirchhoff as Alfonso* and Whitehill as Simone Trovai.* Urban was the designer for this work, as well as for the following *Hänsel,* which remained one of his durable legacies to the Metropolitan. The spacious wood scene, particularly, enhanced the pathos of any Hänsels and Gretels who strayed into it for the next twenty-odd years. On this occasion it was two of the best, Fleischer as a hoydenish Hänsel, Mario as a singularly ingratiating Gretel.* Schützendorf (Peter*), Wakefield (Gertrude*), and Dorothee Manski, who made her debut as the Witch (d), were all excellent. Bodanzky conducted both scores.

Manski was one of the most versatile German singers added to the company in this period, but the season produced three others, of whom Richard Mayr was the most celebrated, Grete Stückgold the freshest talent, and Gertrude Kappel the most welcome. Mayr was a potent Pogner (d) in *Die Meistersinger* on November 2, and Stückgold as Eva (d) impressed Henderson with her "fresh and most agreeable voice." She was called upon almost immediately to prove her ability as a German soprano by singing Aida* on November 8. This produced no strong reaction in the press, whose adjectives of mild approval were pre-empted by the debut of Frederick Jagel as Radames (d). Mayr and Stückgold were heard as Ochs* and Octavian* in *Der Rosenkavalier* on November 17, also as the King* and Elsa* in *Lohengrin* on November 12. In his most famous part, Mayr was the best Ochs* New York had seen, if hardly any longer in the prime of his remarkable voice. He later sang the Landgraf in *Tannhäuser* and Hunding in *Die Walküre,* always as "the really authoritative artist" Henderson had pronounced him at his debut, if with variable vocal sound. Stückgold had Rethberg, Müller, and Jeritza to contend with for prominence in a generally similar repertory, and it took a while for her qualities to be noted. In the *Lohengrin* noted above, Everett Marshall made his debut as the Herald (d), an experience he turned to more practical purposes when he was employed in *George White's Scandals* to sing "That's Why Darkies Were Born."

Kappel was hardly a singer of historic eminence, but she was greatly preferable to Larsen-Todsen, especially as Isolde (d), the role of her debut on January 16. Henderson pronounced it, on the strength of the first act alone, "an exceptionally good impersonation," which was slightly misleading. Isolde was Kappel's best role, the first act itself the best part of it. The same writer paid tribute to her "uncommon command of the piano and moderato which brought really beautiful qualities" from her voice, which in Act I of Isolde she used like a liedersinger. Kappel sang all the Brünnhildes during the month of February, also Leonore* in *Fidelio* on March 14—"generally beautiful singing," wrote Henderson, "and sometimes ravishing"—and Kundry* in *Parsifal* on April 6. In all efforts her intelligence was unrelenting, her artistry compelling, her limitations being those of a voice ample rather than heroic, lovable rather than impressive. The poorish impression of her Kundry was in part owing to lack of physical attraction, in part to a treatment by Bodanzky described by Henderson as "apathetic and resolutely industrious by turns."

This conductor gave the first official signs of the surfeit with opera which led to his "farewell" a year or so later by giving command of *Seigfried* to Serafin for the first time on February 18. The quieter episodes went with unusual lyric emphasis, and the whole profited from the freshening effect of restudy under a new conductor. The big climaxes, however, did not strike most as truly Wagnerian. On March 7 the Brünnhilde was Elena Rakowska, who, in addition to possessing a limited voice and a small sense of style, was the conductor's wife. She had earlier appeared as Rachel (d) in *La Juive* on December 23, and she later sang Santuzza creditably, but she was ill-suited for major Wagner parts.

With Melchior a lamented and Taucher an unlamented absentee Laubenthal and Kirchhoff were an unvaried diet in the tenor roles for Wagner this season. Thus the casting (save for Kappel as Fricka* in *Das Rheingold* on February 24) differed little from that of the preceding season. Fred Patton, an American baritone, was Donner (d) in the *Ring* prelude. Of notable interest was Tibbett's Wolfram* in *Tannhäuser* on December 17, a role he often sang with suavity and expressiveness thereafter. This pointed a way toward such other lyric baritone roles as Sachs and the Wanderer, which, regrettably, Tibbett chose to ignore in favor of the more strenuous Amonasro, Rigoletto, and Scarpia.

The Metropolitan's flickering interest in Meyerbeer was stimulated momentarily with a revival of *Le Prophète* on December 31, in which Martinelli sought further to conquer the Caruso repertory. In Henderson's view "he ascended to loftier heights than he had ever reached" as John of Leyden,* in a manful exhibition of artistry. The cast was otherwise divided among those with voices and those with style, only Martinelli, Matzenauer (Fidès), and Pinza (Zacharias*) providing both. Rothier knew how to sing Oberthal, but his sound was hollow; Schützendorf was a compromise in both respects; and Leonora Corona (Bertha*) had a voice, but little vitality. There was Urban scenery, and Bodanzky conducted.

Corona, Texas-born (Cohron, originally), with a voluptuous voice and a figure to match, had rather more continental background than most American novices of this period. Thus, she made her debut as Leonora* in *Il Trovatore* on November 24, later singing Tosca and Gioconda. The big voice was never disciplined as it might have been, and its promise remained largely unfulfilled. Vettori and Jeritza were other Toscas this season, the latter singing hers on November 9 with blond locks and a picture hat. This was the year also of Jeritza's Carmen* on January 13, with the Urban settings that remained in use till the Gérard production of 1952. She was vigorous, eye-catching, picturesque, but, in Henderson's view, "with all her energy she did not seem to get far beneath the surface" of the part. French was also a trial for her, and the voice responded rather stridently. Johnson was José, Tibbett a passable Escamillo,* and Fleischer a creditable Micaëla.* By contrast with Toscanini's practice, Hasselmans indulged such changes of casts as Bori, Mario, and Morgana as Micaëla, Basiola and Pinza* as Escamillo, Martinelli and Johnson as José—with the purpose which such changes frequently serve, of stimulating attendance.

In addition to his expert Escamillo, Pinza added to Oroveso in *Norma* and Zacharias in *Le Prophète* an impersonation of Don Basilio in *Il Barbiere* on January 2 which attracted much more attention than it had received the year before. Henderson pronounced it "one of the best impersonations . . . since the days of Édouard de Reszke. . . . He sang the famous 'La Calumnia' with a deadly seriousness which carried the air to its exact point." Those who saw Pinza's Basilio, even at the end of his long career, will absorb from this comparison, what made the "Golden Age" golden. He, too, was an actor who could sing, a singer who could act.

The extensive repertory that provided, in steady rotation, such persistent projects as *Boris, L'Amore dei tre re, Pelléas,* and *Der Rosenkavalier* was enlarged by Puccini's *Manon Lescaut* and Mozart's *Così fan tutte,* both absent for two seasons or more. Alda, Gigli, Scotti, and Didur appeared in the Puccini on December 10, with Serafin conducting. *Così* was originally scheduled for mid-March, but Easton's illness, and then Ludikar's, required several postponements. One, on March 24, caused a change of opera, the dread occurrence Gatti had avoided for three years. In the end, *Così* was given but once, on April 11, and then Bodanzky was ill, Paul Eisler conducting. With Fleischer as Dorabella* and Ludikar as Don Alfonso* (Easton, Bori, De Luca, and Meader were as before), the score had its last Metropolitan performance for nearly a quarter-century.

Jagel's lengthy career as a tenor of all work was typified by his first season, which began with Radames (d) on November 8, and continued

with Pinkerton,* Edgardo,* Pollione* in *Norma,* Filippo Mala* in
Madonna Imperia, and Cavaradossi.* None of these roles was sung with
sensuous tone, but it would be unfair to say one was worse than another.
Whether for Rodolfo, Herod in *Salome,* or Peter Grimes, Jagel was both
willing and able for a quarter-century. Louise Homer returned to the role
of her debut twenty-eight years before to sing Amneris in *Aida* on
December 14, and later shared the honors of a *Gioconda* with Ponselle,
Gigli, Ruffo, and Pinza on December 29. Other oddities included Bohnen
as Tonio* in *I Pagliacci* on February 13 (he added handsprings and
cartwheels to the scoring), and Rethberg as Santuzza* in *Cavalleria* on
December 26.

Midseason marked the final rebuff to Otto Kahn's plans for a new
theater, and the Fifty-seventh Street site was put up for sale on February 19. Talk continued, but it had little foundation in fact or in serious
purpose. Meanwhile, on the flood-tide of what Henderson described
as "the two a day business," income and profit amounted to amazing
heights. The former was $3,096,001, the latter $144,378.

1928–1929

The appearance of four contemporary operas in the immediate aftermath of Kahn's failure to make good his promise of a new opera house
suggests, in a historical perspective, some relationship. The evident one
seems to be that despite Gatti's low opinion of contemporary operas—or,
at least, of their performance at the box office—it was the accessible
way to give freshness to the old stage, if no new one was available.

Among them, the works lingered for a total of twenty-three performances. The choice of *Die ägyptische Helena* to represent Strauss was debatable but logical, as it was the newest of his works unheard in New York.
Křenek's *Jonny spielt auf* was a reigning sensation in Central Europe, and
thus of legitimate interest. As for Respighi's *La Campana sommersa* and
Pizzetti's *Fra Gherardo,* they balanced the novelties neatly between works
from both sides of the Alps.

For the hard-working, perhaps over-working Bodanzky, *Die ägyptische
Helena* was in the nature of a farewell gesture to Strauss. Shortly before its
première on November 6, it was announced that he would leave the Metropolitan at the end of the season, his fourteenth. The further news, however,
was not reassuring. Rather than Bruno Walter, Otto Klemperer. Erich
Kleiber, Fritz Busch, or Leo Blech, his replacement was Josef Rosenstock,
from the modest theater in Wiesbaden. Little as the musical press knew of
him, the public knew less. Both were to be illuminated in time.

For some admirers of Strauss, *The Egyptian Helen* had a fair share of merit; others saw it as still another downward step from *Der Rosenkavalier, Ariadne* and *Die Frau ohne Schatten.* None considered Hofmannsthal's book anything but a liability. Henderson said that Metropolitan history had offered some sorry librettos, but "none more puerile, more futile, or less interesting than this." The genius of Strauss flamed in the orchestral score, but all it surrounded was "platitudes of Dr. Strauss's wearied and aging muse." Jeritza, who had been the first Helena* in Vienna, had little grateful music. As Aithra,* Fleischer, who did, delivered a fine performance. Laubenthal was a poor Menelaus,* and was replaced after the first performance by Kirchhoff. Whitehill (Altair*) and Telva (Muschel*) were the other principals. After the *première* the part of Hermione* (badly done by Helen Eisler, and spoiling the final curtain) was deleted. Urban was the designer. In all, the critics' time might have better been spent at Carnegie Hall, where Stokowski was conducting the first symphony of a Russian billed as Szostakowicz.

Since Rethberg, the first Helena in Dresden, had been out-ranked by Jeritza for honors in Strauss, her participation in the Respighi treatment of Hauptmann's *Die versunkene Glocke* preserved peace in the operatic household while favoring a prominent Italian contemporary. Her Rautendelein* was charmingly sung on November 24, though a little portly for an elf. At that, slight musical character emerged from Respighi's treatment of the subject, which would have been more suitable to Weber or the young Wagner. For the cast of Martinelli (Heinrich*), De Luca (the Nickelmann*), Pinza (the Priest*), and Guilford (Magda*), the conducting of Serafin and the scenery of Urban, the highest praise was spoken by the composer himself. Fifteen minutes of the score was eliminated before the repetition of November 30, in which Manski was Magda.*

The general content with Urban's work was marred by faultfinding when *Jonny spielt auf* had its introduction on January 19. The satiric point of the plot was lost in a décor garish rather than gay, and though it was not Urban's fault that the Metropolitan lacked the revolving stage to provide the necessary quick changes, what he provided did not atone for this shortcoming. Also, to avoid offense to white-Negro sensitivities, Jonny* was portrayed by Bohnen as a white entertainer in blackface rather than as the Negro of the original.

Bohnen's Jonny* was grotesque and funny. Tibbett played him with rather more believable character when he took the part on February 27. In any case, it was evident that, for American ears, Křenek's jazz flavor was synthetic, his parody of foxtrots rather naïve. Easton was prim and heavy as Anita,* the principal honors again going to Fleischer for her effective work as Yvonne.* Schorr (Daniello*) and Kirchhoff (Max*) were both miscast. Meader was excellent as the Hotel Manager.* Bodanzky conducted. Aside from Tibbett, the alternates did not improve the kind of performance that prevailed: Laubenthal for Kirchhoff, Manski for Easton, Schützendorf for Schorr. About the only fortunate fact was that they were singing German, not English.

As far as its quality can be discerned from what was written about it, Pizzetti's *Fra Gherardo* was the worthiest of these innovations. At least, Gilman honored the book Pizzetti had written for himself as the expression of a "poetic nature" with "strong convictions," though its exposition on the stage was not "telling," the music being "essentially sterile." The vocal line was in the new mode of spasmodic, almost "song-speech" writing, with an excessive emphasis on declamation. Henderson described the reaction of the first audience, on March 21, as "apathetic," perhaps because the principals—Müller (Mariola*), Johnson (Gherardo*), Pinza (Old Man* and the Podesta*)—had rather hopeless vocal tasks. Serafin conducted, and the scenery was by Urban. Three further performances were all that *Fra Gherardo* received.

Amid these signs of apathy or worse for the works of Strauss, Respighi, Křenek, and Pizzetti, the appearance of *The King's Henchman* in a third season, on February 16, marked a new level of favor for a work by an American. Easton, Johnson, and Tibbett were the principals, and on March 28 Wilfred Pelletier, previously an assistant conductor, was in charge of the performance. Easton also had a try at Turandot,* on March 16, but did not succeed where Jeritza had failed.

The infrequent occasion to compliment a singer as "the best the Metropolitan had seen" came in this season on March 11, when Bori sang the fourth of several performances of Manon in this season. Henderson's opinion, which was emphatic, was that Bori's Manon was "undoubtedly the best the Metropolitan has ever known." He also complimented the luscious-sounding Des Grieux of Gigli, De Luca's sound Lescaut, and the beautifully acted, throatily sung Comte des Grieux of Rothier. Hasselmans gave special care to the preparation, for which there was new scenery by Joseph Urban. If anything, the "fastidious taste" and "aptness of gesture" Bori provided grew more singularly Manon rather than Bori for the next half-dozen years.

Several good deeds of the recent past were given renewed public prominence: Bohnen's classic Caspar in *Der Freischütz* on February 23, with Fleischer singing a delightful Ännchen,* and Müller and Laubenthal as before, and *Ernani* on December 17, when Pinza, as Don Ruy Gomez,* clearly outsang Ponselle, Martinelli, and Ruffo. "Continent" was Henderson's word for Pinza, "more energetic than elegant" his phrase for Ponselle.

Those who heard the Metropolitan's last *Freischütz* (ever), on April 1, also heard a lovely Agathe* from Stückgold.

The notation that Lauritz Melchior returned after one year's absence to sing the elder Siegfried* in *Götterdämmerung* on March 14 and Tristan* on March 20 should suggest a roaring welcome for the gifted artist, but both, truthfully, passed rather quietly. Melchior was still an unformed performer whose lack of physical attraction put a double burden on his singing. In both parts it was considered highly promising, but not more. Kappel was his first Metropolitan Isolde, as she was the Brünnhilde in *Götterdämmerung*. Melchior was scheduled for the presumptive "farewell" of Bodanzky on April 13, but Laubenthal took his place as Tristan. This was one of several occurrences that made parting less sorrow, more sweet, than it might have been otherwise: Kirchhoff was indisposed for *Lohengrin* on November 10 and was replaced by a less than secondary singer, Max Altglass; on January 10 Kappel lost her voice just before the start of *Die Walküre,* and Claussen took her place. A week before, when Stückgold could not perform Sieglinde in the same work, the rearrangement transposed Easton to Sieglinde (from Brünnhilde), and Matzenauer to Brünnhilde (from Fricka), with Claussen at Fricka. On another occasion Jeritza was Sieglinde with Matzenauer (Fricka) and Easton (Brünnhilde).

On the whole, it was a less than happy winter for Kappel, who found a full Metropolitan season rather heavy going, especially when required to sing Ortrud* in *Lohengrin* on March 16 amid Isoldes and Brünnhildes. Stückgold, too, had a share of vocal troubles, with Jeritza as her reluctant replacement as Octavian (a role she had not sung since 1924) in *Der Rosenkavalier* on January 4. One can read Bodanzky's farewell statement, then, as one chooses: "I shall not say I am sorry to give up opera; my work in the future lies elsewhere. In leaving the Metropolitan I am leaving the greatest opera in the world." Bodanzky burned no bridges, slammed no doors shut with these words. Serafin again directed *Siegfried,* and Schumann-Heink returned for another Erda in *Das Rheingold,* an amazing personality at nearly seventy, but hardly a potent voice.

No major new artists were brought to New York in this season, though Marek Windheim, who made his debut as the Lamplighter (d) in *Manon Lescaut,* came to ever greater use as Meader's service in the lighter Wagner tenor roles dwindled. Grace Divine made her debut as a Musician (d) on the same occasion, and the American sopranos of dramatic intentions were made more numerous by the addition of Clara Jacobo and Dreda Aves. Both made debuts as Leonora in *Il Trovatore,* on November 8 and April 6 respectively. Jacobo also sang Santuzza and Aida with big sound, but not more than conventional style. The *réclame* of Moore's debut having vanished, she found her forward progress somewhat slow. As Juliette* on February 13 to Johnson's Roméo, she was admired by Henderson for "a very agreeable quality of voice," but taxed for acting "innocent of all theatrical guile" and for an impersonation in which "the poetic essence of Juliette was entirely missing." Hasselmans conducted.

Chaliapin's final season with the company was neither advertised nor celebrated, but he did not sing again after a Méphistophélès in *Faust* on March 20, with Lewis, Lauri-Volpi, and Tibbett. *Boris* lapsed after his departure, which did not offend those who agreed with Henderson's judgment that the performance of March 4 was "lame." The rumors of a new production were spurs to the hope that it would be something more than "a delineation by Mr. Chaliapin with accessories." Bellezza conducted this performance and the only repetition, on March 14. Two singers who made no secret of their intention not to return were Ruffo and Talley. The latter's last performance was in Cleveland on May 4.

There were days when the characterization of the Metropolitan as "the greatest opera in the world" was honestly justified, as in the opening *L'Amore dei tre re* on October 29 with Ponselle, Martinelli, Pinza a splendid Archibaldo, Danise as Manfredo, and Serafin conducting. A *Tosca* with Corona, Tokatyan, and Danise, an *Aida* with Corona, Claussen, and Jagel, an *Il Trovatore* with Aves, Basiola, and Lauri-Volpi were something else.

The *Herald Tribune* on April 13 gave irritated voice, editorially, to discontent with the limited resources of the Metropolitan's staging, "a lack of co-ordination, of authoritative direction," and "over-frequent appearance of fourth-rate singers in important roles." No rebuttal was offered. On returning from Europe in July, Geraldine Farrar[1] described the Metropolitan as "a well-regulated stock company," giving "the same limited repertory year after year in the same way." The "limited repertory" embraced forty-seven works in this season, with more than two hundred performances (including those in Brooklyn and Philadelphia) in twenty-four weeks. The income—$3,111,805—was the greatest ever, the profit $90,937.

1929–1930

The perpetual question of "the new opera house" was in the mind of at least one person early in the season that began on October 28, 1929. That was Henderson, who had a new but by no means irrelevant thought to

---

[1] One of her old colleagues returned in what Henderson called "astonishingly good condition" when Johanna Gadski sang Isolde in the Manhattan Opera House on January 14. The ill-favored Carl Braun was King Marke, and Ernest Knoch conducted a cast otherwise inconsequential. Gadski was also heard on the 17th as the *Walküre* Brünnhilde and on the 22nd in *Götterdämmerung,* but the strenuous schedule was too much for her, and the company disbanded.

father a wish. "We need a new opera house," he wrote on October 31, "if only to get rid of the ghosts that haunt the old one." The provocation for this was the previous evening's *Die Meistersinger,* in which Henriette Wakefield sang "a routine Magdalene." His thought continued: "For old operagoers, memories of Marianne Brandt and Ernestine Schumann-Heink will not down."

Conducting "one of the most oppressive performances" of *Die Meistersinger* in many years was, for the first time since 1916, a man other than Bodanzky. Not prepossessing in size, Josef Rosenstock did not command, on the podium, an authority he lacked off it. To inquiries of "Why Rosenstock?" the Metropolitan management had a series of stock answers: Bruno Walter wanted fifty thousand dollars, which was too much (but not for Serafin; see page 30); Klemperer was not expensive, but his demands were in other ways "unreasonable"; when Blech or Kleiber or another man of recognized abilities was approached, his contract was immediately extended wherever he happened to be employed.

So it was Rosenstock. "Conservative" was the kindest word for his way with *Die Meistersinger,* which, with Stückgold, Laubenthal, Whitehill, and Mayr, had a share of cordial applause, the New York audience being polite in almost all circumstances. Had his *Rosenkavalier* on November 4 been more vital, things might have worked out differently. Henderson found it "heavy with poppy and mandragora," for which the conductor—"a well schooled Kappelmeister with militaristic tendencies"—was less to blame than a cast that would have resisted "the imagination and temperament of a Nikisch." The names of Stückgold (Marschallin*), Jeritza, Fleischer, and Mayr read well, but Stückgold's Marschallin was pallid at its first venture, Jeritza was ill at ease as Octavian, and Mayr's day as a proper voice for Ochs was drawing to a close.

Rosenstock continued in orderly command of *Die Walküre* on November 9, *Die Meistersinger* on November 14 (with Fleischer a lovely-sounding Eva*), and a *Rosenkavalier* on the 15th, a Friday. Over the week-end Rosenstock developed further symptoms of what the Metropolitan management described as a "nervous breakdown," and his "wish" to be relieved of his contract was granted on the 18th.

Those who had tried to make clear that Rosenstock would not do hardly expected to get Bodanzky all over again. But the "work in the future" to which Bodanzky had so confidently alluded six months before had apparently not matured to his satisfaction, and he was available in New York when Rosenstock found the going hard. Only one shaft of light gave a bright touch to the announcement of Bodanzky's re-engagement. He would conduct an annual uncut *Ring* cycle. The specification that his contract was "for a number of years" actually came to mean the rest of his life. Although his work took an upward surge with the coming, first of Leider and Olszewska, then of Flagstad, it was an enduring indictment of Bodanzky that he did little, in all this time, to effect an improvement where improvement was possible—in the playing of the orchestra. It remained a task undone until George Szell was engaged.

In the interval between Rosenstock's exit and Bodanzky's reentry, Karl Riedel, an assistant conductor for six years, directed *Lohengrin* on November 20 and *Die Walküre* on November 23, the latter with Manski as Brünnhilde.* An efficient caretaker of someone else's performance, Riedel never had full opportunity to show greater capacity. Rosenstock was now able to travel, and he left for Germany with a letter of good wishes from the Metropolitan's orchestra. On November 30 Bodanzky took three bows before giving the down beat for a performance of *Der Rosenkavalier,* and the Metropolitan's German repertory resumed its previous course.

No provision had been made for a German novelty in this season, and the only restoration, other than the usually deleted portions of the *Ring,* was *Fidelio* on January 29. Elisabeth Ohms was a good-looking Leonore,* but no heroic-voiced one. A usual alignment of Laubenthal, Schorr, Bohnen, and Fleischer prevailed, and Urban's scenery was again used. There was pleasure, however, in hearing Beethoven's music, especially on those occasions which placed it in juxtaposition to *Don Giovanni,* which had its first Metropolitan performance in twenty-one years on November 29.

If Eames, Farrar, Bonci, and Scotti—also Mahler—were missing, there was ample promise in the cast of Gigli, Rethberg, Ponselle, Pinza, and Fleischer. But even the literal promise was not fulfilled at the first performance, for Ponselle was ill, and Corona sang Donna Anna.* Musical promise, it soon became evident, was for the future rather than the present, for Serafin conveyed the surface of Mozart's score well, but not its depths; Pinza's was initially a heavy voice for Don Giovanni,* and the only real Mozart style was provided by Fleischer as Zerlina.* It was a beginning, however, if one—in Henderson's words—"not wholly encouraging." Gilman also viewed it unenthusiastically, crediting Pinza with "surviving his ordeal more happily than one had supposed he would," but finding him without "the elegance, the grace, the adroitness, the magnetic charm" a successful Don required. Ponselle's Donna Anna* was finally heard on January 2, when she sang *"Non mi dir"* very beautifully, the "Honor" aria less well. Thanks to Gatti's persistent if sparing attention to the work in the next five seasons, Pinza had the opportunity to improve steadily, until, with such conductors as Szell, Busch, and Walter, he became a Don of sufficient stature to carry a performance. Urban's tasteful production (especially the interiors) made a handsome picture of the stage, and the arias were sung, as they were while the production remained in use, before a forecurtain, downstage.

The extensive experiment of the previous year with contemporary novelties was not repeated this season, nor, on a similar scale, later. The official position that the world's resources of new works offered nothing for the Metropolitan may be debated, but evidence to the contrary is hardly overwhelming. The time of reckoning came later, when the Metropolitan failed to participate in the opportunities afforded by foundation money to broaden its range.

For variety, Gatti turned this year to lesser works by two masters who had served the Metropolitan well. *Simon Boccanegra,* then enjoying a new surge of interest in Europe, might have been a better choice to represent Verdi than *Luisa Miller,* but the production of the latter on December 21 illuminated some recesses of history and the vocal prowess of Ponselle (Luisa Miller*), De Luca (Miller*), Lauri-Volpi (Rodolfo*), and Tancredi Pasero (Count Walter*). The public response was encouraging, but the adverse trend of the Metropolitan in the next season limited the box-office appeal of *Luisa Miller.* Serafin conducted, and the scenery was by Urban.

Rimsky-Korsakov's *Sadko,* with a brilliant décor by Soudeikine, elaborate if conventional ballets staged by Rosina Galli and August Berger, and such melodic attractions as the *"Chanson indoue"* and "The Song of the Viking Guest," was one of Gatti's happiest choices when it was introduced on January 25. Henderson thought the music (aside from the prominent arias) "mostly of small charm," and doubted that the "beautifully made" orchestral score would appeal to American tastes. For whatever reasons, including Johnson's Sadko,* Fleischer's Volkhova,* Bourskaya's Lioubova,* Gustafson's Norseman,* and the Hindu of Diaz,* the production was sufficiently attractive to be given sixteen times in three seasons, a return much higher than provided by the average of such investments.

Also more than moderately successful was the restoration of *La Fanciulla del West* on November 2 after an absence since 1913–14. Gilman was strongly of the opinion that the compulsion given to the original by Belasco and Toscanini was absent, the work therefore lacking whatever interest it once had possessed; but Henderson declared the *"Girl"* welcome "because so many much worse" operas had been seen since it was new. No pretense of realistic drama remained, with a truly operatic emphasis on Jeritza's Minnie* extending to what Henderson decried as "rancid melodrama," with the cowboys of old no more than "brigands of Abruzzi."

Conviction was likewise lacking in Martinelli's Dick Johnson,* Tibbett's Rance,* and Pasero's Ashby,* but by operatic standards they sufficed. Ernst Lert had charge of the stage for the first time, and Bellezza conducted. On January 10 Johnson* was Johnson in fact, and later replacements included Corona as Minnie* and Jagel as Johnson.* The production was executed by Novak.

The growing stature of Bori was honored by a venture on March 1 with *Louise,* not seen since Farrar had sung the title role in 1921–22. Although its settings were newer by years than those for the *Ring, Louise* was freshly produced in an Urban conception that had more use in later seasons. For all the merits of Bori, her Louise* was a characterization Henderson described as "wavering in outline and . . . wholly uncertain of purpose," the production as a whole being "regrettably weak and dull." Antonin Trantoul was a French enough tenor, but an uncompelling Julien,* and neither Rothier (the Father) nor Telva (the Mother*) made much of their parts. Whitehill's Father was an improvement on March 10, but the lack of impact, beginning with Hasselmans's conducting, was not redeemed by such a change. Bori apparently decided that *Louise* was not for her after three repetitions. When it was next given, in 1939, Moore was Louise.

Pinza gave further proof of his versatility in this season when *L'Elisir d'amore* was ventured for the first time since Caruso's death, and the tall basso's oily, amusing Dr. Dulcamara* gave a new interest to Donizetti's work on March 21. Gigli was a foolish enough Nemorino* and one of powerful vocal virtues. Morgana as Adina* was a passable replacement for Fleischer, who was ill. De Luca was Belcore, and Serafin conducted. Novak was the scenic artist.

As the season's subscription books had been closed well before the market collapse at the end of October, the advance of ticket prices to a new high level of $8.25 did not affect the huge audience that attended the *Manon Lescaut* of October 28, in which Bori returned to the role of her debut seventeen years before. As the season progressed and the downward trend of the market accelerated, fears were expressed that the announcement of the Wagner cycle might encounter a serious lack of interest. Actually, however, business was better by fourteen per cent than for the cycle of the previous year, a reaction attributed in part to the promise of uncut performances. *Das Rheingold,* on February 21, showed little deviation from the past: its uninterrupted length is but two and one half hours, and it was usually given full length. Kirchhoff was a wavery Loge (his long years of singing were becoming an increasing liability), Bohnen an ostentatious Wotan. Ohms was the Brünnhilde* of *Die Walküre* and *Siegfried,* with Kappel in *Götterdämmerung.* An early commitment in Europe subtracted

Bohnen from the Metropolitan company in late February, and Hagen (d) was sung by Siegfried Tappolet, a burly, husky-voiced Alsatian who performed with credit if little distinction for the next three years.

Much was expected from Ohms, who was admired for good looks, intelligent action, and serious artistry when she was heard as the *Götterdämmerung* Brünnhilde (d) on January 17. Henderson found her voice "thin at the top and hollow at the bottom, but of very beautiful quality in the medium," and doubted that she had sufficient volume for the Metropolitan auditorium. Her ample experience carried her through all the expectable roles in a matter of weeks—Leonore in *Fidelio,* Venus in *Tannhäuser,* Isolde, Ortrud, all the Brünnhildes, and Kundry. Those of relatively narrow range (Venus and Ortrud) she sang very well, the others in a way to suggest that she was not quite the singer she had been. For this year's *Parsifals* (first on April 16) the conductor was Serafin. His venture with this intractable Wagner score was less satisfying than his *Siegfried.*

Of the new careers initiated this season, the longest was that of Gladys Swarthout, who was heard first as La Cieca (d) in *La Gioconda* on November 15. Her handsome presence and well-placed voice were admired in this role, as in a series of smaller parts—Stéphano in *Roméo,* Siébel in *Faust,* Federica in *Luisa Miller.* The *Faust,* on February 13, was the two-hundredth in the history of the house. With Fleischer a German Marguerite* and Trantoul a not very satisfying Faust (d), the landmark brought "memories tinged with regret" to Henderson. In his one-season tour Trantoul also was heard as Hoffmann, Julien, Rodolfo, and Don José, showing on no occasion more than the "somewhat light and tenuous voice" Henderson noted at his debut. Augusta Oltrabella was heard briefly as Musetta (d) on November 18 and as Liù* in the season's only *Turandot* on January 8. Tancredi Pasero, a well-schooled Italian basso, came to succeed Didur in many low roles, beginning with Alvise* in *La Gioconda* on November 1, and including Ashby in *La Fanciulla del West,* Don Pedro in *L'Africaine,* Ferrando in *Il Trovatore,* Colline in *La Bohème,* and finally Oroveso in *Norma.* Metropolitan opportunities were offered to Santa Biondo as Nedda (d) in *Pagliacci* on December 6 and Edward Ransome (d) as Manrico in *Il Trovatore* on December 14, but both had more success with smaller touring companies.

The complications of critical coverage of New York's music events prevented close attention to several new ventures that may be isolated in time, if not by quality. Rethberg added Leonora* in *Il Trovatore* to her repertory on November 11; Grace Moore sang Manon* on December 21 and Marguerite* in *Faust* on March 7; and on the final day of the season, April 19, Tibbett sang Germont* in *La Traviata,* which became one of his best roles. A trend of another sort could be discerned in the retirement of three singers of celebrity: Alda,[1] who sang last in *Manon Lescaut* on December 28, Galli-Curci, whose farewell role was Rosina in *Il Barbiere* on January 24, and Matzenauer, who retired after returning to sing Amneris, the role of her debut, in *Aida* on February 12. Mary Lewis and Frances Peralta were others who were not re-engaged.

A week before the season's end, Kahn announced that Gatti's contract had been extended for another two years, assuring his direction of the Metropolitan until 1935. To the undercurrent of criticism in the press, Kahn responded that "the attendance of the public . . . this season was but slightly diminished." This, however, did not do much to balance such a statement as Henderson's at the season's end: "The faded works . . . have been performed over and over and over again, most of the time with mediocre singers going through their roles like so many robots." "Dull and stupefying" were his words for the house specialty, *Aida,* in the post-Toscanini, post-Caruso epoch.

A translation of Kahn's description of the attendance ("slightly diminished") into financial terms shows the following: income was $3,052,395, or $59,410 less than the year before. For the first time in twenty years there was no profit. The loss was $14,743, or hardly enough to be considered a deficit. For that matter, it was not regarded as such by Gatti, who reckoned 1930–1 as his first unsuccessful season since 1910. But it was a straw in the wind that soon became a gale.

1930–1931

With $1,100,000 in the bank and twenty years of successful operation in the books, the Metropolitan confidently began its forty-sixth season on October 27 with little thought of difficulty, none of debacle. It was time for another *Aida* opening (the last had been in 1924), and the attendance was set at 4,210. Recalling the old status of the opening as a social function, Henderson took note of the inordinately early date by saying: "It was formerly regarded as the opening of the winter social season when the opera and the horse show arrived, but the lyric drama has pushed its initial date further back than the display of the highly exclusive horse." The critic's last reference (see above) to the company's *Aida* as "dull and stupefying" was not materially altered by the work of Müller, Martinelli, Branzell, and De Luca, the once eminent baritone now being described as a "none too savage Amonasro [who] eschewed all fortes." Serafin conducted.

The hysterical fanfare that had sounded the approach of Marion Talley

[1] Her marriage to Gatti had ended the previous year.

was all but absent when Lily Pons made her debut as Lucia (d) on January 3, 1931. Bitter experience had convinced Gatti that press and public both enjoy making their own discoveries, and the hoped-for success of Pons had been a well-guarded secret ever since the Giovanni Zenatellos (he was the tenor, she was the contralto Maria Gay) had discovered Pons in a provincial French opera house and brought her to Gatti's attention. Her starting fee was $450 a week, of which the Zenatellos' share was more than a trifle.

The preparations for Pons's debut could not escape some eavesdroppers' attention, however, and the grapevine had been busy, resulting in a tighter wedge of standees for this Saturday matinee than might have been expected. But Gatti's main purpose was achieved thanks in large part to Pons's demonstration of "a voice of pure and pleasing quality and a technic far above the slovenly average of today." Henderson further described her *"Spargi d'amaro pianto"* as a "piece of finished singing," adding that "true intonation proved to be one of her valuable musical assets." As for characterization, only Gerster and Sembrich had made Lucia something more than an automaton, and the lack was not held against her. In sequence came Gilda* on January 7, Rosina* on February 4, Olympia* in *Hoffmann* on February 14, and Philine* in *Mignon* on April 6. Her first Gilda was less well sung than the Lucia, but the cadenza ending *"Caro nome"* was sung well enough for Henderson to describe her as "Mr. Gatti's little Christmas gift from a kind providence." By the time of her Philine an arduous schedule had made "thin and acid" a more accurate description for her tones than "pleasing," but the zest and charm of her *"polacca"* drew a warm response from the audience. The favor she found then remained well after the reasons for it had departed.

Bodanzky's first full season of renewed activity brought two fresh undertakings, of which *Der fliegende Holländer* had not been heard since the last Conried season (1907), and Suppé's *Boccaccio* was the first of that composer's works to be heard in the house. Had there been a way to combine them, a good deal of valuable time would have yielded more profit, for the *Holländer* is gloomier than most care about for a whole evening and the *Boccaccio* giddier than many can endure at three acts' length. Soudeikine's handsome setting and the well-spoken Dutchman* of Schorr were prinicipal virtues of the first performance of the *Holländer* on November 1, in which Ivar Andresen made a strong impression in his debut as Daland (d). What Gilman termed a "disconcerting blend of greatness and inferiority" in the score was, as ever, evident, for all of Bodanzky's "inspiring dramatic power and vitality." Jeritza was a picturesque Senta,* rather strident in sound, Laubenthal an Erik* whose best effort Gilman thought "vocally distressing." Telva sang Mary,* and Hans Clemens was the Steersman (d). The need for illusion in the staging of Act I was met by avoiding it. Six repetitions this season dwindled to two in the following one.

Boccaccio in this season, like *Donna Juanita* in the next, was a venture keyed to Jeritza's leggy frame and operetta background in the hope they could give favor to a kind of work not previously successful in the theater. Downes thought that she "scintillated" in the first performance on January 2, but Henderson described her singing as "tentative and at no time brilliant," her acting as "uncertain." Meader was an excellent Scalza,* Fleischer a suitable Fiammetta, with Kirchhoff as the Prince* and Morgana as Beatrice.* Accompaniments for the spoken dialogue had been provided by Bodanzky, who also interpolated a potpourri from Suppé's *Pique-Dame* and *Donna Juanita* for Jeritza in the third act. His idiomatic conducting and the lavish designs of Urban were liked, but the venture disappeared after half a dozen further performances this season.

Likewise short-lived was an investigation of Mussorgsky's *The Fair at Sorochintzy* in an Italian version of Nikolai Tcherepnin. Most auditors of the first performance, on November 29, decided the orchestral *Night on Bare Mountain,* used as a ballet in Act II, was the best music in the performance. Regard for other high spots was tempered by lack of cohesion, and residual pleasure further diminished by a motley cast of which only Bourskaya (Khivria*) had a Russian accent (unfortunately, for the Italian text). Pinza's Tcherevik* "plainly came from Calabria, not from Polodio or Volhynia," observed Henderson, and there were influences of other sorts in Müller's Parassia,* Jagel's Gritzko,* and Windheim's Pastor's Son.* August Berger's Hopak* in Act III was best liked of the several ballets. Serafin conducted, and the staging was by Soudeikine. On December 29 Olga Didur, daughter of the basso, sang Parassia.* She had made her debut as Preziosilla (d) (see page 358).

Following its *première, The Fair at Sorochintzy* was combined with Felice Lattuada's *Le Preziose ridicole,* a one-act adaptation of Molière's *Les Précieuses ridicules.* At its introduction on December 10, Henderson described it as "melodious and apt," if "anything on earth but Molière." Bori was a "bewitching" Madelon," Tokatyan an amusing Mascarille,* and Swarthout an attractive Cathos.* Pearl Besuner, a recent addition, sang Marotte,* with Basiola as Jodelet.* The scenery was designed by Robert Edmond Jones, and Bellezza conducted. Ernst Lert's imaginative direction was above the Metropolitan average for the time. The bill was dropped after the four performances of this season.

February 7, 1931, was a date notable in Metropolitan history not only for the *première* of Taylor's long-awaited successor to *The King's Hench-*

man, but also for the first influence of the Juilliard Foundation on Metropolitan affairs. Although the composer had been "commissioned" by the opera house to do a second work, he had been helped by a grant of $5,000 from the Juilliard Foundation in February 1928 (without specification as to purpose, but generally considered a spur to completion of the opera). Taylor's instinct, in selecting for operatic treatment Constance Collier's dramatization of the Du Maurier novel *Peter Ibbetson,* was generally endorsed. The former attitude of "not so bad," however, for *The King's Henchman* had perceptibly, if unintentionally, veered to "not so good" for *Ibbetson.* Downes commended Taylor, obliquely, for writing music "that does not interfere with the unfolding of the story," adding that he had "assembled a very affecting drama with slow music, and some fast music too." Gilman, more outspoken in denunciation of what he considered a derivative and weak work, absorbed some heavy firing in correspondence from Walter Damrosch, to whom the work was dedicated.

The skillful organization of *Peter Ibbetson* and the prominent opportunities it gave to Tibbett as Colonel Ibbetson* (the inevitable temptation to call it *Peter Tibbetson* was not resisted), Bori as the Duchess of Towers,* and Johnson as Peter* assured audience interest for some time to come. What the critical listeners found wanting was a musical development, a personal accent, which would justify reference to a Taylor style. In the dream scene Claudio Frigerio was Pasquier,* Biondo was Marie,* and Doninelli was Madame Seraskier.* Of other characters, Telva was notably good as Mrs. Deane.* Serafin conducted, and the designer was Urban. Six performances each in this and the next season, and a total of four in Gatti's last two seasons, added to Taylor's record as the American composer most performed at the Metropolitan.

Another attempt to popularize *Iris,* this time with Rethberg in the title role, found no more success than the previous one with Bori. The first performance, on March 6, with Gigli as Osaka,* De Luca as Kyoto,* and Pinza as the Father,* was followed by three others, to the same total of four as in 1914–15. In general, the singers were commended, but Henderson's final opinion of *Iris* as "a pleasing work, not solid in musical content, narrow in style," suggests its limitations. Bellezza conducted, and Novak provided the scenery. The same artist provided two scenic emendations when *La Forza del destino* was resumed on November 21 after an absence since 1927–8. The cloister scene was given in two settings, the latter part inside the church; and the third act opened with an exterior rather than inside the tent. Ponselle's fine Leonora and Martinelli's Alvaro were old friends, Pasero's Abbot* a sturdy new one. Olga Didur sang Preziosilla (d) in her debut. This was directed by Serafin, as was a revival of *Guillaume*

Lily Pons as Rosina
in *Il Barbiere di Siviglia*

Giuseppe de Luca as Figaro
in *Il Barbiere di Siviglia*

Michael Bohnen as Caspar
in *Der Freischütz*

Salvatore Baccaloni as Dr. Dulcamara
in *L'Elisir d'amore*

Characterizations—I

Hans Hotter as the Grand
Inquisitor in *Don Carlo*

Nicolai Ghiaurov as
Philip II in *Don Carlo*

Marian Anderson as Ulrica
in *Un Ballo in maschera*

Regina Resnik as the Countess
in *The Queen of Spades*

Cesare Siepi as
Méphistophélès in *Faust*

Characterizations—II

Emma Eames as Aida

Emmy Destinn as Aida

Zinka Milanov as Aida

Leontyne Price as Aida

Aida

Louise Homer as Amneris

Enrico Caruso as Radames

John Charles Thomas
as Amonasro

Francesco Tamagno
as Otello

Giovanni Martinelli
as Otello

Ramon Vinay as Otello

Otello and *Falstaff*

Victor Maurel as Falstaff

Lawrence Tibbett as Ford

James McCracken as Otello

Geraint Evans as Falstaff

Leo Slezak as Manrico
in *Il Trovatore*

Jussi Bjoerling as
Manrico in *Il Trovatore*

Titta Ruffo as Rigoletto

Verdi

Leonard Warren as Rigoletto

Lawrence Tibbett
as Simon Boccanegra

Carlo Bergonzi as Riccardo
in *Un Ballo in maschera*

Giulietta Simionato as
Azucena and Franco Corelli
as Manrico in *Il Trovatore*

Maria Jeritza
as Floria Tosca

Geraldine Farrar
as Floria Tosca

Enrico Caruso
as Cavaradossi

Antonio Scotti
as Scarpia

Geraldine Farrar
as Cio-Cio-San

Licia Albanese
as Cio-Cio-San

Tosca and
Madama Butterfly

Maria Callas as Floria Tosca and Tito Gobbi as Scarpia

Nellie Melba
as Marguerite

Geraldine Farrar
as Marguerite

Édouard de Reszke
as Méphistophélès

Pol Plançon
as Méphistophélès

Faust

Nicolai Ghiaurov
as Méphistophélès

Gabriella Tucci as Marguerite
and Nicolai Gedda as Faust

Emma Calvé as Carmen

Maria Gay as Carmen

Bruna Castagna as Carmen

René Maison as Don José

Marcel Journet as Escamillo

Giuseppe Campanari
as Escamillo

Carmen

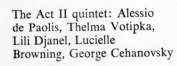

The Act II quintet: Alessio
de Paolis, Thelma Votipka,
Lili Djanel, Lucielle
Browning, George Cehanovsky

Lucrezia Bori as Manon

Beniamino Gigli as Des Grieux

Richard Crooks as Des Grieux

Victoria de Los Angeles as Manon

Manon

Geraldine Farrar as
Caterina Hübscher, Pasquale
Amato as Napoleone,
in *Madame Sans-Gêne*

Rosina Galli

Frances Alda as
the Princess in *Marouf*

Enrico Caruso as Julien,
Geraldine Farrar as Louise,
in *Julien*

Grace Moore as Louise
in *Louise*

Characterizations—III

Jon Vickers as Florestan
in *Fidelio*

Anselmo Colzani as
Jack Rance in *La Fanciulla
del West*

Roberta Peters as Kitty
in *The Last Savage*

Mirella Freni as Mimi
in *La Bohème*

Eileen Farrell as Santuzza
in *Cavalleria rusticana*

Characterizations—IV

Feodor Chaliapin as Boris Godunov

Ezio Pinza as Boris Godunov

Alexander Kipnis as Boris Godunov

Kerstin Thorborg as Marina

Boris Godunov

Lucrezia Bori as Mary,
Edward Johnson as Peter
Ibbetson, in *Peter Ibbetson*

Act II scene from *Peter Grimes*, with Polyna Stoska

Eleanor Steber as Vanessa and Rosalind Elias as Erika,
with (in the background) Regina Resnik as the Baroness

American and English Opera

Marcella Sembrich

Luisa Tetrazzini

Claudia Muzio
(as Norma in *Norma*)

Rosa Ponselle (as Santuzza
in *Cavalleria rusticana*)

Amelita Galli-Curci
(as Violetta in *La Traviate*

Sopranos

Geraldine Farrar with
Mary Garden, right, who w
costume for film of *Thaïs*
she was then making at the
Goldwyn studios in Hollywo

Emma Eames

Louise Homer (as Orfeo
in *Orfeo ed Euridice*)

Gladys Swarthout (as Stephano
in *Roméo et Juliette*)

Marion Talley
(as Philine in *Mignon*)

Ernestine Schumann-Heink
as guest at a "Surprise Party"
of 1932, with Michael Bohnen

Sopranos and Contraltos

In this unusual picture of January 1933 is spelled out Metropolitan history from first to last. Included are Marcella Sembrich (seated, middle), who sang on the second night of the first season in *Lucia di Lammermoor* fifty years before, and three artists who were Honored Guests at the Gala Farewell thirty-three years later. They are Rose Bampton (second from left, standing) and Giovanni Martinelli, next to her, and Wilfred Pelletier, seated at left in second row. The picture, taken at a party in honor of Antonio Scotti, a Metropolitan veteran of thirty-three seasons who had just appeared in a farewell performance of *L'Oracolo,* shows: Queena Mario, with arm around Scotti (seated next to Mme Sembrich), and Lucrezia Bori. Seated on floor left, Giuseppe Sturani, conductor. Standing (in rear): stage director Armando Agnini, Bampton, Martinelli, conductor Vincenzo Bellezza, who had conducted Scotti's farewell, Earle R. Lewis, Metropolitan treasurer, Tullio Serafin, chorus master Giulio Setti, Edward Johnson, and conductor-photographer Carlo Edwards.

Christmas Day 1931. The cast of the very first broadcast (*Hänsel und Gretel*) with other, interested parties. Front row, left to right: M. H. Aylesworth, president of the National Broadcasting Company, which provided the facilities; Deems Taylor, commentator; Henrietta Wakefield (Gertrude), Editha Fleischer (Hänsel), Queena Mario (Gretel). Back row: Karl Riedel, conductor, Dorothée Manski (Witch), Gustave Schützendorf (Peter), and Pearl Besuner (Dewman). At the extreme right, General Manager Gatti-Casazza.

The Metropolitan from First to Last

Tell on March 21, with Lauri-Volpi (Arnold*), Fleischer (Mathilde*), Pinza (Furst*), Danise (Tell), and Faina Petrova (Hedwig*).

None of the restorations attracted so much attention as the perennial *Traviata* when it was given on January 16 with Ponselle as Violetta.* Some opinion took issue with the suitability of her voice for the music. Henderson found it "quite well enough suited" as vocalization went, but thought that only a woman of genius could pursue Ponselle's conception successfully, and that she did not measure up to the description. Her mistake, in his opinion, was to ignore the essentially lyric quality of the role, introducing "spasmodic utterances" into *"Ah! fors è lui,"* dragging out *"Dite alla giovine"* until it lay "cold and heavy" on the stage. Her death scene, transforming Verdi's "plaintively pathetic conception into hard-breathed tragedy," left the ending weakest, the first act her best. Lauri-Volpi and De Luca were the other principals, Serafin conducting. The Ponselle public took Henderson's analysis as a pro-Bori position, and one wrote, chidingly: "Come now—which Violetta do you prefer—Ponselle's or Bori's?" His published answer was: "Neither. Verdi's."

Rethberg also ventured into strange territory when she sang Rachel* in *La Juive* on January 28. To Henderson's mind she "had style and she showed feeling [but] the effort to conquer the strenuous utterances so plentifully scattered through the score may not benefit her singularly captivating voice." The justice of this opinion was all too soon confirmed. The downward trend of standards in other respects was noted in orchestral playing "frequently polytonal, something of which Halévy never dreamed." On March 25 Rethberg was a disaffecting Marguerite* in *Faust,* and George Thill's Faust* made the same critic wonder whether "a less romantic or winning" cavalier had ever been known in this theater. The tenor had made an unimpressive debut as Roméo (d) on January 20, and rarely performed to his Paris capacities at the Metropolitan. Of much more satisfaction was Tibbett's Amonasro* in *Aida* on January 21, giving ever growing evidence of his large abilities. Also a change and an improvement was Müller's powerful Donna Elvira* in *Don Giovanni* on November 7, one of the best performances in a role singularly ill-favored at the Metropolitan. With Ponselle, Gigli, Pinza, and Fleischer as before was Serafin as conductor. Its three performances were the only Mozart heard at the Metropolitan this season.

The matinee performances of Wagner embraced not only the *Ring,* but also a prefatory *Fliegende Holländer* on February 6, in which Bohnen sang Daland,* and a *Meistersinger* on the 12th distinguished by Branzell's comely, well-sung Magdalene.* Following the *Ring,* which deviated little from the previous year, with Kappel as the *Siegfried* Brünnhilde, Ohms as the others, the series ended with *Tristan* on March 20, with Kappel and Maria Ranzow (Brangäne*). Melchior was now beginning to assert some of the mastery for which he became famous, causing Henderson to remark: "Lauritz Melchior looks more like a Tristan than some of those who have been seen here. He is a man of stalwart figure and bears himself well. His singing is what might be expected of the best type of 'heldentenor.' His voice is heavy but agreeable, and he sang . . . with excellent art in the treatment of light and shade." He was also heard in the only *Parsifal* of the season, on April 3, once more conducted by Bodanzky, who directed everything in the German repertory save an occasional *Lohengrin* entrusted to Riedel. One such occasion was January 5, when Manski was Elsa* and Andresen an imposing King Henry.

Several singers, who remained with the company until playing time and personnel were drastically curtailed in 1933, made debuts in leading roles. On November 15 Faina Petrova as Azucena (d) and Claudio Frigerio as Count di Luna (d) were newcomers in *Il Trovatore*. Myrna Sharlow, formerly of the Chicago company, sang Nedda (d) at her debut on November 27. Beatrice Belkin, who had served an apprenticeship at the Roxy Theater, was heard as the Dewman (d) in *Hänsel und Gretel* on October 30.

For some operagoers the season may be best recalled by a happening outside the Metropolitan: the first New York hearing of Mussorgsky's *Khovanschchina* at the Mecca Temple (later the City Center) on March 7. Michel Schvetz (Khovansky), Max Pantelieff (Dosifei) and a Mme Vanentinova had leading roles, with Michael Feveisky conducting. None was remarkable for finish or vocal art, but the performance showed, as Henderson termed it, "the genius of Moussorgsky who had a musical language of magnificent eloquence for just this sort of thing." In the same auditorium (then without pitched floor, adequate orchestra pit, or proper lighting facilities) Johanna Gadski ventured another week of German opera in March. Carl Hartmann, who later sang at the Metropolitan, was the Tristan to her Isolde on March 16, with Max von Schillings conducting. Once more Gadski sang remarkably well, after nearly thirty-five years before the New York public. The company attempted a *Ring* cycle that was little more than a concert presentation of the four works, with Johannes Sembach once more as Loge and Siegmund, Carl Braun as Wotan, Gadski as Brünnhilde. Of new singers, the best was Margaret Bäumer, who sang an excellent Senta in *Der fliegende Holländer* on March 17 and Marta in D'Albert's *Tiefland* on March 19. Marie von Essen, who was the Brangäne of the opening *Tristan,* but was prevented by illness from singing again, was engaged by the Metropolitan.

Following a usual tour to the South, Cleveland, and Rochester, the sub-scription department stated that ninety-five per cent of the seat-holders had renewed for the following season. When options were exercised in the fall, however, the falling off was decidedly more than five per cent. No mention was made, immediately, of the decline in box-office income (from $3,052,-395 to $2,667,062) or the heavy loss of $322,231.

One view of the Metropolitan's plight was offered by Ernst Lert, who left after two years' service as stage director, with the statement: "It is not opera that is dying, only the traditional method of presenting it." Lert was categorized by the management as a man disgruntled because his contract had not been renewed, but an expansion of his views published in the De-cember 1935 issue of *Chord and Discord* is worth consideration. Despite the "most experienced impresario, the most lavishly paid conductor, the most highly publicized star, the most bombastic scenic artist," wrote Lert, the Metropolitan's lack of co-ordination made the results "a variety show." The stage director, he said, is placed "in an impossible position," named as "responsible for the production, even though he [Gatti] has not granted him a single rehearsal for nineteen out of twenty such productions." Even when a new production was staged, the director had no share in choosing the cast and was "required to render the most complicated opera fit for per-formance within ten or twelve hours (three or four rehearsals)!"

The march of events brought a radio microphone onto the Metropolitan stage for the first time on April 21, 1931, during an actual performance, but the adventurous venture was permitted by the League of Composers on behalf of Stravinsky's *Œdipus Rex,* conducted by Stokowski, not for a Metropolitan opera. On January 21, 1927 a network audience had heard the garden scene from *Faust* broadcast from Chicago (with Edith Mason, Charles Hackett, Vanni Marcoux, and Richard Bonelli, Giorgio Polacco conducting). A spokesman for the Metropolitan declared that such a per-formance was "not opera."

1931–1932

Despite the dissipation of one third of the company's reserve fund in the single season of 1930, there was no disposition yet to temper the shorn lamb of opera to the adverse winds. Planning went forward in the spring for a usual period of twenty-four weeks, with quantities of new productions and revivals. As time for the opening approached, two happenings made the future more menacing: one was the falling off, when subscriptions were taken up, of more than ten per cent from the year before. The other was the retirement, on October 26, of Otto Kahn from his position as chairman of the board. Pressing business responsibilities were given as the reason

(Mortimer Schiff, of the Kuhn, Loeb firm, had recently died, and Kahn's responsibilities were greatly increased). Shortly after, he withdrew as a director of the Philharmonic-Symphony Society. His lawyer, Paul D. Cravath, was charged with carrying on his work with the Metropolitan, in which he still retained his stock.

In Gatti's after-view, Kahn's retirement caused "public apprehension" about the Metropolitan's stability. As for the decline in subscriptions, he wrote: "In three years we lost more than thirty per cent of our subscribers. It was clear that the wealthy classes had suffered the largest shrinkage of fortunes, for they formed the bulk of subscribers who cancelled. . . . The general public which purchased its admissions from day to day, continued at about the same level." This, however, was hardly enough.

The question of cause and effect is, of course, interpreted in the only way Gatti could interpret it. On the other hand, it may be suggested that when money became tight, it was easier for some to give up an investment of $400 (for two orchestra seats) a season than save as much by giving up something else. It would also reflect how much such persons cared for opera, how much they cared for Metropolitan opera, and, finally, how much they cared for Metropolitan opera as it had been given during the several preceding seasons.

In any event, the opening *Traviata* on November 2 was attended by a houseful of patrons who paid as much as $11 a seat ($8.25 by subscription), and gave close attention to Ponselle's vigorously unconventional Violetta, to Lauri-Volpi's Alfredo and De Luca's Germont. When it was over, one suspects that more than a few had completed their opera-going for the year.

Gatti notes: "Then came the deluge." But it is not immediately apparent from contemporary accounts of a *Tannhäuser* with Jeritza and Ohms, *La Bohème* with Bori and Martinelli, or *L'Elisir d'amore* with Gigli, Fleischer, and Pinza, which preceded the season's first novelty on November 7. Jaromir Weinberger's *Schwanda* was class of 1927, Prague, as Křenek's *Jonny spielt auf* had been of Leipzig, a thing of "fun and frolic" (as Pitts Sanborn termed it in the *World-Telegram*), which deserved better of New York than it received. Urban's rather joyless production, however, was the key to a generally heavy treatment of a score that has humor of a sort, if not great distinction. Schorr's Schwanda* was beautifully sung by a man who rarely sang another comedy part. Bodanzky's conducting was better than able, and the cast of Müller (Dorota*), Laubenthal (Babinsky*), Branzell (the Queen*), and Andresen (Sorcerer*) had abundant vocal power for *Götterdämmerung*, if not quite the resilience for *Schwanda*. Max Lorenz sang Babinsky after the *première*, the repetitions numbering four.

Max Brod, translator of *Die verkaufte Braut,* also provided the German text for *Schwanda.*

A restricted five performances accrued to Suppé's *Donna Juanita,* given first on January 2, with Jeritza performing an adagio dance and taking part in the English-language "gags" with which the text was sprinkled. In all, the production adhered to no consistent style, though Jeritza was a vivacious Rene,* Manski a Donna Olympia* described by Henderson as a "farceuse of high rank," and Fleischer the Petrita.* The Metropolitan's simulated Theater-an-der-Wien personnel—Laubenthal, Schützendorf, and Windheim—had smaller parts. Bodanzky's early years as an operetta conductor served him well and there was also praise for Urban's evocation of San Sebastián. Henderson expressed a basic reaction when he wrote "some wondered just what this kind of show was doing . . . in the Metropolitan . . . but there it was."

What proved to be the last of Gatti's Italian novelties, Italo Montemezzi's one-act *La Notte di Zoraïma,* was also far from the best of them when seen on December 2. The composer freely confessed that the libretto, based on a revolt among Incas, appealed to him because, in Henderson's words, "it packed into one capacious act every melodramatic antiquity of Italian opera," but aside from some high-flown phrases that permitted Ponselle as Zoraïma* to demonstrate "the grandiloquence of style in which she is so impressive," the score lacked interest. Jagel (Muscar*), Basiola (Pedrito*), and Biondo (Manuela*) were embarrassed not only by poor music, but also by unsightly native costumes. The conductor was Serafin, the designer Novak. Audience attention was shared with *Pagliacci* at the *première,* thereafter with *L'Oracolo,* which had been brought back on November 23 for another round of performances with Scotti.

Considering the number of operas given in New York after Verdi revised *Simon Boccanegra* in 1881, it seems perverse that one of such singular merits should have waited till January 28, 1932 for its Metropolitan introduction. The melodic richness of the score, its solid musical construction, and its strength of feeling were admirably projected by Serafin, and the audience's interest in Tibbett's artistically composed, powerfully sung Boccanegra* was sustained through *longueurs* in the intricate libretto. Pinza as Jacopo Fiesco,* Frigerio as Paolo Albiani,* and Martinelli as Gabriele* all had quality, but the musical line of Maria* fared better when Rethberg replaced Maria Müller on February 24. Camille Parravicini of Milan provided the ornate, old-fashioned, but suggestive scenery. *Boccanegra* wore very well, first with Tibbett, then with Warren.

In two works revived for Pons, her sparkle and charm counted for more in *Lakmé* on February 19 than in *La Sonnambula* on March 16. If she, too, sang the "Bell Song" better than she did the more melodic material of Act I, she dressed the stage better than Galli-Curci or Barrientos, and helped to make Novak's production theatrically valid. Artful work was done by Swarthout as Mallika* and Thill (in better voice than the year before) as Gerald.* De Luca (Frédéric) and Rothier (Nilakantha) were no strangers to operatic India. A lavish, more than usually naked ballet gave unexpected life to Act II, with De Leporte and Kosloff as principals. Jagel and Martinelli were later Geralds, and Hasselmans conducted. For Bellini's music Pons as Amina* displayed a kind of delivery Henderson termed "breathy and tentative," her vocal style lacking finish and ease. Gigli was Elvino* and Pinza a fine Rodolfo.* Urban provided the scenic decorations, and Serafin was the conductor.

Even before the first month of the season was completed, the daily returns had shown such diminished size as to promise a record-breaking deficit. It was then (November 23) that Gatti put forth his plea for "sacrifice" equally shared. As detailed on page 24, virtually all individuals agreed; the unions, for one reasonable reason or another, did not. Subsequently there were rumors that the company would disband and undertake operations elsewhere, in some more financially advantageous setting. These were dismissed by Paul D. Cravath as "quite out of the question," as was the possibility of bankruptcy.

The steady criticism of the German performances in the last several seasons resulted in some alterations of personnel, but no sharp improvement in quality. Kirchhoff followed Taucher out of the Metropolitan, and while Laubenthal lingered, Melchior sang more often and Max Lorenz came to make his debut as Walther (d) in *Die Meistersinger* on November 12. A serious artist and an intelligent musician, Lorenz had a hard, unyielding tone quality that did not alter much in the two decades in which he came and went at the Metropolitan. Marie von Essen, of the previous spring's Gadski company, was a routine Magdalene* (d); Fleischer (Eva) and Schorr (Sachs) were excellent. Hans Clemens was a new David.* On November 14 Lorenz was a creditable Siegmund* and Manski a surprisingly good Sieglinde in a *Walküre* that introduced Carlton Gauld, an American basso of promise as Hunding (d). After Babinsky in *Schwanda* and Erik in *Der fliegende Holländer,* Lorenz sang Siegfried* in a performance of which Henderson wrote: "The scherzo of the 'Ring' became something like a stately minuet." Bodanzky, who conducted, had one of his most unhappy years, for the financial underwriter of the Friends of Music (Harriet Lanier) had recently died and the series came to an end for lack of new guarantors.

What may be noted as a low point of Wagner performances in this period came on November 20, when *Tristan* was given with both Ohms and Laubenthal vocally ailing. By evidence of the *Herald Tribune,* Bodanzky disposed of the first act (uncut) eighteen minutes faster than was customary in Dresden or Berlin. Later in the month, the management announced that Ohms was ill and would not appear again "for some time." She did not ever appear again at the Metropolitan. Her place, physically, was taken by Göta Ljungberg, a commanding figure of a woman, whose debut as Sieglinde (d) in *Die Walküre* on January 20 was admired for picturesqueness, less for a vocal manner that always promised to produce better sound than it did. Her further appearances included Elsa, Brünnhilde in *Die Walküre,* and Isolde, all sung with good detail in what Henderson termed a *"voix de veloute"* that did not quite cut through the Wagnerian orchestra. Her Isolde, in the same critical view, belonged to "the delicately cut intaglio class," sensitive and assured, but with an oboe sound where a trumpet quality was desired. Also of small size in this *Isolde* on February 3 was the Brangäne (d) of Doris Doe, likened by Henderson to the "kind exhibited on the provincial stages of Germany." A hard-working, intelligent singer, Doe had neither the experience nor the vocal plenitude for such roles as Waltraute, Fricka (*Die Walküre*), and Erda (*Siegfried*), her considerable lot in this season.

The Wagner patrons, as distinguished from operagoers, remained remarkably constant, loyally supporting the *Ring* cycle plus *Tannhäuser* and *Tristan.* Bodanzky's share of irritations included a *Götterdämmerung* on March 17 for which Whitehill was ill, with Schützendorf replacing him as Gunther, and Gabor moving up to sing Alberich. Ljungberg, the scheduled Gutrune, was also ill, and her place was taken by Manski. In addition to singing Siegfried, Melchior indicated by nods and gestures where the ill-prepared substitutes should move. The *Siegfried* on March 11 was embellished by the farewell to opera of Schumann-Heink, whose Erda (at more than seventy) "took the breath away," said Downes. In the circumstances, Ljungberg as Brünnhilde* awoke and sang without undue attention. She was a creditable Kundry* in *Parsifal* on March 22. Tangential to the German repertory was Pinza's Landgraf Hermann* in *Tannhäuser* on December 25, sung with beautiful sound if with the lack of ease to be expected in a first venture in an alien tongue.

Lert's replacement as stage director was Alexander Sanine, who gave full evidence of his capacity in a newly staged *Lohengrin* on December 21, which utilized the shabby Urban settings. Plausible groupings and concerted action gave fresh life to the stage, though Lorenz, in Bayreuth style, felled Telramund with a wave of the sword rather than with a blow. A pudgy Swan Knight in appearance, he did not sing very agreeably, a disability shared by Jeritza. For Bodanzky, the tempos were surprisingly deliberate.

With financial problems increasingly stringent, the new source of revenue promised by radio broadcasts could no longer be resisted. The first underwriter was the National Broadcasting Company, whose president, M. H. Aylesworth, prefaced the first broadcast, on Christmas Day 1931, of *Hänsel und Gretel,* with the statement: "The contribution made by NBC . . . helps to maintain the opera." In the column recording "phonograph income" for this season, the company's books show $100,000 more than for the year before, no doubt the earning from the broadcasts.

Riedel conducted the performance, with Fleischer, Mario, Wakefield, Schützendorf, and Manski in familiar parts. Seeking a device to make Humperdinck more palatable than he was, the network offered Deems Taylor as commentator not only before and after the work, but during its progress. The protests that ensued conveyed the listener view that a low voice was an excellent thing in women, but not during an opera. It was soon discontinued in favor of more conventional commentary. Operas continued to be presented regularly thereafter, the first sponsored performance occurring on December 30, 1933 (see page 376).

The steady progress of Gladys Swarthout continued with such roles as Preziosilla in *La Forza del destino* and Mrs. Deane in *Peter Ibbetson,* leading to an Adalgisa* in *Norma* on December 26—the centenary, to the day, of the work's first production at La Scala—which brought from Henderson the praise: "She . . . sang the recitatives with a competence of style which her previous revelations had not led us to expect . . . her warm and lovely voice . . . was heard with pleasure." Arthur Anderson, a basso of excellent voice and bearing, made a debut as Donner (d) in *Das Rheingold* on February 26, and was later heard in *Sadko* (the Norse Merchant*) and *Aida* (the King*). Armando Borgioli and Francesco Merli were new Italian singers of solid ability but no outstanding capacities who sang Amonasro and Radames in *Aida* on April 2 in the same cast as Anderson. (Carmela Ponselle made one of her infrequent appearances, as Amneris, with Rethberg and Pinza.) The baritone Borgioli gave evidence of good capacities in such roles as Don Carlos (d) in *La Forza del destino* on January 22, Barnaba in *La Gioconda,* Tonio, and Count di Luna, and returned for each of Gatti's remaining seasons. Merli, who also sang Edgardo in *Lucia* on March 11 (Pietro Cimara made his debut as conductor in place of Bellezza), Gabriele in *Boccanegra,* and Pinkerton, was not heard after this season.

The confusion and the countercharges detailed elsewhere (see page 25) in the negotiation of new contracts at the end of this season had more than a little effect on the artistic future of the institution. Gigli withdrew defiantly, Clarence Whitehill with mild aspersions on his ability after a long and distinguished career. Bohnen, Lorenz, and Andresen were not re-engaged, and Jeritza decided to sing no more at the Metropolitan. Despite the voluntary cuts and the windfall from radio, the sharp decline in revenue brought the loss to $497,213, the largest in many decades of operation.

3

THE METROPOLITAN OPERA ASSOCIATION

DEPRESSION AND DEFICIT, 1932–1935

1932–1933

THE FORMULA THAT was evolved to facilitate the continuation of opera at the Metropolitan served several purposes. The dominant one was to reduce expenses that had pyramided, through the years of prosperity, including fees approaching $3,000 per performance for Chaliapin and Gigli. By a simple "reorganization," the assets of the Metropolitan Opera Company—but not its obligations—were transferred to the stockless, profitless, and, for some years to come, propertyless Metropolitan Opera Association.

The transformation (see page 26) also gave the Association the status of an "educational" institution and relief, for the while, from amusement taxes. Plainly, ticket prices had to be reduced in accordance with a depressed economy. Elimination of taxes, however, permitted the Metropolitan to reduce its top price per subscription ticket from $8.25 to $6.50 while sacrificing only one dollar per ticket. Almost as much (seventy-five cents per ticket) was saved to the purchaser by elimination of the tax. Ticket prices thus returned to the level that had prevailed in the 1920–4 period. For single-seat purchasers, the top rate was $7 per ticket.

In the spring, Earle Lewis made his usually hopeful prognosis of subscription sales, but this was not justified by the public response in the fall despite the reduced prices and the even more drastic reduction in playing time from twenty-four to sixteen weeks. This was the shortest season of Metropolitan opera since Conried's first in 1903, which had been fifteen weeks.

Even more novel was the prominence of Lawrence Tibbett in the opening performance of *Simon Boccanegra* on November 21, the first time an American male singer wholly trained in this country had been so honored.

Both Kahn and Mackay, veteran first-nighters, were absent, and Henderson observed: "Even to the mere music-reporter it was plain that there were many unfamiliar faces in boxes and stalls." This was Gatti's twenty-fifth opening, and Toscanini, recently reconciled with his old friend, was present. Also present were Serafin, who conducted, Müller, Martinelli, Pinza, and Frigerio.

To fill the need for a leading tenor left by Gigli's departure, Tito Schipa made his debut on November 23, as Nemorino (d) in *L'Elisir d'amore,* with Fleischer, De Luca, and Pinza. His growth since early appearances in New York with visiting Chicago companies was reflected in Henderson's tributes to his "taste, refinement, and elegance," and the statement that *"Una furtiva lagrima"* was sung "as it had rarely been sung" in the house. Among a sequence that included Edgardo and Alfredo, his most memorable effort was an Ottavio* in *Don Giovanni* on December 17, which Henderson commended as "a delight to the connoisseur," the best Mozart singing heard from a tenor since Bonci. With Pinza gaining ease as the Don, Ponselle enjoying one of her best evenings as Donna Anna, and Müller a propulsive if sometimes strident Elvira, the shape of future *Don Giovannis* began to be apparent. Pasero was a rather lumbering Leporello,* Malatesta a poor Masetto.*

The suspension of opera in Chicago the previous January had ended the gentleman's agreement that formerly prevailed, resulting in the availability to the Metropolitan of several fine artists, of whom Schipa was the first and Richard Bonelli the second. The latter's sturdy baritone was heard for the first time as Germont (d) in *La Traviata* on December 1, with Schipa (Alfredo*) and Ponselle, and he gave sound service as Marcello, Tonio, and Valentin in *Faust.* The greatest impact from what Gilman called "the preoccupation of Mr. Insull in foreign parts" followed the debuts of Frida Leider (Isolde [d]) and Maria Olszewska (Brangäne [d]) in *Tristan* on January 16. The quality of their performances (which Chicago had been hearing since 1928) made palpable nonsense of the contention that such roles had been badly sung at the Metropolitan because artists to sing them could not be found. With a revivified Bodanzky conducting, and Melchior, Schorr, and Ludwig Hofmann (Marke*) performing at their best, younger operagoers had a glimpse of what Gilman called "the fabulous days before the war."

Henderson especially admired Leider's first act, which she sang with "passion, variety, and elasticity," though the voice was plainly worn. She had the "indescribable magic of genuineness," however, which transcended vocal blemishes. He also approved Olszewska as "a Brangäne of the first rank," and noted a "vocal finish and depth of feeling" that Melchior had not previously given to Tristan—also Bodanzky's "unwonted fire and feeling." The transformation in Bodanzky had not been suggested by his early-season work, which included a *Götterdämmerung* on November 24 in which Ludwig Hofmann's Hagen (d) was saluted by Henderson as the work of "an artist of authority," Gustav de Loor's Siegfried (d) scarcely saluted at all. A small fee was the biggest merit of this thick-voiced, unimaginative tenor. Hofmann's vocal range and stylistic competence enabled him to perform the work of two such specialists as Bohnen and Andresen, his repertory this season including Landgraf Hermann in *Tannhäuser,* Marke, Wotan in *Die Walküre,* Heinrich in *Lohengrin,* and Gurnemanz in *Parsifal.* He was a commanding figure in any role he undertook, and sang eloquently when his sometimes unresponsive voice was under full command. How such a difficulty might arise was suggested by Henderson in an obituary tribute to Clarence Whitehill, who died on December 19, 1932. He disclosed that the singer had a long-standing difficulty "owing to the supersensitiveness of one vocal chord. When this was slightly congested the singer's tone acquired a little roughness . . . when the congestion was pronounced he became unmistakably hoarse." Only the "thoroughness of his vocal art," said Henderson, enabled Whitehill to sing as long and as well as he did.

The upward curve of Bodanzky's "second" career may be dated from December 3, when he had an unmistakable personal success in the first Metropolitan performance of Strauss's *Elektra.* In Gilman's view, Kappel's Elektra* was "not within a thousand miles of the character Strauss had conceived, Branzell's well-sung Clytemnestra* was temperamentally tame, and Ljungberg's Chrysothemis* was "distressingly self-conscious," but the sustained applause of the large audience was a handsome tribute to Bodanzky's conducting. Henderson described it as "masterful," paying particular tribute to his "communicative temperament." Whatever the lacks of the personnel, the thoroughgoing preparation by Bodanzky began a new period of Metropolitan appreciation for the Strauss of *Elektra,* and eventually *Salome,* especially when Olszewska sang a powerful Clytemnestra* on February 3, with Manski a striking Chrysothemis,* and Ljungberg not less good than Kappel as Elektra.* Schorr (Orestes*) and Laubenthal (Ægisthus*) were constants. Marking the change from the days when "offal" and "ordure" were appropriate terms for Strauss, Henderson noted on February 3 that "there was a daisy chain all around the Metropolitan"—another way of saying that, in combination with *Pagliacci, Elektra* was a benefit for the Vassar College Scholarship Fund.

Leider and Olszewska contributed considerably to the new vitality of the Wagner performances in which they appeared, including a *Ring* cycle that began on January 27 with Olszewska as Erda* in *Das Rheingold*. Unfortunately the soprano began to feel the effects of the New York winter in early February, when *Die Walküre* was given on the 2nd, with Melchior, Olszewska (Fricka*), Schorr, Stückgold, and Tappolet. She sang a highly able Brünnhilde until her throat clogged in Act III and she was momentarily voiceless. Manski, standing in the wings as one of the Walküren, picked up the lines and sang them without lapse till Leider could continue. (The afflicted singer was all for leaving the stage until Manski, during a breathing-spell, hoarsely reminded her she would lose part of her fee if she did.) Although the management virtually denied the incident, thus minimizing Manski's well-earned credit, she was allowed the privilege of singing Brünnhilde* in *Siegfried* on February 9, Leider being bedded with grip. It was hardly for her voice, however. Leider returned for *Götterdämmerung* on February 17, but neither this Brünnhilde nor Kundry in *Parsifal* on March 9 were quite representative of her best. The season's premier cast was reunited for another *Tristan und Isolde* on Saturday afternoon March 11. It was noted as the one-hundredth performance of the music drama during Gatti's direction. Schorr, who had succeeded to one of Whitehill's specialties to sing an eloquent Amfortas two days before, was replaced as Kurvenal by Schützendorf.

As well as singing an able Venus, Brangäne, Fricka, and Erda, Olszewska made her mark as that rare bird who wore German and Italian plumage with equal distinction by performing a powerful Amneris* on February 18, the day after an excellent Waltraute* in *Götterdämmerung*. She won acclaim also for her Ortrud* in *Lohengrin* on February 6, where pertinent action made her a figure in the drama during Act I, though she had no solo music to sing.

The first note of the distant rise of Nazism came to the Metropolitan indirectly on January 7, when Louis Gruenberg's treatment of Eugene O'Neill's *Emperor Jones* was added to the list of the institution's world *premières*. It had been scheduled for prior performance in Berlin, but had been withdrawn when Erich Kleiber, who was to conduct it, decided that a music drama with an American Negro as the central figure would not flourish in the current political climate. Tibbett was doubtless the best non-Negro Jones* one could imagine, close to the dramatic level of Gilpin and Robeson. Gruenberg's monochromatic music gave him little to work with, that little including a heightened use of "Standin' in the Need of Prayer" at the moment of climax. Henderson judged it a "turbulent . . . sometimes frenetic score"; Sanborn in the *World-Telegram* thought it more "a remembered convention" than the product of "an inspired imagination."

Some felt that O'Neill's background drumbeat was more musical effect than any Gruenberg imposed upon it. Jo Mielziner's décor was admired (though it was drastically reduced by the conservative Metropolitan minds from his first bold sketches), and Windheim as Smithers* and Besuner as an Old Native Woman* supported Tibbett splendidly. Serafin[1] conducted, Sanine stage-directed, and Hemsley Winfield, the first Negro to appear in a Metropolitan production, danced the Witch Doctor. *Jones* had nine further performances during this and the next season, usually in the unsuitable company of *Hänsel und Gretel* or *Pagliacci*.

The other unfamiliar work of this season was Rossini's brief *Il Signor Bruschino*. Most knew at least the sprightly overture when the work was served on December 9 as an *apéritif* for *Elektra,* but the historically minded found the ironic jesting of Rossini (a novelty to almost all) amended by an editorial hand, the low range of the soprano and the high tones of the basso parts being restored to more normal ranges. Fleischer (Sofia*), Pinza (Gaudenzio*), and De Luca (Bruschino*) were all skilled in their parts, and Serafin conducted with spirit. It brought to an end the long association of Urban with the Metropolitan, for illness intervened as he was at work on the project, which was completed by Novak. The prolific designer died the following July.

Despite the brevity of the season, Gatti managed to crowd thirty-seven works into the repertory, with restorations of *L'Amore dei tre re* and *Die verkaufte Braut*. The Montemezzi score would have fared better on February 17 had not its able cast of Bori, Johnson, Pasero (Archibaldo*), and Bonelli (Manfredo*) been associated with an orchestra that had spent the afternoon playing an uncut *Götterdämmerung*. Smetana's lark did not ascend so high with Hofmann rather than Bohnen as Kezal* on February 4, but Hofmann was a better than passable marriage-broker in the charming company of Rethberg's Marie, Windheim's Wenzel,* and the chic Esmeralda* of Helen Gleason. Laubenthal, Schützendorf, and Manski (Kathinka) were old hands at the game of barter. Bodanzky played the overture as an overture (before Act I), but the season closed with a mere two hearings each of Montemezzi and Smetana.

An old friend passed from the scene on January 20 when Antonio Scotti rolled his orange for the last time as Chim-Fen in *L'Oracolo,* and pronounced the honest if unconventional valedictory: "I do not want to leave you, but I must." With him in the last performance of his thirty-third season were Mario, Tokatyan, and Pasero. Farrar, whose career had run a romantic course beside his own, was present to throw him a bouquet, as

---

[1] Serafin retained a sufficient memory of *Emperor Jones* to produce it in Italy in 1952, with Nicola Rossi-Lemini as an Italian Emperor.

was Bori. The tears and cheers followed a matinee *Bohème* with Rethberg and Martinelli. Bellezza conducted both.

In deference to the ruthless, sometimes efficient maxim of the theater: "Off with the old, on with the new," an increasing number of young singers came to replace those too old, too expensive, or too independent. The trend of earlier days was slowly being reversed so that it was no longer the exceptional American singer who would be sought out, but rather the exceptional European one. In addition to Bonelli, the new artists included Rose Bampton, Richard Crooks, and Helen Gleason, arranged in order of length of career as well as alphabetically.

The writer in the *Times* (Hubbard Hutcheson), who described Bampton's voice at her debut as Laura (d) in *La Gioconda* on November 28 as "truly contralto," can hardly be blamed, for Bampton so styled herself for five years. Henderson heard a "rich, powerful, sensitive mezzo soprano . . . with a delightful smoothness throughout the scale." She later sang the Sandman in *Hänsel und Gretel* and Amneris in *Aida,* and continued to broaden her mezzo repertory till 1937.

Crooks was much less a questionable quantity at his debut as Des Grieux (d) in *Manon* on February 25, for he had been heard often in concert and on the radio and was well equipped with European experience. "It was a delight to see a young Chevalier," wrote Henderson, "and to hear his music sung with a fresh unworn voice." The critic also remarked a rather needless timidity about high tones, which was a later Crooks characteristic. A standing regret of Crooks's Metropolitan career was his failure to sing either Lohengrin or Walther von Stolzing, for which he was well suited by voice and training. In this year he sang only in *Manon*.

Helen Gleason, who had more prominence on the operetta stage in later years, showed a pretty voice as Bersi* in *Andrea Chénier* on November 25, also as Esmeralda in *Die verkaufte Braut.* Margaret Halstead, a buxom alto, was overmatched as Venus (d) in her debut in *Tannhäuser* on November 26, using her big tones with little discipline. A skilled artist who came by way of Chicago was Eidé Norena, better as Juliette* in *Roméo* on February 22 than as Mimi (d) in her debut on February 9. Her rather limited level of achievement rose somewhat in future seasons. For an oddity, the Ponselle sisters appeared together for the first time in a Metropolitan Opera on December 21, when Carmela sang an eloquent Laura* to Rosa's customarily fine Gioconda. "Together," said Henderson of the second-act duet "they made the fire fly."

Radio broadcasts resumed on November 24 when *Lakmé* was given, beginning with Act II. Conventional summaries replaced the Taylor tones of the previous season. The long-scorned device was gratefully employed for purposes of fund-raising (as noted on page 29), beginning with *Manon* on February 25, in which the honor—a rather ominous prophecy of "appeals" to come—went to Edward Johnson. Geraldine Farrar returned to the Metropolitan stage on March 9, but only to speak on behalf of the fund, and the artists donated their services for two benefits (*Manon* on March 17, *Aida* on March 24), and the entertainment incidental to a ball on April 26. When the goal was achieved, plans were announced for a fourteen-week season for 1933–4. Publicly all was harmonious; in the corridor leading to Gatti's office, matters were sometimes otherwise. Serafin's complaints, for one, were not long suppressed (see page 30). At the year's end Laubenthal, De Loor, Tokatyan, and Lauri-Volpi were not re-engaged. Paul Althouse, in a new career as a Wagner tenor, Charles Hackett, Claudia Muzio, and Max Lorenz were re-engaged; and John Charles Thomas, Lotte Lehmann, and Nino Martini were added to the company.

The usual cheery news of high subscription renewals did not make the customary impression, memories of recent downward trends still being fresh. The sixteen weeks showed a loss of $339,901, an average of $600 a week more than the previous year's weekly red figures of $20,500. As ticket prices were appreciably less, however, the numerical attendance had turned for the better.

1933–1934

The first season of Metropolitan opera underwritten by public funds was unique in more than this single respect. Its fourteen weeks were the shortest period of opera New York had been offered in nearly forty years; and the competition of pre-Christmas shopping was avoided by an opening on December 26. Of itself this indicates the low estate to which interest in opera had fallen in this period; for if there is normally a diversion of attention among New Yorkers at this time, out-of-town visitors usually compensate for it.

In the circumstances, the choice of Taylor's *Peter Ibbetson* for the opening (the first American work thus honored) was an all-round judicious one. It made a comfortable family party of this somewhat depressed ceremonial, especially as its principals—Bori, Johnson, and Tibbett—had been the most active figures in the spring campaign for money. Taylor had amended the work somewhat in search of melodic continuity, but the results did not appear significant. In the juvenile role of Mimsey (d) was a new young actress, June Lockhart. As always, Serafin conducted.

Actually, this was a first night that was not an opening, for Christmas afternoon had seen the customary *Hänsel und Gretel,* and the Philadelphia series had started on December 19 with Pons in *Lakmé.* The old social connections were dissolving faster than any suspected. Those who came through a heavy snowstorm (the curtain was fifteen minutes late in rising) to hear *Ibbetson* were operagoers at least, if not music-lovers. "Going on" once more was legal; but it was to a supper club for a nightcap rather than to the balls or assemblies of old.

The impetus that had been provided to the Wagner literature in the previous season by Leider and Olszewska was continued by the long-delayed but no less welcome debut of Lotte Lehmann as Sieglinde (d) on January 11, in which, with Melchior and Emanuel List (Hunding), she sang a first act of *Die Walküre* not matched in years. In a detailed appreciation of her performance Henderson wrote: "It is no injustice to her predecessors [as Sieglinde] to assert that she must be placed in the foremost rank." Kappel and Hofmann were in their best form, as was Bodanzky. Branzell, who had been ill, got through her Fricka by singing much of the music sitting on a stage rock.

One had to be alert to hear Lehmann this season, for her other appearances were few and widely spaced: Elisabeth* in *Tannhäuser* on February 24, Eva* in *Die Meistersinger* on March 15. The variety of her art and the illumination it shed on these thrice-familiar roles made vibrant drama of what had recently been dull make-believe. Schorr's Sachs reached a new level of eloquence on this occasion, prompting Henderson to say: "He sang all the music like a great artist and some of it as it had never been sung here except, perhaps, by Emil Fischer." Lorenz, Doe (Magdalene), and List (Pogner) were hardly performers to invite historical comparisons.

List appeared first in *Tannhäuser* on December 27, a Landgrave (d) of substantial voice and person. Henderson noted his voice as "not of luscious quality but of fairly good metal," with an artistic sense of "vocal line and color." The Bayreuth recording of the 1932 Festival is still audible testimony to what this critic meant when he termed Müller's Elisabeth "among the best the Metropolitan stage has known." List is best remembered for his Ochs in *Der Rosenkavalier,* which was not in this season's repertory. As Hunding, the Commendatore in *Don Giovanni,* Fafner, Pogner, King Henry in *Lohengrin,* or Gurnemanz, List was invariably a creditable performer, if rarely an exceptional one. As the Tannhäuser* of the performance in which List made his debut, Lorenz was more secure than in his first Metropolitan season, but not much more pleasant to hear.

Pleasant enough, when it could be heard, was the voice of Nino Martini, who profited from the powers of radio to attain a celebrity that would not normally have been his. The big house rather cut him down to size in his debut as the Duke (d) in *Rigoletto* on December 28, his voice striking Henderson as "thin and pallid." A likeable personality rather than a powerful art gave him audience favor in such roles as Edgardo in *Lucia,* Rinuccio in *Gianni Schicchi,* even Rodolfo and Alfredo. Radio itself became a factor of new importance to the Metropolitan with the first Saturday of this season, when *Mignon* on December 30, with Schipa (Meister*), Pons, Bori, and Swarthout, initiated the long sequence of commercially sponsored broadcasts. For the privilege of advertising Lucky Strike cigarettes, the American Tobacco Company paid close to $100,000 to the opera management (much more, of course, for radio time and incidental talent).

As long before as January 4, 1920, the *Tribune* had given favorable mention to a baritone at a Hippodrome concert who "sang the Prologo [from *Pagliacci*] as effectively as it had been heard in New York for years." John Charles Thomas did a number of things well in the next fourteen years, but it was not until February 2, 1934 that he did any of them at the Metropolitan. As Germont (d) in *La Traviata* with Ponselle and Schipa, Thomas left only one question unanswered: why it had taken the leading theater of his native land so long to engage him. In phrasing, style, and action (as well as vocal quality), his was a performance of notable quality. He sang another *Traviata* on March 1 and a Tonio* in *Pagliacci* on April 14 (a post-season benefit for the opera fund), but nothing further till Johnson replaced Gatti.

Also brief was the reappearance of Claudia Muzio, who had been absent for a dozen years (since April 21, 1922) when she sang her fine Violetta* on January 1, 1934. Time had not impaired "the fresh and juvenile character" that Henderson heard in her singing, and her striking artistry was warmly appreciated by a large audience. Her only other role was Santuzza on January 10. Unfortunately she did not sing at the Metropolitan again, for she died suddenly in May 1936.

Two tenors of earlier days reappeared on February 3 when Charles Hackett was an artistic Roméo* to Bori's Juliette and Paul Althouse sang Siegmund* in the afternoon *Walküre*. Both men were fully matured artists, but Althouse had stronger service from his voice in his new career as a German tenor. On March 16 he became the first tenor of American birth to sing Tristan at the Metropolitan, performing in admirable style with Leider, Olszewska, Schützendorf, and Hofmann. Siegmund, however, was better suited to his range than anything else he sang in the next half-dozen years as a Wagnerian tenor. Hardly more than fleeting visitors were Cyrena van Gordon, long with the Chicago company,[1] who sang Am-

---

[1] After a year's lapse, opera had resumed on Wacker Drive, with *Tosca* on December 26, with Jeritza, Dino Borgioli, and Amato. Tickets were priced from fifty cents to three dollars.

neris (d) in *Aida* on January 18 with Carlo del Corso, also new, as Radames (d). Neither returned.

The last influence of Otto Kahn[1] on the Metropolitan was felt on February 10, when Howard Hanson's setting of *Merry Mount* (as adapted by Richard L. Stokes from a story by Hawthorne) had its stage *première*. In rosier days Kahn had accepted the project for the Metropolitan before a note of the score had been written, a recognition of Hanson's stature as a composer for the concert hall. Ann Arbor heard it as a concert piece on May 20, 1933, under the direction of the composer, with Leonora Corona, John Charles Thomas, and Frederick Jagel.

At the Metropolitan, Ljungberg was chosen for the principal soprano role of Lady Marigold Sandys,* mangling further the English text, not very skillfully set by Hanson. Tibbett as Wrestling Bradford* and Johnson as Sir Gower Lackland* were excellent, as were D'Angelo (Praise-God Tewke*) and Swarthout (Plentiful Tewke*). Working, perhaps, on the Mussorgsky model, Hanson made his chorus far more prominent than it customarily is in any except Russian opera. Strongly motivated in artistic conviction, and with some stirring ensemble moments, *Merry Mount* nevertheless suffered from the composer's inexperience in writing for the theater. To Sanborn, the "weight and density" of the orchestral fabric was a critical liability. Serafin's conducting was praised, but not the singularly flimsy scenery of Novak. The latter sufficed for the five repetitions, however, which passed without alteration of basic opinions, despite such cast changes as Corona and Halstead for Ljungberg, Irra Petina for Swarthout, Bonelli for Tibbett, and Jagel for Johnson.

The large opportunities that came to Ljungberg in this period included *Salome** when Strauss's turbulent score followed *Elektra* into Metropolitan favor on January 13. As the Garden performances of the twenties had proved, *Salome* was the bygone scandal of another generation,[2] and Henderson now found the "splendor" of its best pages "not matched by anything else written since Wagner," Bodanzky a conductor who made them sound more "glorious" than they ever had. Once again the triumph was largely his, for Ljungberg sang stridently and with scant illusion. Her dance was little less than ludicrous, for when she shed the last of the veils, she had on as much as before. Schorr was a splendid Jokanaan,* but Lorenz was far from the fine Herod* he later became. Branzell was a victim of indisposition, and Manski substituted as a hardly adequate Herodias.*

---

[1] He died in March 1934.

[2] *Wozzeck,* the scandal of a new generation, had been heard at the Metropolitan in November 1931, with Stokowski conducting the Philadelphia ensemble.

Donald Oenslager's setting (in use until 1964–65) seemed to Downes "nearer Broadway than the River Jordan," but it had architectural impressiveness in its favor. Ljungberg fondled the "head" (a bewigged grapefruit) in the shelter of the prompter's box, risking no offense, giving no illusion. At later performances Branzell strengthened the ensemble as Herodias,* and Jagel was Herod.* Bodanzky's fervent, clarifying work ended any *Salome* problem peculiar to the Metropolitan, leaving only the general one of theaters the world over—where to find a Salome who is young, beautiful, with the voice of a Fremstad and the insinuation of a Garden. *Salome* was given on January 19 with *Gianni Schicchi,* later with *Pagliacci* or *Cavalleria.*

In addition to a customary quota of Lucias, Gildas, and Lakmés, Pons was offered in a production of Donizetti's *Linda di Chamounix* on March 1, its first in the Metropolitan repertory, though both Galli-Curci and Patti had sung it in New York, the latter in the house itself during her special season of 1890. Henderson approved the "brilliancy" of Pons's singing, but not the deliberation with which she prepared her vocal flights. Crooks was a handsome if not wholly confident Vicomte,* Swarthout an excellent Pierotto,* and Pinza a strong Prefect.* With De Luca for Antonio,* Serafin had stalwart support for his good ensemble performance. Novak was the designer. *Linda* had a total of seven performances in this and the next season, none thereafter.

Gatti's favor to Mozart continued with three performances of *Don Giovanni,* in the first of which, on January 3, Virgilio Lazzari (another accession from Chicago) sang his lively Leporello.* His substantial voice did not have the mellowness preferable in the part, but he was a lither, more polished performer than Ludikar or Pasero. Schipa, Ponselle, Müller, and Fleischer did their work well, but it was an off night for Pinza, who had to omit *"Finch'han del vino."* List replaced Rothier as Il Commendatore* on January 20, to the gain of musical sound.

Despite the reduction of playing time, the Wagner cycle continued as before, with six of the largest audiences of the season attending the *Tannhäuser* of February 9 and *Die Meistersinger* of March 15, with the *Ring* between. An outstanding impression was made by Olszewska's Fricka* in *Das Rheingold,* of which Henderson said: "There has not been a better Fricka, and seldom one as good." Leider, who had returned in good voice for her Isolde of February 11, sang all the Brunnhildes in splendid style. List took a strong place in the ensembles with his Hunding, Fafner, and Hagen, and Melchior made himself ever more admired as Siegmund and Siegfried. His Parsifal on March 28 was judged "deeply felt" and "finely wrought" by Henderson, the unusual evening performance also earning Leider's Kundry a larger share of credit than that of the year before.

The closer connection of the Juilliard Foundation with the Metropolitan (see page 28) became artistic as well as economic with the announcement on February 28 that its "artist pupils" would have a more prominent place in Metropolitan planning than heretofore. This was a *quid pro quo* in a contribution of $40,000 for the following year's guarantee fund, which was not raised by a general appeal to the public.[1] Several benefit performances, a "Surprise Party," and a ball in a Louis XIV setting were used for money-raising that resulted in an unspecified but adequate sum to finance Gatti's final season. His next to last one resulted in a loss of $317,582.

Serafin's decision to leave the Metropolitan to become director of the Royal Opera in Rome (see page 29) brought the information, in June, that Ettore Panizza would take his place as chief conductor for the Italian repertory. Later in the summer, Frida Leider decided that alterations in the exchange rate made further trips to America unattractive, and canceled her agreement to return. It was said, also, that she did not look kindly on the engagement of the young Polish soprano, Anny Konetzni. In Leider's place, it was casually mentioned, the Metropolitan had secured a Norwegian soprano, Kirsten Flagstad.

The long years of procrastination about a "new" Metropolitan cost the Opera and Real Estate Company dearly at the end of this season. As discussed more fully elsewhere, various violations of the building code made mandatory the expenditure of more than half a million dollars that added little to the utility of the property or the comfort of the patrons. Including the year's loss, close to a million dollars was spent to keep the theater operating this season.

1934-1935

The formal announcement that Gatti would turn the direction of the Metropolitan over to someone else at the end of his current contract came upon his return to New York in November. Although one hardly needs extraneous factors to explain a retirement after twenty-seven years from such an exacting position, several influences had sealed the inevitable decision. One was the death of Kahn, following the decline of his power before and behind the throne; the other was Gatti's marriage to Rosina Galli in 1930, at which time Gatti was informed[2] that the board would not renew his

---

[1] The Philharmonic-Symphony Society was engaged in a campaign for half a million dollars, which made another appeal to the same general public impracticable.
[2] The authority for this is the first Mrs. Gatti.

contract. Now (1934) he expressed his willingness either to step down at once, or to see the season through. The general sentiment was that he should finish his committed time and be publicly commended for all he had done.

Presumably this was not news to his directors, or to those who had already begun to plan for the future (see page 29). The notion that the city's two principal musical organizations could operate more efficiently under a single roof had sufficient merit for a serious proposal to be made to Arturo Toscanini, the Philharmonic-Symphony Society's musical director. Even before he had rejected the proposition, Bruno Walter had termed it unworthy of New York (see page 31).

For the fourth time since 1908 *Aida* satisfied both a ceremonial and a practical function when it was chosen to open the season on December 22 and to introduce Ettore Panizza as conductor. Henderson gave him a better than passing grade in this examination for Italian conductors in Gatti's time, judging him to be "a fine musician with a keen comprehension of what would be telling in a theater." Rethberg, Martinelli, Olszewska, and Tibbett were all familiar figures greeted by an audience "cool and contemplative," though "richly attired and apparently unacquainted with the sinister word 'depression.' " The first Monday of the season falling on Christmas Eve, the opening was moved back to Saturday.

Those who had heard of Leider's annoyance at the engagement of Anny Konetzni could find little reason for it when the latter made her debut as Brünnhilde (d) in *Die Walküre* on December 26. An artist of experience— "perhaps more than was desirable," wrote Henderson—she sang powerfully but with rather frayed tones. Temperamentally, she was more prosaic than godlike. Althouse was the Siegmund, with Olszewska as Fricka and Schorr as Wotan. Konetzni contributed little of consequence to *Siegfried,* in which she sang Brünnhilde,* on the 28th, to *Tannhäuser* as Venus* (otherwise excellently cast with Lehmann, Melchior, Tibbett, and Hofmann), on January 1, to *Lohengrin* on January 5, as Ortrud.* She did sing an Isolde* on January 26, however, which conformed more closely to her reputation abroad. She sang with much greater freedom and tonal resource than previously, inquiry revealing that she was finally free of a cold that had impeded her work since her arrival. But this was a Saturday-night performance, and few accounts of it appeared in the press. Those which did had to do mostly with Pinza's well-vocalized Marke* and the able conducting of Riedel. Although Pinza could certainly have broadened his repertory in this direction, he decided against activity in a language (German) which he did not speak.

Conceivably Konetzni might have been granted a second chance had not the debut of Kirsten Flagstad on February 2 made other heroic sopranos something like excess baggage for the next half-dozen seasons. What Gatti had tried to do with Pons—introduce a singer of quality who would be a complete surprise to his public—he achieved completely with Flagstad. Although they had auditioned Flagstad together in St. Moritz during the summer, neither he nor Bodanzky had a clear notion of what they had stumbled on till her first rehearsal in the auditorium sent Bodanzky calling for "Mr. Gatti" to hear the prodigy.

It is hard to think of a singer of like importance whose Metropolitan career was so wholly fortuitous. Kahn had heard her (as Tosca) on a trip to Scandinavia in 1929, and had suggested that she was worth investigating. An inquiry through channels (Eric Simon, the Metropolitan's agent for European singers) roused little interest in Flagstad, and the matter lapsed. In the summer of 1932, Oscar Thompson, traveling to Oslo for *Musical America* was warned by the impresario that she was "no Larsen-Todsen," merely a local singer of small celebrity, prior to hearing her as Isolde. His enthusiastic support (qualified only by doubts about the size of her voice) recurred to Gatti when Leider's decision reached him. In the meantime, Flagstad had sung small parts in the Bayreuth Festival of 1933, and Gutrune and Sieglinde in 1934. She was, in fact, seriously considering retirement [1] when a letter arrived inviting her to the St. Moritz audition. When Flagstad had satisfied him that she was worth trying, Bodanzky sent her to George Szell in Prague for intensive coaching prior to her Metropolitan debut. (Nothing about Flagstad appears in Gatti's *Memories of the Opera,* which were finally [1941] published in the form in which he left them in 1933.)

The first act of this broadcast Walküre on February 2 began as Henderson put it, "in a calm, and ended in a storm of applause." Rarely had there been such unanimity in praise of a singer as Flagstad won for her Sieglinde (d). Henderson described her voice as "full-throated [with] richness, abundant power, and a scale that preserves its quality all the way up. It is a fresh, unworn and vigorous voice, showing no signs of wear." Gilman's highest praise was to say that it "recalled to wistful Wagnerites the irrecoverable magic of Olive the immortal." The Gilman audience did not need to be reminded that there was only one Olive, and her name was Fremstad. Downes gave voice to a universal feeling when he wrote: ". . . for once the Metropolitan has engaged a singer who is in her prime."

Any doubts that Flagstad's voice would suffice for the most arduous roles were resolved on February 6 when she was heard as Isolde.* "It is

---

[1] Her husband, as the world well knows from his wartime stigma as a Quisling-supporter, was a man of means.

long since the music . . . has been so well sung," wrote Henderson. "There were moments . . . such as the description of the glance . . . which had a depth of feeling quite beautiful." Gilman saw her Isolde as "a young woman of royal dignity and grace . . . one of the rarest, perhaps the rarest of our time." Drawn by the reports of her Sieglinde, an audience that filled seats and standing room was present. This continued to be an invariable rule for her appearances, suggesting that it was not Metropolitan opera that was depressed, but merely the attractions it offered. In succeeding weeks she sang the *Walküre* Brünnhilde* on February 15, the *Götterdämmerung* Brünnhilde* on the 28th, and Kundry* in *Parsifal* on April 17, with a security and ease that belied the incontrovertible evidence that she had not sung them on any stage before. The *Siegfried* Brünnhilde was announced for February 22, but she was, for a rarity, indisposed. Within the same period she also sang Elisabeth* in *Tannhäuser* on March 15 and Elsa* in *Lohengrin* three days later. Her Kundry was virtually learned in three weeks prior to its performance, for she had not studied the part seriously before.

Those with a mind for comparison found a subtle study in the coincidental appearance of such outstanding artists as Flagstad and Lehmann in common roles: Sieglinde, Elsa, and Elisabeth. The matchless intensity of Lehmann, her consummate underlining of dramatic detail, bring back pictures for every climax. Save for effects of great contrast—the superb repose of her Isolde or the radiant youthfulness of her early Brünnhildes— one *hears* the memory of Flagstad with eyes closed. Including appearances in Rochester and Boston, Flagstad sang twenty-three times during her first season. Not alone for sold-out houses, but also for the modest fee at which she had been engaged, Flagstad was a rich source of income to the company—a legacy that Gatti passed on to Johnson as he himself had inherited Caruso from Conried.

In the wake of *Elektra* and *Salome,* there was thought again of *Der Rosenkavalier,* dormant for five years. Its revival on January 4 had the best of possible reasons—Lehmann's Marschallin,* the Octavian* of Olszewska, and List's Ochs.* The rapport on the stage among these experienced collaborators was not communicated to the pit. In consequence, Lehmann's Marschallin was this time not what it was before and after: Henderson, on the exposed evidence, described it as "singularly cool and dispassionate, apparently well composed . . . but failing to emphasize the gentle pathos" in the role. The Kautsky scenery of 1922, deplored in 1935 as "shabby," was in use years later. On January 30 Kappel was a vocally creditable Marschallin,* a rather dowdy one in looks and dress.

Lehmann had an expectable success with her Elsa* on February 14 (though Bodanzky ill-served artistic ends by retiring after Act II to save himself for the next day's *Walküre,* Riedel finishing the *Lohengrin*), but a rather resounding failure with Tosca* on March 21. Felinity or suppleness was not in Lehmann's movements, though she sang some of the music compellingly. Crooks was unable to sing his scheduled Cavaradossi, and Martinelli replaced him. It was the occasion for Tibbett to succeed Scotti as the Metropolitan's prefect of police, a role he filled with lean efficiency, if not all the subtlety one can impart to Scarpia.* (The effect of costume and make-up which made him look like a dissipated George Washington was first apparent then.) Bellezza conducted a noisy playing of the score. A large audience came for another performance on March 28, but Lehmann being ill, Jacobo offered a conventional Tosca* in her place. This time the Cavaradossi was Jagel.

The stimulating effect of such artists as Flagstad and Lehmann was felt not only by the public, but also by Melchior, who reached a milestone when he sang his hundredth young Siegfried on February 22. Siegmund, Tristan, and Parsifal were more strongly his roles than ever before. Althouse was hardly an ideal complement to him as Walther* in *Die Meistersinger* on February 4, but he offered a satisfactory Tannhäuser* on February 23, with Ljungberg as Elisabeth* and Riedel conducting. Windheim was a new David* in *Die Meistersinger* this season, acting the part well on March 1, singing with a rather strained top register.

Gatti's final season would hardly have been complete without an American novelty, but it was hardly completed by John Laurence Seymour's *In the Pasha's Garden,* which was presented on January 24. A drab tale of a lover buried alive when he takes refuge in a box at the husband's approach, it lacked musical invention or theatrical power. Tibbett performed the Pasha* better than the part warranted, Jagel was a suitable Etienne,* and Helen Jepson made her debut as a likely-looking Helen (d) who had not much useful music to sing. Panizza conducted. As an economy, "projected scenery" devised by Frederick J. Kiesler was utilized for the first time at the Metropolitan, but it was a medium ill-suited to so conventional a score as Seymour's. The composer was present to receive a medal from the American Opera Society and to make a speech. The opera was given twice again, once with *Pagliacci,* and as part of a triple bill on February 13. On the later date Jepson sang an attractive Nedda.*

A final work and composer were added to Gatti's record on February 23 when Giovanni Pergolesi's delightful *La Serva Padrona* was beautifully served by Fleischer (Serpina*), D'Angelo (Uberto*), and Bada (Vespone*). Hardly less welcome was Donizetti's lively *Don Pasquale,* unheard for twenty years, when it was brought back as part of this double bill. Bori was the same superb Norina she had been when Toscanini conducted in 1914, Pinza was a memorable Don Pasquale,* Schipa a perfect voice for Ernesto,* and De Luca a fetching Malatesta.* Bellezza conducted the Pergolesi, Panizza the Donizetti. The attractive double décor marked the first work of Jonel Jorgulesco for the Metropolitan.

Judged by magnitude of reputation, more was expected from the pre-season announcement of appearances by Dino Borgioli, an established Italian tenor, than from the coming of Kirsten Flagstad, a Norwegian soprano. Borgioli came and went after making his debut as Rodolfo (d) on December 31 without leaving behind more than a dim impression of a well-schooled artist of dry voice and limited warmth. He did not shine as Ottavio* in *Don Giovanni* on January 18, and if his Des Grieux* in *Manon* on January 24 was more creditable, it was barely so. Also new were Kathryn Meisle, of long Chicago experience, who sang an unimpressive Amneris (d) in *Aida* on February 28; Myrtle Leonard, a younger mezzo of ample voice who sounded well as La Cieca (d) in *Gioconda* on March 23, and Mary Moore, a small-voiced soprano who sang excerpts from *Lucia* and *Rigoletto* without distinction in a Sunday-night concert on March 17.

The unexpected luster shed by Flagstad, the good things that were said about *La Serva Padrona* and *Don Pasquale, La Gioconda* with Ponselle, and the generally revitalized Wagner works made a picturesque sunset glow for Gatti's last season. Such clouds as a *Sonnambula* on March 2 for which Schipa and Pinza were indisposed and were replaced by Tedesco and Lazzari; an ill-sounding *Roméo* on January 26 with Norena, Hackett, De Luca, and Rothier all suffering vocal afflictions (Swarthout's Stephano was the listenable performance of the evening); or the Jacobo-Jagel-Tibbett *Tosca,* were either ignored or passed off as unimportant. The radio sponsorship was this year purchased by the Lambert Pharmacal Company, for the privilege of advertising Listerine. Geraldine Farrar was the intermission speaker, who added to her spoken remarks snatches of vocalized bits from the day's opera.

As money was once more a pressing concern, Gatti directed that the proceeds of a gala in his honor on March 19 be donated to a "Save the Metropolitan" fund. An audience that paid more than $15,000 heard excerpts from *Norma, Manon, Lucia, Pagliacci, Die Walküre,* and *Otello,* the last not given at the Metropolitan since 1913. Rethberg, Melchior, and Gandolfi were the singers of the Verdi music (Act IV), a fact later explained to me by the tenor as a direct request from Gatti. Always when Melchior's suitability for the part was brought up, Gatti would reply: "I have enough trouble with my Italian tenors as it is." When the gala was planned, Gatti rang up Melchior and asked: "Now that I don't have to worry about my other tenors any more, will you sing Otello for my personal pleasure?" Something of a sensation was created at a "Surprise Party" on March 31 when, in response to calls for the general manager to take a bow, a figure unmistakably Gatti's strode on the stage. Dramatically revealing himself to be, actually, Emanuel List in a perfect disguise, he waved the applause toward the box in which the unspeaking Gatti was seated. During the final broadcast of this season, on March 23, Gatti spoke a few words of farewell in barely understandable English.

The mechanism of selecting his successor has been described elsewhere. What no one could anticipate when Herbert Witherspoon, of long and varied experience in opera, was nominated for the post by the heavily committed Juilliard Foundation was that a successor for him would have to be found when he died a few weeks later, on May 10. Almost automatically the choice fell on Edward Johnson, who had been assigned to organize the following season's experimental spring season. Ironically, he had been Gatti's own first choice as his successor. Shortly after, an Opera Management Committee composed of John Erskine, Lucrezia Bori, Cornelius Bliss, and Allen Wardwell (also of the Juilliard group) was appointed to work with Johnson, whose chief aides remained Gatti's: Edward Ziegler and Earle Lewis. Bori was also made a director of the Association, the first active singer to be honored in this manner.

After a brief tour to Boston and Rochester, a post-season *Tristan* and two performances of *Parsifal* (the last three with Flagstad) brought to an end the long era that had begun in 1908. The loss for this year was substantially less than it had been, but still substantial—$230,538.

In this transitional period the first prospect of city assistance to the Metropolitan appeared when Mayor Fiorello La Guardia—a long-time subscriber to the opera—directed a survey to be made of ways in which the theater and studio space could be utilized as a municipal art center. He conceived of a longer season at lower prices, with the adjacent areas serving as a municipal high school of music. Whatever other problems were encountered, an insurmountable one was the division of control between ownership and operating factions. Eventually the La Guardia ends were accomplished by the establishment of the Municipal High School of Music and Art, and the fostering of the City Center, on West Fifty-fifth Street, leaving the Metropolitan to work out its own means of survival.

Mention, in the next season's prospectus, of a spring season made persons familiar with the auditorium wonder how its notorious lack of ventilation would be combated. The announcement of further renovations to be undertaken by the Opera and Real Estate Company (see page 31) offered little encouragement for those wishing for the all-important air-conditioning system. Two hundred thousand dollars were allocated for an air-*circulating* system, which merely drew outside air of prevailing temperature into the theater.

Amid a flurry of engagements and eliminations (when Flagstad returned to Europe in April, she possessed the only signed contract then negotiated for the next season) Johnson made an announcement of unsuspected importance in August. It stated that a Metropolitan Opera Guild had been formed to stimulate subscription sales and promote interest in the opera. One may regret the necessity that called it into existence, also some dubious influences it exerted in the years to come; but it has accomplished sound public service as instituted and still administered by Mrs. August Belmont, president emeritus in 1966. Her original associates were Mrs. Myron C. Taylor, vice-chairman; Mrs. Herbert Witherspoon, secretary; and Harvey Gibson, treasurer. From a membership of 2,000 in December 1935, the Guild grew to a nation-wide entity of more than 60,000 in 1966.

EPILOGUE

Scrutiny of the whole Gatti period leads inevitably to the conclusion that it was pivotal in one particular aspect of Metropolitan history. When he arrived in 1908, the hand of society was still heavy on the functioning of the Metropolitan. What pleased the Monday-night audience—whether it was *Armide* or *L'Amore dei tre re*—survived; what did not was put aside. To some extent it was "who" as well as "what."

Many things previously unacceptable were done for the betterment of the institution by Gatti and Toscanini, negative and positive in the electrical sense, polar in temperament and action, yet complementary to each other. Within a relatively short time (1908–15), the atmosphere of the Metropolitan was changed and clarified.

For reasons clearly discernible, an economic domination replaced the social one. Kahn's place in this (see page 257) was that of a monarch, but a limited one. He had every power but that of leadership. So long as he obeyed the rules, the ownership faction was quite content that he amuse them, even, on occasions, uplift them. If what was tendered was just plain dull, it disappeared soon enough anyway.

Around a nuclear core of Wagner, Verdi, and Puccini—the Father, Son, and Holy Ghost of Metropolitan orthodoxy—Gatti spun a pattern intricate, diverting, ear-filling, and profitable. When the economic system on which it was based gave way, it followed suit, magnetically, inevitably.

To those who held the critical mirror, the Metropolitan was essentially an entertainment and a diversion in this period. On occasions, the conditions that make opera an art were created by thought, planning, and rehearsal; they occurred repeatedly, let us say, rather than often. On more numerous occasions (still a minor fraction of the whole), a dominating artistic personality—a Farrar, Caruso, Chaliapin, Hempel, Lehmann, Pinza, or Flagstad—by sheer personal force made light where, the night, day, or week before, there had been darkness. For the rest, the opera-mill ground out performance after performance, some fine, some coarse, and most without real distinction.

With the depression came the realization, in slackened support and lessened attendance, that opera could not endure on the patronage of those who supported it by habit rather than volition. Soon enough the most firmly grounded habit—payment on the assessment for boxes— would be uprooted. The roots, it was already evident, would have to be transplanted into a deeper, more fertile soil—the affections of those who valued the Metropolitan as a home of opera rather than of social display.

Long before, with Toscanini's spade work, Gatti had demonstrated how a first-rank opera house should operate. The singers were in large part as good as the world provided; the staging was of the moment; the orchestra compared favorably with the best in Europe. Save for habitual neglect of the French school, the repertory was admirably balanced. Even Russian opera was investigated, if Italianized.

The downward steps are easily recognizable. Toscanini's authority was not replaced; his abilities could not be. The day-by-day and year-by-year struggle against the disadvantages of the auditorium were valiantly carried on even when trends elsewhere, in the postwar era, gave a look of hopeless antiquity to the Metropolitan stage. When the promises of a new theater proved vain, the effect on the morale of those in responsible positions must have been catastrophic. I do not read their minds, but only the results. When the depression set in, the crushing weight of self-interest encountered no solid resistance in practice, tradition, or mere pride, to resist it.

Thus, the money consumed in paying off losses left little but receipts for services, nothing durable in goods, not even the asset of good will. To each successive administration the unworkable stage and its insatiable appetite for human labor were a foe more formidable than any human adversary. It was a sheer miracle that neglect and overuse of the stage machinery did not result in a fatal accident.

By the promise of a new house, also, much necessary replacement of scenery was held in abeyance. That was true not only of the oft-mentioned *Ring,* but also, as the 1920's passed into history, of such standard works as *La Bohème* and *Tosca, Faust, Il Barbiere,* and *Lohengrin.* While the bright new sets for *Jenufa* or *Don Quichotte* or *La Campana sommersa* were rotting in the warehouse, the old tattered ones of *Aida* and *Die Meistersinger* were being exhibited on the Metropolitan stage the necessary six or eight times a season.

The expansion of the repertory to include as many as forty-nine works in a single season put a perilous price on the all too human flesh. Assuming that Europe, in the main, and America, in the little, could produce the personnel qualified to fit into this scheme, New York could not possibly provide the rehearsal time to make the scheme fit the personnel. The system of "half-season" engagements doubtless had its economic justification, but it left the company dangerously shorthanded at best, and subject to the whims of "indispensable" singers at worst. It also led to the "now and then" arrangements that eventually put the management, in Johnson's time, at the disposal of the artists, rather than vice versa.

A summary of the novelties produced during Gatti's time shows a total of 110 works not given previously. Of these, no less than 53, or nearly fifty per cent, were heard in only a single season; 27 were heard in only two seasons. Thus, well over two-thirds of the novelties of this period were failures, at least economically. Variety, one would think, could have been blended with more discrimination.

As well as consuming funds, which for a while were replaceable, the novelties consumed time, which was not. Hence the paradox of the period: what was least worth doing was done well; what was most worth doing was done indifferently. At some point before bad times curbed Gatti's questing spirit, this should have become evident to him. But it did not.

In certain large aspects Gatti and Kahn (to credit the good to those blamed for the bad) established standards that have become traditional. The progress toward internationalism that began with Grau and continued with Conried reached its zenith in these twenty-seven years. The rule of the house that the language of creation should prevail wherever feasible wavered on occasion, but the principle was never disputed. The chorus and ballet reached commendable heights, and for a time the orchestra was excellent. Good designers did good work till the house's old-fashioned facilities rendered them helpless to compete with more modern stages. The smoothly running machine sometimes purred more evenly than the product it turned out.

One contention frequently directed against Gatti must be refuted. The American singer was rarely at a loss for a hearing and, if ability warranted, an engagement. Prudence, if nothing else, made the success story of Talley as appealing as that of Farrar, even if one was as synthetic as the other was genuine. Mention has been made of a number of Americans who reached the Metropolitan only after rather weary demonstration of their abilities elsewhere—John Charles Thomas, Crooks, Bonelli, and others. The number of these was no greater than the number of foreign artists whose engagement was similarly tardy or never consummated.

Whether, under other circumstances, Gatti-Casazza would have acted other than as he did is speculation, not history. By accepting numerous renewals of contract he demonstrated general contentment with his position and the results he achieved. By granting him such renewals his employers unmistakably signed their approval of his actions. Both would be more gratefully remembered had they cherished quality as dearly as quantity.

THE JOHNSON PERIOD, 1935–1950

The way point in history that found Edward Johnson general manager of the Metropolitan on May 16, 1935, invites comparisons with other occasions when such transitions took place. Conried, as successor to Grau, had his own company of financial underwriters who reckoned that desirable social prestige could be achieved while making a profit on their investment. Gatti, as successor to Conried, had a two-year struggle with Dippel and a slightly longer one with Hammerstein before a clear path opened. His backers no longer expected to make money, but in showing that he could manipulate a vastly expanded repertory without losing money, Gatti managed to make a good deal.

It must be apparent at once that Johnson embarked with no such free hand as Gatti was guaranteed by Kahn and eventually received. With Edward Ziegler as his senior counselor, the problem was, largely, how to adapt the well-tried Gatti scheme to the new conditions stipulated by the Juilliard Foundation, with its stress on a budget that would have "a promise of breaking even" and additional opportunities for American singers. The latter was broken down to include the spring-season trials for singers not ready for immediate acceptance as members of the Metropolitan. Eventually it became clear that this function could better be served in another way and another place—The New York City Center.

The ceiling of $1,000 per performance per artist that was adopted to meet the needs of a balanced budget served its main purpose well for a while, if with some unexpected consequences. An immediate one was to deprive the theater of a few (a very few) performers it might have desired. A more subtle one was to concentrate attention on singers of limited celebrity or less mature abilities who would accept a small performance fee (or a weekly salary covering several appearances) in exchange for Metropolitan prestige. Most insidious of all consequences was the relaxation of control over the singers' uncommitted time on the (unspoken) theory: "We're not paying them much anyway."

Add to these circumstances affecting the singing personnel of the Metropolitan the knotty problems posed by the increasing pressure from the unionized factions, and it becomes evident that conducting such an enterprise was becoming as much a study in labor-management relations as it was a struggle for artistic achievement. Add to these backstage factors the menacing developments affecting the real estate occupied by the theater, the taxes it would or would not pay, the storage space it needed or had to make shift without, and the multiplicity of problems the Metropolitan management had to contend with in this period, and those of the past look like child's play.

1935–1936

In more than a figurative sense, the *Traviata* that opened Edward Johnson's first season on December 16 found him carrying on where his predecessor had left off. The principals were Bori, Crooks (Alfredo), and Tibbett, as they might have been in any week of the season before, and the conductor was Panizza. The experiment with the American Ballet, of which George Balanchine was ballet master, began well. Marking a start toward a brave new operatic world was bright if somewhat garish scenery by Jonel Jorgulesco. The staging was better integrated than had recently been customary, and a few new faces in the orchestra (a wholesale revision had been forbidden by the union) made some difference in the sound. A secondary singer, Thelma Votipka, began a career, as Flora, (d) which long outlasted the director's own.

Johnson had, in a sense, taken his oath of office when he said: "Opera depends for its prosperity on Verdi, Wagner, and Puccini." The sequence was honored with a performance of *Die Walküre* on December 18, in which Marjorie Lawrence made her debut as Brünnhilde (d), Meisle sang Fricka,* and Melchior, Rethberg, Schorr, and List carried their usual burdens with credit. Jorgulesco, who had also been commissioned to redesign this work, produced settings of rather commercialized "modernism" that stimulated the eye rather than satisfying it.

The fresh young voice of Lawrence, her vital personality, and her varied background were generally admired in her work of this season. It was a rather bright sound she produced as Ortrud* in *Lohengrin* on December 21, but she showed fine promise as the *Siegfried* Brünnhilde* on January 3 and climaxed a strongly sung Brünnhilde* in *Götterdämmerung* on January 11 by swinging herself to the back of Grane at the end of the Immolation and riding briskly off stage. By the new, exalted standard of Flagstad, some of this was harsh, strident singing, but Lawrence's dramatically poised Rachel* in *La Juive* on January 20 showed the value of several years spent at the Paris Opéra. Also it promised that she could efficiently bestride two repertories while singing such Wagner roles as Flagstad, Rethberg, or Lehmann did not. On the whole, her Rachel was the most even accomplishment of this *La Juive,* for Martinelli's voice had taken on the monotonous coloration that marred the late years of his career, and Cardinal Brogni was not one of Pinza's notable roles. Pelletier conducted.

Two of the younger Americans who had sung with notable success abroad (both Juilliard-trained) were welcomed to the company by Johnson. For Dusolina Giannini, who had attracted attention as long before as March 14, 1923, as a substitute for Anna Case at a Schola Cantorum concert, her debut as Aida (d) on February 12 was almost too late. The bloom was off her voice, and it had both edge and quaver, but she sang with a vitality and pungence that Henderson commended for "the true Verdian grand manner." Martinelli, Tibbett, and Bampton (Amneris) were able associates, with Chase Baromeo as Ramfis. February 26 was assigned for a revival of *Norma* with Giannini, but the announcement was withdrawn without explanation. The common belief is that she could not agree, in rehearsals, with Panizza. *Norma* was given while Giannini was in the company, but she never sang it.

The younger talent of Charles Kullmann had been soundly developed in several German opera houses prior to his Metropolitan appearance, but that hardly argued his suitability for Faust (d) as a debut role on December 19. Edith Mason, absent since 1917, sang Marguerite,* Helen Oelheim was Siébel (d), and Pinza was Méphistophélès. Evaluating this cast, Henderson confessed: "Many years ago this commentator made a German joke about *Faust.* Today *Faust* is no joke." Kullmann's musicianship and good bearing were qualities to value in his Alfredo, the Duke in *Rigoletto,* José, and Rodolfo, but a lack of brilliance in his voice and a feeling that he was always singing at full power to make himself heard made him a dubious asset in such virtuoso parts. Walther von Stolzing or Hans in *Die verkaufte Braut* was something else.

Both Giannini and Kullmann measured up (if only by courtesy) to what was considered a "Metropolitan standard," but the debut of Susanne Fisher as Butterfly (d) on December 26 was another matter. Although she was by no means the least qualified young American of the many to come, Henderson's comment has an inclusiveness worth noting: "It is necessary to keep in mind the radically changed character of the Metropolitan. . . . There was a time when a debut in this theater meant the climax of a career developed upon steadily growing artistic success. . . . Hereafter a few such artists will be heard, while young Americans will be brought forward and permitted to begin their careers on the stage of 'the greatest opera in the world.' "

In this framework, Henderson thought Fisher an "interesting" singer, though light of voice and without power for the climaxes. She later sang Marguerite, Micaëla, and Manon with rather pretty sound, but without notable temperament. Of slighter stature, if more assertiveness, was Josephine Antoine, a direct accession from Juilliard, who had not only "the freedom of the Metropolitan stage," as Henderson put it, at her debut as Philine (d) in *Mignon* on January 4 but also, via radio, the freedom of the air. Bori, Crooks, and Pinza (Lothario*) also participated. Neither Antoine's Gilda nor her Rosina, when it came, was a strong argument in her favor. As Gilda,* Antoine had the staunch support of Tibbett and John Charles Thomas, both of whom sang Rigoletto* for the first time this season, but she lacked such elementary acting skills as listening when her father sang to her and making her betrayal plausible. Tibbett's height made his hunchback a rather grotesque figure when he sang the part on December 28, but it was a remarkably virile conception. Thomas's turn came on March 9, when he showed his training at the Monnaie in Brussels with a beautifully studied, completely integrated characterization.

Also from Juilliard was Julius Huehn, a heavy-voiced, well-built singer whose debut on December 21 as the Herald (d) in *Lohengrin* was followed by good, if immature service as Kothner, Donner in *Das Rheingold*, Sharpless in *Butterfly,* and even Escamillo and Kurvenal. Huehn was on the high road to a notable career when war service intervened, and his voice was never the same thereafter. A brief span of notoriety accrued to Joseph Bentonelli (an American, born Benton) who sang Des Grieux (d) in *Manon* on January 10 when Crooks was ill. According to the Metropolitan's publicity director (Frank Wenker, after William Guard's death in 1932), Bentonelli walked into the theater in search of an audition, was asked if he knew Des Grieux, and was immediately engaged. Even by the standards of the time, that was lax administrative work. His slight voice and intimate manner scarcely did their part to sustain the headlines that recorded his debut, though he was sincere enough in his musicianship. Rinuccio in *Gianni Schicchi* and Pinkerton in *Madama Butterfly* were other roles Bentonelli sang in this and the next season before quietly fading from view.

The return of Flagstad for virtually a full season's service brought with it such feats as an introductory Isolde on December 30 and an Elisabeth in *Tannhäuser* forty-eight hours later, as well as the promise of her first appearance as Leonore* in *Fidelio* on March 7. Challenging as this accomplishment was, it had the unhappy consequence of eliminating the Metropolitan as the scene of Lehmann's fine Leonore (see page 336). As the senior singer in service, Lehmann felt that she was entitled to preference in a part so long associated with her; she rather peevishly refused to sing it afterward. Johnson acknowledged this to be the case, though doubting that Lehmann could still sing the exacting *"Abscheulicher."* The answer is: she never could (with ease) and was still a superb Leonore.

Flagstad certainly could sing *"Abscheulicher."* If she did not act, feel, and live the role as Lehmann did, she sang it cleanly, honestly, even brilliantly, though Henderson noted: "The heroic Leonore of tradition . . . yielded her place . . . to a very dignified, gentle and sympathetic young woman, manifestly glad that she was not obliged to pull the trigger." Gilman termed her singing of the music "at all times nobly beautiful . . . in a great tradition of simplicity and subtlety." René Maison was the excellent Florestan,* with List (Rocco*), Huehn (Minister of Justice*), Hofmann (Pizarro*), and Fleischer responsive to Bodanzky's direction. Bodanzky's recitatives, the Mahler disposition of the overtures, and the Urban scenery were used.

Thanks perhaps to his Belgian birth, Maison had the rather rare trait of equal aptitude in French and German roles. He made a commendable debut as Walther (d) in *Die Meistersinger* on February 3, and was later heard as Loge, José, and Lohengrin, parts that he filled with Slezak-like physical size. The original luster of his voice was well worn when he came to New York, but he is well remembered for sound musicianship and, as Julien in *Louise* (see page 413), for strong characterization.

References to Kullmann and Maison as Don José (Martinelli was another) indicate this as the season in which Rosa Ponselle reached the climax—more accurately, perhaps, the *dénouement*—of her career by singing Carmen* on December 27. Much was made of the long study she had devoted to the part, but the kind of striving for effect that marred her Violetta was even more conspicuous in her Carmen. Said Downes: "We have never heard Miss Ponselle sing so badly, and we have seldom seen the part enacted in such an artificial and generally unconvincing manner." Paul Bekker (the German operatic authority serving as critic for the *Staats-Zeitung*), referring to stories of the French authorities Ponselle had consulted, said that she had overlooked "only the most important one—Georges Bizet."

With Ponselle singing erratically and distorting the drama by overacting, the principal memories of this *Carmen* were balletic—her own carefully contrived dancing in Act II, and the splendid farandole designed by Balanchine for Act IV. It was a highlight of this brilliant choreographer's work at the Metropolitan. (His invention was never at fault, though it often warred with the staid surroundings.) Martinelli, Hilda Burke (Micaëla [d]), and Pinza were the other principals, Hasselmans conducting. Urban's old production was used. Ponselle sang no other role this season, and few others from then on. Her indisposition on January 16 was the cause of bilingual opera returning for a night, for the only available substitute was Gertrude Wettergren, who knew the part of Carmen* only in Swedish. While kicking off a shoe and knocking hats from soldiers' heads, Wettergren sang with little distinction. She was better employed as Amneris, the role of her debut on December 20, with Martinelli, Rethberg, and Thomas (Amonasro*). Neither as Brangäne nor as Venus in *Tannhäuser* did Wettergren have the kind of commanding voice required, though she was no small personality on the stage.

While these oddities were being offered as "interpretations" of *Carmen*, the best voice New York knew for this part in the thirties joined the company, but not as Carmen. Bruna Castagna doubtless erred in coming to New York first to sing in popular-priced opera at the Hippodrome (a huge theater at Forty-fourth Street and Sixth Avenue, now demolished), for the management had secret doubts that people would pay six dollars to hear a singer they had formerly heard for two. (To singers they had previously heard in student opera for nothing, such as Antoine and Huehn, the reasoning did not apply.) Castagna's Amneris (d), however, was richly sung on March 2, as were her Maddalena in *Rigoletto* and Santuzza. A comely if plump woman, Castagna refined her ways as her Metropolitan career progressed, especially in more discreet use of chest tone. When she sang Carmen for a three-dollar top in the spring season (see page 396), some might have wondered why they had paid six dollars in the same theater for Ponselle or Wettergren.

The wise choice between a long career and an overlong career was made by Bori as this season was in progress, and she sang her last on March 29, at a gala in which virtually all the principal artists took part. She was heard in Act II of *La Traviata* and the Saint-Sulpice scene from *Manon*. On her behalf, Johnson restored *La Rondine* for a series of performances beginning on January 17, with Martini (Ruggero*), Windheim (the Poet*), and Fleischer. She had the honor of opening the last season in which she took part (see page 390), and later sang Mimi, Mignon, and Manon. When her appearances came close together, the strain on the voice resulted in sharp tone and flat pitch that suggested the reasons for her retirement. A sentimental plan to present her in a farewell *Pelléas* with Johnson fell through when she pleaded ill health in March. She recovered to sing *La Rondine* on the final broadcast, March 21, and did not fail her avowed intention to work unceasingly for the Metropolitan until her death in 1960.

The minor works of Puccini were also represented in this season by *Gianni Schicchi* done for the first time in an English translation (Percy Pitt's) on January 27. The experiment hardly had a fair chance to succeed, for Tibbett's Schicchi* was grossly overdone and his efforts to articulate rather distorted the musical line. Bentonelli (Rinuccio*) and Burke (Lauretta*) performed clearly enough, but Bourskaya's La Vecchia was syllabic hash, and the ensembles left one uncertain what tongue was being used. Gennaro Papi, who returned with Johnson, conducted.

The Wagner cycle was retained at normal length, and an evening *Ring* cycle added to satisfy the demand from those who could not spare afternoons. Flagstad, however, sang only the *Götterdämmerung* Brünnhilde in this sequence, on March 21. On February 29, Florence Easton reappeared in *Die Walküre* to sing a Brünnhilde described by Noel Straus in the *Times* as "a sympathetic and affecting interpretation, which had thrilling dramatic force." She did not sing at the Metropolitan again. The casting of the *Ring* was varied by the addition to the company of Eduard Habich, a Bayreuth veteran who succeeded to the roles formerly sung by Schützendorf, beginning with Peter (d) in *Hänsel und Gretel* on December 20. His routine was evident, as was a dry, unlikable voice that did not make for interest in his Telramund, Alberich, Kurvenal, or Klingsor. As Beckmesser he revived a crotchety, overdrawn impersonation of the clerk which brought back old, but not good, days. A different kind of contribution was made by Leopold Sachse, engaged to mend the ways in which Wagner dramas had recently been staged at the Metropolitan. Order was certainly preferable to disorder, but Sachse gave earnest Wagnerians an unhappy moment by bringing Melot aboard ship with the welcoming party for Isolde at the end of Act I of *Tristan*. Eventually the "innovation" disappeared as mysteriously as it had come.

The extremes of this season were seven performances each of *Tristan* and *Carmen,* one each of *Cavalleria* and *Tosca* (in which Crooks was Cavaradossi,* with Lehmann and Tibbett, and George Cehanovsky played the fugitive Angelotti in Act I, and his own pursuer, Sciarrone, in Act II); there was none of *Don Giovanni* or *Die Zauberflöte.* Grace Moore was a member of the company briefly, returning after her first film triumphs to sing Mimi on March 14. The attendance was not remarkably large, but a sizable portion of it gathered at the stage door to cheer the soprano's departure. A new saga of heroine-worship was in the making.

FIRST SPRING SEASON

As planning was the weakest aspect of post-Gattian operation of the Metropolitan, it is scarcely surprising that the first spring season gave little evidence of precise objectives. First announced for two weeks beginning on May 11, the season was extended to four. Avowedly undertaken to promote young American talent, it was utilized to give an English-language version of *Die verkaufte Braut* and a sung and danced treatment of Gluck's *Orfeo*. Both had virtue, but not of the sort promised in the season's plans.

The standard of excellence established with the opening performance of *Carmen* had much more to do with the tested Carmen of Castagna and the polished José of Tokatyan than with the *petit-point* Micaëla of Natalie Bodanskaya. A smaller orchestra than usual was employed, and Papi conducted. The house was about sold out at a top price of three dollars. In *Rigoletto,* on May 13, Carlo Morelli and Bentonelli (the Duke) were experienced performers, Emily Hardy (Gilda), Norman Cordon (Monterone), Anna Kaskas (Maddalena), and John Gurney (Sparafucile) in the fledgling class. All save Hardy were passed on to the winter company.

The lively production of *The Bartered Bride* on May 15 had an unexpectedly able Marie in Muriel Dickson, of the D'Oyly Carte Company. Mario Chamlee sang Hans, and Louis d'Angelo was a broadly comic Kezal. George Rasely was well suited to Wenzel. In addition to Kaskas, Gurney, Cordon, and Bodanskaya, as mentioned, Wilfred Engelman and Lucielle Browning of this cast had careers as secondary singers with the winter company. The translation, credited to "Graham Jones," was the work of Madeleine Marshall. It was singable and decidedly gaggy.

A rather obvious contretemps in the polka was later revealed by Lincoln Kirstein (in a brochure entitled *Blast at Ballet*) to have resulted from uncoordinated rehearsals and a Bodanzky cut in the score. None knew this at the time, nor was it known that the highly stylized *Orfeo* (directed by Balanchine, with a décor designed by Paul Tchelitchev), seen on May 22, conceived Hell as a concentration camp, the Elysian Fields as "an ether dream," and Paradise "the Eternity we know from a Planetarium." Lew Christensen (Orfeo), Daphne Vane (Eurydice), and William Dollar (Amor) were the dancers, with the voices of Kaskas (Orfeo), Jeanne Pengelly (Eurydice), and Maxine Stellman (Amor) coming from the pit.

Richard Hageman conducted. It was given once with *Pagliacci,* once with *Cavalleria.* Part of the cost was met by Edward Warburg.

Of the other new singers offered, the most ability was displayed by Rosa Tentoni, who sang Aida and Santuzza convincingly but had no notable Metropolitan history. Joseph Royer, Nicholas Massue, Sydney Rayner, and Arthur Carron also had leading roles. Following Carron's debut as Canio in a performance of *Pagliacci* on May 29, the Metropolitan devoted considerable time and effort to transforming him into a German tenor. (Carron was English, a protégé of Easton's.) The results never justified the effort.

If there was one positive lesson learned from this season, it was the unsuitability of the theater for warm-weather use. As early as May 13 a balmy spring night left the interior far too sultry for comfortable listening to *Rigoletto,* and numerous evenings later on were depressingly soggy for *Orfeo* and *Aida.*

Economically, the season fared not too badly, the loss of $16,331 being absorbed in the pre-season financing by the Juilliard Foundation. Likewise, the regular season was successful in not exceeding its budgeted loss. From the previous season's low income of $1,090,700, the upward turn had brought an additional $140,000 to the box office. With important reductions in expenditures and limited ventures with new productions (*La Traviata* and *Die Walküre*), the situation could be described as stabilized.

1936–1937

In the organization of the first season planned by Johnson, the shape of some future trends of his direction began to emerge. Reorganization of the orchestra went forward at the measured pace decreed by the union, in which no more than one player at a desk (the pairing arrangement in an orchestra) could be changed in a season. This actually retarded the desired end, facilitating replacement of strings—where it was least necessary—impeding changes in the woodwinds and brass, where it was most necessary.

The retirement of Bori, the gradual withdrawal of Ponselle, the need for a strong-voiced mezzo (Olszewska was no longer in the company), the desirability of an alternate for Bodanzky, all brought changes in personnel. But the career of longest duration was initiated by one who neither sang nor played. This was Herbert Graf, who came to the Metropolitan with a curiously mixed reputation as a stage director—experimentation in Frankfurt and Philadelphia where he had collaborated in a memorable series in 1934), traditionalism in Salzburg as associate with Toscanini in the staging of *Die Meistersinger*. On the whole, the traditionalist in Graf predominated during his Metropolitan career, certainly at its beginning with *Samson et Dalila* on December 26. The immemorial problem of animating this work, planned as an oratorio, was solved better by Graf than by most of his predecessors, Henderson commending the staging of Act I as "one of the most memorable achievements of the Metropolitan." Wettergren was an interesting but small-voiced Dalila,* Maison a physically imposing Samson,* Pinza a High Priest* of imposing size if rather rough French style. Maurice de Abravanel made his debut as conductor, leading vigorously, if with scant subtlety.

A limited acquaintance with the peculiarities of the auditorium might have excused this first rude demonstration, but Abravanel's direction of *Lakmé, Lohengrin, Les Contes d'Hoffmann, Manon,* and *Tannhäuser* was much the same. Considering his later career on Broadway and elsewhere, the judgment must be that Abravanel (he dispensed with the prefix "de" a few years later) came to the Metropolitan prematurely. Certainly a more experienced man, such as Alexander Smallens, would have been more useful at this time.

Graf and Abravanel shared a common task on January 14 when *Les Contes d'Hoffmann* was revived, this time for the exhibition of Tibbett, in the Renaud manner, as Lindorf,* Coppelius,* Dappertutto,* and Dr. Miracle.* An inclination to sneering laughter and stagy postures made much of Tibbett's work an embarrassment to observe, and Graf's addiction to the trapdoors in the Metropolitan stage (its only mechanical resource) tended to the ludicrous rather than the effective. The cast was otherwise poorish, with Stella Andreva a thin-voiced Doll (d) in her debut, Irra Petina a nondescript Nicklausse,* Sydney Rayner unappealing as Hoffmann,* and Halstead a thick-sounding Giulietta.* Matters improved when Bovy sang Antonia*, Olympia,* and Giulietta* on January 23, with Maison an excellent Hoffmann.* Still better, on February 8, were Jepson as Giulietta* and Norena as Antonia,* but Rayner reappeared here. On all occasions Abravanel conducted with a vigor befitting *Der fliegende Holländer,* but little alleviating nuance.

The comparison occurs, perhaps, because the Wagner score was again presented on January 7, with Flagstad a notably fine Senta.* In Henderson's opinion, her impersonation shone "with a refulgence quite as brilliant, but more melting" than in more heroic roles. Her treatment of the Ballad was "perhaps the most dramatic the Metropolitan stage has known." With Schorr a moving voice for the Dutchman, and List a strong one for Daland,* Bodanzky had the nucleus of a fine ensemble. Kerstin Thorborg was an uncommonly good Mary,* and when Maison sang Erik* (on January 27) the part was in better balance with the other voices of the cast than it had been with Kullmann. Leopold Sachse managed the staging well enough, save that the ships did not move in Act I, and the heavenly ascent of Senta and the Dutchman was left to the imagination.

This superb accomplishment by Flagstad was a harmonious part of a season that opened with her Brünnhilde in *Die Walküre* on December 21 and extended through a Kundry in *Parsifal* on March 25. Flagstad's repute, coupled with an opening, brought a very large audience to the theater, though the early curtain and the late arrival of the well-dressed customers made a mockery of attention to Act I. Kerstin Thorborg made an admired debut as Fricka (d),* performing in splendid style, though her vocal quality was brighter than the role requires. The resemblance of first names inclined some to think of Flagstad and Thorborg as fellow countrywomen; but Kirsten bespeaks the Norse, Kerstin the Swede.

December 23, 1936, may stand as an occasion to mark an epoch in terms of *Tristan,* reminiscent of the Lilli Lehmann, De Reszke, and Schalk performance of 1899, and the Fremstad-Knote-Mahler performance of 1908. It was now Henderson's judgment that Flagstad's first act "rose to heights . . . not surpassed at the Metropolitan," and Melchoir's Tristan received the final accolade: it was "the best the Metropolitan had known since Jean de Reszke." Thorborg's finely drawn Brangäne* and List's Marke were also in the frame of the major figures, Huehn's Kurvenal definitely outside it. Bodanzky's conducting was notable for the "opulent sonority" he drew from the restaffed orchestra, at last on the way to musical respectability.

This being the fiftieth year since New York had first heard *Tristan* on December 1, 1886, Henderson was prompted to print a summary and comparison of the notable past Isoldes in terms of the reigning Flagstad. Lilli Lehmann ranked as the most powerfully tragic figure, "crushing in the Liebestod"; Fremstad as the most winning and womanly; Nordica as the one who had sung the music with the greatest nuance and subtlety. Historically, she was his parallel for Flagstad, a vocal accomplishment "beautiful in tonal quality, in sustained and exquisitely molded phrasing, and nobility of style." Ternina, Gadski, Kurt, Matzenauer, and Leider were also given prominent rank, with Kappel's characterization remembered as "well-drawn, tender, lovable." For obvious reasons, *Tristan* was the most performed work of this year's repertory. It was heard eight times.

The German personnel was altered this season by the appearance of Karl Laufkötter, who made his debut as the Shepherd (d) in the first *Tristan,* and sang Mime, David, and other roles capably; of Irene Jessner, who began a long career of varied service as Hänsel (d) on December 24; and of Gertrude Rünger, a commonplace soprano (formerly an able mezzo) whose debut as the *Walküre* Brünnhilde (d) on February 3 showed an inadequate range and rather cumbersome movement. Rünger later sang the Fricka* of *Das Rheingold* and Ortrud* in *Lohengrin* with more assurance, but she did not linger. Jessner, however, was a musicianly, hard-working artist who might have had a more prominent career had she been more magnetic on stage.

Flagstad sang all the Brünnhildes in the *Ring* cycle that began on February 9, with Melchior as Siegmund and Siegfried. For her *Siegfried* Brünnhilde* on January 22 (she had sung it during the San Francisco season, in 1935, after missing her first scheduled Metropolitan appearance the previous spring), Henderson had words of limitless praise: "One of the most flawless pieces of pure vocal technic ever heard. . . . No other singer except Melba ever equaled it in liberation of voice, in the utter freedom from all constraint of production and articulation." The oddity that the comparison should be aroused by the very role Melba could *not* sing would interest disciples of Sigmund Freud.

This year's *Meistersinger* performances profited from the vibrant Eva of Lehmann and the youthful, well-phrased Walther von Stolzing* of Kullmann. The latter's rather unforceful sound suffered in the ensembles when he sang the part first on February 12, but it was otherwise a welcome acquaintance. Laufkötter was a conventional David.* Huehn's career expanded with ventures as Telramund and Gunther, both well prepared vocally but shadowy in dramatic detail.

Although neither Bidú Sayão nor John Brownlee came with the *réclame* of a hundred other singers who followed them, both asserted themselves to be the kind of personalities who generate artistic projects rather than merely filling a place in a cast. No one who heard Sayão at a Town Hall recital at this time or even in a performance of *La Demoiselle élue* with Toscanini would venture the guess that she would be long heard in the Metropolitan. But the neatness of detail in her Manon (d) on February 13 and its appealing warmth were merged in a theatrical creation by no means common. Moreover the well-floated sound asserted, again, that purity rather than mass is the touchstone of audibility. No one could say much for the supporting cast of Rayner (Des Grieux*), Baromeo (Comte des Grieux), and Bonelli, or the conducting of Abravanel. Sayão sang Violetta and Mimi this season with credit, though it took some time for the conductors to realize what she could and could not do and to approach the problem accordingly.

Brownlee's art involved something of the same limitation of power, compromised by his introduction on February 17 as Rigoletto (d), a role he seldom sang thereafter and never to advantage. He was admired for intelligent artistry, not for a dry sound and a small one too. As Ashton or Germont, Brownlee was merely another baritone. That character roles were his forte was emphasized by a Lescaut* in *Manon* on March 11 (with Sayão and Maison and by a beautifully dramatized Marcello* in *La Bohème* on March 12. It was the revival of Mozart in the next year or two that gave the measure of Brownlee's worth.

The twenty-year career of Rosa Ponselle came to a double bar on February 15, with no other public emotion than uncertainty whether there would be an eventual *da capo*. Before the season she had become the wife of Carle A. Jackson, of Baltimore, and she was expected to retire, at least temporarily. Her vocal condition was not of the best, but some modifications were approved in her treatment of Carmen on January 9 and 21, and her Santuzza on February 4 was much as it had been. The last *Carmen,* on February 15, ended Ponselle's Metropolitan career, though stories continued to be heard for the following decade and a half that she sang nearly as well as ever, but only for her own pleasure and that of friends.

Most of Ponselle's roles passed to Gina Cigna, a ranking Italian soprano who was first heard as Aida (d) on February 6. This performance supported all claims for her authority, but left some ears disenchanted with the exaggerated vibrato she favored. Castagna, Martinelli, Pinza, and Morelli, with Panizza conducting, made for a relative rarity in these days—an Italian cast for an Italian opera. Cigna had a substantial success as Leonora* in *Il Trovatore* on February 11, but was somewhat out of favor in *La Gioconda* on February 18 and *Norma* on February 20. Henderson described her Gioconda* as "artificial, overwrought, and vocally propulsive," her Norma* as "wanting in the grand line," marred by "spasmodic utterance" and "manifest effort." Panizza, who otherwise conducted very ably, slowed *"Casta diva"* appreciably for her. It was sung in the original key, which, said Henderson "is regarded as an honorable accomplishment." Martinelli was the tenor of both *Gioconda* and *Norma,* Castagna sang Laura and Adalgisa, and Pinza was again Oroveso. Whatever the judgment of the pundits, Cigna was highly regarded by some operagoers, especially those of Italian background.

The hard use of Rethberg's once silvery voice continued apace, with appearances as Sieglinde, Leonora, Aida, and even Santuzza, a part she undertook for the first time in nine years when Castagna canceled a performance. Although a long rest intervened before she sang again, her Sieglinde on February 3 brought Henderson's observation that her voice seemed tired, "without the brilliant tone associated with the creation of its fame." Giannini sang several Aidas in fervent style, but was otherwise heard infrequently. Among other sopranos in leading roles was Vina Bovy, a pleasant-looking, musicianly native of Ghent, whose light, rather penetrating voice did not produce what was desirable for Violetta (d) at her debut on December 24 or as Gilda* on December 28. She was decidedly better in *Les Contes d'Hoffmann* (see age 398), for which, doubtless, she was brought. A final new soprano was an American, Marion Bruce Clark, who was introduced under the name of Franca Somigli, which she had used in Italy. A rather hard-driven quality marred the obvious experience she brought to Butterfly (d) on March 8 and a later Mimi. She did not reappear.

Two influences of the spring season, other than the singers of secondary parts who joined the company, were evident in the addition to the repertory of Richard Hageman's *Caponsacchi* on February 4 and the English version of *The Bartered Bride*. The Hageman score had won some esteem in Germany, and its planned production for the first spring season was deferred when its promise seemed to merit more auspicious circumstances. Based on Browning's *The Ring and the Book,* it had some melodic traits suggestive of Hageman's repute as a writer of songs (a charming *Lullaby,* for one), but the dramatic power to sustain interest in the theater was absent, either in Arthur Goodrich's libretto or in Hageman's elaboration of it. Tibbett's overstrenuous Guido* seemed designed to overcome this deficiency, but the results were mere bluster. Good work was done by Jepson as Pompilia* and Chamlee as Caponsacchi,* and Norman Cordon earned special credit for his characterization of the Pope.* Gilman, frankly distressed by the whole venture, declared that Hageman had "missed his vocation." The composer conducted, and the scenery was by Novak. One repetition completed its history.

The Bartered Bride was presented first on Christmas night, with much the same cast as in the spring. Now, however, the wine of laughter had gone to the heads of the performers, and the broadened business, the playing for comedy, put a final damper on the gentle charm of Smetana's music. Also in English was Cimarosa's *Il Matrimonio segreto* on February 25, coarsely sung by Muriel Dickson (Carolina*) and Irra Petina (Fidalma*). Natalie Bodanya (formerly Bodanskaya) attracted the most attention by losing a petticoat mid-stage and kicking it aside as though this happened every day. D'Angelo (Geronimo*), Huehn (Count Robinson*), and Rasely (Paolino*) were the male performers, and Panizza conducted.

A restoration of *Le Coq d'or* (matinee of February 4) is best remembered for Pinza's clownish Dodon and its raffish dance. Lily Pons danced as well as sang the music of the Queen,* and Votipka did what she could with the coloratura of the Cockerel.* Papi's direction made sober business of the colorful score. Grace Moore was not in the company this year, but Gladys Swarthout returned as a film celebrity to appear as a mezzo Mignon* on March 13. Her treatment of the Thomas music was intelligently planned, but hardly emotional. It was otherwise an undistinguished effort, with Antoine a diminutive Philine, Oelheim a tentative Frédéric, and Hackett a stylish but tight-voiced Meister. Pinza's Lothario was a reminder of how a part should be acted and sung. Pelletier conducted.

The newly founded Opera Guild launched one of its most productive enterprises on March 19 when it invited a houseful of schoolchildren to a performance of *Aida,* with Rethberg, Castagna, and Cordon. Too often these performances have been given in a way to corrupt taste rather than condition it, but the treatment is commendable even if the patient does not always respond. The one hundred fiftieth performance in the series, which had been heard by more than five hundred thousand young people, was given in April 1965.

As Johnson's reward for having taken hold in a generally satisfactory way, his contract was extended by two years in March. Ziegler and Lewis continued as his chiefs of staff. It was also announced that the spring season would be conducted by Lee Pattison, well known as a concert pianist and teacher, but with little theatrical background. To serve the Metropolitan, he resigned as director, in New York, of the Music Project of the Works Progress Administration (WPA).

SECOND SPRING SEASON

Aside from the absurd effort expended on Walter Damrosch's *The Man without a Country,* [1] the second spring season produced rather more interesting young talent than the first. Abandonment of the idea thereafter suggests that the Juilliard people either did not know what they wanted to accomplish or did not realize that they were accomplishing it.

The Man without a Country was not without issue, though hardly of the sort the parent hoped for. Having failed, in turn, to interest half a dozen celebrities, Damrosch settled for an unknown St. Louis soprano, Helen Traubel, as Mary Rutledge. Her splendid sound and strong stage presence were much more affirmative than anything in the score contrived by Damrosch for Arthur Guiterman's treatment of the Edward

[1] Some persons, noting this second Damrosch work to be given at the Metropolitan, wondered how many there might have been had he actually become director of the theater.

Everett Hale story. With her on May 12 were a number of graduates of the previous spring season (Royer as Burr, Carron as Nolan, Gurney as Colonel Morgan, and Rasely as Blennerhassett); also a vigorous young baritone named Donald Dickson (Midshipman Denton), who could have had a worthy career had he not preferred radio with Charlie McCarthy. Most commentary dwelt on Traubel's stunning performance, bypassing the heavy, labored writing of Damrosch. Gilman atoned for his lapses relative to *Peter Ibbetson* by finding the Damrosch score full of "an astonishing freshness of feeling, an infectious gusto." Damrosch made a curtain speech in which he repeated, with apparent approval, a conversational pleasantry in which Deems Taylor likened him to the Verdi of *Falstaff*.

Aside from Dickson (who made his debut as Valentin in the opening *Faust* on May 3, in which the "youth" series was ushered in by the venerable Rothier as Méphistophélès), the newcomers included Ruby Mercer as Marguerite; Lucy Monroe, specialist in *The Star-Spangled Banner,* who sang a Musetta; and Marguerite Daum, another interpreter of the same part. Daum had made a pleasant impression a few weeks earlier when Gian-Carlo Menotti's *Amelia Goes to the Ball* had its New York *première* on April 11 under Fritz Reiner's direction in the New Amsterdam Theater. This was one of the last musical events reviewed by Henderson, who committed suicide (at the age of eighty-two) on June 5, 1937. His appraisal of the work concluded: "It is very probable that Mr. Menotti will be heard from again."

The newly instituted Metropolitan Auditions of the Air produced its first winner when Thomas L. Thomas sang a pathetically inept Silvio in *Pagliacci* on May 15. His rich voice has seen better service since. Much more mature was Robert Weede, of Music Hall background, who sang a strong Tonio in the same performance. On the afternoon of the same day Jennie Tourel made a well-commended debut as Mignon, and later sang Carmen. This was also artistic, but vocally of small size. Rose Bampton marked her gradual transition to the soprano repertory by singing a vocally competent, but unintense Leonora in *Il Trovatore* on May 7.

Perhaps the most ambitious venture of the two seasons was an English-language version of Rabaud's *Marouf* (text by Madeleine Marshall and George Meade) on May 21, with Chamlee as a suave-sounding Marouf, Nancy McCord as the Princess, and Cordon as the Vizier. Pelletier conducted, and the public response was slight. Wagner, too, was undertaken with a motley *Lohengrin* on May 19, in which Agnes Davis was an unsteady Elsa; Dimitri Onofrei a promising Lohengrin; Cordon a solid voice for King Henry; Ernst Fischer a dull Telramund; and Halstead a wobbly Ortrud. Riedel conducted, and a Kautsky setting of 1914 was brought out for all to behold.

The approval earned by such singers as Traubel, Tourel, Dickson, and Weede would have seemed ample reason for proceeding with the spring seasons, but this spring was a warm one and there were occasions when one was uncertain whether to use the hands for applause or for mopping the brow. Without ceremony or post-mortem, the season (and the venture) ended on May 29. Expenditures exceeded income in this whole season by $113,530.

1937–1938

With two years of experiment behind him and two years of security ahead, Johnson began to evolve in this season the strategy and tactics of his campaign as director. The basic concept was a new one for the Metropolitan of the 1930's—that is, the one that had emerged from the trends and turns taken by Gatti. It was that certain "musical" operas not established in the Metropolitan repertory should be given whether they could be cast to ultimate satisfaction or not. Certainly, neither Antoine nor Bovy was an ideal Gilda; then why discriminate against *Don Giovanni* or *Otello* because an ideal Otello or Don was not available? This reasoning was not spelled out in so many words, but another decision was when Johnson told a press conference: "It is our desire to make the Strauss works as familiar . . . as are the music dramas of Wagner."

The tactics to carry out these large ideas included extension of the season from fourteen weeks to sixteen; moving back the opening to a November date (the 29th, but still November); and elimination of the Brooklyn series, which no longer served any worth-while function. The repertory was increased from twenty-nine works, which had sufficed for the fourteen-week seasons, to thirty-five.

The new attitude toward Strauss resulted in the introduction of two characterizations new to New York—Rosa Pauly as Elektra and Marjorie Lawrence as Salome—and the revaluation of Lehmann's Marschallin. Pauly had made a striking impression in a concert version of *Elektra* with Rodzinski and the Philharmonic-Symphony on March 18, 1937, but the full measure of what Downes called the "haunting tenderness" with which she sang some of the reflective music and the bitter eloquence with which she mastered its climaxes could only be taken from the Metropolitan stage presentation on January 7. With Thorborg's Clytemnestra* and Jessner's Chrysothemis* as complementary distinctions (Schorr and Althouse were the male singers), Bodanzky had one of the great moments of his career. Urban's glowering background seemed to have taken on impressiveness as it grew older.

Lehmann's Marschallin was much more what it should have been when she sang the part, with the strong support of List as Ochs, on December 1. But it was a rather dismal *Rosenkavalier* when she was not on the stage, for Thorborg was an awkward, unsuggestive Octavian,* Susanne Fischer a vocally timid Sophie,* and Schorr a ponderously Wagnerian Faninal.* Marita Farell, a new soprano this season, later sang Sophie without distinction.

The limited capacities, in this period, of Metropolitan Salomes continued when Marjorie Lawrence demonstrated a good deal of vocal promise and an attractive physical presence in her attempt on February 4. What she lacked, however, was what no Salome* can succeed without—temperament, abandon, controlled or uncontrolled dementia. Lawrence was much too prim and self-conscious to convince anyone that she really wanted the head of John the Baptist. Panizza conducted with unsuspected flair for the idiom, and there were strong performances of Herod* by Maison, Herodias by Branzell, and Jokanaan* by Huehn. Graf's stage direction was well unified, though he could not prevent Lawrence from wearing an ostentatious, inappropriate headdress. As usual, the setting was Oenslager's.

This designer might have succeeded to the place formerly occupied by Urban, had the Metropolitan had as much money to spend for new scenery in the thirties as it had had in the twenties, for he also executed the décor in which *Otello* began a new quest for Metropolitan favor on December 22. Unfortunately it persisted long after the personnel of this revival had given way to others, for it was a singularly un-Cypriote setting. Nevertheless, with Martinelli's Otello* crowning a worthy career of twenty-five seasons at the Metropolitan and Panizza leading a strong playing of the orchestral score, the great work made a deep impression, especially on the more impressionable, younger operagoers. To be sure, Tibbett again pushed a dramatic character out of focus by excessive facial contortion and exaggerated byplay, but his Iago* was well sung except at the extremes of the *"Credo,"* where it lacked power, and *"Era la notte,"* where it lacked subtlety. Rethberg was a likable Desdemona,* if not a dramatically expressive one. Later cast changes included Jessner as Desdemona,* and surprisingly good, on February 5, with Carron a noisy, immature Otello. In the last of eight performances—the most ever for *Otello* in a Metropolitan season—Martinelli and Jessner were joined by Carlo Tagliabue as a rough but intense Iago.* The smaller roles—Massue as Cassio,* Nicola Moscona as Lodovico,* and Votipka as Emilia*—were mostly mediocre. A beginning had been made, however, and it eventually yielded returns.

This was an eventful as well as a satisfying season for Martinelli. One climax came on February 26, during a broadcast performance of *Aida,* when he suffered an attack of indigestion after *"Celeste Aida"* and had to leave the stage in distress. Jagel was quickly summoned, and replaced him for the remainder of the afternoon. More pleasantly memorable was a concert in his honor on March 20, with gifts for his silver jubilee[1] as a Metropolitan artist. He sang excerpts from *La Bohème* (with Rethberg), from *Otello* (with Tibbett), and from *La Juive* (with Rothier), and other participants included Flagstad, Pinza, and Melchior. He did not hesitate to name his age as fifty-three.

As with *Otello,* the resumption of *Don Giovanni* on January 1 (after an absence of two seasons) expressed a down payment on an obligation rather than a complete settlement of a bill of particulars. Panizza's conducting added a little more in detail and thrust to the previous versions of Serafin (and himself), and Pinza's Don had a stronger dramatic character. For the rest, Giannini did not fulfill expectations as Donna Anna,* her tones spreading to shrillness at climaxes; Cigna was an erratic Elvira*; and Farell a poor suggestion of Zerlina.* Crooks was a passable Ottavio,* though he had the voice to be a distinguished one, and Lazzari's Leporello was acceptable save for bouts of low-comedy clowning with Pinza (the "Serenade" particularly). Two characterizations of greater Mozartian worth, if not so valuable in this theater as they would have been in a smaller one, were Hackett's Ottavio* on January 17 and Brownlee's Don* on March 17. The last of these was admirable for everything save a vocal quality that Oscar Thompson (Henderson's successor on the *Sun*) called "dry and unseductive." Brownlee was at a disadvantage also in being paired with Bampton, whose Donna Anna* had an advantage of several inches in height and reach on her supposed assailant. She sang the music intelligently, if not yet with all the fluency she eventually attained. This time the Elvira was Jessner, vocally rather out of her depth.

As a further suggestion of a repertory trend, Johnson borrowed the Curtis Institute's production of Menotti's *Amelia Goes to the Ball* for introduction to the Metropolitan's public on March 3. Pitts Sanborn in the *World-Telegram* described the scenery as "unimportant and now shabby," but the work gave more than a little pleasure as performed by Muriel Dickson (Amelia*), Chamlee (the Lover*), and Brownlee (the Husband*). In the customary effort to diminish the size of the stage, an

---

[1] He endured to enjoy a fiftieth anniversary in 1963. See page 704.

interior platform and proscenium were used. The partners of *Amelia* in double bills this season were *Elektra, Le Coq d'or,* and *Salome.*

A measure of the changing operatic times was provided by revivals of *Il Barbiere di Siviglia* on January 22 and *Roméo et Juliette* on December 16. Both were works that once could be turned out with facility. Although Pons sang a facile Rosina, this *Barbiere* suffered from a lamentable burlesque of Figaro* by John Charles Thomas, who sang with virtuoso ease and a long list of exaggerations and interpolations. Pinza's Basilio had a new companion in comedy in Petina's delightful caricature of a maid,* but Malatesta was a weak Bartolo, Bruno Landi a wispy voice for Almaviva.* Brownlee showed all the virtues of his art in a Figaro* on February 28, arousing regrets that the Thomas voice was not in the Brownlee body. Papi was a sluggish conductor for *Il Barbiere,* as Abravanel was a rough one for *Roméo.* Sayão as Juliette* had a modest charm, as Crooks as Roméo* had a certain masculine one; but neither could convince the listener that it was this kind of singing that made Gounod's music a connoisseur's delight. Brownlee was Mercutio,* Cordon sang Capulet,* and the Stéphano* was Browning. Bovy was a light-voiced Juliette* on January 14.

The broadening search for vocal talent of an unusual sort (the usual sort was, unfortunately, overabundant) turned, for the first time in years, to the Balkan Peninsula, whence the legendary Ternina had come, and produced the imposing person of Zinka Milanov[1] for a debut as Leonora (d) in *Il Trovatore* on December 17. Her selection to sing the Verdi Requiem with Toscanini in Salzburg had implied a more than casual talent, and it was supported by the range, clarity, and ease with which she performed. It was by no means the Milanov of some later seasons, however, who was heard at this debut, for her uncertainty (especially in pitch) made for alternate sensations of pleasure and pain. Somewhat later one became aware that Milanov had sung her roles almost wholly in Croatian before coming to the Metropolitan, and the problem of coping with Italian texts doubtless affected her accuracy. Those who heard her Aida* on February 2 could hardly imagine that it would eventually become the best of its time, for all the promise in its soaring line and vibrant power.

The notable voice of Helen Traubel was also added to the Metropolitan roster in this season, though the circumstances were the depressing ones of *The Man without a Country* on February 17. Despite the mild reactions the work had encountered in the spring, the token of a single performance in the winter season was granted. Glenn Darwin made his debut as Burr (d), and Daniel Harris and George Cehanovsky divided the music

[1] As noted earlier (p. 166), Milanov was helped on her way by Ternina.

formerly sung by Donald Dickson. Pelletier conducted. It was many months before Traubel had a proper opportunity.

For the while, however, the Metropolitan was better staffed with singers of Traubel's potentialities than it had been for some time, this being a Flagstad-and-Lawrence season. The former, singing with unremitting splendor, added no roles to her fairly inclusive list of Wagnerian heroines. Carl Hartmann, who had been a member of a touring company with Gadski (see page 360), sang a rather impressive young Siegfried (d) on December 3. It was decidedly his best part, for his Tannhäuser, Tristan, and Siegmund were well schooled, but without vocal luster. The Alberich (d) of this *Siegfried* was Adolf Vogel, a capable baritone who was also a well-qualified Beckmesser and Klingsor. Enid Szantho, who had made some worth-while appearances in concert during the preceding winter, was heard as Fricka (d) in *Die Walküre* on February 17. Her vocal art was satisfactory, but her diminutive figure made rather a parody of the enraged goddess.

The continuing need for an alternate to Bodanzky, not satisfied by either Riedel or Abravanel, prepared the way for the debut, on January 21, of Erich Leinsdorf, who had served an apprenticeship to Toscanini in Salzburg, as well as in the usual German theaters. The assured manner in which he took command of this *Walküre* (with Flagstad, Althouse, Rethberg, Thorborg, Hofmann, and List) promised worthy results when he had the opportunity to work out his own conceptions in greater detail. As occasional conductor this season of *Elektra* and *Parsifal* (which he had never directed previously), Leinsdorf performed with vitality and excellent musical taste, demonstrating a control of the unrehearsed ensembles uncommon in so young a man.

Castagna's attractively vocalized Carmen* was admitted to Metropolitan respectability on December 4, and was heard often with pleasure thereafter. The José* on February 14 was Jan Kiepura, a more than commonly vain tenor who had first displayed his hard, unsensuous voice as Rodolfo (d) on February 10. In the latter, he greeted Sayão's introductory words as Mimi with a self-satisfied smirk and a brisk rubbing of the hands, and in *Carmen* he distracted attention from Castagna's card scene with aimless gestures behind her. In all, Kiepura was a positive factor in any performance in which he took part (*Rigoletto* was also in his repertory), but he rarely sang well enough for his presumptions to be condoned. Bruno Landi's intermittent services as a *tenore di grazia* began creditably in *Il Barbiere* on January 22, but he had also been required to sing the Duke (d) in *Rigoletto* (on January 12, with Sayão as Gilda*), and Rodolfo,* for which his vocal displacement was much too limited. Also new were Carlo Tagliabue, a bullish-voiced baritone well schooled at La Scala, who made his debut as Amonasro (d) in *Aida* on December 2, and Nicola Moscona, whose rich bass voice was first heard as Ramfis* in Aida on December 13. Tagliabue's services as Rigoletto, Iago, Count di Luna, Marcello, and Germont had to be ranked relative to his Alfio in *Cavalleria* of which, in power and brusqueness, he was an almost ideal interpreter. Few of his other roles approached it, especially if they called for suavity and projection of line. Moscona, a Greek national originally impeded by limited acquaintance with Italian texts, survived that disability to serve the Metropolitan well for more than twenty seasons.

One of the high points of Dusolina Giannini's career occurred on February 3 when she sang Santuzza* in a manner to stimulate some comparisons with Calvé and Destinn. These had less to do with vocal culture than with an intensity of manner, a bold approach to the music that roused Jagel and Tagliabue (Alfio) to something more than customary tension. Helen Jepson's Violetta* on February 24 brought a new source of operatic tradition to bear on the Metropolitan, for she had learned it in Hollywood incidental to performing excerpts in the *Goldwyn Follies*. She sang the music cleanly, though hardly with dynamic power. Tibbett and Landi (Alfredo) were in this cast. The range of appropriate and inappropriate casting in this season has been noted relative to Szantho and Landi; but it could easily be extended by references to Brownlee as Escamillo; Anna Kaskas, of the spring seasons, as Erda in *Das Rheingold;* or Marita Farell as Sophie in *Der Rosenkavalier*. The failing was one that was to become almost a fixation in the Johnson period.

The end of the season brought an end, also, to the three-year affiliation of the American Ballet and George Balanchine with the Metropolitan. As was shown some years later when Antony Tudor attempted a similar service, distinction as a choreographer does not assure success as choreographer for a repertory opera theater. In Balanchine's case, when his conception accorded with a neutral surrounding, as in the *Carmen divertissement,* the results could well be superb. When it clashed with a stylized one, as in the temple scene of *Aida,* it could well be ridiculous. Balanchine could have made a fresh and vital thing of the danced portions of a Metropolitan production; but the production itself would have had to be fresh and vital for such a departure to be regarded as an adjunct rather than an intrusion. In addition to its part in operas, the American Ballet performed the following ballets as parts of various double bills: *Reminiscence* (music by Godard), *Serenade* (Tchaikovsky), *Errante* (Schubert), *The Bat* (J. Strauss), *Piano Concerto* (Chopin), and *Apollon Musagète*.

Le Baiser de la fée, and *Jeu de cartes* (both by Stravinsky) were danced in a special program with *Apollon* on April 28, 1937, the composer conducting.

This year's income passed the $1,500,000 mark for the first time since 1931, to reach $1,645,329. The lengthening of the season by two weeks, however, has to be taken into account in a comparison with the previous fourteen weeks' total of $1,437,385. The loss remained about the same —$107,000 this year against $113,530 the preceding year.

1938-1939

A new pattern of activity for the Metropolitan began to emerge during the course of this season, which—with Munich before it began, and Danzig before it was over—was the last in peacetime for six years. The opening was inched back slowly to November 21, and the sixteen weeks were followed by the longest tour since the barnstorming ones of Conried. Now, however, in Cleveland and Dallas and New Orleans, the Metropolitan was greeted as the national opera company it had become.

The evident desire for a balanced budget may be seen in the limitation of new productions to a single work, *Orfeo.* On the other hand, the sense of inadequacy in certain important aspects of the company may be read in the engagement of Maria Caniglia, Jussi Bjoerling, Hans Hermann Nissen, Herbert Janssen, and Galliano Masini, all artists of solid European reputation. Even Beniamino Gigli was welcomed for a few performances.

The most enduring artist the Metropolitan acquired in this season was none of these, but a native New Yorker, Leonard Warren, co-winner in the third Metropolitan Auditions of the Air with John Carter, a tenor. Carter had his chance, fell short of acceptability, and departed; Warren moved slowly but very steadily to pre-eminence among the company's baritones. There was no doubt, when Warren sang in the spring of 1938 in NBC's studio 8H, of the power and thrust of his voice. There was some doubt, in his early prominence as Rangoni* in *Boris* on March 7, that he would develop a stage personality to match the obvious star-stature of his voice. The happy fact was that he not only developed the manner for which his noble voice was suited, but also did so while its beauty and expressiveness were still pristine.

As foreshadowed by Gatti in his *Memories of the Opera,* the Metropolitan successor to Chaliapin as Boris* was Pinza, who survived a flood of comparisons[1] to establish a conception wholly his own, more lyric and less pathological than his predecessor's. The transition from authority to

[1] They were heightened by nostalgic tributes when Chaliapin died, on April 12, 1938.

supplication was accentuated by the change in carriage from the tall, impressive monarch of Pinza's entrance to the groveling man at his death. No venture was made toward use of the original score of Mussorgsky, but the first Polish scene was included, as was some music usually omitted in the scene with the children. Thorborg was an excellent Marina,* Cordon a fine Pimenn,* and Kullmann a singularly plausible Dimitri.* The thirty-year relic of a production was renovated by Novak, who also painted the new scene for Marina's boudoir. Panizza took special pains with the chorus, which sang in a manner appropriate to its responsibility. The text, of course, was Italian.

Warren had first sung at a Sunday-night concert on December 25, and he made his stage debut as Paolo Albiani (d) in *Simon Boccanegra* on January 13. His right to blend voices with Tibbett's Boccanegra and Pinza's Fiesco was unchallenged, but his acting was rudimentary. Martinelli's Gabriele was ever less listenable, and Caniglia's Amelia* was disappointing. Nevertheless, the retention of *Simon Boccanegra* and *Otello* in the repertory, and the resumption of *Falstaff* gave a broader vista of the greatest Verdi than Metropolitan patrons had ever known.

Comparatively, the physical attack to make *Otello* effective if not overwhelming was closer to hand than the subtlety to make *Falstaff* winning. Tibbett's lean frame led, perversely, to the most padded, grotesque knight the Metropolitan stage had known when he was first seen on December 16. His dress was modified considerably in later performances, but the inner identification with the character, for all the virtuous singing Tibbett did, was hardly present. A generally competent cast that included Brownlee[1] as Ford,* Castagna as Dame Quickly,* Caniglia as Mistress Ford,* and Kullmann as Fenton* was admirably stage-directed by Graf. Jessner later sang Mistress Ford.* The old Urban sets were utilized. For all Panizza's adroit conducting, the nature of *Falstaff* as an opera that must be played (in the dramatic sense) as well as sung was not sufficiently mastered by this cast to overcome audience inertia.

As the several mentions of Caniglia's name suggests, she was given every opportunity to assert at the Metropolitan the talents that had given her prominence in Italy. She was Desdemona* in the season-opening *Otello* on November 21, and later sang Aida and Tosca as well as Amelia in *Boccanegra* and Mistress Ford. Her best impression was made as Tosca* on December 22 (with Galliano Masini as Cavaradossi,* and Tibbett), a skillful, sure dramatic performance marred by what was at length

---

[1] Warren later told me that he was assigned to this part and participated in all phases of preparation, including the dress rehearsal. He was then asked to step aside. Tibbett's memory of his own success as Ford may have lingered.

accepted as an ineradicable vocal quaver. Her possible future at the Metropolitan was curtailed when the Italian government put an embargo on its operatic artists at the outbreak of the war in the fall of 1939. In the *Aida* of November 24, in which Caniglia appeared, Maria Gambarelli (of Roxy fame) led a new, poor dance ensemble. As *prima ballerina,* she presented herself as a blond Egyptian.

Johnson's choice of *Orfeo* for presentation in a new décor by Harry Horner on November 26 was doubtless designed to show the directors of the departed American Ballet how such a work should be produced. Save for a bleak Elysian Fields (which seemed to have been salvaged from the spring-season production), Horner's work was impressive for spaciousness and clean design. Graf's stage direction had fine mood for Gluck, and Thorborg's noble Orfeo* was the best thing to her credit thus far. Unfortunately Bodanzky had not been able to convey the fervor of his conducting to Jessner as Eurydice.* Marisa Morel as Amor,* and Farell (Un' Ombra Felice*). Jessner was at least efficient; the others were not even that. Dull choreography by Boris Romanoff lent no charm to the dance episodes.

The new prominence of Grace Moore may be dated from her first appearance this season as Louise,* which showed the virtues of careful study and intelligent effort. Any relationship to reality, in the Garden manner, was incidental, but as opera characterizations go, it became one of Moore's best. With her on January 28 was only one authentically French characterization, Maison's Julien.* Pinza performed eloquently as the Father,* and Doe intelligently as the Mother.* Other virtues included the excellent conducting of Panizza, whose direction was rated by some as the best the work had had since Campanini. The many smaller parts were nothing like the vignettes they had been in earlier days. Kullmann sang Julien* appealingly on February 17. The production was Urban *cum* Novak.

The mistake of performing French works without French singers was even more evident in an attempt with *Thaïs* which had the physical advantages of Helen Jepson in the title role on February 10, but also her temperamental limitations. Marjorie Lawrence had been scheduled to take part in this performance, but deferred her effort until March 2. For all her good appearance, it was not much more in her line than *Salome* had been. Thomas was the Athanaël* of the first performance, and a fine-sounding one, if a little dull of action; Brownlee acted the part well when Lawrence sang, and had typical difficulty with the upper range of the music. Tokatyan was as good a Nicias as he had been in 1925; the other performers were close to mediocre. Pelletier directed dutifully. Lawrence was also scheduled to sing Tosca this season, but begged off after a trial in Philadelphia which was received with astonishment rather than delight. Jessner took her place on January 27. In another *Tosca,* on March 8, Thomas performed Scarpia* with notable vocal power, little dramatic subtlety.

Had Risë Stevens been as headstrong about a Metropolitan career as some of her Juilliard classmates, she might have come and gone as they did. Her debut as Mignon (d) on December 17, however, showed the value of several years of European training, her characterization being likened by Thompson, in the *Sun,* to "the cherished Mignons of Lucrezia Bori and Geraldine Farrar." Crooks, Pinza, Antoine, and Gurney (Jarno*) were in the cast, conducted by Pelletier. Stevens gave an even larger measure of her worth when she sang Octavian* in *Der Rosenkavalier* on December 19, thus beginning a lengthy span of ensemble playing with Lehmann and List. Her splendid sense of this role was only an intuition at this time, and Bodanzky's strenuous conducting hardly coaxed the best from her, but the character grew steadily. On the theory that a mezzo who sings German is a German mezzo, the management offered her as Fricka* in *Die Walküre* and Erda* in *Das Rheingold,* but Stevens apparently shared the opinion of her listeners that these were not roles for her and sang them rarely thereafter.

The making of the new Metropolitan company, in which such singers as Stevens and Warren were to be conspicuous, acquired its staunchest European ally in the debut on November 24 of Jussi Bjoerling as Rodolfo* in *La Bohème.* About the age Martinelli had been at his debut, Bjoerling brought with him virtually every virtue a tenor could possess—beauty of sound, range, musicianship—save temperament. His Rodolfo was beautifully sung, as was his Manrico; but if there was a surge of individual feeling in Bjoerling as he sang Verdi rather than Puccini, it did not reach his listeners. Much can be forgiven, however, for an art as sympathetic as his. His Mimi* was Mafalda Favero (d), an attractive performer who might have endured had she not suffered the same fate as Caniglia when the war began. Marisa Morel, who, as Marisa Merlo, had sung with the visiting Salzburg Opera Guild the year before, was the Musetta (d). She was competent, but expendable when Americans of similar abilities clamored for recognition. Lina Aimaro, a light-voiced Lucia (d) on February 2 and Gilda* on February 8, suggested a lengthier career than the management granted her. In another performance of *Lucia,* on December 14, Galliano Masini made as Edgardo (d) a debut that confounded those too young (myself included) to know that *Lucia* was once considered a tenor's opera. Some old-fashioned sobs and tortured high notes offended good taste, but the vigor of Masini's performance was stimulating. Whether his Cavaradossi and Radames might have endured to become irritating as well as stimulating one cannot say; the good, if inconsistent, impression he made in these parts this season was echoed by no others after the onset of war.

Gigli's return occurred on January 23 in the unlikely role of Radames,* but it had been preceded by weeks of self-advertisement by the tenor, prior to an official announcement of his re-engagement. The business he attracted was self-justifying, however; also the ravishing sound he produced in *"Celeste Aida"* and the Nile scene. Elsewhere it was only by calling on the technique and experience of his varied career that he managed the necessary quantity of sound. As Edgardo, Cavaradossi, and the Duke in *Rigoletto,* Gigli was much the superb vocalist of old and a diligent actor. He celebrated his return to Italy with a blast at the Metropolitan, its artists, and its public. With that his American career rested until he returned for a series of "farewell" concerts in 1955.

The coming of Bjoerling and Masini, the return of Gigli, and the retention of Maison, Crooks, and Kullmann in suitable repertory gave the Metropolitan a sounder group of tenors than it had had for some time. For that matter Kiepura transcended his limitations to sing a convincingly dramatic Des Grieux* in *Manon* with Sayão on February 15. It would be easy to say that his self-satisfaction was a natural mate for the young Seminarian, but he also sang the *"Rêve"* skillfully and poured into *"Ah! fuyez, douce image,"* a drama that it rarely possessed. The Guillot of this performance was the able Alessio de Paolis, who made his debut in the same part on December 8, and sang it, and dozens of others, with distinction for decades. A replacement for the seemingly indestructible Angelo Bada, he came close to duplicating the career of his predecessor[1] which began with the first Toscanini *Aida* of 1908 and ended with the Martinelli jubilee of 1938.

In the manner of Favero, Masini, and Caniglia, Hans Hermann Nissen might have become a more familiar Metropolitan name than it did, had the demonstrated abilities of his first season's work led to a normal re-engagement. Plainly, the end of Schorr's notable career was evident in the announcement that he would henceforth spend much of his time coaching younger singers, such as Huehn, who sang Wotan* on February 25. As his possible replacement, Nissen lacked ultimate vocal richness in his *Walküre* Wotan (d) on November 23, but, in such roles as Wolfram, Telramund, Kurvenal, and the Wanderer* in *Siegfried,* he matched every

[1] De Paolis was a member of the company until 1964, when he died after an automobile accident.

reasonable requirement in artistic understanding and skillful projection. The watchdog faithfulness of his Kurvenal is an especial memory. Nissen chose to return to Germany, however, at the end of this season and never reappeared.

By contrast, the more limited Herbert Janssen began a long term of service with an exemplary Wolfram (d) in *Tannhäuser* on January 28, not because he was the best German baritone of the day, but simply because persecution, first in Germany, then in Austria, inclined him to residence in New York. He also sang Kurvenal, Telramund, and Kothner with credit in this season, and many times thereafter. Still to come were Sachs and Wotan, roles for which Janssen's beautiful but rather light voice would have been more suitable in a smaller theater. The Huehn Wotan* (see above) was full of promise, but it did not have adequate chance to mature. Briefly prominent in the German repertory this season were Herbert Alsen, a thick-voiced, tremulous singer of Pogner, Fafner, and the Landgrave in *Tannhäuser,* and Erich Witte, a light tenor, too light for Metropolitan service as Mime or Loge.

The evident trend toward the "musical" works of the musical theater brought such hitherto unknown sequences as those in the week of January 5–12, in which *Don Giovanni* was followed by *Tristan* and *Aida* on the 6th, *Der Rosenkavalier* and *Falstaff* on the 7th, *Lucia* on the 9th, *Elektra* and *Amelia Goes to the Ball* on the 11th, and *Fidelio* on the 12th. In the succeeding period, January 13–20, it was *Simon Boccanegra, Don Giovanni, Lakmé, Tristan, Il Barbiere, Tannhäuser, Falstaff, Elektra* and *Fidelio.*[1] (*Orfeo, Boris, Louise,* and *Otello* came before and after.)

The heavy output of Wagner continued not only with seven performances of *Tristan* in the regular season, but also with three more in two post-season periods that included a week in April and two more in May, the latter in conjunction with the World's Fair. Visitors to the Fair were offered a *Ring* cycle between May 6 and 12, as well as *Parsifal, Lohengrin,* and *Die Meistersinger.* Aside from the *Tristans* only *Götterdämmerung* and *Parsifal* drew strongly, for New Yorkers had been offered forty-one performances of Wagner during the regular season, and the Fair visitors seemed more interested in Flushing Meadows than in the Metropolitan.

As much as in any account of operas and casts, purposes and objectives, the slow restoration of public interest can be read in the rise of income to $1,780,794, the decline of expense over income to $60,492. Thanks to

[1] Somewhere in the house on this occasion was a former Viennese musical agent, resident in England, named Rudolf Bing. He admired Flagstad's Leonore, and deplored Bodanzky's recitatives. That he would some day be in a position to do something about either, or both, would have seemed to him extremely unlikely.

Flagstad and a variety of other artists brought to the Metropolitan in the preceding four seasons, a glow of satisfaction was more often than a flush of indignation a reward for attendance. The transformation could not have happened at a more opportune time, for the season was barely history before a fresh crisis arose. The dilemma in which the Opera and Real Estate Company found itself has been traced in detail elsewhere, as have the tortured means that were devised to resolve that dilemma (see page 35). For this predicament, as well as others to come, the only saving grace was the fanatical devotion of operagoers to their obsession. This, and the immemorial patience of the American public.

1939-1940

Any comparison of the effects on Metropolitan Opera of the 1914–18 war with those of the 1939–45 renewal of it breaks down abruptly because of the vastly different natures of the events themselves. The most conspicuous difference, of course, was the clear distinction that was now made and maintained between German culture and those who sought to manipulate it to their own ends. One member of the Metropolitan board did suggest a boycott on Wagner and Strauss, but his proposal found no support.

In the purely technical detail of running an opera company of the Metropolitan's magnitude, the second war had an influence quite unlike the first. Italy, close to the enemy camp from the start, was soon within it. Hence a vastly important source of talent was this time out of reach. Moreover, if Gatti had a full share of difficulty in bringing his forces together, he had a far more able company to draw upon in 1914 than Johnson had in 1939. Also, the determination to keep the German works in the repertory though new artists from the German area were unavailable posed its share of problems. All of these factors (plus a much more intensive mobilization of American manpower than in 1917–18) exercised new and ever-changing influences on the years ahead.

For the moment, however, immediate difficulties took precedence over those of long range. Virtually without warning, Artur Bodanzky died on November 23, 1939, as the season was about to open. A lean, ascetic-looking sixty-two, Bodanzky had been for so long (twenty-four years) a relentless machine of work that few thought of him in terms of failing health, or of health at all. His recent disposition to share his schedule with Abravanel, Riedel, and Leinsdorf seemed, to the public view, a wise precaution rather than a compelling necessity. The recent upswing of affection for him was reflected in the real sense of loss that attended the playing of Mozart's Masonic Funeral Music between the second and third acts of *Orfeo* (on November 29), in which he would have normally taken his place in the season's routine.

For Leinsdorf, called upon abruptly to add Bodanzky's repertory to his own, this was an opportunity not without hazard. In all, he conducted fifty-five times this season, a back-breaking physical exertion, but by no means the hardest punishment he had to take. In addition to undertaking five works he had never conducted in public previously, he had to withstand an attack from Melchior in the *Herald Tribune* of January 25, 1940. The charges were vague, centering on Leinsdorf's youth and inexperience. Good ground exists for believing that it was part of a campaign to insinuate Edwin McArthur, Flagstad's accompanist, into the company as a conductor. Johnson retaliated with a denunciation of the "old boats" who wanted things their own way, and supported Leinsdorf staunchly—for a while. A public reconciliation was arranged during a performance of *Die Walküre* on January 29 (with Leinsdorf forced to share in burying a hatchet he had not wielded). To judge by the applause, the audience was clearly partial to the conductor.

Meanwhile, out of view, a conflict of equal intensity centered on the steadily maturing abilities of Helen Traubel. Occasional mention in the press showed that her excellent work in *A Man without a Country* had not been forgotten, though she had not been invited to sing anything else. On October 8 of this year she gave a signal demonstration of ability in a Town Hall recital. On the 22nd she was invited to take part in a Philharmonic-Symphony concert dedicated to the memory of Lawrence Gilman,[1] for many years its program annotator. Her performance of Brünnhilde's Immolation from *Götterdämmerung* aroused so much interest that she was invited to repeat it at a later date.

Between October and December the public curiosity as to how the Metropolitan could ignore a singer of such ability had broken down the internal resistance to her, and she was invited to an interview. How she was offered, and turned down, the role of Venus in *Tannhäuser* (which she did not consider suitable for a soprana's debut) not once, but twice, may be left for Traubel's memoirs.[2] She was finally granted a debut as Sieglinde (d) in *Die Walküre* on December 28 (with Melchior, Flagstad, and Schorr), and left no doubt of her powers. An abundant voice and a warmth that communicated through and beyond her obvious limitations as an actress were qualities no singer since Flagstad had presented. Her Elisabeth* in *Tannhäuser* on February 15 was an equally majestic vocal feat, if heavy and awkward in action. With Traubel added to Flagstad and

[1] He had died on September 8 while vacationing in New Hampshire.
[2] They were eventually (1959) published under the title of *St. Louis Woman*.

Lawrence, the Metropolitan seemed to have an embarrassment of riches in dramatic sopranos. The next season had hardly ended, however, when the three stars had dwindled to one.

If Traubel was virtually forced upon him, Johnson did more than a little for his own future peace of mind by engaging three artists who would have been welcome at any time, and in these troubled ones were pearls beyond price. Licia Albanese, Jarmila Novotna, and Alexander Kipnis all had sizable reputations to uphold when they came to the Metropolitan, and none failed. As Butterfly (d) on February 9, Albanese was introduced in perhaps her best part, but the sensitivity and skill with which she used a not exceptional voice were equally evident in her Mimi and Micaëla later on. Kullmann, Bonelli, and Browning (Suzuki*) were the other principals in *Butterfly,* with Papi conducting. Swarthout's rather genteel Carmen* had the headlines following Bizet's opera on March 15, but Albanese's Micaëla* outlived it to embellish many a later performance.

Novotna's debut as Mimi (d) in *La Bohème* on January 5 suggested a well-versed theatrical art, if a rather fragile voice for the big auditorium. Time, and a sequence of such roles as Eurydice in *Orfeo*, Violetta in *La Traviata,* and Cherubino in *Le Nozze di Figaro,* demonstrated that Novotna's forte was not a conventional role done in a conventional way, but character creation in which voice, appearance, and action were equal factors. In *La Traviata,* Novotna matched skills with Giuseppe de Luca, returned at sixty-three to give a remarkable demonstration of artistic longevity. In their scene together, her playing of Violetta, in the opinion of Thompson in the *Sun,* was "the equal of Mr. de Luca's," which exhausted possible praise.

As for Kipnis, the abilities he had demonstrated fifteen years earlier (see page 313) were at least as splendid as before, enhanced by a history of performance in virtually every important opera house abroad. Fortunately, his sumptuous voice was still at his disposal, his introduction as Gurnemanz* in *Parsifal* on January 5 striking Jerome D. Bohm of the *Herald Tribune* as "one of the most impressive" the house had recently had. In his Ochs* in *Der Rosenkavalier* on February 10 the low tones were a bit muffled, but it was a beautifully detailed characterization. Whether as Marke in *Tristan,* Arkel in *Pelléas,* the Landgrave in *Tannhäuser,* or Hagen in *Götterdämmerung* (his roles of this season), Kipnis left the listener with at least one valid reason for spending an evening in the Metropolitan.

In terms of repertory, this season provided one of the major impulses of the decade to come with the long-awaited revival of Mozart's *Nozze di Figaro* on February 20. For artists as well as audience (except those who had nourished their Mozart hunger on the Glyndebourne recording) this was a beginning from scratch, and it took time for the soil to respond. Brownlee's suave, well-sung Count* was the shining deed of this occasion, as it was to be on many others, a model of style on which Pinza's hearty but unperfected Figaro* and Stevens's thickly resonant Cherubino* could well be patterned. Rethberg's fading Countess* would have been a masterpiece ten years before, but was now merely stylish and rather breathy, and Sayão was as yet more minx than maid as Susanna.* De Paolis was a delightfully malicious Basilio,* Lazzari a husky-voiced Bartolo.* The ensemble was sharply improved on February 26, when Novotna's *gallant,* beautifully articulated Cherubino* added a deal of spirit to the performance. (The virtues that made Stevens a delightful Octavian and a rather stiff Cherubino were almost exactly opposite in Novotna's suitability for Mozart rather than Strauss.)

Although Panizza was still, in effect, conducting public rehearsals, the central fact was that a beginning had been made with a major work of the musical theater, one that was unlikely to languish for another twenty-three-year period. Herbert Graf's knowing stage direction tended to broad comedy in consideration of the oversized theater, but later improved under the influence of such conductors as Bruno Walter, Busch, and Reiner. Jonel Jorgulesco's utilitarian if undistinguished settings began their long tour of duty, utilizing an interior platform whose steps down to the stage level required as much agility in maneuver (for the unskilled performer) as Mozart's music. Perhaps the major surprise of this first season of *Figaro* was the responsiveness of the audience, which encouraged more performances in the ten remaining years of Johnson's direction than had been given in the fifty-seven before.

Two works particularly identified with Johnson's own career were ventured by him for the first time when *L'Amore dei tre re* was given on December 27 and *Pelléas* on March 7. What Oscar Thompson called the "nerveless and devitalized" conducting of Papi was an initial liability for the Montemezzi score, which had but a mildly interesting Fiora* in Jepson, a rather phlegmatic Avito* in Tokatyan. In the same critic's view, this was a tale of one king (Pinza as Archibaldo) rather than three, for neither Bonelli nor Tokatyan had regal bearing. One repetition sufficed. As Pelléas (d), Georges Cathelat, of Paris, brought an authentic style if no great persuasion, and the eventual decision to use Jepson as Mélisande* left this shadowy princess a merely good-looking, very palpable opera-singer. Brownlee (Golaud*), Kipnis (Arkel*), and Doe (Geneviève*) had varying esteem with the press, but the opinion of Leinsdorf's conducting was mainly one of objection to the amount of sound he allowed the orchestra and the squareness of his phrasing where a softer curve was desirable. This *Pelléas* passed after one further performance.

Leinsdorf's variable season also included his first effort with *Der fliegende Holländer* on December 14, in which his cautious treatment produced a dull *Dutchman* indeed. Lacking the vitalizing leadership so essential in this work, the superb Senta of Flagstad counted for less than before. Maison was a capable Erik, and List a sound Daland, but Schorr's dwindling range was sorely taxed by the upper tones of his part. On January 8, Janssen sang these creditably enough, but his Dutchman* lacked the resonant low ones that Schorr could still provide. One further performance sufficed for this season and the decade.

The change of responsibility in the Wagner repertory brought some alterations in the often abused "Bodanzky cuts," but not much more satisfaction with the results. *Der Rosenkavalier* on December 4, with Lehmann, Stevens, List, Farell, and Huehn (Faninal*), was modified by thirteen alterations that resulted in a performance fifteen minutes longer than before. When Janssen sang his quiet, rather aristocratic Sachs* in *Die Meistersinger* on December 7, Thompson took ardent issue with the "really inexcusable cuts made in Pogner's first-act address and Sachs's final tribute."

What Leinsdorf did well, like the uncut *Ring* cycle that began on February 2, passed without special notice, as expectable from a man of his promise. Flagstad sang all the Brünnhildes, and Melchior was the unvarying tenor, with Althouse an excellent Loge in the prologue. An evening sequence was also offered, with Lawrence as the *Walküre* and *Siegfried* Brünnhilde. The Venus-in-*Tannhäuser* problem (see page 418) was truly acute, to judge by the use of the well-worn Pauly's voice in one performance and the scarcely opulent Manski's in another. Eventually Thorborg was available for the part, and the Venusberg was a more hospitable place.

In a military figure appropriate to the time, the Metropolitan, more and more, was "living off the land" in using talent at hand ravenously. Norman Cordon, for example, was an excellent Varlaam* in *Boris* on December 1 and a creditable Colline in *La Bohème,* but he was also called upon for Hunding, Pogner, and King Henry in *Lohengrin* while doing duty as Basilio in *Il Barbiere,* Lothario in *Mignon,* and the Uncle Priest in *Butterfly,* along with such secondary roles as Angelotti in *Tosca,* a Philosopher in *Louise,* Sparafucile in one *Rigoletto,* and Monterone in another. Versatility has its virtue, but Cordon would doubtless have matured sooner and lasted longer with more considerate treatment. For that matter, the demand for Bampton to sing Amneris (on January 26) in a season when she was performing Aida (January 19 and March 2) argues a gross deterioration of standards, if nothing more. Brownlee as Iago and Scarpia in a theater of the Metropolitan's size was also a perilous risk of a valuable artist's limited vocal reservoir. Of brighter luster were Giannini's first Tosca*, and a lively Figaro* in *Il Barbiere* by Bonelli.

How planning went in this period may be seen from the acquisition of Raoul Jobin. A French-Canadian tenor with Parisian training, he applied for consideration in the Metropolitan Auditions of the Air and demonstrated sufficient utility to be added to the company forthwith. His first appearance, as Des Grieux (d) in *Manon* on February 19 (with Moore, Brownlee, and Moscona), earned tribute from Downes for a voice "warm in its best registers," though his stage business was "more effusive than distinguished." Jobin was rarely the best member of a cast in which he appeared, never its worst, a mean of ability which assured him Metropolitan prominence despite a colorless sound and little personality.

The remarkable promise that the Auditions had uncovered in Leonard Warren continued to arouse admiration as he added Valentin in *Faust,* Amonasro in *Aida,* Barnaba in *La Gioconda,* and even the Herald in *Lohengrin* to his repertory. His co-winner, John Carter, however, was sadly inadequate for the Italian Singer* in *Der Rosenkavalier* on December 4, and did not excite attention in the smaller bits of Walther in *Tannhäuser* or Froh in *Das Rheingold.* The new Auditions winners to appear this year were Annamary Dickey, who was first heard as the Happy Shade (d) in *Orfeo* on November 29, and Mack Harrell, introduced as Biterolf (d) in *Tannhäuser* on December 16. Dickey, with the inevitable Musetta* on January 27, was the virtual equivalent of numerous other American lyric sopranos who come and go at the Metropolitan. She had more prominence later as a supper-club singer, in the new "of the Metropolitan Opera" style. Harrell's excellent art eventually gave him higher rank as a concert singer than as an opera performer, but he did well with every opportunity he was accorded.

American singers of brief prominence who appeared in this season and no other ranged from Harriet Henders, who was Sophie (d) in *Der Rosenkavalier* at her debut on December 29, to Jean Merrill and Winifred Heidt, semifinalists in the previous year's auditions, who appeared in Sunday-night concerts. Jean Dickenson, of radio background, sang Philine (d) in *Mignon* at a Vassar College benefit on January 26, and occasionally thereafter. Eyvind Laholm (who changed his name from Edwin Johnson for obvious reasons) sang Siegmund and Tannhäuser in an effortful, throaty manner, suggesting no more reason for engagement than for re-engagement. Somewhat more skilled Europeans were Walter Olitzki, a baritone engaged for such roles as Alberich, Beckmesser, and Klingsor when the well-regarded

Hermann Wiedemann could not be brought out of Germany; and Hilde Reggiani, a brittle-voiced coloratura, who made her debut as Gilda (d) on December 7, and later sang Rosina.

Some typical performances by newly prominent members of the company were introduced in these weeks, particularly Faust and the Duke in *Rigoletto* by Jussi Bjoerling, and by Milanov as Gioconda. The life and beauty of Bjoerling's sound made rewarding listening of both undertakings, but Milanov was an erratic Gioconda, if often a greatly promising one. Castagna's Laura was the best effort of this "revival" on December 30, for Martinelli's Enzo was a dim likeness of its best self, Kaskas (La Cieca*) was at most conscientious, and Morelli (Barnaba) and Moscona (Alvise*) were dull in sound. Warren sang an imposing Barnaba* on February 8. De Luca's little tour of triumph (see page 419) included a farewell Figaro in *Il Barbiere* on March 23 which in unction, bounce, and vitality shamed the men of half his years who had been singing it of late. Pons, Martini (an excellent Almaviva), and Pinza made a gala thing of this performance, whose proceeds were earmarked for the fund to purchase the opera house.

This long campaign (see page 37) eventually produced the million dollars necessary to accomplish the purchase. More than a fair share of it was provided by the Opera Guild and its affiliates in such tour cities as Rochester, Baltimore, Boston,[1] Cleveland, Dallas, New Orleans, and Atlanta. Transfer of the property was accomplished on June 27. The loss figure for the year was $171,462, a considerable rise from the preceding season's $60,000. It was absorbed by the operational fund of $500,000 set aside from the public contributions. The satisfaction with the new "security" the institution now enjoyed was widespread. Less happy was the news on September 17, 1940, that Lawrence Tibbett would be inactive for some time to recuperate from "a rare throat ailment" that had interfered with his work for many months and had recently resulted in an operation.

1940–1941

The expectable influences of the war were evident in the first season affected by it; what no one could foresee as the tide ebbed and flowed was the new trend of the unexpected influences. Surprisingly, not all of them were adverse. If, for example, the capitulation of France and the isolation of the Scandinavian peninsula cost the Metropolitan the highly desired talents of Germaine Lubin, a Parisian soprano of repute, and Joel Berglund, a rank-

[1] Flagstad achieved her objective of installing Edwin McArthur as conductor for a Metropolitan performance of *Tristan* in Boston on April 1. Consent was wrung from Johnson when she threatened to abandon the tour.

ing Wagnerian baritone, the curtailment of operatic activity abroad made available Bruno Walter as the first in the series of such conductors as Beecham, Szell, Busch, Stiedry, Reiner, and Perlea, who contributed so much to the Metropolitan in this decade.

Different in so many ways, these were yet men of more homogeneous character than any half a dozen conductors the Metropolitan had known in years, if ever. Virtually all had Wagner, Mozart, and the unconventional Verdi as common grounds of interest, even though the circumstances of the moment did not permit each to perform in all three categories. But they were able, as developments carried one or another in and out of the orbit of the Metropolitan, to pick up the work of a predecessor and carry it forward. In a time when the Metropolitan had to depend more and more on such unformed talents as those of Stevens, Warren, and Harrell (with Steber, Tucker, Peerce, and Merrill to come), it was a providential blessing that the upward curve in standards occurred where it did the most good.

The outcome of the million-dollar fund-raising campaign also afforded some benefits not wholly of a bookkeeping nature (by which ownership of the building was vested in the Opera Association). Designation of $500,000 as an operational fund permitted a measure of sorely needed latitude for expanding the repertory in kind, if not in numbers; and the installation of single chairs for the grand-tier boxes added to the quantity of desirable (hence salable) seats. A Guild room was constructed on the grand-tier floor, and a fresh golden curtain ordered from the loom that, apparently, serves no other purpose. To relieve Edward Ziegler of some administrative detail, Eric Clarke was engaged as administrative secretary to Johnson.

To those whose operatic experience post-dated February 5, 1916, the opening on December 2 marked a fresh beginning in more ways than one, for it brought with it the first hearing of Verdi's *Un Ballo in maschera* in nearly twenty-five years. A curio in 1940, *Un Ballo* has remained a curiosity since in seeming to defy thoroughly satisfactory casting in all roles at the same time—even once. On the rare occasion when everything else meshed, the role of the Page, with its difficult florid air, has remained a grating cog. On this occasion Oscar (d) was sung by Stella Andreva, better, perhaps, than any to come, but hardly a Hempel or a Garrison. Bjoerling was a bright-sounding Riccardo,* Alexander Sved a menacing Renato,* with a bigger voice than he could control at his debut. Milanov was a characteristically uneven Amelia,* Thorborg a capable but un-Italianate Ulrica.* Castagna was much better in this role on December 14, and Panizza did his customarily methodical work with the orchestra.

The perplexing problem of locale was solved by assigning the action to Sweden, though Mstislav Dobujinsky's ornate settings were geographically anonymous. As tended to be a pattern for him, Graf's stage direction was excellent in its handling of masses, less satisfactory where individuals were concerned. On the whole, four performances for *Un Ballo* were a disappointing total for a season in which it had the prestige of opening-night prominence, but it has recurred with tenacious frequency in the years since.

Sved's scattered performances could scarcely be called a season, for he was heard twice more as Renato, once as Di Luna, and once as Amonasro. The vagaries of casting may be judged from the circumstances that when he was not singing Renato or Di Luna with his ponderous, thick voice, Francesco Valentino was singing the same parts with his slim, almost effete one. An American (born Frank Valentine) well schooled in Italy, Valentino showed at his debut as Sir Henry Ashton (d) in *Lucia* on December 9 most of the virtues and limitations that marked his work thereafter. Unlike most of his native-born contemporaries, Valentino had more style than voice in such roles as Malatesta in *Don Pasquale,* Silvio in *Pagliacci,* and Alfio in *Cavalleria.* His Di Luna* in *Il Trovatore* (a new and rather impressive scenic production by Harry Horner) on December 12 was suavely vocalized and well acted, but hard to hear in the large theater. In place of Stella Roman, whose arrival was delayed by transportation difficulties, the Leonora (d) was Norina Greco, a good singer by the standards of the popular-priced companies in which she had formerly been heard, a barely adequate one in the Metropolitan. Bjoerling and Castagna were in the cast well conducted by Ferruccio Calusio. Like Panizza, Calusio was an Argentinian of Italian extraction. He gave good service this season, but did not return.

A new tradition of buffo comedy at the Metropolitan was initiated on December 7 when Salvatore Baccaloni waddled on stage to sing Dr. Bartolo* (d) in *Le Nozze di Figaro.* By no means a stranger to those acquainted with the Italian stage, Baccaloni brought a fresh source of pleasure to the theater in his girthy person, mobile face, and plump voice. He also brought a substantial ego that frequently taxed the laxity of discipline which prevailed on the Metropolitan stage at this time. Certainly he was happiest in such a principal role as Don Pasquale* when the Donizetti comedy was given on December 21, with Sayão (Norina*), Valentino (Malatesta*), and De Paolis (the Notary*) all excellent and Martini (Ernesto*) just fair, for it permitted him, in Oscar Thompson's happy phrase, to "loom sideways" over the rest of the cast. As Benoit and Alcindoro in *La Bohème,* Bartolo in *Il Barbiere,* or even Leporello in *Don Giovanni,* his powerful personality tended to magnetize attention from a more legitimate focal point. When matched with an equal force, such as Pinza's Basilio, his Bartolo could be a comic masterpiece.

Baccaloni gave much, if not always with the right emphasis, to his Sulpice* in a revival of *La Fille du régiment* on December 28, with Pons a lively Marie,* Jobin a sufficing Tonio,* and Petina a delightful Marquise.* As in 1917, its martial coloration suited a time of such preoccupation, though Novak's ornate setting and the occasionally foolish direction (including a prop horse with a working leg to kick passers-by) were hardly stylized. A French text was used, with the recitatives composed for production in Italy interpolated.

Lubin's stature as a dramatic actress was expected to do much for the Metropolitan's first venture with *Alceste* on January 24. It was barely weeks before time for her arrival, however, that she canceled the journey, and Marjorie Lawrence, with her conscientious but rather untemperamental performance, did not give Gluck what was needed in the Metropolitan. *"Divinités du Styx"* was impressively sung, but the nobility of character implicit in the heroine was not conveyed. Maison was an excellent Admetus,* Warren out of his element as the High Priest.* Graf's direction was regarded by some as overelaborate for the problem in hand. Richard Rychtarik's scenery was valued for its spacious architectural design, but not for its inclusion of an anachronistic Apollo Belvedere. Panizza led but did not animate the performance, which also suffered from want of proper emphasis on ballet. In later performances Bampton was a handsome Alceste,* though a variable one vocally. Valentino (High Priest*) and Jagel (Admetus*) were of dubious suitability to their parts. The four repetitions were poorly attended, and the project was abandoned.

An effort to arrest the downward trend of *L'Amore dei tre re* brought its composer to conduct for the first time in the Metropolitan on February 7, with Moore as Fiora.* She had coached the part extensively with him,[1] and they had previously performed it in Chicago. Much of the music was warmly, vibrantly sung, though Moore's actions suggested to Downes "a poor copy of the more extravagant moments of . . . Mary Garden." Orchestrally the work had not sounded so well in years (Montemezzi had restored some cuts, which, with his slower tempos, lengthened the playing time by some twenty-five minutes), but Kullmann was a weak Avito,* and Bonelli a limited Manfredo, leaving only Pinza and De Paolis (Flaminio) as suitable support for Moore. It was not sufficient, as the small total of two repetitions suggests. *Samson et Dalila,* another operatic problem, was given with a largely native cast of Stevens (Dalila*), Huehn (High Priest), and Cordon (Abimelech) to companion Maison's Samson on December 6,

[1] A story of the moment was that Montemezzi had first heard Moore when she was a musical-comedy performer in the 1920's, and urged her to consider opera. She responded by saying that she was hard at work and hoped some day to sing Fiora.

but the central need of *Samson*—a voluptuous voice in an irresistible body —was but modestly present in Stevens.

The other notable occurrences of this season were associated with Bruno Walter, who made his debut (almost inevitably) as conductor of *Fidelio,* on February 14. He received a hero's welcome at his appearance, delivering a reading whose "every phrase," said Sanborn in the *World Telegram* "was a perpetual delight." Much of what Walter was able to do stopped at the footlights, for Flagstad, Maison, Farell (Marzelline) and Laufkötter (Jacquino) were as they had been before. Kipnis was an excellent Rocco,* Huehn a gruff Pizarro.* In its singing eloquence and clarity of texture, however, Walter's treatment of the orchestral score was the most personal the Metropolitan had known since Mahler, and the performance stormed to great heights in the dungeon scene and the finale. Mahler's placement of the overtures was used, Bodanzky's treatment of the recitatives was not. Two repetitions were wholly sold out, enthusiastically applauded.

For *Don Giovanni* on March 7 Walter was able to do more in ensemble preparation, combining the known qualities of Pinza and Schipa (returned to sing Ottavio) with the unknown ones of Milanov (Donna Anna*), Novotna (Elvira*), Sayão (Zerlina*), and Baccaloni (Leporello* in a more Mozartian measure than the work had previously possessed. Milanov's *"Non mi dir"* was sumptuous, her other singing unreliable, and Novotna had a tendency to shrillness, but the authority that emanated from the podium gave new flexibility to Pinza's Don, and a strong guiding hand to such younger performers as Arthur Kent (Masetto*) and Cordon (Commendatore). As the names and descriptions indicate, *Don Giovanni* was tending ever more toward the fine thing it became at the Metropolitan, and Walter's contribution was an invaluable one at a wholly appropriate moment.

The universal esteem for Walter's *Fidelio* and *Don Giovanni* was somewhat tempered by his treatment of *The Bartered Bride* (as the English version of Smetana's work may be properly termed) on February 28. Beauty of statement and warmth of feeling it certainly had, but also a softening curve, a restraining hand on its rhythmic impulse, which tended to refine Smetana's folkish expression. Pinza as Kezal* did not have quite an enchanted evening, for his English was thick, his comedy rather forced; and Novotna's Marie,* for all its sympathy and style, was a rather elegant rustic. Kullmann achieved one of his finest accomplishments as Jenik* (no longer Hans in the Metropolitan program), and all the subordinate parts were expertly treated (Laufkötter as Wenzel or Vashak,* Votipka as Kathinka,* and Kent as Kruschina*). Poor was a flattering word for the ballet work. Cordon was an excellent Kezal* on March 21.

Like Warren, Eleanor Steber had scant stage experience when she made her debut as Sophie (d) in *Der Rosenkavalier* on December 7, but the vocal skill she had demonstrated as winner of the 1939–40 Auditions was sufficiently splendid to condone almost any temporary shortcoming in action. Her debut was made doubly difficult in a perilous part when Lehmann became ill and Maria Hussa, a European singer who happened to be singing *Der Rosenkavalier* in Chicago, was presented as the Marschallin.* She filled the emergency and was never heard again. Steber's security and vocal finish marked her as an American soprano in a hundred, and she steadily, if sometimes slowly, made progress as an actress. In this season such parts as Rhinemaidens, the Forest Bird, and Micaëla in *Carmen* marked the treatment accorded her as more considerate than the lot of many others.

Stella Roman's delayed debut, on January 1, showed her able to sing Aida (d) with assurance and dramatic force, but with occasionally unfocused tone and a varied production that made each performance something other than the one before. In this season, as afterward, she sang Desdemona in *Otello* well, Leonora in *Il Trovatore* erratically. Other singers who came and went included Josephine Tuminia, a diminutive Rosina and Gilda from California who sang both parts cleanly but with miniature volume, and Elsa Zebranska, a Latvian soprano, who had a one-season prominence as Venus in *Tannhäuser,* a Norn, and a Walküre.

Something of more than casual quality was expected from Arthur Kent, a co-winner with Steber in the Auditions, who made his debut as one of the Philistines in *Samson* on December 6. A resonant baritone (brother of the musical-comedy singer Alfred Drake, with whom he shares the family name of Caputo), Kent sang a promising Masetto in *Don Giovanni* and roles of similar scope before his status as a reserve officer resulted in a call to active duty early in the war. He did not find a new start in opera easy going, and turned to other fields. Emery Darcy, who was a Philistine Messenger* in this *Samson,* was a baritone about to become a tenor who actually appeared as both in *Tristan* on December 12, as the off-stage sailor's voice (tenor) and the on-stage Melot (baritone). He was in the cast of a rather historic *Tannhäuser* on January 4, in which virtually all the small parts—Biterolf (Harrell), Walther (John Dudley), Heinrich (Darcy), Reinmar (Gurney), and the Shepherd (Maxine Stellman)—were sung by Americans. This may be endorsed as a sound approach to operatic development, though it must be noted in all candor that none (Harrell excepted) came to lasting prominence as leading artists.

Despite the honors she had won in the last season, Traubel was relatively inactive in this one, singing several Sieglindes while preparing for the *Walküre* Brünnhilde on January 17. She was not ready for it, however, and

Tannhäuser (without Traubel) was substituted. Meanwhile Flagstad moved through another long season that began with a second-night Brünnhilde in *Die Walküre* on December 4 and did not end till a *Tristan* on April 12. As in the two previous seasons, she did not tax herself to sing the top C's as Isolde or the *Siegfried* Brünnhilde.

While a cheering throng remained in the theater, Melchior informed the audience that Flagstad was returning to Norway, and the soprano added that she would be happy to go, but also to come back to the Metropolitan.[1] Among those who hoped she would return was Edwin McArthur, present for the third time in the pit (he had made his debut on February 17), for his career obviously depended on hers. For certain, there had never been such circumspect, subservient conducting of *Tristan* as he provided on behalf of his protectress.

Otherwise mentionable (or unmentionable) in the German repertory were the sagging voice of Schorr (sacrificing a reputation to compensate for Berglund's absence) and the self-saving maneuver of Melchior in deserting the stage during the Grail scene of *Parsifal*. The company being short of Wagner singers, there was no evening cycle, and the afternoon cycle blended Mozart and Wagner, *Don Giovanni* and *Le Nozze di Figaro* being added to the *Ring*.

Louise and *Pelléas* were again in the repertoire, with Moore being noted as the first Metropolitan soprano to sing the Charpentier role in more than two seasons. Such favor, however, did not accrue to Jepson's Mélisande, which was heard again this year, but not thereafter. The Pelléas* on December 20 was Jobin, causing Oscar Thompson to observe that Jobin had made his debut singing Massenet, and still was singing it. Leinsdorf's "operatic" treatment was also found wanting, and the Debussy score was put aside for several seasons. Jobin's varied activities included not only the Singer in *Rosenkavalier,* but also Gerald in *Lakmé* and Don José. In *Manon* with Crooks and Pinza (Comte des Grieux*) on January 10, Novotna was a skilled Manon* if scarcely suggesting the teen-aged schoolgirl. Tibbett, presumably recovered from his operation, returned to the company as Rigoletto on January 3 and managed well enough, even with some uncommon restraint born of caution. Whether the grand gesture was premature or not, however, his voice soon took on a woody, unnatural timbre far from the lyric quality it once had. The company would have been better served by offering more opportunities to Robert Weede, who sang

[1] As early as 1939 Flagstad had told an interviewer (William G. King of the *Sun*) of her desire to retire at the end of the 1939–40 season. She would then have celebrated her forty-fifth birthday, and wanted to spend more time at home with her family.

an excellent Rigoletto* on February 27, and imposing a rigorous, compassionate silence on Tibbett.

The year closed with the debit figure at its lowest point since 1936, a manageable $50,975. Public interest having revived despite the war, a sixteen-week season was announced for 1941–2. The interlude between spring and fall, whatever its technical description, was no off-season for Johnson. Grimly disturbing in June was the news from Mexico City that Marjorie Lawrence, one of the most vigorous, athletic women the Metropolitan stage had known, was a victim of polio. Early in September, Flagstad's management announced cancellation of a concert tour of fifty-four appearances, saying she would be "unable" to return.

1941–1942

The meager information received by Flagstad's management was a volume compared to that received by Johnson—exactly nothing. By the roundabout means of a letter to McArthur, the public learned she was "a virtual prisoner of war in Norway." The immediate consequence was the elimination from the repertory of *Tristan und Isolde* for the first time since 1920. Other consequences became apparent as time passed. For reasons wholly owing to the war, the names of Milanov and Bjoerling were absent from the company list, and Sir Thomas Beecham's was added.

In spite of all difficulties a worthy start was made on a long-range program, incidental to observance of the one-hundred-fiftieth anniversary of Mozart's death.[1] The Metropolitan not only paid a tribute, but also instituted a policy in presenting three of his works in a single season for the first time since 1902. With an English version of *Die Zauberflöte* (*The Magic Flute*) installed beside *Don Giovanni* and *Figaro,* at least two of the three scores were heard in each remaining year of the decade (except for 1948, when Pinza left the company and a new Don was still to be found).

The Mozartian emphasis was symbolized with an opening with *Le Nozze di Figaro* on November 24. Panizza again conducted (though some would have preferred Walter or Beecham), and the strong team of Pinza, Baccaloni, Sayão, Rethberg, and Stevens clearly had strengthened its ensemble

---

[1] Also contributing to pleasure for Mozartians was the launching of the New Opera Company in the Forty-fourth Street Theater on October 15 with *Così fan tutte* directed by Fritz Busch. The singers included Ina Souez, Pauline Pierce (Dorabella), Andzia Kuzak (Despina), Robert Marshall or Eugene Conley (Ferrando), Waldemar Schroeder or Perry Askam (Alfonso). The unconventional repertory also included Verdi's *Macbeth* and Tchaikovsky's *Pique-Dame,* with such later Metropolitan singers as Conley, Regina Resnik, Florence Kirk, and Martha Lipton acquiring valuable experience. Other principals included Jennie Tourel (Lisa in *Pique-Dame*) and Jess Walters (Macbeth).

work, Stevens's Cherubino being notably easier, less constrained. Walter's season began with a sensitively detailed *Orfeo* on November 26 (Thorborg and Novotna were the principals), proceeding to *Don Giovanni* on December 5 and *The Magic Flute* on the 11th. The first honored the day of Mozart's death with a *Don Giovanni* more unified than any since Mahler's time, Kullmann being a new Ottavio* in the company of Bampton, Pinza, Novotna, Sayão, and Baccaloni. Later in the season Kipnis sang a splendid Leporello (not often afterward, however), and Harrell offered a Masetto far too clownish and distorted for this good-natured character.

The use of an English text for *Die Zauberflöte* had its defenders and detractors, though there was general agreement that Ruth and Thomas P. Martin had provided a thoroughly acceptable translation. More than a little blame reposed with such unaccustomed speakers of English as Kipnis (Sarastro*), Schorr (High Priest*), Novotna (Pamina*), Laufkötter (Monostatos*), and Rosa Bok (Queen of the Night [d]) in important parts, but Brownlee's model Papageno* and Kullmann's skillful Tamino* showed the worth of the experiment when it was correctly carried out. In a libretto of Schikaneder's intricacy and with so much spoken dialogue, English is, arguably, the language for Metropolitan acceptability. To be sure, Walter's serenity of spirit and warmth of feeling were all-pervasive, so that the listener came away with the consciousness of a Mozartian experience, if one flawed by Novotna's pallid tones and the wobbly Queen of the Night by Bok. Steber began her career in Mozart as the First Lady,* and Mona Paulee was the Second Boy.* Bodanya did little with Papagena.* Richard Rychtarik's settings had some fantasy, if hardly the solidity wanted for the temple scene. Nadine Conner was presented as Pamina (d) in her debut on December 22, singing neatly but with a lack of presence that was hardly surprising in view of her background (largely radio performance in California).

What Walter succeeded in doing with *Orfeo* and *The Magic Flute*—applying a coat of superior musical varnish to hide the flaws of the basic matter —was not within Beecham's power in a series of projects that included Bach's *Phœbus and Pan, Le Coq d'or, Carmen,* and *Faust.* The first two were given as a double bill at his debut on January 15, with a stylized baroque production by Rychtarik for *Phœbus and Pan* and a cast of Jagel (Timolus*), Brownlee (Pan*), Andreva (Momus*), and Darcy (Phœbus*) ill skilled in singing such music. Only Carron as Midas* made his work amusing, and the ballet contributed little in a dance interlude derived from French Suite excerpts orchestrated by Eugene Goossens. *Le Coq d'or* was done in the traditional manner, but not to the conductor's taste. Sayão was originally announced for the Queen,* but Bok sang the first performance. The uncomplimentary reviews were hardly pleasant, but Bok suffered worse injury when she fell from the wedding cart as it was rolled off stage, and suffered a brain concussion. She seemed to have recovered sufficiently to sing again on March 4, but it was actually six years before she could resume a normal career. Antoine was her alternate as the Queen. Cordon was an excellent replacement for Pinza as Dodon* on January 31, and De Paolis was the admirable Astrologer.* Votipka was again offered as the Voice of the Golden Cockerel.

One able singer per cast was about as much as Beecham had to work with in *Carmen* on January 24 and *Faust* on the 30th. In the first it was Albanese as Micaëla; in the second, Pinza as Méphistophélès. Lily Djanel earned credit for vivid and believable action in her debut as Carmen (d) but not for her erratic singing of the music. Kullmann as José and Warren as Escamillo both looked well, but style was lacking in their vocal work. Kiepura and Jobin also were heard as José this season, but with Pelletier conducting, not Beecham. Albanese was an odd-sounding Marguerite,* Crooks a not very confident Faust, when Beecham applied his surge of feeling to Gounod's score. Only Pinza responded in kind. Illusion was not enhanced when a delayed curtain in the garden scene made farce rather than romance of Crooks's amorous gesture. In all, Beecham conducted too little this season (nine times) to have much influence on the company or its work.

The intermittent career of Gennaro Papi came to a sudden end on November 29, when he died shortly before he was to conduct a broadcast performance of *La Traviata* in which Jan Peerce made his debut as Alfredo (d). Panizza took his place, and the news was withheld from the radio audience and from Peerce lest it should depress the one and unnerve the other. Actually Peerce was told by an unwary colleague shortly after the opera began, and it had no effect on the sincerity or artistry of his performance. Although some doubted that his voice would be audible in the Metropolitan, the solidity of his production has cared for that hazard, his taste and musicianship compensating for shortness in physical stature. His other role in this season was the Duke* in *Rigoletto,* for which his shortness of experience was more a liability than his lack of inches. In the aftermath of Papi's death, there were tales of a prolonged heart condition that illuminated his history of slack, unvital performances. It was also explained that Johnson's devotion to a colleague of Chicago days had provided Papi with sorely needed employment. The humanitarian impulse can be admired, but loyalty to art and to his public might have been better served had Johnson utilized Papi's knowledge in some less critical function.

The emergency brought new prominence to Frank St. Leger, who had joined the company to conduct a Sunday-night concert on December 3, 1939, and to Fausto Cleva, previously an assistant conductor and chorus master. St. Leger directed *La Fille du régiment* on December 19 and *Il Barbiere di Siviglia* on December 24, both with more energy than discretion. Cleva's debut was in *Il Barbiere* on February 14. Their careers followed oddly divergent but related courses, for St. Leger eventually became principal associate to Johnson in the executive sphere, and retired when Johnson did; while Cleva went elsewhere to find the opportunity he did not receive in the Metropolitan, to return as a principal conductor when Johnson and St. Leger departed. Another new conductor this season was Paul Breisach, who directed a Guild student matinee of *Aida* on December 12, followed by *La Bohème* and *The Bartered Bride*. Breisach's lusty feeling for Smetana's energy combined well with the order Walter had instituted the year before, producing superior results.

A new phase of Gian-Carlo Menotti's talent was exposed on February 20 when his one-act *The Island God* was given for the first time anywhere. Rather more ambitious than any previous work by him, and with a libretto of his own creation, it was aptly summarized by Virgil Thomson (Gilman's successor as critic for the *Herald Tribune*) as a work that "sounds like an opera, reads like a short-story, actually is a secular cantata." A rather static creation, its three scenes (played in a setting painted by Novak from designs by Eugene Berman) were bridged by musical interludes. A good cast of Warren (Ilo*), Jobin (Fisherman*), Astrid Varnay (the Wife*), and Cordon (the God*) was well directed by Panizza. Its symbolism and limited musical interest were equal factors in its small total of three performances.

Astrid Varnay's debut as Sieglinde (d) in *Die Walküre* on December 6 (Lehmann fell ill) was the most improbable and, considering its outcome, the most remarkable in the long history of the Metropolitan. It was not only her first venture as Sieglinde, but her first performance of anything on the operatic stage! The tributes earned by Varnay for her composure, musical routine, and artistic purpose were partially explained by her heritage, for she was the daughter of a stage director of the Swedish Royal Opera and had been reared in America by her mother (a singer) after her parents had separated. At twenty-three she had a repertory that the management could not resist in this year of depletion. The *Walküre* Brünnhilde* on December 12, Elsa* on January 9, and Elisabeth* in *Tannhäuser* on January 23 were incidents (while she learned her role in *The Island God*) of an amazing demonstration of aptitude, but she did not long retain the "virginal purity" of sound which Thompson of the *Sun* heard in her Elsa. The unprincipled exploitation of voices which wrecked more than a few in this period merely marred Varnay's, for the bloom was off it while she was still a young woman.

In normal circumstances more might have been made of Traubel's Brünnhilde* on December 6, but Varnay's prodigious feat rather obscured the older woman's merely glorious singing of *"Ho-jo-to-ho"* and her sure command of all that followed. Character in action was still to come. Maria van Delden, a Dutch soprano, and Mary Van Kirk, an Auditions winner, were Walküren in this performance. Neither had a lengthy Metropolitan career. When Varnay sang her Brünnhilde—a task then beyond her resources of vocal strength—the Sieglinde* was Bampton, performing beautifully in a manner modeled closely on Lehmann's. The afternoon *Ring* cycle (in which Lehmann resumed her place in *Die Walküre* on January 28) was marked by the refusal of the stage director to have his name in the program. The man who felt his reputation poorly served by what he had been able to do was the able Lothar Wallerstein, of Salzburg and Vienna. In *Das Rheingold* on January 22, Osie Hawkins made his debut as Donner (d), and in *Siegfried* on February 6, Elisabeth Rethberg reached the *reductio ad absurdum* of her career with a lamentable effort to sing Brünnhilde.* Traubel made an impressive venture as the *Götterdämmerung* Brünnhilde* on February 12, laboring somewhat with the unfamiliar demands of the early acts, singing the "Immolation" superbly. Stella Roman as Elisabeth* in *Tannhäuser* on December 20 was another instance of clutching at vocal straws, but Kerstin Thorborg improved an opportunity provided by Flagstad's absence when she sang a Kundry* of affecting nuance and dramatic detail in *Parsifal* on February 27. Huehn was Amfortas,* and John Garris made his debut as the first Knight of the Grail (d).

A career that was limited to a single Metropolitan stage performance began and ended for Maria Markan, a soprano from Iceland (with a background in Glyndebourne), as the Countess (d) in *Figaro* on January 7. A rather hard voice and some style were remarked. Rather otherwise were the instances of Gerhard Pechner, who made his debut as the Notary (d) in *Der Rosenkavalier* on November 27, and Kurt Baum, who made something of a sensation as the Italian Singer (d) on the same occasion. Both remained with the company for years: Pechner an excellent character actor, and Baum a tenor of all works extending from Radames to Lohengrin. Czech by birth, German by training, an Italian tenor by inclination, Baum sang nothing else in his first season, though his strong voice and potent top tones in the *Rosenkavalier* bit were cultivated as a star part whenever he appeared. The new favor for the Strauss score included occasions when Lehmann could not appear and was spelled by Jessner (first on December 17) with intelligence and musicianship, if scarcely regal grace. Lehmann was the Marschallin on March 13 when Novotna sang her artful, somewhat slight Octavian* and Garris gave polished service to Valzacchi.*

Moore's new attention to her operatic career brought with it on December 18 her first Tosca,* to which her radiant good looks (if not conforming to the textual reference to *"bruna Floria"*), well-studied movement, and caressing vocal quality were equally suitable. With repetition it became very nearly her best part. Kullmann and Tibbett were in this cast, and Sved was a big-voiced, menacing figure as Scarpia* in a performance of January 9. In other performances Roman sang a cultivated Tosca* on February 25, with Kiepura a Cavaradossi* who did his first-act painting in lace cuffs and a formal coat. Baccaloni's Sacristan* on February 7 was a brilliant addition to his list of characterizations. In honor of Moore, perhaps, the first-act scene was redesigned, the rest repainted by Novak. Tibbett's season was intended to include his first Barber in *Figaro,* but he was a victim of appendicitis late in December and was absent for some time. Sved replaced him as Iago* in *Otello* on January 2, and Warren was a rather conventional Germont* in *La Traviata* on January 14.

The variations in repertory included the subtraction of *Madama Butterfly* following the Pearl Harbor attack and the addition of *L'Elisir d'amore* on November 28 to permit Baccaloni the huge opportunity of Dr. Dulcamara* and the audience the pleasure therefrom (Sayao was Adina,* Mona Paulee, an Auditions winner was Giannetta,* Landi was Nemorino,* and Valentino sang Belcore*). Ironically, *Madama Butterfly* was last given on November 29 as the Japanese fleet was on the move. Thereafter it was decided that the American naval uniform and a Japanese geisha were best kept apart for the duration. An effort to strengthen the appeal of *Un Ballo in maschera* brought Martinelli to his old role of Riccardo on February 5, with John Charles Thomas as Renato,* and Roman as Amelia,* but the absence of Bjoerling and Milanov was hardly concealed. Other strains on the thinning ranks were met, with varying success, by having Branzell sing Erda at a matinee performance of *Das Rheingold* on January 22 and Amneris in *Aida* in the evening, and by using Carron as Otello and assigning Kipnis to the seemingly inappropriate role of Nilakantha* in *Lakmé,* which he sang particularly well.

This year's Auditions were decided on the stage of the theater itself in March, when Frances Greer, soprano, Margaret Harshaw, mezzo, Clifford Harvuot, baritone, and Elwood Gary, tenor, were selected from a group of six contestants. Virginia MacWatters, soprano, and Robert Brink, bass-baritone, were the unsuccessful finalists. A momentary flurry involving Ezio Pinza came to light on March 13 when he was taken in custody by the Federal Bureau of Investigation on March 13, charged with boasting

of friendship with Mussolini. His denials were substantiated after internment on Ellis Island, and he was released on June 4.

Birmingham (Alabama), Bloomington (Indiana), and Richmond (Virginia) were added to the tour cities this spring. A final accounting showed
that income had declined from $1,860,511 in 1940–1 to $1,645,000, or
by almost exactly the equivalent of the $214,374 posted as deficit. Re-
viewing the situation in the *Herald Tribune* of March 15, Thomson offered
the view that "the empty seats are not wholly the artists' fault," that the
Metropolitan "needs a reorganization of its direction and management
before any drastic musical improvement can be effected." On June 7 he
discussed a rumor of a shortened season and a reduction of prices, with an
endorsement of the latter course, arguing that a $7.70 top price was no
longer warranted. A few days later the management announced a reduction
to the $5 level that had prevailed in 1910. With tax, the subscriber paid
$5.50, the single-seat purchaser $6.05.

A healthy recognition of the new status of the Metropolitan as an
institution responsible to the public was provided by the publication of a
detailed financial report on August 2. It summarized the year's operations
as stated above, and noted that the cash reserve from the operational fund
of $500,000 had dwindled to $125,000.

1942–1943

The personnel list published on October 25 commanded more than ordinary interest, if only for showing the names of fifty-one native-born
singers. This was virtually half the total of one hundred and five names
listed, and a much larger proportion of those engaged in the day-to-day
operations. Even without this analysis, one can read the changing trend
in the season's record, which notes Traubel as the first American Isolde
since Nordica, Steber's ascension to the Countess in *Figaro,* the use of
Bampton as Elsa, Elisabeth, and Kundry, Cordon as Gurnemanz, and the
appearance of a new Tamino and Ottavio in James Melton.

Fortunately, the other prevailing trend was intensified when Ettore
Panizza decided not to risk a wartime trip from Argentina, and George
Szell was added to the staff of conductors in his place. A share of the
repertory formerly held by Panizza and the deceased Papi went to Cesare
Sodero, a highly qualified musician of long residence in New York, whose
career could have been much longer had he not died in December 1947.

Another phase of transition was dramatized by the retirement of Rethberg and Schorr after notable careers covering almost the same score of
years. Schorr accepted the inevitable with dignity, Rethberg with hauteur.
In fact, the baritone had expressed a desire to slip quietly from sight the

preceding year, but Johnson pressed him to sing a few more times and be properly farewelled. Rethberg apparently felt slighted by the contract offered her, and announced in October that her relations with the Metropolitan were at an end. Her final performance thus was as Aida on March 6, 1942, the role of her debut on November 22, 1922. The last real memory she left was the strained attempt at the *Siegfried* Brünnhilde in February.

The new link in the Metropolitan's Wagnerian chain was successfully forged on March 2, when Traubel sang the *Siegfried* Brünnhilde* in the performance that served as Schorr's leave-taking. Whether by intent or accident, it was his only appearance of this season, for he had had to beg off from singing Wotan in *Das Rheingold* a few weeks before. The audience lavished its affection on Schorr for his strong work in the first two acts, though his voice began to give out in the third. He sustained his responsibility admirably, however, but the gods who preside over matters theatrical made his exit an ironic one. Somehow, the spear with which Wotan seeks to bar Siegfried's approach to the flame-circled mountain came apart without a blow from Melchior's sword. When Schorr strode off stage, some heard the pieces thrown to the floor in an expression of disgust. All was beatific at the end, however, when Schorr spoke his farewell in a blend of quotations from Sachs's "Apostrophe" to the Masters from *Die Meistersinger* and Sharpless's "America forever" from *Madama Butterfly*.

As in her Isolde* on December 4, Traubel's venture as Brünnhilde* was notably cautious. Dramatic action was sacrificed to a concentration on the musical line, much of it delivered with tonal grandeur, if with little that was unbounded or ecstatic. The optional top tones were avoided (as in *Tristan,* where they are not optional). She sang *Siegfried* only once this season, but there were two further *Tristans,* with a marked improvement in her Isolde in each. Melchior and Huehn (Kurvenal) were in all three, Kipnis or List, Thorborg or Branzell appearing alternately. Traubel also took a full share in the other Wagnerian works, singing the *Walküre* and *Götterdämmerung* Brünnhildes and Elisabeth in *Tannhäuser.* On the other hand, Varnay in January sang only three performances of Elsa and one of Elisabeth. Thereafter Bampton embarked on her ordeal, appearing as Elisabeth* on January 22, Elsa* on March 5, and Kundry* in *Parsifal* on April 21. All these parts were new to her. She did not have the dramatic outburst for Elisabeth or the repose for Elsa, but her Kundry was warmly sung from the first, and eventually became an excellent impersonation. Cordon did very creditably as Gurnemanz.*

The poise and refinement that made Steber's Countess* a notable element of many later performances of *Figaro* were remarkably evident in her first effort on December 16. The cast was a customary one—Pinza, Brownlee, Sayão, Novotna, and Baccaloni—with Walter conducting for the first time. Sentiment rather than *esprit* was the dominant quality of his treatment, but as a counteraction to some traits of Serafin's and Panizza's Mozart, this had value. Certainly it helped to shape the unformed conception of Steber. Albanese sang Susanna this season and Stevens Cherubino, but the cast remained unchanged otherwise. (An exception was a student matinee on March 12, when Valentino tried his art as Almaviva,* Brownlee sang Figaro,* and Frances Greer was Susanna,* with Breisach conducting.) Steber was less fortunate with her other new role this year, offering a rather pale and vocally limited Marguerite* in *Faust,* with Beecham conducting, on March 17.

Considering James Melton's beginnings in radio as a member of the vocal ensemble called The Revelers, the tenacity of purpose that brought him to a Metropolitan debut as Tamino (d) in *The Magic Flute* on December 7 must be admired, if not the performance itself. He later sang a small-scaled Alfredo in *La Traviata* and a rather lame Ottavio in *Don Giovanni* with a voice of agreeable quality but gravely limited size. On all occasions [1] the breezy self-assurance that caused Beecham to allude to him, when he could not recall his name, as "the gentleman jockey" tended to make his characterizations a little bumptious.

Pinza's place in the Mozartian renaissance became a predominant one when he undertook Sarastro* on November 27, performing with implacable dignity and nobility of style, helping more than a little to settle the performance as a whole. His English enunciation was improving. Lillian Raymondi, who made something of a specialty of Papagena, made her debut in the role in this performance, further strengthening the ensemble, which otherwise included Brownlee, Novotna, and Kullmann. Antoine was the Queen of the Night.* Harrell's Papageno* on January 16 did not suggest that comedy was his métier, any more than had his Masetto the year before. The return of Milanov was a boon to *Don Giovanni,* as was the continuing direction of Walter. By and large, the school in Mozartian finesse which he was conducting (more than figuratively) at the Metropolitan was the most fortunate thing that could have happened for performers and public.

As supplementary activity, Walter supervised a restoration of *La Forza del destino* on January 9, utilizing the version of Franz Werfel in the interest of clarifying some cloudy points of the drama. Much more contribu-

---

[1] Melton's long tenure and occasionally unwarranted prominence were related to the sponsorship of the Metropolitan broadcasts by the Texas Company, which also presented Melton in broadcasts of lighter music. By putting him forth as a leading tenor, the Metropolitan aggrandized his worth to the sponsors.

tory to this end, however, were the force and vigor of his conducting and his integration of Milanov (Leonora*), Baum (Alvaro*), Pinza (Abbot), and Petina (Preziosilla*) into an ensemble of the first order. Tibbett, as Don Carlos,* was somewhat at a loss for the volume of voice needed, of which nothing was lacking when Warren sang the part on February 11. Baccaloni did one of his characteristic feats in transforming Melitone* from a small part to merely a short big one. Roman (Leonora*) and Jagel (Alvaro) appeared on later occasions, when the ensemble was hardly what it had been originally.

Beecham was truly Beauchamp in this season, conducting only French works—*Louise* and *Manon* in addition to *Carmen* and *Faust*. The strongest impression was conveyed by *Louise* on January 15, which—with a bow to Panizza's effort in 1939—was the most eloquent, orchestrally, that New York had heard. Beecham's special contribution was to build the work to a climax in Act IV, in which with Moore, Pinza, and Doe (the Mother), all capable, he could achieve a real theatrical effect. Jobin was the Julien,* throaty but earnest. Beecham's treatment of *Manon* on December 12 was broader in accent, firmer in outline than the Metropolitan norm, with credit to Massenet if not always to the intimate, piteous Manon of Sayão. Kullmann was Des Grieux,* and Walter Cassel joined the company to make a good impression as De Bretigny* (d). Novotna was a later Manon.

Carmen was substantially what it had been before, with Djanel and Maison, Sved singing a rough, crude-voiced Escamillo.* Lorenzo Alvary began a long tour of service as Zuniga.* On January 1, Petina sang Carmen* intelligently, but, being known largely for comic parts, she exerted little magnetism. Jacques Gerard, a Canadian tenor, was a smallish José,* and Warren sang Escamillo. *Faust* gained a little when Jepson sang Marguerite on December 5, but Jobin, Cordon, and Valentino (Valentin*) hardly gave Beecham adequate straws with which to make musical bricks.

An afterthought to the announced repertory was the election of *Salome* by George Szell as the work in which to make his debut on December 9. New York had sampled his abilities as a conductor with the National Broadcasting Company's Symphony Orchestra and as conductor-pianist in concerts of the New Friends of Music, but that was slight forewarning of the kind of frenzied yet tightly organized *Salome* he delivered. Most of the credit was Szell's, for Djanel was but a fair Salome,* Jagel a limited replacement for Maison as Herod, Janssen a stolid if well-sounding Jokanaan. Garris came to good repute in the short part of Narraboth,* and Branzell made her customary effect as Herodias. What emerged, finally, was a symphonic poem with vocal embellishments. The critical views embraced Virgil Thomson's opinion that Szell did "a virtuoso job on a difficult and complex work," and Oscar Thompson's delight with the manner in which "the score glowed and pulsated." Huehn was Jokanaan* on January 14. At the first and third performance *Salome* was preceded by *La Serva Padrona* with Sayão as Serpina* and Baccaloni as Uberto,* Breisach conducting. On December 28 Sayão was ill, and the second act of *La Traviata* (Albanese, Warren, and Melton) was substituted.

Szell's versatility made him useful as conductor for *Tannhäuser* on December 19 and *Boris* on December 30. Even more, the quality of his art resulted in better performances of *Boris* than the Metropolitan had heard in years. Szell could not transform Traubel, Melchior, Janssen, or Thorborg into something they were not, but his *Tannhäuser* was dramatically just, beautifully organized. *Boris* was planned to be given in English rather than Italian, but the cost of teaching it to the chorus in the "strange" language prevented that. Szell's pacing of the work and his gathering together of the orchestral and choral strands were widely admired, and the cast founded on Pinza, Maison (Dmitri*), and Thorborg (Marina) had uncommon assistance from Baccaloni's Varlaam* and Moscona's Pimenn. A special pleasure was provided on February 13 when Kipnis sang his superbly rich and suggestive Boris* in Russian.[1] Cordon was a gusty Varlaam.*

Cesare Sodero's history in America could be traced back to Hammerstein days in Chicago and Philadelphia, but he was known to the Metropolitan public as a radio conductor when he made his debut in the traditional *Aida* on November 28. With Milanov an inconsistent Aida, Carron a stolid Radames, Branzell a variable Amneris, and Sved a burly Amonasro, Sodero was more concerned with keeping order than with making music. Later *Aidas* (Hertha Glaz made her debut as a rather small-voiced Amneris (d) on December 25, and Baum was an unimpressive Radames* on January 23) hardly gave Sodero workable materials, and a *Bohème* on November 30 in which Frances Greer sang Musetta (d), with Moore, Jagel, and Valentino, was essentially routine. The occasion for the first Violetta* by Albanese on any stage—a statement that seemed unlikely, but was official—gave Sodero better opportunity for preparation when *La Traviata* was given on December 5, resulting in much lovely string sound and a refined pattern of dynamics. Sodero, said Virgil Thomson, conducted *Traviata* "more beautifully than I have heard any other con-

[1] The New Opera Company season at the Broadway Theater included Mussorgsky's *Fair at Sorochintzy* in an edition by Emil Cooper, who conducted. Marina Koshetz, Winifred Heidt, Carlton Gauld, Michael Bartlett, and Donald Dame were in the cast. *Macbeth* was given again, directed by Fritz Stiedry, and the company included several future Metropolitan singers, among them Hugh Thompson and Christine Johnson. This season produced Erich Korngold's version of *Die Fledermaus* (*Rosalinda*), which opened on October 28 and ran for 521 performances.

ductor conduct any opera in many, many years." Albanese's Violetta progressed from a tentative beginning and some wayward sound in *"Sempre libera"* to an intent, expressive characterization that reached a proper climax in a splendid *"Addio del passato."* Kullmann and Tibbett were son and father.

Sodero's other assignment included *Tosca, Trovatore,* and *Cavalleria-Pagliacci,* in which Moore extended her command of Tosca, Peerce sang a promising Cavaradossi, and Warren made first flights as Di Luna* and Tonio.* Jagel also sang a tight-voiced Cavaradossi this season, and Thorborg added to the inequalities of a *Trovatore* with Roman, Carron, and Valentino when she sang Azucena* on March 13. Peerce had a success as Edgardo* in *Lucia* on November 28 with Pons, St. Leger conducting.

A career that began with headlines and dwindled to a footnote was initiated on December 2 by Marie Wilkins as Lakmé (d). When Pons was unable to appear, a managerial mind recalled that Wilkins had sung part of the role for an Auditions of the Air the year before, and she was pressed into service. The audience had a tender regard for her courage, which was great, and her stage deportment, which was good, but not for her singing, which was close to disaster at several points. Jacques Gerard made an understandably distraught debut as Gerald (d). According to an announcement on December 25, Wilkins received a contract as a reward, but she appeared only in Sunday-night concerts and at a Guild matinee of *The Magic Flute* on January 29 (Queen of the Night*).

Pons was doubly honored this season, as Marie in the opening *Fille du régiment* on November 23 and as Lucia when a new scenic production of *Lucia* (by Rychtarik) was offered on November 28. In the symbolic conclusion of the former work, the Cross of Lorraine replaced the Tricolor of the occupation. Military uniforms were ever more conspicuous in the theater, and the Metropolitan Opera Club took a patriotic stand by authorizing guests to wear either white tie or black.

In addition to Cassel, Wilkins, Greer, and Raymondi, the new American singers included Margaret Harshaw, as the second Norn (d) in *Götterdämmerung* on November 25, and Doris Doree as the third Norn (d). Both sang similar ensemble parts in later Wagner performances. Elwood Gary was the Singer (d) in *Der Rosenkavalier* on January 8, and then joined Clifford Harvuot (another Auditions winner) in military service. A hopeful sign of recovery was manifested by Marjorie Lawrence when she was guest at a "welcome home" concert on December 27 and sang the Venusberg duet with Melchior. Though immobilized, she sang so well that she was included as Venus* in a *Tannhäuser* performance of January 22. In another *Tannhäuser,* on January 7, Carron was Tannhäuser,* and he also sang Siegmund* on February 20. The growing impression, however, was that whether as Radames or Tannhäuser, Manrico or Siegmund, Carron was Carron—an unfortunate status for any artist.

Fiorello La Guardia's long desire to stimulate musical activity for persons who could not afford the Metropolitan or the Philharmonic came to fruition this spring with the announcement that the Mecca Temple would be operated as the New York Center of Music, Drama and Art. Built for Masonic use in 1925, it became city property in 1942 through foreclosure of a tax lien. La Guardia attributed the idea for its new use to his president of the City Council, Newbold Morris. Among those who were designated to attend a planning meeting as representatives of the Metropolitan were George A. Sloan, John Erskine, and Morton Baum.

The last of these, a lawyer specializing in tax matters, had been added to the Metropolitan board of directors in January 1943. His activities on behalf of the Metropolitan's campaign for tax exemption had a successful outcome on April 20, when Governor Thomas E. Dewey signed a bill for that purpose (see page 39). As history developed, Baum became much more influential in the City Center than at the Metropolitan.

A curtailed tour was limited to two weeks in Chicago, one week in Cleveland, and a single performance in Rochester, with the prospect that wartime restrictions would probably prevent any touring at all the following spring. To sustain employment at its usual level, a twenty-week season in New York was announced for 1943–4, though the season's income of $1,501,000 left a deficit of $202,607. The decline in revenue (from the previous year's $1,645,784) was a consequence of the lowered ticket prices, for attendance was on an upward curve.

As the season ended, Erich Leinsdorf accepted a three-year contract as conductor of the Cleveland Symphony Orchestra as successor to Artur Rodzinski, who had been appointed music director of the New York Philharmonic-Symphony Society.

1943–1944

Leinsdorf's withdrawal put asunder the indivisible bonds of specialization which had, with few exceptions, governed the Metropolitan's use of conductors since Bodanzky's arrival. With Emil Cooper added to Beecham, Szell, and Walter, there were opportunities for more diversity of leadership than at any past time. As an instance, when Walter was unable to conduct *Tristan* (the first Wagner for which he had been scheduled in the theater), Beecham was available as an eminently qualified alternate.

As a triumphant instance of making a virtue of necessity, this season was designated as a "Diamond Jubilee" for the Metropolitan, though no one could contend that the antiquated pile was either beautiful or functionally satisfactory. In the way of gestures, an opening on November 22 with *Boris* (in Italian) as a tribute to our Russian allies in the war against Hitler had its limitations also.

Save for Norman Cordon as Marke,* and Janssen as Kurvenal, the Beecham *Tristan* of November 24 used the personnel of the previous season (Traubel, Melchoir, and Thorborg), but the general opinion[1] credited it as greatly superior. Traubel had asked that some of the high tones in the "Narrative" be eliminated, and she was accommodated. This compromise and a late, rather noisy audience may have distracted Beecham in the early pages of the work, for they were moodless and rather disjointed; the performance swelled to eloquence with the drinking of the potion, however, and was thereafter of singular excellence. Traubel had more assurance than before, and Cordon's Marke was ably done.

The sixth *Tristan,* on March 14, was notable for the Isolde* of Marjorie Lawrence. Of necessity, the action was revised to cope with her infirmity. Little alteration was required in Act I, the couch on which Lawrence remained sitting being a normal part of the action. In Act II, Brangäne (Thorborg) handed the torch to the seated Isolde, who extinguished it by flinging it aside, and Tristan (Melchior) entered from a front wing so that Isolde could see him approach as she waved the scarf. The third-act problem was poorly solved. After Kurvenal (Huehn) carried her on-stage, he placed her rather awkwardly on the couch beside Tristan. Doubtless this could have been reconsidered for a future performance, but there was none, though Lawrence sang magnificently. Her top C's in Act II rang out brilliantly, and she managed the love duet till her voice began to tire (doubtless for want of such extended use in many months). The house was crowded and the enthusiasm extraordinary, but Johnson has informed me that some patrons considered the exhibition "unsightly." Lawrence also sang Venus five times this season, but she was given no further opportunity after April 6—a sorry discrimination against a woman already so severely tried.

Beecham's busiest Metropolitan season (also his last) included several further performances of *Carmen* (Jennie Tourel sang the role well on March 24) and revivals of *Mignon, Les Contes d'Hoffmann,* and *Falstaff.* In the first of these, on December 4, Beecham had the questionable privilege of presiding at the debut of Patrice Munsel, a recent Auditions winner and, at seventeen, the youngest singer of a leading role in the history of the Metropolitan. Many were charmed by her aptitude, but

---

[1] Army service limited my personal attendance at performances in this and the next season to a mere scattering.—I. K.

her Philine* was a distressing sample of vocal immaturity. Downes thought her "cruelly miscast," and Thomson decried any thoughts of an immediately glorious career for Munsel as "sheerest folly." Thomson also termed Melton's Meister,* vocally, "as always, naif," his dramatic work "vague." Only Stevens and Cordon conformed to a reasonable standard, though Donald Dame sang pleasantly as Laërte (d) in his debut. Better results were obtained on March 16, when Tourel was Mignon* and Gerard sang Meister,* with Lazzari a suitable Lothario.*

With a lavish contract for concert appearances in hand, and a management as eager to exploit her as Gatti had Talley, Munsel sang more often than she should have this season. She was Olympia* in Beecham's treatment of *Les Contes d'Hoffmann* on December 10, performing more than creditably in a cast that gave more style to the work than it had had in years. Martial Singher made his debut (a year delayed by war conditions) as an excellent Dappertutto (d). Djanel (Giulietta*) and Jobin (Hoffmann*) were both schooled in the style for Offenbach, and Novotna was a charming Antonia.* Pinza (Miracle* and Coppelius*) and Glaz (Nicklausse*) absorbed much from Beecham's direction, which was a high point of his Metropolitan effort. Steber sang Antonia* well on December 30, and also Giulietta opposite Gerard, an acceptable Hoffmann,* on February 10.

Falstaff, in an English version largely the conductor's own, was a reasonable project for Beecham, but not for a cast built about Tibbett's uncertain voice and the fading ones of Brownlee (Ford) and Kullmann (Fenton). On the other hand, such fresh-voiced people as Steber (Mistress Ford*), Greer (Nanetta*), Browning (Mistress Page*), and especially Harshaw (Dame Quickly*) lacked the dramatic resource required when they were heard on January 14. The whole project might have matured better had Warren, who sang Falstaff* on March 11, been in the first cast. He had been strenuously coached by Beecham, and used his robust resources well. Four performances in the old Urban settings (touched up at a cost of $5,000 underwritten by the Opera Guild) were all for *Flagstaff* till the Reiner revival of 1949.

Although Singher's voice was less than a match for dozens that had come and gone without stimulating a desire for extended acquaintance, his varied skills made him both a useful performer and an interesting one. Hardly ideal either as Wolfram in *Tannhäuser* or as Pelléas, Singher nevertheless could cope with their vastly varied musical problems intelligently, while singing Escamillo one day, Valentin in *Faust* another, Amfortas in *Parsifal* a third. In the Debussy music on January 26 Singher provided a tone, an accent it had long lacked, performing in a manner Virgil Thomson described as "vocally impeccable and dramatically superb." Sayão, finally used in a part for which she would seem predestined, was a youthful, well-sounding Mélisande,* Kipnis was a sonorous Arkel, and Tibbett managed Golaud* well enough. Harshaw surpassed expectations as Geneviève.* To some, Emil Cooper's conducting in his debut was "Russified," if not "operatized," as Leinsdorf's had been anathematized.

Cooper's career (which ended with Johnson's) is a typical instance of Metropolitan makeshift in this era. Given an assignment that engaged both his abilities and his sympathies—*Pelléas, Boris, Le Coq d'or, Khovanshchina* (even *Il Trovatore*)—and Cooper could be depended upon for artistic, energetic, honestly musical work. Given a task that engaged only his abilities and not his sympathies, his effort could be brutally forthright and uninteresting. In this year his abilities but not his sympathies were engaged by *Parsifal,* which became a problem when Leinsdorf, who had been expected to conduct it after his Cleveland Symphony season, was inducted into the army. Cooper maintained order from start to finish on March 8, but with many misconceptions of tempo, accent, and phrasing. On March 29 there was unexpected merit in Emery Darcy's good-looking, well-sung Parsifal,* a cause for new valuation of this hitherto obscure performer. For reasons known only to the management, Darcy's promise as a *Heldentenor* (at thirty-six he was fully ready for such a career) was ignored when Europeans became available again. Varnay's Kundry* shared the stage with Darcy's Parsifal,* but not its praise. Sensuous beauty was lacking in her tones; allure was absent from her actions.

Except for *Tristan* and *Parsifal,* all the Wagner of this season was conducted by Szell, who did a remarkable work of vitalizing performances grown stodgy under Leinsdorf. In addition to continuing *Boris* and *Salome* (Djanel was indisposed on January 6, and Ella Flesch made an unimpressive debut as a small-voiced Salome* in her place), Szell gave to the *Ring* a personal poetry that had been lacking in Leinsdorf's methodical work, and a new lift and buoyancy to *Der Rosenkavalier. Das Rheingold* on February 8 had the helpful assistance of Baum (Froh*) and Novotna (Freia*) to compensate for the immature Loge* of Garris and the light-voiced Wotan* of Janssen. Nothing, however, could compensate for the meager style and undeveloped art of the Erda (d), an Auditions winner named Christine Johnson, who was asked to sing such a massive pronouncement as *"Weiche, Wotan, Weiche!"* with virtually no stage experience.[1] Small changes in the remaining *Ring* dramas included Frederick

---

[1] Johnson chose a future in musical comedy after this season, and had the livelier experience of introducing "June is Bustin' Out All Over" when *Carousel* was first current on Broadway.

Lechner as Alberich* and Varnay as Gutrune* in *Götterdämmerung,* but the developing artistry of Traubel (she sang all the Brünnhildes) and the compelling direction of Szell brought results that prompted Bohm in the *Herald Tribune* to say (of *Götterdämmerung*): "It is a long time since New York opera goers have heard anything like it."

Szell's contribution to the growing appreciation of *Der Rosenkavalier* (now in a twelve-year cycle of performance in every season from 1937 to 1949) was a lightness of touch, a rhythmic zest, which combined with a luminous treatment of the orchestral score to make the singers audible without vocal strain. Lehmann was absent this season, and Jessner was the Marschallin of an integrated ensemble with List, Stevens, and Steber, with Glaz an insinuating Annina* and Olitzki a more suitable Faninal than Schorr or Huehn. Novotna (Octavian) and Conner (Sophie) appeared in several of the five performances.

The peculiar "career" of Marie Wilkins had a partial parallel in that of Audrey Bowman, who was the Queen of the Night (d) under Walter's direction in *The Magic Flute* on January 22 and once again on April 1, but nothing more at any other time. She sang the exacting, florid music fluently, but the sustained passages were edged and unpleasant. *Figaro* fared much better in its three performances, with Steber, Sayão, Novotna, Pinza, Brownlee, and Baccaloni, a group complimented by Walter in an interview when he stated that he "never had a better cast anywhere." His season was otherwise devoted to Verdi, the works including not only *La Forza del destino* and *Un Ballo in maschera,* but also a benefit for the Red Cross of the "Manzoni" Requiem on March 28. Milanov was a factor of value in several of these performances, singing a superb Amelia in *Un Ballo* on December 17 (with Peerce as Riccardo,* Warren as Renato* and Thorborg) and performing in the solo quartet of the Requiem with great art. Thorborg, Kullmann, and Moscona were the other singers. Walter's dramatic power and his subtle underlining of the orchestral writing in *Un Ballo* were warmly praised. Oscar, the page, continued to be a problem, neither Greer nor Christina Carroll, a new soprano of this season, satisfying its requirements.

The high level to which Johnson's repertory aspired (*Pelléas, Falstaff, Boris,* two Mozart works) was further attested in an effort with *Norma* on December 29. Sodero's direction lacked something of forcefulness, but the sound was beautifully molded. Milanov's long-awaited Norma* did not please in her solo passages, which were lacking in repose and control, but the duets with Castagna (Adalgisa) were well worth hearing. Jagel was Pollione, and Cordon was a dignified if not very rich-voiced Oroveso.* In later performances the part was sung by Lazzari, who gave a superlative demonstration of theatrical art as Simone in *Gianni Schicchi* on January 6. Those who could spare an eye from Baccaloni's masterful Schicchi* observed that Lazzari conceived his character as an epileptic, with a continuous tremor of the hand. The Italian text was restored, and the careful casting of Albanese (Lauretta*), De Paolis (Gherardo*), and Martini (Rinuccio) renewed pleasure in the work as conducted by Sodero. Lauretta* was well sung by Conner on February 11. Brownlee was a rather pawky Schicchi* on March 6.

One of the remaining ties to the old Gatti company was dissolved on January 5 when Karin Branzell, through the agency of her husband and manager, Fedya Reinshagen, said that she would retire at this season's end. Needless to say, there was no mention of waning vocal strength in the declaration, which included the words: "She hopes she is making a place for some gifted American singer." That could well have been Margaret Harshaw, whose new roles included Azucena and Amneris, as well as Geneviève in *Pelléas* and Dame Quickly in *Falstaff.* Harshaw was crude in action and awkward in the use of her voice—she was actually traveling a vocal blind alley, considering her emergence later as Brünnhilde and Kundry.

Another pattern of ascension and decline interacted on December 18, when Leonard Warren sang his superb Rigoletto* for the first time, as a substitute for an indisposed Tibbett. Considering the credit Warren had earned some months before when he sang the part in Buenos Aires, it might have been sponsored under more agreeable circumstances than a Saturday broadcast after he had sung a Friday night Renato in *Un Ballo.* His success was a tribute to personal resource rather than to good planning. Not much of either was evident in Munsel's Gilda* on February 16, which mingled brilliance with ineptitude. Perhaps the management felt that her youth condoned any vocal sins, but this rule of thumb hardly applied to Kullmann as Almaviva in *Il Barbiere,* Melton as Edgardo in *Lucia,* Carron as Herod in *Salome,* or Jobin as Cavaradossi in *Tosca,* all incidents of this season. Baum as Manrico in *Il Trovatore* was a more calculated risk, thanks to his resources in power.

In smaller parts, the fifty-odd American-born singers who sang this season included Thelma Altman, who was Feodor (d) in the opening *Boris;* John Baker, the Morales (d) of *Carmen* on November 29; Donald Dame as mentioned (see page 444); and Christina Carroll, the Musetta (d) of a *Bohème* on December 20, who was later heard as Micaëla. She gave up the Metropolitan struggle after two seasons, as did Ella Flesch, whose Santuzza* in *Cavalleria* on February 23 was a better sample of her ability than the Salome she attempted as substitute for Djanel.

Though memory of the mammoth campaign for one million dollars was still fresh, the management found itself compelled to ask the public for another $300,000. The expected tax relief had not yet become effective, and though income was $300,000 more than the previous year's $1,502,000, it left a deficit of $110,000. Nothing, it may be noted, was spent on new productions or novelties, and even the $5,000 invested in *Falstaff* was a gift from the Guild.

The valuable services that Laszlo Halasz rendered to opera in New York began in the City Center on February 21, with Dusolina Giannini, Mario Berini, and George Czaplicki participating in *Tosca*. The exploratory season also included *Marta,* in English, with Ethel Barrymore Colt, Suzanne Sten (Nancy), Robert Brink, and Edward Kane; and *Carmen,* with Tourel, Berini, Czaplicki, Martha Briney (Micaëla), Regina Resnick (Frasquita), and Hugh Thompson (Morales). In a spring season beginning on May 3, Resnick showed strong talent as Santuzza in *Cavalleria* and Dorothy Kirsten attracted attention with a well-sung Violetta in *La Traviata* on May 8. John Hamill was Alfredo, Mack Harrell his father. Kirsten had previously been heard with the San Carlo Opera Company as Micaëla, but had profited much, in the interim, from study subsidized by Grace Moore.

As some duplicated names (Tourel, Harrell, and others) suggest, the Metropolitan did not prevent its singers from appearing at the City Center, but no effort was made to establish the smaller house as tributary to the larger. The failing was not one-sided, however—the City Center, ambitious and resourceful, did not welcome the stigma of being a mere training-ground. In time, the working relation improved.

Despite the war, the tour was undertaken between April 2 and May 7, and ground was cleared for future activity with the addition to the board of members from Boston (H. Wendell Endicott), Atlanta (Mrs. Harold N. Cooledge), Philadelphia (Thomas S. Gates), Dallas (Arthur L. Kramer), and Cleveland (George A. Martin and Thomas L. Sidlo). A recurrent project that never came to realization was first mentioned this season when the management announced that Serge Prokofiev's setting of episodes from Tolstoy's *War and Peace* was under consideration for production. This intention served some valuable publicity purposes in the next year or two, and was quietly forgotten when the new state of relations with the Soviet Union provided a convenient excuse for abandoning it.

1944–1945

For virtually the first time in history, no singer of foreign birth was added to the company for this season. Of itself this might not have mattered

greatly, with the relation of native to foreign-born singers already disproportionate to merit, but bearable in the circumstances. The addition of
fourteen singers of American birth, however, pyramided problems both
visible and invisible. Sharing, commonly, a lack of operatic experience and
background, they further depressed standards and made heavier the burden on the hard-pressed conductors. Not visible or audible, however, was
the long-range effect, especially in strengthening the bargaining power of
the American Guild of Musical Artists (AGMA). When a new contract
was negotiated, the unnatural conditions of wartime were propounded as
the permanent formula by which three native singers would be employed
for every alien. As noted (page 436), it was a mere few seasons since
Johnson's program had brought American-born singers from a fractional
minority to virtual parity with those from abroad. The new, unrealistic
arrangement should be borne in mind when future complaints are made
about the absence of this or that European luminary.

Included in the freshman class of '44 were Regina Resnik—now so
spelled—(soprano), Morton Bowe (tenor), William Hargrave (bass-baritone) and Hugh Thompson (baritone), all by way of the Auditions. Mimi
Benzell (soprano), Florence Kirk (soprano), Blanche Thebom (mezzo),
Martha Lipton (mezzo), and Richard Manning (tenor) were included in
the list published early in the fall. On October 25 a further group was
announced, numbering Jeanne Palmer (soprano), Beal Hober (soprano),
Richard Tucker (tenor), Philip Witfield (bass), and Frederick Gynrod
(baritone). (The last named was born in Mexico City of German parents.)

The shifting circumstances of the war saw Leinsdorf (unexpectedly
released from the army) once more a Metropolitan conductor. Beecham,
however, could not leave England in time for the Metropolitan season, and
Walter decided to give up public activity for most of this year. Szell's
work of restaffing the orchestra had unlooked-for aid from the musicians'
union. Use of manpower being at its peak, he was allowed to replace
twenty-five players, mostly among brass and woodwinds. By the end of
the season, the quality of performance was better than it had been in
twenty years.

What the young American singer might expect in the way of carefully
supervised progress was demonstrated by the experiences of Regina Resnik (one of the first Metropolitan singers to come from the City Center)
and Florence Kirk. Resnik was awaiting December 9 and *Cavalleria rusticana* to make her debut as Santuzza when Milanov became ill. Without
time for either an orchestral or a stage rehearsal, Resnik took her place
as Leonora (d) in *Il Trovatore* on December 6, and did better than creditably. At this time her voice was large and luminous in sound; when she

had finished singing Leonore in *Fidelio* (see page 452), it had a quaver rarely absent while she continued as a soprano (see page 568). In addition to *Cavalleria* (in which Sved was Alfio, Jagel sang Turiddu, and Paulee was Lola), Resnik sang Aida* at a Guild matinee on December 15.

If the demands on Resnik could be condoned for reasons unforeseen, even this excuse was lacking for the use of Florence Kirk as Donna Anna (d) in *Don Giovanni* on November 29. More than a dozen singers—including Lilli Lehmann, Nordica, Eames, and Ponselle—had preceded Kirk as Donna Anna, but none had attempted it as a debut. Her natural talent was considerable, but of her singing Thomson said: "When she tries to sing fast and loud . . . she executes a line so far from that of the written notes that a listener . . . can derive little enlightenment from what he hears." Szell was the conductor, and shaped a swifter-moving, more forceful version of Mozart than Walter's. The cast included Steber as Elvira* and Conner as Zerlina,* balanced by the Pinza, Baccaloni, Kullmann trio. Kirk's second role was Aida* on December 16, which would seem to foreshadow a substantial career. Actually she did not sing a leading role again for *three* years, replacing Roman in *Aida* on January 23, 1947. In the meantime she appeared at an occasional Sunday-night concert or in ensemble parts.

The equation of opportunity and ability was better balanced when Blanche Thebom demonstrated her striking voice and handsome presence as Fricka (d) in *Die Walküre* on December 14. The conductor was Breisach, Szell being busy with a Philharmonic-Symphony concert. Thebom's dramatic limitations were evident in all her work this season (her first stage appearance anywhere was as Brangäne in a Philadelphia *Tristan* late in November), but her power as a singer sustained interest till hard work and experience made her a competent actress. Brangäne* and Fricka* in *Das Rheingold* were other parts for Thebom in her first season, the first being matched with Varnay's Isolde* (Traubel was indisposed) on February 3, Frederick Gynrod making his debut as a small-scaled Kurvenal (d). On March 21 the Tristan* was Carron, a dull, unpoetic fellow with a weakness for wandering from the pitch. Traubel resumed singing Isolde on this occasion, but Varnay had established herself as a more than creditable alternate with her strongly dramatized, well-phrased effort.

Leinsdorf, the conductor for these performances, was described at his reappearance (December 4) by Bohm of the *Herald Tribune* as "musically maturer and more poised." This Tristan was Melchior's two-hundredth, putting him well ahead of any other interpreter in Metropolitan history. He was Lohengrin on December 20 when Traubel sang Elsa* with strong voice and ample feeling, but the part was hardly suited to her physique. The versatile Varnay obliged by singing both Elsa and Ortrud* (March 15) in this season, and Baum ventured Lohengrin* on January 15. With Bampton an occasional Elsa, Leinsdorf rarely had the same cast—or even one without a "first time"—on successive occasions.

Szell fared somewhat better with his "revival" of *Die Meistersinger* on January 12 (it had been put aside since 1939–40), though not very much so. A brighter setting for the second scene of the third act had been borrowed from the Chicago Civic Opera, but the expected revision of the cast was limited to the good-looking, rather slim-sounding Eva* of Steber, the promising David* of Garris, and the sound Beckmesser* of Pechner. Kullmann (Walther), Janssen (Sachs), and Thorborg (Magdalene) were as before. Some of the most beautiful singing of the evening was done by Harrell as Kothner,* though the general agreement was that real vocalizing was provided by the orchestra, beautifully prepared by Szell. On a later occasion, Baum sang Walther* much as he had Lohengrin—that is to say, with promising warmth in the early acts, diminishing force as the work progressed.

The pattern of odd debuts and miscellaneous casting can be seen in the Wagner repertory, as elsewhere, with Jeanne Palmer, who was one of the Walküren at her debut on December 2, singing Brünnhilde* in *Die Walküre* on January 18. With Flesch as Sieglinde* and Darcy as Siegmund,* it may be doubted that the Metropolitan had ever offered three less skilled principals in this score at the same time. Darcy found the action of Siegmund more challenging than the inaction of Parsifal, Palmer was not a big enough singer for a Metropolitan Brünnhilde, and Flesch's range was unequal to the requirements of Sieglinde. Cordon made a well-studied effort to succeed Schorr as the Wanderer* of *Siegfried* on February 13, but all his resources did not include the vocal power the role requires.

Although Leinsdorf was once again available for *Parsifal,* it continued to be conducted by Cooper. In justice to the latter, it may be noted that he had reconsidered his treatment and delivered something closer to Wagnerian expectations. At the performance of March 28 Darcy was the Parsifal, with Thorborg as Kundry. Melchior appeared at the Good Friday matinee.

With Walter absent, Leinsdorf had his first opportunity as a conductor of Mozart in New York when he directed *Figaro* on December 27. This was an uncommonly virile treatment of the score, much more incisive than those heard previously. Pinza, Stevens, Brownlee, Sayão, Baccaloni, and De Paolis continued to develop their mutual understanding, with Steber as the Countess. On February 17, Singher performed his vigorous Figaro* and Greer was a pretty if thin-voiced Susanna.* Breisach was the conductor for *The Magic Flute* on January 5 when Mimi Benzell made her debut as Queen of the Night (d). Her facility in the high range enabled her to sing the airs in the original key, with no little brilliance, if rather miniature dramatic force. Those who may wonder why Miliza Korjus, who gave a Carnegie Hall recital on October 24, 1944, did not sing at the Metropolitan may be interested in Johnson's opinion that her voice was "too small." But not those of Bok, Antoine, Bowman, or Benzell! Benzell's other roles this season included Philine in *Mignon,* Barbarina in *Figaro,* and Gilda. Aside from the sparkling top, Benzell's voice lacked body.

In response to urgent requests from both the Philharmonic-Symphony Society and the opera, Walter interrupted his year of rest in March, preparing a new treatment of *Fidelio* for his reappearance on March 17. With no Flagstad for Leonore, it was decided to proceed with an English version. The awkward translation by Dr. Theodore Baker was but the initial liability of a production that reached the stage with Resnik an eager, intense, but vocally limited Leonore,* Carron a poor likeness of Florestan,* Thompson a visibly immature Minister of Justice,* and Alvary barely passable as Rocco.* Greer as Marzelline* and Kenneth Schon as Pizarro (d) sang creditably, but the triumph of making a musical experience of these motley elements was wholly Walter's. The new estate of the orchestra was clearly evident from its inspired playing of the "Leonore" Overture No. 3 after the dungeon scene, to actual cheers from the packed theater. A repetition on March 26 was conducted by Breisach because Walter's wife had died the day before after a long illness.

Amid so much vocal dross the voice of Richard Tucker shone as pure gold in his debut as Enzo (d) in *La Gioconda* on January 25. Tucker's scant stage experience was evident in his awkward movements, but the beauty of his voice, its fine ring and expressiveness, won him a long endorsement after *"Cielo e mar."* When Tucker finally decided to give his major effort to opera (at the expense of a highly successful career as a cantor), the Metropolitan acquired its most beautiful tenor voice since Gigli's. Cooper's first *Gioconda* was described by Thomson as "mostly slow, stuffy, definitely pre-Toscanini," but it improved measurably thereafter. In this cast were Roman, a surprisingly steady Gioconda,* and Castagna, an excellent Laura. Harshaw sang La Cieca* successfully, with Bonelli as Barnaba* and Moscona as Alvise. The frequent references to the relationship of Tucker and Peerce (brothers-in-law) were sometimes extended to a likeness of their vocal qualities. This was a coincidence rather than heredity, for they became related only by marriage.

Pons's decision to spend most of this winter on a USO tour of service camps gave Munsel a clear field for a romp through the classic florid roles, beginning with a Lucia* on December 13, described by Oscar Thompson as "a school girl effort." The quaver on every tone was more like "involuntary trilling," in Bohm's phrase, than her actual trills. Munsel had a relative success as Rosina* in *Il Barbiere* on December 28, her pert manner and vocal flexibility being relevant to the problem. Vocal purists gasped when she omitted the section with trills from Proch's "Variations" in the lesson scene. Pelletier conducted. For another *Barbiere* on March 14, Tourel was the Rosina,* singing admirably if not playing the farce to everyone's satisfaction. Thomson's report on Pelletier's conducting called it "vague, careless, sloppy, and slow." On the whole, Munsel had her best success as the Queen* in an English version of *Le Coq d'or* on March 1, delivering the text with a clarity eventually discerned to be one of her great assets. Her ideas of seduction, thought Thomson, came from "the burlesque stage by way of the films," but her sense of the stage was evident. Cordon was Dodon, and Harshaw the Amelfa.* Cooper's conducting was masterful (he had directed the Moscow *première* in 1909), but the translation credited to Tatian Balkoff Drowne was mostly banal. Harrell sang Dodon* at a later performance, with Antoine as the Queen.

The notion that *Faust* would celebrate an anniversary of some sort as the opening opera on November 27 was hinted at but not quite clarified. Allowing for two years of inactivity, this was only the fifty-ninth season of Metropolitan opera, and in any case hardly an occasion for jubilation of any sort. Thomson noted that Mrs. Cornelius Vanderbilt was not in her customary box, with loss to the social glitter, and added that the absence "of Sir Thomas Beecham from the pit was equally unfortunate to the brilliance of the stage show." Martha Lipton, a rich-voiced alto of slight experience, made her debut as Siébel (d) in a cast with Jobin, Albanese, Pinza, and Singher. Conner sang Marguerite* competently on December 29, but with little dramatic force. A similar summation might be made of Steber's Violetta* in *La Traviata* on March 9.

Largely speaking, the Metropolitan was conducting Operation Survival this season, with a quality of performance Thomson was charitable enough to call "dependably second rate." Occasionally, as in the several performances of *Norma* with Milanov (Tourel was an excellent Adalgisa* on December 15), or *Figaro* or *Der Rosenkavalier,* the level was almost first-class, but the sag from a dependable standard was often conspicuous. Thus, Djanel as Santuzza* and Brownlee as Alfio* in *Cavalleria* on March 30, or Raymondi as a minuscule Micaëla in *Carmen* with Swarthout, Kullmann, and Hugh Thompson as Escamillo.

Hugh Thompson had shown a light baritone voice skillfully used in his debut as Schaunard (d) in *La Bohème* on December 1 (with Peerce as Rodolfo,* Moore, and Greer), but hardly the power or personality for Escamillo. Oscar Thompson, of the *Sun,* met a challenge never before posed to a critic of a Metropolitan singer by describing his son's debut thus: "A newcomer, Hugh Thompson, made a very successful debut as Schaunard. His voice is a good one, and for once the musician had the same operatic standing as the poet, painter, and the philosopher." Thompson's season was a mixture of feast and famine, his parts ranging from Nachtigall in *Die Meistersinger* to Papageno in *The Magic Flute,* with the Herald in *Lohengrin,* Prince Afron in *The Golden Cockerel,* the Minister of Justice in *Fidelio,* and Silvio in *Pagliacci* along the way. Richard Manning, the Messenger (d) of *Aida* on November 30, made his debut in company with Philip Whitfield, the King (d). Neither endured for long. William Hargrave sang a Noble (d) in *Lohengrin* on December 22, and such secondary parts as Ferrando in *Il Trovatore* and Monterone and Sparafucile in *Rigoletto.*

The imminent victory in Europe eased transportation restrictions as spring approached, and the Metropolitan toured as far west as Minneapolis, also visiting Baltimore, Boston, Cleveland, Chicago, Rochester, Milwaukee, and Lafayette, Indiana. Including radio income, the season's receipts totaled $2,671,123, the highest total in fifteen years. After all deductions, a net profit of $5,872 was recorded.

Operations at the City Center moved closer to their eventual pattern, with seasons before and after the Metropolitan's. Of special note was the opening *Manon Lescaut* on November 9, in which Dorothy Kirsten's Manon was commended by Virgil Thomson as the work of a singer with a "naturally powerful stage personality" who "should go far." William Horne was Des Grieux, and Thomas Hayward was a member of the cast as a Student. Jean Morel conducted the *Traviata* in which Kirsten sang Violetta on November 12. Polyna Stoska, who moved to the Metropolitan in due course, was Saffi in an English version of Strauss's *Gypsy Baron* on November 14, with Carlton Gauld as Homonnay, and Horn as Barinkay. Marguerite Piazza was charged with a small part in this production conducted by Halasz. The spring season opened on April 12 with a vigorous *Fliegende Holländer* in which Doris Doree, one of the Metropolitan's now-and-then-performers, sang an unexpectedly forceful Senta. Frederick Destal was the Dutchman, and Sidor Belarsky sang Daland, with Horne (Erik) and Enid Szantho (Mary). Giulio Gari was singled out for commendation as the Steersman. Also creditable were Doree's Santuzza on April 19 and Kirsten's Marguerite in *Faust* the day before.

On May 14, with the European war at an end, Johnson was reappointed for two years, and presented by the board with a scroll testifying to his work during ten years' service as general manager. He responded with thanks for being able to take part in "this next decade, which promises to bear the fruits of the sufferings and difficulties of the past war years."

1945–1946

Peace had indeed come to all theaters of war by fall, but not to all theaters of opera. The easy acceptance of incompetence now imposed a period of extrication to balance the one of implication. A new consideration of shortcomings brought the conclusion that the old tattered *Ring* settings would not stand another round of use, and the cycle was dropped for the first time since 1924. An historic point had been reached with the realization that the normal pattern of income and expenditure would not support the burden of a new scenic commission of this magnitude. For this and other purposes, the Opera Guild undertook the establishment of a Production Fund, collecting money from such sources as a pre-season *Roméo et Juliette* on November 23. A large audience paid advanced prices to hear Munsel sing her first Juliette.* The profit to the fund ($15,000) was greater than the profit to Gounod.

Symptomatic of the new and widespread interest in opera was the broadcasting of *Lohengrin* on November 26, the first opening to be thus honored. Ermine was back, as were white ties. The ranking guests were Mrs. Harry S. Truman and her daughter, Margaret, whose musical ambitions were beginning to be known. Mrs. Cornelius Vanderbilt III was again present, and if her return did not bring Beecham's, there was a better than expectable replacement in Fritz Busch. He was warmly received and warmly commended for a *Lohengrin* that had fine lyric flow and, with Torsten Ralf as a new Swan Knight (d), more musical worth than any in recent years. Traubel, Thorborg, Janssen, and Cordon completed a cast whose virtue was solidity rather than brilliance.

With Busch added to Szell, Cooper, and Walter in fairly steady rotation, the day-to-day level of direction was high indeed. If Beecham's flair for the French repertory was absent, so was the French repertory, save for *Roméo, Carmen,* and *Les Contes d'Hoffmann.* Cooper conducted the first rather roughly, Pelletier the others.

As the junior in service this season, Busch was restricted to *Tannhäuser,* a freshened treatment of *Don Pasquale,* and *Tristan* (in addition to *Lohengrin*), of which the first was decidedly the least good. A puzzling lack of cohesion in the first act on December 14 could be related to Melchior's growing difficulty with the music of Tannhäuser and to the tentative

Venus* of Thebom, but reflection yielded the thought that the Metropolitan used the Paris version of the score, with which Busch (of Dresden) had little occasion to be acquainted. On February 2, the Tannhäuser was Ralf, and on March 23, the part of Wolfram was sung by Huehn, marking his return from war service. The tenor fared well, but the baritone's voice had faded distressingly, and he was not heard in a later season.

The warmth and wit Busch imparted to *Don Pasquale* on January 5 were to some a reminder of his status as a Mozartian, to others a flaunting of that skill in an inappropriate place. Donizetti has rarely been so well served at the Metropolitan, however, as with Brownlee (Malatesta) and Baccaloni (Don Pasquale), both of whom had sung the work with Busch in Glyndebourne, and with Martini, Sayão, and De Paolis. Of equal finesse was the Busch *Tristan* on February 2, remarkable for no single feature save a steadily controlled orchestral sound that made for a strong impact at the climaxes. With Traubel, Melchior, Kipnis, and Thorborg on February 2 was Joel Berglund as Kurvenal.*

Berglund, no less than Ralf, was typical of the fine Scandinavian singers who enriched the Metropolitan at this time. Two—Bjoerling and Flagstad —had exceptional vocal endowment. The others had progressed, by carefully supervised steps, to rank as artists thoroughly equipped for a career. Berglund sang a strong, well-detailed Sachs (d) at his debut in *Die Meistersinger* on January 9, an eloquent Wotan* in *Die Walküre* on January 25 (rather drably conducted by Breisach till Berglund took charge in Act III), and Kurvenal (as noted). His tones had lost some of their velvet since he had first visited America as a concert singer in 1938, but their power and modulated resonance were cannily controlled. Ralf was a special pleasure as Walther* in *Die Meistersinger* on February 9, singing the music with more freedom and ease than any tenor the public could recall. Szell had his forces under strong control at all times, even at the broadcast of December 15, in which, with Berglund not yet arrived and Janssen indisposed,[1] Gynrod undertook to sing Sachs,* though his was plainly not the voice for such a role in a big theater. He won the thanks of the management, but not a re-engagement.

Ralf's repute in some of the heavier roles of the Italian repertory was tested if not sustained when he was Otello* in a revival directed by Szell on February 23. In the love duet Ralf sang with freshness and winning style, but there was no *"Sangue"* in his tones, any more than there was the jubilant *"Esultate."* The strong surge of feeling Szell brought to this score counted for much, however, though the erratic cast—Roman was

---

[1] The more than casual number of such occurrences did not increase Janssen's popularity with conductors or management. See page 490.

an able Desdemona, Warren as yet only promising as Iago,* and Lipton feeling her way as Emilia*—was sometimes hard pressed to keep up with him. De Paolis as Cassio and Moscona as Lodovico performed expertly, Schon as Montano* less so. Quite the best of Ralf's roles this season was Parsifal,* which he sang with warmth and musical resource on March 6 despite a return by Cooper to his offhand manner with this score, a voice-weary Gurnemanz by Kipnis, and signs of distress in Thorborg's Kundry. Janssen was the Amfortas of this performance, but he was indisposed for a repetition on March 22, when Hawkins sang the role for the first time, with compelling earnestness.

The upward trend contributed to some tenor roles by Ralf was paralleled elsewhere by the return of Bjoerling, the growing stature of Peerce and Tucker, and the promising talent of Ramon Vinay, a Chilean who had attracted attention as a City Center Don José during the fall. The same part served for his Metropolitan debut on February 22, with Djanel (as Carmen), Raymondi, and Thompson. Vinay looked well and performed with musicianly purpose, but the traces of baritone origin were still in his tones. It was some time before their dark richness came to proper use with Otello and Tristan.

Bjoerling's voice was a shade less brilliant when he was welcomed back on November 29 as the Duke in *Rigoletto* (with Sayão, Warren, and Lipton as Maddalena*) than it had been four years before, but his new-found ability to spread his effort over an evening's length was close to compensation. He sang a boyishly eager, brightly colored Cavaradossi* on December 5 (with Moore and Tibbett) which would have profited from a qualified stage director's supervision; and performances of Rodolfo on January 1 and Riccardo in *Un Ballo in maschera* on April 17 which left but one complaint—the relative infrequency of his appearances. An odd contrast in Rodolfos was evident when Peerce performed the role in the Toscanini broadcast of February 3 with model fidelity to the printed page, only to resume all the tiresome theatrical "liberties" when he was next heard in a Metropolitan *Bohème* on February 18.

A heartening shape of things to come was provided by a *Traviata* of December 15, in which Tucker sang a fine-sounding Alfredo* and Robert Merrill (an Auditions winner) made his debut to sing a Germont (d) far more polished and powerful than one would have expected from his background in radio and summer resorts. Somewhat as with Warren (though gaited, vocally and temperamentally, for another kind of service), Merrill's performances as Ashton in *Lucia* and Escamillo in *Carmen* left only the question whether he would grow, artistically, to equality with his noble endowment.

He had ample opportunity to familiarize himself with the problems of Escamillo, for *Carmen* was given ten performances during this season, and he appeared in eight of them. This was a by-product of Risë Stevens's interest in the title part, which she performed first on December 28. Her good appearance and untraditionally thoughtful singing of the music commanded respect, but repetition did not increase it. The first act was her most successful, her actions thereafter not developing a consistent line of character as, for example, did her Octavian. Jobin, Albanese, and Sved were in this first cast, with Pelletier conducting. At a performance of January 18, Fiorenza Quartararo, a California discovery of Walter, sang Micaëla (d) promisingly. She also sang a creditable Pamina* in *The Magic Flute* on March 4, but her later career embraced only sporadic appearances in principal parts, no steady line of development. Thus the warmth of her voice, the strength of her temperament, achieved no enduring results.

The value of a reasonable progression to prominence was conversely shown by Dorothy Kirsten, whose demonstrations of ability at the City Center earned a Metropolitan opportunity as Mimi (d) in a *Bohème* with Peerce, Singher (Marcello*), and Greer on December 1. Half a dozen years of background in radio, in touring companies, and in Italy gave Kirsten an amount of operatic routine which should always be a minimum requirement for Metropolitan acceptability, but was in fact exceptional at this time. Her strong, well-used voice was more impressive for health than emotion, but she left no doubt of her right to be where she was. In retrospect, Kirsten's ventures as Juliette and Violetta were a digression from her true line of ability. She managed the florid requirements of both well enough, but the differentiation of style was rudimentary. Oddly, the Gounod score had some efficient service from its male performers—Jobin or Gerard as Roméo, Singher as Mercutio, Moscona as Frère Laurent, and Thomas Hayward, another Auditions winner, as Tybalt (d) on November 23—but neither Kirsten nor Munsel as Juliette, nor Greer nor Benzell as Stéphano gave much pleasure. Hugh Thompson later sang Mercutio, and Garris was heard as Tybalt.

A new ceremonial pattern of activity was initiated by Pons in this season. She celebrated Christmas by singing Lucia, and performed the part once again on January 10. Otherwise the Metropolitan saw nothing of her. Thus, though her name on the roster suggested a certain level of coloratura art, evidence of it was a rarity during the season. Tibbett's appearances were also restricted, but hardly for reasons so voluntary. His greatest prominence occurred on January 5 when he added Michele* in Puccini's *Il Tabarro* to his long list of Metropolitan roles. Albanese sang a strong Giorgetta,* and Jagel was an excellent Luigi,* but Tibbett was hard put to produce the vocal power the role required. This laid something of a restraining hand on Sodero's conducting, though he clearly knew what he wanted to do. *Il Tabarro* was directed by Konstantine (Dino) Yannopoulos, who had studied stage direction in Salzburg with Graf and was suggested for the assignment when the latter became ill. His contribution was hardly a major one, however, to judge from Thomson's observation that "the wives of fluvial transportation workers wear pink silk shirtwaists on a day when they are not going anywhere and . . . Notre Dame faces the wrong way." *Il Tabarro* was joined to *Don Pasquale* on later occasions, with Sved singing a powerful Michele* on February 8.

The Puccini repertory returned to its normal course on January 19 when *Madama Butterfly* was resumed after a wartime lapse (see page 435), with Albanese and Brownlee in customary roles, and Melton as a trim-looking naval man. His preference for today's rolled collar rather than the stand-up one of the period was debated and not endorsed. Vocally the day belonged to Albanese, who had developed her fine characterization even more during the years when *Butterfly* was not being given. It was now a work of dramatic as well as vocal distinction. Hawkins sang a strong Uncle-Priest.* Sodero being ill, Cimara conducted capably. Roman sang a creditable Butterfly* on March 9, a really fine Mimi* in *La Bohème* on March 2. Her disposition to dress the part as an impoverished working girl rather than a prosperous prima donna was welcome, as was her clean vocal work. Moore was only occasionally evident this season, resulting in opportunities as Tosca* for Resnik on January 11 and for Ella Flesch on February 23. The former sang powerfully but lacked dramatic resource for the part; the latter combined a reasonable quantity of both virtues, but did not seem to enjoy favor with the management.

The labor that Beecham had expended on *Les Contes d'Hoffmann* was all but forgotten when the work was resumed on January 12 with Pelletier conducting. Pierrette Alarie, a small-voiced Auditions winner, was Olympia,* with Thebom as Giulietta,* Novotna again as Antonia, and Jobin as Hoffmann. Singher undertook the four baritone roles, his Dappertutto remaining outstanding, his Coppelius* being excellent, his Miracle* overacted. As if determined to make things difficult, Thebom, a reasonably suitable Venus in *Tannhäuser,* continued to sing Giulietta, while Djanel, an experienced Giulietta, struggled with Venus* in *Tannhäuser* on January 21. Singher showed his mettle with a lively Figaro* in *Il Barbiere* on December 7, with Sayão, Landi, Baccaloni, and Pinza.

The other new singers this season were Giacomo Vaghi, a bass-baritone from Italy by way of South America, who sang a well-schooled Colline (d) in *La Bohème* on February 18, Don Basilio in *Il Barbiere,* and Alvise in *La Gioconda;* and Wellington Ezekiel, a bass-baritone first heard as the High Priest* in *The Magic Flute* on December 1. Little could be told of his ability in this season (though the fact was established that his name was not, as one paper had it at the time of his engagement, Ezekiel Wellington). With Cooper a more alert conductor than the year before, *La Gioconda* offered some stirring vocalism from Milanov, Pinza (Alvise), Tucker (Enzo), and Warren (Barnaba), with Stevens as Laura* on December 21. Thebom also experimented with Laura* this season and Lipton with La Cieca,* both performances showing vocal promise and dramatic immaturity.

With Frank St. Leger now serving as administrative assistant to Johnson in the place of Eric A. Clarke (who had accepted an assignment with the military government in Germany), the conducting staff was augmented by Max Rudolf, who made his debut as a well-versed interpreter of *Der Rosenkavalier* on March 2. He tended more and more to administrative matters, however, and succeeded to some of St. Leger's responsibilities when Bing replaced Johnson. In the Mozart repertory, this was a *Magic Flute* and *Don Giovanni* year, with the casts much like those of the previous season. Arthur Kent returned from military service to sing Masetto on December 13, but he was vocally unready for activity. Walter continued his performances of *Fidelio* in English, with Resnik again the preferred Leonore. Jagel was Florestan* on December 17, with Hawkins an imposing Don Fernando.*

Melchior and Pinza called attention to their long service with the company with galas, of which Melchior's was motivated by a charitable impulse, Pinza's apparently motivated by Melchior's. The tenor appointed February 17 (a Sunday) for a concert to commemorate his debut exactly twenty years before, and directed that the proceeds ($5,000) be applied to the fund for a new production of the *Ring.* Pinza chose a *Don Giovanni* of March 20 for his anniversary, though the date anticipated the actual event by six months. Both men were in excellent vocal condition, Pinza singing his "Champagne" air with breathtaking *élan.* Joining in his celebration were Milanov, Steber, Conner, and Lazzari, with Garris as Ottavio.*

The expanding activities of the City Center began on September 27 and continued till mid-November. *The Bartered Bride,* in English, with Polyna Stoska as Marenka, attracted particular attention, with eight additional performances in December (some with Brenda Lewis). The repertory otherwise included *Tosca, Pagliacci* and *Cavalleria, La Bohème, Traviata* (with Conley as Alfredo), and *Carmen* (with Winifred Heidt and Ramon

Vinay). Stoska also sang Senta in *Der fliegende Holländer*. During the spring season, which began on May 9, Enzo Mascherini showed good Italian schooling as Marcello in *La Bohème* on May 10, Camilla Williams was introduced as Butterfly on May 14, and Virginia MacWatters added to the zest of a venture into Gilbert and Sullivan with a lively Mabel in *The Pirates of Penzance*. The season was extended one week beyond its announced closing on May 26, when public interest continued strong.

The Metropolitan's well-attended season and the long tour (St. Louis, Memphis, Chattanooga, Dallas, and Bloomington were visited as well as seven other cities) produced an income of $2,251,069. With virtually nothing spent on new productions (the Guild contributed $10,000 to make the restoration of *Die Meistersinger* possible), the year ended with a credit balance of $4,370.

The odd sequence of events involving Leinsdorf and Szell moved a step farther as the season was in progress, with the announcement from Cleveland that Szell would be the new conductor of the orchestra in Leinsdorf's place. Thus, of three contracted years, Leinsdorf actually served one and a fraction of another (he was in the army during the second) before being replaced. Szell's successor at the Metropolitan was Fritz Stiedry.

1946–1947

A review of the two preceding seasons and a preview of this one shows an unmistakable salient fact: that, in this era, Metropolitan opera could be conducted within the framework of income and not sustain a deficit. The two seasons just past and the one that impended all avoided a loss. (They showed a total profit of some $20,000, a negligible amount in a turnover of more than $5,000,000.) In none of them, however, was there more than a token amount of scenic construction; in none of them was a work not previously given in the theater studied and produced without outside assistance; all attracted close to capacity business; and labor demands respected a status quo.

If all four conditions were preserved indefinitely, doubtless the Metropolitan days and nights could be filled with music of some sort without need for public underwriting. But one cannot manage an opera house by that program any more than one can operate a library without buying a book now and then, or a museum without funds for acquisitions. Even if all other factors could be controlled, the long-delayed day of reckoning with the unions could not be put off forever.

In this season, for example, a long dispute with AGMA erupted in a threat by the management to cancel the season when the union bitterly opposed a plan to reduce the chorus. In 1906, when the chorus wage was fifteen dollars per week, there were 29 singers in the German chorus, 43 in the Italian chorus, and 22 Americans who performed with both—a total of 94. Forty years later, when the chorus had long been trilingual, and was paid five times the wage of the earlier day, it still numbered 94, for no reason related to utility, common sense, or musical virtue. It was the management's desire to reduce the total to 78, paying a full year's severance to those with more than twenty years' experience, and proportionate amounts to some others. AGMA's counterproposal was for a status quo on personnel, and wage increases amounting to $151,000.

The final formula saw agreement on the need to reduce the chorus. Those who remained received an eight per cent increase, totaling $30,000. AGMA, however, took the opportunity to rewrite the whole contract governing relations between the Metropolitan and its members—including secondary singers and others on weekly contracts. A strong demand for unemployment insurance (which would cost the Metropolitan $60,000 to initiate) was put aside "for further study." Needless to say, AGMA was not the only faction that felt the time opportune for readjustment. It provided, however, the only dispute that involved more than routine haggling over wages and hours. When all the contracts had been negotiated, Johnson told the press on October 8: "The final settlement of these working agreements has resulted in an enormous increase in the costs of producing opera at the Metropolitan."

Something was made of the difficulty of "organizing a season" under the uncertain conditions that prevailed till the AGMA agreement was signed on September 24, but it does not appear that the eighteen weeks of 1946–7 differed materially from the seasons before or after. Among various changes, only the absence of Kerstin Thorborg could be attributed to a delay in negotiations. Norman Cordon turned to Broadway and *Street Scene;* Julius Huehn, Alexander Kipnis, and Lotte Lehmann for various personal reasons retired from opera. Bruno Walter elected to accept engagements this year in Europe, after a long period of enforced absence.

Thanks to the curiosity of the Northern Ohio Opera Association, which underwrote the Metropolitan's appearances in Cleveland, the season opened on November 11 with Lily Pons in *Lakmé*. If this seems a needlessly roundabout way of describing the circumstances, it is also the only one, for the Ohioans had subscribed a fund of $10,000 to repair the *Lakmé* scenery, replace its worn-out costumes, and finance a modest amount of rehearsing. Although Pons had more than usual difficulty in singing in tune, and the episodes with the cavernous-voiced Vaghi (Nilakantha*) were especially unpleasurable, Jobin sang a robust Gerald,

Singher was an excellent Frédéric,* and Irene Jordan, a new mezzo, sang pleasantly and looked well as Mallika.*

Those who were interested in more general considerations paid special attention to the conductor, Louis Fourestier, the first musician with a Parisian background to occupy the exalted chair (always excepting Beecham) since Hasselmans in 1936. His competence was clear and his forbearance in taking from the singers nothing due them was admired. Unhappily, however, his *Faust* on November 16 and his *Carmen* on November 24 made one aware that his competence was no more than good routine, his forbearance a temperamental inability to rouse these works from the lethargy into which they had fallen. When he returned to France in mid-January, *Carmen* passed to Rudolf, *Faust* and *Lakmé* to Pelletier. So much for authenticity. On Fourestier's behalf it may be said that he was best known in Paris as a symphonic conductor, particularly for Beethoven and Wagner.

An indication that Johnson every so often recalled his own French schooling may be seen in the addition of Renée Mazella, the Marguerite of *Faust* on November 16, to such properly schooled singers as Maison, Bovy, Tourel, and Singher (among many others lacking such schooling). A sweet-looking Marguerite, Mazella displayed a thin reedy soprano and a tight production that did not alter or improve when she sang Micaëla or in repetitions of *Faust*. More vocal competence if less style was provided by Kirsten's Marguerite* on March 5. Jerome Hines, whose big voice and bigger frame had loomed impressively in his debut as the Sergeant (d) in *Boris* on November 21, was not yet ready for the Méphistophélès* he undertook on December 14.

Thanks to outside assistance, the Metropolitan repertory showed its fifth Mozart opera and its second in an English translation when *The Abduction from the Seraglio* was given on November 29. The benefactor was the Opera Guild, but it received scant returns on its investment from the burly conducting of Emil Cooper[1] and a cast scarcely better acquainted with the work than the public. Steber's Constanza* provided present pleasure and promise of future distinction, more than could be said for Kullmann's throaty Belmonte,* Alarie's inadequate Blonda,* and Carter's musical-comedy Pedrillo.* Dezso Ernster might have sung a passable Osmin* in German, but his thick, guttural English made a parody of the text. Alterations in minor roles (Garris for Carter, Benzell for Alarie)

---

[1] The conductor had experimented with the translation by Ruth and Thomas Martin in Central City, Colorado, the previous summer, where some minor parts were sung by Metropolitan personnel.

left the major deficiencies unamended, whether the Belmonte was Kullmann or Felix Knight. Donald Oenslager's picture-postcard scenery was no artistic triumph, but the work might have lasted in the repertory with a new conductor and a group of associates of Steber's quality. Neither was forthcoming, and the whole venture was abandoned after a meager total of four performances.

Likewise subsidized was the production of *The Warrior,* a treatment of the Samson and Delilah legend by Norman Corwin, with music by Bernard Rogers, on January 11. It had been selected by the Alice M. Ditson Memorial Fund as winner in a contest for a one-act work to be given at the Metropolitan. Minimum expense was assured by the use of "projected scenery" by Samuel Lev, and a cast limited to the principal parts sung by Resnik (Delilah*) and Harrell (Samson*). Both applied themselves earnestly to the problem, but neither could make much headway with a musical line derived from *Sprechstimme* and such impossible phrases, for singing, as "the hangdog droop of hopelessness." Rudolf's musical preparation commanded respect, as did Lev's ingenious solution of the scenic problem. *The Warrior* passed after a single repetition.

On both occasions it was given in a double bill with *Hansel and Gretel,* the English title being certified by the adoption of the Constance Bache translation on December 27. How much this added to the attractiveness of Humperdinck's music may be questioned, but it was well served by a largely American cast of Stevens (a lovable Hansel* in still another male-female role), Conner (a believable Gretel*), Brownlee (Peter*), and Claramae Turner (a substantial Gertrude* who had made her debut as Marthe [d] in *Faust* on November 16). Aside from a general disagreement on vowel sounds, the text was cleanly delivered, no less when Lipton (Hansel*) and Harrell (Peter*) were alternates. Conducting with fervor and sometimes with a heavy injection of sentiment was Fritz Stiedry.

This admirable musician shared his debut in *Siegfried* on November 15 with Set Svanholm (Siegfried*) and new impersonations of Mime* by Garris and Erda* by Harshaw. Stiedry's substantial background was well known, but few were prepared for the breadth and vigor of his *Siegfried.* Pleasure in this was extended to something like exhilaration by the limber figure of Svanholm and his musicianly manner of performance. Certainly no young Siegfried in twenty-five years had been so slender-looking a hero as Svanholm, though this became something of a liability in the love duet when he took a step to the wrong side of Traubel (outfitted with a billowing negligee cape by Adrian of Hollywood) and vanished behind her bulk. Garris was a more than creditable Mime,* Harshaw a respectable Erda.*

In a season that embraced *Die Walküre, Hansel and Gretel,* and *Parsifal,* Stiedry sometimes showed himself dedicated to slow tempos as alternates to slower ones, but he restored balance and proportion to *Parsifal* on March 13, especially in a caressing treatment of the strings. Ralf as Parsifal and Bampton as Kundry were joined by Harrell (Amfortas*) and Berglund (Gurnemanz*) in a notably excellent performance. The rapport thus established was absent on April 2 when Svanholm was Parsifal,* but it reappeared two days later when Melchior sang the role (with Ernster a foggy-voiced Titurel). Svanholm's post-Siegfried parts were not so compelling for perfected excellence, but he was an invariably dependable performer as Tristan, Siegmund, or even Walther in *Die Meistersinger.* If he rarely ravished the ear, he rarely offended it, and when he moderated his volume and formed a phrase as well as he could, the results were quite agreeable. An exception must be made for Radames* in *Aida* on December 4 (with Milanov, Turner as Amneris,* Warren, and Moscona), which had no virtue but earnestness. Nothing he did with the part made apparent a reason for Svanholm's being the first tenor of repute since De Reszke to perform Tristan and Radames in the same season (Carron intrudes, but he was in a different category, as his sing-ing of both was altogether indifferent.)

Welcome as they were in themselves, Ralf and Svanholm were a spur to the complacency of Melchior, who was tending ever more to short Metropolitan visits and to extended absences in Hollywood and on concert tours. When he reappeared on January 22, it was as the young Siegfried (a role he had recently professed to dislike), in trimmer physique than for some time past and with a liquid delivery of the reverie in the forest unique for eloquence and lovely sound. Berglund was a fine Wanderer,* and Mihaly Szekely a powerful Fafner.* Benzell was the Voice of the Forest Bird.* Despite a painful foot injury when he leaped from the table to the floor in Act I of *Die Walküre* on February 3, Melchior sang another *Siegfried* on February 20 (Varnay was a sturdy Brünnhilde,* with Ernster as Fafner* and Turner as Erda*), and a customary number of Tristans. Busch being ill on January 30, he was replaced by Wolfgang Martin, a new member of the musical staff. He managed creditably, though Hawkins (Kurvenal*) and Szekely (Marke*) were new here to their roles. A crisis on March 10 (when Traubel was ill and Varnay on tour) was resolved by the use of Palmer as Isolde.* The show went on, but not very far.

Ernster and Szekely were a welcome reversion to the prewar kind of artist who came equipped to sing everything in the range of his voice and the trend of his repertory. The former had spent several of the war years as a captive in a Nazi labor camp and never regained the sonority of voice he had showed on a New York visit with the Salzburg Opera Guild in 1938–9; but his experience was evident in such roles as the King in *Lohengrin,* Pogner in *Die Meistersinger,* and Titurel in *Parsifal.* Ochs, in *Der Rosenkavalier,* which he attempted this season, was less his métier. Szekely, younger and less experienced, had no reputation at all when he entered Hunding's hut in *Die Walküre* on January 17, but his magnificently plangent voice and imposing presence proclaimed him a worthy successor to Kipnis (whose place he actually took). Fafner in *Siegfried* and Marke in *Tristan* were also well sung by Szekely this season, while he relearned other roles he knew only in Hungarian.[1]

The special qualities Ernster and Szekely brought to the low roles were paralleled by Ferruccio Tagliavini in the higher ones following a debut as Rodolfo (d) in *La Bohème* on January 10. As those of the first new Italian tenor in a decade (Masini had been the last) Tagliavini's liquid tones fell on parched ears, but even those not forgetful of Peerce and Tucker and Bjoerling had to agree with Virgil Thomson's statement: "Not in a very long time have we heard tenor singing at once so easy and so adequate." Albanese was Mimi, with Sodero conducting. The immediate esteem for Tagliavini was perhaps not the best reception he might have had, for the excellent discipline and taste of his Rodolfo gave way to gallery-pleasing and forcing of his agreeable but certainly limited sound. Almaviva in *Il Barbiere* and Alfredo in *La Traviata* were followed by Edgardo in *Lucia* and the Duke in a post-season *Rigoletto* (he had been scheduled for this part on February 7, but was replaced by Tucker, who made his first venture in *Rigoletto* a memorably powerful one). Tagliavini did not have the dynamic range this list of parts suggests, but the fire and conviction of his Edgardo made the contract scene a rousing experience. Those who watched closely could anticipate the constrained throaty sounds that intruded upon his otherwise finely spun tone: when he cocked his head on the side and strained for volume, the results were generally unpleasant.

Tagliavini had a rather abrupt introduction into the problems that sometimes beset Metropolitan opera at his first *Lucia,* for a heavy snowstorm delayed Valentino's arrival from his Long Island home. Hugh Thompson, who barely knew the part of Ashton, sang the first act in his place. Valentino was available thereafter, with Munsel a wavery Lucia and

---

[1] What might have been a spectacular career for Szekely ended abruptly after 1949 when he ventured a return to Hungary to visit his family. He died at the age of sixty-two in 1963. Alexander Sved had a like experience.

Vaghi a dull-sounding Raimondo.* On other occasions, Mario Berini, formerly of the City Center, made an abrupt debut as Faust (d) in place of Jobin, and Vinay's Otello* on December 9 was a consequence of Ralf's illness. Considering the stature that Vinay later attained as Otello, it is amazing to recall that his first venture was without any rehearsal at all with Busch, who conducted—merely twenty minutes' conversation before the curtain. For that matter, Kirsten was barely better off for preparation before her excellent Butterfly* on December 28, as replacement for Albanese. The latter's prolonged indisposition also impressed Resnik into service as Butterfly* on February 8, and brought Hjoerdis Schymberg, an experienced but thin-sounding soprano from Sweden, to sing Susanna* in *Le Nozze di Figaro* on February 15. Stella Roman also was unavailable for part of this season, Quartararo singing Desdemona* rather unevenly in *Otello* on January 9, and Daniza Ilitsch coming from Vienna to sing the same role on March 12, Leonora* in a post-season *Trovatore,* and similar roles on tour. A vigorous personality with a powerful voice, Illitsch did not have the later success her first efforts promised. A staggering climax to this series of misfortunes was the news from Denmark on January 26 that Grace Moore had been killed in a plane crash.

For these unavoidable reasons—and some, perhaps, that might have been avoided—the season's total of roles sung for the first time at the Metropolitan was vastly greater than in any normal year. Of 134 performances, a leading role was sung for the first time in no less than 71. The virtuous outcome of such as Thebom's first Amneris, Vinay's first Radames on November 18, or Merrill's Amonasro* on January 11 formed one thread; a longer, more disheveled one found Lipton attempting Amneris* on February 6, Cherubino* in *Le Nozze di Figaro* on February 15, Magdalene* in *Die Meistersinger* the following week, and Laura* in *La Gioconda* later. As for Harshaw, she added such major roles as Brangäne, Fricka, Ortrud, Magdalene, Erda in *Siegfried,* and Gertrude in *Hansel and Gretel* to her repertory, while continuing to sing Amneris and Azucena. For a Matzenauer or a Schumann-Heink this would have been a demonstration of superb versatility; for a singer three years removed from an Auditions competition it could be described as cruel and unusual vocal punishment. Even for a singer of Varnay's experience the command to sing Eva in *Die Meistersinger* and the *Siegfried* Brünnhilde for the first time might have left her wondering just how she was meant to sound.

The passing of Szell gave Busch command of *Die Meistersinger, Der Rosenkavalier,* and *Le Nozze di Figaro,* of which the latter two were especially notable for lightness and finesse. Among those in attendance at his first *Figaro* on November 13 were Secretary of State James F. Byrnes, British Foreign Secretary Ernest Bevin, and Foreign Minister Vyacheslav Molotov of the U.S.S.R. Another member of the Council of Foreign Ministers was Maurice Couve de Murville, of France. Busch also was charged with continuing Johnson's propaganda for *Otello*, which, with *Boris*, two Mozart operas, and a full schedule of Wagner (though neither *Das Rheingold* nor *Götterdämmerung*), attested to the director's determination to maintain his conception of a balanced repertory, come what might. *Boris*, with Pinza, Cooper conducting, sounded much as it had before, though it was if anything uglier to see on November 21. Symbolically, Tucker, who sang a fervent Dimitri,* not only studied the part with the Metropolitan's first interpreter of that role, Paul Althouse, but found himself wearing the identical costume Althouse had worn at his debut in 1913.

One could list indefinitely the names of artists who sang parts they had never considered suitable before, merely to accommodate the management, without providing anything but embarrassment to themselves. A brutal rationale of make-do prevailed, though one performance canceled for lack of suitable personnel would have done more to cultivate good will than the production of six with persons on stage merely because they could sing a fractional number of the notes in a role for which the replacement of the replacement qualified to perform was absent.

The year's tour was the longest yet in Metropolitan history, with fifty-seven performances in fourteen cities. San Antonio and Houston were included for the first time since 1901–2. The tour took in $773,904. Gross receipts, including income from radio, totaled $2,610,618, exceeding expenditures by $11,808. Attendance in New York reached ninety-seven per cent of capacity.

A new trend in the activities of the City Center was manifest on October 10, when Strauss's *Ariadne auf Naxos* received its first public performance in New York. It had been surprisingly well prepared by Halasz, and Polyna Stoska, Ella Flesch, and Virginia MacWatters performed creditably in leading roles. Tchaikovsky's *Eugen Onegin*, in Russian (with Ivan Petroff and William Horne), was another unconventional offering of this series, which also saw the addition of Giuseppe Valdengo to the company. In the spring series, *Salome* was attempted with a reduced orchestral scoring and Brenda Lewis's strained voice for Strauss's music. *Andrea Chénier* was more accessible to the company's resources. On April 20 Kirsten Flagstad gave a song recital in Carnegie Hall, her first New York appearance in half a dozen years.

1947–1948

Compared with the summer before, the interim months of 1947 were quiet ones.[1] Labor problems, if imminent, were under contract control for the while. The official opening was preceded by a benefit *Don Giovanni* for the Production Fund on November 7, in which Polyna Stoska made her debut as Elvira (d). Off-season alterations had not been extensive, but one was significant. The parterre boxes had been hung with fresh draperies, and, in the process, the panels dividing them had been cut back severely to permit better visibility for those in the rear of the boxes.

Don Giovanni, for which Busch was the announced conductor, was conducted by Rudolf, who managed capably till Pinza and Baccaloni took to clowning the "Serenade" in a manner that defied his control. Busch was also scheduled to conduct the season-opening *Ballo in maschera* on November 11, but he was still ailing, and actually did not resume work until January. In his place was Giuseppe Antonicelli, of Trieste, whose attentive manner and occasionally forceful bursts of orchestral sound suggested that he might be the man the Italian repertory needed. Since his time for preparation had been short, and the cast of Ilitsch (Amelia*), Warren, Peerce, Harshaw (Ulrica), and Alarie (Oscar) varied from fair to mediocre, much of the audience's attention was devoted to such other operagoers as Postmaster General Robert E. Hannegan, Frank Sinatra, and Mrs. George Washington Kavanaugh. Mrs. Betty Henderson outshone all others on the front page of the following day's *Daily News*.

Antonicelli did little that was conspicuous and less that was notable in his three seasons with the company. He was, actually, a third choice for the position he occupied, though his two putative predecessors have vanished into limbo with such other members of a phantom Metropolitan roster as Germaine Lubin, Tiana Lemnitz, and Hermann Wiedemann. Antonino Votto, of La Scala, was promised first in 1945 and again in 1946. Then in February 1947 a dispatch from Italy declared that Sergio Failoni, also of La Scala, had been engaged for the Metropolitan. In mid-summer of 1947 a report from Budapest stated that Failoni had suffered a stroke. Antonicelli was thus a successor to Votto, Failoni, and Busch as conductor of *Un Ballo*. His importance to the Metropolitan became even greater when Sodero died in mid-December.

As the most ambitious scenic project in two decades, the wholesale replacement of the venerable *Ring* production was a natural focal point

[1] The thirty-year association of Edward Ziegler with the Metropolitan ended with his death, after a long illness, on October 25, 1947.

of the season. The choice of Lee Simonson for the important task seemed well advised, considering his stature as an æsthetician as well as a practical theater man. When the four works had been unfolded on January 7, 13, 21, and 29, it was all too evident that a whole series of misconceptions had been perpetuated in a project whose magnitude should have called for the closest supervision at every point. Of the basic designs, about half of the ten were acceptable, one or two excellent. But the acceptable ones were barely so, the objectionable ones drastically so. Moreover, it had been a basic premise that the sets should be easily portable, for touring use. The end product was so heavy that none of it could be transported without elaborate reconstruction.

What had seemed, as the project unfolded, the wildest fantasy—the resemblance of the Valhalla projection to the Medical Center on upper Riverside Drive, the suggestion of Fort Tryon Park in the Walküren Rock, the likeness to the Palisades in the scene outside the Hall of the Gibichungs in *Götterdämmerung*—became absurd fact when Simonson confirmed that he had no image of the Rhine on which to base his designs and had utilized the Hudson Valley instead. The settings were never properly lighted this season, though the management had appointed Rychtarik to the new post of co-ordinator of stage matters to oversee such problems.

Stiedry's musical preparation was beset by difficulties, of which the most distressing was the management's decision to produce Benjamin Britten's *Peter Grimes* concurrently with the *Ring*. The principals did not overlap, but the secondary singers did, and of course the orchestra had to be available for both undertakings. Vocally *Das Rheingold* had much virtue in Berglund's Wotan,* Thebom's Erda,* Stoska's Freia,* and the wonderfully realistic giants of Hines (Fasolt*) and Szekely (Fafner*), but the key to a successful *Rheingold,* a fine Loge,* was not provided by the strained voice and unagile body of the aging Max Lorenz. Thorborg returned to sing an authoritative but thin-sounding Fricka, and Garris was a suitable Mime.

The succeeding *Walküre* (with its outlandish tree in the first act, with a veritable flight of steps by which Melchior mounted to the Sword Department on the mezzanine) was much as it had been before, as was *Siegfried*. Stiedry showed more mettle than previously as a dramatic conductor in *Götterdämmerung,* in which Ernster sang a Hagen* to link him with the great ones of Metropolitan history, Traubel was a majestic Brünnhilde, and Melchior an indestructible voice for the elder Siegfried. Stoska was a fine Gutrune.* A new tradition was established when Siegfried and Brünnhilde faced each other in red capes at the scene of denunciation and sword-swearing. By Wagner's text, Brünnhilde gives Siegfried her cape and horse when he sets out on his journey. But Traubel refused to perform unless she, too, had a red cape to drape her ample form. This "tradition" endured as long as Traubel did, and vanished with her in 1953. An evening *Ring* cycle was also given, in which Svanholm sang the elder Siegfried* in *Götterdämmerung* on February 24, somewhat small of voice and definitely undersized, physically, for the armor and plumed helmet of the part.

Peter Grimes reached the stage on February 12, in a rather nondescript setting by Novak and a musical treatment by Emil Cooper that seemed to vacillate between a *Gioconda* treatment of the orchestra and a Mussorgsky-*Boris* attention to the chorus. This latter element is, of course, in the score, and provided the authentic moments of impact and eloquence in the performance. A more pertinent feeling for Britten's orchestration, however, a subtler hand on the interludes (which were, in a sense, leveled off with a bulldozer thoroughness), would have given more profile to the proportions of the score. The dependable Jagel rather than the more illusive Brian Sullivan sang the first Grimes,* with Resnik as Ellen* and Brownlee as Captain Balstrode. Excellent work was done on smaller roles by Hines as Swallow,* Lipton as Mrs. Sedley,* Hayward as Bob Boles,* and Thompson as Keene.* Both physical appearance and sound were better on February 23 when the younger Sullivan, Stoska, and Harrell performed the leading roles. Thus conventionalized by Novak's setting and Cooper's conducting, *Grimes* made only a token impression on the audience: considerable customary first-performance enthusiasm dwindling thereafter. The fervor or conviction that might have turned the tide toward general favor was not offered this season or the next by Cooper.

Although a restaged *Ring* or the production of such a representative new work as *Grimes* would have been a normal incident of a Gatti season of twenty years before, conditions had so drastically changed that they became annoying abnormal ones in this season. Instead of the estimated $100,000, the *Ring* and *Grimes* cost $194,000 to produce. Of this additional sum, $49,245 was also taken from the production fund, leaving it empty. The remaining $45,000 became the single largest element of the deficit, which, with overhead, interest, and depreciation, reached $233,357 —even though income was $195,000 greater than the year before.

In its conventional aspects the season continued the educational process initiated the year before on behalf of such new American singers as Tucker, Thebom, Merrill, and Harshaw—which was understandable if sometimes difficult to bear—and the propagation of inferior Europeans provided with opportunities neither understandable nor bearable. Among the latter were Ellen Dosia, from Greece by way of Paris, who sang a poorish Tosca* on November 15, in company with Valentino as Scarpia* in place of Tibbett (who was indisposed) and Melchiorre Luise (d), an excellent Sacristan. Dosia (sponsored, it was said, by Spyros K. Skouras, president of Twentieth Century–Fox) was inconspicuous thereafter, but she had an opportunity as Mélisande in the next season. Family ties accounted for the debut of Claudia Pinza, daughter of the basso, as Micaëla* in *Carmen* and further opportunities as Mimi in *La Bohème,* though her pretty, lyric voice hardly suggested such immediate prominence, and of Pia Tassinari, wife of Ferruccio Tagliavini, who sang Tosca (d) to her husband's Cavaradossi* in *Tosca* on December 26 and a later Mimi. Tassinari was a thoroughly schooled singer, but her voice was worn beyond real utility to the Metropolitan. An outside limit in barren vocal condition was proffered by Erna Schlueter, who sang Isolde (d) to Lorenz's Tristan* at her debut on November 26. Dry, quavery sound was explained as the increment of a cold, but Schlueter was an awkward, disillusioning figure on the stage both as Isolde and as the Marschallin two weeks later. Her lack of presence could not be explained away, even if either a cold or an arduous recording schedule in London (during which she performed the final scene of *Elektra* with Beecham till it was sung to his satisfaction) could have explained her vocal state.

As counterbalance to these was the dynamic art of Cloe Elmo, who made *"Stride la vampa"* an incitement to arms in her debut as Azucena (d) in *Il Trovatore* on November 19. With Cooper a forceful conductor of a forceful score, and Leonora well sung by Roman, this was an uncommonly worth-while performance. Inge Manski, daughter of the sturdy Dorothee, sang a vocally poised, dramatically appropriate Inez (d). Elmo gave a new shade of meaning to Ulrica* in *Un Ballo in maschera* on December 10 (with Tucker a strong Riccardo*), but she fell far short of acceptability as Santuzza* on December 19. Constricted range and laborious phrasing were explained when Elmo went to the hospital for an emergency operation for appendicitis the next day; but nobody explained how a singer, if so handicapped, could undertake a new part without the management's being aware of it. Lipton sang a good Lola* on this evening, which also saw the debut of Giuseppe Valdengo, imported from the City Center, as Tonio (d) in *Pagliacci*. His creditable, professional work was received with a demonstration suitable for a Ruffo. Elmo resumed activity in February, adding a skillful Maddalena in *Rigoletto* to her other roles. Valdengo's voice was a shade light for the Metropolitan, but he was a reasonably good Figaro in *Il Barbiere,* if mildly endowed for Amonasro or Germont, which he also sang this season.

A lapse in the Auditions series (the long identification with this project of the Sherwin-Williams paint company had ended in 1946 with the selection of Merrill and Hayward) provided no winners for the roster, but the type continued without the label. In addition to Manski, singers who learned their roles as they adapted themselves to the routine of a season's work were Paula Lenchner, who sang the Forest Bird* in *Siegfried* on February 18, and Evelyn Sachs, who was Marguerite (d) in *Louise* on December 12.

This latest *Louise* marked a new acceleration in the career of Kirsten, ironically provided, in part, by the death of her benefactress, Grace Moore. Some of the music was capably vocalized, and Kirsten had every physical attribute for a creditable Louise* save facial mobility and a sense of character projection. Despite coaching with Charpentier, the characterization remained superficial. Jobin (Julien), Brownlee (the Father), and Harshaw (the Mother*) were able enough, and the small roles were done well by such singers as Lipton, Raymondi, Glaz, Hawkins, and Alvary, accustomed to doing larger ones. The unspirited if conscientious work of Fourestier, Parisian though he was, left as much dissatisfaction as the cool, collected singing of Kirsten, American though she was. Vinay was a potent if vocally strained Julien* on February 19. Kirsten best suited her new role of Princess Aurora of the operatic realm when she sang Butterfly, a characterization entitled to the rapturous attention her young fans gave to everything she did.

Steber's developing career encountered one of its most favorable opportunities when she sang a Pamina* of lovely sound and musical excellence in a *Magic Flute* of December 20 directed affectionately by Stiedry. The repose that made this notable, however, was productive of flat, flavorless monotony when she sang Manon* on January 31. Melton was a fatuous Des Grieux, Hines an immature Comte des Grieux.* In another *Manon,* on November 12, Albanese appeared for the first time since the previous January, and showed the effects, in raspy uncharacteristic sound, of a throat ailment that had required surgery. As a characterization, her Manon* lacked lightness and charm, and vocally it could not be fairly judged in the circumstances.

Something like the burden that had been imposed in previous years on Cordon and Harshaw were laid upon Hines this year. He sang for the first time not only the Comte des Grieux, but also the High Priest in *The Magic Flute,* Il Commendatore in *Don Giovanni,* Ramfis in *Aida,* Fasolt in *Das Rheingold,* Swallow in *Peter Grimes,* and Don Basilio in *Il Barbiere.* A good technique and a strong back preserved Hines from permanent damage, but he would have done any four roles better without the other four to fret about. A more judicious attitude—or perhaps a less complaisant nature—limited Merrill's new parts this season to Figaro in *Il Barbiere* and Di Luna in *Il Trovatore*. He delivered Rossini's patter with relevant ease, leaving low comedy to the low voices, and rolled out *"Il balen"* sonorously. In a *Barbiere* performance of January 29 the Rosina* was Carmen Gracia, a youthful Spanish soprano of good appearance and flashy vocal technique, whose sponsorship by Lucrezia Bori was responsible for intermittent prominence in leading roles during this and the next season. She sang difficult music well, but little music musically. Gracia was the Gilda* of a *Rigoletto* on February 25, in which, as the Duke (d), Giuseppe di Stefano (a post-publication addition to the roster showed a lovely tenor quality and a disarming gift for singing, if hardly enough routine to fit the time patterns Cimara was beating.[1] Further samples of his precious vocal endowment were offered in a *Manon* on March 27, in which he sang a suave, well-turned Des Grieux.*

In a myriad *Aidas,* the one of December 5 merits mention for the selfless art of Torsten Ralf, who added to his unlikely pursuit of distinction in an Italian part the musicianship to sing *"Celeste Aida"* as it is written —concluding with a pianissimo B flat. A mere rustle of applause was Ralf's reward from an audience waiting to hear the conventional shout from Radames.* Ilitsch was the Aida,* singing adequately. An uncertain Gioconda* on December 18 presaged her season of rather erratic singing, which included a good Amelia in *Un Ballo in maschera* on February 7 and ended when she became ill during a broadcast of *Aida* on February 21 and was replaced by Kirk. She was rarely heard thereafter, and was not re-engaged.

The conductor for the performance of *Un Ballo* noted above was Busch, who varied procedure by choosing for his Oscar* not the thin-voiced coloraturas recently favored, but the more substantial voice of Manski, who had the necessary top notes to deliver the C of her show piece and also the power to be heard in the ensembles. His season otherwise included several fine performances of *Tristan* (in which Traubel showed an ever deeper comprehension of the meaning of Isolde), *Der Rosenkavalier,* and a well-integrated *Don Giovanni*. Resnik made a valiant try at Donna Anna* and Quartararo had a fling at Elvira*; later, Greer was a vivacious Zerlina,* Thompson a needlessly foolish Masetto.* Stoska's experience in several German theaters was plain in her Eva* in *Die Meistersinger* on November 29 and Elisabeth* in *Tannhäuser,* which, with Varnay as Venus,* Szekely a superb Langrave,* Ralf as Tann-

---

[1] Meeting Johnson in the corridor after Di Stefano's debut, I congratulated him on the acquisition of so spirited a talent, if one hardly broken to the vocal saddle. Johnson said: "What this boy needs is two years of the kind of musical discipline we have in this theater."

häuser, and Janssen in prime voice as Wolfram, was close to distinguished. This was hardly the rule of the house, however, for a week before or after, one might have heard Varnay as a hard-pressed Elisabeth, Lorenz as a dry-voiced Tannhäuser, and Sved as a gruff Wolfram. (He arrived by plane from Detroit an hour before curtain time as replacement for the inexplicable Janssen, indisposed.)

A comparable disparity might be mentioned in the Italian repertory, which could provide a Christmas Day *Rigoletto* with Pons, Bjoerling, Warren a sumptuous-sounding Rigoletto, and Szekely a virtuoso Sparafucile,* and on January 30 the same work with Conner a timid Gilda,* Tucker pushing his voice as the Duke, and Valentino a miniature sound for Rigoletto. Tucker took a turn to a more congenial repertory with his suavely spun Rodolfo* in *La Bohème* on November 22 and the Riccardo in *Un Ballo* mentioned previously.

A revealing index to this complex season is its total of twenty-nine works, far fewer than the colossal forty-nine of Gatti's most active year, and appreciably fewer than the thirty-seven given by Johnson in 1938. The obvious trend downward to accommodate the limitations of inexperienced singers produced twenty-five as the total for 1948–9 and twenty-four in 1949–50. Thus the later Bing seasons of twenty-one or twenty-two were not the whim of an individual, but an inexorable demand of the situation.

The long spring tour carried the company for the first time in nearly forty years to the West Coast, with a fortnight in Los Angeles in early May. Denver and Lincoln were added to cities usually favored by Metropolitan Opera. Although the income of the Los Angeles visit was gratifying, the expense of transporting the company and its effects cross-country was a dismal part of the post-season reckoning.

The ambitious plans of the City Center contributed materially to the pleasures of opera-going in New York during this winter, with Massenet's *Werther* and *Don Giovanni* added to the repertory, *Salome* and *Ariadne auf Naxos* retained. During the spring season ambition became accomplishment when Maggie Teyte sang Mélisande for the first time in New York on March 25, with Jean Morel conducting a remarkably atmospheric performance. Fernand Martel was a wispy Pelléas (followed later by Theodor Uppman), but Carlton Gauld was a surpassingly fine Golaud. Also welcome was a double bill of Menotti's *The Old Maid and the Thief* and *Amelia Goes to the Ball*. Marie Powers was much admired as Miss Todd, the Old Maid.

These and other accomplishments gave Halasz conversational mention as a possible successor to Johnson, who had frequently expressed a wish to retire. When his commitment was about to expire in February 1949, Johnson accepted a final extension to May 31, 1950, to round out a total of fifteen seasons.

1948–1949

The deepening involvement of the Metropolitan with the prevailing labor problems of the day brought with it, for the first time, the threat of a lock-out—suitable, perhaps, to a private enterprise financed by private capital, but hardly to a public enterprise dependent on contributed funds for its existence. Nevertheless the management advised the press on August 4, 1948 that the season had been canceled.

To be sure, the drastic action had been preceded by warnings when July 1, previously agreed upon by the union as the terminal point for negotiations, had passed without contracts being settled. Against the background of a deficit finally audited at $233,357, the management could see no possible way of granting wage increases or underwriting unemployment insurance, as demanded by five unions—Local 1, Theatrical Protective Union (stagehands), Local 764, Theatrical Wardrobe Attendants, the Firemen and Oilers Union, the Union of Operating Engineers, and Local 802, American Federation of Musicians (orchestral players).

To those versed in operatic affairs, a season's lapse for any reason but lack of a place to perform was merely a threatening gesture, no matter how seriously it impressed the public. The break in continuity would encourage the appearance of a competitor, disrupt the carefully nurtured subscription lists, and put at the disposal of the enterprising City Center venture more able artists than it had ever had before. If seriously pursued, it would convict the board of a gross misinterpretation of its function, which was to assure continuance of opera, not to justify discontinuance. If it could not fulfill this function, its only legal course was to vote into existence a board that would, whether by recourse to arbitration or public hearings or by any other means.

At length, after bitter words between management and labor, in which AGMA (which had no current dispute and would be the heaviest sufferer were the season not to be given) acted as conciliator, meetings were resumed with an agreement on August 23 that wages would be held at prevailing levels, and management would provide unemployment insurance "as soon as a plan can be worked out which will be economically sound." The management further placed itself on record as agreeing that any project to put the institution "on a self-supporting basis" involved problems relating to the "physical plant." From this time on, the antiquated structure and its paralyzing effect on efficient operation began to have some part of the attention they had merited, but had not received, for twenty-five years. Another decade passed before it became part of a meaningful plan.

An incident of this controversy was the brief prominence of Billy Rose, theatrical producer, night-club entrepreneur, and newspaper columnist, as an authority on opera. He proposed to operate the Metropolitan for one year without loss, provided he be given "a free hand and allowed to clean house." This, of course, was a guarantee in advance that his proposal would not be accepted. After an agreement with the unions had been worked out, Rose continued to purvey a mass of gossip, misinformation, and sheer misunderstanding of the problems involved, once in the form of a paid advertisement in the *Daily News* when the *Herald Tribune* would not publish it in the space usually allotted for his syndicated column. More than one person came to the eventual conclusion that if Rose was seriously interested in showing how opera should be produced, he could do it effectively, in Hammerstein's way, in his own Ziegfeld Theater. In the fall of 1952, he finally announced his intention to do just that, but he never made good on this promise.

In the plan of operation finally adopted, the season opened on November 29 rather than November 9, for a sixteen-week period. The total of subscription performances, however, was very close to what it would have been in an eighteen-week season. The intervals in the Wednesday, Thursday, and Friday series set aside in the previous season for special performances, benefits, and so on, were utilized, instead, to fill out the subscriptions.

This was an *Otello-Falstaff-Pelléas* season, with *Figaro* the only work of Mozart in the twenty-five-work repertory. Having remained with the company for four seasons, Busch was now senior conductor. He directed an opening *Otello* of refinement and subtlety, if hardly of the driving power of Szell's. Albanese was the Desdemona,* a little wan of vocal strength but excellent in the last act. Vinay was still struggling with the vocal demands of Otello, but Warren was an improved Iago. For the first time, a whole Metropolitan Opera was televised, with unexpectedly absorbing results. The black and white images left much of the Oenslager sets to the imagination—which was, perhaps, just as well.

A revival of *L'Elisir d'amore* (not heard since 1942) on November 30 and another of *L'Amore dei tre re* (absent since 1941) on December 1 were embellishments of the first week. Tagliavini's Nemorino* and Sayão's excellent Adina, the virtuoso Dulcamara of Baccaloni, and the well-sung Belcore* of Valdengo were aptly unified by Antonicelli. The same conductor was much less adept with the Montemezzi score, in which Kirsten was dramatically insufficient for Fiora,* and Kullmann was vocally

swamped by the vocal needs of Avito. Weede was a powerful Manfredo,*
but the best work was done by the veteran Lazzari, singing Archibaldo*
thirty-two years after his first appearances in the part in New York. Paul
Franke made his debut in the small part of a Youth (d). The audience
included Montemezzi, who had come by plane from Italy as a compliment
to Lazzari. At a later performance, Manfredo* was sung by Frank
Guarrera.

The other variations from the usual repertory were much involved with
the vitalizing abilities of Fritz Reiner, who had returned to opera after a
ten-year tenure as conductor of the Pittsburgh Symphony Orchestra. If his
principal sympathies—Strauss, Mozart, Wagner—were too close to those
of Busch for remedying Metropolitan weaknesses, they were decidedly advantageous to its strengths. As director of *Salome* in his debut on February
4, Reiner delivered as tense and comprehending a performance of the orchestral score as the Metropolitan had ever heard and, in company with
Ljuba Welitch[1] as Salome (d), the most absorbing production of the drama
in its considerable Metropolitan history. Certainly no Salome since Fremstad had sung the music with the ease and steely thrust of Welitch, and her
dance, if nondescript in origin, was vastly effective in the sequence
of the action. When the unbroken cumulative tension was finally snapped
by the curtain, the wave of sound from the audience was as much
a release for taut nerves as it was a tribute to an artistic effort. The applause
mounted to cheers and shouts as Welitch came and went in the dazzling
wrap she wore at her entrance. How much her flaming red hair and pudgy
features would suit another character was questionable, but for her Salome
alone, Welitch was a new figure of legend. Under Reiner's fusing influence,
Thorborg (Herodias*), Lorenz, Sullivan (Narraboth*), and Berglund
(Jokanaan*) gave *Salome* the best-balanced ensemble it had known in
years. Later, Jagel was Herod, and Janssen Jokanaan, without damage to
quality, but Harshaw's Herodias* was tame and ineffective.

In his splendidly organized *Falstaff* on February 26, Reiner chose not
to use the English text heard when Beecham had conducted in 1944. This
was justifiable on practical as well as artistic grounds, for aside from
Warren (Falstaff), Resnik (Mistress Ford*), and Lipton (Mistress Page*)
the excellent cast was largely Italian: Albanese (a delightful Anne*), Elmo
(a superb Dame Quickly*), Valdengo (a bright-voiced Ford*), and Di
Stefano (a lyric Fenton*). Vocally, Warren's Falstaff had matured remarkably, though lack of playing experience still left him short of facility
with the text or mastery of the dramatic action such as Baccaloni might

[1] At her debut, she spelled her name Welitsch. Her American managers preferred
to drop the *s*.

have provided.[1] Neither Resnik nor Lipton had quite the vocal flexibility for her role, but the high spirits and excellent musical quality of the performances gave much pleasure to the three audiences privileged to hear the work before it was taken off.

Reiner's assumption of *Parsifal* on March 18 was handicapped by more than the well-known problem of animating this static score, for neither Svanholm, nor Melchoir, nor Ralfls[2] was available. Kullmann undertook Parsifal,* performing in musicianly style and with satisfactory voice for Acts I and III, but lacking the power for Act II. Bampton was Kundry, and Berglund the excellent Gurnemanz on the eve of returning to Sweden to become director of its Royal Opera. To most tastes, Reiner's conducting was slow in pace, dull in color, with limited mood or atmosphere. On April 13 and 15, the Parsifal was Svanholm.

The excitement Welitch generated with her Salome communicated itself to a much wider audience than the usual opera-goers, with seats at a premium every time she performed. This extended even to Aida* on February 9, in which the lyric sweep of her middle voice and the pointed impact of her top register made for exciting service to Verdi. Wearing a tight black wig, Welitch was an obedient if hardly servile slave, with rebellion latent in her characterization from the first. Objections were entered to her poor Italian enunciation, and some complained that the Verdian line was explosively treated, but her pianissimo in the Nile scene was no common experience. Jagel, Thebom, Hines, and Guarrera (Amonasro) were in the cast directed by Antonicelli.

Aside from Welitch, new singers from Europe were limited this season to Italo Tajo and Lubomir Vichegonov, replacements, respectively, for Ezio Pinza (who was making a transition to musical comedy after twenty full Metropolitan seasons) and Mihaly Szekely, detained in Hungary. Tajo was an oddity in this and the next season, for he made, initially, a favorable impression as Basilio (d) in *Il Barbiere* on December 28, and sang creditably as Figaro* in *Le Nozze di Figaro* on January 8, rather less so as Gianni Schicchi* on February 4. A penchant for exaggerated stage action, however, and a faulty singing method in which the music was growled from the side of his mouth rather than projected normally, lessened rather than strengthened his appeal as time went on. Vichegonov made a creditable debut as Sparafucile (d) in *Rigoletto* on December 4, later singing Hunding and Fafner (in *Siegfried*) with good sound and solid schooling.

With no Don Giovanni available to replace Pinza (Brownlee's voice

[1] Baccaloni sang Falstaff in San Francisco and Chicago during the 1940's, but not at the Metropolitan.
[2] This fine artist passed from American view at the end of the preceding season, a victim, according to rumor, of a brain tumor. He died in 1954.

hardly would support the venture any longer), *Figaro* was the only Mozart in this season, given for the most part with the "standard" cast (Steber, Sayão, Novotna, and Baccaloni), with Tajo skillfully molded into it by Busch. A well-phrased performance on January 8 made this Saturday broadcast an appropriate frame for George A. Sloan to speak of high standards and hopes for the future, but a later performance on February 10 was hardly so auspicious. Busch was filling an engagement with the Chicago Symphony, and Karl Kritz, a new member of the conducting staff, replaced him. Later, Anne Bollinger sang Cherubino,* with Greer as Susanna and Valentino as the Count, and Stoska did well as the Countess.* For that matter, *L'Elisir d'amore* was vastly different on January 23 from what it had been during the first week. Tajo was a limited replacement for Baccaloni as Dulcamara, Di Stefano an inexpert Nemorino,* and Marilyn Cotlow, an Auditions winner, a tiny voice for Adina.* Compare, too, a cast of *Gianni Schicchi* on February 4, with Tajo, Conner (Lauretta), Elmo (a superb La Vecchia*), and Di Stefano (Rinuccio*), with one on March 9 in which Quartararo was Lauretta,* Hayward was Rinuccio,* and Turner La Vecchia,* with Moscona as Simone* in place of Lazzari. Without regard for individual merit, the alteration of so many roles in a work so dependent on ensemble as *Gianni Schicchi* could hardly fail to be a distraction for Antonicelli, who conducted.

This year's Auditions winners included Frank Guarrera, a robust baritone from Philadelphia, who was ill served by a debut as Escamillo (d) on December 14, and overmatched in later assignments as Manfredo* in *L'Amore* and Amonasro* in *Aida*. His talent survived the ordeal, however. Less fortunate was Marilyn Cotlow, the co-winner, who sang an assured Philine (d) in *Mignon* on December 4, but whose power was inadequate for Metropolitan service either in this role or as Adina in *L'Elisir d'amore*. Two semifinalists were also given Metropolitan opportunities when Gertrude Ribla sang a strong Aida on January 8 and Anne Bollinger showed a pretty soprano voice as Frasquita* in *Carmen* on January 1. Bollinger made good progress in later seasons, but there was scant reason for her to sing Cherubino* in *Figaro* on March 15 in this one.

Nor, for that matter, was there judicious casting in the use of Dosia as Mélisande* in a production of the Debussy score directed by Cooper on February 16. With or without recollection of Teyte's recent effort at the City Center, it was a colorless, disaffecting performance. Jacques Jansen, of Paris, was brought to sing Pelléas, which he did with sensitivity, but he was wholly out of place in the spacious auditorium. Benzell was Yniold,* with Brownlee, Moscona, and Harshaw in familiar roles. One repetition satisfied interest for this kind of *Pelléas*.

The reduction of the repertory to twenty-five works cut the Wagner list to five. Despite the previous year's investment, the complete *Ring* was not given, *Das Rheingold* being absent. Melchior sang a fine elder Siegfried in *Götterdämmerung* on December 2 with Traubel, Harshaw (Waltraute*), and Ernster (Jean Browning Madeira made a debut as the first Norn [d]), but he left the company before the month was over. Thereafter the Metropolitan's German tenor was Lorenz till Svanholm appeared in mid-January. The latter's season included an interesting Siegmund in *Die Walküre* on February 17, with Ernster as Hunding* and Stoska an able Sieglinde.*

Some effort was made to give *Peter Grimes* a new start on January 21, when Tibbett performed Captain Balstrode* as part of a ceremony commemorating his twenty-fifth season with the company. Sullivan was Grimes, and Stoska sang Ellen Orford, but the desirable force was still lacking in Cooper's conducting. Hines, the Swallow, did not have quite the exacting schedule of the previous year with which to cope, but he added Ferrando in *Il Trovatore*, Lothario in *Mignon*, and Raimondo in *Lucia* to his list. Di Stefano's fine voice was appreciated not only as Fenton in *Falstaff* and Rinuccio in *Gianni Schicchi*, but also as Wilhelm Meister in *Mignon*, Alfredo in *La Traviata*, and Nemorino in *L'Elisir*. There was virtually no expenditure on new scenery this season (*Falstaff* was given in the old Urban production), but a City Center innovation was reflected in a re-designed first act for *La Bohème* on December 16. In the manner of the staging in the smaller house by H. C. Condell, the wall at stage right was cut away, with a staircase showing Mimi and her candle before she knocked at the door.

The rumors and speculations regarding a successor to Johnson were somewhat quelled with the announcement on January 30 that he had agreed to serve another year, thus completing fifteen. The announcement said that his resignation had been reluctantly accepted, also that Johnson had been offering it periodically since 1945. To assure "an artistically outstanding season" for his last, a campaign to raise $250,000 was conducted on the radio and by the Opera Guild, with eventual success. A long tour that carried the company again to Los Angeles encountered a grisly note in Atlanta on April 20 when the body of John Garris was found in an alleyway after the company had departed. He had been shot to death. His assailant remains unknown.

City Center activities began on October 14 with an English-language *Figaro* in a translation by the Martins, under the direction of Joseph Rosenstock. His warm welcome by press and public reversed the unhappy incidents of 1929, and he eventually became the general manager of this company (1952) when Halasz was dismissed. The company also ventured

Aida though the stage was decidedly unsuited for it, while continuing *Pelléas* (with Teyte), *Salome, Eugen Onegin,* and the more usual repertory. Its artistic standards reached a new level of excellence in the spring season with a well-sung, imaginatively staged *Contes d'Hoffmann* vivaciously directed by Morel on April 6. Robert Rounseville was the youthful, well-sounding Hoffmann, with Ann Ayars as Antonia, Gauld (Lindorf, Coppélius, and Miracle), Wilma Spence (Giulietta), Cassel (Dappertutto), and MacWatters (Olympia). Its success, with both the press and the public, offset somewhat the failure of William Grant Still's *Troubled Island.* This was well directed by Halasz, and effectively performed by Weede (Dessalines) and Marie Powers (his wife), but the rebellious substance of Langston Hughes's play was not realized in Still's score.

Among the prospects discussed in New York musical circles this winter was a possible visit of John Christie's Glyndebourne company, under the auspices of the National Arts Foundation. The McCarter Theater in Princeton, N. J., was suggested as a possible place for it to perform. Indeed, the project was sufficiently advanced for the general manager of the company, Rudolf Bing, to make the trip to America to look over the ground. For various reasons, mostly financial, the idea was abandoned in mid-March.

While in New York, Bing looked up his old friend Fritz Stiedry, a colleague of Berlin days, and asked him to arrange a courtesy call on Johnson. Stiedry brought them together and presided over introductions. After some preliminaries, concerned mostly with the difficulties of producing opera in this era, Johnson looked in mock despair at Bing, saying: "How would *you* like this job?" Somewhat startled, Bing replied: "Mr. Johnson, you must be joking." Whether or not he was—and the chances are that he was —Johnson decided that this was an excellent idea, and arranged for Bing to meet Sloan. After much conversation in the next two days, Bing returned to England with a promise of serious consideration for the position.

Sloan had assured Bing that the matter would be settled within six weeks. As the stated time drew to an end, Bing dispatched a letter to Stiedry saying: "The six weeks have passed and no notification. Hallelujah!" At the end was a postscript: "As I am signing this letter, I have received a cable reading: 'Come to New York at once. Sloan.' "

While Bing was in New York for extended interviews with the board of directors in May, Mrs. August Belmont was in London, and was able to satisfy herself that Bing was *persona grata* in every way. Nothing to his discredit being discovered, the board unanimously voted to engage him for a three-year period beginning June 1, 1950. To smooth his way and bridge the transition, Bing was asked to spend the 1949–50 season in New York as a salaried "observer." "He will work with Mr. Johnson," said the announcement, "observing the operations of the Metropolitan Opera and planning the organization of the 1950–51 season." The balance sheet for 1948–9 showed an income of $2,813,835, and an operational loss of $34,346. Adding real-estate taxes, interest on mortgages, depreciation, and other items brought the net deficit to $172,353.

1949–1950

Considering the possibilities confronted by the board of directors in choosing a successor to Johnson, the choice of Bing was both bold and unconventional. Among the known aspirants were Halasz, Lawrence Tibbett, Melchior, Richard Bonelli, and Frank St. Leger. Certainly all would have brought to the position a much more acute knowledge of local conditions than Bing possessed; each would have brought as well a host of preconceptions and friendships acquired during lengthy careers in America. Even in the world of opera it is easier to acquire experience than it is to divest oneself of preconceptions, not to say of friendships.

For its bold action the board eventually had the satisfaction of results in quality; for the time being, it merely had the penalty that accompanies any unconventional gesture in a conventional society. One immediate pang resulted from a rather grandiose description of Bing's background in a biographical sketch tendered to the press after his appointment. It named him as "Director of the Darmstadt State Theater and the Charlottenburg Opera in Berlin" during his German career, and asserted that after the Nazi accession to power in 1933, "John Chrystie, founder of the Glyndebourne Opera, asked Mr. Bing to organize the first season. Since that time—1934—he has served as the General Manager of that company."

When this printed statement reached Bing, he was compelled to write an open letter to the New York press, stating that he had directed only "a certain, though important" phase of activities in Darmstadt and Berlin. It was harder for him to salve the feelings of those wounded by attribution to him of sole responsibility for the good work at Glyndebourne. Bing explained that he had become an artists' agent in Vienna after leaving Berlin, and in 1934 had been asked by Christie to assemble personnel for Glyndebourne. It was not until a year later that he became affiliated with the English venture, when its successful operation had been pioneered by Fritz Busch and his associate in charge of staging, Carl Ebert. Busch apparently took no offense at the error, but the Bing-Ebert friendship was ruptured for years.

Bringing Bing into the New York scene while Johnson was not only still taking his bows, but trying to assure himself bigger and better ones, was sound enough in theory, but it operated poorly in practice. The press, ever alert for what has not yet happened, blandly looked past Johnson's final efforts toward Bing's first ones; the artists, concerned whether they would be getting new contracts, barely bothered to execute the old ones; a sense of impending change pervaded all, to the detriment of the work to be done in the twenty weeks of the New York season.

Had Bing merely "observed" and allowed himself to be led by Johnson, matters might have continued as amiably as they began in November with formal introductions to the press, and innocuous promises of finding out what the job was all about. But this was not in Bing's nature. Rumors that he had not merely thought of engaging Flagstad, but had executed a contract with her began to circulate in early December. The cleavage on this issue being sharp (a considerable number of persons felt she had given dignity to the Nazi occupation of Norway by going to her husband when her government would have preferred her to remain in this country and contribute to the resistance movement), Bing became a focal point of more than conventional opera-house gossip. Almost as in the days attending Gatti's arrival, absurd rumors circulated that he would give nothing but German operas, or everything but German operas; that all Americans would be "out" (impossible even if desirable); that the repertory would be trimmed to a dozen works given over and over again.

Johnson generously recognized that changes would occur, as he told an interviewer for the *Herald Tribune* on January 14: "Naturally a man of experience such as Mr. Bing will come here with ideas. . . . At the Metropolitan we try to hold to the pattern of the past while designing new policies for the future. But all this is done on a trial and error basis—it doesn't change over night, it evolves."

Had Bing intended to "hold to the patterns of the past," matters might have gone more smoothly; but he soon felt compelled to explain his intentions to the press and public, before rumor took complete command of fact. Johnson resisted this request bitterly, but the board, looking forward to a longer association with the new manager than with the old, finally gave Bing his way.

On January 28, the eve of the promised statement to the press, Helen Traubel announced that she would not sing at the Metropolitan in 1950–1. Bing, it appeared, had been discussing contracts and repertory with some of the younger artists, and Traubel felt slighted. (The rumors of the Flagstad engagement did not improve her sense of security, certainly). Two days later Lauritz Melchior (whose manager, like Traubel's, was James A. Davidson) declared himself offended, charging a lack of "natural courtesy" to an artist of twenty-four years' service.

As is well known, Traubel's grievances were conciliated while Melchior's slight was ignored—indicating clearly which artist Bing wanted to retain. The plain fact is that Melchior's rather childish action gave Bing just the opportunity he wanted to rid himself of a troublesome problem—how to enforce discipline in a company of which a leading member was the good-natured, easygoing (but not to rehearsals) Melchior. It would have been more forthright of Bing, however, to have drawn the issue on principle.

The information Bing made public on February 1 clearly balanced Traubel's function in the new season with Flagstad's: each would sing an equal number of *Ring* parts and Isoldes. Flagstad would appear in *Fidelio,* and Traubel would have an important new role, the Marschallin in *Der Rosenkavaliar.* St. Leger and Earle Lewis had both resigned, and Bing had chosen a new "team" of his own. Bing propounded his proposed changes as in no way implying "criticism of what has been done," but the implications were clear to all in the new director's stress on scenic improvement, spacing of fewer productions to intensify rehearsals, division of the eighteen-week subscription into two series of nine weeks to accommodate more subscribers, addition of Tuesday night to the regular plan of performance, the need to attract a younger audience.

While paying tribute to the "high standards thus far maintained," Bing outlined his intention to secure his leading artists for "more weeks and many more performances" than they recently had been giving. "Continuous changes of cast" would be avoided, and in honoring the soundness of many union demands (job security and unemployment insurance particularly), Bing emphasized his position that the artists "must put the Met's interest first." The objective was an "ensemble of stars—not comets." In summation he stated: "Of course I may make mistakes, no doubt I will make mistakes, but I can assure you that I will attempt to run this house —unmoved by promises or threats—on the principle of quality alone."

For all its formal *devoirs* to Johnson, the character of this statement was so clearly analytic of the Metropolitan's shortcomings that Johnson must have found his role of kingmaker a bitterly galling one. As the season progressed and Melchior issued anti-Bing blasts, Johnson forgot his castigation of the tenor as "an old boat" and warmly embraced him at his last *Lohengrin* (page 418). Bing did not attend Johnson's farewell parties, and though they exchanged conversational pleasantries at the last broadcast of the season on March 25, they increasingly went separate ways—Johnson to his traditional office at the Thirty-ninth Street and Seventh Avenue end of the building, Bing to an improvised one in the studio section of the building. Previous ideas that Johnson as a member of the board of directors would smooth Bing's way did not work out. The bulldozer could make its own way, unescorted by the jeep.

Amid these happenings on the front pages of the press, the events that were treated in the music columns only occasionally had the prominence they merited. Perhaps the most seriously affected was Johnson's farewell service to "musical" opera, the first Metropolitan production of *Khovanshchina* on February 16, in an English translation and with Emil Cooper conducting. Even as the work was being rehearsed, it was well known that it would not be included in Bing's repertory. Not only was this compromising to the morale of those working at roles they would perform but a few times; it also caused much grumbling at the investment of $80,000 in a project doomed to early disappearance.

These considerations aside, there was ample justification for serious study of Mussorgsky's powerful, if uneven score. Exercising the traditional prerogative of editing Mussorgsky, Cooper inserted some pages omitted by Rimsky-Korsakov, and puzzled those who tried to trace a dramatic scheme in the story by dropping the scene of Golitsin's exile. Perversely, too, he struck out one of the few portions of *Khovanshchina* known to the musical public—the G-minor entr'acte in Act IV familiarized by Stokowski as a concert piece. The cast entrusted with the performance of a text largely by Rosa Newmarch was almost wholly American. Hines as Dossife* was close to magnificent, Weede was a splendid Shaklovity,* and Sullivan a youthfully lyric Prince Andrei.* Beyond this, the casting was makeshift, for Tibbett, who might have sung a fine Khovansky* in his prime, was dull of voice and exaggerated in action, Kullmann offered little more than good will as Golitsin,* and Stevens had small supply of the wide-ranging alto voice needed for Marfa.* Stoska, who had a bad season vocally, was ill at ease as Susanna.* Thebom was more the vocal type for Marfa* when she sang it on March 6. Other changes included Guarrera for Weede, and Hayward for Sullivan. A prime source of disillusion was the drab, tasteless scenery of Mstislav Dobujinsky. The attractive Dance of the Persian Slaves was ill served both by the interior in which it was danced and by the inept corps that danced it. As a musical experience the Streltsy scene was outstanding (Harvuot did a notable bit as Kuska*), and the duet of Marfa and Susanna acquainted one with a lyric expression of quite unforgettable beauty.

If *Khovanshchina* left one with mingled feelings about the American talents employed, a revival of *Simon Boccanegra* on November 28 might serve as a summation of Johnson's accomplishment in furthering the careers of such native singers as Warren, a splendid Boccanegra* and Tucker, who rose to new esteem as Gabriele.* Varnay sang a powerful Maria.* Stiedry showed a fine hand for the lyric expression of Verdi, and a plastic one for the dramatic, molding Szekely (Fiesco*), Valdengo

(Paolo*), and Alvary (Pietro*) into an ensemble as fine as the Pinza-Martinelli-Rethberg-Tibbett group of 1932. The four repetitions were all excellent, with Sved as an alternate Boccanegra, and Roman as Maria, Thompson an occasional Paolo, and Vichegonov as Fiesco when Szekely made his ill-advised return to Hungary. Those who had not been Metropolitan operagoers when *Boccanegra* was last given in 1939–40 were deeply impressed by the spaciousness and artistry of Parravicini's settings, remarkably preserved, considering their age.

The virtually gala season (two new productions) acquainted New Yorkers with a new scenic artist of note when *Manon Lescaut* was given on November 23 in a compact, fanciful décor by H. M. Krehan-Crayon, of Czech background. Bjoerling as Des Grieux,* Valdengo as Lescaut,* and Baccaloni as Geronte* were by no means unworthy successors for Gigli, De Luca, and Didur, who had sung these parts in 1929–30, but Kirsten's Manon Lescaut,* for all its vocal security and force, lacked feminine softness and believable character projection. Puccini's music was somewhat more idiomatically sung by Albanese as Manon* on December 26, with Tucker a powerful Des Grieux* and Enzo Mascherini as Lescaut.* Another turn of the wheel produced Roman as an excellent Manon* on February 15, with Valentino as Lescaut.* Jagel also sang Des Grieux and Alvary was Geronte. Antonicelli conducted all the performances.

Had it not been for the war, both Erna Berger and Paul Schoeffler might have come to New York long before this season. The latter, indeed, was offered a contract in 1935, but did not accept. Berger established her worth immediately, singing a wonderfully pure, well-phrased Sophie* in the opening-night *Rosenkavalier* directed by Reiner on November 21. This was by no means the conductor's best effort with this score, for Steber's Marschallin* was light in sound, rather tentative in manner, and List's return (after a year's absence) found him limited at both ends of the scale, inducing a good bit of conductorial caution. The last half of Act III was splendidly done, however, the voices of Steber, Berger, and Stevens (Octavian) making for an uncommon blend of sound. Peter Klein, of Vienna, made his debut as Valzacchi,* and Thompson contributed to the youth movement with a well-sung Faninal.* Television cameras were again present: the transmission now extended west to Chicago and Detroit, south to Baltimore and Washington. Berger later sang a notably fine Gilda in *Rigoletto* (see page 489).

By plan, Schoeffler's debut on January 26 would have coincided with Welitch's reappearance, but her journey was delayed, and so Varnay sang an uncommonly strong Salome* (vocally) to his Jokanaan (d). The abandon of the character was not in her, however, nor the kind of hypnotic effect on the audience which Welitch had imparted to the role. Schoeffler's sharply defined characterization was clearly the work of a superior artist, the well-studied Herod* of Svanholm a contribution to ensemble excellence. In a succession of roles embracing Don Giovanni, Hans Sachs, Scarpia, and Amfortas, Schoeffler was good enough to measure up to a high level in each, if in no single one did he surpass the qualities of its best interpreters.

With Reiner as conductor, Schoeffler as the Don,* and Welitch as Donna Anna,* *Don Giovanni* on February 3 was substantially different from the last Busch-Pinza performances of 1947–8. Schoeffler was hardly the dapper charmer Pinza had been, but he played the role with a consistent character and sang the music with vigor and ease. Welitch was an accomplished Donna Anna, though her red hair and aggressive manner suggested a woman well able to care for herself without the token protection of Ottavio* (Peerce). The metallic thrust in her tones gave vengeful fury to the "Honor" aria, but she could not manage the florid passages of *"Non mi dir"* at all. Resnik, previously a Donna Anna, was now Elvira,* and burdened by its demands. Aside from Peerce, who sang with musicianly fervor, the vocal surprise was provided by Munsel, whose Zerlina* gave her the first chance in years to sing a lyric line. She did it with a charming facility that rescued her reputation from near disaster. Reiner's direction was clean-lined, propulsive, and keenly accented, but it did not convey the expressiveness in this score. Stoska later sang Elvira, and Kullmann was heard as Ottavio. For reasons known only to the backstage crew, Urban's scenery no longer lent itself to the swift changes of old, and there were numerous lacunæ.

Little was known of Ferdinand Frantz, a Munich baritone, when he made his debut as Wotan (d) in *Die Walküre* on December 12, but he made a deep impression with his excellent bearing, strong voice, and mastery of the Wagnerian style. Melchior was in remarkable voice for his Siegmund, and Szekely was a commanding Hunding in a performance carried to impressive heights by Stiedry's forceful conducting and the excellent work of Varnay, Traubel (Brünnhilde), and Harshaw. Fortunately Frantz was accompanied to New York by his wife (known to the German stage as Helena Braun), for Traubel begged off from singing Brünnhilde on December 21, Varnay was committed to a Philharmonic-Symphony concert version of *Elektra,* and no other alternate was available. Braun agreed to appear, and sang creditably enough, to the particular pleasure of the non-musical press, which found a husband and wife appearing as father and daughter worthy of front-page pictures. As a further complication, Stoska could not appear as Sieglinde, and Resnik replaced her with a decidedly successful performance. Frantz was later heard as Kurvenal and Hans Sachs. His contribution to a restudied *Meistersinger* was a sturdy voice and no previous history of performance in the role, which made problems for Reiner, who conducted. The work was especially well played by the orchestra, but a big line was not conveyed by Reiner. Varnay was Eva, with Klein (David*), Harshaw, Svanholm, and Ernster. Reiner had more than a normal share of difficulty with *Die Meistersinger* in this season, for Harshaw had to be relieved by Glaz before the second act of one performance, Svanholm tried to sing despite a cold on another occasion, giving way to Kullmann after Act I, and Janssen crowned his history of cancellations by withdrawing from the performance of February 27 in favor of Schoeffler.

A further untapped source of talent for the Metropolitan was revealed on December 1, when Jonel Perlea, a conductor of Romanian birth and recent Italian activity, made his debut as conductor of *Tristan*. (Busch had left the company with the broadening of opportunities in postwar Europe.) The sensitivity of Perlea's "Prelude" and the manner in which he supported the vocalists in the early phases of Act I augured an uncommon artist. Both Traubel and Melchior profited from an orchestral texture that was colorful but not thick, from a leadership that collaborated rather than dominated. Perlea's versatility was evident in a finely dramatic *Rigoletto* on December 4, in which Berger sang the cleanest, most musical Gilda* New York had heard in years, Warren was a vocally prodigious Rigoletto, and Tucker was the Duke. His *Carmen* on December 8 was brilliantly conducted if indifferently sung by Stevens, Kullmann, Singher, and Conner, and he gave a note of believable feeling even to the routine *Traviata* of the Metropolitan on the 22nd, with Albanese, Peerce, and Mascherini (as Germont*) as the singers. Perlea would have adorned any opera company's conducting staff, but his Metropolitan career came to an end when he could not agree on repertory with Bing.

Mascherini (noted above for Germont) was one of two new singers this season who had earned Metropolitan opportunity by superior work at the City Center, the other being the American tenor Eugene Conley. The experience of both at the Metropolitan showed that success in the smaller theater could be deceptive, for neither had the abundance of voice for the kinds of roles they sang this season. Mascherini's debut occurred as Marcello (d) in *La Bohème* on December 7, Conley's as Faust (d) on January 25. Of subsequent roles, the baritone had more to offer as Germont than he did as Rigoletto. Conley's good looks and manly style were appropriate to Pinkerton and Edgardo, but he was inclined to drive his voice hard, with little variation in color or dynamics. Another singer of brief prominence was Elisabetta Barbato, an Italian soprano of talent but limited experience, who sang Tosca (d) at her debut on November 26. Her strong voice was poorly disciplined as Tosca, though it sounded somewhat better in a *Butterfly* on December 29. She thereafter continued her homeward journey from San Francisco, where she had appeared earlier in the fall.

The vitality of Welitch made Tosca* quite another thing when she sang the part for the first time on February 28, a date long set aside for a testimonial to the retiring Johnson by the Opera Guild. To strengthen the attractiveness of a performance for which tickets were scaled to a twenty-dollar top, Schoeffler was promised as Scarpia,* with Tagliavini as Cavaradossi. The incredible came to pass, however, when Janssen reported himself unable to sing Hans Sachs in *Die Meistersinger* on the 27th, and Schoeffler was the only available substitute. Understandably, Schoeffler could not sing two such heavy parts on successive days, and Tibbett was substituted as Scarpia. It was a gallant gesture by Tibbett, for his vocal limitation was all too evident to the listener, and must have been doubly painful for the performer. Because Welitch and Schoeffler were old collaborators in Vienna, little time had been allotted for *Tosca* rehearsals, wherefore the action of Welitch and Tibbett was mostly improvised. Her characterization was an embracingly dramatic one, including a chair flung at the feet of the pursuing Scarpia in Act II, a kick at his supine body when she had stabbed him, and a desperate shaking of Tagliavini (to revive him) when the firing squad had done its work. The music was sung with fervor and brilliance, though Welitch sounded vocally spent halfway through *"Vissi d'arte"* and slid from the pitch at its end. Schoeffler sang his Scarpia* on April 4, impressing more for a rather brutish conception of the pious, wine-sniffing rascal than for his gruff way of singing the music. Stella Roman was another Tosca this season, singing the role competently on February 11, when Tucker was the well-sounding Cavaradossi.*

Welitch was seen two times as Salome this season, retaining all of her power to fascinate an audience, though the vocal strength of her first performances was never quite matched. Hugh Thompson was the Jokanaan* on February 6, singing with more breadth of sound than had seemed to be in his future five years earlier. As before, *Salome* was paired with *Gianni Schicchi,* with Greer as Lauretta* on February 5, and Tajo the prevailing Schicchi. The latter reached a low point of taste for the Metropolitan stage in this period with a coarse (and ill-sung) Méphistophélès* in *Faust* on December 23. Kirsten was Marguerite to Di Stefano's promisingly youthful Faust,* but Manski's Siébel* was poorly sung and Pelletier's mechanized conducting further depressed the level of the performance. On January 25 Hines had another opportunity with Méphistophélès, still but a sketch of a characterization. He was decidedly more at ease with the static requirements of Gurnemanz,* which he did surprisingly well in a *Parsifal* of March 21 with Traubel (Kundry*) and Lorenz (Parsifal*). Stiedry was the conductor for this unfamiliar trio of interpretations, of which Hines's Gurnemanz was the one of real promise for the future.

In addition to Tajo and Hines, a Méphistophélès of this season was Moscona, who sang it for the first time in years on March 11. Steber, Conner, and Albanese were other Marguerites, and Mascherini, Warren, and Guarrera sang Valentin. The impression conveyed is that everybody could sing roles in *Faust* at this time; the fact is that anybody was allowed to. The same could be said for *Carmen* and a "revival" of *Samson et Dalila* on November 26, though neither Stevens, who sang it this time, nor Thebom, who came later, had the ample kind of voice required. Both, however, had expensive gowns to exhibit, as well as rather ludicrous ideas of seduction. For the most part, the men were good—Vinay as Samson,* Merrill an aggressive High Priest,* and Hawkins a sturdy Abimelech,* but that is hardly the reason for giving *Samson*. Baum was also a Samson* this season, likewise a Lohengrin on December 30. This Wagner "revival" (only the remarkable Swan, which turned and flapped its wings before withdrawing, was new) was drawn out to doleful lengths by Stiedry's tempos, and further compromised by lack of a suitable cast. Svanholm's voice lacked lyric suavity for the Lohengrin* he sang on January 18, Stoska was a poor-sounding Elsa, and Thebom's Ortrud* lacked impact. Janssen's was a light voice for Telramund. On February 2 Melchior announced that he had "sung his swan song" in the evening's performance of *Lohengrin*.

From the foregoing it is evident that the trend of the preceding several seasons could hardly be reversed merely to suit the circumstances of Johnson's retirement, that as often as there would be a brilliant performance with Welitch or a well-sounding *Simon Boccanegra* there might be a dismal one of *Carmen* or *Samson*. Nevertheless, in its ceremonial rather than its artistic aspects the year was one of generous rewards for the retiring director. In contrast to the mute, invisible Gatti of fifteen years before, Johnson was audible and visible in the ceremonial that followed the *Tosca* on February 28. A festive audience that had paid $46,000 to be present (the money was set aside as an Edward Johnson Opera Fund) was treated to a ceremony in which such former favorites as Bori, Schorr, and Martinelli, in the costumes of their cherished parts—Violetta, Sachs, Otello— were introduced to the audience by John Brownlee. Johnson was finally brought from the wings by Bori and lavished with gifts from the unions, the board of directors, and the company. He made a brief speech stating that his years as director had been, "in spite of everything, very happy," and, then remarked (addressing, perhaps, the invisible Rudolf Bing): "To be General Manager of the Metropolitan is a great honor, but it carries also a great responsibility. One is not born a General Manager—one learns the hard way, by making mistakes and correcting them." In a final burst of affection the audience joined the artists in singing Rodger's and Hammerstein's "I'm in Love with a Wonderful Guy" (tactfully changed, for the occasion, to the first person plural).

This kind of attention was, perhaps, expectable in New York, where for twenty-eight years Johnson had been a favorite artist and a popular executive, but it was duplicated, with variations, in the fifteen cities visited on the tour. Boston pointed out that his career had really begun as soloist with its choral societies forty years before; Dallas offered him a year's free rent if he would buy a home in Scurry County; and Chicago left no doubt of its belief that Johnson had actually learned how an opera company should be run during his years in that city.

The *Cleveland Press* outdid all others in drawing from Johnson some frank views on Bing's announced intentions. "As to the future of the Metropolitan," the report ran, "he expressed anxiety as to the over-publicized policies of the new manager Rudolf Bing. Despite these doubts, he sincerely hopes his successor will succeed. . . . Johnson can't help but wonder why the new manager announced next year's plans while this season was still in progress. He hopes that Bing will become better acquainted with America. Knowing this country better, he feels, will prevent him from scheduling an opera such as 'Die Fledermaus' which was performed on Broadway a few years back under the name of 'Rosalinda.' Bing's plan to offer it some 20-odd times has prompted Johnson to call it joshingly 'Fleder-Mice.' "

Unjoshingly, Bing went ahead composing his plans in greater detail. *Die Fledermaus,* in an English version by Howard Dietz and staged by Garson Kanin, would be given twenty times or more, thus "buying time" for restagings of *Der fliegende Holländer* and a revival of Verdi's *Don Carlo,* with Margaret Webster as stage director. Rolf Gérard was named as designer for the Strauss and Verdi works, Robert Edmond Jones for the Wagner. The *Ring* would be given entire once again. Antony Tudor was named to revitalize the ballet, and the new members of the administration included Max Rudolf and John Gutman to assist with artistic matters, Reginald Allen (who had come to the organization the year before) and Francis Robinson to supervise matters of finance and ticket sale. A first test of sentiment on the effect of Flagstad's return and the division of subscriptions showed ninety per cent renewals for the full eighteen weeks, and enough interest in the new Tuesday-night subscription to assure its success.

In mid-May, Bing undertook his first series of negotiations with the unions. The only prolonged discussions were those with AGMA, which was bent on restoring to duty some artists whom Bing intended to drop and on circumscribing the specifications he had set forth regarding pre-season rehearsals. In the end Bing persuaded his board to invest nearly $100,000 to underwrite social-security and unemployment benefits, and compromised on some dismissals. He achieved his primary objective, which was control of contractual provisions relating to artistic matters.

The renewal of public interest in operatic affairs was considerably stimulated by the year's accomplishment of the City Center. No longer an experiment, no longer an impromptu interchange of vagrant elements, it had developed not only a repertory, but also a public, of its own. The fall season beginning on September 29 was marked by a new production of *Der Rosenkavalier* on October 6. Prokofiev's *Love for Three Oranges* was successfully launched in an English version by Victor Seroff on November 1. The spring season honored the twenty-fifth anniversary of Puccini's death with *Turandot* on April 6, a staggering assignment on a stage of the City Center's limitations, but an impressive tribute to the hard-working personnel directed by Halasz. A venture to Chicago in the fall was sufficiently successful to justify a return in the spring.

Almost as if foreordained, the Metropolitan's history was left by Johnson exactly where it had begun sixty-seven years before, with a performance of *Faust* in Rochester on May 15. Conner was Marguerite, Di Stefano was Faust, and Merrill sang Valentin. Tajo being indisposed, Vichegonov took his place as Méphistophélès.

EPILOGUE

The fifteen years of Johnson form an entity of Metropolitan history as recognizable as the decade of Grau, the five years of Conried, the first dozen (approximately) of Gatti. In each epoch there was a problem to be faced, a situation to be met, a series of conflicting tendencies to be reconciled. Considering the new factors—artistic, economic, and organizational—which had to be considered, it is evident that the era from 1935 to 1950 had more complexities and perplexities than any preceding one.

In the terms of the largest considerations—the organization of virtually a new company, the stimulation of an interested public, the preservation of a place where opera could be given when the past manner of support had become outmoded, and the adaptation to a prolonged period of change at home and abroad—Johnson's direction was successful to the extent that opera continued to be given without interruption. The popular affection that attended his retirement is proof of a general esteem for the way in which disaster had been fended off.

As the preceding pages indicate, that way was by no means along the easiest or most accessible path. It included the propagation of some highly desirable tendencies for the betterment of the Metropolitan repertory and the taste of its public. A renewal of its contact with the greatest works of Mozart was perhaps the most important; a freshened exposure to *Fidelio, Otello* and *Falstaff,* a reminder that Verdi wrote *Simon Boccanegra* and *Un Ballo in maschera,* something more than lip-service to Mussorgsky, a recognition of the new voice of Benjamin Britten—all these were to varying degrees digressions from the path of least resistance.

The more credit to Johnson, indeed, that these routes of exploration were found despite grave restrictions by financial barriers. Comparisons with what had preceded were as futile as speculations about what might follow. The latitude of choice, the availability of risk capital that permitted his predecessor to range far and wide over the operatic world for twenty years—1910–30—were as remote from Johnson as fifteen-dollar-per-week choristers and thirty-five-dollar-per-week orchestral players. The question was no longer what an impresario wanted to do; it was what he was able to do.

The utilization of native talent was vastly increased, and in ways different from before. As we have seen, in Gatti's operatic scheme a Farrar was as welcome as a Bori, a Whitehill as respected as a Schorr. Box office was box office, no matter whose name sold the tickets. The new thesis was that the house could be Americanized from the bottom to the top, utilizing native singers in all gradations of ability. It expressed, inferentially, the belief that American singers could form the hard core as well as the bright surface of a reputable company.

After fifteen years and some eighteen hundred performances of opera, Johnson turned over to his successor a complement of native talent which included Steber, Conner, Kirsten, Traubel, Munsel, Resnik, and Varnay among sopranos; Thebom, Stevens, Lipton, and Harshaw among mezzos; Tucker, Peerce, Conley, and Sullivan among tenors; Warren, Merrill, Thompson, Harrell, Hawkins, and Guarrera among baritones; and Hines, an outstanding bass. Add to these such usable foreigners as Albanese, Berger, Sayão, and Welitch; Baum, Bjoerling, De Paolis, Di Stefano, Svanholm, Tagliavini, and Vinay; Valdengo, Frantz, Schoeffler, Janssen, Szekely (in theory if not in fact), Vichegonov, and Ernster, and the evidence is ample that Johnson did not leave either a cupboard bare of vocal goods or one bereft of useful properties. The standards of conducting established by Beecham, Busch, Szell, Walter, Reiner, Stiedry, and Perlea are among the brightest memories of the period, if those of Fourestier, Papi, Antonicelli, and Pelletier are something else.

But did this residue justify the vast amount of human talent explored, exploited, tested, and discarded in this period? Had the Metropolitan been a mere artistic laboratory, the vast and sometimes irresponsible experimentation could have been a justifiable indulgence, even one to be encouraged; in a going theater, with a historic standard to uphold, the Johnson period was marked by callousness, practicality, and frequent, previously unknown indifference to enduring values.

In the early reaction to his task, the history of Johnson so bears out the example of Conried and Gatti as to merit recognition as axiomatic: a new man can always see the faults of his predecessors; what he cannot see, after a few years, are his own. In the seasons from 1935 to 1939, Johnson worked steadily and with good effect to rehabilitate the unbalanced personnel he inherited from Gatti. The addition of such Americans as Giannini, Traubel, Kullmann, and Stevens was well advised, if that of Fisher and Marion Clark was not. With the presence of such superior European artists as Caniglia, Cigna, Bjoerling, Albanese, Janssen, and Thorborg, the balance of experienced and inexperienced singers was fairly maintained.

Gradually, however, the pace at which Americanization of the house proceeded wore rough edges around the quality of the work being offered. The wisdom of allowing young singers with no more than a textbook knowledge of their subject the freedom of a stage traditionally the object of a lifetime's progress was dangerous. What should have been the tolerable exception became numbingly regular in a flighty, planless, artistically arbitrary shuffling about of personnel. Who remembers Maria Hussa, Audrey Bowman, Marie Wilkins, Maria Markan, Eyvind Laholm, Jacques Gerard, Maria van Delden, Kirk, or Van Kirk save those who were present when each of them made one or two or three appearances?

Some of these were performers not even on the roster, but called upon to save the show in an emergency. The familiar contention that the nominal "covering" artist was out of town or unavailable does not suffice. Management's job is to manage. When it cannot control its personnel, it is not management, it is mere caretaking. Neither logic nor reason can explain the use of Bampton as Aida and Amneris in the same season, or Varnay as Elsa and Kundry, or Lipton as Cherubino one week and Amneris the next, or Baum as Samson and Lohengrin. Operatic history is barren of singers who made debuts in an important house as Donna

Anna. Why should it be proper for such a young singer as Florence Kirk? Christine Johnson's debut as Erda, Guarrera's as Escamillo, and Berini's as Faust do not argue a conscientious attitude toward either the artist or the art. Often enough there was never again a second chance when the performer was better equipped to meet such a challenge. Sometimes the rule of the jungle prevailed and the fittest did survive. If this is the code by which an opera house should be run, the Metropolitan was well run during these fifteen years.

But the policy was by no means a consistent one. Along with the opportunistic use of young talent went special privileges for a Carmen Gracia, a Claudia Pinza, a Florence Quartararo; sentimental indulgence of a Papi; complacent acceptance of an Antonicelli. The tributes Johnson earned for engaging Bruno Walter and Sir Thomas Beecham were merited; but let us not forget Edwin McArthur.

In non-musical aspects of the artistic endeavor—stagecraft and scenic work—the gestures in the direction of Herbert Graf and Lothar Wallerstein were hardly pursued energetically; the limited funds available for new productions were not always spent well. Harry Horner's *Orfeo* and *Trovatore* and Rychtarik's *Lucia* were promising, as was Samuel Lev's projected scenery for *The Warrior*. The misdemeanor of Simonson's *Ring* continued to penalize Metropolitan audiences until the move to Lincoln Center. Novak's *Peter Grimes* did nothing to assist the possible success of that venture, nor did Dobujinsky's designs for *Khovanshchina*. Crayon's *Manon Lescaut,* on the other hand, was an able accomplishment.

It is this very mixture of good and bad, positive and negative, backing and filling, makeshift and make-do, that gave the Johnson period its characteristic tinge. Improvisation—let's try this, him, her, or it—might be admirable or even amusing if one were discussing a community opera studio in Pasadena; to find it the guiding principle of the Metropolitan in a crucial period of its history is to shame American pride in what is usually called know-how—a synonym for organization, purposefulness, attention to fundamentals.

In train come the idiosyncrasies permitted Baccaloni and Melchior; the numerous blonde Toscas; the extra cape for Traubel's Brünnhilde; the absurd costumes permitted Stevens and Thebom in *Samson* and Steber in *Manon;* the whole idea of letting stars "bring their own" when everyone else on the stage is attired in hand-me downs. The sum of these and a hundred other instances is the measure of *laissez faire* by which the Metropolitan's artistic commerce was carried on in this period.

It has been said that Johnson, after all, was a singer—and what could you expect of such a one? The reply must be, of course, that Johnson was such a very good singer with such a comprehension of his art that one might have expected him to know the weaknesses of the tribe and to deal with them in season and out. The judgment must be, however, that he was never other than a singer at heart; that the special talent for organization, detail, discipline, and creative thinking (in which powers are delegated, but under a watchful eye) which characterizes the able impresario was never in his make-up. More unfortunately, it was not sufficiently in the make-up of his associates, either.

In surveying a decline from previous high standards in his day, W. J. Henderson once disposed of an opera season by saying: "The captains and the kings depart, but the tumult and the shouting do not die." Opera, of itself, has much force and variety, such splendor and fantasy, that there may be glory for corporals and petty princes when captains and kings are absent. But one should not conclude therefore that artistic royalty is in residence, or that the house that it keeps—amid tumult and shouting— merits the blue ribbon for excellence or is even a competitor for high honors.

WITH BING TO LINCOLN CENTER, 1950–1966

1950–1951

Much as he differed from his predecessors, in nationality, background, and personality, Rudolf Bing shared one point of resemblance with those who had occupied the General Manager's office at the 39th Street and 7th Avenue corner of the Metropolitan before him. As Giulio Gatti-Casazza had preferred one work of Verdi (*Aida*) for his first opening in 1908 and Edward Johnson had chosen another (*La Traviata*) with which to introduce himself in 1935, so Bing selected still another, *Don Carlo*. Each choice was an avowal of viewpoint as well as a commentary on the nature of the operatic era to which the manager had succeeded.

In the case of Gatti, it was the belief that such a new conductor as Arturo Toscanini, working in concert with such old favorites as Caruso, Scotti, and Homer and such a favorite-to-be as Emmy Destinn, would provide New York with a new kind of operatic experience. With Johnson, it was less commentary than continuation, for all the principal artists— Lucrezia Bori, Lawrence Tibbett, Richard Crooks, and conductor Ettore Panizza—were established favorites. With Edward Ziegler as his artistic advisor and Earle R. Lewis as consultant on money matters, he could assume that the procedures of Gatti, with which they had all long been associated, would serve them as well, needing only to be adapted to the new conditions of depression rather than prosperity, with stress on a budget that "had a prospect of breaking even."

With Bing, however, the break with the past was not only clean but also outspoken. Those of the old hands who had not decided to retire (such as Lewis) were dismissed (such as Frank St. Leger). Thanks for services rendered were expressed, of course, at the February press conference before Bing's term of office officially began; but the old hands were let go nonetheless. None of the thinking propounded at that January meeting was revolutionary. Singers were to be held to a more responsible attitude toward their commitments; primary attention was to be given to the visual aspects of the Metropolitan's stage; the principle of "quality alone" was articulated as the rule by which the affairs of the theater would be conducted. The iteration of them, however, made clear that such fundamentals had been more often waived than stressed in the period then drawing to a close. If the thinking could be translated into action, the quality of the results might be, for the Metropolitan, revolutionized.

There was as much revelation as revolution when the first Bing-planned production and the first Metropolitan performance of *Don Carlo* in twenty-eight years was shown to an invited audience of press and professionals at a dress rehearsal on November 4, 1950. What they saw and heard was equally evocative of praise from the audience that crowded the theater for the official opening on November 6 and in the press of the next day. Rolf Gérard's handsome settings and strikingly appropriate costumes, it was agreed, proclaimed a sense of style long absent from this stage: the taste and theatrical judgment that had put Margaret Webster among the foremost directors for the contemporary spoken drama had proved equally valid in opera; Fritz Stiedry's secure command of musical values served Verdi, which he had only rarely conducted at the Metropolitan previously, as well as they did Wagner and Mozart. All were made possible by a gift from the children of Otto H. Kahn, through the sale of a Rembrandt.

Though Boris Christoff, the Bulgarian basso who had been promised as King Philip II, was prevented from coming by the restrictions of the McCarran Act,[1] a replacement rather than merely a substitute was found in Cesare Siepi. The rich voice and promising dramatic talents he showed as Philip (d) were well blended by Stiedry with those of such

[1] This first faint flush of the McCarthy hysteria-to-come denied admission to any alien who "holds or has held membership or been affiliated with any totalitarian or communist organization." It was passed over the veto of President Harry S. Truman.

old friends as Bjoerling (Carlo*), Merrill (Rodrigo*), Hines (Grand Inquisitor*), and Vichegonov (Friar*) and the solid sound of Fedora Barbieri (Eboli [d]) to produce an excellently integrated vocal ensemble. Not exceptional in itself, it became so in combination with the visual frame provided by Gérard and the pervasive, well-planned action of Webster. Only Delia Rigal, who made her debut as Elisabetta (d), looked better than she sounded. On the other hand, the young American soprano Lucine Amara, who could not be seen at all in her off-stage debut as A Celestial Voice (d), sounded very well. Television coverage was welcomed, but there was no commercial sponsorship.

To such a veteran observer as Virgil Thomson of the *Herald Tribune,* this *Don Carlo* gave "hope" for other things—"not senseless hope, because he [Bing] is a skilled administrator and a man of taste"—while Olin Downes in the *Times* rejoiced that a fine opera had "come into its own." For them as for others, *Don Carlo* resolved the question of whether Bing could organize the performance of an opera on a level of quality to make him welcome at the Metropolitan. As befits a shrewd impresario, he had seized the opportunity that presented itself to make the eye an equal partner to the ear in the Metropolitan, and had made the most of it. Having put his best foot forward on firm ground, could he pull the other, mired in the old repertory, to a place beside it? One could only speculate as to whether the promise conveyed by "an" opera could be realized throughout the sixty or seventy anticipated in the course of a normal career-span for a General Manager at the Metropolitan (Johnson in fifteen years had been responsible for seventy-odd).

The miraculous did not happen: but the target was struck squarely again before the season was out, giving credence to the view that sharp aim rather than lucky chance had produced a direct hit in *Don Carlo.* This did not happen, however, in the second new production of the opening week, when *Der fliegende Holländer* had its first restaging at the Metropolitan in twenty years, on November 9. Robert Edmond Jones had given up the scenic assignment during the summer, and the execution of his sketches by Charles Elson left the kind of dissatisfaction inherent in divided responsibility. The expected impact of Ljuba Welitch's first Senta was absent (as she was herself for several weeks to come), and the prospect of Mihaly Szekely as Daland vanished when the Hungarian government refused him permission to leave the country. Above all, Reiner's low-key treatment of the score, after a fine performance of the overture, left some listeners becalmed on a sea of declamation despite the superb effort of Hans Hotter, whose Dutchman (d) proclaimed him a singing actor of the first order. Varnay was a variable Senta,* Sven

Nilsson a grumpy Daland (d), and Svanholm insufficiently lyric as Erik.*
In later performances, musical quality was enhanced by the excellent
Senta* of Harshaw, in her first venture as a dramatic soprano on November 22 (she had been heard as Mary* in the previous cast). The project
did not command public response, and it was dropped without Welitch
having sung Senta, or Flagstad having revived the memories of her
superb Senta of another day.

Bing's intention to grant Johann Strauss's *Die Fledermaus* a place on
the Metropolitan stage denied to it since the Conried venture of nearly
half a century before had provided a convenient weapon of attack for
those who had cause to dislike him anyhow. Their contention was that
it was operetta rather than opera and usurped time and money that
might be better expended on something more suitable to the surroundings.
The managerial counter-contention was that production of a masterpiece
was self-justifying, and a proper one of *Fledermaus* (as the new English
version by Howard Deitz was titled) could be given twenty or twenty-five
times in a single season, thus "buying time" for thorough preparation of
other works. Those who were disposed to suspend judgment until the
evidence was presented had their own cause for distress in the report
that Bing was negotiating with Danny Kaye to play the non-singing role
of Frosch, the jailer. Even if the gifted comedian was interested, would
he be likely to play the role more than once or twice as a lark? What
kind of letdown would follow? Was this the kind of front-page play
which could be regularly expected from Bing's Metropolitan, with or
without the advice of his press chief, Margaret Carson (a Johnson
appointee who had been retained)?

The time-buying argument—for this season at least—was weakened by
the obvious fact that much time had passed before *Fledermaus* was first
given on December 20. It came tenth in the sequence, meaning that
seven other operas (*Don Carlo* and *Der fliegende Holländer* were prepared
in the pre-season period) were put on in much the same manner as before.
Fledermaus, too, had its share of organizational difficulties when Fritz
Reiner was "relieved" as conductor just as intensive rehearsals began.
The excuse was the press of other work: the reason, however, was
clear. He had switched record affiliations over the summer, and his new
employers, RCA Victor, had utilized him to direct a competitive, non-
Metropolitan recording of *Fledermaus*. This left him unavailable for the
"official" version by Columbia. Thus challenged, Bing and the Columbia
officials devised their own counter-coups: Eugene Ormandy was "borrowed" by generous consent of the Philadelphia Orchestra.

A wholly unknown quantity in the opera house (his previous experience had been limited to a single outdoor performance of *Madama Butterfly*), Ormandy quickly demonstrated that one Hungarian could be as adept as another with a Viennese score. He fired a resounding command to attention with a rousing performance of the overture, and held it firmly thereafter. The action began well when the fore-curtains parted to permit a top-hatted, white-tailed John Brownlee as Dr. Falke* to deliver a mood-setting prologue by Garson Kanin, who had adapted the book and directed the action. It continued with even more promise when the inner curtain rose on Gérard's evocation of the 1870's and such luminaries as Tucker (Alfred*), Munsel (Adele*), Welitch (Rosalinda*), Stevens (Orlofsky*), and Svanholm (Eisenstein*) gave off their own glow to enhance the candle-power of Haffner, Genée, and Strauss. The rare spectacle of opera performers actually enjoying themselves at their work gave to the performance a holiday aspect that few could resist. Once again the lifeblood of theatrical illusion animated the Metropolitan stage, though Antony Tudor's effort to improvise a ballet around Nana Gollner (Ida [d]) fared poorly. Jack Gilford, an able nightclub comedian, left no longings for Kaye as Frosch (d).

The pleasurable surprise expressed by the press (among some loud but unavailing minority reports—by Thomson, among others) brought enough business to the box office to support eighteen more sold-out performances. If something short of the total projected, this was still more performances than had ever been given of a work in a single season of Metropolitan history. Within days the opportunities of parody provided by Dietz's version of *"Chacun a son goût"* permitted Stevens, as Orlofsky, to compliment the new Manager with these rhymes, at the New Year's Eve performance:

> *The operas that must be your choice*
> *If you like plays that sing*
> *Are solely dependent on one voice*
> *The voice of Rudolf Bing.*

Sometimes, however, it was not the operas but those who appeared in them that came to be described by *chacun a son goût*. In the New Year's Eve performance, for example, Svanholm had already been replaced by the less amusing Charles Kullmann (Eisenstein*). In the weeks that followed, the ranks of those who came and went included Piazza as Rosalinda (d) in place of Welitch; Tibor Kozma (d) as conductor rather than Ormandy (January 4); Novotna as Orlofsky*; Kullmann as Alfred* when Svanholm returned as Eisenstein; Regina Resnik as Rosalinda (March 9), Brian Sullivan as Alfred* (March 9), and Eugene Conley as a fourth

Alfred* on other occasions. Aside from the inescapable effect on ensemble of the alteration of personnel, the changes denatured the character of the original experience and left those who had praised it wondering whose constellation of "stars rather than comets" was being scanned.

For reasons of "time-buying" or others, the season's *Ring* (using the already outmoded though still "new" settings of Lee Simonson) began with an uncommonly tidy *Rheingold* on January 25, with Stiedry conducting and Graf in charge of the staging. Despite evidence of the vocal unreliability that became increasingly acute as the decade progressed, Hotter's Wotan* was massive in its dramatic presence and equally impressive for its intellectual command of the role's purpose, with Svanholm an exciting Loge,* Harshaw as Fricka,* and Pechner's Alberich contributing equally to a satisfying total. The response to the new manager's powers of persuasion brought such acts of cooperation as Novotna as Freia, Erna Berger as the first Rhinemaiden,* with Amara as Wellgunde,* and Glaz as Flosshilde. A plan to reactivate Karin Branzell, who had missed six Metropolitan seasons (see page 447) went amiss when she was unable to perform at the first matinee. Her place as Erda* was taken by her protegé Jean Madeira, a prophetic choice as she has since become one of the role's best performers. Branzell did perform the part at the broadcast of January 27, this being followed on February 10 with an Erda in *Siegfried* which might be described as her second (final) Metropolitan farewell. The other dramas of the *Ring* were much as they had been during the preceding decade, especially with Flagstad as the Brünnhilde of one cycle and Traubel of the other, with Stiedry conducting throughout. Gunther Treptow was only a passable Siegmund (d) at his debut in *Die Walküre* (Ludwig Suthaus had been announced, but he too was a victim of post-war travel restrictions), which left little room for letdown in his later efforts as Tristan and as Florestan in *Fidelio*. Melchior's absence was the more deplorable because of its avoidability: he remained capable, for several years to come, of singing his best parts as well as he recently had sung them.

Part of the satisfaction with this year's *Ring,* and its *Rheingold* in particular, derived from superior lighting. This was owing not to the introduction of new personnel—union restrictions inhibited that—but to the addition of resources not considered indispensable before. These included some additions to the backstage equipment and, more importantly, the installation of frontlighting from masked installations on the audience side of the proscenium. These provided for something more like a bath of light on the stage than the previous isolated spotlighting.

In practice, the juxtaposition of Traubel and Flagstad turned out to be less of a problem than it had appeared to be in promise. The American soprano pursued a more or less normal pattern of performance, with an Isolde on December 1 directed by Reiner[1] in which Vinay showed both the scope and the limitations of his Tristan* for the first time and Schoeffler (Kurvenal*) and Nilsson (Marke*) made an uncommonly gruff pair of low voices. Thebom was the Brangäne. Traubel's non-Wagnerian venture for this year (and one of her few ever) was the Marschallin* in *Der Rosenkavalier,* also with Reiner, on January 5. Fritz Krenn was an active, audible Ochs (d), with Brownlee singing an expert Faninal* in his first Metropolitan venture in German and with Stevens and Berger in their accustomed places. Traubel's bulk disqualified her from competition with such picturesque Marschallins as Lehmann and Schwarzkopf, but she sang much of the music beautifully, with the kind of vocal shading too often underestimated in her treatment of Isolde. For sheer sound, Reiner's blend of her voice with Stevens's and Berger's in the third act had rarely been surpassed.

Flagstad's resumption of activity was, of course, anything but normal. Some of the heat in the objection to her wartime course had waned since her Carnegie Hall reappearance two years before, but the warmth her partisans brought to the *Tristan* of January 22 (her last preceding appearance had been in the same work on April 12, 1941) was all but incandescent. Applause and cheers shattered the mood as the curtain rose at the conclusion of the prelude, leaving Reiner with no choice but to wait. Head buried in her arms, as the action decreed, Flagstad gave no visible sign of response. If this impatient "Welcome home" affected her vocally, it was only toward an Isolde of remarkable breadth, control, and solidity. Temperamentally it had melted somewhat from aristocratic reserve to womanly warmth, but if it ever came close to abandon, it was an abandon wholly relative and always regal. In the circumstances it was hardly surprising that the Tristan of Vinay, as well as the Brangäne of Thebom, the Kurvenal of Janssen, and the Marke of Ernster were somewhat shadowy figures. The curtain-call counters declared Flagstad's total (nineteen after Act I alone) to be the greatest since the farewell of Lehmann in 1944–5. Perhaps they had not been counting after the first Salome by Welitch in 1949.

If Flagstad's Isolde had gained in extroversion during her absence, her Leonore clearly suffered from the encroachment of age and added weight when Bruno Walter returned to direct *Fidelio* on March 6. There was

[1] Bing's question, "With such a conductor as Reiner in the house, who else could do *Tristan?*" may have cost him a lengthy period of service by Jonel Perlea. He had been Johnson's choice the last time *Tristan* had been given. Perlea declined the honor of doing *Fledermaus,* and has not been heard at the Metropolitan since.

no lack of vocal ease in her performance, but credibility was in short supply with a cast that included Treptow as Florestan,* a charmless Marzelline* by Conner, and Ernster's dry-voiced Rocco.* Only Schoeffler's Pizarro,* a veritable *Gauleiter* of Seville, possessed the kind of dramatic impact to make the most of the opportunities afforded by Walter. The upward swing of Hines's career, which embraced such additions to his repertory as Philip* in *Don Carlo* (December 4) as well as the Grand Inquisitor, continued with his first effort as Don Fernando.*

In one respect at least, this *Fidelio* took a place ahead of all others in Metropolitan history—the amount of money paid by the audience, which filled the house. Actually, it was but one-third of an even larger amount, the total of $109,000 exacted from the public by the package of attractions called "Three Firsts." This included Bing's canny separation of the opening night from the body of the season, and the inclusion with it of privileged attendance at the introductory performances of *Fledermaus* and *Fidelio*. The handsome income beamed a strong light on perhaps the least flawed of all of Bing's attributes—ability to raise money in sizeable sums. In time, the opening night would attract almost as much by itself, without necessity for making it part of a package with anything else.

The euphoria induced by the success of *Don Carlo* and *Fledermaus* prompted the addition of still another new production to those planned before the season. Although time for equivalent preparation was lacking, and the money was not nearly so abundant, it was with shock and chagrin that Bing reacted to the (mostly) adverse reviews for the new *Cavalleria rusticana* and *Pagliacci* designed by Horace Armistead when they were offered on January 17. Aside from a magnificent Turiddu* by Tucker, Downes found *Cavalleria* victimized by "the most atrociously inappropriate scenic setting" he had ever encountered, and Thomson noted that "the congregation walked into the church and never came out." Unlike Armistead's Sicily, whose highly specific detail—with Tucker in green shirt, red tie, fawn-colored suit, and buckskin shoes—suggested a hideout for a retired gangster, his Calabria for *Pagliacci* was as barren as a bombed-out village. Rigal sang another of her fluttery-voiced efforts as Nedda,* with Vinay a throaty Canio and Leonard Warren as Tonio alone a sound for which ears were eager. As Santuzza, Milanov made her first appearance since 1947 to begin a second Metropolitan career even longer than her first. One of Bing's choices to conduct the Italian repertory, Alberto Erede, provided a polite push rather than the vigorous thrust wanted in this pairing.

The candid appraisal of Armistead's work by the same press which had endorsed *Don Carlo* prompted a rebuttal by Bing which was all too indicative of other impulsive actions to come. Off the record as well as on, and using the radio as well as the printed page, he contended that his detractors resisted the "modern" approach in the new *Cavalleria* and *Pagliacci,* yearning for more of the conventional manner of *Don Carlo.* This was a misreading, wilful or otherwise, of the opinion in question, which took exception primarily to the quality of the productions, not to their style. In any case, the Armistead *Cavalleria* and *Pagliacci* passed from the scene before their normal life span, to be replaced eventually by a treatment by Gérard in which the congregation came out as well as went into the church, a barber did not shave his customers in the public square on Easter Sunday morning, and Nedda's caravan had a reasonably picturesque place in which to perform.

Aside from Hotter, whose striking Dutchman was followed by such other characterizations as the grandest of Grand Inquisitors* in *Don Carlo* on November 16 and a staunch if somewhat forbiding Kurvenal* on December 16, the most awaited new artist of the year was Victoria de los Angeles. Her qualities as a concert singer were known and admired, leading to the possibility that she might communicate the stage quality associated with such of her countrywomen as Supervia and Bori. Her Marguerite (d) in *Faust* on March 17 did not disappoint the voice-fanciers, but it tempered hopes of those who regard the stage as a place for action rather than inaction. Guarded in movement, and even in the fullness of time not wholly at home in costume and under lights, Los Angeles usually sang too well to be wholly ignored. One of her best roles was Butterfly,* (which she performed for the first time anywhere on March 20) perhaps because it permitted her to assimilate another personality from a wholly different culture. Perhaps, too, Erede's conducting of Puccini and the association with Conley as Pinkerton and Valdengo as Sharpless made for more congenial surroundings than Fausto Cleva provided in his Italianized Gounod. Bing chose Cleva, like Erede, in order to impart something to the Metropolitan's Italian repertory which had previously been lacking. But Cleva, whose Metropolitan career had begun as a young chorus master in the 'twenties, lasted long rather than really wearing well. In the Los Angeles *Butterfly,* Margaret Roggero made a striking success of her first Suzuki,* which developed into a delightful companion for many Butterflys to come. Los Angeles's other role in this season was Mimi* in *La Bohème* on March 30.

Managerial recourse to a "guest" artist—not often invoked at the Metropolitan in recent years—was revived on November 27, when Mario del Monaco, who had been appearing in San Francisco, was introduced as Des Grieux (d) in *Manon Lescaut.* For the most part, his power was under control in this part, which he sang with reasonably lyric freshness, though Taubman in the *Times* described his sound as being "employed always at forte or louder" and Douglas Watt in the *Daily News* said succinctly: "We can forget him." His associates under the direction of Cleva included Kirsten as Manon Lescaut and Valdengo as Lescaut.

Less understandable than the guest engagement for Del Monaco was the extended tolerance, not only in this season but for years to come, of Rigal. Well as she looked in certain "costume parts," she lacked the settled production and assured vocal technic to qualify for leading roles in these surroundings. Whether as Elisabetta in several *Don Carlos* after the first, or as Violetta* on November 19, Leonora* in *Trovatore* on December 28, or Marguerite* on March 1, Rigal was consistent only in the inconsistency that made every performance a measure-by-measure experience. Certainly hers was a case in which the standard of "quality and quality alone" as enunciated by Bing was flouted, if not waived.

With Pinza gone and no other satisfactory alternative yet discovered, the title role of *Don Giovanni* was again entrusted to Schoeffler when it was first given on November 17, and then to the Italian baritone Paolo Silveri in his debut on November 20. Neither in this role nor as Germont* on November 21 did Silveri show the qualities for prolonged Metropolitan service. Siepi, who did, was not yet ready to take on the Don, though the range of his promise was greatly expanded when he followed his substantial Philip of the opening *Don Carlo* with a surprisingly entertaining Basilio* in *Il Barbiere di Siviglia* on December 6 (with Pons, Di Stefano, Valdengo, and Baccaloni), and a capable Méphistophélès* in *Faust* on December 19. The conspicuous memory of this year's succession of *Don Giovannis* was the unexpected debut, in the first of them, of Roberta Peters as Zerlina (d) on November 17. A product of the same William Herman who had trained Patrice Munsel, Miss Peters (born Petersman) was closer to her high school days in the Bronx than to the professional stage when she was pressed into service to replace the indisposed Nadine Conner. Good looks and a secure command of her fresh young voice marked Peters as the exception to the rule of under-prepared, over-exploited American talents. She survived the risky introduction to sing a creditable Queen of the Night* in *The Magic Flute* on January 12 and Rosina* in *Il Barbiere* on February 3 in her first of many Metropolitan seasons to come.

Less favored by unexpected opportunity was Paula Lenchner, who profited from the indisposition of Rigal to appear as Marguerite* on January 24. Insufficient volume of sound and a tentative dramatic effort left her account more minus than plus. A Metropolitan career blighted by other circumstances was initiated by Genevieve Warner, a sweet-voiced soprano, with a debut as the First Boy (d) in *The Magic Flute* on November 25. Miss Warner had the misfortune to be the victim of a purse-snatcher during an engagement in Edinburgh some months later, suffering injuries that curtailed her professional activities. Among her older colleagues who profited by the change in command to perform new roles were Thebom, whose Eboli* in *Don Carlo* on November 14 was more in her vocal line than an Azucena* on February 16, and Tucker, whose fine Turiddu (see page 504) was preceded by a well-sung if indifferently acted Carlo* in *Don Carlo* on December 2 as a complement to his excellent Alfred in *Fledermaus* on December 20. Tamino* on November 25 and Faust on January 14 were other roles he sang for the first time in this season.

Among the decisions by Bing to which some commentators took objection was his reduction of the repertory to twenty-one works (counting *Cavalleria rusticana* and *Pagliacci* each as one). A restricted number for a twenty-two-week season, it nevertheless was not sharply reduced from the number to which Edward Johnson inclined in his final years. What aroused more concentrated objection was the omission of *Parsifal* from the schedule after an uninterrupted run of thirty-one seasons. Its replacement, for the Easter holiday period, by two performances of Verdi's "Manzoni" Requiem under the direction of Bruno Walter and with Milanov, Elena Nikolaidi (March 23, debut), Peerce, and Siepi had its own musical justification, but did not mollify those who found one more Metropolitan habit disturbed.

As a source of operatic experience not provided by the Metropolitan, the City Center fell short, perhaps, of maximum expectations by not venturing *Parsifal* (for Good Friday or any other day), but it did extend itself by adding *Die Meistersinger* to the schedule of the fall season and by inviting Rose Bampton to perform her Marschallin (modeled after Lotte Lehmann's) in its *Rosenkavalier.* Another bygone Metropolitan favorite returned in *Aida,* when Dusolina Giannini (who had participated in the first of all City Center performances on February 21, 1944) reappeared after a considerable absence. Her role was not Aida but Amneris, despite which she was unable to sustain an evening-long effort, retiring after Act III (she was said to be suffering the after-effects of influenza). New additions to the roster included Elaine Malbin, who made her debut in the early fall as Princess Ninetta in *The Love for Three Oranges;* in the spring, Herva Nelli, fortified by singing leading roles in Toscanini's broadcasts of *Otello, Aida,* and *Falstaff,* returned as Santuzza, a role she had sung once in the same theater five years before.

However, it could not be said that changes in habit were wholly on the audience side. Robert Merrill discovered that the kind of willfulness which might have been indulged in the past no longer was acceptable when he broke his commitment to appear in the post-season tour in favor of an offer from Hollywood. On April 8, Bing informed the press that Merrill had been dropped from the roster for the next season. Although Merrill's legal ground for protest was shaky, he made it nevertheless, to no avail. Not until he submitted a written apology the following December was Merrill's case reconsidered, and he did not reappear until March 11, 1952, thus sacrificing nearly a year of his Metropolitan career.

The tightened reins of discipline did not exclude some measure of greater consideration for the performers. An artists' box was established to give those performers who were "covering" the evening's cast a place to sit in dignity rather than lurking in the standing room as before. To bring the behavior of all to conformity with that of the better-disciplined performers, house rules were posted governing response to applause (postures were to be held, there was to be no smiling or nodding, and curtain calls would be subject to strict regulations). The firmness with which this innovation was enforced prompted me to ask one leading artist how he felt about it. With a non-committal if uncontented shrug, Tucker said: "If it's the same for everybody, what's the difference?"

This firm stand on one perennial Metropolitan problem was the public parallel to a firm stand on another problem taken in private. That was the decision, in the spring of 1951, to make a frontal attack on the long-deferred housecleaning of remnants which passed for a Metropolitan stock of scenery for the standard repertory. *Aida, Carmen,* and *Rigoletto* were marked for new productions, and the Mozart list was to be extended by the inclusion of *Così fan tutte* in English.

This was a double tribute to the successful aspects of Bing's first season: first as recognition for the quality of *Don Carlo* and *Fledermaus;* second as token of the popular interest they had aroused. The money for the four new productions was not self-generating: it had been generated by an appeal for $750,000 launched in the aftermath of the early, auspicious Bing weeks, when the impact of his innovations was greatest. The end being worthy, even some of the questionable means, including a benefit performance of *Fledermaus* on February 22 in which Maria Jeritza returned to act if not sing Rosalinde,* could be condoned. The funds required to liquidate the losses of 1950–1 and underwrite the ambitious program for 1951–2 were eventually banked, but not without difficulty and some final intensive effort.

Among those who viewed the results of Bing's first season as, on the whole, a hopeful portent for the future was B. H. Haggin. Writing in *The Nation,* he left little doubt of his respect for the "knowledge, taste, intelligence, standards and convictions" of Bing. "He is," wrote Haggin "the kind of general manager the Metropolitan has never had before; and that even with the inadequacies he will eventually have to put up with, and the decisions that will occasionally turn out wrong, the kind of opera he wants to give is likely to be the kind we will want to have . . ."

That one of the "inadequacies" of the situation might be overcome was suggested, after the season's close, by the newest rumor of a "new Metropolitan," this time in the Columbus Circle area (see page 41). Whether or not it would have any bearing on Bing was at best doubtful, the probable time-lag being what it was. Eventually, of course, it added only one more chimera to the list of "new" Metropolitans which had dotted the horizon over a seventy-year period.

1951–1952

The soundness of Bing's judgement in putting first things first cannot be doubted. More than a decade before, after Johnson had replaced Gatti, I had written: "Little has been done to restore the visual elements of the Metropolitan's productions to a respectable level . . . there has been little attempt to do the staggering job of restoration on the scenery for the standard repertory bequeathed to Johnson by Gatti." By 1950, ten more years of use had made the shabby threadbare, the hard-worn transparent. Hardly more than the fingers of one hand would be needed to enumerate the "new productions" of the Johnson era which had carry-over value—*Lucia, Trovatore, Traviata, Otello, Figaro, Manon Lescaut,* and the *Ring* would about exhaust the list. By 1951 several of these, too, were in need of replacement, further swelling the already long list.

Among first things, *Aida* was unquestionably first of all as the most-played opera in the Metropolitan scheme and one whose last production (by Parravicini) had been put up, taken down, carted out, and carted in more than 150 times since it had been new in 1923. The assignment to Gérard, whose results were exhibited for the first time at the opening night on November 13, was by no means inevitable—Egyptology was not one of his specialities—but was, no doubt, a reward for his striking success with *Don Carlo.* This Gérard production for Verdi had little in common with its predecessor except a shrewd exploitation of the height of the Metropolitan's proscenium to suggest vertical lines soaring to infinity. It offended the musicologically inclined on two counts: the temple scene had been reversed to enable the performers to face the audience for the invocation to Phtha (thus disregarding Verdi's specifications that the image should be at the rear), and the Nile scene, with its barren vista and bales of cargo, suggested some contemporary dock rather than one suitable to the pastoral economy of the Pharaohs. Others took exception to the long flight of steps to be negotiated by Amneris during the Judgment Scene, as they did to other steps in other productions to come, without reckoning with the possibility that it was an elementary defense of the stage director against the flat expanse of a primitive stage without elevators or other adjustable platforms to provide varied playing levels.

The stage director in this instance was, again, Margaret Webster, but without as sound a dramatic plan—not to mention lack of equal opportunity for one—as she had brought to *Don Carlo*. Aside from the solecism of having the King occupy a stage position in the triumphal scene above the High Priest's and putting Amneris on a lower plane altogether, Miss Webster was powerless to make Milanov as Aida other than Milanov was as Santuzza or Norma, or to impel Del Monaco as Radames* into another mold than Del Monaco as des Grieux. Elena Nikolaidi, in her Metropolitan stage debut as Amneris, was a more regal figure than most of her predecessors and sang well, but the strongest dramatic impact was provided by George London's Amonasro (d), a real Lion of Judah in his debut at home after a notable career abroad. Hines as Ramfis and Amara as the Priestess* contributed to a strong musical ensemble that could have given even more than the prosaic conducting of Cleva required. Of large implication toward the long-range well-being of the company was the utilization of Janet Collins (d) as principal dancer. She was the first Negro to be granted a place of such prominence on the Metropolitan stage. The choreography by Zachary Solov was of negligible quality.

There were no complaints, musicological or otherwise, about the suitability of designer, director, and conductor when Gérard's next effort was disclosed on December 28. This was the first Metropolitan venture with *Così fan tutte* since the 'twenties, one that raised it to a place of honor alongside those recently earned at the Metropolitan by *Figaro, Don Giovanni,* and *The Magic Flute*. There were some objections to its performance in so large a house, others to the use of an English translation. The former were somewhat mollified by the use of platforms and an inner curtain (gaily decorated by the intertwined initials WAM) that brought the action as close to the footlights as possible; and the latter were offset, if not contravened, by the well-spoken sound of the Ruth and Thomas P. Martin translation from the cast directed by Alfred Lunt. An inspired choice to stage this comedy of manners, Lunt had supplemented a limited knowledge of music by close attention to the Glyndebourne recording.

Whether there were latent suggestions in this source, or more direct influence from Bing and Gérard (both of whom had been closely identified with the Christie house speciality), Lunt's plan showed many points of resemblance to Carl Ebert's famous staging for Glyndebourne. In any case, the results spoke for themselves.

They also spoke for the absorption of Lunt's agile action and pointed comedy by a mostly American cast, beginning with Munsel as Despina* and continuing with Tucker as Ferrando,* Guarrera as Guglielmo,* Steber as Fiordiligi,* and Thebom as Dorabella.* Mediating their supposed difficulties was the practiced Don Alfonso* of Brownlee. There was not one of them who had every resource the music required—Tucker was a shade heavy, Thebom a trifle light and unfluent in coloratura, Steber troubled by the extremes of register in *"Come scoglio"* and *"Per pietà"* —but there was more than the beginning of a satisfactory ensemble under Stiedry's consolidating hand. As the performers learned, so did the audience, to the point at which *Così* attained a recurrent place in the Metropolitan's revolving Mozart repertory. And, as earnest of Bing's belief in "set" casts, the only changes in this year's half dozen performances came on February 9, when Alvary was Alfonso* and Erede conducted in place of Stiedry, who had spent the afternoon with the broadcast *Otello*. Steber settled in after her matinee Desdemona* to sing Fiordiligi at night.

Somewhere between the glowing *Così* and the glaring *Aida* was Gérard's execution of designs and costumes for a new *Carmen* (the predecessor dated to 1923). Conceived in collaboration with Tyrone Guthrie, whose mental eye saw a choreographic-cinematic statement of Meilhac, Halévy, and Bizet (if not of Mérimée), it substituted a colorful, sometimes garish Spain for the more classical Urban one to which this theater's audiences were long accustomed. It, too, had its share of steps, especially in Act I, which was played on and about a two-level plaza connected by a broad staircase. It also took the liberty of playing the final scene within a room in which Carmen was presumably preparing for her visit to the bullring while watching the procession from a window. This was less a matter of artistic volition than of financial necessity. The funds to do a proper exterior for a *corrida* were lacking when everything else was accounted for, well before the *première* on January 31.

Guthrie's conception had its most active collaborator in Stevens, whose prior venture with Carmen (see page 457) had been amended to sustain in later acts what she did well in the first. However it tended ever more to externals of action rather than to internally generated communication, as her vocal resources steadily eroded under the stress of repetition. Vocally she was least adept where a great Carmen should be strongest, in the Card Scene. Her response to Guthrie's dramatic demands was wholehearted save, perhaps, in that portion of the *Habanera* in which Carmen was held aloft by her swains and toted somewhat uneasily about the stage. Tucker's José* was strongly sung, phlegmatically acted, with Guarrera (the absent Merrill would doubtless have been the first choice) a light-voiced Escamillo and Conner a non-persuasive Micaëla. Reiner, as conductor, left no doubt of his command of the score; but he left some doubt of his enthusiasm for what it contained.

Perhaps the keenest expression to that date of Bing's feeling for style in staging was the assignment of the *Rigoletto* introduced on November 15 to Eugene Berman. It gave this able painter (whose previous scenic designs in New York had been primarily for ballet) latitude in a milieu to which he was well-attuned. The cost for suitability was restoration of the time-period to the Renaissance of Hugo's play rather than the sixteenth century decreed for Verdi's opera by the Italian censor. Most operagoers found no contradiction in the outcome, especially as Berman's somber colors and substantial "architecture" enhanced the values in Graf's staging and Erede's well-judged direction of the score.

It was hardly surprising that the results impelled Downes in the *Times* to describe them as "one of the most interesting and exciting interpretations of the work we have seen." Warren's Rigoletto had progressed from manly to mature to magnificent, and he had, in Hilde Gueden, a Gilda (d) with more voice and a better idea of how to use it than had usually been his fortune during the previous decade. As the Duke, Tucker provided an opposite pole of vocal electricity in the contest to magnetize Gilda from her father's side, and there was also substance in Madeira's Maddalena, the silvery if brief sound of Votipka as Giovanna, and Norman Scott's Monterone (d). Formerly of the City Center, Scott endured to render a long list of solid if unsensational services at the Metropolitan. The Sparafucile* was Alois Pernestorfer (d), a baritone from Vienna who was soon back home on the Ring.

In pursuing his announced plan to restage three standard works, Bing demonstrated a fact about "new productions" which is all too likely to be overlooked, and which had not been conspicuous in the previous season's attention to such non-standard works as *Don Carlo, Der fliegende Holländer,* and *Fledermaus:* i.e., the gain to the ear as well as to the eye. In throwing away the décor (so called, however undecorative) of old, a new plan of action permitted a fresh approach to the musical problem. This was a correction of old habits that had deeper effects than the mere additional amount of rehearsal time provided by a new production.

To be sure, this change had the contrary effect of putting a sharper contrasting light on the quality of performance in works which still awaited their turn in the "new production" sequence. In some degree, this depended on which old rabbits were plucked out of the repertory hat, for some were decidedly more healthy specimens than others. In this season, for example, the choice of *Figaro, Elektra,* and *Salome*—all under the direction of Reiner—restored to prominence three works that had fared well in the Johnson period, and for which the available scenery was acceptable.

In the first of these, on November 17, Siepi made his first Metropolitan venture into Mozart, and though his voice was heavier than a Figaro's* should be and his tread weightier, he gave evidence of a disposition to amend both which counted for much in his future development. The Countess* was a role for which Los Angeles was admirably equipped, and though some would have preferred Sayão (a fine artist who never enjoyed Bing's favor, and soon disappeared) to Conner as Susanna*, the ensemble had the further sustenance of an almost ideal Cherubino.* This was Mildred Miller (née Mueller) who made something of a sensation in her debut, but never performed anything else as well as the boyish part for which she was so well suited by size as well as by voice. Brownlee was again his courtly and countly self as Almaviva, but it was increasingly evident that Baccaloni's days as a first-class Bartolo were beginning to slip behind him. Such people as Madeira (Marcellina), De Paolis (Basilio), Carelli (Don Curzio* [d]), and Alvary (the best Antonio, perhaps, that has ever been seen), together with Peters (Barbarina*), Lenchner, and Roggero as the girlish trio, sustained a standard in the subsidiary roles (there are no small parts in *Figaro*) which had long been a Metropolitan credit.

The Strauss works brought not only some expectable excellences, including the tempestuous Salome of Welitch when her speciality was given on January 10, the excellent Herod of Svanholm, and the strong Narraboth of Sullivan, but also some new virtues. Among them were an imposingly dramatic Jokanaan* by Hotter and an engaging study in degeneracy by Elisabeth Höngen of Vienna as Herodias (d). The latter transferred her special aptitudes from Judea to Greece on February 18, when she inflamed the air with a vitriolic Klytemnestra* in one of the tautest, most explosive versions of *Elektra* the theater had ever housed. Astrid Varnay gave the first of her fine performances to come as Elektra,* with a wel-

come contrast of brightness in the voice of Walburga Wegner as Chrysothemis (d). Hotter was the fine Orest* and Svanholm a capable Aegisth.*
When Hotter was unavailable, there was a choice alternate for him in
Schoeffler, whose Orest* was first heard on February 23. Resnik was
the Chrysothemis* on March 12. In deference to prior policy, Bing
presented *Gianni Schicchi* in English and under the direction of Erede
(with Peters as Lauretta* and Hayward as Rinuccio) before *Salome*.
Baccaloni's verbal virtuosity made every one of the words he mispro-
nounced as Schicchi clearly audible and Armistead's modest set served
its purpose. Eventually, Bing instituted a policy in which *Salome* sufficed
as a stage attraction in itself.

Johnson's barren but not wholly bare scenic cupboard also accounted
for the visual elements in two of the season's other memorable happenings: Gluck's *Alcestis* with Flagstad and a round of *Otellos* in which
Vinay and Del Monaco alternated as the Moor. Perhaps because they
had been used only five times in the 1940–1 season, Richard
Rychtarik's spacious setting for Gluck bore their age with credit when
they were seen again on March 4. Flagstad's broad, well-supported
legato and the majestic character of her declamation, which caused
Thomson to rate her as "unique among living vocal artists," provided
an unforgettable impact to her Alcestis,* also setting the tone for Erede's
conducting and the Admetus* of Sullivan. Though Warren had been
required to struggle with the French text of the High Priest when the
work had last been given, he was excused from this version in English,
thus enabling Schoeffler to declare "Ze zun comes zu zink," one of those
aberrations which will, inevitably, make linguistic hash of most efforts
to give opera in English in an international opera house. When Flagstad
took her last farewell of this stage on April 1 with Valentino as the High
Priest (he had also sung it on March 19 in a cast with Svanholm as
Admetus*), members of the audience cheered, applauded, or stood silent
—according to their preferred way of paying tribute to what they had
heard—for twenty minutes after the final curtain.

In the interval since Vinay had last sung Otello at the Metropolitan
in the 1948–9 season, he had been busy performing it elsewhere. In
consequence, the performance he offered at the opera's restoration on
February 9 was the two hundredth of his career. It found him at an
equipoise of dramatic purpose and vocal power, able to carry the burden
of the tragedy whether dealing with the improved Iago of Warren or the
promising Desdemona* of Steber. Lipton was the capable Emilia, with
Hayward as Cassio* and Franke as Roderigo.* Stiedry had both the
work and the cast well in hand in his first Metropolitan effort with this

score. There was more for him to contend with on February 15 when Del Monaco was Otello* and a vulgar display of undisciplined "passion" was made to pass for a reasoned estimate of Otello's character. It was screamed rather than sung, ranted rather than acted. The musical problem became even more acute on March 13, when Rigal quavered through Desdemona* and Silveri provided a conventional Iago.* He was one of several baritones who profited from Merrill's non-sabbatical "leave," performing a wide range of parts including Rigoletto* on January 16, Amonasro* on February 2, Escamillo* on February 16, Count di Luna* on February 23, Father Germont on February 25, and Rodrigo in *Don Carlo* on March 21. This restoration of Bing's first and, as yet, best production had some unexpected participants—a group of sidewalk pickets from the Holy Name Society who objected to a figure dressed as a "clergyman" who points out Rodrigo to an assassin. They could hardly change the fact that there had been a Spanish Inquisition.

Del Monaco's appeal to a segment of the Metropolitan's public was promoted by liberal use of his talents in a variety of repertory roles, some for which he was suited, some for which he was not. In the first category could be put Radames and Otello, however he abused his voice to make one brassy and the other brazen. Likewise his power counted for something when he was heard as Turiddu* on December 14 and Manrico* on March 11. But not so the Don José* in which he was first seen on February 19 or the vocally inert Edgardo* he performed on January 3 to the Lucia of Pons. The latter's "season" also included Gilda on December 22, in which she turned up in transparent tights rather than the decorous costume decreed by Berman's décor. No one, apparently, had thought to inspect Pons's costume before she appeared on stage, by when, of course, it was too late. In any case, her appearances per season soon dwindled to a token one or two.

For that matter, Bing's efforts to maintain company discipline were severely strained on January 30 when Welitch added a new role to her repertory. This presented her as the star of what could only be described as a hitherto unknown opera of Puccini of which the title role was Musetta.* Though the name character did not appear in Act I or more than occasionally in Acts III and IV, Welitch utilized her prominence in Act II for a full evening's variety turn. Posturing, standing on chairs, and riding Marcello's shoulders pick-a-back, she behaved every way but artistically. Some of it was well sung, but the good she provided was bought at high cost to the prerogatives of conductor Erede, not to mention such other performers as Kirsten, Tagliavini, and Silveri (in perhaps his best part, Marcello*). Bing took what comfort he could in characterizing such behavior as "nasty" and not presenting Welitch another year. However, his motivation was clearly revealed in a radio interview (December 11, 1965) in which he referred to the casting of Welitch as Musetta as purposeful because the other soprano insisted on singing Mimi when he thought her better as Musetta. This must have been interesting news to the Mimi, Dorothy Kirsten, who was still a member of the company.

The multiplicity of *Aidas* (fifteen in New York) brought on by its new production also brought on a multiplicity of performers, in no discernible pattern of logic or quality. For unexplained reasons (some said the size of her fee), Nikolaidi did not appear as often as her initial success seemed to warrant. Nell Rankin was introduced as Amneris (d) on November 22, with but limited command of the sizeable voice which made her a more reliable performer in later years (she was in better control of Maddalena* in *Rigoletto* on November 29). Others who contested for the affection of Radames included Thebom, Barbieri for the first time on January 29, and even Harshaw, whose career was following a path far from the one it had pursued when she first sang the part in 1943–5. By the evidence of the programs, Rigal was an Aida* in this season (December 8) as well as Violetta, Nedda, Desdemona,* and Leonora in *Trovatore,* but the audible evidence always tended to the same query: why such prominence?

The Harshaw path, in this season, took her farther from her mezzo beginnings when she was seen in what could be called the Bing, as distinguished from the Ring, cycle. It began and ended with *Götterdämmerung,* in which Harshaw sang the Third Norn as well as Waltraute on December 13 (with Traubel) before attaining the summit of the final Brünnhilde* on February 1. It suggested that Harshaw had been more successful in altering her vocal center of gravity than in changing her temperamental focus. However well she responded to the vocal challenge (and some of it was very well sung), Harshaw tended, dramatically, to retain the mezzo's secondary status rather than assuming the soprano's primacy. Varnay was another new Brünnhilde* in *Götterdämmerung* this season, adding an emergency journey by air from Dallas (when Traubel was unable to perform on December 17) to the other rigors of performing so large a part for the first time. She had all the dramatic impulse that Harshaw lacked, but not as much of the vocal resource. There were two excellent Gunthers* in Schoeffler (December 13) and Hotter (January 22), each more mindful than the average performer of his status as half a tribal chieftain. Thebom ventured Waltraute* on January 22 with equivocal results; Höngen was heard in the same role for the first time on February 1. Svanholm was the Siegfried throughout, and an admirable one. He also endeavored to sing Walther in *Die Meistersinger* on March 27, but his good days for such a lyric part were past.

Nor were they quite present for Hans Hopf, who was the Walther (d) on March 15 under Reiner's direction. At its best, Hopf's sound was better than that offered by a Metropolitan Walther since Ralf, but it was only occasionally at its best. By contrast, Richard Holm, the new David (d)—Anton Dermota had been engaged but did not come—did adroitly what he had to do in spite of less impressive vocal equipment. Wegner was an able Eva,* Pernestorfer more baritone than bass as Pogner.* Superior to all shortcomings was the Sachs of Schoeffler, always able to spread vocal oil on otherwise troubled waters. At this full tide of his career, he was an excellent alternate for Hotter as Amfortas* in this season's *Parsifals,* though some would have preferred London to either. However, the latter's service in his first season was restricted to Amonasro. Hopf was the Parsifal* on April 12, when the Kundry* was Harshaw, with Svanholm in the performances with Varnay on April 4 and 11. Doubtless Ernster's Gurnemanz* would have made more impression at an earlier point in his career, for what he had to offer in vocal variety was minimal in a part in which it can make the difference between interest and ennui. Of other new impersonations (Pernestorfer as Klingsor* and Vichegonov as Titurel*), there was the longest future in the Klingsor* of Davidson, which he performed in the Ernster-Varnay-Svanholm cast.

The admiration aroused by Gueden in the second night's *Rigoletto* was more often than not sustained by her later efforts. She was a charming Rosalinda* in *Fledermaus* on November 30, when Ormandy returned to the task he had discharged so well the previous season; a coquettish Musetta* in *Bohème* on December 15 with Steber and Tucker (of whom Strauss in the *Times* said "Not since Caruso have we heard a tenor who delivered Rodolfo's music with more fervor or greater accuracy"), and a delightful Micaëla* on March 1. As Susanna* in *Figaro,* however (on January 4, with Singher in place of Siepi), Gueden was as vivacious, coquettish and delightful as she had been in all her other roles combined. Doubtless this was part of some ensemble plan practiced in Vienna, but it ill-suited the kind of performance being given by Brownlee, Miller and Los Angeles.

The Spanish soprano's second season included, beyond the Countess, one other role for which she was well remembered, Massenet's Manon.* When it was first given on December 7, with Albanese, Di Stefano, and Hines, one might have wondered if it wasn't the right cast for the wrong opera (Puccini's *Manon Lescaut* rather than Massenet's *Manon*). There was a better balance with Singher's admirable Lescaut when Los Angeles added her cultivated sense of French style to the undertaking. As of this season, the Metropolitan had not even one proper French tenor, but it did add another Italian one when Giacinto Prandelli shared a debut as Alfredo (d) with Renato Capecchi as Germont (d) on November 24 in a *Traviata* with Rigal. His other roles included the Duke* in *Rigoletto* on December 16, Pinkerton* in a *Butterfly* on January 6, and Rodolfo* in *Bohème* on January 18. He performed agreeably in all, with a voice that was at least one size too small for the theater, especially in its insufficient top range. Capecchi's assignments in this mostly Merrill-less season earned him credit as Marcello in *Bohème* on December 24, Silvio* in *Pagliacci* on December 27, and Ashton in *Lucia* on January 3. Another new Pinkerton* in this season was Brian Sullivan on February 8. His preference for such Italianate roles contested with a managerial belief that he had a better future otherwise (as in the Narraboth he sang on January 10 and the Admetus with Flagstad). He never achieved real fulfillment in any repertory.

This year's "guest artist" was Graciela Rivera of Puerto Rico, who had sung successfully at the City Center, where her slender figure and even more slender voice counted for more than they did on a larger stage. She had a two-night "career" as Lucia,* her debut on February 4 being followed by a single reprise on March 14. Of much wider utility were the talents of Brenda Lewis, whose debut as Musetta* in *Bohème* on February 26 (Sayão's Mimi was her final, unremarked Metropolitan appearance) was a by-product of another, non-New York venture. This was a touring *Fledermaus,* organized in the flush of success at home and designed to benefit from its publicity, with Lewis as Rosalinda. Part of the cost was met by Columbia Records, which had produced the "official" version of *Fledermaus,* but its investment of $70,000 plus an undisclosed amount of additional capitalization was wiped out. Insufficient business (S. Hurok had a rival company in the field), a limited consideration of local conditions, and generally over-optimistic estimates of public interest contributed to the sizeable loss. Bing's esteem for Lewis was frequently expressed and generously documented by future assignments, though hers was a voice not meant by nature or fostered by science for so large a house. Two new Gildas* were heard in the new *Rigoletto,* with more credit for Peters on November 28 than for Warner on January 25. The former survived her premature exposure in so taxing a role, but the latter hardly did. Amara, who had begun her second season with another off-stage role (the Priestess* in *Aida*) came into full view with a creditable Nedda* in *Pagliacci* on December 14, likewise giving a strong thrust of sound to the quintet in act II of *Carmen* as Frasquita* on January 31.

Merrill's period of suspension ended on March 11, when he sang a typical Di Luna in a *Trovatore* with Del Monaco and Rigal. He had fulfilled the Bing formula for reinstatement by submitting a written apology for his failure to appear during the previous season's spring tour (see page 508). Bing then invited him to a meeting to discuss "next season," and Merrill's transgression (on behalf of a non-epic called *Aaron Slick of Punkin' Crick*) was forgiven. However, Silveri still had his place as Rodrigo when *Don Carlo* returned on March 21. Later (April 9) when Resnik was Eboli,* Merrill regained this role, also appearing as Tonio,* Escamillo, Amonasro, and Germont.

Though the soundness of Bing's judgment in regarding, as a prime necessity, more presentable surroundings for the theater's most performed attractions was self-evident, it did not command universal approval. Most outspoken of those who thought otherwise was Thomson, who declared (November 25, in the *Herald Tribune*) "an opera house cannot wait till it gets rich to give modern works, because by not giving them it loses public confidence, which is the source of all financial support . . ." Further, said Thomson "the musical policy of the house shows all the weakness of a non-musician's directorship." As between the two objections, there was more merit in the second than the first, if only because there was a question, after all, of which "public" was at issue. New York has many publics, and if those who cherished "modern works," as Thomson believed, did not find Bing's Metropolitan exciting, there were others whose "confidence" was sustained nevertheless.

The aspiration of the City Center to make itself the civically responsible center for those who found the Metropolitan "retrogressive" took the form, in this season, of its first *première* since that of Still's *Troubled Island* in 1941. This was a treatment of Ansky's *The Dybbuk* by the little-known Dimitri Tamkin (some, of course, insisted on confusing him with the much-better-known Dimitri Tiomkin), whose interest, finally, related more to the situations of the drama than to the manner in which they were treated musically. Patricia Neway made her debut as Leah, in a setting devised by Mstislav Dobujinsky with Irving Pichel (a Hollywood associate of Tamkin) as stage director and Joseph Rosenstock conducting. There were greater animation and more merit in a production of Wolf-Ferrari's *I Quattro Rusteghi* later in the fall, under Halasz's musical direction.

Although *The Dybbuk* had little immediate post-history (or, for that matter, any since), it did mark a turning point in direction for the City Opera. That was the decision of the City Center's board, on December 20, that Laszlo Halasz, who had invented the enterprise and ingeniously preserved it for much of a decade, should be replaced in "the best interests of the company." An immediate factor was an incident of a post-season guest engagement in Chicago during which Halasz, in the heat of a rehearsal, threw his baton at a member of the orchestra. This prompted renewals of charges that Halasz was abusive to singers. But there was also reason to suspect that *The Dybbuk* had been put on over objections by his board and had run up considerable expense. In the words of the late Newbold Morris, principal officer of the City Center's board, Halasz was guilty of "tyrannical abuse of power, duplicitous intrigues, and breaches of contract that had created an atmosphere of hate, unhappiness, and insecurity detrimental to the morale of the opera company." Why these conditions had not been "discovered" during the period in which Halasz was enjoying executive favor is hard to determine: the reason may well have been financial, after all. To the undisclosed quantity of the losses was later added his own demand in a suit, for settlement of a claim of $40,150.35 due him on his contract. Its disposition never found its way into the press.

Shortly after the New Year, Rosenstock—who had been brought to the company by Halasz—was appointed his benefactor's successor. His gambit was to make the City Center's opera as close to that of a German *stadt-theater* as he could contrive, his principal gamble a staging of *Wozzeck* with the best "available" talent, whether suitable or not. (Berg's memorable score had recently had its first New York performance in nearly twenty years in a concert version by Mitropoulos and the New York Philharmonic Orchestra, and thus was ripe for a stage production.) Marko Rothmüller, a baritone well experienced in the title role's requirements from European productions, was the production's principal asset along with the abilities of Rosenstock himself; but neither Patricia Neway nor her alternate, Brenda Lewis, was equal to the demands of Marie. However, the impact latent in *Wozzeck,* plus a successful revival of *Andrea Chénier* (with Nelli, David Poleri, and Walter Cassel, and with Julius Rudel conducting) created the climate of success, and Rosenstock was given a year's extension.

So far as the contention that Bing was "anti-modern" was concerned, it was ill-founded: for even before his tenure officially began, he sounded out Aaron Copland on his interest in creating a version of Thornton Wilder's *Our Town* for the Metropolitan. Copland eventually decided that the theater was too big. And before this second season was completed, Bing reached an agreement for the American *première* of Stravinsky's *The Rake's Progress* (first heard in Venice on September 11, 1951).

Inclusion, in his third season's plans, of a new production of *La Bohème* earned Thomson's scorn as "a scandalous waste of money."

The end of March also brought the end of discussion of the Columbus Circle site as a new home for the Metropolitan. The scheme did not include sufficient provisions for housing to meet legal requirement for public assistance; any other way would have been prohibitively expensive. Those who cherished the old house for its auditorium and unparalleled access by subway turned their thoughts, instead, to renovation rather than relocation. This would require the investment of $5,000,000 (a quarter of the then estimated cost of $20,000,000 for relocation). It provided for the shearing off of the backstage area at the curtain line, and its replacement by twin towers affording not only the comforts lacking in the old theater's dressing rooms but also, more pertinently, modern stage facilities, including storage space for a season's repertory. It provided, also, for air-conditioning of the audience area, replacement of the orchestra circle seats with chairs that faced the stage, etc.

The only positive action at this time, however, was the first increase in the cost of tickets since 1942. They were advanced fifty cents (to eight dollars) at the top of the scale, only a nominal ten cents at the bottom, a departure from the earlier practice of raising the prices of all locations proportionately.

1952–1953

As long before as the fall of 1951—which is to say, nearly fourteen months previously—Bing had made mention to those who collect such information for the press, that planning for the season to begin on November 10, 1952, was all but complete. As he was then less than half way through his first contract of three years, with no assured prospect that another would be forthcoming, there was a real possibility that the third season might also be his last. Thus it would be unrealistic to look to it for major decisions about personnel or long-range planning in repertory.

To suggest that the Metropolitan and its New York public might only have occupied three years of Rudolf Bing's life rather than at least six times that number may seem a fantasy to those for whom the Met has had no other General Manager. He had, after all, given sure evidence of capacity, if not of immunity to error. The concepts of staging which he had introduced, if non-revolutionary, nevertheless brought much attention to the theater, providing the opportunity—even more than great singing might have provided it—for picture magazines to glorify "Bing's Met," for the society press to picture its favorites on parade, and for other

journals to pursue their own interests. All of this was reflected at the
box office, where, for these or other post-war reasons, pre-season subscriptions had moved to nearly $1,400,000 (up $500,000 from 1949 to
1950). Perhaps the only real "failure" had been the modest response to
the management bid for subscribers to take only half a season rather than
the full number of weeks. In spite of the addition of a Tuesday night
series, more than a thousand names remained on the waiting list for
desirable seats.

All of these would appear to represent solid gains for the financial
stability of the house and general esteem (inside if not outside the board
room) for the man whose policies had been on trial. But for all the
plusses, there were offsetting minuses. Bing clearly was what had to be
called an "expensive" General Manager. His requirements, in new productions were vastly greater than Johnson's, and there was little prospect
that they would moderate. Indeed, when questions of retrenchment were
pressed at this time, he might say, as he said to me once: "I am not
interested in the ninth performance of *Trovatore* or the twelfth *Rigoletto*.
If that's the kind of manager they want, let them get Halasz."

"Them," in this usage, meant not the board as a whole, but the faction of it which—absurd term as it is in the context of this theater—was
characterized as conservative. That this faction tended to include most
of those charged with responsibilities for fund-raising was not in the least
mysterious. Among them was the late George A. Sloan, for many years
the board's chairman, who had performed prodigies of resourcefulness in
raising substantial sums during the forties. But when the operation loss
in 1950–1 of $430,502.94 was followed by another, in 1951–2 of
$473,000, which nearly wiped out the $750,000 raised after Bing's
first season and posed the necessity for more fund-raising so soon, longing for a change was by no means a mere carry-over to opera of a phrase
current in national politics.

Aligned as "moderates"—it would be stretching a point to call them
"radicals"—was the other, staunchly pro-Bing faction, of which Mrs.
August Belmont was the most influential as well as the most tenacious.
She had a nucleus of supporters, especially among the younger members
of the board. Included among the youngest was Anthony A. Bliss, son
of Cornelius N. Bliss, a pillar of the "Old Guard" that had supported the
Metropolitan structure in the days of the owning box-holders. The younger
Bliss was just then beginning to acquire rounded knowledge of the
institution's financial situation which qualified him to become president
of the Association a few years later.

Perhaps it would be too much to say that there was a schism in this closed circle. There was, certainly, a division of opinion about the feasibility of continuing on the path that Bing had charted. Those who considered it the right and proper path for the Metropolitan to pursue did not encounter overwhelming opposition on artistic grounds. The consideration, rather, was: how to produce the money to pay the cost of it?

Increased ticket prices was one possibility, and action to that end was taken at the end of the 1951–2 season. Reduction of costs was another (reflected, perhaps, in the restriction of "new productions" to three in Bing's third season). At best, these measures promised only partial gains, leaving a large central sum still to be found. "Public appeals" to supplement the amounts the board could raise within its membership or by personal contacts had become increasingly difficult to mount and even harder to justify—especially as wartime stresses no longer existed and the theater was consistently short of tickets for desirable locations. A conviction that there must be "some other way" was strong among those who pondered the problem.

In the mid-thirties, when the smallest non-urgent expenditure was all but impossible, Mrs. Belmont had conceived the Metropolitan Opera Guild as a means for support on an annual, recurrent basis. At the outset, the Guild had 1,329 members. By the 'fifties, it could count nearly 50,000, with categories of contribution from a few dollars to a hundred. Valuable as these sums were, they could not, in a rising market of costs and services, roll back the losses that accrued from the more ambitious Bing program.

Once more Mrs. Belmont provided the initiative. It was to create a new, more exclusive circle of supporters, a kind of super-Guild to which the entrance fee would be larger and more than nominal amounts could be hoped for. As it was designed to extend nationwide and seek out persons who were known to have both an interest in opera and the means to indulge it, the new group was given the name of the National Council of the Metropolitan. In consideration for contributions of $250 and $500 (eventually $1,000) annually, members of the National Council were offered representation on the Metropolitan's Board of Directors; the creation of a Central Opera Service, which acts as liaison among community enterprises across the country; and supervision of the Auditions of the Air. These had pursued a variable course since their establishment (with a commercial radio sponsor) in 1935. It was proposed to make them, as a function of the National Council, truly nationwide—eventually going beyond continental limits to Hawaii and Puerto Rico—with regional auditions leading to final public comparison of the best.

Within a few years, the National Council had more than 200 members, which made it a source of an underwriting second only to the Guild and, per capita, even more promising for the future. It soon became an adjunct of enormous importance in providing funds for new productions. And it led to the awareness that there were individuals as well as private foundations who might prefer to make a large-scale contribution for the particular purpose of financing a new production. Such a pattern had been established even before the curtain rose on Bing's first season, when the family of the late Otto H. Kahn had contributed funds from the sale of a Rembrandt to finance productions of *Don Carlo* and *Fledermaus*. This led to similar benefactions by others as time passed. Most generous of all, perhaps, has been Mrs. John D. Rockefeller, Jr. (as Martha Baird, she had pursued a career as a pianist before her marriage). Her interest in the Metropolitan was eventually extended to include sponsorship of productions at the City Center.

Thus there was, in all the encircling gloom, a beam of light showing the way to a brighter future. But it was clear that something would have to be done to light the way through the uncertainties immediately ahead. Among the early decisions, made public on December 18, was the extension of Bing's contract for a three-year period. Affiliated with this, as part of the plan to support his continued control, had been the announcement (in mid-November) of the formation of the National Council. It had fifty-nine full and twenty-six associate members. While that growth was developing to the fruit-bearing stage, one more public appeal was made, this time for $1,500,000.

Possibly it had been decided (after the effort expended in 1951 to raise $750,000) that doubling the amount might not really quadruple the effort. This time the larger amount was tied to structural alterations and physical improvements that might appeal to those not approachable for funds merely to meet deficits. As a compromise between relocation and renovation, it was decided to invest $400,000 of the amount in front-of-the-house alterations and backstage amenities. Increased revenue was as much a part of the changes in the auditorium as creature comfort. It was achieved by removing the 315 orchestra circle chairs and then utilizing the space they had occupied for 479 orchestra seats. This was a clear gain of 164 seats in the most expensive area of the theater's capacity, as well as an upgrading of the others. The backstage changes included such essentials as improved plumbing and the installation of a high-speed elevator to the roof stage to replace the old, faltering one. (The new elevator also serviced some dressing rooms, enabling choristers to be moved more quickly for costume changes.) To show that sentiment for a change was still alive, $250,000 of the $1,500,000 was to be used for engineering studies for a new house. The remainder—$850,000—was assigned to "operational expenses," current and anticipated expenditures in excess of income. At the rate of the preceding seasons' deficits, this would hardly see Bing through two years of his new contract, but it could be hoped that thereafter other sources of income (such as the National Council) might provide meaningful amounts. In any case, by renewing their commitment to Bing's concepts, the inner councils of the Metropolitan had given consent to a mode of procedure from which they could scarcely retreat in the future.

While these important decisions were being taken and long-range plans for the future evolved, there was, of course an opera season in progress. It began, for the third year running, with a new production of a Verdi opera. This time it was *La Forza del destino,* or as much of it as could be comfortably accommodated in an evening that included the lengthy intermissions that had become Bing practice (perhaps intended to encourage attendance at Sherry's, with its recently revised décor by Diane Tate and Marian Hall). The role of Preziosilla had been reduced to a sliver by the elimination of the scene in the Inn at Hornachuelos. This also eliminated the need for the kind of substantial mezzo who usually sang Preziosilla and made it amenable to the talents of a Cherubino (Miller) at the first performance of November 10. It was a chilly day, and Bing introduced his custom of serving coffee to the patient customers waiting in line to buy standing room.

Berman's scenery was perhaps not quite so rich in coloration as his *Rigoletto,* even though he exercised the option of placing the period of his designs a hundred years earlier than the mid-eighteenth century specified in the text. However it rated above average, and has worn well. Siepi showed himself a worthy successor to Pinza as Padre Guardiano,* and there was nothing but virtue in the vocal art of Milanov (Leonora) and Warren (Don Carlo). As Alvaro,* Tucker made a brilliant start on a part he sang with distinction many times in the future. The Father was in equally sure custody when Hines* performed it on November 29, but the hero had quite another sound when Del Monaco was Alvaro* on December 4. Some commentators objected to placing the overture as an interlude in Act I (to avoid interruptions by late-comers), though it had been an applauded practice of Walter ten years before. Stiedry did not make so much of a showpiece of it, but his emphasis in the singing of the chorus—well positioned in Graf's staging—was carefully adjusted. Laura Castellano of Rochester, New York, performed the role of Curra (d), Leonora's maid. Valdengo and Silveri were other Don Carlos* in this season (the first on December 4, the second on February 20), but Milanov sang all the Leonoras.

The other two new productions suffered inversion from major to minor importance by the intrusion of extraneous factors. Whether a new production of *La Bohème* was rated a "scandalous waste of money" as it had been by Thomson, or merely a necessary act of mercy, it need not have been more than an incident. It became something else by Bing's decision to give it in both Italian and English, the latter in a new version by Howard Dietz.

Whatever the case for presenting an English *Fledermaus* or *Così,* it was non-existent in *Bohème,* with its clear, familiar story, lack of verbal emphasis, and highly accessible musical content. Nor was an unexpected justification provided by the doggerel tendered by Dietz at the *première* on December 27 in lieu of the text by Giacosa and Illica. His end-rhymes were as feeble as they were unwanted, and a general impediment to enjoyment of the artful singing of Tucker, Merrill (Marcello*), Harvuot (Schaunard), and Hines (Colline*), the less artful but no more intelligible efforts of Conner (Mimi) and Munsel (Musetta). Such phrases as "She really is lovely" in place of *"Che bella bambina"* left no doubt that the Dietz kind of English was a poor substitute for the Puccini kind of Italian. Bing's employment as stage director of Joseph L. Mankiewicz (best known as the director of such films as *All About Eve*) had no lasting influence on the kind of *Bohème* seen at the Metropolitan, aside from such a bit of thundering trivia as having Mimi's muff roll from her lap to the floor as she died. His intrusion of such a questionable license as Rodolfo's sly closing of the door with himself and Mimi *in* the garret at the end of Act I suggested that he knew more about the poet's mind than the librettists did.

The lasting influence of this *Bohème* was Gérard's picturesque production, which succeeded in creating an illusion of a habitable garret on the huge Met stage (lots of space above the visible "roof" helped) and the opportunity for a lively stage picture in Act II. By setting the Café Momus at the apex of a triangle, with streets slanting off to either side, the action was cleverly concentrated down front while leaving room for the comings and goings of Parpignol, the street band, etc.

The official *première* seemed more like a public run-through when the Dietz version (some believed that his text was a commission by the publishers in order to create a new copyright in the Puccini score to replace the one about to expire) was replaced by the customary Italian on January 7. For "authenticity" the Italian Mimi* was Gueden, with

Resnik as Musetta,* Conley as Rodolfo, and Guarrera as Marcello. On
a later occasion (February 13), Amara added Mimi* in English to her
list of stage roles, and Resnik performed Musetta in a second language
(her own) on February 25. As there was no hysterical demand for the
innovation, and some problem (which might have been foreseen) in finding audience-pleasing Mimis, Marcellos, and Musettas who would re-learn
their Italian roles in English, the Dietz text was quietly put aside after
this season, and Rodolfo's *Racconto,* beginning as it always had with
"Che gelida manina," once more flowed unvexed to the high C.

Curiously, the question of opera in English also intruded into *The
Rake's Progress,* which had an expectable audience of *aficionados* when
it was first given on February 14. In this instance, however, it was not a
question of the text's service to the composer, but of the composer's service
to the text by W. H. Auden and Chester Kallman (the interlined German
in the published score has always struck me as a better fit for Stravinsky's
notes). As early as the previous January, Stravinsky had been at the
theater as Bing's guest, and presumably had concurred in the choice of
Reiner, an old collaborator, as conductor. Of his enthusiasm for George
Balanchine, a newer but even more frequent collaborator as stage director,
there could be no doubt. Horace Armistead's settings, especially the drawing room of Act II for Tom's London flat, were attractive.

Whatever the producing group evolved in harmonious agreement on
large matters was offset by such a perplexity as the choice of Gueden for
Anne Trulove.* Charming to see and possessed of a thoroughly appropriate
voice, she nevertheless added an overlay of Viennese inflections to the
uneven scansion of the English by Stravinsky. Mack Harrell's Nick
Shadow* was one of his best efforts, and Thebom made much more of
Baba the Turk* than some later mezzos. Franke was an excellent Sellem*
and Conley a passable Rakewell,* with Scott (Trulove*), Lipton (Mother
Goose*), and Davidson (Keeper of the Madhouse*) well chosen for
what they had to do. Reiner's meticulous balancing of vocal and instrumental elements did not clarify all the subtleties of the writing—first performances rarely do—but he gave a high gloss to the sound of Stravinsky's
evocation of eighteen-century aria opera. Thomson in the *Herald Tribune*
termed Stravinsky's music "enchanting" and thought that the *Rake* rated
"probably among his finest" works. To Downes in the *Times,* "this tedi-
ous labored artificial score" added "nothing to Stravinsky's achievements."
Adversely Auden and Kallman had indulged themselves in too many
esoteric conceits (beyond the grotesquerie of Baba) and "literary" phrase-
ologies to interest an audience of the size that patronizes the Metropolitan.
Performances, in any case, were limited to a total of seven in this and the

succeeding season. Madeira was Lipton's alternate for Mother Goose* on February 27, and also appeared as Baba* in place of Thebom on the same date.

If it did nothing else, the production of *The Rake* gave the Metropolitan a momentary advantage in the prestige sweepstakes, for the two segments of the next season of opera at the City Center were essentially conservative. A new executive arrangement was instituted, with Lincoln Kirstein as "managing director" for City Center activities, including opera as well as ballet. Rosenstock's approach to the opening-night problem was to invite Tullio Serafin to reappear as a conductor of opera (he had left the Metropolitan at the end of the 1933–4 season), directing *Tosca*. Part of this may have been an expression of Serafin's interest in Anne McKnight, an American soprano who had sought broader fields in Italy after being selected by Toscanini to perform Musetta in his broadcast *Bohème*. Her career, however, did not long flourish there or here. A bolder venture was a staging of Bartók's *Bluebeard's Castle* under Rosenstock's musical direction, coupled with Ravel's *L'Heure espagnole*. Among names of later Metropolitan prominence which occured during this fall season for the first time at City Center were those of Laurel Hurley (Zerlina in *Don Giovanni),* Randolph Symonette (Ramfis in *Aida*), Jon Crain (Alfredo in *Traviata*), and Thomas Schippers (conducting *Bohème* and Menotti's *The Consul*). This year's Wozzeck was James Pease. In March 1953, Rosenstock's contract was renewed for a further two years in advance of one of the company's most succesful ventures ever: Rossini's *La Cenerentola,* not seen in New York in 122 years. The excellent staging by Otto Erhardt and the smart performance of Cenerentola by Frances Bible were commonly considered a reflection of Kirstein's initiative. Certainly a byproduct of his interest in things Japanese was the first performance in New York of a production of *Madama Butterfly* by a company native to its locale. This was the Fujiwara Opera Company of Tokyo, which charmed beyond reason with its physical graces and vocal manners, especially those of the fascinating Harue Miyako in the title role. A point of special interest was its use of Japanese words when only native characters were "conversing," a reversion to Italian when Americans were on the scene. Rosenstock's lengthy period of service in Japan (after his expulsion from Germany by the Nazis in the 'thirties) doubtless enhanced his rapport, as conductor, with the performers.

In place of a contemporary "novelty," the company profited by the foresight of Cheryl Crawford in warehousing the scenery for her unsuccessful production (1949) on Broadway of Blitzstein's *Regina* to revive it with a cast that generated unusual credibility—especially Brenda Lewis (Regina

Giddens), Priscilla Gillette (Zan), and Ellen Faull (Birdie). It was an early example of the company's aptitude for portraying persons of similar age and background. (These were adroitly utilized by Julius Rudel, who conducted, when he succeeded to executive control a few years later). William Wilderman, who performed Horace, was on his way to a Metropolitan career, as were such other new singers of this City Center season as Donald Gramm, Cornell MacNeil, and Jean Fenn. Norman Treigle, who found ample career satisfaction in the newer company, showed his talents for the first time as Colline in *Bohème*.

Of uncommon musical interest in this Metropolitan season was a venture to restore *Boris* to something closer to Mussorgsky's original than is found in the customary version by Rimsky-Korsakov. This represented an enthusiasm of Stiedry, who conducted *Boris* for the first time on March 6 in a reconstruction of Mussorgsky's original scoring made by Karol Rathaus. The latter's attention to the unconventional but purposeful scoring of Mussorgsky was a model of respect and restraint. One missed some of the impact that Rimsky imparted to certain sections—especially the Coronation—which meant, really, that the desire for a composite version of some sort still persisted. John Gutman's generally suitable English text was used for the first time, and the lack of funds to spend on a new production was offset by utilization of some scenes from Dobujinsky's *Khovanshchina* of 1949–50 and the reconstruction of others.

George London's European reputation for Boris* had been sampled at a concert performance with Dimitri Mitropoulos and the Philharmonic-Symphony in Carnegie Hall during the preceding fall and found valid. It did not, however, stand up as well in his first effort at the Metropolitan on March 6. Some of his action was stagey and unconvincing, especially in the Clock Scene, and he appeared to be dwarfed by the regal robes and imposing crown of Boris. Much of the music was beautifully sung, however, and he pronounced the English text with the resonant intelligibility that became a characteristic of his later, better efforts in this part. Save for Hines, who sang a splendid Pimenn,* the best work was done in the smaller roles: by Miller as an appealing Fyodor* (in the class of her Cherubino), Madeira as the Nurse,* Lenchner as Xenia,* and Franke as the Simpleton.* This last part had been extended to include a seldom-given scene in which the Simpleton publicly confronts Boris with his crime, in Act IV; but it also had been diminished by placing last the Death Scene in the Duma. Here Schuisky* (an unfortunate choice for the debut of Andrew McKinley, who was best known for his parts in Menotti musical plays) was encouraged by stage director Dino Yannopoulos to steal toward the throne as the curtain dropped. This lurid suggestion of conspiracy further altered

Mussorgsky's purpose in ending the work with the Simpleton wailing his woe for "Mother Russia." A number of others in the large cast were vocally miscast, including Thebom (Marina), Sigurd Bjoerling as Rangoni,* Baccaloni (no longer what he had been as Varlaam), and Sullivan (Dimitri*). Stiedry's careful direction tended to exaggerate the diminished theatrical impact in the Rathaus-Mussorgsky sound.

There were, however, some indications of the better thing *Boris* became at the Metropolitan a few years later, especially when Siepi performed the title role for the first time on March 9. A weightier, more solid vocalization of the music than London's, it added more to Siepi's repute than anything he had done since his Philip II in *Don Carlo*. More by instinct, perhaps, than by plan, Siepi achieved one dramatic stroke of audience identification by a simple gesture. This was the affectionate way in which he let his hand rest on the head of his son Fyodor in the Nursery Scene. He thus unostentatiously identified Boris as a human being with a parent's affection as well as a murderer with a tyrant's neurosis. He, too, grew in the part, especially as he learned to articulate the English text with greater clarity. In the performance of March 21 (with London), Roggero was Fyodor,* with Warner (Xenia*), Franke (Schuisky*), Scott (Pimenn*), Rankin (Marina*), and Carelli (Simpleton*).

The preponderance of familiar names in the preceding summary of new productions and important revivals was a characteristic of a season projected long before against a background of some uncertainty of managerial tenure. There was a scattering of new names, but they were mostly those of supplementary singers, such as Erich Kunz (Leporello [d]) and Hilde Zadek (Donna Anna) in a Reiner-directed *Don Giovanni* on November 26, in which Siepi was the Don,* with Prandelli (Ottavio*), Conner (Zerlina), Rigal (Elvira*), and Ernster (Commendatore*). Zadek performed a powerful, somewhat rough-sounding Anna, and Kunz gave his humorously adroit version of Leporello.* In totality, however, it was much like Gueden's Susanna of the year before: too stylized to blend with the nondescript kind of *Don Giovanni* the Metropolitan was sponsoring at this time. Prandelli's Ottavio spoke more of good will than of aptitude, and Rigal's Elvira* foundered on the optimistic assumption that she could sing either *"In quali eccessi"* or *"Mi tradi."*

Curiously, the virtues of Siepi and London as *Boris* were reversed in their aptitudes vis-à-vis *Don Giovanni*. The boyish charm that served Siepi well as Figaro left him bereft, at this phase of his venture with Don Giovanni, of the passionate fury that would drive a man to kill the father of a girl he craved. In his first Don* on January 14, London's physical magnetism (or what used to be called the *physique du rôle*), his electric action and closely studied conception of Da Ponte's creation were amplified by limber vocal resources for Mozart's needs. Indeed, the good singing in this performance began with the playing of the overture under the direction of Max Rudolf, who made much of the opportunity provided by Reiner's commitment to *The Rake*. The cast (Harshaw as Donna Anna,* Lewis as Elvira,* Peerce as Ottavio, Warner as Zerlina,* Scott as the Commendatore*) was almost wholly different from its predecessor, and in almost every instance an improvement.

In addition to such roles as Boris and Don Giovanni, London's second Metropolitan season enabled him to present his credentials in a sequence of other, equally substantial new roles. Among them were Escamillo* with Barbieri as Carmen* and Los Angeles as Micaëla (she had first sung the part at the Metropolitan on April 4, 1952) on January 20, Scarpia* in *Tosca* on March 26, and, finally, Amfortas* in *Parsifal* on April 3. The last was easily the best of them, perhaps because of its thoroughgoing preparation at Bayreuth, but there were elements of distinction in all. The *Parsifal* of April 1, which was conducted by Kurt Adler in the absence of Stiedry, also offered another chance in the title role to Emery Darcy, who had sung it first in 1943–4. The experiment did not work out well. In this cast Sigurd Bjoerling was the Amfortas,* Harshaw the Kundry.

Harshaw reached the zenith of her career on February 23, when she became the fourth American-born soprano to perform Isolde* at the Metropolitan (her predecessors were Lillian Nordica, Helen Traubel, and Jeanne Palmer). It was in every way creditable to her industry and her musicianship, entitling her to honorable mention in the even smaller company of Isoldes who also had sung Brangäne on this stage (Fremstad and Matzenauer). Of the two acts in which Isolde has a sizeable part, Harshaw was better in Act II, which calls primarily for vocal effort, than in Act I, in which she was required to define a character and create the illusion of irresistible appeal. The Tristan was Vinay, with Thebom as Brangäne and Stiedry conducting in a manner to be described as dispassionately attentive. Hotter notched something of a special category for himself by adding a notable King Marke* to his previous records as Kurvenal, which was performed in this cast by Schoeffler. On March 11 (with Traubel and Svanholm), the Brangäne was Lipton* and on March 27 the Kurvenal* was Sigurd Bjoerling.

Another opportunity for an American in a prominent Wagner role was offered to Steber when she sang Elsa* in *Lohengrin* on November 15 in a cast in which Josef Greindl (Henry [d]) and Sigurd Bjoerling (Telramund [d]) made debuts. Hopf was the Lohengrin* and Harshaw the Ortrud, with Stiedry conducting. Even the Herald (d) was unfamiliar, the role marking a debut for Arthur Budney. Steber sang the lyric music (especially *Elsas Traum* and the Balcony Scene) well enough to merit comparison with some favorite predecessors, but each time a dramatic climax impended, the basis for comparison tended to fade away. This was, on the whole, a prosaic *Lohengrin,* for neither Griendl nor the bass-baritone Bjoerling (no near relation to Jussi) performed with more than sound routine, and Hopf conveyed more of the shining knight by his armor than by his singing. Zadek was Elsa* on December 27 and Sullivan the Lohengrin* on April 11, but neither attained lasting identification with these roles.

What was lasting about this *Lohengrin* came in an aspect where it might have been expected least: the scenic. Without giving much publicity to his plan, Bing invited Charles Elson to strip the old (1920-1) Urban production to its essentials and then utilize the physical materials (timbers and canvas) for a rebuilt, repainted "semi-new" production. The results showed so great an improvement over the drab remnants they replaced that the technique was regularly employed thereafter when some gains could be effected.

In this season, for example, it would not have benefited *La Gioconda,* but it did serve a purpose with *Samson.* In the former, when it was performed for the first time since the 1947–8 season on December 16, the Gioconda was Milanov, with Barbieri (Laura*), Warren (Barnaba), Siepi (Alvise*), Madeira (La Cieca*), and Del Monaco (Enzo*). This mixture, stirred to a blend by Cleva, made a more potent thing of Ponchielli's score than it had been at the Metropolitan in recent years. Even Del Monaco made a conscientious effort to modify the normal volume of his voice for this purpose, but his suavest sound was still rough for *"Cielo e mar."* Solov's choreography for Act III was better than some of his earlier efforts, the smooth execution of it rather beyond the Metropolitan ballet as then constituted. Tucker eventually came to perform Enzo, one of his best roles, on February 2, but the six audiences for *Gioconda* in this season were more likely to hear Del Monaco or Baum (January 3). *Samson* (revamped by Armistead) fared rather otherwise, for a different but related reason—less relevance of direction to subject matter, though the conductor was Cleva when it was first heard on March 3, and weaker vocal elements in a cast of Stevens (Dalila), Vinay (Samson), Sigurd Bjoerling (High Priest*), Scott (Abimelech*), and Vichegonov (Old Hebrew*). There were changes of name (Thebom as Dalila, Moscona as the Old Hebrew) on March 19, but not much alteration of quality.

Also restored after an absence (since 1949–50) was *Tosca.* This brought with it three who sang Tosca* for the first time (Kirsten on November 12,

Albanese on December 20, and Rigal on December 26) and as many unfamiliar Cavaradossis*: Del Monaco (January 3), Conley (January 19),
and Baum (February 18). The number of new Scarpias* was even greater,
including Robert Weede (in his first Metropolitan appearance since 1949–
50) on December 20, Sigurd Bjoerling on January 3, Silveri on February
18, and London, as previously noted, on March 26. Add to these such
familiar Marios as Tagliavini, Tucker, and Peerce, and still another Scarpia
(Schoeffler), and the condition of *Tosca* in this season could only be
called chaotic. Cleva conducted all eleven, but the preferable cast of
Albanese, Del Monaco, and London never appeared together.

The expectation of sustained quality in even the best "new production"
tended to narrow ominously when *Don Carlo* had the first performance of
its third season on December 2. Most of the principals were of tested
merit in their roles (Tucker, Merrill, Hines as Philip II, Schoeffler as the
Grand Inquisitor,* Rigal, and Barbieri), but it was plain that something
had gone out of the cohesion of the ensemble. This could be traced to the
replacement of the conductor, Stiedry, who had a secure knowledge of the
score, with Erede, who did not. Ernster was the Grand Inquisitor* on December 13. On the other hand, *Così,* whose cast and conductor continued
almost exactly as they had begun (Peters as Despina,* rather than Munsel,
was the single change), enjoyed a joyous reunion with its public on January
13. Sullivan was the Ferrando* on January 17, and hardly Mozartian, let
alone Tuckerish. Miller as Dorabella* on February 11 disposed of neither
the vocal weight nor the physical size to balance Steber's Fiordiligi as
Thebom had. Another new Bing production gained a resource when
Merrill was Rigoletto* on November 15, with Tagliavini and Peters.

In this final season of Reiner's productive Metropolitan career (his appointment as the music director of the Chicago Symphony, to become
effective the following fall, was announced on December 10), he left one
durable legacy beyond his part in the *première* of *The Rake's Progress.*
This was the Sophie* in *Rosenkavalier* of Roberta Peters, which he guided
to a successful outcome on January 26. Orchestrally this was one of the
finest *Rosenkavaliers* to Reiner's credit at the Metropolitan, which put it
among the best ever, but it did not have what was required, vocally and
dramatically, in the Marschallin* of Varnay, the Ochs of Endre Koreh (d),
or the Faninal* of Kunz on January 22. Novotna rather than Stevens was
the Octavian on February 4, with Gueden as Sophie* (a fine role for her,
as picturesque as it was well sung), and there was still another Octavian
on February 21, when Miller put herself, with only marginal success, to
that sizeable task. For his farewell on April 11, Reiner was reunited with
Stevens in *Carmen,* with Vinay, London, and Conner. The *Rake* of this

season brought the operas Reiner conducted at the Metropolitan to twelve, the others being *Salome, Falstaff, Le Nozze di Figaro, Parsifal, Der Rosenkavalier, Die Meistersinger, Don Giovanni, Der fliegende Holländer, Tristan, Carmen,* and *Elektra*.

Of these, Reiner's final season also included a *Meistersinger* in which Zadek was an unillusive Eva* on December 8, with Madeira at less than her best as Magdalene,* Kunz as Beckmesser,* Greindl as Pogner,* and Harrell as Kothner (and a very good one, too). Schoeffler was the Sachs with Holm as David. In a theater that strives to present a repertory in the three primary operatic languages, a Metropolitan *rara avis* has always been a singer who can come to rest, with equal comfort, in two or more. And the jewel beyond price—a Farrar, Rethberg, or Tibbett—is the singer who can cope with all three languages and styles. The newest nominee for such triple duty was Los Angeles, whose facility in French (Marguerite, Micaëla, and Manon), and Italian (Mimi, Butterfly, and Mozart's Countess) made a venture into German, as Eva* on January 10, a logical next step. Vocally it also promised well; but the underlying problem with Los Angeles was, and remained, a limited acting technique and no great instinct for character portrayal. Franke was a likeable David* on February 17 (with Hotter as a stately Pogner* and Brownlee as Kothner*), though the range was high for him. Holm had an opportunity as Ottavio* in *Don Giovanni* on December 12 without showing reason for re-engagement when his particular speciality (David) was not required. Plans were pending for use of Sullivan as Walther, but they had not yet matured. His first Rodolfo* on February 13 (with Amara and Lewis) suited him better, vocally, than his Lohengrin. He also sang three-quarters of a Don José* on December 15, replacing Baum after Act I, with Amara as Micaëla.

The Metropolitan's financial needs and the rise of television prompted a new effort to discover whether they could be combined to mutual benefit. The probe, this time, went in two different directions from previous ones. Rather than seeking commercial sponsorship for home showing of a performance from its stage, the Metropolitan accepted partnership in a venture with Theatre Network TV. As the title suggests, this speculative entity had been created to exploit the financial possibilities of closed-circuit television, primarily in the sporting field. For the Metropolitan, theaters in twenty-two cities were to be fed with a live performance from its stage. Prices were adjusted to the local economy, ranging from a low of $1.80 to $7.20 at the Guild Theater on West Fiftieth Street in Manhattan. *Carmen* on December 11, with Stevens, Tucker, Merrill, and Conner, was chosen as the attraction. As seen close to home, the image was jumpy, poorly defined, and not close to the current commercial quality (even with the use of additional lighting, the stage was insufficiently illuminated for television purposes). Color TV still being a laboratory experiment, the image was restricted to black and white, thus sacrificing many of the values in the Gérard production.

For those who took the view that opera staged for 3,500 ticket-buyers could not also serve for home television, the Metropolitan joined in an arrangement with the Ford Foundation. This provided for operatic segments, produced under the direction of Herbert Graf, to be shown on the *Omnibus* program, which was then being sponsored by the Foundation. *La Bohème* and *Fledermaus* were adapted to this purpose, but the affiliation was short-lived.

However great the Metropolitan's financial need, which receded in this season to a deficit of "only" $425,000, it was not so urgent that a bequest of $75,000 be found acceptable regardless of terms. The offer was contained in the will of McNair Ilgenfritz, former occupant of Box I and a dilettante composer. It was dependent on the production at the Metropolitan of either of two operas composed by Ilgenfritz: *Phèdre* or *Le Passant*. However, even need could not strain the Metropolitan to tolerance of the Ilgenfritz literature, and the offer was rejected.

The first public mention of Maria Callas as a performer on the Metropolitan stage also came within the perimeter of the 1952–3 season. She had, as a much younger performer (in 1945), come to the attention of Edward Johnson, who offered her a choice between *Madama Butterfly* (which Callas thought unsuitable because of the weight she then carried) or *Fidelio* (which Callas rejected because it was to be given in English). In the intervening seven years, she had become not only Meneghini Callas but also a world celebrity, with engagements at the Colón in 1949, in Mexico City in 1950, at La Scala in May 1951, and at Covent Garden in 1952. It was Bing's belief that she had committed herself to three performances of *Traviata* for the spring of 1953, but she begged off on the plea that her husband, Giovanni Battista Meneghini, could not obtain a visa, and she would not come without him.

1953–1954

It may have been an accident of chance that Rudolf Bing's new beginning on November 1953 (with a three-year contract based on what he had done at the Metropolitan rather than, as his first had been predicated, what he might do) coincided with a new production of *Faust,* long associated with Metropolitan beginnings and endings. But it was no accident that Pierre Monteux's return to the Metropolitan after an absence of thirty-four years (the 1918–19 season) coincided with the first new production of

Faust at the Metropolitan since the one by Urban which he introduced at his debut on November 7, 1917. A stripling of forty-two then, Monteux had grown to a distinguished *maître* of seventy-eight between Metropolitan productions of *Faust*. Rather than accident, then, it was in a pattern of recurrence foreordained.

It had been said of Monteux's *Faust* in 1917 that it was "well planned," "musicianly," and "finely wrought" (page 271). As much and more could be said of his newest effort, with Los Angeles, Bjoerling, Merrill (Valentin), and Nicola Rossi-Lemeni (Méphistophélès [d]). Despite the lack of a French-speaking cast, Monteux made the orchestra speak French in a way that evoked much of the special sound in the score. Bing's disposition to settle for a wholly non-French cast (even in a new production) was an early instance of an indifference to the subtler aspects of French style which penalized this repertory during his tenure. Bjoerling's Faust was splendidly sung, as were Merrill's Valentin, and, in lesser degree, Los Angeles's Marguerite, giving point to Downes's description of it as "the finest cast in recent seasons." But the whole venture faltered on the limited impact of Rossi-Lemeni in his debut.

One of the well-regarded names of the post-war generation of opera-performers, Rossi-Lemeni (he was born in Constantinople of an Italian father and a Russian mother) had too many solid accomplishments to his credit—including a debut as Boris in San Francisco two years earlier—to be considered a creation of the recording studio. At the Metropolitan, his virtues as a singing actor were inverse to the order of that terminology: and, even so, his acting lacked the subtlety, flair or mobility associated with the best Méphistophélès. Vocally he was short of volume at the bottom of the range, somewhat rough at the top, and without the kind of ring or resonance that carries effectively to the far reaches of a large auditorium.

It is possible that, in another scheme of production than this one, Rossi-Lemeni might have performed with greater freedom, for Peter Brook's staging and Gérard's settings put unusual hazards in the path of the personnel. Moving the time period from the fifteenth century to the nineteenth suggested (in the light of Berman's *Rigoletto* and *Forza,* and others by others to come) as the first commandment in the Bing-Metropolitan's Decalogue for Designers: "Thou shalt not set the stage in the period decreed by the composer." The stated excuse was Brook's desire to put the action in the period of the *music;* but the more probable purpose was to carry out his idea of a Gentleman Devil, with a top hat and Savile Row kind of tails, performing his magic at the flourish of a walking stick rather than of a conventional sword. Whatever virtue there was in the scheme vanished in the clumsy, non-illusive scenery that belied Gérard's earlier accomplishment. Faust's book-lined study was too obviously a painted "flat"; Marguerite's drab garden lacked even the suggestion of a house for Faust to address *"Salut! demeure"* to, and the decision to include a token *Walpurgisnacht* ballet staged by Solov found it performed (poorly) on a nearly bare stage. Best of the lot was the Kermesse, but it did not count for much against the other deficiencies.

Thanks to the enlarged number of orchestra seats, the first-night receipts (at a top price of $30) rose to a new record of $65,336. The cost of the production was cited as close to $85,000. This struck some as expensive for what Thomson described as "the poorest set of decor and costumes yet done for the Met by Rolf Gérard." (His reference to Rossi-Lemeni's "mealy" French vowels was a variant on other expressions of disappointments with the singer's sound.) There was somewhat more style in the action when London took his turn at Méphistophélès* on March 20, but Brook's was not a conception that lent itself to the height of Hines, its other interpreter in this season (with the top hat, he seemed an oversized Lincoln). Siepi did not appear in any of the season's ten performances, though he was present for many weeks beginning in January.

Rossi-Lemeni had other opportunities to improve this first impression, but what he did as Don Giovanni* (December 10) and Boris* (January 11) did not measurably alter the judgment that he was not the kind of vocalist to make a meaningful impression in such roles at the Metropolitan. The repose he conveyed under Rudolf's direction in the role of the amorous adventurer was, in its way, as valid as London's vibrance, and he tied recitative to solo and aria to ensemble in a way that declared the superior artist. However, he never did engage the enthusiasm of the audience. He had his share of problems with this physical design also, for most of Urban's old arrangement had been replaced with one by Elson that featured a U-shaped ramp on which a good deal of action in Yannopoulos's staging was played out. In a realistic sense, it was the performers (Harshaw, Steber, Kunz, Peters, and Vichegonov as the Commendatore*) who tended to be played out after an evening's activity on it. The best Mozart singing of the night, and some of the best that had been heard in years, came from Cesare Valletti in his debut as Ottavio* (d). Light as the voice was, its perfect placement made it consistently audible and always a channel for superior artistry. Also new to Metropolitan Mozart in *Don Giovanni* was Fernando Corena, the Leporello* (d) of February 6, when Siepi was the Don, with Amara out of her vocal character as Elvira.* Corena was clearly the most promising buffo to appear in this decade, but he became a perhaps over-attentive student of Baccaloni at a time when the older singer's excesses were outrunning his good judgment. London was the Don on March 2, with Gueden more a citified than a rustic Zerlina.

As Boris, Rossi-Lemeni did not have an unconventional staging problem to contend with, but it can hardly be said that the English text was to his advantage. His regal bearing and authentically tsarish makeup, plus a grand kind of conviction, conveyed much to those who were willing to accept other shortcomings. These include a lack of fully free vocal production or, at the least, a lack of adjustment to the theater. In either case, the result was rough, growly, and unfocused, meaning that it did not carry well. Kullmann, now turned from leading roles to character parts, delivered a well-considered Schuisky,* and Scott was a convincing Pimenn in a cast with Thebom, Sullivan, and Harvuot (Rangoni*). This was the year for Hines to make a start on his Boris,* but the beginning on February 18 was but a hint of what his conception of the role would later become.

The new talents of Valletti (Almaviva*) and Corena (Bartolo*) contributed to the quality of this year's new production of Rossini's *Il Barbiere di Siviglia* on February 19, as did Cyril Ritchard's stage direction and Berman's new scenic treatment. Both were rather slow to attain the qualities that distinguished them, for Berman's setting for Act I (as given at the Metropolitan) was his weakest, and Ritchard's direction was more to the advantage of comedy than of sentiment. However, at its best, with Siepi as Basilio, Corena as Bartolo,* and Merrill as Figaro restrained from dependence on the oldest of their comic devices (for the while at least) and Ritchard providing them with several new ones, there was a fresh flow of entertainment which carried the spectator with it.

Musically, the "stars" were unfavorable for a dynamic new treatment of Rossini's score, especially as the conductor, Erede, limited himself to the basic function of timebeating. Much was made of the restoration of the Lesson Scene to Rossini's original form, but such concern for authenticity did not extend to the range of the voice which performed it. As Rosina, Peters performed carefully and cleanly, but with the chirping kind of self-satisfaction common to Rosinas of the sort called *coloratura*. At the *première,* Ritchard enacted the mute role of the servant Ambrogio (d), but it passed to the care of the Metropolitan's resident mime, Rudolf Mayreder, on February 25 and so remained. Another Rosina* of this season was Dolores Wilson (see page 543) on March 12, with little variation in quality or emphasis. The presence of Los Angeles (with Capecchi as Figaro*) on April 7 provided for the performance of *"Una voce poco fa"* in its original key of E; also, *"Contro un cor che accende amore"* was sung as written (in the Lesson Scene) in the key of D. Comedy was hardly

Los Angeles's forte, leaving the promise of a wholly suitable Rosina once more unfulfilled. Guarrera was another Figaro in this season (March 12), and Hines made a particularly grotesque Basilio on April 3 in elaboration of a conception first seen in 1947-8. With the passing of Reiner to his new duties in Chicago also passed—for the while at least—the day when the Metropolitan could, or at least did, command the services of a conductor of his qualities on a day-to-day, season-long basis. Formerly it had only been such a highly-prized specialist as Walter or Beecham who was acceptable as "guest" for as long as he chose to make the Metropolitan the scene of his activity. Or, as it often turned out, as long as he could combine a profitable engagement at the Philharmonic with a less profitable but possibly more gratifying engagement at the Metropolitan. That this tended (in the case of Szell, Mitropoulos, Maazel, Bernstein, and Steinberg) to make the Metropolitan a tail to the Philharmonic's kite did not seem to bother anyone at the opera house as long as it was not talked about too much. Tolerable in itself, perhaps, it became intolerable when it brought on the age of the "take-over," with all its dismal consequences.

In addition to Monteux, the revised list of conductors included George Szell in a period that overlapped his Philharmonic engagement starting on December 10 and ending January 10. His resumption of opera in New York was dated December 26 (Bruno Walter was at the Philharmonic that week), when he participated in the first new *Tannhäuser* a Metropolitan audience had seen since the twenties. Some found the first scene (which Downes described as an "odd stage spectacle with its connotations of Venus' shell and perhaps other symbols of a Freudian order") inappropriate, but the other acts pleased the eye as well as the mind in a well-balanced demonstration of Gérard's best abilities. His Hall of Song, for which he created a spacious room, with banked bleachers for the "guests" angling from stage left, front, to stage right, rear, was an outstanding success.

It was elected that the Dresden version, which had been rejected at the Metropolitan since World War I, be used, on the stated ground that it had greater "stylistic unity." This was a euphemism to disguise Wagner's addition in the preferable "Paris" version, of pages and pages of greater music in the Venusberg bacchanale. One could not down the thought that the need the "Paris" version created for an adequate ballet was a count against it.

The decision, apparently, was tolerable to Szell, though the "Paris" version had been in use when he had previously conducted *Tannhäuser* at the Metropolitan (in 1942-3). Whatever the case, there was no suggestion of mental reservation in his conducting, which was typically forthright

and musically well informed. He might, however, have had other preferences than the cast which found Varnay as the only principal who had
sung her role at the Metropolitan previously. With her as Venus were
Harshaw (Elisabeth*), Vinay (Tannhäuser*), London (Wolfram*), and
Hines (Landgrave Hermann*). Of even more critical importance were
such untried subordinates as Sullivan (Walther von der Vogelweide*),
Harvuot (Biterolf*), Franke (Heinrich*), and Scott (Reinmar*). Some
went one way, some another in the quintet at the end of Act I, which came
closer to debacle than any self-respecting theater should permit. At the
third performance, on January 9, the curtain snagged in the transformation
from Venusberg to the outdoor scene that follows, causing some laughter
in the audience. By the fourth performance, when Kullmann took on
Tannhäuser* for the first time in his career (because Vinay was unable to
perform), with Resnik as Venus,* Josef Metternich as Wolfram* and
Varnay now as Elisabeth, Szell had made his decision—no more Metropolitan. As there were no further performances until March, he might
easily have rested on a letter requesting release from his contract, but he
chose to unburden himself of his dissatisfaction with "present conditions"
at the Metropolitan to a reporter from the *Herald Tribune*. Said Szell: "If
the board of directors wants me to give them a report on what I mean by
present conditions, I shall be glad to oblige; but I shall make no statements
to the press or the public at this moment." (Whatever his grievances, the
outburst was curiously kin to the one he made a few years later after a
guest engagement in San Francisco.) Realizing that there remained for
him (publicly), only the gentlemanly side of the argument, Bing took it,
stating: "I am grateful to Mr. Szell for his distinguished contribution to
this season and I regret his departure. He will always be welcome at the
Met." Other things were, of course, said privately. As well as conducting
the two performances in March, Rudolf deputized for Szell at the two
scheduled for the tour.

Monteux's season also included attention to the other French works of
the repertory, of which *Carmen* (on December 12) was much as it had
been previously, with Stevens, Tucker, Guarrera, and Amara. Heidi Krall
made her debut as Frasquita (d). However, by February 16, when Rankin
was the Carmen,* the conductor was Kozma, an arrangement that prevailed for the balance of the season. There was more promise of a gratifying musical experience in Monteux's direction of *Pelléas et Mélisande* on
November 27, when Debussy's music drama had its first Metropolitan
hearing since 1948-9. Singher, who had been a Metropolitan Pelléas on
an earlier occasion, was the Golaud* this time, and a very good one, with
Conner a vocally pale, dramatically insufficient Mélisande.* Hines as

Arkel* and Lipton as Geneviève showed promising aptitudes for these parts, but quite the best impression was made by Theodor Uppman, a light baritone from California, in his debut as Pelléas (d). He had the stature as well as the sound to pursue such roles profitably, building on a background that included appearances with Maggie Teyte at City Center (see page 475). The arts of makeup enabled Los Angeles to make a pretty picture of a Mélisande on December 23, but the wig was blonder than the voice. On January 12, the Arkel* was Alvary. Scenically this *Pelléas* was an Armistead remake of the old Urban settings, with some additions of his own and only fair results.

With the three new productions of this season added to those of *La Forza del destino, La Bohème, Rigoletto, Carmen, Fledermaus, Così, The Rake's Progress, Aida,* and *Cavalleria rusticana* and *Pagliacci,* the preponderance of new vs. old was, for the first time in at least twenty years, on the side of novelty. The venture into revision which had benefited *Lohengrin* the previous year was applied this year to *Le Nozze di Figaro,* of which the results were displayed for the first time on November 20 under the direction of Stiedry. As in the previously mentioned *Don Giovanni,* the new "conception" introduced some elements of staging (by Graf) which offset whatever benefits might have derived from Armistead's "new" scenic arrangement (in this instance, mostly a matter of drapes).

As an example, Graf introduced "aprons" over either end of the orchestra pit which enabled the performers to come closer to the audience from time to time—but also spread the action, laterally, over a wider area than benefited it. It was also evident, from the start, that the auditorium itself was brilliantly illuminated, as if someone had forgotten to dim its lighting when the overture began. Inquiry revealed that this was part of Graf's plan in emulation of some performance of Mozart's time he had read about in which the hall was brilliantly illuminated. What might have been appropriate for a small salon illuminated by candles was not necessarily appropriate for an auditorium holding 3800—a line of reasoning that, of course, prevailed again as soon as this production and its "producer" had run their course.

Of musical illumination there was more than a little in the advent of such celebrated Mozart singers as Irmgard Seefried as Susanna (d) and Lisa della Casa as the Countess (d). The Viennese triangle was completed by Kunz as Figaro,* with Guarrera as Almaviva* taking a new turn in his career and Miller as Cherubino. Not all the promise of these performers was realized in the conducting of Stiedry, whose inclination was to stress musical concord rather than dramatic conflict. What was memorable, then, was the individual efforts, of which Della Casa's was but the first in a succession of beautifully vocalized, carefully acted impersonations. See-fried's exhibition of operatic artifice was, unfortunately, followed by nothing else. Guarrera's resource for Mozart was limited to the manner-isms he had learned for Guglielmo (in *Così*), which were scarcely suf-ficient for the altered circumstances of place and social position. With Steber (January 9) an active replacement for Della Casa and Los Angeles an inactive one, the Metropolitan had richer resources for the role of the Countess than for some time past (the latter limited herself in this season to Rossini's Rosina, depriving those who were interested of the rare op-portunity to see the two Rosinas performed in the same season by the same singer). Hopes for the future of the Metropolitan's *Figaro* were further stimulated on January 28 when London as Almaviva* and Peters as Susanna* initiated an amorous contest renewed many times since. For this first season, Della Casa remained only long enough to perform one other part. Her Elvira* in a *Don Giovanni* (with London) on December 19 was only a suggestion of the characterization she later developed.

The evident effort to add performers who could, like Los Angeles and Della Casa, perform in more than one repertory might be construed as the reason for the debut of Josef Metternich as Don Carlo* in *La Forza del destino* on November 21. By German standards, Metternich had an "Italian" sound, but it hardly rated as such in terms of Warren and Val-dengo, the Metropolitan's recent standards for such a role. In this version, Preziosilla was even more a shadowy part, with the *"Rataplan"* cut and the character of Trabucco restored. Metternich was also heard at a dis-advantage as Di Luna* in *Trovatore* on January 7 and at something like his best as Wolfram* in Szell's last stand on January 14. In physical as well as vocal size, Metternich was better suited to the smaller German theaters than to the Metropolitan.

Neither was a handicap for Gino Penno, a robust specimen of Italian breeding, who made his debut as Alvaro (d) in *Forza* on February 17 (with Nelli as Leonora* and Renato Cellini conducting) after missing his scheduled first appearance as Radames on February 13 because of illness. This opportunity recurred for him on February 27, by which time he had also sung Manrico* in *Trovatore* on February 22. The net of these, to-gether with his Canio* on March 24, was esteem for the promising size of the singer and his voice, distress for his lack of subtlety and mere steadiness of production. The deficiencies rather than the promise domi-nated his Pollione* when Norma was restored for Milanov on March 9, with Siepi as Oroveso.* The notion that Bellini's masterpiece could be "put on" in the middle of a busy season, in a miscellany of ramps and flats by Elson, with a conductor (Cleva) who had never done it previously with the Metropolitan's orchestra and chorus was, perhaps, predicated on the belief that Milanov could "carry" the performance. Creditably as she sang *"Casta diva,"* she lacked theatrical conviction and the vocal resource for the more dramatic portions of the score. This did not, however, prevent her "fans" among the standees from making an inordinate amount of noise about her performance and cueing other singer's "fans" to do likewise. There was some unwanted aggressiveness in Barbieri's treatment of Adalgisa's* music which a more determined conductor would have tempered, but he was not present in Cleva. The role (Adalgisa*) passed to Thebom with some altered emphasis on March 27, and Baum offered his credentials (mostly unacceptable) as Pollione* on April 15.

Another new performer of consequence in this season was Ettore Bastianini, of whom little was known when he offered himself for evaluation as Giorgio Germont (d) in *Traviata* on December 5. The dusky richness of his sound qualified him as a companion for Albanese (Violetta) and Tucker (Alfredo), though it was clear that he was inclined to overplay his voice and underplay his role. The voice remained a source of aural pleasure as Di Luna* in *Trovatore* on December 25 (Nikolaidi was the Azucena*) and as Enrico Ashton* in *Lucia* on January 13 with Pons and Peerce. The only question mark about the Bastianini career related to the performer himself—what he had to work with was unquestionably superior.

American additions to the company in this season began with Jean Fenn on November 21 as Musetta (d) (the Dietz translation had vanished never to return, and all the *Bohèmes* were in Italian), continued with Dolores Wilson (as Lucia [d] on February 8), and also included Jon Crain, who had been a member of the Metropolitan's touring *Fledermaus* company as Alfred [d] in that work on March 10 with MacWatters and Thebom. None of these performers who made debuts in leading roles attained the career goals of another who faced a Metropolitan audience for the first time in the barely noticeable part of Parpignol (d) on November 21 (the *Bohème* of Fenn's first appearance). For all the brevity of the art, it did not escape the attention of Noel Straus, critic of the *Times,* who had heard "big, firm tones" from the newcomer. These were exactly what made James McCracken into an Otello and a Samson.

Both new sopranos added attractiveness to the Metropolitan's stage, Fenn longer than Wilson. The former also appeared as Violetta* on January 27 in place of Albanese, without establishing valid reasons for Metropolitan exposure at this point in her career. Wilson (who had been gathering experience in Italy under the name of Vilsoni) had abundant confidence, well founded on her ability to sing with plentiful power at the top of her range, but her voice was prevailingly edgy in sound and without aural charm. Herva Nelli of Pittsburgh, whose fame was associated with the Toscanini broadcasts of operas and the recordings derived from them, had several opportunities in similar roles, beginning with Leonora (d) in *Forza* on February 17 and followed by Aida* on February 27 (she had been invited to perform the part at a student matinee in the preceding season, on January 23) and Leonora* in *Il Trovatore* on April 17. The quality of Nelli's effort was always expressive of her unusual musical background, but her dramatic projection rarely measured up to the requirements of a large theater. Thomas Hayward, whose career since 1947–8 had been mostly in secondary roles, had a long-awaited opportunity for prominence when he replaced Bjoerling as Faust* after the first act on December 17 and showed himself competent to deal with the emergency. He performed the same role in place of Tucker on January 8 and was also the Alfred of this season's *Fledermaus* cast for the New Year's Eve performance (in which Alicia Markova made her debut as a featured member of the second act ballet). Hayward's vocal quality was pleasant enough and his musicianship was excellent. Personality of the kind associated with leading tenor roles was not in his makeup, however.

The incidence, in the main flow of this narrative, of such names (previously encountered in a side eddy) as Fenn, Nelli, Uppman, and Crain directs attention to the inevitable destiny of the City Center as a tributary to that main flow. It also focuses attention on its need constantly to replenish its own sources and to make the most of them while they remained untapped by others. In this fall season Hurley as Gretel and Schippers as conductor of Humperdinck's masterpiece who profited as they practiced; no special attention, however, was directed to MacNeil as Germont in a seasonal renewal of *Traviata*. Vilma Georgiou, a petite soprano of later note at the Metropolitan, entered in as inconspicuous a manner as possible: as Barbarina in *Figaro*. Much of the season's production effort was concentrated on a venture with Gottfried von Einem's version of Kafka's *Der Prozess* known (in its English version) as *The Trial*. Under Otto Preminger's attentive direction, the drama fared well, and Phyllis Curtin excelled as the much-desired heroine. Musically it did not count for much more during October in New York than it had during August in Salzburg.

Against his better judgment, Aaron Copland was persuaded to permit the City Center to produce his *Tender Land* during its spring season, though he had written it for performance in less exposed surroundings by less sophisticated talents than those of Jon Crain, Norman Treigle, and Rosemary Carlos (Laurie). Schippers conducted. It was substantially revised before being performed elsewhere. Rosenstock's reach exceeded his grasp when he elected Verdi's *Falstaff* for the *Stadttheater* treatment with hardly a suitable performer in the cast. Richard Wentworth earned a new appellation for Sir John by portraying him in an "earnest" manner and Phyllis Curtin was an agreeable Mistress Ford. The English translation by Chester Kallman was well made, assuming that one accepts "With obeisance" as a tolerable substitute for *"Reverenza."* Of rather longer promise was MacNeil's first Rigoletto.

With Schoeffler otherwise engaged during this season, favor reverted to Ferdinand Frantz, who had not appeared during the previous two seasons. His reappearance (as Wotan in *Die Walküre* on February 4) stirred some curiosity as to why a singer of his quality was not steadily employed at the Metropolitan, and his Gurnemanz* in *Parsifal* on March 26 intensified it. With Hotter as Hunding* in the same *Walküre* and the Wotan* of another on February 23, there was substantial vocal matter for conductor Stiedry to work with in these important roles. Harshaw and Varnay were the alternating Brünnhildes and Sieglindes, the former performing both roles for the first time in New York. Her Sieglinde* was learned during the course of the season (because of Resnik's absence), and first performed on February 23. It was musically creditable to her, but the pliant quality of sound wanted (for *"Du bist der Lenz"* in particular) was not hers to provide. Svanholm's declining vocal resource made his Siegmund increasingly trying to hear at this time, but the company had no other. For those who could pick them out of the ensemble, it might be noted that Mariquita Moll was the Waltraute (d) of the February 4 performance and that Rosalind Elias made her initial venture on this stage as Grimgerde (d) on February 23.

The name of Helen Traubel was absent from the Metropolitan's roster and the records of the season for the first time in a dozen years. The cause came to light in the early fall, erupting into an exchange between Bing and Traubel which enabled the press to make much of his "discrimination" against her. Still unattuned to American ways, Bing found inartistic the spectacle of an Isolde and Brünnhilde who clowned on the radio and appeared in nightclubs, thus providing editorial writers with the opportunity to denounce him as "snobbish" and justify Traubel's decision to "give up" the Metropolitan.

In truth, Bing's lack of enthusiasm for her outside activities was the greatest possible favor he could have done for Traubel, whose roles had come to Isolde and virtually nothing else as her top range receded. It enabled her to leave the Metropolitan as an injured party rather than as a performer who could no longer perform, and provided new momentum for her non-operatic career, which she thereafter pursued profitably for some time to come.

With the start of Bing's new contract there was some indication that he meant to validate his promise of fewer cast changes than had been the custom before his arrival. For the first time in several seasons there appeared to be a resolute effort to keep together a cast that had been prepared for the season's first performance of an opera. In a total of approximately 150 performances, a cast recurred without change or with no more than a change in a single role about forty-three times. This meant that nearly ninety performances were spared the kind of multiple changes which afflicted the previous season's *Toscas*. On the other hand, when Stevens performed at La Scala on a Thursday night and flew back to New York for a Saturday matinee of *Carmen* on April 3, one wondered whether there was one rule for "stars," another for "comets."

For an outsider's view of the Metropolitan at this time, attention might be directed to the comments of Desmond Shawe-Taylor in a London publication (*The New Statesman and Nation*) after a mid-winter visit to New York. "Backed by a first-class musical staff and with the amazing wealth of native American vocal talent to draw upon," Shawe-Taylor wrote, "the Metropolitan never seems to descend to the level of an 'off' evening in the famous European houses, while its best is about the equal to the best that Europe can provide." The English critic continued: "Staleness of repertory cannot be mended until the theater receives firm financial backing. In every other respect it has good reason to go on thinking of itself as the world's leading opera house."

The oblique reference might have been more pointed had the report been written after this season's reappearance of *The Rake's Progress,* the most recent effort to freshen the repertory. It returned on January 26 not only to an inordinate number of empty seats, but also to Downes's observation that this was "by no means without justification." Perhaps it was this kind of outspokenness that Bing had in mind when Miles Kastendieck of the *Journal-American* reported: "Bing had never expected 'The Rake' to be a box-office success. . . . He feels, however, that it could have been less of a failure. Both the critics and the public let him down." The possibility that Bing had let the *Rake* down was at least mentionable. The cast was substantially as it had been in its first season, but the conductor was Erede, a questionable choice to replace the unavailable Reiner.

Another kind of comment, reminiscent of Thomson's charge that a new *Bohème* would be a "scandalous waste of money," followed the announcement that *Andrea Chénier* would be included in the repertory for 1954–1955. It came from B. H. Haggin in *The Nation*. He deemed it "a major aberration" that "the Metropolitan not only will revive Giordano's 'Andrea Chénier' but will squander on this rubbish the money for a new production that it would not spend on 'Boris.' "

One of the few remaining members of his administration from the Johnson period left the company at the end of this season with the resignation of Margaret Carson. Her place as head of the press department was taken by Francis Robinson. In an expression of the time it was said that her job had become difficult because "Bing didn't like to take advice from a woman." Soon enough it was apparent that this expression was three words too long.

1954–1955

What happened at the Metropolitan Opera House during the seventieth year of its existence was, on one hundred sixty occasions during the season, of interest to those to whom opera is a compulsion or perhaps even an obsession. But the hundred sixty-first, on January 7, 1955, was one of those landmark occasions when the Metropolitan stage becomes a part of a larger world stage and the drama enacted on it transcends the scope of anything the creators of the nominal "attraction" could invent.

For the first time in the seven decades in which there had been a Metropolitan Opera House a leading role in an opera presented by its resident company was performed by a member of the Negro race. That it came to be Marian Anderson as Ulrica (d) in *Un Ballo in maschera* was, perhaps, inevitable, but it was nevertheless accidental. It was the by-product of an engagement of London's Old Vic Company at the Metropolitan during October and of a post-performance party at the Starlight Roof of the Waldorf-Astoria Hotel. Miss Anderson was present and so was Bing. Perhaps it was an impulse, perhaps not wholly so. Bing asked her whether she would like to appear in the Metropolitan's forthcoming season, and suggested Ulrica for her debut. She said that she did not know the role, but would look at it and let him know. She decided that it was possible for her, and so informed him. The information, when printed, was of course front page news. It was, Bing told me a few days later, done wholly on his own. He was somewhat surprised, he mentioned, that no member of the board volunteered the kind of enthusiastic approval which came spontaneously from all other sides.

However spontaneous the action as far as Miss Anderson was concerned, the thought evidently had been incubating with Bing for some time. For the Gérard production of *Aida* which opened his second season (see page 510), Bing had engaged Janet Collins as *première danseuse*, a departure from custom, but one nevertheless in keeping with the utilization of Negroes as supers and for authentic "atmosphere." More recently, Robert McFerrin, a young Negro baritone, had been included among winners of Auditions of the Air and assigned soon after (in the spring of 1953) to the Katharine Turney Long course, an adjunct of the Metropolitan which had been established (in 1948) for the purpose of providing promising young singers without theatrical experience with fundamentals of posture, stage deportment, fencing, language, and related subjects.

Nor should it be forgotten that there was a more than theatrical context for these happenings. May 17, 1954, was the date of the Supreme Court decision rejecting the concept of "separate but equal" as justification for segregated schools, and the proclamation of the doctrine of "all deliberate speed." There was, in consequence, a movement of the social order as well as the impulse of an individual to be considered. The individual, however, was one who was disposed to advance with the time rather than one who resisted it, as Edward Johnson had a few years before. Confronted with the wider opportunities for Negroes in professional sports in the late '40s than in opera, Johnson had made the plaintive comment: "Don't you think I have enough troubles?"

What was potential "trouble" for Johnson was a beckoning opportunity for Bing. With Tucker (Riccardo), Warren (Renato), and Milanov (Amelia) to sing roles for which they were celebrated, Peters as Oscar,* and Mitropoulos as conductor, *Ballo* had such ample built-in values despite its faded sets (a creation of Dobujinsky in 1940) as not to require more than a qualified Ulrica to make the occasion properly Verdian. Anderson would unquestionably have been such an Ulrica ten years before, vocally; at this debut she depended more on dignity of appearance and the intensity of her dramatic effort in *"Re dell'abisso, affretati"* to sustain her part on the high level of effort around her. Anderson achieved her most striking effect with the startled outcry *"Il coute!"* as she fell into a swift obeisance on recognizing the king as the disguised visitor to her den. However, for those who had waited so long to savor this hour of recognition, there were no gradations of value—the triumph was absolute and they had the applause to prove it, hollow sound and uncertain pitch notwithstanding. The events were re-enacted, with even stronger currents of emotion, when Anderson repeated the role at the Academy of Music in the city of her birth on the Metropolitan's next visit to Philadelphia on January 11. Undoubtedly Bing's well-considered way of handling this particular transition was a kindness for McFerrin when he made his debut as Amonasro (d) in *Aida* on January 27 with Nelli, Thebom, Baum, and Elias (Priestess), Cleva conducting. He was spared the burden of proving a point already proved, leaving him free to concentrate on the still-considerable one of proving himself a proper Amonasro. Some things he did better than others, which could be said of the forty-five men— none of them Negro—who had preceded him on this stage in the same role.

Like Walter's and Szell's before him, the pattern of Mitropoulos's Philharmonic appearances was sufficiently flexible to accommodate some Metropolitan activity. And, though he was not generally thought of as an opera conductor, it was to the advantage of the Metropolitan to have a conductor of his qualities to work with it. He had, indeed, served an apprenticeship in the German theater (Berlin) in his early days and had retained an interest that took the form of notable concert performances with the Philharmonic of *Elektra, Wozzeck, Boris,* and acts of *Die Walküre* and *Götterdämmerung* as circumstances suggested. Had he restricted himself to these and other works for which he had a special aptitude, his Metropolitan career might have more steadily sustained the high level of which he was unquestionably capable.

That it did not may have been owing more to an inability to say "No" than to an overwhelming impulse to say "Yes." Even his debut on December 15 was clouded by this ambivalence, for it was divided between *Salome,* for which he had the well-matched talents of Christl Goltz (Salome* [d]), Vinay (Herod*), Schoeffler (Jokanaan), and Thebom (Herodias*), and an evanescent balletic affair by Solov called *Vittorio,* evolved from oddments of Verdi with a set by Esteban Frances. There was little in the score that another conductor could not have done as well, perhaps—with an experience in ballet that Mitropoulos lacked— even better. Mitropoulos's resistance to the task was well known, but he did not, apparently, choose to make an issue of it. It did not, in any case, diminish the high standard of execution Mitropoulos demanded of the orchestra in *Salome* or the dynamic power with which he animated their performance, but it did recur to mind when he became party to even less suitable things later on. The Salome* of Goltz had many theatrical qualities to commend it, but also some vocal faults (especially in roughness of sound) which left her well short of the still fresh memory of Welitch. Vinay's Herod was perhaps the lasting impression of this whole venture, a characterization that increased in power as long as he had the vocal means to articulate it. As Herodias, Thebom was more vivid in dress and makeup than in voice. Goltz was the Salome through this sequence of performances, and the casting remained substantially the same, save for Kullmann as Herod and Harvuot as Jokanaan* (both on January 10). Mitropoulos's first season was otherwise restricted to *Ballo,* which offered Metternich as Renato* and Madeira as Ulrica* on January 22, the same pair with Laurel Hurley in her debut as Oscar (d) on February 8, and Merrill as Renato* on February 26. In all of these, Mitropoulos's entrance into the Metropolitan's pit carried with it the promise of an effort that would animate routine and transform lethargy into attention, and for this he will be long remembered.

Another conductor who gave promise of amending the Metropolitan's shortcomings in other post-Reiner, post-Szell categories was Rudolf Kempe. He was, indeed, post-Szell as directly as could be contrived, for it was as the conductor of *Tannhäuser* that he made his first appearance on January 26. A former oboe player (in Dresden), Kempe had learned his operatic lessons well, as some had discovered in Munich, were he came to attention after the war. Kempe's *Tannhäuser* was typically urgent in mood and always fluid in manner, to the advantage of a cast that included Vinay, Varnay (Venus), Harshaw, and London. However, all he commanded in plasticity of sound and warmth of impulse did not count for much when Bernd Aldenhoff was the Tannhäuser (d) and Brenda Lewis (hardly a Wagnerian voice) Venus* on February 25. Vichey (a new, shortened form for Vichegonov) took a turn as Hermann* on March 7, with Svanholm as Tannhäuser. Kempe also conducted this season's restoration of *Tristan* on March 3, with Svanholm, Varnay, Hines (King Marke*), Thebom and Metternich (Kurvenal*), in which McCracken sang Melot.* Some found Kempe's orchestral sound somewhat pallid, and it could, indeed, have been stronger without coming close to overpowering his singers. The alternate for an increasingly voiceless Svanholm on March 12 was the Tristan* of Aldenhoff, which was louder, certainly, but hardly more listenable. A diligent but dull performer, Aldenhoff also offered his version of Parsifal* (dry in sound, uninteresting in action) on March 23, with Varnay as Kundry, Ernster, and Metternich as Amfortas.* For those who raised the name of Wolfgang Windgassen in a *Tannhäuser-Tristan-Parsifal* season, the managerial response was a shudder of alarm and the whispered word that he had set his price at $12,000 (plus transportation) for a nine- to ten-week period in which he would sing no more than eight times.

Whether Kempe had been engaged to put on Metropolitan's first venture with a "new" Strauss opera since the *Ägyptische Helena* of 1928–9, or whether *Arabella* became a possibility with the availability of Kempe, the two made a highly compatible pair when the opera had its first hearing in New York on February 10. A fine sequence of stage pictures by Gérard (the second act scene was the least good of the three), a particularly fine assortment of period clothes, and a cast that looked as it should in almost every part gave uncommon theatrical illusion to this production. Moreover, there was a high level of vocal quality in at least two performances, the classic Mandryka* of London and the equally good Zdenka* of Gueden. The level slumped thereafter, especially in the delivery of John Gutman's English text by Ralph Herbert as Count Waldner (d) and Thebom (Adelaide*). Steber was slightly better as Arabella,* but it was not the kind of vocal writing which lent itself to explicit vowels and consonants. However, when the insinuation of Strauss's score was at its most persuasive and Steber's voice was blended with Gueden's under Kempe's knowing direction the *prima facie* case for *Arabella* was made the only way it could be made—musically. For some who were content to remember lines from faded reviews (such as Paul Henry Lang's remarks, as successor to Thomson on the *Herald Tribune,* that *Arabella* was the "tired . . . music of an old man"), it was a closed chapter before it was an open book. To others, however, it was the beginning of a new enthusiasm.

A prime reason for this must be the staunch and attractive Mandryka of London. His broadly based, well-shaded characterization was one of the unmistakable verities of this production, a sustaining strength while others grew, were changed, or matched to it. Not so much could be said of the other men, for Sullivan was a gauche Matteo,* Carelli beset by language difficulties as Elemer,* Davidson an undynamic Lamoral.* Harvuot was closer to the mark as Dominik.* Peters looked pert, but made wiry sounds as Fiakermilli,* a role that sounded better in the voice of Hurley on March 24, when the Matteo* was Gari. Fenn was the Zdenka* on April 4, with Cassel as Mandryka* and Lipton as Adelaide. *Arabella* lasted longer at the Metropolitan than Kempe, but they will always be joined in memory by those who first experienced them together.

If the advent of Anderson opened a door on a host of new, future, possibilities, the debut of Renata Tebaldi on January 31 recalled a time when a leading *prima donna* in Italian opera was also a leading Italian *prima donna.* She might have become a Metropolitan performer half a dozen years before had she accepted an invitation of Edward Johnson when he heard her in Italy in 1948; but she had not felt then that she was ready for New York. She did feel "ready" for San Francisco in 1950, when Bing heard her and offered a Metropolitan engagement as

Elvira in *Don Giovanni* and Mimi in *Bohème,* on the homeward journey. This seemed to Tebaldi less than she was now "ready" to do, and she declined the offer.

Whatever the sequence, the outcome was a suitably substantial success. The size of Tebaldi's voice, its soaring ease and womanly warmth, were of a magnitude not heard in such a role as Desdemona (d) for years, and it responded to a musical discipline that thinned it to the fine line desirable for the *"Ave Maria"* and *"Salce, salce."* A big, handsome woman of gracious presence and good mobility, Tebaldi cherished the beautiful sound more than the incisive accent, which left some illusion lacking. But she wilted gradually under the heat of Del Monaco's rage from imperiously wrathful to wrathfully imperious, and left no illusion lacking in her anguished *"Ave Maria"* and desolating "Willow Song." Warren's Iago was improved by better makeup, a more becoming wig than he had worn previously in the part, and a stronger sense of word values to enrich his always powerful vocal performance. Stiedry was the conductor, with a mostly American group of subordinate performers (Franke as Cassio,* McCracken as Roderigo,* Lipton as Emilia). Downes in the *Times* summed up a general opinion by assessing Tebaldi as "an artist of exceptional quality, intelligence and sincerity." Bing's ban on solo curtain calls was not breached for Tebaldi, with the now customary results: inordinately sustained applause after arias. When the next word had to be spoken, or the next note sung, by the performer who was being applauded, the conductor was powerless to begin until the performer did in fact resume. In other *Otellos* of this season, Amara was afforded an accelerated, unwarranted exposure as Desdemona* on March 17, an occasion brought to a crisis of credibility by the need to employ Svanholm as Otello* *vice* Del Monaco.

Acquaintance with Tebaldi proceeded by way of an old-fashioned, well-equipped opera performer's kind of repertory—Mimi* in *Bohème* on February 9, Maddalena* in *Andrea Chénier* on February 23, and Tosca* on March 8. Her first Aida was scheduled for February 16, but it turned into Milanov's first Tosca* when Tebaldi fell ill. This uncommon change of opera was a gesture of recognition by Bing that those who had bought tickets specifically for Tebaldi's Aida should not be penalized by her illness. House rules stipulated that refunds would be made only when an opera (rather than a performer) was changed, and the gesture of good will was not forgotten (though seldom repeated). Not every Tebaldi role was equally sound from beginning to end—her Tosca, for example, was as yet lacking the playfulness and volatility that the first act demanded, her Mimi physically oversized (for the consumptive), her Maddalena somewhat static at the outset. But there was certain, in everyone of them, to be a moment of vocal abundance (whether in *"Vissi d'arte,"* Mimi's *"Donde lieta usci,"* or Maddalena's *"La mamma morta"*) in which the visual drama was suspended and the ear-filling appeal of a superb voice asserted itself. For the rest, one could hope.

The privilege of being the Metropolitan's first Maddalena* since Rosa Ponselle (and Leonora Corona) in the 1932-3 season was bestowed on Milanov when *Chénier* made its reappearance after twenty-two years' absence on November 16. This was neither the opening night of the season nor even the opening night of the Milanov season, but the furore of her fans—not without some traces of organized effort—pointed to the time not far off when almost every Metropolitan performance would be beset by equally rude noises, which sounded paid for rather than earned. The consequence, of course, was to stimulate the competitive impulse of the Del Monaco partisans, who scarcely needed it. Aside from a compulsion to shout his *"Improvviso"* rather than sing it, Del Monaco had a fine list of attributes for Chénier,* including an ideal appearance for the rebellious poet. For the amount of voice he commanded, Warren's Gérard* should have been better in Act I than it was, but his was, unquestionably, a powerful presentation of *"Nemico della patria."* With a scenic scheme by Frederic Fox well suited to the scope of the Metropolitan stage, an orderly if somewhat tame staging by Yannopoulos, and authoritative direction of the score by Cleva, Giordano's name had a redemption of credit beyond anything associated with it in New York for two decades, including an only fair venture at the City Center in 1947. Glaz made an admirable characterization of her Countess di Coigny,* Madelon* was affectingly sung by Nell Rankin, and the brief part of Bersi* gave more prominence to the outstanding attributes of Elias than anything she had done in her debut as a Walküre the previous year (see page 545). It was noticeable, too, that acknowledgement was gratefully made for a gift from Mrs. John D. Rockefeller, Jr., which paid for the production. In the performance of December 10, the Maddalena* was Nelli, with Bastianini as Gérard* and Sandra Warfield as Madelon (she first showed her substantial vocal gifts in this role on December 4); Tucker provided a ringing sound for the ensemble with his Chénier* on December 23. Baum added another role to his long list when he performed the poet on March 26. Not a little of the atmosphere in the ensemble came from vivid bits of characterization by Baccaloni (Mathieu*), De Paolis (A Spy*), and Carelli (the Abbé*). Consolidating all as a company effort was the performance of George Cehanovsky as Fleville, in which he had appeared when *Chénier* had last been given at the Metropolitan on February 1, 1933.

For the first time ever, the Metropolitan offered not only a star tenor, soprano, and baritone at its opening night, but multiples in all categories. That this event on November 8 began with Warren in the prologue to *Pagliacci* and ended with Warren as Amonasro did not identify some kind of monstrous Leoncavallo-Verdi travesty, but a Noah's Ark kind of gala (two of everything) to test further the appeal of closed-circuit television. Also offered were the first act of *Bohème* with Tucker, Los Angeles, and Guarrera; the second act of *Il Barbiere* (with Valletti, Peters, Merrill, Corena, and Hines); and the first two acts of *Aida* (minus the Temple Scene), with Del Monaco, Milanov, Thebom, Warren, Vichey, and Hines. Though the needs of TV found the audience in the theater (which had paid $62,000 to be present) watching Tucker and Los Angeles search for Mimi's key in a brilliantly illuminated "attic," the results on the screen still did not match accepted visual standards for television. Thirty-three theaters (in twenty-five cities) attracted various quantities of ticket-buyers.

Musically, the season found its impetus in a partially revised *Meistersinger* under the direction of Stiedry on November 11. The old, faded set for St. Katherine's church was replaced by a simpler, cleaner one by Ellen Meyer as down payment on a full, fresh *Meistersinger,* for which funds were not yet available. However, this *Meistersinger* would have counted for as much on a barren stage, for what made it superior to most others of recent years was the excellence of some improved characterizations by familiar singers and some unfamiliar singers also capable of excellence. In the first category were Della Casa as a peerlessly picturesque Eva,* Hopf (Walther), Franke (David), Glaz (Magdalena), and Pechner (Beckmesser); in the second, the redoubtable Otto Edelmann in his debut as Sachs (d) and Kurt Böhme as Pogner (d). It was not unreasonable for the *Weltpresse* of Vienna to spread a headline over three columns declaring *Wiener Künstler triumphieren an der Met.* There were honors also for a file of guildsmen which included such non-Wiener names as Brownlee (Kothner), De Paolis (Zorn), McCracken (Eislinger*), Carelli (Moser), Hawkins (Ortel), Anthony (Vogelgesang), Alvary (Foltz), and Davidson (Schwarz), each given a distinctive characterization by the direction of Yannopoulos. In the role of Nachtigall (d) was a new baritone, Calvin Marsh. It was also an introduction to many for Charles Anthony (Vogelgesang*), who had made his debut the year before as the Simpleton* in *Boris* on March 6 and had also sung Beppe* in *Pagliacci.* He had sacrificed the family name of Caruso on the advice that it would not be an advantage for a beginning tenor. Davidson was the Beckmesser* on November 26.

The importance of Edelmann and Böhme would suggest a broad range of Wagnerian opportunity, but it did not present itself in this season. Neither lingered long. Schoeffler was available for Sachs by November 26, and the five allotted performances ran their course by the new year (among them was an opportunity for Kullmann as Walther on November 15). Böhme's season included the First Nazarene* in *Salome* on December 15, slender usage for so substantial a performer. It was the second time in the current decade that the Metropolitan was denied even the Bing cycle (*Götterdämmerung*) during a two-season *Ring* famine that ended with a feast in 1956-7.

The happy working relationship that had brought Monteux and Los Angeles together in the previous season's *Faust* was resumed with a somewhat revised *Manon* (the revisor was Ellen Meyer) on December 3. Downes thought this "masterly" Massenet, and it was, unquestionably, a firmer, more flavorsome production of the musical score than any in years. Valletti as Des Grieux* was overmatched by the needs of the theater, but he sang a beautiful *Rêve*. Corena as Lescaut* tended to make a buffo of a bravo while substituting a bass for a baritone, more latitude than Massenet's writing could absorb. The Manon of Los Angeles had its earlier virtues of finesse and conscientious musicality, though there was less growth in her dramatic projection than one might have expected. As Comte des Grieux* in place of an indisposed Hines, Alvary made much of posture and lorgnette, but the needed deep sound was absent. Shakeh Vartenissian, a well-endowed protégé of Rosa Ponselle, made her debut as Poussette (d). Scenically, this affair was more *mélange* than *Manon,* for the elements put together by Meyer included the first act of Krehan-Crayon's production for Puccini's *Manon Lescaut* and the second act from Armistead's *Rake's Progress* (Rakewell's London drawing room). Mia Slavenska danced in the *Cours la Reine* scene choreographed by Solov. On February 2, Kirsten ventured Massenet's version of the role for which she was well regarded in Puccini's treatment, but Manon* in French did not become her, vocally, as well as Manon Lescaut in Italian. Other Manons included Albanese and Steber, and there were two new Des Grieux*: Conley on February 21 and Giuseppe Campora on March 31, neither memorable. In all, this venture ended on March 31, with Steber, Herbert (Lescaut*), Campora (Des Grieux), and Moscona (Comte des Grieux) quite differently than it had begun.

As much could be said of Monteux's adventure with Gluck's *Orfeo ed*

Euridice, though its beginnings were lost to sight and sound even before the first rehearsal. It was planned to include Giulietta Simionato as Orfeo, but she left America after participating as Adalgisa in the Maria Callas *Norma* that served as the inaugural performance of the Chicago Lyric Opera early in November, and did not return. Of the possible alternatives, favor finally settled on Risë Stevens, who had neither the top, the bottom, nor much of the middle for this role (after arduous application to Carmen) when she sang it for the first time on February 24. The stance and bearing that had served Stevens well in other "male" roles were also helpful to the picture she made as Orfeo, but she brought little vocal power to her command to the Furies, not enough breath to sustain the legato line later on. Gueden was a comely, well-sounding Euridice.* Peters as Amore,* and Hurley as Un 'Ombra Felice* were both attractive to hear. The one wholly admirable element in the production was Markova, performing beautifully, to Monteux's direction of the music for the Elysian Fields, a better dance conception than Solov generally provided. The Harry Horner sets were used, with Graf directing. On March 11, Hurley was Amore,* Vartenissian Un 'Ombra Felice.*

By far the most durable new artist of this season (more so, even, than Tebaldi, Kempe, or Mitropoulos) was Giorgio Tozzi, who brought a broad but flexible voice and a fine stage presence to the Alvise (d) in *Gioconda* which he sang on March 9 (with Milanov, Warren, Baum, Rankin as Laura,* Warfield as La Cieca,* and Cleva conducting). His other role in this season, April 6, was Ramfis* in an *Aida* with Nelli, Rankin, Bastianini (Amonasro), and Giulio Gari. It was said of Tozzi that when he heard the Messenger for this performance rehearsing his part, he asked himself: "If they have that kind of voice for the Messenger, what must the leading tenor sound like?" It did not take long for Tozzi to discover that McCracken as the Messenger was as superior to the average as he himself was. Another pillar of support for many *Aidas* to come was installed on December 6, when Louis Sgarro, who had made his debut as the Major-Domo* in *Chénier* on November 16, sang The King.* He was a Friar* in *Don Carlo* on December 18, a Jailer* in *Tosca* on February 5, Angel-otti* in the same opera on March 8, a Steersman* in *Gioconda* on March 9, and a Herald* in *Otello* on March 17. The Cavaradossi* of the February 5 *Tosca* was Campora, who sang himself out sooner than he might have otherwise in a futile effort to justify his use in such roles in a Metropolitan-sized auditorium. He was better suited to Rodolfo (d), in which he made his debut on January 20 (with Kirsten, Bastianini as Marcello,* and Fenn) than he was to Faust* on March 22 or Des Grieux* in *Manon* on March 31.

This season's Mozart was restricted to *Don Giovanni* and *Le Nozze di Figaro,* the later cleansed of the scenic "innovations" of the previous year and once more performed in the long-familiar scheme of Jonel Jorgulesco. Stiedry was its conductor and Siepi-London-Della Casa-Miller its roster of principals when it was resumed on December 9. Wilson showed a lively sense of comedy in her Susanna* on December 20 and Amara little sense of aristocratic poise in the Countess* she performed on February 1, with Roggero as Cherubino.* *Don Giovanni,* however, gained something historic in its performance on March 10 under Rudolf. This was the Don* of Hines, unquestionably the tallest grandee ever seen. Much of his action was grotesque, as he slouched nearly double to bring himself to the eye level of Gueden as Zerlina or Amara as Elvira, and his vocal sound was far from the fluidity appropriate to Mozart's rapidly moving line. Further complicating the Hines problem was retention of the unit set introduced the previous year, with its requirement for agile footwork up and down what one newspaper, in an inspired typo, referred to as the "spiral rump." There were other better Don Giovannis on January 12 (London), when Wilson was Zerlina,* and on January 18 (Siepi), when the Donna Anna* was Steber. On some occasions Steber sang this music very well; she always bore herself with the dignity appropriate to the bereaved daughter of a martyred father.

As far as the Metropolitan was concerned, Walter Cassel was an all but forgotten name when he performed Scarpia* on the occasion of Tebaldi's initial Tosca* on March 8 (Corena was the Sacristan, a speciality he had performed first on February 5). Cassel had some recent, worthwhile achievements at City Center to his credit, but it had faded from the memory of most that he was an Auditions Winner who had made his debut as De Bretigny (d) in *Manon* on December 12, 1942, and had sung mostly small roles before terminating this phase of his career as Silvio in *Pagliacci* on January 10, 1945. In the decade that had elapsed, Cassel had made himself into an accomplished operatic performer, and though his voice was voluminous rather than resonant and powerful rather than vibrant, it served him well in Italian, well enough in German (tinged with a mid-American accent). He was a capable Mandryka* in Arabella on April 4, though lacking the London kind of character projection.

Though the season remained at twenty-two weeks, the number of works in the repertory crept up to twenty-seven in contrast with the twenty-one Bing had felt to be sufficient for his first season. One of these was a ballet (*Vittorio*) given in conjunction with *Salome;* two others were the operatic Gemini (*Cavalleria* and *Pagliacci*). The Puccini diet was expanded to include *Butterfly* as well as *Tosca* and *Bohème,* and *Don Carlo* reappeared, as did *Carmen.*

Many of the values in the Metropolitan's *Butterfly* of this period were individual ones, such as Della Casa's charmingly acted Cio Cio San* on November 19, the more familiar conceptions of Albanese, Kirsten and Los Angeles (the last brought along a costume from Yoshimura of Tokyo), a good Pinkerton from Prandelli on January 8, a less good one when Hayward performed it for the first time on February 22, with Harvuot as Yamadori.* It did not, certainly, gain any impetus from Erede, who was in the fifth year of a Metropolitan career that had begun with Bing's. It terminated well before Bing's—indeed, at the end of this season.

As touchstones of quality, *Don Carlo* and *Carmen* had fewer elements of distinction, increasing resemblance to the hand-worn facelessness of more common coin when they reappeared as the fourteenth and sixteenth works of the season's repertory. Much less was heard this season than in earlier years about more numerous performances of popular productions "buying time" to be invested in greater preparation of others. Part of the reason, perhaps, was that only *Faust,* with thirteen performances, was well above the average. *Fledermaus* had receded to three, perhaps for the reason that the best that could be provided for a New Year's Eve "gala" was a cast of Kullmann, Lewis, Hayward (Alfred), Novotna (Orlofsky), Munsel, and Brownlee, with Kozma conducting.

Of the qualities in the original *Don Carlo,* the scenery by Gérard was more nearly what it had been, when it was seen again on December 18, than the musical performance under Stiedry or Webster's action. Both Steber (Elisabetta) and Thebom (Eboli) had sung their roles previously, but neither was equal to making what she did as good as the earlier standard for her part. Tucker was Don Carlo, with Merrill, Siepi, and Schoeffler in roles associated with them. A little more ensemble feeling was drained away on January 28, when Rankin was Eboli* and Bastianini took on Rodrigo,* with Adler conducting. There was still less line of contact with the original vitality of *Carmen* in this season. The performance that Downes saw on December 29, with Rudolf conducting a cast that included Stevens, Baum, Amara, and Guarrera, earned his angry judgment that this was "the worst distortion of book and score that Mr. Bing had achieved," that the "tensions" that had been the "saving grace" of Guthrie's staging were gone. Rankin was the Carmen of January 14 and Thebom had her first opportunity on March 16. Neither sang the music with sufficient style or vocal distinction to make up for other limitations.

Thus, amid admiration for the well-planned *Chénier* and the carefully conceived *Arabella,* there were disquieting symptoms of lax standards and casting decisions that struck one as the product of another mind and taste entirely. Symptomatic of such contradictions was the substitution of other conductors for those who had rehearsed and directed the season's first showing of an opera. In this year, for example, there was Martin Rich in place of Monteux for *Manon,* Adler for Stiedry in *Don Carlo,* Rudolf for *Carmen* and then Kozma for Rudolf, Cimara for Erede in *Il Barbiere,* Adler and Kozma for Erede in *Cavalleria* and *Pagliacci.*

The question was not even the matter of substituting a less well-known name for a famous one, or extolling a "big" man at the expense of a "little" one. The question was, rather, if Kozma, Adler and Rich were good enough to direct the fifth performance of *Manon* or *Don Carlo* or *Carmen,* why were they not good enough to direct the first? Or was it that the first performance was the one that Bing craved to have considered as his standard by the press, and that he therefore sought out a famous man, who might just happen to be a better conductor, for it? It should hardly need to be said that a "high standard" can be established only by exercise of talents superior to the average, that it cannot be sustained by the exercise of average talents or by wishful thinking about talents inferior to the average. To presume that conductor B could "take over" the production created by conductor A and, without his talent, keep it "running smoothly" was evidence of either blind, irrational optimism or equally gross indifference to the distinction between ability and mediocrity.

If any, let alone much, of this disturbed the minds of those who made the Metropolitan's policy decisions or took responsibility for engaging, on the professional level, those who carried them out, it did not weigh materially against Bing. His demonstrated competence, his ability to promote an appearance of vitality and excitement—sometimes, even, the real thing—were sufficient unto themselves. This time his contract was renewed in the spring preceding the final season it covered, a concession to the overtures he had received (Boehm being ill) to consider a return to his native city as director of its rebuilt Opera House on the Ring. That it also coincided with the retirement of Sloan as chairman of the board (on a plea of ill health) had more significance than was, perhaps, generally realized. It meant that a group more sympathetic to the kind of operatic procedures in which Bing believed was coming to have a larger share of authority. This meant, of course, that it also had to assume a larger share of responsibility for raising the money such procedures required.

Sloan's health deteriorated much more rapidly than there was any reason to anticipate at this time, and he died on May 20, 1955, ten days before he would have been sixty-two years old.

"Interim" is an appropriate word for this season's activities at City Center, which offered nothing of moment during its fall season (save for variants in the standard repertory, including Thomas Schippers as conductor of Offenbach's *Tales*). Its *Falstaff* benefited from such recasting as Wilderman as Falstaff and Cassel as Ford, but not by a change where it would have done most good—a conductor other than Rosenstock. By an artful utilization of resources, Nicolai's *Merry Wives* entered the repertory during the spring season without the expense of a new production: the one that had served for *Falstaff* was simply applied to another score and cast. The best Verdi performers were also the best Nicolai: Curtin, Wilderman, Crain. *Don Pasquale* made a brief appearance, but the two seasons were altogether more notable for new names than old works: Morley Meredith, John Reardon, Barry Morell, Emilia Cundari, and Adele Addison were all heard for the first time. Emerson Buckley, who gave the company much good service as a conductor, joined it to direct *Rigoletto* with Crain, MacNeil, and Eva Likova in mid-March.

1955–1956

Between the ending of the Metropolitan's customary spring tour early in June and the opening of the new season on November 14 with a new production of Offenbach's *Les Contes d'Hoffmann,* no single date was marked out as special from another. But October 25 makes its demand on history, though nobody sang, conducted or danced: it was the date for the first meeting of "The Exploratory Committee for a Musical Arts Center."

As had happened periodically in the past, the New York Philharmonic Orchestra was being threatened with the sale and demolition of Carnegie Hall, which would deprive it of the place in which it had long performed. This time the handwriting was blacker, more ominous than ever: those who owned the hall craved a reprieve from the burden of sustaining it, and the Philharmonic was not among those who could realistically be considered a "customer." Would it not be possible, the Philharmonic's board reasoned, for the Metropolitan's need for a new home to be co-ordinated with their own, and a frontal attack made on two of New York's long-standing musical necessities?

Indeed, the groundwork had been laid during the spring when, at the meeting that accepted Sloan's resignation and extended Bing's contract, the desirability of relocating on the West Side was reaffirmed. Interlocking directorates and power structures being what they are, it was no mammoth task to arrange a meeting of individuals from which a meeting of minds emerged. The minds present included those of men representing the Philharmonic as well as the Metropolitan. Not present but participating (in a real sense) were those who had plans for rehabilitation of an area on Manhattan's West Side, a few blocks north of Columbus Circle, where the last promise of a "new Metropolitan" had gone the way of all others. The area bordered on a tiny island-like park at the intersection of Broadway and Columbus Avenue, called Lincoln Square. Out of this initial meeting, the calculations and the planning, the anticipations, and eventually the accomplishments of the next ten years took form.

Whether there would be any accomplishments was, at this date, merely speculative. The projections began to have the sound as well as the shape of reality somewhat later, with a release (dated December 1, 1955) to the press from Room 5600 of 30 Rockefeller Plaza. This identified it as a product of the mystical area of the "Fifty-sixth Floor" from which flowed the actions and impulses of the Rockefeller Bros., Inc. It further identified the Exploratory Committee's members—for the Metropolitan: C. D. Jackson, Irving S. Olds, and Charles Spofford; for the Philharmonic: Floyd G. Blair and Arthur A. Houghton, Jr., plus Robert Blum (Brooklyn Institute), Wallace K. Harrison (architect), Devereux C. Josephs (banker), Lincoln Kirstein (art patron), and John D. Rockefeller III. With due respect for all the others, it is no exaggeration to say that the identification of the last named as chairman was the most hopeful sign of a positive outcome that such a community project could have had. It was an assurance not only of sizeable personal commitment toward the very sizeable amount of money that would be required but also of the will to assist in raising the whole sum as a validation of another Rockefeller initiative of many years before which had not persisted to a positive outcome (see page 21).

It was necessary for the City Board of Estimate to approve a Lincoln Square Urban Renewal Project, with its promise of federal funds for acquisition of property at an advantageous price, before there could be a Lincoln Center or even a Lincoln Center project. But the way ahead was clearer and the objectives were more recognizably defined than in any earlier scheme involving the Metropolitan.

For the supervision of the Metropolitan's first new *Hoffmann* in thirty years (it had not been heard in the theater for nearly ten), Bing made a new blend of talents: Gérard as designer and Monteux as conductor, who had worked together before (on *Faust*), and Cyril Ritchard, who had not worked with either, as producer. Martial Singher, who had made his Metropolitan debut as Dapertutto with Beecham in 1943–4 and had added the roles of Lindorf, Coppelius and Dr. Miracle in a revival of 1945–6, was asked to perform these specialties again, with Tucker as Hoffmann,* Peters as Olympia,* Stevens as Giulietta,* Amara as Antonia,* and Miller as Nicklausse.* De Paolis exercised his virtuosity in makeup in the roles of Andres,* Cochenille,* Pitichinaccio and Frantz. Some of it was good to see and much of it was good to hear, though, as Howard Taubman (who had succeeded Downes on the *Times* after his death in mid-summer) wrote, "it tended to run down hill." A fine setting for Luther's Tavern and an attractive one for Spalanzani's abode gave way to a provocative but incompletely realized vista of the Grand Canal and a disappointingly barren treatment for Dr. Miracle's room in Munich. Whether fantasy or money had run out, the result left a similar sense of unfulfillment. Musically, the evening was Monteux's and Tucker's; dramatically, it was Singher's. Those who sang well (as Tucker did) lacked illusion in their parts (Amara was of this order, somewhat less Peters), while those who had the drama at their command (Stevens, for example) were vocally hard pressed (some of the music was lowered for Stevens's convenience). Though Singher's sound sometimes lost body, his sense of style left him still the most rewarding to hear as well as to see. Ritchard had better success in making a theatrical spectacle of the whole than he did in imparting a sense of character to those who lacked one of their own. He staged the *Barcarolle* very prettily. Aid to illusion came from an unexpected source on December 24, when Hurley sang Olympia* with Novotna as Giulietta.* Those who might assume that Hurley's automaton achieved its faultless mechanics only after long exposure might note the comment, on this first showing, by Jay Harrison of the *Herald Tribune,* that she was "every inch a doll." Campora sang a pleasant Hoffmann* on January 6, with Roggero as Nicklausse* and Anthony *vice* De Paolis. When the conductor became (inevitably) Rich on January 12, the Giulietta* was Lipton. There would have been a third Olympia on February 7, but Wilson was ill and Peters returned to her original place, with Conner as Antonia. With no desire to labor a point, it may be noted that this was barely more Monteux's than Rich's *Hoffmann,* by a margin of five performances to three. *Carmen,* which briefly had been Monteux's not very long before, was wholly Rudolf's (save when it became Kozma's). It began with Stevens, Tucker, Amara, and Guarrera, and proceeded with Baum and Di Stefano (as José* on November 30) as tenors, Thebom as Carmen, etc. On March 17, when Madeira was Carmen, the Don José was Gari.

This was not only a Mozart year, but also a *Così-Figaro-Flute* year, with the two-hundredth anniversary of the composer's birth being observed (on January 27, 1956) with a performance of *Figaro* under Rudolf. It brought together Singher and London as servant and master, with Los Angeles, Conner, and Miller as the ladies. *Così* came early, under the direction of Stiedry on November 26, with the original cast intact save for Valletti rather than Tucker as Ferrando* (with mostly contented smiles among the connoisseurs. This order prevailed for the next little while aside from such acceptable interchanges as Peters for Munsel and Alvary for Brownlee. To be sure, the comedy, especially of Thebom, was broader than when it had been "fresh from the nut" with Lunt, but it remained as enjoyable an evening as the Metropolitan had to offer.

Had certain preferences prevailed, this might have been a Marc Chagall as well as a Bruno Walter *Flute,* but the conductor gently declined the implications of "innovation" which this thought contained. He preferred to work with Harry Horner, a veteran of Viennese associations and familiar with the Metropolitan's stage problems from his work, for Johnson, with *Orfeo* and *Trovatore.* As Walter governed the scenic spectacle, so he governed the musical rendition—it was his "gift" to the Mozart year (he participated in no operatic observation elsewhere), and it was done in his own personal fashion.

The decision having been made to continue the Metropolitan's custom of giving *The Magic Flute* rather than *Die Zauberflöte* (the cost, estimated at $90,000, was borne by Mrs. John D. Rockefeller III), Walter elected a cast that was not only almost wholly American, but also almost entirely Californian—Uppman as Papageno,* Sullivan as Tamino, Amara as Pamina,* and Hines as Sarastro conforming to this singular addition to the Metropolitan's innumerable "firsts." Only Peters as the Queen of the Night and London as the High Priest* were exceptions from the prevailing geographical orientation.

Peters was, indeed, almost an exception from the performance itself, for she developed a fever on the day of the dress rehearsal and had to forego participation. This posed the possibility that the important exercise itself might be crippled, for her alternates (Dolores Wilson and Virginia MacWatters) were also unavailable. While the orchestra waited, an answer was provided from the ranks of the chorus. It was Rose Byrum, a soprano who had sung the part with the Grass Roots Company in North Carolina, but had never expected to sing it from the stage of the Metropolitan. She agreed to "accommodate" the management, performing in her rehearsal wear (black tights and beige sweater) amid the brilliantly costumed regulars. For those who consider "temperament" inseparable from "artistic," it was instructive to note that the venerable Walter, with all his background of association with the world's great singers, was more considerate of Miss Byrum than of anyone else in the cast, breaking no batons and bearing patiently with every inevitable deviation from order.

Needless to say, Walter's mood of benignancy and dedication pervaded the first performance on February 23. Pride of place went to Uppman, a picture of cheerfulness and natural man as a Papageno who spoke as delightfully as he sang, and who looked the part as well. Whether braggart or craven, romantically pursuing a Papagena or hungering for his next meal, Uppman struck a chord of sympathy as resounding as the *Glockenspiel* he carried. Save, perhaps, for Hurley as Papagena,* the remainder of the cast occupied another, and more prosaic, plane of existence. Hines was a solid Sarastro and London an imposing High Priest. For those who searched the celestial heavens behind this Queen of the Night for identification of a truly suitable one, the answer came clear: Maria Callas. That would have enabled Peters to be just what she could be: a perfect Papagena. Sullivan was more lifeguard than prince as Tamino, Amara a lyric soprano rather than a Pamina, and so on. The First Lady* was Krall, companioned by Madelaine Chambers (d) and Warfield; the Three Boys, led by Emilia Cundari, also included Elias and Roggero. Some of Horner's backgrounds were projections (by Leo Kerz), and an effort was made to speed scenic transitions by arranging for set pieces to roll to and from the wings. An artistic triumph it was not, but it had a certain simple relevance to the subject matter and Walter's own way of spiritualizing everything about it. Thus the tinkle of the *Glockenspiel* conveyed more of wonder and magic in this *Magic Flute* than a whole brass choir, and the dance of the animals (in Graf's staging) more sublimity than the solemn tread of the priests. The following three casts were unchanged save for the alternation of London with Schoeffler (no Californian either) and Harvuot as the High Priests.*

Bing's realization that the Metropolitan had a "conductor problem" (as part of a worldwide "conductor problem" that saw the ranks of the revered depleted, almost at once, of such names as Furtwängler, Kleiber, Krauss, Toscanini, Rodzinski, and Dobrowen, among others) took the form of a venture new to the Metropolitan: selection, for promotion, of an American whose talents justified cultivation. For the first time, it was assumed that talent alone was a valid criterion for a Metropolitan conductor, as it too long had been for a Metropolitan singer (the self-willed cause of many of the evil days on which the theater had fallen). The clear difference was, however, there would no longer be a wiser, more experienced head available to fend off disaster—the beginner's errors would be in the pit, the center of operatic authority from which there is no recourse.

In a purely factual sense, it may be stretching accuracy to call Thomas Schippers, to whom the finger of destiny pointed, a beginner. He had "begun" all of five years before as a protégé of Menotti (rehearsal pianist for *Amahl*, alternate conductor for *The Consul* and *The Saint of Bleecker Street*), moving on thereafter to the City Center, where his duties included conducting *Hänsel und Gretel* and the *première* of Aaron Copland's *The Tender Land* in 1954. But he was, in terms of the personalities and performers he would encounter at the Metropolitan, not even a beginner on the international operatic scene.

Of Schippers's talent at twenty-five there was no possible doubt. The possible doubt, rather, was of the wisdom of nurturing it at such a theater as the Metropolitan, which should be, at the least, a finishing school rather than a preparatory center. Three years of learning his trade in a small European theater would have brought Schippers and the Metropolitan more benefit than launching him with a new production of *Don Pasquale* on December 23. That he flourished rather than floundered may be attributed to talent and the capabilities of a cast that included Corena as Pasquale,* Valletti as Ernesto,* Peters as Norina,* and Guarrera as Dr. Malatesta,* well-directed by Yannopoulos. What *Don Pasquale* required in the way of animation and impulse, Schippers provided in ample measure, but he brought less of the finesse it also merited. On the whole, he fared well, no less in the preceding ballet to the Britten arrangement of Rossini called *Matinée Musicale,* but titled *Soirée* in this version by Solov, than in the opera. It was in later, more wideranging undertakings that Schippers's lack of broad experience became first a handicap, then a liability. Principal dancers for *Soirée* included Mary Ellen Moylan (d), Oleg Briansky (d), Margaret Black, and Adriano Vitale, with a décor by Cecil Beaton. *Don Pasquale* benefited from a fancifully witty "duplex" designed by Wolfgang Roth which utilized the first turntable ever seen on the Metropolitan's aged stage. Because of the uneven floor and other technical complications, the dizzying sense of modernity conveyed to the audience by the sight of a Metropolitan scene swiveling around to reveal a new one was accompanied, for those backstage, by a dizzying apprehension that the whole thing might pitch over at any turn. It never did, but it did not enjoy as much favor with those behind the curtain as with those in the auditorium. A delightful variant was provided on March 12 when Hilde Gueden appeared as Norina.*

With or without Schippers, the City Center continued the program projected for it by Rosenstock, opening with what might be called *The Merry Wives of Falstaff*. The visual setting was that introduced for Verdi, the musical setting, on this occasion, by Nicolai. The main production effort was applied to Sir William Walton's *Troilus and Cressida,* which had had its American *première* earlier in the fall in San Francisco. With Rosenstock conducting and Margaret Webster directing the action, the cast was distinguished by an excellent Pandarus from Norman Kelley and a good effort by Yi-Kwei Sze, in his debut, as Calkas. Jon Crain as Troilus and Phyllis Curtin as Cressida were less satisfactory. Much immediate praise was lavished on Walton's "accomplishment," but those with a longer view found *Troilus* more admirable for craftsmanship than for invention. New to New York was Tchaikovsky's *The Glass Slipper,* a work whose fine tunes and lively overture were impaled on a thorny, complex plot. Of more durability than the production was its leading man, Richard Cassilly, who had first earned attention as alternate (on Broadway) to David Poleri in *The Saint of Bleecker Street.* His debut as Vakula was the first in a series of useful services to City Center projects. His associates in this one were Jean Fenn (Oxana), Donald Gramm (The Devil), Margery Mayer (Mother), and Rosemary Kuhlmann (Czarina). Other new personnel included Louis Quilico as Germont, Beverly Sills as Rosalinda, and (probably in the place vacated by Schippers) Herbert Grossman. By the time the spring season arrived, Rosenstock had decided to give up his New York commitment in favor of a return to Tokyo, where he enjoyed solid esteem. The engagement as his successor of Erich Leinsdorf (who had resigned his position as music director of the Rochester Philharmonic Orchestra after nearly a decade) was announced shortly after the first of the new year, but Rosenstock remained to fulfill his spring obligations. Aside from selections out of repertory stock, his closing weeks added only a brief "novelty" (Rolf Liebermann's *School for Wives* in a double bill with Mozart's *Der Schauspieldirektor* in the English guise of *The Impresario*). Best of the new performers was Mignon Dunn, who made her debut as Carmen; the others included Beverly Bowers, introduced as Violetta, and two performers of European background: tenor Piero Miranda Ferraro (Cavaradossi) and Aldo Protti (Rigoletto).

With Monteux, Stiedry, Mitropoulos, and Walter (and Cleva) in rotation, the Metropolitan was better serviced by conductors of quality (including the previously mentioned Rudolf, Schippers, and Rich) than during some of the preceding Bing years. Erede's absence was hardly noted, nor was Szell's. The one kind of ability that this group did not include was one that Reiner possessed in abundance: the ability to tune and align the human gears, pistons, spark plugs, and drive shaft of the orchestral machine as a skilled mechanic tunes a fine car. It was not an easy skill to replace and the orchestra suffered for want of it for years to come.

Mitropoulos's skills, which were of quite a different order, were put to work in a series of projects this season. He began where he had left off, with *Ballo* (on November 26), displaying Anderson to another audience as Ulrica, and Peerce, Merrill, Milanov, and Peters in familiar places. Nelli came into the cast as Amelia* on December 3 (she, like Peerce and Merrill, had participated in the celebrated Toscanini recording of the preceding year), with Warfield—who had recently become Mrs. James McCracken—as Ulrica.* Anderson closed out her ceremonial tour of duty on December 26, and quality went into a series of declines thereafter. Metternich was the Renato and Wilson the Page* on January 17, but the second-rate sound of Mario Ortica resulted in a lower-case king when he performed Riccardo on February 2, with Kozma conducting (Lipton was Ulrica*). The sun shone, however, and monarchy went back on the gold standard when Bjoerling resumed one of his best parts on February 17. The first tall figure to enter the pit before the curtain rose was not Mitropoulos, but Bing. He directed the orchestra in a performance of "Happy Birthday to You" to mark Mitropoulos's attainment of sixty years. (The actual date was March 1, 1956, but Mitropoulos's schedule did not call for another Metropolitan appearance before that time). Perhaps to join in the spirit of the occasion, Bjoerling wore his own medals and decorations in the ball scene.

With Stiedry furloughed for two months in mid-winter (he found the New York cold increasingly difficult to bear), control of *Boris* passed to Mitropoulos (who had been a young "pupil" of Stiedry in Berlin in the twenties) on January 20. In its essentials this *Boris* was much like recent Metropolitan predecessors—Hines, Miller, Kullmann (Schuisky), Rankin, Harvuot (Rangoni), Alvary (Varlaam), and McCracken (Missail) were among its principal performers—but there was no denying the presence of a new drive, a freshly animating spirit. Of special note was the keenness of ear Mitropoulos turned to the advantage of the Rathaus "realization" of Moussorgsky, assigning each instrumental family a separate, audible plane of sonority. Despite the dark of the monastery cell, it was easy to identify Tozzi in his first Pimenn*—that was where the rich, rolling sound came from. Collaterally, one could make out the large frame and equally large sound of Albert da Costa as Dimitri* in place of an indisposed Gari. When Da Costa emerged "plain," in the Polish scene, the illusion was quite different, but he showed a vocal possibility that belied his baritonal background. There was a wholesale shift of personnel on February 15, when London as Boris had another "son" (Roggero as Fyodor), Scott was Pimenn, and Gari came on for Dimitri. Resnik was the Marina,* thus beginning her "second" career as a mezzo. Though Marina is not the exacting test of capacity which some other roles are, Resnik sounded well and gave the role the benefit of her usual intelligent application. Resnik's transformation, impressive as it had been, was not so much a matter of building a "new" voice as solidifying the best parts of the old one and improvising the necessary bottom tones. Once settled, it put Resnik in a category of effort which always seemed better suited to her, temperamentally, than most of the soprano parts she had felt obliged to undertake. It was, in any case, a shrewd and resourceful adaptation. In the third-team *Boris* on March 3, Siepi was associated with Thebom, Davidson (Varlaam*), and Gari.

In addition to Mussorgsky, Mitropoulos turned his attention in this season to Puccini, not the first composer who leaps to mind in association with his earlier career. His music did, however, become more and more a part of Mitropoulos's functioning, perhaps because he always generated theatrical excitement, whether the work was *Tosca* on December 8 or *Manon Lescaut* on March 14. The effect of Mitropoulos's Puccini was invariably stimulating, though one was intermittently aware that much of the flow and flexibility of the music was absent. On reflection, the realization comes that what he provided in Puccini—pulse, animation, drama, instrumental clarity, a persistent quest for precision in execution —was so uncommon in the Metropolitan's Puccini that it fed intellectual taste buds long neglected.

His *Tosca* on December 8 commanded an uncommon amount of vocal strength, for it brought Tebaldi and Tucker together with Warren's first Scarpia.* This was a role, Warren had said to me not long before, "for the end of a career." When he was taxed with this observation, he laughed and said: "The chance to sing it sooner with a real conductor made a difference." As befitted the operatic experience he had acquired in a decade and a half, Warren brought with him, in addition to a solid command of the vocal line, a well-planned dramatic action. It tended to be a little crude, lacking in finesse, but these flaws were in the character-ization rather than in his execution of it. The difference between a strong singer with a carefully planned dramatic action and a masterly actor who also sang was sharply defined when Tito Gobbi made his debut as Scarpia (d) on January 13. With Milanov protecting her virtue in a melodramatic likeness of panic and Di Stefano resting his case on the loudest of *"Vittorias,"* Gobbi had little to play against, save Mitropoulos's direction of the orchestra. There was but one reprise on January 18 (with Tebaldi and Campora), following which Gobbi went back to practicing the operatic art where he had learned it, and the Metropolitan went back to such Scarpias as Cassel. April 4 was notable for a rare appearance in these years of Bjoerling as Cavaradossi (with Milanov and Cassel).

Manon Lescaut was less favored by superior performers when Mitropoulos directed it for the first time on March 14, but his own strong feeling for the score made it perhaps the most productive of any of his ventures with Puccini. Best of the interpreters was Tucker as Des Grieux, with Steber as Manon Lescaut* less good than in Massenet's counterpart, Guarrera as Lescaut* and Corena as Geronte.* Albanese and Bjoerling were an experienced partnership in the leading roles on March 31 and April 13, but time ran out before the possibility of a Tebaldi *Manon Lescaut* could be made a reality.

This fine artist returned for her second season as of the fourth day (November 19), when she sang the postponed Aida* of the previous February, with Thebom, Bastianini, Tozzi, and Sgarro, and against a cut-rate Radames,* Mario Ortica (d). Though one of her most popular roles, Aida was far from a good one for Tebaldi. Much of the music she sang beautifully, especially *"O patria mia"* and the final duet, but much of it lay heavily on her *lirico spinto* voice, especially the ensemble at the end of Act II, with its driving climaxes. It was evident from the overdrive that she had to apply to attain the crest of the tonal mass that there would, eventually, be a day of reckoning. Dramatically, her Aida was stagy and lacking the simple conviction of her Mimi or Desdemona. It also reflected a change of attitude since her appearances of the preceding season, suggesting that she had been feasting on the fruits of success, and had found them a somewhat heady diet (as, for example, the repetition of *"Vissi d'arte"* with which she had made "news" in a San Francisco *Tosca* earlier in the fall). She was much more nearly her prime vocal self as Leonora* in *La Forza del destino* (in which she sang a superb, *"Pace, pace"*) on January 10. Cimara was the conductor, with a cast including Tucker, Hines, Corena (Melitone*), and Metternich (Carlo). The sheer blend of sound currently available for this score approached optimum on January 21, when Tebaldi and Warren were joined by Tucker and Tozzi (Padre Guardiano*). Tebaldi's season also included several performances of Maddalena in *Andrea Chénier,* which continued in the state of musical grace it had enjoyed during its first year, and even improved (on December 2) with the Gérard of Bastianini, one of his best roles. The brief but desultory Metropolitan career of Ortica, a tenor who fumbled *"Celeste Aida"* at his introduction as Radames* on November 19 and showed neither the voice nor the artistic resource to justify such prominence, continued with Don Alvaro* in *Forza* on

December 22, Chénier* on January 14, and Riccardo* in *Ballo* on February 2. He was one of a number of performers who were imported from Italy, in these years, before they had achieved major status at home. This suggested a commendable desire to seek out artistic services *before* the price became too high; but, too often, the services were overpriced even at minimum rates. Whatever the cast appearing in this season's *Aidas,* they were distinguished by the artful dancing of Carmen de Lavallade, who made her debut in the first (November 19). She was a cousin of Janet Collins, who had preceded her, and wife of Geoffrey Holder, who eventually appeared on this stage also.

Kempe's return on January 11 spread satisfaction among those who relished his kind of *Meistersinger,* which he conducted for the first time in company with Edelmann, Della Casa, Glaz, Franke as David, and Pechner (Beckmesser). Planning for this cast included Sullivan as Walther, but he was still not ready for that task and the management found a willing replacement in Albert da Costa. He had competed as a baritone in the Auditions, but had accepted professional advice that he might have a better future as a tenor. He did, indeed, perform commendably in this first major effort (he had sung the off-stage Sailor's voice (d) in *Tristan* on March 3, 1955) with a vocal quality that was both clear and suitably large. His particular problem was that he, himself, was unsuitably large, not so much in height (at six feet three he was an inch short of such a Walther as René Maison, not to mention Leo Slezak) as in girth. Despite conscientious attention to diet, his weight continued to be a problem for Da Costa. Kempe's feeling for clarity of line and transparency of texture worked well with such lyric voices as Edelmann's, Della Casa's, and Tozzi's (Pogner*). For once, also, every note of the overture could be heard without interruption: late-comers were barred from entering. The price for this pleasure was an entrée *en masse* when the curtain rose, with resulting noisy disruption of the chorale. Subsequent performances of *Die Meistersinger* offered Schoeffler and Los Angeles as the Sachs and Eva, with a new Beckmesser* in Ralph Herbert on February 27. This was capably acted along traditional lines, but the long evening's work bore heavily on the singer's not very robust vocal resources.

In place of *Arabella,* which had been retired for the while, Kempe's Strauss in this season on February 6 was *Der Rosenkavalier,* in which Della Casa made a beginning of her Metropolitan career as the Marschallin,* Edelmann sang his Ochs* for the first time, and Stevens continued to show why Octavian was considered "her" role in this theater. Gueden was the accomplished Sophie, and Emilia Cundari made her debut as the Milliner (d). Accompanying these several new beginnings was a "semi-new" treatment for the scenic production, in which Gérard painted over the old Kautsky canvases and superimposed some altered architectural details. He also provided a forecurtain or scrim to engage the eye while the orchestra depicted the nocturnal delights of the lovers. At curtain rise, a "daring" spectacle met the audience eye, for Graf's direction put the Marschallin, with Octavian hovering beside her, in bed (as the script directed) rather than in a chair or *chaise-longue,* as Metropolitan decorum had previously decreed.

Kempe's light-handed way of treating this score recalled the observation of Busch that there was a Dresden tradition of *Rosenkavalier* as well as a Viennese. Kempe's was decidedly in the former, seeking for deftness and finesse rather than sentiment or broad humor. This possibly would have worked better with performers able to sustain their own characterizations and thus provide a suitable blend of elements. However, Della Casa's Marschallin, for all her personal beauty and freshness of sound, was a pale, superficial impersonation, and Edelmann's Ochs had not yet become the many-faceted thing of his later years. Kempe's *Rosenkavaliers* were all worth hearing, especially as the cast was sustained in its major aspects without change on four later occasions. When it became Rudolf's *Rosenkavalier* on April 11 (Kempe had returned to Europe), Steber returned to perform the Marschallin for the first time since 1950–1, the Sophie was Conner, and Da Costa succeeded to Baum's honors as the Singer in Act I. The good promise of Kempe's first two seasons was, unfortunately, not destined for fulfillment; he became ill during the summer of 1956 (jaundice) and Erich Leinsdorf was brought back to take some of his repertory. When Kempe recovered sufficiently to resume work, the explanation went that there was no longer a place for him on the roster. Eventually he succeeded Beecham as principal conductor of the Royal Philharmonic, devoting less of his time to opera.

An attempt at scenic upgrading of *Parsifal* which would not require the money for a new production (the term "new house" began to be mentioned about this time in administrative circles) was disclosed at the first performance on March 23, with Stiedry conducting. It took the form of a neo-Bayreuth use of projections by Leo Kerz (though with no such lighting resources as the Festspielhaus possessed) and a barren central platform that served for temple, woods, garden, or whatever. The vocal components (Schoeffler, Moscona, Harshaw, Svanholm) were much as they had been before, but they were enhanced by the vibrant, well-sung Gurnemanz* of Edelmann. Varnay was the temptress,

Kullmann the "pure fool" on March 30. The performance began with Hines as Gurnemanz, but he gave way to Edelmann for Act III. On April 6, Svanholm returned, with Singher as Amfortas.

The wishful thinking that Edelmann might be capable of duty in the Italian as well as the German repertory had a trial on December 16. With Stiedry conducting, Baum as Alvaro, Metternich as Don Carlo, and Edelmann as Padre Guardiano,* one might have thought this was a gala *Macht des Schicksals* at the Berlin Staatsoper (with Zinka Milanov of Zagreb *als Gast*) rather than a Friday-night *Forza* at the Metropolitan. There was ample weight in the Edelmann sound for the notes he had to sing, but the schooling was as lacking in his case as in Metternich's. In other words, no *bel*, no *canto*. Edelmann altogether posed a problem in efficient utilization, for fine as the voice was at the middle and (when he was in form) at the top, it was deficient at the bottom for some roles that, in normal circumstances, should be the province of an Ochs. One such was King Henry* in *Lohengrin*, which he performed at some disadvantage of range on November 18. However, he was so fine in his specialties (Ochs, Sachs, the *Walküre* Wotan) that he was an "indispensable" (when in vocal health) for years to come. His exposure in Italian roles was not pursued, and the Metternich experiment was also given up after this season. The *Lohengrin* noted above provided for acquaintance with Hermann Uhde, who showed excellent command of Wagner style as Telramund (d). Uhde's voice was the least of his assets, and it eventually became the greatest of his problems, but he was absorbing to observe in whatever he did. (Harshaw was the Ortrud in this cast, Sullivan the Lohengrin, and Steber the Elsa.) Cassel was the Telramund* on January 26, and thoroughly qualified. In Stiedry's mid-winter absence, *Forza* was conducted by Cimara, *Lohengrin* by Adler.

Of interest, otherwise, in the revolving relationships of conductors and repertory was a series of performances of *Samson et Dalila* directed by Monteux, a veteran of Metropolitan *Samsons* stretching back to 1917. There was the beginning of virtue in the blending of his "verve and point" (see page 276) with Singher as the High Priest,* Vinay as Samson, and Stevens as Dalila (on December 29), but the total of performances for this season was only four. Thebom was Dalila in the last of them, with Harvuot as the High Priest.*

An experiment of the Ortica sort produced somewhat better results in Daniele Barioni, whose debut was announced for a *Bohème* of February 9. However, the audience discovered that the Rodolfo was Campora, for a reason quite without precedent—Barioni had been pressed into service to make a recording for the "Metropolitan Opera Record Club" that day, thus qualifying as a "voice" of the Metropolitan even before he had made his debut. When this occurred, on February 20 as Cavaradossi (d), with Rigal and London, Barioni proved to have the size and style of voice to go with his slim, youthful look, qualifying him as perhaps the best young lyric tenor since Di Stefano ten years before. He sang a clear, fresh Rodolfo* on February 22 (with Albanese, Fenn, and Bastianini), leaving a taste for more and the promise of good things to come. Di Stefano himself reappeared on November 30 as Don José,* also performing Faust (complete with a powerful C at the end of *"Salut! demeure"*) on December 9, the Cavaradossi with Milanov and Gobbi previously mentioned, and various repetitions. (In one *Faust*, on February 16, Valentin* was McFerrin.)

Other tenors of the season included Gianni Poggi, whose abilities were given a brief exposure when he sang a "passing-through" Duke (d) in *Rigoletto* on December 14, with Peters and Merrill, and a return engagement for Penno. He missed his Manrico on February 29 because of a vocal complaint (Baum was the replacement, with Madeira as Azucena), and showed the effects of hoarseness or laryngitis when he sang the role on March 5. On April 2, he repaid the favor of Baum when, for once, that veteran of many replacements needed replacement himself in *Forza,* and Penno went on after Act II (Vichey was the Padre*). There were some of the opinion that Penno could have put his physique and vocal strength to better use in Lohengrin and other German roles, but the singer was not, to my knowledge, among them. Of other recent acquisitions, Bastianini was one of the busiest, adding the role of Rigoletto* on March 7. It carried him higher than suited his best vocal range and left him short of the Warren-Merrill standard. The Gilda* of this performance was Wilson, who sang with more weight than the role customarily has, but also more of a metallic sound than became Verdi's line. She overreached herself to attempt an unwritten top E (at the end of *"Caro nome"*), which emerged as a gasp rather than a tone.

Peters sang pleasantly in her first Lucia* on February 1, restricting herself to precision in the execution of the vocal line and a minimum of characterization. This marked something of an overlapping of eras, for Pons, who had sung her first Lucia twenty-five years before, had been honored with a gala on January 3, the date of her debut in 1931. She was joined by Peerce and Merrill for the second act of *Rigoletto* (Cleva conducting) and by Moscona for the Mad Scene of *Lucia,* following which she ranged through arias from *Linda di Chamounix,*

Mignon, Lakmé, and Stravinsky's *Le Rossignol* (Rudolf conducting). There were appropriately inappropriate speeches (by members of the board, by Bing, and by Brownlee), none even suggesting that the recent seasons, which had stretched her string to twenty-five, had seen Pons appearing only occasionally.

Also ceremonial in nature was the happening of April 14, when the public was invited to participate in what was called a "Farewell to *Fledermaus.*" As no one in authority would take an oath that the Gérard production would not reappear (after the forty-one performances it had had in New York), this had to be regarded as an operatic or "Patti" farewell (the reappearance came on November 27, 1958). However, the gambit did, at least, enable the management to persuade Siepi, Bjoerling, Edelmann, and Gueden to participate as performing "guests" in the second act ball, thus selling a few more tickets. In all the planned comedy, the loudest laughter came at the unplanned moment when Siepi, on entering, gallantly kissed the hand of Thebom, at that moment the tail-coated, moustachioed Orlofsky. On a similar occasion, at the New Year's Eve performance, Tebaldi took advantage of her "surprise" appearance to promote a favorite project and cast a shadow of things to come, by performing *"Io son' l'umile ancella"* from *Adriana Lecouvreur.*

Bing's record of success in resolving the Metropolitan's perennial labor problems was threatened, in mid-1956, by differences with the American Guild of Music Artists (AGMA). At issue were the size and personnel of the chorus. Traditionally least favored of the unions with which the Metropolitan did business because it was the youngest in point of organization, AGMA felt the time had come to take a stand. When no agreement had been reached by July 18, the Metropolitan brandished the ultimate weapon: "cancelation." However, before the impasse became a stalemate, a formula was evolved for settlement through the intervention of Local 802, American Federation of Musicians. Agreement was in the air by July 23, and the cancelation threat was itself canceled.

1956–1957

The members of the audience that paid $75,510 to be present at the Metropolitan debut of Maria Callas were much more interested in her and in each other than in either the work (Bellini's *Norma*) or the date (October 29). Yet the last was far from the least. It was the first October date for a Metropolitan opening in twenty-six years, which might mean much or little. But it was also the first opening of a twenty-four-week season in twenty-six years. Thus, finally, had been regained the symbol of public interest which had prevailed in the Metropolitan's period of peak activity (between 1923–4 and 1931–2), when twenty-four weeks had been a "normal" season. It had taken all of twenty-six years and the combined efforts of Johnson and Bing to add, bit by bit, to the scant fourteen weeks to which the season had shrunk in the mid-thirties. But there was very little prospect that the Metropolitan would soon again provide the forty-eight or -nine different works that had made up Gatti's "customary" repertory.

The opera chosen for this opening could hardly have been more inappropriate had there been twice forty-nine to choose from. It had never served the purpose before and the reasons were abundant: its mood is far from the frivolity that makes a ceremonial of this happening; its best-known melody, for the principal performer, comes soon after the evening begins; and the kind of accomplishment that makes a notable Norma demands far more for proper appreciation than can be expected of persons who have paid $35 for orchestra seats and expect a comparable amount of entertainment in return.

Doubtless the choice had been intended as a compliment to Callas, whose engagement had been announced nearly a year before (November 8, 1955), during her second Chicago season. It would have been more of a compliment had Bing provided a new production of *Norma*, opening or no. The curtain rise found the audience facing the same frowsy spectacle that had been in use for years, reconditioned by Charles Elson, but hardly improved.

But Callas was a performer who generated not only her own spectacle but also the electrical charge to illuminate it as well. As with almost any Callas performance anywhere, this had its negative as well as positive poles. The former were more than ordinarily high voltage on this occasion, with Milanov in ermine and the claque in flower. It had also been fed by a specimen of *Time* journalese, more concerned with anecdotage than artistry, the size of her fee (it was reputed to have breached the then Metropolitan top of $1750) and the vigor of her opinions. The most forthright of these was derived from a letter to her mother (from whom her father was separated and from whom she was estranged) replying to a request for financial assistance. As quoted in her mother's hardly affectionate memoirs,[1] Callas wrote: "Money is not like flowers, growing in gardens. . . . I bark for my living. You are

---

[1] Evangelia Callas: *My Daughter Maria Callas* (New York: Fleet Publishing Corporation; 1960), p. 141.

a young woman [fifty-four] and you can work. If you can't earn enough to live on throw yourself out of the window."

Among Americans conditioned to a belief that motherhood is even more sacred than country (and lobby comment indicated that many such were present), this aroused antagonism where nothing else—professional rivalries, personal animosities, artistic differences—would have.

That Callas managed nevertheless to launch her Metropolitan career with a well-controlled, beautifully expressive *"Casta diva"* was a tribute to the hard school of which she was a graduate no less than to steady nerves and iron will that belied inner tensions. It had its edgy, typically veiled sound, and was perhaps not the suavest *"Casta diva"* the Metropolitan had heard in recent times. But unlike those singers for whom a suave-sounding *"Casta diva"* was the beginning and end of suitability for Norma (d), for Callas it was emphatically only the beginning.

As she worked on, the realization soon came that her associates—Siepi (Oroveso), Del Monaco (Pollione*), and Barbieri (Adalgisa) were giving performances of varying degrees of vocal excellence. Callas was creating a character as emphatically her own as Flagstad's Alceste or Lehmann's Marschallin or, in another medium, Markova's Giselle—something seen whole and consecutive from beginning to end. Rounded musical phrases, a musician's way of curving a melodic line, a superior vocalist's sense of dynamics and color—all these were directed by a tragedienne's mind to a single overpowering purpose: realization of everything that Bellini's genius had poured into his sorely tried heroine.

Barbieri, a generously endowed Adalgisa, had her moments of triumph, as did Siepi, a tested Oroveso, and Del Monaco, who could have been a great Pollione and settled for being a merely not bad one. But in the end it was Callas who commanded the longest if not the loudest response from a portion of the audience that lingered on, reluctant to part from her as though this were a vision that might disappear as suddenly as it had appeared. Indeed, for all the Metropolitan had provided in the way of accessories—Cleva as conductor, Yannopoulos as stage director—it could have been a casual "guest" engagement rather than the beginning of a singular episode in Metropolitan history.

In the press, which fumbled for a yardstick and came up with a rule of thumb, appreciation of what had been offered was minimal. Taubman, in the *Times,* thought it a "puzzling voice," while observing semi-sagely that "she brought to the role the concentration of one who had studied it thoroughly." Lang, in the *Herald Tribune,* declared that the voice "had many limitations" and thought the "nicely rolled coloraturas" in *"Casta diva"* were "at times punctuated by high notes that were not well placed." That she moved in a realm of dramatic artistry inaccessible to those whose voices were *not* "puzzling" and all of whose top tones were "well placed" apparently registered not at all. The uncommon talent sought in vain for the uncommon appraisal that was its due.

Four repetitions of *Norma* were followed, on November 15 and 19, by two *Toscas* (both with Campora and London). All that affiliated Norma-Callas in this totally different kind of singing with Tosca-Callas was the same concentration on essentials. The dialogue of Act I was delivered as dialogue, the crisis of Act II was approached as an actress who was the queen of the Roman stage would approach it, with swift, vengeful movement to an unbelieving outcome. Some have made *"Vissi d'arte"* more of a showpiece; none has made it more credible than Callas. As in the previous year's *Toscas,* in which Gobbi's counterforce had been Mitropoulos, so Callas had more to work against in the conductor than she did in her stage associates. (Gobbi was actually on the scene at the time, performing Rigoletto* on December 6, but not Scarpia.)

Withal, there were some for whom Lucia was the prime experience of the Callas "season." For neither as Norma nor as Tosca did she pass the imaginable perimeter of what such a character could be. With her Lucia* on December 3 came a whole new vista of what Donizetti's opera contained in fervent dramatic expression and a poet's view of dementia. Each successive episode became part of a dramatic framework that supported the "Mad Scene" as the logical climax to an illogical happening rather than an isolated capital for a non-existent pillar. Callas sang *"Ardon gl'incensi"* with steady accuracy and strongly executed embellishments, solidly meriting the roar of approval she received. The succeeding *"Spargi d'amaro pianto"* showed signs of vocal weariness, and she barely struck the top E flat (not in the score) before toppling over, ending "life" and all incidental difficulties. The sets were the threadbare ones of old, the "direction" was by Defrère. Cleva conducted, with Campora, Moscona, and Enzo Sordello (Enrico Ashton*) among the principals.

Sordello was a competent but unremarkable baritone who had made his debut as Marcello (d) in a *Bohème* of November 3. He earned a lasting place in the annals of operatic amenities in a later *Lucia* (December 8), when he chose to trumpet, at length, a top note at the end of a duet with Lucia, while Callas ended hers as its time-value decreed. He rejected her angry (off-stage) objection with the accusation that she could not sustain the note properly. Conductor Cleva's prerogatives were also at issue, and Bing decided that Sordello's talents could be dispensed with. By a less than happy coincidence, Sordello turned up at the airport with a booking on the plane that was taking Callas back to Italy. The attention thus focused on the flight revealed that, as prima donna, Callas had first-class passage, whereas her husband, Meneghini, was content with tourist. In all, Callas sang eleven of the twelve performances for which she was announced, canceling one *Lucia*, on December 11. Police had to be called to disperse claimants for refunds when they discovered that they were about to hear Dolores Wilson instead.

With Callas gone her "repertory" returned to its previous status—that is to say, *Norma* vanished, the Pons kind of *Lucia* reappeared, and Tosca became Rigal, Kirsten, Antonietta Stella [on February 15, with Poggi as Cavaradossi*], Tebaldi, or Albanese. Singher was the Scarpia* on one occasion (January 23), and Bjoerling joined Tebaldi and Warren for a singers' festival on February 27. With Pons on March 11 were Poggi as Edgardo* and Tozzi as Raimondo.*

The likeness of this season to some of Gatti's was not wholly a matter of length. There was also an indication that planning took in some of his precedents, especially in the effort to evolve a pattern in which strong works from one season were carried over to the next; also, a cyclic relation among the non-standard ones was established. And, as Gatti had sought to balance his early and late season repertory by concentrating strong personalities in time periods of their own (rather than overlapping them), so Callas was prominent in the first half of this season, Tebaldi in the second.

To be sure, there could be only one opening night a season, and that had gone to Callas. But the Tebaldi partisans did all they could to make an equally momentous occasion of February 21, when she appeared for the first time as Violetta,* in the Metropolitan's first new *Traviata* in twenty years. The scenic opportunity was awarded to Oliver Smith, the dramatic direction assigned to Tyrone Guthrie, and Rolf Gérard was separated from his previously inclusive duties to concentrate on costuming.

However, with Cleva conducting and Tebaldi as Violetta, certain values were pre-determined. Among these, it became apparent as the evening developed, was the personality of Tebaldi herself. All of Guthrie's efforts to animate the opening act (even by recourse to popping champagne "corks" which one doubts that Mlle Valery's French butlers would have tolerated) were frustrated by Cleva's heavy tempos and Tebaldi's voluminous, unagile singing (the cause, perhaps, for the tempos). Other concessions included the lowering of *"Sempre libera"* a whole tone (from A flat to G flat) to bring its top tones within her range. Good as this may have been for her, it was bad for Campora as Alfredo, whose off-stage responses depressed him below a fair tenor range. The later acts were more responsibly sung, the last best of all.

Smith's glass-domed conservatory for the opening act was spacious and visually exciting, and his gambling hall had atmosphere. However his "summer house" for Act II was badly placed, and the huge bed with an even huger canopy towering over it in Act IV suggested a chamber in the Presidential Palace rather than the sick room of an unemployed courtesan. There were ample indications that Guthrie's efforts to separate Tebaldi from some of her "acting" mannerisms were as contrary to natural law as attempts to make water run up hill. For whatever reason, Hans Busch had more part in the staging than an "assistant" normally does, Guthrie rather less than a producer generally must if the result is to be representative of him. Such changes as Poggi as Alfredo* on March 15, Barioni in the same part on March 21, and Bastianini as Germont on March 21 did not alter the continuing elements—Tebaldi and Cleva—which made this *Traviata* what it was.

The disposition of favor to Callas and Tebaldi also gave consideration to Milanov, an old favorite not easily displaced in the affections of her following. She was granted the privilege of being the first Metropolitan soprano in nearly thirty years to sing *"Ernani, involami"* (transposed down), when *Ernani* was revived on November 23. Some might have regarded this as unconscionable propitiation of the opera goddess and gods (Warren as Carlo Quinto,* Del Monaco as Ernani,* and Siepi as Don Ruy Gomez*), but the purpose went deeper. It was part of a program by Bing to investigate some of the less frequently performed works of Verdi, with the hope, perhaps, of finding another *Don Carlo* among them. To his credit, he pursued the plan tenaciously and with benefit to the public.

The beginning was hardly auspicious, for a pair of related reasons—lack of sure knowledge on the part of the conductor (Mitropoulos) of how this opera goes and an unreasonable indulgence of Esteban Frances's impulses in the design of settings and costumes. Included in the former were un-certain tempos, the tolerance of Del Monaco's intemperate yelling and fondness for *fermate,* acquiescence in the downward transposition of *"Ernani involami"* (which skirted the Scylla of a top C but deposited Milanov against the Charybdis of a low A), and participation in the relocation of *"Infelice"* from Act I to Act II (Mitropoulos provided a four-bar conservatory modulation to lower it into its new place). The original placement of this aria had drawn critical complaints for decades, but it had equal incongruity in the altered surroundings of an empty stage.

Among Frances's misdemeanors were a patio, in California-Spanish, for the first act (plainly described in the text as "Elvira's rich apartment in Silva's castle") and another exterior for the second act, which Verdi thought of as "a magnificent hall." Frances's crypt in Act III was imaginatively conceived, and the last interior was creditable, but the damage had been done. Complimentary to his striving for the picturesque was a scheme of action by Yannopoulos which could only be called posteresque. Easily outstanding among the performers was Warren, who took advantage of every opportunity to show why Carlo should be considered the first real "Verdi baritone" part. However, the total of inadequacies recalled the earlier costly misadventure with *Faust*. The evening was extended in length, but not improved in quality, by a Solov ballet derived from *Vittorio* (see page 549), in which Melissa Hayden made her first Metropolitan appearance. In later performances (first on January 3), Tozzi made an appealing study of Don Ruy Gomez,* but Guarrera was overmatched by the vocal needs of Carlo.*

Amid the season's promises and prospects, possibly the least anticipation was attached to a venture with Offenbach's *La Perichole*. A stranger to the Metropolitan's repertory, it was all but unknown to New York operagoers, and the few who knew it from performances elsewhere could hardly relate that knowledge to the Metropolitan's large stage and larger auditorium. Thus the experience that greeted the audience for whom it was first given on December 21 profited as much from novelty as from a gaily fanciful décor by Gérard (one of his best), the lightly pointed direction of the score by Jean Morel (d) (the orchestration had been amended by Julius Burger, of the Metropolitan's musical staff), and a captivating range of performances in a fine, new English translation by Maurice Valency. Very nearly the best was the Viceroy of Peru* by Cyril Ritchard, who directed.

It was Ritchard's wise preference to suppress his parlor baritone to a monotone and "talk" his patter material, leaving the singing to those better equipped, particularly Uppman (Paquillo*) and Munsel (Perichole*). What Ritchard succeeded in doing monumentally well was to impart his own lightness of manner and deftness of touch not only to those who were disposed by nature to be responsive (Munsel and Uppman), but also to others who were not. Among the latter were the Three Sisters (Krall as Guadalena,* Chambers as Estrella,* and Elias as Virginella*), Franke as Panatellas* and De Paolis as a frantically funny Old Prisoner* (in Act III). As a topping to the froth of humor, Ritchard appeared as the "Viceroy's" Jailer in Act III, suggesting a bearded blend of Monty Woolley and Richard Haydn.

By the measure of the original, Munsel should not have sung Perichole, which is best served by a lower voice, but she found the role as suitable, in its different way, as Adele and Despina had been. And if Uppman's baritone lacked robustness, there was nothing but insinuation in his use of it. Hurley was a capable alternate for Munsel as Perichole* on January 11, but other changes were fortunately restricted to small parts that could be assimilated without damage to ensemble. On February 16 an amended version of the Circus Scene was introduced, with Mary Ellen Moylan as the Circus Ballerina* (music for the episode was borrowed from other Offenbach scores).

The lapse of any part of the *Ring* from the repertory in the two preceding seasons made the presentation of the whole of it more than ordinarily difficult in this one. To spread the work burden (which doubtless would have been differently arranged had Kempe been available), Mitropoulos conducted *Die Walküre,* Stiedry the other three scores. As tends to be the case, *Das Rheingold* was the stickiest problem of all, for the cast which was heard on January 18 was almost wholly different from its predecessor of January 1951. Holdovers were restricted to Pechner (Alberich), Ernster (Fafner), and Madeira (Erda), meaning that all the others were in the "first performance" category: Uhde as Wotan,* Budney as Donner,* Mc-Cracken as Froh,* Vinay as Loge,* Kelley as Mime (d), Böhme as Fasolt,* Moll as Freia,* and Krall, Elias, and Warfield as the Rhinemaidens.* The new Fricka* was Thebom. The first performance, thus, was something of a public dress rehearsal, slow-moving and without much dramatic freedom. There was more momentum in later performances, but neither Uhde as Wotan nor Vinay as Loge had the command of his role to provide the dramatic accent wanted. Uhde was limited in physical as well as vocal size, and Vinay was still new to the wiles of Loge, which is exactly what a Loge should not be (Svanholm, the last able exponent of the part, had retired to Stockholm where he became head of the Royal Opera on July 1, 1956). Kelley showed promise as Mime, which was not the same as mastery of the character's craftiness. Save for Davidson as Alberich on January 26 and Lipton as Fricka* on February 18, the performers had the benefit of playing together three times. On its next appearance, in the 1961–2 season, twelve of the fourteen characters were as strange to the house as these had been.

The other three dramas went better, not so much because the Metropolitan's personnel was better suited to their problems, as because the personnel was better suited to the Metropolitan's problem. Wolfgang Windgassen was imported to make his debut as Siegmund (d) on January 22 (his price presumably was as high as it had been before, but his appearances were concentrated in a briefer time span), with Edelmann as Wotan,* Harshaw as Brünnhilde, Böhme as Hunding,* Thebom as Fricka, and Marianne Schech as Sieglinde (d). Windgassen provided experienced service for the Siegfrieds* (in *Siegfried* on January 30 and *Götterdämmerung* on March 2), especially when his partner as Brünnhilde* was Martha Mödl, with whom he had frequently appeared at Bayreuth and elsewhere.

Windgassen's European celebrity was certainly evident in his assurance, authority, and endurance, but he earned limited honors for dramatic illusion or vocal appeal. The big sound was hard, the big body a bar to credibility as the young Siegfried. Mödl's appeal was rather wider, for she looked well as Brünnhilde, limited herself to appropriately plastic gestures, and was never less than an intelligent singer. Her vocal limitation was at the top, a consequence of her beginnings as a mezzo. (These were more evident in *Die Walküre* on February 20 than otherwise.) Edelmann was a promising but not yet masterful Wanderer,* and Kelley's Mime* in *Siegfried* was of the quality of its antecedent. The ample impulse that Mitropoulos showed as conductor of *Die Walküre* would have been welcome in *Siegfried,* but he, obviously, was not (Stiedry was the conductor). For reasons related to Mödl's advent, Varnay was absent, and did not return while the company remained in its old home. Thus the *Götterdämmerung* Brünnhilde was either Mödl or Harshaw. Vinay was Siegmund* and the older Siegfried* when Windgassen was not. For my taste, Vinay was better adjusted to Siegmund (on February 20, with Uhde as Wotan* and Mödl as Brünnhilde*) than to Siegfried, his baritonal background serving him better in its lower range. Schech, who had performed a customary kind of Sieglinde* (as distinguished from the Lehmann or Flagstad uncustomary kind), was a passable Gutrune* on February 7, with Uhde as Gunther,* a part of which he made much. Perhaps if Böhme had stayed longer with the company, his Hagen* would have earned rank with those of Bohnen, Hofmann, and Kipnis, for he had both the sinister sound and barbaric presence. Madeira sang her first Metropolitan Waltraute* on February 23, resorting too often to her vocal overdrive when normal volume (for her) would have sufficed. To round out the Walküren in *Die Walküre,* Gloria Lind as Helmwige (d) and Carlotta Ordassy as Gerhilde (d) were added to Krall, Lipton, Elias, Warfield, Roggero, and Belen Amparan on January 22. On February 25, Warfield had her largest opportunity to date, as Erda* in *Siegfried,* and performed well. Bing rated the preparation required for the four *Ring* dramas as equivalent in time to seven operas of the scope of *Butterfly,* and regretted the small yield in performance thus derived. It was hardly questionable, however, that more sustained attention to *Die*

Walküre or *Siegfried* or *Götterdämmerung*—not to mention a shorter absence of the whole cycle from the repertory—would have diminished the time required to prepare them for sequential performance.

In Kempe's absence, Stiedry also directed *Die Meistersinger* when it was given on October 31 with a mostly familiar cast (Edelmann, Tozzi, Da Costa, Pechner, Lipton, and Franke). The Eva* was Amara, who might have become expert in this part had she performed it more often. On November 17, the Eva was Della Casa, and Amara did not perform it again until March 14, when the conductor was Kozma. Stiedry also brought the Wagner of this season to a close with *Parsifal,* in which Sullivan ventured the title role for the first time on March 30 and Da Costa performed it, also for the first time, on April 19. Neither showed a born or acquired disposition for it. Uhde was the eloquent Amfortas* on March 30, and he also agreed to substitute for an ailing London on April 18. However, he also insisted on performing the Klingsor* for which he had been cast, though an alternate was available. As the victim of his own villainy, Uhde could be described quite literally as his own worst enemy.

Kempe's ill fortune proved an open door to a new career for Erich Leinsdorf, who thus had the distinction of opening and closing his City Center directorship (see page 566) and resuming a place at the Metropolitan within weeks. He had attacked his new assignment with characteristic vigor, "briefing" the press at considerable length on his intention to institute a subscription "base" for City Center Opera, to revitalize the repertory with choice works not seen previously, and otherwise to upgrade its standing, locally, nationally, and internationally.

Unfortunately, much of this foundered before it was fairly launched. Leinsdorf's choice of an introduction was a rowdy version of Offenbach's *Orpheus in the Underworld,* the inept and coarse adaptation of which by Eric Bentley was consistently unfunny (replete with references to bop, high-fidelity, and other topicalities) as well as inappropriately sprinkled with references to "bed," "the hay," and other euphemisms for sexual relations. If the singing cast of Sylvia Stahlman (Eurydice), Beverly Bower (Diana), Jon Crain (Orpheus), and Jacquelynne Moody (Cupid), with Paula Laurence (Miss Public Opinion) and Hiram Sherman (Jupiter) in speaking parts, reflected on Leinsdorf's musical judgment, what they had to do did not. It turned out, also, that his idea of a "unit set" (mostly ramps around a "turntable" whose motive force was manpower and whose lubricant was elbow grease) to serve the whole repertory dis-served such standard works as *La Traviata* and *Mignon* (which introduced tenors Frank Poretta and Richard Verreau as, respectively, Frederick and Meister) as much as it served Leinsdorf's other "innovations." These included a double bill of Stravinsky's *Histoire du soldat* (with Christopher Plummer as Narrator, James Mitchell as the Soldier, Hurd Hatfield as the Devil) and Orff's *Der Mond* (in an English version by Maria Messey, with Donald Gramm, Richard Wentworth, Michael Pollock, and Joshua Hecht); and Frank Martin's *The Tempest* (with Kenneth Smith as Prospero, Richard Cassilly as Ferdinand, Gregory Millar, who later turned to conducting, as Antonio, Donald Gramm as Gonzalo, Cornell MacNeil as Stephano, and Priscilla Gillette as Miranda.

Oddly, the most enduring memory of Leinsdorf's City Center tenure was the work to which the least expectation attached: a first professional production anywhere (it had been ventured previously as a semi-professional production at Florida State University, where its composer-librettist was a member of the faculty) of *Susannah* by the unknown Carlisle Floyd. Its lilt and flow, suggestive of folk materials if not actually based on them, and its honestly homespun way of delivering its mountain-bred "message" profited from an ideal performance of the title role by Phyllis Curtin. Also excellent were Norman Treigle (Blitch), Jon Crain (the brother), and Mignon Dunn (Mrs. Ott). Despite the kudos conferred on Leinsdorf by this successful sponsorship and the praise of the press for his venturesome repertory, there was too little attraction in it for public response in proportion to costs of production, and the season ended with an alarmingly large deficit. Four performances near the end of the season were called off, and there were rumors that the unions (musicians especially) might be asked for a loan—in salaries to members—to tide over the hard-pressed City Center leadership. Eventually the latter managed to expunge its obligations-over-income in the amount of $215,000 with the rueful recognition that opera on the Leinsdorf plan was too rich a diet for City Center's table.

However, the results that Leinsdorf had achieved, musically, in preparing *Orpheus* and *Susanna* for performance persuaded Bing that he was a man for the Metropolitan's needs in Kempe's absence. This provided for his "third debut" at the Metropolitan as director of *Arabella* on January 7, 1957 (the two earlier ones were on January 21, 1938, and, after military service, on December 4, 1944), also paving the way, in the fullness of time, for Leinsdorf's ascension to the leadership of the Boston Symphony Orchestra. Doubtless there would have been some settling of the performance values in *Arabella* in any case, but the surehanded control of its new conductor and some alterations in previous casting which amended previous weaknesses made for superior results. Of outstanding quality was the singing of Della Casa as Arabella,* good enough to inure one to her difficulties with the English text, and the strong effort of Jon Crain as Matteo.* Only four performances were presented (on February 22 Warfield was Adelaide,* Cassel sang Mandryka, and MacWatters returned as Fiakermilli*).

The rising talents of Antonietta Stella were added, perhaps in thoughtful anticipation of soprano problems to come, as Aida (d) on November 13. A young woman of good appearance and strong, adaptable vocal aptitudes, Stella showed herself capable of sturdy service as Leonora* in *Trovatore* on November 16, Tosca* on February 15, and Elisabetta* in *Don Carlo* on March 29. In the last of these, which she repeated on April 4, she showed a sounder, surer command of the vocal line than any Bing-presented predecessor. Neither facial mobility nor character projection was in Stella's line, but she had strong qualifications for an extended Metropolitan career. Her failing was to consider herself a star before she had become a favorite, meaning that a parting was foreordained. With its staging now entrusted to Hans Busch, *Don Carlo* had turned into something like *Gioconda* for demonstrations of partisanship from the standees and *claqueurs* who could afford seats. There was even an outburst for Irene Dalis after she sang the "Veil" aria passably well at her debut as Eboli (d) on March 16. The excellent Inquisitor* of this performance was Uhde.

The *Aida* that introduced Stella also provided for the introduction of Carlo Bergonzi as Radames (d). This was less than the greatest favor to him, for little of the role after *"Celeste Aida"* was truly meant for a tenor of his limited power, for which reason it tended to minimize, in a striving for volume, the attributes of taste, control, and beautifully even sound he commanded. He was also vocally overweighted by much of his next role, Manrico* in an *Il Trovatore* on November 16, conducted by Rudolf. As Bergonzi was an indifferent actor whose good-results-to-come were achieved primarily by voice, it took other seasons and different opportunities to show the best of his talent. In a later *Trovatore* (February 13), the audience made the acquaintance of Mary Curtis-Verna as Leonora (d). (She had sung at the City Center as Mary Curtis, then had ventured a career in Italy, where she married vocal technician Ettore Verna.) She showed a voice of considerable power, especially at the top, and not so considerable control, especially in the middle and lower registers. However, as a determined performer with a willingness to sing anything in her range (whether it was suited to her otherwise or not), Curtis-Verna became a kind of female Baum in Bing's garden.

In this season's *Aidas,* only five years removed from the prime condition of a new production, much had altered, not all for the better. Barbieri wore her own hideous version (bright green) of the proper gown for Amneris at the Stella-Bergonzi performance on November 13, and Nell Rankin, who replaced her at short notice on November 24, seemed a candidate for Queen of the Fireman's Ball in the bright scarlet regalia she affected. The tunic originally designed for Del Monaco had long since vanished, and the dance concept delivered by Geoffrey Holder at his debut on November 13 was unlike anything previously observed in the triumphal scene. Entertaining in itself, it made no particular sense where it was.

Bing's promotion of other Negro talent progressed a step farther when Mattiwilda Dobbs, who had sung with success in Covent Garden and at La Scala, made her debut as Gilda (d) in *Rigoletto* on November 9. She survived scrutiny as the first of her race to perform in "romantic" love scenes on the Metropolitan stage, though her appearance would have been improved by a less pasty makeup than the one she used. Warren was the father, with Peerce as the Duke. A careful and conscientious performer, Dobbs was handicapped in the Metropolitan by the lightness of her sound, especially at the bottom. McFerrin was the Amonasro of an *Aida* on December 25, rather overmatched in the company of Milanov, Barbieri, and Baum.

Schippers's success with *Don Pasquale* (which returned on November 2 with the prior cast of Gueden-Valletti-Corena, but with Merrill as Malatesta)* earned him the further opportunity of conducting *Bohème* on November 3, with Amara, Barioni, Hurley, and Enzo Sordello (Marcello [d]). Schippers applied himself with all vigor, showing his knowledge of score and text by singing virtually every line with the performers. However, the orchestra decided at rehearsal that his knowledge was more related to the piano score than the orchestral, and paid him scant attention. On November 24, Charles Anthony was a commendable Ernesto* and Hurley was Norina* on several occasions, the first on November 14, with Sordello as Malatesta.* Schippers had his first opportunity with *Les Contes d'Hoffmann* on November 29, when London performed the four baritone roles for the first time and Giulietta (d) was impersonated by Belen Amparan, a Texas-born mezzo of ample voice but limited experience. She did better as La Cieca* in *Gioconda* on March 7. London's impersonations at this time ran to a Lon Chaney kind of virtuosity in makeup rather than to anything more penetrating. Though this was only his second Metropolitan season, Schippers was off for guest engagements elsewhere by December 28, when Kozma conducted *Bohème*; Rich was in charge of the following night's *Hoffmann*.

Walter's presence was welcomed again when *The Magic Flute* returned under his direction on March 1. Save for Hurley as Queen of the Night* (Peters was having a baby), the cast of Uppman-Amara-Sullivan-Hines was much as it had been. Hurley's promotion provided an opportunity for

Mildred Allen, a soprano of minuscule size, to perform very creditably in her debut as Papagena (d). As Sarastro, Hines was restricted to virtually no movement, as he had recently suffered a fractured ankle, which was in a protective casing. The nationwide audience that looked forward to hearing a broadcast of *The Magic Flute* under Walter on March 9 was deprived of its pleasure when the eighty-one-year-old master suffered a heart attack a few days earlier. Direction of the performance passed to Kozma, who also directed the remainder of Walter's schedule. On March 23, Irene Jordan, who had given up a Metropolitan career as a mezzo in 1947-8 to essay transformation into a dramatic soprano, undertook to sing the Queen of the Night,* and on March 26, Carelli, an excellent performer in secondary parts, ventured a Tamino* that was penalized by his lack of power. Jordan showed the breadth and weight of dramatic sound some had waited a long time to hear in her role, but was erratic in pitch and insecure in skips. For all the varied services he rendered in this season—in *Bohème* and *Meistersinger* as well as in the *Flute*—Kozma did not find the career opportunity at the Metropolitan that he thought he merited (he was forty-seven), and transferred his activities to the School of Music at Indiana University in Bloomington.

The season's Mozart also included *Le Nozze di Figaro,* for which Rudolf was the conductor on December 1. Ensemble came and went with changes that ranged from Singher as the Count on that date to Singher as Figaro on February 14, when Herbert was the Count*; Hurley as Susanna* on December 12, Tozzi as Figaro* and Elias as Cherubino* on January 12. Albanese, who had previously sung Susanna, ventured beyond her vocal depth as the Countess* on February 1.

The reduction in status of Mitropoulos from a master of special scores to an everyday conductor of almost any found him on December 27 as the spark to ignite the noninflammable remainders of the Guthrie *Carmen* and on December 8 as the impulse selected to make *Madama Butterfly* something other than it had lately been at the Metropolitan. The latter (in which Barioni was the Pinkerton* and Elias sang Suzuki*) had more orchestral definition than for some time past, but the Mitropoulos effect on *Carmen* was to make it nervous rather than animated, tense rather than dramatic. On February 5, eligible Pinkertons* were reduced to Carelli. By March 9 the *Carmen* conductor was Adler (with Cundari as Micaëla* and Bastianini as Escamillo), and on April 18 (when Krall was Micaëla*) it was Rich.

This winter the Metropolitan's pursuit of by-product income took the form of an arrangement to provide Ed Sullivan's televised variety show with segments of opera in costume and with action. It started bravely on November 25 with a generous section of the second act of *Tosca*, with

Callas and London. It retrogressed a few weeks later to a less generous section of *Butterfly* (Act I), with Kirsten and Del Monaco. By the spring, when Tebaldi was scheduled to appear, it had been decided that Sullivan's ratings were suffering from such esoterica, and her performance was restricted to arias. The arrangement lapsed soon after.

As Bing's latest answer to those who deemed him antinovelty was an announcement that he intended to present, during the 1957–8 season, Samuel Barber's first opera. On February 21, the Metropolitan Opera Association, of which Bliss had recently been elected president, became formally affiliated with Lincoln Center as a constituent. In September a further extention of Bing's contract, which would have expired on June 1, 1959, was made public. It reserved his services for a period of five years, with two one-year options. It now extended through 1963–4 when, it was confidently believed, the new house would be not only ready but also operational.

1957–1958

The reasoned relationship of attraction to occasion which traditionally prevails for a Metropolitan opening eludes recognition in the recurrence, on October 28, of Tchaikovsky's *Eugen Onegin* after an absence since 1921. Not much more esoteric, say, than *Norma,* it nevertheless lacked so luminous a personality as Callas in a cast that offered London as Onegin,* Tozzi as Gremin,* Tucker as Lenski,* Amara as Tatiana,* and Elias as Olga.* Tucker's attitude toward the assignment may be read in his later reluctance to perform the part because, he said, "My public doesn't like me in a role where I die in the second act."

A reasoned relationship was not wholly absent, for all the fact that it was not present. *Onegin* was originally intended as a project for Tebaldi, in whom some Metropolitan planners saw a Tatiana on the order of Lotte Lehmann's in Vienna when they were growing up. But Tebaldi finally refused (perhaps because of the decision to use an English translation instead of the Italian in which she had sung it in La Scala), and the role became Amara's instead. The good qualities she had to offer, vocally, were offset by a lack of magnetism to hold the stage during the long "Letter Scene" in Act I and the absence of strong character projection thereafter.

Whether, with all her appeal, Tebaldi would have made the difference between indifference and delight is at least questionable. There would still be the leisurely lengths of Mitropoulos's conducting to contend with, lengths stretched farther by the introduction of instrumental interludes arranged by Julius Burger to bridge scene changes. Together with the repetitions built into Tchaikovsky's score, this made for a kind of tune-plugging less than worthy of the circumstances. As for the scenes themselves, they were among Gérard's poorer efforts, especially the opening act, on Mme Larina's estate. The two grand rooms that followed had spaciousness and charm, but the finale reverted to an outdoor locale (the text calls for a room in Gremin's home) because of a misguided belief that a parting between Tatiana and Onegin would be more "atmospheric" amid falling snowflakes. Nothing in Peter Brook's direction justified this gratuitous "improvement" on a creator's conception.

The robust voices of Tucker, London and Tozzi were as much as anyone could ask for in a Tchaikovsky score, but the characterizations were another matter. The English text by Henry Reese was often as awkward to sing as it was to hear. To be sure, *Onegin* had its staunch defenders to whom none of these objections counted against the appeal in Tchaikovsky's score. However, the money provided by Mrs. John D. Rockefeller, Jr., has yet to find a justification in the quality performances of *Onegin* in this and later seasons.

There was little reason to suppose that a season begun so inauspiciously (for all the $74,777 that was collected at the box office) would take a turn for the better almost at once. The turn it took at the next curtain rise, on October 31, was a turn to the best blend of elements the theater had seen since *Don Carlo*. For the first time in nearly thirty years, the Metropolitan had a new *Don Giovanni,* and one that might have delighted the eye as well as the ear of Mozart himself. Those responsible for the cohesive outcome were Eugene Berman as designer, Karl Boehm in his debut as conductor, and Herbert Graf as director. Underwriting was provided by the National Council and Mrs. Albert Lasker.

Boehm and Graf could have produced a very good *Giovanni* with any qualified designer, but what made this one great was Berman's personal participation in the execution of his designs. "Participation" here went beyond supervision of the work of others, to his own presence on the paint-bridge, day after day to touch in a detail here, highlight an effect there. An old-fashioned approach to scenic execution rarely pursued in these days of unions and craft guilds, it justified itself by the quality of the results that accrued. In addition to evoking a sumptuously colorful Spanish locale (a mixture of many rather than a likeness of any), it was also as practical as it was attractive, with an inner curtain to speed scenic changes and a unit frame which, for once, was an aid rather than a hindrance to illusion.

Boehm's Mozart was not the most dynamic imaginable, but it was rock-solid, thoroughgoing, intolerant of deviation from his conception of balance. This took its measure from the sound of clarinets and oboes, the loudest instruments consistently used by Mozart in this score. As long as they could be heard without overblowing, the voices could also be heard without forcing. His steadying hand lent new distinction to the Donna Anna of Steber (in which she returned after a year's absence from the company), the much-improved Elvira of Della Casa, the Zerlina of Peters, and the Masetto* of Uppman, as attractively foolish as his Papageno. Perhaps the longest stride forward was made by Siepi, whose Don was greatly improved by European experience and his own steady artistic growth. Valletti was the excellent Ottavio, with Corena as Leporello, and Tozzi providing a new order of vocal pleasure as the Commendatore.* Graf's staging was organized and integrated beyond anything seen previously in the *Giovannis* he had been putting together for twenty Metropolitan seasons. There was some cause for apprehension when Corena had to be replaced as early as November 13 (the cast included Hurley as Zerlina* and London as the Don) with the all but unknown Ezio Flagello. However this bass-baritone (New York-born for all his Italian name) performed with such aptitude for Leporello,* in a voice of such resonant fatness, that his future appearances automatically conveyed assurance of a quality effort. The substitution on December 27 of Curtis-Verna for Steber as Donna Anna* and Amara for Della Casa as Elvira brought less cheering results. Curtis-Verna's limitations of control put quavers where a solid sound was wanted, and her lack of florid skill was clearly evident in *"Non mi dir."* Stiedry's performances of *Don Giovanni* on April 5 and 8 were the last (in New York) of a Metropolitan career that had begun with *Siegfried* on November 15, 1946, as he left the company to live in Switzerland at the season's end.

Tebaldi's absence from the opening weeks of the season had been reckoned with (she was busy with performances of her beloved *Adriana Lecouvreur* in Chicago on November 13 and 16), but there was no reason to suppose that she would not take up her Metropolitan appearances as scheduled, beginning on November 21 with *Tosca.* However, her mother, from whom she was inseparable, became ill shortly after their arrival in New York on November 17. The diagnosis of a coronary thrombosis called for hospitalization, but Tebaldi would not consent. Her hotel room became the sickroom, and Tebaldi would not hear of leaving it to perform. The *Tosca* on November 21 was Stella instead. The patient's condition gradually worsened, and she died on November 29. Tebaldi gave herself completely to grief and mourning after the interment in Italy, retiring from public activity for many months.

Tebaldi's absence, which was final for this season, cut across a series of performances for which she had been scheduled well into January. In another year, it might have resulted in wholesale alterations of casts, perhaps

in changes of operas. But with Stella and Curtis-Verna to space out assignments with Milanov, the crisis was surmounted. Curtis-Verna was the
Aida* on November 30, with Dalis as Amneris* and Robert Nagy, a
robust tenor, replacing as the Messenger* an even more robust tenor, Mc-
Cracken, who had followed his star to Europe. On December 5, when
Bergonzi sang a very capable Cavaradossi* (his first Metropolitan venture
with Puccini), the Tosca was Milanov, and so it went with *Andrea Chénier*
on December 11 (Milanov, Roggero as Bersi,* and Flagello as Mathieu*),
another Aida on December 14, and still another on December 20 with
Cesare Bardelli (who had made his debut the preceding April 16 as
Alfio [d] in *Cavalleria*) as Amonasro.* It is worthy of note, as respects
critical opinion, that Tebaldi had come to agree with those who regarded
her voice as too heavy for Violetta's music. After the prior season's spring
tour, she informed her biographer Victor Seroff: "I shall never sing *La
Traviata* again . . . My voice has grown too big for the part."[1] In *Forza* on
January 2, the Leonora* was Curtis-Verna (she had sung Tosca on December 30), with Flaviano Labò, who had made his debut as Alvaro (d)
on November 29, again in this role and Amparan as Preziosilla.* The succession of "firsts" by Curtis-Verna (which also included Donna Anna* on
December 27) did not result in any single performance of outstanding
quality, but it unquestionably enhanced her position with the Metropolitan
management.

If there was a bright side to the dark picture, it may have been that no
novelty later in the season had been created around Tebaldi. Not that this
meant that the scheduled novelty came off problem-free. As time approached for the *première* of Barber's *Vanessa*, it became known that the
announced choice*[2] for the title role, Sena Jurinac, had decided not to
come to America. Despite the short time that remained, Eleanor Steber
welcomed the opportunity to collaborate with the composer from whom
she had commissioned *Knoxville: Summer of 1915* a decade before, and
performed at the *première* on January 15 as though Vanessa* had been
written for her.

Unlike most similar occasions in the past, *Vanessa* had sufficient music
of Barber's best quality not to require qualification as "American." This
justified comparison with contemporary opera being written anywhere,
though so much of its best came so late in the evening that it left a sense
of being only half realized. This included the solo of the Doctor,* beautifully performed by Tozzi, the orchestral interlude before the final scene,

[1] Victor Seroff: *Renata Tebaldi, The Woman and the Diva* (New York: Appleton-
Century Crofts, Inc.; 1961), p. 169.
[2] Callas had been invited many months before, but had declined.

and the quintet. *Vanessa* did, without question, resolve any question of Barber's talent for the theater and make more than a pleasantry the urging that he write another opera . . . soon. Some of the melodramatic situations in the libretto contrived by his close friend Menotti would have been better suited to the latter's own compositional talent, but Barber profited, no doubt, by the guidance provided by so experienced a collaborator.

Outstanding among the characters they mutually evolved was Erika,* who found a perfect embodiment in the sweet-voiced, appealing person of Rosalind Elias. Hardly less good was the caddish breeziness of Nicolai Gedda as Anatol*; Giorgio Tozzi's Doctor was a charming character study. As Vanessa, Steber was heavily engaged with some over-elaborate vocal writing (the "Skating Song" has generally been omitted in recent revivals), but she attained a strategic middle ground between the maidenly and the matronly as the action evolved. Next to the enunciation of the English text by Gedda (a Russian-Swede who brought a gift of tongues as well as a sense of style to everything he did), Steber's delivery was the best of all.

Needless to say, so much that is dramatically good does not come about on the stage (especially the operatic stage) without creative supervision. Menotti's participation as director left some with the strong feeling that it was in this phase of theater that his best qualities asserted themselves (as in the vivid person he and Regina Resnik made of the Baroness,* mostly mute though she was). Framing the action was a superbly atmospheric décor by Cecil Beaton which succeeded in giving reality to the wholly unreal locale: "A country house in a northern country." A richer texture of orchestral sound than Mitropoulos evoked from Barber's not very expert scoring would have filled in some aural lacunae; the later custom of performing Act I as a prologue and proceeding directly to Act II amended a sense of brevity in the original. However, Mitropoulos did achieve a sense of excitement which, at a first performance, is decidedly desirable. Some critical voices deplored Barber's idiom as retrogressive and the Metropolitan as non-progressive for putting its novelty money (actually, the Francis Goelet Foundation's) on so "safe" a choice. However, it clearly rated Taubman's judgment, in the *Times*, as "the best American opera ever presented at the Metropolitan," as well as Winthrop Sargeant's contention in *The New Yorker* that *Vanessa* proved Barber to be "a real master of operatic tradition." The only consequential changes in cast came with Lewis as Vanessa* on February 15 (some of her acting was subtler than Steber's, but she did not sing the music as well) and Harvuot as the Doctor* on February 21.

The affirmative opinions expressed by Taubman and Sargeant (among others) on *Vanessa* and the hope for future production embodied in

Floyd's *Susannah* were not just possibly, but probably, influential on the new turn of direction taken by the operatic enterprise of City Center early in 1958. The drain on resources occasioned by the disastrously expensive Leinsdorf season in the fall of 1956 had come almost as the shock of decisive battle to a weary army. An interlude was declared for retrenchment, regrouping, and possibly restaffing. The City Center put on no season of opera in the spring of 1957, the time being allotted to other forms of activity with a possibility of earning rather than losing money.

As they deliberated on a choice of leadership to succeed Leinsdorf, the City Center's executives were petitioned by the personnel of the suspended "company"—chorus and principals as well as orchestra—to consider the claim of one of their own. This was conductor Julius Rudel, who had begun work, as a young rehearsal pianist under Laszlo Halasz, even before there was a "company" in the fall of 1943 and had spent part of every year thereafter in the generation of the sixty-two different works thus far mounted. This had carried him from his early 'twenties to his late 'thirties.

In the absence of a better alternative, it was decided to "give Julius a chance to see what he could do." It was from this that there emerged the longest tenure of direction the company experienced in its first twenty years of existence, including its historic move from the bourgeois surroundings of the former Mecca Temple on Fifty-fifth Street to the *empire* (appropriate perhaps to the Empire State) elegance of its new home in Lincoln Center in the winter of 1966.

It began, however, modestly enough with a season mostly "out of stock" in the fall of 1957, embellished by a pairing of two Falla works (*La Vida Breve* and *El Amor Brujo*) in a double bill directed by José Iturbi (debut at City Center), a borrowed production (from Stratford, Conn.) of Mozart's *Seraglio* directed by Peter Herman Adler, the safely commercial *Merry Widow* of Lehár conducted by Franz Allers, and, most venturesome of all, the first staging of Verdi's *Macbeth* which New York had seen in a decade and a half (see footnote page 430). At the City Center, Lady Macbeth was the ambitious but unreliable Irene Jordan, with William Chapman as Macbeth, Norman Treigle (Banquo), Giuseppe Gismondo (MacDuff), and Ernest McChesney (Malcolm). Margaret Webster supervised the simplified staging in rudimentary settings designed by Andrea Nomikos, and Arturo Basile directed energetically. The interest aroused by the return to City Center fundamentals (the season opened with *Turandot,* and also included *Faust, Traviata,* and *Butterfly*) drew a gratifying response that justified the addition of a week to the five originally scheduled.

It was, however, with an awareness of the uncertainties of the future that Morton Baum (see page 442), who had assumed a large share of responsibility for perpetuating the operatic activities of City Center, leaving ballet to the flourishing enterprise developed by Kirstein and Balanchine, the dramatic-light opera seasons to Jean Dalrymple's supervision, began to look for outside sources of support. The simultaneous expression of interest in the performing arts by the Ford Foundation and other foundations cast a gleam of hope: but these funds, it had been decided, were not to meet deficits of performing groups, but rather to encourage the creation of new works (preferably works of art, but in any case, new works).

It was this gleam of hope which was fanned into a blazing light to illuminate the City Center's future. The Baum problem, clearly, was to maintain a solvent company: and if the means could be achieved by applying its efforts to four, five, or half a dozen "new" works, the ends could be adapted to them. This was a matter less of cynicism than of realism: that it turned into a fresh source of vitality for the company's better health as well as a sizeable benefit for its public esteem is merely proof that not all the best plans are those carefully laid.

Of critical importance to the outcome was not only the $105,000 made available by the Ford Foundation to mount a season of ten American works in the spring of 1958, but a) the ability of Rudel to seek out produceable works and prepare them for performance in virtually minimal time, b) the identity of the singers at his command with the kinds of works available for performance.

Some of this was apparent in the opening on April 3, 1958, with Douglas Moore's *The Ballad of Baby Doe,* in which the performers included several who had participated in the original production at the Central City Opera in Colorado in the summer of 1956: Walter Cassel (Horace Tabor), Martha Lipton (Augusta Tabor), and the conductor, Emerson Buckley (Beverly Sills was Baby Doe, in place of Dolores Wilson). The physical production also was borrowed from Central City. This lightly cheerful work made an agreeable introduction to the unfolding venture, which proceeded with Mark Bucci's *Tale for a Deaf Ear* (in which Lee Venora made her debut) coupled with Leonard Bernstein's *Trouble in Tahiti* (written for TV), in which Beverly Wolff was the principal performer; Vittorio Giannini's *Taming of the Shrew* (with Chester Watson in his City Center debut as Baptista, Curtin as Katherina, and John Alexander as Lucentio); and the highly original *Good Soldier Schweik* of Robert Kurka, who, tragically, had died a few months before its production revealed the order of talent he possessed. Mixed with them were restorations of *Regina* (Carol Brice made her debut as Addie, with Samuel Krachmalnick conducting), *Susannah,* Menotti's *Old Maid-Medium* pairing, and, because the name of

Kurt Weill legitimatized it, the commercially oriented *Lost in the Stars,* with Lawrence Winters as Kumalo, Godfrey Cambridge as Johannes, and Shirley Carter as Irina. The company acquired one of its most characteristic performers at this time in Ruth Kobart, who replaced Lipton as Mrs. Tabor on April 11. The new identity of the company was officially stamped *Made in the U.S.* when it was sent to Brussels to perform *Susannah* at the World's Fair of 1958 there in June.

Crowning the best sequence of new operatic productions the Metropolitan had presented in more than twenty-five years was Puccini's *Madama Butterfly,* which became, on February 19, something it had not been for even longer—a feast for the eye as well as the ear. The generosity of Cornelius V. Starr, a New York stockbroker, had included a recommendation for the use of such excellent Japanese theater people as Motohiro Nagasaka to design and Yoshio Aoyama to direct the new production, with results that were as close to enchanting as anything the Metropolitan had achieved within memory.

In addition to cleaning up the accrued blemishes of decades (the last new Metropolitan *Butterfly,* by Urban, dated to 1922), Nagasaka and Aoyama eliminated certain traditionally "Italian" devices (such as the fireflies in Act I) which had no validity in the time or place of the action. Everybody, including the director and the designer when the production was being put together, took off shoes before entering the house, and the blend of colors was, like the action, delicate in detail but strong in sum. The costuming was all of a piece and created in the authentic manner.

Good as all this was, it was but a complementary part of a whole supervised by Aoyama. The movements of the "Japanese" characters were carefully distinguished from those of Pinkerton and Sharpless, and as carefully installed on Stella as Butterfly,* Roggero as Suzuki, De Paolis as Goro, Flagello as the Bonze,* and Cehanovsky as Yamadori. They had been thoroughly indoctrinated in makeup techniques to mold their faces into Oriental planes, and the wigs for the women were a crowning touch that made them all but unrecognizable as Italians or Americans. With Mitropoulous to provide the momentum, Puccini's score soared from first to last, with Stella performing affectingly (no top D flat in the entrance, however), an engaging freshness in the tenor of young Eugenio Fernandi as Pinkerton (d), and suitable solidity for Mario Zanasi as Sharpless.* Admittedly no eagle, it was unquestionably a butterfly, which was as much as anyone could ask. Perhaps the best action of all was provided by Roggero, a practiced Suzuki who benefited from the new stimulus of Aoyama to become a practically perfect one. Thanks to continuing supervision, the original qualities were retained when the Butterfly became Los Angeles on April 3, with Bergonzi as Pinkerton,* and when Amparan replaced Roggero as Suzuki* on April 7.

Los Angeles's season was a lengthy one, beginning with her Violetta* in the Guthrie-Smith *Traviata* on November 2 (with Warren and Barioni, and with Robert Nagy making his debut as Giuseppe [d]) and continuing through appearances as Marguerite in *Faust* on November 11 (the conductor this year was Morel), Rosina in *Il Barbiere* on December 2, and Desdemona* in *Otello* on February 27, with Del Monaco, Warren, and Elias (Emilia*). Well as both Verdi heroines were sung, Los Angeles did little to persuade the viewer of a strong identification with the soul-states of the characters. She had more success with Desdemona than with Violetta, but it was all very close to the surface. Under Cleva's direction, *Otello* began assertively enough but, as tended to become his custom, he let the orchestra recede to the status of accompaniment when the "name" singers were performing. On March 17, the Desdemona* was Milanov. To some, including Edward Downes of *The New York Times,* this was the "highlight of her career. . . ."

The dramatic creation of this season was, undoubtedly, the Violetta* of Callas, in which she re-appeared on February 6. Cancelations and incomplete performances abroad cast a shadow of uncertainty on her arrival, but she mustered her strength to perform pridefully and with steadily cumulative dramatic effort. By the word of Taubman in the *Times,* she "sang better than at any time last season." This was flattering if disputable, as the role was quite different from Norma, Tosca, or Lucia. Barioni as Alfredo was hardly equal to the occasion, thus causing Lang in the *Herald Tribune* to accuse them both of singing flat when, if anything, he was slightly sharp. Mario Zanasi, who made his debut as Germont (d), contributed nothing of value, for he was a dull performer at best. At the end, it was the total immersion of Callas in her characterization (for which she had a new wardrobe designed by Gérard) which left a mark on the memory. She was, otherwise, seen in *Lucia* on February 13, with Bergonzi as a superior Edgardo, and Mario Sereni, who had made his debut as Gérard (d) in *Andrea Chénier* on November 9, as a routine Ashton. (He was, apparently, a replacement for the temperamental Bastianini, but lacking Bastianini's voice as well as his temper.) There was, altogether, too much of the Metropolitan routine in *Lucia, Tosca,* and *Traviata* this season, with two other new Edgardos* (Labò on January 20, when Dobbs was Lucia, Fernandi on February 25, with Callas) and Zanasi as another Ashton* on April 5, when Peters was the Lucia. What endured, and distressingly so, was the faded scenery and hardly more animated "direction" of Hans Busch. Bing's desire to perpetuate a Callas relationship and Callas's determination to have conditions of preparation that the Metropolitan could provide only for a new production finally found common ground in Verdi's *Macbeth*. They were, however, still unagreed on many details for this project when she left for Italy after a final *Tosca* on March 5.

In seeking out Boehm to strengthen the Metropolitan's sagging resource of conductors, Bing renewed an association that dated back to Darmstadt in the late twenties. Boehm succeeded, ironically, to much of the Mozart-Strauss-Wagner repertory that had once belonged, at the Metropolitan, to Fritz Busch (a longtime associate of Bing at Glyndebourne). The skein of circumstance that tied them all together had one further knot: when Busch was forcibly removed from his position in Dresden by the Nazis in 1933, it was Boehm who fell heir to this post which, before Busch, had been held by Fritz Reiner, who came to the Metropolitan when Busch left!

In addition to his estimable *Don Giovanni,* Boehm's first season included *Der Rosenkavalier* on November 22, with much the same cast as had been heard two years before: Della Casa, Stevens, Edelmann, and Gueden. If neither inflammatory nor mesmerizing, it was nevertheless a thoroughly Straussian *Rosenkavalier* in its emphasis on theatrical values and in the equal attention to voices and orchestra which carried the momentum of the music forward from one situation to another. On December 9, the Sophie was Peters, and on January 9 it became Hurley for the first time. In a late season performance on March 22 for which Steber was the Marschallin, the conductor was Rudolf.

This was one of the last Metropolitan performances to be conducted by Rudolf, who had come to America as a refugee from Nazi persecution in Prague and had patiently awaited an opportunity to work at the Metropolitan (see page 460). The increasing opportunities he enjoyed under Bing (with whom he, too, had worked in Darmstadt) found him impelled, more and more, by the dream of having an orchestra of his own. This came to him with the exit of Thor Johnson from the Cincinnati Symphony after a decade as its music director. His choice as Johnson's successor coincided with a year of ascension for Rudolf in his Metropolitan career, with the opportunity to conduct so special a work as Gluck's *Orfeo ed Eurydice* on December 16. Unfortunately, it returned with Stevens, whose voice was no more suitable than it had been in 1954-5, an unripe Amore* by Cundari, and, for a novelty, two Happy Shades (*Ombre Felici**) performed by Mildred Allen and Helen Vanni. This arrangement doubled shadiness while having felicity. Basically, then, Rudolf had one

wholly suitable singer, in Gueden (Eurydice). Musically, the performance was at its best when there was no singing at all, as Rudolf applied
himself to providing a suitable background for Markova's dancing in
the Elysian Fields. The staging was supervised by Nathaniel Merrill.
On January 10, the Eurydice* was Amara.

Leinsdorf's new place in the Metropolitan was intimately related to
Rudolf's imminent departure, though this did not become apparent at
once. It proceeded from Bing's decision, in the fall of 1957, to divide the
functions Rudolf had performed between Leinsdorf, as his advisor on
matters pertaining to the orchestra, and Robert Herman, as administrator
(under close supervision) of casting, personnel assignments, "cover" performers, etc. A product of the Opera Workshop at the University of
Southern California, where he had worked with Carl Ebert, Herman
had won commendation by the responsible way in which he had taken
hold of various assignments, beginning in the season of 1953-4 as
assistant stage manager for a revival of *Il Barbiere di Siviglia*. With Herman
Krawitz (likewise class of 1953-4) and Nathaniel Merrill (who came
along a little later), he was part of a group of young associates being
nurtured by Bing to provide the Metropolitan with what it had not recently
possessed—an administrative personnel that would function without respect
to changes on the top executive level.

Leinsdorf's principal assignment in this season was Mozart's *Figaro,*
which he had previously conducted in 1944-5 (see page 451). The
urgency and snap associated with the earlier venture were augmented by
finesse in the orchestral playing which added much (on December 19) to
the enjoyment purveyed by such expert Figarones as London, Siepi, Della
Casa, Miller, and Hurley (Susanna). Resnik was the more than ordinarily artistic Marcellina,* with Kelley as Don Basilio* and Corena as
Bartolo. Changes on later occasions were for the most part in terms of
such readily interchangeable parts as Singher (Almaviva), Peters
(Susanna), and Elias (Cherubino) on January 4, or Gueden (Susanna),
and Tozzi (Figaro) on January 11.

In addition to preparing the new productions of *Onegin* and *Butterfly,*
Mitropoulos continued as director of *Tosca* and *Salome,* also adding
Gianni Schicchi to his Metropolitan repertory as part of a double bill
with *Salome* on January 24. Puccini's comedy was now being given in
Italian, perhaps in deference to Corena as Schicchi.* Conner was Lauretta,
with Carelli as Rinuccio.* The Salome* was Inge Borkh (d) who brought
along, in addition to a powerful projection of the vocal line, a carefully
elaborated action. It was, on the whole, better before the awkwardly

executed dance (of the Wigman school), at the end of which she threw herself across the knees of Herod, than after. The total effect that Mitropoulos was capable of achieving in *Salome* was downgraded more than a little by the vocal insufficiencies of Kelley as Herod* (Vinay was promised, but withdrew) and of Mack Harrell, who looked better than he sounded as Jokanaan.* Thebom was the Herodias, with Crain as Narraboth* and William Wilderman a sonorous First Nazarene.* On February 8, when Hurley was Lauretta* in *Schicchi*, with Anthony as Rinuccio, Vinay performed Herod in *Salome*, with Gari as Narraboth. On February 17, the Lauretta* was Cundari, with Kullmann as Herod. The whole project took on another aspect when Leinsdorf became the conductor on March 1 and the changes in *Salome* included Resnik as Herodias,* Cassel as Jokanaan,* and William Lewis as Narraboth (d). When Mitropoulos returned on March 11, he had still another Herodias,* Madeira.

By contrast with the year before, there was no Wagner at all until the season was more than half over. As this could hardly be attributed to public preference, it must be explained as managerial convenience. The esteem that had accrued to Mödl the previous season earned her the opportunity to perform Isolde* on February 1—unfortunately without a suitable Tristan. Vinay began, but had to retire after Act II, when he was replaced by Da Costa, who had never sung the part on any stage. Dalis performed one of her best parts, Brangäne,* with Stiedry conducting, Edelmann as Marke,* and Cassel as Kurvenal.* Vinay regained his vocal health to sing Siegmund in *Die Walküre* four days later, with Stiedry conducting. Borkh was a powerfully athletic Sieglinde* in appearance and vocally capable as well, Wilderman added his name to the limited list of American-trained Hundings,* and Harshaw performed her capable Brünnhilde. On March 6, the Sieglinde was Schech, who apparently had been brought from Munich for the purpose. This time Da Costa was Siegmund,* with Dalis as Fricka* and Mödl as Brünnhilde. The accelerated exposure of Da Costa continued on March 14, when he performed the whole of Tristan* for the first time anywhere (replacing Vinay), with Harshaw as Isolde. For the final *Tristan*, on March 27, Grace Hoffman, an American-born mezzo who had learned her profession in Germany, was brought in to sing Brangäne (d). It was a serious, thoroughly studied effort, but lacking in vocal weight for the big auditorium. For some, Mödl's best Metropolitan effort was the Kundry* she sang to the Parsifal* of Vinay on March 20, with Harrell as Amfortas, Wilderman as Titurel,* and Hines as Gurnemanz. The principal victim of these uncertainties, next to Wagner, was Mödl, whose artistry (whatever her vocal problems vis-à-vis a particular role) merited something better than the company in which she was displayed.

As a company, indeed, the Metropolitan had become far from the "ensemble of stars, not comets" promised by Bing in 1950. Some of the difficulties were related to the gradual resumption of normal activity in Europe, the competition of German and Italian theaters for talent which had previously been in a buyer's market to the Metropolitan's advantage. But that would hardly explain the sorry condition to which *Carmen* had now descended.

At the first performance on December 4, which was the responsibility of Schippers for the first time, the performers were Stevens, Tucker, Guarrera, and Cundari (Micaëla). A week later they were Madeira, Gueden (Micaëla) and London, then Stevens, Bergonzi, Amara, and Merrill. By February 22, when Schippers had finished his season's work, and Adler was the conductor, the Carmen was Thebom, with Bergonzi, Hurley (Micaëla), and Zanasi (Escamillo*). To complain of Zanasi's lack of French style was to suggest its presence elsewhere in this performance, which would be sheer fantasy. Along with his duties as chorus master, Adler was called upon to conduct Steber's first Tosca* on February 8, an *Aida* on February 24, and even a *Bohème* on March 8, when Marcella Pobbé performed a small-scaled Mimi (d). As Rodolfo was a role for which Bergonzi was showing more and more disposition, his performance of it was the musical pleasure of this occasion. Pobbé came closer to home when she appeared as Marguerite* in *Faust* on March 29, but her operatic home away from home was not destined to be the Metropolitan. Circumstances compelled Adler to conduct a part of *La Forza del destino* on January 13. It began under the direction of Pietro Cimara, who became ill early in Act I and had to be helped from the pit. Concertmaster Walter Hagen stepped to the podium and beat time with his bow until Adler could be summoned to direct the Convent Scene (with which, as chorus master, he was thoroughly familiar). By Act II the conductor was Stiedry, who had been hastily summoned from what was to have been an evening off. After hospitalization, Cimara retired to Italy.

In place of such tenors of the recent past as Poggi, Penno, and Prandelli, the Metropolitan acquired not only the sound if conventional talents of Bergonzi and Labò, but also the unconventional ones of Nicolai Gedda. A product of the Paris Opéra, Gedda resisted the temptation of an offer from the City Center, reserving his first New York appearance for the Metropolitan and its promise of a lasting career. There was some question,

at his debut on November 1 as Faust* (with Gueden as Marguerite,*
Hines, and Guarrera), of whether Gedda had the vocal substance to sustain leading roles in this theater (the top C of *"Salut! demeure"* was,
like the house to which it was addressed, non-existent, being lowered to
B). But Gedda showed qualifications of style, personality, and intelligence
much rarer than vocal abundance. A capable Don Ottavio* in *Don
Giovanni* on November 13 (the best-looking, perhaps, since Schipa) and
a brilliant characterization of Anatol* in *Vanessa* marked Gedda as
versatile beyond the range of most tenors of his time. He was even
amenable to appearing as the Singer* in *Rosenkavalier* on January 18.

Doubtless because the season had been planned to include a series
of *Otellos* with Tebaldi, it was also planned to include a series of *Samsons*
with Del Monaco, the preferable Otello, occupied alternately as Samson.
With him on March 13 were Stevens, Singher as the High Priest, and
Tozzi as the Old Hebrew.* However, it required more than a change
of tenors or an amended Bacchanale with Carmen de Lavallade and
Hubert Farrington to alter the character of the work as long as it was
conducted by Fausto Cleva. His inappropriately Italian emphasis was
not altogether inappropriate for the effort of Del Monaco, a Samson
all ring and virility, but it diminished by much the elements in it which
were personal to Saint-Saëns.

A good deal was made, in advance of the event, of the debut on February 12 of Gloria Davy as Aida (d). This related to her background as a
graduate of the New York High School of Music and Art who had
proceeded from the Juilliard School to success in Berlin. In terms of the
Metropolitan, however, Davy was clearly a lyric soprano who had been
inflated to the status of an Aida largely because she happened to be
a Negro. A conscientious as well as a graceful performer, Davy was
vocally overmatched in the company of Warren, Dalis (Amneris), Baum,
and Wilderman (Ramfis*), especially in the ensembles. She would have
been better placed, for a debut, as Pamina, perhaps. On the other hand,
Helen Vanni, whose debut the season before as the page in *Rigoletto* on
November 9, 1956, had passed without much notice, began in this
season to show the qualities that eventually made her an accomplished
operatic performer.

The end of February was marked, non-operatically, by the official
allocation of a three-block area within the Lincoln Square Urban Renewal
Project for the Lincoln Center for the Performing Arts to include the
new Metropolitan. On July 28, 1958, demolition began of the old brownstones and decrepit business structures which covered the area. It was
believed that the new Opera House might be completed by 1962.

Late in the summer, an Australian soprano en route to England from Vancouver, British Columbia, where she had performed for the first time in the Western Hemisphere, applied for and was granted an audition. The group of Metropolitan officials who heard her (Rudolf Bing was not among them, as he had not yet returned from his European holiday) decided that there was no place on their stage for Joan Sutherland— though the Donna Anna she had sung in Vancouver was at least superior to Mary Curtis-Verna's.

1958–1959

While musical New York was waiting, in 1950, to form an opinion of Rudolf Bing as general manager of the Metropolitan, *The New York Times* provided some foreshadowings of his tastes and inclinations by asking him to identify his ten favorite operas. Not many of them were unexpected, and not all were included among the new productions he sponsored in his first five, six, or eight years. But the ninth season included the least expectable of them—Alban Berg's *Wozzeck*.

For some, this was a deplorably late recognition by the Metropolitan of a work whose importance in the musical panorama of the twentieth century would be conceded by almost all shades of informed opinion. Its first American performance dated to March 19, 1931, when the Philadelphia Grand Opera (an auxiliary of the Philadelphia Orchestra) had performed it under Stokowski's direction. Its first New York performance had followed in the fall of that year (November 24, 1931), when the Metropolitan made its auditorium available for a repetition of Stokowski's Philadelphia production (in which it did not otherwise participate). It had since been heard in a concert performance by the New York Philharmonic under the direction of Mitropoulos in April 1951 and at the City Center, with Rosenstock conducting, in 1952.

Thus Bing's initiative was relative and localized, but, in terms of the institution with which it was concerned, a wide deviation from the kind of experience to which most of its patrons were customarily exposed. The conclusion, therefore, was that they should have the consideration of hearing the work performed in their own language. Considering the nature of the theatrical experience and the power of the music in which it was embodied, the decision was at least debatable. On balance it was determined that theatrical advantage outweighed musical disadvantage.

What eventually proved to be the determining factor of advantage was the foresight of Hermann Uhde in being born of an English-speaking mother and a German-speaking father. He grew up speaking both languages (though a native of Germany, he actually heard his first opera at the Metropolitan when he visited New York with his American-born mother), and thus had the uncommon attribute of understanding the Germanic type of "little man" represented by Büchner's character, and being able to articulate, almost idiomatically, the English translation by Eric Blackall and Vida Harford.

Uhde's work in the previous seasons had certified him as an uncommonly intelligent performer, but it had not probed his capacity to think, to stand, and to act like Wozzeck, even less to provide a dryly accurate re-creation of Berg's musical line. Together they made it possible for him to engage the attention on almost all possible levels of listener awareness. For such a miscellaneous audience as the Metropolitan's, this was of considerable consequence. Of hardly less consequence were the unanimity and the power of the playing Boehm drew out of the orchestra. This was, in part, a by-product of the experience derived from teaching *Wozzeck* to otherwise unindoctrinated orchestras in Vienna, Buenos Aires, and Naples. It enabled Boehm to take maximum advantage of the rehearsal time at his disposal (more than the Metropolitan's customary allotment, but still hardly excessive).

Had everything else been of the Boehm-Uhde quality, the Metropolitan's first *Wozzeck*, on March 5, would have been a string of well-matched pearls. As it was, none, at least, was paste. Steber's well-fleshed outlines hardly suggested a Marie mired in poverty, but she made a searing vocal effect in some high-lying passages and humanized the character she performed, especially in the scenes with the child. A striking study of the Doctor* was provided by Karl Dönch, a Viennese veteran who had made his debut as Beckmesser (d), another of his specialities, on January 22. Graf's direction wove Paul Franke's Captain* and the Drum Major of Baum,* pompous and muscular, into an ensemble that almost reconciled diversities of speech and background. Ezio Flagello as an Apprentice* and Charles Anthony (Andres*) contributed usefully in their roles.

Least persuasive, perhaps, in this production underwritten by the Francis Goelet Foundation were the scenic designs of Caspar Neher. Whatever they might have been in their original form on the German stage, they did not adapt well to the needs of the Metropolitan. The most that could be said was that they were functional, that the scene changes could be accomplished within the time provided in Berg's musical interludes.

The first performance, in accordance with prevailing custom, was a benefit for the Metropolitan Opera Guild. At the prices that were asked, public interest was less than avid. There would, indeed, have been embarrassing patches of empty seats had not a substantial number of professional musicians and others who would not ordinarily have attended been "invited." Uhde's excellent effort, and occasional brilliant moments by the others made a steadily more absorbing effect as scene succeeded scene. Eventually, Boehm's powerful statement of the climaxing interlude (in which Berg laments the collapse of Wozzeck's world) and the anti-climax of the final scene brought an outburst of applause that proved two things—an audience had been waiting for *Wozzeck* at the Metropolitan and it found Boehm's treatment to its taste.

The four performances that followed were neither warmly welcomed nor coldly rejected. There were, inevitably, those who came late and left early; and as many who stayed through, but found the subject matter grubby and distasteful. But an even larger number (or so it appeared to me) derived a measure of contact with Berg's world that otherwise would have been denied to them, and found the experience absorbing. There was no opportunity for Marko Rothmüller, Uhde's alternate, to perform, but Brenda Lewis was the Marie* (dramatically vivid, vocally strained) on March 23. At a later performance (April 1) Da Costa was the Drum Major,* with Alvary as the Doctor* and William Lewis as Andres.*

The public that had been deprived of Tebaldi's presence in the previous season did not have to wait long for a reacquaintance in this one. Together with Del Monaco and London, she was the lure to bring $86,687 for the opening *Tosca* on October 27, with Mitropoulos conducting. Also, Aoyama was again in New York, and spent many hours indoctrinating her in the action as well as the appearance of Butterfly* as he conceived it. The result, as seen on November 8, was to disguise her height and make her a much more believable Butterfly than would have seemed possible. An unexpected factor of quality in this year's series of *Butterfly* performances was the conducting of Leinsdorf, carefully detailed, yet vital. His resourcefulness was tested on more than one occasion, for the understandable impulse to exploit the much-admired new property resulted in ten performances. At the first of these, on November 4, with Los Angeles as Butterfly, the Pinkerton (d) was Barry Morell, a New York-born tenor gifted enough as well as young enough to grow into a sound performer in a variety of roles. In the first Tebaldi performance it was Fernandi, and at the second (on November 19) Morell. In between, on November 15, Leinsdorf had the rare opportunity of supervising the debut of the first Japanese-born performer to appear at the Metropolitan. This was the oval-faced, petite Kunie Imai, who showed a somewhat larger sound as Butterfly (d) than such predecessors—heard elsewhere in

New York than at the Metropolitan—as Tamaki Miura and Hizi Koyke. At maximum it was barely enough, otherwise it was insufficient. But she was an engaging performer. On the first of December, the Butterfly was Albanese, and eventually Stella sang the role again.

Though neither *Cavalleria* nor *Pagliacci* was included on the list of the General Manager's ten favorite operas, they did become the first attraction during his tenure to be provided with a second "new production," on November 7. Doubtless the limited cost of the Armistead treatment (see page 504) made it more dispensable than would otherwise have been the case, for his sets for *Pagliacci* had been discarded, rather than worn out. What had worn out was the older (1924) Novak production of *Pagliacci,* which had been restored to use during recent seasons. Rolf Gérard's settings (the production was sponsored by the National Council) were hardly among his best, tending to the travel-folder school of realism, but they were clean and atmospheric, as conventional as Armistead's were not. For its staging, Bing turned to José Quintero, a Broadway (and off-Broadway) director who provided a well-organized plan for the *Pagliacci,* and some useful guidance for Amara's Nedda. However time seemed to have run out before he could put much of a personal impression on *Cavalleria.*

The suggestion that Mitropoulos could do something with Mascagni or Leoncavallo that another conductor could not do foundered on such immovable objects as Del Monaco's Canio, with its vulgarized *"Vesti la giubba,"* and the standardized exaggerations of Milanov's Santuzza. The good singing of Warren as Tonio and the Lola of Elias were incidental to a substandard Alfio by Bardelli and the lamentable Turiddu* of a transient tenor named Primo Zambruno.

This otherwise obscure performer earned a place on the Metropolitan stage by being "available" when Flaviano Labò decided that Turiddu, which he had contracted to perform, was not for him. This resulted in double punishment for the public: acquaintance with Zambruno and deprivation of Labò in everything else when he was summarily dismissed for failing to perform Turiddu.

Zambruno endured for a second performance on November 10 and even a third on November 20, two more than maximum tolerance would have suggested. On November 28, the Turiddu* was Barioni, risking damage to a voice that was not meant for violent outbursts. When the production returned later in the season, changes included Rankin as Santuzza,* Zanasi as Alfio, and Vanni as Lola* in *Cavalleria,* with Davy as Nedda* (her best Metropolitan effort), Baum as Canio, and Merrill as Tonio in *Pagliacci.* It mattered little, however, how much this cast differed from the one originally rehearsed: Mitropoulos was now hospital-ized, and the conductor was Adler.

The prospect of Maria Callas as Lady Macbeth in the Metropolitan's third new production of this season vanished even more abruptly than it had arisen with the terse words "Bing Fires Callas" in the press of November 7. The justification for this action, the General Manager stated, was the singer's insistence on altering a schedule agreed upon by them only weeks before. It provided for two performances of *La Traviata* on February 13 and 17, between the *première* of *Macbeth* on February 5 and a repetition on February 21. As B. H. Haggin observed in a com-mentary in *The Hudson Review* later in the winter: "Her decision not to sing *La Traviata* in alternation with *Macbeth* was the sort of thing that happens in opera companies all the time, and the sort of thing that is always handled and settled by private persuasion and mutual accommo-dation, not by public martinet-like assertion of power that Mr. Bing seems to like to indulge in when he can. . . ."

It was Callas's suggestion that the *Traviatas* be assigned to another singer and her contract (which called for twenty-six performances divided almost evenly between New York and the spring tour) be amended to deduct them. As for the suggested alternatives, *Lucia* or *Tosca,* she considered them "even worse" between Lady Macbeths, a role which, in her own words, was "very heavy." To her declaration "My voice is not like an elevator going up and down," Bing replied that the eight days allotted between *Macbeth* and *Traviata* was "a pretty long time for experienced artists to adjust their voices."

Beyond standing on the letter of the agreement and imposing a penalty for its abrogation—both, for better or worse, within his prerogative as general manager—Bing added a series of comments which were both gratuitous and self-serving:

"I doubt if anyone will be surprised at the present turn of events. Although Mme Callas's artistic qualifications are a matter of violent con-troversy between her friends and foes, her reputation for projecting her undisputed histrionic talents into her business affairs is a matter of common knowledge." And, as if the dismissal itself were not enough of an affront to pride, Bing found himself compelled to say, also:

"Let us all be grateful that we have had the experience of her artistry for two seasons; for reasons, however, which the musical press and public can well understand, the Metropolitan is nevertheless grateful that the association is ended."

Whatever the feelings of the "Metropolitan" (which, of course, meant Bing), few others could find the dismissal of Callas a reason to be "grateful." To Bing's contention that the issue boiled down to "the question of whether the stars or the management run the opera," the only answer could be: bunk. His disposition to accede in more fundamental matters of musical importance—who sang what high notes, the transposition of arias at the convenience of the performer, the indulgence by even a Mitropoulos of the whims of a Del Monaco—were more important concessions to personal preference than the rearrangement of a performance schedule. Unquestionably Callas had agreed to it; she clearly had had second thoughts on the wisdom of the arrangements. But there seems no urgent reason why Bing should have set a deadline of 10 a.m. on November 6 for the resolution of differences about a happening not days or weeks, but three *months* away. If the deadline was calculated to arouse her resistance in Dallas, where she was preparing to perform Cherubini's *Medea* that evening, it did exactly that. No reply was received (it would have been 9 a.m. Dallas time) and the telegraphed notice of cancelation thus had its legalistic basis.

For her part, Callas did not reap all the benefits that might have accrued to her as an injured party. To the expressions, in print, of hurt feelings for what she considered an unjustified action, she added her spoken preference (in a TV interview), for "doing art" in Dallas rather than appearing in the "lousy productions" at the Metropolitan. And, in the days to come, she contributed to the controversy by collaborating on articles for the Hearst press which were displayed, over her by-line, in banner headlines proclaiming "Maria Callas Tells What's Wrong with Opera!"

Behind the so-called "big issues" lurked smaller ones which might, in the end, have been of controlling importance. One was Callas's reliance upon her husband, Meneghini, in answering telephoned inquiries from the Metropolitan. As he spoke no English or German and Bing spoke no Italian, this required the intercession of Bing's assistant, John Gutman, which irked his superior more than a little. And, having assured himself of the services of Leonie Rysanek, Bing was in the position to rid himself of an annoyance and launch a new career at the same time. In short, the "star" in this instance was Bing himself, who wanted things *his* own way regardless of consequences.

The prospect of *Macbeth* with Callas as Lady Macbeth and Mitropoulos conducting its first performance ever at the Metropolitan promised a certain kind of absorbing experience. The actuality of February 5 was quite another thing. It lacked not only Callas, but also Mitropoulos, who was hospitalized with a heart attack he had suffered on January 23. There being no "logical" replacement to conduct a work so little known as

Macbeth, it became the responsibility of Leinsdorf, whose boldness in performing, at the Metropolitan, works he had never conducted elsewhere was part of his, as well as its, history (see page 418).

In the circumstances, what Leinsdorf did was unquestionably a credit to his determination as well as to his talent for quick study. In terms of Verdi's score, it was no more than broadly approximate, responsive to the black and white of the printed page, but quite unresponsive to the careful markings by which the composer sought to shade black and white into areas of gray. In the instrumental prelude alone there are as many as *fifty* marks of stress to a page, of which Leinsdorf enforced perhaps a minor fraction.

Thus, the skilled hand to reconcile the differences between Verdi's early treatment of *Macbeth* and his revisions of eighteen years later was, in the main, lacking. The result was, in a word, crude. However, it cannot be said that it was out of keeping with the staging. For the production underwritten by The Metropolitan Opera Guild, Bing welcomed his old friend Carl Ebert (see page 483) as stage director and, in turn, united him with designer Casper Neher, who had been Ebert's associate twenty-five years before in a Berlin revival of *Macbeth.* What the Metropolitan audience saw, then, was a revival of a revival, done in an ornate way (an ugly painted flat of a huge staircase dominated the first interior) which suffered appallingly from recent memory of an Old Vic production not many blocks away. The banquet hall scene might have served some operas well, but it was inappropriately bright for this grisly one. Nor was there adequate explanation, theatrical or musical, for the allegorical drop curtain depicting Duncan which settled into place over the heads of the ensemble at the end of Act I for an "oratorio" finale.

Ebert's hand could be discerned in the movement of masses and in groupings of the ensemble, but very little in Warren's Macbeth,* the Banquo* of Hines, or Bergonzi's Macduff.* All of them (also William Olvis as Malcolm*) had vocal qualities to serve Verdi profitably, but they lacked informed leadership from Leinsdorf and creative direction from Ebert to make them more than one-dimensional symbols of the characters they purported to represent.

By much the strongest effort was provided by Rysanek, whose Lady Macbeth (d) defined her as a meticulous and conscientious musician, with a blossoming spread of volume at the top of her range. The sleep-walking scene had a degree of traumatic power in its action and vocalization which proclaimed Rysanek to be that operatic rarity, a true stage personality. She even made the handsome gesture of providing the "thread of voice" that Verdi specified for its top D flat. In later performances, changes were minimal, with Morell as Macduff* on March 16.

It was, in a sense, a fortunate if trying circumstance for Rysanek that she made her debut in a role with the peculiar difficulties of Lady Macbeth. By rigorous diet, she had reduced nearly forty pounds since New York had first seen her in a concert performance of *Macbeth*, in Carnegie Hall under Thomas Scherman, the previous winter, which was all to the advantage of her appearance. Her success with the high range of the writing minimized her weakness in the lower octave and disguised the thickness of sound in her middle register. These flaws of production and her lack of consistent focus through the full range of the voice became more apparent in her Aida* on February 25 (with Rankin, Warren, Bergonzi, and Siepi) and her Elisabetta* in *Don Carlo* on March 14 (with Fernandi as Carlo,* Siepi, Merrill, Uhde, Rankin as Eboli, Martina Arroyo in her debut as the Celestial Voice,* and Cleva conducting). In the light of the Callas controversy, it is worth noting that Rysanek sang no other role in the period of her first *three* performances of Lady Macbeth, and that the hotly argued *Traviata* of February 13 quietly became *Bohème*, with Albanese and Peerce.

The illness of Mitropoulos would have been more than an inconvenience to the Metropolitan in any of his recent seasons. In this one, it was close to a calamity. For two or three seasons, he had gradually been reducing his work load at the Philharmonic, looking to the time when Leonard Bernstein would become music director, and had been increasing his activities at the Metropolitan. This transition came about in the fall of 1958, enabling him to undertake the direction of seven operas, including the new *Cavalleria-Pagliacci* and *Macbeth*.

The subtraction of Mitropoulos and the illness which ended Walter's operatic career, together with the separation of Rudolf (to his new position in Cincinnati) and Stiedry (to retirement in Switzerland), left the Metropolitan less provided with experienced and able conductors than at any time within memory. In a swift reversal of a situation, which as of 1956, or two years before, had seemed stabilized, it recalled the abruptness with which Johnson's resource of Wagnerian sopranos— Flagstad, Lawrence, and Traubel—had dwindled to Traubel alone in 1941 (which is simply to say that no opera company can ever have too much of a good thing).

The immediate consequence was to install Ignace Strasfogel, who had assisted in their preparation, as conductor of *Eugen Onegin* on January 26 (Gedda as Lenski was a welcome addition to a cast otherwise as it had been) and *Vanessa* on January 30. Strasfogel's musical background was extensive and largely operatic, dating (at the Metropolitan) to 1950. Judgment of his capacities, as was the case with Adler, Rich, et al., was sharply limited by the managerial disposition to use them almost exclusively in the role of "takeover" or caretaker conductor of operas that had been rehearsed by others.

The other works for which Mitropoulos was responsible were divided between Leinsdorf (*Macbeth* and *Boris*) and Adler (*Tosca* and *Cavalleria-Pagliacci*). Even more trying, perhaps, was the need to "cover" the performances of *Tosca, Traviata,* and *Lucia* from which Callas had been barred by the impetuous action of Bing. This may account for three appearances of Curtis-Verna as Tosca and a reappearance of Dolores Wilson as Lucia on March 9 (for which Pons had been announced) in a performance conducted by Adler. Since her last Metropolitan appearance (Susanna on March 26, 1958), Wilson had been hospitalized for a neck injury, and the strain of performance bore heavily on her. She managed to finish the "Mad Scene," but collapsed when she reached the dressing room. This was her last performance with the company. For Adler, there was a stretch of unexampled activity. Between March 7 and March 12 (inclusive) he conducted *every* performance given, including, in addition to this *Lucia,* two double bills of *Cavalleria rusticana* and *Pagliacci,* and a *Tosca* with Steber, Morell as Cavaradossi,* and London. In the course of the season, he was also called upon for *Rigoletto* on December 19 and *Traviata* on January 24. The problems incidental to the absence of Mitropoulos were rather intensified by the need of relief, from time to time, for Cleva, whose schedule provided for eight of the most performed works in the repertory. He became ill during the third act of *Manon Lescaut* on December 22, and had to give up in favor of the concertmaster, Raymond Gniewek. The performance continued while George Schick was summoned to the pit to finish the act. Cleva's difficulty was diagnosed as a digestive disorder, and he returned for Act IV. It was a graphic introduction to the problems of the Metropolitan for Schick, an experienced musician with an operatic background in Prague and as assistant conductor of the Chicago Symphony who had been added to the staff when Rudolf left. He had his first opportunity with a full opera on February 18, when he conducted *Rigoletto* in place of Cleva, and he was Schippers's replacement for *Un Ballo in maschera* on March 19, when Morell was the Riccardo, with Sereni, Curtis-Verna as Amelia,* and Resnik (Ulrica*).

Schippers's season added to *Bohème* not only *Ballo in maschera,* for which he had some relevant sense of style, but also *Lohengrin,* for which he did not. His ideas of the latter were first encountered on

December 26, when his mostly experienced cast included Sullivan, Edelmann, Harshaw, and Uhde. Della Casa's first Elsa* was an occurrence to anticipate, for a performer who sang Eva as she did could be expected to do equally well her "older sister." Perhaps for lack of the helping hand she required from a conductor, Della Casa's performance did not realize its promise. Schippers's thoughts on the prelude were sound and well conveyed to the orchestra, but he had little conception of the balance that should prevail between orchestra and voices in Wagner. Where they were loud or soft at the same time, a proper blend was achieved; but where the orchestra should dominate and carry the voices, it was consistently played down. There was little here that could not be improved with experience, but the Metropolitan is hardly the place for a conductor to acquire experience in conducting *Lohengrin*. In such circumstances, *Lohengrin* with Schippers conducting was hardly the work in which to make a Metropolitan debut this season, a fate that befell Aase Nordmo Loevberg as Elsa (d) and Karl Liebl as Lohengrin (d) on February 11. A good-looking young woman with a promising lyric voice, Nordmo Loevberg had made her New York debut with the Philadelphia Orchestra the previous winter when a Scandinavian colleague (Birgit Nilsson) was unable to make the trip to America. Musical visitors to Scandinavia in this period were advised that Nordmo Loevberg was "the next Flagstad," but she did not make the transition from the Verdi to the Wagner repertory well enough even to become Nordmo Loevberg. Though Liebl's sound was smaller than a Metropolitan Lohengrin should have, it was a pleasant sound used with an assurance that qualified him for a lengthy career in these surroundings. The Herald* in most performances was Mario Sereni, sounding exactly as he was— an Italian baritone trying to sing German. Aside from Stella as Amelia,* one of her better roles (on January 2) and the Ulrica* of Amparan (on February 9), most of the singers for Schippers's *Ballo* were as they had been three seasons before. Schick's, however, was different (see page 610).

For reasons that must be related to the competence of their conductor, the productions that most consistently sustained a Metropolitan "standard" in this season were those supervised by Boehm. While preparing his memorable *Wozzeck,* Boehm reinstated the always welcome Berman *Don Giovanni* on January 15 (with Siepi, Corena, Valletti, Steber, Della Casa, and Peters) and rejuvenated the equally welcome *Meistersinger* on January 22. The qualified success of the effort to make an acceptable Wagner tenor of Da Costa could be read in the debut of Sebastian Feiersinger as Walther (d). He was the conventional kind of small-voiced, rather portly German tenor who owed his Metropolitan exposure to the lack of better qualified performers. The winner of the factual contest or song, if not the fictional, this time was Beckmesser (d) as impersonated by the resourceful Karl Dönch. Resnik's Magdalene* was warmly characterized and well sung, if a shade maternal for the David of Franke. Others in the cast included Edelmann, Tozzi (Pogner), Della Casa, and Marko Rothmüller (Kothner [d]). A veteran of the post-war German theater who had now joined the faculty of the Opera School at Indiana University, Rothmüller provided the Metropolitan with an experienced understudy for several roles, including Wozzeck, which he had performed at the City Center. In the matinee *Meistersinger,* on March 7, Nordmo Loevberg was rather more settled as Eva* than she had been as Elsa. The David on March 20 was Anthony, likable in action, a little undersized in sound (he had sung the part previously on February 21), with Wilderman as Pogner and Da Costa as Walther.

Except for *Lohengrin* and *Die Meistersinger,* the Wagner repertory was conspicuously absent. In place of the semi-customary *Parsifal,* the Easter season offered two performances of Verdi's *Requiem,* with Bruno Walter conducting. His preferred soprano was Milanov, but she became ill the day before the first performance, on March 27, and Krall was considered the best qualified replacement. She met the emergency with commendable poise, but neither the sound of the voice nor the way it was used was really suitable for this work. Bergonzi's effort qualified him as the best tenor for this music since Bjoerling, and Elias made much of the opportunity to display her rich middle register. The art of Tozzi was more of a contribution than his sound to the quality of the quartet, because he lacked depth and impact for such phrases as *"Mors stupebit."* By March 29 (Sunday) Milanov felt able to take part in the Requiem as well as the Convent Scene of *Forza* which preceded it, but she became faint after the *Dies Irae,* and Krall took over. This was, incidentally, Walter's final appearance as a Metropolitan conductor.

Unlike some seasons that had offered three or four works of Mozart, his repertory this year was restricted to *Don Giovanni* and *The Magic Flute,* the latter conducted by Leinsdorf when it reappeared on November 18. Dignity rather than fantasy was the tonality of this *Flute,* in which Tozzi was a welcome addition as Sarastro,* Gedda spread charm with his appearance, pleasure with his singing, and clarity with his command of the English text as Tamino,* and Davy as Pamina* had an opportunity more in keeping with her abilities. The lively tenor sound of William Olvis was heard in his debut as the Second Priest (d), though lack of experience limited the profit he could derive from it. Uppman and Allen were excellent, as before, but Peters fared poorly as Queen of the Night. On January 9 Valletti sang a characteristically capable Tamino.*

What had been publicized three seasons before as a "Farewell to *Fledermaus*" turned out to have been merely an *auf wiedersehen* when the masterful operetta and its familiar production by Rolf Gérard returned on November 27. Doubtless it was owing to the influence of Leinsdorf, who conducted, that the treatment was marked by such touches of scholarship as the use of an accordion in an interpolated performance of *Tales from the Vienna Woods* for balletic purposes in Act II. Less scholarship and a more flexible beat would have been preferable. John Brownlee, who had gracefully achieved a transition from singing to other activities, was engaged as stage director to indoctrinate Guarrera (Falke*), Valletti (Alfred*), and Uppman (Eisenstein*) with some of the humor that came so easily to him. The results were variable, especially with Valletti, whose artistic intelligence appeared to rebel against the caricature of it he was required to provide. Such others as Gueden (Rosalinda), Peters (Adele), and Harvuot (Frank) were already indoctrinated, as was Thebom as Orlofsky. On December 31, the Orlofsky* was Resnik, who was joined by Hurley as Adele* on January 10 (Munsel was no longer a member of the company). On April 8, Jean Fenn made one of her infrequent appearances, as Rosalinda.* John Butler devised a showy ballet for the ballroom scene, in which Lupe Serrano and Jacques d'Amboise were guests of the management as well as of Prince Orlofsky.

Concern for the Metropolitan's dance component was evident also in the engagement of Alexandra Danilova to supervise the "Dance of the Hours" in *La Gioconda*. What was seen at the first performance on December 11 was more than creditable to her influence, but it required a better disciplined ensemble than the Metropolitan possessed to support the standard of the imported soloists, Serrano and Scott Douglas. The enduring memories of this *Gioconda* were, musically, the Barnaba* of Merrill, not so much for the power of *"O monumento"* as for the lightness and agility with which he led *"Pescator, affonda l'esca"* in Act II, and dramatically, the obedient way in which the good ship *Hecate* blew up on schedule though the torch tossed into it by Tucker (Enzo) was obviously a dud. What Cleva had to conduct was, if not an all-star cast, an all-strong one: Milanov, Rankin (who sang an excellent *"Deh! non turbare"*), Tozzi as Alvise, and Amparan as La Cieca, in addition to

Merrill and Tucker. On March 18, the Laura* was Elias, with Mignon Dunn, who had made her debut as the Nurse (d) in *Boris Godunov* on October 29, as La Cieca.

The notion that the Metropolitan might, somehow, produce a tenant for the dance theater that was now a part of the Lincoln Center plan may have been part of the impetus for a full evening's performance by its ballet on March 22 (a Sunday, when the theater was otherwise unoccupied). The curious combination of elements brought together new ballets by John Butler (*In the Beginning*), Herbert Ross (*The Exchange*), Danilova (*Les Diamants*), and Tudor (*Hail and Farewell*), with a cross section of well-known dancers including Nora Kaye, Bambi Linn, Bruce Marks, Tommy Andrew, Serrano, and Douglas. For all the stimulation that the visiting notables provided, the performance of the *corps* left little doubt that there could be no miracle on Thirty-ninth Street until a good deal more effort had been applied to fundamentals under thoroughly qualified direction.

With Callas banished and Rysanek still to be established in public favor, a heavy burden of sustaining the standard repertory was put upon Tebaldi. In addition to her first Butterfly (see page 604), the season also provided for acquaintance with her Manon Lescaut* when the Puccini score was given on December 3 under Cleva's direction. This was, on the whole, one of her most appealing conceptions, well suited to her vocally (especially in Act II and thereafter), and dramatically within her capabilities. Tucker was Des Grieux, with Guarrera as Lescaut and Flagello as Geronte.* It was, indeed, intended to serve as her farewell for the season on January 23, but Tebaldi was unable to perform. Substitution of another singer would have fulfilled the management obligation to the houseful of ticket-holders, but it was deemed wiser, in the interest of public faith, to change the opera (it became a Curtis-Verna–Tucker–Cassel *Tosca*), thus enabling those who had bought tickets specifically for Tebaldi rather than Puccini to request refunds. The cost of the gesture was $11,000. On March 13, when the Manon Lescaut was Albanese, Bergonzi sang a particularly good Des Grieux,* with Sereni as Lescaut.*

For many, the first of Tebaldi's roles remained her best, as the return of *Otello* on November 15 recalled. With her as Desdemona were Del Monaco and Warren. She was also in the cast on December 9 when Tito Gobbi performed his craftily calculated Iago* in a performance commemorating the 150th anniversary of the founding of G. Ricordi, publishers of this and many other scores. Funds from the large audience that paid benefit prices to be present were divided equally among the

Henry E. Abbey

Edmond C. Stanton

Walter and Leopold Damrosch

Maurice Grau

Heinrich Conried

Managers of the Metropolitan—I

Giulio Gatti-Casazza

Andreas Dippel (as Raoul in *Les Huguenots*)

Edward Ziegler, Earle Lewis, Edward Johnson

Managers of the Metropolitan—II

Herbert Witherspoon

Rudolf Bing (right) with Mrs. August Belmont, founder and president emeritus of the Metropolitan Opera Guild, during intermission of 1961 opening performance.

Anton Seidl

Alfred Hertz

Gustav Mahler, from a
mezzotint by Emil Orlik

Arturo Toscanini

Artur Bodanzky

Metropolitan Conductors—I

Tullio Serafin

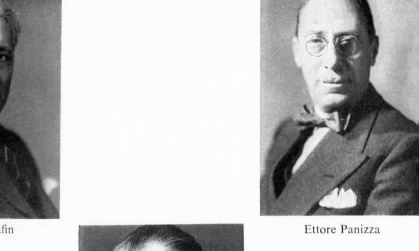

Ettore Panizza

Erich Leinsdorf

George Szell

Bruno Walter

Metropolitan Conductors—II

Fritz Stiedry

Sir Thomas Beecham

Fritz Busch

Fritz Reiner

Jonel Perlea

Metropolitan Conductors—III

Dimitri Mitropoulos

Karl Boehm

Thomas Schippers

Georges Prêtre

Zubin Mehta

Metropolitan Conductors—IV

Enrico Caruso as Radames, Adamo Didur as Ramfis, in the consecration scene of *Aida* on the first Toscanini opening night (November 16, 1908)

Angelo Bada as Prince Shuisky, Adamo Didur as Boris Godunov, in *Boris Godunov*, first American performance (March 19, 1913)

Productions—I

Final scene from *L'Amore dei tre re* (1917-18 season), with Pasquale Amato as Manfredo, Claudia Muzio as Fiora, José Mardones as Archibaldo

Scene from Act II of *Fidelio* (1914-15 season) with Arthur Middleton as Fernando, Otto Goritz as Pizarro, Jacques Urlus as Florestan, Margarete Matzenauer as Leonore, Elisabeth Schumann as Marzelline, Carl Braun as Rocco, Albert Reiss as Jaquino

Productions—II

Opening scene from *Le Nozze di Figaro* (1948-9 season), with Alessio de Paolis as Basilio, Jarmila Novotna as Cherubino, John Brownlee as the Count, Bidú Sayão as Susanna

Act III scene from *Il Barbiere di Siviglia* (1940-1 season), with Irra Petina as Berta, Josephine Tuminia as Rosina, Ezio Pinza as Don Basilio, Salvatore Baccaloni as Doctor Bartolo, John Charles Thomas as Figaro, Bruno Landi as Almaviva

Productions—III

Joan Sutherland as Amina and Nicola Gedda as Elvino in *La Sonnambula*

Maria Callas in *Lucia di Lammermoor*, with Nicola Moscona as Raimondo, Paul Franke as Arturo, and Thelma Votipka as Alisa (background)

Productions—IV

Otto Wiener as Hans Sachs (right) and Karl Doench as Beckmesser in Act II of *Die Meistersinger*. At left, Sandor Konya as Walther and Ingrid Bjoner as Eva

Risë Stevens (Carmen) and Richard Tucker (Don José) in Act I of *Carmen*

Productions—V

Entrance of Butterfly in Act I of *Madama Butterfly*, with Antonietta Stella as Cio-Cio-San, Eugenio Fernandi (left) as Pinkerton, and Mario Zanasi as Sharpless

Birgit Nilsson as Turandot (Act II). In the background, Alessio de Paolis as the Emperor

Productions—VI

Franco Zeffirelli directs Anselmo Colzani as Falstaff in the wooing of Mistress Ford (Gabriella Tucci) in Act II of *Falstaff*. Looking on, Leonard Bernstein

Tyrone Guthrie (rear) and Hans Busch, who assisted him in the staging of *La Traviata*, attempt to exercise persuasion on Renata Tebaldi (Violetta)

Rehearsals—I

Alfred Lunt demonstrates an action to Eleanor Steber
as Fiordiligi for his staging of *Così fan tutte*

Lotte Lehmann, as consultant for the staging of *Der Rosenkavalier*,
pantomimes an attitude. At left conductor Lorin Maazel

Rehearsals—II

Margaret Webster studies an effect in her staging of *Simon Boccanegra*

Rehearsals—III

Farewell to the Old Met. Cesare Siepi sings his part of the Gala Farewell before a stage full of past performers. Left to right, front row: Risë Stevens, Marjorie Lawrence, Elisabeth Rethberg, Martha Lipton, Lotte Lehmann, Helen Jepson. Across the aisle: Ruth Miller, Hertha Glaz, Vilma Georgiou, Anna Case, Rose Bampton, and Marian Anderson. In the second row: Alexander Kipnis, Raoul Jobin, Frederick Jagel. Across the aisle: Richard Crooks, Eugene Conley, Mario Chamlee, John Brownlee, and Richard Bonelli

Final Curtain Call. A stage full of performers and other company personnel leads the audience in the singing of "Auld Lang Syne"

composer's favorite charity, the Casa Verdi, and the Metropolitan Employees' Welfare Fund. Quest for an alternate to Del Monaco (Vinay did not perform in New York this winter) brought on Dimiter Uzunov, whose vigorous but undisciplined talents were heard as José (d) on December 10 (Stevens was the Carmen) and Otello* on January 24 (with Milanov and Warren). Aside from not having a very good voice (more volume than quality), Uzunov indulged in all the trumpery substitutes for acting technique.

With the new *Cavalleria* and *Pagliacci, Macbeth,* and *Wozzeck* added to such prior Bing productions in this year's repertory as *Madama Butterfly, Rigoletto, Contes d'Hoffmann, La Bohème, The Magic Flute, Carmen, Die Fledermaus, Eugen Onegin, Vanessa, Aida, Don Giovanni,* and *Don Carlo,* the balance sheet showed a further upswing in the preponderance of new–sixteen—over old–ten. In addition to the benefit in sightliness, the steady expansion of the list of newly produced works further endorsed the principle that expenditures for such a purpose were inherent in the upkeep of an operating establishment that aspired to high rank.

But other lessons were to be learned as well, for the process of operatic education, like any other, is never-ending. The mere presence on the stage of a production that had, in the recent past, been carefully planned, thoughtfully executed, toiled over, and laboriously brought into being was no assurance that it remained what it had been. In a rare instance, an *Arabella* improved with recasting; less rarely, a *Don Giovanni* or *Butterfly* retained the virtues for which it was admired. More often, and too frequently for any sense of self-satisfaction, regression set in within a season or two, as though the way the work was being given—whether *Aida* or *Carmen, Fledermaus* or *Don Carlo*—was the concern of another theater, with another director and another taste altogether.

The tale of *Carmen* (now directed by Jean Morel) has already been told. In this season the regression was especially evident in *Aida.* A cast that included Davy as Aida and Uzunov as Radames* on January 3 was hardly made up of "personalities" whose preferences in costuming needed to be indulged. But the principal thing absent was the color scheme conceived by Gérard, as Davy slunk in under a blue sheath. Thebom (as Amneris) preferred orange, and even Uzunov turned up in spangled armor that he obviously "brought along." This was exactly the kind of thing that Bing had observed and denounced in the Metropolitan of Johnson's time, but if he observed it now, he was no longer denouncing, or even renouncing, it. For a final indignity, the performances of this season offered, for what is clearly described in the score as the

"Dance of the Moorish Slaves" in Act II, a single muscular male adult, who would hardly have been allowed on the premises while Amneris was being prepared for the processional that follows.

As the thoughts belonged to the time, so did a conversation during which Bing was asked whether he felt he was anywhere nearer to the solution of the Met's basic problem. "What problem?" he inquired, as though, if it existed, he had never heard of it. "The problem," I stated, "of maintaining the day-to-day repertory on a level of performance comparable to, or within reasonable range of, the level of the first performances, new productions, etc." "Oh," Bing said, "that is simple. Merely a matter of money." If the Met had unlimited funds, he could have Tebaldi for twenty weeks, not ten; or Bjoerling, or Tucker, or whomever. Opera performers, he went on, go where the money is, unlike those who are concerned with "art" (recent press comments were still fresh in mind). The Met cannot have all of them all of the time, he added.

If this reply did not beg the question, it certainly did not answer it. Clearly the presence of a Tebaldi or a Bjoerling, or their mezzo and baritone equivalents, would not alter the performance level of an otherwise poorly conducted *Aida* or of a *Carmen* with disreputable stage direction. Nor was the question merely one of money, in a season in which the Metropolitan had an operating deficit of $528,823. It was, rather, a question of how one allocated the money one had. Elementary logic suggests that it is easier to find an individual who would be present to enforce a quality standard at thirty performances a season than the numerous individuals to bring along their own quality standards for 160 performances a season. That is to say that the money spent on acquiring a sound and responsible group of conductors *who would merit respect as well as demand it,* would yield vastly more widespread results than the money spent on a new production (the second!) of *Cavalleria rusticana* and *Pagliacci.*

If Bing belonged to that school of thought, there was little evidence of it in the work being done as his first decade as general manager drew to a close, or through much of his second. The presence of a flashy "name" for a week or two or three weeks did no more to guarantee a sustained quality standard than a drenching rain in May provides for adequate moisture in July. Without continuous supervision, the quality standard might as well never be instituted.

As far as the response of the Metropolitan's public was concerned, the standard was not so inferior as to discourage attendance. In this season of 164 performances, the last *La Gioconda,* on April 11, with Tucker, Milanov, Merrill, Resnik, Roggero (La Cieca*) and Wilderman (Alvise*), brought to 110 the number of performances for which every seat was sold.

On May 14, the Lincoln Center for the Performing Arts moved a long step closer to realization with the formal ground-breaking. The first shovel of earth was turned by President Dwight D. Eisenhower in the presence not only of city and state officials, but also of a large number of persons in a musical and artistic life of New York. Leonard Bernstein conducted a musical program by the New York Philharmonic Orchestra in which Risë Stevens and Leonard Warren participated as representatives of the Metropolitan.

The growing importance of foundation support for opera, especially of the contemporary kind, overshadowed any other single happening of the two segments of performances given by the New York City Opera Company under Julius Rudel in the City Center during October and November 1958 and March and April 1959. Rudel's inspection of the broad perspective of the contemporary operatic literature provided the first New York hearing of the Strauss–Stefan Zweig *Die schweigsame Frau* —Peter Herman Adler conducted, with Joan Carroll as Aminta, Herbert Beattie as the Admiral, John Alexander (the Nephew), Paul Ukena (Barber) and Ruth Kobart (Housekeeper)—early in October and Britten's *Rape of Lucretia*—with David Lloyd (Male Chorus), Brenda Lewis (Female Chorus), William Chapman (Tarquinius), Frances Bible (Lucretia), Lee Venora (Maid) and Kobart (Nurse)—later in the month, without altering much the known quality of either score. (The Britten was advertised as the "premiere" of a revised version, but the changes seemed to be related mostly to the use of a larger orchestra in the pit.)

Whatever credit accrued to the company for these innovations and repetitions of such recent productions as *The Ballad of Baby Doe* and *Susannah,* its cash position profited materially from the announcement, while the season was in progress, that the Ford Foundation had made a further grant of $310,000 to implement its prior benefactions. It was specified that $155,000 of it was earmarked for another spring season of works by Americans; an equal amount was to be utilized for a similar season in 1960 to be followed by a tour of cities in the Eastern half of the country with a repertory emphasizing works fostered by Ford Foundation funds.

In a pattern that was to become a fixed mode of procedure for the future, the spring season was devoted almost entirely to works of contemporary origin, some not previously produced, some not previously heard in New York, all new to this stage. Included were Menotti's *Maria Golovin,* with key members of the cast—Richard Cross (Donato), Patricia

Neway (Mother), Norman Kelley (Tutor)—with whom it had fared poorly on Broadway during the preceding November (Ilona Kombrinc was the new Maria, with Regina Sarfaty as Agata and Herbert Grossman conducting) and Weill's *Street Scene,* neither of which could be called "experimental"; and Moore's well-regarded *Devil and Daniel Webster* (Cassel was the new Dan'l, with Kelley as Scratch and Joshua Hecht as Jabez Stone). However, there was a mounting sense of discovery that there were native composers of little reputation but considerable gift for the stage with the introduction of Lee Hoiby's *The Scarf* (Neway as Miriam, John Druary as her husband, and Richard Cross as the vagrant); Hugo Weisgall's setting of Pirandello's *Six Characters in Search of an Author* (Ernest McChesney was the Director, with Patricia Neway, Paul Ukena, and Adelaide Bishop among the Characters); and Robert Ward's version of Andreyev's *He Who Gets Slapped* (Lee Venora was Consuelo, David Atkinson the Pantaloon, and Regina Sarfaty the lion-taming Zinida). The adaptation of Norman Dello Joio's *The Triumph of St. Joan* (Mack Harrell was Cauchon, with Venora as Joan) also worked well, in partnership with *The Medium.* Much less gratifying was Floyd's successor to *Susannah:* a treatment of *Wuthering Heights* that spared him indictment as a "one work" composer, but also found him engaged with a subject beyond his musico-dramatic capacities. Phyllis Curtin was Cathy, John Reardon Heathcliffe, Jon Crain Hindley and Patricia Neway Nelly. New additions to the company in these two seasons included Regina Sarfaty and Russell Christopher in the fall weeks, Joy Clements, Richard Cross, and Craig Timberlake in the spring.

1959–1960

During the days of November 1958 when the press was trying to uncover the root reasons for the dismissal of Callas, unbelieving that a mere disagreement about two *Traviatas* was sufficient crime for the penalty, some attention was directed toward Callas's expressed discontent with the "old routine," her desire to appear in "new productions." Bing's response ran: "This is a free country, and we have no contract with her for next season. The Metropolitan has only two or three new productions a season, after all . . ." (New York *Herald Tribune,* November 7, 1958). The implication of this was that, having been favored with a new *Macbeth* in 1958, Callas would have to wait her turn while the Metropolitan considered the claims of other singers, at the rate of two or three new productions a season.

When the controversy had subsided and time was at hand to present his plans for the forthcoming season, Bing's budget of new productions showed not two or three, but six—the largest number by far for any season in his first decade, and more than the Metropolitan had been able to afford in a single season since the carefree days of the 1920 boom. A further sign of progress could be noted in the addition of another week to the season's schedule, bringing the total to twenty-five, the most ever.

Perhaps the most eagerly awaited of the new productions was the restaging of *Tristan und Isolde,* the first time a Metropolitan audience would see a new frame for Wagner's action in decades of Isoldes dating back to November 20, 1920. And the musical prospect of Birgit Nilsson's debut on December 18 was brightened by promise of the first Metropolitan appearance of Otto Klemperer, whose abilities as a conductor had been esteemed by New York concertgoers since the mid-twenties.

The possibility, indeed, that Klemperer might, with Boehm and Mitropoulos, give the Metropolitan three conductors of the first rank for the first time in years was not beyond hope. But it had vanished, one may say in smoke, on October 23, 1958, with news from Zurich announcing that Klemperer had been severely burned after he fell asleep with a lighted pipe in his mouth, and would be hospitalized for an indefinite time to come. No date could be set for resumption of his activity.

By readjustment of some other commitments (including the assignment to Leinsdorf of responsibility for the season's performances of *Der Rosenkavalier*), Boehm cleared time to participate in the preparations for the new *Tristan*. With Nilsson in the country to fulfill her obligations in Chicago (where her debut had occurred as long before as October 20, 1956, as the *Walküre* Brünnhilde), no other misfortunes seemed possible. But Vinay's year of absence from the Metropolitan had not made his vocal condition any more reliable than it had been previously. He was replaced by Liebl, who had, at least, the advantage of the dress rehearsal a few days before the first performance.

For all its curiosity about the new staging and its possible doubts that a not very robust Lohengrin could qualify as a competent Tristan, the attention of the capacity audience at the Opera Guild benefit on December 18 clearly was concentrated on the new Isolde (d). When Nilsson had raged and stormed, hated and melted through but one act, the audience left no doubt that this was a performer they would cherish, not merely for the rest of the evening, but for years to come. They literally threw their thanks to her at the end of the act in a welcome such as no new singer since Welitch had received.

As it turned out, even those who had heard Nilsson elsewhere had to admit astonishment and disbelief. For she had proved herself, in that limited but exacting stretch of singing, to be the greatest of rarities, a performer—like Flagstad before her and Caruso before *her*—to whom the size of the Metropolitan was not a hazard, but an advantage. It enabled her to demonstrate an amplitude of sound as well as a healthy freshness of quality which actually searched out the far reaches of the gallery. Attractive in appearance and intelligent (if hardly inspired) in action, she was clearly the kind of singer of whom Willa Cather was writing when (in *The Song of the Lark*) she wrote, in a fictional version of another singer's debut at the Metropolitan,[1] "At last somebody with *enough!*"

Under the stimulation of such aural adrenalin, the others in the cast surpassed themselves under Boehm's carefully cumulative direction. Where the requirements of Tristan* were within Liebl's dynamic range, there were a lyric line and sensitivity to meaning in his sound. At other times, he vanished from audibility, especially in Act III, which had been considerately reduced to eliminate a good deal of Tristan's delirium. Dalis sang and acted a more than respectable Brangäne and Cassel performed a swaggering kind of Kurvenal. With his assets of size and sound, Hines should have been a superior rather than merely a good Marke. Franke was at his best as the Shepherd, and the orchestra rose to the occasion with more glow and flexibility of sound than it ordinarily musters. But the single overriding fact was that a new, powerful embodiment of Wagner's heroic sopranos had come to join a company that the Metropolitan could proudly call its own, from Lilli Lehmann, Nordica, and Fremstad to Flagstad and Traubel.

Ironically, the one remnant of Klemperer's association with this project (underwritten by the four daughters of Mrs. Elon Huntington Hooker, in tribute to her) could outlast all the others. This was the scenic production of Teo Otto, whom Klemperer had suggested as a designer with whom he would be happy to work. There was a certain measure of regal fitness in the "barque" Otto provided for Act I (its visible portion, stretching from front stage right to rear stage left, suggested an over-all craft of dreadnought size, but quality dropped sharply thereafter, with a metallic kind of Jackson Pollock moon dominating the sylvan scene of Marke's garden and with a stunted growth in Act III as a forlorn suggestion of the "great lime tree" specified in Wagner's stage directions. At later performances, the participants were mostly familiar, save on January 21, when the Brangäne* was Christa Ludwig, and on January 30, when Kim Borg was King Marke.*

Though it should follow that the Metropolitan management would react favorably when the debut of a new singer became front-page news, the stories about Nilsson in the next day's *Times* and *Tribune* were not greeted,

[1] By general consent, Olive Fremstad's.

executively, with unmingled joy. What was wanted, apparently, was a success but not a sensation. The sentiment seemed to be that it was all very well to have a new public favorite, but not, on the basis of a single performance, a new star.[1]

The price to pride if not to purse became an unpleasant reality on February 15, a Monday when Nilsson was scheduled to sing Senta in *Der fliegende Holländer* for the first time. She spent the previous day preparing for her debut in another, more profitable medium, as a participant in the TV variety show of Ed Sullivan. Pleading fatigue the next day, she refused to perform, and Harshaw was called upon to take her place. The nettled management could do no more than fume and be nettled.

But as this followed an occasion on December 28, when Nilsson had every right to be more than nettled, the balance would appear to be fairly even. Vinay had managed to perform (variably) on December 23, but could not guarantee an evening-long repetition of Tristan five days later. By this time Liebl, too, was voice-weary, and Da Costa, the only possible alternate, did not seem the right choice for a full Tristan with Nilsson. After studying and discarding the available options, Bing decided to serve the public its paid-for portion of Nilsson—with three Tristans: Vinay for Act I, Liebl for Act II, and Da Costa for Act III. I do not regret my inability to provide an ear-witness account of this travesty: my best judgment was

[1] In pursuance of the sound precept of his mentor at Glyndebourne, Fritz Busch —"When a new singer has a success, sign a new contract immediately"—Bing undertook to secure Nilsson's services for the future, only to discover that her value had appreciated considerably overnight. By this time, the Metropolitan's success in maintaining $1,000 per performance as the top fee (instituted by Johnson, and perpetuated by him through his period of direction) had long since become history. It was undermined, first of all, by the resumption of activity in Italy and the substantial sums paid by La Scala; and it collapsed altogether with the renewal of activity in Chicago and the large amounts expended there to lure "name" talent. By the mid-fifties, the Metropolitan's most wanted artists (Mario del Monaco first, and then Risë Stevens) were asking and getting $1,750 per performance. This remained the honorary honorarium through the first Callas engagement and the peak celebrity of Milanov and Tebaldi. It is believed that both Nilsson and Sutherland began their Metropolitan careers at this figure, meaning that a new round of raises was inevitable when they became established attractions. The advent of Corelli and the buyer-response that his talents aroused at the box office created a new high of $2,750 in the early 'sixties. Under the stimulus of demand from elsewhere for their services, the fee per performance for both Nilsson and Corelli has since risen to $3,750. In such matters, the governing principle is parity: with or without the impulse of cupidity, professional pride dictates that those who are in a position to demand it receive *no less* than any other performer in the same opera house. Thus when one demands more, the manager must resign himself to the inevitability that the other will ask as much, immediately. However, the real money value or purchasing power of the top amount cited herein is substantially less than the $2,500 per performance paid to Caruso between 1914 and his breakdown in 1920. The largest real amount ever paid to a performer for a single Metropolitan opera was the $3,500 commanded by Chaliapin for a single Boris in Philadelphia during the boom period of the later 'twenties.

to stay away, the first—perhaps the only—time in thirty-five years I have deliberately absented myself from a Metropolitan performance. Bing's willingness to pose, after the final curtain, for newspaper photos of himself, the three-thirds Tristans, and Nilsson was evidence of his satisfaction with publicity for an event that should have been suffered in silence, if at all.

The measure of Nilsson's competence in the Wagner repertory was documented one part more with her first Brünnhilde in *Die Walküre* on February 9, also conducted by Boehm. Radiant to see, powerful to hear, Nilsson gave a well-tested estimate of the girl goddess, as attractive in its suggestion of youthful freshness as Flagstad's had been when it was first seen in New York. Some opinion marked her down for a clean attack on the top C's of *"Ho-yo-to-ho"* rather than the swooping ascent that is customary. (It would seem to me hers was the harder, more demanding way of doing it.) The performance provided opportunity also for acquaintance with the fervent, well-sung, and picturesque Siegmund* of Jon Vickers, the picturesque if neither fervent nor well-sung Sieglinde* of Nordmo Loevberg, and the imposing but effortful Wotan* of Hines. A major accomplishment for a basso who had started his Metropolitan career with a minor role in *Boris,* it carried Hines uncomfortably higher than he could produce a full-throated sound. Ernster was Hunding, with Dalis as Fricka. In a later performance, Rankin was Fricka,* with Harshaw as Brünnhilde, and on March 2, Liebl worked hard to make his vocal means serve him as Siegmund,* as Rysanek sang her impassioned, thoroughly convincing Sieglinde.* By March 7 the Brünnhilde was Mödl, with Uhde a less than wholly audible Wotan.

A second new production, justified by the presence of Nilsson, though not technically "for" her, was Beethoven's *Fidelio,* first seen on January 28. The settings by Horace Armistead (underwritten by Mrs. John D. Rockefeller, Jr.) were reminiscent of various classical approaches to this subject, including a stage-wide "gate" that rose, symbolically, before the scene of celebration at the end. It was, for the most part, spaciously atmospheric, especially in the Prison Scene of Act I.

Despite the presence (for "name appeal," perhaps) of Siepi as Don Fernando* in a style of singing for which he had little preparation (the German text was used) and the large opportunity provided for Nordmo Loevberg as Leonore,* the real gratification in this *Fidelio* came from the darkly brooding, musically superior effort of Vickers as Florestan.* This quixotic singer had elected to make his debut as Canio (d) in *Pagliacci* (a style of singing for which he was as unsuited as Siepi was for Fernando) on January 17. He survived this misadventure to prove himself the nearest thing to a serviceable *Heldentenor* since Svanholm, and the best Florestan since René Maison. His qualification for this high rank became more glowingly apparent on February 13, when Nilsson supported the requirements of Leonore* with far more dramatic power and vocal eloquence than Nordmo Loevberg had. Her trim figure, admirable deportment, and wideranging vocal resources painted exciting possibilities of things to come in the Verdi, Puccini, and Strauss repertory. With Edelmann absent in this season because of the death of his wife, Oskar Czerwenka performed a light-voiced Rocco,* with Hurley as Marzelline,* Anthony a very likable Jacquino,* and Uhde as Don Pizarro.* Most of these parts remained unchanged in the few other *Fidelios* the season produced—Wilderman was the Fernando* on February 2 and Tozzi succeeded him on February 13. Aside from its musical qualities, the Boehm *Fidelio*—he was faithful to the tradition of the *Fidelio* overture as prelude and the *Leonore No. 3* before the final scene—had a place in history not wholly of his own making. The demands this score placed on the horn choir resulted in wrong notes and uncertain right ones at almost every performance. Angry complaints in the press were frequent, and desire for replacement of the erring performer widespread. How it became a *cause célèbre* emerged in due course.

The premise that Ritchard had proved his deft touch for operatic comedy in *La Perichole* and thus could be entrusted with such an operatic comedy as *Le Nozze di Figaro* was put to the test on October 30 when the new production by Oliver Messel, on which Ritchard collaborated with Leinsdorf as musical director, was publicly displayed. A syllogism at best—operatic comedy and Mozartian operatic comedy being as widely separated as a guffaw and a smile—it failed for specific as well as for general reasons: Ritchard's knowledge of Italian was scant, meaning that he had to find out, from those he was supposed to be directing, what an idiomatic expression meant. The gaucheries and extravagances that emerged, such as the stamp of Susanna's foot on Marcellina's toe for a crude "laugh" at the fall of the second-act curtain, usurped attention from many quieter touches of wit which were creditable to him. Nor for the direction to say: "Look— servants' quarters!" was it necessary for a pair of Susanna's underpants to be displayed on a washline in Act I.

One consequence of the annoyance aroused by Ritchard's directorial lapses was the downgrading of Messel's scenic conception, though much of it was apt, and the second-act scene in the Countess's boudoir was far better than any the Metropolitan had had in decades. It was particularly well planned to accommodate the necessary relationships among the performers and the conductor as well as the relationships of the performers to other performers, and thus achieved two purposes simultaneously—as well as looking the way one imagines a Countess's boudoir should. Money for these unaccustomed luxuries was provided by Mrs. John D. Rockefeller, Jr., bringing her benefactions for this single season (*Fidelio* was the other) to two.

Leinsdorf's tested feeling for this score was not only a factor of quality, but also a proper cohesive among vocal and instrumental elements. Of the former, the best was Della Casa's Countess, matured from the role of her debut in 1953–4 to rank as a charming character study, closely followed by the adroit Susanna (d) of Elisabeth Soederstroem, a servingmaid who knew her place not only in the Count's household, but also in Mozart's score; Siepi as Figaro, now beginning to struggle a bit for the top F in *"Se vuol ballare,"* and Miller as Cherubino. The Count (d) was Kim Borg, suitably aristocratic in bearing, but of rather plebeian vocal quality. Ritchard's handling of situation was best when it was least obtrusive, especially in the *commedia dell'arte* playing of Resnik as Marcellina and Flagello as Bartolo. The long-lived career of Charles Kullmann was prolonged by his willingness to assume the responsibilities of Basilio.* John Butler supervised the dancing.

On December 10 the Figaro was Tozzi, more labored than laboring man. Amara was the Countess, and Christa Ludwig displayed her lively talents for the first time in a non-stop performance of Cherubino (d). She was, perhaps, the only mezzo to sing Cherubino and Brangäne (not to mention Octavian) in the same Metropolitan season, a measure of the uncertainty that beset her own estimate of a "settled" performing future. An unexpected touch of comedy intruded into the performance of November 11, when Kullmann found himself voiceless minutes before the curtain was to rise. In the brief time before Basilio was required to appear on the stage, Carelli slipped out of his costume as Don Curzio, arranged his appearance to fit Basilio, and went on in Kullmann's place. The most surprised man in the theater was Leinsdorf, who looked up to give a cue to Kullmann and found himself confronted by Carelli. It was a minor triumph in adaptability for Carelli, who held his place in the ensembles successfully. Nagy, in turn, replaced Carelli as Curzio.

Some portion of this comedy, unexpected or otherwise, would have been welcome on November 25, when Bing disclosed his second venture with a work of Johann Strauss, Jr. This time it was *Gypsy Baron,* for which Gérard, designer of *Fledermaus,* was given the scenic opportunity, Ritchard was appointed to direct, and Leinsdorf supervised the musical interpretation. Seeking, perhaps, to recapture Ritchard's own impact as a speaking rather than singing performer in *La Perichole,* Bing engaged Walter Slezak to fondle the pig and speak the lines of Szupan (d).

In the opinion of many, the star performance was given by the pig, whose part should, perhaps, have been beefed up, or at least, pigged out. Aside from Gérard's two pastoral views, which had an almost edibly operetta quality, and his last imperial ballroom (at Schönbrunn), the production was a chaotic complex of miscasting, misdirection, and plain misconception of how to proceed with this subject—assuming that it was suitable for the Metropolitan's stage to begin with. Unlike *Fledermaus,* which has an endless river of enchanting music to support the flimsiest kind of dramatic craft, the flow of *Gypsy Baron* is episodic and non-consecutive, putting much more of a burden on the text. Though prepared by the same Maurice Valency who had done so well with *Perichole,* the English version was infirm and unfunny from the start.

The miscasting began with Leinsdorf as conductor, and continued through Della Casa as Saffi.* It was Leinsdorf's inclination to substitute speed for brio, the discipline of the paradeground for the fluidity of the ballroom. Della Casa was far too chic and ladylike for a proper stage gypsy, well as she sang, and such performers as Hurley as Arsena,* Roald Reitan as Homonay,* and Dunn as Mirabella* were miles removed from the atmospheric center of Strauss's fantasy, without a proper guide to show them which way it lay. If anything, it was Ritchard's perverse impulse in this season to make *Figaro* a farce rather than a comedy of manners, *Gypsy Baron* a comedy of manners rather than a farce. Those who survived the general confusion to earn credit for good individual efforts were Gedda as an engaging Barinkay,* Resnik, who made a roughly swaggering gypsy of Czipra,* and Alessio de Paolis who outdid himself to present in the ballroom scene a veritable likeness of Franz Josef as the Emperor of Austria.* This scene offered an interpolation of the *Emperor Waltz,* with Violette Verdy (d) and Scott Douglas leading the choreography devised by Danilova. She was appointed, no doubt, because of the memories that lingered of her charming part in Massine's *Le Beau Danube.* What was wanted, rather, was Massine himself.

The plain evidence of the mild public reaction and such press opinions as Jay Harrison's (in the *Herald Tribune*) that the production possessed "neither zest nor flavor" confirmed the fears of the management that *Gypsy Baron* would fall short not only of *Fledermaus* but even of a moderately successful entertainment. It made its round of the subscription and an additional performance or two with substantially the same cast (changes ran to such roles as Szupan* by Herbert on January 9, Kullmann as the Emperor of Austria,* Olvis as Barinkay,* Votipka as Mirabella,* and Amparan as Czipra* on February 11). It did not appear in a second season while the company remained in its old home.

The two remaining new productions were of works by Verdi, both welcome, both overdue. The first brought forth a new vista of J. P. Morgan's favorite opera (see page 58) when *Il Trovatore* was elected for the opening night (October 26) for the first time in Metropolitan history. It served the occasion admirably, not only in providing a score that made the least knowing feel erudite (by recognition of the *"Miserere"*), but also in bringing together a quartet of performers with at least suitable, and in one instance brilliant, qualifications for Verdi's requirements.

Even more resplendent than the bright if flimsy-looking designs by Motley (a theatrical trade name for Elisabeth Montgomery) was the jet of sound poured forth by Giulietta Simionato as Azucena (d) and the shaping artistry with which it was formed. Of much the same physical as well as vocal type as her illustrious predecessor, Cloë Elmo, Simionato gave ample cause to regret the lost years since her first, nonproductive Metropolitan engagement in 1954–5, but gratitude, too, that she had as much, both in sound and skill, to work with as she poured forth without stint from *"Stride la vampa"* on. Bergonzi, as her "son" did not show quite the likeness of temperament that kinship would suggest, but he performed beautifully in the lyric passages, in company with Stella as Leonora and Warren as Di Luna. Roald Reitan, of American birth, made his debut as the Gypsy (d). Not the most bountiful of recent Metropolitan productions (a B—or Budget—production, no doubt), Motley's construction lacked the substance that comes from set pieces of solid construction, tending rather to flats and painted drops. But it was clean and tasteful, qualities that had long since departed from the Metropolitan's prior *Trovatore*. Cleva conducted energetically, and Graf's direction kept the members of the ensemble moving on well-defined paths. The first cast change came where it hurt most when Madeira replaced Simionato on December 3. By April 6, the luminous sound the production had possessed at the beginning was definitely dulled as the ladies became Curtis-Verna and Amparan (Azucena*), with Bastianini as Di Luna.

The quality of Simionato's art was even more graphically revealed on October 31, when she was Santuzza* to Peerce's Turiddu.* As the symbol declares, this was Peerce's first Turiddu in a Metropolitan career moving toward twenty seasons and proved to be an ideal mate, in temperament as well as physical size, for Simionato's peerless Santuzza. If the idea of depicting Santuzza's frantic despair by hanging on to Turiddu's wrist as he dragged her across the stage on the way to the church was Simionato's own, it was brilliantly original: certainly the despair that haunted her voice in *"Voi lo sapete"* was uniquely her own. Here the likeness to Elmo would have to be amended, for Simionato proved herself capable of doing superbly what her predecessor had attempted, but failed, to do. A well-matched cast provided Elias as Lola and Cassel as Alfio,* with Votipka a Mamma Lucia cut from the same cloth as Simionato. The following *Pagliacci* brought on Cornell MacNeil to begin his first full season as Tonio*—he had advanced the date of his debut to the previous March 21 in order to replace Merrill as Rigoletto (d). His trumpet blast of a voice made a spectacular effect in the prologue, but neither in this role nor in any other of the season did he mount a characterization to match the possibilities in his heroic sound.

Amara and Uzunov were well matched on the lower levels of distinction as Nedda and Canio,* with Sereni as Silvio. The conductor was Nino Verchi (d) of Trieste, who spread a quieting oil of competence on what might otherwise have been a troubled sea of temperament. Passing note may be given to more than a scattering of empty seats at this performance on an early fall Saturday afternoon despite the quality of the vocal art provided. A later Nedda* on December 5 was Maria Nache, a Spanish soprano who had made her debut as Micaëla (d) in *Carmen* on October 31. The voice was small and of ordinary quality.

For the final new production of this bounteous season, Bing turned on March 1 to *Simon Boccanegra,* a Verdi score of proved popularity at the Metropolitan. To give its pageantry and drama some of the values that had ennobled *Don Carlo,* Bing re-employed Webster as stage director, working now with Fox (whose *Chénier* had earned credit) the Mitropoulos. Not all of Fox's designs were equally well motivated—cutting away a corner of Fiesco's house so that the audience could see Boccanegra discover the dead body of Maria rather downgraded the onlooker's awareness of what he was supposed to *know*—but his Council Chamber was colorful, his great hall of suitable proportions.

Musically the night was Leonard Warren's. His Boccanegra marked the unquestionable high mark of a career that had begun in the subsidiary role of Paolo in the same opera in January 1939. As well as providing the sound wanted for Simon, something within his power on other occasions dating back to 1949–50, Warren now possessed the dramatic means to create a full-length likeness of the Doge's character in all its shadings from triumph to despair. Doubtless a part of this was contributed by Webster, who worked uncommonly hard at making the most of her opportunity and succeeded brilliantly. Unfortunately, Tebaldi was not able to reach America in time to participate in the rehearsals, and was replaced by Curtis-Verna, whose performance as Amelia* was, on the whole, above her average. Tucker was again a superior Gabriele, but Tozzi as Fiesco* lacked depth of sound for *"Il lacerato spirito."* The Paolo* was Flagello, which left this cast altogether short of the standard of Johnson's final year (Varnay, Tucker, Warren, Szekely, and Valdengo). Aside from another of Mitropoulos's concessions to managerial convenience—a cut, this time, at the end of Scene I, Act I, which eliminated Paolo's plot to abduct Amelia—he delivered a powerful conception of the score, especially in that prime moment of Verdian profundity, the revised Council Scene.

By contrast with the problem that the Metropolitan was having during these years, of assembling a wholly competent corps of conductors, the City Opera added another of indisputable quality with, apparently, no great difficulty. This was Leopold Stokowski, who accepted the honor of being lion of the fall opening on September 24. For the purpose he put together an attractive double bill of Stravinsky's *Oedipus Rex* (Richard Cassilly and Claramae Turner were the principal singers, with Wesley Addey narrating) and Orff's *Carmina Burana* (with Johns Alexander and Reardon sharing attention with the debut of Reri Grist). And it acted shrewdly in utilizing the gifts of Robert Irving (in time off from his work with the New York City Ballet) to vitalize a new production of *The Mikado.* For the company's first venture with *Così fan tutte,* in which Judith Raskin added to the qualities she had shown in televised (NBC) operas a lively talent for the stage in her debut as Despina, Alexander sang a capable Ferrando to Reardon's Guglielmo, and James Pease presided over the intrigue with Curtin as Fiordiligi and Bible as Dorabella, all under the direction of Rudel. The promise of John Macurdy was heightened with his good effort as Colline in a *Bohème* of mid-October, and he later sang a good Timur in *Turandot,* with Gertrude Ribla in the title role. This was one of several occasions on which the company profited from Flaviano Labò's exclusion *chez* Bing to provide a quality of tenorizing as Calaf which was well above the house level. It was notable, too, that more Italian was heard in the lobby on Labò evenings than was customary at City Center, suggesting that "Mulberry Street" (the generic term for the Italian population of New York) would find its way anywhere its interests were well served.

If the foregoing citations digress rather decidedly from the path that the City Center had marked out for itself in recent seasons under Rudel, it signified not a change of direction but a temporary side excursion. Indeed, the high road to new uncharted ground was clearly defined in an announcement from the Ford Foundation, during the fall season, that it had set aside $950,000 to further the program of promoting American opera it had instituted in 1957. All of the opera organizations in the country with a claim to permanence—the Chicago Lyric, the San Francisco, the Metropolitan, and the New York City Opera—were invited to participate. The intention now was to increase the number of performable works by Americans by making available funds to commission new operas. The Metropolitan, rather more wary of the results than some of its contemporaries elsewhere, did not actually present such a Ford-commissioned opera during the years in which it continued to perform on Broadway, though one grant was made to Marc Blitzstein for the treatment of the Sacco-Vanzetti case on which he was at work at the time of his death in Martinique on January 22, 1964. All the others moved much more quickly, with the New York City company showing the swiftest results of the most intensive interest. While these plans were maturing, it presented a brief season in early 1960 in which the only happening of consequence was a production of Blitzstein's *The Cradle Will Rock* in fully staged form set in a brilliantly economical surrounding of fresh-from-the-mill red "girders" by David Hays. Tammy Grimes was Moll, with David Atkinson in the role of Larry Foreman created by Howard da Silva, who directed the production, for which the conductor was Lehman Engel.

In the later period when the company would normally have been performing on Fifty-fifth Street, Rudel led them on a month-long tour sponsored by Ford Foundation money to show a representative segment of the repertory developed under those auspices. It opened on February 23 in New Brunswick, N.J., with *Susannah* and closed on March 26 in Hartford, Conn., with *The Ballad of Baby Doe*. The tour included visits to Baltimore, Philadelphia, three days in Washington, D.C., three more in Chicago en route to St. Louis, and then back through Cincinnati; Bloomington, Indiana; Detroit; and Boston to Hartford. The repertory also included *Six Characters in Search of an Author* (given only in Boston) and *Street Scene*. A post-mortem showed the greatest interest in such collegiate communities as Lafayette, Indiana; East Lansing, Michigan; and South Bend, Indiana (as well, of course, as Bloomington), and a dismal lack of response in some much larger centers.

Frustrated though Bing's plan was for adding a conductor of Klemperer's stature to his company's resources, the span of the season was for the most part encompassed in better order and with fewer improbable combinations of conductors and what they conducted than during several past seasons. Part of this related to the repertory itself, which, in a revolving pattern of change brought back such scores as *Manon* and *Pelléas* to join *Carmen* and *Faust* under the direction of Morel; and part to Mitropoulos's larger participation in the work load. If far from wholly well, he was wholly disinclined to spare himself. Also available was Leinsdorf, who had both health and energy to dispense. The nominal addition, Verchi, had little more than a trial run with a smoothly routine *Traviata* (with Los Angeles, Valletti, and Sereni) on November 4 succeeding *Cavalleria rusticana* and *Pagliacci*. Direction of *Traviata* passed to Cleva, and Mitropoulos resumed as conductor of the "twins" when Verchi departed in late December.

The commendable effort of the Metropolitan management to share with its patrons some of the decade's developments in talent resulted in debuts not only for the well-known Simionato, Nilsson, Vickers, and Ludwig, for all their diversity of age, background, and experience, should Elisabeth Soederstroem, and Kim Borg. The oddity that Simionato and Ludwig, for all their diversity of age, background, and experience should cross paths on the Metropolitan's stage came to happen in the role of Amneris,* which both sang in this season. Ludwig's, on January 14, with Amara (whose first Aida* had been heard on November 9), MacNeil as Amonasro,* which he had sung previously on December 19, and Uzunov as Radames, was another instance of her doing well with a part which she should not have sung at all in this theater. That this related to other things than physical size was underscored when Simionato (hardly as tall as Ludwig) stretched her inches to queenly bearing on February 18. Here was an incandescent example of will in ascendancy over natural endowments, for she took and held by assertive use of voice and a singular command of dramatic means the place that Amneris should have but rarely has in Verdi's creation.

Though Soederstroem had been a successful Octavian in Glyndebourne's *Rosenkavalier* during the preceding summer (and also sang the Marschallin at home in Stockholm), it was as Sophie in the Strauss-Hofmannsthal comedy that she was seen when it returned under Leinsdorf's direction on December 26. Perhaps this was a consequence of Peters's absence for much of the season (see page 586). The Octavian* was also new, this being the scarcely repressible Ludwig, who swarmed all over Della Casa as the Marschallin, pulled "boyishly" at her knee britches from time to time, and in short, acted as though a lady's boudoir was a rumpus room. The music lay well for her, and she sang much of it with supple, warm sound, which made the trio of Act III, with Soederstroem and Della Casa, worth enduring the bumptious Ochs (d) of Oskar Czerwenka to hear. The fault, in fact, was hardly the performer's, for he was ill-suited by size of voice to make a legitimate impression in a theater of this size and had to resort to clowning. The fault was, rather, in the choice of him as a plausible alternate for the unavailable Edelmann. The Singer* of this performance was Fernandi (as ill-suited to the surroundings as he was to Radames's). On February 5, the Valzacchi* (*vice* De Paolis) was Kullmann, and Gedda was the Singer. By February 27, the whole cast had been switched about to present Steber, Miller, Hurley, and Rothmüller (Faninal*), and by March 17 one might have thought it a visiting company that offered Rysanek (Marschallin*), Stevens, and Gueden as the trio of ladies. The first of these could reasonably be characterized as a rough diamond, for it had many carats of quality, all in need of polish. The best of these was her spirit of play in the part, even at the moment when Mariandl (Stevens) upset the chocolate pot in Act I. This Marschallin enjoyed her discomfiture as much as she did the *gaucheries* of her cousin. Those who saw it also saw the last Stevens Octavian in a sequence that had begun almost twenty years before. She was not in the cast when *Rosenkavalier* was next given.

Between her first role in Italian and her third in German, Soederstroem showed typical Scandinavian adaptability by singing another in French on December 8, when *Faust* reappeared under the direction of Morel, with Bjoerling once more as Faust (and showing a master's command of vocal technique to offset some small evidences of creeping vocal decline), Siepi (Méphistophélès), Merrill (Valentin), and Reitan (Wagner*) all in prime form. The male performers, at least, were all responsive to Morel's able direction. As Marguerite,* however, Soederstroem was a white-voiced, rather pale-appearing performer. Nathaniel Merrill's direction was not yet his own, nor was it altogether's Brook's, with inevitable cost in quality. In later performances Fernandi sang a strained Faust* on January 8, Morell was not appreciably better on January 27 in his first try (Sereni was the Valentin*), and Conner had a final opportunity as Marguerite on March 12. Her stated reason for terminating a Metropolitan career that had begun as Pamina in *The Magic Flute* on December 22, 1941, was a desire to spend more time at home (Compton, California) with her husband and children.

The opportunity for indulgence in the Bjoerling order of operatic artistry included a fervent Turiddu on November 16, with Simionato; another Faust; a fine Cavaradossi, and a final Turiddu on December 22 (Curtis-Verna was the Santuzza*). This represented not so much a renewal of enthusiasm for the operatic stage as a response to a suggestion of RCA Victor when he found the sales of his records sagging. It was thus as Turiddu that Bjoerling made his final Metropolitan appearance: he did not appear in opera again in New York before his sudden death in Stockholm on September 9, 1960.

The name of Anna Moffo had meaning for a few who had been paying close attention to happenings in the world of records when she made her debut in *La Traviata,* but even they had had no opportunity to evaluate her qualifications for singing Violetta (d). These, it turned out, included the good looks and lively personality to be a sightly courtesan, plus well-placed sound and well-schooled agility to deal with the florid as well as the legato challenge of the part. Like many before her who could sing the first act well, she could not fill the dramatic demands of succeeding acts, especially the last, which asked a weightier sound than she could provide. However, as she was only twenty-five and had relatively little professional work behind her, there was still the possibility that the broader sound would come in time. Valletti's Alfredo was no more able to provide the dramatic accent wanted than in prior efforts, but MacNeil, as replacement for Merrill, showed a full range of vocal resources for a better than fair Germont.* The sequence of *Traviatas* which began on November 4 (Los Angeles, Valletti, and Sereni) included a common kind of personnel instability, but also an uncommon kind when Curtis-Verna, responding to an emergency created by the illness of Los Angeles, put off departure for Italy to venture Violetta* on January 7, with Gedda as Alfredo* and Mac-Neil. This is the kind of effort that qualified Curtis-Verna for high marks in trouping, but the heavy, unagile singing she offered was a sad commentary on the Metropolitan's inability to do better.

Hardly more could be seen of Teresa Stratas (a recent Auditions' winner) as Poussette (d) in *Manon* on October 28 than could be heard of her in the trio with Javotte* (Vanni) and Rosette* (Wall), but the large voice in the deceptively small body and her ability to magnetize attention to its point of origin made hers one of those names to note. For the moment there was much more to note in Gedda's Des Grieux* and the polished Comte des Grieux* of Tozzi (Los Angeles was the Manon), but in the weeks to come, Stratas provided a point of interest, whether as a Peasant Girl* (with Wall) in *Figaro* on October 30, Annina* in *Traviata* on November 4, Frasquita* in *Carmen* on November 12, Barbarina* in *Figaro* on December 10, or even a Flower Maiden* in *Parsifal* on March 21.

The last of these found Leinsdorf in the midst of the fairly formidable problem of trying to conduct *Parsifal* without a Parsifal. On this occasion, for which the Kundry was Mödl, with Uhde as Amfortas and Hines as Gurnemanz, he had the appealing sound of Liebl to work with in Act I, but its appeal diminished as the dramatic burden on Parsifal* increased. For the April 15 (Good Friday) matinee, the manpower for Parsifal was reduced to Kullmann, whose name as of this season had been associated with such roles as Valzacchi in *Rosenkavalier,* Basilio in *Figaro,* and Goro in *Butterfly*. The Amfortas* this time was Kim Borg, with Harshaw as Kundry.*[1]

The odd circumstance that Rysanek had been introduced in her first season as a singer only of Italian roles called for consideration of her as almost another performer in her second season. This provided, in addition to repetitions of such earlier roles as Aida and Lady Macbeth, opportunities in the repertory she had been born to perform: Senta* in *Der fliegende Holländer* on January 13, Sieglinde* in *Die Walküre* on March 2, and (as already noted) the Marschallin* in *Der Rosenkavalier* on March 17. It would be an exaggeration to say that the voice was freer or more even in production in these than in the Italian repertory, but it was no exaggeration to say that what she had to offer counted for more. What counted most was the immersion of all her blood and being in a trance-like evocation of Senta's mystical essence, the fervor in Sieglinde's transformation from slave of her husband to free spouse of her brother. That she managed to convey her hynotic conception of Senta despite the uncouth conducting of Schippers was a tribute to superior indoctrination as well as to the strong support of London's fine Dutchman,* the jovial, well-sung Daland of Tozzi,* and a better than average Erik* by Liebl. Olvis was the Steersman* and Amparan out of her element as Mary.* Later *Holländers* included one on February 12, with Harshaw (Senta) and Wilderman (Daland*), and another on February 15, with Da Costa (Erik*) and Dunn (Mary*). Rysanek's occupation with the German repertory provided the opportunity for Dalis to appear as Lady Macbeth* on February 4. She did better than might have been anticipated, though her sound was hard for Verdi.

Aside from *Der fliegende Holländer,* which had been absent since Bing's first season, the least frequently performed work to be heard again was *Pelléas et Mélisande*. The conductor on December 2 was Morel, an assignment for which he had more than ordinarily promising credentials in the memory of his fine participation with Maggie Teyte at her memorable City Center performances of March 1948. However, Morel's *Pelléas* at the Metropolitan never came close to its quality elsewhere (he had also done better in a concert version with the Philharmonic), either because it was no more suited to the "repertory" treatment than *Parsifal* or because his dynamic values were not drawn on a sufficiently large scale for the theater. Uppman as Pelléas and Los Angeles as Mélisande resumed rôles they had performed previously (with Monteux), with more that was meaningful vocally than dramatically. London made much of his opportunities for

---

[1] This performance was publicized as "uncut," meaning that approximately twelve minutes of music were restored to the part of Gurnemanz and the duet of Klingsor and Kundry.

Golaud,* Tozzi was a superior Arkel,* and Resnik a convincing Geneviève.* Together with Allen as Yniold* and Harvuot as the Doctor,* the cast should have added up to more than it did. On January 2, Borg was Golaud,* but there were, miraculously, no other cast changes in the five performances. (At the other extreme of Morel's experience in this season was *Carmen,* which began on October 31 with Madeira, Olvis as Don José,* and Merrill as Escamillo; altered to Stevens, Uzunov, and Sereni on November 12; proceeded to Elias as Carmen,* with Baum and Zanasi on November 18; and took a turn to Amparan as Carmen,* Uzunov, and Guarrera on January 1.)

Otherwise restored in this season was the Berman production of *La Forza del destino,* which had last been performed on January 25, 1958. Its return on February 1, with Schippers as the conductor, provided for the first Leonora* of Rysanek. She presented a more than ordinarily convincing illusion in the male costume of the Convent Scene, but sounded uncomfortably strained by the middle and low range of the part. Tucker performed with his customary quality as Alvaro, as did Siepi as Padre Guardiano, but there was rough going for Corena as Melitone. He had to be replaced by Pechner after Act I. Nor was it a good night for Bastianini, performing his first Metropolitan role in three seasons. He was plainly out of voice as Carlo.* Schippers's treatment of the overture earned cheers after its noisy conclusion, though one doubts that Verdi would have been among the cheerers. Dunn was Preziosilla,* and Reitan had the small opportunity provided by the role of the Surgeon.*

There were expectations of improvement in detail if not in sum for the *Forza* of March 4, in which Tebaldi made her seasonal reappearance as Leonora. Tucker and Warren, fresh from their triumph in *Boccanegra* four days before, were reunited as Alvaro and Carlo, with Baccaloni as Melitone. The evening began not too well for Tebaldi, whose sound was beginning to take on the heavy, inert quality that became a chronic condition in a year or two, but her Convent Scene was freer. How she might have sung *"Pace, pace"* this night will never be known, for the curtain that fell on the crumpled figure of Warren lying face down on the floor near the middle of Act II (in this version) did not rise again.

To some in the audience, the abrupt forward motion that followed his *"Oh gioia, oh gioia"* was a vivid bit of stage action, or perhaps a stumbling lunge from a misplaced step. But to horrified others, including conductor Schippers, his colleagues in the wings, and the better-versed public (including his wife in a box), this was no make-believe or casual accident. The performer nearest to him was young Reitan as the Surgeon. He looked at the limp form on the floor, then with helpless disbelief at Schippers, who motioned the orchestra to stop, as the curtain fell.

The first to reach Warren from the wings was Tucker, crying "Lennie! Lennie!" Closely following him was the stage manager, Osie Hawkins, who attempted artificial resuscitation by mouth-to-mouth breathing. Within a minute and a half of Warren's collapse, Dr. Adrian W. Zorgniotti, the physician in attendance, who had been a witness to the occurrence from his seat in the auditorium, had pushed his way through the crowd—Tucker, he says, was the most difficult to move—and began his examination. Oxygen was administered and an ambulance summoned. Warren was removed, unconscious, from the spot on the stage where he lay (the only sign of the happening was a patch of blood from the broken nose he suffered when he crashed to the floor) to a dressing room. He died eight minutes after his collapse, at 10:03, but efforts to revive him went on for half an hour. Cause of death was ascribed by Dr. Zorgniotti, in the first flush of the happening, to a massive cerebrovascular hemorrhage. In a more reflective second thought, he now says, it would be more accurately described as myocardial infarction with ventricular fibrillation. Though the fact was unknown to his closest colleagues, Warren had been receiving treatment for high blood pressure, and his personal physician was present (in a box with Mrs. Warren) at the moment of the tragedy.

Meanwhile the stunned spectators, unaware of what was happening behind the lowered curtain, lingered in their seats or gathered in the lobbies to smoke and wait. After a brief interval, Bing appeared to settle the unrest of the audience by an assurance that the performance would continue. But even before Mario Sereni, who had been summoned to assume Warren's role, could reach the theater, Bing appeared before the audience again, this time with grim face, a slip of paper in his hand.

"This," he read, "is one of the saddest nights in the history of the Metropolitan"—a prologue to doom that brought outcries of "No!"

"May I ask you all to rise," he continued, "in memory of one of our greatest performers, who died in the middle of one of his greatest performances?"

After a pause, he concluded: "I am sure you will agree with me that it would not be possible to continue with the performance."

As the bad news spread, bits and pieces of detail began to accumulate as background to a tragedy unlike any the Metropolitan had witnessed since the death of Armand Castlemary on its stage in 1897 (see page 128). In a rehearsal preceding his splendid success in *Boccanegra* the previous week, Warren had exploded in an irascible tirade at the orchestra and its conductor, Mitropoulos, which suspended the session for a lengthy interval. The orchestra felt that not only its members, but also Mitropoulos, to whom they were devoted, had been demeaned in a fashion that demanded more than a second-person expression of regret. Only a verbal apology from Warren himself cleared the air and permitted the rehearsal to proceed. Those with an eye to the circumstances of the *Forza* itself surmised that the tensions of the week and Warren's desire to outdo himself resulted in an explosive effort at the climax of *"Urna fatale"* (up to a G) which triggered the fatal attack.

Thus, after a time too long to allow memory to recall a predecessor, a Metropolitan performance terminated before it was concluded. But, the next day being Saturday, there was another to be given almost immediately. As it could hardly begin as if nothing but the afternoon's effort was on the mind of the performers, Bing addressed both the visible audience in the theater and the invisible audience of the radio in these words:

"Ladies and gentlemen, I am sure that all of you—far away as well as here—know the heavy loss we suffered last night. I am equally sure that all of you share our grief, as, indeed, you share that loss. There can be no more fitting tribute to Leonard Warren than the music of the composer he loved and served so well. In his memory, our orchestra will play the prelude to the fourth act of *La Traviata.*"

Oddly, but fittingly, the conductor for the matinee of *Der fliegende Holländer* was Schippers, who had conducted the last note that Warren sang. He and many other colleagues, friends, and mere admirers attended the Low Mass that was held for Warren, a convert to Catholicism from the Jewish faith in which he had been born, on the following Monday at St. Vincent Ferrer's, Lexington Avenue at Sixty-sixth Street.

Thus the closing weeks of a season that had begun with the bright promise of six new productions and had included the highlight of Nilsson's Isolde, Simionato's Azucena, and Warren's own Boccanegra, were played out by a company in a state of semi-shock and a dull awareness rather than a keen realization of what really had happened. Perhaps only Rudolf Bing and his close associates knew what it meant to write the name of Warren twenty times a season on a cast list and be assured of results by which the efforts of others could be measured. But, in the immediate happening, it was, by common agreement, Bing himself who faced the grim fact of Warren's death with the most composure and the least sign of panic and spoke the words he had to speak, when he had to, with simplicity and self-control.

According to the canons of those reared in its faith, the theater resumed its functions undaunted if hardly unaffected. Direct effects of Warren's death bore heavily, first of all, on the numerous performances of *Bocca-negra* (on tour as well as in New York) that followed the normal schedule of an important *première*. The first, in Philadelphia on March 8, was taken by Guarrera, the appointed alternate, as was the second in New York on March 15 (Tebaldi was the Amelia*). But neither in vocal size nor in dramatic pith was Guarrera a Boccanegra* to sustain the place of prominence he had inherited. This, if any, was the ideal moment to add the sound and stimulating artistic talents of Tito Gobbi to the Metropolitan's assets, but Bing did not choose to go that route. He chose, instead, to engage Anselmo Colzani, a younger Italian baritone who was, no doubt, more amenable to what the Metropolitan could offer in a time of dire need than Gobbi might have been. He made his debut more than creditably on April 7 in a *Boccanegra* with Tebaldi as Amelia (Milanov had sung two intervening Amelias,* with Bergonzi as Gabriele* on March 25), Tucker, and Hines as Fiesco.* The voice was big if not lustrous in sound, the manner of using it altogether dependable, if scarcely distinguished. He was, to be sure, not a Warren, which was hardly possible; but he was also no Gobbi, which was possible.

There were, in other roles that Warren might have sung, the make-do of Sereni as Carlo in the next *Forza* on March 12 (Tebaldi, Tucker, Baccaloni, and Hines repeated their paces of the fatal night with professional composure if private woe); Cassel as Scarpia on March 19 and MacNeil as Scarpia (with Stella and Bergonzi) on March 22; and another "emergency" baritone, Piero Cappuccilli, as Germont* (d) in *Traviata* on March 26, followed by Uhde as Scarpia* (with Tebaldi and Morel) on March 30. In his lean posture and head-hugging wig, Uhde conveyed an uncanny likeness to Conrad Veidt of silent films, but the vocal power to support his action was hardly what Puccini-in-Italian required. Before the season was over, the schedule also included a *Forza* on April 13, with Tebaldi, Bergonzi and Siepi, in which the Carlo* (d) was sung by Aurelio Oppicelli. Which was Cappuccilli and which was Oppicelli would be difficult, indeed, to determine. Neither returned for another season, and the total of their appearances at the Metropolitan in this one was two.

As if the unpredictable crises were not sufficient unto themselves, a relatively predictable one erupted before the season finished. It came when Stella took the occasion of a *Butterfly* on March 24 to press a demand on Bing for a solo curtain-call after the second act. In the test of wills that ensued, Stella did not have her solo bow and the Metropolitan did not have Stella after her Maddalena* in *Chénier* on March 31. No formal explanation was made of the rupture, but Curtis-Verna was in Stella's place for *Trovatore* on April 6 and in *Chénier* as Maddalena* on April 12. On

April 16, the final matinee of the season, Kirsten was brought back for the first time in three seasons to sing her expert Butterfly. As the door revolved, it was Stella out and Kirsten in.

In another season of less incident, and, alas! accident, there doubtless would have been more attention to the debut on March 3 of Pavel Lisitsian as Amonasro* (d) in *Aida*. He was a baritone of the Bolshoi Opera who had come to America for recitals under the cultural exchange program and been invited to share the stage of the Metropolitan in what turned out to be a veritable UN of talent (Simionato and Stella of Italy, Baum of German extraction, Moscona of Greece, and the Americans Sgarro, Nagy, and Vanni as King, Messenger, and Priestess). He thus became the first People's Artist of the Soviet Union to perform at the Metropolitan, with as much professional composure and artistic attainment as the usual experienced Italian would bring to a similar debut, plus the qualification of a voice "a little light for the theater." Though it was said that Lisitsian knew the role in Italian, he favored Russian as more comfortable for him in these circumstances. As the debut occurred on the night preceding the *Forza* of Warren's death, memory of any other baritone in that week was almost automatically obliterated.

1960–1961

The cause to mourn Warren's absence was not delayed long after the beginning of the new season. Indeed, it was in part because of him that the opening night had been set aside, long before October 24, for the first performance in the Metropolitan of Verdi's *Nabucco*. Neither the unfamiliarity of the work nor the increase of the top price for tickets to $45 (including a tax-deductible donation) affected the public response, which brought $91,482—a new record—to the box office.

It was venturesome of Bing to undertake a work from the very beginning of Verdi's career, and risky to make this tale of Nebuchadnezzar's tragedy a subject for display on an opening night. Perhaps that very risk invited Bing's action, as an inverse return on the display itself. In any case, the audience and the work were far from coalescing, with results that perhaps influenced its reception generally and lessened its chances of acceptance.

Somewhat as in the instances of *Ernani* and *Macbeth,* Bing had neglected to provide a central, pervasive authority who would communicate the unfamiliar work to the performers to whom it was unfamiliar. The conductor this time was Schippers, who functioned efficiently on the whole, but without that compelling conviction based on thorough knowledge which communicates itself to an audience whether it is aware of the reason or not. The stage director was Günther Rennert, a product of the German theater who brought to his task a good sense of groupings for the chorus, but only limited animation for the principals. The scenic design, by Teo Otto and Wolfgang Roth, provided risers and platforms that satisfied the functional needs of the chorus, but did little to provide credible surroundings for the action. Funds for the production were provided by the National Council.

Those to whom the action itself was unfamiliar may have had no cause to question the occurrence of the great chorus *"Va, pensiero"* at the opening of the final act (the third in this version) rather than at the place Verdi decreed for it later in the act. The notion that this would make for a better "picture" did not reckon with the file of latecomers straggling to their seats, especially at the first performance. And no one seemed aware that as Verdi had positioned it, it separated the two stretches of heavy singing for Nabucco, providing a welcome interlude for rest. In the amended form, they followed close together. In any case, Schippers got so little from the chorus that it passed almost without notice.

Whether Warren's presence as Nabucco would have made more than a marginal difference in sound is debatable, for MacNeil had warmth and volume in abundance. Where one might have looked for a difference would have been in the strength of feeling that Warren could communicate by presence as much as by voice. This was largely lacking in MacNeil's effort. Of the others, Siepi was a resonant Zaccaria* and Fernandi a better Ismaele* than might have been anticipated, while Bonaldo Giaiotti produced a bass sound of promising richness as the High Priest* (d). In the smallish role of Fenena,* Elias had a part cut to her measure.

However, where this venture sagged most was in the lack of a soprano for whom the searching requirements of Abigaille would provide an opportunity for greatness rather than merely a challenge to survival. Modified though the part was to remove some of the demands Verdi had put upon Strepponi, and diligently as Rysanek applied herself to the problem, Abigaille* proved, in the course of the season's performances, to be beyond her capacities to deal with on even terms as it would have been beyond any contemporary soprano, save, perhaps, Callas at her pristine best. Some of the high-range writing was accurately, even powerfully accomplished, but elsewhere the voice was typically undependable, and characterization was restricted to the broadest terms.

Thus, however much the hearing of *Nabucco* gratified those with an interest in Verdi's development and in the first crude eruptions of the impulses that were to dominate his life—love of country, filial devotion, defiance of oppression—the demonstration of it on the stage lacked too much in power, conviction, and dramatic compulsion to make an effect on the average (Metropolitan) operagoer.

The lack of interest on the part of those present and its echo in the press of the following day, in which the opinion of Rysanek's performance was largely adverse, aroused Bing to a retaliatory action unmatched, perhaps, since Conried had chided the press for not listening to Caruso sing *"E luce-van le stelle."* It was directed not toward individuals, with whom he had differed in the past, but against the whole writing corps. It took the form of exclusion from all further dress rehearsals of new productions (a privilege in effect since his arrival). It was based on the premise that because Rysanek had—admittedly—been off pitch and below form at the dress rehearsal on Friday, that impression had colored the judgment of her (somewhat) better performance at Monday night's *première*. In his coolly courteous letter to each critic, Bing wrote: "An unfavorable impression is usually the most lasting: to revise such an impression perhaps only a day or two later may be asking too much . . ." It was, however, not asking any more than discrimination between a privilege and a performance, which most of the press recognized and respected.

Whatever the justice of Bing's complaint (in which Rysanek's distress undoubtedly had a part) or the wisdom of his counter-action (he could endure bad relations with the press more easily than bad relations with an important, insecure performer), *Nabucco* went its round of the subscription cycle with little evidence of enthusiasm or, even, of appreciation for the effort expended on its preparation. In the total of nine performances (including a benefit, on January 7, in celebration of the centenary of the unification of Italy), the Abigaille on every occasion was Rysanek. Otherwise, changes included Tozzi as Zaccaria* on November 11 and Hines in the same role on December 7, when the Nabucco* was Colzani; Dunn as Fenena* on November 21 and Olvis as Ismaele* in the same performance. Despite Bing's efforts to interest other leading singers in the role of Abigaille, none matured sufficiently to justify another venture with the work during the next five seasons.

The season thus begun with less than happy results tended, for weeks, to pursue a stubbornly unsteady course of difficulty and dilemma. Some of this came from over-estimation of the new talents to which important responsibilities were entrusted. Among these was the Swedish mezzo Kerstin Meyer, who was introduced as Carmen* (d) on October 29, presenting a curiously Germanic view of the character (in make-up and action) and insufficient vocal appeal, and the French Jane Rhodes, who followed her in the same role on November 15 with another list of liabilities—a small voice and a highly personal estimate of the part which accorded with nothing else on stage. The low estate to which Bizet's masterpiece had descended as the animation of Guthrie's original effort faded caused it to be characterized as "shabby" by Watt in the *Daily News*. Possibly the death of Bjoerling (whose contract called for ten appearances in this season) resulted in a series of new Don Josés,* of whom Vickers was the best in his first effort (with Meyer). He was followed by the Bulgarian Nikola Nikolov, crude and unappealing at his debut on November 7, and the all but unmentionable Leonard del Ferro, who had a one-performance Metropolitan career on November 30. Who had certified him for this stage was never disclosed, but it was the function of the General Manager to prevent such an imposition on an audience paying Tucker prices.

Such an excuse as Bjoerling's death could hardly explain the presence of Lorenzo Testi, who made his debut as Marcello* (d) in *Bohème* on October 28 (Reitan was Schaunard,* with Amara, Tucker, Hurley, Siepi, and Kelley as Alcindoro*). His debut dated to 1956 at Spoleto, which may have commended him to its resident maestro, Schippers, who also conducted this performance. Testi's good vocal material was offset by a gaucheness of manner and a lack of stage discipline which testified, in his Escamillo,* Sharpless* (brown shoes with a seersucker suit), and Lescaut* in *Manon Lescaut*, to the laxity that afflicted the Metropolitan at the time. Among the *Carmens* of this time, the memorable effort was a Micaëla* by Stratas on November 15. However, all was not bleakness. There was a newcomer of the quality once considered "Metropolitan" in Gabriella Tucci, a little-known Italian soprano who paused en route home from engagements elsewhere to take her place as Cio-Cio-San* in *Butterfly* on October 29 with practiced professionalism and a sound of likeable timbre. Bergonzi's Pinkerton and the freshly spirited effort of Morel in his first *Butterfly* contributed to a happy result. It suggested that Tucci's only role in this season would be followed by many others in the future.

Those who believe in a rule of threes for misfortune found their worst fears justified on November 2 with news from Milan that Dimitri Mitropoulos had suffered a heart attack during a rehearsal and died en route to a hospital. This came only weeks after Bjoerling's equally sudden death in Stockholm in early September and while the memory of Warren's collapse was still fresh. By the evidence of letters written to Bruno Zirato, his friend and associate in New York, Mitropoulos's strength had been waning steadily during the summer. But he had persisted with a heavy schedule of work, hopeful that he could survive the strain and return to America without being hospitalized again. However, his first rehearsal of Mahler's Third Symphony with the Scala Orchestra was his last. The place he filled for any and all services from *Cav.* and *Pag.* to *Salome* instantly fell vacant, with no ready prospect of a replacement then or perhaps—in all his variety—ever.

The preparations in progress for Donizetti's *L'Elisir d'amore,* the season's second new production (paid for by the Metropolitan Opera Club, Mrs. John Barry Ryan, and others) could thus hardly be called lighthearted. But whatever it was by November 22, it was something else by the first performance on November 25. Between the final rehearsal and the performance, Valletti's participation as Nemorino was canceled and the obscure Dino Formichini substituted. Oddly enough, in view of Bing's recent admonitions on the fallacy of judging a performer by a dress rehearsal, it was Valletti's performance at rehearsal that aroused managerial dissatisfaction. Rather than participate in a face-saving story of "indisposition," Valletti considered his position in the company gravely compromised, and resigned. Nor did he, despite efforts to smooth over the difficulty, perform at the Metropolitan in the next five seasons.

For whatever reasons, *L'Elisir* proved to be more for the eye than the ear. There was a good deal to enjoy and some things to admire in the scenic concept, which began with the arrival of Fernando Corena as Dr. Dulcamara* in a "balloon" that swung in from the wings, and continued— with caster-mounted set pieces swiveling around a central, elevated island of playing space—to be airy, light and highly functional. It was the work of Robert O'Hearn, a young designer new to the Metropolitan. He thus embarked on a career of mutual profit with Nathaniel Merrill, who had graduated from acting as "stage director" of productions by others to directing one of his own. Merrill solved the immediate problem of arousing laughter by means of gags and tricks that frequently rubbed roughly against the humorous but always aristocratic spirit of Donizetti's music. Of *character* there was barely a trace, whether brought along by Corena (a small doctor by contrast with such predecessors as Baccaloni and Pinza), Guarrera (Belcore*), or Soederstroem (an admirable artist whose gift was not for the florid singing required of an Adina*), or provided in the direction of Merrill.

As for Formichini, the best he could provide was a thinly sweet trickle of sound that made Nemorino* (d) unhappily synonymous with *tenorino.* When the orchestra under Cleva's direction was sufficiently subdued, he could be heard if he expended full power; in the concerted numbers, or ensemble, he was all but inaudible. By *"Una furtiva lagrima"* he sounded vocally fagged and was cooing, rather than singing, it. Dramatically the short pudgy Formichini's efforts were of the sort that aroused laughter because they were ridiculous rather than because they were comical. There was no cast change in the next five performances, but the Adina* on January 28 was Moffo; on February 1 it was Peters, and on April 4 it was Hurley, with Gedda as Nemorino* on January 28 and Sereni as Belcore* on February 1. Of these, the Adina of Moffo was a gratifying improvement, but the audience was not permitted to have it become habit-forming.

As well as subtracting the talents of Valletti, the substitution of Formichini resulted in the addition of his talents to roles for which they were even less suited than they were to Nemorino. In this season they included the Duke* in *Rigoletto* on January 19, for which he had neither the *brio* nor the volume to match Moffo's Gilda,* and Rodolfo in *Bohème* on April 10, with Los Angeles and a youthful American, Dorothy Coulter, as Musetta.* It may be noted without comment that Schippers became ill after the first act and was replaced by Schick.

Mitropoulos's death did not affect the immediate, day-to-day functioning of the Metropolitan as the date for his return was still a time off; but it left a large vacuum of leadership in a project as ambitious as any yet sponsored by Bing—the first performance of Puccini's *Turandot* since the season of 1929–30. The extraordinary equipment of Nilsson gave the project the shining kind of vocal spearhead it required, but the large dimensions of the score called for a conductor with the thrust to follow through. Where to find one above the average *routinier* posed a needle-and-haystack problem, for it was all but certain that any one of the desired quality would already have his year's work laid out, and be unable to accommodate the period of rehearsal required for a *première* on February 24. Even such an illogical one as Victor de Sabata, on leave from Scala because of uncertain health was approached and found (regretfully) unavailable.

Eventually the solution was found no farther away than an apartment on upper Fifth Avenue, where Leopold Stokowski was enjoying the company of his two young sons and filling his choice of orchestral engagements here and there. As noted earlier (page 628) he had been lured back to the theater by the City Opera in the fall of 1959, and had taken another turn on the same wheel in the fall of 1960, when he presided over a double bill bringing together Monteverdi's *Orfeo* (with Gerard Souzay making his New York stage debut in the title role and Judith Raskin as Euridice) and Dallapiccola's *The Prisoner*. The latter was given in an English translation with Anne McKnight as the Mother, Norman Treigle impersonating the Prisoner, and Richard Cassilly as the Jailer. Aside from a sprightly production of Werner Egk's *The Inspector-General,* for which the composer was the conductor and Jon Crain was cast in the title role, it was by much the most interesting offering of the fall season (for the first time since the post-Leinsdorf period of 1957, it was decided to forego a spring season).

Perhaps the memory of Stokowski's presence in the City Center pit presented the necessary impulse to the idea that here, close at hand, was the liveliest of possibilities. His co-operation was invited and eventually secured, but before it became operative, another calamity seemed to foreclose this solution to the dilemma posed by the sudden death of Mitropoulos. While romping with his sons in Central Park, the seventy-nine-year-old conductor suffered a back injury that required hospitalization. Within a few weeks, however, he was back home, strapped and braced to permit mobility on sticks, and ready to begin work.

There were, however two other plateaus to be attained on the way to the summit of *Turandot*. Waiting at the first was the long-deferred debut of Eileen Farrell, an American soprano who had defied categorization for most of twenty years during which she had appeared on the radio, ventured pop music, made occasional records, reared a family, sung a sound track for a film based on the sad history of Marjorie Lawrence, and, while her voice blossomed to majestic size, done everything but perform in opera. Under the stimulus of reviews of her recent concert appearances and a few tentative ventures on the stage elsewhere, Bing invited her to participate in Gluck's *Alcestis,* in which Flagstad—to whose sound hers had often been compared—had made her final Metropolitan appearances. Embellishing the occasion was a new production, paid for by the Fisher Foundation of Marshalltown, Iowa, for which Michael Manuel, a member of the Metropolitan's backstage *entourage,* was stage director as well as designer. Best of his visual efforts was a highly successful temple scene, with a high platform in mid-stage and pillars receding into the distance. As director, he expended his main effort on limiting the action of the short (5 feet 5½ inches), broad (180 pounds) Alcestis to as few steps as could be contrived. When she had to do more, in Act III, she moved well enough to suggest that Manuel had been over-considerate.

Vocally, Farrell met every requirement of *Alcestis* on December 6 with the kind of vocal art of which no opera house ever has an excess, and with a fluent command of the English text which spoke of a varied, demanding background in concert and radio. What was lacking, only, was what that same background had denied her—the settled ease and assurance of the practiced opera-singer as contrasted with one who has, merely, appeared in opera. The prognosis was that Farrell had an operatic future in special projects devised to exploit her strengths and minimize her weaknesses; but hardly as a regular performer in the day-to-day repertory. Associated with her under Leinsdorf's sober direction were Gedda as Admetus,* Cassel as a dry-voiced Priest,* and, in smaller roles, Olvis (Apollo*), Marsh (Herald*), and Scott (Leader of the People*). Tudor's choreography, though promising, was in that state of semi-completion all too frequently associated with his *premières*. After several performances by the original cast, Sullivan returned on January 30 to the role of Admetus, which he had sung with Flagstad. Marsh was the High Priest* with Nagy as Apollo. Farrell's other role in this season was La Gioconda* when Ponchielli's work was given on December 26. Her enviable endeavor to respect the letter of her part was somewhat roughly treated in the battle royal this score may become with such seasoned competitors for applause as Tucker (Enzo), Rankin (Laura), Merrill (Barnaba), and Giaiotti (Alvise*). Dunn as La Cieca* sang *"Voce di donna"* very well. Changes were rampant as the season progressed, with Baum as Enzo on January 15; Resnik as Laura, Siepi as Alvise, and Colzani as Barnaba* on January 20; Milanov, with Resnik, Tozzi, Mary MacKenzie (La Cieca*), and Morell (Enzo*) on March 2.

Some of the most agreeable sound that could be imagined from four principal singers was the special dispensation of January 26, when Flotow's *Martha* had its first Metropolitan performance since December 29, 1928, in a production underwritten by the Opera Guild. Comprising the well-matched quartet were Tucker (Lionel*), Tozzi (Plunkett*), Los Angeles (Lady Harriett*), and Elias (Nancy*). The order of vocal effort was consistently high, the scenic effort of Oliver Smith was often pretty (save for a rather drab Richmond Fair), the stage direction of Ebert skillful, the musical direction of Verchi as good as anything he ever did. What was most to the detriment of this venture was the cheap, barely literate English "version," which remained without attribution on the program because some of its lines had been changed during the rehearsal period, and the author had deemed this sufficient cause to prefer no credit. But the libretto, with its full quota of "looker-cooker" and "hurry-scurry" rhymes, bore the name of Ann Ronell, whose ASCAP credits included the texts for "Who's Afraid of the Big Bad Wolf" and "Willow Weep for Me." The crassest chore, whether the responsibility of Ann Ronell or Ann Onymous, was the substitution of new words for "The Last Rose of Summer" in place of Tom Moore's. Los Angeles sang it beautifully nevertheless. On subsequent occasions the cast remained the same, save on March 27, when the Plunkett* was Flagello, without penalty to the beauty of the ensemble sound. On April 13 Tucker added to the linguistic confusion by singing *"M'appari"* in Italian in order, he said, to "let his fans know how Caruso sounded."

As the restriction on press attendance at dress rehearsals remained inflexible, what was in store for *Turandot* when Stokowski, half hobbling on crutches, made his way laboriously to the conductor's desk on February 24 was as much a surprise to the critics as it was to the audience (receipts totaled $46,000, or more than was earned by an opening night when Bing was new). The clangorous chords of the opening affirmed Stokowski's ability to transform the sound of any orchestra with which he was associated, and the choral singing that followed was no less than arousing. But what was even more transforming was the sight that greeted the eye—a *mélange* of vivid colors harmoniously blended by Beaton into a composite that most would have considered impossible on this stage. Completing the illusion of another time and place were the skin tints and pigmentations of the makeup (including body paint, moustaches, and pig-tailed wigs) created by Yoshio Aoyama of *Butterfly* fame in collaboration with Beaton. Even this aspect of the whole had not been achieved without a share of the adversity that characterized this season, when Aoyama was suddenly hospitalized while rehearsals were in progress. Fortunately, Merrill was able to carry on his work from Aoyama's detailed "plot" of the action.

However much his accident impaired his ability to walk, Stokowski was all thrust and animation once on the chair that had been provided for him on the conductor's stand. The authority he exerted over the orchestra served also to bend the strong voice and stronger ego of Franco Corelli as Calaf* to his will, meanwhile preparing a suitable frame for Nilsson's glinting high-register sound for *"In questa reggia."* Giaiotti as Timur* did well what was needed and Anna Moffo as Liù* was sufficiently disguised to look her humble part while providing, vocally, for an appeal equal but opposite to Nilsson's. Mattyln Gavers contributed a plan of choreographic action which insinuated grace into the actions of Ping* (Guarrera), Pang* (Nagy), and Pong* (Anthony), as well as in those episodes which lent themselves directly to dancing. A final touch of artistry could be heard in the aged voice summoned by Alessio de Paolis for the venerable Emperor.* Musically, the performance adhered to custom in shortening the scene of Ping, Pang, and Pong, and deleting about ten pages (Nos. 428–437) from the concluding scene evolved by Franco Alfano from the sketches left by Puccini at his death.

Some part of *Turandot*'s effect, no doubt, was owing to the impact of a great if flawed work which had not been heard at full value in New York for thirty years (a venture at City Center in April 1950 was no more than half way successful). But it was owing even more to the rare combination of star talents—Beaton's, Nilsson's, Aoyama's, Corelli's, and Stokowski's—coalescing into a constellation of values. The common suggestion that there is something evil in the "star system" was properly refuted by this demonstration of what can be achieved when there are both a system and stars.

Even more, it attested to the benefits that can be conferred on the routine of an opera house by a conductor with the gifts to transcend it. Curiously, the performance itself was only half over when some "voices of authority" undertook to decry the contribution of Stokowski. He was no opera conductor, it was said; he didn't give enough cues to the chorus, he forbade the prompter—who ordinarily transfers the beat of the conductor to the singers, who can see him better—from doing anything but prompting. The causes for this kind of sniping came out later, in the aftermath of Stokowski's angry exit from the Metropolitan. He had, it seems, sought to exercise some influence on lighting, and had openly criticized the long waits imposed on other personnel while production details were being arranged on stage. This, it seems, was not what conductors were supposed to concern themselves with at Bing's Metropolitan.

However, while Stokowski performed at flood tide in this season, the results were, also, beyond what one had been conditioned to expect at the Metropolitan, Bing or otherwise. The principals remained mostly unchanged for the succeeding seven performances, save for the role of Liù,* which was performed by Stratas on March 9, Amara on March 24 (when Wilderman was Timur*), and Leontyne Price on March 29 (when Gari was called upon to finish what Corelli had begun as Calaf but couldn't sustain beyond Act I), and Albanese on April 8. The combination of Nilsson-Price-Corelli made a particular effect on March 21 in Philadelphia's Academy of Music, when Stokowski faced his old friends for the first time as conductor of a Metropolitan Opera performance in the scene so long familiar to him. It also closed a circle of association for the Metropolitan, whose management decreed an end to the long history of visits to Philadelphia because of increasing costs and a preference to devote all future Tuesdays to performances at home.

The history of *Turandot* would be incomplete without reference to the source of the benefaction that made this production possible. It came in large part from John S. Newberry, a Detroit art patron and opera enthusiast, who had presented the Metropolitan with the proceeds from an unexpected stock dividend. For a while, it was earmarked for use at Lincoln Center, but as that prospect receded into the future, it was decided to proceed with the plan while Nilsson was at the height of her career. It was well that the schedule was altered, for Newberry might otherwise never have seen the *Turandot* he made possible. He died in Paris on October 24, 1964.

The new talents of Corelli were certainly of prime value to the success of *Turandot,* but the evening of his debut as Manrico* (d) in *Il Trovatore* on January 27 was even more memorable for its Leonora* (d), Leontyne Price. Here, after an interval of too long a time, was a leading soprano of American birth with the means as well as the ambition to sing leading soprano roles at high-quality standard. That she was, as well, a Negro added to the lustre of her accomplishments, which had been pursued from Laurel, Mississippi, through the Juilliard School and a widely traveled production of Gershwin's *Porgy and Bess,* to opera. Either by sound advice or good fortune, Price's Metropolitan debut had been deferred until she had acquired, elsewhere, the operatic indoctrination to make her completely at home once she had reached its stage.

This *Trovatore* was hardly the most orderly imaginable—Corelli had his coterie of enthusiasts to exult at the first blast of loud sound he uttered from the wings, and Price was equally attended by friends and well-wishers—but it ended better than it began. After some early uncertainties (caused mostly by shortness of breath), Price displayed a sound command of the line and meaning of Leonora's part, and Corelli survived a crude *"Ah si ben mio"* and a stentorian *"Di quella pira,"* to show qualities of voice to match his formidable good looks. Cleva conducted, with Merrill (Di Luna), Dalis (a strident Azucena*), and Wilderman (Ferrando).

Much of Corelli's later effort was committed to *Turandot,* in which he made a dashing Calaf to see and a potent one to hear (he sang everything better than what should be the high point of the part, *"Nessun dorma"*), but he did show his qualification as Don Carlo* before the season's end (first on April 3 with Curtis-Verna, Tozzi as a rather gruff King Philip, Sereni as Rodrigo, Rankin as Eboli, and Uhde as the Grand Inquisitor). A striking figure of a young Prince, and possessed of all the vocal resources to be an equally fine-sounding one, Corelli insisted on squandering them on blatant bids for applause, meanwhile taking whatever negligent postures suited his mood. There was little else to be hoped for from this *Don Carlo,* whose earlier performances showed its conductor, Verchi, to be largely uninformed on the speed, power, or weight of sound appropriate to Verdi's highly specific intentions. Earlier the Carlo had been Fernandi on March 16 (another Bjoerling date?), overburdened in this venture, with Wilderman as the Inquisitor, the whole of it justifying Lang's comment in the *Herald Tribune* that of *Don Carlo*'s original glory "all that is left are the sets and costumes." Some effort was made to interest Boris Christoff in taking up, ten years later, the role of King Philip, which he had been scheduled to perform in 1950, but it was said that he specified a rehearsal schedule that Bing could not meet.

The cost to Price, in effort and money, of the time she had invested in preparation abroad yielded handsome dividends in the succession of roles she assumed with confidence and performed with distinction during the next month: Aida* on February 20, with Fernandi, Dalis, and Merrill; Butterfly* on March 3 with Olvis and Testi; and Donna Anna* in *Don Giovanni* on March 25 with Curtis-Verna as Elvira,* Anthony (Ottavio), and London. She was least suited, physically, to *Butterfly,* which she nevertheless sang affectingly, but the excellent formulation of the vocal line in Mozart was even exceeded by the thorough match of dramatic and vocal abilities she brought to Aida. In a carefully developed arch of effect from humility to self-assertion, Price put her strongest effort where it counted most, on *"O cieli azzurri."* Not all her vocal effects were equally good, for she inclined to awkward phrase endings and the gaspy glottis stroke, but there was much beautiful detail in the final duet and a full reserve of power for the ensembles. The Radames was the unfortunate Fernandi, who was first put to the test of this role on November 19 (in place of Bergonzi) and, despite obvious shortcomings, was subjected to the same strain several times later. Perhaps this was a consequence of a mid-season ailment of Vickers, but it was hardly a fair requirement for a young tenor who was also called upon for Ismaele in *Nabucco,* Rodolfo in *Bohème,* Pinkerton in *Butterfly,* Enzo in *La Gioconda,* and the title role in *Don Carlo.* There were almost equal demands on Olvis, an even less experienced tenor who was called upon for Gabriele* in *Boccanegra* on January 12 and Radames* on March 14, with Elias as Amneris.*

The elusive "standard" returned briefly on December 17 when Georg Solti's debut in *Tannhäuser* provided the kind and quality of vital, alert, and informed leadership which the Metropolitan's Wagner had lacked for some time. But he had only time to prepare the first performance (with Hopf as Tannhäuser,* Rysanek as Elisabeth,* Hines as the Landgraf, Dalis as Venus,* and Hermann Prey in his debut as Wolfram* [d]) and to conduct it three more times before he was off to other engagements elsewhere. Certainly it is not merely hindsight to say that the Metropolitan could have moved sooner to secure the services of so able a young conductor (his Chicago debut dated back to October 20, 1956) before he was absorbed by commitments elsewhere. The Rysanek of *Tannhäuser* was the Rysanek of *Der fliegende Holländer* and *Walküre* rather than the Rysanek of *Don Carlo,* which is to say a performer with the fire and determination to make a meaningful person of Elisabeth.* It was not so well sung, note for note, as the Elisabeth* of Los Angeles on January 16 or of Nilsson on January 25 (by which time the conductor was Strasfogel), but was the most persuasive in action since Lehmann's. The casts, otherwise, were undistinguished, for Hopf's Tannhäuser strained him, vocally, the Venus of Dalis was vigorously sung but without much dramatic illusion, and Prey's Wolfram was light. The Wolfram* with Los Angeles was Cassel, and Eberhard Wächter (d) had the "passing-through" kind of exposure in the same role with Nilsson. Prey had slightly more substance to his sound than Wächter, but neither was at ease in a theater of this size. Solti's dynamic performance of the overture—a product of a concentrated energy which, some members of the orchestra thought, made "unreasonable" demands on the players—flowed on into the Bacchanale, thanks to his preference for the Paris version and the additional amount of fine music it provided. Not much, however, could be said in praise of Tudor's choreography for the Venusberg episode. The scenic designs of Gérard retained the qualities originally admired in them.

Even while some were congratulating themselves on the addition of a Solti to a conducting corps depleted by the death of Mitropoulos, it suffered a still further depletion. As Boehm was about to transfer his activities from the Philharmonic, which he conducted for the first time near the year's end, he found himself afflicted by an eye ailment. It was his preference to have it treated in Vienna, which left his budget of work as unaccounted for as Mitropoulos's. What was probably intended to serve for his resumption of activity on January 14 turned out to be, instead, Leinsdorf's *Don Giovanni* (Steber, Siepi, Della Casa, Gedda, Corena, Hurley, and Uppman), but the schedule left no such latitude for improvisation with *Tristan* impending.

By a tortuous series of circumstances (which could, conceivably, be tracked down to produce a sequence akin to the Reiner-Busch-Reiner-Szell-Boehm chain), the die came up Joseph Rosenstock. There were, probably, very few in the audience that greeted him cordially on January 31 who recalled his earlier Metropolitan experiences in the fall of 1929, but they could hardly have been forgotten by the one to whom the second chance meant the most, Rosenstock himself. There was nothing at all in his *Tristan* to alter the judgment passed thirty-one years before that, as a conductor of Wagner, Rosenstock was "conservative," but, at least, he conserved the strain on his singers to the extent that Vinay sang a full performance with Nilsson, Dalis, Cassel, and Hines. Uhde's eagerness to make himself of use could be read in his willingness to perform the role of Melot.* Dunn was the Brangäne* on February 16, and on March 1 the lovers became Liebl and Harshaw.

What Rosenstock had gained in security and poise emerged in his direction of *Elektra* on February 13, in which Borkh added action to the qualities of voice she had demonstrated in a concert version directed by Mitropoulos in 1956-7. It all worked out well enough to be rewarded by ear-shattering applause, but the aural scheme drawn by Rosenstock made its best effects in the most accessible areas—the climaxes—while slighting some important transitional passages. Frances Yeend, well-known for her work at City Center, provided a strong sound for Chrysothemis* (d), with Madeira raging wrathfully as Klytaemnestra,* Cassel a less than satisfactory Orest,* and Da Costa a passable Aegisth.* Mary MacKenzie made her debut as the first serving woman. On March 4, Gladys Kuchta, an American soprano who had earned attention in Berlin, performed capably as Chrysothemis* (d), with Resnik as Klytaemnestra, Uhde as Orest,* and Liebl as Aegisth.* When *Elektra* was heard again on March 25, the Chrysothemis* was Rysanek, who had been originally nominated for the part, but had withdrawn because of illness, with Vinay (who had first sung Aegisth* on March 17). The action generally, and especially the interaction of her part with Klytaemnestra's, gained much.

Fortunately for the budget, Boehm's health improved sufficiently for him to resume work when *Wozzeck* returned on March 10, thus averting the expense of having it prepared by another conductor. Uhde's excellent Wozzeck and Steber's Marie were of their prior quality, but Herbert's Doctor* was no substitute for the absent Dönch's. In a later performance (March 30), the Doctor was Alvary.

The prime need of the Metropolitan's *Parsifal* was adroitly evaded when its reappearance on March 22 offered a new conductor (Boehm) rather than a new Parsifal (Vinay). There were strength, knowledge, and deep motivation in Boehm's leadership, of most benefit to Hines, but the limited service Vinay was able to provide put an unbreachable perimeter around the liberties Boehm could take when he was performing. The Kundry* on April 7 was Dalis, a role which she had prepared well and for which she had more than adequate means.

Some of what had been considered the "Mitropoulos repertory" passed to Leinsdorf in this season, including *Boris* when it was first given on October 27. This was, however, no improvised assignment, but obviously part of a plan, for it was given in the Shostakovitch version rather than in the Rathaus realization introduced by Stiedry and perpetuated by

Mitropoulos. The new edition doubtless countered some dissatisfaction with the occasionally thin sonority of the Rathaus compromise, but it introduced others, such as Shostakovitch's "innovation" of a stage band for the Coronation Scene and an inappropriately noisy background for Varlaam's *"Town of Kazan."* To Lang in the *Herald Tribune,* the results were "well sounding and very impressive . . . something like Mozart's version of Handel's Messiah. . . ." But there was nothing in the least impressive about Leinsdorf's idea of shifting the Polonaise from the middle of the Polish scene to the end to provide a "brilliant curtain" for the episode while violating a story point. The sequence of roles followed much the same course as before, with London as the first Boris and Siepi following him on November 14. Gedda was a good-looking, rather white-sounding Dimitri* on December 9. For those who inquired about the continuing absence of Boris Christoff, whose performance of the Czar was considered, by some, to be unexcelled, Bing had a standard answer— the unhappy experience with Rossi-Lemeni and the ruffled feelings among his other bassos with the favor to this "outsider." However, other sources recount the negotiations at this time for Christoff to appear in *Don Carlo,* and the reasons for their non-success (see page 649).

Among Leinsdorf's other responsibilities, which included *Nozze di Figaro* (Ludwig made a fleeting appearance as Cherubino* in the first on November 6, with Dunn as Marcellina,* and Vanni was Cherubino* on January 3) and *Don Giovanni* (see page 650), he applied himself most profitably to *Arabella.* His feeling for the structure of the score provided a refinement in the orchestral sound to complement the addition of Anneliese Rothenberger as Zdenka* (d) on November 18. Also upgraded was the role of Matteo,* now being sung by Morell. With such performers of established excellence as London (Mandryka) and Della Casa (Arabella), this Strauss score began to take on some of the character of a house specialty. It would be too much to say that Rothenberger sang her music better than Gueden—difficult if not impossible—but her compact frame and small features made her more believably a girl-raised-as-a-boy than her altogether feminine predecessor. Rothenberger sang no other role in this season, but she was destined for a prominent part in the Metropolitan company-to-be.

The range of Colzani's duties expanded with Amonasro* on November 5, Nabucco* on December 7, Barnaba* on January 20, and Rigoletto* on January 24, most of them on the order of serviceable rather than distinguished. New names included Nerina Santini, a small-scaled Gilda* (d) on March 11, Gianna d'Angelo (born Angelovich in Hartford, Connecticut) in the same role for her debut on April 15, and Biserka Cvejic, whose first opportunity came as Amneris* (d) on April 14. She had the formidable competition of Nilsson's first venture in New York with a work of Verdi, but her promising vocal material was commended nevertheless. Nilsson's Aida* suggested that she could sing it very well were it to become a regular part of her repertory; in a season in which she had been singing Isolde and Turandot, the sound was frequently overproduced, searing rather than merely powerful and brighter than it should be. At an extreme of new and old, Risë Stevens made but a single appearance in this season, that on April 12, when it was all but over. For all its hard use, Stevens's voice nevertheless enabled her to come closer to the needs of Carmen than any prior performer of the season. Thus ended the Stevens career on this stage, for she was not presented in a subsequent season. And rather than making a formal farewell, she preferred to assume executive responsibilities as co-manager (with Michael Manuel) of the Metropolitan Opera National Company when it was launched in 1964.

With the addition of *Turandot* and the return of *Manon Lescaut,* the Puccini works in this season totaled four. Together they had forty performances, or nearly twenty-five per cent of the 178 given in New York in this winter. *Bohème* alone had fourteen, or nearly as many as ALL of Wagner put together (a mere fifteen for three works). This was not only grossly disproportionate to any conception of a balanced repertory, but also the personification of the easy way out. Della Casa was a new Mimi* in this season (on December 10), along with Amara, Albanese, Tebaldi and Los Angeles; Soederstroem joined the long list of Musettas* on January 9.

1961–1962

Nothing would seem more logical, after the prominence of Leontyne Price and Puccini in Bing's eleventh season, than an opening for the twelfth which would bring them together, preferably in a work as long unheard as *Turandot* had been. As if predestined, there was such a work: *La Fanciulla del West,* which had its first performance in nearly thirty years on October 23, with Price as Minnie,* Tucker as Johnson,* and Colzani as Rance,* under the direction of Cleva. For a Negro to appear in a leading role on a Metropolitan opening night marked a social change as significant as any in years, and there was an appropriate number of prominent persons present to participate in it. Few of them received as much attention from reporters and photographers as the Secretary of Labor, Arthur J. Goldberg.

Had there been no Secretary of Labor Goldberg or, more specifically, had there been no President John F. Kennedy to appoint him, it is possible that neither the predestined nor the logical would have come about—no *Fanciulla,* no opening, even no season. As early as May there were rumors that this year's confrontation between labor and management had more ominous undertones than any in the past. At the end of June, I was advised by a member of the Metropolitan's administration: "Don't bet on a season" (I did, and won). As late as August 17, the Metropolitan's board stood on the position, taken ten days before, that a season was "no longer a possibility."

Short of disaster to the building itself or a war that forbade public gatherings, there appeared no rational reason—other than a will to that outcome—why something scheduled to begin on October 23 should be deemed "no longer a possibility" on August 17. As with Bing's deadline to Callas in November for a schedule that did not become operative until February, the wish appeared to be father to the thought.

Between May and August, negotiations with ten of the unions whose contracts required renewal had been concluded successfully. Still as far apart as ever, however, were the demands of the orchestra, as represented by a committee of its membership, and the negotiators for the Metropolitan. In terms that labor relations experts apply to such matters, there had been no "movement" by either side. The opening demand of the players for a wage increase from a minimum of $170.13 per week for seven performances to $268 (an increase of nearly $100 per week) for six performances per week had been countered with an offer, from the Metropolitan, of $176 in the third year of a three-year contract. Other issues, relating to year-round employment, grievance machinery, the rights of management to dismiss a player for cause, and fringe benefits, could hardly be approached while the distance between wages asked and wages offered was so astronomical that each side considered the position of the other no basis for rational discussion.

At this point, public sympathy inclined to the side of the Metropolitan. However valid the contention of the players that they were overworked and underpaid, the demands they had put to an institution whose annual deficit had risen to $850,000 could only be considered provocative and arrogant. Satisfaction of such demands (including the number of extra musicians to make possible a weekly schedule of six performances per man) would, the management contended, increase the deficit by $750,000 a year.

By long-observed custom, July 30 is the date on which the Metropolitan annually dispatches its "letters of intention" to inform those on weekly contracts (chorus, ballet, and "principal" singers who are not on a "performance" basis) that their services are reserved for the following season.

When the date had come and passed without a settlement of the contract dispute with the orchestra, the Metropolitan advised such "weekly" personnel that they were released from further obligation. This impelled the American Guild of Musical Artists (AGMA), to which most such personnel belongs, to join with five other unions in putting pressure on the musicians to moderate their demands. Their response was to retreat to a minimum of $248 per week.

More than summer heat and frayed tempers contributed to the atmosphere in which the "negotiations" (anything but calm and reasonable) were conducted. An aggravating factor to the Metropolitan's representatives was the presence, on the other side of the table, of one player (a member of the French horn section) whose own job was at issue. He had been nominated for replacement many months before, because of difficulties with conductors (particularly Karl Boehm), but had been reinstated on a plea that his performance would improve. The renewed effort to replace him was now attributed by his fellow negotiators to his union activities rather than to his shortcomings as a horn-player. This obviously made a side issue of greater prominence than the main business of negotiating a contract.

By August 7, a sharp trend in another direction set in. As proof of the urgency of the situation, Bing returned to America from his usual summer holiday in Europe to attend a press conference on that date (Monday). In the judgment of some, the only proper place for a press conference bearing on continuation of opera would be in the Opera House itself. It was, however, called for the Rockefeller Center offices of Milbank, Tweed, Hadley and McCloy, the law firm of which Anthony A. Bliss, president of the Metropolitan Opera Association, was a member. The purpose of the meeting was soon apparent. Bliss read a statement announcing the cancelation of the season and Bing then took over to answer questions bearing on the organizational problems that justified this decision.

According to Bliss, the cancelation was final and irrevocable. If the musicians "came in tomorrow morning, Mr. Bing would certainly make every effort to get the singers back," Bliss said. "But we have no reason to believe that this will occur." In Bing's opinion, "nearly twenty" of his important singers had dropped their Metropolitan commitments in response to offers of engagements elsewhere. He would not put on a "patchwork season." There was no likeness, he said, to the situation of 1946, when a "canceled" season could be reinstated because there was then no activity in Milan, Vienna, or Germany—singers would wait. His best hope was to get on with arrangements for the 1962–3 season.

If some of the prior statements bearing on contracts and cancellations, were colored to serve the Metropolitan's purpose of proving that a season was no longer possible, the last was, at the least, wildly unrealistic. Perhaps, as a foreigner, Bing might have thought that musicians deprived of a year's work would meekly drop their demands and negotiate in a better spirit for employment twelve months later. There is, indeed, evidence for the belief that he counseled firmness as a tactic to root out the troublemakers. But it was not to the credit of the board—which, being composed of Americans, should have known better—that it accepted his leadership in taking such a stand.

By Wednesday, when the news had circulated worldwide, concern began to deepen. In Europe, where Price was looking forward to her cherished opening night opportunity, she told a reporter: "They should send for Secretary Goldberg," alluding to his success earlier in the year in settling a strike of airline engineers. It is a fact, reported in the press, that later the same day Secretary Goldberg did tender his good offices to Bing and was politely informed that there was nothing he could do. Then having failed to heed the warnings of persons better posted on American affairs (general as well as operatic) than himself that there *would* be a season—despite his angry iteration "But I said there would be no zeason"—that the minority of 100 could not deprive the majority of 700 of a year's work and that some way would be found to restore working relations, Bing flew off to Siusi, near Bolzano (in the Dolomites), to finish his vacation.

In a progression that had begun with the dismissal of Merrill and Sordello, Bing had worked up to the state of mind in which he could "fire" Callas. A season before, he had excluded the press from dress rehearsals. Now, finally, he had reached the point of autocratic independence at which he could "fire the public" and keep the theater dark for a year because he found the tactics of the musicians not to his taste.

However convinced Bing may have been that this course was correct, it served merely to arm further those who felt that he had, right along, been "playing for a cancelation," perhaps because of the preceding, death-afflicted season. Nor did it help that in the absence of a senior spokesman, authority for answering questions about the Metropolitan's future was left to various "anonymous" spokesmen (generally either Krawitz or Herman) who were quoted as saying that thirty or so members of the "staff" would "remain on the job" planning the 1962–3 season, that it might be necessary to raise $400,000 for overhead and maintenance costs. Had they thought it through, they might have realized that, together with the bill to the state and the community for relief and unemployment insurance (supposing it became necessary for 500 of the 800 employees to require such public assistance) at $40 a week for a six months' period, it would cost the public nearly $1,000,000 for the Metropolitan *not* to give opera.

At the instigation of Mayor Robert F. Wagner, negotiations were reinstated, but it soon became apparent that what the Metropolitan representatives were empowered to discuss was not 1961–2, but the putative season of 1962–3. By the seventeenth, when "movement" was all but meaningless, and the Metropolitan board issued its position-paper stating that there was "no possibility" of a season, the press began to apply the pressures that were latent in its power, and should have been anticipated by any executive worthy of the name. It was, perhaps, a simple story of nothing being missed until its deprivation was threatened—but it was a story with which every American, if not Rudolf Franz Josef Bing, was familiar.

Now the sentiment swung to the side of the musicians, who were described, in a *New York Times* editorial of August 19, as "conciliatory," the management being called "high handed." Said the *Herald Tribune:* "If it [the Metropolitan Opera] cannot save itself, others must." That was precisely what happened. In an article by myself published at this time, it was noted that the musicians' union was under contract to S. Hurok to provide an orchestra for a Leningrad Ballet season in the Metropolitan at a base pay of $26 per performance, as contrasted with the opera's base pay of $24.60. Certainly this was a much more realistic figure for a settlement than anything like the $248 per week ($41.80 per performance) which was asked—or even $220, which the union posted as its rock bottom ($36.50 per performance). Nor could the union renege on its Hurok contract and picket the theater (as had been threatened) without intolerable international embarrassments.

As the pressures accumulated, the White House began to feel that the time had come to act—that, indeed, a point of no return might soon be reached. Though her own future was in no way at stake, Risë Stevens was one of those who asserted leadership when a spokesman, or even a spokeswoman, was urgently required. According to one newspaper, it was in response to a telegram from her suggesting that a call from the White House to the leaders of the two parties to the dispute would go a long way toward unblocking the deadlock that the vital initiative was taken.

When at last such a call to Bliss alerted him to a pending approach from Goldberg, who was under orders from the White House to "get this thing settled," it came upon Bing to utter the most offensive, obstinate, and intransigent statement to come from either side in the whole long wrangle. Under date of August 20 (Sunday) *The New York Times* reported from Italy that the news of Goldberg's intervention had prompted Bing to the comment: "It will not help a bit. At best they could decide to arbitrate—

and then what? . . . I see no chance for a season. I can't ask any singers to hold back any longer, nor can they be blamed if they signed with other houses. It is too late." Bing concluded what *Time* described as a "contemptuous dismissal" of Goldberg's efforts by saying: "I am deeply appreciative of efforts by Mr. Goldberg and President Kennedy, but the basic issue remains."

From Denver, however, where Goldberg had gone to address a meeting of Hadassah, Bliss was getting a different message at his ranch in Montana. It was to come to Denver for a meeting. By Monday (August 21), the word was out that Goldberg had had a "very constructive" conversation with Bliss. It was too early, perhaps, to breathe easily and forget there had been a crisis, but the way out was at last apparent. Labor's representatives felt that Goldberg was "one of them" and welcomed his participation as arbitrator. The Met, though fearful of what such a dictated settlement might cost (it accepted on condition that the Secretary act personally as arbitrator), had at last been brought before a bar of public accountability which it could not evade. By August 29, when representatives of both sides convened in Washington, Goldberg had in his pocket a letter from the President "thanking" the participants for demonstrating "statesmanship" in accepting "voluntary and binding" arbitration even before they had signed an agreement to that effect. Among those present to sign and be photographed—not wholly of his own volition—was Bing.

When the cables rescinding the "cancelation" had gone out and replies had been received, the list of prominent artists who sent regrets because of commitments contracted between August 1 and 29 had dwindled from Bing's figure of twenty, based on his "firm knowledge," to less than half that number. The most conspicuous absentees were conductors Francesco Molinari-Pradelli and Karl Boehm; sopranos Helga Pilarczyk and Sena Jurinac; baritones Hermann Prey and Walter Berry; and mezzo Giulietta Simionato. Tebaldi would also be absent, but not for the common reason. She had made her return contingent on a production of *Adriana Lecouvreur* (see page 574). When the season was restored, she informed Bing that she could perform during the season, but not on tour. It was the management's contention that Tebaldi's appearances on tour were essential for a revival of *Adriana*. Lacking them, it decided to shelve the project, and Tebaldi refused to come without it.

Thus Bing's twelfth season began unlike any other—which is to say with the promise of only one new production. Even the scenery for the opening *Fanciulla* had been acquired on loan from the Chicago Lyric Opera, and was noted, in the program, as having been "redesigned by Gerald L. Ruitholz." This lack of commitment could be interpreted in two ways: as an example of Bing's foresight in not obligating the Metropolitan to heavy expenses for productions that it might not be able to use, or as proof of his conviction that there could, and would, be no season. Which view holds more credibility may be left for the reader to determine. (The "inacceptable" demands of the orchestra were not tendered until April 6, by which time plans for the impending season are generally far advanced).

As for *Fanciulla* itself, it proved to have much more merit than demerit for those who had been denied its suave tunes and sonorous choruses for a generation. Unlike the original appraisers (see page 224), to whom the "cowboys" seemed more like "brigands of the Abruzzi" and the Puccini *cantilena* inappropriate for so "realistic" a background, those of 1961 found Belasco's West as much a dream world of romance and fantasy as the Nagasaki of *Butterfly* or the China of *Turandot*. As Minnie, Price dispensed vocal abundance and not much dramatic credibility, especially when she entered on a white pony in the final scene. Tucker looked little like an outlaw, but sang with piercing power, and there were moments of touching finesse from Flagello as the camp Minstrel* and Andrea Velis as Joe* (d). Harvuot played Sonora,* with Roggero as Wowkle.* The direction by Henry Butler* was his first in a sequence that spoke more for managerial tolerance than for discrimination.

The surprising performance, both for vocal impact and dramatic flair, was the Rance* of Colzani, big in stature as well as in voice. It was, in a way, an anticipation of how he might perform Scarpia (his first came on January 27), for he succeeded in making the crude venom of the character credible and his passion plausible. For Price, however, the bright promise of the opening night faded almost immediately. She had begun to feel the strain of international prominence (including a misguided effort to sing Leonore's *"Abscheulicher"* from *Fidelio* in a Carnegie Hall concert with the visiting Berlin Philharmonic under Karajan late in October), and was forced to retire after two acts of her next Minnie on October 31. Kirsten was the hastily summoned replacement. It was a role well within Kirsten's resources, and she sang almost every performance thereafter, save the one of December 4, for which Price was present. The latter also performed as scheduled in *Turandot* (Liù) on December 1, *Aida* on December 13, and *Butterfly* on December 20, but she was forced to defer to Curtis-Verna in another *Aida* on December 23 (Elias was the Amneris for Acts I to III, but Dalis finished in her place). On doctor's orders, she gave up further performances and, indeed, left the country for a long rest in Rome. When she did return, it was as Tosca* on April 1, with Tucker and MacNeil (see page 670).

Two of the performances for which Price was scheduled but did not appear were enhanced by the efforts of as versatile and well-equipped a tenor as the Metropolitan had acquired since Gedda. This was Sandor Konya, Hungarian-born, German- and Italian-trained, who made his debut as an uncommonly sympathetic, vocally sound Lohengrin* on October 28. As Schippers had decided during the period of the "cancelation" threat to spend his winter elsewhere, this *Lohengrin* was under the direction of Rosenstock. The Elsa* (d) was Ingrid Bjoner, with Dalis as Ortrud* and Hines as King Henry.* Bjoner was probably a replacement for Nordmo Loevberg, who also gave up her season before it began. This was a net gain for the Metropolitan, as Bjoner was, on the whole, a more settled, more professionally capable performer. Konya's competence in a variety of styles—more legato than the average German tenor, more musicianship than the average Italian—soon qualified him as the rare vocal bird who could shed the plumage of the Swan Knight and adapt himself to the varied feathers of Johnson* in *Fanciulla* (on November 23) and be a reasonably good Radames* (on December 8) or a respectable Calaf* in *Turandot* on January 8. His fascination with the vocal "catch" or "sob" was to be deplored, especially as it seemed to express Konya's belief that this was an authentic part of Italian singing rather than merely an authentic part of bad singing, Italian or otherwise. Another Johnson* on December 30 was Barioni, whose fine fresh sound of 1955–6 was considerably worn when he reappeared as Cavaradossi on November 2. Guarrera was Colzani's deputy as Rance* on December 30.

For the single *new* production that time permitted, Bing elected a continuance of his Verdi re-stagings, this time a reconsideration of *Un Ballo in maschera* on January 25. The funds provided by Mrs. John D. Rockefeller, Jr., were entrusted to a joint effort by Günther Rennert as producer and Ita Maximowna as designer. Her effort was crowned in a regal way by the ball scene in the Stockholm Opera House (where the assassination happened, historically), but it had its share of miscalculations along the way. Included was a poorly realized setting for the den of Ulrica (how the king could escape recognition in it eluded comprehension) and a merely ugly rather than eerie *"campo abbominato"* (apparently a crime wave was in progress, for it had five gibbets in readiness). Her costuming had some merit, but not the gaudy gown in which Amelia was supposed to escape recognition by her husband.

Aside from moving his characters about with more or less facility, Rennert did little to make a plausible stage being of Bergonzi's Riccardo,* which was beautifully sung, or of the powerfully projected Renato of Merrill. However, where the production faltered most was in the uneven effort of Rysanek as Amelia.* Attractive to see and acted with her customary conviction, it did not gain sufficiently from her power at the top to compensate for lacks elsewhere. Jean Madeira's exaggerated, unlovely way of performing Ulrica was another blemish, as was the barely audible Oscar* of Rothenberger. Probably this was meant to be conducted by Molinari-Pradelli, but his absence brought on young Nello Santi (d) instead. He showed a good ear for the blending of sound and quick, active reflexes. What he lacked then, and did not demonstrate later, was the authority to make celebrities go his way rather than their own. Vichey returned to appear as Tom, with Giaiotti as Sam.* On a later occasion (February 12), the Ulrica* was Rankin, and on February 27, Claudia Parada of Chile was Amelia* (d), with Schick conducting and Hurley as Oscar. Even in the stringencies of this season, Parada did not show qualifications for Metropolitan acceptability—the voice was of limited size and her use of it merely well routined, thanks to Italian training. She was also the Amelia on March 7, when MacNeil assumed the privileges of *"Eri tu"* with more honor than he did the dramatic responsibilities of Renato.* And there was always Curtis-Verna (April 6).

This was, in its other respects, more like a Johnson season than any of its predecessors, with a quota of new singers, a sequence of *Ring* performances (the first since 1956–7) and, for some stretches of time, a more even average of quality than had been attained in seasons not fated, as this one was by Bing's word, to be a "patchwork." Some of this was the increment from seasons immediately preceding, of *Turandot, Butterfly, Tosca,* and *Bohème*—which, with *Fanciulla,* made up a kind of super-*Ring* by Puccini (five works to Wagner's four); the restoration of such gay favorites as *Così fan tutte, La Perichole,* and, in lesser measure, *Contes d'Hoffmann;* and a strong *Elektra. Macbeth* was also seen again, this time under the direction of Rosenstock on February 24, with Colzani as Macbeth* (solid but hardly gripping), Rysanek, Tozzi (Banquo), George Shirley (Malcolm*) and Bergonzi.

Easily the most eagerly awaited of the new singers was Joan Sutherland who had progressed in the short span of three years from a soprano who had auditioned in vain (see page 602) to a celebrity for whom managers paid top dollar (it would soon cost the Metropolitan $1,750 *per performance* for a singer whose services might have been secured three years earlier for $500 a week). Her first Lucia* (d) on November 26 had been preceded by sufficient evidence of ability (including a concert performance of Bellini's *Beatrice di Tenda* in Town Hall the previous February) to leave little doubt of her extraordinary command of florid singing. This brought an audience with an unusual awareness of what it was about to hear to this unusual event (a Sunday-night benefit for the Opera Guild), and it greeted her accordingly. As was to be remarked many times in the future, it was among Sutherland's remarkable attributes rarely to vary from her self-set standard. This tended, after a bit, to take the edge of expectation away—the hope that *this* time she might outdo herself—but it gave ample cause to marvel at her security. Dramatically, she was square, heavy, and not very suggestive of the temperament that would produce Lucia's kind of dementia. Her Mad Scene was not only much the best-acted episode of the role, but also almost a thing apart, thanks to the coaching she had received from Franco Zeffirelli for a production at Covent Garden. Tucker as Edgardo sang scene for scene on Sutherland's level, which was several floors higher than Testi's as Ashton.* Silvio Varviso, a young Swiss conductor who had been performing with Sutherland in San Francisco prior to her Metropolitan debut, had been observed there by Bing and engaged forthwith. For this kind of assignment, he qualified as discreet, flexible, and musically responsible. This being a *Lucia* season, there were other Lucias*: Moffo, on December 25, offered a Sutherland-cum-Callas conception, heavier than the former, more accurate than the latter, but without the mastery of what was best in either. Colzani was a rough Enrico* (his talent was scarcely for *legato* singing). Near the end of the season (April 17), D'Angelo offered her version of the old-fashioned, bird-like Lucia,* pecking at it prettily. The Edgardo (and excellent) was Bergonzi, with Rich conducting. Morell had his first opportunity as Edgardo* on April 4.

Though Sutherland's "season" was limited to a mere five performances (all as Lucia), it did last long enough for her to participate in one of the great days of singing in the post-war history of the Metropolitan. That occurred on December 9, a Saturday when the afternoon's broadcast of *Lucia* was followed, in the evening, by Nilsson's first Brünnhilde* in *Götterdämmerung*. Here, for those who could find the means to be present, was a re-creation of some golden times of the past—physical prowess mated with the mental discipline to produce the kind of sound (sad, joyous, or vengeful, to order and without disorder) that the composer specified.

There was, even, a mounting climax from *"Regnava nel silenzio"* to the Immolation. Sutherland's order of achievement of Lucia was, by now, relatively familiar, whereas Nilsson's mature Brünnhilde was a new experience. As Leinsdorf insisted on doing *Götterdämmerung* uncut, it provided even more test for her stamina than Isolde or Turandot. She sustained the part with forthright response to the letter of the score and no deviation from vocal virtue, though some dramatic details were as yet underemphasized. For the rest, this *Götterdämmerung* was rather too much a dialogue between Nilsson and Leinsdorf, whose new status as conductor-elect of the Boston Symphony was reflected in the bigness of his orchestral design, especially in the funeral music. Hopf was a hard-pressed Siegfried,* Dalis vocally and physically undersized for Waltraute,* Ernst Wiemann (who had made his debut as the King* in *Lohengrin* on November 17) crafty rather than barbaric as Hagen,* Herbert a routine Alberich,* and young Norman Mittlemann (the Herald* [d] of the October 28 *Lohengrin*) a promising but immature Gunther.* Dalis was also the second Norn, with Dunn and Martina Arroyo, and could, conceivably, also have turned into a Rhinemaiden along with them. But Elias made their third instead. The Gutrune* was Bjoner.

Unlike some other recent *Ring* cycles (the last full one had been in the 1956-7 season), this one began relatively early in the season, spanning December and January. It opened with *Götterdämmerung* as a review course in advance on December 9, with the first *Rheingold* on December 16. London lacked the physical stature of a Hotter for his first New York Wotan*, substituting an appealing likeness of a vigorous young god. Also good were Dalis (Fricka*) and Liebl, who showed promise of becoming the best Loge* among contemporary performers. However, the memorable virtuoso performer of this *Rheingold* was Paul Kuen, a Bayreuth Mime* (d) who lived every moment of the role. It had everything—manner, vocal flavor, restricted physical size—to make the character believable. Wiemann was an able Fafner* to Hines's Fasolt, Herbert better attuned to this Alberich* than the one of *Götterdämmerung,* and Madeira approaching her best as Erda. Intelligently staged by Merrill, it added up to one of the better *Rheingolds* of recent years.

With the two ends of the cycle accounted for, it would not appear that the interior parts would cost too much effort, but the now common "Siegfried problem" had also become a "Wotan problem." Some of this was owing to a year in which Edelmann was off form, but some of it also was due to misplaced faith in his alternates. With Edelmann in *Walküre* on December 23 were Vickers, Nilsson, and Dalis as before, plus Kuchta (barely acceptable as Sieglinde*) and Wiemann (not an impressive Hunding*). Before the first *Siegfried* on January 2, a second cycle brought a *Rheingold* cast as before, on December 27, save that it offered the debut of Gottlob Frick as Fafner* (he had been engaged for Bing's first season, but had not come), with Wiemann as Fasolt* and Olvis as Froh.* It was followed on the 29th by a *Walküre* in which Edelmann was unable to perform and was replaced as Wotan* by Randolph Symonette. Like Telramund* (d), in which he had made his debut on November 17 (with Bjoner,

Liebl, and Rankin), Wotan was a part for which Symonette had substantial routine. However, the burden of singing these long, arduous parts in a large theater seemed to weigh heavily on him. He also served as Amonasro* on December 23, on the way to taking part in one of the most bizarre episodes in the Metropolitan's recently bizarre history.

This was the celebrated "double Wotan" *Walküre* of January 10. It began with Harshaw substituting for Nilsson (who may have had a premonition) as Brünnhilde, Kuchta replacing Harshaw as Sieglinde, Dunn as Fricka,* and Ethel Greene, a member of the chorus, taking on Schwertleite* (d) in place of Gladys Kriese. (When Kriese had been unable to appear on December 29, Madeira generously had consented to step backward from the big roles she had been singing recently and join the Walküren again). It ended with Edelmann, who had begun as Wotan and been replaced by Symonette at the beginning of Act III because he was weakening vocally, on stage to finish the act because Symonette could not. In justice to the latter it should be said that he had been assured that his services would not be needed, and he had dined accordingly. Probably there was some wine, too, for he appeared to be uncertain of his place on the stage and unsure of his entrances. Arriving at the line in the text reading *"Aus meinem Angesicht bist du verbannt,"* Leinsdorf decided that this was an appropriate moment to ring down the curtain and consider his next course (it means "From my presence you are banished"). The decision was to put Edelmann back on the stage, begin at *"War es so schmählich"* and let nature take its course. More speaking than singing his part, Edelmann made it to the "Magic Fire" music.

The program for the first *Siegfried* on January 2 began in the customary way with the names of London (the Wanderer*), Hopf (Siegfried*), and Nilsson (Brünnhilde*), but the one that made the performance was Kuen's as Mime.* A superb physical simulation of the conniving Nibelung, it also offered a lesson in vocal production and textual enunciation for any singer wise enough to listen. The Wanderer suited London well, and Nilsson took the long ascent to the crest of the duet without appearing to call upon her last reserve of power. As a performance, this suffered from the lack of a truly qualified Siegfried, for Hopf sang the music fitfully, with a burst of quality now and then, but with more vibrance in the low register than the high. Eventually the climax was an anti-climax, for he had little lyricism to offer in the duet. In another *Siegfried,* on January 29, the Wanderer* was Symonette, with Harshaw as Brünnhilde, and a *Götterdämmerung* of February 1 was dignified by the expert Hagen of Frick (he had done the part for the first time on January 5). As Siegfried,* Liebl extended himself to produce a sound hardly believable for one of his known limitations, but it did not match Wagner's needs even so. The Gutrune* was Krall. The sum of it, really, was that "cancellation" or no, the Metropolitan had not provided itself with the manpower for a *Ring,* and should not have attempted it in this season. The womanpower, which it possessed in some depth, was augmented on January 23, when Anita Välkki, a Finnish soprano hitherto unknown to New York, performed a *Walküre* Brünnhilde of considerable vocal distinction. There was no great dramatic projection, either by voice or by body, but the possibilities for it to develop appeared to be present. The very good Hunding was Frick, the strained Wotan was Hines, who had performed the *Rheingold* Wotan,* not very comfortably, on January 15. With the burning of Valhalla came, also, the end of the Wagner, for this season consisting wholly of the *Ring* and *Lohengrin.*

For the restoration of *Così* on October 24 after an absence since 1955–6, Bing provided not only a new conductor (Rosenstock) and a new Fiordiligi* (Teresa Stich-Randall [d]), but also a new producer. It was, more accurately, an old *Così* producer, Carl Ebert, whose carefully plotted, drolly humorous direction at Glyndebourne had contributed much to the rebirth of international favor for *Così*. It may be imagined, then, with what surprise he read in *The New York Times* report of Harold Schonberg (Howard Taubman's successor as music critic): "While Carl Ebert has been responsible for the staging, his direction follows, if memory serves, that of Alfred Lunt very closely." The practiced Fiordiligi of Stich-Randall was, like Ebert's direction, better suited to a smaller house, but its finesse and closely crafted detail were a pleasure when they could be heard. She could, however, do little to upgrade the Dorabella* of Elias, who played her part for archness and easy laughs, while lacking dramatic impact in her aria. Uppman, as Guglielmo,* carried forward the likable qualities of his Papageno and Masetto, with Guarrera making a mostly successful transition to become Brownlee's successor as Alfonso.* The scheduled Ferrando* was Charles Anthony, but he was replaced by George Shirley, who thus made his debut in as difficult a role (musically) as a tenor can undertake. He made the necessary basic points by exertion of maximum power, but he was hard to hear in the ensembles.

When Shirley reached the role scheduled for his debut on November 13, the veteran operagoer had a problem in adjustment to make. That was: did the obvious incongruity of a Negro naval lieutenant, at a time when there was none such in the United States fleet, invalidate the use of Shirley as B. F. Pinkerton* in *Madama Butterfly?* Those who dared to think so were plainly in the minority, for the spirit of the moment was that such thinking was a product of "bias." Where such opinions related to dramatic credibility, in the same way that such other physical factors as height, weight, or facial conformation generally did, such "bias" is cheerfully acknowledged. (As Alfredo* in *Traviata* on November 30, Shirley was somewhat better vocally and dramatically.) Andrea Velis gave promise of quality service to come in character roles with a spirited Goro.* Kirsten was the Butterfly. The continuing prominence of *Così* also provided for the debut on December 19 of John Alexander (Ferrando*), whose City Center background prepared him for a varied career that since has prospered. Anthony finally performed his Ferrando* on January 1 (with Amara as Fiordiligi* and Hurley as Despina*), at a volume level even below that of Shirley. Another Fiordiligi* (d) in this season was Phyllis Curtin, whose attractive appearance and sound musicianship lent lustre to her effort on November 4. She, too, was lacking in the kind of projection which counts in this theater, and has not been heard again. Some thoughts of an earlier, brighter time for the Metropolitan's Mozart were stirred on February 17 when word was relayed from Beverly Hills, California, of the death of Bruno Walter at eighty-six. The performance of the 19th (*Rigoletto*) was preceded by the Priest's March from *Magic Flute* in tribute. No other part of this score was heard in the Metropolitan this year, for the Mozart was otherwise restricted to *Le Nozze di Figaro*. In the first performance on January 11, Rothenberger was a rather fluty kind of Susanna*, with Della Casa, Miller, Borg, Tozzi as Figaro, Velis (Basilio*), Flagello (Bartolo), and Dunn (Marcellina). On February 23, the clear sound and good sight of Judith Raskin as Susanna* (d) added to the Metropolitan's resources another performer of excellent quality by way of City Center. Cassel was the Almaviva*, offering an impersonation that may have been countly but was not courtly. On March 6, when the conductor was Strasfogel, the cast had been amended to provide Siepi as Figaro, Hurley as Susanna, and Elias as Cherubino.

Of the musical as opposed to the specifically aria-oriented operatic repertory, the season included, otherwise, a revival of *Orfeo* and several performances of *Salome* and *Elektra*. Apparently the Metropolitan was not destined to hear Simionato as Orfeo, for the "cancelation" had rubbed her name from the list of availables and substituted Meyer's. Her Orfeo* on March 3 could not be faulted for dignity or serious effort, and the totality was much more to her credit than the Carmen of the year before. What could be said, however, was that she did not substitute for what was lacking in vocal richness or substance a rapturous identity with Gluck that can be conveyed even by a limited voice. Morel's conducting gave shape and color to the score, but the shape was small-scaled, the color pale. Amara (Eurydice) and Rothenberger (Amore*), with Violette Verdy, and Arthur Mitchell (d) as the solo dancers for the choreography of John Taras were about at the level of the whole. Later, Gabriella Tucci, who had given up the Eurydice* of the evening of March 3 in order to sing Aida the previous afternoon added some to the total of sound in the music when she sang the part on March 21.

With Pilarczyk unavailable, the *Salome* conducted by Rosenstock on February 2 took its character from the princess of Rhodes. This meant that it was calculated to make up for the eye what it lacked for the ear, stressing as near a simulation of nudity as flesh-colored leotards could provide. Vocally it ranged from unlistenable to inaudible, with *"Eid"* (oath) coming out "aid" in her French-German, and an encore of her "nudity" (though the purpose for which the exposure had been justified was already accomplished) when she cradled the head of Jokanaan in her arms. Here Rosenstock took the applaudable course of giving Strauss his due, orchestrally, and Rhodes was left to pantomime what was not worth hearing anyway. In a cast that included Thebom as Herodias, Olvis as Narraboth,* and Cassel as a short-ranged Jokanaan, the most mentionable matter was the Herod of Vinay. Its worn, tortured sound was audible evidence of why he had, after tortuous years of cancelations and replacements, decided to forego the tenor repertory and return to the baritone range from which he had ascended in 1943. Brenda Lewis acted a sightly Salome* on February 17, but was no more audible than Rhodes, who returned to the role on February 22, with Morley Meredith as a hollow-sounding Jokanaan* and Alexander as Narraboth.* In the performance of March 5, when Rankin was the Herodias,* Vinay closed out his career as a tenor. In the Bing view, *Salome* was sufficient unto itself for the evening thereof.

The sequence of *Elektras,* also directed by Rosenstock, was on the whole on a higher artistic level, owing in large part to the participation of Gerda Lammers. Though her intent, musically absorbing, and dramatically compulsive Elektra* (d) on March 16 merited comparison with Pauly's it made no concession at all to eye appeal, even in curtain calls, in which she was the same unsightly hag as before. In any case, the qualities that earned her ovations at Covent Garden in 1957 as a replacement for Goltz did not impress the New York public or press. Most of the other performers were holdovers from the previous year's *Elektra,* including Madeira (Klytaemnestra), Yeend (Chrysothemis), Da Costa (Aegisth), and Cassel (Orest). On April 3 the Klytaemnestra was Resnik, with Liebl (Aegisth) and Meredith (Orest*).

The last named, a well-built man with a highly developed stage sense, made his debut on January 3 in the four-way requirements of *Contes d'Hoffmann* (Lindorf,* Coppélius,* Dappertutto,* and Dr. Miracle*). He performed with elaborate action and equally dense sound in all. Neither as Jokanaan nor as Orest did Meredith show the kind of service for which he was best equipped—an acting role such as the Majordomo in *Ariadne* or the Speaker in *Magic Flute,* for which singing was minimal. This was, on the whole, not a rewarding year for Offenbach. It started on November 11 with Moffo's attempt to perform Olympia,* Giulietta,* Antonia,* and La Stella,* a feat last ventured by Vina Bovy (see page 398). By the middle of her Olympia, it was evident that Moffo was running down more than artificially, with a sticky note here, an unformed one there. After a verbal announcement that she was "too ill to continue," she did—unsteadily. She did not appear for the scheduled repetition on November 18, Mmes Hurley, Elias, and Amara replacing her. On December 22, Alexander performed a strong, well-acted Hoffmann* *vice* Gedda (with Gladys Kriese making her debut as an off-stage Voice* [d]). Moffo returned on January 3 to make good her four-part feat, but it was a one and only, there being no reprise. As for *Perichole,* it was missing more than Munsel when it returned on November 25 after an absence of several seasons. It did not possess the blithe spirit that had prevailed when it was new, even though Ritchard returned to supervise the action, act his old part, and indoctrinate Moffo in hers. The latter tended to overstate the emotional content of the letter and understate the spoken dialogue, manifesting, in all, a limited sense of operetta or *opéra comique* style, especially in comparison with Paquillo (Uppman). There was, indeed, an improvement when Hurley applied her likable talents to the problem of Perichole* on January 16, with a success that earned her the part from then on.

The absence of Valletti doubtless had a part in the effort to make a Ferrando of Shirley, Anthony, and Alexander, and probably could account for the return of Tagliavini to enhance the attractions of *L'Elisir d'amore* on January 13 as Nemorino. Somewhat pudgier than when he had last performed on this stage in March 1954, Tagliavini sang his Donizetti artfully and acted it entertainingly. Moffo was the Adina, with Guarrera as Belcore and Baccaloni joining the reunion as Dulcamara. Tagliavini also sang Rodolfo in this season (February 9 and 26), a role whose demands made more apparent his decline in vocal power.

There was no Leonard del Ferro in this season, but there was another transient tenor or two. The first was Giuseppe Zampieri, en route from San Francisco to Europe, who took on a Cavaradossi* (d) in *Tosca* on November 20, when Tucker was unable to perform. His better than average qualities did not make a "lasting" impression—which is to say that he did not last beyond this season. Later, Umberto Borsò performed a loud, unappealing Enzo* (d) in *Gioconda* on April 16, in a cast with Farrell, Elias,

Hines, Rankin, and Lili Chookasian (La Cieca, the role of her impressive debut on March 9). Borsò earned his opportunity in New York by substituting for Tucker in a Boston *Forza* on April 12 (this being a year in which the company returned to New York for Easter week before continuing its tour in Atlanta).

The short, mostly unhappy history of Eugenio Fernandi as a Metropolitan tenor reached its end this year, an end brought on by his endeavors to meet requirements such as Radames and Don Carlo, which should never have been put upon him. His reappearance occurred on February 21, in *Traviata* with Tucci (she first performed Violetta* on February 10 with Formichini), and I do not find that he performed thereafter in New York. There was another Radames* not to be forgotten on November 6, when Vickers gave a strident, unlovely performance of *"Celeste Aida"* and advertised his self-satisfaction by grinning at the applause. A warrior in physique, he had too little sense of what to do with his body for it to be an asset. Of considerably greater artistic quality was the Aida* (d) of the Russian soprano Galina Vishnevskaya. This was skillful, well-vocalized Verdi, a little light in weight for the Metropolitan, but powerful at the top. Dramatically it derived from a stylized scheme of action which did not blend with anything else on the stage. Her Butterfly* on December 5 was better (Olvis was Pinkerton, with Vanni and Harvuot). Her role was all performed in Russian, save for *"Un bel di"* for which, it was said, there was no translation.

However, a Russian Aida for the Metropolitan's increasingly disorderly production was no more unstylistic than the Italian but un-Verdian Radames* of Corelli on February 16. He made a shambles of legato in *"Celeste Aida"* and sang much of the rest of the role in a loud, uninflected *tenore robusto*. Few who saw it will forget Corelli's battle dress, described by Watt in the *Daily News* as "a heel length robe of bright red velvet with a sparkling yoke over a short tunic made up of some sort of dazzling silver pieces about the size of halved golf balls, plus a conical helmet composed of the same stuff." The Aida was Rysanek, with Dalis, Flagello (Ramfis*), and Colzani. Verchi by this time having found the Metropolitan road too rough for his mental shock-absorbers, the conductor was Schick. Corelli's virtuosity in costuming was by no means exhausted by his Radames. As Enzo* in *Gioconda* (a role he might have sung very well had it not included *"Cielo e mar"*), Corelli was clad on March 9 in what appeared to be paratrooper boots embellished by gold buckles. At a later *Gioconda* on April 5, Hines performed his first Alvise* anywhere, and did it handsomely.

This being a year in which Puccini works equaled those of Wagner (five each) and far exceeded them in quantity of performances (forty-five to twenty-one), it is hardly surprising that all sorts of people sang all sorts of parts for the first time. On the theory, perhaps, that fish who are avid for the hook will go for any kind of bait, there were seven different Toscas, including performances by Nilsson on January 31 and Price on April 1. These had the justification of being associated with attention-drawing individuals, though neither of them was truly gifted for the role. But what is one to say of Tosca as a debut role (opposite Corelli as Cavaradossi*) for a small-scaled soprano billed as Margherita Roberti (better known to home folks in Iowa as Margaret Roberts) on January 27? She was, by virtue of the casting department, an Aida* on February 20. In the case of Meredith as Scarpia* on February 6, the question can be more simply put: why? When Formichini sang Rodolfo on February 3, there was a cogent reason. He was about the right number of inches for Stratas, whose Mimi* deserved more prominence than it has enjoyed since. The appearance of Curtis-Verna as Turandot* on March 12 could have been accurately forecast by any qualified operatic stargazer. Like the unseen planet Pluto, predicted to exist (by Camille Flammarion) before it became visible, it was off there someplace and would appear sometime.

On the whole, the quantity of Puccini performed in New York during this winter—taking in the extensions provided by the fall and spring seasons of the City Opera—very likely exceeded anything heard even in the days of his double duty at the Manhattan Opera House and the Metropolitan. For its opening on October 5, the City Opera elected the first sequential performance of the *Trittico* which New York had heard since its introductory season of 1918–19. Something was made of the tour de force by Claramae Turner in taking part in all three works (she was best as the Principessa of *Suor Angelica,* good as Frugola in *Il Tabarro,* not very conspicuous as Zita in *Schicchi*), but the virtue of the evening's endeavor derived from an uncommonly suitable concurrence of good young singers. Other than the well-seasoned William Chapman as Michele in *Tabarro,* they included John Alexander as Luigi and Arlene Saunders in her debut as Giorgetta in the same work, Gladys Kriese as La Badessa in *Suor Angelica* (also her debut), and Doris Yarick (Lauretta) and Frank Porretta (Rinuccio) in *Schicchi*.

Rudel also chose wisely in bringing together the talents best suited to his renewed promotion of new works for which Ford money was responsible. In the first, Douglas Moore's treatment of a text by Ethan Ayer derived from Henry James's *The Wings of a Dove,* it was the talented young Dorothy Coulter (on loan from the Metropolitan), a Milly Theale to the life, in company with John Reardon as Miles Dunster, Regina Sarfaty as Kate, and Martha Lipton as Mrs. Lowder; in the second the operatized version of Arthur Miller's *The Crucible* by Robert Ward (the text was made for him by Bernard Stambler), the sizeable figure of Chester Ludgin as Proctor and the apt talent of Ken Neate, an Australian tenor, as Judge Danforth balanced the more familiar abilities of Frances Bible (Proctor's wife), Norman Treigle (Reverend Hale), and Patricia Brooks (Abigail). Emerson Buckley made a propulsive thing of Ward's fine choral writing (much of it hymn-tune-derived) and wove a well-balanced ensemble from the others in a large cast that included Norman Kelley, Maurice Stern, and Eunice Alberts.

Memories of the unfortunate venture with Tamkin's try at making an opera of Ansky's *The Dybbuk* recurred in the spring production of Abraham Ellstein's singing version of H. Levick's *The Golem* (as adapted by Joseph Buloff). Perhaps it was no more than the kinship they have as part of Jewish literary lore which affiliated them in retrospect, but it was also a common trait that Ellstein no less than Tamkin over-reached himself in his choice of subject matter. John Fiorito attracted attention to himself as the Shames; Ludgin extended the good impression of his Proctor in *The Crucible* with his impersonation of the Golem. Jon Crain made a dominant figure of the Maharal, Rabbi Levi Bar Bezallel, and Lee Venora did well what was required of Deborah, the Rabbi's granddaughter.

The all-contemporary repertory of this spring season also included a venture with Benjamin Britten's *The Turn of the Screw,* its first professional presentation in New York. Patricia Neway found a rich role for her own kind of aptitude in the Governess, and there were able performances also by Richard Cassilly (Quint), Janice Martin (Mrs. Gróse), Jean Kraft (Miss Jessel), with Michele Farr (Flora) and Bruce Zahariados (Miles) as the beautiful, devious, devil-ridden children. Of even more significance than the presentation of the work, with a production derived from one the company had presented in Boston during the summer, was the source of the funds that made it possible. These were made available to the City Opera by Mrs. John D. Rockefeller, Jr., the first in a series of benefactions that underscored her disposition to be equally helpful to New York's two sources of operatic experience. There was no need for philanthropy on behalf of the season's other "novelty": an inclusion in the Opera's repertory of the preceding spring's "operetta" production of *Porgy and Bess.*

As far as the most distinguished of all the contributions to this out-pouring of Puccini was concerned—the Metropolitan's *Turandot*—its grand design began to crumble before the season was many weeks old, with the replacement of Stokowski as conductor by Adler. In this second season, Stokowski's participation was limited to the performances of November 4 (in which Tucker as Calaf* sang impressively in everything save *"Nessun dorma"* and Flagello performed as Timur*) and November 7. By the time it was next given on December 1, the chorus master had taken the place of the orchestra master, and so it remained. The presumption had to be that Stokowski would sooner or later tire of this latest toy; but the exchanges of opinions in the press (see page 647) left little doubt that each party to the controversy had ample reason to find fault with the other. Simple justice would be, however, to record that the Metropolitan's public benefited more from Stokowski's assets than the performers suffered from his liabilities, and that the cost, in effort, of living with his services was more than Bing chose to pay (money could hardly have been a factor). At another extreme of ability, the *Traviata* on November 24 led by Strasfogel marked the termination of the tenure of Verchi, who had begun the season conducting *Bohème* and *Aida*. Someone concerned with the unvital, rather than the vital, statistics of the Metropolitan might find in this season that a paralyzing proportion of performances was conducted by such now-and-then directors as Schick, Adler, Rich, and Strasfogel. I restrict myself to the week of March 10–17, which went as follows: *Rigoletto* (Rich), *Turandot* (Adler), *Bohème* (Rich), *Macbeth* (Rosenstock), *Tosca* (Adler), *Elektra* (Rosenstock), *Ballo* (Santi), and *Nozze di Figaro* (Strasfogel). Schippers's absence for *Lohengrin* was made good by Rosenstock, but either Schick had insufficient time to prepare *Forza del destino* before it was given on December 12 (with Farrell mostly an unhappy choice for Leonora,* Merrill as Carlo,* Tucker as Alvaro, and Hines as Padre Guardiano) or it was simply beyond his sympathies. On the other hand, *Traviata,* which Schick later directed capably, was conducted by Strasfogel when Tucci was the Violetta* on February 10.

When the Secretary of Labor's initiative cleared the way in late August for the season to proceed, Price expressed her gratitude by forwarding him as a gift a recording of Bach's Aria with Thirty Variations dedicated to another Goldberg. However, the Goldberg variations on the theme of arbitration which were published on December 14 hardly struck a harmonious note with the orchestral musicians.

Their first fallacy was the presumption that Goldberg was "one of ours." He was, rather "one of *ours*," meaning the public's. What he offered was rational, reasonable, and non-parochial in that it did not overtly favor one side or the other.

The musicians were loud in cries of "sellout" when the award stipulated a first season's salary of $180 a week, or almost exactly the amount paid to the orchestra for the Leningrad Ballet (see page 657). It went up $5 a week in each of the two following years, with $190 as the minimum for the third year (it should be understood that many of the players received *more* than the minimum, and that they all were paid $28 a week additional for the Saturday-afternoon broadcasts and more for rehearsal time). This left them still short of the $220 which had been their last "demand." Goldberg did, however, categorize the per diem, during tours, of $10.25 as "plainly unrealistic." He increased it immediately to $13 and stipulated that it equal the government allowance of $16 per day in the second and third years. The same "award" went also to chorus and ballet members whose contracts entitled them to parity should any other union be granted an increase. However, this amount was relatively easy for the Metropolitan to absorb, as it could call upon the cities it visited on tour to meet the added cost.

The complicated agenda of fringe benefits, grievance procedures, and management-labor relations in general was turned back to the participants themselves for further discussion. As for the musician the Metropolitan wished to dismiss, this problem was assigned to Theodore W. Kheel to arbitrate. After hearing testimony, on February 28, 1962, he upheld the Metropolitan's right of dismissal.

An imperishable addendum to this phase of the management-labor controversy and an appalling indication of the new performer-conductor relationship was provided by a report in the theatrical trade publication *Variety* for May 23, 1962. It recorded the intention of the discharged musician described above to bring "charges" against conductor Fausto Cleva as a "fellow member of the union." It was his contention that Cleva's testimony that he should be dismissed did not "advance nor protect" his interests and "did not enforce good faith, fair dealings nor adherence to union practices." The essence of the doctrine thus promulgated was that a conductor's first allegiance was not to art or the organization by which he was employed as a responsible specialist, but to those with whom, by union pressures, he was obliged to be affiliated. No disposition of the "action" was ever disclosed, but it is believed that Cleva was required to make an appearance before a board convened for the purpose of hearing the charges.

1962–1963

No earlier Metropolitan Opera season had begun as early as September 29, but the Metropolitan's personnel, especially orchestra and chorus, was busy even earlier than that in the fall of 1962. Any public activity at that uncustomary time would have had significance as bearing on the possibility, much discussed during the labor crisis of 1961, of extending the season to provide year-round employment for those on salary. The activity of September 1962 was not only a short step in that direction, but also another one, in the direction of things to come, for it took the Metropolitan to Lincoln Center for the first time, as a participant in the ceremonies inaugurating Philharmonic Hall.

The first structure to be made ready for use at Lincoln Center, Philharmonic Hall had its formal dedication on Sunday, September 23, with a concert by Leonard Bernstein and the orchestra for which it was built. This was followed by a ceremonial week of concerts by such regular tenants as the Philadelphia Orchestra under Eugene Ormandy and the Boston Symphony with its new music director, Erich Leinsdorf. The Metropolitan's turn came on Saturday, September 29, when it chose to offer, for the first time in America, Parts I and III of Manuel de Falla's *Atlantida*. Ernest Ansermet, whose operatic debut at the Metropolitan was scheduled for later in the season, prepared and conducted the orchestra, chorus, and soloists Eileen Farrell, Jean Madeira, and George London. The all-Falla evening began with *El Amor Brujo,* with Madeira as soloist. The concert did not offer basis for a conclusive estimate of *Atlantida*. The omitted parts added up to 165 of the 340 pages in the piano score, and there were cuts within the 175 that were covered. It was clear, however, that *Atlantida,* on which Falla had been at work for much of the last decade of his life (1936–46), embodied his faith as a musician, much as an architect might dedicate the last years of his life to the creation of a cathedral. An unexpected by-product of this performance was the end of Victoria de Los Angeles's affiliation with the Metropolitan. As the most prominent soprano of Falla's native country and a principal member of the company, she felt that she should have been invited to participate in the American *première* of his last work (as she had in Barcelona). The choice of Farrell cooled considerably her enthusiasm for further appearances at the Metropolitan. In fact, she made none during the last four seasons in the old theater, leaving her Mimi on April 10, 1961, and Lady Harriet in *Martha* on April 13 the last in the sequence that had begun in March 1951 with her debut as Marguerite.

The haste and considerable added expense with which Philharmonic Hall had been made ready to meet a deadline also had an influence on the planning for the new Metropolitan. Some of the dissatisfaction with the acoustical characteristics of the new auditorium was attributed privately to the lack of time to conduct tests *after* all the other work had been done. There had been a well-publicized "tuning week" in June, but the unrealistic conditions of the unfinished auditorium made it all but worthless as a guide to the responses that would prevail when all the furnishings, lighting fixtures, organ bay, etc., were in place.

Thus, before the winter was out, it was decided not to risk such a result with the new opera house which was, as of January 1, 1963, no more than a huge excavation at the west end of the Lincoln Center plaza, with enough water in it to be known as Lake Bing. Instead of proceeding with all haste to have the theater ready for the beginning of the World's Fair in the spring of 1964, it was decided to give priority in construction to the smaller New York State Theater. A simpler building, it could be comfortably accomplished within the period available. Opening of the new Metropolitan was set back to September 1966, permitting a pre-opening period of occupancy and trial operation after the delivery date of March 1, 1966. In due course, options were added to Bing's contract to cover the first year of occupancy—whenever it should be— and one beyond it.

Thus, instead of restricting himself to a ten-year commitment, as seemed his preference in the later 'fifties, and ending his New York career with the last season in the old house, Bing was, in effect, electing to identify himself with the Metropolitan for the remaining years of a normal work- ing life. As the new stage would duplicate almost exactly the playing area of the old (the vast improvements were to the sides, below, and above), new productions could continue to be built for the old house with a view to use in the new. With the same general manager overlapping old and new, the transition could be smooth, devoid of unwanted rivalries, and with a possibility of on-the-job training for a successor even before he was designated as such.

There was, however, no immediate evidence of this in the opening on October 15. This found the Metropolitan in what could be described as mid-season form, with a thoroughly routine performance of *Andrea Chénier* directed by Cleva. It also found Farrell out of her element as Maddalena,* Corelli a physically imposing poet, but otherwise not much of a Chénier,* and Merrill rather on the way of being a Gérard than one having arrived at that destination. The distinctions then were all statis- tical: earliest opening ever, for which the largest income ($99,202 at a top of $50 per ticket) had been collected, at the beginning of the longest season (twenty-six weeks) in Metropolitan history.

The sequence that followed—*Butterfly* conducted only moderately well by Varviso, with Kirsten, Morell, Sereni, and William Walker as the Imperial Commissioner* (d) on the sixteenth, *Aida* with Rita Gorr in her debut as Amneris* (d) and Santi conducting on the seventeenth—was much in the mold of what preceded. The more wonder, then, that what followed on the 18th was nothing less than the best production of *Die Meistersinger* which New York had seen in a generation. This was a Robert O'Hearn-Nathaniel Merrill collaboration (the funds were provided by Mrs. John D. Rockefeller, Jr., in the amount of $125,000) which excelled in imagination and suitability any Wagner staging offered by the Metropolitan in decades. What was most gratifying about the O'Hearn conception was its blend of tradition and freedom. Everything about Old Nuremberg was richly picturesque and realistic save the scene on the Peignitz at the end, which was in a freer, more symbolic spirit. Easily the best of his settings was that for Act II, in which the cobbling shop of Sachs, at the center of the stage, was isolated as an island, around which the action of Eva and Walther, Beckmesser's serenade, the entry of the Nightwatchman, and the street riot could flow unimpeded. A curving "street" on one side, a flight of stairs on the other provided for the necessary entrances and exits. It might be noted, too, that the total production—scenery, costuming, props., etc.—was created under the Metropolitan's roof, by its own personnel. The economics of such work had turned about to the extent that it was cheaper, once again, for the Metropolitan to build a production with its staff employees than to contract for it elsewhere in New York or import it from abroad.

As much as this *Meistersinger* appealed to the eye, it had quite as much to offer musically. Soundly conducted by Rosenstock (though with a degree of deliberation which echoed the descriptions of his previous Metropolitan *Meistersinger* thirty years before), it provided three performances of the first rank: Konya as Walther,* Murray Dickie as David* (d), and Dönch as Beckmesser, with Bjoner as Eva* who might, in time, sound as well as she looked, Flagello a worthy Pogner,* and Mittlemann a crusty Kothner.* In the Viennese Otto Wiener, it had what a proper *Meistersinger* cannot do without—a sizeable embodiment of Sachs* (d). His was a big rather than a rich voice, but he created scene by scene a character study that pivoted neatly on the drama's focal point: a man vigorous enough to justify Eva's thought of him for a husband, old enough to explain his wise refusal. Vanni as Magdalene* was a little light in sound, but a pleasantly youthful contrast to the matronly 'Lene sometimes seen.

Despite Wiener's qualities, opportunities to see him were limited. He endured for only four performances (Wiemann was the Pogner* on November 3) and has not been heard since. Edelmann was the Sachs on November 29, followed by Schoeffler on December 11. With this grand veteran (now sixty-five, but bearing his years as well as Sachs himself) was the able American Jess Thomas as Walther* (d). That some considered him as good or better than Konya testified to a greater resource for the lyric Wagner roles than the Metropolitan had possessed in a decade, considering the quality that Liebl provided as Walther* when it became his turn on December 28. On January 14, when the Sachs was Schoeffler and the Eva was Della Casa, Robert Patterson made his debut as Kothner* (d). There were, in all, ten performances of *Meistersinger* in this season, enabling those long on a starvation diet (the last performances had been in 1958-9) the opportunity to gorge.

The other new productions of this season (which lacked the customary press coverage because of a newspaper strike lasting 114 days, from early December to late March) were equally divided between the purposeful and the obligatory. In the first category were those produced for the works themselves, in the second, those produced for the singers who would appear in them.

Of primary interest in both categories was the first venture in the theater with Strauss's *Ariadne auf Naxos* on December 29. A prevailing doubt that the intimate work, with its instrumental complement of only thirty-eight, would sound well in the big auditorium was dispelled by the expert direction of Boehm. His sense of the euphony in Strauss's score provided a wave of resonance on which the voices floated easily and securely. More of a complication was incurred by the decision to present the prologue in an English translation as a way of "explaining" the circumstances to those who were too lazy to read a libretto, but preserving the German text of Hofmannsthal for the "opera" . . . on the theory, perhaps, that the intermingled plot and action were too silly to be understandable anyway. But, as tends to be almost inevitably the case, the European performers selected because of their ability to deal with the musical problem—especially Meyer as the Composer* and Rysanek as Ariadne*—were ill equipped to deal with the English language problem. A higher level of quality was attained by Meredith as the Majordomo* and Cassel as the Music Master*, especially as directed by Ebert, an expert on this subject, in the attractive décor of Messel. Francis Goelet provided the underwriting. The "opera" was more of a musical pleasure than the prologue, not only because Rysanek could deal powerfully with the flights of Ariadne's music, but also because Thomas was a qualified Bacchus,* D'Angelo a pert, resourceful Zerbinetta* (the usual amended version of *"Grossmächtige Prinzessin"* was used), and the female trio (Jeanette Scovotti as Echo,* Kriese as Dryade,* and Hurley as Najade*) was vocally well matched. The male members of the *commedia dell'arte* troupe were all skillful farceurs—Uppman (Harlekin*), Velis (Scara-muccio*), Flagello (Truffaldin*), and Anthony (Brighella*)—and vocally adept as well. To deal with the problem of so special a work in a reper-tory theater, Bing had provided alternates who were, in some instances, better than their predecessors. When the work was given on January 16, Konya was Bacchus,* with Peters as Zerbinetta,* and on January 22, the Ariadne* was Della Casa (not quite the sweep at the top, but beautiful to see), with that grand master of a Music Master,* Schoeffler, being heard for the first time. Despite Meyer's lack of either the voice or the manner, she continued to perform until March 2, when Miller was the Composer* and equally ill-suited in different ways. On March 8, the Zerbinetta* was Dobbs, agile but tiny in volume.

The saga of success stories at the Metropolitan added a new, uncom-mon chapter on March 10 when James McCracken, who had last been heard as the off-stage voice of a singer in *La Gioconda* on April 20, 1957, returned in the full glory of Otello,* with Solti conducting, Graf directing, and a new production by Berman. In the years since his last (invisible) Metropolitan appearance, McCracken had taken his talents, and those of his wife, Sandra Warfield, to Europe. Especially in Zurich (where he profited by working with Graf), he carved out a career that would, in all likelihood, never have accrued to him had he remained at the Metro-politan. He had, moreover, acquired such stature as Otello that the Metropolitan could hardly ignore his claim to be the first American to sing the part on its stage. Despite his 270 pounds on a 5 foot 10 inch frame, McCracken moved with surprising mobility in response to the goadings of Merrill as Iago.* This villain was as yet better sung than it was acted, but Merrill's slender frame balanced well, physically, against the bulk of McCracken. Both profited from the exacting leadership of Solti, who struck fire at the opening and sustained appropriate heat throughout. In place of Tebaldi, who was unable to perform (see page 680), the Desdemona* was Tucci, in some awe, apparently, of the person she was replacing. Franke was Cassio, with Dunn as Emilia* and Giaiotti a better than average Lodovico.* Rather than *Otello* being a climax, in quality, to Berman's succession of fine décors for the Metropol-itan stage (*Il Barbiere* had been the first, *Don Giovanni* the most recent) it was, on the whole, one of his least distinguished. (The two interiors were closest to the quality expected of him, the exteriors lacking in spaciousness and the architectural values of his *Rigoletto* and *La Forza.*) The whole result betrayed one basic difference in procedure from his *Don Giovanni:* Berman did not participate in the painting himself. After several performances with the cast of the first, Janis Martin (who had made her debut as Flora* in *Traviata* on December 19) was the Emilia* on March 23; Milanov was the Desdemona on April 4, with John Macurdy as Lodovico; and on April 9, Colzani was an unsubtle, gruff Iago.* McCracken performed all seven Otellos.

Of the obligatory offerings, the more purposeful, on February 21, was Bellini's *La Sonnambula*. Unlike its last revival in March 1932, which took its tone from the *petit point* Amina of Pons (see page 364), this new one for Sutherland was on the order of a Gobelin tapestry. In addition to performing the printed text with a facility rarely heard, Sutherland added a shower of embellishments and ornaments (collated from traditional sources by her husband-coach, Richard Bonynge) which was both tasteful and in the style. She also mustered the stamina to run the full course and take the most arduous hazards—*"Come per me sereno"* (hedge) and *"Ah! non giunge"* (water jump)—in stride.

Of her associates, the heaviest burden was borne by Gedda as Elvino.* He put himself out to make up by zeal and self-sacrifice what he lacked in natural resource, especially in the high range of the part. Tozzi as Rodolfo* was dealing with a more accessible problem and solved it, on the whole, well. Scovotti was a capable Lisa,* Chookasian a suitably maternal Teresa.* The scenic problem was entrusted to Gérard, whose Swiss landscape belonged to the Lindt, or candy-box, school. This did not do disservice to the direction of Butler, which was lamentably lacking in flair for the subject or resourcefulness to make up for the lack. Some intrusive dance action by Mattlyn Gavers, imposed on instrumental preludes and postludes to the vocal "numbers" could have, should have, been resisted by a more determined conductor than Varviso. On March 14 the Elvino* was Formichini (whose small tenor would have gone better with the Pons order of Amina than the Sutherland), with Hines as Rodolfo.* Flagello was Hines's successor on March 23.

The season's final new production was the inevitable, unavoidable, but still-to-be-resisted *Adriana Lecouvreur*, on January 21. A work of incontrovertible mediocrity, which had been tried and found wanting more than fifty years before (see page 191), Cilèa's score received a second Metropolitan production only because Tebaldi had embraced it as a "cause." To some the cause related more to the opportunity it presented for the title performer to impersonate a celebrated actress, to recite lines from two plays of Racine, wear four different costumes, and be described by her fellow mummers in such terms as *"magnifica"* and *"splendida"* than it did to the quality of music for Adriana to sing. This was mostly of the syrupy sentimentality that prompted reference to Cilèa really being a *nom de plume* for Massenini or Puccinet. Though Tebaldi had slimmed by more than twenty pounds since her last New York appearance (February 1961), there was no remission of the vocal decline that had been apparent even then. Now constriction set in about A, formerly a bell she rang with consistent clarity; the voice was heavy and unlovely in sound, the security of old had given way to effort and unease. What had seemed an outside possibility at the first performance became an inescapable certainty after but a few of the ten performances that had been scheduled. Tebaldi asked to be excused, and Bing decided that she would have to withdraw for the remainder of the season. Albanese replaced her as Adriana* on February 23, and Tebaldi retired to mull her vocal problem, see no one, and brood.

Thus, for having accepted the dictate "No Adriana, no Renata" at considerable cost to the contention that *he* and not its "stars" controlled the Metropolitan, Bing was rewarded with a production built around a star for which there was no star. Albanese performed with unflagging intensity and strained, tortured sound for all the remaining performances, save when Curtis-Verna had her opportunity as Adriana* on April 13, the last night of the season. Ironically, the whole project from the start was more to the glory of Corelli as Maurizio* than to that of Tebaldi. His replacement on February 23 was Morell. The first Princess* was Dalis, who lacked magnetism for such a "personality" part, a quality that Cvejic provided in some measure on February 1 and most succeeding occasions (Dunn had an opportunity on February 13). Colzani did well with the acting problem posed by Michonnet,* less so vocally. As conductor, the supple Varviso sustained his status as a prima donna's best friend. Although the production (imported from Naples at a cost of $50,000 to the Opera Guild) may not have added to the season's financial cost, the time committed to its theatrically vapid, musically void content could have resulted in something of more durability. *Adriana* has not been seen in another season, nor is it likely to be.

By contrast, when the City Opera decided to venture something from relatively the same period of the operatic past, it found it possible to combine novelty with quality in a venture with Charpentier's *Louise* to open its fall season on October 4. It would be idle to contend that the unwieldy "scenery" devised by Gordon Micunis evoked the image of Paris suitable to the circumstances or that every part was faithfully recreated. However, in Arlene Saunders, a pretty-sounding if insufficiently mature Louise, Claramae Turner, an excellent embodiment of the mother, and Norman Treigle, ideally suited for the father, conductor Jean Morel had more than a modicum of usable talent at his disposal. John Alexander's Julien was more proletarian than poet, despite director Christopher West's intelligent efforts to Gallicize him. In small roles, there was promise in the colorful mezzo sound of Joann Grillo in her debut as Gertrude. At the least, there was more musical return on this investment than on the Met's *Adriana Lecouvreur*.

From its own, so-to-speak composer laureate, Carlisle Floyd, the City Opera derived its *première* of the fall season: an invention wholly his own entitled *The Passion of Jonathan Wade* which turned out to have unlisted collaborators in the many prior writers who have dealt with a love affair between a Northern officer and a Southern belle in the Reconstruction period. As far as the emotional aspect of the subject was concerned, Floyd had made Columbia, South Carolina, as believable a locale as the area of the state represented in *Susannah*. However the ideational content was much less well represented, his carpetbaggers, scalawags, and Negro politicians "on the take" being as thin as the cloth from which they were cut. Theodor Uppman was a perfect figure of a Jonathan Wade, gentleman officer, and Phyllis Curtin a charming figure of the Celia Townsend he married. Norman Treigle performed a beautiful portrait of her father, Norman Kelley scathed away as a cardboard "moralist" from New England, and Julius Rudel made as much of the score as the composer permitted. But the clear fact seemed to be that Floyd was no longer content to treat subject matter he could handle and not able to handle subject matter with which he was content. Other events of the season included the debuts of Alpha Brawner, a large-voiced Negro soprano as Aida, and the evenly controlled artistry of Sara Mae Endich as the Countess in Mozart's *Figaro*.

The good results that attended the offering of Britten's *Turn of the Screw* in the preceding spring created a virtually read-made response for his *Midsummer Night's Dream*, which opened the second segment on April 25. Its virtues were admirably expounded by Rudel at the conductor's desk, and Robert Fletcher's production ideas were mostly to the good of William Ball's staging. The performers varied from excellent, in cases of the new Tatiana Troyanos as Hippolyta, Nadja Witkowska as Titania, Spiro Malas (Bottom), John Fiorito (Quince), and Richard Krause (Flute), to inadequate, William McDonald as Oberon not being the counter tenor Britten proposed. Julian Miller was a lively non-singing Puck. The repertory otherwise was very much the mixture as before, with revivals of *Love for Three Oranges* (Ara Berberian made his debut as Leandro) balanced by *Street Scene, The Ballad of Baby Doe, Susannah,* a Menotti double bill, etc.

What Varviso could not do to animate *Adriana* he did not, in the absence of Leinsdorf, Stokowski, Morel, and Verchi, provide to the gain of *Butterfly* on October 16 (see page 674) or *Fledermaus* on October 24, in which Formichini was a travesty Alfred,* and Rothenberger (Adele*) and Soederstroem (Rosalinda) contended unsuccessfully with the English text. It fared better from Uppman as Eisenstein, Guarrera as Falke, Velis as Dr. Blind,* Reitan as Frank,* and Madeira as Orlofsky.* A recollection of the early, original spirit of *Fledermaus* was provided by the reappearance of Jack Gilford as the Jailer. Varviso attacked the overture as though this were going to be one of his better efforts, but what followed was lacking in stylistic distinction. Kirsten was another Rosalinda* on November 3, and Alexander ventured an engaging Eisenstein* on November 15 in a cast that included Jeanette Scovotti as Adele* (d). Each had something of value to offer, Alexander continuing to win esteem in such roles as Pinkerton* on December 15 and Alfredo on January 12, Scovotti for a variety of services that included Echo* in *Ariadne auf Naxos* on December 29, Lisa* in *Sonnambula* on February 21, Oscar* in *Ballo in maschera* on February 25, and Xenia* in *Boris* on March 25. In the kinds of assignments for which he was suited by background and temperament, Varviso functioned efficiently, but this was, as yet, a narrow range for the Metropolitan.

The return of Schippers and the first appearances of Lorin Maazel and Ernest Ansermet pitched some standards a bit higher. The first Schippers assignment for this year was the vivification of *Ernani,* which had a mostly new cast of Price (Elvira*), Corelli (Ernani*), and MacNeil (Carlo*) when it was restored on November 10 after a lapse of five years. *"Infelice"* (the Silva* was Hines) occurred at the place where Verdi had provided for it, but what counted more was Price's healthy vocalism in *"Ernani, involami,"* the power of Corelli and MacNeil, and a surer direction of the action by Butler than had previously prevailed. Schippers's season was otherwise restricted to a series of performances of *Il Barbiere di Siviglia,* of which the first on November 25 had the uncommon interest of Simionato's Rosina.* Vocally this made for a lightly ornamented capstone to her prior achievements as Amneris, Azucena, and Santuzza; dramatically, she retained the vivacity of mind and the flexibility of body to suggest the youthful heroine despite the years she had invested in learning how. Formichini as Almaviva* had perhaps the most appropriate role of his Metropolitan career. There was familiar quality in Siepi's Basilio, Corena's Bartolo, and Merrill's Figaro (when it was not overly busy in action). Neither Schipper's direction nor Simionato's Rosina remained a season-long attribute of this *Barber:* the latter vanished after a single repetition, to be replaced by the conventional, bird-like Rosina of Peters (on December 21, with Shirley as

Almaviva*) or D'Angelo (on March 9, when the conductor was Strasfogel).
On March 26, Sereni was the Figaro with Giaiotti (Basilio*) and D'Angelo.
On April 8 the conductor was Rich. In such circumstances, talk of
ensemble was as meaningless as reference to a Metropolitan "standard."

The endeavor to find a conductor of the younger generation who would
eventually become a dependable part of the Metropolitan's resources
(in the sense that Schippers was an undependable one) turned in this
season to Lorin Maazel. His debut on November 1 as conductor of
Don Giovanni (with Siepi, Steber, Tucci far off sure ground as Elvira*,
Peters, Gedda, and Flagello) had its share of shortcomings, related to
his tend to drive, to rush, to hustle his singers from one phrase to the
next. But there were, at bottom, a strong feeling for Mozart and a sense
of the conductor's craft developed over a twenty-year span that had
begun before he was in his teens. His second assignment was *Der Rosenkavalier,* in which Régine Crespin made her debut as the Marschallin*
(d) on November 19, as did Hertha Töpper of Munich as Octavian,* with
Rothenberger as Sophie.* It was the original idea that Lotte Lehmann
should direct this production, which interested her as far as the principals
were concerned. A dual arrangement was arrived at, in which Ralph
Herbert supervised all else. What she had to offer was more to the gain
of Crespin than to that of Töpper, who resisted or rejected the older
woman's unsurpassably knowing advice. Rothenberger was an excellent
Sophie, Edelmann more a comedian than a singing actor in this season
as Ochs. As for Maazel, he was alternately riding the crest and foundering
in the troughs of Strauss's carefully crafted score, pushing the strings,
driving the brass, and otherwise imposing his inexperience on his associates. Included in his offences was a disregard for the distress of
Barioni in *"Di rigori armato"* which did not help the singer or improve
the performance. Maazel conducted the next *Rosenkavaliers* on November 24, 27, and December 7 (Soederstroem was Sophie), but by December 14, when Della Casa was the Marschallin, the conductor was Strasfogel. The Metropolitan was sharing Maazel's services with the Philharmonic, and he did not feel up to an evening opera after an orchestral
matinee. The *Rosenkavaliers* of November 19 and 24 were notable for
the Marianne of Votipka, her last performances at the Metropolitan in
a history of excellent service going back to the opening opera of Johnson's
first season, nearly thirty years before. In later *Rosenkavaliers* directed
by Maazel, Elias ventured Octavian* on January 17, sounding well but
offering little that was boyish in the characterization. In his *Don Giovannis,*
Maazel had the advantage of a superb Donna Anna by Price on December 5, showing a command of the vocal line as good as any the Metro-

politan had offered since Ponselle's. However, by December 20, when Price made her next appearance, the conductor was Schick. Deviations from previous casting included Reitan as Masetto on December 25 and Stich-Randall as an impassioned, vocally adroit Donna Anna* on February 9. This time the conductor was Rich. Maazel was announced for the season of 1963–4, but he sustained an arm injury while performing in Japan during the summer and had to be replaced.

Ansermet's activities were not subject to the pattern of interruption and replacement typical of other Metropolitan guest conductors at the time for a simple reason: he confined himself to preparing *Pelléas et Mélisande* for a performance on November 30 which commemorated the hundredth anniversary of Debussy's birth (the actual date was August 22) and did nothing beyond four repetitions of it. In his hands, it was in every way distinguished Debussy, beautifully built to the scale of the large auditorium in a sonorous scheme that conceived the orchestra as one of the physical facts of the drama. Ansermet's ablest allies were London (as Golaud) and Uppman (as Pelléas). Moffo's promise as Mélisande—youth, pliable voice, musical intelligence—was offset by her technical limitations as an actress and a fatal disposition to lapse into attitudes and gestures all too plainly of the here and now. It is noteworthy that in a season of his Elvino in *Sonnambula*, Ottavio in *Don Giovanni*, and Dimitri in *Boris*, Gedda was also a very good Pelléas* on December 10. Stratas as Yniold,* Thebom as Geneviève,* Hines (or Tozzi) as Arkel were all able adjutants to Ansermet's command function. Moffo's shortcomings altered little in the span of the five performances allotted to *Pelléas;* there was no other Mélisande in this season.

Along with preparing the new production of *Otello* (see page 678), Solti made himself available for *Tristan* beginning on March 8 and *Boris* (the first on March 16). Hopf was engaged to provide Nilsson with a proper partner in Wagner, but as the date approached, it became known that he had begged off (the reason was unspecified, but the presumption was that he did not feel ready to sing Tristan). Thus it was Liebl again, with Hines, Cassel, and Dalis, a combination that Solti tended to react against rather than with. In any case, the qualities that contributed favorably to his *Tannhäuser*—animation, energy, a relentless pressing forward—tended to be disruptive of mood and eloquence in *Tristan*. The broadcast performance of February 23, it should be mentioned, was more supple, less insistent. On March 9, with the *première* of *Otello* impending on the next day, it became a Rosenstock *Tristan* again (Dunn was the Brangäne*). For his *Boris* on March 16, Solti retained the Shostakovitch instrumentation and made a powerful sound with it. When

London was working out his characterization or Solti had the chorus under ringing discipline, the satisfactions were many; however, it did not sound as though Solti had had sufficient time to work with the numerous other characters in Mussorgsky's score, especially such newcomers to their roles as Flagello (Pimenn*), Dunn (the Innkeeper*), Cassel (Rangoni*), Blair (Xenia*), and Chookasian (Nurse*). In consequence, this *Boris* ran a course from expert (London, Gedda, the chorus) to uncertain (almost all the smaller roles enumerated above). At the next performance, Alvary was the Varlaam in place of Corena, and Martin was the Innkeeper.* By March 25, the changes ran to ten, with Hines as Boris, the young American Arturo Sergi as Dimitri* (d), Roggero as Fyodor, Scovotti as Xenia,* and Tozzi as Pimenn. There were another five on March 29, when Tozzi performed his thoughtful, well-conceived Boris* (a conception he had introduced in an NBC telecast the year before), and Hines returned his colleague's compliment by appearing as Pimenn. This time the Dimitri* was Olvis. Probably the only reason there was not a fourth Boris this season was that Siepi was busy with a Broadway "musical," and restricted himself to a few performances as Don Giovanni, Ramfis, and Basilio.

Sutherland's success as Lucia and in *La Sonnambula* projected the possibility that she would, in seasons to come, assume, with Nilsson and Price, the share of prominence that had formerly been occupied by Tebaldi, Callas, and Milanov. Of Nilsson's capacities the passage of time only revealed more and more. Her earlier venture in Verdi (as Aida) was followed in this season by an Amelia* in *Ballo* on January 9 which was, perhaps, the best singing in this part during the current revival (Tucker, Merrill, and Chookasian as Ulrica were well chosen, for power, to match her). Singing Verdi always poses a problem in adjustment to Nilsson but it is one she usually solves in relatively short order, in this case by the middle of her duet with Riccardo. By comparison with Crespin, whose endeavor with Amelia* on December 13 found her struggling for a middle ground between *fortissimo* and *pianissimo,* Nilsson had all the desirable dynamic variations at her disposal. Such resource also added to the interest of her Leonore in *Fidelio* on January 26, in which Vickers was the excellent Florestan, Wiemann a dullish Rocco,* and Raskin a beguiling Marzelline* under Boehm's direction (Meredith as Pizarro* and Flagello as Fernando* both excelled their immediate predecessors). Whereas *"Abscheulicher"* had previously been by much her outstanding achievement, it was now part of a consistent performance in which she blended well with the other voices in the *"Canon"* quartet and spoke lines as well as she sang notes. Her selfset standard was so high, however, that when she was otherwise occupied, the Kuchta kind of Leonore* (with Robert Patterson as Fernando* and Herbert Fliether as Pizzaro* [d]) on February 15 or the Curtis-Verna kind of Turandot sounded even poorer than it might otherwise have sounded. Rysanek was the Leonore* on February 7, with Thomas as Florestan.* His sturdy effort commanded respect, but if one could sympathize with the diminishing vocal powers that left Rysanek well short of the standard she had achieved on a recording a few years before, one could only wonder at her inappropriate costume and the managerial indulgence that passed it on to public view. She remained supreme as Senta, however, which had the additional impact of Boehm's first Metropolitan performance of the score on January 11, with Konya as Erik,* Chookasian as Mary,* and Shirley as the Steersman* abetting the classic Dutchman of London and Daland of Tozzi. Crespin was the Senta* on January 19, performing it for the first time anywhere and doing better than might have been anticipated. There were no *Ring* dramas in this season, whose Wagner was confined to *Meistersinger, Holländer,* and *Tristan.*

As an example of what makes the Metropolitan a proud name in the operatic world, this year offered—as a parallel to the preceding year's *Lucia-Götterdammerung* day—another Saturday (January 26) with an afternoon *Fidelio* (Nilsson, Raskin, Vickers, etc.) and an evening *Meistersinger* (Thomas, Schoeffler, Della Casa, and Tozzi) directed respectively by Boehm and Rosenstock. Here, in terms of two productions suitable to their purpose, was a summation of what makes distinguished opera: good singers directed by able conductors. When one is present but the other is lacking, the results tend to become uneven, uncertain, or undistinguished. If—as had become too often the case with the Metropolitan lately—both are absent, the outcome can, by a process of elimination, result only in the inept, the uninteresting, and the unworthy.

Thus in the shadow of the brilliant *Meistersinger,* the powerful *Otello,* and the admirable *Sonnambula* were the commonplace *Aida* of October 26, with Borsò as Radames* impeding the efforts of Price to resume her superior standard, and the *Cavalleria rusticana* and *Pagliacci* of the next day, in which Gorr was strained by the demands of Santuzza,* Testi was an inadequately provincial Alfio*, and Morell was required to perform Turiddu* after a matinee as Pinkerton in *Butterfly.* Or another *Aida* on January 4 for which there was no qualified Radames when Corelli was unable to perform, and Thomas, who had learned his Verdi in Munich, was pressed into service. Thus a Metropolitan audience had the questionable privilege of hearing *"Celeste Aida"* as Verdi set it, and the rest of Radames's lines in German because Thomas had not yet completed learning the role in Italian. A certain kind of administrative virtuosity in solving another "crisis" was demonstrated on February 2, when Konya pleaded laryngitis on the morning of a broadcast of *Der fliegende Holländer* and no other Erik could be found. With Boehm and Rysanek as pivot points and a dozen administrative assistants busy on telephones, the *Holländer* was turned into *Ariadne auf Naxos* by two p.m.

The addition, in this season, of one week to the twenty-five of the season before may not appear significant, but the increase in numbers of performances from Bing's first twenty-two-week total of 154 to the 201 given in this season is. Enlarging the number did not add materially to the total of *good* performances (let alone very good or great ones), but it did increase the number of indifferent or poor ones. It did not add, in a season, to the total number of performances of outstanding or unusual operas, but it did swell the number of those easiest to give. Least of all did it add to the number of the good or above average singers, but it did add incontestably to the number of those on the borderline of acceptability or dangerously beyond it. *Need breeds tolerance* may be offered as a three-word summation of many of the Metropolitan's ills at the time.

Aside from *Die Meistersinger*, whose ten performances in New York were of consistent quality, the widest fluctuation of quality might be found among those works given with the greatest frequency—*Aida* (twelve), *Chénier* (eleven), *Fledermaus* (ten). The *Chénier* sequence, for example, included Farrell as Maddalena* on the opening night, Milanov (the performance of December 17, in which Mariano Caruso made his debut as the Spy,* was celebrated as her twenty-fifth anniversary at the Metropolitan), Tucci (her first on November 10 included Barioni as Chénier* and Chookasian as Madelon*), and Parada on January 25, also for the first time, with Schick conducting rather than Cleva. Borsò was the Chénier* on October 30, as Bergonzi, Corelli, and Tucker (in addition to Barioni) were on other occasions. For the *Cavalleria-Pagliacci* pairing, the Santuzzas ranged from Simionato, Gorr, and Farrell (the last-named's first venture on November 25 showed her in a role closer to her instinctive sympathies than anything she had performed in her Metropolitan career) to Curtis-Verna and to Dalis on April 1. With the last as Santuzza* was Labò, whose Turiddu* could be construed as penance for the performance he had declined to sing five seasons before. Vocally it was a part for which he was well-disposed, though at barely more than five feet his stature was against him.

Labò had resumed Metropolitan appearances on November 24 as

Radames,* with Vladimir Ruzdak, who had made his debut as Amonasro* on November 20, portraying the Ethiopian monarch in a cast with Curtis-Verna, Gorr, and Tozzi. Physical size aside, Labò performed more than creditably in a season's work that included Radames again on February 14, with Nilsson, Cvejic (Amneris), Ruzdak, and Flagello; Calaf* in *Turandot* on February 26; Riccardo in *Ballo* on March 15 and again on March 27, when Tucci was Amelia.* In the earlier *Ballo,* the part of Sam (known in this production as Count Warting) was performed by John Macurdy. His substantial bass voice had first been heard when he made his debut in the same role on December 8. The numerous *Pagliaccis* of this season provided for the introduction as Nedda* (d) in the first on October 27 of Raina Kabaivanska, whose attractive appearance and bright lyric voice promised more than it produced in this or the next season. Her successors in the part included Amara on December 24 (the Canio was Borsò) and both Stratas (with Vickers and Colzani on January 31) and Hurley (with McCracken as Canio* on April 1). In addition to Labò, the Turiddus* of the season included Morell on October 27 and Olvis on November 13. Of a higher quality altogether was Konya's Pinkerton* on January 13.

While the company was pursuing its customary tour (minus, it might be noted, *Adriana Lecouvreur*), progress toward the new structure in Lincoln Center continued. On May 9, Milanov was invited to participate in a ceremony marking the installation of the first steel and to be photographed with a riveting gun.

1963–1964

If a season is known by its peak accomplishments, 1963–4 was one of Bing's most successful; if it is known by the inadequacies of which it was guilty, it could also be described as one of his least notable. Perhaps it is just because of the distance between its extremes that it can also be described as among the most characteristic in this period of his direction.

It was, for example, a formidable accomplishment to achieve a complete reversal in the quality of one much-performed work, *Aida,* which had reached Johnsonian depths of dramatic and scenic infidelity when last heard in the season of 1962–3. The turnabout was not accomplished by the addition of new names to the cast, or even by the addition of a conductor not available before. Rather it derived from the decision that the only way to dis-establish the abuses of the existing conditions was to create new ones whose abuse would not be tolerated. By the standards of some other works, the Gérard *Aida* still qualified as "new" in the sense that it had originated in Bing's own time, but twelve years of use and some 150 performances in New York and on the road certainly qualified it for replacement.

The designer this time was O'Hearn, with Nathaniel Merrill as stage director. For the opening night, October 14, income rose to a record $101,108, which still did not equal the $135,000 it cost to dress the stage and its occupants and finance the rehearsals. For the first time ever, the expense was not underwritten by an individual or a foundation, but by a business organization. The farsighted firm was the American Export and Isbrandtsen Lines which deemed the investment desirable for general good will and of particular appeal because it identified its area of operation—ports of call in the Mediterranean—with the locale of the opera. Realistically, too, it had its appeal, for if the production had the same use as its predecessor, it would work out to little more than $1,000 per mention in the program.

O'Hearn's shrewd utilization of the height and depth of the Metropolitan's stage created a wholly new atmosphere for this *Aida,* with spacious temple scenes, a broad plaza for the procession, and picturesque surroundings for the boudoir of Amneris and the Nile Scene. Its one deficiency was a nondescript treatment of the crypt, which emerged as little more than a dark area. It was, on the whole, generally admired, the inevitable qualification coming from Schonberg in *The New York Times,* who found what he saw to be marked by "vulgarity and a lack of imagination characteristic of some recent Metropolitan efforts." This complaint was provoked in part by the choreography of Katherine Dunham, whose vitality, ingenuity, and interest had not been matched in any Metropolitan *Aida* within memory. For her pains in extending the danced episodes beyond the range of operatic Egyptology usually seen, Dunham was rewarded with complaints of their "African" character. However, she had ample, and cogent, reasons, for her assumptions on a locale (the Egypt of the Pharaohs) for which there were no surviving eyewitnesses and few living experts. Among other improvements on its predecessor, O'Hearn's scheme restored the statue in the temple scene to its proper position vis à vis those who venerated it, and his costumes were tailored to suit the many who would wear them in the future as well as to the particular singers of the first cast.

Musically, the distinctions of this *Aida* stemmed from the ability of Solti to treat the score as an expert restores a painting—by erasing accumulated grime from the sound of the orchestra, bringing "up" the color values, and making fresh the sense of a whole. Had he been provided with the best cast the company could assemble, he doubtless could have made as fine a totality of the vocal ensemble as he did of the instrumental. But it could hardly be contended that Bergonzi, Nilsson, Dalis, and Sereni were the best the company could provide as Radames, Aida, Amneris, and Amonasro. (Only Tozzi as Ramfis and Macurdy as the King qualified for rank as "best.") With the others, selection was conditioned by other considerations—who had, or had not, performed on a recent opening night, whose good will might be cultivated by this honor, etc. For the while, Bergonzi consented to end *"Celeste Aida"* with a sigh rather than a shout, though it was not quite the piano specified by the composer. Nilsson performed with typical concentration, better in the ensembles than in *"O patria mia"* and the rest of the Nile Scene.

There was provision for nearly twenty performances of *Aida* in the course of this season (which included an extra two weeks to coincide with the opening of the World's Fair), thus permitting latitude for other tastes to be satisfied. But it could contribute only to bafflement rather than satisfaction that the first change provided Curtis-Verna (on November 1). Price made her first, exciting appearance in these new, exciting surroundings on December 7, with Gorr as Amneris. By the time of her next Aida on December 30, Solti was gone and the conductor was Adler, with Gorr as Amneris, Labò (Radames), London (Amonasro) and Justino Diaz (a young Auditions' winner from Puerto Rico who had made his debut as Monterone* [d] in *Rigoletto* on October 23) as the King.* Even this change was subject to change, with Varviso in charge for the performances on May 1, 6, and 7.

The choice of *Manon* for the second new production was both merited and welcome, recent performances (see page 555) having been given in a collection of scenes made for other purposes. But it was making an evil of necessity to affiliate a non-French conductor (Schippers) and a non-French group of principals with a German director (Günther Rennert) and a Russian designer (Ita Maximowna). From the charmless courtyard at Amiens through a cheerless apartment for Manon in Paris and a colorless rendering of the Cours la Reine, Maximowna's settings gave little of the atmosphere suitable to Massenet's score. The St. Sulpice scene was better, the Hôtel de Transylvanie best, but much of what is crucially important to *Manon* had, by then, been ill-served. Schippers's conducting could be termed spirited, in the sense of animated; but of the true Massenet spirit—refined, worldly, insinuating— there was all too little. And though Moffo had the physical advantages and the sound to make a Manon,* her effort with it was unhappily similar to her Mélisande of the previous season, her Pamina* and Marguerite to come in this one. More performances of few roles would have served them, and her, better than the steady succession of different parts which she performed too seldom to develop ease and assurance, let alone mastery. Gedda's Chevalier des Grieux was less than had been remembered from his previous performances, which may have been caused by concern for his father, who was ailing in Sweden. He left for home soon afterwards, resulting in an unwarranted use of Shirley as Des Grieux* (the *Herald Tribune* described the results as "distressingly adolescent") on October 25. Neither surroundings nor lack of direction could discourage a practiced performer such as Tozzi from being a superior Comte des Grieux, but the roles of Lescaut* (Guarrera) and Brétigny* (Walker) needed more to make them credible than the performers alone could provide. In addition to Scovotti as Poussette,* the first act trio included the debuts of Marcia Baldwin (Javotte* [d]) and Joann Grillo (Rosette* [d]). There was no other Manon than Moffo in this season; on October 30 the Lescaut* was Ruzdak, who had little more than a hearty voice to offer. Moffo's not very expert Marguerite* was first seen in a *Faust* on November 6, in which Campora, in vocal straits, attempted to make good the absence of Gedda. Alexander was more successful on March 17.

For his third venture with a work by a living composer, Bing had some time earlier committed the Metropolitan to a project in which Menotti returned to the light manner of his early *Amelia al ballo* and *The Telephone.* Originally entitled *The Last Superman*, it was called *The Last Savage* by the time of its American *première* on January 23. Also by that time it had had its unhappy *première* in Paris (where Menotti's best was disparaged and his second best denounced), which did not promote optimism. That it nevertheless held the attention of the audience and provided some pleasure even for the more discriminating portions of the public was a tribute to two things: Menotti's able mounting of his own work and the range and depth of the theatrical talent in the company.

Mounting, in this instance, included not only the artful direction of the performers, but also the provision of Beni Montresor, a young designer little known by operagoers, to provide an enormously cheerful, adroitly contrived décor. Beginning with an almost bare stage, Montresor engaged the viewer as a participant in the process by which artfully arranged drops, set pieces put in place by costumed supers, and interior changes were achieved. This kind of whimsicality added as much as the thin line of music they were given to perform to the efforts of London (Abdul*), Stratas (Sardula*), Peters (Kitty*), Flagello (Maharajah*),

Chookasian (Maharanee*), Gedda (Kodanda*), and Meredit (Scatter-good*) to make Menotti's satire on contemporary civilization entertaining. Much of it was cleverly instrumentated, but it was ill served by a translation by George Mead of the Italian text into libretto-English which bore heavily on such rhymes as "laddie, daddy," "money, honey," "torso, more so." The final episode of Abdul and Kitty when all the other performers had left the stage recalled Hofmannsthal's ending of *Rosenkavalier* for Octavian and Sophie, but the music did not reach any comparable distinction. Variations in casting provided Donald Gramm as the Maharajah* and Cassel as Abdul* on February 14, Hurley as Kitty* on February 22, and Alexander as Kodanda* on February 26, in most instances without cost to quality of performance.

Periodically during Bing's first decade, as his affection for the works of Verdi became increasingly manifest, the question arose: "Why not *Falstaff*?" The answer probably dated back to the last Metropolitan occurrence of Verdi's comic masterwork in the next-to-last Johnson season, for it ran: "I won't give it with Warren, and I can't give it without Warren." When *Falstaff* finally reappeared after an absence since March 7, 1949—a date during the period when Bing, still general manager of John Christie's Glyndebourne company, was in New York and met Johnson for the first time (see page 478)—the Falstaff* was Colzani, whose access to America had been promoted by Warren's death.

With or without Colzani, what made this *Falstaff* on March 6 memorable was the indomitable spirit of the man who wrote it and the aspiration to excellence it inspired in Franco Zeffirelli as designer-director and Leonard Bernstein as conductor (their combined ages were scarcely more than Verdi's when he wrote the work at eighty). Zeffirelli's scenic conception, perfected by six prior efforts in Europe and England, evoked the spirit of Elizabethan England in a Verdian way possible, perhaps, only for one who was both Italian and a Shakespeare student. Bernstein's conducting transcended any of his concert hall achievements in the creation of a musical ensemble that defined his biggest, truest gift as theatrical.

There was the danger that so much mutual stimulation might result in a broadside attack on a work that courted delicacy as much as it did brio, but what there was of exaggeration could be described as the right kind for the Metropolitan. Once the initial impact was dispersed, Bernstein's musical direction was deft, discerning, and unfailingly musical, as Zeffirelli's staging, after a few too many tricks at the beginning, was unswervingly resourceful. The best of which both were capable showed itself in the lightly pattering ensemble of Raskin (Nannetta*), Tucci

(Mistress Ford*), and Elias (Meg*), with Resnik as a broadly con-spiratorial Dame Quickly,* Luigi Alva a Fenton* (d) who sounded as well as he looked, and a sound collection of rascals in Velis (Bardolph*), Scott (Pistol*), and Franke (Dr. Caius*). They were, together, worth every dollar that was spent of Mrs. John D. Rockefeller, Jr.'s financing.

There were some circumstances, perhaps, in which Colzani could be considered the best available Falstaff, but not those in which Gobbi was available to the Metropolitan to perform Scarpia concurrently, or Geraint Evans could be presented in succession to Corena on March 12. In any case, those who were only mildly aroused by the unknightly *roué* of Colzani and not at all by the grossly clownish lecher of Corena did not wait in vain for the grandly artistocratic Sir John* (d) of Evans on March 25. He produced maximum results from a smallish voice by restricting its full power to moments of climax, and varying its color adroitly to the quantity required otherwise. In all cases, the production reached an unforeseeable resolution in the evocative setting Zeffirelli made of his Windsor Forest, and the pageantry with which he filled out the implications of text and music. Last because he did least with a rich opportunity was Sereni as Ford,* a stock Italian type rather than the English model desired. Guarrera, with much less voice to dispose of was capable of more of the character wanted, but it did not materialize until the following season. Other changes were restricted to Caruso as Dr. Caius* on March 16, a part he performed several times thereafter. The nine performances were more than *Falstaff* had been accorded in any prior season, perhaps because there was more in it for the audience to enjoy, visually, than in any prior production.

With *Otello* held over and *Macbeth* once more in the repertory, the pro-duction of *Falstaff* enabled Bing to present, in this season, what had never previously been possible at the Metropolitan: all three of Verdi's operas on Shakespearean subjects. This was put in the framework of the quatercentenary of the playwright's birth (1564–1964). During one mid-March interlude, *Otello* was given on the eighteenth, *Macbeth* on the nine-teenth, and *Falstaff* at the matinee of the twenty-first. This enabled Colzani to sing Iago and Falstaff with only two days' interval. Nilsson was the Lady Macbeth* between. Hers was an impressive example of vocal virtuosity, with gradations of volume and finesse (up to a D flat) which made one momentarily forget that she had ever sung Isolde, Leonore, or Turandot. And she exhibited a sense of dramatic suitability dating back to her first operatic venture in Stockholm (1947) in the same role. MacNeil's Macbeth* was vocally weighty, dramatically light, and Franco Ghitti did little to demonstrate why he should have been imported to sing

Malcolm.* Hines (Banquo) and Shirley (Macduff) were of their previous quality, but Santi's capacity to animate this score was several shades lighter than Rosenstock's or Leinsdorf's. Dalis was Lady Macbeth on April 4, but the part was not ventured at all in this season by Rysanek. The latter's delayed "season" did not begin until February 8, when she performed Desdemona* (with a sound described by Ericson in the *Times* as "hollow" and "blurred") in company with McCracken, Merrill, and Alexander (an excellent Cassio*). Because of telephoned "threats" received by Rysanek, together with some noisy, derisive reactions to her performance on this date and on February 12, Bing ordered all standees excluded from the theater on February 15, when Rysanek sang Desdemona in a broadcast performance of *Otello* with McCracken and Colzani.

The announcement posted at the window where standing room tickets were ordinarily sold read:

> RECENTLY A NUMBER OF DISTINGUISHED ARTISTS HAVE BEEN THREATENED AND INSULTED. WE HAVE DEFINITE REASON TO BELIEVE THAT THIS EMANATES FROM SOME STANDING ROOM PATRONS.
>
> CONSEQUENTLY STANDING ROOM IS CLOSED UNTIL FURTHER NOTICE.
>
> RUDOLF BING
> GENERAL MANAGER

When Bing was queried on the length of time the suspension would remain in effect, he speculated that it might be a matter of weeks. However, before the afternoon's performance was over, the standees who had gathered outside the theater were visited by Maria Jeritza (a regular Saturday-afternoon visitor at the Metropolitan from her home in New Jersey). They pleaded with her to intercede with Bing. Later she was seen entering his office. Whether this was a factor or not, the ban was lifted in time for the standees to be admitted to their regular places for the evening performance of *Onegin,* with Price, Thomas, and Dooley. It was not re-imposed.

As far as a gesture was concerned, the grouping of Verdi's three "Shakespeare" operas did more honor to the poet than to the composer. With or without comparison, Santi's *Otello* and *Macbeth* were on another level of interpretative effort altogether from Bernstein's *Falstaff* (or, for that matter, from Solti's *Otello,* which he did not conduct in this season). The complaint, indeed, was less against Santi—who doubtless did the best of which he was capable—than against those who assumed this best was "good enough." Milanov was another Desdemona in this season, and, in the absence of McCracken on February 25, Otello* was entrusted to Sergi. Power he had in abundance, but neither the range of vocal effects for this complex role nor the dramatic resources to sustain it. On April 4, Tebaldi returned to the role of her debut.

However, Santi's *Otello* and *Macbeth* were by no means the most untoward combinations of work and conductor in this season, which began with Maazel's accident, continued with Reiner's death in November, and proceeded for its full length without Boehm. As the beginning of the Metropolitan season overlapped the reopening of the National Theater in Munich—Boehm was a participant—he was under prior obligation for part of the winter. Whether he might have come later is debatable —there was some opinion that he was offended by the assignment of *The Magic Flute* to Maazel, and preferred to remain away. In the end, the Metropolitan had neither Maazel nor Boehm for the *Flute* or for anything else.

It was Reiner's retirement from his position in Chicago that made him available for at least part-time service at the Metropolitan, but the cause of that retirement (a series of heart attacks and related illnesses) made it unlikely that he could direct a lengthy opera without real danger of collapse. Thus the choice of *Götterdämmerung* (as lengthy an opera as the repertory contained) for his reappearance on November 14 appeared as unrealistic as numerous other command decisions of the time. The worst possible did not happen in the theater: but it came as a direct result of his exertions at rehearsals. Reiner came down with a cold, contracted pneumonia, and died within a week. Rosenstock agreed to replace him, even though this meant that he would have to pick up the rehearsals with Act II.

Aside from Nilsson, and perhaps Dalis as Waltraute, there was not a wholly sound performer in the four performances of *Götterdämmerung* heard in this season (another was scheduled for November 22 but canceled in mid-afternoon when reports of the assassination of President John F. Kennedy were received from Dallas). Hopf was not much more of a Siegfried than he had been two years before, or Liebl a qualified alternate in this part; Wiemann was an unconvincing Hagen and Mittlemann not yet a fully formed Gunther. The obvious endeavor to cast this *Götterdämmerung* as far as possible with "resident" talent was reflected in the election of Curtis-Verna to sing both the Third Norn* and Gutrune* (her first efforts in German), with Pechner as Alberich. Nilsson's redeeming superiority was absent on November 29 when quality retreated to the Kuchta level of Brünnhilde* with Liebl as Siegfried and Gorr as a strong-willed rather than strong-voiced Waltraute.* On December 4, the Gunther was Cassel, with Yeend as Gutrune* and Ernster, who once could sing Hagen impressively, restricted largely to an acting performance. On December 14, the order reverted to the cast of the first performance, save for Dunn as Waltraute.* Madeira appeared as Orlofsky in *Fledermaus* on November 30 and December 7, but in none of the *Götterdämmerungs*. For Johann Strauss if not for Richard Wagner, change resulted in improvement, for the emergency re-assignment of Varviso to *The Magic Flute* brought on Franz Allers, a conductor with a flair for the style. He made his debut as director of *Fledermaus* on November 30 with rousing results. On December 12 the Rosalinda was Fenn, a role she also performed well on later occasions.

For the rest, outside aid was not solicited though it could well have been used. In such works as *Meistersinger, Don Giovanni,* and *Götterdämmerung* (likewise the later *Lohengrin*), Rosenstock performed with solid competence, but he was not available to deal with *The Magic Flute* and *Ariadne auf Naxos* as well. It was, in all, not a prime year for Mozart, as much because of constant shifts of cast as for any other single reason. Leopold Simoneau made a welcome, belated debut as Don Ottavio* (d) on October 18, and there was attractive quality also in the Zerlina* (d) of Neyde Thomaz, a Brazilian soprano, to balance an ensemble of Stich-Randall, Amara, Siepi, and Corena. They barely had time to settle to mutual understanding (two further performances) when Tozzi was Don Giovanni* (his first effort sounded as though he were no more comfortable as a Mozart singer in this role than he had been as Figaro). Della Casa was Elvira, with Scovotti as Zerlina* on November 12. Exit Simoneau, enter Dickie on November 16, as a David-sized Ottavio* with or without juxtaposition to Hines as Don Giovanni. The Donna Anna* was Kuchta, with Della Casa, Scovotti, and Macurdy as the Commendatore* en route to a combination of Bjoner as Donna Anna* (she had neither the dramatic force nor the florid technique for this music) and Peerce as Ottavio on December 20, with Diaz as the Commendatore.* Rosenstock was somewhat, though not much, better off with *Lohengrin*, in which Crespin performed with more will than adaptability as Elsa* on February 1, in a cast with Konya, Rankin, Cassel, and Wiemann; later Lohengrins* included Jess Thomas, who had the means to perform this part well, and Sergi, on February 17, who did not. With Thomas, on March 10, was Rysanek, whose days for controlling the line of Elsa* appeared to be running out.

The view that Varviso could equalize the loss of both Maazel and Boehm while attending to his own work left, in the aftermath, only one uncertainty; whether the results were less good when he conducted, or when he did not conduct. In *The Magic Flute,* when he attempted it for the first time on November 30, were such excellent performers as Gedda, Uppman, and Siepi as Sarastro* to form a strong central core of male talent, and Scovotti as Papagena* to keep pace with them. But Moffo's Pamina* lacked character in both sound and action, and D'Angelo was a much too small-sounding Queen of the Night* to support the dramatic demands upon her. Harry Horner, the Viennese artist who designed this production, was also named as the stage director this time, but evidence of his effort was limited. Varviso's credits included courage, musicality, and a measure of taste, but hardly the authority to produce a convincing performance of the overture or to propel the scenes that followed. Even in Act II, where he was better adjusted to his surroundings, there was too little of the symphonic interplay of orchestra and voices to make a weave of Mozart's tonal texture. On December 16, the High Priest* (d) was Kenneth Smith, who had joined the company during the spring tour at the end of the previous season; on December 24, when the conductor was Strasfogel, changes included Shirley as Tamino*, Walker as Papageno,* Blair as Papagena,* and Meredith as the High Priest.* By January 3, when the conductor was Varviso once more, he faced another unfamiliar group of principals: Price (Pamina*), Alexander (a potentially fine Tamino*) and David Ward (Sarastro*).

Here, in being, was a compelling example of the favorite executive jest of the time at the Metropolitan, the *Wiener Schnitzel* story. It concerned the patron of a Viennese restaurant who settled back to study the bill of fare, only to be told by the waiter: "I am sure you will enjoy our *Wiener Schnitzel.*" "But," said the patron, "why should I enjoy the *Wiener Schnitzel* when I don't like *Wiener Schnitzel?*" "Because," said the waiter, "that's all we have." At twelve dollars a ticket, the Metropolitan was asking *filet mignon* prices for a *Magic Flute* whose shortcomings were, in some backstage areas, considered amusingly represented by the *Wiener Schnitzel* story.

For its part, the City Opera continued to offer a standard that was, if never as good as the Metropolitan's best, more consistently compatible with its ticket prices. For its opening, a new pairing of Stravinsky (*Le Rossignol*) and Honegger (*Jeanne d'Arc au bûcher*) was devised, with the first performed in Russian—a rather fussy bit of pedantry, as it had begun its life with a Paris *première* in French in 1914—and the second in English. Musically, the Honegger was better performed under the direction of Leon Barzin, with Elisabeth Carron (Virgin Mary), Juanita King (debut, St. Margaret), and Mauro Lampi (Cauchon) than it was spoken by Jacqueline Brookes and Douglas Watson (Dominic). Nor did the introduction of a group of soldiers uniformed to suggest Nazis add to clarity. Patricia Brooks was heard as the voice of the Nightingale, with Arthur Graham as the Fisherman and Donald Gramm as the Emperor. Other than a new production of *La Traviata* costumed to suggest the 1890s (Franco Patané conducted, with Beverly Sills, John Craig, and Igor Gorin as Father Germont), the principal interest of this playing period attached to a work by Jerome Moross and librettist Edward Eager entitled *Gentlemen, Be Seated.* As the title suggests, it was derived from the modes and manners of the minstrel show, against which was set a retrospect of history from Fort Sumter to Reconstruction days. Unfortunately the idea was better than the execution of it, and there was evidence that rehearsals were proceeding up to a few hours before the curtain rose. Aside from praise for Dick Shawn, a versatile kind of song-and-dance man who was at one moment a Pinkerton man, at another the photographer Matthew Brady, and at a third a gentleman officer of the Old South, most critical reactions to *Gentlemen Be Seated* were negative: but it showed to advantage Moross's knack for elevating the vocabulary of the popular song into something like an art expression. Others in the cast included Avon Long (Tambo), Charles Atkins (Bones), and Alice Ghostley as a female counterpart to Shawn. Emerson Buckley managed by main force to hold together a sketch for a score rather than what could be described as a finished product. A final venture in this fall season (the spring period was devoted largely to Gilbert and Sullivan) was a *Don Giovanni* in English for Norman Treigle rather than merely with him. By much its most memorable feature (more so than the Commendatore, who arrived at the dinner on his "horse" or than the omission of *"Dalla sua pace"*) was the Zerlina of Judith Raskin. Beverly Bower was the Donna Anna, Arlene Saunders the Elvira, and John McCollum made his debut as Ottavio. Rudel conducted.

In terms of musical standard, the Met's *Ariadne auf Naxos* was not even up to the best heard at City Center when it reappeared on December 25 under the direction of Varviso. The effort to find a suitable Composer* settled this time on Stratas, who had something of the vocal range it required and, if one thought of the character as the young Mozart, something of the physical size as well. What she needed was guidance and leadership, neither of which was provided by Varviso. As Ariadne,* Kuchta was less gifted, if more experienced. In later performances, the aspirants to Ariadne* included Amara on January 10 and Bjoner (who had stayed on to help fill a gap caused by delay in the arrival of Rysanek) on January 27. Among the other, incessant shifts of casts in this season were Donald Gramm as Truffaldin* (d) on January 10, Scovotti well beyond her coloratura depth as Zerbinetta* on January 18, and Soederstroem as the Composer* on February 20, when Rysanek was once more Ariadne, with D'Angelo as Zerbinetta. On Varviso's behalf it was said that he had directed *Ariadne auf Naxos* at Glyndebourne, which left him wanting in just the requirement this project required at the Metropolitan—the skill to enlarge the aural dimensions of the score to the needs of the large theater. In the midst of the strains thus produced, Varviso had to absent himself periodically because of fatigue, with Rich succeeding him as conductor of Act III of *Sonnambula* on January 8 and directing the whole of that work on January 14, Strasfogel taking over *The Magic Flute* on January 16, and Rich directing *Ariadne* on January 18 (the blend of sound was better because he had assisted Boehm the season before in preparing the production for performance). Varviso resumed with *The Magic Flute* on January 25 and *Ariadne* on January 27, but Rich did the later performances of *Sonnambula* and the *Ariadnes* of February 20 and March 3. The list of Metropolitan conductors for this season also included the name of Jan Behr, a *repetiteur* and coach who succeeded to the direction of *Fledermaus* on January 15, when Allers, who had succeeded Varviso, was off to engagements elsewhere.

The reference to "incessant" shifts of cast in a theater where they are to be anticipated as "constant" suggests a more than normal number of insertions, extractions and alterations. Where they involved such contingencies as Gedda's absence because of family illness or the delay in Rysanek's arrival, a veil of tolerance could be drawn over the untidy picture that presented itself. But there were scarcely such exigencies to be contended with in this season's scheduling for *Bohème* (as an example).

The sequence began on October 16, with Shirley (not a leading tenor for this theater) as Rodolfo,* Kabaivanska as Mimi,* Marsh as Marcello,* Anton Diakov of Bulgaria as Colline* (d), and Maria Gray, of parts unknown, as Musetta (d). Diakov's gifts, by measure of the Metropolitan, were modest; Gray's Musetta was not only immodest in manner, but also brassy in sound. By November 8, the Colline was Giaiotti, and the Musetta* (d) was not only *not* Gray, but was another new singer, Janet Pavek (reputed to be an understudy in a Broadway musical). The Mimi* (d), and promising, was Nicoletta Panni, a grand-niece of Giuseppe De Luca. (She was also heard as Marguerite* on November 28, but has not been heard since). By December 3, the Mimi was Kirsten, the Musetta* Rothenberger, and at another performance, on January 7, the Mimi was Amara, with Musetta as unsuitable a role for Jolanda Meneguzzer as it had been at her debut on December 23. Later on, the limitless resources of the casting department produced Amara and Hurley (January 30),

Tucci and Soederstroem (February 29), Tebaldi and Hurley (on March 14), and still another Musetta (Fenn) on April 10. To the bewildered observer, the conclusion had to be that such tolerance was bred by something more than need.

For one variation on this theme, there was at least the compelling reason of Tebaldi's first appearance on the Metropolitan stage since her withdrawal from *Adriana*. She had, in the interim, found a vocal adviser in whom she had faith. The results were eagerly awaited on the afternoon of March 14, in a cast that also offered Konya's first Rodolfo* (Guarrera, Hines, and Hurley were the other principals).

To those familiar with the Tebaldi Mimi, it was like watching a familiar figure on the TV screen accompanied by an unfamiliar soundtrack. The actions were as they had been, but the voice was distinctively different— farther forward, leaner, without the full-voiced throb of earlier days, but also without the heavy, strained production of her last preceding appearances. What she still had to work with, it appeared, would enable her to display the artifice, the winning ways, and the traits of character that her audience had grown to love in her favorite characterizations. Her vocal stride grew progressively easier in a combustible *Tosca* on March 22 with Corelli and Gobbi and a sometimes strained but eventually affecting Desdemona on April 4 with Colzani and McCracken.

For a part of the Metropolitan public, perhaps a large part of it, the circumstances relating to Varviso and Maazel, Boehm and Rosenstock were of small consequence. They were the ones to whom the performances with Price or Nilsson, Tebaldi or Sutherland atoned for all ills, made good all other shortcomings. There was no new production for Sutherland in this season, which began, for her, with a resumption of *La Sonnnambula* on December 5, with Tozzi, Scovotti, and Alexander (a reasonable replacement for Gedda, save for greater difficulty in the top register) as Elvino.* The decision that *Sonnambula* should be a repertory opera brought with it the lighter kinds of Aminas* from D'Angelo on December 27 to Peters on February 6. Both were charming to see. (In a later *Sonnambula* with Peters on March 7 the Elvino* was Shirley.)

Before the resumption of her Metropolitan activity, Sutherland had invested time in a venture with *Norma* in Vancouver, B.C., a place deemed suitably far off to discourage critical eavesdropping before she was ready for it. It was the joint Sutherland-Bonynge decision that she was not yet ready to perform the role in New York which called for a revision in Bing's plan to open the 1964–5 season with a new production of *Norma*. This, in turn, called for an alteration in the then current season's repertory, as Bing decided to substitute a new *Lucia* (Sutherland would have preferred *I Puritani*) and therefore withdraw that opera from performance (save at a gala on January 5 in which Sutherland performed the Mad Scene between the first act of *La Traviata* and the third act of *La Sonnambula*). Her first Violetta* on December 14 produced a predictable division of opinion. Those who valued vocal virtuosity above all else deemed it something special, especially in Act I (Konya was Alfredo* and Sereni the elder Germont, with Schick conducting). Those who looked for some degree of believability in Verdi's heroine and a progressive dramatic development to a climax found the vocal arcs and parabolas elements of a design rather than aspects of a characterization. For a singer of such celebrity, whose professions of faith included high fidelity to the composer's purpose, Sutherland's Italian enunciation was unpardonably inept.

By comparison, the Violetta* (d) of Mary Costa on January 6 (with Labò and Sereni) earned no such consideration from vocal connoisseurs, but it probed much closer to a credible character. A dazzling picture of blonde beauty, Costa surprised those who knew of her only as a high-priced demonstrator (on TV) of motor cars by projecting a full-ranging soprano sound of manifestly Metropolitan quality. Her immediate activity was limited to one more Violetta, but her eventual destination seemed close to that once achieved by Grace Moore, a native of the same part of the country (Tennessee) in which Costa originated. With her on February 10, with Alexander as Alfredo, was Igor Gorin as Germont* (d), making his debut many years too late. He performed creditably, but hardly with the bravura sound or the mastery of character to push aside those who had become entrenched during the years when he was otherwise occupied.

Quite another kind of American performer introduced himself on February 15. This was William Dooley, whose activity, like that of Jess Thomas, had been mostly in Germany. This did not seem the most suitable preparation for the debut as Onegin* (d) in another effort with the Gérard-Brook production of Tchaikovsky's opera. No specific connection between qualifications and requirements was established, but his general ones—physical size, healthy sound, and stage assurance—encouraged the belief that Dooley might prosper in other circumstances. The Lenski* this time was Thomas, willing enough, but not possessed of the kind of voice one associates with a predominantly lyric role. Finally, and this was a double disservice, the Tatiana* was Price, poorly costumed and lacking the dramatic resource and vocal flexibility to do justice either to herself or to Pushkin's heroine. Henry Butler's direction was of little help to those who needed it most. Tozzi as Gremin and Elias as Olga had the means to make their way, but Schippers's conducting did not provide the flexible kind of stimulus all the performers required. In later *Onegins,* Grillo was an at-

tractive Olga* on March 5, with Morell (Lenski*); Meredith acted
Onegin* well on March 13 (when Schippers became ill just before curtain
time and Strasfogel replaced him); and Amara returned as Tatiana on
March 24, with Macurdy as Gremin,* a role sung by Diaz on March 31
when the Onegin* was Guarrera. When Dooley was not singing the title
role in *Onegin,* he was performing in a far from title role, as the Herald*
in *Lohengrin* (on February 17 and after).

For reasons previously stated (see page 588), Tucker rejected the appeal of Onegin, even at the cost of foregoing Lenski's air, but he did direct
himself to a new challenge as well as to the resumption of an old one. He
made an occasion of the season's first *Trovatore* on December 11 by adding
Manrico* to his repertory, thus making a bountiful blend of sound with
Price, Dalis, and Merrill (the Ferrando* was Diakov). Like almost all of
his contemporaries, Tucker preferred *"Di quella pira"* in a downward transposition, but he performed the preceding *"Ah! si ben mio"* with more
grace than most Manricos since Bjoerling (Bergonzi would be the single
exception). Schippers made the anvils ring in the appropriate places, but
lashed about rather too strenuously elsewhere. For whatever reason that
attracts untoward events to one particular opera, in this season that opera
was *Trovatore.* On December 26, Merrill, who had injured an ankle in
an off-stage accident, played Di Luna while hobbling about with a cane
(Gorr was the vengeful Azucena,* Luisa Malagrida a strident Leonora*
in her debut); on January 25 Labò replaced McCracken, who had turned
an ankle, as Manrico,* in a cast with Cvejic as a vocally unstable Azucena,* Merrill, and Malagrida. By February 4, McCracken had enough
mobility to go on as Manrico,* though not to leave the stage after *"Di
quella pira."* The endeavor to find another role in which McCracken could
piece out a season when he was not performing Otello encountered the
same obstacle as his Canio: inability to modify on behalf of less strenuous
music the vocal output that made him an outstanding Moor. Tucci was the
Leonora* on February 21, with Corelli, Rankin, and Marsh, in his largest
undertaking to date, as Di Luna.* Its sound was less good than had been
hoped.

Tucker's other "new" role was the Duke in *Rigoletto,* a part in which he
had not been heard since the spring of 1956 when he appeared on November 5 in a cast with D'Angelo and MacNeil. The conductor was Strasfogel. Apparently Tucker found the experience to his taste, for he repeated it later in the season as well as participating in the broadcast of
February 22. Other new Gildas* included Scovotti on November 21 and
Meneguzzer (her first, and very light) on December 13, with Morell. On

February 3, when Alexander performed variably in his first venture as the Duke*, Dobbs was the Gilda.

With new productions of *Aida* and *Falstaff* added to the recent ones of *Otello* and *Macbeth,* which were restored for the Shakespeare "season," the Verdi works in the repertory numbered eight, or a third of the Metropolitan total. The aggregate of eighty-four performances could not be decried on musical grounds, but it supposed a quantity of talent that was not truly available. *Don Carlo* was one instance of a work in which talent was sometimes spread thin, beginning bravely on October 31 under the direction of Solti, with Tucker, Merrill, Hines, and Schoeffler affiliated with Gorr as Eboli* and Kabaivanska as Elisabetta* (Junetta Jones was the offstage Celestial Voice* in her debut). But it settled to the lower level of Curtis-Verna as Elisabetta, Ernster in vanishing voice as the Grand Inquisitor, and Labò as Carlo on December 17, with Adler conducting. It produced Ward as the Grand Inquisitor* and Cvejic as Eboli* on January 11 before touching lower levels of uncertainty on March 7, with Corelli, Uhde (no longer a voice for the Grand Inquisitor), Rysanek as Elisabetta, and Dalis as Eboli. Nicolae Herlea, a Romanian baritone, was above this average in his debut as Rodrigo* (d).

Herlea and Corelli were also collaborators, if that is the word, in a *Pagliacci* on March 11. The former sang his *prologo* well, but Corelli's Canio* was a preposterous mixture of ego and bathos, including a *"Vesti la giubba"* that roused laughter as the tenor launched a barrage of sobs and crying noises. Amara was Nedda, with Franco Ghitti as Beppe* (d). In the *Cavalleria* of the same bill, Farrell, Bardelli, and Grillo (Lola*) were under the strain of a Turiddu* (Sergi) described by Schonberg in *The New York Times* as a striking likeness of Oscar Wilde, with "dark velveteen jacket, flowing black tie, a fine head of hair and rather generous proportions." Corelli turned his attention to Turiddu* on March 28, with generally better results (McCracken was the Canio this time). Farrell's Santuzzas (including one in the World's Fair season, on May 5) were her only appearances of the season. She was nominated for the title role in *Ariadne,* but canceled that commitment.

The post-season of two weeks was tendered to World's Fair visitors to New York (tickets were sold nationwide to provide priority to those who did not ordinarily have the opportunity) in place of the previously projected, long-since-abandoned plan to have the new Metropolitan in Lincoln Center available by this time. It began with *Falstaff* (the cast of the first performance) on April 27 as validation of a "Shakespeare commemoration," but the final arrangement showed only two *Falstaffs,* two

Otellos, and one *Macbeth* (a second *Macbeth* was altered to another *Aida* shortly before time for the performance). There was also a scattering of the best the company had to offer in other directions: *Don Giovanni, Sonnambula* with Sutherland, *Aida* (with Nilsson on May 1 and 6, Price on May 7). The last two works were conducted by Varviso. Alva was the Ottavio* in *Don Giovanni* on May 10, and on May 4, Resnik, who had started her first Metropolitan career with Leonora in *Trovatore* in 1944, continued her second with Azucena.*

In the plan for the season made many months before, it had been decided to exclude *Parsifal* from the sequence and substitute the Verdi *Requiem,* which Solti returned from Europe to prepare. The selection proved to be unhappily forehanded, for the two performances (on March 27 and 28, the latter broadcast) were given in memory of the late John F. Kennedy. The excellent quartet was composed of Price, Elias, Bergonzi, and Siepi, and the performances directed by Solti—his last in the old house—were much to his credit. The Verdi was prefaced by the Good Friday scene from *Parsifal,* with Hines and Thomas, and with Marcia Baldwin interpolating the *"Dienen, Dienen"* of Kundry.

Some of the greatest singers ever to perform on the Metropolitan's stage gathered on November 20 to commemorate the fiftieth anniversary of Giovanni Martinelli's debut on that same date in 1913 (see page 246). A few of them—Milanov, Siepi, Merrill, Tozzi—were among the dozen or more who participated in the musical program (a benefit sponsored by the Metropolitan Opera Guild). But the larger number were among those, now mute, who surrounded the smiling, white-haired guest of honor as he spoke his thanks. These included Karin Branzell, Anna Case, Bidù Sayão, John Brownlee, and Rose Bampton, as well as Eva Turner, a frequent partner of Martinelli at Covent Garden but never at the Metropolitan.

The accession of Mariano Caruso, Paul Franke, Andrea Velis, and Gabor Carelli to the many roles formerly sung by Alessio de Paolis was inner evidence that the latter's long career as a peerless *comprimario* was, at seventy-one, approaching its end. It was wholly unexpected however that he would be the victim of a fatal automobile accident on March 9. His final appearance, in a Metropolitan career that began on December 3, 1938 (Cassio in *Otello*), was on March 5 as Triquet in *Eugene Onegin.*

1964–1965

For the thousands who assembled on October 12 when a Metropolitan Opera season began as early as Columbus Day for the first time, this was an opening not unlike many others, with a new production in which to admire a star and an adequate number of intermissions in which to admire each other. For a few, however, there were some other circumstances to consider. The labor agreement so painfully achieved only three years before had run its course, and no new one had been negotiated. Nevertheless the orchestra was in its place, ready to perform on the existing terms —which argued a change of mind on tactics if not a change of heart on issues.

The season also marked the fifteenth under Bing's supervision which, with three more already contracted for and a lively probability of an additional renewal or two, left him second only to Gatti-Casazza as the Metropolitan General Manager with the longest, most profound influence on its affairs. Reviewing the period since 1950, the question might be asked: to what extent was the Metropolitan in Bing's fifteenth year as he might have foreseen it to be in his first? How did the range of reforms he had then considered essential compare with the degrees of difference for which he had since settled? Were the gains fundamental or superficial, permanent or transitory, the losses of lesser or greater consequence, the net results affirmative or negative?

If statistics are irrefutable proof of the validity of a contention, they can also be quoted to deny its validity. Thus the success of Bing's fifteenth season could be expressed in terms of length (five weeks longer than his first, three weeks longer than the longest prior to his arrival); of attendance (the prognosis was for 97 per cent of capacity for more than 200 performances, or a demand for all but seventy-five of the poorest locations every time the curtain was raised); and a steady addition to the number of works redone during his tenure (to a total now of nearly fifty).

But the statistics of changes in cast and "first performances" were directly contrary to the values by which success was measured in Bing's own statement of 1950: "I have attempted to come to somewhat different arrangements with some of our leading artists . . . instead of only a few short weeks and only a few performances, some of these artists will be available to the Metropolitan for more weeks and many more performances than they ever have been. This will also to some extent avoid *continuous changes of cast, which must be detrimental to the quality of performances* [italics mine].

The extent to which "continuous" cast changes had become constant and then incessant has been indicated from time to time in the preceding pages. To determine whether they merely matched or greatly exceeded those in prior seasons would require the intercession of a computer. But there was no parallel to or precedent for the extent to which, in Bing's time, the shifting about of conductors had been first a necessity, then a habit, and, finally, a custom. Taken together with cast changes, they rendered a Metropolitan "standard," elusive at best, now as variable as the New York weather.

Instead of *Norma,* which Bing had chosen, or *I Puritani,* which she preferred, the production in which Sutherland had her opening night opportunity might be described as the *Lucia* nobody wanted. This became even more inclusive after the heavily ornate, unillusive scenery by Attilio Colonnello was revealed. Outdoors or in (and it was sometimes difficult to tell, from the unit pieces employed, which was which), the Ashtons dressed better than they lived, which was hardly in keeping with a concept of Scotch thrift. It was, to be sure, a different kind of spectacle than the remnants of the Rychtarik production long in use but hardly a full use of the opportunity offered by its replacement. Margherita Wallmann's staging produced some picturesque groupings among the supers and chorus, but did little to make the principals other than as God had made them.

Indeed, there were some who would have preferred what Zeffirelli had previously made of Sutherland in the Mad Scene to the results that were seen now. As before, the score had the rocket-like thrust of her singing to lift it from the ground, but it tended to trail vapor otherwise. Konya's Edgardo* required him to adapt himself to a vocal manner that did not much advance the cause of *bel canto*; Merrill was placidly Merrill as Enrico Ashton, and Giaiotti was a summation of all Italian (or Greek) bassos who had ever sung Raimondo, as Varviso was of accompanist-conductors. A briefly pleasant choreographic interlude was provided by Markova. All this was done on funds made available by Mrs. Izaak Walton Killam of Montreal. Changes were minimal in the first four performances (Sereni as Ashton on October 24), but D'Angelo was the Lucia on November 5, with Sergi an Edgardo* who merited ! as well as * . On November 14, the Ashton* was Herlea, with Labò and Sutherland, who on December 14 was heard with Alexander (Edgardo*) and Colzani. On January 4, when the Lucia was Moffo, the Edgardo was Bergonzi, and at the next performance, on January 23, it was D'Angelo, Morell, and Merrill. By February 10, nothing was left of the original principals, the values being on the order of Peters-Bastianini-Labò-Diaz (Raimondo*).

A substantially higher level was attained in the season's second new production, when Saint-Saëns's *Samson et Dalila* followed later in the opening week, on October 17. This was so much the inverse, qualitatively, of its predecessor that it might almost have been cited as an example of how things were better ordered "elsewhere." In addition to O'Hearn's excellent designs (they had some of the spaciousness of his *Aida*, but with a character equally suitable to the different locale) and Nathaniel Merrill's well-conceived action, *Samson* profited from the leadership of the rising French conductor Georges Prêtre. It was his shaping of sound, instrumental, choral and solo vocal, which prompted more than a few to revise their opinion that *Samson* was not an "opera." Under Prêtre, the musical matter asserted its own kind of drama, without respect to the action on stage. Its flow and flexibility contributed much to the excellent efforts of Rita Gorr as Dalila* and Gabriel Bacquier as the High Priest* (d). Though the German-trained Thomas was not up to their level as Samson, the totality amounted to more than any Metropolitan treatment of this score in years. Not much could be said in praise of the conventionalized delirium that Solov provided for the *Bacchanale,* but it was better performed than most similar matter in recent years. The quality of this *Samson* remained firm as long as Prêtre was its conductor, which included the first eight perform-ances. In one (on November 3), Mittlemann was the High Priest,* and in two (the first on December 17), Dalis was Dalila.* However, when it reappeared on March 17, virtually all of its musical refinements had van-ished, for the conductor was now Cleva, with Elena Cernei, a newcomer from Bucharest, as Dalila* (d), Vickers as Samson,* and Walker a stolidly low-level High Priest.* Here was the institution of the "take-over" at its cynical worst: aside from not preserving the virtues that Prêtre had striven so hard to perfect, Cleva introduced vices of his own which put too many false emphases on too many inappropriate places. Vickers could well have been an improvement on Thomas in the original cast, but the planning did not go that way. In later performances, all directed by Cleva, the Dalila* on March 26 was Dunn, and on April 16, Cernei again.

The season's final new production on February 3 had an assurance of interest in Birgit Nilsson's first Salome,* whatever might meet the eye to replace the long-used Oenslager settings for 1934. For ease, the security, for purity, this was the finest singing of the music since Welitch's, and the diligence that had made Nilsson a Turandot as well as an Isolde was re-flected in an appearance—a face-hugging wig and well-conceived makeup —that was credibly that of a willful young Princess. The action, in which she was coached by Rennert, made artful use of the interlocking ramps around the cistern at stage front, and even the dance contrived by Markova served a dramatic, if not a choreographic, end. Nilsson was more con-vincing in projecting Salome's stubborn desire for the head of Jokanaan than pleasure in the trophy after she possessed it, but the compulsion of a great vocal effort so long sustained had its reward in a roar of applause that persisted through twenty-six curtain calls. Boehm was fortunate in his Herod* (Liebl) and Herodias* (Dalis), not so fortunate in his Jokanaan* (Dooley), who did not possess the rolling sonority that the music of this character requires. Alexander was the excellent Narraboth. Of unexpected quality was the setting by the young German designer Rudolf Heinrich, not only in a floor plan that aided the drama by keeping Herod and Herodias in the same line of spectator vision as Salome, but also in the darkly brooding set and the projections displayed at the rear. To provide for the inevitable circumstances in which Nilsson and *Salome* had to be separated, Bing succeeded more than moderately well with Maria Kouba, a slight, well-proportioned German soprano who gave a wholly different accent to the role at her debut on February 12. She was much more the adolescent, and provocatively so, performing with assurance against the handicap of a vocal sound too small for the theater. What could be heard was not bad in quality. Cassel was the Jokanaan of this performance. On all occasions, *Salome* was preceded by Boehm's direction of Strauss's *Don Juan,* which compromised the difference between something before *Salome* and nothing before *Salome.* This struck some as an imposition on the hard-working orchestra, especially as the sound out of the Metropolitan's pit could hardly be measured against the concert hall criteria that were, all too obviously, invited.

Boehm's ability to produce dramatic results had an earlier demonstration on January 19, when he returned from his year's absence to give the measure of *Der fliegende Holländer* as he conceived it. This was in terms of its ardent expression of the mind of the twenty-seven-year-old Wagner, without regard for anything he might compose in the future. Not only did Boehm believe in every note of it—he made the listener a believer too. With London, Rysanek, and Tozzi as extensions of his impulse, Konya an excellent Erik, and Shirley a very good Steersman (Kriese was Mary,* and rather conventional), it was all of a piece. Some opinion gave high marks to Ward for his Dutchman on February 5 (with Wiemann as Daland), but the sound was thick and non-compulsive. On February 20, Välkki's power aroused more hope for a quality Senta than she was able to realize in creation of a believable character. Cassel, rather light of sound for the part, was the Dutchman* on February 25.

The best of which Boehm was capable in *Wozzeck* (and the memory of it was too recent to require recapitulation) was not equal to restoring to Berg's work its original effect in the circumstances that governed its return on February 19. The "repertory" treatment—once, or at most, twice over, lightly—did not suffice to restore the common impulse that had previously permeated the orchestral performance, and the cast changes further dissipated recollection of what had previously prevailed. One, which went unfulfilled, promised Stich-Randall as something else than a performer of Mozart. However she suffered a painful injury in a fall in her Vienna apartment shortly before time for her departure for New York, and a substitute Marie had to be found. In her place as Marie* (d) was Helga Pilarczyk, given a second chance (she was one of those who withdrew after the "cancelation" scare of 1961) and did not make much of it. To judge by comparison with some of her other efforts, Pilarczyk had retrogressed vocally in the preceding few years, and the English text was clearly inhibiting to her. No less of a recession from the prior level (of Hermann Uhde) was the Wozzeck* of Dooley, too mechanistically inhuman, insufficiently animated by the passions that Wozzeck conceals until driven beyond restraint. The good order of the first performance was further impaired by the inability of Paul Franke to perform. His place as the Captain,* in a feat of musical resourcefulness comparable to some others of the past (see page 624), was taken by Gabor Carelli, who had never performed the role in public before. Martin was an inferior, stereotyped Margret,* and the whole project came to be what Watt in the *Daily News* described as "sloppy," Schonberg in the *Times* considered "limp," and Rich in the *Herald Tribune* found a "supreme experience." On February 24, the Marie was Brenda Lewis, with Franke as the Captain, and in the performance of March 10, with Pilarczyk, Nagy replaced Baum as the Drum Major* and Alvary was the Doctor.

Unfortunately, not all the Strauss of this season was directed by Boehm, for he arrived too late for the sequence of *Rosenkavalier* performances which began on October 13. Fortunately, Schippers did less to offset the splendid qualities of Elisabeth Schwarzkopf's Marschallin* (d) than might have been feared, a tribute—perhaps—to the effect of superior will and the extraordinary illusion of a regal presence she conveyed. The Schwarzkopf voice was hardly what it had been ten years before (when Bing's reactions to queries about her engagement had been on the order of icy disdain), but there were a vocal nuance for every gesture and an unfailing reserve of power when needed. Faultless in manner as well as in manners, Schwarzkopf's Marschallin was the first truly great one the Metropolitan had seen since Lehmann's, as valid in its more brittle way as her predecessor's. However, when Schippers was not rushing one scene, he was dragging another, adding to the limitations piled upon a total result by the inept Octavian* of Della Casa (who seemed impatient to get back to doing the other character herself). Rothenberger was the excellent Sophie, Mittlemann a good Faninal,* and Konya an unexpected boon as the Singer (in place of Morell) after his leading role in *Lucia* only the night before. Close to Schwarzkopf in quality, and surprisingly so, was the Ochs of Edelmann, who had made an astonishing return to vocal health in a characterization much more refined than it had previously been. Those who thought they had seen as much as a stage director could do to distract from the drama of the principals in Act I found a new intrusion invented by Dino Yannopoulos—a "second" chamber maid, dressed in the identical uniform being worn by Octavian-Mariandl, to "help" her make up the bed, thus compounding the obvious. Lynn Owen was the Marianne* (d), Velis an excellent Valzacchi.* Schwarzkopf had all of two further performances with the same personnel (Morell was the Singer*), but by the fourth, the Ochs* (d) was no longer Edelmann but Michael Langdon. What the tall, English-trained Langdon had to offer in his one-performance season on November 2 was more on the order of the Good Squire Ochs than a *Herr Baron,* a country cousin from Yorkshire rather than from Lerchenau. However, nothing at the Metropolitan is ever so bad that it cannot get worse. When the next replacement for Edelmann was required on December 30, it was the American-born Elfego Esparza, a small, not very accurate carbon copy of Corena, who substituted grimaces and laugh-getting "business" for the vocal range required of an Ochs,* in a manner that could be called *bluffo* rather than *buffo.* By this time the Marschallin was Della Casa, with Elias as Octavian and Strasfogel conducting. In a prior performance on December 8, the Sophie* was Raskin, and very good. Before Schwarzkopf finished her season, she participated in a momentous "gala" on November 29 which brought $93,000 to the company's Welfare and Pension Funds. It was conceived on a novel plan (attributed to the fertile mind of Eleanor Belmont) which brought together three reigning queens of the stage, each in a province of her realm: Schwarzkopf in Act I of *Rosenkavalier,* Tebaldi in Act I of *Bohème,* and Sutherland in Act I of *Traviata.*

Schippers's season was otherwise devoted to *Otello,* which he directed for the first time on November 7, *Manon,* and *Ernani.* The conductor's disposition to seek the fount of all that is Verdian (Toscanini) as guidance to *Otello* could not be denigrated, but it did not have very much relationship to what Kabaivanska (Desdemona*), Uzunov (Otello), and MacNeil (Iago*) were able to provide within the time allocated for preparation. On November 21, the Desdemona was Milanov, and on December 4 McCracken made his only appearance of the season, a shamefully restricted schedule for so capable an artist, with or without regard for rumors of disagreement with management on other assignments, fees, etc. By December 23, when the Desdemona was Tebaldi and Merrill was Iago, *Otello* was on the Adler plan. A popular Metropolitan formula for reviving an ailing production—change the performers, not the production—was applied to *Manon* at its reappearance on November 18. It called for an infusion of *elisire de Stratas,* but the young lady was herself ailing, and was replaced by Fenn as Manon*. She had neither the dramatic presence nor the vocal art to help much, though there were substantial qualities of both in the Lescaut* of Bacquier and the Comte des Grieux* of Macurdy, less in the Chevalier* of Richard Verreau. The sound and look of the stage were decidedly better on December 22, when Costa performed her Manon* with vocal ardor and dramatic assurance, Tozzi returned to play the Count, with Gedda as his "son," and Bacquier had a Frenchman's pride in his cousin, Manon, which was warming to see. However, this barely lasted long enough to be reported, for by January 1 the conductor was Rich, and Guarrera was Lescaut. For whatever reason—and some odd inclinations on the part of Price would have to be considered—*Ernani* under Schippers's direction on March 4 was something less than it had been before. Part of the problem may have been the emergency replacement of Corelli by the unready Sergi as Ernani,* with some dramatic contretemps (he slipped on a staircase in Act I and sent a "wall" askew) to complicate a lack of preparation for his grave vocal problem in such music. MacNeil performed valiantly in his third act aria (*"Oh! de' verd'anni miei"*), and Hines was of his customary quality as Silva, but the strong central impulse to draw all the elements into a tight ensemble was rarely present. Price sang all the four following performances, all of them with Corelli, some with Siepi and Sereni.

The infectious spirit of the previous season's *Falstaff* was severely moderated when it returned on October 31, no longer as the Bernstein-Zeffirelli *Falstaff,* but as the Bernstein-Rosenstock-Zeffirelli *Falstaff.* This related to Bernstein's long-planned sabbatical from service with the New York Philharmonic, which carried with it a prohibition—implied if not factual—on other activity in New York. Whether or not no other conductor of stature could be found to take on this responsibility, the results available to Rosenstock were destructive of just the qualities that had made his predecessor's outstanding—volatility, lightness, and, above all, musical character. Falstaff was once more Colzani on October 31 and Evans on November 11 (the latter on forty-eight-hour leave from San Francisco to enable Colzani to replace an ailing colleague in Philadelphia).

The casting was largely as before, save for Miller as Meg* (not nearly so good as Elias). On November 23, Guarrera added a note of authentic drama with his Toscanini-trained Ford.* The Alicia* this time was Kabaivanska. These roles were similarly cast on December 2, when Flagello ventured Falstaff* for the first time and showed excellent qualities to serve it well in the future. Scovotti was Nannetta.* On January 5, when Chookasian had her first exposure as Quickly,* Corena was Falstaff, with Curtis-Verna as Alice.

Counting Rosenstock's series of *Meistersinger* performances, which began on October 21 (Konya as the excellent Walther, Edelmann in fine form as Sachs, Bjoner as Eva, Dönch as Beckmesser, Flagello as Pogner, and Kriese as Magdalene) and a student matinee of *Der fliegende Holländer* on April 13 (in preparation for performances of it which he conducted on tour), he shared with Cleva the distinction of being the company's only season-long regular conductor. Among later *Meistersinger*s was one on December 5 in which Sergi maintained a sturdy level of competence as Walther* and Macurdy showed the vocal stuff of which Pogners* are made, with Walker as Kothner.* Schoeffler sang Sachs still another time on November 14, again on November 24, when Fenn was the Eva,* and yet again on December 11.

As well as venturing *Falstaff* for the first time, Rosenstock undertook *Le Nozze di Figaro* on December 2, with Hermann Prey barely substantial enough in sound for Almaviva,* Stratas a delightful Cherubino,* and the admirable Countess of Della Casa, Raskin's Susanna, and Siepi's Figaro to offset a clownish Bartolo by Esparza.* Those who had found the display of feminine lingerie a crudely ostentatious way of calling attention to locale of the first scene (servants' quarters) at earlier performances found this *Figaro* amended by a line of freshly washed handkerchiefs instead. This did not represent a change of heart on Bing's part; it was rather, a response to pressure from one of his board members. Rosenstock's sound sense of *Figaro* produced better results on December 15, when Bacquier was Almaviva* and Tozzi was Figaro. The passion for change paired Evans as Figaro* and Dooley as Almaviva* on January 16 in a cast with Bjoner as the Countess,* with predictable cost to anything like a settled ensemble. A venture with Gérard Souzay as Almaviva* (d) on January 21 was unfortunately conclusive proof that his light voice, like Prey's, was not suitable to these surroundings.

Still another effort to restore *Così* to its original status as an elegantly amusing experience was made in this season by persuading Lunt to supervise his own original staging, and by providing Rosenstock, as conductor, with a mingling of old and new performers. What emerged on January 30 was akin to the "revival" of a successful comedy, in which the laugh-getting effects tend to be broadened and the participants are so amused by their own actions that they forget to be believable characters as well. Indeed, some new bits of business which Lunt had thought of intruded on musical areas (ends of phrases, postludes, exits, etc.) which Stiedry had held inviolate. Thus it was all less elegant and not nearly so amusing as it had been previously. Musically, the largest gain was provided by Donald Gramm as Don Alfonso* in place of an indisposed Guarrera, for

Price was not yet up to the requirements of Fiordiligi* and Elias put more effort into being flirtatious than into being Dorabella. Oddly, too, the blend of sound was an inversion of what was wanted, for Price in the middle register of her soprano sound had more mezzo weight than Elias. Tucker's Ferrando, Uppman's Gugliemo, and Peters's Despina were all of practiced quality. Price improved steadily in her command of the Mozartean line, and by the broadcast of February 20 she had it under sure control. Dramatically, however, the requirements of light comedy were a trial for her. On February 26, the small-scaled Dorabella* was Vanni, a forerunner of a wholly new shuffle of players which produced herself, Amara, Hurley (Despina), and Meredith (Alfonso*) on March 8.

By an odd dictate of fate, Rosenstock's direction of the matinee performance of *Figaro* on January 2 was followed that evening by the Metropolitan debut of a conductor with whom he had not shared an affiliation since they had been reduced to touring Germany as a two-piano team under the Nazi proscriptions of the thirties. This was William (formerly Hans Wilhelm) Steinberg, who was following the pattern of Walter, Szell, Mitropoulos, Maazel, and Bernstein in dividing his New York season between an engagement at the Philharmonic and assignments at the Metropolitan. His first task was intended to restore *Aida* to the musical level at which the new production had been pitched by Solti in 1963, but the result turned out to be more of an experience in scholarship than musical theater. Steinberg's quiet, painstaking treatment of the score was doubtless to the advantage of Tucker's first Metropolitan Radames* (which did not honor Verdi's request for a quiet ending to *"Celeste Aida"*) in underlining the lyric rather than the dramatic, but it left more than a little lacking, as sound, to support the pageantry and excitement of the action. For Tucker, it was the twenty-seventh leading role in a Metropolitan career that had begun with a command of hardly any. Price was at her best on this occasion, with Dalis as Amneris and Sereni as Amonasro.

Of his two other enterprises in this season, Steinberg unexpectedly contributed more to Barber's *Vanessa* when it reappeared on March 13 than to Wagner's *Walküre,* which was first performed on February 22. Steinberg's probing treatment made audible rather more of the internal lines of Barber's orchestration than its previous conductors (Mitropoulos, Strasfogel), and he made a fine blend of sounds with the voices. These included, in addition to the indispensable Erika of Elias and Tozzi's Doctor, the Vanessa* of Costa, Alexander as Anatol,* and Thebom as the Baroness.* Some tastes preferred Costa's kind of barely muted glamour to the mere remnants of that quality in Steber's Vanessa, but there was general agreement that the believable irresponsibility Gedda conveyed as Anatol eluded

Alexander. In any case, Menotti's text was harder to hear from these per-formers than from their predecessors. According to a sadly recurrent trend of the operatic theater, Thebom, who had begun as a fine singer with little acting technic, had now become a resourceful actress with steadily dimin-ishing vocal strength. *Vanessa* possibly established a record for these Bing seasons in being performed five times without a single change of cast.

Considering his known qualifications as an orchestral conductor, much was expected from Steinberg when he directed *Die Walküre* for the first time on February 22. All the performing personnel promised well also, from such known quantities as Rysanek, Vickers, Nilsson, and Dalis to the less-known but eminently able Ward as Hunding* and London as Wotan.* But it was curiously undersized, unintense Wagner that was heard. Ward's Hunding was an impressive woodsman to see, but not nearly so formidable to hear, and London's range was much less suited to the *Walküre* Wotan than it had been to the comparable roles in *Siegfried* and *Das Rheingold*. With or without respect for these deficiencies, Steinberg's tendency to re-strain the orchestra left a link lacking in the composer-listener relationship. Beverly Bower was the Ortlinde* (d). When Dunn moved from the obscurity of Waltraute among the Walküren on March 24 to Fricka (with Hines, Välkki, and Wiemann), her place was taken by Patricia Berlin (d), a member of the chorus. A rather more conspicuous change on that date brought Crespin as Sieglinde,* with an abundance of voice to match the power of Vickers as Siegmund. They did not, in truth, have much of subtlety or lyric urgency between them, but the sheer volume that they produced brought cheers as the first act curtain fell. Kuchta was the Sieglinde on April 2, but on April 10, it was Crespin again with Kriese as Fricka.* This last performer, who had been trained by Karin Branzell, learned to mimic many of her mannerisms but not much of her teacher's vocal mastery.

Other variations from recent repertory (*Walküre* had been absent for three years) included a renewed opportunity to see Wolfgang Roth's attrac-tive décor for *Don Pasquale* on November 13. A pleasure denied since 1956–7, this was doubly welcome under the shaping hand of Varviso, to whom the Donizetti style was congenial, and with the addition of Alva as Ernesto* and D'Angelo as Norina* to the continuing quality of Corena as Pasquale and Guarrera as Malatesta. An indulgence was asked on behalf of D'Angelo, who had turned an ankle during rehearsals, but it slowed her down just enough to make her actions credible. Velis was the excellent Notary,* and the ensemble was cheerfully efficient as directed by Yannopoulos. On November 30, the Norina was Peters, and on January 14 Moffo for the first time, with rather better results than accrued from

Esparza as a substitute Pasquale.* On each occasion, the opera was preceded by something a Metropolitan had not seen in years—a performance
by the resident ballet which was enjoyable of and by itself. The close to
miraculous results were achieved under the demanding direction of
Markova, who had chosen the Fokine-Chopin *Les Sylphides* (the simple
setting was by Rolf Gérard) to demonstrate her contention that style
could be transmitted by example (her own) and application to detail. She
was not, of course, able to create "ballerinas" for the solo dances, but Hans
Meister performed the partnering function with credit, and the ensemble
was both steady and unified. Varviso was the musical director. The success of Markova in building pride-in-accomplishment among her charges
was recognized by an opportunity for the ballet to have an evening to itself
on April 11. Repetitions of *Sylphides* (conducted by Behr) and the
Bacchanale from *Samson* were augmented by a staging of Bartók's
Miraculous Mandarin under the direction of Joseph Lazzini in a highly
atmospheric setting by Bernard Dayde of the Marseille Opera, the "Blue-
bird" variations from Tchaikovsky's *Sleeping Beauty,* and Pugni's *Pas de
Quatre* (staged by Markova, after Dolin). Of the new efforts, the most
successful was *The Miraculous Mandarin,* with Meister in the title role and
the Bartók score under the able direction of Robert La Marchina. He had
made his debut on December 31 in a restoration of Menotti's *Last Savage,*
which he served well. This being New Year's Eve, Price was persuaded to
appear as an "added attraction" in the Cocktail Party (Act II), performing
"Vissi d'arte" from *Tosca,* which prompted some to describe it as the best
Puccini in the score. In the last of the season's three performances, the
Sardula* was Joy Clements, who had moved from the smallest to the
smaller roles since her debut as the Countess Ceprano* (d) in *Rigoletto*
on October 23, 1963.

Clements was but the most recent of former City Opera singers to be
accepted by the Metropolitan at this time. Indeed, when a cast brought
together Hurley, MacNeil, and Morell, or Alexander, Reardon, Dunn, and
Raskin, it might seem that Fifty-fifth Street and Thirty-ninth Street were
but a step apart. Meanwhile, the best of the City Opera's performers—
Norman Treigle—remained faithful to it, possibly because he was repeatedly presented in the most cherishable roles of the bass-baritone's
repertory. The preceding season it had been Don Giovanni; this year it
was Boris. If Treigle's performance of one was nearly as creditable as of the
other, it was clearly evident that with the exception of Norman Kelley as
Schuisky and Jon Crain as Dimitri, most of the performers were feeling
their way (not necessarily toward each other). Thomas Paul (Pimenn),
Spiro Malas (Varlaam), and Tatiana Troyanos (Marina) made some

sounds of the right quality, but with more than a little tentativeness. Walter Susskind conducted a project in English made possible by the underwriting of Mrs. John D. Rockefeller, Jr.

This season's derivative from Ford Foundation funds was Lee Hoiby's version of Turgenev's *A Month in the Country,* which in this treatment of a text by William Ball bore as title *Natalia Petrovna,* the name of its leading character. This bore out, in occasional felicities of mood and atmosphere, the sympathy for things Russian manifest in Hoiby's shorter treatment of Chekhov's *The Scarf,* which had been introduced by the City Opera in the spring of 1959. He did not, however, show the intellectual stamina to support his purpose over a three-act course, though what he did was clearly an advance over his earlier effort. Of the cast, the most suitable was the American-born, German-schooled Maria Dornya, whose attractive appearance and good sound were advantageous to Natalia's requirements. Others in the ensemble put together by Rudel, who conducted, were Richard Cross (Rakitin), John Reardon (Belaev), John McCollum (Arcady), and Patricia Brooks (Lisavette).

By a curious coincidence, the next event of more than common interest at the City Center—though across a turn of the year—was also an opera with a Russian female name: the erstwhile *Lady Macbeth of Mtsensk* by Dimitri Shostakovich in its revised form as *Katerina Ismailova.* It would, perhaps, have been simpler to identify had Shostakovich called it *Lady Katerina,* for it was, on the whole, a gentler echo of its raucous predecessor, especially in the deletion of the trombone smears connoting the pleasures of the bedroom shared by the loving, if unwed, couple. Other changes included (orchestrally) an interlude added to Act II and an orchestral prelude for Act III; and (vocally) a solo for Katerina to render her a more "sympathetic" character. More than anything else, it recalled that the work that had followed official censure of *Lady Macbeth* was the Fifth Symphony subtitled *A Soviet Artist's Reply to Just Criticism,* and that Shostakovich had not written a real opera since. The title role was reasonably well performed by Eileen Schauler (something of a younger Patricia Neway), though her voice was not quite large enough, with Richard Cassilly as Sergei, Richard Krause as the husband, and William Chapman particularly good as the father.

Mayhem was also a prominent part of the spring season's new American work, a treatment of the Lizzie Borden axe murders by Jack Beeson (text by Kenward Elmslie working from a scenario by Richard Plaut). The invented detail which provided three characters of each sex in principal parts (among them a "boy friend" for Lizzie's "younger" sister, who was, in historical fact, older) served theatrical convenience more than it did dramatic truth. Beeson's growth as a composer from the work entitled *Hello Out There*, produced by the Columbia University Workshop in 1953, was gratifying to observe, but it did not carry him the distance to deal justly with his grisly subject. Where the subject had a lyric character, as in the earlier episodes, Beeson's smooth-flowing texture suited it well; but the dramatic climaxes tended to arouse echoes of *Wozzeck* and of Britten's *Turn of the Screw*. As Lizzie in a Brenda Lewis type of part was (surprisingly) Brenda Lewis, with the former servant Abigail, who becomes her stepmother, admirably embodied by Ellen Faull, Anne Elgar as a convincing "young" sister, and Herbert Beattie as the father-husband. Richard Fredericks was an apt choice for the invented suitor, and Richard Krause served sufficingly as the Reverend Harrington, who balanced the three pairs. Anton Coppola directed efficiently in his City Opera debut, with Nikos Psacharopolous in charge of the stage set by Peter Wexler. Completing the spring's roster of novelty was a curiously diffuse version of Weill's *Dreigroschenoper*. It was, presumably, in the manner of its early Berlin production, with a German-speaking cast especially assembled for the purpose. Stefan Schnabel and Lilia Skala were cast as the elder Peachums, with Kurt Kasznar as a rather too engaging Mack the Knife and Martha Schlamme beyond her musico-dramatic depths as Jenny. Ralph Herbert (Brown), Anita Hoefer (Polly), and Marion Bash (Lucy) were other principals. Adolph Rott directed the action in Wolfgang Roth's unit set and Julius Rudel proved himself as adept with the eight-piece band required in this version as he had with Shostakovich's large orchestra.

Indeed, some Metropolitan operagoers had cause to regret that Rudel had not accepted a Bing offer to take on a production in the big old house— or, perhaps, that Bing had not tendered Rudel a production he felt inclined to accept (the invitation, it was generally understood, related to *Fledermaus* in one of its post-"Farewell to *Fledermaus*" revivals). He certainly would have been welcome as relief from a steady diet of Varviso, which began with the season-opening *Star-Spangled Banner* as preface to the new *Lucia* and continued not only with the double bill of *Les Sylphides* and *Don Pasquale,* but also with a restoration of *Les Contes d'Hoffmann* on December 18. Some of Offenbach's score was well-savored, but Varviso tended to equate haste with high spirits.

This *Hoffmann* was rather perilously founded on the presumption that Dooley, as a performer of Lindorf*-Coppélius*-Dappertutto*-Dr. Miracle,* was somewhat on the order of Singher or London. It turned out that he substituted, for the acting style of the one, an elaborate reliance on makeup and costumes, and for the voice of the other, a dry quality that took most of the glitter from *"Scintille diamant."* The female roles were distributed among Scovotti as Olympia,* Cvejic (Giulietta*), and Amara (Antonia), with varying quality, and Gedda was not in good voice for Hoffmann. The pleasure content was augmented substantially on December 28 when Hurley performed her exceptional Olympia, but the whole venture sagged seriously on January 27, when Giuseppe di Stefano's bid for reconsideration as a Metropolitan tenor found him short of breath, short of range, and shorter still of style as Hoffmann* (he began by bowing ostentatiously to a part of the audience that extended a friendly greeting in recollection of his past services). Meredith had the four baritone roles, with Stratas as Antonia,* Rankin as Giulietta,* and Hurley in her speciality. Di Stefano was announced for a further appearance as Hoffmann on February 11 (with Fenn as Antonia*), but he withdrew in favor of Alexander and has not been heard at the Metropolitan since, a sadly deflating outcome for a career that had begun with such abundant promise at the age of twenty-seven only seventeen years before.

With more weeks to fill with more performances, the number of operas (five) in double figures[1] was very probably more than in any season for years. The fourteen for the first new production (*Lucia*) and eleven for the second (*Samson*) were to be expected, but not the sixteen for *Tosca,* which led all. It began as early as October 23, with Santi conducting, Rysanek as a heavy voice for Puccini and with acting style that recalled silent movie days, and Merrill performing a well-studied Scarpia* at his first try (Labò was Cavaradossi), and it was still being given on April 17, with Cleva conducting, Crespin as a vigorous rather than mobile Tosca (her first had been on April 3), and Konya as Cavaradossi.

Between October and April the church of Sant'Andrea della Valle was visited three times again by Rysanek (on November 4 the Scarpia,* modeled closely and profitably on Gobbi's, was Bacquier), by Kirsten (with Konya as Cavaradossi* and Colzani), on November 19, by Tebaldi (with Morell and Merrill) on December 12, by Tebaldi again (with Tucker and Colzani) on January 12, and also on January 18 (with Labò and Colzani), by Tucci (with Tucker and with Bastianini as Scarpia*) on February 13, and by Kirsten on March 3 and 6 (the Cavaradossi* [d] in the latter was Bruno Prevedi).

For many, however, there were only two performances of *Tosca* this season, those on March 19 and 25, in which Callas made her first appearance at the Metropolitan since being "fired" by Bing in 1958. As mutual inconvenience drove them apart, so mutual convenience brought them together again: his the need to "pick up" a season when its interest

---

[1] *Der fliegende Holländer* is not included because seven of its fifteen performances were in the student series.

should lag, hers the desire to renew the momentum of an American career which had been mostly a matter of hearsay for half a decade. All the circumstances (including reports of her recent appearances in London) contributed to a demand unprecedented for any pair of Metropolitan performances in years. The first, at extra prices, a Metropolitan Opera Guild benefit for the production fund, was sold out weeks before it occurred; the second, in the Thursday-night subscription series, left few locations unspoken for even before this particular attraction was announced early in the fall.

Though it was understood that the Metropolitan would not, even for Callas, provide an orchestral rehearsal for an opera already in the season's repertory, it did not prove possible to meet her other, reasonable request—to have the same tenor (she did not care which one) for both performances. The possibility turned on Tucker's availability for the performance of Friday, March 19; but he would not forego the opportunity to sing Radames at the broadcast performance of *Aida* the following afternoon. Hence it was Corelli for the first, Tucker for the second. Cleva conducted both.

What preserved the heart of the performance and enabled Callas to build her conception to its full, forceful climax was the fortunate presence of Gobbi as Scarpia each time. For much of Act I and the beginning of Act II, the accumulated tensions (some of the standees had endured a forty-eight-hour vigil for their places) tended to isolate the performers from each other rather than draw them together. But when Cavaradossi (Corelli or Tucker) had been dragged off in Act II and the stage was cleared for action, it was no longer Callas and Gobbi matching thrust and riposte, but Tosca and Scarpia at their immemorial contest. Inevitable as the outcome had to be, when the curtain fell on the retreating figure moving silently from the room where Scarpia lay dead, everyone knew why Callas was Callas.

One finally comprehended, too, the range of emotions she displayed, from irritation to tenderness and from suspicion to loathing, and the volatility with which one gave way to another. It was part of a carefully calculated plan to prepare the observer for Tosca's sudden, super-volatile act when the inner core of hate erupted through the outer cloak of sanctity. Among more than a score of Toscas seen at the Metropolitan since the 'twenties, Callas alone persuaded the viewer that she had not discovered the knife—the knife discovered her in her moment of extremity and need. And she used it as this Tosca had to use it, in a lightning-swift lunge, thrust, and shuddering rejection of her own act.

Every bit of it would have been as vivid without a note of vocalizing, but her play with words, with vocal color and emphasis was more meaningful than the best that could be achieved by her fresher-voiced contemporaries. Even her *"Vissi d'arte"* was more a cry of despair than a well-formed vocal expression—despite the applause it aroused in some areas—but it filled the composer's purpose of breaking one tightly drawn situation and preparing the way for the next. Gobbi was not quite so resolute in protecting his vocal means—he sometimes resorted to volume for the sake of volume—but he had, at his disposition, as many subtle variations of mood (sanctity for venom, gentleness for brutality) as Callas, every one of them contributory to drama. It was, unquestionably, a night to remember, especially on the nights to come when *Tosca* seemed lackluster and dull, for no reason attributable to Sardou, Illica, and Giacosa or, least of all, Puccini.

As far as the Verdi of this season was concerned, there were not very many nights to remember. One came on February 6, when Nilsson's unwillingness to perform Verdi between Salomes on February 3 and 9 brought on Martina Arroyo as Aida.* She had, in her two seasons' absence from the Metropolitan, attracted considerable attention in other activities, especially as soloist with orchestra. The grateful carry-over of this experience in the power and assurance of her performance was bolstered by an inbred awareness of Aida's place in this drama. Labò was the Radames, Rankin the Amneris. Arroyo had another opportunity on April 1, when Bruno Prevedi was the Radames.* This tenor's prior performance in Verdi was on March 20, when he was heard as Alvaro*—rather hard going for one whose baritonal origins were still audible—in a *Forza* with Amara, Sereni, and Siepi. The conductor was Rich. *Forza* was, altogether, one of this season's distressed areas, lacking either the leadership or the manpower to make it prosper. It began, on November 26, under Santi, with Bergonzi as Alvaro associated with Tucci (Leonora*), Herlea (Carlo*), and Siepi. The Leonora* on December 16 was Kabaivanska, and on January 29 Corelli added Alvaro* to the roles in which he performed with power but little finesse. On February 17, when Santi had gone and the conductor was Rich, Kostas Paskalis, a well-schooled baritone from Greece by way of Vienna made a successful debut as Don Carlo.* Also of instable quality was *Simon Boccanegra,* for which Cleva was the conductor for the first time on December 9, when Shirley made a valiant if losing effort to meet the needs of Gabriele* in a cast with Tebaldi, Colzani, Tozzi, and Walker (not yet ready for such a character study as Paolo*). There was more substance to Paolo* when it was performed by Diaz on December 19. On January 6, the Gabriele* was Campora, now striving to attain by force as a dramatic tenor what he could no longer sustain by art as a lyric tenor. The best balance of vocal capabilities was achieved on February 23, when MacNeil as Simon* was joined by Milanov (Amelia), Tucker (Gabriele), and Siepi (Fiesco). In an early-season *Rigoletto* (October 14), the name of Nedda Casei (born Casey in Baltimore, Maryland) was entered on the records of Metropolitan Maddalenas* (d) in a cast with Herlea (Rigoletto*), Bergonzi (the Duke*), Peters (Gilda), and Diaz (Sparafucile*). She was also seen as Suzuki* on October 31.

The day of *Turandot,* which had, in the words of Kipling, come up like thunder only four seasons before, dimmed to something like a sunset glow in this one. When it returned on January 13, with Nilsson at her unvarying best, with Giaiotti as Timur and Amara as Liù, the Calaf* was Thomas (loud enough, but not of the quality for Puccini) and Mariano Caruso was the Emperor* in succession to De Paolis. Cleva conducted. As the season wore on, so did *Turandot*—with Curtis-Verna in the title role on January 28 and February 1, Nilsson with Corelli and Albanese on February 14, and, after a lapse of weeks, Kuchta as Turandot and Konya as Calaf on March 27, and then Välkki as Turandot* on April 7, with Konya and Moffo.

The career of Eileen Farrell, which had begun auspiciously in December 1960 and had included the opening night of the 1962 season, yielded only silence in this one.

For the first time in Metropolitan history, the end of the spring tour did not mean the end of employment for the company's salaried personnel (orchestra, ballet, chorus, etc.). With the withdrawal of Philharmonic personnel from summer activity at the Lewisohn Stadium to newly created projects of their own in Philharmonic Hall, the Metropolitan assumed responsibility for continuing the traditional outdoor attractions. This provided many weeks' more work on the way to the goal of a year-round contract. The public response to the sequence that began on June 11 with the appearance of Renata Tebaldi was successful beyond the most optimistic expectations.

1965–1966

There was no foreordained reason why the last season of Metropolitan Opera in the theater on Broadway should have been designated 1965–6. It might, with but slight changes in existing circumstances, have come out 1964–5 or 1966–7. That it began and ended as it did produced a concordance of numbers in which the eighty-third year of occupancy was the last at a theater built in eighty-three, thus giving an impression of inevitability to what was, at the least, coincidence. For those who pay attention to some sciences other than musical, it might be interesting to note (according to Olive Adele Pryor's article devoted to "The Golden Horse-shoe" in the spring 1966 issue of *Fate's Astrology*) that "Uranus requires 84 years to transit a chart completely and return to its own place. Uranus rules the new, the unusual and it returns to its own place in the chart of the Metropolitan Opera in the 1966–7 season."

Whatever the interaction of these forces, there was nothing but volition in the choice, for the final season's opening on September 27, 1965, of Gounod's *Faust,* which had opened the first season on October 22, 1883. This was an interesting evidence of the general awareness of Metropolitan Opera history which had come about since the publication thirty years before of the first volume on the subject (by the present writer). At that time, and for many years before, the only one concerned with, or aware of, the reason why one opera rather than another was chosen for an opening was the incumbent executive. He had to exercise caution lest a favored work be repeated too often and thus incur the displeasure of those who were neither Aidas nor Amonasros. Now there were squads of official experts and divisions of correspondents to them ready to accuse General Manager Bing and his associates of dereliction of duty should such an important opportunity for invoking the Metropolitan's past be ignored.

As far as the past was present, it was exclusively on stage. No survivor of the celebrated event of 1883 made an appearance, and the descendants of the families that created the theater were conspicuously absent from the boxes they had ordered into existence. Those whom George Warren (page 4) had identified as the leading participants in the plan—"Roosevelts, Iselins, Goelets, the Astors, the three Vanderbilts, the Morgans, myself . . ."—had no close kin with sufficient affection for the old ways to expend the cost ($650) of a box for eight. Among the moneyed and the merchants who did, only the occupants of number 17 had a nominal identification with the old order. They were the Cornelius Vanderbilt Whitneys. The ranking government official in attendance was Vice-President Hubert H. Humphrey: but he and Mrs. Humphrey were the guests neither of General Manager Bing nor of the Metropolitan Opera Association's president, Anthony A. Bliss. Their host in box 33 was Roger L. Stevens, whose other guests included Mr. Justice (Abe) Fortas and John Walker, director of the National Gallery.

The production of *Faust* was among the least retrospective matters of the whole occasion. Mindful of times past when his treatment of French opera had been chided for lack of French influence, let alone French-trained singers, Bing utilized the funds provided by Mrs. John D. Rockefeller, Jr., to make a banner (tricolor, of course) showing from conductor

Georges Prêtre, Jean-Louis Barrault as stage director, and Jacques Dupont as designer. Any two without the other would have diminished the total, but the absence of Barrault would have robbed the evening of more than his nominal third of what the headline writer for the *Staats-Zeitung*'s review termed a *"sehr französischer Faust."*

What Barrault brought to his first important venture in opera direction was not merely knowledge, imagination, and a superior sense of the theatrically appropriate, but also the ability to convey them to his performers. A superb actor himself, he shared the Lunt-Webster-Ritchard-Zeffirelli ability to act out the posture, stance, or stride appropriate to each character's place in the drama. He thus provided a visual model for the opera performer whose instincts are all toward the audible. When, as in the case of Siepi, Barrault had a Méphistophélès with the figure and the agility to reproduce such "choreography," the result was a singularly French kind of devil. He hummed along sardonically (as though to say: "Don't we all?"), when Faust sang of his longing for youth, made a mocking sign of the Cross in the Garden scene, playfully whacked Marthe Schwerlein on the bottom, and otherwise acted the part of a debonair, urbane Prince of Darkness.

The other characters provided Barrault with less opportunity for creative improvisation, but Nicolai Gedda's Faust was attractively youthful; Gabriella Tucci's Marguerite,* transformed by a blonde wig, looked an appealingly *bürgerliche* heroine, and even the members of the chorus each had an identity to fulfill. The action was played on a sharply raked stage before a series of colorful settings much above the Metropolitan's average (though some opinion found them over-reminiscent of Breughel, Hals, Bosch, etc.). From these, and such able others as Merrill (Valentin), Baldwin (Siébel), and Kriese (Marthe), Prêtre evolved a musical ensemble on the order of his *Samson et Dalila*. For a change, a Metropolitan ballet aroused comment for daring rather than for the lack of it. Flemming Flindt, on the verge of becoming director of the Royal Danish Ballet, was engaged to provide what was necessary, which meant a conventional Kermesse and an unconventional *Walpurgisnacht*. The latter was given the title of "A Night at Mephisto's" and provided the visiting Faust with the kind of well-spiced fare to be expected from such a host. However its lifts and splits with their anatomical suggestion of sexual relations, roused some jeers and boos, also charges of vulgarity and tastelessness in the press.

Withal, this was the best-planned and artistically best-executed *Faust* in more than a decade. It retained that distinction as long as the cast remained intact or the inevitable replacements had profited from Barrault's guidance. This endured for all of six performances (something of a Metropolitan miracle) with the same central trio (Sereni replaced Merrill as Valentin in the sixth, on November 1). But the spell was shattered on November 8, when Jean Fenn was the Marguerite, Barry Morell the Faust, and the Bulgarian basso Nicolai Ghiaurov (d) made his debut as Méphistophélès.* The latter's striving for the Chaliapin kind of personality projection— which was, on the whole, more suitable for Boito's score than Gounod's —not only showed little awareness of, or interest in, Barrault's conception, but a coarseness of tone that had little contact with French style generally.

Indeed, as the season progressed it became increasingly difficult for one who had praised Barrault's production to justify that esteem in circumstances when the Marguerite* was Mary Costa in distressingly poor voice and Justino Diaz ventured Méphistophélès* on December 2; or when the Marguerite* (Montserrat Caballé [d]) and the Valentin* (Sherrill Milnes [d]) were strangers to the production, to each other, even to the theater itself, on December 22. The debut of the much-acclaimed Spanish soprano and her only appearance of the season[1] left some equivocal impressions of her stageworthiness, but the tall, vocally well-endowed young American baritone made an excellent first impression. It was echoed and extended in a substantial range of roles thereafter, including Yeletsky* in Tchaikovsky's *Queen of Spades* (December 28), Don Fernando* in *Fidelio* (January 8), Amonasro* in *Aida* (January 22) and Gérard* in *Andrea Chénier* (February 15).

Reference to *Queen of Spades* identifies it as the second new production of 1965–6. Oddly enough, though there were twenty-eight weeks to follow, it was scheduled not only for the same week as *Faust,* but on the following night (September 28). This imposed considerable penalty on preparation of a work not performed at the Metropolitan since March 9, 1910, especially as the conductor, Schippers, was ill prepared for this task and the stage director, Henry Butler, could not decide on stage business even *after* the dress rehearsal. Robert O'Hearn's sets were rather splashy and ostentatious for a designer of his customary good judgment (it was all paid for by Mrs. Albert D. Lasker and Francis Goelet).

It was all too reminiscent of such other Bing-decreed ventures as *Ernani, Nabucco,* even *Onegin,* even to the extent that a "version" prepared for use in San Francisco, with certain passages deleted to reduce the size of the ensemble required, was accepted for use at the Metropolitan, where no such problem existed. Among them was the chorus of children in Act I, and another segment of chorus in Act II, both ex-

---

[1] Caballé was offered a Metropolitan engagement after her unexpected success as replacement for Marilyn Horne in a Carnegie Hall concert version of *Lucrezia Borgia* in late April 1965, with a view to a debut in Lincoln Center. However Caballé expressed a desire to perform at least once in the old house, and the debut in *Faust* was accordingly arranged.

plicitly provided by Tchaikovsky for necessary contrast. Taken together with the inappropriate choice of Jon Vickers for Hermann* (Butler insisted that he be called Gherman, because there was no "H" sound in Russian, for all the fact that an English text was utilized), Teresa Stratas as a Lisa* of appealing youthfulness and insufficient vocal maturity, a hearty but unsubtle Yeletsky* by William Walker, and a labored Tomsky* by John Reardon in his debut, it sagged much more than it soared. The scene was dominated by the one performer with a sure sense of purpose which, needless to say, Regina Resnik had brought along from elsewhere on behalf of her regally decaying, enormously impressive Countess.* Rosalind Elias had the means to develop into an attractive Pauline* (she did, soon enough), Gene Boucher (d) did well what needed to be done in the small role of the Master of Ceremonies* and Markova arranged a pretty pastorale on the subject of *The Faithful Shepherd* for the ball of Act II. But, like other worthy endeavors of the recent past, *Queen of Spades* was penalized by lack of authoritative direction in the pit and on the stage.

By the third performance, on October 16, the jagged edges began to fit somewhat more smoothly together. But the improvement was offset by the next performance, on October 21, when Stratas was otherwise engaged and Lisa* became a debut role for Felicia Weathers, a young Negro soprano with some record of performing the part in smaller European houses. Even slighter in size than her predecessor (it appeared that the gowns worn by the compact Stratas had to be taken *in* for Weathers), she had neither the vocal weight nor the physical displacement to carry such a role in so large a theater. Apparently she pleased someone in authority, for she reappeared as Lisa later in the season. With Weathers's debut was a second newcomer, a former member of the chorus named Loretta di Franco (d), who sang a sweet-sounding Chloe* in the pastorale.

To judge from the pattern of casting in the half-dozen further performances of this season, the Metropolitan's IBM machine specially designed to prevent the same principals from performing more than once together was operating at peak efficiency. On November 20, Cassel was Tomsky* (with Stratas) and on November 24 it was Weathers, with Grillo as Pauline.* There was only one further *Queen of Spades* during the next four weeks (it was on December 3, with Thebom as the Countess*), by which time the principal male role had been recast to provide McCracken as a heavy, non-romantic-sounding Gherman* on December 28, with Milnes as Yeletsky* and Meredith as Tomsky.* The last of these gave the most impact to his role in the season's sequence of ten, which went forward doggedly on January 6 to muster Madeira as the Countess* in company with Weathers, Grillo, McCracken, Meredith, and Milnes. By January 15, when the opera was broadcast and Schippers was in full command of the balletic idiom that Tchaikovsky called upon in this work, the cast consisted of Stratas, Elias, Madeira, McCracken, Cassel, and Walker, who had not performed as a unit previously! Thus the conductor's hand was hampered by a wildly shuffled deck lacking the highest ranking of its face cards, Resnik's Queen of Spades.

Reference to new singers of the quality of Ghiaurov and Caballé within the framework of the season's two new productions (plus such others as Milnes, Reardon, and Weathers) may suggest several things. One was the desire to end the last season in the old house on what might be called, in movie land, "a note of hope." Another might have been the showmanly purpose of providing through new personnel what was lacking in new repertory. A third could have been a response to the printed grumble of recent months that without a generous number of replacements for those who had become superannuated and others who had never been annuated, the removal to Lincoln Center would be less an advance into a Promised Land than a retreat to previously prepared positions. Whatever the motivation, the note that was sounded, in some instances, was largely promissory. A finite fact, indisputably, was that no such quantity (thirty-odd) of quality names had been added to the Metropolitan roster for any single season in most of a decade.

Months after the event, the most vivid memory still attached to the slightest, as well as one of the earliest, of them. This was Mirella Freni, an Albanese-Bori-Sayão order of Latin soprano whose Mimi* in a *Bohème* of the first week (September 29) was one of the most polished and yet non-obtrusive the role had had in many a season. The polish was buffed to a glow of vocal gold rather than merely glinting with highlights, the characterization as simple as it was affecting. Providentially provided with a new tenor of sympathetic artistry with whom she had frequently appeared in Italy, Freni was able to work consistently for the fine line and the cultivated phrase, whether performing with Rodolfo* (Gianni Raimondi [d]) or alone. When she was confronted by the brassy, hard-hitting Musetta of Heidi Krall, the results were otherwise.

The full range of Freni's abilities was only suggested in this season, her other roles being restricted to Adina* in *L'Elisir d'amore,* which she sang with charm and finesse on November 12 in company with Gedda (Nemorino), Sereni (Belcore), Corena (Dulcamara), and Joy Clements (Gianetta*), Schippers conducting. For the while, Adina* was a role uncommonly favored, for it also had expert treatment from Renata Scotto in a

Christmas Eve performance in which George Shirley showed an engaging comedy flair as Nemorino.* Unfortunately neither Freni nor Scotto was heard in collaboration with the best possible Nemorino,* for when it became the opportunity of Bergonzi to spin out a fine thread of sound in *"Una furtiva lagrima"* on March 5 for the first time, the Adina was Peters.

Though not so personable a performer as Freni, Scotto earned an increasing esteem for expert vocalism in a sequence of performances that began with her debut in a carefully elaborated Butterfly* on October 13 and also included several fluent performances of Lucia,* the first on December 13. Scotto's special order of accomplishment related to her start as a performer of coloratura roles, and her success in broadening her sound to encompass lyric (*spinto*) parts as well. Thus she had more security at the top than the average Butterfly, more breadth at the bottom than the usual Lucia. Also, she gave evidence of having thought her parts through thoroughly and embellished them with the kind of dramatic artifice that would seem accessible to many, but appeared to elude most of her colleagues.

The Scotto debut was accompanied, rather quietly, by the first appearance of John Robert Dunlap (d), a rare kind of specialist not only in a single composer (Puccini), but even more, in a single character (Sharpless*). Plain in appearance and unburdened by the kind of vocal quality that needed suppression lest it overflow the requirements of a secondary part, Dunlap characterized the Consul as a Midwestern type, even to black bow tie and Hoover-high collar of the period (1900). Interesting in itself, it scarcely satisfied the focus that was needed when Dunlap's sound vanished in the ensembles. New, too, was the American-trained Goro* of Robert Schmorr (d). On October 30, Raimondi was one of the best sounding Pinkertons* in years, in a cast with Albanese, Grillo (Suzuki), and Dunlap. Most of these *Butterflies,* including the first on October 13, were conducted by Schick, in place of Cleva whose recurrent spells of ill-health required frequent changes of assignment and, eventually, a protracted leave of absence (see page 728).

Even more tantalizing than the few glimpses of Freni and Scotto was the brief prominence of Grace Bumbry. A St. Louisan by birth, Bumbry had first come to prominence in California and then as the *Schwarze Venus* of Wieland Wagner's Bayreuth *Tannhäuser* of 1961. Her first Metropolitan season was restricted to the role of Eboli,* which she performed at her debut on October 7 in the first *Don Carlo* to be directed by Schippers. Not only by the vigor of her temperament but also by the vitality of her voice she made a more potent factor in the drama of this character than almost any predecessor in the Bing revival. She was particularly successful with the Veil aria, rather less so with *"O don fatale,"* an inversion of usual emphasis, but no less positive in total effect. Also unfamiliar were the Carlo* of Prevedi (which like his Manrico* in *Trovatore* on November 15 was dramatically immature and vocally undistinguished), the likewise immature but much more promising Inquisitor* of Diaz, Pracht as Theobald,* and Margaret Kalil in her debut as the offstage, barely audible Celestial Voice.* Raina Kabaivanska gave some signs of filling out the weak spots in her voice as Elisabetta, but Ettore Bastianini's recession continued in his Posa. As it was not one of Hines's better nights as Philip, the promise of a new start under Schippers was only intermittently realized. As was the case with *Queen of Spades,* the Metropolitan's roster contained the necessary names for a good *Don Carlo,* but they were never allowed to perform on the same occasion. That preferential privilege would have offered Martina Arroyo, a powerful Elisabetta* in her first effort on October 30, as the soprano; Tucker as Carlo (he sang it only once this season, as replacement for Vickers, whose first appearance in the part was promised for November 16 but did not come to pass then or any time later in the season); Ghiaurov as Philip,* a part he portrayed with sharply defined dramatic means, rather less of the bottom sonority required on November 16; and Ward as the Inquisitor. The mad pace of change provided Giaiotti as a tentative Philip* on November 10, Flagello in a lyric statement of the same part for the first time, and still another Inquisitor* of limited resources when Dooley was offered his opportunity, both on November 29. Such formulations could hardly be arrived at without the intent to frustrate the best combination possible.

Of the thirty new names in this season's listing of personnel to bear the asterisk signifying "new artist," the record for singularity unquestionably accrued to Ion Piso. He was a Romanian tenor who was confidently nominated for other roles prior to his debut on September 30 as Edgardo* in a *Lucia* with Moffo, Sereni, Giaiotti, and Dan Marek (Arturo* [d]). Perhaps Piso could have survived a) lapses of participation in the visual drama and b) deviations from grace in tone production and fidelity to pitch. However the combination of the two resulted in so dismal a showing that he was relieved of further responsibilities and quietly returned whence he came. In the third *Lucia** on October 16, the Edgardo,* and a very good one, was Raimondi.

For a season as long as any in history and with a substantial share of Italian works he was accustomed to conduct, heavy reliance was put on the durability of Cleva. However, the ailment which had impeded his efforts in other recent seasons (it was finally acknowledged that he was suffering from impaired vision due to cataracts, which not only reduced his contact with the stage but made for dizzy spells and unsteady balance) all but terminated them in this. As he was able to begin and finish only seven performances in the first three months of the season (an eighth, the *Bohème* of December 30, had to be completed by Schick), the emergency called finally for an action that was affirmative rather than apologetic. It took the form of an invitation to Lamberto Gardelli, who had come to New York to conduct a concert performance in Carnegie Hall of Boito's *Mefistofele* on January 25 (with Bergonzi, Tebaldi, and Ghiaurov) to prepare and conduct the season's performances of *Andrea Chénier*. He drew a strong outline of the kind of sound he wanted in his first effort on January 30, kept the rhythmic detail sharp and, in general, gave a shape to the score it had rarely possessed in recent seasons. Most of the applause went to Tebaldi, Corelli, and Colzani (Gérard), but they were more in the picture—as well as better framed—than on some other occasions when Cleva was absent.

If Gardelli was the common kind of competent operatic conductor who, one had reason to suspect, was available in Italy when the Metropolitan was "making do" with inferior others, Francesco Molinari-Pradelli was well known to be the uncommon kind the management coveted but failed to obtain through no fault of its own. He had been engaged for the season of 1961–2, but made other plans when the Bing "cancelation" was promulgated. It was unlikely that he had been waiting, since, for the same work (*Un Ballo in maschera*) to be revived for his debut, but it worked out that way when he finally appeared on February 7.

For some with useful standards and a long memory it was the best conducting of middle period Verdi to be heard in the Metropolitan since Panizza and Walter, or for twenty-five years. Others might have stopped simply with Perlea; but there was little question that the articulation, definition, and character of the orchestral sound were more appropriately Verdian than the work had had in years. This was to Price's advantage as Amelia* no less than to that of Bergonzi and Merrill, resulting in a generally superior performance. Dunn was the Ulrica, with Peters as Oscar. Molinari-Pradelli did not have an all-round good cast in his subsequent *Ballos* (Crespin was the alternate Amelia, with Scovotti replacing Peters as Oscar on February 19, and Milnes rather than Merrill as Renato* on March 25) or in *Rigoletto*, which he conducted first on February 16. The latter's principal interest, aside from the conductor's refined sense of orchestral values, was the Duke* of Alfredo Kraus (d), whose Spanish-derived style (he is a native of the Canary Islands) found little sympathy with the public or press. His sallies up to D suffered from strain induced by want of the volume for so sizeable a house, but much else about his effort was ingratiating. Joined with the familiar Gilda of Peters and the increasingly imposing Rigoletto of MacNeil was an above-average Maddalena* by a comely mezzo, Ruza Pospinov (in the announcement of her engagement on the previous March 17, the name had been spelled Pospis). She also made a good sound as Ulrica* in *Ballo* on March 25. Whether in these or in *Andrea Chénier,* which he made his own in March when Gardelli left (in the performance of March 14, Eileen Farrell made the first of only two appearances of the season to perform a Maddalena that was considered as good as any she had ever sung), Molinari-Pradelli demonstrated the professional's concentration on the problem before him rather than the dilettante's concern for the impression he was making on those behind him.

For those to whom virtue in a conductor relates to how he looks rather than what he is doing, the consequential addition of the season was doubtless Zubin Mehta (d) who was introduced as conductor of *Aida* on December 29. What the young (thirtyish) Bombay-born Mehta had to dispose in the way of impulse, drive and musical perception did much to pick up a production that had most recently languished under the sober guidance of Steinberg (see page 713). However his inclination to treat the ballet music as orchestral interludes—he did not even bother to watch the dancers in the *ballabile* in Amneris's boudoir, hence could hardly observe that feet could not fly fast enough to cover ground at the pace he conducted the score—and to clutter the eye with cues that the performers could more conveniently take from the prompter, left some doubt whether what was happening on his stage was his first, or second, concern.

In his relationship with the singers, Mehta appeared to proceed on the basis of an armed truce, in which they would follow his tempi when they were unconventional (mosty faster than customary) and he would accept their prerogatives in blasted top notes (Corelli's B flat at the end of *"Celeste Aida"*), disregard for dynamics (Rita Gorr's explosive lurches for dramatic effect as Amneris), or indifference to note values (Tucci's exaggerated high C at the end of *"O patria mia,"* where Verdi does not permit even the latitude of a fermata). A seemly enough sort of complaisance for the average *Aida* conductor, it hardly was consistent with the formidable disciplinarian face that Mehta turned toward the orchestra. In the otherwise familiar cast were two performers who promised much in categories where the Metropolitan had need of their services: the tall Bulgarian-born Nicola Ghiuselev, who made his debut as Ramfis* with assurance and a good firm sound, and Raymond Michalski, who came from no further away than Bayonne, New Jersey, and performed his King (d*) with a shade less assurance but even richer, more commanding sound. Mehta conducted all but one of the season's nine *Aidas,* the sequence ending on April 14 with a Price-Cernei-

Guarrera-Diaz-Michalski cast under the direction of Varviso. Between these dates, Michalski made a secure place for himself with his equally capable efforts in such roles as Benoit* in *Bohème* on January 11, Mathieu* in *Chénier* on January 30, and Monterone* in *Rigoletto* on February 16.

On a basis of musical justice rather than name value, a share of credit for some of the season's most satisfying results would have to go to the previously inconspicuous Jan Behr, one of the company's associate conductors. It was a consequence of Cleva's intermittent absences (which lengthened into a leave of absence after the first of the year) that Behr drew the responsibility for *La Fanciulla del West* on January 8, which was also a broadcast. It was hardly surprising that he was well acquainted with the score, for he was in charge of what was currently termed "musical preparation" (which is to say coaching and rehearsing the ensemble); what was surprising was the sense of orchestral drama with which Behr infused the opening and the strength of purpose with which he sustained the singing of Corelli, Kirsten, Colzani, and Macurdy (Jake Wallace*).

Previously Cleva had the baton when Corelli performed his tall-in-the-saddle, non-Presidential Johnson* for the first time on December 1, and Kirsten was honored on the twentieth anniversary of her Metropolitan debut. But it was Behr who was in charge on January 17 when Kirsten was unable to perform and her "cover" performer (Beverly Bower) was also unavailable. A searching of memories produced the recollection that Steber, who had sung the part in Chicago but not in New York, might consent to breach the gap (she had last sung at the Metropolitan on November 23, 1962). Though the change was decided upon only one day before the curtain, sufficient of Steber's ardent admirers had assembled to greet her with cheers and bravos and make a disproportionate show of enthusiasm for the loud, quavery sounds she produced—though, it must be said, with enormous good humor and a superficial show of enjoying herself. For one reason or another, Corelli decided that he was unable to continue after Act I, a piece of news that aroused groans when it was communicated before the curtain rose for Act II. Those who returned belatedly and missed the announcement discovered to their amazement, upon the character's entrance, that Johnson* had shrunk by a third in physical size and by half in vocal output over the intermission. This was by far the greatest prominence the season provided for Gaetano Bardini (d) until unexpected circumstances gave him, together with Behr, access to a historic first some weeks later (see page 742).

Partially by design—a prolonged period of service by Schippers, and the engagement of Molinari-Pradelli—and partially by accident (the availability of Gardelli), the conducting of this season was, on the whole, of more consistent quality than for several years past. Part of the result to be attributed to design was the enlarged repertory for Prêtre, who moved in two directions from his geographical base (such French operas as *Samson* and *Faust*): south for *Il Trovatore* and east for *Arabella* and *Parsifal*. He achieved the best results where they might have been least expected, recalling that the score of *Parsifal* had more than its share of admirers among such French musicians as Debussy. The lovely sheen of sound that was heard on March 10 during the beautifully paced prelude gave rise to hopes that something uncommon might follow. Intermittently, and for much of Act II and the beginning of Act III, it did, especially where Prêtre was working with the lyrical talents of Konya as Parsifal* and Crespin as Kundry.* The latter's characterization was altogether individual (a product of Bayreuth conditioning by Wieland Wagner), much more feminine than is commonly seen, and with an insinuating treatment of *"Ich sah das Kind"* that was more akin to a *chanson* than to a *lied*. What Prêtre had to offer was rather less apropos to the lengthy philosophical ruminations of Gurnemanz or the sufferings of Amfortas, especially as Hines was in poor voice for the former and London had not sufficiently recovered from an operation (said to involve his diaphragm) to do himself justice in the latter. Assistance to the quality of Act II came from Meredith, undertaking his first Klingsor.* He declaimed the music with baleful power and projected the action impressively. This being the first *Parsifal* at the Metropolitan since the 1960–1 season, there were new impersonations in a host of subsidiary roles, beginning with Diaz as Titurel,* and progressing with Pospinov (A Voice*), Goodloe (Second Knight*), Pracht (First Esquire*), Love (Second Esquire*), Marek (Fourth Esquire*), and, as flower maidens, Clements, Di Franco, Baldwin, Casei and Lillian Sukis, the last also making a debut. The Kerz ramps and benches were no more illusive than they had been, but the projected backgrounds appeared to be in somewhat steadier focus than during earlier viewings. But the whole of it, clearly, was headed for discard against the opportunities soon to be available for a properly staged *Parsifal* in Lincoln Center.

Crespin's order of artistry was missed when she was spelled by Välkki (Kundry*) on March 16, for most other "spell" was missing in her vigorous, hard projection of the vocal line and nonillusive stage deportment. Cassel was the Amfortas,* also replacing London in the later performances for which he had been scheduled. In his other assignments, Prêtre applied himself with the vigor and spirit admired in *Samson, Faust* and parts of *Parsifal*, but not always with equal command of substance. In *Arabella,* which he conducted for the first time on October 1 (with Della Casa, Rothenberger, Thebom, Cassel, and Gramm as Waldner*), a real balance between vocal and orchestral elements was never attained, and in *Trovatore* (October 20, with Tucci, Dalis, Labò, Merrill, and Macurdy) he had more control of the ensemble—as, for example, in the opening scene—than he did of the "name" performers. This suggested that it was done on an insufficient budget of time, and the "soloists" were just that, rather than part of a unified conception. In later performances of *Arabella*, Reardon was Mandryka* on October 14 (Scovotti was Fiakermilli*) without having the vocal displacement it required, with Dooley following him on November 23, also for the first time (he had the displacement but not the personal appeal to make much of the character). The most notable of the *Trovatores* this season was the one scheduled for November 9, for the simple reason that it did not happen. This was the occasion of the power failure that paralyzed the Northeast, and the Metropolitan was no exception. It was rescheduled for December 19, which moved the date for Colzani's first Di Luna* from November 9 to November 15, when Prevedi was the Manrico.* When Prêtre's first sequence of performances ended on December 22, *Trovatore* reverted to the care of Schippers. However when MacNeil offered his sturdy Di Luna* for the first time on February 28 (with Arroyo, Rankin, and Tucker), the conductor was Schick. One Prêtre project that languished in this season was *Samson,* for the reason that he did not conduct it after the three performances of December. When it returned to the repertory on December 6, it was with McCracken as Samson,* Gorr as Dalila, and Bacquier as the High Priest. The subsequent performances were assigned to Cleva, but in his absence they passed to Kurt Adler with the matinee of January 1. Thus the six performances were divided between Prêtre and Adler.

Among the pre-season promises of Prêtre's *Parsifal* was the prospect that it might bring Wolfgang Windgassen to the stage of the Metropolitan in one of his most celebrated roles. However this prospect, together with the possibility of seeing Windgassen in anything else, vanished early in March when it was discovered that he had decided not to come to America at all. A plea of illness was entered on his behalf from Paris, where he had been appearing as Tristan to Nilsson's Isolde, but it was well known that he had been thoroughly unhappy on his prior stay in New York, and this doubtless weighed against his making the trip again.

This, in turn, promoted what had been one, if a double-edged, interest of the Metropolitan's first *Tannhäuser* since December 1960 to virtually its only one. That was the double undertaking of Nilsson as Elisabeth, which she had sung before in New York, and Venus,* which she had not, on March 19. The challenge would have been more meaningful had it involved the full-formed Venus of the Paris version rather than the incompletely characterized Venus of the earlier Dresden version: there was no doubt that Nilsson could have sung either—or both—on the same evening had she been asked. What was lacking in her Venus* was neither vocal strength nor plausible appearance, but the kind of complete command which had brought her Elisabeth to a level on which it merited comparison with Lehmann's or Flagstad's. In the circumstances, it was just not a very good Venus by the standard of the Nilsson Elisabeth, whether sung by the same person or not.

The default of Windgassen brought on not only the scheduled known new performers of Wolfram* (Thomas Stewart, and a promising one) and Landgrave Hermann* (the best effort to date of Macurdy), but also a Tannhäuser* who was neither scheduled nor known. It was Pekka Nuotio, of Finnish birth, who was promoted from standby to stand-in, and in the difficult circumstances of such a debut, earned friendly esteem for musicality and manly bearing. Doubtless his voice would have been more impressive in a smaller house (also measured against a Venus-Elisabeth with less heroic output than Nilsson's), but he did better than some tenors of the past with bigger names. In the final two performances of the season, casting reverted to custom, with Rysanek as Elisabeth, one of her best roles, and Välkki no more distinguished as Venus* than as Kundry (on April 4). Rosenstock conducted all the performances, with an uncommon command of the work's more than patches of problems.

With no *Ring* dramas in the schedule, Nilsson's season was divided between an early phase, in which she spaced several performances of Leonore in *Fidelio* (the first on January 8, with Boehm conducting, James King making his debut as a loud but not appealing voice for Florestan,* Geraint Evans miscast as Pizarro,* Edelmann as Rocco,* and Milnes as Fernando*), with Salomes and a Tosca; and a later phase in which *Tannhäusers* were spaced by *Tosca*. In one remarkable sequence of slightly more than a week, she sang Leonore on January 22 (Saturday), Tosca on January 25 (Tuesday), Salome on January 28 (Friday), and Leonore again on the following Monday. When she was otherwise engaged, Leonore was performed on January 12 by Ludmila Dvorakova (d), whose rouged cheeks and well-coiffed head left little doubt that she was a good-looking woman, *Hosenrolle* or no. Vocally, it was of the "promising" order, though not with enough easy power to perform an effective *"Abscheulicher"* in these surroundings. With her on January 27 was Dooley as Pizarro.* His sound was more appropriate to Beethoven's purpose than Evans's had been, but a real malevolent characterization—of the Schoeffler-Uhde variety—was not in him.

Some, to be sure, thought well of Evans's martinet bearing despite his lack of the requisite voice, but there was no less than universal praise for his Leporello,* first seen on January 29. It was by no means the most anticipated effort of this occasion, which also promised the first Elvira* in New York by Schwarzkopf, but by the end of *"Notte e giono fatticar"* it was clear that nothing else would be needed to make the afternoon memorable. Not only was Evans's Leporello the most artfully sung servant in decades; it was also acted with typically English conviction that to be a fine servant is no less a distinction than to be a worthy master. Not all the other drama of this performance was provided by Da Ponte and Mozart, for Schwarzkopf's interpretation of her best part was hampered by a vocal malaise that made almost every note an effort. Fine artist that she is, there was abundant compensation in the quality of her acting and ensemble effort; but by the end of the afternoon she had exhausted the vocal reserve at her command, and did not reappear thereafter. What seemed an improbable presumption turned into an occasion for congratulations when Elias slimmed her vocal sound (and dimmed her ordinarily luminous personality) to the needs of Zerlina.* With Siepi as an uncommonly frisky Don, Stich-Randall performing her practiced Donna Anna (companioned, unfortunately, by an Ottavio who had begun to look the years of his performer, Peerce), Uppman as Masetto, and Ghiuselev presenting the likeness of a grandly set-up Commendatore,* the sense of *dramma giocoso* expressed in the work's subtitle was more consistently honored than for a decade at least. "Frisky" was not the word that automatically comes to mind to describe Rosenstock's conducting, but it was animated. The intent to keep the cast intact for a few performances at least was undone by Schwarzkopf's cancelation, and her immediate replacement (Amara) soon gave way to other changes, including eventually, such undistinguished elements as Bjoner for Anna and Esparza for Leporello on February 21. Kraus was a fair Ottavio* on March 8.

In the performances of February 11 and 14, Schwarzkopf's replacement was Pilar Lorengar,[1] whose scheduled debut on the second of these dates was advanced three days to meet the emergency. Against the recollection of a sweet sounding, light-voiced soprano heard a decade before when Lorengar made her New York debut in a concert version of *Goyescas* in Town Hall, the actuality produced a broader sound used with no little temperament but a quaver now on, now off, the pitch. She managed the florid line of *"Mi tradi"* better than most recent Elviras, but at a cost to the dramatic urgency in the music. Need also prompted the use of Lorengar as Mistress Ford* (a part sung for the first time, and not well, by Costa on

[1] Her countrywoman, Teresa Berganza, was also scheduled for a Metropolitan debut in this season, but it was deferred when she became pregnant.

October 29) in the absence of Schwarzkopf, for whom it had also been scheduled. As Lorengar had been singing it recently in German, she was granted the indulgence of performing in that language when she joined the cast of Evans-Alva-Guarrera-Chookasian-Miller on February 17. She later re-learned it in Italian, but the sound—whatever the language—remained spread and unfocused. On the whole, the first flush of *Falstaff* had faded more than a little, with Tucci occupied by *Faust,* Rosenstock providing much less of the wanted *brio* than Bernstein had.

However, Evans's Falstaff remained a substantial delight whenever it was offered, sustaining a standard of quality by which even so respected a performance as Tito Gobbi's appeared insufficient when it was first seen on March 5. What Gobbi had to offer in verbal facility and physical vitality might have earned cheers a few years before, but it was, by the measure of Evans's Shakespearian figure, much more *cavaliere* than knight. Kostas Paskalis, who had been announced for the Ford* of this cast, did not appear to perform it or any other part in this season, and Thomas Stewart, whose debut was scheduled for *Tannhäuser* a week later, agreed to replace him. However he too found himself vocally ill disposed, and it eventually became Guarrera. Stewart did make his debut as Ford* on March 9, showing a lean, active figure, a good stage presence, and a sure command of a strong voice. Not yet a finished artist, he had all the equipment to become one.

Like such other debutants of this season as Bumbry and King, Stewart was an American who had pursued the fellowship-Fulbright route to European opera houses and the benefits to be derived therefrom. Of the same general background was Reri Grist, an elfin coloratura who made her debut as Rosina*(d) in a restoration of *Il Barbiere di Siviglia* under Varviso's direction on February 25. It was neat, well-finished vocal work she offered, but undersized even by the measure of such small voiced singers as Peters and D'Angelo (in the lower register, she was hardly audible). Dramatically, Grist carried on a considerable flirtation with the audience, to whom she gave much more attention than she did to her nominal suitor (Shirley, as Almaviva). Herlea's Figaro* was a compound of all the stock gestures and vocal flourishes, but there was not much real artistry in the mixture. Kriese was Berta.* For those who paid attention selectively, the real source of pleasure came from the duel of comedic devices between Corena as Bartolo and Tozzi as Basilio, the latter making one of his few operatic appearances in a winter he devoted largely to operetta. On March 12 the Almaviva was Alva, with generally good results. The same could not be said of Vinay's effort to launch a "second" Metropolitan career (actually a return to the low range in which he had begun) as Bartolo* on March 31. The sound was dry, the action unfunny.

Along with Bumbry and Grist, another American singer to find a wider range for her talents in this season was Martina Arroyo, building on the success of her recent Aidas. In addition to the admired Elisabetta* in *Don Carlo* on October 30 (see page 728), she had the range of sound as well as of sympathies to convey conviction with her Butterfly* on November 20 (assuming one did not notice that the kimono was oversized and concealed her considerable bulk) and dramatic fervor with her Leonora* in *Trovatore* on Christmas night. Another Butterfly* on January 5 was drummed into prominence by the publicity that its performer had been "promoted" from the National Company (see footnote, page 738) by reason of her success with it. Actually, the performer in question, Francesca Roberto, had been awarded an engagement with the Metropolitan Company as an Auditions winner in the spring of 1961 and had failed to take it up for reasons of her own. What she did five years later was commendable but not really significant of anything.

As if the grueling demands of Lisa in *Pique Dame* were not sufficient focus of attention for a single season's effort by a young singer, Stratas was also called upon to fill the role of the frolicsome street singer when *Perichole* returned on December 18. Not merely for her spirited acting but also for her fluency in singing the music, Perichole* proved to be much more in her line than the heavier parts to which she had been recently assigned. She was much the best performer for Offenbach since Munsel and Hurley, with the advantage over both of a much more substantial lower range (to meet the needs of the composer's conception). The best of the previous casting—Uppman as the practically perfect Paquillo and Ritchard as the Viceroy—were artfully integrated by its new conductor, Allers, with such new impersonations as Don Pedro* by Gramm, Guadalena* by Clements, Virginella* by Baldwin, Estrella* by Pracht, and An Old Prisoner* by Velis. When Allers's engagement ran out, the project passed to Strasfogel on January 18.

By contrast with the previous season's effort to improve the quality of balletic performance available to the company's requirements, this year's emphasis went in another direction altogether. As expressed in a Sunday evening (March 27) program largely devoted to works of Antony Tudor (including the first performance anywhere of *Concerning Oracles* to music of Jacques Ibert and the American *première* of *Echoing of Trumpets* based on Martinu's *Fantaisies Symphoniques*), the intent seemed directed toward providing the Metropolitan Opera Ballet with an independent identity.

Whatever the merits of such a program, it did not in the least advance the Metropolitan's needs for a better ensemble and more adept soloists than those commonly seen in *Traviata, Aida,* or *Samson.* The quality of effort on this occasion was most nearly satisfactory among the female members of the group, but it was deemed desirable to import an outsider, Lance Westergard, to meet the male requirements for *Concerning Oracles.* This indeed the talented Westergard did well, but it could hardly have added to the self-esteem of those he superseded. Strasfogel conducted *Echoing of Trumpets* and the evening-ending *La Ventata* (after Bournonville), with Alain Lombard, a Mitropoulos competition winner and assistant to Leonard Bernstein, added for a debut as director of *Concerning Oracles.*

While one pattern of activity was running its prescribed course at Thirty-ninth and Broadway, another, converging one began to take shape at the Amsterdam Avenue end of the Lincoln Center Plaza. As the external structural work was rounded off by the installation of the glass panels that made an airtight chamber of the huge interior area, the time of occupancy began to be reckoned not in months or weeks but in days. It became an informal actuality on October 25, when Herman E. Krawitz, who had served as liaison between the Metropolitan and the contractors of the new building, took possession of temporary offices. This was to provide an on-site base during the final work of "finishing" (painting, decorating, carpeting, etc.) and to expedite the sequence of movements by which the old building was evacuated and the new quarters occupied.

By mid-March the auditorium had reached a state of readiness to permit inspection by various factions—ranging from board members and their friends to press representatives and *their* friends—who had been petitioning for such privilege for some time. The date for the press tour was set for the afternoon of March 22, with a series of inspections as visitors accumulated, and a press conference at the end. There were, finally, nearly a hundred representatives of domestic and foreign press and periodicals in the assemblage that gathered in what would eventually be the Grand Tier Restaurant to query Messrs. Bliss, Bing, Wallace K. Harrison (architect), Schuman, and Krawitz. Edgar B. Young presided.

However even before these portents of the "new" Metropolitan would produce, finally, the New Metropolitan long awaited, Lincoln Center's history as a scene of resident operatic activity was begun by the City Opera Company in the New York State Theater on February 22, 1966.[1] This was

---

[1] The touring Metropolitan Opera National Company, made up of younger singers, which had opened its first season on September 20 at Butler University, Indianapolis, Indiana, invited the attention of the New York public with a season of twenty-three performances in the State Theater between November 3 and 19. The repertory embraced two works given exclusively in English (Rossini's *Cenerentola,*

in conformity with the agreement covering the theater's future following the twenty-month period (beginning in April 1964) in which it was operated by Lincoln Center in conjunction with the World's Fair. There was a spate of noisy dispute between official Lincoln Center, represented by William Schuman, and official City Center, represented by Morton Baum, as to control of the theater when it was not required for City Center purposes (ballet and opera). In the end the legalities favored Baum's position, as well they should have, as he virtually devised the language of the law.

Before the turn of the year provided the turn of the key that saw the control of the State Theater pass from Lincoln Center to City Center, there was a season's work to be done on Fifty-fifth Street. Its most publicized feature was the first American production of Prokofiev's *Ange de Feu,* introduced on September 22 as *The Flaming Angel.* It scored high marks for Rudel's ingenuity in getting the work on despite a constricted playing area (ramps were in again this season), but not so high for his success in casting it. Eileen Schauler's success as Shostakovich's Katerina Ismailova prompted her choice for Prokofiev's Renata, which was beyond her, temperamentally as well as vocally. Sherrill Milnes gave little warning of success to come at his Metropolitan debut with his crudely acted, not very well sung Ruprecht, and the scenic effects devised by Will Steven Armstrong were both skimpy and non-illusive. Rudel shrewdly added weight to the musical substance of the opera by utilizing, for interludes, portions of Prokofiev's Symphony Number 3 based on materials of the opera.

As the final production, on November 4, of an American work commissioned for the Fifty-fifth Street stage by Ford Foundation money, Rudel gave his favor to Ned Rorem's treatment of a libretto by Kenward Elmslie based on Strindberg's *Miss Julie.* Whatever the weaknesses of the libretto (in omissions and relocations of material in the play), it was fundamentally a mismatch between Rorem's rather gentle order of expression and the naturalistic passions depicted by Strindberg. Here and there a lyric episode emerged with the shape and flavor Rorem imparts to settings of song texts, but the strong spinal column of an operatic structure was missing. Donald Gramm, borrowed from the Metropolitan, made a real character study of John (the Groom), and Elaine Bonazzi, in her City Opera debut, did well as the housemaid to whom he is "engaged." Marguerite Willauer was small of sound for Julie (she was said to be vocally under the weather for both

---

billed as *Cinderella,* and Floyd's *Susannah*) and two others sung alternately in their original language and in English (*Madama Butterfly* and *Carmen*). The performances varied in quality (*Susannah* and *Butterfly* were, by common agreement, on the higher level), but all were adversely affected by the acoustical surroundings as they then existed.

the dress rehearsal and first performance), but she acted it well. Robert Zeller conducted, zealously.

The quality achievement of this playing period came, improbably, in the first professional staging in New York of Strauss's *Capriccio* on October 27 (it had been given by the graduate students of Juilliard in May 1954). Against the well-known difficulties of a work with scant "action" and no pause to break its two-hour length, the ordinary resources of City Opera seemed insufficient. This, however, reckoned without such extraordinary resources as the Vienna-born Ernst Märzendorfer (debut), whose conducting showed a penetrating knowledge of the work, and the Dutch basso Guus Hoekmann, who not only commanded the vocal problems of La Roche but also delivered the English text by Maria Pelikan with barely a burr. Donna Jeffrey did better with the Countess than might have been expected of so young a performer, and David Lloyd was a musically expert Flamand. Christopher West's thoughtful direction made an intimate house party of the other, assorted talents, including John Reardon (Oliver), Marija Kova (Clairon), and Robert Trehy (Count). Ellen Faull and Enzo Citarelli made light, as it should be, of the Italian opera burlesque.

When the curtain fell for the last time on a performance by the City Opera in its long-familiar home, the totals showed that 115 works had been produced since the introductory *Tosca* of February 21, 1944. The total became 116 immediately on resumption of activity in the State Theater, for Rudel chose to open on February 22, 1966, with another unfamiliar "American" score (South, rather than North). Thanks to the generous purse of Mrs. John D. Rockefeller, Jr., he was able to consider a venture with Alberto Ginastera's *Don Rodrigo,* which had first been performed at the Colón in the composer's native Buenos Aires on July 24, 1964. Doubtless such requirements as the four horn quartets scattered through the theater for the hunting episode of Act II inhibited production elsewhere, but Rudel took it in a giant stride that advanced his company to a new position of artistic esteem.

Whether or not one agreed that Ginastera's treatment of the voice against the limitations of the twelve-tone system and a heavy orchestral scoring made for repeated hearings, it was clear that the production problem had been met with uncommon success by Ming Cho Lee, designer, and Tito Capobianco, stage director. Of outstanding quality were the Mexican tenor, Placido Domingo as Rodrigo and Spiro Malas as his tutor Teudiselo. Jeannine Crader excelled the best to be expected of so young a singer in the difficult music of Florinda, but it may have cost her more than the applause of an evening repaid. The Spanish text of Alejandro Casona was utilized, and the total effect was so stimulating that two additional performances were added to the three originally scheduled.

Successful as it was, *Don Rodrigo* roused some expectations for the subsequent productions (also for the first time on a New York stage) of Poulenc's *Dialogues of the Carmelites* (on March 3, in English) and Gottfried von Einem's *Danton's Death* (also in English on March 9) which could not be fulfilled. Rather than having set a new, consistent standard for City Center productions, the effort of Rudel, Capobianco, and Lee (with Ginastera) was seen to be the result of an all-out expenditure of time and money that left too little of both for the other works of the repertory. Alain Lombard conducted Poulenc knowingly and Märzendorfer did his best on behalf of Einem, but neither cast measured up to its responsibilities and the production in each case was drab. Indeed, the tepid response to *Danton's Death* caused one performance to be canceled on behalf of an additional *Don Rodrigo*.

On the whole, the State Theater proved a more attractive, audience-inducing locale for such other works of the repertory as *The Ballad of Baby Doe, The Consul, Love for Three Oranges,* and *Street Scene* than the City Center had been in some recent seasons. Such was the stability now attained by the company Rudel had inherited at low ebb a decade before that it could give eighty-six performances of twenty-eight works between September 1965 and March 1966. This made it the largest source of operatic activity in the United States next to the Metropolitan.

The problems persisted, though Rudel continued to deny that the acoustical environment of the State Theater was one of them (see footnote, page 738). His observation on the difficulties experienced by the Metropolitan National Company was that "quality voices" would make the difference. If so, he did not have enough of the requisite quality to conquer the bounces and buffeting the sound took from the flat undersurfaces of the boxes and the curves around the proscenium. As Philip Johnson, architect of the State Theater, had tailored his design to the needs of dance, it was hardly surprising that it did not suit, without some adaptation, the needs of another art altogether. Doubtless it would in time, but it was merely stubborn of Rudel to pretend that there was no problem.

Taken together with prior complaints about the original acoustical environment of Philharmonic Hall (though the two cases were quite different) confidence in the ability of acousticians to produce a desired result had been replaced, generally, with concern verging on pessimism about the biggest gamble of all in Lincoln Center, the new Opera House. Months before it was ready for inspection, let alone use, Harold Schonberg filled a column of *The New York Times* on a January Sunday with ominous forebodings based on the cubic air space of the auditorium. It was, he warned, bigger than any other auditorium save that of the Colón, and the bigger the space, the larger the hazard. Schonberg neglected to mention that the architects of the Colón had solved the problem so well that it was famous as a singer's favorite and also enjoyed a reputation as the best concert hall in most of South America.

Even those who took the view right along that the new Metropolitan was designed on the lines of the old, and thus was following a known pattern for quality results, could have little sense of certainty without a full-dress trial. This meant not a random run-through of excerpts, but a full performance with scenery, costumes, *and* an audience. It was later revealed that plans to utilize, for this purpose, one of the annual student performances, had been in existence for some time. It was eventually decided that the auditorium and lighting facilities were in order for the afternoon of April 11, and the necessary instruction were issued for the participants to report uptown rather than at the old house. Word was passed to the bus companies that transported the students to deliver them to Lincoln Center, and invitations were extended to a segment of the press to attend as guests of the management. That is to say, with the understanding that the performance was "off the record" and that the impressions they gathered would be available (informally) to the management for guidance, or at least consideration.

Thus the choice for the long-awaited preview, which might be one of the most memorable performances of opera in New York's history, came to be *La Fanciulla del West* because it had been selected by the Opera Guild for its annual series of student matinees. In accordance with the custom of these events, it began at 1 P.M., which offered scant opportunity for customary lunches by those who were deskbound during usual hours. (Most of those with sufficient interest to be invited to attend cared little about a "customary lunch" on this particular day.)

Thus in the continuing absence of Cleva, it came to be the name of Jan Behr that was inscribed on the record as the first to conduct a performance in the Metropolitan Opera House at Lincoln Center. It also became Gaetano Bardini as Dick Johnson, when Robert Nagy, who had been scheduled for the part, came up hoarse and could not perform. Beverly Bower was Minnie, with Cesare Bardelli as Rance. Following the performance of the National Anthem—clear, crisp, cleanly sonorous—Executive Stage Manager Osie Hawkins appeared to ask the audience's indulgence for tests designed to promote measurements of reverberation, rate of decay, echo, and sound reflection. These took the form of blasts on a shotgun and the sounding of a chord by the full orchestra (it was duly noted that Puccini had acted with forethought in providing just such a chord to open *Fanciulla*).

For those who poke around for such details, it was noticeable that the spacious pit made possible an orchestral arrangement long cherished by Metropolitan conductors but never possible in the old house: eight double basses facing the conductor from the rear of the pit, rather than being shunted to a corner far on his left. Strings and woodwinds, brass and percussion were also ranked according to an ideal of balance rather than by necessity of available space.

The opening pages of *Fanciulla* being the scrappily scored things they are—calls from right and left, offstage, the onstage "Allos" of Joe, Harry and Sid (in all probability their performers had never before been listened to with such critical attention)—not much could be gathered in useful judgment for some minutes. It was, indeed, not until some seven minutes had passed that a sound which could be grasped as a touchstone was heard: the introductory measures of the Puccinicized "Old Dog Tray." It needed no reference to the program to identify this Jake Wallace as Louis Sgarro, nor too many bars of listening to conclude that it was the kind of solid Sgarro bass sound familiar elsewhere. As to be expected, it was with a shading of color and timbre distinctively conditioned by the particular surroundings, but without loss of character or resonance. Moving about in the dark, it was possible to determine that the sound followed the auditor to the back, or from one side to the other, without falling off in volume or definition. The structural features built in to enhance sound distribution— especially the wide flaring proscenium frame, which served as a trumpet bell does the sound from its tube, and the curved wooden panels that lined the huge auditorium on all its walls from floor to ceiling and faced all the exposed surfaces around the boxes, grand tier, dress circle, and balcony— had apparently been accurately calculated to perform the desired function. And when one ascended to the least-favored area of all—top row of the balcony, extreme side aisle—it was clear that architect Harrison had made good on his primary promise, which was to provide an environment that would not favor the expensive seat-holders at a penalty to those in the less costly locations. The *full* stage, as exposed in *Fanciulla*, was universally visible, thus rectifying a condition that had plagued every performance of opera in the old house since the very first. The only exception was in some upper boxes along the side walls, which were "marginal" capacity at best and destined to be the last to be sold in most circumstances.

By the end of the first act, it was clear that a standard above minimum acceptability had already been attained, meaning that trial and error—the elevators for the floor of the orchestral pit were not yet operational and the scene loft above the stage was empty—could only result in improvement. Among those encountered in the semi-darkness as the curtain fell was General Manager Bing, who had rare recourse to an Americanism to express his own reaction of relief: "Well, I think we are out of the woods."

Proceeding "out of the woods" and into the lobby, a sampling of the total mood—the audience included tenors Tucker and Corelli eavesdropping on their home-to-be, conductors Molinari-Pradelli, Rosenstock, Adler, and Schick, as well as sound engineers busy with their metered boxes and other measuring devices—suggested that certainty had replaced uncertainty, and content was much more evident than complaint. Indeed, it was the opinion of some press and administrative personnel that the vow of silence could be rescinded, that word-of-mouth would travel even faster than printed opinions. In the end, it was decided to allow individual judgment to prevail. The consensus was put into type in the following day's *Daily News* with Douglas Watt's observation: "The general reaction to the acoustics of the new Met was highly favorable." In *Variety* of April 20 R. J. Landry reported: "Musicians who recently played in the new house during the student test (of acoustics) agreed that the new stand is far finer than the old."

For those who participated in this interaction of old and new, it was an extraordinary, almost a fatalistic coincidence that the two lines of history moved toward an interaction during the same seven-day period, with the curve of the new moving upward from Monday, April 11 to meet the downward drop of the old toward the final Gala Farewell on Saturday, April 16. What might have been, in other circumstances, a question-laden evening of parting with the known to embrace the unknown became, in these circumstances, an occasion for a fond retrospect of the past against high promise for the future.

What made it a farewell was evident enough in the creeping grime that had been allowed to accumulate on the exterior walls against the imminent removal, the broken bits of plaster here and there where cracks had not been repaired in recent weeks, a rent in the gold curtain which had gone unsewn, and no less in the foyers denuded of pictures against the temptation they might present to souvenir hunters. Staff offices were nearly empty of furniture as well as occupants as removal uptown went forward on a schedule designed to terminate occupancy with the season's end, and vacant stores on the Seventh Avenue and Broadway corners gave mute evidence of terminated leases.

What made it "Gala," however, was something else again. It began of course as the kind of dress-up occasion which is *de rigeur* for anything in New York costing two or three times the usual price of admission. For this particular occasion, for which top seats were priced at nearly twenty times the usual ($200) to produce a gigantic revenue of $290,000 (the largest in the history of the theater and possibly the largest in the history of a theater anywhere), the *couture* was not merely *haute,* but, in some instances, excessively so.

The opening night of the Metropolitan in 1883 was half an hour late in starting: so, too, was the closing one in 1966. There were pictures to be taken, and latecomers to be ushered to seats. To Leopold Stokowski, oldest as well as most famous of the conductors participating, went the honor of opening the evening, receiving the first ovation, and directing a vital, pulsating performance of the Entrance of the Guests and Greeting to the Hall of Song, from *Tannhäuser.* He also provided the evening's first flavor of personality. As he turned to leave the pit, he added the special Stokowskian touch of a verbal appeal to "save this beautiful house," a cause to which he had given his name as chairman. This evoked some cheers from passionate others, especially in the upper areas of the theater, but also a little resentment among those who realized that Stokowski had used his invitation to denounce by implication those who were hosts to the party.

Stokowski's extempore was obliterated by the succeeding segment of the program, conceived in sentiment but productive of a result no one could foresee. It was the presentation by name and in alphabetical order of nearly forty past members of the company who had been invited as Honored Guests. That the sequence began with Anderson, Marian, was no more than an accident of the alphabet: but it was no accident that her appearance set off a tempest of applause that could only relate to one of the most meaningful happenings in Metropolitan history, when her debut in 1955 opened the way for all the others of the Negro race who had followed her. As the list went forward from Baccaloni (ill, and unable to be present) to Stevens and Swarthout, it became a kind of *tableau vivant* of many moments to remember (and a few to forget). When Richard Crooks entered, the tenors in the chorus seated on the stadium-like tiers of Gérard's Wartburg setting, applauded with extra vigor; when the great Boris and Hagen, Alexander Kipnis, strode in, all the bassos stood up. There was but a patter of applause for some half-forgotten conductor, but a roar for Martinelli and Rethberg. When Lotte Lehmann, proudly erect beneath her years, came forward, everybody stood up.

What followed was, true to the surroundings, like a gaudy sound montage of all the operas ever written, pieced together from the choicest morsels of Verdi, Wagner, Mozart, Rossini, Puccini, even Giordano and Ponchielli. Merrill performed *"Eri tu"* from *Un Ballo in maschera* not so much to the audience out front as to Richard Bonelli, his boyhood idol, sitting among the Honored Guests in a semi-circle behind him. And when Licia Albanese launched into *"Un bel di,"* it was against the critical judgment not of some contemporary journalist but of such perfectionists in Puccini as Rethberg, Sayão, Martinelli, and Crooks. For Dorothy Kirsten, the *"Depuis le jour"* she performed more beautifully than anything she had sung on this stage in a twenty-year span was not for herself alone, but also for Grace Moore, her benefactress and Metropolitan predecessor in the part. She sang it well enough for both.

As a program, it was overlong, unimaginative, full of too many *devoirs* to company convenience (solos by people who should have been content to take part in an ensemble in these circumstances, a *Carmen* quintet with a Carmen, Regina Resnik, who had previously sung part on this stage only in a student performance). What redeemed it, in spite of its lumpy contrivance, was the natural impulse of the human being, especially the performing human being, to respond to a challenge. In a single span of minutes during which Leontyne Price spun out a superb *"D'amor sull' ali rosee"* from *Trovatore* and Birgit Nilsson (wearing in pride the gold wreath[1] that had been presented to Christine Nilsson on the night the theater opened) poured out vocal abundance without stint in the Immolation Scene from *Götterdämmerung,* the flame leaped high with the best the present-day Metropolitan had to offer. But within minutes after an intermission, there were reminders that the blaze flickered as often as it flared, that there were Metropolitan evenings when the Triumphal Scene from *Aida* brought forth not Price (or Nilsson) and Corelli, but Curtis-Verna and Baum (as this one did, with Madeira, Sereni, Macurdy, and Scott). Eventually the evening's greatest cheers were accorded to Milanov and Tucker, with a duet from *Andrea Chénier* which reprised her formal farewell to the house a few nights before (April 13) with the same tenor in the same work.[2] And, as must happen on the best-regulated operatic occasion bringing together sixty or more "names," there were the inevitable cancelations: Lucine Amara could not perform her part of the *Forza* trio with Peerce and Tozzi (Delia Rigal, who came as an honored guest ended as a somewhat less honored performer in her place), and George London decided not to try to sing his excerpt from *Boris.*

Almost any time a person of prominence in the annals of opera has died in these last decades—a Caruso, a Chaliapin, a Toscanini, or a Bruno Walter—it has been sagely said, and with some justice, that it "marked the

---

[1] It was located in the Museum of Musical History in Stockholm and flown to New York for the occasion.

[2] She had made a total of 424 appearances in fourteen works (including the Verdi *Requiem*) in New York and on tour, over a twenty-eight-year span (she missed four seasons in that time).

end of an era." What is there left to say, then, when the place in which these and hundreds more of almost equal note spent some of the most productive years of their lives, itself dies? Only, perhaps, that it marks the end not of an era but of an epoch, which by dictionary definition, connotes "a moment of time when a varying quantity had a certain given value."

So, with the singing of "Auld Lang Syne" by all those who waited for the final curtain of the final night to fall at approximately 1:05 Sunday morning passed an epoch of opera in New York. It passed though Stokowski sought to stem the tide with his Canute-like gesture; it passed as Licia Albanese, with an excess of Latin sentiment (and an eye for a *Life* photographer in the wings) transferred a kiss from her lips to the floor of the stage with a pat of her hand; it passed as conductors from Molinari-Pradelli to Rudolf (present "on loan" from Cincinnati), Schick, Rosenstock, Varviso, Cleva (who managed to take his place in the sequence), Mehta, Kurt Adler, Leinsdorf, and Prêtre exchanged batons in relay formation.

The given value in this interminably inconvenient, unquestionably difficult, and withal unforgettable place was the power of the human voice to arouse, to excite, to inspire. Whatever the varying quantity (opera itself) may be in the next, uptown arena, it will be different—as different from the old as its massive resources of staging and lighting are from a theater meagerly equipped with both.

If we are fortunate, the opportunities for good work will be no less favorable: if we are thrice blessed, they will be even better. But it is a future to which all, including the General Manager who used the words in his speech at the Gala Farewell, can look forward with confidence. That is written in the stars, human as well as astrological, under which, as one epoch ends, another begins.

EPILOGUE

In common with the General Managers who preceded him, Rudolf Bing confronted certain conditions that were hardly more mutable by him than by them when it became his turn to continue and, as it happened, to close out the epoch of opera associated with the theater at 1423 Broadway. In order of magnitude they may be itemized as follows:

I) *The house itself, of a size and character which put priority emphasis on:*
   a) Big voices rather than small.
   b) Singers rather than actors.
   c) Vocal-instrumental values rather than scenic illusion (difficult or impossible to achieve with its limited facilities).

II) *The opera-going public of New York, with its disposition toward:*

a) Italian and German opera rather than French (or Russian or Slavic).

b) The lyric-tragic appeal rather than works with a comic, satiric, or even folk emphasis.

c) The conventional repertory rather than the unconventional.

III) *The geographic location, with its remoteness from Continental sources of supply, which made mandatory:*

a) Maintenance of "cover" personnel for the whole range of current repertory (that is, substitutes available on daily call for rehearsals as well as performances).

b) The obligation thus assumed to provide performing opportunities for the "cover" personnel, as few will accept engagements merely on "stand-by" status.

c) The inevitable consequence to performance standards when the desirable artists of the first or second rank cannot be obtained, and an artist of the "third" rank is covered by an artist of the "fourth" rank, and so on.

Like the accomplishments of his predecessors, Bing's must be related to the extent to which he improved the opportunities presented by the vocal talent available in his time, or neglected by oversight, prejudice, or indifference, to take advantage of other resources—repertory, scenic designers, conductors—generally available on the operatic scene. Money is, of course, a factor not to be ignored: but it is clear enough that he had more at his disposal than Johnson, if not so much as other predecessors, especially Gatti. Tenure is also a factor: but when a General Manager has endured for sixteen seasons with a clear run at twenty, the judgment must be that he has come to accept the results as representative of his standards, as those who employ him accept them as representative of theirs.

In his year of observation and preparation, Bing had the outsider's advantage of judging the extent to which the practices of the past had become habit, and the procedures possible at one time had become obligations indefensible at another. Among them were the yearly *Ring* and *Parsifal,* the widely spaced repetitions of repertory, the "traditional" series in Philadelphia, and the omission of its night (usually Tuesday) from the New York schedule. His first evaluation of the flaws and fallacies in the *status quo* as he found it, especially in the long neglect of theatrical values in the most performed repertory, were not only keen and competent, but also provocative of a positive counterinfluence long required.

It was out of these observations and the means to implement them that there arose what was recognized as the "Bing standard," typified by new productions of *Don Carlo* and *Fledermaus, Così fan tutte, Don Giovanni,* some aspects of *Carmen,* the memorable *Butterfly,* etc. These managed, by the exercise of skill and planning, to evade or overcome certain hazards related to the "immutables" enumerated above. Americans in larger number than hitherto engaged could be marshaled for a better grade of "cover" talent in some works. The alteration of the "traditional" schedule to provide more frequent performances of the same work within a shorter time than was hitherto deemed acceptable might help: the reduction in quantity, or the omission altogether from a given season's repertory, of certain demanding works permitted concentration on others with more compatible demands.

These evasions and innovations were helpful for a time, but the dividends to be derived from them tended to diminish and, indeed, to disappear altogether when the lengthened playing schedule built up the number of performances that had to be given, when the hoped-for carry-over value of a brilliant new production proved illusory and it regressed to the category of "day to day" with its perilous effect on quality.

There were some countermeasures to be instituted against these unexpected increments of success, but there was none at all to diminish the discovery that the "Bing standard" was one thing when personally administered, another thing when the maintenance of it was delegated to others. One accepts as fundamental the proposition that it is beyond the competence of any single individual to oversee the casting and preparation of four, five, or six new productions, as many revivals (sometimes a more difficult category of effort than wholly new productions), and a hundred or more performances of works carried over from year to year. But one does not accept the proposition that the level of taste should vary from one to the other, or that a man capable of pronouncing judgment on the shortcomings of his predecessor should be immune from judgment of his own shortcomings.

It was in line with his acute evaluation of the Metropolitan as he found it that Bing saw the need for the creation of an administrative cadre that would function regardless of change in the top command. It was under his urging that such a staff was created where none had existed previously. But it is also evident that the quality of advice on practical musical matters was better when it stemmed from Max Rudolf—whom he had inherited from the previous administration—than it has been since Rudolf left. In other words, the façade of a functioning administration has been created, but the implementation of it has been open to question. Rudolf's order of ability has not been replaced in his Bing-chosen successors, with the result that Bing has relied too heavily in recent years on persons lacking adequate qualifications, or the influence, or the forthrightness, to make their advice meaningful. Herman Krawitz was well above this average.

Setting aside for the moment such *minutiae* as who sang what and when, it is not too much to ask that in any and all circumstances an operatic venture of the Metropolitan's prominence should be at the very least what professionals call a "musical house." That is to say, whether or not a production be scenically right and vocally strong, that at bottom it be, according to the composer's prescription (this, certainly, is not a matter of cost). But all too often Bing (and inferentially the house he serves) has exposed himself to the charge of being musically negligent—by indulging a truncated *Forza del destino,* a *Eugene Onegin* tied together by "interludes" not of the composer's creation and with its final scene relocated, an "edited" *Queen of Spades,* a rearranged *Ernani, Nabucco,* and *Boris.* Credit for enterprise may be awarded in the instance of *Perichole,* where a weak original was made strong by editing, but it is a mere matter of history to observe that the most acclaimed new productions of his sixteen seasons on Broadway were those—*Die Meistersinger, Falstaff, Così fan tutte, Arabella, Salome, Turandot, Samson*—in which the musical foundation was sure and secure enough to bear whatever scenic or dramatic structure was reared over it and no "improvements" on the composer's conception were tolerated.

It has been Bing's counterposition, when some contentions attacking the musical premises of his administration were advanced, that he was not out to "change the world," that if a Rigoletto sang an (unwritten) high A-flat in Act II at La Scala, he could jolly well sing it at the Metropolitan, too. But it did not always work that way. Too often, a "star" has been granted one right, the satellite restricted to another, as in the last notes of *"Caro nome"* in *Rigoletto* or *"Sempre libera"* in *La Traviata.* I am certainly not arguing for any more interpolated high notes than are unavoidable: I am merely citing this as one, among other, instances of lax musical standards and inconsistent procedures.

On the other hand, when "changing the world" called for the courage to go to the roots of certain prejudices in the society as he found it, Bing was not in the least remiss. His hospitality to Negro talent may well have begun as enlightened self-interest. But in following his beginning through to its logical conclusion and joining such self-interest to that of the institution he served, Bing made the Metropolitan of the 'fifties and 'sixties a responsible participant in a nationwide upheaval.

The more contrast, then, with the instances of individual prerogatives accepted or rejected according to the prestige or drawing power of the individual in question which have been sufficiently enumerated in the preceding pages not to require recapitulation here. But it is certainly a fact that baritones are held on a shorter rein than tenors because there are more of them, and a big name bass or soprano can exercise (without penalty of reprisal) more "individuality" than a mezzo. This does not involve a pox on what is injudiciously denounced as the "star system." As everyone who has seen a Callas-Gobbi-Corelli *Tosca* or a Siepi-Evans-Schwarzkopf-Elias-Peerce *Don Giovanni* or a Nilsson-Price-Corelli-Stokowski *Turandot* will understand, there is nothing at fault with the star system as long as there is a system as well as stars. My complaint about the Bing Metropolitan is that on too many occasions in the last sixteen years there has been neither.

Opera managers no less than other mortals are susceptible to natural laws, among them the proposition that Nature abhors a vacuum. In the Metropolitan's affairs there has, in my judgment, too long been a power vacuum between performers and administration. In the best operatic times at the Metropolitan, that vacuum has been filled by a strong executive on the musical side, such as Mahler, Toscanini, Serafin, or Bodanzky. Edward Johnson was supremely fortunate in having a world situation in which a Beecham, a Walter, a Szell, a Stiedry, Busch, or Reiner were available to him, at once or sequentially. Whatever the reason, when those he inherited left or died, Bing's replacements were rarely given a similar share of executive responsibility. Along with the baleful influence of the "take-over" went an expansion of his own range of influence to fill the vacuum that thus came into being.

The real thrust of these comments at a midpoint in the Bing management is not the plusses and minuses of his total achievement—that can wait until the achievement is totaled—but the question of whether he is capable of seeing them as clearly (and in as just perspective) as he did the merits and demerits of the institution as he found it. The time may be at hand, for example, not only for the company to broaden the range and variety of its repertory but also to administer it according to another system altogether. That is to say, instead of the semi-*stagione* system now in vogue, to go over entirely to that mode of scheduling.

For those unacquainted with the term, it may be defined as follows: in the *stagione* (the word simply means "season") system in vogue at La Scala, when a new production of *Aida, Turandot, Gioconda,* or whatever is put on, it is given ten, twelve, or sixteen times in a period of weeks and then taken off. The advantage, of course, is that the same performers take part in all or most of the performances, the director's influence remains strong, and the values of preparation are retained through the run. In Bing's time, this procedure has obtained in some instances (a *Pelléas,* a

Così, or a *Martha*) but not in others (especially in a new production of a popular piece like *Faust, Bohème, Aida* or *Contes d'Hoffmann*). The argument to the contrary has been that too-frequent repetitions discourage single seat sales. There is, however, little validity in such arguments when desirable subscriptions are subject to a long waiting list and even standing room may be sold in advance of a performance, as is proposed for Lincoln Center.

Musing on the experience of a long lifetime in music, a critic of a prior time came to the conclusion that there "are no perfect opera singers," that flaws can be found in the best of them. As much certainly is true of General Managers, charged with administering the inequalities not only of the near perfect—those rarities in any generation—but also of the imperfect, the unperfect, the competent, the incompetent, the tolerable, and the all but intolerable. We can ask, however, that the mirror he holds up to his own abilities be neither slimming—where faults are concerned—nor fattening—where virtues are reflected—but a true likeness of them as they exist or do not exist. The place in opera for fantasy, dreams, and illusions is not in the General Manager's office, but on stage.

If a single thread runs through the checkered—and excheckered—history of the Metropolitan, it is simply that its times of greatest glory and peak accomplishment have come when it was infused by the idealism and energies of a Seidl, Mahler, Toscanini, Bruno Walter, Reiner, Boehm, or Stokowski, in whom the desire to excel was not merely inordinate but also unquenchable. For them, the good was only one step above the poor, on the way to the better as the kneeling approach to the altar of the best. For the Metropolitan to be "as good as" its contemporaries is for it to accept a common standard of limitations and restrictions in which complaints about today's jet planes no less than those about yesterday's steamships and the day before yesterday's steam engines have had a disproportionate part. To excel in opera, as in everything else, the wish must be father to the thought—in the board room as well as in the general manager's office, in the closed circles in which budgets are calculated and plans laid as well as in the public arena where efforts are assessed and judgments rendered.

THE METROPOLITAN REPERTORY
1883–1966

IN ORDER TO ESTABLISH a uniform record of opera performances at the Metropolitan Opera House, the author has accepted a compilation undertaken by
Gerald Fitzgerald of *Opera News*. In expressing his appreciation for this long-
needed service, the author notes that the Fitzgerald totals differ from his own
earlier ones by the inclusion of certain categories of performance hitherto
omitted. Among them are the so-called "Patti" season of 1891–2, the spring
seasons of 1935–6 and 1936–7, and the World's Fair seasons of 1938–9 and
1963–4. In addition, the compilation includes student performances since their
inception. It does not include partial performances in "galas," concert performances of operas, or performances by visiting companies. It is thus wholly and
exclusively a record of the performances presented by and with the Metropolitan Opera Company in its various transformations. Operas are listed alphabetically under the names by which they have commonly been billed at the
Metropolitan. The seasons are given thus: 1883–4 as 83; 1900–1 as 1900;
1965–6 as 65. The numbers in parentheses tally the performances of the single
season; at the end of each listing the total number of times the work has been
sung is given together with the number of seasons in which it has been sung.

Compilation of Works

The Abduction from the Seraglio:
46(4) = 4 performances in 1 season
Adriana Lecouvreur: 07(2); 62(10)
= 12 performances in 2 seasons
Die ägyptische Helena: 28(5) = 5
performances in 1 season
L'Africaine: 88(5); 90(3); 91(4);
93(1); 94(1); 96(1); 98(1);
99(1); 1900(1); 06(2); 22(4);
23(4); 24(4); 25(3); 26(3); 27-
(2); 28(3); 29(1); 30(5); 31(3);
33(3) = 55 performances in 21 seasons
Aida: 86(4); 88(3); 89(3); 91(2);
93(1); 94(4); 95(5); 96(3); 98-
(4); 99(5); 1900(4); 01(5); 02-
(7); 03(6); 04(5); 05(4); 06(6);
07(7); 08(8); 09(7); 10(8); 11-
(7); 12(5); 13(7); 14(8); 15(7);
16(7); 17(8); 18(8); 19(5); 20-
(10); 21(8); 22(8); 23(6); 24(8);
25(8); 26(9); 27(5); 28(8); 29(7);
30(6); 31(7); 32(7); 33(5); 34-
(5); 35(9); 36(8); 37(6); 38(7);
39(6); 40(4); 41(6); 42(6); 43-
(4); 44(9); 46(7); 47(6); 48(6);
49(9); 51(15); 52(9); 53(6); 54-
(8); 55(7); 56(7); 57(8); 58(7);

59(11); 60(8); 61(11); 62(12); 63(19); 64(11); 65(9) = 511 performances in 74 seasons

Alceste: 40(5); 51(5); 60(7) = 17 performances in 3 seasons

Alessandro Stradella: 09(3) = 3 performances in 1 season

Amelia al ballo: 37(3); 38(3) = 6 performances in 2 seasons

L'Amico Fritz: 93(2); 23(3) = 5 performances in 2 seasons

L'Amore dei tre re: 13(5); 14(5); 17(5); 18(3); 19(3); 20(5); 21-(4); 22(1); 23(2); 26(3); 27(2); 28(2); 32(2); 39(2); 40(3); 48-(4) = 51 performances in 16 seasons

L'Amore medico: 13(4) = 4 performances in 1 season

Andrea Chénier: 20(5); 21(4); 22-(5); 23(4); 24(6); 25(5); 26(3); 27(5); 28(3); 29(2); 30(1); 31-(1); 32(2); 54(8); 55(6); 57(6); 59(7); 62(11); 65(8) = 92 performances in 19 seasons

Anima Allegra: 22(5); 23(4) = 9 performances in 2 seasons

Arabella: 54(6); 56(4); 60(5); 65-(7) = 22 performances in 4 seasons

Ariadne auf Naxos: 62(8); 63(7) = 15 performances in 2 seasons

Ariane et Barbe-bleue: 10(4); 11(3) = 7 performances in 2 seasons

Armide: 10(3); 11(4) = 7 performances in 2 seasons

Asrael: 90(5) = 5 performances in 1 season

Un Ballo in maschera: 89(4); 02(1); 04(2); 13(5); 14(2); 15(3); 40-(4); 41(2); 43(4); 45(6); 47(5); 54(5); 55(7); 58(6); 61(8); 62-(9); 65(6) = 79 performances in 17 seasons

Der Barbier von Bagdad: 89(5); 90-(4); 25(5) = 14 performances in 3 seasons

Il Barbiere di Siviglia: 83(3); 91(1); 98(5); 99(4); 02(3); 03(4); 04-(2); 05(2); 07(6); 08(2); 09(3); 12(3); 15(4); 16(3); 17(4); 18-(5); 19(4); 20(3); 21(6); 22(3); 23(2); 24(3); 25(2); 26(2); 27-(3); 28(2); 29(3); 30(3); 31(2); 37(5); 38(3); 39(3); 40(3); 41-

(4); 42(4); 43(3); 44(4); 45(8); 46(4); 47(6); 48(3); 50(12); 53-(8); 54(9); 57(7); 62(15); 65(7) = 200 performances in 47 seasons

Boccaccio: 30(8) = 8 performances in 1 season

La Bohème: 1900(5); 02(3); 03(3); 04(3); 05(5); 06(7); 07(7); 08-(7); 09(7); 10(6); 11(8); 12(6); 13(8); 14(7); 15(5); 16(5); (17-(5); 18(6); 19(4); 20(9); 21(7); 22(7); 23(8); 24(7); 25(8); 26-(7); 27(4); 28(6); 29(7); 30(6); 31(4); 32(7); 33(3); 34(6); 35-(6); 36(4); 37(5); 38(6); 39(5); 40(3); 41(4); 42(6); 43(7); 44-(7); 45(7); 46(5); 47(7); 48(10); 49(8); 50(5); 51(11); 52(11); 53-(15); 54(5); 55(6); 56(14); 57-(9); 58(17); 60(14); 61(9); 63-(19); 65(16) = 444 performances in 62 seasons

Boris Godunov: 12(4); 13(6); 14(6); 15(6); 16(4); 17(6); 18(4); 19-(3); 20(1); 21(5); 22(5); 23(4); 24(4); 25(3); 26(2); 27(3); 28-(2); 38(2); 39(4); 42(4); 43(3); 46(5); 52(5); 53(9); 55(6); 58-(8); 60(7); 62(6) = 127 performances in 28 seasons

La Campana sommersa: 28(5); 29-(2) = 7 performances in 2 seasons

The Canterbury Pilgrims: 16(6) = 6 performances in 1 season

Caponsacchi: 36(2) = 2 performances in 1 season

Carmen: 83(4); 85(2); 90:(3); 91-(1); 93(15); 94(6); 95(14); 96-(8); 98(3); 99(10); 1900(1); 01-(7); 02(3); 03(4); 04(4); 05(2); 06(1); 08(6); 14(10); 15(5); 16-(8); 17(7); 18(5); 19(7); 20(7); 21(8); 22(6); 23(8); 24(5); 27-(6); 28(5); 29(6); 30(3); 31(3); 35(11); 36(7); 37(6); 38(1); 39-(1); 40(6); 41(5); 42(6); 43(7); 44(6); 45(10); 46(6); 47(7); 48-(6); 49(9); 51(9); 52(13); 53(9); 54(7); 55(8); 56(8); 57(14); 58-(7); 59(10); 60(8) = 380 performances in 59 seasons

Cavalleria rusticana: 91(4); 93(8); 94(4); 95(8); 96(3); 98(1); 99-(6); 1900(4); 01(4); 02(1); 03-

(8); 04(4); 06(1); 08(7); 09(7); 10(7); 11(6); 12(5); 13(3); 14-(3); 15(4); 16(3); 17(6); 18(6); 19(5); 20(3); 21(6); 22(6); 23-(7); 24(6); 25(5); 26(7); 27(6); 28(7); 29(4); 30(3); 31(3); 32-(1); 33(3); 34(2); 35(3); 36(5); 37(2); 38(2); 40(4); 42(2); 43-(4); 44(5); 47(5); 50(9); 51(9); 52(6); 53(4); 54(6); 56(4); 58-(8); 59(10); 62(9); 63(6) = 290 performances in 59 seasons

La Cena delle beffe: 25(6); 26(2) = 8 performances in 2 seasons

Le Cid: 96(2); 1900(3); 01(2) = 7 performances in 3 seasons

Cleopatra's Night: 19(4); 20(3) = 7 performances in 2 seasons

I Compagnacci: 23(3) = 3 performances in 1 season

Les Contes d'Hoffmann: 12(7); 13-(2); 24(5); 25(3); 26(4); 27(3); 28(3); 29(4); 30(1); 31(4); 36-(3); 43(5); 45(6); 55(8); 56(6); 58(6); 61(7); 64(7) = 82 performances in 18 seasons

Le Coq d'or: 17(6); 18(5); 19(7); 20(5); 23(9); 24(5); 27(5); 36-(5); 37(2); 41(3); 44(3) = 55 performances in 11 seasons

Così fan tutte: 21(4); 22(3); 23(2); 24(2); 27(1); 51(6); 52(6); 53-(5); 55(6); 61(8); 64(6) = 49 performances in 11 seasons

Crispino e la comare: 18(3) = 3 performances in 1 season

Cyrano de Bergerac: 12(5) = 5 performances in 1 season

La Dame blanche: 03(1) = 1 performance in 1 season

La Damnation de Faust: 06(5) = 5 performances in 1 season

Diana von Solange: 90(2) = 2 performances in 1 season

Dinorah: 91(1); 24(2) = 3 performances in 2 seasons

Don Carlos: 20(6); 21(3); 22(2); 50(10); 51(4); 52(4); 54(5); 56-(4); 58(4); 60(5); 63(7); 65(9) = 63 performances in 12 seasons

Don Giovanni: 83(5); 84(2); 89(2); 91(3); 93(1); 94(4); 95(1); 96-(3); 98(5); 99(1); 1900(2); 02-(1); 05(2); 07(4); 29(5); 30(3);

31(2); 32(2); 33(3); 34(2); 37-(4); 38(2); 40(2); 41(4); 42(3); 44(5); 45(5); 47(7); 49(4); 50-(8); 52(7); 53(8); 54(5); 57(8); 58(6); 59(14); 60(5); 62(10); 63-(10); 65(8) = 178 performances in 40 seasons

Don Pasquale: 99(3); 01(1); 02(1); 04(2); 05(2); 06(1); 08(1); 09-(2); 12(2); 13(2); 34(3); 40(4); 45(3); 55(5); 56(6); 64(6) = 44 performances in 16 seasons

Don Quichotte: 25(4); 26(1) = 5 performances in 2 seasons

Donna Juanita: 31(6) = 6 performances in 1 season

Le Donne curiose: 11(5); 12(3) = 8 performances in 2 seasons

Elaine: 94(2) = 2 performances in 1 season

Elektra: 32(6); 37(4); 38(3); 51(5); 60(5); 61(4) = 27 performances in 6 seasons

L'Elisir d'amore: 03(4); 04(1); 05-(2); 08(2); 09(1); 16(5); 17(5); 18(5); 19(5); 20(1); 29(3); 30-(2); 31(3); 32(3); 41(4); 48(6); 49(5); 60(9); 61(7); 65(9) = 82 performances in 20 seasons

The Emperor Jones: 32(7); 33(3) = 10 performances in 2 seasons

Ernani: 02(3); 21(4); 22(4); 23(3); 28(4); 56(7); 62(7); 64(5) = 37 performances in 8 seasons

Ero e Leandro: 98(2); 02(2) = 4 performances in 2 seasons

Eugen Onegin: 19(4); 20(3); 57(7); 58(5); 63(8) = 27 performances in 5 seasons

Euryanthe: 87(4); 14(5); = 9 performances in 2 seasons

The Fair at Sorochintzy: 30(5) = 5 performances in 1 season

Falstaff: 94(5); 95(4); 08(3); 09(2); 24(6); 25(6); 26(4); 38(4); 43-(4); 48(3); 63(9); 64(8); 65(8) = 66 performances in 13 seasons

La Fanciulla del West: 10(9); 11(5); 12(4); 13(4); 29(8); 30(2); 31-(2); 61(8); 65(15) = 57 performances in 9 seasons

Faust: 83(6); 85(5); 86(3); 87(4); 88(4); 91(11); 93(10); 94(8); 95-(9); 96(12); 98(8); 99(8); 1900-

(7); 01(5); 02(7); 03(4); 04(4); 05(5); 06(4); 07(6); 08(7); 09-(5); 10(4); 11(3); 12(4); 13(1); 17(6); 18(6); 19(6); 20(4); 21-(5); 22(4); 23(5); 24(4); 25(5); 26(6); 27(6); 28(4); 29(3); 30-(6); 31(3); 32(5); 33(3); 34(3); 35(3); 36(5); 37(1); 39(5); 40-(3); 41(3); 42(7); 43(2); 44(5); 46(8); 49(7); 50(10); 53(10); 54-(13); 55(6); 57(7); 59(7); 63(9); 65(13) = 362 performances in 63 seasons

La Favorita: 95(2); 96(2); 98(1); 05(4) = 9 performances in 4 seasons

Fedora: 06(4); 07(3); 23(6); 24(5); 25(3) = 21 performances in 5 seasons

Fernand Cortez: 87(4) = 4 performances in 1 season

Fidelio: 84(3); 86(3); 87(5); 88(2); 90(4); 91(2); 95(1); 99(1); 1900-(1); 03(1); 04(1); 07(3); 08(1); 14(5); 16(3); 26(3); 27(2); 29-(3); 35(2); 38(3); 40(3); 44(2); 45(4); 50(5); 59(6); 62(7); 65-(9) = 85 performances in 27 seasons

La Fille du régiment: 01(3); 02(6); 17(5); 18(4); 40(3); 41(4); 42-(2) = 27 performances in 7 seasons

Die Fledermaus: 04(4); 05(1); 50-(19); 51(9); 52(4); 53(5); 54(3); 55(3); 58(7); 62(8); 63(6) = 69 performances in 11 seasons

Der fliegende Holländer: 89(5); 90-(4); 91(1); 99(3); 1900(2); 07-(4); 30(7); 31(2); 36(4); 39(4); 50(8); 59(8); 62(7); 64(15) = 74 performances in 14 seasons

La Forza del destino: 18(6); 19(5); 20(3); 21(3); 22(2); 26(3); 27-(3); 30(5); 31(4); 34(3); 42(5); 43(4); 52(8); 53(8); 55(7); 57-(6); 59(7); 61(9); 64(7) = 98 performances in 19 seasons

Fra Diavolo: 09(3) = 3 performances in 1 season

Fra Gherardo: 28(4) = 4 performances in 1 season

Francesca da Rimini: 16(5); 17(4) = 9 performances in 2 seasons

Der Freischütz: 84(1); 09(2); 23(3);

24(5); 25(3); 28(3) = 17 performances in 6 seasons

Germania: 09(5); 10(2) = 7 performances in 2 seasons

Gianni Schicchi: 18(6); 19(4); 25-(4); 26(2); 27(2); 33(4); 35(5); 37(3); 43(3); 48(5); 49(3); 51-(5); 57(6) = 52 performances in 13 seasons

La Gioconda: 83(4); 04(4); 05(4); 09(6); 10(6); 11(6); 12(5); 13-(5); 14(2); 24(7); 25(7); 26(8); 27(4); 28(5); 29(6); 30(4); 31-(3); 32(2); 33(2); 34(3); 36(2); 39(3); 44(4); 45(6); 46(3); 47-(4); 52(6); 54(3); 56(4); 58(5); 60(7); 61(5) = 145 performances in 32 seasons

I Giojelli della Madonna: 25(6); 26-(5) = 11 performances in 2 seasons

Giovanni Gallurese: 24(4) = 4 performances in 1 season

Das goldene Kreutz: 86(4) = 4 performances in 1 season

Götterdämmerung: 87(7); 88(4); 89-(5); 90(4); 98(4); 99(2); 1900-(3); 01(1); 02(2); 03(2); 04(2); 05(3); 06(1); 07(1); 08(5); 09-(2); 10(1); 11(3); 12(4); 13(3); 14(2); 15(3); 16(1); 24(4); 25-(2); 26(4); 27(3); 28(2); 29(3); 30(4); 31(2); 32(4); 33(2); 34-(2); 35(4); 36(2); 37(3); 38(4); 39(3); 40(4); 41(2); 42(3); 43-(2); 44(3); 45(3); 47(2); 48(4); 50(2); 51(5); 56(4); 61(5); 63-(4) = 156 performances in 52 seasons

Goyescas, o Las Majas Enamoradas: 15(5) = 5 performances in 1 season

Guillaume Tell: 84(3); 88(3); 89(2); 94(3); 22(5); 23(4); 30(2); 31-(2) = 24 performances in 8 seasons

La Habanera: 23(3) = 3 performances in 1 season

Hamlet: 83(1); 91(3); 93(1); 95(1); 96(1) = 7 performances in 5 seasons

Hänsel und Gretel: 05(11); 06(8); 07(5); 09(4); 10(6); 11(7); 12-(4); 13(6); 14(4); 15(4); 16(1); 27(8); 28(5); 29(4); 30(5); 31-(3); 32(3); 33(2); 34(1); 35(2);

36(1); 37(1); 38(1); 46(5); 47-(2) = 103 performances in 25 seasons

L'Heure espagnole: 25(5) = 5 performances in 1 season

Les Huguenots: 83(2); 84(5); 88(5); 90(3); 91(4); 93(2); 94(7); 95-(5); 96(3); 98(6); 99(2); 1900-(4); 01(3); 02(3); 04(4); 12(5); 14(3) = 66 performances in 17 seasons

In the Pasha's Garden: 34(3) = 3 performances in 1 season

Iphigenia auf Tauris: 16(5) = 5 performances in 1 season

Iris: 07(5); 14(4); 30(4) = 13 performances in 3 seasons

The Island God: 41(3) = 3 performances in 1 season

L'Italiana in Algeri: 19(4) = 4 performances in 1 season

Jenufa: 24(5) = 5 performances in 1 season

Jonny spielt auf: 28(7) = 7 performances in 1 season

La Juive: 84(5); 87(3); 88(3); 89-(2); 19(7); 20(2); 24(3); 25(5); 26(4); 27(2); 28(3); 29(3); 30-(2); 31(1); 35(3); = 48 performances in 15 seasons

Julien: 13(5) = 5 performances in 1 season

Khovanshchina: 49(4) = 4 performances in 1 season

The King's Henchman: 26(6); 27(5); 28(3) = 14 performances in 3 seasons

Die Königin von Saba: 85(15); 86-(4); 89(5); 05(5) = 29 performances in 4 seasons

Königskinder: 10(11); 11(7); 12(6); 13(6) = 30 performances in 4 seasons

Lakmé: 91(2); 06(3); 16(3); 31(5); 32(4); 33(3); 34(3); 35(2); 36-(2); 38(2); 39(3); 40(2); 41(3); 42(3); 46(5) = 45 performances in 15 seasons

The Last Savage: 63(7); 64(3) = 10 performances in 2 seasons

The Legend: 18(3) = 3 performances in 1 season

Linda di Chamounix: 33(3); 34(4) = 7 performances in 2 seasons

Lobetanz: 11(5) = 5 performances in 1 season

Lodoletta: 17(5); 18(3) = 8 performances in 2 seasons

Lohengrin: 83(5); 84(9); 85(4); 86-(4); 87(6); 88(2); 89(5); 90(7); 91(4); 93(5); 94(6); 95(9); 96-(6); 98(9); 99(7); 1900(8); 01-(4); 02(7); 03(5); 04(6); 05(5); 06(5); 07(2); 09(6); 10(6); 11-(6); 12(3); 13(6); 14(5); 15(5); 16(5); 20(7); 21(7); 22(3); 23-(5); 24(6); 25(6); 26(5); 27(5); 28(5); 29(7); 30(6); 31(5); 32-(4); 33(2); 34(4); 35(6); 36(6); 37(4); 38(8); 39(6); 40(3); 41-(6); 42(4); 44(5); 45(4); 46(5); 49(6); 52(6); 55(6); 58(5); 61-(6); 63(8) = 341 performances in 63 seasons

Loreley: 21(5); 22(3) = 8 performances in 2 seasons

Louise: 20(7); 21(4); 29(4); 38(5); 39(3); 40(3); 42(3); 47(4); 48-(4) = 37 performances in 9 seasons

Lucia di Lammermoor: 83(4); 91(1); 93(3); 94(4); 95(4); 96(2); 98-(2); 99(2); 1900(2); 03(3); 04-(3); 05(5); 06(4); 07(1); 08(2); 11(3); 13(1); 15(4); 16(2); 18-(1); 19(4); 20(3); 21(4); 22(2); 23(2); 24(5); 25(6); 26(6); 27-(2); 28(3); 30(4); 31(4); 32(5); 33(4); 34(2); 35(2); 36(1); 37-(2); 38(4); 39(2); 40(2); 42(4); 43(5); 44(5); 45(6); 46(5); 47-(4); 48(9); 49(4); 51(7); 53(6); 55(5); 56(7); 57(9); 58(4); 61-(9); 64(14); 65(9) = 234 performances in 58 seasons

Lucrezia Borgia: 04(1) = 1 performance in 1 season

Luisa Miller: 29(4); 30(1) = 5 performances in 2 seasons

Die lustigen Weiber von Windsor: 99(1) = 1 performance in 1 season

Macbeth: 58(6); 59(5); 61(6); 63-(6) = 23 performances in 4 seasons

Madama Butterfly: 06(5); 07(6); 08-(8); 09(6); 10(8); 11(7); 12(8); 13(8); 14(8); 15(4); 16(5); 17-(6); 18(8); 19(8); 20(7); 21(7); 22(6); 23(7); 24(5); 25(5); 26-(5); 27(4); 28(5); 29(6); 30(3);

31(3); 32(3); 33(3); 34(3); 35-
(7); 36(3); 39(4); 40(5); 41(1);
45(5); 46(6); 47(5); 48(5); 49-
(7); 50(2); 51(8); 52(8); 54(8);
56(7); 57(8); 58(10); 59(12); 60-
(11); 61(8); 62(10); 64(8); 65-
(10) = 325 performances in 52
seasons

Madame Sans-Gêne: 14(6); 15(2);
16(3); 17(3) = 14 performances
in 4 seasons

Madeleine: 13(4) = 4 performances
in 1 season

Madonna Imperia: 27(5) = 5 performances in 1 season

The Man without a Country: 36(4);
37(1) = 5 performances in 2 seasons

Manon: 94(4); 95(2); 98(1); 08(6);
09(4); 11(3); 12(5); 13(4); 14-
(3); 15(1); 19(4); 20(5); 21(4);
22(4); 28(5); 29(5); 30(4); 31-
(5); 32(4); 33(4); 34(3); 35(3);
36(4); 37(4); 38(4); 39(4); 40-
(2); 42(4); 47(7); 51(7); 54(8);
59(7); 63(6); 64(5) = 145 performances in 34 seasons

Manon Lescaut: 06(3); 07(5); 12(5);
13(4); 14(3); 15(3); 16(4); 17-
(4); 18(4); 19(4); 20(4); 21(2);
22(2); 27(3); 28(2); 29(4); 49-
(6); 50(6); 55(4); 58(5); 60(7);
65(8) = 92 performances in 22
seasons

Manru: 01(4) = 4 performances in
1 season

Marouf: 17(6); 18(3); 19(2); 36(2)
= 13 performances in 4 seasons

Marta: 83(2); 91(2); 96(2); 98(2);
05(4); 06(3); 07(3); 15(4); 16-
(3); 17(5); 18(5); 19(4); 23(6);
24(2); 25(1); 26(2); 27(3); 28-
(2); 60(7) = 62 performances in
19 seasons

Masaniello: 84(3); 86(2) = 5 performances in 2 seasons

Il Matrimonio segreto: 36(2) = 2 performances in 1 season

Mefistofele: 83(2); 95(3); 96(4);
1900(2); 07(7); 20(7); 21(6); 22-
(5); 23(3); 24(3); 25(3) = 45
performances in 11 seasons

Die Meistersinger von Nürnberg: 85-
(8); 86(5); 87(1); 88(5); 89(3);

90(6); 91(3); 93(2); 94(1); 95-
(1); 96(3); 99(4); 1900(3); 01-
(1); 02(2); 04(7); 05(5); 07(4);
08(5); 09(2); 10(5); 11(3); 12-
(5); 13(4); 14(3); 15(4); 16(5);
23(6); 24(5); 25(5); 26(6); 27-
(5); 28(5); 29(6); 30(5); 31(3);
33(5); 34(4); 35(4); 36(3); 37-
(3); 38(2); 39(5); 44(4); 45(5);
46(3); 47(5); 49(4); 51(4); 52-
(5); 54(5); 55(4); 56(5); 58(5);
62(10); 63(7); 64(6) = 243 performances in 57 seasons

Merlin: 86(5) = 5 performances in
1 season

Merry Mount: 33(6) = 6 performances in 1 season

Messaline: 01(3) = 3 performances
in 1 season

Mignon: 83(4); 91(2); 94(1); 99-
(1); 07(5); 26(4); 27(4); 28(2);
29(3); 30(3); 31(4); 32(1); 33-
(1); 34(2); 35(3); 36(3); 38(3);
39(3); 43(8); 44(5); 48(4) = 66
performances in 21 seasons

Mireille: 18(4) = 4 performances in
1 season

Mona: 11(4) = 4 performances in 1
season

Mona Lisa: 22(5); 23(1) = 6 performances in 2 seasons

Nabucco: 60(9) = 9 performances in
1 season

La Navarraise: 95(5); 21(4) = 9 performances in 2 seasons

Norma: 89(1); 91(2); 27(6); 28(5);
29(2); 30(4); 31(2); 36(2); 37-
(3); 43(4); 44(4); 53(4); 56(5)
= 44 performances in 13 seasons

La Notte di Zoraïma: 31(4) = 4 performances in 1 season

Le Nozze di Figaro: 93(3); 94(1);
98(3); 99(4); 01(2); 02(1); 03-
(1); 04(2); 08(6); 16(3); 17(2);
39(3); 40(6); 41(4); 42(6); 43-
(3); 44(5); 46(6); 48(5); 49(4);
51(8); 53(8); 54(5); 55(6); 56-
(6); 57(5); 59(8); 60(8); 61(6);
64(6) = 136 performances in 30
seasons

Oberon: 18(6); 19(5); 20(2) = 13
performances in 3 seasons

L'Oiseau bleu: 19(8); 20(4) = 12
performances in 2 seasons

L'Oracolo: 14(6); 16(2); 17(6); 18-(3); 19(5); 20(5); 21(3); 22(1); 23(5); 24(2); 25(1); 31(4); 32-(1) = 44 performances in 13 seasons

Orfeo ed Euridice: 91(4); 93(1); 95-(1); 09(5); 10(5); 11(5); 12(2); 13(3); 35(2); 38(5); 39(3); 41-(3); 54(5); 57(5); 61(5) = 54 performances in 15 seasons

Otello: 91(1); 94(4); 01(3); 02(3); 09(6); 10(5); 11(4); 12(3); 37-(8); 38(4); 39(3); 40(2); 41(4); 45(3); 46(6); 48(5); 51(5); 54-(6); 57(5); 58(6); 62(7); 63(13); 64(7) = 113 performances in 23 seasons

Pagliacci: 93(4); 94(2); 95(2); 99-(1); 1900(1); 01(1); 02(6); 03-(5); 04(3); 05(3); 06(4); 07(4); 08(5); 09(7); 10(8); 11(9); 12-(9); 13(9); 14(7); 15(4); 16(5); 17(5); 18(6); 19(6); 20(6); 21-(6); 22(7); 23(4); 24(8); 25(7); 26(6); 27(6); 28(6); 29(6); 30-(8); 31(6); 32(6); 33(5); 34(3); 35(7); 36(7); 37(1); 38(4); 40-(4); 41(3); 42(2); 43(4); 44(5); 47(5); 50(9); 51(9); 52(6); 53-(4); 54(6); 56(4); 58(8); 59(10); 62(9); 63(6) = 319 performances in 59 seasons

Parsifal: 03(12); 04(8); 05(4); 06-(2); 08(5); 09(3); 10(4); 11(3); 12(3); 13(3); 14(4); 15(3); 16-(3); 19(6); 20(4)(; 21(3); 22(4); 23(3); 24(3); 25(2); 26(1); 27-(1); 28(1); 29(2); 30(1); 31(2); 32(2); 33(2); 34(4); 35(3); 36-(1); 37(3); 38(4); 39(5); 40(2); 41(3); 42(2); 43(3); 44(2); 45-(3); 46(3); 47(3); 48(3); 49(3); 51(3); 52(3); 53(3); 54(2); 55-(3); 56(2); 57(2); 59(3); 60(3); 65(4) = 169 performances in 54 seasons

Les Pêcheurs de perles: 95(1); 16(3) = 4 performances in 2 seasons

Pelléas et Mélisande: 24(4); 25(4); 26(4); 27(4); 28(2); 29(2); 30-(2); 31(2); 32(2); 33(2); 34(2); 39(2); 40(2); 43(3); 44(4); 48-(2); 53(5); 59(5); 62(5) = 57 performances in 19 seasons

La Perichole: 56(11); 57(8); 61(7); 65(5) = 31 performances in 4 seasons

Peter Grimes: 47(4); 48(4) = 8 performances in 2 seasons

Peter Ibbetson: 30(6); 31(6); 33(3); 34(1) = 16 performances in 4 seasons

Philémon et Baucis: 93(4); 95(2); 98(1) = 7 performances in 3 seasons

Phoebus and Pan: 41(4) = 4 performances in 1 season

The Pipe of Desire: 09(2) = 2 performances in 1 season

Pique-Dame: 09(4); 65(10) = 14 performances in 2 seasons

The Polish Jew: 20(3) = 3 performances in 1 season

Le Preziose ridicole: 30(4) = 4 performances in 1 season

Prince Igor: 15(5); 16(2); 17(2) = 9 performances in 3 seasons

Le Prophète: 83(1); 84(9); 85(3); 86(5); 87(2); 88(3); 90(1); 91-(2); 94(1); 98(2); 99(2); 02(5); 17(5); 18(6); 19(5); 27(4) = 56 performances in 16 seasons

I Puritani: 83(1); 17(4) = 5 performances in 2 seasons

The Rake's Progress: 52(5); 53(2) = 7 performances in 2 seasons

La Reine Fiammette: 18(4) = 4 performances in 1 season

Das Rheingold: 88(9); 89(3); 98(4); 99(2); 1900(2); 01(1); 02(2); 03-(2); 04(2); 05(2); 06(1); 07(1); 08(1); 09(2); 10(1); 11(1); 12-(1); 13(1); 14(1); 15(3); 16(2); 24(1); 25(1); 26(3); 27(1); 28-(1); 29(1); 30(1); 31(1); 32(1); 33(1); 34(1); 35(2); 36(2); 37-(2); 38(3); 39(2); 40(1); 41(1); 42(1); 43(2); 44(2); 47(2); 50-(2); 56(3); 61(3) = 85 performances in 46 seasons

Rienzi: 85(7); 86(5); 89(1) = 13 performances in 3 seasons

Rigoletto: 83(3); 84(1); 91(2); 93-(2); 94(5); 95(1); 96(1); 98(2); 99(1); 1900(2); 02(2); 03(5); 04-(2); 05(5); 06(2); 07(4); 08(3); 09(2); 10(4); 11(5); 12(1); 15-(5); 16(5); 17(5); 18(3); 19(5);

20(5); 21(4); 22(3); 23(5); 24-(6); 25(5); 26(7); 27(5); 28(3); 29(2); 30(4); 31(5); 32(5); 33-(2); 34(4); 35(8); 36(4); 37(5); 38(3); 39(4); 40(3); 41(4); 43-(5); 44(5); 45(6); 46(6); 47(4); 48(7); 49(7); 51(11); 52(12); 53-(8); 55(15); 56(8); 58(7); 60(8); 61(6); 63(10); 64(7); 65(6) = 312 performances in 66 seasons

Robert le diable: 83(3) = 3 performances in 1 season

Le Roi de Lahore: 23(5) = 5 performances in 1 season

Le Roi d'Ys: 21(5) = 5 performances in 1 season

Roméo et Juliette: 91(4); 93(7); 94-(5); 96(6); 98(7); 99(5); 1900-(5); 01(3); 02(2); 03(2); 04(4); 06(5); 10(3); 22(10); 23(6); 24-(3); 25(4); 26(2); 27(2); 28(3); 29(4); 30(6); 31(3); 32(3); 33-(1); 34(1); 37(3); 45(6); 46(4) = 124 performances in 30 seasons

La Rondine: 27(5); 28(3); 29(2); 35(3) = 13 performances in 4 seasons

Der Rosenkavalier: 13(9); 14(5); 15-(5); 16(3); 22(4); 23(3); 24(2); 26(3); 27(4); 28(2); 29(4); 34-(4); 37(5); 38(3); 39(4); 40(5); 41(5); 42(4); 43(5); 44(3); 45-(5); 46(5); 47(5); 49(6); 50(6); 52(7); 55(6); 57(7); 59(5); 62-(9); 64(10) = 153 performances in 31 seasons

Le Rossignol: 25(4); 26(3) = 7 performances in 2 seasons

Sadko: 29(8); 30(4); 31(4) = 16 performances in 3 seasons

Saint Elizabeth: 17(5) = 5 performances in 1 season

Salammbô: 1900(3) = 3 performances in 1 season

Salome: 06(1); 33(7); 37(3); 38(3); 42(3); 43(3); 48(5); 49(3); 51-(5); 54(6); 57(6); 61(5); 64(8); 65(5) = 63 performances in 14 seasons

Samson et Dalila: 94(1); 15(5); 16-(5); 17(4); 18(5); 19(5); 20(4); 21(1); 22(5); 23(5); 24(3); 36-(4); 37(1); 40(2); 41(3); 49(6); 52(5); 55(4); 57(4); 64(11); 65-

(6) = 89 performances in 21 seasons

Schwanda, der Dudelsackpfeifer: 31-(5) = 5 performances in 1 season

Il Segreto di Susanna: 12(4); 13(3); 20(3); 21(1) = 11 performances in 4 seasons

Semiramide: 93(4); 94(1) = 5 performances in 2 seasons

La Serva padrona: 34(4); 42(2) = 6 performances in 2 seasons

Shanewis: 17(5); 18(3) = 8 performances in 2 seasons

Siegfried: 87(11); 88(6); 89(2); 90-(4); 96(7); 98(4); 99(2); 1900-(2); 01(1); 02(3); 03(3); 04(2); 05(3); 06(4); 07(4); 08(2); 09-(3); 10(2); 11(3); 12(2); 13(4); 14(3); 15(4); 16(5); 23(2); 24-(2); 25(2); 26(3); 27(4); 28(3); 29(2); 30(5); 31(3); 32(2); 33-(2); 34(3); 35(3); 36(4); 37(5); 38(6); 39(2); 40(3); 41(2); 42-(1); 43(2); 44(2); 46(4); 47(2); 48(3); 50(3); 56(3); 61(3) = 167 performances in 52 seasons

Il Signor Bruschino: 32(4) = 4 performances in 1 season

Simon Boccanegra: 31(6); 32(4); 33-(2); 34(2); 38(2); 39(2); 49(5); 59(6); 60(6); 64(7) = 42 performances in 10 seasons

Snegurochka: 21(7); 22(2) = 9 performances in 2 seasons

La Sonnambula: 83(2); 91(2); 05-(2); 09(1); 15(3); 31(3); 32(3); 34(2); 62(10); 63(10) = 38 performances in 10 seasons

Suor Angelica: 18(6); 19(4) = 10 performances in 2 seasons

Il Tabarro: 18(6); 19(4); 45(3) = 13 performances in 3 seasons

Tannhäuser: 84(9); 85(4); 86(6); 87(4); 88(5); 89(5); 90(7); 93-(2); 95(3); 96(3); 98(7); 99(5); 1900(5); 01(2); 02(4); 03(5); 04-(3); 05(4); 06(5); 07(4); 08(7); 09(4); 10(6); 11(4); 12(6); 13-(3); 14(5); 22(3); 23(5); 24(5); 25(6); 26(4); 27(5); 28(3); 29-(5); 31(7); 32(4); 33(5); 34(6); (35(5); 36(2); 37(5); 38(7); 39-(4); 40(4); 41(5); 42(5); 43(5); 45(5); 47(8); 53(6); 54(4); 60-

(7); 65(6) = 263 performances in 54 seasons

The Temple Dancer: 18(3) = 3 performances in 1 season

Thaïs: 16(5); 17(6); 18(5); 22(7); 23(6); 24(3); 25(1); 38(4) = 37 performances in 8 seasons

Tiefland: 08(4) = 4 performances in 1 season

Tosca: 1900(3); 01(3); 02(4); 03-(4); 04(4); 05(2); 06(6); 07(5); 08(6); 09(6); 10(6); 11(5); 12-(5); 13(7); 14(6); 15(3); 16(5); 17(6); 18(6); 19(5); 20(6); 21-(9); 22(7); 23(7); 24(5); 25-(5); 26(4); 27(7); 28(7); 29-(4); 30(2); 31(3); 34(2); 35(1); 38(4); 39(3); 41(7); 42(4); 43-(4); 45(5); 47(6); 49(7); 52(11); 54(7); 55(10); 56(18); 57(11); 58(12); 59(9); 61(12); 63(4); 64-(16); 65(10); = 326 performances in 53 seasons

Die tote Stadt: 21(6); 22(4) = 10 performances in 2 seasons

La Traviata: 83(4); 94(1); 95(4); 96(3); 98(3); 99(2); 1900(1); 01-(1); 02(4); 03(3); 04(4); 05(2); 06(3); 07(6); 08(5); 09(3); 10-(3); 11(2); 12(3); 13(4); 14(5); 15(2); 16(2); 17(3); 18(3); 21-(3); 22(6); 23(6); 24(4); 25(6); 26(4); 27(4); 28(6); 29(6); 30-(5); 31(5); 32(5); 33(5); 34(4); 35(4); 36(5); 37(5); 38(2); 39-(6); 41(5); 42(8); 43(6); 44(6); 45(6); 46(9); 47(7); 48(6); 49-(6); 50(14); 51(10); 52(4); 53-(8); 54(7); 56(9); 57(10); 58(7); 59(9); 61(16); 62(10); 63(9) = 339 performances in 65 seasons

Tristan und Isolde: 86(8); 87(3); 89-(5); 90(3); 95(7); 96(2); 98(5); 99(3); 1900(4); 01(3); 02(4); 03-(4); 04(2); 05(3); 06(4); 07(6); 08(4); 09(5); 10(4); 11(5); 12-(5); 13(5); 14(4); 15(5); 16(5); 20(6); 21(4); 22(5); 23(2); 24-(2); 25(4); 26(2); 27(5); 28(4); 29(6); 30(6); 31(6); 32(5); 33-(5) 34(7); 35(7); 36(8); 37(9); 38(10); 39(7); 40(7); 42(3); 43-(6); 44(4); 45(3); 46(6); 47(5); 48(6); 49(3); 50(8); 52(4); 54-

(3); 57(5); 59(8); 60(5); 62(5) = 299 performances in 61 seasons

Der Trompeter von Säkkingen: 87(7); 89(4) = 11 performances in 2 seasons

Il Trovatore: 83(3); 88(5); 89(3); 91(2); 94(4); 95(2); 96(2); 98-(1); 99(3); 1900(1); 02(1); 05-(4); 07(6); 08(5); 09(6); 10(6); 11(4); 12(4); 14(6); 15(4); 16-(5); 17(3); 18(2); 19(2); 20(3); 21(2); 22(2); 23(1); 24(1); 25-(1); 26(2); 27(3); 28(5); 29(4); 30(3); 31(4); 32(3); 33(2); 34-(1); 35(3); 36(4); 37(3); 38(3); 40(4); 42(4); 43(3); 44(4); 46-(5); 47(5); 48(5); 50(13); 51(4); 53(8); 55(5); 56(6); 59(8); 60-(14); 63(11); 65(9) = 242 performances in 59 seasons

Turandot: 26(8); 27(6); 28(6); 29-(1); 60(8); 61(8); 62(7); 64(9) = 53 performances in 8 seasons

Vanessa: 57(6); 58(4); 64(5) = 15 performances in 3 seasons

Der Vasall von Szigeth: 90(4) = 4 performances in 1 season

Die verkaufte Braut: 08(7); 09(1); 10(4); 11(2); 25(5); 26(3); 27-(2); 32(2); 35(5); 36(4); 40(3); 41(3) = 41 performances in 12 seasons

Versiegelt: 11(4) = 4 performances in 1 season

La Vestale: 25(5); 26(3) = 8 performances in 2 seasons

La Vida Breve: 25(4) = 4 performances in 1 season

Le Villi: 08(5) = 5 performances in 1 season

Violanta: 27(4) = 4 performances in 1 season

Der Wald: 02(2) = 2 performances in 1 season

Die Walküre: 84(7); 85(4); 86(3); 87(4); 88(4); 89(3); 90(4); 95-(2); 98(7); 99(6); 1900(5); 01-(3); 02(3); 03(5); 04(4); 05(3); 06(2); 07(4); 08(5); 09(4); 10-(5); 11(5); 12(6); 13(7); 14(7); 15(5); 16(4); 21(6); 22(5); 23-(6); 24(4); 25(5); 26(5); 27(4); 28(6); 29(7); 30(7); 31(6); 32-(3); 33(5); 34(5); 35(4); 36(6);

37(7); 38(6); 39(7); 40(4); 41-(3); 42(3); 43(4); 44(5); 45(2); 46(5); 47(3); 48(4); 49(5); 50-(2); 53(4); 56(4); 57(4); 59(5); 61(4); 64(6) = 292 performances in 63 seasons
La Wally: 08(4) = 4 performances in 1 season
The Warrior: 46(2) = 2 performances in 1 season
Werther: 93(1); 96(1); 09(2) = 4 performances in 3 seasons
Der widerspenstigen Zähmung: 15(2) = 2 performances in 1 season

Wozzeck: 58(5); 60(5); 64(4) = 14 performances in 3 seasons
Die Zauberflöte: 99(5); 01(3); 02-(2); 03(4); 12(9); 13(6); 14(6); 15(4); 16(3); 26(5); 41(4); 42-(6); 43(4); 44(3); 45(5); 47(6); 50(10); 55(6); 56(5); 58(5); 63-(7) = 108 performances in 21 seasons
Zaza: 19(7); 20(7); 21(6) = 20 performances in 3 seasons
Der Zigeunerbaron: 05(1); 59(9) = 10 performances in 2 seasons

This tabulation is as accurate and complete as possible in view of the incompleteness of early Metropolitan records. It shows the following totals: 218 separate, fully staged operas, for a total of 11,078 performances.

INDEX

by Martha W. Arnott

EXPLANATORY NOTE: The following abbreviations are used in this index: (d) for a Metropolitan debut; (b) for ballet; (f) for footnote; (cond.) for conductor; (des.) for designer. Titles of works (but not personal names) beginning with such articles as Da, Das, Del, Der, Die, Die, I, Il, L', La, Le, Les, The, Un, Una, and Une are alphabetized under the first word following the article: *Das Rheingold* under *Rheingold, Das, L'Africaine* under *Africaine, L'*. Names of New York City newspapers are alphabetized without the name of the city: *Post* and *Times*. Names beginning with Mc are alphabetized as though spelled Mac. Names containing Van and Von are alphabetized under the element following the particule: Weber, Carl Maria von. Quotations from critics and reviewers will be found under the name of the person or work dealt with: *Tristan und Isolde*, Henderson on; Toscanini, *Times* on.

A NOTE ABOUT THE AUTHOR

IRVING KOLODIN was born in New York in 1908. He served on the music staff of the New York *Sun* from 1932 to 1949, being its music editor and music critic from 1945 to 1949. Since 1947 he has been editor of the Recordings section of *Saturday Review*. He became its music editor and critic in 1949 and is now one of its associate editors. In addition to earlier versions of this book on the Metropolitan he has published books on recordings and *The Musical Life* (Knopf, 1958); he was co-author of *Saturday Review Home Book of Recorded Music and Sound Reproduction*. Mr. Kolodin is married and lives in New York.

A NOTE ON THE TYPE

THE TEXT of this book was set on the Linotype in a face called TIMES ROMAN, designed by Stanley Morison for *The Times* of London, and first introduced by that newspaper in 1932.

Among typographers and designers of the twentieth century, Stanley Morison has been a strong forming influence, as typographical advisor to the English Monotype Corporation, as a director of two distinguished English publishing houses, and as a writer of sensibility, erudition, and keen practical sense.

The text and illustrations were
composed, printed, and bound by
The Haddon Craftsmen, Scranton, Pa.

Typography and binding
based on designs by W. A. Dwiggins